GRAENUM

An Autobiography by Graenum Berger

Graenum Berger (photo by Tim Gidal—1986)

GRAENUM

An Autobiography by Graenum Berger

KTAV Publishing House, Inc.
Hoboken, New Jersey
and
John Washburn Bleeker Hampton Publishers
Pelham, New York

Copyright © 1987
GRAENUM BERGER

Library of Congress Cataloging-in-Publication Data

Berger, Graenum.
  Graenum, an autobiography.

  Includes index.
  1. Berger, Graenum. 2. Jews—United States—
Biography. 3. Community centers, Jewish—United
States. I. Title.
E184.J5B45   1987   973'.04924024   87-3819
ISBN 0-88125-123-2

Manufactured in the United States of America

Tribute to Matthew Penn

THIS BOOK WOULD not have been written had it not been for Matthew Penn's amazing persuasiveness. A close friend and colleague of more than forty years, he has always seen in my spoken words and writings thoughts that he felt deserved a wider audience. He involved me in the writing and editing of *The Turbulent Decades*, which took two years of my life. It was well received. So he couldn't be altogether wrong. He not only inveigled me into writing this text, which would have been quite enough, but on his own went out and found the money to assure its publication. What more could anyone else do for another person? May he be granted long life, for in everything he touches, he enriches the community.

To My Wife of Fifty-Eight Years
EMMA BERGER

Who has been my constant and staunchest supporter, my severest critic and loving companion, always enduring the isolation that I imposed on myself when engaged in any task and particularly when writing; and then critically examining the text to tell me what I should eliminate, what I should tone down, and what I must write in.

And to My Children and Grandchildren

Ramon, Michael, Anita, Sandra, Elisabeth, Bonnie, Judith, Gideon, and Deborah, who I hope will read this autobiography with keen interest, for in many respects it was written for all of them.

* * *

My deepest appreciation to Prof. Dr. Nachum Tim Gidal of Jerusalem, distinguished author, teacher and photographer, my long-time friend, who was responsible for the portrait frontispiece and for the arrangement of the photo-section.

My thanks to Nathan Kolodney and the Bronx House staff for assisting with important administrative procedures; to Merwin Rosenman, Ruth Rafel, Seymour Kameny, Dale Lewis, Lewis Stolzenberg, Philip Cohen and David Berger for providing me with materials essential to this book.

To My Patrons

YOU ARE IN that glorious tradition that has made possible the writing and the printing of literature in many ages.

I hope that this modest volume will live up to your expectations.

My thanks to all of you for your interest, your generosity, and your friendship.

  Dr. Charles and Maryann Ansell
*Stanley and Ruth Beckerman
  Edwin Berger
*Stanley and Sally Berger
  Leonard and Adele Block
  Milton Bluestein
  B'nai Torah, (Highland Park, ILL.)
  Richard W. Dammann
  Henry and Edith Everett
  James J. Fuld
  Lester and Sylvia Gerson
  Drs. Morris A. and Rose Goldberg
  Louis C. and Celia Grossberg
  Bernard Levy
  Leon and Hortense Lippman
  Haim and Judith Morag
  Dr. Theodore and Jane Norman
*Max Orenstein
  Matthew and Aviva Penn
  Mrs. Ruth Rafel
  Daniel Rose
  Frederick P. Rose
  Roger Seasonwein
  Samuel J. Silberman
*Rose Stockhamer
  John Trubin
*Morris Weil
  Robert and Peggy Wolf
  Mrs. Marjorie Wyler

*Deceased.

Table of Contents

FOREWORD	xii
1908—A FLASHBACK.	xiv
CHAPTER 1—*Where It All Began*	1
Family background—The Kindergarten trauma—Cultural milieu—Sacandaga—Ike Cohen Family—My Brother Morris—The name Graenum—The War Ends—Gloversville—Drinking Liquor—Back to School—A Tragedy—Caroga Lake—Sex—A Spelling Bee	
CHAPTER 2—*College—Reporter—College*	52
New York University—New House on Bleeker Street—Newspaper Reporter—Emma Finestein—University of Missouri—Married—Politics—Jewish Student Organization—Ramon is born—Last Year in Missouri.	
CHAPTER 3—*The Graduate School*	89
CHAPTER 4—*Staten Island*	99
Jewish Studies—Gambling—A Black Girl—Family Memberships—Soviet Russia—The Catholic Church—National Youth Administration—Taint of Radicalism—Anti-semitism—Emma—Leaving Staten Island	
CHAPTER 5—*Moving To The Bronx*	124
A False Arrest—Milton Married—Sam and Margaret—Baruch Michael is Born—Peace and Pacifism	
CHAPTER 6—*Bronx House*	133
The Union—Budget—Disciplines Cooperate—Claremont House—Father Divine—"Slave Market"—Public Schools—Music School—Italian Community—World War II—A Neighborhood Organization—Assistant Headworkers—Camp Bronx House—The Jewish Flag—Zionism—Kansas City—Center for Aging—Nan Langman—The Janowsky Survey—Albany—Should I Become a Rabbi?—President of the NAJCW—Leaving Bronx House	
CHAPTER 7—*Germany and Europe*	191
Germany—Emma and Michael in Europe—To England—To France	
CHAPTER 8—*Federation*	209
Early Years—Origin of the Associated Ys—Tempting Offers—Camps—Henry Kaufmann Campgrounds—An Arts Day Camp—Sabbath and the Rabbis—The Fourth Force—J. O. T. S.—Jews and Communism—Pelham Jewish Center—Burlesque—Federation	

Moves—Pulling Out of a Community—Fund-raising—Government Funds—Efforts to Make Federation Non-sectarian—Jewish College Youth—Jewish Gambling—The Jewish Poor—Blacks and "Black Jews"—Chicago's Black Israelites—Training Staff—Jewish Education—Autonomy and Centralism—Rabbi Isaac N. Trainin

CHAPTER 9—*Israel: 1955 and 1959*   314
The Seminar—Jerusalem YM-YWHA—Cyprus Adventure—Greece, Italy, Belgium and Holland—Israel 1959—Greece, Spain, Portugal

CHAPTER 10—*The Early 1960s*   354
Ramon and Anita—Baruch Michael and Sandra—A Man is Killed—Dogs and Canada—The Orient in 1962—Hawaii, Philippines, Hong Kong, Taiwan, Japan, Hiroshima, Korea

CHAPTER 11—*Ethiopia: 1965*   396

CHAPTER 12—*Israel: 1965*   410
Gettye Benjamin—Turkey, Switzerland, Italy, Portugal

CHAPTER 13—*South America—Central America—Mexico: 1966*   425
Venezuela, Brazil, Uruguay, Argentina, Chile, Peru, Colombia, Panama, Mexico—The Washington Conference—Papers written in 1965-66—The Brandeis Institute

CHAPTER 14—*The Latter 1960s*   446
Margaret's Death—Israel in 1967—The Rones—Sicily—Student Teaching—The Wiener Educational Center—No Assistants—Helsinki—Stockholm, Denmark—Israel in 1968—A Menorah and a Psalm—Yugoslavia—Austria—Long Island—Labor Zionism—Camping

CHAPTER 15—*Around the World: 1971*   483
The Ansells—Honolulu—Vietnam—Henry Kissinger—Cambodia, Thailand, Burma, Calcutta, Nepal, Benares, Khajraho, Agra, Jaipur, Bombay, Cochin, New Delhi, Iran, Israel, Rumania, Rome, Portugal

CHAPTER 16—*Readings and Travels—1972*   526
Readings—England—David Kessler—Israel in 1972—Capri, Sardinia, Southern France, Spain, Portugal

CHAPTER 17—*The Dyarchy*   546
Hexter and Willen—Federation Leave Taking—The New York Board of Rabbis—The Yom Kippur War

CHAPTER 18—*Formation of the American Association for Ethiopian Jews*   557
The AAEJ—Lebanon—England-Israel in Spring: 1974—Ethiopian Jews—Funerals—The Cemetery—Burglaries and Security—Israel in Summer and Fall: 1974—Yitzhak Navon—Uzi Narkis—Pincus Sapir—A Pictorial History—Guatemala, Mexico, Yucatan, New Orleans

CHAPTER 19—*Israel: 1975 and a Safari*   590
Israel—Chicago Black Israelites—Dr. Salo W. Baron—Chief Rabbi Shlomo Goren—Rabbi Mordecai M. Kaplan—Henry and Mildred

Rosenberg—The JDC Breakthrough—A Safari—Accident in Nairobi—Ethiopia—The Bi-centennial—Philip Habib

Chapter 20—*Israel: 1977* 618
ORT—August 15, 1977—Ethiopian Jews Arrive in Israel—"They May Have to Kill You"

Chapter 21—*The Year 1978* 631
Menachem Begin's Letter—Sudan—"Black Jews in America"—"The Turbulent Decades"—Morocco

Chapter 22—*1979: A Breakthrough* 650
Sudan Rescue—Israel—Montreal—William P. Halpern—U. S. Senators and Congressmen—World ORT in Ethiopia—Baruch Tegegne—Caribbean Islands—Dominican Republic—Jamaica—Ethiopian Embassy—Sam Died—Sam's Letters

Chapter 23—*In Search of the Origins of Graenum* 678
Sources for name "Graenum"—Milton's Death—Orphaned

Chapter 24—*Ethiopian Jewry* 692
Frustration and Success—Meyer and Tereska Levin—U. S. Jewish Organizations and Ethiopian Jews—Matti Elias and Mizrahi—St. Louis General Assembly—Return to Missouri—"Last Flight from Ambo Ber"

Chapter 25—*1982* 704
Ethiopian Jews—Mayor Koch—Simon Wiesenthal—Moshe Gilboa—Israel—The NJCRAC Mission—Rabbinical Assembly—A Congressional Hearing—Los Angeles Conference—Ireland, Scotland and England

Chapter 26—*1983* 725
Ethiopian Jews—Israel—A Concentration Camp—The Jacobovici Film—NBC Television—Advertisements

Chapter 27—*1984: Haiti* 736
Haiti—Elderhostel to England

Chapter 28—*Operation Lion's Cub* 744
Operation Lion's Cub—Rescue from Sudan—Illnesses—Cancer—An Autobiography

Chapter 29—*1985* 763
Tudor Parfitt—Louis Rapoport—The Testimonial Dinner—Racism—Martinique—London—Chagall—Thyroid—Bonnie Widowed—Perugia—Brussels—Pulmonary Embolisms

Chapter 30—*Cancun, Mexico* 788
Cancun—JDC and Ethiopia—Financing our Life—Helpful Friends—Gifts—Art—A Medal?

Chapter 31—*Summing Up* 801

Index 807

Foreword

DECIDING HOW TO write my autobiography was not easy. While I had collected miscellaneous material for years with the thought of writing something, I did not contemplate anything as formidable as a life history. One suggested that I interview people that I had known over the years, accumulate firsthand data, how they remembered me as a youngster, as an adolescent, as a college student, as a professional, as a teacher, as a writer, as a traveller, as a leader in the Ethiopian Jewish movement. I had no desire to undertake such a vast assignment and the subsequent editing of taped records. Another, thought I should confine my energies to describing and evaluating my professional career, that I have in mind the prospective reader, who could benefit from my experience, if either planning to enter the social welfare field or who wanted to know more about it as a practitioner. Another that I should concentrate only on the Ethiopian Jewish cause. One advised that I write a travelogue with interesting adventures. I was urged by a few to make it "sexy," to invite curiosity, make it easier to sell, perhaps have parts of it reproduced in magazine articles, attract interviewers on the radio and TV. My family wanted me to leave out, no matter what I wrote, anything that might be embarrassing. I was warned by everyone not to make it too long or I would repel all readers.

My natural style is chronological, informal and narrational. I like a beginning, a middle and, with a few permissible digressions, a summing end. I began to write with a simple outline, often a single word. One event led to recalling another. This is how the book developed. My problem was how to cut it to the barest descriptions, eliminate every unnecessary adjective. Otherwise, it would have been endless.

Actually there are four themes. In some instances they are interwoven. One is my personal history. The second is my professional career of work, teaching, writing, building, at times battling, creating. The third is adventures in travel, a search for new vistas, meeting different people, their land, their economy, what they ate, their religion, their art and culture—in 85 different countries. The fourth is the Ethiopian Jewish affair with which I have been occupied for thirty years and particularly since my retirement in 1973.

The book might have been written in four separate sections, perhaps in four separate books, thus appealing to different audiences. Rather than address it to one or several prospective readers, I have written it without regard to any specific peruser. In some respects, I unconsciously wrote it for myself, perhaps to discover the forces or factors that made me do what I did. I'm not sure that I found them. Whatever I omitted has not fundamentally altered my overall story. Whatever is related is largely from my memory, my eyes and my ears, supplemented on some occasions from my files. A few critical friends read brief sections and reacted positively. This made me convinced that I was on the right track. Except for Emma, who read the first draft and made important deletions, corrections and suggestions, and my editor, Robert J. Milch, who improved the last draft expertly, I have asked no one else to examine it. What you will read is what I am responsible for writing.

My editor perceptively commented, that it is a life story told in a "grandfatherly" fashion, as though I was narrating the story to my grandchildren, who would then know much more about their grandfather. If it accomplishes only this, *dayenu*.

Graenum Berger
Sacandaga, NY July 1986

It is better to take refuge in the Lord
Than to trust in man.
It is better to take refuge in the Lord
Than to trust princes.
—Psalm 118:8–9

I am neither a mystic, nor a trusting person.
I trust my own judgment.
I assume responsibility for my own actions.
—Graenum Berger

1908

A flashback review of national and international events in the year that the subject of this book was born.

AN EARTHQUAKE KILLED one hundred thousand people in Calabria, Italy, and across the Straits of Messina in Sicily.

King Carlos I and his son were assassinated in Portugal.

Russia with its newly elected Duma strenuously suppressed all revolutionary outbreaks and disorders.

Austria annexed Bosnia and Herzegovina, which was a prelude to World War I in 1914.

Ethiopia engaged in a dynastic struggle for power as King Menelek was paralyzed.

Pablo Picasso exhibited his first painting in the cubistic manner.

Paul Ehrlich won the Nobel Prize in the field of medicine-physiology.

The United States, with a census of 90,000,000, had not yet recovered from the financial panic and depression of 1907.

Admiral Robert E. Peary embarked on an expedition to reach the North Pole.

The Chicago Cubs defeated the Detroit Tigers four games to one in the baseball World Series.

A fire in a theater in Boyertown, Pennsylvania, killed 170 people.

A mine disaster in Mariana, Pennsylvania, killed 154 workers.

The U.S. Supreme Court upheld the ten-hour-workday law for women in Oregon.

William H. Taft was elected as the twenty-seventh President, succeeding Theodore Roosevelt.

1

Where It All Began

JOHN STREET IN Gloversville, New York—a village in 1847, a city by 1890, nestling in the foothills of the Adirondack Mountains—was only two blocks long. It peaked in the middle of the second block, directly in front of the house in which I was born. A dirt road, muddied every time it rained, it became deeply rutted when the ice of winter began to melt. Macadam paving was to come decades later. But on April 21, 1908, the day I arrived in this world, at 15 John Street, if you walked out of the house on to the knoll and looked northward, you first glanced down the hill and then across Cayudetta Creek, then up the long treeless hill, which we called a mountain, and you could observe the meadow that served as a grazing pasture for the Westland Farm Dairy, owned by the Thompsons, and from where we later purchased our milk. My mother bought milk in quantity, turning it into cream, cheese, and butter. At the top of that rise was a pine tree crown. In the dead of winter, sometimes the snow fell to a depth of eight feet. During a few winters we actually had to tunnel our way out to the street. Annually, the ice never thawed until the end of April. We skiied down that slope in the distance, even piled up snow for jumps. Our skis were made by hand from old pieces of wine barrel staves that we sanded smooth, with heavy harness nailed on, not so firmly, holding our high-laced, almost knee-length, boots. When the crust froze, one could slide down the half-mile hillside on one's back, suffering a few minor face lacerations or cuts on one's hand when a glove or mitten was lost en route.

I was born in this two-story, white-painted clapboard house, which my father had rented in 1907, after the family moved to Gloversville from Barnesboro, Pennsylvania. Some years later he bought the house as an investment. I was delivered at home by Dr. Peters, who subsequently brought into this world my two younger brothers—Samuel and Milton. Their births occurred at 15 Washburn Street, three blocks away. That was another clapboard house with a flat roof and a porch which my father bought in 1911. No one in our family was born in a hospital, whether in Europe or the United States.

My father, Yitzhak Ber, transformed in America to Harry Isaac, was born in Kupishik, Russian Poland, in 1869. He was one of six brothers and sisters. My grandfather was Graenum Falk Berger, after whom I was subsequently named. His claim to fame rested on an event in the 1860s, when the Russian Czar came to his village on a tour of the countryside, and he presented His Majesty with a resolution of welcome on behalf of the Jewish inhabitants.

When Emma and I visited the Theodor Herzl Room in Jerusalem in 1955, she related that my mother, Hannah Batya Cohen, who became Bessie in the States, had told her in 1930 that her uncle, who was a rabbi in Vilna, had accompanied Herzl on one of his trips to Palestine around the turn of the century. Herzl was highly regarded by the Zionist Ashkenazi Jews.

My father married Riva Fine in 1891, and after bearing two children, Shifrah, who became Sadie (1892), and Moses, who became Morris (1894), she suddenly died in 1895. At the age of twenty-six, he married my mother. The year was 1895. She was born in Vilna in 1875 and was an only child. Since her mother had died at her birth, she was raised by an uncle and aunt, Wolf and Batya Cohen.

I have a photograph of my mother's father seated at a table. It portrays a formidable, full face, small eyes, angular nose, fully bearded. There was a resoluteness about his presence. He was not slim, appeared to be of medium height from his sitting position. Over his suit was draped a large *tallit* (prayer shawl), and his head was partly covered by a *kippah* (*yarmulke* or skullcap), testimony to his traditional religious practices as well as his scholarship. My mother was able to read Hebrew and was literate in several European languages. She resembled him in many ways.

My mother bore two daughters who passed away in infancy. The first child to survive was my sister Rachel, born in Russian Poland in 1902. Around the turn of the century, my father and his siblings—Hyman, Morris, Pauline, Sarah Ethel, and Fannie—embarked one by one for America. All but one of them were married, some had children. All apparently had just enough money for the transatlantic passage and to get started in the New Land. My oldest uncle, Hyman, with whom I had the most contact, migrated to the United States in 1894, bringing with him, along with his wife, three sons, Moe, Max, and Henry. Graenum, a fourth son, was born in the United States on March 25, 1901. He was the first of the family to be named after my grandfather, who had died several years before. I do not know how Graenum spelt his name originally, but he decided in adolescence to spell it Graenum. His name might have been spelt either as Granum, Gronum, or Gronem, which later research on my own name turned up. The rest of us emulated his fancy, Latin-like spelling and pronunciation.

My father had already served in the Russian Army for five years thanks to the "liberal" policies of Czar Alexander. With the threat of being recalled for another term, something which he dreaded, he cut off the top of the middle finger of his right hand, so that physically he would not be able to pull a trigger on a gun.

My father was of medium height, walked erect with an aristocratic bearing (based on pictures taken in Russia and the United States shortly after his arrival in 1904), and had a trim moustache. He wore a beard in Russia, but there is no evidence of *payot* (side curls). While he was an observant Orthodox Jew, he did not bear the signs of many of his co-religionists. Perhaps all this had disappeared when he was in the Russian Army. I suspect that my father would have preferred to be an intellectual, but was forced to make a living in business due to the constant urging of my mother. In Russia they had a small *kremel*, a neighborhood store, which my more businesslike mother, who never exceeded four feet ten inches in height, managed. Their stories of Russia in the late nineteenth century, and even the early twentieth, were not filled with any affirmative nostalgia. It was a hateful place to Jews, subjected daily to insults, discrimination, and periodic pogroms, some of which ended in widespread killings by brutal, drunken townspeople or peasants, egged on by officials and lower-echelon priests. It was an environment from which they wished to flee, and my parents began to lay such plans in the 1890s. They sought safety, freedom, and opportunity in a new world.

All of my father's family had preceded him to the *goldene medina*, the golden land, of America. His older brother Hyman and his wife Debora and their three sons came first, settling in New York. There Hyman became a cigar maker. Short, bald-headed, slow of speech, with a philosophical turn of mind, he held your attention as he told a tale or gave you sage advice. In their crowded apartment, they offered hospitality to each family on their arrival in New York, after battling their way through Ellis Island.

Pauline, an unmarried sister, arrived in New York with her mother, my grandmother, in 1898. Pauline met her future husband, Jacob Kanster, a dark-hued, moustached Palestinian Jew, whose family, originally named Kansteroom, had migrated to Palestine from Holland in the early 1800s. Their numerous descendants live in Israel and occupy prominent positions in many walks of life. They were married in 1900 at Uncle Hyman's apartment on Hester Street. Ceal, their first daughter, was born in the United States. They always spoke of coming from the province of Kovno. Jake, as he was affectionately called by everyone, became a copper maker in Newark, New Jersey, and brought up a fine family with whom my parents were most intimate over the years.

My uncle Morris and his wife Fannie settled in Spring Valley, New York. He started out as a peddler and later opened a small general store from which they made a living and raised two daughters.

My aunt Sara Ethel also settled in Spring Valley with her husband, Israel Shapiro, who at first peddled and later opened a candy shop. They had two daughters and a son. My grandmother, Nachama Yochevet lived in Spring Valley until her death in 1909. She was buried in Spring Valley in the Jewish cemetery off Brickchurch Road.

My father's other sister, Fannie, married Joseph Brickman, who became a tailor, settled in Baltimore, Maryland, and brought into this world three daughters and three sons. We also had a great deal of contact with this branch of our extended family.

All were traditional Jews, maintained kosher homes, attended the synagogue, sent their children to Hebrew schools, and in various ways were identified with the Jewish community.

For the first eighteen years of my life, I remember our uncles and aunts and cousins visiting us in Gloversville, or else we made the trek to Brooklyn, Spring Valley, Newark, and Baltimore. We traveled by train on the Fonda, Johnstown and Gloversville Railroad, picking up the New York Central in Fonda, the railroad junction nine miles away, and ending up at the Grand Central Station in New York, having eaten all the way to the metropolis on food prepared in advance by my mother. Then we somehow found our way to Newark and Baltimore via the Pennsylvania Railroad, trying to make the long trip in one day, instead of spending the night in New York. Occasionally we sailed the night boat from Albany, fifty miles from Gloversville, landing in the harbor in New York after a beautiful trip down the Hudson River with its green shadowy shoreline until we reached the stately Palisades, which a geology instructor told me some years later, while I was attending New York University, resulted millions of years ago from the upending of layers of igneous rock.

After 1913, when we acquired our first Model A Ford, we went by car to all of these places, a twelve-hour ride to New York, again during which my mother prepared three full meals for the appeasement of our perpetual hunger. We started eating almost as soon as the vehicle left Gloversville. The roads were narrow, with rounded macadam surfaces, that perilously tipped the car on one side whenever we passed another auto. Gasoline stations were few and far between, but we got good mileage from the light vehicle. If we had punctures, and they were frequent, it was a relatively simple matter to lift the tire off the rim, repair the tube, and pump it back to workability.

All the families seemed to be making a satisfactory living. They lived in good, well kept, and large rented apartments or houses, houses which they subsequently bought. There was plenty of food. The atmosphere was noisy, with a mixture of banter and earnest conversation. Four of us, sometimes sexes were mixed, slept sideways across the beds, so as to accommodate everyone who came and stayed for a day or two, or for a week.

Our extended family maintained close ties in the early days. Some thirty years later, these ties had to be restimulated by the creation of a Berger Cousins' club, because the second generation, now well established, was scattered throughout the United States. Some had graduated from colleges and were now professionals, others were successful businessmen, but all wanted to retain something of the old family, hearthside intimacy. I became the first president of the club.

Since all of the Bergers left Russia, long before Hitler's rise to power, we were one of the exceptional Jewish families that had no Holocaust victims or survivors after World War II and the Nazi depredations. Nor did we have any sentimental memories of the bare earthen floors in our *shtetl* homes, the muddy streets, and the constant fear of Russian intrusions. There has never been a desire on the part of any member of our family to return to the "native" land and see the old country, which had changed so radically as a result of the Russian Revolution and the Second World War.

My father arrived in the United States in 1904. At first he lived with his older brother Hyman on Hester Street in Lower Manhattan. He was apparently able to earn and save enough money, because in less than a year my mother and their three children arrived at Ellis Island, traveling in steerage on the S.S. *Blucher,* which had sailed from Hamburg, Germany, on August 23, 1905, and docked in New York Harbor on September 3. Shifra was only thirteen, Morris was twelve, and Rachel was three years old. This information was gleaned from the ship's passenger manifest.

They brought with them few possessions—a pair of brass candlesticks to celebrate the Sabbath and holy days, a heavy brass mortar and pestle for grinding everything from food to medicine, and some heavy silver-plated knives, forks, and spoons. Photos taken shortly after their arrival and settlement in Pennsylvania reveal that both my father and mother had fur-lined coats, and that my father wore a gold watch and chain, the latter partly crossing his vest, all articles which they must have brought from Europe. They were well dressed, so I'm inclined to believe that they lived quite well in Russia and perhaps brought some money with them, although the ship's manifest disclosed that they had a total of $11 in their possession.

The journey to America was not an easy one. First they traveled by horse and wagon from Sowalki, about one hundred miles south-southwest of Vilna, followed by the long train ride to Hamburg, where they embarked on a ship.

They did not linger long in New York. My father had made arrangements to settle in Houtzdale, Pennsylvania, about twenty-two miles north of Altoona and twenty-five miles northeast of Barnesboro, where they took temporary roots. He had communicated with a brother of his first wife, by the name of Fine, who lived in Barnesboro. I mention Houtzdale because that was where they had a picture taken, although it is possible that the photographer was itinerant and actually photographed them in Barnesboro.

My mother did not like the area and suffered from inhaling the pervasive coal dust that polluted the local air. A decade later the damage to her lungs developed into cancer. I also suspect that she yearned to be closer to her kinsmen in Gloversville. My mother's uncle and aunt, who had raised her as a child, lived there, along with other cousins like Mary Pozefsky, who had married a leather dealer, and another cousin, Isaac (Ike) Cohen, who after a brief sojourn as a peddler had opened a clothing store on Church Street. My father was apparently not doing too well as a peddler in Pennsylvania, for this was a depressed period in the American economy. Anticipating better prospects in Gloversville, they moved there and found the house on John Street.

I was never able to obtain many details about my early years, except one—that while I was still in a carriage and left outside a store while my mother and sister went in to do some shopping, I was reputed to have eaten a number of bananas left in a bag at my side. Despite their worst fears, it had no impact on my health. I have loved bananas all my life, eating them as is, with cereal, in fruit salads, and above all with ice cream in what was and is still called a banana split with all the trimmings.

We were the only Jewish family on John Street, but there were clusters of Jewish families several blocks away on North Street, all of whom worked in the glove industry. Later, when we moved to Washburn Street, our next-door neighbors were the Sacks, the grandparents being milk dealers, while the son worked in a glove factory. Others were the Cashinskys, changed to Cash, who dabbled in insurance and later operated a country hotel in Cashville.

Washburn Street

Within four years, in 1911, my father bought a two-family flat-roofed house with a side porch at 15 Washburn Street at a cost of $1,500, paying $300 down. The property was a corner plot, one hundred by three hundred feet, and included a large barn, where my father housed a horse and cow, with a hayloft in which we often played, after pushing the hay down into the bin for the animals' feeding. My father built coops for chickens, geese, and turkeys, and hand plowed a plot to grow a variety of vegetables. The yard already boasted an apple and a cherry tree.

The kosher meat market, the kosher ritual slaughterer *(shochet)*, and the only synagogue (Orthodox) were in the eastern end of the city, two miles away, a pleasant stroll in the summertime, but an arduous, bitter cold trek on Sabbaths and holidays in the fall, winter, and spring. Since my parents did not ride on the Sabbath (my mother did some years later), we walked with them. My father strode alone to the end of his days. When services ended after nightfall, we picked them up with our car.

My father never violated the Sabbath by riding on any vehicle. This story was related to me by my nephew Edward Finn, having been told to him many years before by my brother, Milton. An elderly man was sitting in a kosher restaurant in Gloversville. Milton was waiting for a table. The man invited him to join him. The man asked if his name was Berger, because he looked like a peddler who knocked on his door in Vail Mills one Friday just before sunset and asked whether he could put his horse and wagon up for a night. The stranger told him he was an observant Jew and did not work or ride on the Sabbath. The farmer told him to put the horse in the barn. My father walked alone the five miles to Gloversville. He returned on Saturday night to pick up the horse and wagon. For a number of years thereafter my father drove us by horse and wagon, and later we went by car, to visit the Lingenfelter farm, where we purchased eggs and vegetables, partially in appreciation for the courtesy that had been extended that Sabbath evening. Milton, who was not born when this incident took place, looked more like my father than the rest of his children, and the face lingered in this elderly farmer's memory.

My father walked many miles on Friday nights and Erev holidays later on, when we started out too late by car, and had not reached our destination. It was evidence of the strength of his commitment to the performance of Jewish mitzvahs as an early immigrant and later as a well adjusted American citizen.

Neither of my parents, although well educated as Europeans, ever learned to write more than simple English words, and they always spoke with a distinctive accent. Conversations were invariably in Yiddish, which later became liberally sprinkled with Americanisms. My parents could speak Yiddish, Polish, Russian, and some German; both could write Yiddish, both could read Hebrew, so in some respects it was a multilingual household. When I left home to enter college, and thereafter until their decease, I corresponded with them in Yiddish, which I had learned to read, write and speak.

When I was four, my father decided I must initiate my Jewish studies.

In 1912 there was no daily and permanent Hebrew school associated with the synagogue. That was to come a year later. The synagogue was for me an imposing building. It was built of great blocks of gray stone, and one walked up the steep steps to an exterior that had four tall columns, with a Romanesque arch under which there was a stained-glass window with its large Star of David, under which there was the replica of the Ten Commandments in Hebrew lettering. The interior was attractive, with its decorated *bimah*, raised above the floor level, which housed the ark and its Torahs, the podium from which the prayers were chanted. The second-floor balcony was reserved for women, since in this sanctuary it was forbidden for men and women to sit together. I was always awed as I sat next to my father on the wide, dark-stained oaken benches. The synagogue was located on East Fulton Street, where a large Jewish population lived on the contiguous side streets, and where kosher food could be purchased.

Four late afternoons a week, after he returned from peddling (Friday he ceased work at noon to prepare for the Sabbath), my father brought home a *melamed* (teacher), who also was a *shochet* (ritual slaughterer), to spend one hour teaching me the Aleph Bais, the ABCs of the Hebrew alphabet, so that I could begin to read the prayers and eventually the Humash, the Five Books of Moses. We sat in the dining room at the round oak table with the large multicolored glass shade (now a Tiffany antique) which clothed a gas lamp, as I repeated after the teacher each of the Hebrew words, for we were taught to commit everything to memory rather than rely on the text or book itself. My father sat through this torturous hour as I stumbled over the words, but I can still recall the way he smiled with pride as I finally mastered each word and later whole sentences and paragraphs, no mean accomplishment for a five-year-old. The teacher received 50 cents for each lesson.

A year later, I was sent to the newly established Hebrew school, where the teachers, whether bearded and traditional or more modern and clean-shaven were changed every year or two, usually because of problems with the synagogue leadership rather than the students. Rabbi Katz sat us at a long table and taught us in pairs for ten to fifteen minutes, testing us on our reading and translation from Hebrew into Yiddish, and then gave us some homework and dismissed us. Whoever made a mistake incurred his wrath and was rapped on his knuckles with a long ruler. We were publicly admonished and shamed. Luckily I escaped both his tongue and punishment, because my partner was inferior to me in this setting of sheer rivalry. But the white-bearded, elderly rabbi was also a scholar and well informed on what was going on in this world. I remember June 28, 1914 as though it was yesterday. He told us that the Archduke Ferdinand of Austria, the oldest nephew of Emperor Franz Joseph, had been assassinated in Sarajevo (now Yugoslavia). He mourned this tragic event, extolling the benign Austrian Emperor because he had treated the Jews so well. He predicted that the assassination would bring about a *milchomo,* a war, which would have serious implications for Europe, the Jews, and the whole world.

Moving to Washburn Street gave us Jewish neighbors, also a Jewish tenant on the second floor, who helped pay the mortgage, interest, and taxes. Our first tenants were the Spinacks; tragically the mother died, and the father, left with very small children, put one out for adoption and left the city with the others. The child was adopted by one of the leading and wealthiest Jews in the city, and grew up to be a fine citizen, active in the Jewish and the general community. Later, one of the other sons returned to the city, established a thriving business, and became president of the synagogue.

Our second tenant was the Rosenbaum family. They came from Warsaw, and I remember the endless quarrels between them and my parents over distinctions among Jews, the pronunciation of Yiddish, and political issues. The Rosenbaums had three daughters, two about my age with whom I went to school and socialized. They eventually left the city, and from reports we received prospered elsewhere.

My father peddled his wares (pots, pans, cloth, needles, thread, and other household items) to the farms and isolated families that lived on the outskirts of the city, making himself sufficiently understood in English to do rather well financially. He was a genial, outgoing person friendly to every stranger. He was always an early riser; he began each day by donning his *tefillin* (phylacteries) and *tallit* (prayer shawl) and reciting the morning prayers, then would feed the animals and tend the garden, using selected garbage, including egg shells, to nourish the earth. After preparing a simple breakfast and some food to take with him for the day (a crust of bread, a hard-boiled egg, a whole tomato or cucumber, a jar of cold coffee), he harnessed his horse and was off before any of us had risen.

While peddling, he would pick up whatever junk—iron, copper, brass—he found lying in someone's yard, paying little or nothing, and would bring it back to our yard, where he piled it in ever higher heaps behind the house. In 1914, when World War I began in Europe, there was a need for scrap iron. The Kramers from nearby Amsterdam, who were in the scrap metal business, came over one day and bought the junk, piled fifteen feet high and occupying a yard forty by sixty feet. It undoubtedly provided my parents with a lot of money and changed our lifestyle.

We children eagerly awaited my father's return at the end of a day of peddling. Running down the street, we would jump on the back of Nellie and triumphantly ride into the barn, where we unharnessed her and fed her oats, hay, and water. This came to an end when my father sold the horse and bought a Model T Ford.

It was also the end of the huge and interesting junk pile, where we found hidden treasures to play with. We converted these items into useful toys. I recall making wheeled carts and even sleds with brakes to slow us down on the snow-covered hilly streets.

Leather Business

While peddling, my father had begun to dabble in leather hides. The major industry in Gloversville and all of Fulton County was tanning leather and manufacturing leather gloves.

Sir William Johnson, an Englishman, had borrowed an Indian trade in the eighteenth century and with English ingenuity converted it into a thriving business. The local forests abounded with conifers, whose bark was indispensable in the tanning of leather. Gloversville was originally called Stump City. The area was overrun with deer, whose skins were useful for coats, pants, hats, and gloves. The water was unusually pure, and in combination with nature's other elements led to the economic development of an entire county. First came the English, then the Germans, then the Russian-Polish Jews, and finally the Italians, to enter in and dominate this industry. While all finally came to work in the leather business, the Italians had originally settled in Gloversville in order to build the Fonda, Johnstown and Gloversville Railroad. The city reached its largest population of approximately 25,000 persons in the 1920s, and since has been in a steady decline, the glove and leather industry was gradually displaced by other industries.

When I went to high school in the early 1920s, I was taught how to skin rabbits and actually tan the hide in my chemistry class. The chemical tanning process had superseded the aboriginal method of preparing leather. Until the depression of the 1930s, Gloversville was a one-industry town, and that is what the town officials and the manufacturers wanted it to be, in order to prevent the unionization of labor, keep wages down, and prevent competition with other types of work.

While there were already many factories in my youth, a good deal of the process of making gloves was performed at home by piece work, employing female and even child labor. My mother, my two older sisters, and I, before I was seven, performed some of these relatively simple tasks, which we classified as "pulling ends." Embroidery of the back of the glove was somewhat more complicated with its stitched decorations.

The sale of our junk apparently gave my parents enough money to fix over our house in 1915. A new front entrance was built to the tenanted second floor. The porch was shifted from the side to the front. Electricity replaced the gas fixtures. A hot air furnace with a maze of pipes in the cellar provided heat through floor ventilators, replacing the wood- and coal-burning potbellied stoves, and an up-to-date gas stove took the place of our old kitchen stove. The floor heat warmed us and dried our clothes when we came in from the cold and wet.

The wooden water closet, which hung three quarters of the way to the ceiling, with a long pull chain and wooden handle, made the water rush down, filling the room and house with noise. It was a Mott's Primo, imported, direct action, then in vogue. We replaced it with the modern type, where the tank, sitting on the stool, responded to a pressing of the handle, and was much quieter.

Until this time I had been sleeping on a makeshift bed, which came down over the bathtub at the rear of the house. When we replaced this with a modern bathroom and added two bedrooms, my isolation ended and I began to share a bed with my older brother, Morris; after he left our house to get married, Sam replaced him. New furniture took the place of the former furnishings, which, if we had kept them, would now be worth a fortune as antiques.

There are other memories connected with that bed over the bathtub. On Friday nights my father often brought a stranger into the house on his return from the synagogue. He was wont to do this because he was not only hospitable but he hungered to learn more about the outside world. We subscribed to two Yiddish newspapers, *Der Tag* ("The Day") and the *Morning Journal,* which he often read aloud to us at the table and elsewhere, when an interesting item was printed. He had a thirst for knowledge and quizzed every person with whom he came into contact. This trait was one that he inculcated in me.

One Friday night—the year was 1913—a black man appeared at the synagogue wearing a robe, a *tallit*, and a *kippah*. He claimed to be a Falasha, an Ethiopian Jew. He spoke Yiddish. He had come to the city like many itinerants, collecting money for Falasha relief. He walked home with us, had dinner, and occupied my bed. He remained over the Sabbath, went to shul with my father and me on that day, and in the evening he was given money for both the relief fund and his carfare, so that he could reach Utica, the next Jewish-settled city.

This was my first contact with a black person. There were a dozen black families residing in town, who belonged to the A.M.E. Zion church, which was a block east of the synagogue. Some of their children attended school, but none were ever in my classes. Many decades later when I became involved with Ethiopian Jews, this flashback came to mind. My studies have revealed that the visitor could not have been an Ethiopian Jew.

How am I so accurate as to dates and what my family and others looked like? I have dated pictures taken in front of the house before it was remodeled. In one I am wearing a blue sailor suit, mounted on a pony, with my sister Rachel, in her white dress and stockings, standing majestically at my side. The year was 1914. An earlier photo (1911) showed me wearing immaculate white short pants and jacket.

My mother, by 1913, had six children in the household, no help, no electric machines to wash and dry clothes. I still recall the long lines of clothing hanging outside on a sunny day. In the coldness of winter or on a rainy day, lines were hung in the kitchen over the stove or in the cellar. We did have a hand wringer, and I remember losing a nail of my finger while clothing was mangled. It eventually grew back as good as the old one, but I never lost another. The whiteness of my clothes was due to her cooking the wash in a huge copper tub filled with steaming water.

My mother arose just before we were off to school, preparing our breakfast while still wearing her robe. Some years later, when she became ill, we were taught to be self-sufficient in getting our breakfast meal, so as to spare her from having to perform this task. I have a vague recollection of my mother holding my young brothers in her arms as she went about preparing meals. She was an excellent cook, but not so good as a baker, but there was always a bounteous and varied feast at dinner and supper. On Friday nights, we ate after my father and I returned from the synagogue. Candles had been lighted at nightfall. There were the prayers over the wine and challah, chicken soup, chopped liver, boiled or roasted chicken, compote, cake, and tea. We were never allowed to mix meat and dairy dishes, pots and pans. Meats were always kashered with salt and thoroughly rinsed. The two sets of dishes were easily distinguished and separated on the shelves. So were the towels used to dry the dishware—one red and the other blue. For Pesach (Passover) there were completely different dishes and some pots and pans. Others were made pesachdik with red-hot stones to scour their sides. The children joined in this ritual act.

The main meal was served at noon, after we returned from school or work. My father was always present at this meal once he gave up peddling, since his business was in our home, his leather stock in a shed at the rear of the house. It was a family meal twice a day. There were no packaged lunches in brown bags to take to school, and no food was served in school. Restaurants were available, but those nearby served only nonkosher food, which we were not allowed to eat. Some years later a kosher restaurant was opened in Gloversville which we frequented.

When our coal stove was a source of cooking and of heat for the rear part of the house, I can still inhale the pungent smells of a matzes herring, carefully selected by my mother at the delicatessen, being wrapped in newspapers and baked over the coals until hot and done, served with homemade cold sauerkraut for a Sunday breakfast or lunch. And how can I possibly forget the bakery smells on a cold day when we returned from school to find a dish full of cakes and cookies that we quickly devoured with a cup of hot or cold cocoa.

When guests dropped in on a Sabbath afternoon, a custom that regrettably has been abandoned except in sizable Jewish neighborhoods, there was always cake, fruit, and tea. No milk was permitted with coffee after meat was served. It was many years later, when my older siblings could no longer abide having their coffee without milk or cream, that a reform was permitted, providing they drank it in another room and not at the dining table.

My mother was an extremely efficient and productive *baaleboste,* the one Yiddish word which describes her concisely. While there were stores and bakeries, she preferred to make a great deal of what we ate. Milk products and bakery goods were daily delivered to the door. I vividly recall the large, heavy black bread baked in an immense pan, whose fragrant odor permeated the house for the better part of the day. Challah was baked before the Sabbath, along with cakes and cookies, *kichel* being my mother's and our favorite. There was often enough to last the better part of the week. Later when a kosher bakery opened up, we bought seeded rye and pumpernickel bread and challah from that outlet, but it was either a long walk or an auto ride to Washington Street.

Pickles were put up in great crocks (where did they disappear to, for they would now also be valuable antiques). The crock was covered with a board to keep the pickles wading in the brine. A heavy stone topped the board. They were best when immersed for a week or two, what is now called fresh dills, and the smell and taste of dill are still more than a memory. We still seek out dill in season and freshen our salads with this aromatic herb.

Sauerkraut was made in similar large crocks. When my family bought the first cabbage shredder, it made the rounds of our neighbors, who also welcomed this early time-saving device. The fragrance of the kraut embraced the household and enhanced many a meal.

When eggs were plentiful and cheap, my parents put the eggs in another large crock in a solution that was then called water glass. It had an odd odor. When I reached into the crock to pick out the eggs for a meal, there was a gray, gooey mass which you had to wash off your hand. When I went to Hong Kong in 1962 and tasted the "hundred-year-old eggs" that the Chinese took such pride in preserving, the taste had the same flavor as the preservative that we had used forty years earlier. To my horror, I later learned that the preservative was actually 40 percent sodium silicate ($Na_2Si_3O_2$), a chemical that is also used for fireproofing fabrics, a detergent in soaps, adhesives, waterproofing walls, in cements, in cold water paints, for abrasive wheels, and to weight silks. That we survived this chemical preservative is a miracle.

It may have had some effect on the health of members of my family who died of cancer.

When the canning season came round in the fall, my mother with our help put up all kinds of fruits and vegetables—peaches, pears, beans, corn, peas, strawberries, black berries, blue berries, raspberrys (always my favorite)—some of which we bought, some we grew, and some we picked in the woods. We bottled our own ketchup. We made our own sarsaparilla and root beer.

My father was an intellectual. He was also a farmer. When our back yard could not produce enough, he bought a half-acre tract about three miles away in east Berkshire, just over the city line, and we drove there by horse and wagon several times a week in late spring to plant potatoes, beets, carrots, and corn. We weeded the fields, and harvested the crops, storing the food in a cold cellar. Much of it lasted most of the winter.

In winter, the wagon was changed to a sled, which my father also used for peddling. It was a great treat to bundle up and go for a ride around the city and into the countryside. If we pleaded long enough, my father would sometimes permit us to take the reins and lead the horse over the snow-covered roads. We would come home half frozen and gather around the potbellied or kitchen stoves to warm ourselves, and be served hot foods and drinks.

Lincoln Street, which bordered our house, was great for sledding. There was little auto traffic in those days, so it was relatively safe coming down a half-mile hill without having to worry that cross traffic might suddenly issue from the side streets. One of our friends had a huge sled steered in the front by a wheel and at the back by another fixed sled with a steel brake. A dozen people could sit on the sled and take perilous rides, singing or screaming all the way.

The year 1912 marked a momentous event for me—my sister Sadie's marriage. She was twenty, a beautiful woman, articulate, with a sharp tongue, biting wit. She never went beyond sixth grade in school for she had to work to help the family and herself. Sadie fell in love with Samuel Finn, twenty-seven, a glove cutter with great expertise. He had come with a large family from Vilna, Russia. They all settled in a large house on Summer Street. For a number of years after they were married, the respective families would visit each other's homes, attended by much talk, noise, and tables laden with food.

The marriage ceremony was performed in Amsterdam, fourteen miles away, because we had no rabbi to perform this ritual in Gloversville. The wedding party travelled there in a number of automobiles. Neither I nor my young brother attended the ceremony. I distinctly recall the feast after all returned, the guests crowding our original house on Washburn Street. The rooms were still lit by gas, with their small fragile mantles, so that it had the eeriness of semi-darkness. After a few drinks, my father was the life of the party. He could easily compose two-line rhyming couplets in Yiddish for any special event, and everyone in attendance was mentioned in his long, pleasant-voiced, sing-song recitation.

Then my father, in his Judaic and familial generosity, made an extravagant toast to my sister and her new husband, and donated the magnificent sum of $25, which seemed to everyone a fortune, to a yeshiva, a Hebrew school, in Palestine, which he had never seen, and a land, regretably, that he would never reach, for he died in March 1947, a year before the State of Israel was established. We were always taught that some part of our resources, no matter how small, must be given to charity, preferably a Jewish charity, each week, each holiday, and for very special occasions, which he labeled *simchas,* joyous events. There were several *pushkes* (charity boxes) on the wall of the kitchen to remind us to perform these benevolent acts.

My father had a fine voice, and during Yom Kippur (Day of Atonement), when we spent the entire day in the synagogue, he would be called on to *duchan* because he was a *kohen,* priest, when the *kohanim* blessed the entire congregation. He stood on the *bimah,* the platform where the services were conducted, alongside of the other *kohanim,* in stocking feet, for one could not wear leather shoes in that holy place, his head covered with a *kippah,* wearing a huge *tallit* with black stripes, swaying with the chanting of each prayer, then bending on his knees to the floor in supplication for himself and the congregation, always an awesome sight for me even as an adult. It made me intensely proud of my father. On a few occasions in my life, I have been called upon to perform the identical ritual act.

My father became a citizen of the Untied States on January 12, 1915, and it was a momentous day for him and for our household. We hung the American flag in front of our house for this singular happening, and subsequently for all patriotic occasions—Decoration Day and July Fourth.

The Kindergarten Trauma

I put up no resistance to going to school, initially. In 1913 I was five and eligible for kindergarten. In that large room, we always seemed to be sitting around in a semicircle on small, heavy oak chairs. We walked to school about a half a mile away, down Washburn Street, turning right on Grand, crossing West to Orchard, then left past Christie to Spring Street, where the Spring Street School was situated.

We were given a penny each day for candy, which we spent at the red store at the corner of Spring and Orchard, owned by a man named Freeman. We lingered long in making a decision, exasperating the owner, who did not have much patience with his young customers. I liked chocolates with white sprinkles and jelly beans. I disliked licorice, which most of the children bought, because you got a lot more for your money. I have carried that distaste for licorice into my adult years.

After making our purchases, we took our last steps, half a block to the school, set back at least 250 feet from the road, built of red brick in the

Victorian style. It is now gone, replaced by a playground, where other generations have come to rest and cavort.

In the second semester, I had a hateful experience. I was sitting in that semicircle with a twelve inch by twelve inch slate in my hand on which we wrote or made drawings. For some unaccountable reason—perhaps I was bored, perhaps I was already given to that curmudgeon streak that has turned up on occasions in my life,—I sailed my slate across the room and it struck a little girl schoolmate.

Before I knew what was happening, I was hauled by my irate teacher to the principal's office. Miss Prager, of medium height, was wearing a tight-fitting black dress, of shiny material. I looked up at her with tears, almost pleading. She had black, shiny hair tied in a bun at the back, a mole on the right side of her upper lip with black hairs conspicuously growing around it. I was severely admonished for this unforgivable sin of striking another child. I stopped crying as much out of fear as the severity of the lecture. The teacher escorted me to the kindergarten room. When her back was turned, I fled from the room, ran home, and thereafter refused to go to school.

Each morning my father drove me to school in the horse and wagon, with me crying all the way, and left me in the yard. Then I ran home. I did not go to school for over a year, missing the second half of kindergarten and all of the first grade. How I got away with it, I do not know, but the experience must have been traumatic enough, for my parents finally gave in to my unchildlike resistance. How I spent that time I do not recall, except for two things—I went to the daily Hebrew school across town, and I went to the Carnegie Library on the way to the synagogue, because they were both on East Fulton Street, a few blocks from each other. I apparently borrowed and read a lot of books, which in the long run may have been even better for me than attending the classes. My mother used to say that maybe the absence from school wasn't so terrible, because when I finally returned, I kept going to school until I was twenty-four years old and had completed my graduate studies in social work.

* * *

My brother Sam (Samuel David) was born December 4, 1911. There was excitement in the house when he was delivered. I do not recall suffering from any sibling rivalry, even though I was my mother's favorite above all her children until the day she died. Sam was tiny, but very early showed the feistyness which was to mark his life. Blond and small of build (he never grew beyond five feet five inches), he was a coxswain on the crew of the University of Wisconsin, which he entered at the age of sixteen in 1928, having graduated from high school at fifteen, working for a year as a newspaper reporter before matriculating. I still see him in that picture taken in 1912 at the side of our house, looking alert and older as he sat up in a baby carriage, flanked by my sister Rachel in a white dress and white socks, with a white ribbon in her hair and with handsome patent-leather sandals. I stood next to the other side of the carriage in a white suit and white knickerbockers, wearing long black hose to the knee and black shoes. I had a grim look on my face. My father was behind the carriage, his face thin and boney, adorned with a moustache, standing dignified in a trim suit, stiff collar and tie, topped with a jaunty derby.

In 1914, along came my youngest brother, Milton Eugene, born on the first day of spring, March 21. His arrival was noted by all of us, as he too was born in the house, delivered by the same Dr. Peters who had, as an obstetrician—general practitioner, delivered Sam and me. Now we were six plus my parents, but we had also taken in a boarder, Nellie Weinstein, a daughter of a friend in Europe, who wanted to live in a house where she could be part of a family. She lived with us for a number of years.

* * *

We lived in a period when there were no antibiotics and relatively few illnesses could be prevented by inoculations. We were vaccinated against smallpox, but suffered through all the other childhood diseases like measles and chicken pox. It seems, in retrospect, that we were always either underclothed or overdressed. During the bitter winters, we often came in nearly frozen. I recall several times being frostbitten on my fingers and toes. Our house was always overheated. The fear of too much fresh air kept the windows tightly closed in the colder periods. We lived close together, usually slept two in a bedroom, and we caught each other's illnesses.

Colds, sore throats, and chest coughs were frequent, along with many stomach upsets, the latter, I suspect, from the too heavy diet. We ate raw meat, freshly chopped, at least every other week, a delicacy, served with onions and sometimes a raw egg, usually spread on pumpernickel bread. My mother thought it was good for our constitution. I continued eating raw meat as an adult, even when I went out to good restaurants in the United States and abroad, and only gave it up in 1973, at the age of sixty-five, on doctor's orders, that it was a dangerous food. I recall ordering it in a famous restaurant in Brussels, Belgium, where it was garnished with mayonnaise and labeled *"steak americaine."* I had expected a real steak, but this was a delicious nostalgic substitute. But that was 1955, when my stomach still performed perfectly.

When we were ill, chicken soup was a standard prescription and remedy for anything from a cold to a stomach upset. For the normal sore throat, my mother would heat salt, put it in flannel, and wrap it around our necks. Another household recipe for illnesses was honey heated in tea or, better yet, a sweet raspberry jam. Lemon was added to give it some tartness. It seemed to possess magical healing powers. Hot cocoa, hot milk, hot postum, but no coffee was served while we were convalescing. I actually never tasted coffee, of which I am an addict, now in my later years using the best decaffeinated brands (Colombian water-processed), until I went off to college in 1925. My parents prepared it with chicory, which I have tried and found interesting. I do not know whether it was used to stretch the pound of coffee or just to give it a European flavor, because this is something that they brought with them from the other side of the ocean.

Getting back to illnesses, if we had a chest cold, it was treated by rubbing in hot chicken fat as a poultice. Later this was changed to store-bought salves with equally aromatic odors. For cuts and bruises, apart from iodine, which stained the injury, there was always Antiphlogistin, a sure-fire remedy that invariably cured. Dr. Rose Koblenz-Goldberg, Emma's doctor in Pelham, was still using it in 1985.

The first serious illness struck our family when Milton contracted diphtheria. Only two years old, he had raging fevers, which medications at first seemed unable to control, and the doctor sadly informed the distraught family that he might pass away. But thanks to the European antitoxin developed in 1890, the fever eventually subsided and the disease was overcome, so that he could continue to live, play, and grow to manhood. It was a scare that did not leave us for a long time.

During the dreaded influenza epidemic of 1917–1918, when huge numbers of Americans died, the scourge struck our entire family, sparing only me. All were bedridden, with an overtaxed doctor dropping in from his exhausting calls to medicate them. I had to do all the household chores—buying food, preparing meals, and seeing that everyone took their medication. The disease was so widespread that the local armory was converted into a temporary hospital. In those days the doctor carried all kinds of pills with him, so that we seldom had to go to the drug store, except for unusual medical orders. Gradually the disease subsided, and all returned to their normal pursuits. School had been cancelled during the period when the disease was rampant. The malady spread during the period when America was involved in World War I.

We, like most Americans, had prospered from the war which began in Europe in 1914. In that year my father went into the leather merchandising business, a field which profited from the demand for leather and gloves for soldiers overseas. We rebuilt our house and refurbished its interior with new rooms and furniture. We acquired an automobile, installed electricity, and put in the first telephone on our block. Within a year, my father purchased the house in which I was born on John Street. These were all marks of economic success and a higher social status. With our new telephone, we undertook additional responsibilities. Our neighbors told their relatives and friends of this technological innovation. We began receiving calls for them. It was a nuisance to summon them for each call, so we introduced a large bell on the front porch with the appropriate number of peals for six of our neighbors. Within a few years, happily, they installed their own telephones, and this clanging and bother was abandoned.

Business proved so good that my father took his son-in-law, Sam Finn, in as a partner, and there was benefit for both families. Sadie and Sam had added two sons to their ménage by the end of the war.

After America entered the fray in 1917, shortages began to develop in many commodities, but particularly coal and flour, which had to be rationed. When my family was ill with influenza, I pulled a cart or sled, the latter in winter, down to the railroad yard, where one could purchase a bag of coal at a time. Fortunately the yard was less than a half mile from our home, so that the task was not too difficult for a lad of nine or ten. However, getting that rationed bag of flour was another thing, since the source was easily a mile away. I had to perform these onerous chores, for even my brother-in-law, Sam, was laid up with the flu, and there was no one to drive the car.

We were patriotic. Bought Liberty Bonds. Displayed the American flag. We were overjoyed when the war ended on November 11, 1918. I ran down to Main Street early that morning and joined the impromptu parade that was rapidly mobilized to celebrate the Allies victory.

When the veterans of the war returned home, we welcomed them with a huge parade that passed under a large replica of the French Arc de Triomphe, which had been built on North Main Street. All the buildings were decorated with bunting.

As soon as he obtained citizenship, my father enrolled in the Democratic party, and in 1916, his first presidential election, he voted for Woodrow Wilson. Why he became a Democrat in a Republican town is attributable to the independence that he always exhibited on political and all other matters. He had a critical and rebellious nature, deepened by an emotional sense of justice, particularly for the have-nots. Unlike many other Jews from Eastern Europe, who were Bundists and socialists, he never moved that far left. He was not given to sloganeering or easy solutions to difficult problems. He was essentially an individualist and entrepreneur. He could not identify with the Republicans in Gloversville, who were led by businessmen, factory owners, and had a stake in maintaining the status quo. He could not understand why the majority of workers, afraid of being dubbed "foreigners" or "radicals," chose to vote Republican. The workers changed their political allegiance only in the 1930s with the depression. In any event, Pa, as we called him (and we called our mother Ma), remained a staunch Democrat all of his life, and two of his sons, Sam and I, imbibed that political philosophy and with some modifications pursued that position. Wilson was a hero in our household, and we mourned his death. My father supported Wilson's Fourteen Points and regretted the president's failure to get them into the Versailles peace treaty. We also rooted for the League of Nations, which America refused to join. Politics was not a foreign subject in our home.

Cultural Milieu

Our parents did many things to give enrichment to our cultural lives. There were not too many books in our house in the early years, and those that found their way on to the shelves were either religious or written in Yiddish. Although we all spoke this language with some fluency, I was never attracted to reading them until I was much older and could appreciate the writings of a Sholom Aleichem or an Isaac Leib Peretz, both of whom were alive in my early years. My father spoke of them with respect. I was, frankly, not too interested in their description of Jewish life in Eastern Europe, an environment from which my family had escaped and which even they were not prone to describe to us. For them it had neither romance nor nostalgia.

My father wrote a number of witty pieces that were published in the Yiddish press. He pasted them into a little notebook, which I kept in my files after he passed away.

The witticisms that my father wrote usually made reference to a Rebbe, who was the dispenser of advice and wisdom, to someone who came to him with a knotty problem and a humorous but moral solution. The following piece is a good example.

> A woman once hauled her husband before the Rebbe, accusing him of beating her. When the Rebbe asked: "Why do you beat her?" the man replied: "Because she drinks too much." Thereupon the Rebbe told the woman that she was not to drink anymore, while the husband was instructed never to beat her again. The wife, obeying the Rebbe's injunction, took to dunking in place of drinking, and the husband ceased to beat her and resorted to pinching her instead. (Trans. by Carl Urbont.)

Since we were a family that had "arrived," we bought an upright Wing piano in shiny mahogany which sat solidly in our front living room. Rachel and I were introduced to the instrument when she was eleven and I was just five, but it never quite took with either of us. After a few years, lessons were abandoned. I can still see the teacher, a man solemn in mien, looking more like an undertaker, utterly bored as he half listened to me punching out the scales, fingering too many musical errors. He received 50 cents for the hour's lesson divided between Rachel and myself. He was a competent musician, for he made his real living as an organist in one of the Protestant churches. But I did learn to read music, and all my life I could somehow transpose simple compositions in my own rhythm and style. Years later when I sat down at a piano either in our own home or elsewhere and started to play Irving Berlin's "Remember" (he is still alive at ninety-eight as I write) and Billy Rose's "You Tell Her, I S-T-U-T-T-E-R," my total repertoire, people would gather round me and ask for more. I obviously and successfully begged off, for that was it. I was able to finger out the melodies of most of the popular tunes of the day. When we were young, at a party, or at college, or in a fraternity house, or at the community center or in a camp which I directed, if there was no other real pianist in the crowd, I would play the tunes and keep them singing into the wee hours.

But music we had to study, so my parents bought me a small, inexpensive violin. If I couldn't be a great virtuoso at the piano, perhaps they might arouse the musical genius which was supposed to lurk in every Eastern European Jewish boy, and thus I might become another Mischa Elman. But my technical skill was poor, my interest in the violin approached the zero mark, I had to be constantly harassed to practice. I never realized my parents' ambition that I might someday be a concert artist, even if only for a local audience. I wasted two years. Yet in my adult years I loved to listen to the great violinists, and I think that I heard most of the great play—Kreisler, Heifetz, Elman, Zimbalist, Menuhin, down to the more recent celebrities.

I then tried the banjo and that didn't take either, but I did learn to play the ukelele, which was popular in my youth. Later on, as an adolescent, I bought a set of drums and made a good deal of my expenses during my high school years playing in an orchestra.

We had a Victor phonograph with a large horn, on which we played records of Jewish cantors singing religious music, of operatic stars like Enrico Caruso, and disks from the current musical comedies as well as band music. We turned in that Victor about 1915 for a modern mahogany Victrola, hand-wound with a convenient section to store records. Popular records were added to our collection, so that we could dance and sing.

Movies and vaudeville were the most popular forms of entertainment. For five cents, we would usually be shipped off to either the Family or the Darling theater, where we might sit through several performances lasting all afternoon until nightfall and see a full-length movie, a serial with Pearl White or Ruth Rolland, and a few vaudeville acts. Later, after Meyer and Louis Schine came to Gloversville in 1919, the Hippodrome was added to the movie houses, and finally they built a luxury theater, the Glove.

From time to time a touring group of Jewish actors would appear and the entire Jewish community seemed to turn out for such a special event. As a child I was taken to see the *Yiddish King Lear.* Only when I went to high school did I learn that the original had been written in Elizabethan

English by William Shakespeare and that he wasn't a Jewish playwright.

There was an electric trolley car system that enabled one to get around the city of twenty-five thousand people, but we seldom used it. Despite the terrible accident in 1902 that killed twelve people, we took the trolley out of town to Mountain Lake for picnics until 1916 when this line was terminated. The site was beautiful and cool.

We walked or drove out in horse and wagon to Wohlfarth's Pond at the western end of the city for day picnics. Occasionally, we made similar visits to Myer's Park on a hill at the eastern end. In winter we walked to the nearby playground, which was flooded and frozen for ice skating.

A major event to which we looked forward each spring was the arrival of the circus. I would run down to the railroad yard before dawn, often with my father, to watch them unload the animals and vehicles. Then we would walk at the side of the animals, particularly the huge elephants, to the circus grounds a mile away and observe the workmen erect the massive tents. Later in the afternoon or evening, we would witness the bizarre and spectacular events under the canvas.

The periodic parades on Decoration Day and July Fourth were experiences we did not miss as spectators. We frequently marched in them during the early years. Dressed in our best clothes, carrying an American flag, we paraded through the streets. On Decoration Day, we would end up in a cemetery where the veterans of previous wars (this was before World War I) were honored. They marched in their uniforms or at least wore a soldier's hat of their service period. On July Fourth we terminated in a park, where the classical orations, at some length, were delivered by former soldiers, or the mayor, or a prominent clergyman—their speeches seemingly shortened only when the crowd began to thin. Our parents encouraged our participation and usually accompanied us, for the events had meaning to us developing Americans. Today, the holidays are a day off from work, the holiday not even coinciding with the original date, so that it has little or no significance. Yet, in Pelham, a tiny village, these events are formally executed each year across the street, in front of our high school, so I still see some adults and children gather for these unique events, and for the hour of the parade, again observe the same enthusiasm I experienced as a child.

Sacandaga

Sacandaga became our second home. Sixteen miles from Gloversville, which, before the fifty-five-mile-an-hour limit on driving imposed by law in the 1970s, and of course when we were younger, we boastfully drove in sixteen minutes. The development of the railroad in the nineteenth century speeded up transportation and opened up this vast country. It also had a great deal to do with the expansion of recreational facilities and pursuits. Spurs of the New York Central Railroad made accessible the interior of the Adirondack Mountains with its multitudinous parks and lakes, green covered year round because of the conifer forests. This preserve allowed wealthy New Yorkers to acquire huge tracts for a song, on which they built rustic-looking but extravagant homes, in one of which I once played billiards in a room the size of a farmer's house. The railroads encouraged the development of camps for children, first for the upper classes to give their children a sense of the wonders of nature and to balance or counter their already developing urban lifestyle. Toward the end of the nineteenth century, with millions of immigrants streaming into this country and confined to the stifling, unhealthy, overcrowded city slums, philanthropic organizations saw an opportunity to provide some health-giving care under the slogan that the poor needed "sunshine and carrots" for a week or two in the same rural atmosphere. It was hoped that this brief exposure to nature would give them enough healthy stimulants to survive the rigors of city dwelling for the rest of the year.

The area north of Gloversville also benefitted from the railroad. A connecting spur with the New York Central was opened in 1870, taking three years to build. It was called the Fonda, Johnstown and Gloversville Railroad (FJ&G), its rails running from Fonda through Johnstown and Gloversville to Northville for twenty-five miles, ending in the Adirondacks. Northville was on the Sacandaga River, named after an Indian tribe. Another branch of the railroad led from Gloversville to Broadalbin, a village which our family frequented. Apart from the railroad's aiding the growing industries in these relatively small communities, its management created a delightful recreational resort called Sacandaga Park to which the steam-driven engines with a train of cars brought the wealthy from New York, including many well-to-do German Jews, all of whom stayed in typical large inns, where waiters served them day and night, good food was purveyed, and chamber music played during the day, while another orchestra entertained with dancing in the evening. There were also band concerts on a rustic bandstand amongst tall pine trees. For those in the middle and somewhat lower classes who still did not own cars, there were smaller hotels, rooming houses, where one could stay for a week or two. A number of privately owned cottages were sprinkled about this large area on the banks of the river. On the weekend, huge trainloads of people from as far as Poughkeepsie and Syracuse would come on excursion to swim and boat in the river, play ball on Sports Island, reached by a wooden bridge, or enjoy the midway originally called the Bowery, which included a Ferris wheel, roller coaster, carousel, pony and burro rides, a miniature railroad, bowling alleys and pool tables, a dance hall, a movie theater, and scores of games of chance, which tested one's skills in ball rolling and horse racing. Restaurants abounded for the quick snack, but most people brought their own full day's food supply.

The Bergers used the railroad for day outings. They began to go there more frequently after acquiring an automobile. The train stopped for us, much as a bus does today, only two blocks away on Lincoln Street, so it was easy to lug our overloaded baskets for an outing. We rented rooms in large cottages for a week or two and then for a whole summer. In 1917, my father bought an eight-room cottage, where we not only spent the summer but began to come up before or after most of the summer vacationers had left. The cottage was painted green, quite simple, with furniture of the 1890s pattern, when the cottage was first erected. That it had a large *B* decorating the pediment was an added attraction. Actually, this initial was the first letter of the name of the previous owner, but it gave everyone the feeling, as well as us, that we had actually built the structure. The only heat was provided by a coal-wood stove in the kitchen. One bathroom served as many as fifteen or twenty people when the cottage was filled to capacity. Scheduling its use was a top priority in our day's activities. Our relatives from New York, Newark, and Baltimore would visit us during the summer. Since we were one of the few families that owned a cottage, our friends from Gloversville, who usually came by train, would undress for swimming and leave their gear in the house. It was always a busy second household for my mother, who seemed to be the only one cleaning, straightening out the messes, and cooking for a multitude.

Some of us caddied on the golf course, where we were paid 50 cents for nine holes, and thus we had some spending money. I learned golf at the age of ten. Caddies were allowed to play for nothing after 5 P.M. I still have some of the old wooden-shafted clubs and use the putter even with my up-to-date professional steel clubs, housed in a massive bag that no caddy would want to lift today, no matter what I paid him.

I also learned how to play creditable tennis on the nearby courts. We shilled for the games of chance on the midway, developing enough skill, before any of us was even a teenager, to win games from strangers, so that we would be paid to play for the house.

I set up pins in the bowling alley and learned how to play that sport, but never developed any proficiency. I racked up the balls in the pool hall and mastered that game, winning many a dollar from my friends. There was no stigma attached to either sport, when played in the country. It allowed us to earn some money. It was not a place infested with "drunks" and "bums." My parents would never have allowed us into a pool hall or bowling alley in the city.

When I was a little older, we worked in some of the restaurants, making and selling hamburgers and frankfurters for the Zuckermans, who operated two establishments. My sister Sadie and her hsuband managed such a stand for the Zuckermans one summer. They hired me. I disliked the work. But since the money was pretty good, about $10 per day, I remained at my post for six weeks, then took off the last two of the summer for a complete holiday.

There were hordes of kids our age at Sacandaga, so we never wanted for friends or company. Many a night, without the benefit of liquor or drugs, we just decided to become mischievous. We would untie all the boats at the river dock and let them float to the dam a half a mile downstream. Or we would upset the tee boxes on the golf course, for in those days, they had not yet invented the wooden or plastic tee. One had to make his own out of wetted sand. Lije (Elijah) King, the hunchbacked park caretaker, was led a merry chase, as he pursued and even tried to arrest some of us. In later years, when he was our neighbor in a different location on Hampton Road, we would laugh about those childish escapades three decades before. Lije's family had settled in this region after coming from England in the eighteenth century. He worked hard all of his life to make a living. His wife died, and then his only child, a son, committed suicide. He became a lonely man, rowing alone on the lake, fishing, sawing wood, or carrying a gun to hunt for fowl and animals during the hunting season. He lived to be over eighty.

Among our neighbors in the Circle at Sacandaga was the large Lurie family, who operated apartment stores in Gloversville, Amsterdam, Schenectady, and Utica. They were a religious and Zionist family, and I recall the many discussions on both subjects that the elder Lurie had with my father. Of their children, Ted became the publisher-editor of the *Jerusalem Post* and a president of the Jerusalem YM-YWHA, in which Emma and I had an intimate interest. Jesse became the editor of *Hadassah* magazine.

After a few years my father rented the large summer cottage and purchased a smaller one on the Circle, which was sufficient for our family. Fewer of our relatives came to visit us in the summertime, since they had closer places which they could now enjoy, once they had acquired their own automobiles. While we always loved the park, and always came there for part of the summer, as we got older, and after I left for college, we had to earn more money, and so we usually worked in Gloversville after school, Saturdays, and during the summer season.

In the 1930s, the state decided to impound the Sacandaga River, so that it could control the waters flowing into the Hudson River. It built a huge dam at Conkingville, creating a large lake about thirty-five miles long and at its widest stretching for five miles across near Mayfield. With the widespread purchases of the automobile, the park, which remained popular through the 1920s, became less and less crowded. No longer did the Surpass Leather Company have its annual fireworks display on a Friday night across the street from our home on Washburn Street, and then take its hundreds of employees to the park to spend a busy Saturday. Similar excursions were abandoned by other groups that formerly could only transport themselves by train.

The hissing steam railroad engine and its cars gave way to a solitary diesel train, which often made the trip with only a handful of passengers. When the lake was impounded, the midway and its fifteen-foot-high bridge, from which we used to dive into the shallow water with expertise, and Sports Island, were inundated. The park lost its visitors and its attendant pleasurable pursuits.

Actually we never owned the land on which the cottages were situated, but only the structures built upon it. The land was owned by the railroad, which decided not to lease it, but instead to force each person to buy the property at inflated prices. Despite the depression year of 1938, my father sold one cottage, dismantled the other, bought a half-acre of land about one mile down the road amongst a group of farmers, rebuilt a cottage on one floor, pulled in electricity, and dug a private well—all for the cost of $800, less than what he would have had to pay for the tiny piece of property in the Circle.

My mother had died that year. I always wondered whether she would have approved of this move had she lived. She liked to be in the thick of things. The cottage became a place for those of us who had moved away from Gloversville to come back for a short vacation, usually at the end of the summer. It became the permanent summer residence of my brother Milton and his family, who with their boat on the lake, docked at the end of Hampton Road on our small private beach, made it a gathering place for the Berger clan. In 1938, when the cottage was first built, my father and I planted lilac bushes on the front to screen the house from the road traffic. We set out about forty pine, spruce, fir, and maple trees, some of which have since grown to a height of one hundred feet, giving us shade, beauty, and a sense of isolation, as the land near the cottage began to develop with new houses. When they hard-topped Hampton Road, it allowed access to the lake front, where expensive summer and year-round homes began to rise. We have since had to cut down many of our trees, which grew too thickly, a sad act that of necessity had to be performed.

Over the years we improved the house, finally adding a fireplace, but we never insulated it so that it could be used year-round. Some years, the snows in that area are so heavy that the cottage is covered. For those of us who loved to ski, it was not the place for such an activity, so it couldn't be used as a lodge in any event. But for either the long or brief periods when it was used, it was a delight, particularly when we had a glorious Indian summer in September.

The Ike Cohen Family

The major reason for settling in Gloversville was that my mother had relatives there, including a cousin, Isaac Cohen, known to everyone as Ike. A medium-tall, thin man with a sunken face and prominent moustache, always smoking a cigar, which he smoked in serial from morning through the night, given to taking more than a nip of whisky, he was a unique character.

Ike arrived in Gloversville with a wife and two sons, Abe and Phil, born abroad, in 1906, and settled on the corner of Kent and North Streets, where a number of other Jewish families were living, only a block and a half from John Street, where I was born. Ike became a peddler with a horse and wagon, going out to the countryside, but had made enough money in a year or two to open a shoe store in the front half of 46 Church Street, the rear being a pool room run by Charles Persico, who owned the building. Ike peddled the first half of the week and then opened the store nights and Sunday morning. When asked how he made money, he said that he operated on a one percent markup—"I buy for one dollar and sell for two dollars." He later bought the whole block, opened a series of stores selling men's merchandise at first, later expanded to include women's wear. Three children were soon born in Gloversville, Izzie, Fannie, and Sadie. Everyone, when old enough, worked in the store, except Mrs. Cohen.

Ike had a hearty laugh, intervened in all and any sales of his employees, including his own children. I worked there for several years from the age of eleven through thirteen, at first for $1 for an 8 A.M. to midnight Saturday shift, finishing up the last hour taking inventory of the shoe stock. I asked several times for a raise in the second year and was finally upped to $1.50. I am sure that my mother must have said something to him to get this increase. For Christmas, I received a belt as a gift, worth 25 cents. I left after the second year, because I could make more elsewhere, of course based on the valuable experience I had obtained with a master salesman. Ike would sell to the customers, mostly farmers, on credit and load them up with more merchandise than they had originally come into the store to buy. While he bought all kinds of job lots (I recall trying to sell shoes all for left feet for 50 cents a pair without too much success), most of his merchandise was of good quality. He would keep me busy, when I wasn't selling, putting the stock in good order or running out to buy him cigars at a neighborhood store.

Ike was the first to buy a Chalmers car with what he called a "self-commencer" (self-starter), for in 1913 most cars had to be cranked from the front to start. I remember his taking our family for a ride. He wore a duster coat, cap, goggles. He made quite an impression as we drove through the streets and nearby villages with the top down. He was the first among the immigrant Jews to sail off to Europe in the early 1920s, and my family posed for pictures before he left. That picture shows my handsome father with a modish cap, my mother looking intensely with her straight, smoothed-down hair, and my sister Rachel was robed in a striking dress with a belt circling her garment below the waistline. Rachel has been stylish in dress since her adolescence.

Cohen spent his surplus cash buying up other properties, then extending his business to Johnstown, Northville, and Corinth. I worked in the Northville store, about seventeen miles north of Gloversville and two miles north of Sacandaga, during the summer of 1931, between my first and second years at the graduate School of Jewish Social Work and the New York School of Social Work.

One thing that still sticks in my mind is the sign in front of the store on the second floor. Cohen owned the building and rented out the second floor to an evangelical Christian group. In their window, directly above the display "Cohen's Department Store," they had a sign reading "Jesus Saves." In 1985, at my son Michael's housewarming, in Vienna, Virginia, one of his house guests was a man who was born in Northville, and we had a good laugh recalling this juxtaposition of markers.

We were close to the Cohen family. Ike often visited our home to play checkers with my father. Although my father usually won their games, he did so in silence; when by contrast, Ike would exult in his occasional victories. Emma and I were closest to Phil. Phil was four years older and ahead of me in high school. Short, wiry, and shifty, he made an excellent basketball player and was a member of the high school varsity, which went off by train in a blaze of glory to Walla Walla, Washington, to play in the national championships in 1922. Phil also played on the 1923–24 Gloversville YMHA team, of which I was the captain.

My Brother Morris A. (Moshe Aaron)

My brother Morris, who was nine years old when he arrived in the United States in 1905, had only a brief schooling through the sixth grade, sold papers, and then went to work as a teenager with the F. S. Mills Company, which manufactured pocketbooks and pouches with pull strings and assorted locks. Everything was made of leather in a limited number of hues. Morris was bright, spoke slowly and deliberately before giving you his opinion, and enjoyed the confidence of the owners, the elder Mills and his two sons, who had recently completed their studies at Cornell and Princeton. From mechanical work, including the use of a sewing machine, he moved on to become a salesman on the road.

One day, in 1916, a tramp inventor from Meadville, Pennsylvania, came into the factory and was showing his newest creation, later known as the zipper throughout the world. He did not impress the Mills brothers, but my brother by chance walked into their office, saw the zipper, went up to the sewing machines on the second floor, and very quickly sewed together a pouch with a radically new and different way of closing. Within a few years it was internationally acclaimed. The Mills Company, which had the exclusive use of the zipper for ten years, offered my brother a partnership on the basis of his bold imagination, ingenuity, and $1,500 which he borrowed from my father.

When war came in 1917, Morris was inducted into the army and assigned to the chemical division to supervise the production of gas masks. While he wore a uniform, he never left these shores. After the war, he returned to the factory, which had changed its name to the Locktite Company, the name given to the pouch, which was sold worldwide. Its sales made Morris well-to-do and the other partners richer, because they had both already inherited considerable wealth.

Morris had met Florence Blue, a firm, well-dressed, and attractive woman in New York, while he was serving in the army. They were married in 1919 and bore two sons, Howard and Richard. Morris later was elected a councilman, and due to his sound fiscal views, acquired entirely by self-study, he steered Gloversville out of bankruptcy during the depression and put every municipal department in efficient, self-sufficient operating order. He became a trustee of the Carnegie Library. Earlier he had been one of the organizers of the YM-YWHA in 1912, was a founding board member of the Jewish Community Center in 1918, and in every way was associated with Gloversville's civic and Jewish life, including membership in the War Veterans and Masons. He moved into a fine house on stately Kingsboro Avenue, and for a number of years enjoyed a small country home on the outskirts of Gloversville, where the family visited.

I still remember my first violation of the dietary laws, which occurred when I was with Morris and his bride-to-be, Florence. They had taken me for an automobile ride during the week of Passover and stopped at an ice cream parlor for some refreshment. I was reluctant to order, let alone eat, *trefe* (nonkosher now multiplied by its being non-Passover), but somehow I was coaxed into it, and at the age of eleven, it was hard to resist my favorite dessert. When the wrath of God, through bolts of lightning, did not descend upon me with my first mouthful, I quickly learned that he was an understanding God, or perhaps he was not as all-seeing as our prayers would indicate. Violation of the laws of kashrut became easier to adopt over the years, despite the rigidity with which they were enforced while I was living at home.

I worked at the Locktite factory when I was fourteen and fifteen years old, after receiving my first official working certificate. I operated a skiving machine, which thinned leather to a point where it was malleable and sewable. It was a tricky device, and I always had morbid thoughts of what might happen if my hands slipped and were caught in the razor-sharp knives. I also worked on the stamping machine, which embossed the word "Locktite" on all of the products. I was well received by the older employees, who treated me as a youngster, but nonetheless were mindful that I was the brother of the boss. My pay was 20 cents an hour,

I usually worked for three hours after school, five days a week and during the holidays. It provided me with spending money, but after two years, I left to take a better-paying job in a shoe store.

One story of the zipper comes to mind. It dates to around 1926, when for the first time, one began to see zippers on traveling bags, women's bags, women's dresses, and replacing the buttons on the flies of men's pants. A man was sitting comfortably in the Glove Theater, and when the lights went out as the film came on the screen, he relaxed even further by pulling down his zipper and loosening his belt. A woman walked into his row and as she passed his seat, he hurriedly rose and pulled up the zipper, catching her dress in his fly. Needless to say, this caused her great consternation, as she could not extricate herself. The manager was called, and they were both ushered into his office, where nothing could be done, as she did not want to cut her dress, nor did the hapless man want to destroy his trousers. It was 9 P.M. Suddenly the manager remembered that Morris knew all about zippers and phoned him. Morris hurriedly came down to the theater to separate these two strangers out of their hopeless predicament. He unzipped them without injury to either garment.

The Name Graenum

A radical change in my life, or at least in my name, occurred when I was in the fourth grade and all of nine years old. One day the teacher called me to her desk and asked me to write my name. Until that moment I had been going under the name of Abram, often called Abe or Abie by my parents, siblings, friends, and schoolmates. I had always assumed that that was my legal name and nothing else. When the teacher examined what I had written, she then read me a letter from my sister, Rachel, which revealed that my correct name was Graenum and advised the teacher to alter the records. My sister and I had quarreled, as siblings are wont to do, but I do not recall the nature of the argument that could have led to such a "punitive" reaction. Anyway, the school authorities immediately changed my name. It was extremely difficult to tell everyone about the reason for this alteration, particularly classmates and close friends. For many years thereafter, they continued to call me by the original Abe or Graenum Abe. Apparently the mixup took place, after I was born, because it is clear from my birth certificate that Abram was not the name listed. It was Graenum. Even my parents were never clear in their explanation of how the error occurred. There are four other Graenums in the Berger family, all named after the same grandfather. In Hebrew it would probably have been pronounced Gronem or Granum, but my oldest cousin chose to spell it Graenum, and since I was next in line, I adopted his version. Several of my cousins changed their name from Graenum to George, but one later restored Graenum as a middle name. Another cousin, a psychiatrist, has always used the name Graenum.

The War Ends: Its Aftermath

The year 1918 and its aftermath made some changes in our family life. Our fortunes, which had improved with the course of the conflict, were now altered, for my father was left with large leather inventories that he was not able to sell for many years, and then at prices that did not recapture the original investment and additional expenses like insurance. I do not recall any changes in our lifestyle, but money was always much tighter.

My sister, Rachel, had finished high school, and although she was very bright, articulate, and provocative, and wanted to go to college, the finances were not forthcoming, and she settled for a clerical post. While she did get away for a summer at Syracuse University, and did manage to attend a dancing school, where she studied briefly with Ruth St. Denis and Ted Shawn, it never quite fulfilled her ambitions. She was popular with young men, but had set her sights on an ideal who would be a professional, well educated, and of good family. Over the years she turned down a number of men who had made it financially, but did not have the other background qualifications. She did not get married until 1929, but when she did, it was to someone who fulfilled her criteria.

In the 1920s, Rachel left her secretarial duties and went to work as a reporter on the *Gloversville Morning Herald*. When she resigned this position, the job was filled by me, later by my brother Sam, and then by my youngest brother, Milton. Rachel was a reporter with a good writing style and a flair for newsworthy stories. Her adventures led to a flight in a barnstorming airplane that came to town, recorded in detail in the press. My father, brother Sam, and I also took the same brief flight for five dollars in 1925, and it was quite a daring experience. When Rachel returned from her studies with the dancing teachers, she practiced with me, and we became rather expert in ballroom dancing, entertaining on several occasions and winning awards for our twirling, bendings, and intricate steps. While we both remained good dancers, we soon gave up these public displays.

* * *

In 1919, I became ill and had to be taken to New York for an examination by a famous specialist, Dr. Libman, who diagnosed my illness as some liver complaint. It was treated by my taking the nasty-tasting mineral oil. The illness cleared up shortly thereafter, because I would not continue spooning this remedy.

* * *

That year my mother became ill for the first time. After many physicians had examined her in Gloversville, New York, and Albany, it was finally diagnosed as cancer of the lymphatic glands in the chest. She was then treated by Dr. Ordway at the Albany Medical College, where he was experimenting with the use of radium. Although her chest thereafter showed the scars of this treatment, the radium being applied in heavy lead bars, she recovered sufficiently, so that the disease was in remission until sometime in 1935, when it recurred. It gradually led to her death in 1938 in the Massachusetts General Hospital, where she had been sent for treatment.

Her illness extended for two years. She was frequently absent from home and hospitalized. It took place when I should have been preparing for Bar Mitzvah. I had been trained for this *simcha* very rigorously by my Hebrew teacher, Haim Grant, a red-headed man, who though quite young had a kind of gnarled face. He was vigorous in speech and used his hands and arms to emphasize what he was verbally communicating. He was enormously influential in interesting us in Jewish life and particularly Palestine and Zionism. But with my mother ill, no one paid any attention to my birthdate nor this Judaic rite, and I suspect that I was always pleased to have it pass by without any fuss. While I continued my studies in the Hebrew school until I was fifteen, I was never motivated by my family or personally to undergo this ceremony.

Grant was also trying to persuade me to become a full-fledged Zionist and go with him to Palestine. The Balfour Declaration was issued in 1918, through which the British government promised to help the Jewish people reestablish a homeland in Palestine, the ripple effect being felt even in a small town like Gloversville. Although many local Jews did not subscribe to the idea of a Jewish state, particularly Jews who believed that we were only a religion and not a nation, or, like the Bundists, who believed that Jews should have a domestic political orientation that would seek the improvement of the status of Jews in the Diaspora by working toward a just, more democratic society, some of us were taken with the ancient dream of the restoration of Zion. Regrettably, Grant left the city for a better job elsewhere, never went on aliyah to Palestine, and his influence, to which my family strangely responded, died in its incipiency. Yet he left a mark on me that never completely eroded. I met Grant again in Jersey City in 1931–32, when I was doing field work at the local YM-YWHA and supervised his work in teaching Hebrew and other Jewish studies. We spoke of the past, but it had become another interesting, unfulfilled memory.

The year 1918 and thereafter also brought a deep blemish in my life. I broke out with acne, and the scars of those years never left me. My father had also had acne in his youth, so it was just assumed that it was inherited and I would outgrow it. Both of my brothers suffered from the same ugly fate, but not quite as deeply as I did. I was eventually taken to a physician, who looked up the disease in his huge medical volume, showed me the disfiguring pictures, and prescribed bay rum, which men used after shaving. While the aroma was not unpleasant, the liquid did nothing to cure the ailment and instead aggravated it by practically tanning my skin to the hardness of leather. To overcome this development, he then prescribed various creams, but they too had no effect except softening my skin once more. We then went to another physician in Amsterdam, who was reputed to work miracles with acne patients, and he made a culture out of the acne deposits, from which I was given injections for the better part of a year. Nothing happened. My mother, who by then was under treatment for cancer with Dr. Ordway, asked him what might be done, and he decided to experiment with radium treatments on my face. While they seemed to have some modest effect, they inhibited the growth of facial hairs, which pleased me, because I had begun to shave and it was a difficult thing with acne scars. One radium application was on a few seconds too long and resulted in burning my chin and creating a visible indentation to this day. It matched the mark on my forehead, which had come about when I was delivered at birth with forceps. These enduring features have been the cause of endless inquiries both from friends as well as physicians. So I was a burdensome problem coming into this world and in my adolescence.

One night I went to the YMCA for a lecture presumably on the evils of sex, but the announcement indicated that it would also deal with curing acne. The speaker spoke in a semi-darkened room, where he showed slides, but it also relieved anyone of any embarrassment should he elicit questions from the floor. He railed against masturbation as a sin, as a destroyer of one's health, and as a contributor towards the development of acne. He was opposed to any kind of sexual relations without marriage, and said that any violation of this covenant would consign one to perdition forever. When someone asked him about acne, he replied that this came about when young people thought too much about sex. This was nature's way of damming up the flow of the natural secretions, and in turn producing those unattractive pimples and even boils. Obviously abstinence from anything sexual was the cure-all. When pressed by some adolescent for a more immediate cure, he related that in his travels around the world, he had heard that in one country, those afflicted with acne bathed their faces in the urine of cows. I recall fleeing from the room after listening to that sage piece of medical advice.

Ultimately the acne began to clear, but there were residual emissions until I was at least twenty-five years old, after I was married. But I had reminders of my malady when my youngest son, Michael, developed an even more grievous case. When we took him to doctors some thirty years after I had gone through a variety of so-called treatments, the eminent specialists in dermatology did not seem to have arrived at any better cures than in my day. They had added vitamins to the list and the use of X-rays, but nothing worked on Michael and his face became even more scarred. I have given up on dermatologists, who with all their new found nostrums neither cure you nor kill you.

Gloversville: A Small Jewish Community

The Gloversville Jewish community, with which I was to maintain a relationship all my life, played a significant role in my development. The city's Jews never constituted more than 15 percent of the population in its heyday, and the figure has now shrunken to less than 5 percent. The origins of the Gloversville Jewish community date to the arrival of Nathan Littauer in the United States in 1846, at the age of seventeen. He became a peddler, then worked in a store in Albany, where he married Harriet Sporborg. With his new bride, Littauer opened a store in Gloversville in 1856. A few years later he established a glove factory. Word was sent to the "Old Country" that there was a need for glove workers, and Jewish immigrants began to arrive, at first to work in the factories and later to build their own.

Littauer became wealthy, turned over his business eventually to his sons Lucius (born 1859) and Eugene. The family contributed immensely to the business life and other services that Gloversville needed.

The Littauers were followed by other Jews from middle and eastern Europe, who built tanneries and glove factories and opened department stores in both Gloversville and the older neighboring city of Johnstown.

The earlier settlers, who became wealthy, were considered aristocrats by those who came later or were pejoratively considered capitalists by Jews who arrived from eastern Europe and started out as workers in these Jewish establishments. Many of the newcomers were outright socialists and occasionally were antireligious. The older, well-established Jewish families leaned toward Reform Judaism, which had already established a foothold in the country. The newcomers were traditionally Orthodox and built a substantial synagogue. It was not until 1920, after the Jewish Community Center was established, that regular Reform services were initiated. They succeeded quite well on the High Holy Days, but there was difficulty in getting a sufficient attendance on Friday night or the Sabbath. Rabbi Maxwell Dubin, a Reform rabbi and the executive director of the center, officiated.

Before the Orthodox synagogue was built, Jews conducted prayer services in each other's homes. In 1905, an imposing building was erected and named Knesseth Israel. It had grown out of the Hebrew Mutual Assistance Association, formed in the 1890s to aid Jews in need of financial or other forms of help. The Fulton County Hebrew Cemetery Association was organized earlier, in 1884, because Jews needed a plot of ground in which to bury their dead. In the history of American Jewish communities, the establishment of a cemetery very often came even before the building of a central facility to pray.

While my father was not listed among the original members of the synagogue, since he had not yet moved to Gloversville, he joined the synagogue immediately after his arrival in 1906, becoming not only a member but, shortly after that, a board trustee and officer, posts which he continued throughout his lifetime. He was an active member of the Hebrew school committee, because he firmly believed that this was even more important than a synagogue. My mother became an active participant in the relief society. When she was done with her household chores for a family of eight with an additional boarder, she baked a cake and carried it to visit a sick person at home or in the hospital, or she would make a visit to a home in need of money, food, and coal and see that these necessities were immediately provided.

My father was a critic of the management of synagogue affairs, often questioning the honesty and the integrity of some of the officers. Sometimes, when he came home after a vitriolic meeting at which there was name calling and, on several occasions, the throwing of a chair or two, he was so overwrought that he had to relate the whole incident to us before he went to bed. We would also hear about the episode from others the following day. Nevertheless, he had such a reputation for honesty in speech and the conduct of his business and personal affairs that he only alienated a few of the *baalabatim*. When he passed away in 1947, he was honored by having his casket borne into the synagogue, a rare happening in Gloversville, where part of the eulogistic service was rendered. He did not live to see the synagogue rebuilt next to the Jewish Community Center in 1963. His youngest son, Milton, was the president of that religious body, and was a prime mover in bringing about the creation of one of the handsomest buildings in this country.

I attended the synagogue from my youngest years, and as long as I remained in the city, or when I returned to visit my parents, particularly during the Jewish holidays. I would always attend services with my parents, usually sitting in the first row with the male members of my family, while my mother and sisters sat in the balcony. It was always a noisy sanctuary, because of the indecorous manner in which traditional Jews prayed. Children ran around the sanctuary, from their male parents downstairs to the mothers in the balcony, or out of doors, since the services seemed interminable to a young child. The honors of reading from the Torah were in former days auctioned off, and it was of interest to me to follow the spirited bidding, particularly for *Maftir,* the concluding section of the Sabbath or holiday Torah portion. Most of the cantors had good, clear, melodic voices. All foreign born and trained in the old country, they often also served as *shochetim* (ritual slaughterers), or *mohelim* (circumcisers). Some members of the congregation, including my father, had good voices, and frequently uttered the chants with beauty and dignity. My father was a *kohen*, reputed to be a lineal descendant of the High Priest Aaron, a distinction which I inherited and later readily accepted.

While as children we were quite restless with the long drawn out ritual, most of which we could not understand, even though we could read the Hebrew in the prayer books with facility, nonetheless the ceremonial—the taking of the Torah out of the ark, the parading around the sanctuary while chanting, the unrolling of the scrolls—all had a pageantry that one could never forget. In our travels to eighty-four countries around the world, we never failed to look for a synagogue, particularly on the Sabbath and holy days, and found ourselves quite comfortable in strange lands, despite the differences in style and ceremony, because basically they were the same prayers and rituals.

In the old days, there was no role in the synagogue for the children, with the exception of Simchat Torah and especially Purim, when because of the special joyous nature of the holiday, we could make as much noise as we wanted with hand, foot, voice, or grogger every time the name of Haman was uttered in the reading of the *Megillat Esther*.

Drinking Liquor

Until recent years, Jews have been marked by sobriety. The Torah permits us to drink wine as a sacrament to the Lord, and there are injunctions against the drinking of too much hard liquor. Aaron's sons were struck dead because they approached the altar with liquor on their breaths. As a descendant of *kohanim*, I am constantly being reminded of this ominous event. Yet the eight-day-old son who has just gone through the rite of circumcision and cries from the pain of the cut is given a bit of wine on a cloth to soothe him. Wine is offered at the beginning of the *Kiddush* each Friday night and on the eve of every festival, and whenever one sits down to meals in these Jewish calendaric events.

On Pesach, we are mandated to drink four cups of wine. Most Jews with whom I have annually enjoyed this festival seldom drink that quantity. In my childhood, when we recited the Ten Plagues visited on the Egyptian Pharaoh and his people, and ritually spilled a bit of wine on our plates, someone always told my mother, as a joke, to collect the spilled wine in a pitcher, since it was a shame to waste it, and give it to one of our non-Jewish neighbors, who staggered home many an evening after having used a great deal of his painter's wages in a saloon. My mother always indignantly refused this suggestion, because the wine had been cursed. My mother also reminded us that she had an uncle who became an alcoholic and died in a sanitarium, after developing cirrhosis of the liver. She always discouraged excessive drinking and only took sips of wine herself.

On warm summer days, my father sent me with a two-quart tin pail and a cover and handle to a nearby saloon to purchase cold beer, a refreshing beverage on a hot day tapped out of a barrel. In those days it was sold to minors.

After the Prohibition Amendment was passed in 1919, the sale of both liquor and even beer was forbidden. So my father, who always liked two thimbles of hard liquor each day, and said it kept his mind and body in good health, was forced to make his own liquor. Usually he used cherries or plums to make his own brandy or slivowitz, mixing it with pure grain alcohol, which was legally purchasable. Sometimes he touched up the brew with kimmel (caraway seeds) to give it an added or different flavor. We of course made our own wine in the fall, when purple grapes were harvested and in the market, and made enough for an entire year. Down the street, an Italian family went through the wine-making process openly, in the street. With great ceremony, they crushed quantities of grapes in large wooden vats, stamping out the juices with their bare feet. By contrast our wine was made with a small wooden press, then poured in small wooden barrels and later bottled for storage.

My father frequently went to the synagogue during the week in the early morning for *yahrzeit* prayers, where at least ten men must gather for an authentic service. At such events, the individual who had the *yahrzeit* provided kichel, herring, and some liquor, which my father always enjoyed.

At any *simcha*, such as a wedding, my father, a spontaneous poet after a few drinks, would rise to toast the honored ones with his ready-made two-line couplets rendered in Yiddish. He told me that the liquor helped stimulate his imagination.

Strangely, we did not have a single silver wine cup in our household, unlike today when we, like so many other Jewish families, collect large numbers of varied wine cups for just such a ceremony. Our favorite gift to a new child, or for a Bar or Bat Mitzvah, or even for a wedding, is to present the honorees with sterling silver, beautifully decorated wine cups. Since 1955, when we made our first trip to Israel, all these cups have been purchased and made by Yemenite craftsmen in that country.

Friends in turn have given us a number of wine cups for special occasions. On my sixty-fifth birthday, a group of intimate friends tendered me a party at which I was given a magnificent modern-style cup designed by the celebrated silversmith Ludwig Wolpert, who before he died, was working at the Jewish Museum in New York, where I visited with him on several occasions. I had first met him and seen his silver smithy in Jerusalem in 1955.

In my high school years, at parties, we occasionally drank to show off.

We drank a bit more on New Year's Eve. While a few of us got sick, and even that was rare, I do not remember anyone actually getting drunk. We never patronized saloons or the speakeasies that had sprung up to accommodate those who wished to violate the Prohibition Amendment. So if and when we wanted to drink, we always took a little of something from our homes, sometimes with and sometimes without our parents' permission. My father was more understanding than my mother about such consumption.

At college drinking was part of the Saturday night ritual, and especially at fraternity parties. One could always manage to buy a pint of pure grain alcohol with which to spike 3.2 percent near beer that was all one could purchase legally. In our Jewish group, there were few who ever got drunk, so that habit was not deepened during this academic exposure.

In our home, after Emma and I were married, there was always wine and liquor. We did not consume it as daily fare but, it was always available when guests were present. While drinking in larger quantities became popular after World War II, the amount consumed, which at first began to rise, then tapered off, switching from ryes, to scotch, to gin, to vodka, to wine, mostly white. Now, in our seventies, we drink less and less, until we have stopped drinking altogether, substituting grape juice for the *Kiddush*.

Our children and grandchildren are light drinkers, not because we have ever asked them to drink in moderation, but, we believe, from the example that we set throughout our lives.

Alcoholism has become a serious problem in the Jewish community in recent decades. Regretfully, the official Jewish community has never taken a strong position against the consumption of liquor, we observe how hard liquor and wine flows at every *simcha* from a *brith milah*, heightened at Bar Mitzvahs, unbridled at weddings. One finds it served even during *shivah*.

Back to School

I completed the fourth grade at Spring Street School without any further incidents and with pleasanter memories than in kindergarten. Mrs. Rice, in the third grade, was portly, cheerful, and buoyed our spirits by her friendly openness to her students. She knew our family and greeted them warmly when they visited the school or when she met them on the street. Mrs. Tygart, older and gray-haired, was a kindly teacher, interested in each pupil, and never uttered a sharp word. Her husband was in the candy business, and from time to time, we were rewarded with some sweets.

Then I was transferred from the Victorian red brick school, with its high ceilings and well-lighted rooms, to the North Main Street building, built of dirty white brick, flat-roofed and nondescript. The interiors were drab, neglected, peeling, and shortly after, it was demolished, having outlived its usefulness. I spent two years there in the fifth and sixth grades, but I cannot recall a single teacher's name.

I do remember one incident, however. During the recreation period. We were lined up in a makeshift gymnasium in the cellar of the school, waiting our turn to bat a ball thrown by a pitcher. Each youngster at the plate had five swings of the bat and then moved to the end of the line. I was pushed forward by a boy behind me, so that I was much too close to the plate. The right-handed batsman took a tremendous cut at the ball, and the end of his bat caught me on the nose, just between my eyes. I was knocked to the floor. The coach bent down, ran for a towel and cold water to press over the injured organ. I was never unconscious, soon revived, standing a bit dizzily. But my nose was swollen and blue. I was taken to the principal's office, where the coach made a report. No nurse or doctor attended me. No one thought of taking X-rays. When I felt better, I was excused for the rest of the day and told to go home. After my mother's initial alarm when I came into her presence, she applied cold and hot compresses, not quite knowing which was best. The next day I was back in school with my discolored nose and forehead. Luckily, there was no eye injury. I still have an indentation at the bridge of my nose, which I attribute to that accident. How different it is today, when the school marshals all of its resources to treat any injury that might befall a student while under its ministrations, hoping that there will be no lawsuit.

The city had just constructed Estee Junior High School, a new, large, and handsome beige brick four-story building, and as a junior high, an innovation in education at that time. I spent my next two years in grades seven and eight in that bright atmosphere.

While I had improved my vision with the acquisition of spectacles, so that I could see clearly both the blackboard and the books that I was reading, it had given no spur to my scholarship or my reading interests. I had stopped going to the library to select books. I was content to read the typical, superficial books that one could read through at a sitting— Horatio Alger and Victor Appleton's "Tom Swift." I looked forward to the next one, but I do not recall being inspired by reading about these fabulous boy heroes.

I was apparently bright enough, learning without too much effort, but since no one was driving me, even at home, I took the easiest way out, satisfied with slightly above average grades and no really bad marks. So there was no complaint when my parents read my report cards, no summons to see the teacher. This encouraged me to coast even further.

I recall that whenever I finished a reading assignment or examination in the classroom, and I always seemed to perform these exercises quickly and with ease, the teacher, noting some restlessness in me, invited me to come up to the front of the room and sit at a large table with a huge globe and thick dictionary. I browsed and indirectly added to my knowledge by examining both closely. I was always an A student in geography and could rattle off countries and their capitals or major cities with accuracy. I like to believe that this motivated my later interest in travel. I was also able to use multisyllabic words with facility. I am not sure that I would have been able to define each word if I had been challenged but nobody did. It undoubtedly made me a champ speller in my senior year.

I had lots of friends, saw them before and after class, and these friendships led to other developments in my life. We often called each other over the phone in the morning to arrange to meet at school. I can't remember the name of a single teacher in the junior high school, evidence of either a faulty memory or else a failure to develop any intimacy with my teachers.

The move to high school was accompanied without too much ceremony, although I vaguely remember going through a graduation exercise of some kind. The handsome high school was housed in a formidable, well-designed beige stone and brick building, contiguous to the junior high. It fronted on Main Street, set back on a well-kept lawn several hundred feet from the thoroughfare. I was thirteen years old. I already had developed a kind of sophistication with boys and girls my age. There was a large group of Jewish youngsters who knew each other from their association in the Hebrew school, the synagogue, and the Jewish Community Center. While we had daily contacts with our non-Jewish fellow students, all of our intimate relationships were exclusively with Jewish young people. We never had any negative attitudes towards non-Jews, but just kept ourselves segregated voluntarily. On the other hand, the non-Jews never made any overtures to us either.

I never proved to be a good scholar in any of the four years that I attended high school. It was a good school directed by one of America's finest educators, Julius E. Warren, who left Gloversville during my last term and built up a superlative reputation in other posts around the country. In my senior class yearbook, *The Oracle* (1925), someone wrote about me:

> As a scholar you are fair.
> As an actor you'd get no letter.
> But as a speller,
> You know there is none better.

The class prophecy indicated that I would become the "successor to Webster." I was pleased with these statements.

I was already articulate, yet I had a curious lack of confidence about getting up and speaking before an audience. My exposure to drama consisted in playing some minor part in Shakespeare's *Midsummer Night's Dream*. In the presentation, I forgot some lines, so other actors were not properly cued. I assume that is why the editor questioned my acting ability. Frankly, I thought the play silly, and still do. I was bored witnessing it in later years, despite the star actors and the rave notices of the drama critics.

In my second year at high school, I sang in the choir because one of my teachers said I had a fine tenor voice. We presented a cantata, *The Man Without a Country*, which was very well received by an appreciative student and parent audience. I was able to sing many of the lines for years thereafter. As a member of the French club, I tried to improve upon my three years of that foreign langauge, following two years of Latin. I can still recall some of the important Latin phrases.

French has been useful when we travel in foreign countries, although I have the habit of using the wrong language in the wrong country, for which I would need an analyst to explain. With some difficulty, I can read a newspaper in other countries with a Latin or Romance language base, indicating that my learning was not entirely wasted. However, I do not risk entering into any conversations with either natives or others who speak with fluency.

I went out for track and basketball, but these sports demanded too much of my spare time, so I dropped them. Since I had to work after school and Saturdays, I had insufficient time for practice and, if I had made the team, for participating in major events. I also tried football, but it was too rough a sport. I tried boxing, and that proved to be even rougher when I took on an opponent who knew how to deliver punishing blows.

Basketball was the sport in which I thrived. I played it almost daily in the very late afternoon or evening at the YM-YWHA. For three years I was a member of the Y team, and from 1923 to 1925 was its captain. Although I was far from the best player, they all thought I had a good, sobering influence over the players and could resolve disputes and make quick and successful decisions.

Since I wore glasses, which I had to cover with a steel and leather cage, and was comparatively light and not too tall, I had to develop a specialty to be part of the five. I had extraordinary skill in shooting fouls. In those days, one member of the team shot all the fouls for his team, something like a designated hitter in American League baseball. One season I shot ninety-nine fouls before I missed. I would be rushed in as a substitute and as quickly ushered out of the game after I had done this important scoring job. Since some of the courts did not even have a backboard, shooting fouls had to be done with unerring expertise.

The Y often played preliminary games to the professional teams that came to Gloversville, and as a youngster I saw and met all the great, particularly the original Celtics. Years later in New York I had the pleasure of working with Nat Holman, famous coach of the City College of New York championship basketball teams and an active volunteer in Jewish philanthropies and Israeli sports. Whenever we met, we would kibbitz about the good old days, when his team had played in Gloversville.

While I was far from an intellectual, I was thought worthy of inclusion in a somewhat snobbish Jewish cultural club called Mefitzah Daath. We would meet periodically to listen to some lecture on a Jewish theme by an alumnus of the group, such as Harry Starr, the butcher's son, who had studied at Harvard and its law school and eventually became head of the Littauer Foundation, a dispenser of philanthropic funds, and with whom I had periodic contacts during my professional years.

My closest friend was Charles Finkle. His father had passed away, and his mother supported the family. Charlie had to supplement her income. He did this by creating an orchestra. Charlie was its violinist. There was at first a black by the name of Leroy who played the piano, and he was succeeded by Louis Tremonte, who later became a local doctor. Paul Husek played the saxophone and clarinet. What they needed was a drummer. I had accumulated enough money to buy a bass drum, a snare drum, cymbals, and some other noise-making equipment; within a matter of weeks, after taking a few lessons, I was a full-fledged drummer, even able to toss and twirl the drumsticks to the amazement of dancers and even my friends. When I did not have access to a car, it was a troublesome chore dragging all of these items to a performance on a cart or sled. Since we had a piano, all rehearsals were held in our home. When I could borrow the family car, we were able to go out of town, and many of our engagements were conditioned by its availability. I began driving the family car at the age of eleven. There was no problem getting and driving it when I was fourteen through seventeen. These were the days before it was necessary to have a license or arrive at a minimum age.

I played music with enthusiasm, learned all the tricks, and on top of that was the singer for the group. In the summer, we played in the country, mostly at a speakeasy hotel in the Adirondacks, where we offered both popular and country square-dance music. I learned to call the squares, largely by default. No one else in the orchestra wanted to do it, and we frankly could not afford to hire a caller.

Some Saturday nights, when the crowds were slim, the hotel owner suddenly disappeared, for he was reluctant to pay us. We had to stay overnight in his lodgings. Then he would deduct the cost of the room and breakfast from our fee, so that we had little left for our strenuous efforts. We slept two in a large bed, and while I would have preferred to sleep with Charlie, my bedmate was always Leroy, the black pianist, to which I offered no objections.

Apart from my family's positive attitude towards black people—there were only a score or so in Gloversville—I had developed a similar regard for them. They lived quietly and gracefully, were hard-working, and what I remember sharply was how well dressed they were on Sundays, when they went to church. I believe that this intimate contact with Leroy, a fine, light-skinned young man, helped nourish my affirmative views towards blacks all my life. Sometimes we played for special groups, and I recall how we prepared our music for a very large black assembly. The women came in their long dress finery, the men in their tuxedos. We played into the wee hours of the morning the kind of jazz music they liked. We introduced "April Showers" to Gloversville and other audiences with music and lyrics by Louis Silvers and B. B. De Sylva. When Al Jolson sang it the opening night of the musical show *Bombo,* he drew thirty-six curtain calls. When I sang it, nobody paid much attention, although they politely applauded the orchestra after completing the dance. This number allowed me to do a number of drum solos, as I dramatized the scenes reflecting thunder and lightning. For this exhibition, I regularly received some hand claps.

Tragedy on a Hike

One of the popular programs initiated by the Jewish Community Center in 1919 was the Boy Scouts, an all-Jewish troop. Most other troops were affiliated with churches. The variety of activities, the uniform, the merit badge aspirations all were attractive to the forty boys enrolled. We met weekly, made our scout pledge, and then turned to an evening of activity—knot tying being one of the first. The scouts encouraged patriotism, good deeds, and physical exercise. Our leader was Sol Sackheim, a businessman, slightly bent over, lean, and with sunken dark eyes along with a baritone voice that barked out instructions and warnings.
 One Sunday during the winter we undertook a round-trip ten-mile hike to Mountain Lake. Dressed in our heaviest clothes and high top boots, we trudged through snow up to our knees. Streets and highways were not readily cleared. It was a gray day, not warm, and our breath could easily be seen in the cold air. We reached our destination in two hours, but stragglers were stretched back over a long distance, and we waited impatiently for them to arrive. When we finally assembled, our first task was to build several fires on which to broil our lunch, consisting of frankfurters and potatoes. We milled around standing as we consumed these delicacies, although in our hurry to eat we had to content ourselves with half-baked spuds. The franks we would have eaten raw. We tramped down a snowy field and began to play ball and running games.

Teddy Morein, tall, lean, always pale, with a good sense of humor, was one of the popular scouts. Suddenly, while running in a race, he fell to the ground and died instantly, the victim of a heart attack. We were stunned. A few scouts ran to the nearest house, nearly a mile away, to summon a doctor. Others bent over him to administer artificial respiration, pounding on his chest, but to no avail. When the doctor finally arrived he could do nothing. We just stood around silent, in grief, helpless.

After the doctor pronounced Teddy dead, I was one of the boys who picked up his body and started for the city, the doctor having promised to send out an ambulance, which would meet us en route. With the scoutmaster, a number of us, who knew the family, trekked to the house to relate what had happened and provide whatever comfort we could to the shocked and grieved. Everyone turned out for the funeral and at the cemetery. It was my first experience with death, and a sad one, for he was a good friend.

The scout troop survived, but the pall of Teddy's sudden death always hung over the group, and it never seemed quite the same attractive youth organization again. I dropped out within the year.

* * *

Death seldom comes singly. A few days later, we heard a shot, and ran out of the house to see what it was all about. Four houses down the street lived a family by the name of Johnson. For reasons that I never learned, Mr. Johnson had decided to commit suicide. He had taken his shotgun, put the barrel in his mouth, and blown most of his head off. The neighbors gathered and watched the gruesome scene from the sidewalk, as his bewildered family wailed. When the police arrived, we were all told to go back to our homes. The family quickly moved out of the house, as mysteriously as Johnson's death.

Caroga Lake

During the summer of 1921, my brother-in-law Sam opened a hot dog, hamburger, soda, and candy stand in a tent at Caroga Lake, about ten miles north of Gloversville. Around this lake, the area was being transformed into a summer resort to attract more people owning automobiles. A man by the name of Sherman had built a large dance hall and restaurant a bit down the road, which attracted mainline dance orchestras. In the evening and on weekends throngs came to the resort. While there had been a number of large cottages on the lake for years, people were buying up the remaining land and building new and smaller ones. In back of our fly-front tent stand was another tent, where I slept alone most of the week, since Sam showed up only on the weekends. He had hoped that there would be a thriving business to supplement his income working in a factory, but it was a rainy summer, and business was not good. We ended the season with a small profit.

I bathed in the lake each morning, a refreshing swim that woke me up as well as cleaned my body. The nights were cool and I slept well under blankets. Young girls my age were a constant attraction. I gave away some free ice cream cones from time to time, when it led to some amorous adventures. On a few occasions I went fishing with Sam for pickerel up at undeveloped Pine Lake, a half dozen miles to the north. A picturesque lake with stumps of cut-over pine trees around the water's edge, testifying to that summer's high rainfall. We tied our lines to the stumps and let them out just before dawn with long, juicy worms as bait. By the time we had run out a dozen lines, we returned to find most of them with fish 24 inches long, which we packed in grass, and Sam took them to the city for delicious meals.

What I experienced was the responsibility he imposed on me as a mere adolescent to run a small business in all of its aspects. I had to do not only with sales, but also with ordering supplies from the salesmen, keeping accounts, and maintaining the place in apple-pie order. Sam did not continue the stand in the second year, as I was beginning to work for my father during the summertime, driving the car, preparing and delivering leather, I had already learned how to type and do simple bookkeeping. Each evening we drove to Sacandaga, where, if we arrived early enough, I played golf, and on weekends I caddied, not only to earn money, but so I could play for free.

My mother's health had improved. She once again resumed all the burdens of running multiple households. We didn't make her life any easier by inviting our friends to change their clothes when they came up for a day's outing, and somehow they always managed to stay for supper.

On occasion I would go out with my parents early in the morning to pick fresh mushrooms, a skill they had acquired in the old country. The mushrooms sprung up overnight in the moist, mossy soil under the tall conifer trees back of the Sacandaga Inn. My mother cooked the tasty and delicate fungus, pink or tan, with potatoes and savories, so that a rich, thick soup was created, whose special aroma permeated the cottage as it simmered over the coal stove. Gas and electric stoves came into vogue later. When she cooked mushrooms, she always put in a silver spoon. If it turned black, it was a poisonous variety, but I never recall either of my parents making an error.

Who can forget the sweet corn, which came to fruition in August? Whether it was the soil, the water, the altitude, or the latitude, I still contend that the fresh-picked corn bought from local farmers equaled that of any other corn that I've eaten in many parts of the world. It was so tender that it could be eaten raw. My mother bought a sackful, one hundred ears or more, cooked them in a large copper boiler, and corn with mushroom soup made a full meal, along with good seeded rye bread, for a Saturday or a Sunday night. It was finished off with coffee, cakes, and cookies.

Sex

Sex was not taught or discussed in our house. I had personally witnessed the delivery of my two younger brothers at home. I knew where babies came from long before I learned how they were created. As children of six and seven, the boys sometimes played doctor and nurse with little girls, examining their respective sexual regions, but it was play without any significance. Sometimes, when a group of boys were up on the hill playing ball, the non-Jewish boys would gather in small circles and indulge in individual masturbation, an intriguing sight to behold, but one which I did not emulate. A teenage non-Jewish girl named Red, who lived next door, introduced me to the mysteries, as well as the ecstasies, of sexual relations. She met me in my father's barn in the hay loft, played with my penis, which was easily aroused, made me don a condom, which she had somehow obtained, and then we did it. While this did not become an obsession, over the course of my adolescent years, I had opportunities to enjoy this titillating pleasure with other girls, some Jewish. I never went out with the boys on a sex party, preferring always to keep it a private matter. I never boasted of my sexual exploits to my friends, nor did I give them any clues as to whom I was seeing. In our earlier years, we did have parties with girls, and if permitted by the parents, who may or may not have been at home, the lights were always turned down or off, so that we could engage in kissing games—a kiss won in the process of spinning a bottle. Obviously we would try to do more than kiss the girls, but we were not always successful, unless we had one of the bolder females, who enjoyed this type of contact. Most girls were afraid to engage in the actual sexual act, but would let you do everything else except the climactic event, leaving the eager male with a feeling of frustration. After a few dates, such teasing girls were abandoned for those who would provide fulfillment. Dancing with girls often involved the execution of dance steps that brought the two bodies tightly together, particularly at the loins, which the girls did not object to, but they would not permit such closeness when you met them alone.

I was street-wise enough to know all about "blue balls," gonorrhea, and syphilis, as well as pregnancy. I was always sheathed in any sexual act. It was against the law for a minor to purchase such a protective device. If one overcame his embarrassment, looked a bit older, and had no fear about approaching the druggist, the instrument could be purchased and no questions were raised about age or motive.

My parents, I believe, were totally unaware of my mischievous sexual escapades. Otherwise they would have sternly lectured me on its evils. Yet I suspect that at least my father may have had a premonition of what I might be doing. When I went out on a date, he would always say: "Remember, you are a Jew!" thrusting the whole moral tradition of the Jewish heritage on my mind. While this always made me feel guilty, it did not deter my enjoyable evening.

Later, when the family's status had risen, he would tell me as I left the house, "Remember, you are a Jew and a Berger!" adding the family's reputation to what I had to bear, lest I violate the ethical code and bring shame on my immediate kinsmen.

* * *

Having a car was a decided asset, since one could not easily find a place in your own home or that of the girls, to pet, let alone press to the limit. Our original Ford, had given way to a second-hand Dodge with a California top. While I was in high school, we purchased a second-hand Buick. We could not yet afford new vehicles in those days. I needed a car for "socializing" as well as to cart around my several drums.

I had been driving a car since I was eleven, and by the time I was thirteen, I thought I should own one. With two other friends, I purchased a used Ford for $35. We fixed and polished it, and then were able to pick up nice girls from Gloversville or Amsterdam with whom we ate, danced, and petted. The car suffered many mishaps, such as burning out the bearings and losing a wheel while going up a hill, and after a year or two, having spent so much of our money and time in making our own repairs, we junked it, going back to begging for the use of the family car.

While I was a reasonably good driver, I had two mishaps before I was fourteen. One day, as I was passing a car on a narrow road which was barely wide enough for one vehicle, the driver of the car that I was about to pass suddenly decided to pass the one in front of him without bothering to even give the customary hand signal, for there were no directional flashing lights until decades later. I ended up in a ditch with the auto on its side. My mother suffered some minor bruises, which were immediately tended by a doctor in Mayfield. I got a garage to right the car and tow it back onto the road, replaced the oil, which had leaked out in the tumble, and then proceeded to our destination. No one reprimanded me for bad handling and I continued driving our car.

A year later, I was driving a full car of folks in Gloversville, when a dog suddenly darted across the road. Having always been mindful to be kind to animals and certainly not kill them, I applied the breaks with undue vigor, skidding the car onto the sidewalk and ending up at a sign advertising cigarettes. Everyone was shook up and frightened. Despite the absence of seat belts, no one was hurt. I backed off to the street and proceeded. But I have never braked for any animal on the highway since, including a chicken, whose feathers I can still see flying skyward.

* * *

Going out with girls, playing in an orchestra, dressing in style, driving and owning a car required money, and that had to be earned. While my parents provided most of my essential needs, including clothing, the extras had to be found elsewhere. I left Cohen's department store, where in my second year my wages were $1.50 for a twelve-hour day and obtained a job at Beck's shoe store, where, with a basic $5 a day salary, I could earn as much as $7.50 to $10, the extras coming from the sale of PMs ("post-mortems")—shoes that were so out of style that with a lot of talking and finagling I was able to convince even wary buyers that they were, in fact, unique and in "season," and what is more, fit them well. The orchestra provided me with additional sums. As soon as I was fourteen, I obtained official working papers and was employed after school and could earn another $2 per week. I was a crack shot in shooting a basketball into a hoop and developed expertise in playing pool, and since as youngsters we gambled for small sums on everything, this also added to my till. Playing cards on Saturday night was another minor vice, but my skill and luck also fattened my pocketbook. I had enough to meet all my requirements, but it meant being active and productive.

* * *

Some part of my earnings were expended in buying modish clothing. I bought my first suit with a Norfolk jacket at Barney Galinsky, the best men's store in town, featuring Kupfenheimer clothing. Later I acquired a magnificent brown herringbone weave, with a long coat that flared when I danced and pants that were in the bell-bottom fashion. When I twirled and dipped with my sister or any other worthy partner at some event or at a 10-cents-a-dance hall, everyone watched as we made a superb dancing couple along with our clothes. My sister Rachel, six years older, was always the most fashionably dressed young woman in town. I gave up wearing mackinaws for real adult coats. For a time I wore spats for special affairs and even donned a homburg hat in my last year in high school.

I recollect having given up wearing short pants with long black socks when I left North Main Street school and entered Estee Junior High. But I had a hankering for short pants too, even when long pants were the vogue, for with the introduction of knickers (knickerbockers) I had several outfits of plus fours and later even longer ones called plus eights. They were cut from attractive plaids, but in the summer I usually wore white linens. Long Argyle socks were fashionable, and I had an assortment of patterns. Like Bobby Jones and Gene Sarazen, I also wore the knickers on the golf course.

* * *

Our family fortunes began to improve as the 1920s advanced. My brother Morris was already married and lived in his own home. My sister Rachel, who wanted to go to college but couldn't afford to, was working full time. I was totally self-sufficient as far as my expense money was concerned, and by the time I left high school, I was earning from a variety of sources up to $25 per week, I could do anything that my heart desired without plaguing my parents for money.

* * *

My adolescence took place during the days of Prohibition, an era of bootlegging and gangsters. While I never had the opportunity to visit the notorious Cotton Club in Harlem in the 1920s, I saw the movie of the same name toward the end of 1984 and was immediately reminded of an experience a few of my friends and I went through with a reputed bootlegger in Gloversville back in 1924, sixty years earlier. We had left the Jewish Community Center after an evening of basketball and stopped at the ice cream parlor for a banana split, never counting our calories or worrying about our weight. Then, as we were just driving about town, we stopped at a corner next to a large car driven by a local man who, everyone said, transported contraband liquor from Canada and sold it in one of the speakeasies which could be found in every rural hamlet as well as larger cities.

For some incomprehensible reason, the driver of our car, always irrepressible in his speech, blurted out as we started to pass the vehicle, "Bottlegger! Bootlegger!" not once but twice, then stepped on the gas and sped down the street. I turned in my seat to see whether this foolish remark had any consequences and to my horror discovered that the bootlegger's car seemed to be pursuing us. Dave, our driver, in a small Ford, pressed the gas pedal to the floor and at the first cross street made a wheel-screaming left, then proceeded to slow down a bit, only to learn that the other car had skidded around the same corner in hot pursuit. The three of us were stupified with fear. Dave shot up the street, made another left and then another, with the other car gaining on us only half a block behind. I pleaded with Dave to drive into a large garage, which we knew was open, and after a few more turns we entered this building, jumped out of the vehicle, and ran into the manager's small office beseeching help. The bootlegger, alleged or true, meanwhile was still on our tail. Driving into the garage, he quickly and literally jumped out of his car. A youngish, tall, handsome man, whom we all had known as a fine athlete, and whom we often passed on the street, even addressing him by his first name, grabbed Dave, lifting him off his feet, and shouted, "Don't you ever dare say that again!" He let him down slowly, returned to his Cadillac, and drove out. We were trembling afterwards as we contemplated our narrow escape from injury and even death. The papers were filled with stories of the ruthlessness of such illegal operators. Being shot to death movie-style did not escape our thoughts. I learned a lesson, and so did Dave, for ever after, he was more circumspect even in his off-the-cuff speech.

A Spelling Bee

An important businessman, who found that his son, a senior in high school, and in my class, was a poor speller, offered a prize of $25 to the high school if it would conduct a spelling contest. Every senior had to go through some preliminaries, and twenty-five students were selected to participate in the final event. I went off to the contest that evening. I didn't bother to tell my parents or siblings, as I had no expectations of winning. But as the evening progressed and one contestant after another was forced to drop out for failing to correctly spell the word given, I found myself matched with one other speller, Alfred F. Patten, valedictorian of our class, an excellent pianist, and handsome to the point of seeming effeminate, so that the editor of *The Oracle* wrote: "We wonder if Al makes all his own dresses." The editor also wrote "A great pianist rivaling Paderewski." Al missed on the word "irascible." I had never even heard the word before, let alone know what it meant. But perhaps I had come across it one of those days when I was sitting at the front desk in the classroom thumbing through the dictionary, and if so it must have impressed itself on my unconscious. In any event, I spelled it correctly. I modestly accepted the $25 prize in cash and mumbled a thank you. When I reached home, told the story to my family, and gave my mother the $25, they were more amazed than I was at my victory. Now at last I had one accomplishment of some merit for my four years in high school. Forty years later, the *Leader-Republican*, the Gloversville newspaper, recorded this accomplishment in its column "Ten, Twenty, Thirty, Forty, Fifty Years ago." The event had a kind of immortality.

High school did not make much of an intellectual impression on me. I only recall a few of my teachers. For typing I had Miss Murphy, who was very pretty. I had a secret crush on her and as a consequence learned how to type fast.

She gave me a 100 for the term. It is a skill which I have used productively all my life. I still type fast, but not always with accuracy. There was Wiggins, who taught business subjects. He was blond, feminine, middle-aged, with a good sense of humor. He also gave me passing grades, because I was attentive and made out well in his examinations. Vickery was a tall, lean, sourpuss professor of physics and chemistry, who made the abstruse sciences simple, practical, and interesting. Under his tutelage I learned how to make batteries, built a radio crystal set, and mastered the art of tanning rabbit skins. Mrs. Yerkes taught Senior English and concentrated on Shakespeare. For the first time I began to appreciate this genius, as she illuminated his characters, but above all explained the magnificence of his quotable phrases. But none of my teachers trained me either to study or even to read, important skills that I had to develop for myself some years later.

2

College—Reporter—College

College—New York University

I WAS NOT ACTUALLY interested in going to college, but my mother had other plans and insisted that I should make something of myself. She even suggested that I should become an engineer, a field which was not exactly hospitable to Jews. Why she suggested that discipline I do not know, for I was not interested or talented in either mathematics or science. My father gave only reluctant encouragement, for he thought I ought to stay home and help him with his business.

As usual, my mother, a persistent woman, won out.

It was suggested that I matriculate at Columbia University. I discussed this with Harry Starr, and he told me that he would contact the dean of admissions, a personal friend. The dean examined my record, which was not distinguished academically (I had a 77 average), and then, to my great surprise, told me that I would not be eligible for the 1925 fall term, because the Jewish quota had been filled. The Ivy League schools, led by Harvard and Yale, had adopted a policy of limiting the number of Jewish students, because they were seemingly already too numerous as well as promiscuous. Jews, who were ambitious academically, socially, and professionally, wanted to study only at the best universities. The universities responded with restrictive admission policies fully in line with the pervasive bigoted attitudes and open anti-Semitism that had emerged in the 1920s. The federal government had legislated severe restrictions on the immigration of foreigners from Eastern and Southern European countries, which obviously affected Jews. Henry Ford, through his newspaper, the *Dearborn Independent*, was spewing its noxious anti-Semitic venom throughout the country and in addition was widely circulating the spurious *Protocols of the Elders of Zion*. Not being as well informed, combative, or sophisticated as I later became, I accepted the dean's verdict without a whimper and left. He could have rejected me on other grounds, but in candor he told it like it was.

I was again to run into anti-Semitism some years later when I tried to obtain a position as a teacher in the Gloversville school system and was told by the superintendent of schools that the Jewish quota for teachers was also filled. The quota was one Jewish teacher.

My revenge came in 1938, when the faculty of the New York School of Social Work (later a division of Columbia University) asked me to teach and I accepted.

After consulting with my parents and friends and other relatives, I decided to enroll at New York University, located in Manhattan's historic Washington Square. This college, I was informed, would take anyone who paid the fee. David Pontak, a student at the university, was helpful in arranging my registration, and I stayed at his home in the Bronx while executing these steps. My parents paid my tuition and gave me $50 per month to cover all of my other expenses. To cut costs, I always hitched back and forth to New York. It was difficult to get a ride directly into or out of the city, but a five-cent subway dropped you in Yonkers; a five-cent trolley took you to the outskirts of that city; and a few more nickels brought you to Peekskill and the open highway.

Where to live? A cousin from Gloversville, Harry Pozefsky, who was a junior at NYU, approached me about living with a group of five other students, who wanted to rent an apartment back of a beauty parlor at 50 West 8th Street in the heart of Greenwich Village. The others included his wild older brother Joe, who had just graduated from Cornell and was entering the NYU Law School; Joe Weisman from St. Louis, a serious student in his junior year, who read poetry out loud by the hour and later became a schoolteacher; a sophomore named Manny Goldstein from Nyack, undisciplined and garrulous, who became a lawyer and a judge; and Harry Shertzman of Gloversville, a portly, tallish fellow with a Falstaffian sense of humor, who decided at the last minute not to go to school and eventually entered the business world. The Pozefsky brothers ended up as lawyers in small towns. I was the only lowly freshman. To the best of my knowledge, all of them have passed away.

It was an unforgettable year, in which I learned little at the university, but a great deal about New York, about the behavior of college youth in the roaring twenties and about theater, poetry, and the bohemian world with which I came into daily contact.

A score of students hung around our house, as though it were an extention of the university. Some came to study or talk. Some came to gamble. Some tried to use it as a place of assignation for girls they picked up. Some were brilliant students. Others were top athletes. They were rich, middle class, and poor. All eventually did quite well with their lives. In retrospect they were a fair cross-section of the Jewish community.

I enrolled in these courses—geology, trigonometry, ancient history, English composition, and French. Geology was at 9 A.M. I liked the course, particularly the field trips to the Palisades, standing gray, tall, and majestically solid on the Hudson River. We were taken to Connecticut to see the drumlins or terminal moraines, pileups resulting from the melting of the ice age. I also learned about the theoretical origin of the universe, an especially fascinating subject, since the Tennessee "monkey" trials were being conducted during this very period, with evolution having to defend itself against creationism, and Clarence Darrow matched against William Jennings Bryan, who spouted, "I am more interested in the 'Rock of Ages' than in the Age of Rocks." When I went home during the Thanksgiving holidays, I recall relating my new, discovered knowledge to my father, that evolution contradicted the information that I had obtained in Hebrew school about the biblical origins of the universe. He asked me a number of questions, but he did not argue with me even though the views I was expressing were diametrically opposite to his. He commented that what I had learned was very interesting, but he would prefer to retain his previous beliefs.

My father was intelligent enough to know that what I was saying had merit, but he did not want to disillusion me by challenging the new learning that I had just acquired, but had not tested against positions that he had repeatedly told me were thousands of years old.

Mathematics was always a dull subject for me, and while I usually passed, I am afraid that its mysteries and complexities eluded me, although my instructors and learned friends always insisted that it was the simplest of courses. The laws of probability intrigued the class however, because the professor used gambling devices, such as one's chances of winning at the dice table or on a wheel, to illustrate certain key principles. Nonetheless, math left no lasting impression on me. French was more involved, since with three years of high school French behind me, I was put into an advanced class with a Frenchman as a teacher. He did not think highly of my accent or my grammar and would embarrass me in class by calling upon me to read aloud from the *Bourgeois Gentilhomme,* which I falteringly read and translated. I did much better on written examinations, when I did not have him haughtily staring at me in an open class.

History, I loved. That is the correct word. I easily identified with the older periods and their events. I had always had a historical sense, believing that everything had a beginning, middle, and end. The professor, a tall, rather thin man with a beard, made the ancients come alive and stimulated me to take many courses in history and continue to read history all of my life.

English composition was an outright bore, for the professor was more concerned with grammar than with the literary creativity in the writings we read and wrote. I really never gave a damn about syntax, and since I had already developed what I believed was some talent for writing, exhibited in an article I had written in 1924–25 for a Gloversville Jewish journal, and could use words handily, I would have preferred a different kind of English course.

Because of my other diversions, my semester ended with a lot of cramming. My report card showed four A's and one F, the latter for cutting too many of my 9 A.M. classes in geology. I was called in, put on probation, which I felt unjustified, and told to mend my erring ways.

My final year ended with three A's and two F's, one for cuts in my 9 A.M. geology class, where I really had learned enough and tried to convince my professor of my knowledge on the final exam, to no avail. The other F was in French, where I did miserably on my written examination. I failed to identify properly a passage from some French novel, misinterpreted the whole story, and translated it with a number of mistakes. I had the same experience in "Chaucer" at the University of Missouri, but this story I will relate later.

When I reached home in June, I intercepted my report from the university, which had indicated that if I returned, I would have to repeat two courses. I had failed. Flunked out. Tearfully I revealed my derelictions to my parents, who for some strange reason were not angry, but very disappointed. Since I had already made up my mind not to return to school, I looked for a job in Gloversville, and was not considered a dropout by anyone except myself.

But if my academic work at the university was a mixed bag, for I did get seven A's along with three F's, proof that I wasn't a complete dullard, my life that year made me grow twelve years in twelve months.

With five exotic roommates, and all of us having the capacity to attract many friends, our apartment was always an overfilled campus stopping place. We were only two blocks away from the university, and numerous fellow students stopped in on their way to and from class. One turned off West 8th Street, into the Mews, which crossed into and backed up the handsome row of early nineteenth-century houses made of red brick, facing Washington Square North. That Henry James and other distinguished families occupied them was of more than passing interest.

Most of us were card players, playing late at night or on weekends, and particularly after football games. Cards often changed to dice, and the place always seemed to be a gambling den, with the carpet rolled back and a dozen young students on their knees, rolling the ivories back and forth with cries and prayers that the numbers would be in their favor. As the year progressed, students dropped in and gambled most of the day in between classes and on their way to and from classes. While I added to my income by my skill and luck at pinochle, I was literally forced, because of flaws in my character, to engage in other gambling pursuits, where fortune did not favor me. Sometimes this was at the expense of my studies.

When the apartment wasn't used for gambling, then our pals would troop in with girls, some of whom did not mind going to bed. The place took on the smoked-filled, gloominess of an amateur whorehouse. Some nights I would come home and find my bedroom preempted by an amorous couple, and very often, to add insult to injury, the male wasn't even one of my permanent roommates. While I was not exactly innocent in my relations with girls, I literally abhorred promiscuity and was never a party to such sexual ventures. These so-called extracurricular activities were not an inducement to study.

On such occasions I had to turn elsewhere—to the university library or on the second floor of the all-night restaurant next door, where the operators were tolerant of our using it for such nonrestaurant purposes, if we bought some food. There were even nights when I returned home to find an SRO sign in the window, which meant that even though I was the legal occupant of the flat, I had to wait outside until some of our friends finally decided to leave.

In our apartment in Greenwich Village, I never knew what I would find when I returned home. Six of us lived in a three-bedroom flat, and each of us had a bedmate, all male. One night I came home rather late, let myself in with the key, and found the place in darkness. I undressed quietly, walked into my bedroom on tiptoe so as not to awaken anyone, and crawled into my side of the bed. I found myself next to a warm, cuddly woman's body. I grasped the situation immediately—they had had their fill and were both purringly asleep. Not wanting to spend the night on an uncomfortable chair, I decided to make the best of it, even though it was a bit crowded with a trio. Nothing happened sexually. I slept soundly. The next morning no one remarked about this strange happening. I put the incident behind me. The young woman never showed up again at our apartment. I suspected that it was a chance encounter between my roommate and this girl, whom he might have picked up on his walking-searches through the streets of the village. Girls were always available. They were not prostitutes, just adventurous amateurs.

Every Monday night without fail, we religiously attended the Palace Theatre at 48th Street and Seventh Avenue to witness the opening of the new week's program of the best vaudeville in the world. For 25 cents we walked up to the top gallery. Our eager eyes and ears took in every movement and word uttered by the sparkling comedians, marveled at the acrobats and dog acts, and almost got up in the aisles to strut with the dancers, whether one, or two or in a line. It would take a page to list all the greats that we saw: Eddie Cantor, Al Jolson, Jimmy Durante, Sophie Tucker, Fannie Brice, Jack Benny, Ed Wynn, W. C. Fields, and Will

Rogers. Some of these popular stars were in between their major roles in Broadway spectaculars or on their way for cross-country tours.

It was the theater that I also found most influential in my later life. Tickets were cheap and easily obtained. I saw many of Eugene O'Neill's plays: *The Emperor Jones, The Great God Brown, The Hairy Ape,* and *The Fountain,* based on Ponce de Leon's search for the Fountain of Youth. Eugene O'Neill, despite his gloomy outlook, his unusually long works, his digging into the interior lives, the psychological attitudes, the conflicts between people even in the most intimate families, appeared to me as America's outstanding dramatist, and I sought out his new plays and revivals whenever they appeared in the Greater New York area. Whenever young people or foreigners want to get a deeper and richer insight into America's cultural life and particularly its theater, I alway advise them to read O'Neill or better yet see the revived performances.

Not long ago, while reading Burns Mantle's *The Best Plays of 1925–26,* and realizing how many of them I had seen, I was astounded to learn how much of my time had been spent in the theater. The other plays I saw were *The Green Hat, The Butter and Egg Man, Craig's Wife, The Dybbuk, The Jazz Singer, Last of Mrs. Cheney, Lucky Sam McCarver, No, No Nanette,* and *The Student Prince.* No wonder I had so little time for study; and no wonder there was never enough money to last the month.

Meanwhile, about four months after we moved into the West 8th Street apartment, our landladies, who ran a beauty parlor in the front, decided they'd had enough of our shenanigans, and one day we found all of our personal possessions in the alleyway.

We scoured the neighborhood and rented an apartment on the first floor of a Greenwich Street house near Seventh Avenue, across the street from the theater where O'Neill's plays were performed. Our friends soon found us, and the same kinds of activities were renewed in our new quarters, but since the apartment was smaller, we had to impose some severe restrictions.

While some of us received an allowance, our money never seemed to hold out and was gone by the end of the third week of the month. All of us worked somewhere, usually on Saturdays, selling shoes in stores that were always in the process of going out of business with the customary "come-on" sales. A few times, we traveled by train to Stamford, Connecticut. We made about $15 a day, and that plus occasional gambling winnings carried us through the month. During the last two months we could not scrape enough money together, so they cut off our electricity and telephone for not paying our bills. A diet of rolls costing 2 cents and milk about 9 cents a quart kept us going for the last few days of the month. Once in a while we got a free meal by accepting invitations to the homes of college friends who exploited our lodgings. That involved a long 5-cent subway ride to the interior of Brooklyn or the Bronx. My relatives invited me to Brooklyn or Newark, and if it was for an entire weekend, I would be well provided for and even brought back something for a day or two, which was shared with my companions. My brother Morris came to New York once in a while for business and treated me to dinner at a top-flight restaurant. My sister Rachel visited me at the Greenwich Street residence and was repelled by the bohemian atmosphere, although, knowing her adventurous character, I believe that she secretly wished that she too might have gone through such extraordinary experiences.

We also went to the Yiddish theater, then in its prime, with stellar actors like Maurice Schwartz. We could see them through the window enjoying a drink or a meal at the Cafe Royale on Second Avenue, a haunt for thespians who had arrived. Our experiences with the waiters at Rappaport's or Ratner's, whose English was liberally sprinkled with Yiddishisms, was also something to talk about beyond the food. Impatient and arrogant in taking our order, they also forced you to endure their off-the-cuff, snide and humorous comments about what you were eating or perhaps the party at the next table. When you asked for the specialty of the day, you would be answered: "I do not have time to advise you." Books on Jewish humor are full of remarks made by the fabulous waiters in the old Jewish restaurants. But the rolls and sweet butter, the mushroom and barley soup, the cheese blintzes smothered in heavy sour cream, the savory shmaltz herring compel one to go back to the remaining Jewish dairy restaurants to order the same dishes. It is rare to find one of the old-time waiters. They have long since gone.

We walked the streets of New York. We knew each block intimately. We relished the piquant smells of the different cultures occupying the Lower East Side, Chinatown, Italian Greenwich Village. We took in museums and movie houses. But it was the street cultures that remain vivid. I still like to walk through the side streets of the city, gazing at the architecture that sprung up in the nineteenth and early twentieth centuries. Downtown, the Woolworth Building was still the tallest skyscraper. Steadily Wall Street and the contiguous areas were becoming canyons without a bit of sunlight. Now with even taller buildings, that section of the city has become a spectacle.

Our own Greenwich Village had its share of celebrities. Early some mornings, I saw Texas Guinan returning with her entourage from night club speakeasies to her apartment east of us on Eighth Street. Maxwell Bodenheim, the flamboyant poet, could be seen parading the streets with his cape flying in the wind. Actors and artists were pointed out to passersby as they walked through the streets, for no one lived in privacy during the hectic 1920s. Crime was literally unknown, and we came home in the dark by subway and walked the intervening blocks without fear of molestation.

Our last night in New York was unforgettable. To celebrate it, during the days of Prohibition, we decided to forgo baths in our tiny bathtub, scrubbed it clean, and used it to make beer according to someone's formula which required only a week of brewing. About a dozen of us gathered for the party with an assortment of crackers and cheeses. Since our electricity had been cut off, the apartment was dark except for candles and flashlights. Every so often someone would step into the bathroom and bring out fresh pitchers of beer. I had not yet learned to appreciate the taste and effect of that kind of homemade beer, although I did drink beer at home or in a saloon, usually limited to one glass or mug. This concoction I did not find to my liking, so that I was the only one who remained sober. In the early hours of the morning, as the hilarity increased and the beer had almost been consumed, some of the boys forced portly Shertzman, who was glowingly drunk, into the tub, clothes and all, and because it was a tight fit, there he remained for some hours until he sobered up.

The year ended. I was not to see New York for another four years, when it and its environs came to be my permanent residence.

We Buy a New House on Bleeker Street

As our family fortunes improved, it became obvious, particularly for my mother and sister, that we had to live in a better neighborhood. My mother was pressing Rachel to get married, and Washburn Street was not the most prepossessing address.

While I was off to college my father, mother, and sister, after searching the town, found a customer for our house, garage, and barn. A Syrian immigrant family named Toney had done well; they bought the property and converted the barn into a grocery store. The son, Anthony, later became a well-known artist and teacher in New York. We purchased a handsome, large two-family house on upper Bleeker Street, a street with a number of imposing structures occupied by prominent professionals, business, old-line families, all non-Jewish. The Livingstons, who ran the town's largest furniture store, lived next door. The Murphys, who operated the best shoe store in town, lived directly across the street. His wife's maiden name was Cohen. Her grandfather, a Jew who settled in Gloversville in the mid-1800s, had converted to Christianity, but the family retained the avowedly Jewish name. His granddaughter married a Catholic businessman. We were friendly as neighbors and were buyers of his fine footwear.

Our new house, which dated from the turn of the century, was built entirely of wood and clapboard, with an L-shaped porch covering the front and side. Stained-glass windows adorned the front entrances on both levels. The downstairs interior included four bedrooms, kitchen, dining, living, and sitting rooms, high ceilinged, covered with embossed metal. The walls were half-wainscoted in oak panels. Gas fireplaces provided additional heat for the living and sitting rooms, but steam heat kept the house warm for three quarters of the year. The upper level had similar quarters. It was a fitting place for Rachel to invite her beaux, and she had a number of them, for she was a pretty, well-dressed, smartly coiffeured young woman. At that time she was working as a reporter and writer for the *Morning-Herald,* and her special pieces were written extremely well and read widely. Later she would leave to take a position as secretary to the president of the Fulton County National Bank, where she remained until she was married.

Our upstairs neighbors were the Antevils, who owned a successful glove-making factory. The older son attended Yale University. They moved out in a few years and built a new home on Kingsboro Avenue, the finest residential section. Their rooms were quickly rented to the Nissenbaums, who had recently moved into town to open up a large fur tannery.

We had no sooner moved in than my always early-rising, part-peasant, prudent father hand-plowed a small garden at the rear of the house, where he grew a variety of vegetables, nurtured partly by garbage which he carefully selected from the kitchen, such as peelings of vegetables and fruits, leftover bones, and egg shells, which in his compost heap added considerably to the quicker growth, size, and even taste of his produce.

When I came home from New York University in June 1926 with four friends as guests, it was to our new house at 187 Bleeker Street. Gone was the Tiffany lamp overhanging the round oak table and oak chairs in the dining room, replaced by a modern walnut set of table and matched chairs, buffet, and a simpler, less colorful, modern, hanging chandelier. Gone were the mahogany, green velvet sofa and chairs in the living room, and in their stead was a modern stuffed sofa and large chairs, which we all agreed were more comfortable. Gone was the mahogany upright piano, and various tables filled in the spaces. The old pictures were also gone, shipped to the cottage at Sacandaga, where they still hang. The kitchen had a modern gas range and sink. The bathroom now had flush toilets instead of the long-chained pull handles, which when tugged let down a rush of noisy water into the bowl. The porch had modern wicker furniture. Only the bedrooms were the same, assuring us of old comforts and memories. But modernity finally won out, for even those old brass and white iron beds were to be displaced by up-to-date wooden bedsteads, then in vogue. They of course included matching bureaus and tables. So the old order finally did change completely. My mother and sister were pleased. It was now a house fit to entertain the finest suitors or visitors, even to impress visiting relatives. My father, who first balked at the expense and debt, finally accepted it and exhibited it with the same pride as the females. My brothers Sam and Milton and I liked it too, albeit there were items from the past that I missed.

As Sam and I and our wives, and for that matter Rachel too, became collectors of antiques, developing a new appreciation for the types of articles that had once been our commonplace possessions, we were retrospectively annoyed that all that older furniture and the Tiffany light fixture, which were so quickly sold off, had now become rarities for which we had to pay extravagant prices. Still worse, the things we purchased, however similar to the ones that once adorned our house, were like intruding strangers, without that old nostalgic aroma.

I Become a Newspaper Reporter

My sister Rachel had been working at the *Morning Herald*, the ten-thousand-subscriber morning newspaper owned by Emmett Cullings. There was a rival paper, the *Leader-Republican*, with a larger circulation, that appeared in the afternoon. Years later they were merged into the *Leader-Herald*. Rachel left in 1926 to work for the Fulton County National Bank, so there was a vacancy, and she recommended me for the job. Cullings, a short, portly, cigar-smoking officious man took me on without too much of an interview, after I agreed to work for $15 per week. Since this was a morning paper, my shift was roughly from 4 P.M. to 3 A.M., but it could sometimes be longer when there was special news or problems arose in the mechanical department. The editor was Beach, a serious, talkative alcoholic, who was constantly pushing his hair around his head and was possessed of a great deal of wisdom. He taught me how to write succinctly and accurately, always insisting that the basic copy, as far as possible, should go into the first paragraph, so that if the story had to be cut, the reader would still have gotten the main elements in summary. Beaman, a younger man, who always wore a green vizor, edited all the material that came over the wire service. He too was a constant drinker. Often, when both Beach and Beaman wound up in the speakeasy across the street on the third floor, I, just nineteen years old, turned out the paper by myself, even writing the headlines for the first page, which they suggested in their stupor.

Bess Marks was a graduate of the University of Missouri's School of Journalism. She had worked for the past year learning the business, and was about to move to another larger paper in western New York. She eventually became her own publisher-editor. Bess told me about Missouri and recommended it as a good university and inexpensive, whether I wanted to study journalism or anything else.

Obviously, I had no previous training as a journalist, but I quickly learned the craft from day to day by gritty experience. Since I was the only reporter, I did most of my work on the outside, then typed the story. If I had free time, I edited a lot of the mail that came from nearby villages—Stone Arabia, Ephratah, Vails Mills, Broadalbin, Perth, Oppenheim—because this was an important source of news for our out-of-town subscribers, who, like everyone else, liked to see their names in the paper. Church news, covered-dish suppers, literary clubs, births, marriages, deaths, changes of ownership of a business, and occasional crimes—on the whole, misdemeanors—made up the bulk of the copy.

While from time to time the editor and even the publisher gave me a lead for a story, I was literally on my own. I made the daily rounds of city hall, reported the meetings of the Board of Aldermen, read the police blotter, checked in at the fire department. Occasionally the hook and ladder vehicle on the way to an important fire stopped in front of the office, and if I was free and had heard the alarm, I would hop on the back to get a first-hand look at a fire. On the most memorable occasion of this kind, I helped to rescue a large number of distraught horses from a barn that subsequently burned to the ground.

I made the rounds of the churches in my search for news—and there were numerous and substantial edifices of every denomination—interviewing clergymen and sometimes editing some of their sermons for publication. I met with the superintendent of schools and different principals to get a story. I looked in on the Nathan Littauer Hospital to get a list of who was sick, babies that were born, those released and those who had died. I wrote hundreds of obituary notices.

For a nineteen-year-old, this was heady stuff, as I met the entire leadership, and many of the rank-and-file citizens, of a small community and its environs.

The *New York Daily News* called me on two occasions in connection with celebrated stories. The Rev. Mr. Snyder had run off with Mrs. Gray after killing her husband. The police were searching for them everywhere. It was believed that they might have stopped off in Gloversville on their flight to Canada. I studied the hotel registers, interrogated the desk clerks, and with pictures of the infamous couple, found that they had indeed stopped overnight at the Kingsboro Hotel. So the police search was intensified northward.

An elderly woman, who ran a boarding house in Brooklyn, was found hacked to death in a gruesome murder. The *Daily News* labeled it "Hatchet Murder" in huge type on the first page. That paper learned that she had relatives in Cranberry Creek, twelve miles north of Gloversville. I drove out with the boss's son, Emmet Jr., a classmate in high school, to interview the dead woman's relatives. I discovered that the victim had a close relationship with a Norwegian seaman who boarded at her establishment. She had repeatedly refused to marry him. He was also known to have a fierce temper and a tendency to violence. I reported my findings to New York. The sailor was picked up as a suspect and subsequently was convicted of the heinous crime.

The Irish Catholics dominated the Catholic scene in Gloversville, due to their longer residence, the wealth and standing which they had acquired, and the Irish priests who officiated in their handsome church. The Italians and the Slovaks, latecomers, but growing in numbers, considered themselves by treatment as second-class Catholics. The Italians finally engaged an aggressive Italian priest by the name of Father Ottaviano to serve their needs in makeshift quarters. Interviewing him one day, I learned that it was his ambition to build a distinctive Italian Catholic church. As I drew him out, I saw a good story in the making, told him I would help, and wrote a major, first-page account with a three-column headline, indicating that the Italians were going to build their own church. It disturbed the Irish, but did not deter the Italians. In the course of time the money was raised and a large building was erected on South Main Street. The father told me that my story was the starting point for his successful campaign.

The Jewish Community Center was housed on the top floor of the *Morning Herald* building, where I worked. While the several rooms were spacious and even included a gymnasium with an eighteen-foot ceiling, it was hardly a suitable facility for a growing and wealthy Jewish community of fifteen hundred people. The old synagogue was imposing, but it had limited use as a religious sanctuary and Hebrew school. There were hundreds of young people who wanted a more commodious center with a real gym, a swimming pool, an auditorium, and all the other requisites. I taunted the leadership, whom I saw regularly and knew intimately, as I visited them at the center, or at their businesses, or even in their homes. It was decided clandestinely that I was to write a story stating that plans were afoot to raise money and build a major structure which would provide all the facilities that a respectable Jewish community needed. When the story appeared, in part on the first page, it caused quite a storm. I was even accused of writing an untrue story about what the Jewish leadership was thinking and planning. The story was never publicly denied and finally forced the center's leadership to create a committee, and two years later, in 1929, a magnificent building was dedicated with all the facilities they and I had envisioned. Instead of a routine auditorium, a real theater and stage were constructed.

Clarence Darrow

The center conducted an annual lecture series in which prominent Jewish and other personalities were brought to the city. If there was a large advance ticket sale, the program might be held in the Glove

Theater. It was really too large for such purposes, but the soft seats were much more comfortable than the hard wooden chairs at the center.

In 1926–27, Louis Schine, one of two brothers who owned and operated the local theaters plus a growing chain all over the state and elsewhere, became the chairman of the lecture committee. I was invited to the planning committee meeting and remember Louis, who was not the most elegant speaker, stating that he wanted "speakers who would pack them in." After a number of suggestions had been offered, I spoke up and strongly recommended that we bring Clarence Darrow, the eminent Chicago lawyer, who had attained international fame as the defense attorney in the Loeb-Leopold case, where two young, rich Jewish youths were tried and convicted, but not executed, for the murder of a young Jewish child named Frank, who came from a well-to-do family that the senseless murderers knew. On top of that Darrow had been the attorney for the defense in the equally well publicized Scopes trial, where he defended a teacher who was subsequently convicted of teaching evolution in the classroom. William Jennings Bryan, lawyer, politician, presidential candidate, provided the oratory for the state, as an archexponent of the biblical account as the only, approved document on the creation of the universe.

Darrow was accepted and agreed to come. The advance sale was so phenomenal that over a thousand tickets were sold, and in consequence the site of the lecture had to be changed from the theater, which did not have enough seats, to the armory, a cavernous hall, where major sport events as well as military drills were held. What was surprising about the response was that Gloversville was a most conservative community. While there was some fear, which never materialized, of a possible backlash of the Christians against the Jews for bringing this outright radical atheist to the community, the event went off without incident. I wrote an eight-column story on Darrow and his speech, wherein he castigated the religious establishment for deceiving people with myths rather than facts. He claimed that they had failed to get across to their parishioners the ethical message that was embodied in religion itself. He was violently opposed to capital punishment, claiming that a civilized citizenry had no right to take another person's life, even if an individual committed murder. He spoke of the many injustices in our society toward the working man and minority groups. He answered questions until the chairman finally called a halt. It was a night that Gloversville never quite got over.

The committee had decided to pick up Darrow in Fonda, where the New York Central train from Chicago, where Darrow lived, made a stop. I was asked to accompany the committee. When we reached Gloversville, we dropped him off at the Kingsboro Hotel. After lunch he asked to be excused, because he wanted to rest. He requested that I go with him to his room. He was a man a little above medium height, already in his seventies, with a wrinkled face and twinkles in his eyes. His clothes were sturdy but unpressed. When he took off his jacket to lie down on the bed, he revealed the suspenders which signatured his dress style, always a distinguishing feature in the movies and on stage, and which, he told me, were "to keep my pants up." He was thirsty for some real beer and was sure, since I was a reporter, that I could find some—and I did, across the street in a clandestine saloon.

We talked for over an hour, as he quizzed me about my young life. I told him I had left college, decided I might become a journalist, and was learning the trade in the field. He broke in to tell me I ought to go back to college and complete my education. I reminded him that H. L. Mencken, the celebrated *Baltimore Sun* reporter who covered the Scopes trial, had never gone to college and had become a famous writer as well as a newspaper man. Having read a bit about Darrow's background, I also reminded him that he had read law in an attorney's office and never went to law school. He replied crisply, "Those days are over." He advised that the future would be in the hands of the college-educated and not in those of the rare, exceptional individuals who made it on their own. When a great man talks, you listen, and I did. I am convinced that this counsel made me return to college, reinforcing what my mother, father, and sister had been urging upon me for the whole year.

One morning at the newspaepr office in walked Lucius N. Littauer, the most famous man that Gloversville ever produced and was the first Jewish child born in the town. It was my first face-to-face contact with him. Littauer had graduated from Harvard, where he had pulled an oar on the Harvard crew and played football, and he subsequently became Harvard's football coach, in fact the first college football coach in the United States. A successful businessman, he represented our district in Congress for seven terms and was an intimate of President Theodore Roosevelt. Wealthy beyond his needs, he decided to devote his life to philanthropy. He had already established a hospital in memory of his parents. He built a park, then a swimming pool, and contributed to all major charities, including the Jewish Community Center and synagogue. Later he was to do this on a national scale.

The city of Gloversville, deciding that it was time to honor Littauer, began to raise money to erect a life-size bronze statue and put it in a public place. When this medium-height, slightly stocky, white-haired distinctively moustached mogul walked in and without any ado asked me to accompany him, I readily accepted. He was on his way to the railroad freight station to witness the arrival of his crated statue. Then he wanted me to help him select a site for its permanent display. Overwhelmed by the invitation, I walked back with him to his chauffeured limousine. While he never told me why he had selected me, and I was too timid to ask, I was not entirely speechless. I asked him why he had to choose a location, when this would usually be the responsibility of the prominent committee that had been set up to pay honor to his benevolence. To my surprise, he related that the statue cost $40,000. The city in its generosity had only raised $20,000; he had contributed the balance and then felt he had some right to recommend a site. We drove around to several places and finally drew up to the lawn in front of the high school. He pointed to the corner of Main Street and Prospect Avenue as the most desirable spot. There would be a lot of traffic, schoolchildren would have to pass it daily, and that is where it was placed for posterity. The city, at the statue's dedication a year later, made quite a fuss: parade, speeches, photographs, brochures. None of Littauer's subsequent reporters or biographers ever mentioned this incident.

While I went to the movies nearly every day, since I had a free pass, I also often dropped into a gambling joint at the Four Corners, Main and Fulton streets, to spend an hour or so before going to my office down the street. I bet on horse races, played poker, occasionally rolled the dice; I won some, lost some, but on the whole broke even. Once a month, I played poker with the boys from the backroom of the newspaper, linotype operators and pressmen, in a speakeasy across the street, and I am sorry to say for them that I took away a good part of their wages, since I had unusually good luck.

I led a reasonably active social life, in spite of the restrictions posed by my working six nights a week. It was also a year that marked the beginnings of my intellectual awakening. I read a number of books, among them Lewis Browne's *Stranger Than Fiction* and *This Believing World,* one a popular history of the Jewish people and the other a readable companion piece on the better-known religious groups. Since Browne mentioned William James's *Varieties of Religious Experience,* I borrowed that from the library and read it with interest. I was at a stage where I was questioning all absolutes, including Judaism. An examination of the various faiths, which I had a chance to observe closely in my journalistic wanderings amongst the local church denominations, accompanied by these readings, ultimately led me to reaffirm my Jewishness. It was now reinforced by historical and sociological concepts rather than theological preachments.

I remember reading Ben Hecht's *Count Bruga,* which subsequently led me to read many of this journalist-writer's provocative works. I wrote a book review for the paper, and my first effort was Struther Burt's *The Delectable Mountain.* When none of the readers of the paper bothered to comment on it, the editor decided that the paper's readers were not ready for that "intellectual stuff." I wrote a long piece on the celebrated murder in our area that Theodore Dreiser described in such vivid detail in his novel *An American Tragedy.*

I also wrote some nature poetry in classic style as well as some verse that didn't rhyme and received my first rejection slips, which included one from F.P.A. (Franklin P. Adams), who wrote an extraordinary column, "The Conning Tower," in the now defunct *New York Herald-Tribune*. Since the nights were long and I couldn't leave the office until the paper was on the press at 3 A.M., I even undertook a novel dealing with the sexual vagaries of a teenager. I read parts of it to a long-distance female telephone operator, whom I never met, but who relieved the monotony of a long night by listening. She was my severest critic and told me that while the events I described had a certain interest, the story that enfolded did not grip her. I finally chucked it into the wastebasket.

After Emma and I were married, my sister Rachel told Emma to save every scrap of paper that I wrote, because someday "he will be famous and whatever he wrote will be valuable." Regrettably, I did not begin to save my writings until some years later, not with the thought of fame, but just to have a record of my doings should I ever want to look back on my life.

However, rejections ultimately led me to wait until I was invited to write or speak, rather than commit anything to spontaneous efforts, which had proved to be frustrating.

My brother Sam, diminutive, brilliant, sandy haired, was already distinguishing himself in high school as a student and as an orator. The year I worked on the paper, he was entered in several oratorical contests and needed copy, which I readily provided. My vocabulary was extensive, and I incorporated words in the text that Sam had to look up in a dictionary to understand both the meaning and the pronunciation. He won the local high school prizes, then went on to win additional contests on a state level. This began to further deepen our relationship intellectually. We saved each other's letters for decades, a chronicle of our respective views about personal matters as well as world events, as he rose to become an ambassador for the U.S. State Department.

My newspaper exposure taught me to look behind the surface of even a simple meeting. One night I wandered into a hall where an assembly of glove cutters was just finishing a meeting. I talked briefly to the chairman and typed up a story that was just six inches in length, indicating the workers in the glove factories had met and were scheduling a follow-up session within a fortnight.

My editor, Beach, instantly called me to his rolltop desk and quizzed me for a half an hour. Who was there? How many were there? Did they say anything about a union? Did they say anything about wages, working conditions, the possibility of a strike? I replied in all honesty that I didn't know and hadn't asked. Beach went to his writing pad, for he could not type. The next day a front-page three-column story was printed indicating that the meeting might be a prelude to the formation of a union. Such an organization would be fought both by the owners of the factories and by the officials of the city, which had for decades prevented the formation of such a workers' organization. The story recalled a bloody strike that had taken place years before, which had once and for all destroyed any prospect for such an association of employees. The grim story frightened off any possibility of such a development. It was not until the depression and the NLRB that a union found a receptive response from the factory workers. I learned from this experience that two things were necessary—one, to prepare myself on the background of any issue, and second, to be probing in any interviews that I conducted.

* * *

Having decided to go back to college, I explored the catalogue of the University of Missouri, finding that it had the courses that I wanted to pursue and, what is more, that the tuition would cost only $80 for a whole year for out-of-state students. I had saved enough money for a year's expenses, which I estimated would be about $1,000. Through a mutual friend, Harry Unterfort, whom I had met in New York during my year at New York University, I was put in touch with Irving Epstein, who was completing his sophomore year at Missouri. That summer I visited him at a summer camp in Massachusetts, and he assured me of a hearty welcome, even inviting me to send my trunk to the Zeta Beta Tau fraternity house, until I made up my mind where I wanted to live. The university gave me credit for the courses I passed at NYU and wrote that I would have a wide choice of studies, since it was committed to an elective system. Nothing could have been more satisfying, for it would give me greater freedom to explore a world which was just beginning to emerge and expand for the increasing curiosity of my mind. When I enrolled, I found that I would have to make up some language and science courses that I had failed at NYU, so I didn't have the flexibility I wanted until I entered my junior year.

Emma Finestein

The year 1927 brought Emma Finestein into my life for an enduring and loving relationship of more than half a century. A young, beautiful well-dressed teenager from Albany, accompanied by her girl friend and two young men, who by chance I had known for years, drove up to Gloversville one Sunday afternoon for an outing. I was standing alone in front of the newspaper office on a dreary day with little traffic of any kind to disturb whatever thoughts might have occupied my mind.

When the men in the auto saw me, they stopped. I walked over to the car, and the next thing I knew I was in the rumble seat of the vehicle next to Emma. They were all on their way to a party on Christie Street. That was the beginning of a romantic passion. We were on the phone each night. I drove down to Albany on my free days, or else Emma would find someone to take her to Gloversville.

While the newspaper had increased my salary to $18 per week—not voluntarily, but only after I had pursued the matter from week to week—I decided to leave the paper at the end of June and took on the responsibility of being the head counselor of a two-week boys' camp run by the Jewish Community Center. It was located on a Boy Scout campsite on a mountain at Stony Point about twenty-five miles north of the city. The elevation was three thousand feet. That gave me part of the summer free to court Emma with unremitting diligence. Even when I was at camp, she found ways and means of having other boy friends bring her to that spot.

Camp was another unforgettable experience. The tent colony was pinned into the bare ground a half mile from the end of the road, so that every piece of equipment and food had to be carried on the backs of staff and counselors. The fog and cloud bank did not rise until 9 A.M. We slept in winter pajamas and wore heavy clothes until the radiant sun brought warmth to the mountaintop. The rest of the sunny day we could walk around without shirts, in shorts and bare-feet. To bathe, we walked a short distance to a twenty-foot natural waterfall, which had created a pool for swimming in the dimension of seventy-five by seventy-five feet. In the pool were flat rocks just above the water level, where we left our towels and soap and bathed in almost ice-cold water. Toileting was primitive in a hand-dug latrine a short distance away, screened for privacy by pine trees, and where we shoveled over our several movements. Food was turned out by a former navy chef, whose menus were decidedly limited. Oatmeal, cocoa, hamburgers, and salads seemed to constitute our daily diet, with eggs and pancakes thrown in for good measure once a week. We cleaned up after each meal. The director, Isadore Solomon, who headed the Jewish Community Center in Gloversville, had never had any camp experience, so he had to rely on me. While my knowledge as an outdoorsman was extensive, at the age of nineteen, I hardly had the knowhow to operate such a complex service, which has to be concerned with the total life of a small community—housing, health, food, program. Athletics, swimming, and hiking made up the bulk of the activities, I had invited Harry Starr, an attorney, who later became head of the Littauer Foundation, to try and introduce more profound educational fare through lectures and discussions during the course of the day, in which we were moderately successful. It was a busy and intensive two weeks in which I learned a great deal about camping, but more than that, about the behavior of people—youth as well as adult. I was happy with its termination, because I had some unfinished social things to do as well as prepare for my college year.

My parents, particularly my mother, were not happy about my energetic dating. They thought I was too young to be serious about one girl. They did not want anything to interfere with my studies. Besides, if I was going steady, why couldn't I pick out a girl from a rich home? Emma came from a poor family. Her mother had died in her presence when she was a preteener. She lived with her widowed father and a younger sister. Her father trudged five days a week to a slipper factory to eke out a living. A quiet, kindly, scholarly, cigarette-smoking man, he was religiously observant and kept his financial condition to himself. From his modest earnings he contributed more than his share to charity.

My parents thought that I would forget Emma when I went off to college and phased into new studies and a new life twelve hundred miles away in the Middle West. Our parting was tearful. We pledged our undying love to each other and promised to write frequently and fully. Our letters had to be destroyed after receipt, because they were the freest expression of our torrid feelings, and if found by anyone else would have proved most embarrassing.

Missouri

My trunk was shipped by railroad express to the Zeta Beta Tau fraternity house in Columbia, Missouri. I took the long, tedious Pennsylvania train that ended in Missouri and then transferred to the Kansas, Topeka line, which dropped me at the university town. It was a sunny day in September. Unexpectedly, I was picked up at the station by Myles Friedman in his gray Packard sports car. Irving Epstein had accompanied him to identify me.

The fraternity house on Hitt Street was in the center of the campus, across the street from the Bell Tower, around the corner from the library, and near book stores, a barber shop, and a refreshment parlor, which I regularly frequented. The house was decorated with banners, as were all the other fraternity and sorority buildings, because this was pledge week, when newcomers to the university were interviewed as prospective members.

ZBT was the only Jewish frat; and since there were 125 Jewish students at the university, and its membership was limited to 40, it tried to do a selective job. The members were mostly from the Middle West, warm and boisterous in their welcome.

While I had made up my mind that I would not join the frat, which I could not afford, and aside from that I did not like congregate living, particularly after my NYU experience, tremendous pressure was put upon me to pledge. They liked my looks and my clothes (which many of them later borrowed with or without my permission), and assured me that I could leave if I did not like the club and its members, if and when I could find quarters elsewhere. So I weakly resigned myself to stay.

It was a mixed experience during the first year. I was older than half the fraternity members, but as a "freshie," they tried to treat me like a first-year novitiate. To get out of cleaning the house on Saturday mornings, a chore for the newcomers, I conveniently enrolled in classes that removed me from this unwelcome task. I tried to absent myself by studying in the library on Monday nights, because after the fraternity meeting, the sophomore hooligans, led by Gene Bain, would come rushing up the stairs to the dormitory looking for hapless pledgees to paddle them with a flat wooden stick—and paddling on the ass was the real thing. I vowed to have it eliminated if I ever lasted the year and became a member, along with the other stupid initiation rituals.

This was my first crusade, and I succeeded in the following year in eliminating paddling. The other "fun" torments designed for the pledge about to become a brother I did not succeed in extirpating from that annual practice. That came later, after individuals on other campuses were actually killed during such antics. I became a member by bringing to my savage brothers six cow flops, all of the same size, six inches in diameter, which I found in the agricultural school's cow field, hardly an elevating exercise in proving one's worthiness. Yet, apart from these primitive rites, the young colleagues were congenial; some were intellectually stimulating students and conversationalists. When I delved into their history and lives, I learned a great deal about the middle and southwestern parts of the country. A few became close friends, all from the east.

I came with a trunk full of clothes, excellent in cut and quality, a good deal of which my brothers borrowed, including my shoes. One item, a handsome purple sweater, was never returned, the borrower claiming that he had somehow mislaid it. But that was part of group living. I therafter kept my more valuable items locked in a trunk. While I insisted that I came from a lower-middle-income family, the general impression from my clothes and my manner of speech, for I had a decided northern New York State accent, was that I was concealing my family's assets. I was forced to buy my first pair of white buckskin shoes, a kind of upper-class college uniform. When I went to St. Louis for the Christmas holidays, staying with Jean Charak, a fraternity brother, I had to buy my first tuxedo, a luxury I could ill afford. I had to give up a lot of other things for this second part of my formal equipment. I grew accustomed to these luxuries and wore them at every opportunity. The shoes wore out and had to be replaced in a few years from constant shuffling. The tuxedo was part of my wardrobe for two decades, after I had become an executive of agencies in Staten Island and the Bronx, and was finally abandoned when I began to put on weight.

There were fraternity parties and dances. Since there were not enough Jewish girls on campus or in town, we were persuaded to invite non-Jewish girls, which the brothers understandingly welcomed, else you might be a wallflower. That is, unless you aggressively cut in on other partners. Illegal booze found its way into some of the bolder fraternity brothers' stomachs, befuddling their minds and behavior.

Some of us had to help them get over their hangovers and sometimes even more serious disorders.

The first year's school curriculum was restricted, because I had to make up some subjects. I enrolled in botany, learning a great deal about plant life from a distinguished professor. In German, I was able to decipher the decorative script and how to read and speak it with some fluency, abetted by the Yiddish which I had never forgotten. My course in psychology was novel. Professor Max Meyer did not permit us to speak of mind, spirit, consciousness, feelings, and so forth, since he believed that man was a behaviorist and that we could only understand him from the outside. He could not understand himself. His text for the course was his own work, *Psychology of the Other One*. In English we read masterpieces, a stimulating subject. Along with all undergraduates, I had to take ROTC military study and drill. Assigned to the Artillery and Cavalry, I became both a half-baked pacifist and a semi-hater of horses, at least as far as cleaning them was concerned.

In my second semester, since my brother Sam in the following year would be entering the University of Wisconsin Experimental College headed by Dr. Alexander Meikeljohn, a distinguished, innovative educator, I decided to study Greek life. I took courses in ancient Greek history and Greek literature, since Sam's first year at college would be devoted to Greek civilization and I wanted to communicate with him on that subject. In addition, I was enrolled in two courses in English, masterpieces and the novel. Other subjects included philosophy, French painting, and the ROTC stint.

In my junior year, I selected Chaucer, the Age of Reason, the French Revolution and Napoleon, German history, and ancient philosophy. In that second semester I studied contemporary Europe, American literature, Samuel Johnson and his time, Spanish American life and literature, English painting, and the history of education.

In my final year, my courses covered the romantic period in England, short story writing, modern American literature, Shakespeare, the history of eighteenth-century England, the Renaissance, the history of the Hebrews, general sociology and social pathology, high school economy, and practice teaching in high school.

Beyond my Bachelor of Arts degree, I was awarded a certificate to teach in the public school system. I was usually on the dean's honor list. I always took more courses than were required, satisfying majors in both the English and history departments.

I began to collect books, especially old ones, and found a mine in the bookshop around the corner. If one wanted to wade through the dust and come out blackened in body and clothes, one could find old copies, as I did, of Flavius Josephus' *Antiquities of the Jews,* Boswell's *Life of Samuel Johnson* and some of Johnson's other eighteenth-century writings, and a great deal of early Americana, all probably cast off by former and deceased professors and book collectors. These volumes could be bought for pennies, all I could afford. During the Christmas holidays, which I spent in St. Louis, I uncovered other old bookshops and added to my store.

My social life was limited before I was married. I found few girls to my liking, and if you dated them it did not lead to any sexual fulfillment. There was no place to take them, even if they were willing. Who could afford a hotel room or rent a car? If you took a girl out to a restaurant, usually before and not for dinner, you drank Coke, ate olives, and nibbled on chips. Sometimes you took her to a movie, then walked her home and stole a good-night kiss on the steps of the dormitory. My roommates blamed my abstinence on my enraptured love for Emma, because one of them had discovered a letter she wrote, which I had not yet disposed of, and this proved my undoing and subjection to constant teasing. After that I read and reread her flaming missives and destroyed them, albeit with great reluctance. Those letters would have made marvelous mementos for later-day rereading and even incorporation in an autobiography.

Once I entered into a conversation with a pretty student who sat next to me in a history class. I learned that she was a Baptist from a small Missouri town and was studying to be a teacher. When I volunteered that I was Jewish, her reaction was dramatic. She looked intently at my head and asked me to turn around. While I had heard that uninformed Christians believed that Jews had horns, this was my first object lesson. When she discovered that I was normal physically, she became a bit more curious about me and friendlier. We dated a few times, but I found her totally devoid of knowledge and sadly lacking in imagination, so we parted.

Although I was aware before I enrolled that Missouri was a border state, I was totally unprepared for the separation of the races in every aspect of life. Our fraternity employed a black woman cook and a black male houseman, with both of whom I developed a good relationship. Sometimes I found a snack in my bed and I knew its source. Once I loaned an item of clothing to the houseman, who was acting in a church play, after he had seen it in my wardrobe. I was constantly reminded by my brothers that I should keep blacks in their second-class roles or else they would get uppity.

One day there was a report that a Negro had been lynched, and some of us ran to the town center to find out what it was all about. There was a huge crowd. The body had already been taken away by the time we reached the scene. It was quite clear from the conversation I overheard that there was no sympathy for the black man nor any condemnation of the inhumane act. I was never quite clear whether he had committed a criminal act or had just entered into an exchange of words with a white woman. Nonetheless he was killed. When I raised the issue at the fraternity, no one condoned the lynching, but I had the feeling that most secretly felt that the Negro had gotten what he deserved. The brothers did not want to discuss it at all. The memory of that experience, albeit I was not an eyewitness, never left me.

Later in the year, an epidemic of smallpox broke out. Vaccinations were immediately provided for the white constituency, including white students and faculty. There were no blacks enrolled at the college and certainly there were no black instructors. When the few and inadequate Jim Crow clinics could not accommodate all the blacks, and they appeared at the university hospital for vaccinations, they were turned away. I was outraged, as were a few other students, but sadly not including any of the brothers. We screwed up enough courage to tell the university officials that medical care for the Negroes was imperative, not simply for humanitarian reasons, because if the disease spread into an epidemic amongst them, whites who had not been inoculated might also suffer. Our simple argument, not complicated with any civil rights advocacy, seemed to have sufficient merit. Steps were taken immediately to give the vaccine to the black community. Why a few liberal students had to educate officials and doctors on the menacing aspects of their bigoted attitude was something that has always been difficult for me to understand. Appealing to one's self-interest worked—sometimes. My brothers did not commend me. They looked at me as though I was an odd ball for getting involved in matters which did not touch them and that were none of my business. Years later, when the civil rights movement invaded all the universities and fraternities north and south, Zeta Beta Tau not only adopted a pro-civil rights position but changed its policies to include anyone as a member, white or black.

The first school year was ending. My grades were quite good. I had begun to develop a relationship with a few instructors, whom I found much more stimulating than my fraternity colleagues. I frequently raised a Jewish point of view in the classroom, which at times seemed to puzzle and even confound them. There were few Jews on the campus. They were a kind of curiosity. A few instructors went out of their way to talk with me outside of the classroom. During my last two years, I was invited to their homes, where I met other faculty members. A good deal of the evening was devoted to questions about Jews. As our relationship grew even friendlier, they offered me part-time employment in grading papers. Before I completed my studies, two of them even offered me instructorships in their departments. All of them were non-Jewish. In their homes I was introduced to classical music, the intricacies of research and writing books, good bootleg scotch and beer (even during Prohibition), campus gossip, and worldly ideas.

When the first year was over, I hitched home with Is Willner, a brother, tall, handsome, a tackle on the football team, who lived in Kansas City, and another student by the name of Geller, who lived in

New York City and later became a doctor. The trip was at times an ordeal. We thought we'd never get out of Effingham, Illinois. When we reached Pennsylvania, no driver wanted to take us over the Appalachian Mountains with an overloaded vehicle. After many hours along came a crazy-driving Irish Catholic student, who not only picked us up, but sneaked us into the seminary where he was studying and provided beds for us to sleep on, under the watchful surveillance of Jesus on a cross. The beds had straw mattresses that were uncomfortable even for a single night. We finally reached Pittsburgh, where we had our first real scrubbing in a Turkish bath. After parting with Geller, Willner and I turned south to Baltimore, where I was to meet my family, who had driven down in their new Marmon to spend time with the Brickmans, our relatives. After a few days, all seven of us crowded into the car, which normally held only five people, finally arriving in Gloversville safe, but thoroughly uncomfortable.

During the summer of 1928 I worked for my father, driving the car, picking up and delivering leather. Business was good, but I still could not bring myself to become interested in making his business my livelihood. I was not driven by the desire to make big money, although the speculative spirit that ended in the 1929 tragic economic bust was already in full swing. I was thinking seriously of becoming a teacher, preferably on the university level or at least high school, even though I had not yet tested myself in a classroom exercise. I had found that I could be influential with people. They listened to what I had to impart, more so when I quoted some writer or authority to support my views. I had begun to make use of my readings. I had not received any inner call to turn to this or any other profession. It just evolved out of my experiences. Little did I know, when I finally entered the social welfare field, that I would be running an enterprise that entailed buying, selling, managing, and communicating. My exposure to the business world helped me weather my first years as an executive.

Instead of my involvement with Emma cooling down in our year of separation, it was resumed at the same heated pace. Whenever I could tear myself away from my father's work, we would see each other. I had the use of the family car, so the one-hundred-mile round-trip drive to Albany was an easy run. My parents were even more wary about the deepening relationship, and prayed that during my stay at college, the ties would weaken and lose their ardor.

My brother Sam, who had finished high school in three years in 1927, at the age of fifteen, had taken my place on the *Morning Herald* and then had been accepted in the new Experimental College at the University of Wisconsin. This college followed a European plan of education, using the tutorial system, seminars instead of classes and students living in a dormitory together with faculty. The first year was devoted to Greek civilization, and the second to the comparative American culture. In our letters and conversations, I had decided to develop a curriculum at Missouri that would parallel his Greek program. I looked forward to returning to the university with added eagerness.

Sam and I were hitchhiking cross country to our respective colleges. We set out with the blessing of our parents, found easy rides across New York and Ohio, and ended up the first night in Elyria, Ohio, a dreary town. We had some difficulty getting rides the next day. One driver finally stopped and we got in; as I closed the front door, the window shattered, and he pushed us out with foul curses. The next lift had room for only one person on the front seat, and I elected to lie flat on a pile of lumber in the back of the covered small truck.

My father had given me a fine silver flask filled with homemade brandy, in case either of us "caught a cold" on our journey. Being in good health, we didn't drink a drop. When we reached the Indiana-Illinois border, we noted that cars were being stopped and searched. We immediately assumed that they were looking for illegal liquor, so I hurriedly ran out of the car and emptied the flask, hiding it in a bag that we were carrying. When our car finally reached the police, we discovered that they were looking for certain vegetables that had been quarantined. What a waste.

In Illinois, Sam and I separated, as we were going in opposite directions. I found a driver, who wanted to sleep, and so I drove his immense Cadillac at high speed to St. Louis. Eventually I reached Columbia for a reunion with my fraternal associates. I was now a full-fledged member, who would be permitted to paddle the incoming class. I battled to abolish this brutal and childish activity, which the conservative members saw as a way of disciplining younger recruits and exercising authority; it was only a playful sport, they insisted. I eventually succeeded, but not until the next term, when I no longer lived at the house.

I Get Married

After a few weeks at school, I found that I could not live without Emma at my side, and in our nightly phone conversations she said she felt the same way. My limited resources were being eroded by these long-distance conversations. We finally decided to cast the die, throw caution to the winds, elope. Emma would immediately come out to Missouri to marry me and study. Neither of us would tell our parents what we proposed to do, and we would wait to see what the consequences would be after the final act. If my parents wanted to cut off my allowance, so be it. We would somehow find our way, and both of us would work as well as attend school.

I arranged with two of my fraternity brothers, Irwin Fane, whom we called Shug, a law school senior, who would later become a prominent Kansas City attorney, a trustee of the University of Missouri, and president of the Union of American Hebrew Congregations, and Jules Fogel, my roommate, who later became a publisher of newspapers in the midwest and south, to find a rabbi in Kansas, to marry us.

Emma took the train to Kansas City and had as a seat companion the famous Warden Lawes of Sing Sing Prison in Ossining, New York. When he gracefully turned her over to me at the station, he warned me to take good care of this beautiful girl or else. We checked in at the Hotel Muehlbach and hurriedly signed for a marriage license at city hall. Luckily for us, Emma was old enough to pass the age test in that state, which was seventeen years. (She was eighteen eleven days after our wedding.) We bought a sterling silver ring in a pawn shop for $2. (She still has it and wears it occasionally.) On October 6, 1927, in the residence of Rabbi Samuel A. Mayerberg of Congregation B'nai Yehudah, Kansas City, we were married. Fogel, Fane, Gertrude R. Mayerberg, the rabbi's wife, and Bernice Louis Smith, who later married Fane, were the witnesses. We went out to dinner with the three observers of the wedding scene, returned to the hotel, and the next day took the bus back to Columbia.

The fraternity welcomed us raucously. The elopement and secret marriage of a brother was something that had never happened before, and none of them could believe that I had actually gone through with such a daring escapade. The fraternity generously offered us free board and room for a month or until we could find an apartment. It was not easy living in the house, so we moved out within a week, having found attractive quarters on the other side of the campus, some distance from the fraternity.

I wrote a long letter home in English, not Yiddish, to my parents, trying to explain what we had done. Emma and I could not live without each other, I said, and if they disapproved of our action, they were free to sever my allowance and we would find some other way of supporting ourselves.

To state that they were shocked is to give the mildest construction to their reaction. Despite my mother's tears and their displeasure at what I had done, they nonetheless continued the same allowance, but no more, and wished us well. My sisters Sadie and Rachel and brothers Sam and Milton, who were all fond of Emma, sent us their congratulations, but my brother Morris was indignant, and it would be some years before our weak but correct relations, for they were never really ardent, were restored.

I like to believe in retrospect that what we did was not impulsive, that we knew what we were getting into and were prepared to take the consequences. Amongst many of our friends, the opinion was that we were both too young, that we were irresponsible, and that in view of our electric, emotional qualities, the marriage would not last. (In 1986 we celebrated our fifty-eighth year of marriage.) It was not always easy. It was not made easier when after a few months, despite the precautions we thought we were taking, Emma became pregnant. Abandoning all thought of continuing her studies, she took a part-time job to add to our always modest income, as our household took on a dimension that we had not quite planned for in advance.

* * *

I was a serious student, highly motivated, doing well in my courses, gaining intimacy with a number of professors in philosophy, history, literature, and art. One professor found employment for me as a reader of papers in the Extension Department, and the 25 cents I earned for each of the often dull and ill-written papers came in handy. Moreover, constantly rereading so much material that I had already studied fixed it more firmly in my mind. As a result, my professor friends recommended me to tutor students, particularly young women who were not sure why they had come to college and neither read nor studied. The $2.50 that I earned for each hour of tedius instruction was a God-send. Occasionally I went out to Booneville Academy, an hour's bus ride west, to teach Sunday school and earn another $5. Before each term came to a close, I would tutor larger groups in history and literature, adding over $100 to my income from each four-session program. Somehow Emma and I were able to pay our bills.

Politics

I was not yet twenty-one in November 1928, when I became somewhat more involved in politics. I belonged to a small group of serious students, who met once a month in an attic to discuss the issues of the day—economic injustices, war and peace, race problems. The major presidential candidates that year were Herbert Hoover, an engineer and standard bearer of the Republicans, running against Alfred E. Smith, the first Catholic to win the nomination of any party, now the choice of the Democrats. In our view, neither man would be able to influence either the domestic problem of runaway speculation or the ominous situation on the international scene, resulting from Japan's emergence as a world power and Germany's dissatisfaction with the consequences of the Versailles treaty at the end of World War I. The League of Nations, without the United States as a member, was a weak instrument incapable of imposing its will on nations always eager to assert their own precious autonomy or lust for power. There was already a naval race with Japan, as it began to assert its growing martial strength on its neighbors. While Hitler had failed in his earlier putsch attempt in Germany, his movement was steadily growing and creating an uneasiness not only in German political circles but throughout Europe.

So who to vote for? I would have cast my first presidential voting ballot that year for Norman Thomas, the Socialist, a brilliant speaker and debater, who seemed to have the best answers both of American society and the world at large. I had heard him speak several times at Cooper Union, when I attended NYU in 1925–26 and he was most impressive. Hoover was overwhelmingly elected with 444 electoral votes and almost immediately ushered the United States into a catastrophic economic depression, which affected our lives for the next decade.

Jewish Student Organization

Because I knew how to read Hebrew and the prayers, and since ZBT "controlled" the presidency of the Jewish Student Congregation, a group that met several times during the year, with rabbis from nearby communities delivering sermons, I was persuaded to take over this office for the year 1928–29. The organization had been founded in 1915, but it drew a slim attendance at its sporadic meetings. I soon discovered that there was another small Jewish group on the campus, made up entirely of students not affiliated with ZBT, then the only Jewish fraternity on the campus. This was the Menorah Society, an important national college association. With my burgeoning organizational powers, skills which I had never known I possessed, I arranged a merger, and we became one overall Jewish Student Organization by name and program. Lillian Viner of Oklahoma City, who led the Menorah group, became the vice-president of the combine. (Years later, when I was with the Federation of Jewish Philanthropies of New York, I arranged a number of mergers between centers and between camps. Someone arose at a meeting and called me Merger Berger.) We established a policy of one meeting a month on a Sunday night to which we would invite rabbis and other Jewish professionals.

The first meeting was a disaster. I had put up a few notices in places frequented by students announcing that a speaker would be present at our first combined meeting. Emma and I joined him for dinner and then brought him to the meeting hall, but not one person showed up. It never happened again. To ensure an audience, I provided a role for a lot of students to participate. I pressured the ZBT leaderhsip that every member must attend and, what is more, bring a female companion. As a result, meetings that had rarely attracted more than a few handfuls grew to an audience of thirty or forty at each session.

We met at the Christian Bible College, an independent organization on the university campus, which offered courses in the Bible, Hebrew, and Christian theological subjects that were accepted for degree credit at the university. As president of the Jewish students, I automatically became a member of the Student Religious Council, wherein I was the only Jew. I introduced a four-page newspaper, the *Scroll,* which brought information about the organization and outside Jewish affairs to the attention of the Jewish students.

What the Jewish students lacked was a mentor. There was only one Jew on the faculty, but he had nothing to do with Jewish student life. Columbia had five Jewish families, all in business, but it was not a large enough community to afford a synagogue, and none of the heads of these Jewish families was equipped to give leadership to the Jewish students. When Emma and I were invited to their homes, they often called me "Rabbi," because I presided over the Sunday night services and conducted several holiday programs. Besides, we were married and thus appeared more august in their eyes, despite our youthful looks and actual years.

Many of the students sought our company, and a steady stream of visitors dropped in, often without notice. Our resources were always strained. Pennies counted. We served ginger snaps, a large box for only a nickel, and tea without either milk or lemon. No one complained about the meager offerings. At times we received a package of food from my parents, and the contents—salami, cake, cookies—became a feast for those who were lucky to come in that night or week. Several times a week we ate herring, which could be purchased for five cents apiece, served with boiled potatoes, a carryover from the immigrant days of my parents. We ate other things, like eggs, chicken, and occasionally meat. But we ate simply, and our perfect weights were partly a reflection of a well-controlled diet. Once the package that arrived was broken. Unhappily my mother had included a jar of pickles, which she had put in a tin in the event that it spilled. But the can also leaked, so a large chocolate cake was drenched in pickle juice. We told the hungry students what they were eating, but they ate it nonetheless—and with gusto.

Several months after I became president of the Jewish students, I took the liberty of seeking out Dean G.D. Edwards and suggested the possibility of the Bible College adding a Jewish faculty member, who would not only immeasurably increase the range of subjects, but at the same time would be available to the Jewish student body. We were both standing as I made this daring proposal. The dean responded quite sternly, even though we were on friendly terms: "The Christians of the state of Missouri would never allow a Jew on the faculty of the Bible College." I explained to him that we would raise the money to maintain the incumbent, but he was unshakable. I left feeling utterly defeated, although I really had no right to believe that my engaging proposal would meet any other fate.

Months later, in midwinter, around 11 P.M., I received a phone call from Dean Edwards, who always called me Mr. Berger. I detected excitement in his voice. He told me that he had finally screwed up enough courage to present my suggestion to his board, and to his surprise it had been unanimously approved. I was elated, of course, and asked him what it meant. He instantly replied that I would have to raise $100,000 as an endowment, which would be invested at 6 percent, the income of which would be used to employ a professor at $4,000 per year, a secretary at $800 per year, and the balance would cover the expenses of the department. Space would be provided by the college. I gave him no inkling that I was overwhelmed with what I now had to do, thanked him and sat down to think. I didn't have the slightest notion where such funds could be obtained. Emma and I could not sleep that night.

The next day I dispatched letters to the Hebrew Union College in Cincinnati and to the Hillel Foundation, care of Abram L. Sacher, who taught history at the University of Illinois at Champagne, asking for help. Within a few weeks I received replies that funds were not available and with no suggestions as to where I might seek them.

Meanwhile, I had taken advantage of Rabbi Mayerberg, who had performed our wedding, and invited him to speak to the students on a Sunday night. He accepted my invitation. At dinner before the meeting, I unburdened myself on the Bible College's acceptance of my proposal and my negative results in finding funds. I can still see and hear his knife and fork drop out of his hands to the table.

In his fine oratorical style, for he was a formidable speaker (west of the Mississippi he was considered to be a counterpart of the crusading Rabbi Stephen Wise, not only for his speaking ability, but also for his interest in social and political reform), and with his dark, penetrating eyes looking at me intently, he said: "Young man, you have performed a miracle. The rabbis and Jewish leaders of the state of Missouri have been trying to achieve this for twenty years. I shall have the funds for you by tomorrow night." He called the next day to say that the monies had been underwritten by a Mr. Hartman, a wealthy merchant of Kansas City, and he urged me to see that the program was initiated in the fall of 1929. (Several years later a Jewish committee was set up to supervise and support the program. It eventually became a branch of the Hillel Foundation, as the Jewish census increased. A handsome building was finally erected for the Jewish student body.)

Academically I had another good year at the university in 1928–29. My marriage deepened my sense of responsibility in study. I was becoming known around the campus by faculty members, who liked to show off a bright Jewish student whom they could quiz about the Jewish people. All of them were quite ignorant of the subject and had little or no contact with Jews. I was taking many courses each semester, some for no credit, but just to broaden my knowledge. An example, a course in Latin American life and literature. My library on all subjects was steadily growing, as I liked to own books as well as read them.

Emma was well into her pregnancy, the baby due in August. That summer, after a brief stay in Gloversville, we moved in with her father in Albany. Since I was still embarked toward a career as a teacher, I enrolled into summer educational courses at the Albany State Teachers College. To earn some money, I sold magazines and books, but my parents continued their allowance. We lived frugally.

Ramon is Born

Ramon Francis (Reuben Ephraim) was born on August 23, 1929, in the Albany Brady Memorial Hospital. He was a bouncing, healthy boy. My father was so impressed by the Rev. Shapiro, the *mohel* who circumcised Ramon, that he induced him to come to Gloversville to fill the fourfold post of rabbi, cantor, *mohel*, and *shochet*. Shapiro remained there for the rest of his life. A tall, bearded, imposing, yet gentle man with a fine voice, he served the community well and always had close ties to our family.

As the opening of school approached, we had a difficult decision to make. Would we all go back to Missouri, or should I accept the invitation of my parents to have Emma and the baby stay with them? While I knew that my parents had not yet forgiven Emma for marrying me and interrupting the kind of life that they had envisioned for me, they were willing to undertake this obligation. Although they offered a good home, my mother was not always kindly to Emma. My sisters Sadie and Rachel and my brother Milton, who lived at home, went out of their way to compensate for my parents', but mostly my mother's, incivility.

My sister Rachel married Sidney Rosenthal in June 1929, a marriage which brought together two radically opposites, but the marriage was durable and productive. Rachel was bright, loquacious, and lively. Sidney, a Harvard Law graduate, son of a well-to-do manufacturer of gloves and a prominent person in the county, was well educated, well read, laconic. He was an archconservative and differed with me on every political and social issue. He puffed away at his pipe, read extensively, and was not given to an active physical life. They produced three fine children, who studied at Hamilton, Vassar, and Northeastern. Edward, the oldest, became a Foreign Service officer. Ann and Albert married and between them bore seven grandchildren, most of whom have already turned out to be unusual.

Last Year at Missouri

I returned to Missouri in September 1929 with many misgivings about my family left behind in Gloversville. I was partially relieved by our long letters to and fro and occasional phone calls. Emma wrote me almost daily. I rented a room with the Kopel family, not too far off the campus. They were kindly people. I spent relatively little time in my room. Apart from a heavy academic schedule, which included practice teaching in a public school, something I had to do in order to get a teaching certificate, I was grading papers in several university extension programs, tutoring individuals, and conducting a series of end-of-the-term tutorial sessions, so as to earn money to meet expenses. My monthly allowance had been severed, because my parents were supporting my wife and child. When the baby was a few months old, Emma left the child with my mother, who loved Ramon, and took a job in a local department store, so that she would have some money of her own.

During the previous spring, I had helped in the selection of a Jewish faculty member for the Bible College. Dr. Isidore Keyfitz, an eminent scholar associated with Professor James H. Breasted of the University of Chicago, had been engaged to fill the post. A medium-sized, moustached, round-faced, always smiling man, he and I hit if off from our initial meeting at the train pulling into Columbia on a sunny afternoon.

I was deeply involved with the Jewish student organization, spending a great deal of time with Dr. Keyfitz, the director of Jewish studies and mentor to the students. I enrolled in his course in Hebrew history. Now there were all kinds of committees, and the congregation met weekly on Sunday nights instead of monthly. It published a news bulletin. For all the Jewish holidays there were special programs, including a Passover Seder of such dimensions that it burst the hall where it was held to accommodate the unexpected reservations.

In addition, I was doing research for Professor Cochran, a Scotch-Irishman with no religious affiliation. He taught German history and was assembling material for a book he was writing titled *Germany—Not Guilty: 1914*. It was a provocative, revisionist volume, which placed the blame squarely on the British rather than the Kaiser for the start of World War I. His view essentially was that Germany had been challenging Britain's worldwide power by establishing its own colonies on many continents, and the war in Europe was initiated to bring an end to Germany's growing economic and military strength. I read everything that was available on the subject in English and found a number of items to footnote his case, although I never did or could accept his thesis, nor the consequences for Europe and the world, had the war ended with Germany the victor.

Although I could ill afford it, I traveled home during the Christmas vacation. On the way I was stuck in a train for twenty-four hours as a result of a snow storm in Illinois. The train turned on its heat periodically. Food ran low. We played a great deal of poker. My reunion with Emma and Ramon was joyous, but altogether too short.

While at home, I approached the principal of the high school about a job in the fall of 1930. He had been appointed the new principal, when I was still a senior student. Though he might have rejected me on the grounds that there were no vacancies, or that my academic record was not up to his standards (although I had been regularly on the honor list at college), or that he just didn't like my looks, instead he told me that there was a Jewish quota on teachers and there were no openings. The quota was one.

I also made an effort to obtain the position of executive director of the Jewish Community Center in Gloversville. The new building had just opened and it was looking for a professional to head the operation. I felt that I was qualified by my participation as a member over the years. My head counselorship in the camp was excellent administrative practice. My two years as president of the Jewish student organization had given me a great deal of program, executive, and public relations experience. Practice teaching had developed some good teaching skills, which I knew I could translate into programs for young people.

I went to see the president of the center, Albert Rosenthal, my sister Rachel's father-in-law. My brother Morris and my brother-in-law Sidney Rosenthal, the son of the president, were also members of the board. After a long conversation with Rosenthal, who did most of the talking while lying on a couch, recovering from a broken leg, he told me that as a local boy, I should first of all not work in my hometown. Furthermore, it was better for me to get more experience elsewhere and then apply for the position, should there be an opening in the future. I told him that I had applied not only because I felt competent, but it had been at the suggestion of several members of the board, none of them my relatives. He finally said categorically, "No." While I did not accomplish anything for myself, I did persuade them to engage my schoolmate Isidore Willner to fill the position of athletic director. Willner had finished school in 1929, but despite his prowess as a football and track varsity star, the only job he could get was pumping gas in Kansas City. Is was engaged, did exceedingly well, and after a few years resigned, went into the insurance business, married, and became a prominent political figure. I see him whenever I am in Gloversville.

The members of my family on the board did not give me the support, which might have assured me the position. Perhaps they did not like the bold strokes in my life-style. Perhaps they did not want to get involved in any conflicts with the upper socio-economic Jewish leadership that might arise during my incumbency. I knew all of them by their first names. In later years, as I develoepd a reputation in the field, the heads of the center did not hesitate to call me frequently for advice on staff, program, building construction, and finding funds to meet their deficits. I gave my counsel freely, including the preparation of memoranda and letters, which they usefully translated into money, and rejected their offers of compensation. Perhaps I was paying the center back for all that it did for me as a youth. In retrospect, this turn down was the best thing that ever happened to me, for if I had taken the job, I might have been stuck in this small town the rest of my life.

On my return to Missouri, I sent out letters looking for teaching jobs. The depression was beginning, and while layoffs were not yet taking place, there were few vacancies. The best job offer I had was in Independence, Missouri, to teach five high school subjects, including bookkeeping, and coach the basketball team, all for $800 per year. If I had taken the post, perhaps I might have gotten to know Harry Truman and taught his daughter, Margaret, and who knows where fortune would have taken me.

Dr. Keyfitz was beginning to insist that my field was the Jewish community and not teaching in a public school. He claimed that I was a born executive, with true potential to influence people and institutions, so I should change my profession from education to social work and management. His wife, Sarah Feder, who had remained in Chicago, where she headed the Pioneer Women, reinforced his views whenever she came on weekend visits. I had never felt a calling for any profession, whether journalism, education, or social work. While I was seeking a life where I would be useful, my preoccupation in the last year at college was how to make the best living for my family. I listened to their suggestions, and began to think about taking some courses that might better equip me for social work. I had attended two courses in behavioristic psychology but knew nothing of Freud, Jung, or Adler, and while I was enrolled in a course in sociology, the professor was more of a Christian minister than a social scientist. Thus I had not only a limited but also a warped view of the disciplines which were slowly coming into academic fashion in the latter 1920s.

In 1926, Dr. Maurice Karpf created the Graduate School of Jewish Social Work in an effort to professionalize Jewish communal institutions, particularly those dealing with families and children, the community centers, and other community organizations. He had campaigned for such a program for years and finally brought it into being with the financial aid of some wealthy Jews. By and large, the individuals who managed Jewish institutions at this time were rarely trained or properly educated for these positions, so that the services that emerged rarely reflected a social science point of view, but one that grew out of the interests of well-meaning laymen. There was little planning. If individual clients were helped, it was as much by chance as the kindliness of the managers or their staffs.

Karpf's school was small. My entering class enrolled thirty-three individuals drawn from the entire country. The second-year class had fifteen students. Since great emphasis was placed on scholarship as well as a desire to help people, many of the students exhibited their Phi Beta Kappa keys. The school's faculty was mostly part-time instructors, but several already had distinguished reputations. The school itself, at 71 West 47th Street in Manhattan, was located in a building owned by the Federation of Jewish Philanthropies and offered courses in Jewish subject matter and research. For the general courses in psychology, case work, group activities, and community organization, we attended the New York School of Social Work (later to become the Columbia University School of Social Work). The program led to either a certificate or a master's degree in social service.

When the school's representative, Frances Harrison, arrived in Missouri, I was one of several students interviewed. I made it clear that I could only attend if I obtained a generous scholarship. I took the necessary examination, which required that we offer solutions to four problems with which social workers were confronted. To my surprise, I was awarded the $2,000 per year Drachsler Memorial Scholarship, and my future career was decided immediately.

My last year at Missouri was intellectually most rewarding. My professors were among the best that I ever encountered. Pickard, the white-haired, white-moustached teacher of all the art courses that I took, not only gave us the facts embellished with hundreds of stories, but stimulated an interest in that cultural field that has never left me. His field trip to the State Capitol in Jefferson City to study the murals that Thomas Hart Benton had recently painted were dramatic in color and story. Some years later, when I accidentally met Benton at an exhibition of his work in New York, and he found out that I had seen his work in Missouri, he eagerly engaged me in conversation about Pickard and my art interests.

One incident worth recording was my course in short story writing with a bearded professor, a bit pompous but knowledgeable, named Ramsay. He hurriedly passed you on the campus without a nod. I had written two short stories for him, neither of which he liked. One, titled "Marriage à la More," was inspired in part by my reading of Sir Thomas More's *Utopia*. A college instructor is at the altar about to marry a woman whom he has never seen in the nude. He recollects that in *Utopia*, one didn't even buy a horse without examining all of its parts. Afraid of what he may be getting into without a thorough inspection of his future spouse, he bolts from the church and disappears. Madly in love with the young woman, at night he passes her house in the hope that she will somehow appear. One night, as she is preparing for bed, she forgets to pull down the shade. He creeps up to the window and gapes as she goes through motions that revealed her entire body. He quickly knocks on her door, commands her to dress, and rushes her off to the justice of the peace. They live happily ever after. Ramsay's comment was, "Learn to walk before you run," and marked it with a D.

Another story, titled "Gershvinsky's American Tragedy," related a story with a musical arrangement, modern of course, in the margins.

The story was influenced by Theodore Dreiser's *An American Tragedy*, except for the names, the location, and the manner of death, wherein a contrived auto accident instead of a drowning was used to kill the unwanted love affair, an auto being more in keeping with the 1920s than Dreiser's version in the early twentieth century. The cause of the accident had to do with the growing hedonism, women's emancipation, the flapper age, and Prohibition. The musical notes on the side of the pages, which I developed with Samuel Sandmel, a big, burly, likable freshman from St. Louis, who played the clarinet, was in keeping with the already famous George Gershwin and Igor Stravinsky, and reflected that period of both the blues and musical discordancy. (Sandmel later became a Reform rabbi, teacher and scholar, and the author of books on Judaism's relationship to Christianity at its very incipiency. Keyfitz thought that Sandmel and I were his two top graduates.) Ramsay wrote on the paper "Unacceptable" and again marked it D.

I related my unfortunate experience with Ramsay to Keyfitz, never asking him to intervene. But some days later Keyfitz met Ramsay by chance at a faculty party, where quite informally Keyfitz told him that he had learned a great deal about him from one of his students, who spoke of him most favorably. Ramsay was taken aback and asked Keyfitz how he knew Berger. Keyfitz related my background telling, how I literally had created his department single-handedly, and adding that I was an imaginative leader, as well as an excellent speaker and writer, to all of which Ramsay listened with no comment. After our next session, Ramsay asked me to stay a moment after class and told me that he had thought again about the stories I had written, and while they were still not of top grade, he had changed my marks from D's to C's. So I passed the course. Ramsay only gave an A to students who could write like Edgar Allan Poe; a B if you created stories like O'Henry's. He gave a C if you wrote like Octavius Roy Cohen, then a popular short story writer, whose works were published in the *Saturday Evening Post*. He did not like Cohen, but I did, so my mark was not only passing but flattering, admittedly thanks to Keyfitz's interposing on my behalf.

Some years later, when I taught at graduate schools of social work, I gave students an A only when their papers were publishable in a professional journal; a B if they indicated research, thoughtful analysis, and were well written; a C if they were quite pedestrian but well written. I never gave a D. I gave an F to any paper not worthy of a graduate student.

Rankin was my professor of Chaucer. I knew the *Canterbury Tales* almost by heart. I memorized the "Prelude" to the *Tales*, which opens with these famous lines:

> Whan that Aprille with his shoures sote
> The droghte of Marche hath perced to the rote,

And bathed every veyne in swich licour
Of which vertu engendred is the flour.

I recited these opening lines on many occasions, and with renewed enthusiasm when Emma and I attended an enjoyable, farcical, musical version of the poems in London in 1972.

Yet when it came to the final examination, the only basis for the semester's grade, of the three questions—(1) identify the tale for which an obscure quotation was given; (2) relate the rest of the story based on this quotation; and (3) evaluate its significance—I erred in identifying the tale, wrote extensively about the wrong quotation, and therefore evaluated it unsatisfactorily, thus I received a 66, an I grade, the lowest passing mark, the only blot on my Missouri record. I learned a lesson which I never forgot. Read every label carefully before consuming.

The Jewish students gave me a testimonial farewell party on May 16, 1930, along with many speeches and a handwritten placard:

> For your admirable leadership on the campus of the University of Missouri, both as President of the Jewish Student Organization in the years 1929 and 1930 and as organizer of several activities including the Scroll.

Keyfitz remained on campus until he retired in the 1950s. His wife, Sarah, joined the faculty as a sociologist and retired with him. We corresponded for a number of years, but then it lapsed. Keyfitz was not a letter writer. I saw them occasionally at Jewish communal events in and out of New York. Their one child, a daughter, married and with husband and child settled on Kibbutz Urim in the Negev of Israel near the Gaza border. By chance I met the entire family at the kibbutz in 1965. Keyfitz and Sarah (she called him Keyfitz) went on aliyah to Israel, where I saw them several times, and where both passed away.

Emma and I did not return to Columbia, Missouri, until 1981. During that visit I attended services at the Hillel House on a Shabbat morning and afterwards told the rabbi and the small congregation who I was. They were fascinated to learn the story of the origin of the Jewish student organization. No one had ever heard of me. Even the memory of Keyfitz had begun to fade. Such is the fate of pioneers, unless their contributions are chiseled in marble in large letters at the entrance of buildings for future generations, if interested, to stop and read.

I didn't bother to stay for the graduation exercises and rushed home by train to see Emma and Ramon, growing up a beautiful, bright child. I worked for my father that summer, supplementing my income by working in Cohen's store on Saturdays. After considerable discussion, it was decided that Emma and Ramon would remain in Gloversville with my parents for another year, so that we could better manage economically during my first year at graduate school in New York.

3

The Graduate School

I ARRIVED IN New York in September 1930, planning to stay with relatives for a few days while I looked for a room in which to live. But at the graduate school registration, I found that Sam Rabinowitz and Al Erlin, two of the students, were looking for a third roommate, and I brought my bags to their apartment on East 36th Street off Park Avenue, not too far from the school in West 47th Street. I threw myself into an academic program in two schools that was highly demanding. I had a field assignment in casework during the first semester. In addition, I was a paid club leader at $2 per session at the Central Jewish Institute on East 85th Street on Wednesday and Saturday nights and performed similar duties on Sunday mornings at the 92nd Street YMHA. On Saturdays I occasionally worked in a shoe store.

The school was a revelation with both its Jewish and general content, bright students, and a unique faculty. Professor Salo W. Baron, who had come to the United States from Austria a few years before, to teach in Jewish religious institutions, was still at the onset of his career, a long one, during which he would become the foremost Jewish historian of the twentieth century. He lectured in impeccable English with a pronounced European accent, never using notes. His material, heavily illuminated with political and economic facts, placed Jewish life in the context of the larger societies in which Jews dwelt. As each session ended he responded to questions, few in number, with tolerance. It was always obvious that no matter what the student body had learned beforehand, we were all literally ignoramuses. At the end of the second semester, I asked Dr. Baron, who entertained us at his home during the course of the year, with his future wife Jeanette acting as hostess, what I should read to become better informed. He suggested five volumes of Heinrich Graetz and all of Simon Dubnov, both Jewish historians, but with different approaches to the subject. In the summer of 1931, while working at Cohen's department store in Northville, I actually finished this massive assignment, getting a grasp of the vast Jewish experience which has always stood me in good stead.

I had occasional contacts with Baron over the years and read all of his books, including his eighteen-volume *Social and Religious History of the Jews*. The eighteenth, published in 1983, carried one through the middle of the seventeenth century. Now, having reached ninety, he still planned to bring the story of the Jewish people up to date. In 1974 Emma and I lunched with the Barons, at their country home in Connecticut. While we were there, Jeanette Baron asked me to persuade her husband to write a one-volume summary, as time was running out. I did not even make the effort. He would only have laughed in reply.

On the occasion of Baron's eightieth birthday, I happened to be in Jerusalem, where his friends and colleagues were honoring him. I represented his old students at the Graduate School, paying tribute both to his masterful teaching and to his influence on my own thinking.

In 1974, I was one of the lecturers of a seminar for postdoctoral students that Baron directed with a group of major scholars at Tel Aviv University on the subject of "Violence and Defense in the Jewish Experience." I led a session on "The Role of Communal Workers in Jewish Self-Defense." My lecture was included in the volume of seminar papers, published in 1977.

The other major personality on the faculty was Rabbi Dr. Mordecai M. Kaplan, the maverick in the American rabbinate, who created the Jewish Center and founded the Reconstructionist movement. As his text in the classroom, Kaplan used the material for his forthcoming book, *Judaism as a Civilization*. Of medium height, bearded, with a deep resonant voice, he read aloud from his manuscript, resentful of all interruptions to ask questions or make comments, because, as he put it, "Since you do not know my entire thesis, you have no right to question its separate parts until I am through."

While personally a kindly man, Kaplan was an arrogant teacher, and some few students, who rebelled about most things Jewish, were put off by his manner. He approached Jewish life in a mental-hygiene, sociological context. Jews had become a "sick" people, because of too rapid assimilation and the steady loss of their Jewish identity. In his view, we had to become knowledgeable about our entire history, abandon outmoded religious notions, such as the alleged theophany on Mount Sinai, approach God rationally, and make Zion (Israel) a cornerstone of our devotion, yet at the same time find firm roots in the Diaspora by developing strong, democratic communities. He was also ethically concerned with all the major problems that confronted society outside of the Jewish framework.

Kaplan had a long-time impact on many of his students, as he did on a large section of the American rabbinate. Much of what he taught fitted in with what we were being taught in other areas of the school's curriculum. A piece of one of the papers I wrote for his class found its way into his major work, for which I earned a footnote. We met many times since those school days and on several occasions participated on the same platform. He also wrote prodigiously, and I read most of what he published. While I accepted his general thesis, I could not completely identify with all of his views. For example, he never convinced me that the Jews were not the "Chosen People." I still recite the plagues on Pesach, which he deliberately excised from the Reconstructionist Haggadah.

The other instructors were Karpf, his wife Faye, Samuel Kohs, Mordecai Soltes, and Ludwig Bernstein, all competent, but without the scope and imagination that Baron and Kaplan brought to an impressionable group of students.

At the New York School, I was introduced for the first time to the mysteries of Freud, largely through the stimulating presentations of Dr. Marion Kenworthy, a psychiatrist. It was heady stuff, as I not only read but ingested Freud. His rivals, Jung and Adler, were held in lower esteem, and we had to read their works almost surreptitiously. Freud's influence had already pervaded the casework agencies. It was reinforced in the field of practice. Freud was penetrating the theater (Eugene O'Neill's *Strange Interlude*) and the literary world (through James Joyce's *Ulysses*), which I had seen and read.

The dean of the school, Porter Lee, was a talented teacher. In his course, "Interviewing," he preferred to use parts of English novels of the nineteenth century, rather than case studies, as illustrations of how we were to get into the insides of people's thoughts and feelings. He found novelists superior probers and recorders than current practitioners. Coming from a literary and humanistic background instead of the social sciences, I more readily appreciated what a social worker should be seeking in his efforts to resolve human problems.

The other teachers were sometimes too theoretical or too practical and did not have the same impact on me nor among the other students. Some of these non-Jewish teachers were surprised that we were so well read. One professor met with several Jewish students to criticize our role in the classroom, claiming that we raised too many questions, challenging the instructor's point of view and even the "facts." She didn't like it. Next semester, I changed to another teacher, but her successor was no better.

I recall an interesting episode one morning in a class devoted to recreation. The instructor, with a book before him, asked each student in the class what he thought was the most important leisure-time interest of Americans. He went around the room and everyone answered, but no one gave the correct response. When he came to me at the end, I responded: "Reading the comics." He looked up at me and said: "Correct." Then he went around the room a second time asking the class for the second most important recreational interest. Again all the answers were wrong. When it was my turn, I responded: "Going to the movies." "That is extraordinary, Berger." "No, professor, I read the same book that you have before you."

The year 1930–31 was an eye-opener for embryonic social workers. The depression was beginning. Ever larger numbers of workers were unemployed. It would be several years before the national government stepped in to provide wide-scale work and adequate relief. The situation offered a field day for radicalism, particularly the spread of communistic ideas among Jewish social workers. While I never bothered to determine whether my coworkers were dues-paying, card-holding members of the party, they talked and acted identically with the official line. In the field, my supervisor placed all kinds of literature in my hands and took me to a John Reed Society meeting one night, where one speaker after another harangued us about the failures of the American capitalistic system and the virtues of Soviet Communism. Even in handling our clients at the Jewish Social Service Association located in the Bowery, I was advised not only on ways to provide aid and counsel, but also how to stir them up to protest and join left-wing unions and groups.

Some of the students at the Graduate School were more amenable than I to this propaganda, and they raised and provoked discussions in the classroom. Our class only behaved this way at the Jewish school, being reserved when among the non-Jewish students and faculty at the New York School. These continual and controversial pontifications became, during the course of the year, a disturbing issue for Dr. Karpf, who was personally conservative and probably did not wish to antagonize the chief benefactors of the school, men like Felix M. Warburg and Louis E. Kirstein. In his tight-lipped way of speaking, he became critical of some students, and I am convinced that of the fifteen who were dropped at the end of the first year, it was due more to their political commitments than any academic deficiencies.

While personally a nominal socialist, but never a card-carrying one, nor attending their meetings or participating in their demonstrations, I was deeply concerned with the plight of the unemployed and the growing relief rolls. Yet I could not take the absolutistic, strident, pro-Soviet, anti-American party line that was spewed forth by the more extremist groups, although as a student leader at the school, I defended the other students' right to be dissidents.

My casework exposure often put some of my liberal views to the test. I had a client on the Lower East Side of Manhattan, where the father had deserted his wife and two children of eight and ten, and had run off with a young woman to Atlantic City. There they had an out-of-wedlock child. He supported his common-law wife and child as a waiter. My instructions were to see if I could get the father to return to his original family, or at least assume support for the abandoned woman and her children. Financial aid to the family was being provided by the Jewish agency. My visits to the wife and her always dark apartment were not pleasant. Not only had I to listen to her diatribes against her vagrant husband, always accompanied by continuous crying, but she personally was unattractive and unkempt, exuding a noxious odor that forced me to talk to her from a distance. The apartment was no cleaner than her person. I got nowhere with her over the four months of visits in improving her appearance, tidying her apartment, or ever going out to find some part-time work, difficult as that was becoming, or think of training herself for some kind of work in the future.

I took the train to Atlantic City to see what I could do with the husband. I found a quiet man, reasonably well dressed, clean, who had a very attractive younger woman living with him. She held the baby throughout our hour-and-a-half long conference and never said a word. The furnished apartment was well kept, even if it was not elegant. He clearly indicated to me why he had left his wife—she was dirty, always cried and complained, withheld sexual relations, was never satisifed with what he earned—and after twelve years, he had had enough and deserted her. Now he was happy and was trying to rebuild his life. My sympathies were with him, despite my attempt at objectivity and my outright pleas that he had a responsibility to his wife and children, at least to send them some money and to visit them, or at least his children occasionally, which fell on deaf ears. I left knowing that I had not influenced him either. My record to my student supervisor was most detailed. She sided with my evaluation and we both wrote off the original family as one doomed to separation and suffering, at least on the wife's part. I recall having invoked Jewish morality and the sanctity of maintaining the Jewish family, but that made no impression, because neither of them were religious Jews or Jews with a firm Jewish identity. I had some success with my three other cases.

In my second term I was given the experience of working with homeless Jewish men, an old problem, which became more of a phenomenon with the depression. More men deserted their families. More single men could not find work. Included amongst them were Jewish homosexuals, my first contact with such individuals. The four months I spent working on this assignment did not lead any of my clients to change their style of living. Some of them liked to be wanderers, working whenever they were impelled to, in order to keep from starving, and moving from city to city. Some had left their homes, their families, or their jobs. They were unhappy and could not accept the responsibility of working out their problems. I tried to use a psychoanalytic approach to get at more deep-seated problems, but ended nowhere due to my own inexperience and their outright refusal to reveal their life histories and their feelings. They were content with the modest sums that we provided for food and shelter.

Dr. Karpf urged that I go into research rather than direct service, because he thought I had both a good inquiring mind and a facility to write clearly. I had made up my mind to follow my original inclination for the community center field, with which I had more than a passing acquaintance, rather than embark on a discipline where it would be more difficult to find work and make a living. My decision proved correct during the years of the depression.

In between the first and second years at graduate school, I worked at Cohen's department store in Northville. Then Emma and I decided that she would return to New York with me. Ramon was now three years old and needed to be closer to his father. Since I had the minimal money to support all of us, it would be a joy to live together. We found a pleasant apartment on West 156th Street in Washington Heights and rented one of the bedrooms to Harry Barron, a first-year student, and his wife. Within a few years after graduation, Harry became a Jewish Federation executive, and later headed the National Foundation of Jewish Culture. I was invited to serve on its board and saw Harry quite frequently. When they left, we leased the room to another student, an incredible individual named Joe Lebo. A reader, a soap-box orator, and political enthusiast, he was oftimes very funny, but it was a trial to survive the six months we had to live with him. He promised to write the definitive book on a variety of subjects, but never did.

The second year was, if anything, more demanding on my time and energies. Apart from the numerous courses at both schools, each of which required many papers, I had to work on my master's thesis; and the task of developing my methodology and collecting the necessary material was a formidable one. After consultation with my thesis supervisor, Dr. Kohs, I decided to study the "house organs" of Jewish community centers to determine whether one could evaluate the purposes and program of any agency by reading its published, periodic bulletins. With the help of Kohs and George Wolfe, another member of the faculty, Ezekiel J. London of the National Jewish Welfare Board, one of my roommates during the first year, Sam Rabinowitz, and Emma, I finished the thesis before the year was over. While I found that one could not completely evaluate an agency through this medium, it did clearly reveal that athletics and social activities were the dominant programs and that both Jewish and cultural activities, as well as news about domestic and world Jewry, were at a minimum, revelations that have been reported in later years through studies by Oscar I. Janowsky and Carl Urbont.

My fall fieldwork assignment took me to the JCC of Yonkers, which was already suffering from lack of funds due to a burdensome mortgage and the failure of the members to pay their dues. Under the supervision of Gertrude Carnovsky (the sister of the famous actor, Morris Carnovsky), a very intelligent woman, I led an adolescent and a young adult group, and organized some agencywide programs. I learned some elements of administration through consultation with the executive director, Isidore Beierfeld, the building superintendent, the department heads, and a few board members, I often returned home at 12:30 A.M. after a long trolley and subway ride.

During the spring term, I was assigned to Jersey City's YM-YWHA, an even longer ride by subway. This agency was in even more serious trouble due to an even larger mortgage on its Italian Florentine-style structure, so that it could not pay its help. As a consequence, I was given administrative duties and supervision over programs formerly directed by paid workers. Among my supervisees was Irving Stone, who was then a part-time worker directing the drama department. This was before he became one of America's most successful novelist-biographers with a long list of best sellers. My relations with him were purely administrative—schedule, supplies, payroll, etc. We never seemed to find the time to discuss drama or literature, because both of us worked on restricted schedules. Another supervisee was my old Hebrew school teacher from Gloversville, Hyman Grant, who had not gone to Palestine, but instead was trying to make a place for himself as a Jewish educator in the States. I was supervised by Charles Nemser, the executive, a tall, lean man with a hoarse voice, down to earth and competent, wearing himself out fighting against financial obstacles. Here, too, I learned something about mortgages, special campaigns for funds, membership drives, and public relations, but never how to resolve a perpetually unbalanced budget. Both Yonkers and Jersey City prepared me for the equally difficult problems that I was to confront on Staten Island—big mortgage and lack of funds. The ride back to Manhattan brought me home at 1 A.M. three nights a week.

I continued to lead clubs at the 92nd Street Y and the Central Jewish Institute, in the latter receiving acute supervision from Miriam Ephraim, who became one of the top women professionals in the Jewish communal field, educational director of the Pittsburgh YM-YWHA, then a leading professional within the Jewish Welfare Board. After her retirement Miriam brought to life the International Conference of Jewish Communal Service. She has been a lifelong friend.

At the CJI I led the Balfour Club, named after Lord Balfour, who was responsible for the British pledge to make a homeland for the Jews in Palestine. All clubs had to have "Jewish" names and conduct some programs of a Jewish character. The Balfour Club, at my instigation, assembled a scrapbook of items of Jewish concern, which were discussed at each meeting for at least half an hour. When the boys played basketball, I was young and vigorous enough to join in and compete with them. On warm nights I often took them for peripatetic tours of Central Park (the Institute was on East 85th Street between Park and Lexington), where in the dark they would ask me all kinds of personal questions, including sex. The club was involved in the annual drama competition and won the second prize. I was their coach.

My club at the 92nd Street Y was of a different character. No matter how hard I tried to infuse an interest in intellectual and Jewish affairs, the members were only interested in athletics and social activities. That is where they began and that is where they ended when I left. My supervisor, Herman Jacobs, was too overwhelmed with work to give me much help. The executive director, Jack Nadel, to whom I was never introduced during those two years, but whom I later came to know intimately as a fellow executive in the field, could always be seen, with his thin body and distinctive bald head, patrolling the building. He managed to talk to everyone, and with his prodigious memory for names and great gift of humor, he knew each member and contributed immensely to building this outstanding institution. He had grown up in the Y as a youth; after finishing law school, he decided that he would like to work there and did so for more than sixty years.

During the second year my extracurricular activities increased at the graduate school. I was president of the student body, and in the course of that year and subsequently, also became one of the leaders of the alumni. In both capacities, as a member of various committees, I tried to influence the school to make fundamental changes in its top leadership, or at least to change its dictatorial attitude toward students. The school was inculcating no loyalty in its students and future graduates. Such devotion was imperative if funds were to be forthcoming for the support of the institution, particularly since the depression was not waning.

Karpf, short in stature, sharp and critical in speech, without a touch of warmth or humor, was reluctant to have the students, and even the more mature alumni, share in the making of any decisions on program, student schedules, or scholarships. Whenever students articulated personal grievances, they were handled roughly by warnings and even dismissal. Collectively, we didn't get any further.

Karpf believed definitively that the future of Jewish communal work in the United States was related to the school's existence and the students it would graduate. They would translate his views into the institutions where they worked. While he personally understood the need for government to take over work and relief problems facing the country, which had now reached catastrophic proportions, he saw the private, Jewish sector as a necessity in order to experiment and demonstrate new methodologies and set standards for higher-quality service. In all this he saw himself as the determiner of what students would think and do. In a speech he made before the alumni on October 2, 1933, he was clearly disturbed by the critical atittude of the alumni toward the school.

At a joint meeting of the alumni and the entire faculty, at which I was present, on April 26, 1934, the hostility between both parties was patent. We had opposed the type of study being undertaken by the school as being self-serving and felt that another mode of evaluation should be made that would reach into the interior of the mounting problems. The breach was never healed. The school, while having made an important contribution to the development of professionalism within the American Jewish community, failed to attract support and ceased to exist. A totally different relationship with the alumni might have saved it, for many of its graduates were now influential enough to have inspired large donations. It would take several decades before comparable schools and programs were established to achieve the same purposes.

I was a member of the alumni committees, which after the school's demise, met with officials of the Hebrew Union College and the Jewish Theological Seminary to see whether they would take over the program and the substantial library. Neither was in a positon to undertake such a financial liability. In later years, after World War II, the seminary introduced a partial program, so as to give social work training to all of its rabbis and Jewish educators. In the 1960s, the HUC-JIR initiated a full-scale school on its western campus in California.

But in 1931–32, we were not always battling with the administration. We had meetings with a lot of fun. I recall presenting an amusing piece entitled "Brave New Graduate School," a parody of Aldous Huxley's popular *Brave New World,* set in the year 186 A.K. ("after Karpf"), which was enthusiastically applauded. At Purim, I wrote an original version of how the word "Purim" came into being, a far cry from the conventional treatment in the Book of Esther. I was both booed and cheered.

As the term came to its inevitable end, we were all concerned about jobs, and the pickings were lean. We were all being educated as line workers, or at best as lower-level supervisors, but certainly not as executives. As it turned out, the only position open for me was as an executive at the Jewish Community Center of Staten Island. I was twenty-four, married, with a four-year-old child, and needed a job desperately. After a long interview that lasted several hours, a small committee of the center's board decided to hire me as of September 15, 1932, at the salary of $2,000 per year. I grabbed it.

I filled in the balance of the summer working as head counselor at the Council House Day Camp on Forest Avenue in the Bronx, a program operated and supported by the Council of Jewish Women. The settlement house was directed by a sharp, critical, imperious woman, Lillian Strauss. She not only found no fault with my work but, on learning that there were no limits to my capacity and productivity, loaded me with a schedule that kept me occupied five full days a week. I learned a great deal about day camping, which was to come in good stead for the remainder of my professional career. In 1932, the Bronx was still a teaming Jewish community. The depression had hit hard, and all the children came from families of the unemployed, on relief, where conflicts were already searing and disrupting many of them. The staff had to function not only as educators, social workers, and recreational leaders, but actually as surrogate parents.

In the spirited election of 1932, I voted for Norman Thomas, the Socialist candidate, because I did not believe that Franklin Delano Roosevelt, the patrician from Hyde Park, would want to take the Democratic Party and the country through the tortuous measures necessary to pull the country out of the unemployment morass and equally severe financial problems. I was, of course, absolutely wrong in my evaluation, for Roosevelt, as President, rose to every challenge—the bank holiday, establishing the Reconstruction Finance Corporation, the National Labor Relations Board, the Social Security system, the regulation of the stock market, WPA, CCC, NYA, federal cultural programs in art, music, drama, dance, writers. All proved to be the kinds of measures necessary for getting the country back on its feet. I voted for Roosevelt in 1936, 1940, and 1944, even though I did not always agree with all of his policies.

Pronouncing Berger

Sometime after we reached New York, there was a change in the pronunciation of my last name. In Gloversville and Missouri, I was known as Berger with a soft *g*. In New York, the rest of the Berger family used a hard *g*. Rather than try to explain the difference, since everyone was curious, I began to use the hard *g*, and that is how it has been ever since.

4

Staten Island

THE BOARD OF the JCC of Staten Island did not help us find an apartment, but by walking the streets near the center, we found one in a new apartment house at 125 Silver Lake Road for $25 per month. Nor did the board offer to pay our modest moving expenses. We had no furniture and less money. I borrowed $75 from my bother Morris. When it arrived, we hailed a taxi and moved all our worldly goods. On time payments we purchased a bridge table and three folding chairs for the kitchen, a sleeping couch which we opened each night for the two of us, and filled part of the rest of the living room with a modern maple chair and one lamp attached to a small table. We bought a beautiful single maple bed for Ramon, who occupied the bedroom. Later we added a dresser. We gradually bought some pillows, and visitors sat on the floor.

As the walls were bare, we cut out modern French and other impressionist paintings (Van Gogh, Cezanne, Matisse, Rouault) from a magazine and after shellacking them, we found some 10-cent frames and hung them on the walls. Later, when the center was months behind in payment of my salary and we had no money to live on, a board member was overheard saying: "What can you expect? They squander their money on art." Visitors to our home, who thought we were original, quaint, and bohemian, enjoyed the novel atmosphere.

I arrived at the center the first day to find it a beehive of activity. A large committee was preparing for the annual gambling bazaar, which provided a great deal of money to support the budget. No one paid any attention to me. The president had not yet called to either greet or brief me. Saturday night was the gala opening, and hundreds of people crowded the facility to play the spinning-wheel games of chance, buy food and drinks, all well organized, in the large gymnasium. I walked around the building to imbibe the hectic atmosphere, smiling to people, who returned their smiles. I shook hands with a few and told them who I was, but apparently my youthful appearance did not make them recognize me as an executive director. I entered a large, noisy room, where some fifteen men were on their knees shooting craps. Innocently, I thought this was a rump game diverting money from the center's operations. I tapped a man on his shoulder and boldly stated: "You can't roll dice here!" "Who are you?" he sharply replied. "The new executive director." He curtly answered: "I'm Ben Cantor, the president. This game pays your salary." He resumed playing. That was my introduction to the head of the center.

If I had been vocationally sophisticated and not so hungry for a job, I might have learned more about the center the night I was interviewed. It might even have deterred me from accepting the position. Built in 1928, when the leadership was well off, the center was saddled with a $250,000 mortgage. By the time I arrived, it couldn't pay even the interest, let alone the amortization. Unpaid debts of tens of thousands of dollars had piled up. The center lost its first executive after two years. Then it engaged a mature Jewish educator. He was not strong enough to weather the continuous financial headaches and the personal storms at board meetings. His position was terminated in 1932. I still blame the Jewish Welfare Board and E. J. Londow, my supervisor, for not revealing the facts, for the center was on the verge of bankruptcy.

Had it not been for my efforts, even as a neophyte, to prevent foreclosure, forcing the board to work out some better arrangements for payment of the mortgage and going out to solicit members and funds, the center would never have survived. Some of the board were unable and/or unwilling to pay their building pledges. But a small group, constantly urged on by my pleas and hard work, developed a renewed feeling that there was still a future and helped it continue, although on the barest level. My family and I paid a price for all this. From the very first payroll, the center fell behind, and in the course of years, up until the day I resigned, and finally left in 1938, they always owed me six months' back salary. Since rent, food, and clothing were cheap in the thirties, $38 per week might have met current expenses at the minimum, but I never received it on time. I borrowed small sums from the bank and from friends, pawned a few items of value, and managed to pay it back in time to make further loans. When Emma told one of our rich board members that we couldn't live on this part-payment plan, she replied, "I thought you had an independent income."

My first task at the center was to build program in order to attract members. The staff consisted of a secretary, a building superintendent, and part-time gym and swimming instructors. The entire budget was less than $12,000. When our telephone bill reached a staggering amount and was not paid, service was disconnected. I used a five-cent pay phone in the hall for the years I was on Staten Island. While a phone was essential, I saw more important priorities. I often worked seven days a week, including nights, leading many programs personally. I led one of the Sunday school classes. I led youth groups. I led adult study units. In time, I found and developed volunteers to cover many of these programs. Since I was one of the few professionally trained group workers in the field, the Graduate School and the New York School of Social Work gladly sent me two students a year. I supervised their training and used them instead of paid program directors, whom we could not afford in any event. I started a Friday night group in our home for college graduates, a group that in the ensuing years became the presidents and board members of the center and leaders in the Jewish and general community. We met in our living room, dimly lit by one bulb, and sat on the floor. There was only one couch and one chair. Sometimes someone brought some cake, so we had a feast; otherwise we served store-bought cookies out of a box and plain tea. We discussed the major issues of the day: "How to Deal with Unemployment," "Technocracy," "The Menace of Fascism," "Anti-Semitism—The German Bund and Father Coughlin." We also dealt with literary subjects like Walt Whitman's poetry, Browning's "Rabbi Ibn Ezra," and the dramatic writings of Eugene O'Neill.

Another group that I led was composed of selected undergraduates, a number of whom later became social workers and executives of agencies, and one became the dean of a school of social work. In retrospect, while I was not much older than the group, I served as a role model and in a few cases as a surrogate father. A few walked me home late at night after the center closed, and we stayed up for many hours discussing everything from personal matters to dialectical materialism. Abraham Fleischman and Simon Slavin were members.

I introduced courses of study for the Council of Jewish Women dealing with Jewish history, anti-Semitism, Christian-Jewish relations. The courses involved the perusal of Jewish historical works and Jewish novels, the latter an interesting way of enticing the women to read. The women presented papers on the author, the book itself, and the contemporary problems that might be remedied through our discussion. The program was the equivalent of a college course.

I was invited to lecture before synagogues, Hadassah, Jewish War Veterans, and even the "Jewish" section of the Knights of Pythias. The local librarian used me several times a year to review books for the general public on art and literature, including such books as Franz Werfel's *Forty Days of Musa Dagh*, the tale of the destruction of the Armenians by the Turks, and Robert Briffault's *Europa*. I usually received the book I reviewed as a gift.

All of these contacts with groups in and out of the center were undertaken for the purpose of bringing the center to their attention and to recruit members and other forms of support.

* * *

An effort was made through the local library and the museum to improve the quality of the arts on the island. A Council of the Arts was formed, and Mrs. Jacques Marchais, the wife of Harry I. Klauber, a well-to-do chemist-businessman, was elected chairman. She asked me to be her vice-chairman, and I accepted. Mrs. Klauber, a former opera singer, was a flamboyant woman in speech, manner, and dress, and most persuasive for any cause she adopted. The Klaubers lived at the lower end of the island in an unusual house situated on a bluff overlooking Lower New York Bay. She was also a leading collector of Tibetan art, and after both of them died, they left the house and collection for a permanent museum open to the public.

Mrs. Klauber was also an extraordinary entertainer of the famous. I met celebrities at her house. She had invited Claude F. Bragdon, an outstanding architect, stage designer, and Theosophist, who authored a number of books on these subjects. He was to lecture on "The Fourth Dimension," an abstruse theme, and a mixed international guest list of some twenty persons had been invited to listen to him and then indulge in a fabulous feast, displaying exotic foods that I had never seen.

When I entered the room, I noted a man with a shock of disheveled gray-white hair sitting in a corner by himself. He looked like Albert Einstein. My curiosity led me to him. I introduced myself and he identified himself simply as Einstein. He told me he had been invited to listen to Bragdon, whom he had not met, but with whose works he was familiar. He was eager to get the program started, as he had to return to Princeton. Others gathered around, so our brief conversation came to an end. Einstein listened to Bragdon, asked no questions, made no comments, excused himself, and left. He ate nothing.

Another well-known person who was present, and with whom I chatted for a short time, was Benjamin de Casseres, a journalist who wrote a column "On the Nail" for Hearst's *New York American.* He authored poetry and essays. Casseres, from a Sephardic family, was a descendant of Spinoza and wrote a book about him, which was the subject of our conversation. There were also guests from China and Japan.

I visited the museum decades later and could not help recalling vividly the night of that meeting amidst the two thousand ritual and other objects Mrs. Klauber had collected. She has been called "the greatest disciple of Tibetan culture in the United States."

* * *

Staten Island was a locale where a number of German Jewish refugees had settled after Hitler came to power. No committee was ever organized to receive and help absorb them. Several, who lived in the vicinity of the center, dropped in to find out about the program, so that I knew a few of them intimately.

During the depression, among the great contributions to our country's culture was the Federal Art Project, part of the much maligned WPA, which gave artists, actors, dancers, producers, and writers a chance to work and create with a stipend of only $25 per week. A traveling drama group scheduled a performance of *Professor Mamlok*, the story of a Jewish doctor who was forced to leave Germany during the Nazi regime. One of the local "refugees" whom I had met was Dr. Hans Mamlok, a tall, heavy-set man, formerly a famous dentist and teacher of dentistry in Berlin. I invited him to view the play with me. He was deeply absorbed as it unfolded, and was visibly, emotionally moved. While he said that the name of the play was fortuitous, in some ways it paralleled his unhappy experiences. He died shortly afterward. I became friendly with his widow, who made a living in a fashionable department store reading palms and fingernails. She had learned how to diagnose illnesses by such readings as part of her hospital training in Europe. From this she believed that she had developed insights into people that enabled her to help them. She persuaded me to let her read my hands. While I have little faith in such mysteries, she was uncanny in relating my past and even foretelling events that took place in my life in future years. She upbraided me for not having pursued a musical career, because she said the lines and color clearly delineated that I had talent to succeed in that art form. Even after I told her about my meanderings through the piano, violin, and mandolin, and drum, she firmly stood by her evaluation.

The Federal Art project assigned Samilla Love Jameson, a middle-aged artist, to the center. She had been the recipient of honors and important commissions earlier in her life. We advertised her classes in the *Bulletin*. I turned out this four-page house organ each week, along with other copy for the *Staten Island Advance*, letters to the editor, articles and speeches in quantity. No one enrolled in her class. I decided to become an art student on exhibit. I bought an easel, canvas boards, paints, and brushes and went out in the park with my teacher to learn how to paint. The magic of juxtaposed colors on canvas produced a painting that I thought crude, but she said it indicated that I had art potential. What was more magical, several passersby, including some members of the center, decided to join the class after watching me paint. That picture which I painted has been on loan exhibition in the homes of a number of our friends.

The weather cooled, so the class moved indoors, and there I painted a portrait of Emma from a photo taken shortly before our marriage. The instructor thought it was good and urged me to continue painting seriously. But I had too many other things to do, and that was the end of my studies. Emma's portrait hangs in our bedroom contiguous to a portrait of me that another Federal Art teacher assigned to Staten Island painted. Wallace MacBeth, a Yale Art School graduate, was more of a perfect copier than a creative artist. While I never had enough money to pay bills, his needs as a husband and father were so great that I gave him some business. Paying $10 or $15 a piece, I had a half dozen copies of interesting paintings made, some of which we have since given away. One included Modigliani's *Dr. Deveraigne,* which is such a remarkable likeness of the original that he insisted on painting in "Copied by Wallace MacBeth."

Mike (Meyer) Barkin was a local young man striving to be a sculptor rather than run his father's profitable restaurant. He volunteered his services. We advertised in the *Bulletin,* and again no one enrolled.

I became his first pupil, working in clay between 6 and 7 P.M., often forgoing supper at home. I sculpted a head in clay of Henry, the center's black porter, then a head of my young son, Ramon. I learned how to cast the model in plaster. The latter head was highly praised by my instructor, and is now prominently displayed in Ramon's home amongst the many art treasures that grace the residence. I made one more piece and stopped. I had accomplished my purpose, for members came down to watch me work and enrolled in the class. Barkin became a well-known sculptor, selling his creations for large sums. He died in Florida in January 1985.

Among the events which were held to raise funds was an annual musical show directed by Ernest Gluckman, who later became a prominent producer in Hollywood. Scores of people learned to sing, dance, act, and tell jokes, to the amusement and wild applause of a large, friendly, paying audience. I played minor roles in several productions.

The center also had a dramatic group, which produced a few plays during the year. In the first season of my incumbency, the group under the direction of Mrs. Elias Bernstein, wife of one of our important board members, selected Sholom Aleichem's *Hard to be a Jew (Shver tzu zein ah yid).* I was coaxed into a minor role and performed creditably, although no agents sought me for either Broadway or the cinema.

I personally led a stamp club for a group of teenagers whom everyone thought would turn out to be at least delinquents and at worst felons. They grew up to be respectable citizens, married, and acquired wealth, but none ever continued with stamp collecting.

On Tuesday nights, I could usually be found playing basketball with one of the adult teams. Basketball was a prominent activity at the center, and we even brought top New York college basketball teams to play before crowds of yelling spectators, so that we could add a bit to our treasury.

All of these activities brought me close to the membership.

Jewish Studies

While the center had operated a Sunday school designed to serve a population that was not always identified with synagogues (all the synagogues in the area were Orthodox), the program, like most one-morning-a-week curriculums, was superficial. There were several afternoon schools associated with synagogues, where a longer and somewhat better education was provided. Many of the Jewish children were so tied up with music lessons, dancing lessons, Boy and Girl Scout troops, that their parents did not want to subject them to a four- or five-day-a-week afterschool schedule.

I conceived the idea of a six-hour, Saturday and Sunday morning school, which would fill the gap. It would actually provide more hours of study than even the afterschool programs. There would be no writing on the Sabbath. On that day the program would conclude with a half hour religious service. I recruited a committee, found an imaginative educator, David Rudavsky, enrolled twenty children, and we were in business. The children ranged from ten to twelve years of age. All pre-Bar and Bat Mitzvah, although Bat Mitzvahs were not popular during this period. The program had to be self-sufficient, as the center's budget could not afford a penny of subsidy. We could not offer any scholarships either. It functioned for two years and then ceased, because the parents felt that while the school better fitted into their schedules, it still did not provide a deep enough learning of Hebrew and preparation for Bar Mitzvah.

In my next-to-last year on Staten Island, I pushed the board into introducing a five-day-a-week afterschool and Sunday morning program with a full-time teacher, who also served as an assistant in other program areas. Our budget had risen, and this was no longer considered a luxury, but essential for a Jewish community center.

I must add that both programs—Friday night services and Jewish schools for children—were vigorously opposed by the synagogues. I won out on the talmudic principle that while no Jewish community should permit a craftsman to set up a shop in competition with a similar worker in the same neighborhood, every encouragement should be given to adding to the Jewish educational resources in any community, because there were never enough.

My real battle with the rabbis came over the establishment of a Friday night religious service at the center. No local synagogue had services that evening. Thus young and old alike had either to find their own way of observing the Sabbath or else resort to other means of entertainment not in consonance with the Sabbath.

A few parents were also concerned with what their teenage young people were doing. I gathered a small committee of parents and older teenagers and asked their reaction to having a different type of Friday night service in which they would be the principal participants. There would be no rabbi officiating. No visiting speakers. They could use the existing prayerbook or, if they preferred, we could fashion and mimeograph one of our own. Sermons would be offered by members of the group, and I would help in preparation. They asked for music. why not an organ? While we knew this would create controversy, we decided to combat criticism and bought a handsome, old oak one from the local Catholic girls' school, thus compounding our blasphemy. The program was an instant success with an attendance of seventy-five to one hundred people, mostly young ones. From time to time I was asked to deliver sermons.

The rabbis and their synagogue presidents insisted on meeting with the center's leadership and me. It was a stormy session. We refused to back down, because we fervently believed that the program fulfilled a basic Jewish need. There were long-term consequences, for after I left the island, other synagogues established programs on Friday night, more in the traditional and not in our innovative manner. The center finally dropped it—in part, I suspect, because my successors did not have the same enthusiastic commitment that I had to Judaic programs. (After I left and the program was abandoned, I purchased the organ and for some years I enjoyed playing it. Later I gave it to Bronx House camp.)

Gambling

One of the first issues that I got entangled with was whether the center should cease the gambling bazaars. I told the board that it was difficult for me to prevent young people from wanting to gamble at the center with both cards and dice, when their leaders and parents condoned it in an open communal event. I did not argue on moral grounds, but held that it was just a bad practice. I believe that centers and synagogues should not be supported by such means, but should depend on membership dues and fees, or on a Jewish Federation that would provide Jewish communal funds. Money should have a direct relationship to the purposes of an institution.

I got nowhere the first year on Staten Island, because the board was not prepared to find alternative means of funding. But in the second year of my incumbency, Fiorello LaGuardia became mayor of New York and decided to clean up gambling in the city. Thus, when it came time for our next bazaar, and there was a prospect that the formerly cooperative police might now have to close us down, the board decided that they would get a court order to restrain such a police action and that I was to serve the order to the local police captain. I adamantly refused. There was some talk about my looking for another job, but most of the board were deeply impressed by what I had already accomplished for the center, so someone else was selected to serve the judge's order. I did not let the issue die. The bazaar as a means of raising money by gambling was forsaken. The next year we sponsored a large outdoor carnival to obtain money. This introduced new problems. The carnival stands were often so dishonest that the center received complaints from irate citizens who had been swindled. By the fourth year of my presence, gambling in any form was proscribed. Private gambling at home was another matter.

While I was not a regular card player, I always had some good fortune when I played. I never sought such opportunities, but I occasionally accepted an invitation. One night at the center after we had finished playing basketball and handball, a half dozen men, all professionals (doctors, lawyers, dentists, accountants), dropped into my office for a chat. Someone suggested poker for two hours from 11 to 1 A.M. and invited me to come along. I had $20 in my pocket for more important bills at home, which I dared not lose. But some malevolent voice, the death knell of inveterate gamblers, told me that this might be my lucky night, so I accepted with a 1 A.M. deadline. Since I often returned from the center about that time, I didn't even bother calling Emma to tell her I would be home late or what I was doing.

Lady Luck occupied my seat, and by 1 A.M. I had won over $100, which at that moment was a fortune. I felt guilty calling the time to their attention, and after some pleading, I agreed to one more hour.

My winnings were further augmented. No matter how many cards I drew, I filled inside straights, flushes, four of a kind. At 2 A.M. they asked for another half hour, extending it, because they were all losers, until the clock finally ticked to 4 A.M. and my winnings were still over $100. I rose and told them I must go home. I even offered to return the money. Like good gambling gentlemen losers, they refused.

When I opened the door, Emma was waiting and in tears. She had called the center and there was no answer. Thinking I might have been held up, she notified the police. They searched the center and the streets on which I walked home and notified her there was no trace. Even my prodigious winnings could not pacify her.

I never played cards again at such an hour, nor did I ever go anywhere without first notifying her. I always learned my lessons the hard way.

A Black Girl in the Pool

One of the most attractive facilities at the center was the swimming pool, at that time the only indoor pool on Staten Island. The center rented it to the Boy Scouts and Girl Scouts and other organizations which used it for handicapped individuals. This was done as a community service and to obtain additional revenue. There were no religious or racial restrictions on who the organizations could bring to the pool.

The center had a policy that each member could invite a nonmember without charge in the prospect that this might induce the visitor to become a paying member. A few non-Jews became members only to use the gymnasium and the pool.

One day young Pescha Rosenholz stopped by my office after school and wanted a pass for a classmate, a black girl. Without hesitation, I wrote out the pass and both went for a swim. An hour later, a howling mother, the same person who thought we lived on a private income and were not dependent on the center for our sustenance, the same person who was the ringleader in using gambling and carnivals to meet the center's budget, rushed into my office. She was tall, good-looking, and articulate. "How dare you allow a black person in our pool with my child!" She had gone to the pool to pick up her daughter and was horrified to see a black swimming among the whites.

While I defended my action courteously and vigorously on both the grounds of humanity and the center's policy, she would have none of it. She threatened to bring charges against me before the board and did. I accepted the challenge. The issue was raised at the next meeting. While my antagonist was not quite so vociferous before the board as she had been in my office, the subject was debated with considerable heat. The meeting ended with the board supporting me and reaffirming our policy that a member had the right to bring anyone in as a guest, including blacks. In the six years that I was at the center, not a single black applied for membership and not another one was brought in as a guest.

A year later, Rabbi Philip Goodman, director of programs at the Institutional Orthodox Synagogue in Harlem, brought a large group of children to spend a day in our outdoor summer day camp. We poached on the wooded lot next door, which did not belong to the center, and used the gym, pool, and other rooms to provide a good recreational experience for fifty children. As Goodman's group stepped off the trolley car in front of the center on Victory Boulevard, amongst his youngsters were a number of black children, all of whom had been formally converted to Judaism and were members of his congregation. The program proceeded throughout the day without incident. I waited that day and a few days thereafter to learn whether there would be any reaction, but there was not even a ripple of criticism. The "racial" battle of the year before had established a policy which was permanent.

Family Memberships

My difficulties in collecting dues from the young people who were the main users of the building convinced me that not the children but their parents should be held accountable for payment. The policy in all centers was for individual affiliation, and the agency looked to the person who was registered and in attendance for his dues and other fees. When I approached the parents, they often balked about payment, putting the responsibility on their children, for in most instances, they were not users of the center's facilities. Once I took the trouble of explaining what the center was all about, they paid up.

I made a proposal to the board that our method of affiliation should be altered—that only families and not individuals under twenty-one years of age must be the registrants as a unit, and that we should set a dues scale that had some relationship to the cost of services, adjusting our rates for those who could not afford to pay. Even on Staten Island, considered a middle-class Jewish community, there were some unemployed, and a few families received public welfare. Individuals twenty-one and over could enroll as individuals, for they were either through with college or working. Family enrollment would obligate us to provide programs for all members of the family. I considered this an opportunity to introduce a wider program, reach out to the parents, better interpret what we were doing for their children, and initiate more services on an adult level.

The subject, as usual, underwent intensive debate at a number of meetings, for in a sense it was a revolutionary concept. I finally convinced the board that a system of family memberships would provide larger and stable revenues. They agreed to try it out in the next annual membership campaign. It was not easy to persuade most families to join and pay more. However, some did, and they were enough to make a significant difference in our membership and income and ultimately the entire program.

On this issue, I met considerable opposition from my colleagues in other centers and even from the National Jewish Welfare Board. Everyone accused me of overthrowing a tradition that was fifty years old. When I read a paper on this subject at the annual conference of center executives, my first encounter (there were to be many more later) with fellow professionals, they all resisted the idea and it was categorically rejected. Within a decade, I was happy to note that the family membership idea was being widely adopted, and today it is universal. The need for more money and stable financing brought about the change. My paper is now just a historical memory. No one ever recalls that I initiated the concept.

Soviet Russia and the Center

The recognition of Soviet Russia by the United States in 1933 had an immediate impact on our center. Heretofore the center had been largely proscribed by those Staten Island Jews who had Communist leanings and affiliations. Suddenly I was visited by representatives of ICOR, a Soviet-endorsed Jewish organization interested in settling large numbers of Soviet Jewry in Biro-Bidjan, far out in Siberia, which the Soviet regime offered as an autonomous Jewish republic. It was also secretly conceived as a Soviet barrier against incursions by China. ICOR wanted to meet in the center. Its constituency would become members. In principle, I could see no objection to bringing another Jewish group within our confines. While I suspected that we would be exposed daily to their propaganda, I also felt that we might have some influence on some of the not-so-diehard party members, particularly their children, who would intermingle with all the others on other than a political basis.

Their propaganda began immediately. I found the *Daily Worker* on my desk. Soviet magazines and books were presented to me as gifts and for my edification. Their leadership dropped in to see me frequently, not only to arrange their own meetings, but to suggest topics for exposure to our wider membership. They inveigled the Zionists into a debate on "Palestine or Biro-Bidjan—which would be a better and safer haven for the Jews?" I chaired the meeting. It was a strident affair, which I tried to keep within reasonable bounds. Jews do not always discuss vital issues with calm, objective detachment.

When the Kirov trials took place in Russia, accompanied by a revival of anti-Semitism, ICOR members tried to rationalize the forced confessions of Jews by claiming that I did not understand the Soviet mind; furthermore, since in their view the confessions were true, they felt that Soviet Jews would have to pay the price for their perfidy. They found no support for such a position from me.

When the Spanish Civil War began, they supported the extreme left, again following the strict Soviet line.

In meetings organized against Nazism and anti-Semitism, they were in the forefront, marshaling attendance, suggesting speakers, and getting up from the floor to make long speeches. On the whole, they began to behave much better, and they came to understand that to attract followers or even fellow travelers, they would have to adopt some bourgeois, civil practices. Eventually, several ICOR members were elected to the board, where their "rough edges" were somewhat modified in speech and behavior. I was correct in my original evaluation of the consequences for their children, who began to adopt attitudes that were no different than those of non-Communist and anti-Soviet members. These young people became an integral part of the center; some became group leaders and in time were elected to the board.

The Catholic Church

In looking for programs for the center, I was always seeking subjects and speakers who could bring a fresh point of view and shake up the conventional thinking of the membership. Scott Nearing and Margaret Sanger were good examples.

I remember Nearing with his sun-tanned, lean, lined outdoor face, who appeared at the lecture in a blue chambray workingman's shirt and a tie, wearing a rumpled suit. I spoke with him at some length before the meeting began. He gave a straightforward talk on what I would term socialist technocracy, a subject in vogue at the time. I read with sadness about his death in 1983. He lived in Maine for the greater part of his later years, a believer that man could sustain himself by growing his own vegetables and other foods, and could clothe himself with homespun garments made from the shearings of his own animals. He was as true a native American as I had ever met, but in the 1930s he was considered a "radical."

Margaret Sanger addressed a small audience on birth control. A goodly number of her auditors were sympathetic, both sociologically and medically, to her way-out position, and there were none of the fireworks that I had anticipated. Of course, except among some clergymen, particularly Catholics, the Right to Life movement had not taken on the violent role that some of its adherents advocated and practiced in the 1980s.

By this invitation to Mrs. Sanger, I incurred the wrath of the local monsignor, whom I never met, and eventually I paid a price for my daring.

During the Spanish Civil War, I was approached by the Socialist group (in contrast to the pro-Soviet Communists) to see what I could do on Staten Island to help the cause. In assembling a group to sponsor a meeting and raise money, I inevitably had to come in contact with other groups more to the left, eager to associate themselves with anything that would help the Spanish Republic defend itself against the reactionaries who were trying to overthrow it. Among the supporters of the Republican cause were a number of Protestant ministers, who saw the alignment of the Catholic Church with the reactionaries as a threat to the democratic forces in Spain. Before I knew it, I was asked to preside at a boroughwide meeting to take place in October 1936. I was told that all the details would be handled by a committee. Unfortunately, without consulting me, they, all non-Jews, set a date on the eve of Sukkoth. When I learned about this, I told them I could not attend. However, by now they had already distributed press releases and other literature indicating that I was to preside. The major speaker was a prominent Protestant minister. His attack on the role of Germany and Italy as well as the Catholic Church in the overthrow of the Spanish democratic government was recorded in headlines in the local press. The local Catholic hierarchy immediately assaulted the meeting in the *Staten Island Advance* as "intolerant" and "unchristian." (This paper was owned by S. I. Newhouse, who later became the head of the largest combine of newspapers, magazines, and assorted related businesses in the United States. I met him once to raise money for the center. This diminutive, dynamic executive handed me a check for $1,000 without comment. I am not sure he even looked up at me as he continued to edit some material on his desk.)

The report in the *Advance* stated that "Sebo acted as chairman of the session in place of Graenum Berger, executive director of the Jewish Community Center, who was supposed to have presided but was unable to attend."

I took exception to this piece of reportage, wherein an absentee got more space than the acting chairman, and wrote a letter to the editor revealing my displeasure. The absence of a chairman was hardly news, I said. Moreover, I had become a member of the committee and agreed to preside not as the executive director of the Jewish Community Center, which was not a sponsor or participant in the proceedings, but as a private citizen.

The *Advance* answered me in a long column indicating that it was only as the head of the center that I was significant in the community and that I would always be identified as such no matter what other activities I participated in. Therefore I was not a private person any longer. While I considered both the original statement and the reply as cunning prejudice, I learned that you never could win when you tangled with the press.

Some of the center's board members were disturbed by the battle in the newspaper, and I suspect more so, because they feared it might create a cleavage with the Catholic community, with whom a few of the center's leaders were identified politically. I fought for my right to be a person apart from the center, and in the end I was supported and not even warned or censured. But the Catholic Church never forgot.

National Youth Administration

The National Youth Administration (NYA) had just been created to find useful work for young people of high school age and a bit older who were either unemployed or qualified by poverty for some supplementary assistance from the government. Unlike the Civilian Conservation Corps, which took this same age group out of town, where they rebuilt our national parks and other recreational properties and made them a major national resource for all Americans to this day, this program would be confined to nonprofit agencies, schools, hospitals, children's institutions, community centers. Mark McCloskey, a craggy, histrionic social worker-educator, who grew up in Hell's Kitchen in Manhattan and made good, had been appointed director of the Metropolitan Region. He chose to call me, because in checking he learned that I was one of the few professionally trained people on Staten Island, and he had a dim recollection that I had been one of his students at the New York School of Social Work, where he had been a lecturer. He asked me to chair a local committee and present a proposal for projects that he could act upon and fund. I assembled a committee, but to lose no time, I called a number of agencies that might be interested in and able to use and supervise NYA assignees, and within a fortnight McCloskey received a detailed request. The local committee hurriedly endorsed my report, as I told them that time was of the essence.

McCloskey, apparently impressed with my rapid and detailed memorandum, invited me to his office and offered me a job as his assistant. The salary was twice what I was earning at the center, and along with other perquisites, it seemed like a fortune, since the center was always months in arrears in meeting its payroll. I was prepared to leave, but I did not want to discuss this with my board and give them notice until I received a formal contract.

A week later McCloskey called to tell me he was having difficulties with my appointment. He had asked his volunteer chairman, who lived on Staten Island, to check into my credentials. His chairman, a leading Catholic layman, turned to the monsignor of the Catholic church, and received a report that I was an out-and-out radical, for I had brought a birth control speaker to the center and was active in the campaign to support the democratic regime in Spain.

Sometime later, our landlord told me that I was being tailed by the FBI. In my innocence, I was never aware of their secretive presence. I am sure that their search for evidence of my radicalism was fruitless. Someday I will check the government files, now that such documents are available under the Federal Freedom of Information Act. I know that whatever they wrote, it was never used against me, for on later occasions I was offered jobs by the federal government.

The church's position was against McCloskey's Ethical Cultural grain. He did not want to knuckle under to the appraisal his chairman revealed. He was even more convinced when I leveled with him about my views on many social issues. He told me that he was willing to fight it out with the hierarchy, if I concurred. I thought it over for twenty-four hours and called McCloskey to say that the new program should not be initiated with a lot of redbaiting, and that if employed, I would be working under a cloud. I was willing to forgo the appointment. However, I made one condition: if he appointed a Catholic as his assistant, then I would raise my personal issue publicly. I had been working with a fine Protestant, formerly a YMCA worker, named Carroll Gibney, and I strongly recommended him for the post. He got it and performed very well for years. Gibney became a good friend. We met, wrote to each other, and when he got older, he telephoned me regularly from his native town, Marlow, New Hampshire, to which he had retired and where he died in 1975 at the age of eighty-three.

McCloskey's and my paths crossed over the years. When he became the director of the New York City school recreational program, he made several schools available to Bronx House for extension programs. He always seemed a bit apologetic when he met me, as he probably recalled the injustice that had been done and his need to back off in the face of religious and political prejudices.

The Taint of Radicalism

The charge of radicalism continued to plague me. In 1938, when Harry Glucksman was the executive director of the Jewish Welfare Board, he personally arranged an interview for me with the board of directors of the Newark YM-YWHA, one of the most important and larger centers in the country, which was searching for an executive. Glucksman met with a small group of handpicked executives who he thought might be the future leaders of the movement and had taken a liking to me. He was at the interview, which went exceptionally well. I left with the feeling that the job would be offered to me. I was just thirty and ready for bigger game. The next day an agitated Glucksman called to tell me that a Newark Y staff member, who was himself interested in the position, had accused me of being a "Communist," and the board had called him asking for information on that score. I wrote a letter to Glucksman in which I said: "I have not been and am not now a member of the Communist Party. I am an enrolled Democrat. I will always oppose forces that make for tyranny, exploitation, corruption, persecution or war, when an intelligent examination of the facts reveals such injustices."

I sent the Jewish Welfare Board the names of sixteen individuals, all but one non-Jewish, including Catholics and Protestants, who were willing to give written references as to my behavior and character. The names included the president of a Lutheran college, the president of the Borough of Richmond, the pastors of two churches, top public school officials, the head of the Boy Scouts, heads of public and voluntary social service organizations, lay leaders in public and higher education, and outstanding philanthropists.

I did not get the job. My accuser did. Perfidy pays off. Glucksman was crestfallen about the false accusations and the board's decision. He died shortly thereafter.

Attempts to Leave Staten Island

In 1935, I decided to leave Staten Island, because no matter how the program improved and the membership grew, and no matter how long my working days, my salary was still only $2,000 per annum and, to boot, six months in arrears. I received an invitation for an interview for the executive directorship of the Springfield, Massachusetts, YM-YWHA. I spent two days in that city talking with all the leaders of the center. We reached an agreement that I would take the position for $3,250 per year and would begin work on September 3, 1935.

When I reported this decision to the board on Staten Island, they were thunderstruck. I just couldn't do this to them. A campaign was immediately initiated, particularly among the younger people, to have me remain. On September 2, 1935, the night before I was to leave, over five hundred people assembled at a meeting, at which one speaker after another rose to extol me and, if this is the proper word, beg me to stay. The leaders of the board promised to pay off the mortgage, an act that I had been strenuously urging for years. The board publicly promised to match Springfield's salary and pay the unpaid portion of my salary at once. I was listening not so much to the promises of the board as to the youth in whom I had invested so much of my energies and whom I had grown to love. I knew that I had already had a substantial influence on their lives. How could I desert them? So tearfully, after this outpouring of promsies and affection, I told them I would remain. I honestly believed that the center would collapse if I left, since I thought that I was the bond that really held all the fragments together. I telegraphed Springfield that I had to turn down their kind and generous offer.

The board did fulfill one promise. An editorial in the *Staten Island Advance* on August 8, 1936, a year after I had agreed to remain, stated: "The required cash sum was raised at the eleventh hour, and prevented the property from going under the hammer. Under the able leadership of Mr. Graenum Berger, it has become a real cultural center, as well as a center for recreational and social activity."

As to my salary, the board asked me to accept $3,000 instead of $3,250, to which I protestingly agreed. But it never caught up with my back salary. When I finally resigned in 1938, they still owed me for six months.

* * *

In 1938 my colleagues elected me to the presidency of the Metropolitan Association of Jewish Community Center Workers. I was thirty years old, and the youngest professional to hold that office up to that time. No significant changes took place in the association during my incumbency. My major stress was on improving the professional standards of personnel and, even more importantly, on attempting to improve the salaries and working conditions of those employed in the field. While there was general acceptance of such programs, it was not until after World War II, when a large group of new professionals entered the field, that both of these desired goals began to have an effect on the field at large, and then on a national rather than a mere local level.

I recall having arranged an all-day meeting and outing in one of the public parks. It included a baseball game in which William (Bill) Kolodney, an artistic intellectual and hardly an athlete, played in his first baseball game.

Anti-Semitism on Staten Island

Anti-Semitism again raised its barbarous, ugly claws all over the United States in the 1930s. The hooligan German-American Bund and Father Coughlin's savage radio messages, which reached tens of millions instead of the small numbers who could formerly hear such scurrilous harangues only in an auditorium, square, or open field, were poisoning the American polity—particularly against Jews. Immigration was cut off due to unemployment and the opposition of labor unions and reactionary, nationalistic groups. There was no sympathetic outreach to the Jews, who wanted to escape at first from Germany and then from the other European countries that Hitler's army was steadily absorbing, without too much protest.

The center had become a forum for speaking out against Nazism and anti-Semitism. I was active with a small group of young Jewish professionals called together by Judge Jonah Goldstein under the aegis of the American Jewish Congress to develop the apparatus for countering the insidious propaganda and provocative street actions by the Bund. I was the only member from the social work fraternity.

Staten Island was singularly exposed to German-inspired anti-Semitism. There was a large German-American population along with several Lutheran churches, which gave hospitality to the Jew-haters. The older German population had a close kinship with the Fatherland. The well-to-do German-American families sent their children to Germany for study, so that they would never lose touch with German culture. The Lutheran Church had created Wagner College on the Island, where not only the religion, but the culture of Germany was disseminated.

Only the Jews were concerned with combating this menace. It bothered me that apart from the Jews, only a few Christians—some Protestant clergymen with whom I had worked on various issues—had spoken out against anti-Semitism. There was no spokesman for the German-American constituency who could project a positive attitude toward Jews.

I had met Clarence C. Stoughton in his capacity as director of the Staten Island Chamber of Commerce, and we had both helped organize the first Community Chest. He was a prominent Lutheran layman, active in the national movement, and had just become president of Wagner Memorial Lutheran College on the Island. I sought him out at the college one day and we had a long conversation on the issue of local and native anti-Semitism. He was a man concerned with human problems, and I found him to be sympathetic to my request that something must be done quickly to contain and attack the problem. When he asked me for suggestions as to how we could work together, I presented a verbal plan—hastily improvised, I must confess, because I had not really come prepared for anything so concrete and immediate.

I told Stoughton that the center conducted a cultural series each year, bringing speakers of prominence, usually Jews, who spoke on vital issues. Perhaps, I timidly suggested, we could follow up these major speakers with smaller group meetings at the center or at the college, in which his professorial staff might be the discussion leaders. Thus two institutions from different faiths would be joined together in the sponsorship of the forum. In fact, as my enthusiasm and imagination grew, I saw this as a means for the college to offer extension courses for college credit. His faculty would, of course, be paid for their services.

Further, I suggested, we ought to have a joint committee in charge of the entire event, drawing its representatives from the college, the center, and the Jewish and general community. We would not ask the college or the community to assume any of the financial obligations. This would remain with the center, primarily from the fees it charged for the lectures.

My vision now had no bounds. Before each event, I suggested, the main speaker should be invited to have dinner with the committee. This would give them an opportunity to dine in a congenial social setting with a celebrity. This was not a common thing on Staten Island, where at the time, Jews were barred from membership of social and golf clubs.

Mr. Stoughton, who soon became Dr. Stoughton, but whom we all called "Prof," bought the program as I outlined it on the spot. I also suggested the theme of the first community forum series as "Is America Changing?" Rabbi Stephen S. Wise, one of the most imposing personalities on the Jewish and general scene at the time, was invited to speak on "Religion: A Force for Social Change." Other speakers on that year's program were Ludwig Lewisohn, a distinguished writer and teacher, and James A. MacDonald, a well-known statesman. Alertness credit was offered to students who attended the main and subsequent lectures and did some additional study.

A vicious anonymous circular was widely distributed on Staten Island shortly before the series began in a crude attempt to stir up racial prejudice. The first test of our non-Jewish friends came in their resolute and public repudiation of the leaflet in the press.

The entire program, from the meetings of the committee to the follow-up discussion groups, was an extraordinary success in both content and attendance. It continued for several years until I left in 1938. Professor Stoughton wrote me a letter (August 18, 1938) regretting my leave-taking of the center: "And now about the Forum. Somehow I am not at all excited about it without you at the helm. I take it for granted that no letters have been sent to prospective speakers. No matter what happens, thanks for the very careful summary and set of instructions you made."

I never left a job undone and throughout my career always provided detailed instructions for my successors—both professional and laymen—so that they would not have to start from scratch.

Anti-Semitism was not easily extirpated, but I had created a device by which it was at least restrained.

* * *

Throughout my stay on Staten Island, I had been urging not only the board, but non-Jewish community leaders as well, to establish a Community Chest, a method by which nonprofit organizations could benefit from a central fund collected from business, industry and government, along with gifts from the general public. I saw this as one way of providing some financial underpinning for the agencies in emergency as well as normal times. The board was not interested. Its members saw the idea as another appeal to their pocketbooks, something which many of them had strenuously avoided over the years, contributing minimally, never up to their wealth or capacity.

So when a meeting of community leaders was called to establish the Community Chest, I went to the meeting on my own, for none of the center's board members wanted to accompany me. I was elected to the Community Chest board, the only professional to fill that role, and incidentally the only Jew on that body. I actively participated in the first campaign, after which an allocation was made to the center. While not large it still represented 20 percent of the center's budget. The center board's only reaction was that it was not enough. After I left Staten Island and had to be replaced on the Chest board, members of the center board vied for my position, for the Community Chest had already become a most important civic organization. It provided an essential source of support in all the years that the center functioned, until it was finally admitted as a constituent member of the Federation of Jewish Philanthropies of New York. This is something which I brought about as

Federation's consultant. Thus the center's historic financial problems were finally resolved.

* * *

During the six years that I was working on Staten Island, we frequently traveled to Gloversville to stay with my parents, sometimes on my vacation at the end of the summer and definitely on the major Jewish holidays. More than anyone else, my father had a deep sense of esteem for my status as an executive of a Jewish institution, for in his eyes this meant that I had made it. He convinced the synagogue to invite me to deliver the sermons on Rosh Hashanah and Yom Kippur, in part because he thought that it would save the synagogue money, since I would accept no fee, not even my expenses, which they would have had to pay someone from out of town, but he also wanted to show off his son. He coached me on the things that I should say, although I was sufficiently well versed in Jewish thought and the significance of the holy days to write my speech without any assistance. It went off well. I was complimented profusely by people who had known me as a young boy but not as a respected adult and public figure. The synagogue sent me a modest gift in appreciation. But my father had something to *kvell* ("boast") about for many years thereafter.

My parents also visited us several times a year, and what they brought as gifts was always deeply appreciated. My mother had begun to accept Emma with greater warmth, although Emma still rankled from the treatment she had received because she had deigned to marry my mother's first and favorite son. My mother may have had some private dreams of my marrying a rich girl with a great deal of *yichus* ("prestige"), but she had never shared such visions with me. I suspect now that she would have resented anyone removing that first male child from her bosom. I was told by my sisters later that my mother loved me more than she loved my father. That explains a great deal of her behavior.

When I went out on a date in the car, she would always wait up for me to return, not to talk with me but simply to know that I was safely home, going to bed only when she heard the car in the driveway. We never shared too many intimacies about our inner feelings and thoughts. She knew from my hugs and kisses my deep respect for her, just as I was part of her mind and body.

Cancer began to afflict her again in 1935, so that she was thereafter under a physician's care, frequently hospitalized, and in the last year moved about only in a wheelchair with a woman attendant to help her and relieve her of all domestic chores. While it was clear that the disease was terminal, it was difficult for me to make frequent visits. My work consumed every minute of my time, and I could ill afford to leave. I did see her several times during the winter of 1937–38. She was finally taken to the Massachusetts General Hospital in Boston, where some new therapy was being tested. Her stay was brief and she passed away on March 8, 1938, with my father and me at her side. I had flown up to Boston by airplane, my first commercial flight, and my stomach was queasy. We accompanied her body back to Gloversville for burial in the Knesseth Israel cemetery. I remained with my father, brothers, and sisters during *Shivah*. It was a tragic end for a woman who so loved life and her children. She always sought to look well and improve herself, held out the highest standards of conduct and achievement for us to pursue, was concerned with helping her less fortunate neighbors, and earned all the necessary rewards in the next world for the mitzvahs that she regularly performed. She was a mother of whom I was never ashamed. Her image often appears before me in my mind and eyes.

Emma

In all the years on Staten Island, I devoted most of my waking hours to the center in an effort to keep it alive, develop it, and make it pay for our needs. This was often to the neglect of my family. While I was at home before Ramon left for school and had dinner at home most nights, my absence was marked during the evenings as well as many weekends, during which I was necessary for programs I had initiated.

Ramon was involved in the summer day camp, in Sunday school, in afterschool athletics, and in the last year in the Hebrew school, so I would catch glimpses of him as he flitted in and out of the building or as I toured the building to observe activities. But it was insufficient, and my influence was not as pervasive as I would have liked. I recall one time quarreling with him about not wanting to go with us on a visit to someone's house. He balked every argument and entreaty. He just wouldn't go. In desperation I shouted at him that thousands of people from the community came to me for advice and followed my counsel, but my own son wouldn't listen to me and do what I asked. He quietly went into his room, dressed himself, and came out ready to go—all without saying a word. Somehow that plea reached him.

Emma reminded me that Ramon's favorite game, when we were at home together, was to tie me up with a rope. The symbolism was clear.

Emma decided that if she was to see more of me, she had to be involved in the center's life. She became an active participant and officer of the Council of Jewish Women, the most important Jewish women's organization on the Island. She learned how to translate Braille for the blind. She served as a recreational leader. When the Hebrew school was established, she became the organizer and chairman of the Parents' Association. She attended all of the major events, even though she sometimes came late and rushed home earlier, because we could rarely pay for a babysitter. She left Ramon at home alone with the telephone numbers of the center and our doctor, Herman Friedel. He was a kindly man, and after his wife died he consoled Ramon in their mutual loneliness. Friedel became one of the presidents of the center. Emma learned my business thoroughly and became an articulate interpreter of everything that I was trying to do as a professional.

* * *

While I saw something of my relatives in the 1930s, we most frequently visited my cousin Max A. Berger and his family in Bensonhurst, Brooklyn. He was a dynamic, successful businessman, president of a Reform synagogue, and member of the board of the Jewish Community House of Bensonhurst. He persuaded me to call together all of our relatives and form a cousins' club. Over sixty people gathered at his home for the first meeting, bringing together three generations, each one relating the experiences of their lives and achievements. All the families were cohesive. There were no intermarriages, no divorces—facts which were to change radically in the next few decades. Most of my generation have since gone, but the Berger Cousins still meet irregularly. We now resort to impromptu luncheons, dinners, phone calls, and letters to maintain our cousinly relations. In 1982, our son Baruch Michael, who was not yet born when the club was organized, compiled a record of the entire family from the time of my grandfather and grandmother, so that anyone who wants to contact a member of the family now has the information. The list has over one hundred names. The cousins are scattered over the entire country, and some live abroad.

Leaving Staten Island

While the budget grew as program and staff expanded, the basic financial condition of the center did not improve. A temporary financial crisis in the spring of 1938 necessitated an extraordinary board meeting, wherein a committee suggested that to help economize, I take a cut of $400 in my $3,000 salary. At that time they owed me $1,500 in back pay and had never reached the $3,250 figure which they had promised when I gave up the Springfield position in 1935. I resented this ungenerous suggestion. With tongue in cheek I indicated that I would be willing to take the cut, provided the fifteen people in the room would make the same sacrifice by each contributing $400 to the treasury deficit. The board members were affronted by my "offensive" suggestion. Then and there I made up my mind that it was time to leave and look after my own welfare.

I advised the Jewish Welfare Board that I was looking for another position. They contacted Bronx House, which had an opening, and three representatives of the settlement house, Mortimer Fox, Frederic Stettenheim, and Arnold Weisberger, came to Staten Island to interview me. They wanted to see how I actually functioned. I responded to the multitudinous questions they had outlined on a sheet. Fox kept detailed notes on my responses. They told me the job would pay $4,000, and that they had no indebtedness on the building or the annual budget. The agency was funded by the Federation of Jewish Philanthropies of New York. The board consisted of many wealthy individuals. They wanted someone for September 15, 1938. I told them that if they were impressed with me, I would look no further. I had previously checked on Bronx House and learned that it had a good reputation. I received a phone call the next day that the position was mine. I told my Staten Island board I was leaving. There were some efforts once again to persuade me to change my mind with promises of meeting the salary of Bronx House. I had had enough. My decision was irrevocable.

* * *

What were my contributions to the Jewish Community Center of Staten Island? While I came there as a novice, I was a quick learner and acquired skills in administration, finance, public relations, law, building management, program development, civic contacts. No one could have given of himself more than I did in thought, time, and energy. During my incumbency, the membership increased substantially, the budget expanded considerably, the mortgage and other indebtedness were resolved, and the Community Chest provided a God-send in additional monies. While I never totally settled my own fiscal problem until after I left, and only by threatening suit for the $1,500 still due me, what I had to endure never occurred again with future executives. When candidates called me about an opening, I told them to get everything in writing. A written contract ensured a definite obligation, which the center never felt toward me, since our original agreement was oral. The building had been repaired and improved, so that it could function serviceably. The roof had leaked like a sieve during the first three years of my incumbency, but I had raised the money for repairs from a nonmember benefactor with whom I developed a good relationship. All in all, the center had become the foremost institution on the Island because of the cultural events I had introduced. Moreover, relations with the general community, except for the Catholic church, reached almost optimum levels. A Jewish Community Council covering the entire island had been established to give some coherence to the competing schedules of different Jewish organizations. The center was now firmly established as a distinctly Jewish institution. Many young people had been educated to take major responsibility for the center in the future, and some became future presidents. Whether anything more could have been accomplished, I do not know. But the record was clear for each of my successors to emulate.

I was repeatedly invited to come back to the center and the Island to make speeches, to help raise money for an expanded building, and to attend social events. I was visited to obtain information on the same subjects as well as for the center's historical records. They had begun to collect data about my years of service. My name was not forgotten.

Yet when I asked people at the center to tell me what I was best remembered for, it was almost always as a liberal activist. Many had to be reminded of my battles for Jewish programming, the one enduring memory that I wanted to leave behind.

What I got out of this experience that was most compelling was the awareness that an executive of a Jewish center must be first and foremost a Jewish educator. Yes, he could also be a social worker, a manager, a recreational leader, a cultural resource, but above all he must be a model teacher. This role I carried forward in the two other posts I held until my final retirement. It became a subject that I wrote about and spoke about to such an extent that it embroiled me in controversy during and after my active professional career.

5

Moving to the Bronx

WE FOUND A desirable elevator apartment on the corner of Pelham Parkway and Matthew Avenue in the Bronx, where we would dwell for the next two years. This was a teeming Jewish community with synagogues, stores catering to Jewish appetites, and a wide tree-and-grass-covered parkway that was a favorite place for sitting in the sun or for recreation. Nearby was Pelham Bay Park, City Island, Orchard Beach, the Zoo, and the Planetarium. There were no indoor Jewish recreational facilities. Young Jews took the subway down to the YM-YWHA on 92nd Street and Lexington Avenue. Our apartment was several miles away from Bronx House, accessible by bus. On many late nights, I walked home from Washington Avenue—unafraid. It was to be our home until we moved into the newly created Parkchester, a huge housing project built by the Metropolitan Life Insurance Company, in 1940.

A False Arrest

We decided to spend our intervening weeks before going to the Bronx at Sacandaga Park. My father had moved and rebuilt our summer cottage a mile away from where it was originally situated. The land was bare, so we set out lilac hedges in the front, planted maple trees at the corners of the property and pine and fir on three sides, with a cluster in the front to provide shade for the porch. I missed my mother, but my father, brothers, and sisters were constant visitors along with many old friends.

But the tranquil holiday was interrupted with a horrendous event. I had decided not to shave for the duration of our vacation, possibly grow a beard. I looked a bit unkempt. Emma was pregnant and due in December. She was plump and uncomfortable. Ramon, now nine years old, was a true joy, as we could play sports together, ride horses, go berry picking, and cook out of doors.

We went to the beach in Sacandaga Park, where many people gathered, although we had our own beach and boat landing two hundred yards down Hampton Road, because there were no companions for Ramon. I had driven onto the beach with an old blue Plymouth. After a while I noted that the car had attracted the scrutiny of a state trooper and another person in plain clothes who turned out to be a deputy sheriff, a fellow I knew from the old days, when the Gloversville basketball team played against the Northville five. I walked over and indicated that the car was mine. They asked whether I would mind driving to Northville, where they were investigating some matter and thought I might be helpful. They did not describe what it was. I resisted at first, but they were firm and even threatening. Since I was not aware of having committed any crime, I said I would go with them, but first wanted to return to the cottage and get dressed, since I was wearing a bathing suit. Emma and Ramon, already somewhat anxious, rode with me, all of us wondering what it was all about. When we reached the cottage, the trooper asked me whether I had a yellow T-shirt. I said no. But without further ado, he went into the house, turned the bedroom and the dresser and closet upside down, and found nothing. Now I was getting anxious; I kept asking was I was supposed to have done, and was told it would be revealed in Northville.

We drove to what turned out to be the courthouse. Three other people, two men and a woman, were seated inside. The trooper removed his jacket and started to ask me questions from a form. Now I insisted on knowing what I was going to be charged with. The trooper came over to me, grabbed my shirt, and threateningly told me to shut up and just answer his questions. I demanded a lawyer. The young justice of the peace, against whom I had also played basketball in my youth, recognized me and asked who my lawyer would be. I replied, Sydney Rosenthal, my brother-in-law, an attorney for the county. They whispered to each other and it was agreed that he could be summoned. I went outside to see Emma and Ramon, because they had been barred from the courtroom, and told her to call Sydney. They were in tears. I still could not tell them what the charges were.

On my return, I was informed that I was being held on an attempted rape. It was alleged that at 12:15 P.M. that day, on the road to Sacandaga, I had stopped my car and tried to attack the woman sitting in the room. She identified me as the culprit. I denied the charge, pleading not guilty, but had to await the arrival of my attorney, who had to drive twenty-one miles. I was released in his custody without bail and the trial was set for ten days hence.

We were overwhelmed. How was I to prove my innocence? Even my brother-in-law felt that I was in serious trouble. A New Yorker, a social worker, and a Jew violating the morals of a married woman! This charge of attempted rape could have grave consequences, possibly including a long jail sentence, not to mention the disgrace and the loss of the excellent job that I was about to begin.

I met with my brother-in-law and my brother Morris, who thought we ought to hire the best non-Jewish local lawyer to defend me. I agreed. The next day, when I had gotten a grip on myself, I began to search for witnesses who could verify my whereabouts at the time of the crime and thus establish my innocence.

On the morning of the alleged crime, some well-diggers were in our back yard deepening the well, because we were short of water. They left at 11:50 A.M. for lunch. They signed an affidavit that I was in the back yard all morning, at times working with them.

At 11:50 A.M., as they were leaving, I had started mowing the lawn. The man who ran the stable down the road was just returning with some riders, and I stopped mowing long enough to make an appointment for the next day for Ramon to ride one of his horses. He signed an affidavit that he had talked with me between 11:50 A.M. and noon.

A neighbor from down the road had stopped and chatted for a minute, wondering why I was mowing on such a hot, humid day. She was on her way to get some sugar at the store to bake a pie. She returned about 12:10 P.M. When I interviewed her, she was not sure of the time, but the facts were correct. So I interviewed the storekeeper. He told me that he was just sitting down to lunch at 12 sharp, his regular midday eating time, and was annoyed that he had to leave his dining room, go into the store, and sell my neighbor her sugar. He knew the transaction was not later than 12:10 P.M. He signed an affidavit to that effect. The woman, with this information, also signed a paper confirming the times that she saw me while going to and coming from the store.

A young man was parked at the next house one hundred feet away, waiting for his girl friend, who was doing some housework. He signed an affidavit stating that when he left at 12:15 P.M., he saw me at home and the car parked in the driveway.

When the well-diggers returned at 12:30 P.M., they noticed that my car windows were steamed from the heat and asked me why I didn't open them. I did. They signed the affidavit with this information. It was obvious that the car could not have been driven elsewhere and returned in the time when the alleged criminal act was averred to have taken place.

Armed with these statements, I felt that I had established an iron-clad alibi of my innocence. But when I met with Morris, Sydney, and the attorney, they were not so sure that these documents would stand up in court. It was then decided that the best approach was to meet with J.

Ledlie Hees, the president of the Fonda, Johnstown, and Gloversville Railroad, who lived at the Park. Since the railroad owned the Sacandaga Inn, and the woman who had made the charges against me was the wife of the manager, we hoped that Hees could induce her to withdraw her accusations. It was a friendly meeting and Hees agreed to see what he could do. He was apprised that the Berger family was quite prominent in the county and, in light of the affidavits I had assembled, that this would be a serious miscarriage of justice. It wasn't even necessary for me to indicate that I would sue for false arrest, but that is what I intended to do, whether my family or the attorney rejected the idea. It was my only counterfoil.

In any event the charges were withdrawn. There was never any publicity in the press. But a pall hung over my life for a long time. I now knew the suffering that one goes through when one is falsely accused of a crime.

Milton Married: The House Divided

Within a year after my mother's death, my brother Milton married Harriette Weisman of Amsterdam. This presented a problem in privacy, since my father lived in the same household. It was decided to remodel the house, so that my father could occupy his own apartment with a separate entrance. While they saw each other daily and my father often shared meals with them, he preferred to live alone, manage his own rooms, and even cook for himself. Whenever I made visits, I straightened out his clothes and closets, buying new items to replace the old. A maid came in once a week to clean the rooms, but due to his advanced age—he was in his late seventies—he sometimes thought she was stealing things and went to great lengths to keep his effects locked up, even though he had little of great value in either cabinets or chests. Actually nothing disappeared. Just mislaid.

Milton was now running my father's business, so my father had a good bit of free time, which he did not altogether welcome. The business practically ceased when World War II was declared in December, 1941. Milton was assigned to factories, where he supervised workers turning out leather for our war needs, and he remained there until the war was over, then returned to manage the business by himself.

My father made visits to us in the Bronx, and during the summer months he would spend two weeks with us at Bronx House Camp. There, we utilized his skill as a fisherman, and he regularly caught enough large carp in our lake to feed a population of over 250 persons. As my father got older, he spent some of his time visiting several buildings that he owned and always seemed to be repairing them whether they needed it or not. My brothers finally took this responsibility away from him, since the buildings were not producing any income and thus not worth maintaining. He still walked slowly to the synagogue a mile and a half away. He maintained a small garden, which provided the families with vegetables. When he got a lift, he went fishing, and always seemed rewarded for his patience. He lived gracefully, in good health. He made no demands on his children.

Sam and Margaret

My brother Sam was graduated from Wisconsin in 1932, stayed for a year to get his master's in labor economics, and taught as a part-time instructor, since no full-time positions were open. He managed to get an assignment in Rochester studying the unemployment situation, then became the director of the Chicago Labor College, and for the year 1938–39 he obtained a fellowship to do graduate study at the London School of Economics in England. During that year he made valuable contacts with union leaders, university professors, and politicians, two of them future Prime Ministers, that would serve him in good stead when he returned to England in 1941.

While Sam had been dating girls for a number of years, he finally found the woman of his heart in Margaret Fowler, and they were married on September 27, 1937. Margaret was a small, pretty, freckled, bright student of Sam's at Wisconsin with a specialty in economics. She graduated Phi Beta Kappa. Margaret was not Jewish. She was a descendant of English settlers who came to the colonies before the American Revolution.

How were we to handle this with my father? Margaret's mother had died in childbirth, and she had been raised in Kansas by relatives. We invented a story that she was originally a Jewish child, brought up by Christians, and therefore knew little about the Jewish experience, except what Sam had taught her, including Yiddish expressions, during their courtship. They were married in a civil ceremony.

Whether my father ever believed the story, we'll never know. He was very fond of Margaret, and they had many long talks together. My father was the kind of person who did not question our cuisine or utensils when he visited our home, which was not kosher. Whenever he stayed with us, we bought only kosher products, cooked everything in separate utensils, and served in glass dishes with silverware that met the religious test. We would tell him: "Pa, you can eat everything. It is strictly kosher." He would invariably reply: "Who asked you?" implying that he assumed that we would always respect his dietary practices.

In any event, he, like all of us, loved Margaret, who was a remarkable wife and companion in all the years she and Sam shared together when he was in the diplomatic service—London, Washington, Tokyo, New Zealand, Greece, Korea. She died in 1967 before he went to Vietnam.

She watched and helped him rise to the rank of ambassador, when he always was handling difficult assignments for the State Department.

Baruch Michael: Born Christmas Day

December 25, 1938, was a banner day for us. It was not a celebration of Christmas. Baruch Michael was born, named after my mother, Batya, and Emma's aunt, Mary Ryan, both of whom had recently passed away. Emma loved her aunt, who had helped her in many ways after her mother had died. When Emma's father passed on, Mary continued living in his home in Albany, and from time to time Emma visited her. Michael was delivered at the Harkness-Presbyterian Baby's Hospital. Unlike Ramon, who had been sent during the winter school recess to Johnstown, New York, to spend this time with my sister Rachel, Michael was given a distinctively Hebrew name, partly because we had become "more" Jewish in our practices, but also because we had finally been blessed with another child after a nine-year interim. He was unlike Ramon in every respect from birth and thereafter. Dark instead of blond, feisty (a term which will come up several times in the course of this book) instead of calm, he added mischievous color to our household. He always claimed that he lost out as a child born on Christmas Day. We never celebrated Christmas and thus never distributed gifts on that Christian holiday. We told him that he was doubly lucky, for he received presents for each of the days of Hanukkah and also received a birthday gift on his day of coming into this world.

Ramon and I set up electric trains, which we had given to Ramon as a gift some years before, on the eve of Michael's birthday. Additions to the system were made periodically, so that each year was a special event. Eventually Michael "inherited" them. When I thought Michael had outgrown them, I gave them to the son of a close friend. Michael has never quite forgiven me, because he asserts they would now be worth a "fortune."

Until he was almost a teenager, he could not understand why he couldn't have a "Chanukah bush" if we wouldn't have a Christmas tree.

He hung out with a group of Jewish and a few gentile boys, whom he described as a "gang." He still looks back with horror on his two-day-a-week program in a disorganized "storefront" Hebrew school in one of the recently organized synagogues. I had complained about both the teachers and the content of the school's educational program, but it was to no avail. I finally withdrew him, much to his joy.

* * *

My sister Rachel knew that I was fond of spicing my food with bay leaves. Whenever we were at her home for dinner, she would always prepare something seasoned with bay leaves for our meal—beef and veal particularly. Rachel was also a practical joker. One night when we were staying over at her home, we turned back the covers on the bed and immediately sensed the piquant fragrance of bay leaves. We picked up the pillow, and there were the leaves arranged carefully to spell out the word *Welcome.*

* * *

Sam and Margaret returned to the States early in 1939, after a year in England. Sam had no job, for the universities had not yet begun to recover from the depression and Jews still found it difficult to get faculty appointments. Since they had no funds, we invited them to stay in our three-bedroom apartment in the Bronx. I introduced Sam to the personnel director of the National Refugee Service, and in short order he was hired as a statistician. Sam hated the job from the beginning, because his forte was in conceptual studies and being with people in a political and academic context, not working on dry-as-dust data compiled by hand or by the simple machines available long before the age of computers. As soon as Sam and Margaret had enough money to meet all of their obligations, they found their own apartment.

In June 1940, I was attending a conference of Jewish communal workers in Atlantic City. A group of us went to some well-recommended restaurant, and when we were seated, I introduced myself to the man alongside me. "Berger," I said. He replied, "Perlman." Looking at him carefully, I thought I had met him before and asked whether he was Selig Perlman of Wisconsin, the distinguished professor and writer on economics and labor unions. When he acknowledged that he was, I told him I was Sam's brother. He asked where Sam was, because he had a job for him in Washington with Isidore Lubin. I wrote down the information, left the dinner table, and phoned Sam. The next day he left for Washington, was hired on the spot, and for the rest of his life his destiny was to work for the government.

From the War Manpower Commission Sam was picked up by Averell Harriman, who headed the Lend-Lease program, and went to England with him. After the United States entered the war he was commissioned a captain in the army and was assigned to the U.S. Embassy in London, headed by John Winant, where he became the Foreign Service's first labor attaché. He remained in England until 1950, after the war became a specialist on the coal industry, an outgrowth of his earlier study of the British miners' union. Foreseeing the coal crisis that would develop in the postwar period, he wrote the paper that led to the creation of the European Coal Organization.

On his return to Washington, Sam worked with Harriman in the Mutual Security Administration, after which he was assigned to Japan as the deputy chief of mission, a great post, where he developed a relationship with the emperor's son. In 1953, when Richard Nixon, the new vice-president, went on a sight-seeing trip to Japan, Sam was his escort, and they seemed to get along splendidly. However, Nixon learned that Sam was not only a Democrat and a close friend of Harriman, but also had views of his own about foreign affairs. Without forewarning, Sam was reassigned to New Zealand, the bottom of the world, and served under a political-appointee ambassador who was more interested in toasting the president who had appointed him than in carrying out his diplomatic responsibilities, which in any event were minimal. Sam and Margaret endured their stay, relieved by tending to their garden and making a lot of friends. He had one great adventure, hosting the Antarctic "Deep Freeze" expeditions and visiting McMurdo Sound and Little America.

Because of this shabby treatment, for a time Sam thought of resigning from the Foreign Service. During the McCarthy period, due to political prejudice, he was constantly hounded by the FBI to determine whether he had a subversive background. He was prevailed upon to remain in office, and finally was posted to Greece, where, from London, he had earlier performed special services for the U.S. government in countering the Communists. Sam's undergraduate studies of Greece at the University of Wisconsin were invaluable in his role as second in command. Shortly after he landed in Athens, the ambassador left, and it was several years before a new one came on the scene, so that Sam was in fact acting ambassador for a good part of his stay, developing close relations with the king and queen of Greece. We had a wonderful visit with Sam and Margaret in 1959, which is described elsewhere.

After his tour of duty in Greece, Sam returned to the United States to head the National War College and finally was appointed ambassador to South Korea, immediately after the coup which brought Park Chung Hee to power. After exciting years in the Far East, he was appointed assistant deputy secretary for Far Eastern Affairs, during which he had an interesting argument with President Johnson over the *Pueblo* affair, urging no direct military action to free the crew captured by the North Koreans. With the war in Vietnam heating up, Sam was appointed deputy chief of mission in Saigon under Ambassador Ellsworth Bunker. Those trying years (which I also describe elsewhere) were brought to an end when he returned to Washington and was put in charge of various State Department training programs for high-level personnel.

Peace and Pacifism

My involvement with pacifism began during my experience with compulsory ROTC in Missouri. While I learned something in the cavalry-artillery unit—namely, how to ride and take care of a horse, and how to become a good marksman (I was awarded several medals)—the endless and sometimes senseless drill, marching, and saluting, and the dirty job of cleaning the horses, didn't make me either more patriotic or a stouter defender of America. It took too much of my time, which I was eager to devote to other academic and collegiate matters.

Furthermore, my courses in modern European history (although earlier histories taught me the same lesson), and particularly my research on the origins and consequences of World War I, and the failure of the League of Nations, convinced me even further that wars solved no problems, but frequently served as the pretext for starting the next conflict. I was convinced that once Germany reestablished itself economically, it would seek revenge for the defeat in 1918 and another world war would eventuate.

That was part of why I found pacifistic socialism a more acceptable political philosophy.

As I read about the naval arms race between the great and emerging great powers and their inability or unwillingness to put limitations on heavily armed vessels, as I read and saw on newsreels Japan invading the mainland of Asia with little protest, as I observed Italy rape Ethiopia with no one listening to the voice of its Emperor Haile Selassie in the League of Nations, as I noted Germany and Italy supporting a reactionary force overthrowing the first democratic government in Spanish history, as I clipped reports of Senator Nye's investigations of the U.S. munitions industry with its corruption and fraud, I could not help but throw my support to the American peace movement, weak as it was. During the depression I preferred "scholarships rather than battleships." But I was never a single-minded pacifist, for I did not undervalue the need for police protection on a local level, nor an adequate national armed force on land, sea, and air. But I viewed it more as a defensive instrument than a means of aggrandizing American commercial, industrial, colonial, and ideological interests.

The rise of Hitler, particularly after 1933, gave pause to both my pacifistic views and my affiliations with bodies promoting peace. In the mid-1930s, it was already obvious that peaceful approaches would only lead to appeasement rather than contain the spreading Nazi political and war machine. As one nation after another was absorbed in Hitler's expansionist movement, as his military, with the most modern hardware on ground and air and even the sea, was invading Poland, northern Europe, France, and now threatening England, I abandoned socialism and pacifism and became a supporter of aid to Britain as a first step toward the containment of Hitler on the European continent.

When the Nazis and Soviet Russia signed a mutual-security pact, I would not associate myself with those who suddenly put on buttons bearing the slogan "The Yanks Are Not Coming." This was one of the crises I had to resolve as an administrator at Bronx House, where the politically-minded staff had totally different views.

6

Bronx House

MY INCUMBENCY AT Bronx House was not my first contact with the Bronx. I had friends living there. I had dated girls from the Bronx when I was a student at New York University. I had worked at Council House during the summer of 1932. Yet I knew little of its history; for example, that it had been aboriginally occupied by the Siwanoy Indians; that the colony of Connecticut had claimed it, as did the Dutch; that Sir Thomas Pell, literally the founder of Pelham, where we bought a house in 1953, had bought a huge tract of land from the Indians in 1654 and most of the Bronx was included in the deal; that it was part of Westchester until it was annexed by New York City between 1874 and 1897; that the Bronx, named after a Dutch farmer, Bronck, was once covered with farms, market villages, "embryo" commuter towns, and country estates; nor that it had ever been referred to as a region of "rural delights."

The Bronx rapidly changed with the extension of the subway system in 1911. Bronx House was established in that very year. Henry Morgenthau, Sr., had grown rich by buying up properties where subway stations were being located. His wife Josephine and he had been active at the Henry Street Settlement on the Lower East Side. Lillian Wald, its famous and influential director, persuaded the Morgenthaus to establish a similar institution in the Bronx to help in the adjustment of the many newcomers, particularly Jews, who were beginning to move into this still rural borough, with its extensive parks and beaches on Long Island Sound. The settlement originally functioned in a frame house at 1637 Washington Avenue, but this soon proved inadequate, as the Jewish population of the Bronx, and concomitantly the settlement's membership rolls, steadily increased. Thus, in 1928 a four-story brick building was erected, with a gymnasium, a music school, and residence and dining facilities for the executive and staff.

I was the first executive who elected to live out of the building (all the previous incumbents were either single or, if married, had no children). I was looked upon with some suspicion by the board for having broken a tradition, especially since it was believed that the directors and staff had to live in the community in order to understand and serve the clientele. Within two years, however, all residence use was abandoned, as was the dining room, in order to make these spaces available for the growing program I initiated.

Bronx House was totally different from Staten Island. The building was larger (even though it had no swimming pool); so was the membership, and, what is more, it was poorer, for our rolls included hundreds of unemployed and hundreds who were receiving public welfare. The board, in contrast, was composed, with some exceptions, of very well-to-do Jews, all of whom lived in Manhattan and none of them users of its facilities. The board wanted, above all else, to raise the standards of behavior and the aspiration level amongst those being aided. Within a few years, I would break other traditions by bringing formerly impecunious members who had become respectable professionals and businessmen, and generous contributors, on the board. I recruited some of them from an alumni association which I established in my first year as head of the house. Later I convinced the board to permit representatives of the Youth Council and the Adult Council to attend board meetings, in order to establish direct contact between clients and board, so that those who used the center could have some voice in decisions that had formerly been made only by the board.

The building had no mortgage encumbrance. The budget of $33,000 was subsidized by the Federation of Jewish Philanthropies, of which Bronx House had been a charter member since 1917. If there was a deficit, the board was obligated to meet it. From the first payday to the last, it was my delight to always receive my full salary—and on time.

The building operated seven days a week, and while I would ordinarilly not have worked on Friday nights or Saturdays, the demands of an ever expanding catalogue of activities, with every room occupied for the entire weekend, required staff to be scheduled for a forty-eight hour week, and for the executives, especially the headworker (my title at Bronx House), to put in seventy-two hours.

The Union

Shortly after I arrived, the staff confronted me with a series of demands: they wanted a forty-hour work week, five-day schedule, increased salaries (full-time workers were receiving at most $1,080 per year), longer vacations, and sundry other benefits. They had also decided to form a union and wanted recognition. My own sympathies were with the demands. I had become partial to unions during my previous incumbency at the JCC on Staten Island, but this was my first experience with having to deal with one. I presented this important matter to the board, as a first test of my leadership. While a few younger members were also sympathetic, the old-timers were not so liberal and generous in their response. I went to see a number of them personally to try to convince them that times had changed. The National Labor Relations Board was handing down opinions which had become facts of life, and we could no longer treat workers as though they were individual contractors, but had to deal with them collectively. While nonprofit agencies were exempt under the act, I stressed the point that as Jews we had an ethical obligation to see that workers were paid adequately and worked under reasonably fair labor conditions. Furthermore, if the workers wanted to meet with us as a group, we should not oppose such an approach.

The board, after a great deal of discussion, finally agreed to meet with the staff, even as a union, and eventually, after many difficult meetings with the workers, the board and the workers signed what became the first union contract with a community center in the U.S. It was not always easy to deal with the staff as a unit, and when negotiations took place, their initial (and supposedly "final") demands often went far beyond anything that the board was able or willing to accept. As a result, there were occasional slowdowns and work stoppages, but as long as I and a few board members like Richard Dammann and Arnold Weisberger handled the negotiations, we always ended up with an amicable and fair settlement and no strike.

In 1947, it was recommended that we add several labor relations specialists to our board, and we elected Theodore Kheel and Howard Lichtenstein, both of whom later rose to the top of their profession. Coincidentally with their handling the negotiations, we had our first strike, with pickets in front of the building, and the membership torn between their need for the agency's services and their basic working-class sympathies with the employees, who they knew intimately. It was not a happy situation for me, because while I was fond of the staff, I thought their decision to strike unreasonable; and so I identified with the board and the agency, and maintained a program through the duration of the short walkout.

I left Bronx House in 1949, before the two-year contract had expired, with a sense of relief that I would not have to participate in such a wrenching experience again. As many of the workers walked out to the picket line the first time, they stepped into my office and either kissed me or shook hands. They could not yet identify me with the unhappy decision that they had come to. I crossed the picket line because I had to open the building and see that the furnaces were heating the plant, for we maintained a large nursery school for the children of working mothers, and if the nursery wasn't open, they would have to stay home and lose their meager wages. Most of the workers later forgave me for violating that holy union law of not crossing a picket line. Yet I felt neither shame nor guilt. I learned from that experience that not every strike was valid. This one wasn't. The final settlement was no different than the last offer made by the agency. I would hereafter choose which picket line to honor or trespass.

One of my earliest innovations was to make it possible for the board and the staff to meet on other than formal occasions. Previously there had been few such contacts. A board member who chaired a committee concerned with a particular department might know the supervisor of that department, but would not be likely to meet other staff members, and those board members who were not committee heads never even had this opportunity to meet individuals who, under their aegis, had been engaged to exercise a significant influence on the lives of hundreds of members. When the union issue came to a head, I was afraid that even these limited contacts might be vitiated. Therefore I suggested that before each board meeting at the house, there should be a one-hour dinner, attended by several staffers, who could use this time to make a presentation about their departments and any problems they were facing. During the course of a single year a staff member might make several such appearances. As a consequence, a much closer relationship developed, often on a first-name basis, between board and staff.

Budget

Another major problem that brought me into conflict with some of the conservative members of the board was the first budget. While the expenditures agreed upon were met, it was only because the agency was staffed with thirty WPA workers and eighty NYA assignees. Some of these workers were excellent, and a few were subsequently engaged full-time on our payroll. Others, however, were just filling in until a better job came along, and did not see social welfare as a career opportunity, so that there were always shifts in personnel, which did not make for continuity in leadership for the members.

As economic conditions began to improve in 1939, I felt that the members could pay a bit more, and they did. I thought that if we presented a better case to Federation, clearly demonstrating our need for more full-time, professionally trained staff, who would stay with us for a number of years, Federation might help us with a larger allocation. I was putting more emphasis on professionally trained supervisors and paid club leaders who had an interest in pursuing social work as a career. This obviously meant a larger budget.

When I finally convinced a majority of our board to go ahead with these increased requests, my treasurer and another member of the board resigned in protest about my extravagance. Happily, Federation increased our allotment and we were on our way to implementing a larger and better program. When I left Bronx House in 1949, the budget exceeded $350,000 per year.

While I have pointed out a few areas of conflict, I always had the support of a remarkable group of presidents—Dolly Marcuse, Richard W. Dammann, Lillian Riegelman, and Anne W. Langman. With all of these fine people I developed the closest personal relationships, and under their banners, Bronx House undertook a tremendous expansion of its services.

Since I am basically an educator, the weekly staff meetings and the monthly club-leaders sessions became instruments for developing a group of people who later moved out to become major executives, professors, and deans of schools of social work, spreading the outlook and the programs of Bronx House around the country. The staff called the institution "Bronx House University." Staff not only participated in decision making, but willingly accepted special assignments, preparing detailed papers on forthcoming events, such as Jewish and American holidays, the Sephardic Jewish community, the Italian community, the needs of the blacks who were moving into the neighborhood, housing, and so forth. These were major contributions.

Bronx House was accepting graduate students from the New York School, Pennsylvania, and Atlanta, Georgia, the latter a black school. Eventually we engaged a full-time professional whose sole duty was to supervise twenty students. This too was a measure of how highly regarded the institution had become. All of the top staff, including the executive, supervised students. I had some problems with the director of the student-training program, because too much emphasis was placed on overly liberal social work principles, and not enough attention to the cultural arts, administration, fund-raising, and community relations, all duties that workers had to assume immediately upon graduation. When I left Bronx House in 1949, these differences had still not been resolved, and the ideological battle would continue to befuddle the field and Bronx House for another decade, until the agencies began to demand that the schools change their field work assignments, so that students would get the full benefit of their graduate training opportunities.

I had been supervising students since 1933 and continued this practice at Bronx House. In addition, from 1938 on, I had a part-time instructorship at the New York School of Social Work, teaching one course a week in group work. Thus I had an opportunity to combine theory and practice in my teaching and as a supervisor of students. This kept me up to date with the literature in the field as well as with the changing attitudes of students over the course of years. Students were never the same in 1938, in 1942 during the war, nor in 1946 after the war was over.

In 1944, I initiated an undergraduate course in social group work in the sociology department of the City College of New York (CCNY), and the next year I introduced such a course for students preparing for the rabbinate at Yeshiva University. In addition to administering Bronx House and Bronx House Camp, I was teaching in three separate schools, one session in each per week. At CCNY I had a number of students who came out of the membership and club leadership of Bronx House. Later, some of these undergraduates became my students on a graduate level at the New York School. My educational influence on some of them extended over a number of years. Many of them attained eminence in the field.

At Bronx House, I also continued the practice I had established on Staten Island, that all executives and supervisors had to lead groups—and I assumed my share of this load. One group of mine was composed of young non-Jews, mostly Italians, some of them adjudicated delinquents. I decided after meeting with them for many weeks that the group had to be terminated, because its members were infecting each other, and, in effect, breeding a criminal culture. It took a while to achieve this end, but nonetheless, a few of the boys continued their criminal acts. I went to court to plead for one, but when the parents told the judge that their son had learned how to be a thief at Bronx House, which was hardly the case, I knew that working with the boys alone, without intimately involving the parents, was fruitless. Since the boys all came from Catholic families, and since the local churches had proscribed Bronx House because we operated a birth control clinic (35 percent of the users were Catholic), I never got any cooperation from the parents or the priests. Luckily, in the course of time the group disintegrated. Yet, curiously, they trusted me to the point that when one of them was hot, he left his killer knife and loaded gun in my office for me to protect. Some days later he called for his equipment, and I returned both objects to him, but I removed the bullets and warned him that I would never be a repository in the future.

My other groups, entirely composed of Jewish youths, fared better. Some of the members grew up to be successful professionals and businessmen, and also board members of synagogues and philanthropic organizations. One became the president of a federation in the Midwest. All married and had children. Some still keep in touch with me.

My office always had an open-door policy, and you did not have to go through a battery of secretaries to talk to me. My secretary always objected to this arrangement. While at times I had to lock the door, when I was holding certain types of meetings, my openness and physical availability made our staffers and clients feel "important," as one told me, and it left its mark.

Bronx House received all kinds of referrals from social welfare agencies and schools: delinquents under parole, school dropouts, children orphaned when a parent died or was institutionalized, the physically handicapped. I met many of them personally. Years later I frequently gave lectures all over the country, most of them after I was retired, and very often well-groomed individuals would come up afterwards to identify themselves and relate their experiences at Bronx House or Staten Island: how I, or another staff member, or the overall agency, had an impact on their lives, helped them make friends, almost compelled them to return to school, urged them to finish college, aided them in finding their first job. Now they were married, had children and grandchildren, and were living constructive lives by identifying themselves with institutions offering the same things for them and others as when I was the director.

Social researchers have spent a lot of time and money trying to determine whether social work and educational methodologies have an impact on their clientele. Somehow they can never isolate the factors that would prove or disprove their theses. Intensive interviewing of such individuals as I have described might reveal the amount of influence exercised by professionals, teachers, and the agencies with which they were affiliated. I have a few detailed biographies of such individuals in my files, but not enough to make a case. However, the collection of such materials from a thousand individuals might give the organization a much better argument for support from the community than the artificial hype worked out by public relations firms. It might also reveal much better ways of selecting teachers and social workers than the random means employed to date, and usher in better content in the curriculum and the field work assignments, and, I should add, even in the selection of the persons who should supervise students.

Two Disciplines Cooperate

Group workers—that is, professionally trained social workers who work with groups, usually in community centers and settlement houses—had a difficult time establishing their legitimacy. The earliest professionally trained social workers were in the social casework field, working with people in trouble, and, whether the problem was emotional, familial, or financial, placing the emphasis on the kinds of psychological and emotional difficulties that could be resolved through the methods developed by Freud, Adler, and Jung. Freud was the most influential in the education of social case workers. Such workers joined cooperatively with psychiatrists and psychoanalysts, who were beginning to enjoy a lofty status on the American therapeutic scene. Caseworkers, with their special conferences and their professional magazines, held themselves above other social work disciplines. Some professionally trained social workers, like myself, had been educated in both classroom and field assignments in both social casework as well as social group work, and we felt competent to handle many of the same problems. Or if we couldn't work with all clients ourselves, we knew where to refer those who required more attention and time than we were able to provide. The group workers finally established their own professional society, the American Association for Group Workers, in the mid-1930s, in an effort to be treated on a par with their more distinguished colleagues. Some felt that their agencies were equipped to handle many of the problems confronting individuals and families, and, what is more, thought there were many pluses in having such individuals placed in community centers.

I was one of the early exponents of the theory that the end object of casework treatment was to get the client functioning in a more normal environment, where one could test whether the problems had been resolved. This test would always be activity- and people-centered. As more people trained in group work were introduced into the group work agencies, they espoused cooperative relationships between the two disciplines, so that it would not be necessary to establish more casework agencies, when auxiliary services were already available.

A few of us, to test out this approach, met with casework agencies and initially worked out an inter-referral process for the benefit of our varying clienteles.

I suggested at first to Frances Taussig, head of the Jewish Family Service of New York, that it place a part-time worker in Bronx House. One of its caseworkers was assigned to Bronx House one day a week to test the waters, following which the Family Service turned down our request. The JFS could not see the value in such a relationship, and believed that any person who needed casework service should be sent directly to an appropriate agency.

I was more successful with Dr. John Slawson, director of the Jewish Board of Guardians, which placed a worker at Bronx House at once. The contact between our two agencies continued for decades. As his agency learned more about a center, it used it more frequently for the referral of its own clients both during and after completing treatment. They found the art classes, the music school, Hebrew school, social groups, athletics, camp and day camp excellent auxiliary outlets for children in trouble. The caseworker at the center also observed groups and could often detect behavioral and emotional problems in their incipiency, thus heading off difficulties that might have been aggravated by neglect. Early interviews with individuals and/or their families led to counseling or even more extensive treatment. It was a mutually rewarding enterprise.

Since I supervised the caseworker's program in the center, I had intimate knowledge of what she was doing. I usually gave reports at joint staff meetings of both agencies for their respective edification. I recall that in one report, I told about an eight-year-old boy whose behavior in the group was uncontrollable. The group was led by a woman leader. It was difficult to get male leaders during the war, so male groups sometimes were assigned to females. As we studied the boy's life patterns, we discovered that his teacher in school was a woman, that he slept in the same room with an older sister, and that his mother was his parent model, because his father worked a twelve-hour night shift, six days a week, and seldom saw, or talked to, or played with his son. We changed the boy's group leader to one who was a young man. We suggested that the room which he shared with his sister be divided, so that he could have his own niche; and we convinced the father to come to the Bronx House wood-working shop on his day off to build the partition. We also persuaded him to spend more of his spare time with the youngster, who liked to go to ball games and enjoyed all athletics. We counseled the mother not to be too demanding of him to avoid further alienation. Within six months, the boy's behavior underwent dramatic changes.

A full account of this collaboration between two disciplines and the resulting benefits for individuals and their families was recorded in *Group Work–Case Work Cooperation* by Ruth Slutzker, Yonata Feldman, Anne W. Langman, and Graenum Berger. It was published by the Association Press (1946) and received considerable attention.

Shortly thereafter I was asked to deliver a paper at the National Orthopsychiatric convention on the same subject: "The Group Worker and Psychiatry." It was subsequently published in the *American Journal of Orthopsychiatry*, vol. XIX, no. 3 (July 1949).

This innovative spirit of Bronx House thus made another contribution to the field of social work.

Claremont House: An Interracial Experiment

Toward the end of the 1930s, any Jewish family that had improved its economic condition was ready to vacate the neighborhood of Bronx House. The area then developed a reputation as housing only the poor and declassed. The Jews moved steadily to where they could find better housing and what was then a stable Jewish sector, such as the Grand Concourse, the West Bronx, or Pelham Parkway. When Parkchester, a huge housing complex for nearly fifty thousand persons, erected new and inexpensive, excellently built apartments in a park-like atmosphere in 1940, hundreds of families also applied. In fact Emma and I were so impressed with the units that we left Pelham Parkway and for thirteen years thereafter lived in Parkchester, enjoying a five-room apartment for less than $80 per month rent, including gas and electricity, and also including an indoor garage.

The vacancies in the Bronx House area were being filled slowly and steadily by blacks and some Hispanics, who had also improved their lot and were seeking better neighborhoods, where they hoped they might live alongside whites. The Bronx was a step up from Harlem, as it had been for the Jews who had left Harlem for the Bronx decades before.

While the policy of Bronx House was to serve all who applied, after the first few black applicants became part of the membership, some Jewish members began to question their presence. I realized that we had a growing problem and that we must prepare our members for what would surely be a greater influx of blacks in our neighborhood as well as amongst our membership. I therefore instructed our intake staff to defer acceptance of nonwhite members for a year, while we undertook an educational campaign. The board and the staff then took the following steps: A brochure was written setting out the history of the blacks and the type of programs we would have to initiate to tell their story. We decided that we would show our members that blacks were not all poor, nor did they all have families without fathers, nor were they all delinquents and criminals, but that they had made a significant contribution to American life, despite the discrimination and disabilities they had undergone for hundreds of years. We would constantly emphasize their positive side, what they had accomplished in the fields of art, drama, music, writing. We arranged a concert with a major black chorus, an exhibit of black artists, whose works were already in museums and private collections. We brought in black speakers, who eloquently related the black contributions to America. However, we did not ignore the serious problems of racial prejudice, nor the behavioral problems that blacks did present in the community, for these issues had been constantly raised by members and others in our discussions and when speakers were questioned.

Two young blacks had been brought into Bronx House at the suggestion of the local school social worker. We had varying degrees of success with them, and both turned out to be respected citizens in the end. Amelio Sanchez was an extremely hostile young adolescent who challenged everyone. We thrust him into the art department under Bert Jahr, an unusual artist, teacher, and person. There Amelio could pour out his wrath into inanimate objects rather than people. I still have his first painting, actually his father in a Cossack uniform, which he gave to me on impulse, unfinished, after I told him I admired it. It is a powerful portrait. He later became a distinguished artist; his works are shown at many exhibitions and command high prices.

Roger Furman was not doing well in junior high school. Teachers claimed that he was deficient in reading and writing. Roger was also placed under the direction of Jahr, and quietly developed as a competent artist. When he entered the Navy during World War II, he burgeoned as a writer of drama, and won a prize. After the war, he turned to the stage, developing the theater in Harlem. When he died in 1984, he was acclaimed in an obituary in the *New York Times* as an important force in black drama.

In these instances, Bronx House made the difference in their lives. We opened up new vistas, gave them concrete skills and opportunities, and proved to them that the white and Jewish world was not indifferent to their ambitions, inner drives, and talents. While these individuals lived out their lives mainly in the black community, they actually found support for their varied occupational endeavors in the white world.

One of the speakers at a Bronx House meeting devoted to the blacks was Lester Grainger, a consultant for the New York Welfare Council and in later years a leading American social worker and president of the National Conference of Social Work. Grainger approved of what we were doing. He agreed with me that Bronx House would have a problem absorbing any large number of blacks unless the blacks proved themselves first in a special setting. He therefore supported my proposal that it would be better to set up a separate agency, hopefully interracial, in which a mixed board and mixed staff, as well as a mixed clientele, could start from scratch, rather than attempt to foist blacks on a well-established white, Jewish agency. Thus we might avoid any resistance and residual prejudices. He agreed to find some money for this purpose—and he did—and that is how Claremont House was born.

I gave a great deal of time to recruiting a board. While we had some good black names—a judge, a minister, a teacher, along with neighborhood residents of quality—it was the white component that did most of the work, attended most of the meetings, and found all of the additional money to pay for the modest program that was initiated in a rented private house. The mixed staff of two people worked well, although the black lacked administrative, fund-raising, and public relations talents and was always hesitant about reaching out to the white community. I was their community contact in that respect.

At first there was a mixed clientele, but it soon became obvious that the blacks considered the place their own. They literally took over, and within two years there was not a single white person in the membership. The building was inadequate, and since we were already using the school for athletic activities, a relationship was worked out with Junior High School—P.S. 55 across the street, and the entire program was moved into that structure after school and evenings, with considerable financial support forthcoming from the school system. By the time I left Bronx House in 1949, our agency no longer had any direct relationship with the program. We had tried to do the impossible, yet we succeeded in developing a new service for the incoming community.

There was a tidal wave of black migration into that part of the Bronx in the next few years, which determined both the character of the neighborhood, the composition of the schools, and the future of Bronx House itself.

I have always believed that social workers must be able to anticipate events, so as to plan better for the handling of social problems that have not yet blossomed to their fullness. However, there was no effort on the part of public officials to deal with this population change in any comprehensive manner. Within less than a decade, relatively good housing became slums, most buildings had to be demolished, new housing on a massive scale had to be erected, and various new services had to be created, but for an exclusively black constituency.

Father Divine

Father Divine was very much in the news in the 1930s and 1940s. This self-appointed black clergyman had recruited thousands of followers—black and white—meeting with them or accommodating them in various "Heavens" in a number of eastern cities and suburbs. He lived and traveled flamboyantly, supported by his worshippers. His black adherents had a reputation for being honest and reliable house workers, attributing their ethical and productive labors to his mystical influence.

When I was asked in 1940 whether I would like to meet him, I readily accepted the invitation. Escorted by the black director of Claremont House, I drove down to upper Madison Avenue in Manhattan's Harlem. We entered the well-kept building and stepped into a lobby where a number of his flock were sitting in silence. The center table and the walls were decorated with Father Divine's photographs, his head encircled with a halo.

We knocked on his office door and went into a room with lots of furniture, book-lined shelves, and more pictures of the leader. Father Divine greeted us warmly. He was short, squat, with a rounded pleasant face, topped by close-cropped hair. He did not wait for our questions, because, having been interviewed countless times, he anticipated what we might have asked: When did he get started? What motivated him? How many followers did he have? What was his distinctive theology? Would the movement grow?

All of these questions were answered in a long, chaotic harangue, which he interspersed with complaints about being persecuted by black rivals, the police, and the religious establishment. His English was often garbled, and one had to listen intently. Some of his words veered on sheer gibberish, incomprehensible. He spoke quickly, never pausing for questions or comments. When he was through, he arose and asked whether we would like to see the rest of the building. As we walked through the rooms, his worshippers fell to their knees in ecstatic devotion, murmuring his name and clutching at his garments. He accepted their words and touches with a soft pat on their heads. He told several women that he had found employment for them.

He showed us small cubicles where individuals could pray in complete isolation. There was only enough room for one to sit. Several other cubicles had a table with a typewriter, where one could learn the skill or just type. He steered us into large, immaculate, tiled bathrooms, with no walls or doors separating the stools for privacy. He told us that one should not be ashamed when one had to perform natural acts. He showed us similar bathrooms on each of the other floors. The only gathering place was the top-story dining room, where large tables were set with fine cloths and gleaming silver that flashed before your eyes. Food was apparently served to those who were part of the Heaven.

The talk and tour took two hours. Father Divine spoke continuously as we walked, although at times it was difficult to hear or understand what he was saying. We left the building literally to obtain a breath of fresh air. We could not comprehend why he had succeeded in attracting so large a following. Yet he must have some esoteric powers that eluded us. The message, if there was one, that came through in his unrelieved presentation included such words as "cleanliness," "honesty," "naturalness," "faithful worker," and "Father Divine will take care of you." Apparently he did, and they worshipped him.

The "Slave Market"

One scene that outraged me the first time that I witnessed it was the "slave market" on the Grand Concourse in the Bronx, where black women would congregate in search of day work as maids, and Jewish women, during the latter part of the depression, would bargain the price of an hour's house labor with them. The black women often competed with each other, beating down the wage, because they desperately needed money to feed themselves and their children. Often, before making a final deal, and it could be as low as 20 cents an hour, the Jewish woman would feel the arms of the black woman to make sure that she was muscular enough to perform the strenuous household chores. A rabbi on the Concourse brought this degrading scene to my attention, and I went to observe the setting in which the black women were forced to "sell" their services. Some of us brought this to the notice of the press, government officials, and the police. I don't think we eliminated the unsavory practice, but we did succeed in pushing it off the main streets, so that henceforth such deals had to be made in alleys, clandestine and private.

* * *

In Parkchester, Emma decided to enroll Michael in a nursery school. There he spent several days, but was obviously bored, as he seemed to be throughout his elementary school years, because no one fully challenged his energy and intelligence. He dropped out after a week, saying: "All they do is give you a little piece of clay. You can only make a little frankfurter."

* * *

Ramon was twelve years old. I took him away with me for an interesting holiday, starting with the inauguration of Franklin Delano Roosevelt for his third term. It was January 1941. The parade strode down the avenue on a bitter cold day with snow and slush on the ground. Despite our frostbites, it was a memorable sight observing the president riding by in his open-topped limousine, the vehicle passing only a few feet from where we were standing.

I thought this would also be an appropriate time to augment Ramon's knowledge of American history, so we drove south through Richmond, Williamsburg, Jamestown, all centers in our country's past, crossed into North Carolina, and ended our southern journey at Chapel Hill, where we met Rabbi Samuel Sandmel, whom I had known as a freshman at the University of Missouri. He was now ensconced as the director of the Hillel Foundation at the University of North Carolina. Although we did not keep a kosher home, Ramon was shocked to see a rabbi ordering *trayfe* when we dined with him.

We drove back through the off-beat roads and towns of Carolina and Virginia, where we saw the daily life of black residents, existing at a pitiable level on muddy streets and ramshackle houses and farms. While Ramon was not a talkative companion, he observed and absorbed everything quietly, and this fortnight's journey made a deep impression on his attitudes regarding blacks and politics that has remained with him throughout his life. Ramon was disappointed to find only a marker at the place where the Appomattox Court House once stood, the scene of Lee's surrender to Grant, which ended the Civil War. The South preferred to forget that bloody defeat.

Bronx House and the Public Schools

From the outset in 1911, Bronx House developed relations with local school leaders. Angelo Patri, a distinguished educator, and Simon Hirsdansky and Jacob Shufro, principals of nearby schools, were members of the board from its inception. The latter two were still serving on that body when I arrived in 1938. I decided to further our relationship with the local schools. To this end we regularly invited the principals of P.S. 2, 4, 42, 55, and 58 to luncheons at Bronx House. Minnie Obermeier, the assistant superintendent of schools for our district, and later elected a member of the Bronx House board, also attended. Two other school personnel who were invited to some of the luncheons and later became the spearheads for innovative programs, were the dynamic Viola Mitchell, a visiting teacher in the Bureau of Child Guidance, whom I saw almost daily as she brought countless problems to my attention, and her equally imaginative sister, Lillian Rosenson, wife of a physician, and teacher of so-called health classes at P.S. 4. If a child was below the average weight for his age, he was automatically thrown into her class of assorted children with all kinds of problems. Bronx House established seminars for teachers in all five local elementary schools, introducing them to our philosophy, program, and method of handling children and their parents. Teachers visited our center to observe the program and talk to our staff. They began to make referrals of children in their classes who were in need of specialized services. Teachers told me that this exposure led to their better understanding of children's needs and had an impact on the behavior and learning abilities of some of their students. Bronx House leaders wrote reports for teachers on children who had been referred, from which the teachers learned how to prepare reports with a social work ring. The seminars eventually led the schools to initiate similar meetings within the system.

Shortly after I came to Bronx House, it was converted from an individually oriented institution to one that served the entire family. We had an opportunity to introduce teachers to this approach. Some of the enterprising teachers began to use parents in different ways to help them in the classroom.

Later developments with the school system included cooperative summer play schools, special afterschool programs in the arts, a better appreciation of the older Italian and newer incoming black residents, and an inter-referral process for children with problems. While all teachers did not participate, since this was a voluntary experience, enough of them did partake, so that this small circle had a ripple effect on the entire school. A paper on this subject, "A Community on the Alert—Child Growth in a Great City," which I wrote in collaboration with Lillian Rosenson and Violet M. Mitchell, was published in the *National Elementary Principal* (September 1945). My niece, Natalie Finn Oppenheimer, told me how proud she was, when this article was given to her, when she was training to be a teacher in college.

I am and always was a strong supporter of the public school as the only way to educate the masses of Americans. I believed in this and I acted on my belief, sending both of our sons to public elementary and high school, even though it was clear that they might have profited from more individual tutelage and the contacts with a higher-aspiring class of students in a good private school.

Yet I wanted to determine whether a private institution like Bronx

House could bring some improvement to the local schools, in the hope that such successes could be extended to the larger system. Regretfully, the schools were not prepared for the mass of unexpected problems that arose after the war and were soon overwhelmed by them: the uprooting of whole neighborhoods, accompanied by vast changes in population and student enrollment; the post-1954 racial revolution which forced integration on reluctant and resistant communities; the loss of experienced teachers to more rewarding fields. Moreover, the reduction in student expectancy as education had to become more pleasurable, replacing the former more rigid requirements, did not help. Even to this day, the schools are struggling to determine their true function in our society, how to recruit and train better teachers, and how to achieve more demanding standards in science, languages, and the humanities—and in many instances, alas, how to improve instruction in the three basic R's.

The schools must require more. But they also must work more closely with the parents if they are to fulfill more of their objectives. This was one important lesson Bronx House tried to communicate to the teachers and their principals along with better use of other communal resources.

The Bronx House Music School

A music school was an integral part of Bronx House from its inception. I recall Mrs. Henry Morgenthau, Sr., telling me that she played the piano, preferring four-hand playing with a partner, and felt that all immigrant and poorer children should be exposed to music, as it would help educate them to the higher values of life. Classes in voice, piano, violin, and wind instruments were offered, often with distinguished teachers, supplemented by classes in theory. An orchestra was assembled and presented periodic concerts. These classes were conducted during the week and on Saturdays and Sundays. The House always seemed to sing with music. The Morgenthaus were the benefactors, in the sense that they picked up the deficit. By the time I arrived in 1938, the school was directed by Andrew McKinley, who felt that he had no responsibility to either the board or to me, but conceived of the music school as an independent entity using the building as a free convenience. McKinley reported only to his patrons. When Mrs. Morgenthau appeared at the center once a week, she paid me a courtesy call and then went up to see him. Emma and I were invited to the Morgenthau home for dinner several times. We listened to the ambassador reminisce about his interesting life abroad. Mrs. M. was proud of her son, who was then the secretary of the treasury. The ambassador gave me copies of books that he had written, and I read them with interest.

One day, I received a report that the ambassador, after dreaming that he had lost his fortune, had called in his attorney and cut Bronx House and the music school out of his will. McKinley was beside himself and for the first time came to seek my counsel. Some of our board members, who felt that the school was really a luxury and not a social work necessity, were ready to abandon the enterprise. I saw the school as essential, perhaps due to my interest in the cultural arts. Convinced that music was an important ingredient in the education of all people, and particularly those who could not afford to pay for such opportunities, I campaigned for the school's continuation, insisting that we should seek support from Federation and make it part of our overall program. At first Federation was not sympathetic, because it felt that the Morgenthaus had no right to desert a program which they had intitiated and sustained for more than thirty years. The board finally decided to incorporate the music school if it could become more self-supporting. A new committee of parents was created to work with McKinley. It sponsored fund-raising activities and raised the fees; thus the school not only continued but grew, a number of its students finding musical careers and some going on to distinguished positions in the music world.

My efforts to keep the music school reflected my personal and professional philosophy that the arts must be an organic part of a Jewish center. Music, fine arts, poetry and literature, dramatics, and dancing were indispensable in the development of modern man and both socialized and humanized him. I was beginning to put increasing emphasis on the Jewish arts, because they were one of the instruments through which one's identification with the Jewish people could be more deeply etched. I insisted upon ever better teachers, who would be role-models as well as instructors. I also demanded that the level of instruction should be demanding rather than merely entertaining, and that artists who were invited to the institution should be of high caliber, so that the listeners would always hear the best. Staff members were inclined to contract for artists on the basis of price rather than talent.

As radio, television, and the growth of new art centers proliferated after the war, the centers temporarily suffered from this superior competition. Yet it is still possible for a center to be a general and Jewish cultural center, even in a city like New York, if the standards are not compromised. Witness the continuing success of the 92nd Street YM-YWHA in Manhattan.

The Italian Community

North of Bronx House lived a large Italian community. The parents were immigrants, Catholic schools and churches abounded. An increasing number of children were going to the public schools. There were no recreational resources under Catholic auspices, except for modest programs conducted by the Catholic Youth Organization. Delinquency was frequent amongst their youth, and adult crime was not uncommon.

Several Italian-American social workers employed in public welfare agencies came to see me about doing something more for Italian youth. Concerned with how to develop services that would appeal to the youth, and how to influence the parents to deal with their children's misbehavior, they sought our experience. Italian parents had not yet created a single institution to deal with this problem, because they did not want to do anything that was not under the aegis of the church. The priests were opposed to any competing influences; and since social services would be costly to maintain, there was no support from the Italian community's businessmen and professionals. So the social workers knew from the outset that they would be undertaking a task that would not be well received.

Italian-Americans had established no centers, no child care institutions, no family casework agencies, no homes for the aged, no hospitals. Despite the frequent charges leveled against the infamous Mafia, they had not yet developed a communal relations organization to defend their good name as Italians. It would be another decade or two before such an organization came into being, following a federal investigation revealing the prominence of Italians in crime.

I felt from the start that all our efforts on their behalf would be in vain. Nevertheless I worked with a small group that saw the problem clearly, although they could find no way of breaking through the community's resistance to efforts to change its behavior patterns.

In the 1960s and 1970s, the Italians had arrived and conquered. Their leadership was then associated with the highest levels of American finance, industry, government, medicine, law, public relations, and teaching (one became the president of Yale University), as well as sports and restaurants (Italian food had become part of the daily diet of American families). In 1984, Geraldine Ferraro, a woman of Italian descent, became the first woman candidate for vice-president in a major party, on the Democrat ticket. As I write, an Italian-American has been appointed to the Supreme Court. Forty years earlier, in 1944, things were rather different. The Italian social workers with whom I was working arranged a dinner and invited a leader of the local Italian citizenry as the guest of honor. The dinner, however, was suddenly cancelled when it was discovered that the honoree was a middleman for stolen goods.

The Impact of World War II

The war produced some radical changes at Bronx House, and as a result, in many ways it soon ceased to resemble the agency I had first come to head in 1938 or even the agency as it was in 1941, the last year before the war.

When I assumed my duties in 1938, Mrs. Alexander M. Marcuse—Corinne was her first name, but she was Dolly to all of us—had been the president for twenty years. A beautiful woman with a soft but firm way of speaking and always dressed impeccably, she had given extraordinary leadership during her long reign. The board she had assembled were all, with few exceptions, millionaires of the German-Jewish stratum in Jewish society. With Dolly as guide, our new building had been constructed in 1928, and Bronx House had been transformed from a conventional settlement house interested in "doing good" for poor Jews to a professional agency. Samuel Levine and Moses H. Beckelman, the agency headworkers who preceded me, had also received their professional training at the Graduate School of Jewish Social Work. She had given them unstinting support, and similarly she assisted me wholeheartedly when I plugged for a larger budget, a full-time professional staff, and the acquisition of the camp in 1940.

With the outbreak of war imminent, the USO was reestablished to assist the soldiers in their extra-curricular military life. Dolly offered her services to the USO, was accepted, and after a period of training was assigned to Chicago, where in addition to her job, she had roots and family. I continued my contacts with Dolly until her demise, seeing her from time to time, writing to her, and seeking her good counsel. She left a large legacy to Bronx House.

Who would we turn to as her successor? We had a number of older and experienced board members, but the lot fell to young Richard W. Dammann, tall, handsome, vigorous, articulate, liberal. A Princeton graduate, a lawyer, married to a graduate of the New York School of Social Work, he was made for the position. For years he had been spending at least one night a week at the House as the leader of a boy's club, and after the meeting he usually played basketball with them. Like Dolly Marcuse, he also had a vision of making Bronx House the premiere center in the country. In the brief time he served as president, he gave full support to its continued professionalization, broadening the services to new areas and neighborhoods and influencing Federation's direction in the development of centers in Greater New York. While he had been opposed to accepting the burden of the music school, he went along with the decision of the board. When war was declared, Dick did not think that he should stay out of the conflict. He volunteered for the navy and served for the duration. Another war loss to us at a crucial time.

Mrs. Charles Riegelman—Lillian, as we knew her—a relative of the Morgenthaus, had been on the board for many years. Sharp-featured, extremely well organized, full of knowledge, and also articulate, she made her own mark on the agency. Her husband, a prominent attorney, was the chairman of the all-important distribution committee of Federation. At several dinners at her home, where her husband was present, I took the liberty of telling him that the New York Federation was not granting sufficient monies to the centers, and I cited figures to show what Federations around the country were allocating to similar institutions. This undoubtedly influenced the New York Federation to make increased appropriations to Bronx House as well as to other centers in the city.

Lillian called me at 7:30 A.M. every morning to discuss Bronx House affairs. It was under her leadership that the Bronx House Camp expanded its facilities and clientele by acquiring a large contiguous piece of property. She supported our pioneering senior citizens program and at my suggestion became the first president of the William Hodson Community Center for older people, which had an enormous influence on the development of similar centers in New York and over the country. With Dolly Marcuse she played an important role in developing extension centers in the Bronx and Brooklyn, which eventually became full-fledged independent institutions. Lillian served until the end of the war with devotion and distinction. While with her critical mind, she always argued against every new program as a means of understanding it better, in the end she was supportive of me as a professional.

Some of our staff were also called into service. Jerome Goldsmith became an officer in the army. Later he was appointed to top administrative positions in Jewish agencies in New York. Arthur Katz obtained high army rank and then entered key positions in the general social work field. Michael Rand saw service in the navy. After the war he returned to work at the house and camp, then left to become a consultant at the National Jewish Welfare Board, specializing in physical education. David and Emanuel Hallowitz, David Steiner, and Irving Kaplan also served in the military. After their discharge their social work careers led them into the universities and high administrative posts.

The young men from our membership were called up one by one, so that we were soon denuded of all eighteen year-olds and older. This changed the composition of our membership. Young women of that age, who previously had sought male companionship through our extensive club programs, now found other avenues of interest and also left. Many of our soldier members dropped into the House and my office while on furlough, because I had known all of them personally, and some of them I knew intimately as the leader of their clubs. I had listened to their personal problems, attended their social functions, sometimes even dealt with their parents. A few corresponded with me when they went overseas. Although some two hundred went off to war, we had an unparalleled record in that we didn't have a single casualty. Mothers and some of the older girls were induced to send packages from Bronx

House. Some of the women were recruited as volunteers, to help the Red Cross roll bandages and perform other chores.

A unit, made up mostly of fathers, was organized to protect the neighborhood in the event of air raids and other forms of sabotage. They learned first aid, how to put out fires, how to use oxygen and stretchers, and how to rush victims to the hospital.

The Bronx public officials organized a Civilian Defense Volunteer Organization (CDVO). As a member of the organizing group, I was appointed chairman of a committee for the training of volunteers. In this capacity I prepared a manual for such programs, assembled the teachers, and also taught the personnel who would be training other units over the Bronx.

Bronx House was, of course, subjected to the same rationing of gasoline and other commodities in short supply that was in effect throughout the country. The House also acted as an office for the distribution of ration coupons.

During World War II, there were few dissenters and conscientious objectors, so there was no need to provide counseling to anyone who didn't want to serve. This was quite different from what centers had to do during the Vietnam War. Occasionally I was asked to write letters in order to help a draftee obtain a deferment because of special problems at home, but such requests were rare.

While I was registered for the draft, like every other eligible male, my form indicated that I was married with two children. I received a notice of deferment and never heard from the draft board again for the rest of the war. If I had been called, I might have asked for a deferment on the grounds that I was my family's only support and was working for an agency that performed vital civilian functions on the home front. I was never put to the test. I never entertained any notion of volunteering.

Near the end of the war I was approached by the American Jewish Joint Distribution Committee about taking on an assignment in Southern Europe (Italy or Yugoslavia) to work with the refugees being freed from the concentration camps and other parts of Europe formerly under Nazi domination. After considerable discussion at home, Emma convinced me that I should not leave our family and that I had equally important unfinished business at Bronx House. Ramon was fifteen and Michael was six. I have often wondered whether my life would have been different if I had accepted this challenging offer. In retrospect, I believe that I made the correct decision.

The tragic story of the Jews of German-dominated Europe began to filter into the American Jewish consciousness after 1942. The tragedy began with Hitler's accession to power in 1933, and from then on, wherever I worked, I had always sought to bring home to the membership the need to combat this evil, although none of us recognized in advance the full consequences of his ascendency. At Bronx House we initiated programs which revealed the grim story. We sent letters off to the President and other officials in Washington, urging them to open our shores to the refugees and later the war victims, to barter materials for Jewish lives, and toward the end of the war, to destroy the railroad lines leading to and feeding the Jews into the fires. We felt so helpless, because our appeals and protests were ineffectual. Six million Jewish lives were lost. We obviously did not scream loud enough at the massive outrage. Our leaders, both American and Jewish, always urged caution, telling us that winning the war was the first priority, or that more Jews might be massacred if the truth were widely revealed. I am not sure, as I write this, that we learned anything from this horrible experience. Recent studies of the Holocaust assert that as Jews we did not do enough. As Edwin McDowell, a non-Jew at that, put it in a *New York Times* article (Nov. 6, 1984): "Too few schedules were rearranged. Vacations were seldom sacrificed. Too few projects of lesser significance were put aside." American Jewish leaders were "unable or unwilling to break out of a business as usual pattern."

The lesson was not even remembered, because we repeated this unconscionable inaction when it came time to save the Ethiopian Jews in the 1948–1977 era, as I will recount later in this book.

The Jewish community held President Roosevelt in the highest esteem. He was revered. During his lifetime, nobody blamed him for what was not done for the Jews, but instead we put the onus on anti-Semitic or pro-Arab officials in the State Department. Hence, when he suddenly died on April 12, 1944, a pall fell over the membership of Bronx House. I can recall the standing-room-only turnout for a memorial meeting that was held shortly after his death and that I addressed. Our American flag was lowered to half-mast for a month of mourning.

When the war ended, few of the veterans returned to Bronx House. They went off to school, got married, had children, and lived in better sections of the city. Their parents had already made the same move, for the war had provided employment, higher incomes, and different aspirations. Bronx House was left with a large number of the residual poor, more older people, and a few families that had given up on improving their lives. Yet in his 1943 study *Unemployed,* which was researched in part at Bronx House, Eli Ginzberg revealed that the unemployed in the 1930s managed better than any casual observer of the scene would have expected. Most families did not disintegrate. They did not give up the belief that there was still a future for them and their children. When opportunities began to emerge with the advent of the war, they seized them. A success story developed for the mobile, aspiring Jewish residents.

In the postwar years, some of those who had moved to better neighborhoods continued to send their children to the music school, the art classes, for dancing and to the summer camp at Copake, New York.

Gradually, instead of serving only the poor and the aged, Bronx House now also started to serve the middle class. As a result, our program began to change to meet new requests and needs. Ultimately the change in clientele also altered our goals. Bronx House sold its property on Washington Avenue, where it had operated a program for fifty years, and moved to a new building in a new area, where it now offered the same program to a somewhat different clientele.

Bronx House: A Neighborhood Organization

In addition to my interest in the schools in the vicinity of Bronx House, the agency and I were interested in the entire neighborhood. I had close ties with the local police, occasionally visiting the precinct house to talk with the captain, and similarly the police sometimes dropped into the agency to see what was going on. We permitted policemen to use our gym facilities as a courtesy. There were a few times when some youngster we knew was arrested, and if the crime was only a misdemeanor—and it usually was—we got him released without difficulty. I do not recall a single Bronx House girl ever running afoul of the law. When we learned that the nearby movie house was being used as a place for promiscuous sexual activities, we got to the police quickly to eliminate that nuisance. We were instrumental in getting traffic lights at nearly every intersection to protect pedestrians. If there was a meeting at the House with an unusually large attendance, we could always get the police to patrol the streets in front of the building. The police were always cooperative.

The neighborhood streets were never clean when I arrived. The many markets on Bathgate Avenue contributed to the unsightliness, but landlords and storekeepers on Washington Avenue were equally negligent.

A visit to the Sanitation Department a block away led to several neighborhood cleanup programs, which not only improved the cleanliness of the streets, but motivated some of the shops to paint their fronts and landlords to improve the appearance of the entrance to the walk-up apartment houses.

Only in housing did we fail to make a dent. Many buildings in our area had been adandoned and thereafter vandalized. Some old wooden houses from the early nineteenth century were unsafe and unattractive. I wrote a letter to Mayor LaGuardia to see whether the area could be designated for some of the new housing that was springing up in many other parts of Greater New York. Apparently the Bronx was not yet a high priority and thus was ignored. I also felt that the political leaders were not doing enough to promote such construction. I began to pester them about the need to do something to change the appearance of the community and provide better housing for the people who needed a decent place in which to live. Nothing was done until a decade or more after I left Bronx House. By then the deterioration was almost universal. Vandalism and the burning of hundreds of abandoned apartment houses had made a vast sector look like scenes that I had observed in bombed-out Germany after the war.

I also visited the local fire houses to urge an increase in the number and frequency of inspections to avoid fires and loss of life. I do not recall a single fire or death during my eleven years at the House. Perhaps our appeals had some effect.

Assistant Headworkers

During my years at Bronx House, I worked with four assistant headworkers, three of whom went on to most distinguished careers in the field of social work.

After I was engaged in 1938, I was visited on Staten Island by Sanford Solender, a twenty-four year-old occupying the assistant's post at Bronx House. I had known Sandy for a number of years, first when he was on the New York University debating team, which used the Jewish Community Center of Staten Island as its home base for in-town debates, principally because Professor Williamson, the team's mentor, lived on Staten Island and made such arrangements with me. It was an interesting activity for our community. I was also a colleague of his father, Samuel, the executive director of the Washington Heights YM-YWHA, which we visited when we lived nearby in upper Manhattan in 1931–32. Sandy brought me copies of reports on the programs and budget at Bronx House—something the board of directors, who had met with me several months before, did not think necessary for my preparation for Bronx House leadership.

Sandy was a tall, articulate, bright, aggressive young man, who had made a good record at NYU as a student leader, devoting himself to liberal causes. He had obtained a master's in psychology rather than a social work degree, although that never hindered him in his ever-climbing carrer. He was a born executive, highly organized, knowing precisely what he wanted to do and achieve. He assertively advanced his programs at staff meetings and in supervisory conferences with key personnel, confident that he would get his way. He kept careful notes in tiny lettering on very small note pads, a practice which he continued throughout his long professional life. We got along quite well during the first year I was headworker.

It was my view that Sandy was ready, despite his age, for his own post as an executive. I also felt that he would be restive under my different kind of leadership and program goals, if he continued under my incumbency even for another year. I recommended him highly to the Jewish Welfare Board. Regrettably, the personnel department did not view Sandy in the same light, so he found employment directing a settlement house in Lower Manhattan. From there he went to a center directorship in Cleveland, then to a sub-executive post at the JWB, which had finally discovered his talents, rising to its executive vice-presidency. He was finally chosen head of the Federation of Jewish Philanthropies of New York, ending up as my boss during the last four years of my consultantship to that major philanthropy. He has been the head of major Jewish and non-Jewish professional organizations, posts which he earned as the result of being an active, hard-driving member or chairman of subcommittees.

When Sandy left I engaged the short, bright, imaginative Norman Lourie. While we had originally seen eye-to-eye on policies and program, he really wanted to change the agency in ways that I deemed and knew were not in the best interests of the membership and the community. He also exhibited the capacity for being a top executive and after two years left for such a post, but finally ended his career as commissioner of welfare for the state of Pennsylvania. Like Sandy, he also headed up several major nonsectarian professional organizations in this country. I liked his keen mind and youthful enthusiasm, but it was my conviction that the staff was confused by our ideological differences and our conflicting administrative styles.

To replace Norman, I sought an experienced educator with a good Jewish and mental hygiene background, rather than a person trained in social work. I could supply social work knowledge when needed, but since our programs were veering in a somewhat different direction, I thought a good disciplined educator was necessary.

After a long search, I thought that I had found him in European-born Dr. Maurice Shore, a scholar, the author of several books, and already experienced as the educational director of a large midwestern YM-YWHA. I engaged him to develop educational materials for the staff and membership. While he had all the qualifications, and a touch of academic arrogance to boot, he lacked the ability to communicate with and influence the unusually gifted substaff which I had painstakingly assembled. They could work with me, but not with Shore, so I let him go at the end of the year.

I began to realize that what I really needed was not another conceptual social worker or an educator or even a program specialist, for these were the very skills that I was proficient in. Most of all, I needed someone who could relieve me of the host of administrative details that were taking up so much of my time as the agency grew by leaps and bounds. Bronx House had added a country camp, a number of extension services, and a variety of specialty activities. I needed someone to handle these multitudinous details. I found him on my staff.

Sol Rafel originally wanted to be a doctor, but the depression and the restrictive quotas against Jews trying to enter medical schools had prevented him from realizing his goal. He earned a master's degree in psychology, but when he could not find work in that field, he went into commerce. Unhappy in the world of business, for he wanted above all to work with people rather than commodities, he became a volunteer in the group therapy unit meeting at the House, and that is where and how I met him. In 1940, I engaged him as a counselor at the country camp. After the season he said he would like to work with me, and I hired him as a full-time membership-intake worker, where he did a good job. He had an easy relationship with members and especially with new applicants. He knew where best to refer them in the multi-faceted program we were offering. He knew how to negotiate with them about dues and fees (our agency was always generous in reducing fees for individuals and families in the lower-income categories). His reports were accurate and on time. In the next few years I tried him out as the head counselor of the camp and in program supervision. He did well.

When I elevated Rafel to be my assistant, his duties were both administrative and supervisory, and he proved thoroughly competent and trustworthy. I still conducted staff meetings and trained key personnel, but Sol supervised staff in need of administrative control and watched budgetary expenditures. I went off to camp during the summer for three months. Even though I came back to the city two days a week to check on house matters, Sol had the opportunity to learn every aspect of our comprehensive operations.

When I resigned in 1949 to go to the Federation, the board did not interview any outside candidates, since Sol was the obvious choice. As the executive director of Bronx House, he moved the agency to its new location and there built up a large facility. When he died in 1981, I lost a good friend. During his years at Bronx House, he had obtained recognition from the field, heading one of the national professional organizations and winning several awards.

Camp Bronx House

For more than a century, American children had been going to country camps. At first these camps were designed only for the rich, to give young people a nature experience to counter growing urbanism. Their parents had already built large residences in the mountains and at the seashore to bring their own lives closer to nature. After the huge immigration to this country before and after the turn of the century, philanthropic agencies decided that it was essential to get the children of the poor out of the disease-ridden ghettos in the larger cities, so that their health might benefit from sunshine in the out of doors and and a better diet. Before long, camping had become as fashionable in America as apple pie. Upon analysis of its abiding values, it has proven to be America's most original contribution to the education of children during the long summer recess. Later, camping benefits were extended to working girls, adults, families, and in recent decades to the growing population over sixty-five years of age.

For many years, Bronx House children had been referred to camps conducted by other organizations. In 1936, the parents of Bronx House children, not the board of directors, rented a camp for the summer and operated their own enterprise. They persuaded the board to provide some staff and even support for the program. In 1939, the parent group was able to acquire a campsite for nothing, because the New York Society for the Deaf was giving up its 165-acre site at Copake, New York, with a 30-acre lake on its edge. The site was satisfactory, but the parents, through poor management, ran up a debt of $10,000, which they could not meet. I suggested to the parents that if they donated the project to Bronx House, we would assume the debt, manage the camp, and even enlarge the enrollment.

While some of the parents were loathe to give up the camp's operation, the majority finally decided to turn it over on the conditions I had outlined. I recall going out in the winter of 1940, with three feet of snow on the ground, to inspect the site, which I had never seen. In the spring, Dolly Marcuse and Lillian Riegelman made the first board inspection.

Raising money for the camp was an experience in itself. I went back and forth amongst some of the wealthy members, to obtain most of the money needed not only for purchase, but to open the camp and subsidize children whose families could pay nothing or very little. In early June, I went to the camp again to make an inventory of what we had and needed, ordered food and other supplies, engaged a staff, began to enroll children, and we were open for the season before the month ended. That summer we took five groups of 165 children aged eight through fifteen. Each group spent two weeks in the wonderful setting.

The magnificent campsite, almost in the tri-corner where New York, Connecticut, and Massachusetts converge, looked up at the Berkshire Mountains across a green, farmed valley. Located on a knoll, the camp area dropped down toward the deep and pure Drum Lake, where the campers swam. Some lived in tents, others in cabins. Unfortunately, my inspection failed to detect the porous condition of the building roofs, and we had a rainy summer that first year. The roofs leaked like sieves. But no one complained. The staff was warmly interested in the children. The summer prospered without a serious accident or illness. I was the only casualty, breaking my ankle while chasing a fly in a game of baseball between the staff and the older campers. I walked on crutches for six weeks—never missing a day's work. Food was simply prepared and plentiful. Emma, Michael, and I (Michael being only one and one-half years old) shared a cabin. Ramon, eleven years old, went into a unit with his age group, but was soon made an assistant counselor.

From the outset I put the camp's emphasis on out-of-door living, hikes, cookouts, and the assumption by campers of all camp chores. There was to be no social dancing and singing of popular songs, duplicating city life. Instead, we created an atmosphere for American folk songs, and everyone became adept at square and country dancing. The group rather than the individual was important, so there were no free-choice activities. We chanted Hebrew prayers before meals, and on Sabbath eve we dressed up in our finery, usually white clothes, and ate a typical Sabbath meal, concluding with a religious service. At the end of each two-week session, there was a grand banquet, following which each group put on a show of some kind. There were the usual tearful goodbyes.

The children traveled by train from Grand Central in Manhattan to Copake Falls, where buses picked them up and drove the five intervening miles through farm country and a village. As one group arrived, the other left, so changeover day was quite a hectic event. When the last bus left in September after ten weeks of constant activity, we heaved a sigh of relief. Those were the days before the polio vaccine had been invented, so we lived all summer in fear of an epidemic. A few of us remained afterwards for a week to close up the buildings for the winter.

I had taken on the additional responsibility of camp director in order to learn the business thoroughly, for my only previous camp experience had been my summer as a head counselor in a small camp out of Gloversville. I quickly learned about planning mass menus and buying food in quantity. When one of the cooks got drunk and I had to fire him and could not get a replacement for several days, I donned a kitchen apron and in between all of my other duties, cooked for over two hundred campers and staff. I was roundly cheered after each meal. When the doctor had to make an emergency trip to New York for several days, I put on a physician's white coat and administered aid to the children and staff, only calling the village doctor in an emergency or to prescribe medicine. I learned all about the problems of overflowing sewage and inadequate water supply, and, as well, how to dispose of garbage, maintain buildings, and deal with homesick children. The director of a camp administers a small village, except that every person in it is his personal responsibility.

I went to the city each week to find out how things were going, driving a one and one-half ton truck, dressed in my best summer suit and a straw hat, and came back the next day loaded with items which we could buy more cheaply.

Over the course of nine years, through our unique program and method of training, which included educating our staff in administrative practices as well as creative programming, a number of our counselors and supervisors became camp directors. Others called and taught country dancing and singing professionally. Many entered the social work field. A few became cooks, well paid, after their experience in mass cooking in our kitchen. The alumni campers would faithfully come back before and after the season for a holiday with their friends and to help us open and close the camp. In subsequent years, when I visited the camp as a consultant for Federation, I met their wives and husbands, their children, and eventually even their grandchildren. While initially, most of the campers were from lower-income families, I always sought to recruit a mix from higher-income levels. As the camp's reputation grew, we had great success in attracting children from such backgrounds. In addition to providing us with more income, their presence heightened the cultural and social plane of the camp population. I never encountered any problems in such a commingling.

But a summer is never without some unexpected incident. When Michael was three, I took him with me in the station wagon to Copake Falls, where I was to pick up some freight. He stood in the back and, holding on to the front seat, began rattling away in his usual manner. Michael began to speak before he was a year old. As I was going up the hill and making a sharp turn, the right rear door suddenly opened and Michael fell out, rolling on the macadam surface. Luckily there was no car behind us. I braked almost in panic, an unusual thing for me, because I am always at my best in a crisis. Michael was bruised from head to toe, with his clothes torn in many places. I picked him up, put him in the front seat next to me, secured the door, and rushed back to Copake to Dr. Bowerhan, the only local doctor and also the camp physician. Luckily again, he was in; he examined Michael thoroughly, but found no evidence of fractures or internal injuries. Michael, who had stopped crying on the way to the doctor, took it all like a veteran. The doctor covered the bruises with tinctures and salves, so that he looked like a clown. When we got back to camp, Michael walked on his own to our cabin, where his mother in fright embraced and kissed him and put him to bed against his will. There were no aftereffects.

Some years later in Gloversville, I had a car full of people, including my sister Sadie. As we were turning a corner, she apparently put her hand on the handle of the door; it opened and she fell out, and the rear wheel rode over her arm, but fortunately, I was traveling very slowly at the time. I immediately stopped, put her in the car, and rushed to the Littauer Hospital. While her clothes, including a coat, were torn, she only suffered minor bruises. Ever since that second accident with an open door, I always make doubly sure that all doors are locked before I start driving. Not so incidentally, Michael was in the car.

Emma and I loved the camp. I saw the enormous educational possibilities for young people. More happened to them in two weeks of camping than in a whole year in a community center. For those children that we held over for an entire summer, I even saw their emotional problems ironed out. But it was their cultural growth that touched me.

Each Saturday morning during the music festival at Tanglewood, Massachusetts, I drove a group of campers by truck to sit in on the morning rehearsals. For most, this was their first exposure to great music and musicians at close range. Serge Koussevitzky conducted the inspiring Boston Symphony Orchestra. Celebrated soloists in voice or instrument walked by as we sat in the shed or on the grass. When I occasionally meet some of the campers, now adults, they often reminisce about that rough truck ride of some thirty miles.

Now they go to the festival for a week-end, as full-paying customers. Music has become part of their lives. Perhaps we inspired them.

Once I took a truckload of teenagers to Hyde Park to see the grave of Franklin D. Roosevelt and the house and environs in which he had grown up. At the grave site, without coaching or coaxing, the group spontaneously began to sing "The Lonesome Train," a cantata about Abraham Lincoln's funeral train puffing back to Springfield, Illinois, which the campers had rendered the previous Saturday night before the entire camp. A piece of American culture was no longer something they had learned for a single performance. It came to life when they mysteriously felt the connection between two of the great presidents in American history, both of them victims of war, of course in different ways, both of whom died in office, veritably giving their lives for their country.

The camp added to its economic and social mix in future years by taking in deaf children. Our program, in consequence, expanded to include instruction in sign language and new ways of integrating the handicapped with the so-called normal. I also experimented with a few epileptics under good control and found that they too could function without mishap. One unit was set aside for partially sighted children, who could avoid accidents by walking on terrain that was not exactly a paved playground. Referrals began coming in from varied social work agencies, as they learned that our staff could handle deviant behavior problems, and could write valuable reports on how a child adjusted away from his family or the institution in which he was living year round.

But the camp was too small. The New York Bible Society owned two hundred acres, with several buildings situated across the lake from our camp and bordering on another, even larger lake a half mile away. We bought the property for $10,000 with the help of Samuel Gould, whom I met on a train going to Copake one afternoon. Gould owned a vacation farm adjoining our property and became a superb board member. The new site was used as a work camp for adolescents. I strongly believed that such youngsters were ready for a work experience under good supervision. They built facilities, worked on the farm, learned good work habits, and enjoyed the products of their labor. Some of them became counselors and eventually went into the social work field.

To help us erect additional facilities, we found an elderly English-born carpenter by the grandiloquent name of Gibson Marlborough. Gibby, as we called him, lived next door with the Drums. With Gibby directing—working and smoking his pipe—our work campers, including the executive director, who wanted to demonstrate that manual work was not beneath the dignity of a leading professional, built a dozen buildings from scratch. When wood was in short supply during the war, we cut thousands of board feet of thirty-year-old pine trees, thinning out the woods around the teen site. After the cut-up lumber had weathered for a season, we used it to construct new buildings.

We had an unusual caretaker in Jack Elfers. German born, he came to the United States in the early thirties and had been employed as a porter at Bronx House. He taught himself carpentry, plumbing, and electicity. He knew every aspect of farming from his homeland. Under his direction, the work campers laid our sewage and water lines. But Jack was more than a manual worker. From time to time he was assigned difficult youngsters and in his intuitive way, he had a direct effect on their behavior. They became his close friends, visiting him for the many years he tended camp.

With some preliminary training, the teenagers were ready to work on the camp farm, raising enough potatoes, tomatoes, and corn to feed a population that had reached 350 persons. These vegetables were ripe for the last six weeks of the season. Chickens, ducks, and several sheep were paraded around the camp grounds to teach campers a bit about domestic animals. Wild game and birds could be seen in profusion during the summer.

A number of mothers with children under eight years of age petitioned the camp to create services for them. Mr. Drum, who occupied the north end of the lake and owned a three hundred acre tract, wanted to sell his land and buildings for $25,000, and with a gift from Frederick Stettenheim, one of the board members who originally interviewed me, the property was acquired. This area was turned into the camp for mothers and children and was later developed for senior citizens. We now owned 650 acres, all the land around one lake and bordering another.

Somehow I managed to operate the camp on a self-supporting basis, some years even having a surplus that could be used for capital improvements. Yet the one year when I had a deficit of $5,000, the board was annoyed at my extravagance. They were always worried about my plans for expansion or the possible acquisition of new parcels of land. The board understood that we were now serving fifteen hundred different individuals in one season, and that we had acquired a valuable piece of property at comparatively little cost, but they did not quite appreciate how this had all come about. Perhaps it would have been better if I had asked them to raise the money for all our expanding facilities and services; then they would have been educated in the process of what it takes to get things built and done. I had built the camp steadily with little indentation of their personal pocketbooks.

I had fallen in love with the camp and its possibilities, so much so that in 1944 I came up with a scheme that would have kept me there all year: I would run the camp for ten weeks in the summer, take small groups of children and adults for weekends and holidays during the off-season, and raise vegetables, fruits, chickens, and sheep that could be consumed during the summer season. I wanted to do all this for $5,000 per year. My salary for running the house and camp at that time was only $4,000, as I had not taken an increase for six years. The board thought the amount I asked was more than they could afford, so this romantic dream of being a country farmer–educator–social worker never came to fruition.

My family and I had wonderful summers at the camp, because we saw each other all the time. Emma was involved in intake and camp administration, and while she had no title and received no salary, she, rather than the head counselor, was put in charge on the two days each week that I spent in the city. She performed superbly.

Actually Emma was the "assistant director," although her duties more closely resembled that of a camp mother. She was concerned with the campers' health, seeing that they ate properly, dressed in consonance with the weather and had clean clothes. She inspected bunks to see that they were swept and mopped, that beds were made and clothes neatly stored. When a child had a crying spell, or became homesick, she took him to our cabin, talked to him, fed him candy and fruit, gave him things to do until the spell was over. When the children went home, she made sure they were fully dressed and had not forgotten too many items in their hurried, unskilled packing. She added to camp life all those things that made a difference to the child and to the parents.

Emma had a beautiful voice. It should have been cultivated professionally. She could always be distinguished from those singing around her, whether in informal group singing or with an organized choir. Yet she was always embarrassed when asked to sing. Although I never told her, I loved to hear her when she sang spontaneously, usually accompanying a voice she heard on the radio or a record. I was afraid that if I commented on its quality, she might clam up.

Ramon grew up to be a junior counselor, a counselor, and a pioneering specialist. He was paid. After receiving his bachelor's degree, he later earned a master's degree in education with a specialization in camping administration and made this field part of his professional career, developing an expertise in every aspect of this complicated operation.

Baruch Michael became a troublesome camper. Having sprouted on the grounds, he knew better than the counselors that no one should sit down to a picnic in a poison ivy patch. When the cabin went out on a hike, he refused to make the right turn where the counselor was leading the group, insisting that the turn was to the left. He was always right.

By 1949, as Bronx House continued to expand, it was evident that I could not do everything, and so for that summer, a director was appointed to run the camp. Although it was only a summer job, he received more than the sum I had asked four years before, when I proposed my all-year-at-camp idea. Since this occurred in the year that I was leaving Bronx House, my break with the house and the camp was complete. When I looked back over my investment of nine years in the camp, I saw that the site and population had grown, the camp's reputation had been firmly established, and many new innovations in camping and counselor training had been initiated, tested, and proven sound. Walking over this square mile of wooded land, in which I felt I knew every tree and path and waterhole, I had a feeling of accomplishment. My only regret was that I had not been able to introduce the camp unit for senior citizens, although I had recommended it to the camp committee the year before I resigned. That was left to my successors.

One additional note: Everyday at the morning flag raising, we gave a brief news report to the assembled campers, which included the baseball scores for the Yankees and the Giants. On August 6, 1945, I reported what I had just heard over the radio. The Americans had dropped a bomb on Hiroshima. I recall sermonizing on this gruesome military event that would soon bring the war with Japan to a close. While I indicated that tens of millions had died during the war, and that whole cities had been destroyed by saturation bombing, there was nothing quite as ominous as what had happened at Hiroshima. No longer would any part of the civilian world be safe. (In 1962, when we toured Japan, we went out of our way to visit Hiroshima. It was already rebuilt, but the epicenter, where the bomb fell, had been made into an eternal memorial for those who died. We had already learned of the six million Jews who died in the Holocaust. The two events were the two most awesome aspects of global World War II.)

The Jewish Flag Incident

In 1938, during my first year at Bronx House, we celebrated our tenth year in the new building. All of the board members were there, and the honored guests included the newly elected Federation president, Benjamin Buttenwieser, whose father, Joseph, had been an earlier president of Federation, and whose son, Lawrence, would preside over Federation's destinies after my retirement. Hundreds of our members were sitting in the audience. On the stage were two flags, one the American, and the other the emblem of the Jewish people. A breeze was blowing from an open window, and the Jewish flag's furls annoyed one of our board members. I was sitting next to her when she asked: "What is that thing?" I replied in a whisper: "The Jewish flag." "Well, get it off the stage, it doesn't belong in this building." I didn't remove it, but moved it back a bit, so that it would not disturb her. After the meeting, she told me in no uncertain terms that the flag should never be flown again at Bronx House. I tried to pacify her by stating that the flag had always been part of Bronx House, even before my coming, and that it was proper to display it on all important public occasions. Her reply: "I shall have this matter taken up at the next board meeting and see that this flag is removed."

At the next board meeting, the subject was on the agenda, and there was a spirited debate as to whether the Jews were a nation, whether the Jews had a flag, and whether it should be flown even subordinately to the American flag. While a few could see no harm in displaying the Jewish flag, there were no supporters of our doing so in the future. Rather than have them make a decision on the spot, for a vote would have certainly eliminated the flag forever, I suggested that we appoint a committee to check into what other centers and Federation institutions were doing, and surprisingly the board adopted that course.

A committee spent several months gathering data. We learned that many Jewish institutions in the Federation family displayed a Jewish flag on special occasions, but the practice was not universal. The committee report, which gave the facts but no recommendations, was debated at several meetings, where I stoutly defended its use. By a narrow margin, a motion was passed that the flag was not to be displayed at official Bronx House board meetings or events, but that any member group that chose to could exhibit the flag even at meetings held in the house. The Jewish flag was officially banned. I tried to get the issue reviewed several years later, but without success.

Now it was 1948. I was leaving for a conference of Jewish professionals in Atlantic City. It was momentarily expected that the State of Israel would be declared as a result of the vote taken by the United Nations the year before. On May 14, the State of Israel was established. I had left no instructions about flying the Jewish flag either inside or outside of the building in that event, not risking the chance of being turned down on a request to display it.

On the day the state was declared, the American flag, as usual, was on the mast in front of the building. The neighborhood, still largely Jewish, was celebrating the great event in the street. Someone noticed that the Jewish flag was not being displayed, and a delegation went into the house to demand that it be immediately hung, or else. By sheer coincidence, I was talking with my secretary over the phone, checking on agency affairs, when the delegation invaded my office. I gave instructions to display the flag at once; this appeased the residents and no rioting ensued.

At the next meeting, I reported what I had done. None of the board members, including those whose objections had been so vehement years before, criticized my action. They rationalized that the flag was now legitimate, since it represented an official state instead of something so indefinite as "the Jewish people." The flag flew forever after. It is another demonstration of how things somehow work out, if you only have patience, and if, as a director, you are willing to make an instant and proper decision, come what may.

Zionism

I have been a lifelong Zionist. Perhaps it started at the time I first learned how to translate the Hebrew text into English with "Next year in Jerusalem." My family contributed to Palestinian institutions. I found amongst my father's effects, stock that he had purchased in a flour mill in Palestine. (I checked on it on my first visit to Israel in 1955, and it didn't exist.)

As a youth, I was a member of a Young Judea group, and I still recall the rabid speeches made by the representatives of that organization who came to Gloversville once a year. My Hebrew teacher, Hyman Grant, had almost convinced my family to permit me to go to Palestine with him after my Bar Mitzvah, but my mother's illness prevented this journey from taking place. Grant left Gloversville. When I met him again in 1932 in Jersey City, he had still not gone on aliyah.

At the University of Missouri, quite naturally in view of my inclination toward socialism in domestic politics, I became a Labor Zionist, and in New York, as a graduate student, I joined the League for Labor Palestine along with a few other interested Jewish social workers. On Staten Island, and then at Bronx House and the summer camp, I introduced numerous programs on Zionism and the need to create a Jewish state. I waited with baited breath as the United Nations voted for the creation of Israel. So my interest in the Jewish flag was more than casual. When one had a board composed of many anti-Zionists, one had to operate with the foreknowledge that he might encounter opposition. I could easily have rationalized, both as a group worker and as a progressive educator, that our program always permitted the membership to determine what they would like to believe and support. This was acceptable even to skeptical and resistant board members. I recall talking one of our well-to-do board members out of making a large contribution to the American Council for Judaism, an anti-Zionist Jewish organization.

Subsequently, I headed a committee of Labor Zionists that held meetings in New York and at major social work conferences. Distinguished Israeli leaders often addressed these gatherings. Emma and I have helped raise millions of dollars for the United Jewish Appeal, Israel Bonds, and the Jerusalem YM-YWHA building, all for the benefit of Israel. We have a swimming pool named for both of us at the Jerusalem YM-YWHA. We established a playground in Jerusalem in memory of my brother, Sam. We have visited Israel seventeen times, during which I was a group leader, a consultant to several organizations, participated in a university seminar, and labored on behalf of Ethiopian Jews. I have a large library on Zionism and Israel. I have written on the subject. Emma and I have convinced hundreds of people to visit Israel, buy Israeli products, and do everything possible to defend the country. If this is not being a Zionist, then I do not know what the word means.

* * *

While I make no claim that I fought as vigorously as I might have for the rescue of the victims going to their death in Hitler's extermination program, even after it was known that the Nazi genocide machine was operating at full force, I tried to do something through private talks and occasional organized meetings at Bronx House.

I recall attending the March 9, 1942, rally at Madison Square Garden, together with tens of thousands of other Jews, to protest the European Jewish catastrophe. There we witnessed a pageant entitled *We Will Never Die,* organized by an activist group that was decrying the lack of action by the Jewish establishment. Brilliantly written by Ben Hecht, with stirring music composed by Kurt Weil, and the first-class talents of Edward G. Robinson and Paul Muni as narrators, it was directed by master showman Billy Rose and the prize-winning dramatist Moss Hart. All were outstanding luminaries of the American stage.

The event had been organized by Peter Bergson, a nephew of the former Chief Rabbi of Palestine, Abraham Isaac Kook. For attending this meeting, I was looked upon with some suspicion by some of the leaders of the so-called more responsible Jewish organizations, who gave this dramatic presentation little or no support.

I think the memory of that experience shaped my position when it came time to do something for the Ethiopian Jews. My guilt over not having done enough for the Jews during the Holocaust would not permit me to repeat such a calamity again.

Kansas City

For six years, I had directed the Bronx House and never gave a thought to leaving the institution. My mind was buzzing with plans for the expansion of facilities and the enrichment of its program.

In 1944, I received a call from Frank L. Weil, the imaginative and energetic president of the National Jewish Welfare Board, whose fertile imagination and public relations sense made the name of the national organization known to every Jewish community in the land. He told me that I was to take the position of executive director of the YM-YWHA in Kansas City, Missouri. He had just spoken to the board and informed them that I was the man for the post. I protested that I was content at Bronx House and wasn't looking for another job. Furthermore, I just couldn't consider his bartering me like a baseball player. He angrily told me that I could not let him down. He had promised to deliver me, as they had an important vacancy to fill. After a long and argumentative long-distance phone conversation, I finally agreed to go to Kansas City for an interview. If the board there wanted to look upon me as a serious candidate, I said, it could do so—but I agreed to this only to bail him out.

I took the lengthy train ride to Kansas City, which I had not revisited since my marriage to Emma in 1928. I was greeted by a committee of three at the railroad station. They took me to lunch at a fancy hotel, and when they asked me who I wanted to see, I suggested the heads of the Jewish Federation, the leaders of the Community Chest, and Rabbi Samuel Mayerberg, who had officiated at our wedding, and was the city's most important rabbi. I saw all of them the following day. That evening I was entertained royally at the home of one of the officers.

In the late afternoon of the following day, I reported to a personnel committee composed of eight people on what I had learned and what I would do if I were to become the executive. I recall being especially lucid, which I should not have been, if I wasn't going to accept the position under any circumstances. I indicated the kinds of programs I had instituted at Bronx House—Jewish, for the aged, for the emotionally disturbed, training of graduate personnel, extending activities into other institutions like synagogues, building facilities, raising money, etc. Some of these services would have been brand-new to a midwestern town. From the applause, the questions, the individual comments after the meeting, I knew I had made a good impression.

That evening I dined at another board member's home with a few more people whom I had not met before. I recall one approaching me and asking whether I would come and work for his large drug store chain, where he thought I would make a superb director of personnel. He couldn't understand why I would want to waste my talents in charity work, when I could do so much better in the business world. He offered me $10,000. per year to start. I smiled and told him I would think it over, but knew that I would turn down this tender too.

The Kansas City Jewry that I saw glittered. The YM-YWHA was in a large and attractive building, with extensive facilities, including a theater for the presentation of major plays. I also became acutely aware that Kansas City was a Jim Crow town, which treated its blacks badly, and that its welfare program even for poor whites left much to be desired. It was not a community in which I could feel comfortable, and I knew I would end up with confrontations that would force me to leave.

The next afternoon, I was to meet with the board at noon. When I entered the hotel dining room, I discovered some forty people present for what appeared to be a banquet rather than a meeting. The chairman, Joseph Lerner, who ran a chain of women's hosiery shops—bouncy, loquacious, with a good sense of humor—opened the meeting with a toast to the "New Executive Director." In my embarrassed response, I told them that I was seriously considering their offer and would let them know in a few days. I then went on to repeat many of the things I foresaw for Kansas City if I accepted the position. The chairman whispered to me that the starting salary would be $7,500.

I left the meeting escorted by the chairman, who drove me to the railroad. I already knew that I was not going to accept their invitation. As we talked, I was thinking about all of the unfinished business and opportunities awaiting me at Bronx House. Besides, I could never rid myself of the notion that New York was the only exciting location for anyone who wanted to work in the social welfare field. On the train I began composing a telegram to say no. When I reached home, I found a telegram from Lerner stating that in addition to the salary, the Y would pay all of my moving expenses and there would be a rent-free house available for a year. Emma would never have to buy a pair of hose as long as I worked in the center. It was all tempting, but we decided to risk it in New York.

When I told the Bronx House board that I had been offered $7,500, they raised my salary to $6,000, my first increase since 1938. Kansas City found another executive and that romantic three-day visit was soon forgotten. Frank Weil never forgave me.

A Center for the Aging

Back in 1943, I was looking out of my office window at Bronx House and noticed for the first time that elderly people, mostly women, were sitting on soda water boxes in the sunshine, moving the boxes from one spot to another and even across the street as the sun shifted its heating course. I mused why they had to spend their waking time that way. As I reviewed our program, I realized that we did nothing specifically for them. They sat mute and inglorious as spectators at lectures, concerts and other major events, but they didn't actively participate. There was not a single elderly person on the adult council, one of the most important bodies in our house. The subject of their interests and needs had never been raised at our regular or special staff meetings. The topic had never come up at a board meeting.

Lying on my desk was a recently purchased copy of the 1940 census.

Thumbing through the charts and accompanying text, I noted with surprise that the number of aged in our population was growing, and there were projections that their numbers would continue to increase in the years to come. But despite my transient thoughts, neither the scene outside my window nor the statistics that I had perused moved me to take action of any kind. Nonetheless, most of what we experience through our eyes and mind is not extinguished, and remains in our consciousness to someday be acted upon.

Not long afterward, Beatrice Brown, a former teenage worker on our staff, and the first head counselor at the camp back in 1940, dropped in to see me on one of her walks through the neighborhood visiting clients. She had resigned from our staff, because she could not afford to work for a salary of $1,200 per year, and had taken a job with the Department of Welfare, where the pay was several hundred dollars higher. This day, when she dropped in, she told me that her case load was increasingly made up of older people, and she thought that I ought to be doing more for them. Furthermore, since we were known as an innovative agency—and she complimented me on my far-sighted leadership—she thought that she could provide us with enough clientele to start a program. This chat rekindled my memory of the scene outside the window and the census report.

But more than that, Beatrice said that the director of the welfare center on nearby Arthur Avenue, Harry Levine, had discussed the possibility of the city doing something for the aged in the field of recreation, and she thought it would be a good idea if we met. I told her to arrange a meeting. Several weeks later, we lunched in a delicatessen on Claremont Parkway, around the corner, and talked. Levine was a bit shorter than me, a bit older, and a lot more talkative. But over a corned beef sandwich on rye bread with seeds, thickened with mustard and with celery tonic to wash it down, we hit it off immediately, and before the luncheon was over, we made some definite plans to help the aged. I said that we would set up a club for them and study how we could absorb them in the agency, using the insights and skills of social group work and education, as we were doing with other age groups. I told him we would start on this as soon as a leader could be lined up to recruit and program for this assembly.

Levine told me that he had already started some modest programs for the aged, but was looking for a separate and larger location and would try to persuade the department to provide a worker and some funds for its operation. I told him that if such a site could be found, it would be better, since I thought like a private agency person, that we set up an independent board of directors, composed of professionals and lay people, from the volunteer and the public sectors, who would look after the service and try to find additional money for the program, since the city was not likely, at least at the outset, to make available all the funds that would be needed. What was more, if there was a board, it could, if the program succeeded, become an instrument for advocating public support for this and additional projects. While Levine was not at first willing to relinquish any control of the undertaking to a private board, he nonetheless saw the wisdom of at least trying to get such aid. We shook hands and agreed to proceed in our separate ways.

On my return to Bronx House, I raised the question with our board president, Lillian Riegelman, an elderly, vigorous woman herself, who was quick to realize the value of both enterprises. She put it on the agenda of the next board meeting, at which there was a spirited debate, opposition coming strangely from two social work professionals, both on the faculty of the New York School of Social Work, Drs. Philip Klein and Nathan Cohen. Cohen questioned whether group work principles could be applied to the aged. Klein, a social welfare researcher of note, thought that considerable study should be undertaken before the house ventured on such a new course. The board approved the motion to go ahead with the venture, but since the summer was approaching, and I would soon be burdened with my added duties at camp, it was suggested that I not implement it until the fall. Klein was so adamant on the question that he made a trip to camp to dissuade me. Like Cohen, he had to learn that on this board, he had only one vote, and had been voted down. Klein tried to get me to change my mind, but the more I thought about it, the more convinced I was that we should proceed with dispatch.

Our sizable staff had recently been joined by a young woman, volunteer, Beatrice Roberts, who was intrigued by the prospect of doing something new and interesting, although her original assignment had been in the field of consumer problems. After we worked out the preliminary details, and informed the staff of our plans, she started to recruit older people from the membership and referrals from the Welfare Department.

In short order the Friendly Folks was born and prospered. A full account of its development was published in the *Jewish Social Service Quarterly*, in June, 1945, under the title "A Recreational Project for Older Persons," authored by both of us. We tried to present this paper at the annual meeting of the Jewish Communal Workers, in 1944, but there was no interest on the part of the program committee. I did read a paper before an all-Philadelphia conference on October 4, 1945, with the grandiloquent title "The Significance of a New Era for Older People through Leisure Time Activities." The subject was now slowly entering the social work consciousness. *Recreation Magazine* published an article of mine, "The Human Problems of Old Age," in its October 1945 issue. Both articles dealt with both the Friendly Folks and the William Hodson Center. Beatrice Roberts later became the director of Camp Bronx House and eventually ended up as the assistant dean of the Columbia University School of Social Work.

The William Hodson Community Center, named after a New York welfare commissioner who had been killed on a wartime mission to

North Africa, found a new home for itself in the Old Boro Hall Building on Tremont and Third Avenue in the Bronx. The building was quickly transformed into a suitable meeting place for the aged. With the aid of a host of volunteers, 350 people were quickly enrolled in its miscellaneous programs. A board was created, with several members of the Bronx House providing the leadership. Mrs. Riegelman became the first president. She brought a number of downtown volunteers to assist her in the program, raise money, and even lead some groups. Emma immediately joined the volunteer corps.

The center was most fortunate in having as its first director Gertrude Landau, a social welfare investigator, whose intelligence, imagination, and around-the-clock productivity made the center an instant success. While she was directly responsible to Levine, I supervised her regularly for six years, until I left Bronx House in 1949. She kept good records, recruited other board members, and gradually assembled a staff as the program expanded. A record of the early days was published in 1945. Later she wrote a book about the center's philosophy and program.

The role of the Bronx House in the formative years was pivotal, for it gave the project a much wider horizon, attracted influential and informed volunteers, and brought resources to supplement the city's contribution.

I gradually dropped out of direct contact with the center, but remained on its board and from time to time saw Miss Landau. She had greater visions not only for the center, but for similar developments throughout the city and country and even the world. She wrote, lectured, sat on important government committees, and influenced the course of this movement for decades.

In 1984, the Hodson Center celebrated its fortieth anniversary. It was clear that the constituency, originally Jewish and white, was now almost entirely black. The building had been relocated in a special structure in an exclusively black neighborhood. The new president was black, replacing a series of Jewish women leaders. The staff was black. The transition was complete.

Today, the subject of the aged is on every agenda. It is estimated that within a few decades the majority of Americans may be in this age bracket. There is now no difficulty in attracting money for programs and buildings for the aged. What is more, there are no longer any obstacles to putting this item on the agenda of a conference or to getting a paper on this subject published.

The Era of Nan Langman

Anne Wertheim Langman, daughter of Maurice Wertheim, Wall Street banker, art collector, deeply involved in international chess, and Alma Morgenthau, a daughter of Mr. and Mrs. Henry Morgenthau, Sr., was elected to the board in 1943. A graduate of the New York School of Social Work, married to a physician, and the mother of four children, she came well equipped by heritage and training for her board role. She literally threw herself into the Bronx House program, when her husband enlisted for military service. She had ideas and drive. She was systematic in her approach to every problem, had a close relationship with the staff, established her influence over the board and beyond that to Federation. She had a good public relations sense, spoke well, wrote better, and some years later became the successful author of several books.

Nan was elected president in 1945 and came to the meetings with a well-developed and extensive program for the future. Some would assert that during her incumbency, Bronx House attained its zenith. Certainly it became even better known. Yet I believe that the earlier period, 1938–45, was the era of greatest creativity. Her regime, which began in 1945, was an epoch marked by expansion, consolidation, and public interpretation. My own energies were now exerted in an enlarged program and board structure. But I had also taken on outside duties. During this period I served for two years as president of the National Conference of Jewish Center Workers, a post which consumed a great deal of my time, and also had teaching positions at three colleges. In addition, I played an active role, as did Nan, in the highly publicized JWB Survey.

Our first concern, however, was to recruit new people for the board. The death of Henry Morgenthau, Sr., on November 25, 1946 brought to an end the foundership of 1911 and the traditions associated with that past. From a largely voluntary enterprise, Bronx House had grown to one that was now highly professional. It had moved from a relatively modest list of programs confined to a small wooden builidng to a venture that reached into extension services far beyond the confines of the neighborhood. Its financing had increased from a few thousand dollars in 1911 to $30,000 when I arrived in 1938, and by 1947 it was $200,000. When I left in 1949, it exceeded $300,000 per year.

The board added Julian Lazrus, Merwin Rosenman, and Dr. Abraham B. Tamis, all of whom would become presidents in the next decade. Dr. Tamis, a product of the earlier Bronx House membership, had already attained high distinction in the medical field as well as for his voluntary work in Jewish philanthropy. Peter A. Cohn took on the chairmanship of Bronx House Camp, Joseph F. Cullman III spearheaded the West Bronx extension program in cooperation with the Bronx YM-YWHA. Phoebe (Mrs. William) Stein headed an expanded child care committee and later became head of the city-wide Play School Association. Aaron Samuelson and Hyman M. Resnick, former members, and both now lawyers, invested their energies in strengthening the alumni association. Dr. Jacob I. Miller, a psychiatrist, whose children attended the music school, headed a Parent Association that assured the financial stability of that unit. Miss Minnie Obermeier, a district school superintendent, intensified the relationship of Bronx House with the neighborhood schools and the Board of Education. Theodore W. Kheel and Howard Lichtenstein became the key bargainers in the biennial negotiations with the staff labor union. Drs. Philip Klein and Nathan Cohen of the New York School of Social Work ensured that the agency would get professional social work counsel. Anne (Mrs. Henry) Weintraub, Abraham Haham, Morris Hirsch, and Jacob Cohen served on the board as adult and youth representatives, so that the out-of-neighborhood board members could be fully cognizant of who the membership were, and what they needed and expected.

We had succeeded in obtaining a grant from the Hebrew Technical Society for a fully equipped craft shop. An Oneg Shabbat program had been introduced, headed by Marshall Sklare, then a student, who went on to become one of America's foremost Jewish sociologists.

The student-training program underwritten by Frederic R. Stettenheim grew apace, with a full-time director and students drawn from a number of graduate schools, many of whom went on to distinguished careers in the future—heads of agencies, deans of schools of social work, authors. I continued to supervise two students each year. Along with my teaching duties at Yeshiva University and the College of the City of New York, part of which I gave up as my duties at Bronx House increased, I continued one course at the New York School until I left Bronx House in 1949. Some of my students were former members of Bronx House, whom we had nourished and stimulated for years. Several of our Bronx House alumni also went on to become teachers, deans, authors, heads of national social work agencies. I encouraged my students to visit the agency and even my home to discuss their course material or the projects that I gave them to write on. One of them, Dr. Harry Specht, later attained the deanship of the School of Social Work of the University of California at Berkeley. Another, Dr. Carl Urbont, became the executive vice-president of the 92nd Street YM-YWHA. Teaching and supervising students along with leading membership groups gave me an opportunity to test out theories in practice and kept me current with the profesional literature, all of which I was able to translate into programs for the benefit of our membership. I wrote articles, reviewed books, spoke at major conferences, led sessions at training institutes.

My salary was finally raised to $7,500, I suspect in part because I was being solicited for other positions. While I invariably found some reason for turning these job offers down, I always advised the board what was happening.

Going to camp became ever more a burden, as the camp was now larger, covering 650 acres, and had a daily enrollment of over three hundred campers, with nearly fifteen hundred different people accommodated over the ten week summer season. After the 1948 season, a full-time director was chosen to take over this considerable task. I still went up to see what was going on, because the camp was part of the total Bronx House complex and expanding.

In my tenth year, the president and some board members felt that there should be some celebration of the decade of my professional leadership. Although I have always been wary of such events, because they so often become superficially laudatory rather than a genuine expression of what was actually performed, I found it easier to give in than to protest. The final part of the evening turned out to be fun, as well as congratulatory. Apart from my family, including cousins, and the board members, there was a large representation from the membership and the alumni, as well as old friends from Staten Island, my first post, and Federation and its constituent agencies plus professional colleagues from the settlement house field, the Board of Education, the schools of social work, camps, the Jewish Welfare Board, and former students, some of whom were now full-time professionals. Beatrice (Mrs. Isaac) Landman organized the details. Dr. Nathan E. Cohen was chairman. The speakers and entertainers (and it was hard to tell which was which, because so much humor attended the event) included Dr. Charles Ansell, then at the Educational Alliance, later to head Bronx House Camp, and subsequently, after his move to California, an analyst, together with his wife, Maryann, now life-long friends; Jack Nadel, the irrepressible jokester who headed the 92nd Street YM-YWHA; Matthew Elson, who had succeded me at the Staten Island Jewish Community Center, and at that time was director of the Metropolitan Section-NJWB; Joseph Willen, executive vice-president of the Federation of Jewish Philanthropies; Elly (Mrs. Leonard) Bernheim, president of JANC; and Elly (Mrs. Randolph) Guggenheimer, a volunteer leader who was unparalleled at writing scripts for such an occasions, and who became most prominent in the child care field as well as New York City's commissioner of consumer affairs and a TV personality. (In 1986, we attended the marriage of her grandson, Randolph III, to my niece, Elisabeth Miller.)

Someone later wrote to me that it was the adult groups of Bronx House who stole the show with their eloquent speeches, relating how Bronx House and its staff had shaped and enhanced their lives. The sterling silver service for twelve which they gave to Emma and me is still in use decades after the event.

The board gave me a handsome Mark Cross alligator-skin wallet with edgings of solid gold. Enclosed was a check for $600. It was leaked to me that the board had hoped to raise enough money to enable me to buy a car of my own. I had been using the camp station wagon for eight years. In 1948 I inherited $2,000 from my father's estate, and with that sum and the gift, we bought a brand-new Plymouth.

In addition, the board paid for the publication of a collection of my writings *Adventures in Group Work* which had a rather wide circulation.

The Janowsky Survey

When the war ended, the NJWB undertook a survey of its constituent members to determine what philosophy should guide their destinies in the postwar years. The war's aftermath had wrought many changes. Old Jewish neighborhoods were being abandoned as the better-circumstanced Jewish population sought new locations within the five boroughs or else began to move out to the suburbs. New institutions were needed. Would they be synagogues or Jewish community centers, or both, or a combination of both? If they were to be Jewish, with which "denominational" group would they affiliate, Orthodox, Conservative, Reconstructionist, Reform, or community center—or something else? What would happen to the agencies left behind? Should they serve the remaining few Jews, or should they begin to enroll a non-Jewish membership? Could they be Jewish and serve the others? If they became non-sectarian, did they belong within the Jewish framework? If the centers remained Jewish, should they provide a program with Jewish content or concentrate mainly on the popular athletic and social activities? Since the future almost guaranteed an upwardly mobile Jewish population that was American born, better educated, and better circumstanced economically, should the centers pay more attention to the interests of the growing middle class and not concentrate only on the lower-income Jewish population? Should a center move out of a poor area while some of its clients still lived in the old neighborhood? These were among the many fundamental questions faced by the committee chaired by Professor Salo W. Baron, distinguished historian and my former mentor, and directed by Professor Oscar I. Janowsky, a well-known social scientist teaching at City College of New York. A preliminary report was presented in Pittsburgh at a meeting of the NJWB on May 10, 1947.

I had, of course, been interviewed by the researchers, and was somewhat disturbed by the premises of the survey. What concerned me was their seeming effort to define the Jewish center as a monolithic institution. There had always been a strongly individualistic tendency in the field, particularly among the executives, each seeing his own center as uniquely different despite the many features that all centers had in common; but at the same time, any effort to impose an overall ideology would limit functions, eliminate flexibility, and create unnecessary divisions among centers with different tendencies. I thought the findings did not correctly view membership interests and needs, and saw Jewish content only in the narrowest definition. If the survey's recommendations were adopted, the centers, instead of being more openly democratic, would become doctrinaire and parochial. I felt that the JWB was trying to cast the centers into a synagogue, or at least a synagogue-Center mold, a pattern that was already a growing and competing phenomenon nurtured by the religious movements. I incorporated the above sentiments in a speech at the annual meeting of the Metropolitan Section–NJWB on October 20, 1947, subsequently published in the *Jewish Center Worker.*

Regrettably, my ideas were picked up by several well-known scholars, among them Oscar Handlin, historian at Harvard, and Louis Wirth, social scientist at the University of Chicago, who had been retained by several federation and center leaders. Handlin, Wirth, and their colleagues held strongly that the centers ought to adopt a more nonsectarian approach in the future, or at the least did not want to exclude nonsectarian institutions from the fold.

Janowsky gave extensive recognition to my position in the book that was finally published, *The JWB Survey* (1948), citing at length from a paper I had presented in 1940 at the annual conference of the NAJCW.

Writing in 1940, I had seen the centers as having, according to Janowsky, a "mission in America," not only to fulfill the needs of Jews as "mere centers for Jewish survival," but to work "with Jews, all Jews—and even with non-Jews," for the betterment of society as a whole, for the promotion of social justice. I thought Jewish idealism should be utilized "to improve the character of American civilization." He quoted: "Let not Jewish leadership be jealously reserved for the Jewish group. . . . but encourage Jewish leadership for the social edification of the larger community." Janowsky summed up my views as follows: "The primary purpose of the Jewish Center is to serve humanity, and not the specialized needs of the group which maintains and directs it. Apparently it must remain a Jewish Center—a Jewish sponsored institution—in order to preserve the inherited purity of higher ideals." Janowsky described me as "a sincere and able center executive, who enjoys a large following in the field."

The debate was a bitter one. My reputation was tarnished by the charge that I had sold out to the nonsectarianists and to "Jewish anti-Semites." In any event, while some changes were made in the final report as a result of our criticism, I did not see eye-to-eye with my compatriots in the opposition and soon severed my relations with them.

The survey established that the Jewish Center was by and for Jews in order to ensure their continuity as a people in a culturally pluralistic society. This necessitated the primacy of Jewish programming. There was no place for the affiliation of nonsectarian agencies even under Jewish sponsorship in an all-embracing Jewish center movement. The center was seen as an instrument for Jewish identification, Jewish integration, and Jewish personality development, all to be operated under the schema of a democratic way of life. While Jews should be concerned with public issues as American citizens, social action was not the primary nor even one of the main functions of the center.

In my directorship of both Staten Island and Bronx House, I had actually adhered to most of these principles, for I had endeavored to make both of these institutions more Jewish over the years. At the same time I had also sought to make them concerned with the major political and social issues confronting the larger community. Moreover, I still maintained that Jewish centers should not be forced to adhere to a single rigid pattern, and that the individuality of each institution should be protected.

When Samuel Gershowitz, then the executive director of the NJWB, came to Bronx House, a year later, to see whether the board was following the mandate made by his organization following the acceptance of the Janowsky report, he was surprised to learn how well informed the board, staff, and membership were about the survey. We had used this subject, like many other themes over the years, to educate these three interacting elements in our structure. He was also amazed to learn that the trio also felt strongly about maintaining and expanding the Jewishness of the agency.

Some years later, when I was fully ensconced at Federation and learned how far most of the affiliated agencies were from following the JWB recommendations and practices that I had incorporated at Bronx House before the survey, I began to write and speak out for Jewish primacy. This provoked the professional leadership, including some on the NJWB staff itself, to attack the positions that I was advocating. I had come to realize that I was closer to the Janowsky principles than I had thought, while the field was with few exceptions not following it at all. It would be some years before the NJWB became a firm advocate of Israel and of Jewish education.

A Study of Albany

I had never made a systematic study of a community. On Staten Island I had periodically collected data on the Jewish community, so that I had a fair estimate of the population and the number of members in various institutions (synagogues, philanthropies, fraternal groups), and some approximation of their employment and income status, but the material had never been gathered, put down, and analyzed in a comprehensive document.

At Bronx House, when I first arrived, we had invited Dr. Charles Bernheimer, the venerable elder on the JWB staff, to study Bronx House. I aided him in collecting data, but the study was limited to one institution in a large and complex Jewish neighborhood. While we gathered demographic data about Jews, Sephardic Jews, Italians, and blacks, our effort never attained the level of a community study.

Thus in 1945, when the Jewish Welfare Board asked me to participate in a Jewish Community Survey of Albany, New York, I welcomed the opportunity. As part of a team of specialists on community organization, family, children, and aged institutions and Jewish education, I was to focus especially on the need for Jewish Center services. The study also touched on Jewish communal relations. In the course of this study I made a number of visits to Albany, meeting with its lay and professional Jewish leadership, and with representatives of public and non-Jewish agencies, such as the mayor's office, the Community Chest, the YMCA, etc. I also met with all the rabbis, because if there was to be a new center, located elsewhere than on its present site, this would impinge in some part on their domain. Some of the synagogues, as they built new structures, were already beginning to term themselves centers and had added center functions to their religious educational services.

While I had grown accustomed to resistance over the years, I had rarely encountered such universal blockage to any kind of change as I met in Albany. This included members of the board of the center itself. Most seemed content with the status quo. Building any new or larger facility was considered an unnecessary invasion of their pocketbooks. The synagogues, too, were opposed to a new center in any new location. Only individuals without wealth or influence welcomed the changes I recommended.

It was clear from our data that the Jews of Albany were rapidly moving from the areas of primary residence to new areas on the city's fringes, building larger and finer homes than they had originally occupied. In light of this, the center and all the synagogues were poorly located to meet the requirements of the dispersed Jewish population, who were reluctant to travel downtown to neighborhoods from which they had fled.

Despite the opposition, I recommended that the center be relocated in one of these budding areas, and that it should initiate extension services in several of those sectors immediately. In addition I suggested the creation of a central day camp and a central country camp, the latter in cooperation with other cities, such as Troy and Schenectady, all three comprising the Capital district. For the center itself, I recommended a preschool, a comprehensive program in the arts, more professional staff, more and better Jewish educational programs, and changes from an individual to a family membership system.

Regretfully the recommendations that all of us made fell initially on deaf ears. Action was delayed for several years, so that when the proposals were finally seen as imperative and inevitable, the costs were substantially greater than we had estimated. Even the synagogues accepted our data and suggestions and eventually built new facilities.

The lag between making sound recommendations and achieving action within a reasonable time has continued to bother me all my life. I blame part of this lag on the professionals. If professionals are to be more than mechanical operators of existing services, they must be able to forecast future population movements, services needed, and facilities in which to house them. How to shorten the time between projection and implementation is the problem. Albany could have easily afforded the changes recommended. But it took years to bring them about, and because of the delay, the community was deprived of valuable facilities and services urgently needed.

One incidental story is worth recording. One of the individuals who gave me a great deal of difficulty during the study was a young traditional rabbi. He objected to the center on two counts: first, that whatever the center could do, the synagogue should be doing and could do better; second, that the center was negative toward the tradition and its strict observances, such as Kashrut and the Sabbath—and because of this bias, those attending the center became more assimilated and alienated from historic Judaism.

Several years later, while dining in a New York prestigious nonkosher steak house, I saw this rabbi walk in with a few friends. It is questionable whether even the water served could meet the test of Kashrut, let alone the other items on the menu. There were no vegetable or dairy dishes. I could not resist getting up and greeting the rabbi rather volubly, to his utter embarrassment. He and his party left the restaurant.

Should I Become a Rabbi?

In 1947, I was approached by Nan Langman and Phoebe Stein, both members of the Bronx House board, about conducting a seminar for a group of their women friends, all mothers, who were trying to cope with bringing up their children in a modern Jewish fashion. The war was over. The revelations of the Holocaust were having a telling effect on them, because most of them were of German-Jewish extraction, and they were beginning to feel guilty about not having done enough to save their kinsmen. The United Nations was engaged in a bitter debate to determine whether Palestine should be divided into separate Jewish and Arab states. While none of them were Zionists, they could not but feel that there must be some just solution for the benefit of the Jews. Most of them belonged to the prestigious Reform Temple Emanu-el on Fifth Avenue in Manhattan (one of them used the term "pew holder" rather than "member" to describe her affiliation), where some of them had studied in the Sunday school. They were not regular attendees, and were not sure they were even religious Jews, but of one thing they were certain: that they knew little about Judaism and the Jewish people. Even being identified with the Federation of Jewish Philanthropies had given them little background, nor had it deepened their identification. Nan had been exposed to my own view that being a Jew meant that one had to be knowledgeable, identified, and committed to an ethical life-style. She had learned a great deal about the complexities of Jewish life while engaged in studying the Janowsky report.

While I considered myself an informed and earnest Jew, I was sure that I should not be leading this group. So I sent them to Dr. Louis Finkelstein, the head of the Jewish Theological Seminary, and to Dr. Israel Rappaport, a professional Jewish educator, who was making some waves with notions of his own how Jews should be educated. They saw both men, but came back to me reinforced in their initial resolve that I should be their seminar leader. I was finally persuaded after they accepted certain conditions: that the husbands must attend as well as the wives, because unless they were both of the same mind, an educational program for their children would not work; that the meetings should take place once a month in different homes, starting with a buffet dinner at 6 P.M. and ending not later than 10 P.M.; that they would have to read books that I would suggest: and finally, that the seminar should be limited to twelve families, as twenty-four was the optimum size for a group of this kind. The conditions were accepted, a schedule was worked out, and they undertook to enroll a dozen couples. The roster read like a list of the leading Jewish families in New York. They were all rich, all active in philanthropy; some were quite well known, scions of the Morgenthaus and the Baerwalds. All were searching for something they were not sure of. While the women were involved in Jewish and other philanthropies, this was not true of the men. All were college graduates, some with advanced degrees. One of the men was a scientist who later became a Nobel Prize winner in chemistry; the others were doctors, attorneys, stock brokers, and important businessmen heading substantial concerns. Some had attended Ivy League schools.

At the first session I provoked them with a challenging question: "When did you decide that you didn't want to remain a Jew?" While this unnerved a few, confessions began to pour out, more from the men than the women. It appeared that such self-questioning had become a factor when they left the bosom of their families and went off to college. There they were confronted with outright prejudice and anti-Semitism. They had played down their own Jewishness on the campus, which meant not going to temples, not being a Zionist, not subscribing to or visibly reading Jewish books and periodicals. With few exceptions, all of their intimate friends were Jewish. Their only active affiliation was with

Federation and its agencies, which they considered more a nonsectarian than an avowedly Jewish cause, since most of the New York Federation's affiliates offered their services to non-Jews, and while the Federation supported domestic Jewish organizations, it had nothing to do with the United Jewish Appeal, Israel, overseas Jewish relief, or other national Jewish organizations. If the members of my seminar saw anything uniquely Jewish about their association with Federation, it was precisely its ethical character, in offering its bounty to the non-Jew and more specifically the poor, someone on a social scale below their own status, which they enjoyed through inheritance or by dint of their own vocational talents.

After this initial expurgation—and it was something remarkable for these individuals to do publicly, for it both educated the others and told me a great deal, although I had suspected in advance that they would expose themselves—our other sessions were less dramatic.

On succeeding evenings, I gave them a brief history of the Jewish people, a history of the Jews in America, a list of books they should read and have in their home libraries. In addition I gave them books, games and records for their children. Their questions expressing doubts about why they should become full Jews were not easily answered, nor were all their reservations dispelled. Yet I began to feel that they had moved from "Why should I remain a Jew? to "Try and make me a Jew!"

As spring approached, the women suggested that we should end the season with a party, something in which their children could participate. I suggested a Passover Seder. This took off like wild-fire. They engaged the Harmonie Club, the premier Jewish social club, of which all of them were members, for this festive event. I learned that the club had never had a Seder before. A committee met with me to rewrite the Haggadah, so that there would be twelve questions raised by twelve children and answered by twelve fathers. I obviously included the four original questions. I asked my colleague at Bronx House, Leah Rosen, a professionally trained social group worker, and a very knowledgeable Jew, to work with the children in developing a pageant with costumes.

One mother brought a candelabra that had been used in her family for over a century. Another brought in a beautifully engraved silver wine cup and said her grandmother had told her that this was used in the service to entice some angel into the household—the cup of Elijah.

The Seder, over which I presided, was a phenomenal success. Even the most skeptical of the fathers felt that it had not only brought them all together around a major Jewish event, but that it had given them insight as to why Jews would want to continue this ancient festival year in and year out, when they were no longer, as one put it, "Slaves in America."

Within a few days, a committee of women came to my office arguing that the seminar and Seder should not be the end of it. They had determined that what they needed was to continue with this group under my leadership, that I must become their "rabbi." I could see all the implications of this—a radical change in the way I had to operate in my free time, weekly synagogue attendance, setting up and supervising a Hebrew school for their children with creative programming, conducting adult studies for parents, and creating the image that I was indeed a "rabbi," at least in the sense of "teacher," because I had never been either trained or ordained for that post, a post in which I would have been most uncomfortable. I begged off, indicating that it would be an impossible task and obligation, requiring me to give up most, if not all, of what I was doing at Bronx House. I recommended that their best course would be to affiliate with a synagogue, advising them to talk to the rabbi of Temple Emanu-el to determine how their group could play a special role in that vast cathedral, perhaps as a *havurah*, a type of group structure that later became a popular mode of congregational affiliation and participation.

This suggestion they categorically rejected, but they responded favorably to my suggestion that their children should attend a special school for which I would find a teacher and a location. It was easy to obtain a room at the 92nd Street Y within walking distance of their apartments. A teacher was another thing. After considerable search, we found a woman who had all the qualifications—she was a Jewish educator, experienced with children in schools and camps, a writer of Jewish books. The school was initiated. The year was 1948, when the Jewish world was in constant ferment about the creation of the State of Israel. The teacher, inevitably because of her own leanings and the currency of the subject, began to introduce activities about Israel. The children made the Zionist flag of blue and white. They turned out Jewish ritual objects in clay. They collected money for Zionist organizations. They began to learn Hebrew, as well as Jewish history with a Zionist emphasis. But the parents, who were still troubled about the conflicting duality of being Jews and Americans, with all of its implications, felt their children were being exploited, and so the venture ended just as suddenly as it had arisen.

I have often wondered what would have happened to this group of twelve families if I had indeed become their "rabbi" and had found a teacher who might have handled the vital subject matter with a little less original zeal. Would I have enrolled in a seminary and eventually ended up with ordination? How would I have developed in that profession? Would the group have grown larger? But of course, none of this happened. While a few of the families subsequently became interested in Israel and other Jewish matters, my efforts proved to be ephemeral, largely because the program had been designed around my personality and my relationships with them, and not through any full, inner, personal commitment on their part.

President of the NAJCW

The National Association of Jewish Center Workers came into being when professional Jewish center executives decided to form a national organization, so that they could meet annually to discuss their common problems, enjoy a social reunion, and elect officers to conduct business between annual sessions. The staff of the Jewish Welfare Board provided whatever administrative assistance was required. The JWB recruited, trained, and placed personnel in available jobs. The JWB also provided consultation to the boards of affiliated societies, to enhance programs, and help design and construct facilities. As new and larger buildings were created in the 1920s, more individuals below the executive level were recruited as members of the national association. While still dominated by the executives, its membership included physical educators, specialists in youth programs, adult educators, and workers associated with the arts.

When I attended my first NAJCW conference in 1932, shortly after completing my studies at the Graduate School of Jewish Social Work, I met some of the personalities with whom my fortunes would be linked for many decades. I was one of the few professionally trained people at the conference. Most had entered the field from other endeavors, and had been educated as rabbis, teachers, lawyers, accountants, physical educators, businessmen. They had been drawn to this work for a variety of reasons. Some had actually grown up in the Ys, and while trained for other professions, eventually found this field more to their liking.

For the executives, the NAJCW was a club. If you decided to be active in the club, serving your apprenticeship by working on committees, you would very likely be elected to the board, then could work your way up the ladder of various offices, and if you behaved yourself and played by the rules of the game, you might end up someday as president. While the quality of the presidents varied, one did not necessarily have to be a great conceptualist, nor an orator, nor have made any unique contribution to the field, nor distinguished oneself in one's own institution nor even have presented a paper, to reach this exalted office. You only had to live long enough and wait your turn.

I became an activist, working to change all this from the beginning of my career. I was made a member of important committees, was invited to present papers at conferences, and was elected to the board of directors while still in my twenties. I was not a clubby member. I thought recognition should be given only to those who made or might make leadership contributions to the field. I asserted that presidents should not be elected solely because one was part of a fraternity, out of sheer loyalty and friendship to his colleagues.

At each convention, a nominating committee would present the members with an "official" slate of approved candidates, and these would in due course be elected to office. At the 1939 annual meeting, however, I led a revolt against this practice. Armed with a list of signatures written on a napkin at breakfast in Child's restaurant in Atlantic City, we nominated our own list of candidates and overruled all efforts to declare our impromptu list illegal, unethical, and downright indecent. Upsetting decades of unchallenged tradition, we succeeded in electing the rump candidate Julian L. Greifer as president. Julian, a rabbi by training, scholarly, witty, articulate, seemed to me and others a better choice than the official candidate. I had no personal dislike for the official candidate, but he had achieved nothing to warrant his election. He was elected president at a later convention, because the boys in the back room made sure that there would be no last-minute opposition and made doubly sure that they had the votes in advance.

While I was reasonably well regarded and respected, there was no desire on the part of the old-time insiders to violate the code by presenting me as a candidate. I was now thirty-eight years old, too young to be considered for the office. But a group of young turks thought differently, and took it upon themselves to present my name with everything but a ticker-tape parade and marching bands. I was elected in 1946.

I took the job seriously. The organization had created chapters throughout the country that met several times a year between annual conventions, but no one had drawn them more closely into the national fabric. Moreover, not all Jewish center workers were members and participants. Many did not understand what the organization was doing for them, even though they benefitted from all the improvements in standards and salaries that the national organization fought for. If you were not an executive, and the annual conference was distant from your city, the chances of your attending were nil, unless you were prepared to pay your own expenses. Lower-echelon personnel were not sure that the organization was fighting hard enough to improve their salaries, fringe benefits, and pensions, nor to ensure paid conference expenses.

Over the next two years, I arranged visits to New England, New York, and the midatlantic states, the southern states, and the midwest (I never got to the far west), and spent several days with my colleagues dealing with the problems that concerned them most. This led to the enrollment of many more members and greater interest in the association's activities.

It was my view that the annual conference in 1948 should be different than the conventional formula. There should no longer be a presentation of a miscellany of papers on specialized themes, often inspired only by the author's vigor in getting on the program, nor should we have several commentators on these papers plus a chairman and a recorder as political handouts or to swell attendance. While the formula worked, many complained that the papers were dull or that *they* should have been invited to read one instead of the selectee. I urged that the entire conference be devoted to a single, circumscribed theme. In that way, those who attended, would obtain a thorough grounding in a universal subject that they could more easily translate for their membership when they returned to their respective communities.

The whole concept was radically different. It took me almost two years to persuade the officers and the program committee to experiment with this approach. I called it a "college course in five days." The association finally agreed to devote itself during my last year in office to the subject of Jewish Youth, with three subtopics that we believed to be of the greatest importance and interest—Recreation, Sex, and Judaism. Task forces were set up, detailed manuals were prepared summarizing the problems confronting Jewish youth and how the center might contribute toward their resolution. Bibliographies were assembled. Machinery was set up to make the presentations through plenums and workshops. Books were brought to the conference, so that conferees could add to their store of knowledge. The publication of the Alfred C. Kinsey's *Sexual Behavior in the Human Male* (1948) added zest to the program.

But the conference was not a success. While the few colleagues who took the trouble to read everything got something out of the experience, most of the people who came to the conference wanted to relax, not study. Too few even read the well-prepared manuals, and even fewer borrowed from the shelf of books. Hence their contributions in the workshops were a recitation of what they already knew, rather than an effort to shake and disturb well-entrenched notions and sterile programs, and to think in a different way. There was little conceptualization of the theme. Thus there was little immediate impact, but in the course of years, as the ideas raised at this conference were implemented by enterprising center workers, they finally came to realize and understand the dimensions of the new program concept. It was years ahead of its time both as a method and as subject matter.

One unhappy revelation about workers in the general social welfare field was that most are not readers of solid works. If they read anything at all, it is the fugitive articles that are printed in professional journals. Workers like few demands to be made upon them intellectually. If they have to learn something more, they prefer a short course with experts and teachers whom they like, where they take notes and do not have to read texts in the long bibliographies. Even when they take such courses, they want, sometimes demand, that their agencies pay for the tuition and give them time off.

This is as true for Jews as for others, even though we are supposed to be the "People of the Book." I repeatedly had the same experience as an instructor at several undergraduate and graduate schools. Part of this was due to the students' educational backgrounds, for very often reading was not stressed or tested. This is especially true of students who majored in a social science. Those with a humanities undergraduate degree usually were forced to read a great deal of literature, history, and philosophy, where books instead of excerpted pieces were assigned. This perforce developed reading habits, which ultimately stood them in better stead. With the advent of TV, and of digest literature after the 1940s, the reading problem was further exacerbated. In the 1980s it is still a major problem in the public schools as well as the universities.

My term of office wound to its end in 1948 in Atlantic City, just as the State of Israel was being established. In the euphoria of the moment, my final message to the membership was titled "Birth of a State—A Presidential Message." Whereas my address in 1947, in which I dealt with the uncertain future of the Jews, had been described by one of my colleagues, in both compliment and criticism, as "lyrical pessimism," this one was subsequently referred to by another colleague "as one of the most inspiring messages he had ever heard." Since one of the other speakers at the 1948 convention was the outstanding orator Abba Eban, I felt quite elated by this colleague's evaluation.

Leaving Bronx House

I am still not sure whether some outside force propelled me from Bronx House to Federation, or whether this dramatic move in my career resulted from some initiative on my part. In any case, during my eleven years at Bronx House, I had achieved everything on my agenda. The agency had changed, had grown, and was serving an ever larger constituency through extension activities and the summer camp. Moreover, I had trained and inspired scores of professionals, had developed an amazing board of directors, and at the end was earning a salary that was one of the highest in the field.

In a sense there was nothing left for me to do at Bronx House. If I had been content to rest on my laurels and to simply superintend what I had built, I could have followed the example of many other directors of distinction, remaining with the same agency for my entire working life. Mary Simkovitch of Greenwich House and Helen Hall of the Henry Street Settlement come to mind. Both were already legends in their lifetime. Both invited me to speak about my views on how the settlement houses of the future might be fashioned. Jewish colleagues like Jack Nadel of the 92nd Street Y and Rabbi Alter F. Landesman of the Hebrew Educational Society were also content to spend their entire professional life in one setting. But this was not for me. I was restless and ready for a change.

As far back as 1940, when Richard W. Dammann was president of Bronx House, he told me, after attending his first budget conference at Federation, that Federation needed a consultant on centers, because neither Dr. Maurice B. Hexter, the executive vice-president, nor the budget director at the time, seemed to have more than a superficial appreciation of what really went on in an institution like Bronx House. The institutions were rarely visited. Federation relied almost entirely on written requests with accompanying financial data and a listing of services rendered. I suspected that it evaluated an agency more by the quality of its board of directors and perhaps its executive than by its program.

In 1945, as Federation was initiating its first postwar building-fund campaign, it decided to engage several consultants, one of them a center director and private camp owner, to compile material on what Federation's affiliated societies needed in the future. The center and camp consultant was Abraham W. Rosenthal, who left his post at the Bronx YM-YWHA after many years of service. The Bronx Y was six blocks east of Bronx House in what was still a large Jewish area of residence. Rosenthal worked with the Jewish Welfare Board, the centers, and the camps in assembling a report which was issued in 1948, just in time for the second building-fund drive. Unhappily, so far as earmarked support was concerned, the 1945 campaign was a failure for the centers and camps. This was not entirely Rosenthal's fault. Over the years the type of leaders that these institutions attracted were not people of great wealth, so the results were meager. The report recommended too little for centers and camps, did not make their services seem dramatic enough to compete with hospitals, child care, and the aged, and it totally ignored future population trends, which made many sections of the presentation obsolete before it was printed. In the years when he served, Rosenthal neither succeeded in elevating centers and camps to the position that they eventually attained, nor did he endear himself to his colleagues and their boards of directors.

In 1948 several high-level volunteers and professionals in a few centers initiated a movement to convince Dr. Hexter that he needed a new, dynamic assistant, who could change the attitude of Federation about these low-image fields. Hexter, an imaginative, productive, and powerful executive with a distinguished history, had been with Federation since 1938, first as an assistant to the head of Federation and since 1942 as co-executive with Joseph Willen. Hexter felt, at least at that time, no need for any aides and at first resisted the badgering appeals. When he finally assented, not one but three "consultants" (note the term) were engaged to cover hospitals, family and children services, and centers-camps. Rosenthal was released from his post, because he had been engaged only for the building-fund study and not as a permanent member of the staff. I was later accused of having been responsible for his termination, but I had nothing to do with it and tried in later years to get him a pension for his years of service—not out of guilt, but as an act of justice for a fellow worker. Rosenthal had alienated most of the center professionals and presidents by submitting a proposal that all the centers be merged into a single agency, so that each of the centers, now pristinely independent, would become merely a branch operation. This idea had actually arisen among a few top leaders in Federation, and when I came to Federation, I was instructed to carry it out. I resisted. Although I went through some of the motions, I never translated the proposal into reality.

A small group of lay and professional people approached Hexter. They told him that he must hire a consultant, and that their unanimous choice was Graenum Berger.

Hexter interviewed me several times. Despite my capacity for almost total recall, I do not remember very much of what we talked about. I do not recall any discussion of what I thought the field should look like in the future. I do not recall any listing of what my duties were to be. Yet I was one of those executives who always thought about the future; I had definite ideas in which direction I should move, and had come prepared in my mind, if not on paper, with the course we should pursue and how my duties would bring it about. He was still trying to decide whether he wanted a potentially volatile person as one of his assistants, for I am sure that he did not want to disrupt the tranquility of his office. I do recall his telling me in no uncertain terms at each of the interviews that if I worked at Federation, "there was only one boss." The last time he made that comment, I calmly replied that I thought the opening was for a consultant and not for his position. He accepted my response in good spirit. We agreed on a starting date. I preferred a higher initial salary, but finally accepted $13,000. I subsequently received a letter with few details addressed to "Mr. Graenum Berger." During the years that we worked together, he always addressed me (and my other colleagues), whether at Federation or in any informal setting, as mister. It was not until he retired from Federation that we spoke to each other on a first-name basis. He was indeed the "boss."

7

I Go to Germany and Europe

IN THE SPRING of 1949, I was visited by two tall, interesting women, Katherine Taylor, daughter of Graham Taylor, the founder of Chicago Commons, the rival to Hull House, and director of the well-known Shady Hill School in Cambridge, Massachusetts, and Helen Fogg, a professional on the staff of the Unitarian Service Committee. They asked me to be a member of an American team that would go to Germany and educate a large number of German social workers and educators who had either been driven out of Germany during the Hitler regime or had been forced underground, so that they had not been exposed to current social work and educational thinking and practice for a long period. My first reaction was to say *no*. I hated Germany for what it had done to the Jews and the world, and therefore had no wish to visit it in any capacity. I felt that trying to educate German social workers in a brief summer institute would be futile. They wanted me to teach group and settlement house work, along with American folk music and dancing. I further protested that as a Jew I would be looked upon with suspicion. I would find it difficult to develop a relationship with the *teilnehmer* (students). The two women were not persuaded by any of my arguments and asked me to think it over for a few days. They wanted me.

The more I thought it over, the more attractive the opportunity became. I had never been abroad. That alone was alluring. Perhaps I could learn more about the mentality of a people that had so completely succumbed to the Hitlerian mania. I might even be influential, precisely because I was a Jew. There was no salary. The Service Committee would provide all expenses for travel and room and board, plus $150 for incidentals. Not very much, to say the least. Emma and I talked about it, and while I could not take Michael and her with me, maybe I could arrange to meet them for a holiday in England and France during two recesses.

When the women came to see me for a second time, I succumbed and became part of a nine-member team of Americans for an educational child care institute sponsored and paid for by the American Unitarian Service Committee in cooperation with the Arbeiter Wohlfart, a labor-socialist welfare organization in Germany. The detailed report, on this institute, published in 1949, is still worth reading.

Since I was resigning from Bronx House and wouldn't start at Federation until mid-September, there was no problem of leave. While I had taken one semester of German in college and could read German and even the script with halting difficulty, I was relying on my Yiddish to carry me through. To practice German, I spoke to one of my pre-school teachers at Bronx House in German each day. She was a refugee from Deutschland. In addition, I attended German-speaking movies in Yorkville on East 86th Street in Manhattan, at least once a week, to get used to at least hearing German spoken. I was advised that my lectures would be given in English and a suitable translator would be available at all sessions to translate difficult words and phrases.

Our team—consisting of a psychologist, five teachers, two social workers, and the director—flew on a propeller plane via Gander in Newfoundland, a primitive halfway outpost used for refueling on transatlantic flights. Our first European stop was in Prestwick, Scotland, where we had our first taste of British food under the stringencies of rationing. The restaurant meal consisted of a tiny, stringy piece of tough beef, three kinds of potatoes, brussels sprouts, and tea, all served by a headwaiter in a swallow-tail suit, a subsidiary waiter in a tuxedo, and three waitresses dressed in starched black-and-white garments, all appropriate to the trade, but in marked contrast to the spartan diet.

We then flew to Frankfurt, which had not yet been reconstructed after the bombardment suffered during the war. I was put up overnight in an apartment which I approached by walking on wide boards covering the rubble from the front part of the building, which had been destroyed. It was intact in the rear. The kind landlady provided tea and toast before I went to bed, the teapot covered with a well-worn cozy. We had little time to see Frankfurt, but one got the quick impression that it had been a beautiful city with handsome buildings, wide boulevards, and many parks. Next we flew north to Bremen, a city which had suffered almost total destruction, with debris still piled high in areas that had been only partially cleaned up.

I will always remember the reception given to us by the burgomeister at the Rathaus the first evening, where we were to meet with the seven

German members of the team to discuss our joint program. We were greeted by the Bremen City Council, composed of a number of men and women sitting in a huge, ornate hall at round tables, which were covered with fine linen, with a service of gold plate, sterling silver, and innumerable cut-glass goblets. Since the government was socialist, I asked my partners on the right and left why the councillors were putting on such an extravagant party in a country and city still gripped by extreme scarcities and rationing. The reply that I received—not wholly unexpected, because I had always been aware that the party in power always benefited from the spoils of victory—was: "There is nothing too good for the working-class leaders." We were not quite prepared for the pageantry of ten waiters walking in with their black patent-leather slippers, white hose, black knee breeches, white blouses, and red waistcoats, at first carrying large flagons of wine, then repeatedly returning with soup, meat, vegetables, dessert, and coffee throughout the long evening. It was quite an introduction to postwar Germany.

We then traveled to our eventual destination by bus through the Rhineland to Hesse, everywhere seeing evidence of destruction by the Allied Armies. On July 5, we reached Voehl, a beautiful countryside village, and drove up the hill to a two-story building that had been built as a labor barracks by the Nazis. After the war, it had served as a shelter for DP children, and part of it was now being used as a conference center. A large camp for children had been erected behind the center. Some of the signs and symbols from the Nazi period had not yet been removed.

Four of us could not be accommodated at the main center, where meals and classes were held, so we were billeted in a *gasthaus*, the Stiegmuehle, down the hill about a quarter of a mile away. It was a charming old stone house with a brook running by from which we brought up pails of water each day for washing and toileting. It was run by a widow named Hagenfeld, whose aviator husband had been killed during the war. She had three daughters and an elderly father who had once been superintendent of the district schools. Summer boarders also occupied rooms in the house. I had a room to myself and enjoyed this privacy. I was able to provide my landlady with precious items, hard to get, such as coffee, cocoa, chocolates, and other luxuries, because we enjoyed U.S. Army PX privileges. She went out of her way to see that I was well fed at supplementary dinners in her home, where she served goose, wild mushrooms (which I helped her pick), home-baked cakes, and real coffee, since the food at the main center left much to be desired. I never knew there were so many ways to prepare potatoes, or the various ways of serving raw and cooked cabbage, along with tiny slices of meat, poultry, and occasionally eggs. The chauffeur for the institute took a liking to me. After hours, (the programs began at 7 a.m. with exercises and ending at 9 p.m. with singing and dancing), he would take me to butcher friends of his for some fresh liver or steak, always washed down with good German wine or beer.

The program consisted of three three-week seminars, each enrolling thirty students. The age range was from twenty to fifty, although most were in their twenties and thirties. It was difficult for me to believe that the participants had not been part of the Nazi structure, and subsequent questioning revealed that some had been members of the Hitler Youth. Contrary to what I had been told when recruited, most of them had not gone underground or fled the country, nor were they necessarily in conflict with the Nazi ideology and regime. They were not all innocents.

I lectured each day on group work and settlement house practices. Initially, I started my talks in English, but the translations were so long and tedious that the class preferred to listen to me in ungrammatical German, with the translator correcting some of my humorous lapses. I made it clear that I was a Jew, so that they were fully aware of my identity, although in the several seminars some of the students asked whether I or my family came from Hamburg, because of the peculiarities of my accent.

The institute was uniformly successful. All the Americans, and even the German instructors, presented material that was brand-new, such as psychology and psychoanalysis, which had been "banned" under the Nazis. An effort was made in 1984 to indicate that psychotherapy was not eradicated in Germany during Hitler's regime (Geoffrey Cocks, *Psychotherapy in the Third Reich*), but this was a rationalization. All Jews were eliminated from the German General Medical Society for Psychotherapy, directed by a cousin of Herman Goering. One could discuss Freud, if his name was not mentioned and his classical terminology omitted. Yet the society served the regime without reservations, and the psychiatric profession participated in the murder of 200,000 persons through the mental-patient euthanasia project. Even if psychiatric services of some sort were maintained during the Nazi regime, in 1949 thorough exposure to at least an American point of view was still essential.

The material we presented came as a refreshing stimulant, for the Germans, if given material and direction, were, as a group, good and earnest students. They liked our informality and responded to our urging them to react. None of us put on any formal professional airs. Since we ate with them, played games, danced, and sang with them, we were, without exception, well liked. Some students sought me out for more data and books, and at times revealed a little bit more about themselves. At the end of each seminar, there was a final party, a bit better food, speeches, and tearful goodbyes.

Two episodes are worth reporting. One night, Edward T. Ladd, who taught at Yale University, and I decided to invite anyone who wanted to attend a meeting devoted to the Hitler period. Nearly everyone showed up. We had a large blackboard on which we had written in separate columns: "What was *Good* about the Nazis?" and "What was *Bad* about the Nazis?" We thought that this would be the best way to get their views as a basis for discussion.

There was an amazing rush to fill up the blackboard on the first question. In rapid succession they listed "Restored pride to the German People," "Built superhighways," "Built the Volkswagen," "Provided employment for everyone," "Paid and longer vacations," "Made the Germans physically strong and courageous," "Stressed comradeship," "Pride of the Race," "Stressed discipline and obedience," "Restored our military power," "Wiped out the memory of the defeat in World War I." There was no room left to chalk in other favorable phrases.

Then Ladd, who spoke German fluently, turned to the other column, "What was Bad?" A young woman blurted out, "We lost the war!" No one challenged her. No one added anything about the savagery, the racism, the madness of the period, the death camps or the Jews. Ladd and I felt that there was no point in going on that evening, and the session came to an end. William A. Shirer, the author of important books on Germany before and during World War II, in a letter to the editor of the *New York Times* (Feb. 18, 1985), wrote: "Their chief complaint was not that their Fuhrer had imposed on them a mindless tyranny and on the conquered Europe a savage barbarism, or even that he had started a murderous war of naked conquest, but that he had *Lost* [emphasis added] it and that it had left their land utterly ruined and occupied by foreign troops." They "*Lost*" it. Later that night and for the duration of that seminar, individuals would come up to me to confess that they had been Nazis, that they had been caught in a no-win situation, that they had never heard about the death camps nor the persecution and execution of the Jews, that they were unhappy about the past—and some even told me that Germany would have to make amends for many years. But I did not get this view collectively. In the main, the subject was taboo, to be avoided as too painful.

At my *gasthaus*, there was a boarder, a man in his sixties, elegant in manner. Though his clothes were well worn, they were pressed. His shirts were starched. He usually wore a jaunty gray felt hat. As I talked with him on several occasions, I learned that he had been a concert pianist, but since the war had been unable to resume his career. Life in this bucolic village, where every farmer stacked his animal manure, a sign of wealth, in the front yard, was hardly exciting. I asked him whether he would play for us, and he agreed after much coaxing, provided I could find a grand piano. I spoke to our landlady, and she located one in the home of the new principal of the school. A concert was arranged. Apart from Dr. Clemens E. Benda, the psychologist on our team, and our landlady, I asked no one else. The principal invited the burgomeister, the village druggist, and their wives. With our pianist, we constituted a small group of ten.

He played the first piece, and it was evident that this man was an accomplished artist. There was an intermission, during which the first round of coffee and cake were served. When I audaciously raised the question of how a group of people like those sitting at this concert could have accepted a leader like Hitler, the pianist, who was still sitting on the bench, turned and pressed down thunderous chords. "No politics. I want no discussion of politics." As a courtesy, I said nothing further at this point.

He resumed playing a second piece of moving music, further demonstrating his talent. When he was done, he lit a cigarette and moved to a chair, so that he could enjoy a cup of coffee. I apologized for bringing up the subject again, but I reminded the artist that music and politics do mix, and that the U.S. government had, a few months earlier, refused to admit Gieseking, the great German pianist, because of his association with the Nazi regime. The pianist did not answer. Others did. One said that the U.S. did not realize that the true enemy of civilization was Soviet Russia and not Germany and that someday we would understand the error of our actions during the last war. I commented that this was not the burden of my question. "How could an enlightened, scientific, educated German people accept the rapaciousness of a leader who brought them utter defeat?"

This time the answer was not by diversion, but was self-abasing. "We were not responsible for Hitler. We had no power. We were little people."

He played once again. There was no further political discussion. I had heard everything I expected to hear. We thanked our hosts and left. Later I heard from our landlady that the pianist was in disgrace in contemporary Germany, because he had played for Hitler.

* * *

It was a cold and rainy summer. Yet the area was beautiful, and when the weather was salubrious, we took long walks in the woods to see the Edersee, a huge artificial lake. The forests were immaculate, almost as if they had been swept clean. If a tree had to be cut down, it was cut up and neatly piled for the park tenders to dispose of and another tree was planted to replace it. This general sense of orderliness and cleanliness I found wherever I traveled in Germany. Occasionally, we rode into Marburg, a solemn, high-walled university town, where the Army PX was situated. This was also where I caught the train for Frankfurt.

During the third seminar, I was asked to do some work for the U.S. Cultural Centers that were being established in various German cities to point up the virtues of the Americans who had so soundly trounced them during the war. I visited Fritzlar, Hanover, and Luneberg. Accompanied by a young American as the driver of our Volkswagen, we set off for Fritzlar. During the war it had been a large municipality of several hundred thousand people, and its factories had turned out tanks and other equipment for the military. Not a building was standing. Everything had been leveled by the Allied bombings. We stayed overnight in a hostelry built by the Nazis under the railroad station (*Bahnhof*). We descended by elevator to subterranean levels. Our bedroom was livable until midnight, when the air conditioners were shut off. We soon began to feel clammy and eerie. About 3 a.m., in an almost suffocating atmosphere, for we had exhausted all the oxygen, we dressed and spent the rest of the night in the *Bahnhof* restaurant, after walking up many flights of stairs.

In the morning, I went into the makeshift wooden shack that served as a barbershop for a shave and massage. As he worked on me the barber prattled about the barbarity of the Allied saturation bombing of the city, which was so intense that those who sought sanctuary in their cellar shelters were either burned or boiled to death by the fires that consumed the city. I made no comment, for with a razor in his hand, I was not in a mood to be challenging or provocative.

In Hanover, we had a sumptuous dinner with superb Moselle wine. We dined with Lotte Lemke, who was the liaison leader between the German organization and our institute. A middle-aged woman, bright and articulate, she spoke with directness and firmness. She had been a refugee from Germany during the Hitler period and had returned after the war to provide leadership in welfare and education, two of her specialties. A year later she visited us in Pelham and we reminisced about the 1949 seminars, which had initiated a number of changes in German welfare practices and programs.

In Hanover, I was asked to visit a refugee center, where escapees from East Germany were being housed. Most were young people, men. I suggested some activities that might improve the existing, limited program. I was also taken to a Salvation Army (*Heilige Armee*) shelter to meet girls who had become prostitues, whom the Army was trying to rehabilitate. They asked me what we were doing in the States for prostitutes. There I was not helpful. Our American record on this score was a dismal one. We take them to court, lock them up for a night, fine them, release them. The cycle is repeated over and over again.

We then drove to Luneburg, a quaint old tenth-century German city with a distinctive architectural style. The extraordinary *Rathaus* had superb stained-glass windows portraying famous warriors, among them David and Judah Maccabee. On bicycles we rode out into the heather fields, which were then in full bloom, and observed the crowds of youth and families getting the same pleasure out of picnicking in the woods as all of us do elsewhere in the world. On my return to Voehl I wrote a report for the government.

German government officials and leaders in the welfare field visited the institute, and we had interesting exchanges with them. They invited us to stay longer and implement our suggestions. Several did stay, and others returned in future years to staff the courses offered.

At a final banquet in Frankfurt for all the institute leaders and the officials involved in our work, we summarized our experiences. I indicated that I had come to Germany very skeptical about the possibilities of changing the German people and their institutions. But I had learned from my exposure, and felt that if Germany followed the educational and social welfare principles we enunciated under a democratic aegis, it would in time be restored to the community of civilized nations. I indicated that Germany would have to prove itself over and over again. I still think that is true thirty-five years afterwards. My remarks aroused no comment.

The interpretation of the settlement house that Miss Taylor and I presented had concrete results: similar institutions were established throughout Germany under the multi-syllabic term *Nachbarschaftheim* ("neighborhood house"). My individual contribution was to introduce the words *Grupen Arbeit* ("group work") into the vocabulary of the German social work profession.

One humorous incident occurred during one of my lectures on the financing of social welfare agencies. I had referred to government tax funding (*steuergelt*), but I couldn't think of a German word for private donations, and the word that slipped out of my mouth was *Gift*. First there was a look of consternation on my listeners' faces, and then I quickly remembered that *Gift* meant "poison" in German. I laughed and told them that we didn't have to poison Americans to force their donations or write their wills in favor of charities.

While I had given of myself completely, my visit to Germany was in turn a rewarding experience. I found the Germans individually like people elsewhere. While I was convinced that Nazism had by no means been completely extirpated from the German mind and polity, yet if given the continued stimulation of democratic forces, changes could be made in their way of life. They were genuinely courteous, amazingly well informed, and their young people much more broadly educated than those in the States. Adult professionals whom I met spoke with expertise and authority on many subjects beyond their field of employment. They had considerable knowledge of music and the arts. The reputation that Germany had built up before the Hitler epoch of being well-educated, scientific, cultured, artistic had not evaporated. But I was puzzled then, and am to this day, as to how a whole people could have succumbed to the Nazi incubus.

Thus I have never wanted to return to Germany as a tourist, to study or to lecture. I have never bought a German automobile. I have never bought a bottle of German wine. So in the last analysis, I am continuing, in a sense, to "boycott" Germany, and I can never forgive its destruction of six million Jews.

* * *

While my colleagues used the intervals between seminars to see other parts of Germany, I took leave to go to London for one period and to Paris for the second break to be with Emma and Michael.

When the decision was made for me to go to Germany, the question arose how would Emma spend the time during my long absence, since spouses, unless involved professionally in the institute, were not allowed to accompany them. After some persuasion she agreed to go to England and France with Michael, although she was fearful of undertaking a voyage to strange lands on her own.

* * *

Ramon

Ramon didn't want to go at all. Almost twenty now, he was finishing up his second year at New York University, after having studied during his first year at Mohawk College in Utica.

In 1946, when Ramon was seventeen years old, he was emotionally moved by the struggle of the Jews of Palestine to create an independent, albeit partitioned state. He had learned a great deal about the Palestinian situation at home. The papers were full of the subject. So was the radio. It was ever a topic of conversation amongst his friends. While he was not a martial person—in fact I would have to describe him as being pacific—nonetheless the battle for Jewish freedom and statehood moved him. He came to us with an overwhelming, unexpected suggestion that he be allowed to go to Palestine and fight with the Haganah. None of his friends had any such plans. His dramatic proposal took us wholly unaware. In one sense we were inwardly proud that we had raised a courageous Jewish son, who was prepared to make such a sacrifice. At the same time we were not ready to lose him. The matter was churned without heat for some months, after which he decided not to pursue it further.

He had become interested in an attractive young woman and in an adventurous moment became engaged. If we thought he was not ready to go to far away Palestine, we were even more protective about his leaving home and getting married. I presume both gestures were an effort to break away from the "tyranny" of his parents' household. The engagement was undertaken, notwithstanding our ineffective protests. He accused us of a double standard: "You both were not much older when you eloped and married." The engagement did not last too long, since the young lady wanted to get married without delay. He said no. We were happy.

He had to wait until he went off to college in 1947 before separation from his parents, if you can call it that, fully took place. His sterling qualities always were manifested in his desire to be independent. He always worked, so that he would not have to be completely dependent on us for his personal expenses. I was earning by the social work standards of the day, a good salary, and we were catching up with our debts and for the first time trying to furnish an attractive home. There were no reserves. When he went to college, we paid for his tuition, room, and board, and gave him a small allowance of $50 per month. Emma would send packages with food and in her letters she included a $5 or $10 bill. She would always get the money back with a note that he didn't need it.

Ramon was never garrulous, at least to his parents. We had to initiate the conversations and press for information. This was a pattern all of his life. Yet on rare occasions there were good exchanges. We frequently drove up together to Camp Bronx House, where he helped with all kinds of chores. Many years later, he told me that he remembered "the cold, crisp sunny days and the serenity of small towns" (Millerton, Pine Plains, Copake). "I liked the people you met with, the Kaufmans at the drug store, the folks at the Holsapple House, the Rockefellers and their ice cream parlor and the town gossip—the barber," he once wrote. Another time he told me about a small restaurant in Pine Plains, New York, something which he always looked forward to on our trips to camp. I remembered it for its wholesome but undistinguished cooking. He recalled specifically the juicy hamburgers and the thick, sweet apple pie. "Those were fun years."

While Ramon spent an interesting year at Mohawk, the school closed, and as a result, he had to make a change. Eager to be in New York, a city which he had already come to love, he enrolled at NYU and pursued a program in industrial arts. When he was five years old, we bought him a real carpenter table and tools for his birthday, so that as a child he had developed good skills with these instruments and materials. He not only did good carpentry, but gradually extended his talents to mechanical things and could build, take apart, and fix a radio and most other electrical appliances. It was not surprising that he turned to this field with a possible career in teaching.

At Mohawk he had become active on the campus. Coming from a liberal tradition, he became involved with a group concerned with political issues. The group was dominated by "progressives," not uncommon on and off the campus, and they decided that Ramon should be their representative at a meeting in Buffalo, where vital national and international political topics were being considered. Ramon had written me about the group and the causes it espoused, and wondered whether he should accept the assignment to represent them. The group was supporting Henry A. Wallace in the 1948 presidential election, and opposed Harry Truman because he had dropped the A-bomb. They were exposed constantly to Communist Party speakers.

I wrote him a long letter about radical groups, indicating how they had always tried to exploit me, and how they were ever on the alert to find earnest innocents and get them more deeply enmeshed in their movements. I wrote that if he firmly believed in these intriguing concerns, then there was no reason for him to refuse the tender. But he should be aware that his name would be publicized, and that he would thereafter be identified as a radical by the university, and perhaps even by the government, through the FBI, which was always penetrating radical groups to determine their membership. I questioned whether he would profit personally from such an association. I wrote that if he wanted to have his fling with radicalism, now was the time, because it is only youth that has the courage, the idealism, and the adventurism, and he might someday regret it if he turned down this opportunity. He didn't go.

Instead of accompanying Emma to Europe, Ramon wanted to work in the summer of 1949. He had been offered a good supervisory job at Camp Bronx House, which he had been attending since 1940, first as a camper and then as a counselor, and now he saw an opportunity to develop administrative skills, planning programs for larger units and the whole camp. Later he took a master's in camping and counseling at the university and made camping his first professional career. His decision to go to Bronx House bore a new romantic contact. He met attractive, intelligent Anita Fink, and within two years they were married.

Emma and Michael—Europe

In planning Emma and Michael's trip to Europe, I wrote to my brother Sam, who was the labor attaché with the U.S. Embassy in London. Sam was enthusiastic about their coming. Margaret and he were very fond of both of them. They sailed from New York on the S.S. *Washington,* a luxury liner that had been a troopship during the war, sharing a cabin. (Since the ship had not yet been completely reconverted for the civilian passenger trade, on the return voyage, when I joined them, males and females were separated.) Michael roamed the ship freely, and made some money playing "horse racing." When he reached London, eager to spend his winnings, he wanted to buy an old firearm. Aunt Margaret took him to an antique shop, where he acquired his first "lethal" weapon, a nineteenth-century cap-and-ball single-shot pistol. Later he accumulated other old guns. He haunted gun and antique shops, often buying pieces that he completely restored to usable condition.

As an aside, I must tell this story. A few years later, when Michael was not doing well in a junior high school, I went to see the teacher. She said that he did not write very well and wondered whether his home environment provided him with the proper literary objects and stimulation. I told the startled teacher that his room was filled with books, as was our whole house, that he was a constant reader, that I was a writer, teacher, social worker, and administrator, and that the ambience of the home in which Michael lived was highly cultured with a stream of interesting visitors. Furthermore, holding her silent attention, I informed her that Michael had been exposed to the theater, ballet, museums, and assorted cultural institutions both in this country and abroad.

Emma and I decided that perhaps Michael needed counseling, and we arranged for a meeting with an outstanding adolescent psychiatrist with whom I had some institutional contacts. The psychiatrist asked us to remain in the room while he conducted his first interview. He was short, sharp, and provocative, but in resistant Michael he met his match. Michael had protested all the way to the office that he was O.K. and didn't need an outsider's help. After a few perfunctory questions about his age and year in school, the psychiatrist asked Michael if he had any hobbies. Michael replied curtly that he collected guns. The psychiatrist then shot this question: "Why? Do you want to shoot your father?" Michael rose from his chair, and shouted back, "That's a stupid question," and left the room. That was the end of his psychiatric consultations. The doctor was provoking and stupid, hardly the shock question technique to use before he even knew the first thing about Michael. I don't know whether Michael ever thought of shooting his father or whether I was the cause of his problems, but as the years went by, our relations continually improved, especially after he grew up, married, had children, and served in the army. Eventually Michael became a colonel in the reserve, with tremendous responsiblities, as well as a top civil servant in Washington. Contrary to what his junior high teacher probably expected, he also began to write extensively on military history and other subjects, and was paid for a chapter he wrote in a book published by the City University of New York.

* * *

When Emma and Michael disembarked at Southampton, Sam and Margaret met them. Their bags were handled with dispatch, diplomatic courtesy, and immunity. Sam's first remark after kissing Emma was to say: "Little Emma from Clinton Street, Albany, finally arrived." To which Emma replied "Little Sam from Washburn Street, Gloversville, also made it." The exchange was related to their humble origins and the not very prepossessing streets where each had lived in earlier days. The whole party traveled by car to London, where Sam had found a pleasant apartment.

While awaiting my arrival, Emma and Michael saw a good deal of London, which was still living under rationing and food coupons, not yet recovered from the devastating effects of the war. Michael, although only nine years old, was able to negotiate the two-tier buses and the Underground system, traveling alone (with his name, address, and telephone number attached to his shirt), spending time at Madam Tussaud's wax gallery and rowing in St. James's Park.

* * *

I left Voehl with Strauss, the chauffeur, who drove me to Marburg, where I caught the only available train, sitting in a third-class seat in a pig-sty coach to Frankfurt. I strolled around that city, tasted pastries, had a shave and haircut in a PX barbershop, dropped into a movie, and then flew to London, where Emma and Michael picked me up in an embassy car and then drove to 19 Salisbury Place, our apartment. Sam and Margaret were up north attending a miner's convention. On our own we visited Petticoat Lane, the Bernard Baron Settlement House in the Jewish ghetto, and Toynbee House, the first and most famous settlement house. We toured London to witness where the ravages of the German bombs had burned out large sections.

On their return Sam and Margaret arranged a round of entertainment. One night we dined with Irving Brown, the AFL representative in Europe. (In 1984, he presented the annual memorial lecture for Sam at Georgetown University and publicly recalled our meeting him in London.) We spent the better part of a day in Parliament and heard Clement Atlee, the prime minister, debate an iron-and-steel bill. Atlee, thin, short, and wizened, had his feet on the table in front of him and jumped up from time to time to answer some challenging or nasty question from the opposition. He later walked out with Anthony Eden, both bowing out before their colleagues. We then met and lunched with Hector and Sheila McNeil, he a member of Parliament, eating egg and cucumber sandwiches with tea, preceded of course by a drink. We toured an old section of London and ate fish and chips at the famous Prospect of Whitby Pub overlooking the Thames. One day we passed 10 Downing Street, the seat of power in the British world. Another afternoon we went to the international horse jumps, where amidst royalty and wealth the jumpers competed for the King George and Princess Elizabeth Cups. One night we had dinner with Sam Watson, white-haired, suspender-wearing Scotsman, head of the Durham miners and leader of the British Labour Party, a self-educated miner who had risen to the top.

Food was rationed, and as visitors we were entitled to coupons, but Sam had access to the American Army commissaries. Furthermore, he and Margaret were both extraordinary cooks, aided and abetted by their housekeeper, so for anyone dining in their home there were no shortages. Nor was there any absence of good food in some of the excellent restaurants like Cunningham's, where all the costly items in short supply were available.

We got a taste of England's socialized medical program when Michael needed an allergy injection and Emma required medication for a cold. The doctor's offices were like those anywhere else in the world.

One evening we went to the theater to see *The Beaux Stratagem,* a George Farquhar play that I had read at the University of Missouri along with the dramas of Congreve, Sheridan, and Goldsmith. The night was not complete until we had dined at the Hotel Savoy. We were served food, but since we were not dressed in tuxedoes and long gowns, we were not permitted to dance.

We visited the Tate Gallery and saw at firsthand the works of Blake, Reynolds, Hogarth, Constable, Turner, Sargent, Manet, Degas, Modigliani, Rouault, Breughel, Durer, Goya, and above all Rembrandt, some of which I had only seen on slides, when I was studying at the University of Missouri, or in book collections. We didn't miss the National Gallery or the British Museum.

One night, at the Royal Albert Hall, we heard Sir Malcolm Sargent conduct the music of Rachmaninoff, Sibelius, Brahms, and Respighi with an audience composed of royalty and others dressed in finery. Another night Sam and Margaret had an elaborate cocktail party for us. Among the guests were Hugh Gaitskill and Harold Wilson, both of whom later became prime ministers, and other members of Parliament, several enjoying high rank in the Cabinet. It was a stirring evening in that these gentlemen and their wives were content to sit on the floor, since the modest apartment did not have enough chairs to accommodate everyone. There was a great deal of inside story telling, friendly banter, and even serious discussion about England's future and America's role in world affairs.

We also picnicked in the Cheltenham Hills on the way to Oxford, where we walked through the gray-stone Tudor Gothic buildings with the well-worn interior woodwork and furniture, were told about the famous men who had studied in these chambers. We peered at the books in the Bodleian Library. On the way back along the Thames, we stopped at Henley, where the annual regattas took place, and then at the Hampden estate, where friends of Sam, the Noel Halls, were running a school for government and business administrators. Michael had a great day—swimming in the pool and playing with the dogs. The day culminated with an unusual dinner at the Fitzroy Club in Marlowe.

On Sunday morning we walked through Hyde Park and listened to the debate of a Catholic priest arguing for government support of parochial schools. On another stump, a Jewish ex-serviceman was haranguing his listeners about the inevitable recurrence of war and fascism.

I had a rough flight back to Frankfurt, especially over the Channel, caught a military train en route to Marburg, and finally returned to Voehl for my second institute exhausted, yet refreshed.

To France

Emma and Michael planned to spend the second month of the trip in France. We communicated with Judah and Ida Shapiro. Judah, a colleague and friend of many years, was now working for the American Jewish Joint Distribution Committee, an international Jewish welfare organization, with an office in Paris. The JDC, or Joint, had been created in 1917 to help Jews during and in the aftermath of World War I. Judah was part of a team reconstructing Jewish communities in Europe, some of which had been completely eliminated. The Shapiros found a small, inexpensive hotel, Mont Fleury, 21 Grande Armée, a block from the Arc de Triomphe, where Emma and Michael were living when I arrived in Paris to join them.

I left Voehl during my second break by taking a train at Herzhausen, which literally crawled to Marburg, riding through attractive farmlands, woods, and small towns with the distinctive big clock, always giving the correct time, at each station. The people on the train were poorly yet neatly dressed. Through the windows I could see men and women working in the fields, hand raking and plowing with animals for the coming harvest. I luckily found a seat on another military train to Frankfurt, where the food was good and cost very little. Dinner was only 40 cents. Every American soldier I talked with disliked the German tour of duty and wanted to return home.

In Frankfurt I was ticketed on a night train to Paris. A partly drunk young American woman was ushered into my compartment with friends, who were bidding her farewell. I thought it strange that they were mixing sexes, but since I found that sex was easy and free in Germany, perhaps this was it. *C'est la guerre.* It turned out that her ticket was for the following night, so I was deprived of her potentially enjoyable company.

My firm companion was a Czech, who came in with a huge valise, which he said was filled with German cameras. At the border, guards came in to search our compartment, and the last I saw of him he was seemingly under arrest, his oversize bag confiscated. The police neither searched nor talked to me, but I was anxious nonetheless until they left. The conductor told me that my roommate was a notorious smuggler. Riding on night trains between Germany and France can be quite an adventure.

The rest of my ride to Paris was through the attractive French countryside. I could detect from the windows no sign of the impact of the war. Emma, Michael, and Judah Shapiro met me at the Gare de

L'Est, and a JDC station wagon carried us to our hotel through beautiful Paris. Our hotel was small. A quaint circular elevator lifted us to our two rooms, each with its separate bath and douche. Both rooms together cost $8 per night. The meals, some of which we ate at the hotel, were excellent and inexpensive. You could eat rather well for $1.50 per person.

We toured Paris, often on foot, other times by Metro, occasionally by taxi, so that we saw a great deal of Paris in ten days. The beauty of the city, its boulevards and parks, its attractive homes and public buildings, lived up to all that I had read and been told by earlier visitors. The Palais de Chaillot, the Eiffel Tower (we rode to the top, had lunch, and then Michael and I raced down the many flights of stairs), the Ecole Militaire were seen on the first day. We relieved ourselves in the convenient pissoirs.

My three years of high school and college French, despite my bad grades in this subject stood me in fairly good stead in reading signs and other instructions. I could even with some difficulty make out the daily newspapers. Yet I was tongue-tied in speech and could not understand more than a few words of what anyone was trying to tell me. They spoke too rapidly..

August was a holiday period for the French, so many shops and even restaurants were closed. One of the humorous remarks we heard in Paris was that Moses had given us Saturday off, Jesus had given us Sunday, and Léon Blum was trying to add Monday for a three-day holiday. Curiously, all three were Jews.

Another day was spent walking down the Champs-Élysées, visiting shops, being overwhelmed with the art in the Grand and Petit Palaises. We toured the Louvre with its exceptional collections, again recalling my studies at Missouri, only this time I saw the original Nike of Samothrace rather than the plaster cast which I had studied at the university museum. The Seine, crowded with boats, the Quais, Notre Dame, the Invalides. Our boat ride down the river passed the French version of the Statue of Liberty resting on the Allée des Cynes at Pont de Grenelle, finally turning back at the red-tiled roof tops of the beautiful suburb of Saint-Cloud. (In 1986, the statue in New York Harbor was rehabilitated and rededicated with pomp and ceremony.)

Our day at Versailles was memorable. After walking through the handsome but extravagant buildings and grounds, I still had to admire the imaginative King Louis XIV, for despite his arrogance, oppression of the poor, and ruthless treatment of his subjects, he was a builder of taste, beauty, and art for all time. It seems that talented dictators and exploiters have the gift to erect enduring monuments.

We spent still another day taking a picture of the Danton statue, recalling the bloody excesses of the French Revolution. Walking through the Cluny Museum we noted some of the pieces that dated back to the

Roman conquest. Then to the Pantheon, the Halles de Vin, the Jardin des Plantes, and the building where radium was discovered by the Curies. Michael liked the Vincennes Zoo.

One night we went to the Théâtre Marigny to see Roland Petit's Ballet de Paris and gaped as he danced with Renée Jean Marie, two stars who later became famous around the world. Elisabeth Bergner (who died in 1986 at age eighty-five), Lily Pons, and Andre Kostelanetz sat directly in front of us. We entered some of the luxurious shops for which Paris is so well known, but we did not buy—couldn't have afforded it.

While Michael easily found his way around Paris, through the Metro and interchanges, at times he needed us. While unaccompanied children could see the sexiest of films, they could not enter movie houses with films of violence unless they were accompanied by parents or adults. So we had to escort him to view *La Rivière Rouge (Red River)* in French with English subtitles, which we had seen in the States and would see for a third time in a theater in Shikoku, Japan, in 1962.

Michael repeatedly tried to get us to go to the Folies-Bergere, which was flamboyantly advertised all over Paris with the dancers kicking their feet, revealing their legs and underpants. He wondered whether the play was owned by someone in our family (Bergere). He was obviously intrigued by the sexiness of the ill-concealed nudity of the women dancers. Emma tried to put him off, saying that he had already seen naked women, in fact had seen her undressed, to which he offered his usual decisive and rapid reply: "Oh, it must be different."

We went to see an exhibit of Émile Antoine Bourdelle's sculpture and the paintings of David, Ingres, and Delacroix, all of whom were previously known to me. We bought books from the Bouqinistes des Quai, and a few antiques, such as a pair of old opera glasses that we still use in the theater, in the Village de Suisse, a junk market. We took Michael for an injection against hay fever in a French clinic. It was not as inexpensive or up to the standards of American and English medical offices.

We spent time with Carl and Genia Urbont. Carl had been a student of mine at the New York School of Social Work and now was a colleague, having headed up one of Federation's agencies in Manhattan. He would be spending several years in Paris working for the JDC and assisting Judah Shapiro. Both the Urbonts spoke French fluently and made excellent guides. We met other colleagues like Joseph Schwartz, Moses Beckelman, my predecessor in Bronx House, Philip Klein, Herman Stein, and Henry Selver, all exceptional social workers, and dozens of English, French, and Americans with whom we had pleasant conversations.

One day Michael and I rented bicycles and rode through the Longchamps woods.

I left Paris, like everyone else, in love with the city, its curious people, its attractively dressed women, its free and easy manners. It was an eyeful to see the boys and girls with their tiny string bikinis lying on the Quais overlooking the Seine.

After I left, Emma and Michael went on a tour of eastern France and Switzerland with the Shapiros. In the Alps, Michael forced Emma to accompany him on a ride over the mountains on an open swinging lift, a feat she never wanted to repeat. They spent the last weeks of their holiday in Trouville, where they rested up after a strenuous two months of vacationing.

After I completed the third seminar in Germany, I made my final farewells to my colleagues, took a series of trains back to Paris, and, having a few hours before my train left for Le Havre, I rushed to the Jeu de Paume galleries to see how Turner had influenced the Impressionists in the early nineteenth century, and the works of Lautrec, Van Gogh, Manet, Monet, Cézanne, Rousseau, Sisley, and Pissarro, all of whom I had missed on my earlier visit. I lunched with Judah Shapiro, who told me how difficult it was to rebuild the Jewish communities destroyed by the Germans. Some Jews had returned to Germany to reclaim their property and, despite the Holocaust, were remaining for the many business opportunities. At the same time Zionists were conducting campaigns everywhere to entice Jews to live in Israel.

I bought eight bottles of Grand Marnier cognac for a song. (They were all broken on board ship, so the Cunard Line had to reimburse me at American prices for the breakage.) I boarded the train to Le Havre, where I was reunited with Emma and Michael, walked up the steps to the S.S. *Washington* for our voyage back to New York. Michael and I were bedded in a room with two adult men. Emma slept in a room with three other women. The ship was not luxurious, but the food was good and plentiful. It was an uncomfortable sailing only for me. I was partly drugged with dramamine to relieve sea sickness. If someone had only told me to avoid too much liquids, the voyage might have been more pleasant. I ate less, walked the decks constantly, and read a book a day from the ship's library. I had been told by American doctors that I had a malady called otitis media, a problem in my middle ear, that induced *mal de mer*. It was years later, after a week of examinations in a hospital, that I learned that my middle ear was O.K., but that I had other complications that brought about vertigo.

We landed. Ramon met us with the car and brought us back to Parkchester with memories of a remarkahble summer that made us constant travelers ever after. Michael's comment as we sailed by the Statue of Liberty was that he was overjoyed to get back to the "good old U.S.A."

8

Federation

WHAT WERE NEW YORK, the United States, Israel, and the world like in 1949, when I reported for work at Federation? New York was undergoing shattering changes. Many old neighborhoods were disintegrating. Newcomers, mostly non-white, were moving into these abandoned sections of the city. Apart from developing new parts of the five boroughs, there was a steady exodus from the city to the suburbs. Nassau, Suffolk, Westchester, and Rockland counties were unprepared for the influx. This meant that synagogues, centers, and even hospitals in the old neighborhoods would be discontinued and rigorous planning for new facilities in the suburbs would have to be initiated. There was a vast change in the economic condition of Jewish families. With college opportunities available to most returning veterans, with new industries flourishing in TV, plastics, ceramics, aviation, and travel, new businesses developing or enlarging in real estate, construction, public relations, advertising, and the stock market, and cultural institutions flourishing, additional opportunities arose in abundance and new fortunes were being made by new people. Young people were not returning to the bosom of their families and neighborhoods and instead were scattering all over the country—with shattering effects on the nuclear family. Europe was about to begin its spectacular recovery from the war, with the victors aiding former enemies, largely through the Marshall Plan. Israel was accepting refugees from the Holocaust regions and from the Arab countries, where they were no longer welcome, which required massive financial assistance from the Western and American Jewish communities. It was a time for thinkers and planners to provide the kinds of facilities and services needed to meet the requirements of new places, new times, new populations in ever upward, optimistic, and aspiring communities. Money could be found for any idea. All went around with faith in the future.

Always an early riser, I took the elevated train from Parkchester to Grand Central, then walked across the business streets to 71 West 47th Street in Manhattan to start work at Federation. I was there at 8:30 A.M. The building was well known to me, because that was where I had attended the Graduate School of Social Work in 1930–32, and since then I had attended numerous meetings in its chambers. The block between Fifth and Sixth Avenues had not yet become the diamond and jewelry center of America. It had interesting shops, excellent restaurants, and an old book store for browsing. Rockefeller Center was a few blocks north. Broadway and its sparkling theatrical district was one block west. The 42nd Street library was a few blocks south.

My new office was a long, corridor-like room. It had not been painted for years. The office looked out on 47th Street, but it could hardly be seen, because no one had bothered to clean the windows. These neglected maintenance items were soon corrected with the first memo that I sent. A secretary was assigned to me later in the day.

I recall looking at my unused diary, turning the pages, and not finding an entry. I waited for several hours to see whether I would receive a call from the intramural offices upstairs or from the outside. When none came, I took the elevator to Dr. Hexter's office, said hello, reported that I'd had a good summer, and asked whether he had anything for me to do. He replied that it would all come in good time. I went back, started to make calls to friends and colleagues, and before the day was over my diary was filled for weeks.

When I arrived at Federation, I assumed that I had at least two duties. One was to organize separate functional committees for centers and camps. I would have to start with the appointment of several chairman. My other presumed duty was to provide professional staffing for the distribution committee's subcommittees on centers and on camps. I gave Dr. Hexter a list of suggested names for the functional committee chairmen, and they were soon officially appointed by the president of Federation, Ralph Samuels, an important, independent stockbroker, talkative, positive in his point of view, whom I had never met before. My candidate for the chairmanship of the functional committee on centers was Anne W. Langman, the president of Bronx House, with whom I had worked for years. Nan knew centers inside and out. While Hexter and Samuels assented to my recommendation, they warned me that she was a bit difficult to handle, even if her credentials were impeccable. While my relations with Nan had been extremely close all the years we were together at Bronx House, in my new assignment there was bound to be a different quality of tie, because she was not prepared to give the same time and energy to the committee as she had and would still offer to the

House. But with our usual cooperative efficiency, we called a meeting of the lay and professional representatives of all the centers, determined what interests the constituents had, and rapidly organized a number of subcommittees, which apart from the monthy meetings of the entire body, kept me busy.

The functional committee was essentially an advisory body to Federation's board and other overall committees. It had no power of its own. It could only study and recommend, exercising all the pressure that it could muster to see that recommendations were implemented. Programs that it evaluated included pre-school care, adolescent activities, adult education, senior citizen units, day camping. New facilities were in time translated into realities. We influenced the board to adopt programs that they had never heard of before. Over the years a number of strong chairmen helped to bring about many changes. Among these chairmen were Ben Touster, Leo E. Frenkel, Harold Levin, Robert Wolf, and Daniel Rose.

One of my functions was to define the respective jurisdictions of the Metropolitan Section Jewish Welfare Board, which in the main duplicated the constituency of the functional committee, plus a few centers that had not yet either applied or been admitted into the Federation family. The latter did not receive any central communal support. Numerous meetings were held between the two groups, but nothing actually materialized, since the various benefits being funded by Federation outweighed all the functions offered by the NJWB. In time its staff and program underwent attrition and the issue became moot. Federation continued to support the NJWB for the personnel, program, and other services rendered by that body. There was always consultation to avoid duplication, but it became clear that Federation's functional committee was the essential and influential body in planning for Greater New York.

In my first month I was called by Ralph Samuel, the president, to meet with Dr. Hexter and Joseph Willen, the two executive vice-presidents, and was told that high on Federation's agenda was the merger of all the centers. Under this plan there would be a central board, and each affiliate would constitute a branch. I had strongly opposed this move when I was the director of Bronx House. While I raised all the objections I could muster against the proposal, because of its size, the concentration of power, the reduction of flexibility and originality, the loss of interest on the part of staff and local boards, the possible reduction in financial support, it was not only evident that Federation's leadership thought the concept desirable in itself, but that only through centralization would money be attracted or allocated to this field. Centers had fared badly in the 1945 campaign, and the prospects for the future were only slightly better—and then only if this development took place. I told them I would put my mind to the subject and prepare a memorandum.

When I said there was a prospect of improvement in obtaining funds,

I had in mind the recently established "Free Fund," which siphoned off a percentage of all large gifts, including those earmarked for specific agencies. This fund would be distributed amongst the have-nots, whose priorities would be determined by Federation's building committee. I like to believe that the fund came into being as a result of my many discussions on the subject with Nan Langman while at Bronx House. Our discussions influenced her to take the matter up with her father, Maurice Wertheim, who had been appointed chairman of the 1949 campaign. I had an interesting meeting with him. Wertheim was a short, slight, brilliant man, whose brain was ticking away before you as you advanced a problem. When he presented the notion of a "Free Fund," it was fought by the big agencies and the big givers, but eventually fair-mindedness prevailed and the fund was established. In two building-fund campaigns, only $750,000 had been earmarked for the centers, and two-thirds of this sum had been committed to one institution. The question then was, how would the committee set up to evaluate Free Fund allocations arrive at a decision as to who would get the money? As the professional consultant for centers, I presented a case for three centers, none of which had received very many earmarked donations, and all of which had substantial needs. The Bronx YM-YWHA had to move to the Grand Concourse, because its own neighborhood had become non-Jewish, and those remaining could be served at Bronx House only five blocks away. The Concourse had a large Jewish population without any facilities. The East New York YM-YWHA had to move from its horrible rented quarters because of the encroachment of non-Jews on the area which it served, and locate farther east, where there was a large Jewish concentration. The Washington Heights YM-YWHA had been forced to give up its rented building to make way for the George Washington Bridge. I recommended that it move farther north and merge with the small Inwood YM-YWHA. After several tough, sharply debated meetings, $1,250,000 was finally set aside for these three institutions from the Free Fund.

While free funds and the earmarking of some of the money for these three facilities was a good start toward new buildings, the board of each institution had to raise at least one-third more to complete and furnish such structures. While there was some wealth on the Bronx and East New York boards, Washington Heights and Inwood were not as well circumstanced. It took the utmost pressure from Federation, at meetings in which I was principally involved, before this money was raised and the buildings were finally completed years later. I recall telling three men on one board, when Ben Touster, the chairman of the functional committee at the time, accompanied me to a luncheon, that unless the trio first donated $10,000 each, their project was dead. They were astounded by my effrontery, but eventually they gave such sums to fulfill the building program.

Forcing centers to move, after they had outlived their usefulness in a section of the city which they had served faithfully for many years, was another difficult problem. The Bronx Y would have preferred to leave behind a phasing-out operation, but since Federation thought this costly and unnecessary, it was forced to close down the original plant when it moved into the new one.

The surroundings of Bronx House changed radically after I left that post. Federation urged the agency to move to Pelham Parkway, where a large Jewish census was without any services. Federation, at my instigation, finally told Bronx House that unless it moved immediately, its appropriation would be cut off for the following year. This accomplished the ends we sought. While some old members would be temporarily deprived of activities, even those residents finally moved to new areas, where similar programs were being developed.

Another problem we had with some of our agencies then and even later was how to dispose of their structures. Some felt that the building should be given as a gift to a private or public group that wanted to continue services for the newcomers. It was my opinion, based largely on the experience of Council House in the Bronx, that a Jewish organization that turned its facility over to a nonsectarian group for nothing and even supported the program for some years thereafter earned no good will from either the agency or neighborhood beneficiaries. In fact, when the Council of Jewish Women decided to discontinue its support of Forest House, the new name for the enterprise, they were publicly accused of defaulting on their responsibility. No promises had ever been given for permanent contributions. I insisted on outright sale to a private agency or a long-term lease to a public one like the Board of Education or the Department of Welfare. Generally, when a public agency took over the property, it was well maintained and the program itself was usually well supported and supervised. This policy was pursued when it came time for the East New York Y and the East Tremont Y to close their doors, after the Jewish residents literally moved out en masse. It proved most advantageous in financing new structures elsewhere.

When Federation made large-scale capital funds available to the centers, its standard contract provided that in the event that the buildings terminated their services, and did not relocate elsewhere, the proportion toward the cost of construction which Federation had provided would revert to Federation. Agencies at first resisted this type of contract, on the historical grounds that until now, once a gift had been made, the board and its corporate entity were the owners of the property and had the right to dispose of assets in any way they deemed fit.

I brought to the attention of Federation the unhappy experience with Federation Settlement House. Federation had provided all the money for a building erected in 1923, when Harlem had a large Jewish population. In time the area changed completely. The Jewish board attempted to serve the new clientele, but it soon became obvious that an all-white, Jewish board and professional staff were hardly equipped to deal with the needs and demands of a non-white census, aching for its own kind of program and its own leadership. When the settlement, which no longer enjoyed a grant from Federation because it had refused to dispose of its building and move elsewhere into a needy Jewish neighborhood, finally sold its building, note that it did not give it away, it refused to make any grants for either capital or program purposes to any Federation agency, arguing that Federation had no right to the money and had disassociated itself from the agency by disaffiliating the settlement. I know all this because I had several meetings with a few key board members on this issue. The board had shrunk to a handful.

Federation's leadership stated repeatedly that the reason the centers had failed to raise large capital funds, either in the Federation campaigns or on their own to supplement the Free Fund grants, was that centers were no longer the type of association commanding the interest of large donors. When Federation first began, this had not been so. Of the first eleven presidents of Federation, four had formerly been presidents of centers—Felix Warburg, Irving Lehman, Joseph Proskauer, and George Z. Medalie. Several more former center presidents became presidents of Federation during the period when I was employed.

In the aftermath of World War II, the dominant charities were the hospitals, homes for the aged, and child care institutions, all of which attracted the wealthy, the large donors, and the more influential Jews. The capital needs of these agencies were large—in fact, huge. Their services were more dramatic what with all the new inventions and tools in medicine, surgery, and other therapies. The aged were becoming a burden, even for the rich, so that services took on greater personal importance for them. Child care, orphans, the neglected and abused, the child in need of a foster home or institution, the emotionally disturbed child, the retarded child, the physically handicapped child were receiving ever greater attention as psychiatry made impressive presentations of what ought and could be done for them under the aegis of well-trained, well-staffed, well-housed institutions.

Centers, by contrast, were seen largely as recreational resorts, despite the efforts of some of us for years to give them an aura of professional social work and progressive education, with emphasis on the family and group as well as to make them an oasis for the arts and a facility for developing Jewish life.

It was part of my task, self-imposed, to see that the message of the modern center was given greater urgency than it had previously obtained in our public relations programs. I spent a great deal of time interpreting the centers to Federation's staff, including the fund-raisers, and the specialists who were called in to lay out major campaigns.

I devoted some of my energies to recruiting and referring individuals of the wealthier classes to our center boards, which needed strengthening and diversity. The centers, in an effort to become more democratic, had been turning to their local constituencies for most of their board members. In some cases, with new and smaller centers, even the top leadership was selected locally. In many instances these leaders were splended in force, influence, and aspirations, but none of them had the capacity to fund their agencies adequately, and they lacked the resources and contacts to achieve a major physical facility. Such boards eventually had to be mixed, and in most instances the leadership was transferred to well-to-do non-residents as the only way to achieve these larger objectives.

The acquisition of major building funds was another task in which I was engaged. Tipped off to a large foundation that had just been created through a multi-million-dollar legacy, I introduced the executive of the fund to Dr. Hexter, and as a consequence, millions of dollars were eventually allocated to Federation projects, including centers, camps, and day camps. I spent time with the fund's executive and his committee, taking them to visit all kinds of institutions and areas where facilities were needed.

I recall one chairman of a large foundation who was primitive in his knowledge as far as modern philanthropy was concerned. When I took him to dilapidated centers in cellars and lofts that cried out for better buildings, his first reaction was that the children were well dressed. Therefore, why did they need help? He didn't see anyone in rags, or with dirty faces, as in the photos of needy children taken in the early 1900's. I explained to this Upper East Side Manhattan resident that today even people who received relief funds were suitably dressed and not suffering from malnutrition. I told him that there were stores on the Lower East Side and 14th Street where people with low incomes could purchase merchandise of style and quality. I told him that they shopped for food in large markets, sometimes at the end of the day, when prices were marked down.

He constantly reminded me, in the tours I took with him, that the donor of the fund had accumulated a fortune by doing business in a small office, using an old rolltop desk in need of revarnishing, that he had kept every piece of cord that came in the mail and rolled it into a large ball, boasting that he had never bought a packet of string in his lifetime; quite a feat, since the donor lived to be more than eighty years of age. It was clear that at times one had to begin from the beginning to educate a potential donor, or one who controlled large assets, as to the character of life today.

* * *

The YWHA, a Jewish girls' residence and center on West 110th Street in Manhattan, closed its doors in the 1940's, sold its building, and looked elsewhere for the continuance of its programs. Young women no longer wanted to live there, because the area had completely changed and it was deemed unsafe, particularly at night.

A merger was arranged with the 92nd Street Y, and young men and young women were housed in the Y's formerly all-male residence. Part of the YWHA board, after a study, felt it had an obligation to poor Jews, and in the old settlement house tradition began to establish small centers in lower-income neighborhoods, where there was still a residual Jewish population. It was called the Jewish Association of Neighborhood Centers (JANC). The areas selected included a section near the Montefiore Hospital and East Tremont Avenue, both in the Bronx, as well as Upper Williamsburg and East Flatbush in Brooklyn. All sections were underserviced. When some locations were rapidly changing, JANC reached out to new sections in Queens and Brooklyn. Federation agreed to support these centers. JANC, led by influential volunteers and good professionals, was effective in its presentations. There were voices in Federation who felt that centers were moving ahead too fast and making too many claims in ever larger amounts of the limited available funds that Federation collected annually.

I was not happy with the facilities of JANC centers or with centers in Brooklyn and Queens operated by other boards. Their quarters were poor, in basements, over restaurants, amidst other commercial ventures, sometimes in apartment houses, all unattractive, lacking sufficient room space, overcrowded, unsafe. Yet none of these institutions mounted a campaign for a major building. In fact, JANC, which had an affluent board, had resigned itself to acquiring buildings that would not cost more than $50,000 (at most $150,000), all of them inadequate to begin with, limiting the character and quality of the services. JANC was not prepared to undertake a capital campaign and preferred to use its resources for direct service.

There was no predisposition on the part of Federation to encourage large capital gifts for centers. Nor was there any likelihood of tapping the Free Fund for more center structures. What to do?

Meanwhile, Bronx House, with the help of Free Funds and a number of donors recommended to the board by Federation, finally made the move from Washington Avenue to Pelham Parkway in the Bronx. It purchased the steel skeleton of a synagogue that had failed to raise enough money to complete the structure. It then built the first stage of a modern building. Later, thanks to a fortuitous gift and legacy, it enlarged the building. Finally it added a swimming pool.

The addition came about when an elderly man named Harris Lichtman walked into the Bronx House and asked Sol Rafel, the executive director, what it would cost to have the building named for him and his deceased wife. Rafel, not knowing whether Lichtman was serious or not, spoke to me, and I suggested that he bring his potential donor with $150,000 to my office and we would work out the deal. He did, and Lichtman turned over to Federation, to hold in escrow, savings bank books valued in excess of the sum Bronx House required in return for its naming of the structure for Mr. and the late Mrs. Harris Lichtman. Lichtman had come to the U.S. as a young immigrant, alone. He had learned early that you could make more money lending than by doing other forms of work, and apparently had accumulated enough money to sustain him in his older years. I tried to convince Lichtman to make out a will, to ensure that the funds could be used for this purpose in the event of his decease before the project was completed, but he was opposed to writing such a document. Several months later, Rafel called to say that Lichtman was in a hospital and seriously ill. I urged Rafel to come to Federation immediately, and with our legacy department, I wrote out a will, in which I specified that Federation should receive one-third of his estate, assuming that there was more than the $150,000 which he had already turned over to Federation for the Bronx House account. Rafel told me that Lichtman was also interested in a synagogue on Pelham Parkway, where he worshipped. So it was split three ways. I told Rafel to make sure that there would be two witnesses to the signing, preferably doctors or nurses, who would testify that Lichtman was of sound mind and had not been coerced into putting his signature on this testament. Lichtman signed the document. A few days later he passed away. Rafel, as one of the executors, visited his residence and found other bank books and negotiable instruments worth in excess of $750,000. That was how Bronx House completed the second stage of its expanding building. Federation eventually received a quarter of a million dollars.

The pool was added following another accidental meeting. Simon Scheuer, the well-to-do realtor and philanthropist, was visiting the area looking for locales where aged services might be established. He walked into Bronx House, met Rafel, and discovered that the building had no pool. This led to a large gift that produced that much-needed and much-used facility. Before making the gift, Scheuer called me to obtain Federation's assurance that the pool was needed, would be erected properly, and thereafter would be supported by Federation. I confirmed Federation's responsibility in writing.

Another incident is worth recording. A member of the Bronx House board came to see me from time to time asking how she could dispose of relatively small sums of money left over at the end of the year, when she had completed her normal charitable list. I would give her suggestions and then carry them out for her. One year, when we were through determining how $2,500 was to be spent for a children's playground in memory of her husband, I unabashedly asked her how she was disposing the money in her will. She was then approaching eighty, and to the best of my knowledge had no close relatives. She sat down and asked me what I had in mind. I told her of various Federation agency unmet facilities and said that I would be happy to escort her to visit organizations that needed large sums for buildings and services. I had no idea how much she possessed, but I assumed that it was considerable because of her history and lifestyle. I took her on a tour of agencies that were servicing either the aged or children, her preferences. After many days of sightseeing, we ended up at Bronx House, which she had not visited in years, and I told her that Bronx House was eager to acquire a certain building in the neighborhood that would be suitable for an extension center for the aged. Rafel filled in all the details.

A few days later her lawyer, whom I knew, called me, and we worked out the details of a new will that she was writing. As a consequence, after her death, Bronx House received $500,000 and Federation received an even larger sum. Long-term contacts and respect for the individual and his profession by a potential donor can lead to projects and legacies of enduring value.

* * *

Origin of the Associated Ys

In 1953, I decided that something must be done to improve the image of Federation centers, in order to help the have-not agencies attract large capital funds for new buildings. On my own initiative, and mostly at home, I wrote over some months a detailed report which recommended a major campaign to provide center facilities that would literally rim Greater New York. The centers would be located in areas now served by four separate organizations, Rhoda Schapp Council House, the Jewish Community Center of the Rockaways, the East Tremont Y, and all the units managed by JANC. My report provided for buildings costing upwards of $500,000. I suggested that it would be advisable to have such a program under one corporate entity, thus subscribing to the principle of a merger of some, but not all, of our centers. My document indicated that if the merger did not work out, any of the merged bodies could secede after five years.

This seemed like a reversal of my previous position about total merger, and in a sense it was. I had rationalized a merger of the weaker institutions as the only way of achieving their primary objective—having a decent building in which to operate. A fine building is a symbol, as banks well know, and programs should be housed in a good structure to attract people, create a better ambience, and offer a wide variety of services. The building should be well designed, safe, properly lighted and heated, with space for offices where workers could meet individuals and small groups, and be centrally located.

The report was at first roundly condemned: Unauthorized! Unwanted! Those agencies that did not benefit from its findings and recommendations had no interest in seeing it furthered. Those who would benefit didn't know where they would end up in a merger, so they were suspicious and also opposed it. Some, like JANC, felt that such large structures were unnecessary and in conflict with their ideology about what a center should include. Actually the buildings were not large enough. While they included gymnasiums, no provision was made for swimming pools or for large auditoriums. (These facilities were added to some of the buildings at a later date.) Altogether I recommended fifteen buildings, which would require a campaign totaling $7.5 million.

When I first wrote this report, Federation showed little interest in its recommendations, but I gradually obtained support from both executives. Then Federation came forward with an even more exciting proposal—a much larger venture. Willen suggested that the campaign should not be only for Jews, but it should be a three-way drive that would include Protestant and Catholic centers, Y's, and youth agencies, with fifty centers covering all of Greater New York. This would have a more dramatic appeal, as it would up the amount to be raised to $25 million. Major foundations and the wealthiest individuals could then be approached for seven-figure gifts.

Since there was no single Protestant address, and the Rockefellers were not prepared to speak for all the members of that faith, one-third of the partnership proposal was out at the start. To work out a relationship with all the independent protestant YMCAs, YWCAs, settlement houses, and church groups would take years, and we were unwilling and unprepared to undertake such a long and uncertain mission. Judge Joseph Proskauer, Joseph Willen, and I met with Cardinal Spellman of the New York Catholic diocese, but it was clear that they had not given any thought to such a building enterprise and that their cooperation could not be assured until a great deal of exploration was undertaken by the several dioceses having jurisdiction over their numerous churches and parishioners. I thought he showed little enthusiasm for this venture. We finally resigned ourselves to going it alone.

Undaunted, I went to work on the agencies singly. At the first meeting my proposal was endorsed by Murray Handwerker, of Nathan's famous frankfurter restaurants, the president of one of the centers, and Harry Rothman, the well-known discount men's clothier, a former president of another center. Both men were personal friends of mine, and they persuaded their reluctant executives to go along. At Far Rockaway, while there was no opposition from the executive, John Karpeles, he was not in a position to influence his board. I went to see the president, J. Lewis Fox, Abraham Margulies, and Judge Irwin Shapiro, and they bought the deal as the only means for the realization of a building in that part of New York. At the East Bronx Y, May Stroock, the president, and the late Barnett Lambert, the executive, were at first opposed to the merger, but they finally accepted the plan, if I would personally guarantee that a building would be erected in the neighborhood. This was the one area about which I had reservations, because of the rapid changes in the composition of its population. Nonetheless, I agreed. If the building could be erected quickly, it would still have ten years of life in that community.

The major problem was JANC, the largest and most important component. When Dr. Hexter and Joseph Willen asked what I could do to break the impasse with JANC, I imaginatively suggested that if Irving Brodsky was made the executive, a deal could be consummated. Brodsky, probably the best of the four executives, was administering a larger program than any of the others, and while I did not always see eye-to-eye with him on many aspects of center work, I thought he was the only man who could implement the merger and fulfill the program. He had toughness. He worked well with high-level board members. He was the only one who had the potential to organize a drive for large sums of money. Given the sign to proceed, I called Brodsky and asked him what commuter train he was taking back to Rye that night. It coincided with my travel plans to Pelham. We both rode on the same railroad. We boarded the 5:35 P.M. and when I got off at Pelham thirty-one minutes later, we had reached an agreement. JANC would go along with the proposal if he became the executive.

Salem L. Lewis, the dynamic and straight-shooting president of Federation, a great fund-raiser, was retiring from office. He wanted a rest and to go back and devote his time to his stock brokerage firm. Being president of Federation was a demanding chore in terms of sheer time. Willen was convinced that success would be guaranteed if Lewis undertook the presidency of a new, merged society, if only to get it started. Lewis was persuaded, in part because of the size and the boldness of the undertaking. He liked to work on big things. The merger would create an agency of the magnitude of a major hospital or a combination of family and child care services. As a condition of acceptance, he wanted assurances that considerable money would be forthcoming and that Federation would go all out. He was given such guarantees.

We were assured of a gift for one building from the Henry Kaufmann Foundation. Federation had already persuaded the Hirschmann Foundation to provide a second structure. The Gustav Hartman Home for children was merging with the Jewish Child Care Association, and part of the deal was to divert over $1 million from capital funds to name one building after the late Gustav Hartman and another for the last president of the home, Samuel Field. The JANC board promised to raise funds for still another building on land next to the Montefiore Hospital.

With money for five buildings in sight, the papers were drawn, a merger effected, and the Associated YM-YWHA's was born.

Two sticky points were written into the final plan. One, the executives of the other Ys were to become assistant executive directors of the merged organization to give them status as well as a role beyond that of being the directors of their formerly independent institutions. I thought this a fair proposal, and while it was resisted at first, it was finally accepted and proved no problem in overall administration. Second, the agreement provided an escape clause, in case things didn't work out. While the JANC representatives stubbornly fought against anything except an unequivocal, irrevocable merger, we finally achieved a protocol specifying that five years following the completion of a building, a review would be made to determine whether it should remain with the Associated Ys, become an affiliate of that overall body, or split off and become independent again. While no group ever split off, this item in the constitution continued to annoy the leadership of the Associated Ys, who wanted this resolved. Federation leaders like Samuel Lemberg and Edward Isaacs of the distribution committee raised the issue over the years as the Associated Ys grew ever larger. The Associated Ys also assumed that all new Ys in the future could only enter the Federation family by becoming part of its complex structure. These problems were never decided until I left Federation, because I kept these constitutional issues alive. After I left, the Associated Ys always got its own way in dealing with its branches and with Federation.

* * *

In some respects I remained a kind of partisan theoretician about the ways centers ought to operate, perhaps because I visualized them as functioning in the manner that Bronx House had functioned during my days there. The center was not merely a service agency offering programs to its constituency. I saw it as having a radiating influence on the total area to which it could reach out. This required an educated and influential board, an executive with imagination, productivity, and independence along with administrative skills, whose concern must always be with the total scene. On the other hand, an executive who was only a branch administrator had a different set of relationships and duties, which impeded that larger view and obligation. With few exceptions, the Associated Ys rarely attained that end, and if so, did so only by the fortuitous accident of having an executive of independent talents. With few exceptions, however, most executives, at best, developed a pretty good intramural program, but rarely had a significant influence on the larger neighborhood. I do not in any way wish to impugn a single institution under the aegis of the Associated Ys, but I know from my intimate contacts with some of the executives, which predated their employment under the banner of the Associate Ys, that they were not always free agents after the merger took place.

Barnett Lambert of the East Tremont Y, who grew up and struggled with the agency from its humblest beginnings in 1938 as a kind of offshoot of Bronx House, always thought of his neighborhood in terms far beyond his limited institutional facilities. In his last center post, he tried to save the deteriorating area. He inspired a huge housing project to upgrade and rehabilitate the region. He was suitably honored by having this public housing project bear his name. I encouraged him in every step of that difficult, often frustrating effort.

When Lambert's last center finally acquired enough money to purchase a former popular movie theater and remodel it into a useful facility, it was my view that it was opened too late. The Jews had moved out at a pace that could not be slowed, even by the erection of a reasonably good plant. The Associated Ys, to the last, differed with my projections. To prove me wrong, they hired an expert in community studies, Blanche Bernstein, who later became commissioner of the huge Human Resources Department of the City of New York. Her report indicated that the rate of exodus was much slower than I had predicted, and the center was built. Within a few years, though, I was proven correct. The building, at my insistence, was leased to the City of New York, so that the general community could continue to be served. This turned out to be financially beneficial. The Associated Ys recaptured its total investment of $650,000.

I was vitally interested in protecting Lambert's professional position. I had been his consultant throughout his years as an executive, and had supervised him one summer when, as a student at the New York School of Social Work, he had been assigned for field work to Bronx House Camp. Lambert was placed in charge of camp development for the Associated Ys and ultimately became director of the large Block-Hexter camp for senior citizens, located in Pennsylvania. He had been the director of Ella Fohs, another Federation camp, for a number of years, helping it grow from an elementary school-age program to one that included adolescents and older people. I had arranged for Federation's acquisition of Camp Ella Fohs, having worked out the gift with the original owner of the attractive property, Julius Fohs, and in addition obtained support for its maintenance for a number of years. The family preferred to work with me rather than anyone else at Federation. Unhappily, on Barney's first joyous trip to Israel, he suffered a heart attack, died, and was buried there, but his life work and dreams had been fulfilled.

In 1958, I was designated by Federation to be the Coordinator for the day to day operations of the Demographic Study of the Estimated Jewish Population of the New York Area 1900–1975 and worked intimately with two research specialists, C. Morris Horowitz and Lawrence J.

Kaplan. For years thereafter, all questions on the Jewish population were directed to my office.

* * *

Tempting Offers

Shortly after I was ensconced at Federation, the leadership of HIAS offered me the position of executive director. The chairman of the functional committee on community centers was Ben Touster, at the time president of HIAS. We had become good friends. I was offered the position at twice the salary I was earning at Federation, plus substantial perquisites. Thinking this over with Emma for a day, I decided not to take it. This job would require a lot of traveling, often out of the country, and this would disrupt our family life. I turned it down. Then I told Hexter what I had done. He was not angry at me, but took out his rage on Touster for having dared to interview me without consulting him first. Touster never rose very high in the Federation volunteer hierarchy, but found other outlets for his talents and largesse.

A year later I was invited to dinner by Dr. John Slawson, executive vice-president of the American Jewish Committee. He was looking for a key staff member who could be groomed to someday fill his chair. He went over a number of names with me, because he had been told that I not only had a wide acquaintance with the field, but that I had the ability to evaluate people honestly with respect to their abilities, their character, and their potentialities. I didn't leave him until eleven that night, four hours following our dinner.

Some weeks later he called me and said that he was close to a decision and wanted to discuss a few more names. Again the dinner started at seven; we went over the same names and a few others. I appraised each one carefully, and even recommended the one person whom he should appoint. About 9 o'clock, he suddenly turned and said, "When are you ready to start working for me?" I was startled. Slawson had cleverly been interviewing me both evenings without my having the slightest awareness of what he was up to. I told him that I was not interested—that I had initiated a program at Federation and had to finish by my own will, and not because I had any contractual obligations. He told me that I was not a slave and should consider his offer, which, while not as generous as that advanced by HIAS, might nonetheless have led to one of the most prestigious positions in the field of Jewish communal work. The next day I called him and told him that he should not consider me for the post.

When I reported this to Hexter, because I did not want him to learn or interpret this meeting and offer from any other route, he was irate. He called Slawson and not only gave him a bitter piece of his mind, but for some time actually broke off relations with his old colleague.

Incidentally, the man I recommended for the job, who turned it down at the time, later succeeded to Slawson's position.

Years later, Slawson called me for lunch on several occasions. We spoke about our visit to Bardin's camp in California, and how such an enterprise might be developed on the east coast. He gave me one of his books. He tried to convince me that he had always been pro-Jewish, even interested in Jewish education, and was not the nonsectarian that I had labeled him. Slawson was a keen professional. I first met him when I was director of Bronx House and he was the executive of the Jewish Board of Guardians. We joined forces in one of the first case work-group work programs in the country. The year was 1940.

* * *

While my life at Federation was fertile and reasonably free of criticism from the powers at the top, I had a few experiences that, if I had not acted with expedition and fearlessness, might have cost me my job. The president of the Educational Alliance, Frank Weil, an important contributor to Federation, later to occupy a high position in the Carter administration, walked into Joseph Willen's office one day and accused me of trying to force the Educational Alliance to raise its dues to members, so that the new rates would drive out the non-Jews—blacks, Hispanics, Chinese—who were becoming the largest component of its registrants. What I had actually told the Alliance, in the presence of members of its board and representatives of the distribution committee, was that it should have a graded membership-fee scale, because a large number of its members, who were mainly middle-class white Jews, could afford to pay more than the minimum schedule the agency was charging. In this way, it could become somewhat more self-sufficient and not have to rely on Federation to meet the largest part of its deficit. The Alliance received one of the biggest institutional grants from Federation. Weil told Willen that a man holding such prejudiced views should be fired. I demanded an immediate meeting with Weil, who had not been present when I made the suggestion, together with all the people who had attended that meeting. Such a meeting was arranged. No one confirmed Weil's allegations and the matter was quickly disposed of. At the meeting, I suggested that Weil be appointed to the distribution committee, where he could closely observe my conduct. He accepted the appointment, but learned that being a member of this committee required giving up a tremendous amount of time. He quickly resigned.

I was called in one day by Willen, who informed me that a serious complaint had been leveled against Federation by a member of one of the most prominent and generous Jewish families in the city. This woman, a leader in the Women's Division, had objected with strong emotion to Federation's supporting a Zionist organization like the Jewish Education Committee. I was implicated, because I was a consultant to the committee and was doing nothing to restrain this organization. I explained to her very soberly that the committee was all-embracing; the schools it coordinated had a variety of points of view on Jewish life from Reform to Orthodox, from secular to religious, and thus it could not be classified as totally Zionist. She held up an issue of *World Over*, a newspaper published by the committee, that was entirely devoted to Israel. She was unequivocally opposed to Israel as a Jewish state, and her family refused to support anything having to do with Israel. Willen asked me how we could change the newspaper's policy. I answered that *World Over* was a newspaper for children and covered subjects of concern in the Jewish world. While it carried news of Israel, we had no right to censor what it printed. Our critic asserted that she questioned giving any more money to Federation if it supported such a vehicle. She intended to withhold her annual donation and would raise the issue at the next board meeting.

I suddenly recalled that *World Over* threw off a profit from its sales in excess of $100,000 annually. I boldly replied that Federation did not give one penny to the financing of this newspaper and, in fact, if it wasn't for this paper's surplus, which the committee used to pay for other items in its budget, we would have to allocate over $100,000 for Jewish education. Willen's jubilant comment was: "I knew Graenum would have the answer. We don't spend any Federation money for this newspaper and its Zionist views." Believe it or not, she was completely satisfied with my comment. Thus Federation avoided another confrontation with the segment of Federation supporters who were anti-Zionist, nonsectarian, and not too avowedly Jewish in their ideological ways.

* * *

Camping

When I arrived at Federation in 1949, there were a dozen camps on the roster, mostly for children, several for emotionally disturbed referrals, some still catering to poor children or children from broken homes, who came from the Hebrew Orphan Asylum or other child care agencies. Another took care of the physically handicapped, two served working girls; only one camp, the oldest, Surprise Lake, going back to the turn of the century, utilized its facilities beyond the normal eight, nine or ten-week summer season. Some of the camps were on sites owned by the operating society. Several, in poor condition, were on poorly located properties. A number were rented, several in beautiful Bear Mountain Park, where the facilities were primitive, often lacking in decent amenities. Each camp provided its own unique program, reflecting the views of its independent board. They were interested only or primarily in poor or problem children, and there was a reluctance to enroll even lower-middle-class Jewish children, who could not afford private camping, but would be able to pay the costs charged by Federation camps. A superficial survey revealed that these children were the most neglected group in the Jewish community. There was a feeling of guilt about taking care of anyone but the poor, and about setting top fees at the level of cost per camper. As a result, such camps generally had poor facilities, inexperienced staffs, and inadequate programs in the arts, crafts, nature, and music, with dining rooms that served a routine diet, in modest quantities. I had the task of trying to improve the overall quality of most of the camps.

It was evident that there was a need to relocate some of the camps. The concept of putting several camps on one large site appealed to Federation, particularly Dr. Hexter, who spent each summer at Saranac Lake and loved the out-of-doors. It also later appealed to the Henry Kaufmann Foundation, which was prepared to put up the money for a major site. I spent a considerable amount of time exploring huge tracts of land and walked over many properties in New York, Connecticut, New Jersey, and Pennsylvania. They all lacked something. In some instances, the lake was not large enough. In others, the sites were so far from New York that the trip to and from camp would be costly and even uncomfortable to travel. Federation actually never acquired such a property until a few years before I retired. Located near Monticello, New York, the property was purchased at modest cost after I had conducted lengthy negotiations with the owners. Regrettably, instead of setting up an independent board to administer and develop it, Federation turned the site over to the Associated Y's, which brought in some architects who had won numerous prizes but had never planned a camp, and with their grandiose ideas, an investment of nearly $2 million would have been required for raising the lake, for water, electricity, roads, and the construction of a second lake, without providing for a single person to be bedded down, a sum far beyond what Federation wanted to invest and support. The property still lies fallow. My notion had been to develop it camp by camp instead of planning for seven units in advance. Several units could have been provided for quickly, if there had been less emphasis on centralization. Funds could have been found for this more limited exploitation. This was an instance where overplanning became self-defeating.

* * *

During my search for a large camp property, I received a call one day from Dr. William Sharpe, a septuagenarian brain surgeon, who wanted to give Federation a tract of hundreds of acres in the Adirondack Mountains. A tall, lean, healthy-looking man, with a Falstaffian sense of humor, who in his college days had pulled stroke on the Harvard crew, this son of a Scotch Presbyterian minister had over the course of a long and apparently lucrative career acquired a number of properties all over the United States, and he was now disposing of them. The well-known *Herald-Tribune* camp, at Fishkill, New York, which survived the newspaper, bears his name.

When I asked him at the Harvard Club, where we first met, why, in view of his background, he wanted to give the land to a Jewish organization, he told me that he had been working on his autobiography and had learned that his Scotch ancestors had come from Holland, where their name was Scharf, and that his Dutch forefathers had come from Spain, where their name was Sherif, so he suspected that somewhere in his past there was Sephardic Jewish blood, of which he was quite "proud." He told me that if we could use the site, it was ours for the taking.

I explored the land with Sharpe and a camping specialist, Julian Salomon, on a four-day weekend in the fall. In addition to examining the grounds and its possibilities, we were coaxed into hunting for deer each bitter-cold morning. Neither Salomon nor I was a hunter, and we did not like to shoot at anything, including handsome wild animals. Yet we arose at 4 A.M., donned our red jackets and red caps, stationed ourselves at strategic points, and waited. I am happy to say that we never saw a deer, never fired a shot. Still, we worked up a healthy appetite trudging over the mountain terrain and returned to eat a hearty breakfast and listen to Sharpe's adventurous tales.

I recommended that we turn down his property, because it lacked a lake and there were no streams to impound. I learned a great deal about this fun-loving, great story-telling, interesting physician and researcher—Dr. Sharpe, some of which was later incorporated in his autobiography, *The Brain Surgeon*. We corresponded for a number of years, and I sent him many volumes about the Jewish people, particularly the Jews of Spain.

* * *

In the first few years, I visited each Federation camp accompanied by members of Federation's distribution committee and at times by the chairman of the functional committee on camping. This was the first time that the lay leadership performed this task as part of their duties before making allocations. Going to one or more camps was an all-day affair, and if we wanted to see all of them, one would have to spend the equivalent of a seven-day week. I usually planned two-day outings. We would stay overnight in one of the camps, so that the camps could be seen in more than a superficial manner.

In addition, I thought that I ought to visit the best camps in the business, not only those under philanthropic auspices, but also those privately run. I compiled a list, and in the first five years I drove to some forty camps from southern New Jersey, as far west as eastern Pennsylvania and as far north as Maine. I learned a great deal about standards in personnel, unusual programming, buildings, water systems, lake maintenance, and health provisioning that helped me evaluate and improve the Federation camps.

I was strengthened in my views developed earlier at Bronx House, that not enough emphasis was placed on recruiting much better personnel and keeping them for more than one season. I was convinced that facilities should be simple in design to asssure low-cost construction and for easier maintenance and repair. I was reinforced in my belief that more attention had to be placed on using the outdoors for nature and science programs and for exploring native American folklore; otherwise, why bother to haul people a hundred miles from the city, where the conventional programs could be better produced? I emphasized coeducational camping, extending the programs for teenagers into work camps. I was responsible for initiating and getting Federation to support bicycle trips—hosteling, which was carried on with considerable appeal and success. Unlike the original programs, which kept the hostelers within one hundred miles of New York, today buses, trains, and planes take them to the far west and to Canada.

I helped convert the female-only camps into young adult resources for both sexes, pushed for the introduction of family camping and camping for the aged, the latter becoming one of the most important camping services, with large and modern facilities built to accommodate the ever increasing demand. I urged and succeeded in getting camps to extend their seasons year round and helped camps find the funds to winterize their buildings, water and sewage systems. With some pressure, I convinced camps to abandon their totally inadequate sites and helped their boards find locations and obtain funds for the acquisition of better properties. I persuaded several individuals, who at first wanted to sell their properties to Federation, to donate them as tax-free gifts for use as camping locations.

I was a stickler for cleanliness both as a camp director and as a Federation consultant. I can't stand the sight of a gum wrapper on my own front or back lawn. I could not tolerate unclean kitchens and dining rooms. I thought toilets and showers ought to be immaculate. I did not like to see garbage uncovered and fly-ridden. I did not like debris anywhere, and particularly at the waterfront, where everyone walked barefooted. After I visited a camp, I usually sent the director a letter giving thanks for his hospitality and courtesies. I also included comments on cleanliness, programs, personnel, buildings—matters which I had already mentioned to the director during the visit.

Some, perhaps all, camp directors resented such criticism, and especially when they thought I shared my observations with my volunteer committees, which I did. Volunteers always said this about me—that I treated them like adults and professionals, not attempting to conceal the disagreeable, and never failing to point out significant camp achievements. I always believed that volunteers must know as much as I did; otherwise they would not be qualified to make judgments about annual grants for maintenance or capital funds.

One day I received a letter signed by all the camp directors with a list of complaints, demanding that I appear before them at a supper meeting to be held outside of Federation. The chairman of the aggrieved was one of my closest friends, and after forty years still is. I listened quietly but impatiently to the criticisms, the major one being that I shared too much with lay people, including their own boards, and this reflected on their professional competence and status. I waited for everyone to speak and then answered without fear or favor. I like to believe that I think more clearly, answer more firmly, convincingly, and eloquently, when backed against the wall. At the end of this spirited meeting, while they hoped that I would be a little kinder in my formal letters in the future and not confide everything to my volunteers, they accepted my critical remarks as true, whether oral or written, and acknowledged that my comments were given without malice. What is more, they pledged to correct their own shortcomings. Some of them did.

Examples of how volunteers could perform like professionals occurred on two occasions when I decided to take a ten-week summer holiday, vacation time that I had accumulated as a result of working almost year round. Vacations were contractually for only four weeks, but in lieu of unpaid overtime, executives received six weeks each year. Since my summer and winter programs often blended, I never could take all of it in any one year, and it accumulated.

During the summer of 1955 and again in 1959, I went to Israel and Europe. I needed someone to cover my summer visits to both resident and day camps. In 1955, I asked Louise Shwartz, a member of the distribution committee on camping, to visit all these agencies, and she did most creditably, writing an excellent report on her observations. I received laudatory reactions from the camp directors. For one thing she was less critical. When the budget conferences were held, she asked all the right questions and made cogent comments, so that my role that year was diminished, something which I did not resent but felt good about, for I had helped train an informed lay person. Louise later decided to become a professional, and until her premature death, she held both line and executive positions in non-Jewish and Jewish agencies.

Four years later, I asked Myron Mayer, president of Bronx House-Emanuel Camp and chairman of the functional committee on camping, to undertake these visits for me. Mickey, as he was called, was a lot more informal than Louise, but faithfully saw each of the agencies and prepared a less detailed, yet good report. During the following year it served him in good stead as chairman, because now he knew intimately all the camps over which he was presiding. Mickey later became an influential person on Federation's planning committee and committee for the aged. He was a founder along with me of the Vacation Services for the Aged, a nonsectarian organization that raised money to support camps that were expanding their services to senior citizens. Mickey died prematurely, a loss to the volunteer, philanthropic community.

Among the many excellent volunteers with whom I worked on both the functional and distribution committees, who were devoted to the camps were: Marian Hess, Helen Witty, Edna Erdman, Marjorie Wyler, Billy Tisch, Adele Block and Doris Rosenberg.

I actively participated in the merger of several camps, usually a Federation with a non-Federation organization. Camp Emanuel, which for many years provided camping for children, was joined with Bronx House. This brought an excellent group of volunteers and their money to Bronx House Camp, which was going through the throes of expansion. The merger required little persuasion, since Emanuel had no physical site to dispose of. Eventually, it led to the severance of the camp from Bronx House, although the camp continued to house its offices with its former parent sponsor.

Ray Hill, a Federation camp, had disposed of its valuable property at Mount Kisco, because there was no longer a need for a camp for working girls, and the camp property could not be adapted for other age groups. It had money and an active board that wanted to use its expertise elsewhere. Poyntelle, an independent camp on a desirable site in Pennsylvania, was well suited for expansion. The camp needed an infusion of new blood and money in order to improve and develop its facilities. It also needed guaranteed annual funds for its maintenance. There were the usual fears among the Poyntelle board and its executive on the possibility of the camp's being "dominated" by Federation and coming under the aegis of the Associated Y's and its assertive executive and board, to whom the camp would also have to account, since Ray Hill had been part of that domain. My relations with both groups were of such a positive character that eventually I brought about an uneasy merger, yet one that had beneficial consequences. True, in such new and different relationships, Poyntelle did not retain its autonomy. Fearful people always feel that this is a precious state that should not be forsaken. The long-term advantages ultimately proved that their suspicions and fears were ill-founded.

New camps emerged during my incumbency largely for the traditional Jews. They had previously been ignored by Federation. This was a new constituency that arose after World War II with the influx of such Jews from Middle Europe. Hassidic Jews under an aggressive rabbinic leadership had already established enterprises of their own, because they wanted absolute control over every aspect of camp life. Their camps were literally a transposition of the city yeshivah to the countryside. While standards at times left much to be desired, on the whole they were providing services badly needed by oversized families living in crowded city apartments, which offered little comfort during hot and humid summers.

Rabbi Isaac N. Trainin, my colleague at Federation, was a major factor in bringing about several of these camps. The dramatic story of how he obtained $20,000 in needed funds for the opening of the first ultra-Orthodox camp under Federation auspices was revealed in his volume *From the Pages of My Communal Diary* (1977). He was not daunted by a snowstorm that brought the city of New York to a halt. This so impressed the potential donor with whom he had a meeting that he readily provided the funds. This marked the birth of Camp Mogen Avraham. It was my task to see that such camps were fully supported by Federation. It was not always easy. In this instance I had the aid of several influential members of the distribution committee.

Rabbi Trainin conducted an around-the-clock campaign during my years at Federation to make the non-kosher camps kosher. Most of them originally were not. The decision to make the change was entirely within the province of the individual boards. Some were ideologically opposed to such a radical move. Making a camp kosher involved the expenditure of considerable sums for changing the kitchen, nearly doubling every type of equipment, maintaining two sets of dishes and silverware as well as pots and pans. In some instances it required enlarging the kitchen and storage areas. It required using different foods that met the kosher test, higher-cost items. The kitchen staff had to be sympathetic to these fundamental alterations. While a few camps seemed ready to take this step, in part because Rabbi Trainin said he would find the money, Federation also had to make provision for the changeover, because the costs would be higher from year to year. Some camps were resistant to having a *mashgiach* (religious supervisor), who would have to be on the premises at all times to ensure that the foods and equipment met kosher standards. This meant having a conspicuous religious person, often with his family, on the grounds, and who by his presence often recommended other changes in practices, such as strict Sabbath observance, no promiscuous use of vehicles on the Sabbath, abstaining from food and certain activities on Tisha B'Av, a holiday in the summer time commemorating the destruction of the ancient Temples in Jerusalem. With Trainin's persistence and my support, some of the camps went kosher. The presence of the dietary supervisor, or what a Jewish comedian once termed an "inside picket," led eventually to more Jewish programs, since the resident rabbi or Jewish educator was free to conduct a class or two, give a lecture, and enrich the Sabbath services.

One of the early organizations in Federation was the Jewish Vacation Association, chiefly a registry for Jewish children whose families wanted to be directed to the proper camp. The JVA sought to enlarge its functions by visiting the camps and evaluating them. It felt that it should not refer individuals to camps that did not meet minimal standards. New York State had passed legislation aimed to improve conditions, but its agents were mainly concerned that camps should be safe and sanitary, that there should be sufficient toilet and washing facilities and a sufficient number of counselors to protect the children. State inspectors annually visited the camps to ensure compliance with the laws. In addition the American Camping Association sent volunteer evaluators (I was one of them) to inspect both private and nonprofit camps. Finally, Federation's representatives made annual visits, and their regular educational meetings with the boards of camps were another means of raising standards. Thus there was little need for a fourth agency like the JVA to harass the camps on the same theme, so it was decided to limit the JVA's functions to that of referral of campers.

Because of the ever-increasing cost of camp operation and out of zeal to satisfy the demand for service from a lower-middle-class and middle-class clientele who either could not afford private camping fees or actually preferred the type of program provided by nonprofit camps, Federation camps began to charge fees which met the full cost of operation. To encourage Federation camps to take more lower-income campers, a scholarship program was introduced. Admittedly, the program was a headache, although I undertook to administer it and assembled the annual data as a basis for making special allocations. Yet as a result of the program, it can be said with accuracy that no Jewish child in the city was deprived of a camping experience because his or her family could not afford to pay the fee in whole or in part. Fees were adjusted on the basis of "ability to pay," and I brought in accountants, economists, and specialists on family budgets to work out fee scales that were fair. Rarely did my office receive a complaint about an agency overcharging, and when I did, a phone call to the camp resolved the problem immediately.

When the retirement of the executive of the JVA led to the dissolution of that agency, some of its services were picked up by a new camp organization that Federation created—the Association of Jewish Camps. It not only dealt with the referral of the campers, but attempted to coordinate a group of camps that were not supported by Federation. Such camps needed access to consultation and to the central purchasing of supplies that was provided by Federation's Joint Purchasing Corporation. The director of the AJC, in effect, gradually provided the same kind of help to non-Federation camps that I as the consultant was giving Federation affiliates.

After I relinquished my responsibilities for camping in 1969, the new camp consultant incorporated both functions into one office.

While it would have been advantageous to bring more of the unaffiliated Jewish camps into the Federation family, some of them did not qualify because of their idiosyncratic boards, who preferred not to be beholden to any higher authority. Others were of a special religious character and were affiliated with national religious bodies that provided them with whatever funds they needed.

One day I was called in by one of our most dynamic presidents, Lawrence Wien, who told me that he had promised the president of a camping society, a personal friend, that Federation would accept it as an affiliate. While the board of this camp was Jewish and raised most of its money from Jews, and its director was Jewish, I told Wien that the camp was nonsectarian in its philosophy, program, and clientele, and therefore was not eligible for admission. Wien was a man of iron will and fiery speech, yet could always relate a good joke to disarm you. He was visibly and verbally annoyed by my judgment and effrontery. My view of the camp was based on visits I had made there to review its reports in detail, for I had evaluated this society for the Henry Kaufmann Foundation, to which it had applied for funds. Since the Foundation had no sectarian restrictions, I had recommended that it approve such grants. Wien immediately called in Hexter and Willen, and said that I was too narrowly judgmental and someone else should make a study of the camp's eligibility for affiliation. He wanted a report at the earliest moment. The executives defended me, as they always seemed to do publicly. Willen declared, in his soft, seemingly pleading voice, that Berger was a man who would always prepare a report that was factual, but that the final decision to accept or reject the camp was not in his province. Wien seemed mollified and accepted the suggestion that I prepare the document.

That very day, I wrote the report, since all the relevant data were in my files. I started out by stating Federation's criteria for accepting a new agency for affiliation. I wrote this without comment. Then I described the purposes, the program, and the clientele of the camp by quoting from the literature it circulated to the public and from reports it had made to its board, to which I was privy. I stated that the board without exception was Jewish and that it solicited funds largely from Jewish sources. I described its program and revealed the absence of any Jewish content or symbols, even though on some trips, half of the campers were Jewish. I described the camp's physical facilities, income, and expenditures, including its indebtedness. It was a thorough report, but there were no recommendations at the end to accept or reject. I did indicate that I was prepared to provide any further data, if requested. I sent it to Wien immediately.

Every Wednesday morning Wien held a session at Federation, where whoever he wanted to talk with, including the two executive vice-presidents, responded by appearing in his presidential chamber. He was alone when I came in. He told me that he had read my report and added: "I will not recommend the camp for membership." "Anything else, Mr. President?" "No, that will be all."

Our relationship was not jeopardized as a result of that episode. Shortly after, I visited some agencies with Wien, including a camp that had requested a large Federation grant with which to acquire a sizable piece of contiguous property. Without having seen the land, Wien thought it might be a worthy addition. He listened attentively to my discussion about camping and sundry other matters in the three hours we spent driving back and forth from New York. I pointed out that this property was not needed, and if acquired would add little of camp value and yet make for expensive maintenance, further burdening the board and Federation. After Wien saw the acreage, he went along with my opinion. Wien had a bright, hard, articulate mind of his own as a most successful attorney and realtor of major properties (he was one of the owners of the Empire State Building) and a force in philanthropy at Brandeis and Columbia Universities, but he could accept a judgment from someone else, including a social work professional, if it was based on knowledge and the legalities, and was practical.

During my incumbency I saw camps go from the traditional part-time camp directors to the employment of full-time managers who were paid respectable salaries. They were employed full-time, even when the camp was not operating for more than a nine, ten, or twelve-week season. Part of the reason for engaging full-time directors was the size of the camps, for many now had 250 to 400 beds and served fifteen hundred to two thousand individuals during a summer. Registration and the determination of fees became more complex and began as early as February 1. Recruiting a staff was a time-consuming, almost a year-round affair, due to the heavy turnover in personnel each season. Being a counselor was often a one-summer job. Even supervisors did not return from year to year, unless there was a large increase in salary or assurance that the job would be a stepping stone to a directorship in that camp or elsewhere. A large camp with scores of buildings and utilities had to be maintained, and if the work was to be done properly, the director had to make trips to the camp out of season. Boards were growing weary of interviewing new directors every year or two, since the better ones were offered higher-salaried jobs elsewhere in an expanding camp market. So they capitulated to their directors, who after contracting for the position, usually stayed on until they retired. It took quite a bit of interpreting for Federation's distribution committee to accept this new trend and the additional costs it entailed, which required larger subsidies from Federation.

Even for me this was quite a change. I recalled my own nine years at Bronx House Camp, which I directed along with the agency in the city and its many appendages. For years, my running of both enterprises was not even reflected in the salary I received. At camp I occupied a small one-room-and-porch cabin, where Emma and Michael also lived, and where we often held smaller staff meetings. We had a stool and washstand, but took our showers with the campers and staff. We ate our meals with everyone else. The full-time directors changed all that. Large residences were newly built for them with all the amenities, including refrigerators to store any food that they would like to eat on their own or with their guests. Camp directors were no longer workhorses; now they often had several assistant directors, in some instances also year-round. They could now go around camp properly dressed all day long. Camp directors now referred to themselves as professionals. They had status. They had arrived.

* * *

The Henry Kaufmann Campgrounds

Day camp was not a new phenomenon when I arrived at Federation. Its origins were in World War I, when centers had to provide services for children of working mothers. Then called play schools, they were conducted in schools and centers, using their buildings as a base. Often they utilized nearby swimming pools or beaches, and took periodic side trips to places of interest. The term "day camp" was coined in the 1930's to give it the competitive aura of the outdoor camps. I had supervised a play school at Council House in the Bronx during the summer of 1932. On Staten Island, I used the building and its pool, preempted the neighboring wooded lot for out-door activities and cookouts, and took groups into Manhattan to visit museums or major league baseball teams. The ferry ride passed the Statue of Liberty. Each summer that was another stop. We arranged overnight hikes on the still-forested Staten Island, although the Jersey mosquitoes discouraged second trips by the same youngsters. The day camps at Bronx House utilized the entire building, used the public swimming pool in nearby Crotona Park, and made trips to Yankee Stadium and the still-existing Polo Grounds, with occasional overnight trips to Westchester. With a camp of our own, schedules were arranged in both programs. Day camping, by the time I reached Federation, was a large program, often the most important activity of the year, and for some Centers throwing off a surplus that helped finance part of the year-round service.

Normally when one thinks about how an unusal institution was born, one assumes, as a social planner, that it went through the drawn-out, conventional planning process. A need had been articulated; a long and careful study was executed by a committee and professionals; an evaluation was made of the findings and recommendations. Once approved a campaign was undertaken to raise funds for its completion.

The Henry Kaufmann Campgrounds, however, was created by sheer accident, or if one doesn't believe in the accidental theory in history, then it was brought to life through a desperate, spontaneous, creative suggestion as to how we could avoid losing $1 million.

I have previously mentioned that Ralph Samuel, the president of Federation, wanted me to merge all the centers under one banner. To sweeten this proposal, Norman S. Goetz, a former president of Federation, a partner in the prestigious law firm of Proskauer, Rose, Goetz and Mendelsohn, dangled in front of me a $1 million grant for such a program, the funds to come from the Henry Kaufmann Foundation, of which he was the chairman. The late Pittsburgh department store owner had bequeathed a fortune to be distributed to worthy charities. I breakfasted with Norman, whom I called by his first name, to relate how I was getting along with Samuel's merger request. In each merger agreement, I explained, I always included an escape clause, so that if the merger didn't work out, the individual center could resume its independence.

Norman, totally dissatisfied with my equivocal memos, one morning said: "Let's forget about centers. Bring your wife and spend a weekend with us at Deal, New Jersey, and maybe we will come up with something else."

We spent a delightful couple of days in their late-nineteenth-century white house with its porches, turrets, and other trimmings overlooking the ocean and beach. We avoided the subject the first day. Lunched at the club with other Federation friends, then dined at the Stephen Strooks' in the evening. Sunday morning, breakfasting on the sunny porch, we finally returned to the object of our weekend. Once again, he reiterated that I seemed to believe that a merger of the centers was both undesirable and difficult to execute, but at best it would take many years to bring about. So what else did I have on my mind? I cited the recommendations of Federation's building fund committee for millions of dollars to be raised to rebuild and create several new country camps. I had started to describe the program when I was abruptly interrupted: "I never went to camp as a boy and I am not interested." In such a manner are great decisions made and disposed.

Veritably in desperation, for I have no other words to describe my frustration at that moment, I turned to his wife, Mildred, and said: "Perhaps we ought to acquire a large site for day camping?" I reminded her that when she was president of the New York Section of the Council of Jewish Women, she and several other women had visited me at Bronx House, to enlist my aid in putting pressure on Robert Moses, the city's imperious commissioner of parks. He was giving the private agencies a hard time about their use of public parks and beaches as swimming and athletic facilities for their children. "Why not a large Federation day campground to which we could send our children in the summer months?" Norman turned to Mildred and asked what she thought of my proposal. Mildred instantly replied: "It is an excellent idea!" And that is exactly how a major Federation development was spawned. Suggestions began to flow. I thought Staten Island was a possibility, since I knew there was plenty of open space and it was accessible to the other boroughs by ferry. I romantically told of ferry rides passing the Statue of Liberty, Ellis Island, and Governor's Island, which could be a daily added history lesson. The twenty-minute ferry ride could be an occasion for singing, telling stories, giving instructions. No time would be wasted.

Goetz told me to call James Felt, an important real estate developer, to help locate available properties. I began to think ahead about who should operate this new enterprise. "Let us start with a new group, involve a lot of young people, the sons and daughters of Federation leaders and major contributors. Mildred, you should be its first president." She accepted the assignment on the spot, and no better choice could have been selected.

The next day I reported what had happened to Dr. Hexter, and I am not sure whether he was enthusiastic or not, but since "this is what Goetz wanted, this is what Goetz gets."

I met with James Felt, a genial man, who looked nothing like the aggressive real estate developer I had read and heard about. Soft-spoken, always putting his arm around your shoulder, strongly committed to Judaism, Felt became a good friend over the years. He was appointed commissioner of city planning and grew in stature and reputation. He died prematurely. I traipsed over a lot of properties with him during the years, when and where we often talked more about Jewish life than real estate. He always deferred to my judgment as to whether a site would be useful as a day camp. His contribution was to determine a reasonable price and conduct most skillful negotiations for its purchase.

We quickly learned that the city was planning to put up for auction a thirty-five acre tract on Staten Island, which had fallen into its possession through a tax default. The site was excellent for our purpose, although smaller than I would have liked. I found that the contiguous lots might also be put on the auction block for the same reason at a later date. I recommended that we acquire it at an upset price of some $45,000. William (Bill) Higgins of Proskauer, Goetz, Rose and Mendelsohn legal firm was assigned to assist me and deal with the legal problems. We set out for the auction, which was to take place on the steps of the Borough Hall on the island. There we learned to our dismay that the auction had been called off and a deal was being made with the Boy Scouts of America to sell it to them without bidding. The Scouts owned a large neighboring tract and wanted to expand their holdings. I could write a book about the many meetings with the Scout officials, where we finally convinced them to let us buy the lots. After this delicate feat had been accomplished, we lived next to each other as good neighbors. Yet I never got over the feeling that they felt we had talked them out of something that they wanted for themselves.

We readily obtained tax exemption as a nonprofit agency. Additional properties were added in one- and two-acre parcels as they came up for public auction. I attended all of these sales alone and usually made a brief speech before the desired parcel was put on the block, indicating that I represented a Jewish charity that wanted to build a day camp for lower-income children. With one exception there were never any competitive bidders, so we purchased parcels at low upset prices. The one violator of my request consequently doubled the price before I acquired it. When I bid above the sums approved by Goetz and Hexter, I always first got their questioning looks, but received their approval. No matter what I spent, it was a bargain, even in the early 1950's. We acquired seventy acres for a total of $135,000. There was another tract of some thirty acres adjoining our grounds, which was offered for sale at $40,000. I wanted to buy this land to round out our holdings and wrote long memos pleading for its acquisition. I can still hear Hexter asking me: "What do you want to do, buy all of Staten Island?" I wish we had. In the fall of 1984, on a visit to Staten Island, I learned that the property, if offered commercially, would bring over $7 million. Today it is worth much more. In retrospect I thought that I should have made a stronger pitch or at least put together a group of people to buy it for speculation. I never thought of the latter, as I was only concerned with what it would do for Federation and the children that would be served.

We engaged a camp specialist, Julian Salomon, to supervise the construction of simple wooden shelters and a swimming pool, leveled areas for athletic fields and parking, built a medical clinic and administration building and a house for a caretaker. None of the structures could be seen from the street, because they were set back and screened by trees. I recall walking through the campgrounds with Edgar Kaufmann, son of Henry, who lived in a house in Pennsylvania, designed by Frank Lloyd Wright, that became a national showpiece and was frequently photoed in magazines devoted to architecture. He told me that he was impressed with the simplicity and thought that had gone into our planning and stated that the Kaufmann Foundation could be proud of having made it possible. My input into this development was considerable, both in the ground layout as well as the type and style of buildings constructed.

As the director of the day camp we engaged Monte Melamed, who had grown up on the Lower East Side and was a group worker at the Grand Street Settlement. Short, lean, intense, a twenty-four-hour-a-day producer, he guided the destinies of the ever-expanding day camp development until his retirement in 1981, and without him it would have been quite difficult to maintain all of these properties.

The camp served seventeen hundred children brought from Federation centers in Brooklyn and Lower Manhattan. Later Staten Island was added. The buses made the trip by ferry, since the Verrazano-Narrows Bridge, spanning New York Bay, had not yet been built.

We were dependent on preferential loading and leaving at both ends of the ferry in order to get the children back and forth for a full day from 10 to 3 P.M. On the first day, the truck drivers who were forced to wait while our buses bypassed them began to honk their horns. Indignant at the delay, they made their views known to public officials, and the *Staten Island Advance* came out with a strong story objecting to this favoritism, which interfered with the business community.

Monte called me in desperation. "What can we do?" Unless we had preferential loading he said, the children might arrive as late as 11 A.M. and have to leave at 2:30 P.M. Hardly a worthwhile program day for all the costs that had gone into building the day camp and maintaining it thereafter. I rushed over to the Island and contacted the commissioner of hospitals, Dr. Morris Jacobs, who lived nearby. He intervened with the commissioner of transportation, and the matter was internally resolved in our favor. After that horns would toot from time to time, but there was no further interference. What might have been turned into "Berger's white elephant," as someone termed it that difficult day, did not eventuate. The day camp became a model for the country, as a stream of visitors came to see what we had wrought.

We had some problems. City-born day camp directors were not trained to use the out-of-doors. They usually planned the same programs for the woods that they provided in their in-city buildings. The day camp had to introduce nature and outdoor instructional programs to broaden horizons.

One day, when I arrived at my city office, I found a committee of indignant mothers awaiting me. Led by one of the day camp directors, they criticized Federation, but especially pointed their fingers at me, for opening a camp where there was still a lot of poison ivy that could afflict their children with painful itching. It appeared that the director had led the children to a nice green picnic site, and when they sat down, it was in a virulent poison ivy bed. If you have never had this rash, which at first seems to defy all treatment, you cannot fully understand the justification of their complaint. We had been aware of this menacing leaf, and had already undertaken spraying to kill the plants, but its elimination could not be accomplished overnight. I suspect that over the years, in all of the Federation day camps, well over $100,000 was spent to get rid of this scourge. Eventually we did.

But what do you do to assuage the mothers and the professional all yelling at the same time? I finally calmed them down and made this imaginative statement: "I don't know what you expect your children to learn over the summer, but I know that if they only learned how to detect poison ivy and how to avoid it, it would be worth the entire fee that you paid." I never really know what will influence anyone, but I never saw a quicker transformation. The parents looked at each other, said "Berger was right," and then turned on the poor day camp director as the guilty one, for his not knowing the difference between poison ivy and benign plants.

While the overall program was named, quite properly, the Henry Kaufmann Campgrounds, the specific site was named after Flora Haas, whose foundation provided a great deal of money for the development, and during all the years I was at Federation continued to provide annual maintenance grants.

The construction of the site created another problem. Day camps in the Bronx, Upper Manhattan, and Westchester wanted to know why we were ignoring them. With encouragement from the Foundation, we began to look for sites in Westchester and then in Rockland County, across the Hudson River, and finally purchased a commercial day camp in Pearl River, New York. This served as the basis for an ever-larger population. Mildred Goetz had unfortunately passed away, and the new site was properly named in her memory.

Before we could use it, we had a legal battle with the local zoning and tax officials, who did not want the land taken off the rolls. Escorted by Bill Higgins, our attorney, I appeared before the zoning board and after a long evening meeting, convinced them that even without our taxes, the town would be better off. We intended to spend hundreds of thousands of dollars for food and other materials in the local stores. Our vehicles would be purchased and serviced in the village. We would allow the local school children, their parents, scout and church groups to use our grounds on weekends and off-season, when our normal programs were not operating. That evening I witnessed a group of initially hostile officials change their minds and vote to grant us tax exemption. They never regretted it, because an excellent facility was being created without the town or county having to pay a penny for its purchase and construction.

The reason I was so deeply involved in this development was that Federation owned the property and the encumbrances, even though the Campgrounds had its own board of directors. The Henry Kaufmann Campgrounds also wanted me present on these important occasions because I had somehow come through many difficult situations with what someone termed "flying colors."

Over the years we added acreage to the Mildred Goetz site. New wooden buildings were constructed, following the Staten Island pattern, and a large swimming pool was built to replace the inadequate small lake used by the commercial enterprise. As expensive houses were built around the periphery of the site, the camp could not grow beyond the original 150 acres. It served some twenty-four hundred children daily, with additional groups camping out overnight, Sundays, and during the winter. One building was winterized to provide comfort for thirty individuals in the most severe weather. Later, the day camp added a large unit for the elderly with model facilities and programs.

I recommended that all food served at the day camp be kosher, so that there would be no difficulties with the religious authorities and to respect observant Jews.

Individual centers began to develop special programs of Jewish interest on Friday afternoons and for other occasions, thus giving the day camps more of a Jewish ambience.

While this site never appreciated in value as much as the ones in Staten Island and Suffolk County, its value as real estate is far beyond the capital investment in land and buildings.

Large sites for day camping were being developed in the commercial and philanthropic spheres. The growth in the child population, and the desire to provide an all-summer experience for children who were not ready or willing to go to a country camp or travel with their parents, made the day camp alternative more attractive. Pressure was put upon Federation to do something for the centers in burgeoning eastern Brooklyn, Queens, and Nassau, where the demand and registration was even larger than elsewhere in Greater New York.

With Bill Lese, a member of the Campground board, I began exploring sites, actually large estates, first in Queens, then in Nassau, and finally moving out to Suffolk County. The properties in Queens and Nassau were too small in acreage; the buildings that encumbered the property were too magnificent and expensive to be used for day camping and too costly to maintain. We had to move farther eastward, where there were still large tracts of undeveloped land waiting for exploitation. We located a 750-acre tract, originally owned by the Catholic Youth Organization, which had sold it to a Jewish developer. The wooded land rose to 210 feet, the highest point on Long Island, and lent itself admirably for day camping. Initially, Hexter and Goetz thought we should buy no more that 100 acres, which I regarded as a serious mistake. This was later changed to 200 acres, which I still thought insufficient. I hired a small airplane, picked up Mr. and Mrs. Goetz (he had remarried), and with Frederick Rose, the incumbent president of the Henry Kaufmann Campgrounds, we flew over Queens and Nassau, where I pointed out below how large green areas had practically disappeared, and then over the site in Suffolk between the cities of Huntington and Babylon, where there were still only clusters of small settlements. Goetz was sufficiently impressed to authorize the purchase of 450 acres with funds that his foundation would provide. I still argued for 750 acres, but got nowhere. James Felt and I negotiated the sale with the owner and purchased the land for less than $1 million.

The Long Island Expressway was still in the planning stage, but it would eventually pass alongside the remaining 300 acres which we did not acquire. When the expressway was completed, within a year after the day camp was opened, land values skyrocketed. In 1973, when I was about to leave Federation, a real estate dealer came to see me and offered $45 million for Federation's tract. What the site is worth today I do not know, but certainly considerably more.

It was decided to develop one portion of the large tract for recreational purposes, like the other two properties. Edward Larrabee Barnes, a prize-winning architect, was engaged. He designed cement-block structures, unlike the wooden buildings at the other two locations, giving it a modern, rather than a rustic, look. The camp was laid out for three thousand children daily, with a complex of three swimming pools, athletic fields, and sundry other structures for administration, medical care, and overnight camping. The land was actually a sand bank, and we sold off tens of thousands of dollars' worth of sand in the course of leveling off areas for parking and athletics, but the hill was left standing as a potential ski slide, if enough snow ever fell on the Island.

Luckily, the Long Island Expressway opened at the same time as we inaugurated the camp. As a result, driving time was cut down, and day camps as far away as Westchester, the Bronx, and Manhattan could reach this day camp within an hour.

The camp development cost $1.5 million. We had been looking for a donor after whom it could be named. One day I was sitting in the office of the late Harold Levin, a partner of Proskauer, Rose, Goetz and Mendelsohn, who was also president of the YM-YWHA of 92nd Street. Levin had been a member of the Y as a youth and had risen to its highest post. Proskauer had been the president of the Y when Levin was a young member. Levin was chairman of the functional committee on community centers, and I saw a great deal of him.

Judge Proskauer, who roamed around the many offices during the day, happened to come into Levin's office. Seeing me, he asked whether I had any ideas for a memorialization for his wife, Alice N. Proskauer, who had recently died. "You know," he said, "she was very much interested in children." With my usual quick response, I said that I had the ideal memorial for her, the new Henry Kaufmann Campgrounds in Suffolk County. Proskauer was a trustee of the Henry Kaufmann Foundation, so he knew about its development. "What will it cost me?" I replied: "$150,000." "Oh, I can do better than that with Maurice Hexter. Tell him to call me." Hexter did, but the price was the same, and Proskauer donated that amount.

When Proskauer walked out of the room, I thought Harold Levin was going to have a heart attack. "You know," he said (in fact I didn't know), "that the 92nd Street Y was trying to get him to give a big gift as a memorialization. After all, he was a former president of the Y. You had no right to make any other suggestions than the Y, sitting in my office." I tried to mollify him, but failed. I do not believe that Levin ever forgave me for taking this large donation out from under his nose. It was another of my experiences where a considerable sum was obtained without a plan or long drawn-out interviews, but spontaneously. Site number three was now funded and on the way to completion.

* * *

Purchasing the site was one thing, but getting it off the tax rolls was another, difficult matter. A community of German-Americans owned property contiguous to our tract. I learned that this had been a colony of the German-American Bund, a Nazi, anti-Semitic organization during the Hitler period. Their dislike of a Jewish group moving into their precinct led them to protest to the Town Board that the property should not be taken off the tax rolls. They also objected to the noise and the molestation they would face if a large number of children occupied the land. I appeared before the town officials and spoke at length on how the Jewish Federation was engaged in an important delinquency-prevention program. I explained that our groups were well supervised, with one counselor for ten children, and that all our programs would be at least one hundred feet from the property line. Apart from the many trees already growing on the site, I said, we would add others, which would serve as a sound barrier and cut noise to a minimum; furthermore, there would be no loudspeakers and all traffic would enter from a street a half mile away from this community. We were granted tax exemption and had no further problems with our neighbors.

* * *

Before we signed papers for purchase, there was a report that we were acquiring property in an area near a Negro settlement and that this would have an impact on the safety of our children and the value of the site. Monte Melamed and I made a study of the neighborhood. We found that there were about one hundred black families, all home owners, living in an area about three-quarters of a mile away, where they had been at peace with their white neighbors for over twenty-five years. I discovered that the original black colony had been initiated by "Rabbi" Wentworth Arthur Matthew of the Ethiopian Hebrew Congregation of Harlem, who hoped to develop a large, self-sufficient community of "Black Jews." The elaborate plans never eventuated. When I made inquiries as to whether any of the present residents had black Jewish connections, the answer was in the negative.

Suffice it to say the entire area between the black residents and the day camp in Wyandanch was completely built up with middle- and upper-class housing ranging in price from $75,000 to $250,000. This story is related in my book *Black Jews in America.*

An Arts Day Camp

For a number of years, I had been badgered by Andrew McKinley, the director of the Bronx House Music School, about creating a performing arts day camp with music, dance, arts, and drama along with recreation.

The idea took root in my mind. I flew out to the National Music Camp at Interlocken, Michigan, with McKinley and his wife, a concert pianist, to study this unique operation. I came back with greater enthusiasm and notions on how to translate this exciting summer camp into a day camp.

The board of the Henry Kaufmann Campgrounds was less enchanted with the prospect of building a fourth day camp, let alone an arts camp. They were already burdened with raising funds to complete the third unit and felt that I was too quickly forcing another major venture on them. Despite their sophistication, they felt that recreation was what "poorer" children needed and not the arts, which seemed more suitable for the upper class, with whom they were less concerned. I tried to persuade them that while the upper-class children could afford private arts camping, poorer children had no such opportunity and we should find a way to give it to them. Adjusted fees would enable many children from this economic category to attend.

The other half of the Suffolk property was waiting for exploitation. I found both Hexter and the foundation interested in the arts idea. I suspect that in some part this was because Hexter had become a sculptor, a field that he was still pursuing at ninety-five years, as I write this volume. We persuaded Samuel Lemberg, a wealthy realtor, who had already given large sums to Federation agencies, Brandeis University, and the Albert Einstein-Yeshiva Medical School, to make another large initial gift. He wanted the new camp named not for him and his wife, but for his daughter, Susan, and her husband, Nathan Usdan. Susan was added to the campgrounds board. I had worked closely with Lemberg since my coming to Federation in 1949. He was chairman of several committees that I serviced. He also had confidence in my views.

While there were objections to engaging Andrew McKinley, it was my opinion that he alone had the imagination, the zeal, the contacts with the art world, and the twenty-four-hour-a-day administrative productivity to bring the camp into realization. After interviewing a number of candidates, the board engaged him, but with reservations. Since he was a do-it-alone man, he had difficulty with the incumbent president, Stanley Beckerman. I arranged a dinner at our home so that the antagonists and their wives could socialize and iron out their differences. There were other problems. The board decided to engage a new and distinguished architectural firm to design this new set of buildings for the varied arts, structures which were to be scattered in the woods. The architects created modern, attractive, yet simple buildings, shingled from peaked roof to the ground. I argued that they would leak.

I have had trouble with most of the architects designing structures for centers and camps. They all claimed that I was not an architect to begin with, and that I was not familiar with all the new materials being used to provide unusual and modern aesthetic designs. My long experience in the actual construction of camping facilities and the supervision of camps, day camps, and center buildings, my ability to read blueprints, my knowledge of maintaining structures, I thought, gave me sufficient background to evaluate anyone's architectural plans. The buildings leaked.

I recall reading a blueprint for a new building and discovering, to my dismay, that one had to walk outside to get into the engine room. The architect was flustered by this revelation, blaming it on his new associate. On another occasion, I pointed out that there were no stairwells between the first and second floors, and again an embarrassed architect put the blame on other members of his staff. There never was enough foresight to provide for adequate ventilation which I always insisted upon, since the architects mechanically used space measurements rather than also take into account the number of individuals, all generating body heat, who would occupy the room.

Architects designed buildings with new materials and new heating and ventilating systems, large window panes, new types of roofing. I always looked at plans not only from the point of design and aesthetics or their being modern, but from the aspect of utility, lesser costs in repair and maintenance, security—items which always burdened the agencies. Sad to say, I was usually correct. When I didn't convince either the board or the architect to modify the plans, repairs a few years later proved to be most expensive. I finally got to the point where I advised all boards and architects to design buildings in a 1928 or earlier model, because I knew such solid buildings had fewer problems compared to the modern structures.

My concerns about the exteriors of the Campgrounds buildings proved true. They leaked like a sieve and ultimately required costly recovering materials. The buildings, despite this problem, were beautiful.

Opening day finally arrived, with fifteen hundred children marching through the woods. But the camp was not quite finished. Buses arrived late, having to master new routes. It was a hot day, with temperatures in the 90's. Some of the water coolers were not working. Yet within an hour of opening, the orchestras were playing music. Those in the band shell were rehearsing. The chorus shelter emitted voices. String instrumentalists, pianists, wind instruments, percussion instruments were making their characteristic sounds. The four dance studios were already exercising bodies. In the art studios, children were painting. It was all so unbelievably astounding amidst the trees in this forest that I cried, an emotion that I am not easily given to.

Later I had to sit down with all the directors of the various camp units to placate their petty protests as to why everything was not ready as promised. As usual I had to appeal to their sense of balance. I reminded them that their own operations were not perfect on my visits—and that this was only the first day.

As I took scores of visitors through the camp, year after year, I was always amazed at what so few of us had wrought despite the objections of so many. The Usdan committee finally became independent of the Campgrounds board in order to eliminate a great deal of personal conflict and because the financial needs of the arts site were ever increasing as more buildings had to be erected. The Campgrounds board, despite its initial resistance to this severance, was actually relieved.

The arts camp had no sculpture and ceramic units. Riding home from a visit to the site with Hexter, I asked him whether he would mind, if I could find the money, for erecting such units in his name. He smiled and raised no objection. The next day I called up his good friend Lemberg, and before the next season rolled around a whole new program was added. One of Hexter's modern obelisks adorns the arts compound.

We needed an administration building. I had a flash about approaching a specific individual. At the time, I was also directing the William E. Wiener Education Center in an effort to recruit and develop better middle- and upper-echelon personnel for Federations. I decided to use my meeting with this prospect to demonstrate how fund-raising is done, even though I did not have the slightest assurance that I would succeed in such a public manner. I invited my friend Frederick Naumburg to lunch with me and asked whether he would mind my bringing along four students to whom I was teaching administration and how to raise money. He had no objection. At lunch, Naumburg talked unceasingly about his success in the market and how much money he made. I let him speak without interruption. When our lunch was consumed, I broke in to say that I wanted to discuss a project in which I was deeply interested. "I'll give you $50,000" was his instant reply. "But Fred, I haven't told you about the project, and besides, it will cost $75,000." "I'll give you $75,000, but it will be over three years." I was obviously grateful. I could only tell him a bit about the building, as he was in a hurry to get back to his office. As we rose from the table, I told him I would take his wife and him out to the campgrounds to see what he was giving his money for.

When we returned to my headquarters, I sat down with the four students to evaluate the meeting. I asked, "How long did it take me to raise the $75,000?" One replied, "Two minutes." The others thought it took a few minutes longer. They were impressed by my demonstration. I told them that it had taken ten years to develop the kind of relationship that could bring about such a quick and generous response. I went into the history of this relationship.

Naumburg had a piece of property in Putnam County which he used as a country home. He wanted to give it to Federation on his demise to be used as a camp for children or older people. I worked out the arrangements. While this item was being incorporated into his will, I asked him whether he had made provision for Federation in this final testament. He said he would give it some thought. His greater interest was Yale University, from which he graduated. He told me that the president of his alma mater made quite a fuss about him whenever he made a large gift. A few weeks later he called to report that he had written Federation into his will for one-third of his estate. Then, strangely, he asked whether I was aware how much this might be. I answered that I had no knowledge of his fortune. He replied that the bequest would be in the millions. Obviously impressed, I thanked him profusely. I subsequently suggested his name for one of our camp boards, and he became a most generous supporter of that agency. I would annually approach him for his maintenance gift to Federation and usually received an increase from year to year. One day he called me to ask whether I would be a character witness for him at a trial in the federal court. I accepted, and when I went to court found that I was the sole witness. Naumburg had few friends. I testified that I had known him for some years and that he was a very philanthropic person. There were no further questions. He was acquitted. He was extremely grateful for my appearance. For a person of his wealth, he lived modestly, traveled little, and always admired the world-wide traveling that I had done.

* * *

I had other ambitions for the Suffolk County site. Amongst them was the building of a science-nature-ecology unit, and I wrote up a detailed proposal. There was no interest on the part of the board in finding the money for such a project. I thought it was crucial, because in those days the protection of the environment was becoming a stormy issue, particularly after Rachel Carson published her book *Silent Spring* (1967). This field would have commanded the interest of young people.

In 1970, recovering from my first prostate operation, I took off three months from going to the office, but continued my daily labors both in the hospital and at home without losing any time. I received a sick call in Pelham from Frederick Rose, a young man whom I had recruited for the board of the Henry Kaufmann Campgrounds after he had finished at Yale and the Army. His name had been advanced by his uncle David Rose, an important realtor and philanthropist. Fred had been president of the Campgrounds and one of the movers and shakers in its expansion and fund-raising. With his two brothers, Daniel and Elihu, and his uncle David, Fred directed the tremendous development of Rose Associates, builders and managers of skyscraper properties in New York, Boston, Philadelphia, and elsewhere. Fred later became a president of Federation and a director of the Metropolitan Museum of Art and other important philanthropies.

As we sat together in my back yard in the shade of a crab apple tree, Fred asked me why I had not approached him about having either the

Proskauer or the Usdan sites named for his family. I answered that I hadn't thought, from what I had heard, that he was prepared to make a gift of that dimension. He had made many gifts, but none of them singly was in the six-figure range. Fred said he could afford it and wondered whether I had any other project in mind. I recalled from our conversations over the years, usually when we were walking in the country looking for camp sites, that he was interested in nature. He had once given me an interesting book about flora and fauna. I thought such a project could easily be added on the grounds of the Suffolk property. I reminded him that I had brought such a proposal to the attention of the Campgrounds board several years before. "What will it cost?" I replied: "About $250,000." "You can have it" was his instant answer. That is how the Rose Nature-Ecology Center came to be built.

When we were looking for an additional large donor for the Usdan development, I drove Horace Goldsmith, a well-known broker and philanthropist, and his wife out to the Suffolk property, in the hope of enlisting his support. Goldsmith had been giving away large sums for avowedly Jewish projects and always wanted his name conspicuously displayed on any of his benefactions. A bachelor until his early seventies, he was a healthy-looking, pink-cheeked, sprightly man, who seemingly knew what he liked and disliked. The day camp held no interest for him. The arts were not up his alley. When I drove him back to the city, he suggested that I join them for lunch. There he quizzed me about what else I did. I mentioned my interest in building the Jerusalem YM-YWHA. He had been approached for a donation, but had turned down the solicitor because the Y was not prepared to have a synagogue as part of its program. I rekindled his interest by my knowledge of Jerusalem, stating that there were more synagogues in that city than were actually needed and another one would be unnecessary. He asked me what it would cost to have his name incised on the front of the building. I told him $150,000, the sum that the building committee had set forth. In a conversation that could not have subsequently lasted more than five minutes, we made the deal. In 1968, I was with him at the dedication of the new building in Jerusalem.

One project that I never realized at the Suffolk day camp was a language arts program. Deficient in foreign languages myself, although I had studied Latin, French, German, Hebrew, and Yiddish, I had always been concerned about this lack in the American educational system. It occurred to me that a day camp in which groups of children spent eight weeks together studying a language of their own choosing would be an ideal setting for learning a new tongue quickly. I was hoping that emphasis would be placed on Hebrew, since more Jews were traveling to Israel and the day school movement had given impetus to learning how to speak as well as how to read Hebrew. But it has not yet come to pass.

One of the delights at the Usdan arts camp was the daily treat of an outside artist or group of artists, who would entertain the entire enrollment of fifteen hundred children between noon and 1:00 P.M. in the great shed. Some of the world's great artists in voice, violin, piano, and other instruments; duets, trios, quartets; dancing groups—all appeared each day to the plaudits of a youthful and enthusiastic audience. Many of the performers lauded the camp and its objectives. During the month of August, the day campers were ready to perform themselves, and day after day the orchestra, ensembles, the chorus, individuals played before their fellow campers. I spoke at a final session, when the orchestra of over one hundred, a chorus of over one hundred, and a dance ensemble of fifty gave a performance in which these three elements in the arts were coordinated.

One potentially dramatic project fell through at the last moment for lack of sufficient funds.

The director of the music program for the New York State Department of Education at Albany visited the Usdan site. She was overwhelmed. Yet she was unhappy that children from outside the Greater New York area could not take advantage of this unique program. She believed that if some way could be found to bring in and house the best talent from around the state, some money might be available.

At the same time the New York Philharmonic Orchestra approached us as to whether we could find some useful employment during the month of June, when the orchestra was unscheduled. The musicians would expect to be paid for any services or performance.

McKinley and I were enthralled. I prepared a most imaginative memorandum suggesting that the 270 best high school musicians in selected instruments (the Philharmonic complement was 135) be chosen from around the state. They would spend ten days, Monday through Friday, over a fortnight, each pair of students practicing alongside a musician from the great orchestra. This association would culminate in a massive concert on the last day. The orchestra would be bused out each day, but the students would be billeted and fed in a nearby agricultural school, which had no students during this period. Obviously the stimulation the students would receive from such an exposure would not only be memorable, but might be the decisive influence that could determine a young person's career. The total cost would be $275,000. In my mind, even if this was only a short-term educational stunt, it would have far-reaching public relations benefits for the Usdan arts camp. It would be easier to enlist top-level teachers, enhance enrollment, and attract artists for the daily concerts. Not to forget fund-raising.

The state was ready with $25,000. I found another source for $100,000, but this was far short of our goal. There was little enthusiasm in the lay and professional hierarchy at Federation for spending so much money on such a limited venture. The program was dropped.

But the spectacle of 375 artists and students playing before a shed full of listeners and the press reports which would follow was something that never left my mind.

* * *

In subsequent years a large theater complex was added to complete the four arts originally envisaged for the project. Later photography and creative writing were introduced. The enrollment has swollen to eighteen hundred children.

A plaque has been placed on one of the dance studios paying tribute to my role in bringing this program into realization.

During my tenure at Federation, the day camp was blessed with a number of devoted presidents—Mildred Goetz, Edna Erdman, Frederick P. Rose, Walter Bluhm, and Stanley Beckerman. With a director like Monte Melamed, who always supported any expansionist project I might dream up, even though it would always mean a greater load on his lean shoulders, the day camp became a model for other communities to emulate. There was nothing comparable to it on the American and world scene.

The Sabbath and the Rabbis

While I was able to read Hebrew (though I had difficulty in translating it), and was familiar with the rituals, the customs, the holidays, and many of the laws, my not being a traditional Jew, nor a regular attendant at daily and Sabbath services, was always a problem when I had to deal with traditionalist rabbis. I developed a strong position on introducing Jewish educational and some religious programs in centers and camps, and particularly programs centered around the Sabbath. I have already written about my difficulties with the rabbinate on Staten Island when I initiated Friday night services and Jewish educational programs. On Staten Island, the only rabbi who did not make any pronouncements against me was the venerable and scholarly traditional rabbi at the Jersey Street Synagogue, Rabbi Roshgolin. Perhaps his attitude was favorable because I had brought several difficult cases before him when Jewish couples wanted to become divorced. His distinguished son, Hillel Bavli, poet, educator, philosopher, occasionally dropped into the center to talk with me. I once arranged for him to give a lecture there on Hebrew poetry.

At Bronx House, I had similar difficulties when some of the local rabbis, all traditional, objected first to our music school functioning on the Sabbath and then to our introduction of lectures, often on Jewish subjects, on Friday nights. They objected to our Oneg Shabat program on Saturday afternoons. Rabbi Simon Kramer of the Hebrew Institute of University Heights in the Bronx was a vocal critic until we finally met, after which his personal evaluation of me brought about a change of mind. As he was an active rabbi on the Commission of Synagogue Relations at Federation, we crossed paths frequently. In 1966 he gave me a copy of his book *God and Man in the Sefer Hasidim*, as a gift, inscribing it with the words: "A friend and devoted public worker and in many ways a kindred spirit." He cooperated with the Bronx House and the Bronx YM-YWHA by making facilities at his synagogue available for a West Bronx Extension Center supervised by both Federation agencies.

None of the rabbis in the neighborhood of Bronx House ever invited me to pray or speak in their sanctuaries. All were rigidly traditional. Most were European born. They were mainly concerned with maintaining their institutions and positions, for the continuity of these religious institutions depended solely on their administrative ability and zeal coupled with their authoritative knowledge of the sacred text. Some of their congregants were members of Bronx House. I do not know of any ban (*herem*) that they ever put on such participation, as some of the local Catholic priests had done to their parishioners.

While we invited local rabbis to attend agency events at Bronx House, I do not recall any of them accepting our invitations. Only at the memorial service for President Roosevelt in 1945 and at a celebration of the founding of Israel in 1948 did they make an appearance at these extraordinary events, where they delivered appropriate prayers. In retrospect, it was a failure on my part not to have reached out sufficiently and persistently in order to develop closer ties between these important institutions in Jewish life.

On April 2, 1962, I was invited to present a paper before the Social Work Alumni Association of Yeshiva University on the "Implications of Sabbath Programming for the Jewish Community Center." My thesis was that even though the Jewish religious tradition had many restrictions in order to make this day sacrosanct, and perhaps as much as any other factor the Sabbath had kept Judaism alive, so many Jews had stopped observing it, either as a day of prayer for self-improvement or rest, that measures had to be undertaken by Jewish institutions to counter the trend. I thought this could be done by introducing programs of Jewish interest as well as providing activities of a higher cultural standard, which might attract elites and ordinary Jews and elevate their spirits, encourage their study on the Sabbath. While I was not enthusiastic about initiating athletic and ordinary social activities on the Sabbath, I could see the value of music, visits to art museums, folk dancing, if they could be conducted with a Jewish tone. I even justified travel, if the end object was to find one's self in a synagogue or to attend a Jewish educational program. The paper was vigorously opposed by Rabbi Herschel Schachter, a traditional scholar, although he said that he did not want to quarrel with its contents, which he admitted were well researched. He dealt with the general theme, which he believed would not encourage too many people to become more Jewish, but would further justify abandoning the sanctity of the traditional Sabbath.

As I was advocating the intensification of the Jewish experience, I began writing and presenting more papers on this subject. The opposition to my position shifted from the rabbis to my fellow social workers, and this continued up to the time I left the field in 1973.

The Fourth Force

It all began with a paper I wrote in January 1956 entitled "The Jewish Center as a Fourth Force in American Jewish Life." This paper eventually became the title of a book of my collected papers that the Jewish Education Committee, at the instigation of its executive director, Dr. Azriel Eisenberg, published in 1966. Eisenberg had asked me for some material on the Jewish centers, and I gave him a sheaf of articles I had written over the years. As a prolific writer himself, he undertook to get a series of the papers I had written since 1940 published by his organization.

In June 1969, it was a delight for me to read that the literary group at the Jewish Community Center of Staten Island had decided to publish a magazine entitled *The Fourth Force*. It printed items of arts, poetry, and literature based on the views I had propounded in my 1956 paper and my 1966 book. It quoted from my paper the following:

> The word, "Force," as I would like to use it, is that in Jewish life there are now three main vital forms to find salvation for the individual Jew and the Jewish group . . . Orthodoxy, the Conservative Movement and Reformism . . . We [the Jewish Community Centers] should be another institutional device and movement in which Jews may find some degree of comfort, some security in the American scene and still have it meet the particular needs of individuals in a flexible, free ever-developing atmosphere.

Regrettably, as a result of the departure of the charismatic leader of this group, no more than a few issues were published.

My essential theme was that the Jewish centers were part and parcel of the long religio-ethical tradition of our people; thus they should not be identified only as a social welfare instument, but rather the center should become the "Synagogue of the Twenty-First Century." Hence, along with Orthodoxy, Conservative, and Reform Judaism, we should now become a "Fourth Force."

The paper so disturbed my colleagues that I had to read it again at a meeting in April 1956, where it could be roundly, more than soundly, assailed. Not so incidentally, I could never get this thirty-page paper published in any professional Jewish social work journal.

Strangely, it was also attacked by representatives of the National Jewish Welfare Board, who had only a few years earlier forced upon the centers the acceptance of the Janowsky study, which declared that centers were exclusively Jewish agencies, committed to serve Jews, and thus these institutions were compelled to provide programs of Jewish substance. The study aimed to educate Jewish constituencies in a profounder Jewish fashion. The social work clique which had come to dominate both the NJWB and the center field wanted to see no deviation from the open-ended, multisectarian, social-action-oriented institution which had begun to emerge once again in the 1950's with the introduction of many more professional trained workers, whose inspiration came not from Jewish sources and educated Jewish leaders, but from the nonsectarian schools and their well-assimilated Jewish professors.

I suspect that the rabbis and some Jewish educators saw the adoption of my position as a threat to their establishments, for now I was invading their ideological sphere—and if we got a toehold, this might even threaten their jobs. I was met with outright hostility by fellow professionals whenever I spoke on this subject.

I presented a paper at the annual meeting of the New York Metropolitan Section of the NJWB on November 24, 1958, entitled "What Have Jewish Centers to Offer Future Generations?" I had been invited to speak and was not imposing myself on this audience. The paper stirred up further animosity amongst my colleagues, some of whom I had once considered good friends, some whose very growth in the field had involved my intervention. Walking out after the meeting, one was heard to say, in a voice that was far from sotto voce, "Graenum is still peddling that Jewish shit."

JOTS

It had been clear from the outset that if the centers were to fulfill the mission that I prescribed, they would have to do something about filling the Jewish lacunae in the backgrounds of their workers, from the executives down.

Meetings with Dr. Leon Feldman, a rabbi, scholar, and Jewish educator associated with the Board of Jewish Education, beginning as early as 1953, eventually led to the creation of the Jewish Orientation Training Seminars (JOTS), which has continued to this day. A small committee of laymen and professionals headed by Earl Morse, a businessman with strong interests in mental hygiene and Judaism (he later became president of the Union of American Hebrew Congregations) and a fabulous collector of Oriental art, introduced this program to the Jewish communal workers in various disciplines, with surprising results. It was clear from their own confessionals that they personally profited from exposure to some of the most seminal minds in Jewish life, Rabbis Joseph Soloveitchik and Emanuel Rackman to mention just two. What is more, the agencies in which they worked were also affected. Once the head professionals were more comfortable with a rationale as to why they should be "Jewish" professionals, it was easier to get staff members to attend these short-term Jewish seminars. In some instances an agency's overall philosophy was influenced. JOTS made an effort to extend this influence into the education of the boards of directors, but it never got off the ground. Whereas professionals, including executives, were not loathe to expose themselves to these courses, they did little or nothing to encourage their lay volunteers to follow their example. I suspect that this was partly due to the fact that policies were in reality made by professionals, and a too-well-educated Jewish volunteer leadership might have wanted to push for a more sectarian character for the agency.

Dr. Feldman maintained the highest standards in attracting lecturers for the seminars, and he also made sure that the content was relevant to the interests and needs of the enrollees. Having sat in on lectures by Rabbi Soloveitchik, I can attest that it was a phenomenal intellectual exposure to the thinking of one of the leading Jewish minds of the twentieth century, albeit a highly traditional mind.

The successors to Dr. Feldman, Herman L. Sainer and currently Dr. Norman Linzer, maintained the seminars in the original mold, although in later years it became more closely related to the Wurzweiler School of Social Work of Yeshiva University than to the Board of Jewish Education. Annually, I saw to it that an earmarked fund was provided to the Jewish Education Committee for the subsidization of this program.

How to extend the training of Jewish communal workers in Jewish subject materials was a larger problem, since the creation of similar JOTS around the country was difficult. There were few partisans willing to risk their necks to establish such seminars. Most of the leaders and their staffs were deficient in Jewish learning. The closing of the Graduate School of Jewish Social Work had not led to the creation of any substitute. A short-lived Training Bureau for Jewish Communal Service was established in 1947 for the supplementary training of executives only. But the emphasis was on training in administrative skills rather than in Jewish subject matter, even though excellent instructors and detailed manuals were prepared for the students on Jewish themes. Something had to be done. In the mid 1950's, it was finally decided, after pressure by a few of us, that the National Conference of Jewish Communal Service would appoint a committee on professional training. I became its first chairman, and Dr. Feldman was vice-chairman.

At the National Conference of Jewish Communal Service held in Pittsburgh on June 1, 1959, I read a wide-ranging, major paper on

"Professional Training for Jewish Communal Services" before a well-attended plenum session, with the president of the NCJCS gracing the podium.

My thesis was that the overwhelming number of professional workers in the field today have a limited Jewish background. My recommendations therefore called for intensive recruiting of the ablest, Jewishly educated students. It would be necessary to create Jewish schools of social work, because the nonsectarian schools were neither interested nor prepared to provide any Jewish orientation even for Jewish students. If no distinctive school eventuated, then graduate students should be enrolled simultaneously in courses of Jewish studies elsewhere, such as religious seminaries or universities with departments of Jewish studies. Jewish students should be assigned to field work placements in Jewish agencies that espoused Jewish purposes and placed with supervisors, who had a knowledge and affirmative interest in Jewish affairs. All Federations and large Jewish agencies should be encouraged to establish in-service training programs comparable to JOTS, and the lecturers and the content should be on a high intellectual and not on a "digest" level.

I would like to report that the paper was received with enthusiasm, but the reaction was quite the contrary. The president, a strict nonsectarian, stalked off the platform with a look of disgust. While there were a few supporters among the attendees, in the main it was attacked without quarter as being sectarian, medieval, narrow, not in keeping with the times. At the time most Jewish social workers still advocated integration (particularly after the Supreme Court decision on school integration in 1954). They believed that agencies should accept more non-Jewish clientele, more non-Jews on their staff. Most were for soliciting more money from non-Jewish sources, especially government departments.

I vigorously answered the attackers with my own philosophy and long experience, always fortified by facts, but it made little impact.

Again the paper was never published in the *Journal of Jewish Communal Service*, a deliberate slight, because most papers, whether worthy or unworthy, found their way into that quarterly. This rejection was an "official act" of the editor and the magazine's management board.

* * *

My tenure as chairman of the professional committee was coming to an end. I had suggested that Dr. Feldman succeed me, as the best-qualified person for that post. We were both invited to a meeting of the top leadership of the National Conference, where this decision was to be made. When Feldman and I arrived, we discovered that the meeting was already underway. The discussion that followed was acrimonious. Harry Lurie, one of the prominent professionals in the field, argued that rather than Jewish studies, his own recent investigations revealed that it would be better if the professionals in Jewish agencies learned Spanish, because their customers now and in the future would be bound up with recent immigrants who spoke that tongue. Several stated that it would also be necessary for more professionals in Jewish organizations to learn more about the Negroes, their problems and their culture, since they too would comprise a larger portion of the future clientele of Jewish agencies. Then, to our dismay, we learned that Donald Horowitz of Philadelphia, an inner-circle professional, would become the new chairman, and that he would appoint his own committee and develop whatever programs and policies the new crew would determine. We sat through the meeting in disbelief, boiling inwardly, but restrained until we obtained the full picture.

Then I let loose an attack on each individual in the room, seven in all, all of whom I knew intimately. I indicated that they were voting their historical prejudices, which completely misinterpreted the needs of American Jews and their institutions. They would now deliver the final coup, which would inevitably recommend that our agencies become nonsectarian. Under such circumstances I was resigning from the committee. I would not accept the high office to which I had been elected by the National Conference. (If I stayed, I would have been the president in one or two years.) To my amazement, Dr. Judah Shapiro, a learned Jew, an intimate friend from the mid-thirties, the newly elected president of the conference, the executive director of the National Foundation for Jewish Culture, an organization that he helped create and that was devoted solely to the furtherance of the very objectives I espoused, assailed me for not listening to the members of the conference, who were expertly informed on the character and development of the Jewish community and its social welfare institutions. He told me that I should stop trying to impose my own philosophy on American Jewish institutions, something they were not willing or prepared to accept. I replied to Shapiro, "Et tu, Brute," stalked out of the room, and did not speak to him for many years. He approached me six years later at a conference and told me that I had been right and he was wrong. He had become a commentator on the radio and invited me to speak over the air on several occasions.

The Professional Committee on Training did nothing in either a Jewish or a nonsectarian direction, leaving the field leaderless in this respect for years. But nature abhors a vacuum. The need was there for what I advocated. The Wurzweiler School of Social Work was established at Yeshiva University, the first "Jewish" school in a university setting, and what is more a Jewish university. It had a slow and hard time at first, because it was not only Jewish, but in an Orthodox milieu.

Meanwhile, events in Jewish life began to make demands on Jewish institutions for more Jewish focused services. The integration of American schools and the disintegration of the public school system created a backlash, triggering a quick dispersal of the Jewish population. In their new locations they wanted Jewish intitutions with Jewish programs. The major factor in the change of Jewish Federations and their constituent societies was the Arab-Israel War in 1967. At first it looked as though the Jews would suffer another Holocaust. Yet the extraordinary skill of the Israeli army instead brought a quick and resounding victory with the conquest of the Sinai, Gaza, the Golan Heights, and the West Bank. In the euphoria of victory, the Federations and many of their agencies reversed their attitudes toward Israel, now vigorously espousing positions that were the diametric opposites of what they had stoutly defended only a few months before. Missions to Israel of Jewish professionals brought them back converted to a new cause. Soon everything had to be nearly one hundred percent Jewish.

In 1969, the School of Jewish Communal Service of the Hebrew Union College—Jewish Institute of Religion matriculated its first class. Brandeis University was quick to follow with the Hornstein-Lown Center. The Council of Jewish Federations set up a program to recruit students and provide scholarships for professional training, and after graduation from an accredited school assured them of good positions in Jewish agencies. Baltimore and Cleveland developed special programs with local schools where social work was taught supplemented by Jewish programs in Bureaus of Jewish Education and local Hebrew colleges.

So historical events, domestic and international, forced dramatic changes that I had foreseen years before, but which had been heretofore categorically rejected. Perhaps my "prophetic" insights had been premature. Perhaps my method of communicating my ideas was too abrasive. I could not change my tone nor my timing. I had been deeply moved by Abraham J. Heschel's description of a prophet in his book *The Prophets* (1962), in which he wrote:

> The prophet seldom tells a story, but casts events. He rarely sings, but castigates. He does more than translate reality into a poetic key: he is a preacher whose purpose is not self-expression or the "purgation of emotions," but communication. His images must not shine. They must burn.

Jews and Communism

In his article "The Menorah Journal—A Literary Precursor" in *Midstream* (October 1984), Louis Harap referred to Elliott Cohen, a former editor of the *Menorah Journal* and the founding editor of *Commentary*. Reading this I was reminded of a visit that Cohen had made to me at Federation accompanied by the sociologist Nathan Glazer. Glazer was compiling material for a book on the Jews in the Communist movement in the 1930's, a movement with which Cohen himself had been intimately identified. Disillusioned with its dishonesty and rigid parochialism, he broke with and then began to attack the party from every vantage point.

They had come to see me because they had heard that I too had been "identified" with the Communists and had "broken" with their positions. So they thought I would be an excellent source for revealing who was a Communist among the Jewish social workers during those decades. I told them they they had been misinformed about my affiliations; that I had never even flirted with joining the party, nor had I even contributed to its causes, subscribed to its papers or magazines, or even signed their petitions. I stated that I had been a Socialist up to 1936, had sympathized with the recognition of the Soviet Union in 1933 by the U.S. Government, and had allowed the followers of ICOR, a pro-Soviet organization of Jews interested in the Soviet Jewish Republic being established in Biro-Bidjan, to meet at the center on Staten Island; that I had attended one meeting of the United Front American League Against War and Fascism, but when I saw that it was Communist-controlled from top to bottom, never attended another session; that I had helped the democratically elected regime in Spain, but under the banner of Socialism.

While I knew scores of Jewish communal workers, who I was sure were closely identified with Communist movements, and how they tried to insinuate their point of view in the deliberations of the Conference of Jewish Communal Workers, and in the programs of agencies, and in the seduction of both members and staff to their point of view, I had never seen their Communist Party membership cards, nor had any of them ever admitted to me that they were party members, so I was in no position to give anyone their names. I could only discuss what they did collectively and how effective or generally ineffective they were. I told them that since I had been tarnished with the Communist brush to the temporary cost of my early professional career, and knowing that I was innocent, I was loathe to tincture anyone that I knew with an uncertain coloration. Cohen and Glazer were both disappointed, Cohen more so than Glazer, because he had been led to believe that I not only knew the facts, but I would tell all.

The Pelham Jewish Center: Native Anti-Semitism

Our son Michael was getting along in Public School 106 in the Bronx, but was not thriving, even though he was always in the special program for gifted students. I believed strongly in the public school system, even to the point where I thought that our younger son ought to study both in a junior high and senior high school that already were highly integrated, even though class size was unduly large, and behavior problems interfered with the quality of the school both in and out of the classroom, obviously downgrading the educational process. While he learned easily, he never felt the school challenged him. He was always bored.

On several occasions Michael had been molested by non-whites holding him up for whatever money or articles they could force him to turn over. When he was threatened with a weapon, we knew it was time to move elsewhere. Emma suggested a private school, which our modest rent in Parkchester ($85 per month for five rooms, including gas and electricity plus a garage, and immaculately maintained) would have permitted us to afford, but I still had an antipathy toward private schools, even though I acknowledged their superiority. But any extension of the private system would alter the number and quality of the public schools. More and more upper and middle class families with higher education, and even those on a somewhat lower economic level, were enrolling their offspring in private schools. The implications of this move for housing and the character of whole neighborhoods were obvious. As we computed our expenses, we decided we could afford to buy a house in the suburbs, preferably Westchester, and still have our son attend public schools.

The better public school systems in 1953 were in Scarsdale and Chappaqua. We could not afford Scarsdale. Chappaqua turned out to have affordable housing, but we were apprised of considerable anti-Semitism by the agent who showed us some homes. The distance from New York, where I worked, was too time-consuming. We finally concentrated on Pelham. It was Waspish, although as we learned later, it had a large Italian Catholic census. There were even a few middle-class blacks. It enjoyed a good school system with small classes and mature, caring teachers. The principal of the high school assured us there was no problem of anti-Semitism in the schools, and the real estate agents gave us the same impression.

Before we moved to Pelham, Michael had complained of a knee problem. Our Parkchester doctor assured us it was nothing and that he just liked to gripe. Shortly after we moved to Pelham, the pain became severe. A Jewish friend suggested that we have her husband look at it. Dr. Henry Jaffe was already a world-renowned bone pathologist, researching at the Hospital for Joint Diseases in Manhattan, a Federation institution. After a careful examination, he suggested that we see Dr. Joseph Milgram, a distinguished orthopedist, who headed the the orthopedic department at the same hospital. Milgram over some years has treated every member of our family. He told us that Michael should not be operated on until he had attained physical maturity. Michael was now fourteen years old. Milgram fitted him with a brace from his ankle to his hip, which obviously immobilized him for sports, except for swimming. Yet he moved around with amazing agility.

Our purchase of a house in Pelham directly across from a school at 340 Corlies Avenue was most convenient for him. It was a handsome eight-room house, Dutch colonial in design, half brick and half stucco, a common pattern in Pelham when it was built in 1927. We paid $24,000. We had only saved up $6,000, borrowed $6,000 from a special interest-free fund at Federation, took out a mortgage for an unbelievable 4.5 percent for five years, 4 percent for five years, and 3.5 percent for the last seven years.

The school turned out to be excellent for Michael. He did reasonably well in his studies, but never up to his I.Q., which was in the top classification.

He managed athletic teams. He acted in plays, learning his part virtually overnight. He was always a quick study. While his brace was a handicap socially, nonetheless he found it possible to have a reasonably active social life, particularly after he learned to drive and was permitted to use the car. In his last term in high school, his knee underwent surgery. He recovered completely.

We knew only two families when we moved to Pelham. Emanuel Schwartz, an attorney, lay leader at the Mount Vernon YM-YWHA, and Louis Kraft, who had retired from the National Jewish Welfare Board and the European office of the American Jewish Joint Distribution Committee. Initially we had no idea whether there were other Jews in Pelham. There were no outward symbols like a synagogue or other Jewish organizations. Since Pelham was squeezed in between Mount Vernon and New Rochelle, with a YM-YWHA and many synagogues all within a three-mile radius, we assumed, after making the rounds, that we would affiliate with one or more.

Shortly after we had settled in, the Krafts and the Schwartzs introduced us to other Jewish families. We were invited to a meeting of an organization called the Pelham Community League—all Jews. We were not happy with this group, wherein Jews were trying to establish a "nonsectarian" Jewish organization, in the hope of breaking down some of the social barriers. No Jews were admitted as members or even as guests at the Pelham Country Club (golf, tennis, swimming, restaurant, and bar). No Jewish children were admitted to Barclay's dancing classes with side excursions to skating, skiing, and other resorts. No Jewish women could become members of the Manor Club, a fashionable group that conducted excellent educational and social programs. While the league was not prepared to combat these restrictions, its members hoped to develop desirable substitutes for their children and themselves.

There was a flurry of activity in the fall to create something distinctly Jewish. A group appeared at our house one Sunday morning in early November, seven months after we moved to Pelham, urging me to take a more active role, since I was a "Jewish organizer." Meetings were quickly arranged at the home of Drs. Morris A. and Rose (Koblenz) Goldberg, who subsequently became not only our physicians, but also amongst our closest friends for over thirty years, to determine whether we should be a B'nai B'rith branch, a YM-YWHA or a synagogue.

While I was extremely burdened at Federation, I met with a committee to arrange a meeting to determine how many Jews would respond. Emma and I, along with others, researched the Pelham telephone book and picked out all the Jewish-sounding names. We made a few mistakes, but on the whole we were quite accurate. I sent out a letter to over one hundred people for a meeting at the local high school, which the officials were initially happy to offer us.

Ninety enthusiastic Jews showed up. It was quickly agreed that we should not set up a synagogue, but rather a Jewish community center, although the center would program a Hebrew school, Jewish educational activities, and sponsor religious services if the membership requested same. Every family paid $100 dues for the first year on the spot, even though we had not yet been incorporated or developed more than the paper program I circulated. Someone rose and said we needed a building at once, and $10,000 was additionally pledged for such a structure.

I appointed a committee to search for possibilities, appointed an attorney to file for our charter as a nonprofit membership corporation, appointed a committee to develop a program and another committee to engage a youth worker.

We publicized the results of our first meeting in the local press, stating that we were looking for property and planned to build a library and a swimming pool, indoors of course, for the three villages which composed our town had neither of these facilities. Then the roof caved in.

The school would not let us meet there again, as we were now categorized as a religious organization, and that ran counter to the school's policy on use. I met with the Board of Education, some of whom were high-powered executives of major American industrial and commercial corporations; the chairman was a vice-president of the *Saturday Evening Post*. I argued that we were like a YMCA, a secular rather than a religious organization. That argument did not impress them. Hanukah was drawing near, and one board member asked me whether we would celebrate that festival. I said that we would and pointed out that the holiday had both a religious and a secular aspect. They would not buy that either. I then riled them by asking why the school permitted the Men's Club of Pelham to hold a Christmas Carol Sing at the high school, since a program of that kind had a distinctly religious element. The meeting was adjourned. We couldn't use the high school again. Prejudice rather than principle prevailed.

As our committee began looking at properties, we noted in the local paper that the Village of Pelham Manor had inserted an advertisement to publicize a proposed amendment to its zoning laws. During the summer of 1953, less than six months before, the village had adopted a new zoning ordinance, after an expensive five-year study, which permitted clubs, religious institutions, libraries, and swimming pools to be built within prime residential areas. When we inquired about the proposed changes in the zoning laws, we learned to our dismay that these items were to be eliminated. This was obviously in response to the article in the newspaper. We went to the hearing and spoke against the proposed amendments noting that churches and social clubs were now located in the best residential sectors, but that did not influence the passing of the zoning amendment. We had the same experience in North Pelham, after we found a desirable property, which already included an outdoor pool and a garage large enough to serve as a gymnasium. Joseph Mandell, a resident and lawyer, and I appeared before that village's zoning board and made an impassioned plea, but nonetheless the zoning ordinances were also amended to prevent our acquiring the property.

Meanwhile, we rented quarters in the Community Church (Protestant), where we had a number of meetings and activities for our children. We engaged Ira Moss, an attractive physical educator whom I had known for many years, to provide activities for the children. Before the year was out, we were told that the church would not renew our use of its facilities. Apparently the congregation had overruled the wishes of its liberal minister, who welcomed our presence. Next we rented quarters on the second floor of a commercial building at the corner of Pelhamdale Avenue and the Boston Post Road. Our legend on the door was frequently defaced or destroyed, but we persisted in remaining there.

It was abundantly clear by the end of 1954, one year after we founded the PJC, that we would never be able to acquire property as a secular Jewish community center. Many of the leaders of our organization felt that if we became a religious institution, a synagogue, the villages could not prevent us from obtaining a building. At a stormy meeting, the change was made. I gave way to Louis Schrag as president, a businessman and the strongest proponent of a synagogue. The board gave a great party for me on my retirement from office. My friend Dr. Nahum Tim Gidal, a photojournalist, art historian, and greatly honored in Europe and Israel in recent years for his books and photographs, put together, with David Jae's expert technical assistance, a film tape on "This is your life." They presented me with a marvelous painting executed by Victor Trasoff, an important commercial artist, which still adorns our home. It is dedicated to "Graenum 'Moses' Berger." The attendees all wrote their signatures on the back.

In 1954, Pelham was celebrating its three-hundredth anniversary. Since 1654, when Pelham was founded, was also the year when the first twenty-three Jews had come to New Amsterdam (later New York) from

Recife, Brazil, I wrote a letter to the local newspaper, noting this coincidence, and pointing out that Lord Pell, the founder of the community, might well have bought his pots and pans, cloth and thread, even rum, from Jewish peddlers who had to sell their wares beyond the confines of the Dutch seaport, for they could not engage in retail trade in the first year of their residence. The paper did not see fit to print it.

However, in 1976, when the United States was celebrating its bicentennial, I recommended that we have a special program at the synagogue commemorating this event. I wrote a long pageant in words and song that related the story of the Jewish contribution to the development of this country before and since the Declaration of Independence. I included the reference to the Jewish peddlers and Lord Pell. Present were a number of village officials and clergymen from other faiths. I am sure that the recitation of this section of the pageant made some impression on their sensibilities. But this historical presentation came some years after a long court fight with the village of Pelham Manor about our right to worship in a synagogue of our own in Pelham.

Our rented quarters were inadequate. We changed rabbis nearly every year. The board, in the early years, was unable to find a rabbi who could duplicate the inspiring High Holy Day services which Charles Bernstein, Dr. Julius Fink, Louis Kraft, and I had conducted at the home of Charles and Celia Bernstein in 1953. We tended toward Reformism, although some of the members were Orthodox. After a year of debate, during which all of the denominations were evaluated, we decided for the Conservative identification. Men and women would sit together in worship. We would observe *Kashrut*, the Jewish dietary laws, in the synagogue, and not depart from the traditional conventions on the Sabbath, festivals, and the High Holy Days. It took several years to codify our practices. We engaged student rabbis who were in training at the Jewish Theological Seminary as our religious leaders.

Charles Feinstein, the diligent and generous chairman of the building committee, finally found a handsome residence on the Esplanade, one of the finest residential districts in Pelham. Although we had no assurance that we would be able to use it as a synagogue, in view of the zoning restrictions, a group of us decided to buy it and quickly raised $40,000 to consummate the sale. We applied for an occupancy permit. A public hearing was scheduled. Meanwhile petitions were circulated and signed by hundreds of citizens to prevent our use of the building even as a religious institution. I am unhappy to state that there were some Jewish names amongst them. They also did not want any more Jews settling in Pelham. Abuse and anti-Semitic diatribes were publicly heaped upon us to discourage and prevent our utilizing this structure. The school auditorium was packed when the zoning hearing took place, and the whole scene was unbelievable in the United States in 1956. Our small committee of nine, Emma and I amongst them, felt as if we were walking through a Nazi gantlet when six hundred people rose to their feet, booed, told us to go back to the Bronx.

The committee had decided that I should not present our case, because my style was unafraid and caustic. We left it to our mild-mannered attorney, Edward Winkelman, a member of our board. He handled it soberly.

Seventy-five families, he said, wanted a dignified building in which to pray in Pelham. We had found one in a desirable location. We planned to maintain it in such a way as to enhance the appearance of the neighborhood. We were certain that any additional traffic we might bring to the area would not constitute a hazard. We asked for permission to use the building and modify it to accord with the building code.

The charges leveled against the use of this building as a synagogue were fantastic. Noise, traffic (children would be killed), unsightliness, unsuitability, and many other obscure excuses were cited. It was obvious that the people did not want Jews or a Jewish institution in the village, particularly one that might attract more Jews as residents and thus change its pristine Christian character. The village board turned down our petition. We had no other recourse but to go to court. In passing, it is worth noting that thirty years before another effort had been made to start a synagogue in Pelham. When the villages turned it down, the Pelham Jews had accepted their fate, and helped establish a synagogue in neighboring Mount Vernon.

Dr. Morris Goldberg and his wife, Dr. Rose Koblenz, who had played a most important role in the organization and continued support of the synagogue, and I underwent some interesting experiences while trying to obtain a building. I was invited to the home of the village president to discuss why we insisted on having a building in a residential area. He pointed out some vacant land in the industrial zones and wondered why we didn't acquire those parcels. In my nicest manner, I replied that all the churches were in fine residential districts and that is where we wanted to be. Furthermore, we could not afford to build a new structure and therefore were constrained to purchasing a large existing dwelling. I was told to my face that if the others were like me (I had good manners and a northern New York State accent) it would be different, but that they did not want people coming in from the Bronx, which bordered Pelham. I then confounded them by stating that I had moved from the Bronx. I told them that doctors, lawyers, accountants, teachers, and businessmen in our congregation were all from the Bronx, and that a finer assembly of people did not exist. I finished my drink and left—leaving them unhappy with the interview. The Goldbergs were told by the village leadership that if we were really serious about practicing our religion, we would even worship in a cellar rather than alienate a whole community, and we didn't need the fine building on the Esplanade. Morris never forgot these outrageous anti-Semitic remarks.

Some of us, with me playing a major initial contact role, appealed to the B'nai B'rith Anti-Defamation League, the American Jewish Committee, the American Jewish Congress, and the National Conference of Christians and Jews to provide legal talent or use their influence to override this local blockage. One sent an observer to public meetings. Another unctuously advised us to abandon the building and join congregations in contiguous cities. Another said it was too busy fighting against the display of a crèche on Christmas to take on this case. It was embarrassing to meet with such indifference from well-financed organizations that had been established to fight for so-called Jewish rights. All felt that we should not argue the case in court on the basis of discrimination against religious observance or anti-Semitism, but that at best we should try to overcome the adverse administrative decision of the village zoning board. We obtained the services of Samuel Gottlieb of Larchmont, an attorney who had fought and won a similar case for that community. Gottlieb gave of his time without compensation. The synagogue only paid for incidental costs, which, as the case wound through the courts for many years, turned out to be expensive.

We regrettably followed the advice of the Jewish communal relations agencies and did not raise the issue of religious discrimination or anti-Semitism. We lost in the State Supreme Court. We went to the Appellate Court, where we were turned down again. We carried the case to Albany in the Court of Appeals, where we lost for the third time. One of the judges asked our attorney why we were not arguing this case on the basis of religious discrimination.

We took the hint, filed again in the county Supreme Court, and won. The village appealed the case to the Appellate Division, where the judgment was reaffirmed. The village intended to carry the issue to the Court of Appeals, but was stopped by the threat of a taxpayer's suit initiated by some Christian friends, headed by William Peters, a television producer, who charged the village board in their petition with religious discrimination and wasting the taxpayers' money.

We finally won the case. Yet our difficulties were not over. The village engineer made so many recommendations about alterations in the building that we would have virtually had to tear it down and start from scratch. One vital condition of its use was adequate parking.

There was a vacant lot, two hundred by sixty feet, contiguous to our property, which would have been ideal for parking. Feinstein approached the owner, who was willing to sell it to us for $6,000. Before we could meet and act, although our action would have been for purchase, we read in the local paper that a group of citizens had purchased the land and were giving it to the village to be used as a park in perpetuity.

This would prevent our acquisition. While grass had been grown on this land and cut, it has never been converted into a playground or park.

My long experience with buildings used for similar purposes convinced me that we did not have to make all the changes nor provide as much parking space as demanded. We had the right to use the streets surrounding our property for parking, just like all the churches in the villages. We proceeded on our own modified plans, which were finally accepted by the authorities. We told them that if they didn't accept, we would take them to court again. It was obvious that the intent was to discourage us from using the building. We raised the money for repairs, made the alterations, and dedicated the building, carrying the Torahs through the streets of Pelham from our rented quarters to the new sanctuary.

Since then we have had no trouble with the village officials or citizen organizations. Our rabbis and laymen participate in interreligious programs and committees. Ministers on occasion speak from our pulpit. When we wanted to build an addition, we had no trouble with the authorities. Life has also changed in Pelham. The Country Club and Manor Club now accept Jewish members, and a number have joined. The civil rights legislation of the last twenty years has had an impact on their policies. The three villages are still predominantly Christian. The Jewish population has not increased appreciably. In 1985, there are only seventy members, and some of them live in neighboring cities. We have had some able rabbis like Bernard Eisenman, now head of a large congregation in Massachusetts, Benjamin Hollander, now a teacher in Israel; Yaakov Rone, leader of a sizable synagogue in San Diego, and Hillel Friedman, now with New York's Federation. These young rabbis made a deep impression on our synagogue membership.

Apart from services and meetings, my continued contribution to the synagogue has been the creation of the Book Readers, which since 1975 has been reviewing important Jewish books, attracting a group of up to fifty people, urging them to build their own libraries of Jewish works. We have also been instrumental in developing an excellent Judaica library through my personal influence on the late Celia Greenfield, who originally established the library in memory of her first husband, Charles Bernstein, a founder of the synagogue. Since her death, it has been rememorialized in both their names. Each year on Yom Kippur, I have been honored with the reading of the Book of Jonah. Each year I have been invited to install the newly elected officers. Emma is active in the sisterhood, and both of us attend services and most synagogue happenings.

* * *

For the first twenty years of the Pelham Jewish Center, its presidents were all men who had been founders of the synagogue or had joined its ranks shortly after its initiation. With one exception, the son of a founder, all had been conventionally married to Jewish women. The exception was married to a convert, who opted for a total Jewish life and had become active in every phase of the center. From the outset, we knew that a large number of residents in the community were intermarried, and while some had joined the center and a few others had supported it from time to time, most never indicated that they were interested in living as Jews, nor did they become active in the institution.

Ten years ago, this changed, following a steady influx of new and young families, many of them intermarried. While in some cases Jewish women had married non-Jews, by and large, the Jewish partners were mostly men. Among the first was an able, articulate young man who was critical of the center for not having better rabbinical leadership and better Jewish educational programs for children. He and a few others were on the verge of leaving, when I invited him to a meeting in our home along with former presidents of the center. We listened carefully to his "fourteen points" (I remarked that he was a "Wilsonian") and an agreement was reached, whereby he would assume the presidency in another year, and we would undertake most of the changes he recommended. We did. He served well, revitalized the organization, brought in many new members. His son now attends a day school, because he still thought the educational program in the center was not good enough. His wife, a convert, became an active participant. He was succeeded by another male president whose wife had been converted. She even went through a second conversion and a formal Conservative marriage. Later she became chairman of the sisterhood. He was followed by still another man whose wife did not convert, but who nonetheless became an active member of both the synagogue and the sisterhood. His successor will be a man married to an aboriginal Jewish woman. In the years ahead, it looks as though the center will be led more and more by intermarried couples, with the possibility of one convert, a woman, even rising to the helm. In this latter family, after her conversion, the family introduced one of the few kosher kitchens in Pelham, and the children of her first marriage, who had also been converted, are being given an intensive Jewish education.

In 1985 Charles E. Silberman's *A Certain People* was published. He was one of the few writing about Jewish life today who did not see intermarriage as a tragedy, but rather as an opportunity. If the Jewish community couldn't stem the tide of these burgeoning relationships, he said, then it should turn these units into a positive force, which would increase rather than diminish the Jewish census. Many intermarried families in Pelham have not yet joined the center. We hope they will. Of those who have become members, their children have been exposed to a Jewish education. A number have had a unique Bar or Bat Mitzvah, where they chanted their portion of the week from the Torah scroll. In some instances both parents have been for the first time formally identified with the Jewish community. Their interests are, however, broader. They actively participate in Pelham organizations, the art museum, the Junior League, the family service agency, the Manor Social Club, and the Country Club.

Silberman, who has been faulted for having Pollyannish rather than the more conventional lachrymose views on the future of Jewish life in America, may be a better prognosticator of the future than most of the Jewish sociologists, communal workers, and other leaders who have viewed this growing phenomenon with anguish.

While I advised my children and grandchildren that I would look with disapproval on their marrying anyone who was not a Jew by birth or conversion, the evidence, at least in Pelham, points to the possibility of adding to our Jewish ranks if a kindly hand is proffered to those who have intermarried.

* * *

I joined the Pelham Men's Club, a civic organization, at the suggestion of a Jewish neighbor, but after the incidents with the various village officials in 1954, some of whom were also leaders in the Men's Club, I resigned. Several years later, I was appointed to the nominating committee for the Board of Education. I accepted the invitation, because I thought I might be able to influence the election of members who were competent to serve in that unsalaried capacity. While on the nominating committee, I developed an outline for prospective nominees. It was unlike anything they had ever used before; I gathered that the committee usually selected people they knew and trusted—a kind of club affair.

To my surprise, I was approached and asked if I would accept a nomination for the board. It seemed that I had made a significant impression through my knowledge of education, social work, administrative management (including fiscal operations and management of buildings,) so that the criteria I had expounded had an impact. I thought it over and decided against accepting the tender. Although it would have given some kudos to me and to the rest of the Pelham Jews, the demands that would have been put upon my time were far beyond that which I was able and willing to give. Once my name was publicly associated with the court fight the Pelham Jewish Center undertook against one of the villages, I was sure that such an offer would never be made to me a second time. It hasn't.

In the late 1970's a Jew was not only elected to the board, but also became its president. He used his association with the PJC to get elected. In 1983, for the first time, a Jew was selected to be the superintendent of schools. Prejudice on religious grounds had seemingly disappeared.

I attempted on several other occasions to join civic groups, but my experience was always negative. I met with a human rights group that wanted overnight to change Pelham into an interracial community. There were and are now several score blacks in Pelham, mostly middle class, who apparently moved here to escape from the "Harlems" in which they had been forced to live. They wanted a quiet niche for themselves in an upper-class village. They lived inconspicuously. Their children benefited from a superior school. They were not consulted about changing Pelham. It was a naive, white, non-Jewish, liberal assembly, who had decided to join the stream of advocates for instant integration. I dropped out after one meeting.

At the invitation of the local librarian, who knew Emma and me as constant readers and generous supporters, we were invited to a meeting of a group studying Mortimer Adler's "100 Great Books." I went alone to the first meeting, where they were reading Aeschylus' *Oresteia*, a superb Greek trilogy and tragedy. A summary of the play was presented and the chairman called for discussion. I saw the group struggling to interpret the text as written. I always read these plays as important documents in Greek history. Aeschylus had been arrested, despite his literary gifts, and was pleading through the plays, particularly the third one, for a trial by a jury of his peers, which would have been a landmark legal development twenty-four hundred years ago.

In the *Eumenides*, the third play, Orestes, who murdered his mother, Clytemnestra, because she had killed Agamemnon, her husband and his father, so that she could marry or at least disport openly with her lover, Aegisthus, is pleading for his life before the goddess Athena, and asks not to be disposed of without a trial. Athena is impressed with his plea. She replies:

> Judges, I will appoint for homicide,
> A court set up in perpetuity.
> Meanwhile do you call proofs and witnesses.
> As sworn supports of Justice; they, having chosen
> The best of all people, I shall cause
> To pass true judgment on the present cause.

Thus was trial by jury of one's peers initiated at least in literature. The chairman and several others chastised me for departing from the rules of not referring to any other works or sources for interpreting the text. We were to use only our own limited imaginations. Such a proscribed method I could not accept. I never returned to that group.

When we came to Pelham, we had been enrolled Democrats for many years. We unhesitatingly registered in the party so that we could vote in the upcoming primaries. We subsequently learned that while most Jews usually voted Democratic, they chose to enroll in the Pelham Republican Party, as Pelham was Republican and rarely elected or voted for a

Democrat even for local offices. I attended several meetings of the Democratic party at people's homes and came away with the decided opinion that it was more of a social organization than a serious political group. We stopped attending meetings, although we still continue to support the party.

I believe that my unsympathetic attitude toward non-Jews in our community and elsewhere was decidedly influenced by our trials in court in our effort to establish a synagogue. While the people in the various forums that I briefly attended might not have been the perpetrators of the attempt to keep a synagogue out of Pelham, I also found out very quickly that none of them had done anything to further our cause. I suspect this was my reason for not wanting to associate myself intimately with them even in civic endeavors. It also influenced how we spent our philanthropic dollars, which have gone substantially to Jewish organizations.

Yet we love our immediate non-Jewish neighbors, exchange gifts, and bring them matzos and wine on Pesach.

Burlesque

Back in the early 1930's, my sister Rachel came to New York. In the course of a conversation she had with Emma, the subject of burlesque shows came up. The Minsky brothers had made this form of entertainment quite popular, and performances were attended even by curious intellectuals. Mayor LaGuardia conducted a vigorous campaign during his administration to outlaw these displays of sex, gags, and brassy music. Emma suggested that Rachel join her at a performance in Manhattan, as part of her exploration of the New York theater and shows of an unusual character. One afternoon, they bought tickets in one of the sleazy houses, found themselves in the sparsely populated stalls almost entirely occupied by men. The performance began with the usual sexual and obscene references, although in those days they were double entendre rather than explicit, as today. Then the strippers appeared with their bumps and grinds. They were about to start discarding their scanty clothing when Rachel rose in disgust and fled from the theater, stepping all over the men seated in her row. She never made another comment on this unhappy afternoon in the demi-world of Broadway. She was a lady through and through and no longer had any sympathy for such manifestations of adulterated fun.

I relate this story because Michael confessed many years later that he kept secrets from Emma and me when he was growing up. While in Pelham High, he related, "a bunch of us used to go to New York City, allegedly to see a legitimate show, then take the bus to Union City, New Jersey, to attend the burlesque at Minsky's, located in the Hudson

Theater." I laughed when he revealed this clandestine act, telling him that I too had kept many secrets from my parents, including having gone to similar trashy performances—seeking, I presume, some kind of vicarious sexual pleasure—when I was a freshman college student in New York. Tony Pastor's burlesque on East 14th Street was one of our occasional haunts. One memorable performance was billed as "Tilly Pipick from Peru." Gloversville and its environs and Pelham offered no such off-beat frolics.

Federation Moves Its Offices

Federation decided in the early 1950's that its original building at 71 West 47th Street was no longer adequate. It sought a new location and finally purchased a large lot near the corner of 59th Street and Lexington Avenue, facing both arteries. The corner building was acquired a few years later, remodeled, then demolished in 1984, when a new building was architecturally tied in with the original structure.

In 1955 a debate ensued as to how the building, comprising some seventeen stories, was to be utilized. I was amongst the few who felt strongly that the building should not only house Federation's expanding operations but that it should also be the headquarters for the total Jewish community, or at least all those services that wanted to be under one roof. A number of Federation's affiliates were renting space, and they could have been easily rehoused. I saw it as a way by which Federation could exercise a great deal more influence on its members through physical proximity and more frequent contacts. Since I was an early advocate of the merger of Federation with the United Jewish Appeal, I also visualized the possibility of bringing that organization into the building in the future. But none of these "radical" views prevailed. It was decided to rent out the space that Federation did not use, so as to pay off the mortgage quickly. While a prudent step, this was unnecessary in view of Federation's sound financial condition, considerable reserves, and the possibility of even running a special campaign for the new edifice.

In the course of years, the property appreciated tremendously in value. As tenants moved out when they needed more space than Federation could provide, Federation began to turn over the vacated square footage to its own societies. In 1973, when Federation and the UJA entered into a joint venture, after which the UJA sold its own building and moved into the 59th Street address, the expanding role of both organizations required even more space, so that the addition was constructed. Regrettably, all of the organizations that rent space elsewhere or were required to purchase their own buildings have not been relocated in the Federation Building. It was a serious mistake not to have adopted the policy some of us strenuously recommended in 1955. It has foreclosed using this building as the central address of the Jewish community of Greater New York.

Pulling Out of a Community

Although all social welfare and community planning should take into consideration that there may come a time when it will be necessary to pull out of a community, the textbook has not yet been written on that subject. There is an assumption that an institution should remain where it is forever. But, perhaps because a Jew can never feel permanently settled, it always seemed to me that there should be an element of foresight, and contingencies should be planned for well in advance, before one is forced to close down.

On several occasions I was involved in disputes about when the Bronx Y should terminate its program on the Grand Concourse. The conflicts arose in part because of different perceptions. My views eventually became Federation policy. Jewish organizations often had other interests, such as remaining to help in the integration of a neighborhood or rigidly staying there to prevent them from becoming all black.

The Grand Concourse was an elegant thoroughfare with elevator apartment housing built in the 1920's. It also included a number of recently built structures, such as a Catholic high school, large Borough Hall, a new synagogue. Nearby was the famous Yankee Stadium. Originally it was predominantly a lower- and middle-class Jewish neighborhood, where younger Jewish families had moved on their way up the economic ladder. In the early postwar period, when it looked like there might be some intrusions at the lower end, sporadic efforts had been made to upgrade and try to save the area above 158th Street to Fordham Road. But politicians caught up in the integration struggle had no stomach for maintaining the status quo. They allowed events to drift. As apartments became vacant, landlords perforce rented to anyone who applied. Few if any Jews or whites moved in. At first efforts were made to rent only to a few of the better-class non-whites. When the exodus took hold, entire apartment houses were abandoned by whites, as though they were in flight. Overnight, entire houses became non-white. The Welfare Department began to place more families on relief into the apartments. The area changed completely. Graffiti appeared on the walls, garbage was not picked up with care, the area deteriorated.

Literally seeing the handwriting on the walls, I began a concerted campaign to get the Bronx Y to dispose of its building as quickly as possible, while there was still a potential market. I wanted them to move to Riverdale, where there was a stable Jewish community in need of service. Board and staff opinions were divided. Some believed that the Y had an obligation to remain in the neighborhood as long as any Jews, and particularly the older ones, had need for its services. As past experience in other areas had demonstrated, closing the center was an important factor in finally compelling relocation even by those hardy older Jews who had still not moved because their incomes were low and they had few surviving friends. Even without resorting to elaborate and expensive surveys, the demographic impression was clear. Synagogues were closing. Kosher butchers had exited. Small Jewish storekeepers and Jewish professionals were rapidly abandoning that part of the Bronx.

While this ferment was going on, along came the American Jewish Congress, which was actively concerned with maintaining, perhaps developing, integrated neighborhoods. In the face of Jews moving out in record numbers, it published a report which indicated that there were more whites in the area than some of us thought. Whites were equated with Jews, but this was not necessarily so. Actually, on analysis, the population data in the report did not reflect the boundaries within which most of the Jews lived. The AJC's effort to keep the Jews in the Grand Concourse section was for nought. The flight was inexorable. Within a few years, the Bronx Y had to sell its building and luckily found a customer in a nonsectarian girls' club. Thereafter the Y operated in rented space in order to maintain a modest service for the elderly Jews in their seventies and eighties who still lived there.

A similar development took place in the East Bronx-Westchester Avenue region. After the war, it was still primarily a lower-middle-class Jewish neighborhood. A small center was established in rented quarters under the aegis of JANC. Then a large public housing project was erected. Efforts to hold the poorer white families, mostly non-Jewish, failed, despite efforts by the center, which had moved its programs into the project. It also failed to keep the Jews in the area. The center then rented another commercial facility farther east, but the encroachment of non-whites, mostly Hispanics, led to more Jews moving. Several synagogues closed. A new center building had been recommended for this district in 1949, but Federation and I opposed its construction. Federation made it clear that it could not afford to support programs in areas where only small pockets of Jews remained when so many large Jewish-populated communities still remained unserved.

Along came the American Jewish Committee this time, and contrary to our plans for leaving this area, it tried to initiate an interfaith and interracial program. We maintained indignantly that no such group should be created under voluntary auspices, that no such mixed organization could find the funds to sustain any kind of decent operation, and that it would end up with the Jews forced to provide all the resources on the fiction of intergroup cooperation, when it was obvious that the Jews were leaving. We recommended that our Jewish center close down. It did.

While it may be theoretically desirable to have Jewish organizations participate in a program of city-wide Jewish social planning, an organization that has to cater to all of its constituent members, even if they have strong ideological differences, is bound to run into trouble on long- or short-term Jewish interests. Of one thing I am certain: Jewish institutions must move with expedition to salvage part or even all of their original investments. They have no right to squander limited annual maintenance funds. While population trends are sometimes reversed (note the West Side of Manhattan), when that occurs over some decades, the Jews who return are usually upper-class, better educated, and their needs can probably be satisfied within the framework of existing synagogues. If more is eventually needed, then that class is in a position to build a new and satisfactory facility, after which it can come to Federation for support for its year-round program.

Fund-Raising Within Federation's Staff

When I arrived at Federation in 1949, I was surprised that the staff gave little to the Federation campaign. The argument was that "we work here and therefore should be exempt from giving." There was no feeling that they were also independent members of the Jewish community, users of Federation resources, and that they had an obligation to support Federation as part of the time-honored Jewish principle of personal *tzedakah*. As a staff member of Bronx House, I contributed, often more than some of my board members, and annually conducted a campaign amongst the staff.

I decided to see what I could do at Federation. I raised the issue at one of the earliest overall staff meetings. While there was some resistance, a committee was appointed. I was on it. After several meetings we came up with a fair formula for contributions based on gross salaries earned only at Federation. I became chairman of the first campaign. I took the cards for the two executive vice-presidents. While we did not succeed in getting most workers to give according to the formula, we raised considerably more than was ever given before. In each succeeding year more pressure was put on each worker, and the amount keep mounting until the receipts began to approach respectable levels. We extended our efforts to the staffs of the member societies of Federation with the same intitial resistance and ultimate success.

As to the annual United Jewish Appeal, the results were worse. No such formula was ever developed. It was not until the 1967 Israeli-Arab War that significant sums were collected from Federation's personnel. After 1973 (and that was the year that I retired), with the advent of the Yom Kippur War, when Federation and the UJA conducted a joint campaign, the whole contributing scale was lifted to higher levels.

In 1949 and for many years thereafter, UJA was anathema to many of the top leaders of Federation and amongst the staff as well. There were sharp ideological divisions, which the creation of the State of Israel in 1948, the year before I arrived on the scene, had not dispelled and possibly exacerbated. Furthermore, there was unbridled competition for funds. Hexter was a non-Zionist. I would have to describe Willen, the other executive vice-president, as an anti-Zionist. So professional support from the top for a pro-UJA campaign was not forthcoming. Hexter knew Israel (actually Palestine when he was living there) intimately, for he had represented the non-Zionist faction on the Jewish Agency and did this most capably for ten years before coming to Federation. He saw it as a haven for distressed Jews who had no other place to go or who wanted to go there voluntarily. He did a great deal to develop settlements in Palestine. It was a philanthropic and not an ideological concern for him.

Being a Zionist and a believer in the basic principle that Jews should support generously all legitimate Jewish ventures beyond the pale of Federation—locally, nationally, internationally, and Israel—I pushed for more generous support of the UJA campaigns. I could never quite see why the two organizations were separate, conducting two competing drives and maintaining duplicate structures with all the costly overhead.

An arrangement had been made for two discrete campaigns, with Federation controlling the turf from September through January, and the UJA taking over from February through August. There was always a little cheating on the time schedule. I often heard complaints that one or the other had the best time frame. This was true only when some critical event, like a war, occurred during the Federation season. Some of the lay leadership, who participated in both campaigns, also objected to being exploited for fund-raising year-round. Publicity-wise, Federation felt that it was at a disadvantage, because the UJA always seemed to benefit from the crises that plagued Israel. First the wars before and after the state was established. Then the unprecedented influx of impoverished refugees from Europe, victims and survivors of the concentration camps, or those who had become displaced persons when new states arose. Then came the refugees from Arab countries, victims of Moslem hatred. Then the war in 1956. There was a need for housing, schools, hospitals, philanthropic institutions, universities, centers. Then the war of 1967. All of these critical events made for dramatic demands for funds from the Jewish community. A host of satellite Israeli organizations sprang up, expanded, needed large-scale funds for the vast network of additional services required by the burgeoning population. Missions of volunteers went back and forth to Israel and could see with their own eyes most vividly the needs of this exploding country. They also saw how their funds contributed to the construction of facilities and the additional services. They personally noted how this frail land not only survived, but was blossoming. Great pride was felt about these visible achievements.

Federation, despite its accomplishments, did not always have such eye-catching projects. It did not have so many visibly poor Jews. Instead, everywhere there was evidence of Jewish prosperity. While there was a documented need to provide more and better facilities to meet the spreading Jewish population, to meet the ever higher standards of care which medical and social welfare agencies emphasized, it was never quite the same as showing a graphic picture of impoverished Jews, who needed everything, arriving daily by sea and air. New public relations techniques would attempt to dramatize Federation's needs, but they were not comparatively the same. What is more, most Jews already knew that poor American Jews were supported mainly by the government and not with Jewish money.

In the middle 1950's and the early 1960's, it was recommended that we feature photos of non-whites in some of our publicity to appeal to the pockets of potential givers. I tried to counter this, at least for the centers, and had some success.

On the other hand, each year Federation raised more money, due in great part to the steady improvement in the economy. Part of the increase could be attributed to the generosity of the Jews generally, which our public relations department played up. Part was ascribed to the favorable tax laws, and we did not hesitate to apprise all givers of how "little" it cost them to give away ever larger sums. I must also mention that part resulted from the Federation-invented system of "card calling." Thus a giver would be "lured" to a meeting or dinner or luncheon by friends or his financial peers, members of his trade or profession, or synagogue affiliation, or area of residence, and then would be pointedly asked to announce his gift publicly. It worked. This required a great deal of preliminary organization, pre-meeting solicitation, telephone followup by either his peers or a professional. When Federation was founded in 1917, a list of donors was published, and this acted as another incentive, a form of public pressure to contributing, for not to have one's name on the list was tantamount to lacking philanthropic generosity. Attempts to revive this method failed, except for one year, the fiftieth anniversary of Federation, after which it was not repeated. I advocated the printed list.

To have two drives in virtual competition with each other irked me. I made no bones of my views on the issue, to the displeasure of my indifferent and opposing listeners in Federation.

I recall talking to Jack Weiler (who in 1984 was hailed as one of American Jewry's greatest philanthropists) in the early 1950's about the need for such a union, and he agreed without reservation. He told me that there would be a saving of several millions of dollars a year. On December 12, 1984, I ran into Weiler again at a JDC luncheon. He was a former president of that organization. Recalling our conversation years before, he told me that he had approached Milton Weill, the president of Federation from 1951 to 1954, on such a joint program, but without success. So he gave up. He then devoted more of his tremendous and influential energies to the UJA and other appeals than to Federation, a leadership that we sorely needed and missed. He represented a large bloc that we did not recruit into Federation until years later.

When Federation was thinking of changing its focus in the middle 1960's, I pursued this subject of merger once again in written memos, hoping that it would have an impact on some members of the study committee that was considering alterations in Federation's purposes. I was still unable to elicit any support on that score, yet steps were taken toward better cooperation. We can attribute this development to the coming of the Computer Age, for the cooperation was more mechanical than ideological. Both organizations had introduced computers to keep abreast of the growing volume of business and to analyze more quickly the information assembled. Even this presented difficulties of location and type of equipment, but it was finally instituted at Federation's headquarters. It took years to straighten out and harmonize different methods of collecting and recording data.

Nothing further developed until the sudden and grim Yom Kippur War, which the Arabs launched precipitously on October 6, 1973, just as the Federation campaign was getting under way. Previous wars had come at times that did not sharply conflict with the fund-raising schedule. Israel's financial needs were now so urgent that a campaign for that country could not be delayed or ignored. This crisis, as all the others, generated a vast outpouring of money. The groups met hurriedly, in panic, and agreed to a joint campaign. They soon began to quarrel about the division of the receipts, and were still suspicious of each other's motives, but nonetheless this marked the first and what proved to be a most successful joint fund drive. The continuing crisis forced the two parties to maintain their relationship. The ties could not be unbound. The UJA finally sold its own buildings, moved into Federation's headquarters, and their joint activities were sustained from year to year. As I wrote this in 1986, a final merger took place. Why did it take more than a decade to effectuate? There were numerous problems about union contracts, titles and status, and the equitable distribution of funds raised. Problems arose over Israel's recurrent economic and security requirements, which were ever more costly, and over the economic problems faced by Federation agencies in light of cuts in government grants. Somehow everything was resolved.

Government Funds for Jewish Agencies

Government funding of voluntary and especially Jewish agencies has always been an ambiguous problem. Every institution has a natural desire to expand and improve both its facilities and its program. With government aid easily available, organizations were willing to make compromises in order to put their hands on this largesse. In child care, public support for individual children was available for a long period in American philanthropic history. It was not until the 1950's that legislation made it possible for a variety of other institutions—hospitals, homes for the aged, child welfare, and even centers—to become eligible beneficiaries. Centers for the first time were qualified through pre-school, aged, antidelinquency, and antidrug programs.

The problem became more complicated when government began to intrude into the agency's policies as a condition for making grants. If an agency discriminated against clientele, staff, and board on the basis of religion, race, or country of origin (later sex), it was deemed unworthy of government allotments. This forced agencies to make choices—either conform with the directive, find some way of evading it, or turn down the offering. (See my "Historical Overview" in *The Turbulent Decades* [1980], pp. 74–83.)

In 1984, a well-publicized dispute arose between Mayor Koch of New York and Cardinal O'Connor of the Roman Catholic Diocese about a directive from the city that institutions receiving municipal funds could no longer discriminate against hiring homosexuals. The list had now grown to include sexual orientation and the handicapped. An article in the *New York Times* (December 14, 1984) indicated that the church might be prepared to forgo $73 million (the sum was actually twice that amount) rather than bow to the city's demands which conflicted with the traditional policy of the Catholic church.

In the last three decades, hospitals, homes for the aged, and child care have become overwhelmingly dependent on government grants. This included grants for buildings, payments for services via Medicare and Medicaid, and large research stipends. Of necessity, there were radical changes in clientele and staffing. While in homes for the aged, it was somewhat easier to maintain both a Jewish clientele and a Jewish ambience, this was not true for hospitals and child care. The fortuitous location of a hospital in a Jewish or segregated neighborhood, or the predominance of Jews on the staff, might still give it a high ratio of Jews. This was not so when the neighborhood became non-Jewish. Then Jews no longer wanted to use its services. Child care agencies have fought an ever retreating battle for the right to determine who their clientele should be. The pressure of the public authorities to force the taking of children at random, which in New York meant mostly non-whites, and the sharp reduction in the Jewish child population that needed such services, led these institutions to become more non-Jewish in all aspects.

The centers, catering largely over 90 percent to Jews and housed in areas still predominantly Jewish, had less difficulty resisting compromises. Some centers refused to take public money. Some would take it only if it could be used for Jews. A few, situated in low-income areas, like Williamsburg, had no problem meeting the government criteria that the services supported by its funds would be for the poor. There were enough poor Jews.

Some centers, prepared by their own "nonsectarian" philosophy of offering service to anyone who applied, could easily sign the necessary documents required by the governmental bodies. A little later, this same policy of non-discrimination was exercised by the Greater New York Fund, a voluntary community chest, to ensure that contributions drawn from the community at large were being distributed only to agencies that followed the government's prescriptions, using the funds for the poorest and the neediest.

In the centers, public grants were initially in the fields of pre-school and afterschool children's care. These grants became very large. The centers had to set aside a substantial part of their facilities for such purposes. New buildings were designed with modern child care rooms and outdoor playgrounds, because the facilities would be supported by government funds. The clientele, children of working mothers in the main, was often non-Jewish. Where there was a majority of Jews, efforts were made to observe certain Jewish practices—Kashrut, closing on the Sabbath and Jewish holidays. Public authorities accepted these Jewish rites.

In such instances the quality of the program was often superior, and there was no evidence of real discrimination against non-Jews. The problem became more difficult to resolve when the clientele was substantially non-Jewish, and when parents requested some recognition of their dietary preferences and the celebration of their own, usually religious, holidays.

With respect to the aged, the large numbers of Jewish older people who flocked to the centers gave the agency a Jewish aura. Few questions were raised as to the dominant Jewish clientele or the Jewish character of the program. The Jewish elderly changed over the years only from a European to an American origin.

Centers like the Educational Alliance, and those located in public housing projects in heavily integrated neighborhoods (Jews, blacks, Puerto Ricans and other Hispanics, Chinese), which accepted large sums from the government, were visibly affected, and despite efforts to maintain some Jewish atmosphere, it was only the presence of the Jewish Senior Citizens that gave the institution any justification to be classified as a Jewish center.

My personal attitude was that we should never take money from public sources unless the program was exclusively for non-Jews; nor accept any grants if it meant changing the character of the center. An open-door policy would steadily force the Jewish membership to look elsewhere for services which were more congenial, or where there was some surety of security. My warnings were often heeded, so that during my tenure the amount of money received by all of our affiliated centers was relatively modest in comparison with their overall budgets, and even those public sums were concentrated in a few agencies.

It would only be fair to state that my views on this subject were singular, except for the support of Rabbi Trainin. I don't know of anyone else on the staff who shared my position. Some of my colleagues wrote extensively in support of public funding. The key lay and professional leadership was committed to this as a means of enlarging and improving the agencies. Eventually Federation created a department for the exploitation of public funding. It was designed to help both Federation and its institutions make the best presentations and contacts with city, state, and federal officials, so as to assure their getting their share of whatever public monies were available. And they got it. I am not sure that they always understood the ultimate consequences of their advocacy; or whether they cared. They saw the money, and that was more important than any other consideration in fields where you don't want to be smaller than your competitor. It led to excesses in facilities and budgets. A few scandals arose that were quickly nipped. Costs of operation and salaries rose to proportions which quickly influenced the demands of other agencies not so fortunate as to receive government support. But above all, it changed the relationship between Federation and its constituent societies. They were not quite the same as in the more intimate days, when they had a greater dependency on Federation and Jewish money. Some changed their charters to conform to the demands of the government. Some even dropped their Jewish names.

After I left Federation the picture changed radically. Some centers, including the 92nd Street Y, received far more money from the public purse than from Federation.

While there have been periodic cuts in government grants to social services in the Jewish community since 1980, the full impact of cuts due to the passage of the Gramm-Rudman Act in 1985, which proposed to eliminate the federal deficit by 1991, could be devastating. It was speculated that the New York Federation agencies would lose millions of dollars, which would be impossible for Federation to replace. In 1986, it was already drawing on its reserves to meet the increasing costs of operation of affiliate societies. Continued dependency on government grants was an uncertain way to assure stability in an enterprise that still relied largely on sectarian relationships.

As more money was received from public sources and non-Jewish foundations, the influence of Federation on these agencies began to wane. This was most apparent in the hospital and child care fields. Federation grants, in comparison to the sums realized from public and third-party sources, were trivial. This loss of influence also had some bearing on the support that Federation received from the board members of those societies, who were usually amongst the wealthiest in the community. When money was raised centrally, it could be distributed more equitably, particularly to those who had great needs and could not find the money on their own. That is the great value of a Federation. The need for unlimited, large-scale capital funds to match the offerings of the government, and the tremendous annual deficits rolled up each year, some with budgets in the tens of millions, taxed the wealthiest board members and diverted their contributions from Federation.

On the other hand, the positive effects of government and other outside support eventually led to a reduction of the sums annually allocated by Federation and permitted their diversion to agencies that were not always so fortunate and to those which were more Jewish in purpose, program, and clientele. Thus I noted a shift of Federation support to Jewish centers, which became one of the largest bloc beneficiaries, as well as to Jewish education.

It had always been my view that more Federation money had to be allocated to those fields to assure the continuity of the Jewish community. This was in Federation's own self-interest, for it would assure a future constituency of Jewishly educated and committed individuals and families, which would produce future leaders and contributors.

I had also tried to develop an attitude in Federation that if the synagogues would be willing to provide services similar to those offered by Federation affiliates, such as pre-school education, youth programs, adult education, and programs for the aged, then they too might be eligible for Federation support. For many reasons—as much due to the indifference and resistance of synagogues to submit to some Jewish authority, preferring to maintain their own pristine independence, and the unwillingness of Federation leaders to recognize the synagogue as a "communal" institution on a par with all other Jewish organizations—this type of relationship or financial allocation was never permitted to develop. If a large number of synagogues had opted for this proposal, the immediate financial burden on Federation would have increased, but in the long run Federation's problems would ultimately have been relieved by an ever larger group of supporters from the synagogue and the overall community.

Whether the synagogue will ever be recognized as this type of communal institution, bound by the same type of community discipline, is far from certain. Obviously the right of any collectivity of Jews to establish their own form of worship, with a rabbi of their own choosing, is not likely to change in the foreseeable future. While the independent synagogue adds a creative dimension to the Jewish community, it also leads to unplanned developments, makes demands on other Jews for building funds, and creates problems within those synagogues that never have enough money to develop the comprehensive programs that their American-born, well-educated, but economically not well-endowed, members expect. Some fortunate synagogues have magnificent programs that surpass the offerings of most centers. They obviously do not feel the need for Federation support or supervision. This was not the case for the largest number of synagogues. Particularly those in neighborhoods with few Jews or with primarily older Jews. There will never be enough Federation-supported centers to meet the needs of the Jewish census.

Efforts to Make Federation Nonsectarian

In 1967, Federation's communal planning committee circulated a memorandum "On Goals and Purposes" to the board of trustees and staff, clearly designed to alter Federation's historical character. This idea had been occupying the minds of some of Federation's leadership, who believed that the number of Jewish poor was "declining." Since Federation had originally been established as a charity "primarily" for the benefit of needy Jews, it was time to review the purposes of Federation, for life had changed considerably since its founding fifty years before in 1917. Now the poor were no longer from the Jewish community. Most agencies had begun to accept non-Jews through an open-door, nondiscriminatory policy, and in some instances they were served in overwhelming numbers. Non-Jewish staff were also being engaged. Public funding had reached a point in some agencies, that by comparison the Federation grant was insignificant. The new poor in the city were blacks and Hispanics, for whom neither public nor voluntary funding and services were adequate. Some Jewish leaders deemed this a new and most important responsibility to be assumed by voluntary groups and by the Jewish community which in this instance meant Federation. Furthermore, studies indicated that Jews were amongst the wealthiest, the best-educated, the least needy, and the most philanthropic. It was incumbent on them to look beyond Jews, if they wanted to continue in business.

It was also time, they said, to recognize that integration was a fact, not around the corner, that acculturation as a process for Jews had been fully achieved. Sectarianism no longer had any justification. Now Federation should not be primarily for Jews, but for all the residents of New York. The memorandum formalized a development that had taken place slowly and informally. It recommended as a cardinal proposal that "professional and/or financial contributions to establish programs and services for the benefit of *non-Jewish* clientele, together with other groups in New York or *alone*" (emphasis added).

While there was seemingly to be no diminution in support for existing Jewish agencies, and an invitation was to be extended to selected unaffiliated Jewish philanthropic societies, it was evident that nonsectarianism was the wave of the future, even if it would dilute the historical Jewish philanthropic organization.

I had several forays on this issue in previous years, which contained, but never eliminated, the nonsectarian infiltration. Several years before, Joe Willen had called me to his office, where I met Lawrence Buttenweiser, a future president, and Frank Weil, an important contributor. They had jointly recommended that Federation hold up building any more centers in Jewish areas, but that instead we should erect a demonstration center in Harlem, as an indication that the Jews were concerned with the welfare of the total community and not only their own people. They even indicated that special monies would be raised from amongst Jews, so as not to interfere with solicitations for centers now on Federation's drawing board. How I restrained myself I shall never understand. I indicated my opposition to the suggestion as something a Jewish Federation should not undertake or support. I saw nothing wrong in a group of independent Jews, not as Jews per se, but as American citizens, building a center for anyone in the greater community, but I firmly maintained it would be a serious violation of Federation's historic policy to do it solely or even jointly with other groups as a *Jewish* expression of its philanthropy. I stated that I would oppose it should it come before Federation's board. For whatever reasons, which I never bothered to unearth, the suggestion was never implemented.

Jacob Glazer, a sociologist who had a great deal of influence among some Jews, had written an article in *Commentary* indicating that there were no longer significant numbers of poor Jews to take care of, and that the Jews should shift their interests and concern themselves with the non-Jewish poor. This would give them an outlet for their voluntary energies and their abundant financial resources.

I had anticipated the communal planning committee's memorandum by more than a year, for on June 5, 1967, at the very moment of the Six-Day War in Israel, I had addressed a five-page statement to Dr. David G. Salten, the new executive vice-president of Federation, stating that since Federation must plan for the next fifty years, and we were in the midst of celebrating a half-century of service, we should advocate the further Judaization of every aspect of our activities. I called for a merger with the United Jewish Appeal. I wrote that if we were looking for the Jewish "poor," a native group that was *not* taken care of by the local Jewish community, for the burden had been transferred to the public agencies, then we should support the Jews who were still suffering in many countries abroad and the poor Jews who had recently arrived in Israel, whose needs were far from being adequately met.

Furthermore, I saw the need for greater coordination amongst all Jewish organizations, including those that were not yet constituent members of Federation, for the outsiders were conducting major fund-raising campaigns, including building drives of such a magnitude as to impinge on Federation's own efforts. Only by developing a community discipline could well studied and approved efforts be realized in some orderly, efficient, and economically prudent fashion. Better planning would result through the elimination of unnecessary agencies—and there were some, through the merger of others for more efficient operations, and through better coverage of services for the many Jews now sprawling out to the suburbs.

Would such joint ventures save money? My contention was yes, for it would eliminate costly duplicative fund-raising operations. Would it raise more money? I was sure that it would, because its very inclusiveness would permit reaching out to every section of the Jewish community. That was the experience everywhere else in the country where such an apparatus existed. It would have had the same effect in Greater New York.

I presented this document as a challenge to Federation's leadership for the forthcoming fifty years. Nothing was done about it.

When the committee's memorandum was issued at the end of 1967, it was in the aftermath of the Six-Day War, which really shook up American Jewry as nothing had stirred it since the creation of the State of Israel in 1948. In the weeks before the war, American Jews lived in dread of what it might mean to have a second Holocaust in their lifetime. We were not prepared for the quick and decisive victory which followed. The outpouring of funds for Israel was phenomenal. Even non-Zionists and anti-Zionists contributed, with a mixture of guilt, relief, philanthropy, and genuine pride in what Israel had accomplished. There appeared to be an unabashed renewal, reaffirmation or affirmation of Jewish identity. Shortly after, Jews flocked to Israel to witness how this tiny army had conquered the Sinai, Gaza, Golan, Samaria, and Judea (West Bank). No one, except for a few disgruntled intellectuals, was concerned about the responsibilities and consequences of this unparalleled military conquest.

Before and after the victory, it was plain that Jews and Israel had little support from the Christian world, and that the radical and youthful leadership of the black community, with whom Jews were embraced in the 1950's and 1960's, had now deserted them and unequivocally sided with the defeated Arabs, who were now elevated to the status of underdogs, despite their territorial vastness, numerical strength, and prodigious oil wealth.

The reversal of attitude shocked the Federation leadership hell-bent on advocating a Federation that would be interested in the larger community with its unmet needs rather than Jews alone.

I wrote another five-page memorandum to Dr. Salten on January 15, 1968, reinforcing what I had sent him seven months before. I insisted on our "divesting of all nonsectarian agencies and services." I indicated that "all organizations that wished to remain in the network, must offer more services to Jews and they must stress Jewish identity, association, program and continuity." Federation should "admit only new applicants which clearly subscribe to this mandate." Federation institutions should "accept public funds only when they are given through individual beneficiaries or only where they will not alter the Jewish character of the agency." I urged that we broaden our concept of Federation to include other than so-called philanthropic agencies. We should "emphasize in the recruitment of voluntary leadership . . . that we are an instrument for the development of Jewish life and not a network of service that merely renders service to any one who knocks on our doors." "We shall have to develop and support academies for the training of Jewish professional personnel." My peroration was:

> This will make for a larger and not a smaller Jewish Federation, if mere size or scope is important in this age. It encompasses Jews all over the city, the nation and the entire Jewish world. It embraces Jewish education as a fundamental and not a peripheral service. It reaches into normative Jewish life, into the universities which matriculate hundreds of thousands of Jewish students, and into the Jewish cultural arts now burgeoning but sadly undersupported—and at the same time, it does not neglect the Jewish sick, the orphan, the widow, the disturbed nor the problem ridden. A union with local, national, and global Jewish organizations will provide a discipline for Jewish communal planning and fund-raising now so conspicuously absent.

This time I made sure that many of the Federation leaders, whom I knew intimately, would receive copies of both of my statements, originally sent only to Dr. Salten. Whether the recipients agreed with me or not, I did not care, but at least they would have a point of view which the Commission on the role of Federation was continuing to reject for one reason or another. As late as December 1971, the commission submitted a report which took little note of what I had been proposing. The commission had taken insufficient account of the 1967 war, of the uprising of Jewish college students in 1969 at the Council of Jewish Federations Assembly in Boston, the revelations that there were more Jewish poor than the Jewish community had hitherto realized, that there was a need to democratize the Jewish community of Greater New York by developing small neighborhood councils that would protect the interests of Jewish constituences in the sections of the city that were rapidly changing, that the needs of Jewish education were mounting, and that a community the size of New York could not keep its hands off the growing concern with helping Soviet Jews leave the iron-bound Russian tyranny.

The report of December 1971 was not pigeon-holed, but was bitterly debated and finally rejected. In a statement on December 17, 1973, a few months after the Yom Kippur War, Lawrence Buttenwieser, the president of Federation, wrote: "It became evident that the community developments were outdistancing the Report of the Commission." The board agreed to support the New York Conference on Soviet Jewry, created a Program Development Fund for Jewish Education, and changed its relationship to the United Jewish Appeal, which would thereafter bind these two organizations closer together.

True, unforeseen events always have a more immediate impact on philosophy and practice than sociological analysis or ideological forecasting. Yet I like to believe that I had a little influence, along with some other stalwarts in Federation, like Rabbi Trainin and his lay and rabbinical supporters, in making these long-opposed, neglected, and deferred functions of Federation come into being.

Jewish College Youth

Jewish college youth was one of the groups most neglected by Federation, even though they constituted an ever-growing census. The B'nai B'rith had long been concerned about the lack of Jewish influence on Jewish youth in college and as far back as 1923 had organized the first of the Hillel Foundations, which in the course of decades brought a rabbinical and Jewish educational impact on the campus. Not only did Hillel attempt to organize Jewish students and persuade them to maintain a Jewish existence in the college setting, but it also added academic courses that provided Jewish learning in a broader aspect for the total university. Yet in 1927–28, when I was at the University of Missouri, I had to personally create a permanent Jewish organization on the campus, because no help was forthcoming from any national source. I was told we were too small a Jewish student body. Occasionally Jewish communities in which universities were located lent a hand, or an individual Jewish philanthropist provided a building or endowed a chair of Jewish studies, but in the main, Jewish students, despite the presence of Hillel Foundations, were largely neglected. There were never enough Hillels or money or interest to deal with the ever-blooming situation.

After World War II, there was an enrollment explosion on the campuses. By the 1970's, it was estimated that there were more than 325,000 Jewish college students over the country. At the same time, a huge number of Jews were hired as faculty, which proved a doubtful benefit as far as Jewish students were concerned, since relatively few of them were interested in the students as Jews or in furthering Jewish education or fostering Jewish life.

After the Six-Day War, the New York Federation began to receive requests from Jewish college students. They were not asking, and later demanding, that the Jewish Federation get involved in racial integration, or the anti-nuclear war movement, or the protest against the war in Vietnam, or environmental protection—causes which were attracting millions of college young people—but they wanted the Jewish community to expand programs like Hillel and to foster Jewish education on a college level. Most found themselves in college ignorant of their Jewish background, due to poor education or even to a total lack of Jewish pedagogical experiences in their youth. They wanted support for their newspapers, magazines, conferences, study projects, libraries. In the Greater New York area, where there were more than one hundred colleges and universities and an estimated Jewish enrollment of 125,000, they were serviced at most by less than two handfuls of Jewish leaders, most of them paid for by Hillel.

In 1969, the students came to Boston spontaneously to bring their vital appeal to the attention of the twenty-five hundred Jewish leaders at the General Assembly of the Council of Jewish Federations. When the leaders, both professional and laymen, denied them a hearing, the students picketed in front of the hotel. I joined the line, along with Rabbi Yitzhak Greenberg, an activist rabbi and professor at CCNY. Joe Willen of the New York Federation and John Slawson of the American Jewish Committee, observing the pickets, asked me what it was all about. When I explained the cause, they went in and spoke to the leadership of the council, who reluctantly agreed to give the students an audience at the business meeting the following day. Exploiting Robert's Rules of Order, the chairman tried to limit their speeches and resolutions, asserting that the students were not bona fide delegates of Federations or other affiliated organizations. Despite the ensuing chaos, the message got through. The council and its affiliates all over the country could no longer ignore the legitimate and neglected needs of Jewish college young men and women.

The following year—1970—and since then, Jewish youth, including college young people, have been officially invited to and provided for at these conclaves. But in 1970 the relationship had not yet firmly jelled. At the annual banquet-meeting, which took place on a Saturday night, a group of students felt that the program ought to be introduced with a *Havdalah* service, that brief and colorful religious rite which separates the sacred Sabbath from the profane days to follow, as Jews begin another "good week." The same bureaucratic rejections of previous years took form. No provision had been made for it, so it was out. Several students came to ask my assistance, relating that they were contemplating a formal protest that would hold up the proceedings. Elie Wiesel was the major speaker of the evening. I suggested that a small group, not more than three, approach him at the head table, since the dinner session had not yet begun, and request his intercession. From my seat at a nearby table, I could see what took place, as Wiesel turned to the leadership on the rostrum and asked them to accede to this request as being reasonable, beautiful, and thoroughly Jewish. The five-minute discussion, with a lot of headshaking, resulted in a hurried search for a couple of candles (no twisted ones were available), a cup of wine, some spices, and the ceremony took place fittingly and without further incident. Most of the twenty-five hundred people assembled never knew what had happened. The introduction of this ceremonial event became standard practice thereafter as other Jewish rites found their way into such assemblies over the years.

The New York Federation was adamant about not accepting any responsibility for Jewish college youth. Thus it invited picketing and sit-ins, the latter requiring the police to arrest these young people, who wanted nothing more than help to further Jewish education on the campus. Some of the pickets, like Hillel Levine and Stephen Cohen, are now highly respected college professors and are used by Federations as speakers or to conduct studies of Jewish life.

I was not only sympathetic to their cause, but friendly with the protestors. I strongly urged Federation to set up a committee to meet with them, listen to their requests, and do something about meeting these pleas. I don't recall getting a brotherly response from any of my Federation colleagues except Rabbi Trainin. Alan M. Strook, a prominent Jewish leader, whose family had long been associated with Federation and the Jewish Theological Seminary, was appointed a one-man committee to study the situation and summit a report. I was asked to service the committee. I found him indifferent to such a responsibility being undertaken by Federation. The project, in his estimation, should be continued by Hillel, or interested parents, or private philanthropists, or students themselves, but not by Federation. He didn't like the strident tones uttered by students at the several meetings he conducted. I had provided him with all the pertinent facts, the number of colleges, the number of Jewish college students, the kinds of programs they conducted, the kinds of projects they requested, and the anticipated costs. The sum total of my efforts and these meetings resulted in a one-man decision not to make even a report, but to forget about the whole venture.

I succeeded in bringing this cause directly to the attention of the distribution committee, which also heatedly debated the issue, but finally decided, with many reservations, that it would provide $75,000 to set up a department of Jewish College Youth, supervised by Federation, which would study the problem and come up with further recommendations.

The JCY got underway just as I was leaving Federation in 1973, struggled for a few years, finally attained permanent status with an ever-larger grant and a respectable budget. I know that it has had an impact on Jewish college students.

In the intervening years, there have been amazing developments on the campuses around the country. Hundreds of departments of Jewish studies have been established as integral parts of the university. Hundreds of Jewish scholars are employed as directors and teachers. Thousands of students, Jewish and others, are enrolled in these courses, which have, as a by-product, been a source of recruitment and the education of future academics and volunteer Jewish leaders. Libraries, art salons, exhibits, conferences on Jewish themes have spawned. There is now a universally respectable Jewish presence and influence on the American college campus.

The question that must be raised again: Why the long delay?

Jewish Gambling

I grew up with no prudish attitude toward gambling, although neither my father nor my mother ever played any kinds of games that involved gambling. My older brother and my oldest sister's husband gambled, my brother with his friends, one brother-in-law did it for a living for several years. As teenagers we gambled on everything—shooting basketballs, playing pool, pitching pennies or nickels, bowling, cards, and occasionally dice. When I studied at New York University I made a modest bit of my expenses playing pinochle. As a reporter on the *Gloversville Morning-Herald*, I occasionally put a $2 bet on a horse race at a local gambling parlor. Some Saturday mornings from 3 to 6 A.M., after we had been paid and the press run had finished, I went across the street to an all-night speakeasy and played poker with the newspaper mechanics, where I was frequently the winner. My parents, who did not approve of gambling, alluded to individuals whose families and fortunes were dissipated by compulsive gambling. There was one graphic example, where a Jewish man shot a player at the gambling table and spent the rest of his life in prison.

At the University of Missouri I gambled in a setting where the "sport" was a daily exercise. When you walked out of a barber shop or some of the smaller restaurants, you dice rolled the owner to pay double or nothing. I stopped playing cards and dice after my first year at college, because I could not afford to lose, and on two occasions I lost a considerable amount of money. Thereafter, it was only an occasional social experience. I never could join a card-playing group, although I was invited to many. In latter years, if we were vacationing in the Adirondacks, Emma and I would make a single summer visit to the track at Saratoga Springs and place our maximum $2 bets. On a trip abroad to Prince Edward Island, off the Canadian mainland, we went to the track one night, as there was nothing else to do. Another night in Geneva we crossed the border into France and played at a fancy gambling casino run by the Rothschilds, losing some money on a variety of games, most of which were novel. At Monte Carlo, in Atlantic City, and in Costa Rica, we inserted coins in slot machines without much success. While I liked to win—who doesn't?—I really never played with great intensity. I quit when I lost. Yet I suspect that if I had kept an accounting of my wins and losses, I probably broke even. In the 1980's, when Lotto was the rage and one potential winning pot was in excess of $40 million, I bought dollar tickets on several occasions and fantasized what we would do with our fabulous winnings: make our children and grandchildren independent financially and give away the rest to our favorite charities. We never talked of what we would do for ourselves. We never won—and there was no after disappointment, since we knew that our chances were one in several millions and our investment insignificant.

Yet I have always opposed gambling as an activity in the Jewish centers or as a means of financing an institution's budget. I risked my job on at least one occasion on Staten Island, when I opposed the leadership on this issue. I finally won. Gambling was no longer permitted.

At Federation I disapproved of any center using bingo or any other gambling device to finance any part of its operations, even though in my incumbency, nonprofit agencies, including churches and synagogues, were permitted by law to conduct such events. Eventually the state itself began to operate betting parlors on horse races and then introduced the lottery, the surpluses going to the maintenance of public functions, such as education. Gambling casinos leaped from the Southwest to the East and added another popular means of extracting money from helpless victims. All of these forms of gambling induced many new people to this social vice, specifically women. It often ruined households when the habit became expensive and overwhelming. It has led to the creation of therapeutic organizations like Gamblers Anonymous, following the Alcoholics Anonymous pattern, including Jewish Gamblers Anonymous. It has not yet produced an outcry for reform or the elimination of this widespread vice. Government bodies are ever exploring other ways to make these popular, "innocuous" activities instruments for raising money to conduct public business.

An issue arose as to whether the Jewish community and specifically the rabbinate should endorse these gambling ventures. Many synagogues found gambling an easier way to finance their mortgages and year-round program. They discovered many willing volunteers amongst their membership to manage the enterprise. If they couldn't get volunteers, they contracted with outsiders to operate the business—professionals who made a good living exploiting the unwary customers.

Among the major participants in many of the bingo gambling events, which offered modest money prizes, were senior citizens seeking to fill in their empty schedules by attending such programs with regularity, always hoping to win, but usually squandering their limited and never sufficient resources.

When a prominent Conservative rabbi and scholar, Seymour Siegel, a leader of the Neo-Conservative political movement, saw no serious problem in the aged and the synagogue indulging in such pastimes, because it does little harm and was one way with which the poorer synagogues could support themselves, I answered him in an article in *Sh'ma* (February 19, 1973) titled "Gambling for the Shul Is Still a Vice." I pointed out historically that gambling caused obdurate problems in Jewish communities, even infesting prominent rabbis, so that rabbinical bodies had to take extraordinary steps to halt such practices. I was incensed about the notion of financing impecunious synagogues through this means. These synagogues, often in neighborhoods undergoing population changes, where the wealthier supporters had either died or moved away, now required communal support. I proposed then, as I had earlier, that such synagogues should become legitimate beneficiaries of the Jewish Federation on the sound ground that they served a major Jewish purpose and generally provided for a Jewish clientele that was either marginal or poor and could no longer provide such programs on its own. Regrettably this issue was never seriously considered. Federations never wanted to provide any support for services conducted by and in synagogues, unless the service was actually operated by a nonecclesiastical body. Synagogues did not seek official Jewish communal support, because their own leadership preferred to maintain their precious independence rather that be accountable to a responsible central Jewish authority.

Some synagogues continue with bingo, raffles, annual journals with advertisements, second-hand goods sales, auctions, soliciting merchandise and contributions from the business and professional community—Jewish and non-Jewish—a precarious way of maintaining an institution, but hardly Jewishly edifying, more akin to the old-fashioned, partly abandoned *shnorrer* method, which nice Jewish institutions came to disdain. People should pay directly for what they get; and if the membership cannot afford to maintain the institution, and the institution is needed for Jewish continuity, then it ought to be supported by a central Jewish Federation.

The Jewish Poor

I do not remember any signs of poverty in our home in my youth. Our home was not a palace, but it had everything we needed. My father did not earn or ever make a fortune, but our bills were always paid. We all worked from our earliest years to provide additional income for the family or ourselves. I do not remember ever being hungry, or suffering from a cold house, or being in need of clothing.

Yet that there were other poor, I can remember from childhood.

Older people, usually men, filthy, often drunk, staggered by our home on the way to the city poor house. My mother and father were active members and supporters of the Fulton County Jewish Relief Society and the Hebrew Ladies Aid Society. My mother was a visitor to families reported to be in need of relief. After lunch, when she was through with all of her household chores, she would visit families. Our dinner table conversation after such a visit was at times a discussion of the poor family's need for coal, food, or money to pay rent, buy clothes. All the professional standards of confidentiality were violated by these revelations, but we learned about poor people, that their neighbors or the Jewish community helped. There was no slum section in Gloversville, so there was no concentration of the poor for either the general population or for the Jews. The Jewish poor were recent immigrants, or the victims of changing industrial conditions and, at times, personal ineptitude. I heard that some people drank or gambled away their meager income.

When I studied in New York in 1925–1926, it was my first contact with huge poor ghettos and massive poverty. The Lower East Side and Harlem gave me visible evidence of this condition.

As a student of social work in 1930–32, at the onset of the depression, I witnessed poverty on a widespread scale with long lines of the unemployed seeking work, and equally long lines at feeding stations and soup kitchens, with people sleeping on the sidewalks and in doorways, hundreds of them in the Bowery, near where I was assigned as a student. As a case worker in a Jewish family service, I dealt with individual instances of poverty amongst Jewish families and homeless men. I was moved to seek political solutions, because generous individuals and well-established voluntary agencies could not cope with this human disaster. It required government aid in dimensions hitherto never projected.

During the 1932–38 period on Staten Island, while there was a substantial population receiving relief, there was no concentrated Jewish slum and relatively few Jews had to turn to the public agencies. If unemployed, their families made provisions for them.

When I arrived at Bronx House in 1938, it was different. Large numbers of the Bronx House membership were receiving relief or other forms of government aid. Jewish families suffering the most were those where a husband had lost his job and was too old or did not have the skills to find work, even when conditions began to improve. They were in the fifty- and sixty-year-old range. Some had already given up on life, and were often dependent on their wives and children to support the family. The area surrounding the Bronx House was deteriorating, so that the lack of hope found expression as one looked about the neighborhood. With the right programs, even a seemingly empty life can become more fulfilling. Bronx House gave thousands of such people an opportunity for constructive activity; encouragement to learn a new trade, go back to school, or remain in school to ensure one's future;

exposed them to social issues and the arts, helped them make friendships; and give them avenues for leadership. It was interesting to observe how in the senior citizen's group old trade unionists came alive again through programs that gave them a chance to speak and to run for office. Retired cantors could chant again. Parents, rejected at home, found leaders, usually much younger, who treated them with respect.

When I moved on to Federation in 1949, I found that the question of poverty was often played down. True, the clientele of hospitals, homes for the aged, child care institutions, employment services, even centers and camps, could not always pay the fees charged, but government support, union, and other third-party funds hid their poverty from our agencies. Fee adjustments were made for those who could not pay the full sum or who wanted to contribute something toward the cost of service. In some cases, after embarrassing questioning or a grueling examination, the fee was waived.

In the post-war period, the economy was in an inexorable trend upward. It was felt that the millennium was near and that poverty might be eradicated. Since the public agencies took care of the primary needs of the poor—shelter, food, clothing, and health care, the Jewish agencies became even more dimly aware of the existence of a large class of Jewish poor. There were poor aged, poor large religious families. There were more broken homes, where wives and children were suddenly left without resources. Yet somehow the statistics were never added up to a cumulative total that would reveal a substantial number of Jewish poor.

Whenever I called the public welfare office to find out how many Jewish poor were on its lists, even when I spoke in confidence to Jewish executives, I was given the impression—no facts—that the number of Jewish poor was small. Since they did not keep records on religious affiliation, these were understated guesses.

In the mid-sixties the government decided once and for all to wipe out poverty with massive sums of money that would be given, in most instances, to minority groups, so as to develop self-help organizations, which would meet the problem head on at the grass roots.

As a member of Mayor Wagner's Committee on Poverty, formed to distribute huge sums for New York City with expedition, I waded through the hundreds of applications from organizations. There were few requests from Jewish agencies to relieve any segment of the Jewish poor, and if an application did come from a Jewish source, it was rather to provide service for non-Jews, blacks and Hispanics. It was as though the Jewish poor either did not exist or the facts had to be hidden in favor of other minorities. Sociological and demographic surveys continued to report that Jews were in the highest income brackets, the best-educated, employed generally in business, the professions, and white-collar trades. So the illusion was furthered that Jews had few poor, who, if they existed, were somehow being taken care of in ways that did not demand extraordinary Jewish financial support or special services. In some Federation campaign advertisements to reveal our interest in the poor, we would show an older person sitting alone in the park, or a group of teenagers, one of whom might be a black, sitting on the steps of a rundown tenement with nothing to do. The size of the problem of the Jewish poor was never properly explored or pointed up.

Shortly after the antipoverty program got underway, James Dumpson, the black commissioner of welfare of New York City, was invited to speak before a Federation young leadership group. I was also a participant. Dumpson made no mention of the Jewish poor. He indicated that this time the government meant business, and he optimistically believed that if enough money was pumped into the enterprise, poverty could be wiped out. He said that the government was concerned with getting people off the poverty rolls into self-sufficient jobs, where they would enjoy status. He said that the sums to be allocated this time would not be on an emergency basis, but that the grants would be continued each year until the lingering problem was resolved.

When I spoke, I pointed out to the Jewish audience that Dumpson had just given them the cardinal principles of Jewish philanthropy, a tradition that went back to biblical times. The main points were:

1. Help should be such as not to demean the poor through any kind of test.
2. It should be administered by people or organizations in which the poor themselves participate.
3. The amount should be sufficient and continuous to sustain the person until he is self-sufficient.

I ended by stating that the Judaic rather than the Christian attitude toward the poor and poverty seemed to be the guiding influence in the government's program.

The young leaders subsequently invited me to give a lecture on the principles of Judaism and philanthropy.

My views on the poverty problem were thoroughly aired in my review of a book entitled *Poor Jews: An American Awakening* in the Winter 1974 issue of the *Journal of Jewish Communal Service*. The persistence of poverty in American Jewish communities despite the historical concern with the Jewish poor, I wrote, "is due in large part to abject negligence, delusion about the distribution of Jewish wealth resulting from faulty sociological studies, and total reliance on the government rather than the Jewish community to take care of the Jewish poor." Jews somehow preferred to "blot out the ugly picture of an abandoned elderly, the under-financed large religious Jewish families and the growing number of broken homes occasioned in part by the easy divorce laws often legislated with considerable Jewish sponsorship."

I observed that our sophisticated Jewish social service agencies thought it beneath their professional dignity to deal with a Jew who "only" had a financial problem. "They preferred to reserve their newly acquired insights for the intra-psychic, the inter-personal, the dysfunctional, through intensive individual therapy, or encounter groups or community social action."

I related how little was being done for the aged and especially for small Jewish businessmen "trapped in rapidly changing neighborhoods, their meagre and shrinking financial resources further reduced by daily theft by marauders and their lives in constant jeopardy." Jewish agencies saw these as individual cases, or conditions that required police action, but not as a matter of major Jewish communal concern.

When I suggested at a small group meeting of professionals dealing with the aged that Federation must go into the real estate business and buy up entire apartment houses to preserve Jewish neighborhoods and to rehouse the Jewish aged, neighborhoods which had enough stability to ensure a large Jewish presence for a generation, it was viewed as a pipe dream, an unrealizable objective. The only reaction to those Jews, who had to be rehoused to actually save their lives, was to recommend further study, which resulted in bringing more "band aid" services to some of these isolated elderly Jews. The agencies experimented by renting a few apartments to determine whether the plan had long-range validity. I saw the project on a domestic level, in the same dimension as the relocation of tens of thousands of Jews from Europe and Arab countries to Israel and elsewhere after World War II. Taking poor Jews out of deteriorating neighborhoods required equally radical measures. I thought that the Jewish community could afford it and that, if necessary it could even obtain government funds to make these transfers and partly support these dramatic moves. A few Jewish agencies finally got around to it, when there was no alternative. Great suffering could have been avoided with less of a foot-dragging approach.

The assault against Jewish poverty did not come from the well-established Jewish agencies, but from the religious segment of New York Jewry, which had a large number of the Jewish poor. It demanded large-scale government help for vocational and other projects to help these Jews become self-sufficient in the same way that the government was providing huge sums for other ethnic groups. A young, upstart antipoverty worker named Elly Rosen, on June 25, 1971, had the temerity to assert before a federal committee that "Jews in New York city are systematically denied participation in antipoverty programs." He was at first greeted with suspicion and derision by recognized Jewish agencies for preempting their terrain. But the Jewish Federation was forced to cope with his revelations. In New York alone, it was divulged that there were over 250,000 Jews living below the official poverty line—and that was a low level. Federation then made some modest appropriations, later enlarged, to begin to deal with the problem, but in the course of a few years, it was back to the government again. Grants were made in large sums to the "unprofessional" and aggressive religious organizations, which did not always know how to use these funds with propriety, but they learned quickly enough. There are still many Jewish poor unprovided for in Greater New York.

The difficulties have not been resolved in the wake of sharply reduced federal grants, in part due to disillusionment with many of the badly planned and ineptly supervised antipoverty programs, in part due to the reactionary attitude of the Republican administration after the election of President Ronald Reagan, in part due to the straitened financial circumstances of a government burdened with multibillion dollar annual deficits. So the needs of the poor, the poor Jews amongst them, will once again be deferred. Perhaps the Christians, who still run this society, are right: "The poor shall always be with us."

Blacks and "Black Jews"

In the opening chapter of my book *Black Jews in America* (1978), I described my first meeting with a black "Jew," which affirmatively colored my attitude toward blacks and black Jews throughout my life. There was a long hiatus between this first encounter in 1913 and 1955, when I first met black Ethiopian Jews in Israel, and the mid-1960's, when black Jews in the United States were brought to my attention by Rabbi Isaac N. Trainin, whose Federation Commission on Synagogue Relations set up a subcommittee to deal with problems that were emerging.

There were a number of black "Jewish" congregations and a number of black "rabbis" in Greater New York that attracted occasional newspaper articles, a few studies, and occasional white visitors to their synagogues. No one seemed to question their authenticity as Jews, except the New York Board of Rabbis, which had twice, in 1931 and 1952, turned down the application for membership of "Rabbi" Wentworth Arthur Matthew, founder and leader of the Ethiopian Hebrew Congregation in Harlem, and who had ordained scores of "rabbis" around the country, even though he could submit no proof of his own Jewishness or ordination. No one else bothered to disclaim publicly the Jewishness of the rabbis or their congregations or their synagogues. If there was some skepticism amongst the cognoscenti, they kept it quiet for fear of being accused of racism.

A fresh wind swept into the black Jewish movement in 1964. It created an instant stir among blacks and Jews that lasted for several years, under the inspiring leadership of a young Jewish educator, Yaakov Gladstone, a Canadian, who relocated in New York. He had heard of some black

Jews meeting in a basement of an apartment house in the Bronx. An inquisitive and compassionate man, he volunteered to teach them Hebrew songs and dances, and secured the help of the Jewish Education Committee in furthering their cultural programs, so that in the annual celebration of Israel Independence Day in May 1964, black Jewish young people for the first time danced horas and sang Israeli songs along with their white Jewish brethren.

With the help of a sympathetic rabbi, Irving J. Block of the Brotherhood Synagogue in Manhattan, Gladstone organized the Hatzaad Harishon (Hebrew for "First Step"). Esther Bibbin, a black convert to Judaism, was elected chairman. A mixed group of black and white Jews, including some black "rabbis" and white rabbis, were elected to the board with Gladstone as the director.

While the immediate aim was to bring Jewish community assistance to the black Jews, it also had a second objective of drawing the black and white Jewish communities together.

There was considerable resistance from the major black rabbis against obtaining funds for and making services available to black Jews through the new organization. Members of the new association were also affiliated with black synagogues, which were afraid of losing control over their constituents. If Hatzaad Harishon would offer programs, scholarships, introduce their children to good white Jewish day and afternoon schools, enroll them in white Jewish camps, they saw this as a threat to the continuity of their own limited enrollment and struggling schools. They refused to participate in a census of black Jews that would determine how many needed and wanted the new services. I suspect that they were afraid the census would disclose a total number much smaller than they claimed. They also feared that it might disclose that many, perhaps most, had not met the official test of Jewishness, either by birth to a Jewish mother or by conversion. Lastly, it might reveal their own questionable status as rabbis, for none of them had ever been ordained according to Jewish law and by an authentic rabbi.

I found a meeting place for Hatzaad Harishon in one of the centers. Rabbi Trainin obtained scholarships for a number of children in reputable Jewish schools. I pressed some of our camps to accept black Jewish children, particularly Camp Hatikvah. This was when I met Henry and Edith Everett, members of the Williamsburg Y board, and developed a close relationship with them, as we served together on the board of the American Association for Ethiopian Jews. The Everetts made a donation to send black Jewish children to Federation camps.

Hatzaad Harishon looked like it was on its way to prosperity. Several of its members spent a summer in Israel. Several enrolled in seminaries to study Jewish education. Fund-raising activities obtained the support of prominent Jewish entertainers like Theodore Bikel, Herschel Bernardi, and Shlomo Carlebach, who appeared gratis.

The organization printed a mimeographed newspaper with a national circulation. For a time, between 1966 and 1972, it appeared as though the organization would make a major impact on interracial Jewish communal affairs.

I gave a slide lecture before a large group of black Jewish adults and youth, some months after my return from Ethiopia. It was in the spring of 1966. There was intense interest in the subject, since some black Jews claimed an identity with ancient Ethiopian Jewry. One question stood out during that lecture, addressed to me by an elderly black woman. "Where is Israel?" she asked. I was puzzled by the query, as I did not immediately grasp the point she was making. I answered in classic, academic style: "Israel is in Asia Minor, a bridge between Europe and Asia." She repeated the question: "Where is Israel?" I searched for another identifying mark: "It is in the Middle East." She curtly replied: "You don't know your geography. Israel is in Africa!" Then it dawned on me. She was seeking to identify her own black Jewishness with Israel, and thus Israel had to be in Africa to establish her legitimacy. I did not argue her point. American blacks who are trying to create a new identity for themselves by reviving their old identity with Black Africa, yet also want to disassociate themselves from the heritage of slavery that this may imply, often insist that they are the original Jews, and actually of Ethiopian Jewish stock. This gives them an origin associated with ancient Israel and makes them descendants of King Solomon and the Queen of Sheba (Ethiopia), adding to their Jewish lineage a royal ancestry.

Despite Federation's support and that of congeries of blacks and whites, Hatzaad Harishon was beset with problems from the outset. Its numbers were never large. The movement was opposed by the black "rabbis," who saw it as a menace to their own influence and membership. The organization stimulated a number of blacks to undergo authentic conversions. This question of who was a real Jew soon became a searing issue. The white director resigned, and his replacement was a converted black Jew. With his presence, the conflict did not disappear and in fact was exacerbated, because he too pressed the issue of genuine conversion.

Rabbi Avraham R. Coleman, an articulate black, not only converted to Judaism but also obtained rabbinical ordination. He had been employed briefly by the Synagogue Council of America, and under his direction the council sponsored a national meeting on black Jews. When money ran out, he lost his post, and organized his own Brooklyn congregation, attracting a large number of black Jews, all legitimized by authoritative conversion. Coleman muddied the waters by declaring that most of the blacks who professed Judaism were not bona fide Jews, and except for himself, he stated, there were no other truly ordained black rabbis.

The budding organization fell into debt. With the bitter backlash following the 1967 war and the rejection of the white Jewish community by young, charismatic black leaders, many blacks were fearful of any kind of affiliation with a Jewish organization. Its problems became unsolvable and the group dissolved. A few of them joined predominantly white congregations and were accepted. Others went back to their relationship with their own black "Jewish" synagogues, but they too were shrinking in the number of worshippers. Others were reabsorbed in the black community.

Over the years, I visited black synagogues in the Bronx, Manhattan, Queens. I met with some of their religious leaders and congregants. I developed a relationship with Moshe Hailu Paris, whose career I later described at some length in my book.

In the spring of 1976, Rabbi Trainin asked me to write a chapter for his first autobiographical volume, *From the Pages of My Communal Diary*. This first volume had grown to six by 1985. Emma and I spent that summer at our camp on Greater Sacandaga Lake in the Adirondacks. I thought I would do some research on my holiday and visited the Gloversville Carnegie Library, which I had used as a child. All libraries, even in small towns, now had shelves stacked with books on blacks, for Black studies had become the vogue in the preceding decade. There was no room to work, so I took an armful of volumes at a time, off the shelves, sat on the floor, and began to read and make notes.

I literally skimmed through a hundred volumes that summer—histories, sociological studies, biographies, autobiographies, novels. While I found references to the impact that biblical Judaism and even Herzlian Zionism had made on black leaders and their struggle to obtain civil liberties and equality before the law, there was not a scintilla of evidence that blacks were aboriginally Jewish, that black slaves had been converted to Judaism by Jewish masters, that American blacks had an Ethiopian Jewish connection, or that many of them had ever converted to Judaism. This was in contradiction of what I had been lead to believe by my contacts with some black Jews and the limited number of articles and books that I had previously read.

I then decided not to write a chapter for Trainin's book, but instead to do more research and write my own book, preferably in documentary form, which would tell the story from the record. I spent long hours at the Schomburg Center for Research in Black Culture in Harlem, almost going blind examining rolls of microfilm reaching back to the turn of the century. I read in other libraries, contacted Jewish historical societies for their archives, read and reread scores of American Jewish histories, including books on Jews in the Caribbean region, searching for evidence of ties between Jews and blacks, who might have become Jews. Everything I examined revealed the absence of such data, except for isolated incidents.

I came to the painful conclusion that there were and are relatively few legitimate black Jews in America—perhaps five thousand, half converted, and the other half the offspring of Jewish mothers (usually white), who were intermarried with or lived with blacks. I projected no increase in their numbers in the foreseeable future, even though some might want to link their fate with the historical Jewish people and convert. It must be recognized that some black Jews have invented and accepted a mythology about their origins, that makes it more difficult for them to achieve acceptance or integration within Jewish communities, whether in America, Ethiopia, or Israel. Those who elect to convert should be welcomed with total hospitality into the House of Israel. Those who are repelled by this formal act of identity should not be treated like a dissident sect. There are no partial Jews. There are only two tests for either a white or a black.

The book, the first of its kind, was well received by a limited audience. I was interviewed on TV and the radio a number of times. A trio of black radio interrogators tried to break down my thesis through tough and rough questioning, but ended up accepting my analysis and conclusions. Blacks who claimed to be Jews in audiences that I addressed, often challenged my overall views and my writings about specific individuals, but I never wavered from my documented position. Some told me the book was out of date. On closer questioning I learned that some people I described had since gone through formal conversion to Judaism.

Several questioners protested that I was wrong on my data about the Caribbean region and that there were large numbers of black Jews on these islands, some with a historial Jewish background. Emma and I decided to arrange a trip to the islands, even though my previous research had disclosed no significant numbers. We went to Curaçao, Trinidad, Antigua, Nevis, St. Kitts, Barbados, St. Thomas, the Dominican Republic, and Jamaica, all locations where at one time there were black slaves of Jewish masters or where it was alleged that a black Jewish community had once existed. In the course of that month I think I met with all the black Jews in those islands, a total of 17. Despite the stories they related of their origins, all proved to be recent converts to Judaism. They were often the only ones in their family to have forsaken the Christian faith. In the instance of the small black Jewish congregation in Barbados, they were natives who had lived for some years in Manhattan, became part of Matthew's congregation, and after retiring returned to practice his version of Judaism. The local Jewish community did not recognize them as Jews.

If I were to issue a second edition, for which so far there has been no demand, I would not change the body of the text, except to correct a few typographical errors, but I would add a short postlogue indicating the few conversions I noted above. There are now a few bona fide black Jewish congregations as a result of wholesale conversions of the original members in several congregations. One is in New Jersey and the other in

Chicago. There are some additional recruits from the outside, but the overall picture had not changed. Blacks are not likey to become Jews in large numbers in the future.

My book was dedicated to Rabbi Isaac N. Trainin. A number of generous patrons paid for its publication. I received no fee for researching or writing the book. All income from the sale of several thousand copies was donated to the Federation of Jewish Philanthropies of New York, as I had done for another book I had written previously.

Chicago's Black Israelites

From periodic stories in the press of Israel and the United States, the world learned that several groups of black Americans from Chicago had ended up in Israel after a brief but unsuccessful attempt to establish a unique independent community in Liberia. Their imaginative ideological leaders wrote that this was a return to the Promised Land after wanderings about the world, reminiscent of Moses and the Jews some thirty-three hundred years ago. They claimed that Israel rightfully belonged to them. They were the aboriginal inhabitants of that region and had been there before the other so-called Jews had arrived on the scene. They did not claim to be Jews or Zionists, but called themselves Black Hebrews or Black Israelites.

While some American black Jews, all Jews by conversion, have made it to and in Israel, often as celebrated athletes, the Chicago Hebrews imposed themselves on a country that didn't want them. Israel might have expelled the smaller groups arriving in 1968 and 1969, had it not been for the intervention of major American Jewish communal relations organizations, who asserted that such a racial act would sully Israel's reputation as a democracy and would exacerbate black-Jewish relations, which had reached their lowest ebb at that time. I have included a chapter about these Black Hebrews in my book *Black Jews in America*.

In 1975, I was providing consultation service to the community center in Dimona, the city in which most of the Black Hebrews lived. The center was used by some of the Chicago blacks in limited ways. For example, they used the electric washing machines and dryers. The women gathered around these utilities in their colorful dresses and turbans, gossiping. They refused all offers to involve them in other center activities. The sect, apart from the limited separation forced upon them by Israeli officials, self-segregated themselves, ran their own schools, ate special foods, and ministered to their own medical problems, so that their leaders could exercise complete control in every area of their lives.

By chance, while visiting the center, I met their dictatorial leader, Ben-

Ami Carter, as he was sitting in the lobby. I introduced myself as an American educator and social worker who headed an organization aiding Ethiopian Jews. I told him that I had read about him and his group in the press. Carter was less than medium in height, young looking, dressed in a white robe with swirls of cloth, a leather sash holding it together. A turban graced his head, a beaded chain rimmed his neck with a nondescript symbol hanging at its center. He walked with a wooden cane and an ivory top piece, a symbol that was unfamiliar to me. In any event they were not Jewish signs.

My efforts to elicit information from him about his sect proved unfruitful. I had neither pen nor pad in my hand, but he managed to evade every question as to how many there were, what their program was, what success they'd had with Israeli officials in resolving their "temporary" status. There was no animus in his voice as he spoke. He exuded confidence. His dressed-up presence was dignified, but not awesome. After fifteen minutes of fencing, I left him. But I felt that it would not be easy to dislodge him from his role as leader and force the group to leave Israel. They aimed to stay.

On later trips to Israel, I met small groups of Black Hebrews in various places—on the street, in restaurants (they were all vegetarians). A trio attended a dance recital at the Jerusalem Theatre. There was no mistaking them, thanks to their distinctive dress worn both by men and women. However, all efforts to find out more about them in conversation were unrewarding.

Stories appeared in the press that some were criminals and after prosecution had been deported to the United States. Their numbers grew, but no one could ever provide an accurate count. They lived in overcrowded conditions, some of their children died of faulty cultist diets. They sought better housing, and some found space in Arad and Mitzpe Ramon, but nowhere did they integrate with the community. Somehow they obtained jobs, but how they all supported themselves was a mystery, except that individual earnings were turned over to their leaders for redistribution.

The government of Israel was unable to make a decision about their future, because it frankly did not know how to deal with this complex situation and feared to create a racial incident.

My position over the years was that they should all be deported—that they were unassimilable because of their ideological views, reinforced by the tyranny of their leaders, and were a potential "fifth column" should there ever be an internal uprising by the Arabs in Israel or an invasion of Israel by its ever hostile neighbors. There was no positive contribution that they could make to the country. I doubted that their expulsion would precipitate a widespread reaction among blacks in the U.S. or Africa, or any other unsympathetic group anywhere in the world, or would have any material or long-lasting effect on Israel's reputation, status, or economy.

On June 12, 1984, George E. Gruen, director of Israel and Middle East-African affairs for the American Jewish Committee, issued a paper on "The Position of the 'Black Hebrews' in Israel: An Examination of the Complex Issues Involved." I wrote him on August 3, addressing him by his first name, since I had known him off and on for several years:

> I was under the distinct impression that after the Black Hebrews arrived in Israel in 1969, that the Israelis wanted to deport them immediately, but that the consortium of American Jewish communal relations organizations urged Israel not to do so, because of the implications it might or would have for relations between Jews and Blacks in the United States and United States Black and white attitudes toward Israel. Why wasn't that early aspect of the initial problem included in your paper?
>
> It would appear that this was their attitude for the subsequent support in 1978 of the "Histadrut Recommendations" and their and your own attitude as reflected in the last two paragraphs of your paper.
>
> From what you wrote, you see no solution to the problems of their presence, except to have them remain in Israel. Is this conclusion based more on what all of you deem best for Black-Jewish relations in the United States, rather than on what might be in Israel's short or long term best interests?

On April 6, 1984, I received the following letter from Dr. Gruen, addressed "Dear Graenum":

> Thank you for your thoughtful letter on my recent paper .... You are quite right that the AJC was involved from the beginning, urging the Israelis not to deport the group, because of the mistaken impression it would create among the Blacks and the general community in the United States. But these concerns were also shared by the Israeli administration on its own. An added consideration for the Israeli government, as pointed out in the Glass Commission Report, was Israel's concern re the impact on its relations with Black African countries ....
>
> As for my personal preferences, I don't see the solution as necessarily keeping them all in Israel. Those who wish to return to the U.S. should be aided to do so. Any criminal in the group should obviously be deported, and safeguards have also to be worked out to assure that the human rights of the remaining individuals are protected from the arbitrary authority of Ben Ami Carter as well as from hostile actions by their neighbors.

I replied on August 8:

> I value your personal candor about the interventionist role played by the major American Jewish defense organizations in protecting their rights in Israel.

(Then I could not help adding:)

> To the end of my days, I will never understand the total lack of any such interposition on Israel to rescue the Black Ethiopian Jews and for continuing to allow 10,000 Ethiopian Jews to suffer and die every day in Sudan and for permitting 8,000, that is all that are left in Ethiopia, to live in poverty, disease and discrimination.

The presence of the Black Hebrews in Israel constituted a problem for the Ethiopian Jews. It would not be amiss to state that some efforts have been made to obscure the complete differences in origin, belief, and lifestyle between these two black groups. The unfortunate presence of the Black Hebrews may have further prejudiced the leadership of Israel against admitting Ethiopian Jews, and it might have influenced Israelis, who did not know each group initimately, from accepting either of them. Action by the Israeli government in 1968 and 1969, when the Black Hebrews first appeared on the scene, to force them to return to the U.S. might have hurried the influx of thousands of Ethiopian Jews, if the government really wanted these Jews to migrate.

During the summer of 1977, which I spent in Israel, I was told by a number of Ethiopian Jews who had lived for some time in Israel that representatives of the Chicago group had flown to Ethiopia in the previous year to establish their credentials as "true Falashas." No leader of Ethiopian Jewry in Ethiopia was prepared to certify such a linkage. It was curious that they resorted to this tactic, since at the time there were only 165 Ethiopian Jews in Israel. But it was a year after the Israeli government had finally acknowledged that the Ethiopian Jews were indeed Jews and therefore eligible to come to Israel under the Law of Return, despite the fact that up until 1977 no effort had ever been made to stimulate aliyah amongst bona fide Ethiopian Jews. Ethiopian Jews living in Israel told me that they had no contact with the Black Hebrews and had no intention of developing any relationship.

Training Federation's Staff

Always a believer in furthering the education of staff, I used my skills, wherever I worked, to offer courses for my colleagues, the subject matter being determined by whatever I considered to be the gaps in their background. Sometimes they lacked administrative deftness, at times it was special professional dexterity, at times it was programming, and most often a lack of knowledge of Jewish history and contemporary Jewish problems, which they needed if they were to work on the Jewish scene.

At Bronx House, the agency developed a reputation as a kind of "university," because so much supplementary education was provided for the personnel. Specialists were occasionally invited to enrich their capabilities.

Federation was a more difficult area to penetrate, since I was neither the top executive nor the overall program coordinator. Whatever was finally offered had to be suggested in a roundabout way. In other words, I was available should the call come. On a few occasions I led seminars for volunteers, particularly in the young adult division. The subjects ranged from the New York Jewish community to wider problems, such as relations with other ethnic communities and the antipoverty program. I always tried to put a book in the hands of my "students," such as *God, Jews and History*, a popular, concise, and readable history of the Jewish people, in the hope that this would inspire them to do other reading on their own.

In my latter professional years, I was invited to lead a number of discussions with the fund-raising staff, which, in the main, found itself deficient in both Jewish history and the sociology of the contemporary Jewish community. Though these personnel worked almost exclusively with Jews, Jewish issues were not usually raised, and when they were, help was always needed in answering such inquiries. They often worked with synagogue leaders, where their approach was essentially administrative fund-raising. A worker did not bother or had little time to learn even the character of the religious institution with which he was engaged. He might wear a *kippah*, depending on the denomination, or even quietly pressure for a kosher meal, if that was not the practice of some synagogue or organization. But he would do it under instruction rather than from knowledge or conviction. Workers' knowledge of other Jewish organizations or even of Israel was minimal, unless they were personally involved with such organizations or had a personal interest in Israel.

For several years, I led a number of seminars, of six to eight sessions each, spread over a period of several months. I provided some books to deepen their backgrounds. Usually, my lecture would be followed by a torrent of questions about matters pertinent and useful in the trade. The response was generally good, more so from the middle and lower-level personnel than from the upper-echelon executives. The executives were busy, often called away from a session, not to return. Frankly they had less interest in the subject. I was given a beautiful *Kiddush* cup and tray by the class of 1971, for what they called the "Federation Enrichment Program." I know of no better way than such courses, short of enrollment in a complete university program, for workers to develop greater knowledge and skill. I do not believe that the occasional one- or two-day or even weekend session does the trick. They are too short. The experience must be dispersed over at least six to eight weeks, with reading assignments, and with opportunities not only for discussion, but for further contact with the seminar instructor during the intervening weeks. Whenever a "student" walked into my office with a question or comment, he not only received my respectful attention or an answer to his query, but I usually gave him a book or a pamphlet from my well-stocked shelves and files, with the admonition to read it and not return it.

During the course of my career, I participated in institutes at the National Jewish Welfare Board, the Metropolitan Association for Jewish Center Workers, at schools of social work in Cleveland, at the New School for Social Research, and before many other social work, educational, and camping bodies. The results were mixed. I found the one-session institute a waste of time. Panels of speakers were an ineffective educational tool. In later years, I turned down many invitations, because of the limitations of the media.

Furthering Jewish Education

My interest in furthering Jewish education had been evident ever since I undertook the presidency of the Jewish student organization at the University of Missouri in 1928. I tried to improve the quality of monthly meetings by getting better speakers and asking them in advance to raise the level of their presentations. In my inspiration for the creation of a department of Jewish studies at the university, and in bringing Professor Isidore Keyfitz to the campus, the content and the variety of Jewish subjects offered and the other auxiliary Jewish activities initiated also underwent a radical ascent. I taught in a Jewish Sunday school at the Boone Academy in Missouri, which required me to prepare more adequately before facing the indifferent students.

At the Graduate School for Jewish Social Work, my exposure to outstanding scholars like Salo W. Baron and Mordecai M. Kaplan, and the readings they motivated, deepened and widened my Jewish background. When I directed the Jewish Community Center of Staten Island, I introduced a novel Saturday and Sunday morning Hebrew school, then a daily afterschool program, Friday night services, and conducted a seminar or two each year, the subject matter being exclusively Jewish. In arranging the annual lecture programs, even in cooperation with Wagner Lutheran College, the subjects were Jewish as well as the lecturers. I brought educators like Rabbi Ira Eisenstein and Dr. Abraham Duker for special sessions of three lectures each to stimulate the membership.

When I reached Bronx House, the content of the Jewish holidays and other major Jewish events took on a more profound aspect. As the staff was not specifically trained to execute these programs, they had to be provided with a great deal of knowledge. The one-afternoon week-day Jewish school, the Sunday school, and the Oneg Shabbat on Saturday afternoons attempted to be more than perfunctory programs. I consulted with the Jewish Education Committee representative at the time, Ben Edidin, for both advice and materials. As our relationship developed, he suggested that we should collaborate in writing a book on group work in Jewish education, because he thought I had a contribution to make to the Jewish educational experience. Regretfully, time did not permit us to consummate such a venture.

At Camp Bronx House, a variety of Jewish educational materials, programs, prayers before meals, Friday night services, Israeli campfires, songs, drama, and art with a Jewish substance were also introduced over the resistance of disinterested staff members. The campers accepted these programs without reserve.

So I arrived at the Federation of Jewish Philanthropies in 1949 with sufficient equipment, albeit I was neither a Hebraist nor a trained and recognized Jewish educator. I was mostly self-taught. Yet I was prepared to bring these subjects to centers and camps. Very early, I began to suggest the introduction or the enrichment of Jewish content. I wrote many papers and gave many speeches advocating similar themes, including a greater intensification of programming around Israel.

Jewish education was not on my original work assignment at Federation. Before the first budget conference rolled around in 1950, I was asked to work with the subcommittee on Jewish education, which for years had been under the one-man domination of Dr. I. Edwin Goldwasser, one of the founders of Federation, who served as its first professional and then for many years as a volunteer. I found little interest in promoting this field on the part of Federation and even the subcommittee. I would be charitable in stating that their attitude was at best tolerant, but never enthusiastic.

The executive of the Jewish Education Committee was Dr. Azriel Eisenberg, a passionate spokesman, articulate, informed, already a writer of many books on varied aspects of Jewish life, who was struggling to improve the quality of Jewish education in the hundreds of schools to which his staff offered consultation. He wanted to make his agency a more potent force in the Jewish community, but there were few listeners to his story. Salaries for his staff were low, including his own. Salaries paid in the schools were even lower. While there were a few excellent schools—day schools, afternoon schools, and Sunday schools—it would be fair to state that most schools rated from poor to fair. Schools suffered from a large turnover in personnel and student body. Teachers usually worked in this field as a second or part-time job and did not look upon it as a profession or a lifetime career. Many of the principals were superannuated. Jewish education was supplementary in every respect. At Federation it was an unwanted orphan.

My task, as I saw it, for no one encouraged me to make the distribution committee better informed on the subject, was to get them to visit the offices of the Jewish Education Committee and meet more of its staff, and urge them to visit some of the schools, the good ones and the worst ones, so as to better appreciate the needs and what could be done. I did get the chairman at least to visit the committee's offices, but no one wanted to see the schools.

Federation, which had started out supporting Jewish schools in 1918, abandoned this direct contact in 1938, when the Jewish Education Committee was formed. After that Federation permitted the committee to allocate some of its funds to schools, but it was an insignificant amount. Technically Federation had wiped its hands clean of direct support. It turned a deaf ear to pleas for more money to maintain the schools, for it suspected that large sums would be necessary to upgrade even some of them. There was always an open hostility to the existence of the day school movement. Any mention of it at a distribution committee hearing would lead, in the early years of my incumbency, to a tirade from some of its members.

Each year, as we evaluated our grants to each society—and in most years there was an increase—I always had a struggle with the subcommittee to include the JEC for its entitlements. I always felt that the denial of such an addition was motivated by a secret hope to strangle the operation. But I saw to it that these measures were granted, if for no other reason than decent equity.

When I first came to Federation, its grant to the JEC was under $400,000 per year. For several years, the annual cost-of-living supplement to the JEC was denied, so that percentagewise it fell even further behind.

The case for Jewish education was made annually before the committee by a group of men, occasionally a woman, long-time advocates. I was invited by its board to attend an evaluation meeting in the Catskills. Looking over the assembly, I told them that they must recruit young people of wealth and promise, because this was what would give Federation a sense that Jewish education had a future and not only a past. I emphasized young people because they would ultimately be leaders in the broader Jewish community and more generous supporters of Federation. While the donations of the board members to Federation were objectively supposed to have nothing to do with the grants, unwittingly this did influence the grantors. In later years, the staff was given lists of every agency board's contributions (and some did not give), which we followed up to make sure that every board member became a contributor. This move sparked a larger financial response.

When the JEC pressed Federation for much more money to support some of its most needy 750 schools—so that they could eliminate fire and health violations, hire more and better teachers, obtain better teaching materials, retire superannuated principals and teachers, or meet the annual increases in enrollment resulting from the postwar baby boom—there were spirited debates at our committee hearings as to whether the schools ought to be supported at all.

As new members were added to the distribution committee, often individuals with little knowledge of and sympathy for Jewish education, the debates were sometimes vicious. That did not mean that all felt that way. Members like Samuel Lemberg, Clarence Unterberg, and Edward Isaacs were ardent supporters of this functional field and spoke up vigorously for Jewish education. It was necessary for me—without instruction from anyone—to prepare an important memorandum for the distribution committee, which revealed that Jewish education and even direct support for schools was part of the original Federation program. This revelation helped stifle some of the agitation against the JEC and the schools. A few members of the committee were partial to other services and outrightly antagonistic to Jewish education in any form; when money was tight, they seriously proposed cutting out Jewish education entirely. At one meeting, I blurted out that I could not serve on a Federation that would make such a move. Luckily for me and my career, the committee disregarded or forgave my passionate outburst. Yet the tone of my uncontrollable comment had some effect on the decision not to bring that resolution to a vote.

Another move on my part, again spontaneous and at no one's urging, was to put together the figures on the total cost of Jewish education in Greater New York. I pointed out that it summed up annually between $150 and $200 million, the largest costs due to the constant growth in the enrollment for day schools. At the time Federation was providing only $750,000 of this overall amount out of the $25 million that was raised, insignificant as compared to the overall expenditures. I think this made the committee have much more respect for the size and significance of the Jewish educational field. The bulk of Jewish educational income came from student fees, all kinds of fund-raising activities, generous benefactors, and even some aid from governmental sources for food and transportation, sums which Federation, again at that time, could not replace. Only substantial donations through a special fund for Jewish education could have made a dent in this enormous financial problem. Just before I left Federation, such a fund was finally established, but not before some of the most vicious exchanges that I ever witnessed at Federation meetings took place. Due to the magnitude of one donor in recent years, this fund has grown enormously, and vast improvements are said to have taken place in many of the schools.

I had prophesied during my Federation incumbency that Jewish education would someday have to become Federation's major concern. I have lived to see the day when this was fulfilled. In 1984, about $15 million was allotted to education through the Federation budgetary process and special funds, a sum which exceeded that received by any other Federation beneficiary.

This has come about gradually as a result of the presence of Israel, the joint operation of Federation and the UJA, the introduction of more pro-Jewish education leadership on Federation's board and its major committees, a gradual turning inward within New York's variegated Jewish census, and an enhanced appreciation of the values of Jewish education itself.

But my struggles were not with Federation officials and volunteers. At times I had to get involved with what was happening within the Jewish Education Committee itself. When cutbacks were to be made to keep the committee viable, the easiest targets were the drama and art departments. I believed that these departments were essential for the Jewish educational process to have an emotional hold on the students. I threw my support in favor of their retention. I even had Federation provide earmarked grants to retain the drama department. I not only saw the arts as essential for the Jewish school system, but for other institutions like centers and camps, child care, and the aged. There has been an explosion of interest in the Jewish arts over the last few decades, inspired in part by the National Foundation for Jewish Culture, where I was a board member.

While a few Jewish day schools are on a par with the best private and public schools, producing top scholarship winners in state and national competitions, most still have a long way to go. There is need for the judicious consolidation of many schools as the Jewish child population declines and neighborhoods change. There is still a need to recruit, train, and provide more full-time competent principals and teachers, so that Jewish teaching truly becomes a profession, a career, and not a congeries of teachers drawn to it for supplementary earnings. There is still a need to enrich the programs with all of the Jewish arts. As the number of Jewish scholars graduating from universities increases, there is a possibility that many of them may throw in their lot with the Jewish primary and secondary schools rather than teaching in the universities or doing research. If that happens, there is every prospect of a Jewish renaissance in the Jewish community as it approaches the twenty-first century.

Autonomy or Centralism?

In the early 1950's, shortly after I arrived at Federation, I was called into Joe Willen's office one morning, where he was just concluding a meeting with short, wiry, well-tailored Victor Riesenfeld, president of Montefiore Hospital, one of Federation's major affiliates, and president of Broadstreet's, a chain of fashionable men's clothing stores. They had met because Riesenfeld, a defender of his agency's autonomy, was concerned about Federation's efforts to encroach upon the destinies of its member societies. This reaching out for control was a subtle outgrowth of the recent building campaigns, where Federation, in its allocation of capital funds, was endeavoring to tell the agencies what kinds of institutions they should build. Riesenfeld was opposed to this on the ground that "Federation was a creature of the agencies, and not the other way around."

Willen told me he had suggested that a committee be set up to study the problem, and he wanted me to service the committee. He introduced me to Riesenfeld as a "thoughtful professional." Riesenfeld told me that he would call for an appointment after he checked his calender.

Presuming that a committee would be set up, I jumped the gun and wrote a detailed memorandum, indicating how the issue had come to the fore, listing the benefits and defects of autonomy and/or more centralized Federation control. I sent it to Riesenfeld and Willen for their comments.

Riesenfeld called me a few days later and said he would be at Federation in a few days and wanted to talk to me. His voice sounded sharp, if not indignant. Not having worked with him before, and having been given no clues as to the way he behaved, I didn't know whether he was reacting to my memo or whether that was the manner in which he usually spoke and acted.

We met alone around a large table in one of Federation's meeting rooms. He started off by telling me the facts of life. "There is going to be no committee. There is no need for any memorandum. Federation is not going to put anything over on us." I was taken aback, expressing my surprise at his definitive position. I told him that I had written the memo on my own with no instructions from anyone. "Didn't Willen tell you to prepare it?" I said: "No." "Well, let's forget the whole thing." He rose and left. That was the end of the issue and the committee.

When I told Willen what had happened, he laughed it off. "Typical Victor." I heard nothing further from him about the subject. Occasionally a lone agency would raise this issue, when it felt that Federation was intruding on its domain. While Federation's influence, even domination, over some of its agencies grew over the years, autonomy still prevailed as a principle. I learned from that brief encounter that with some lay people who have "power," one should not run too fast. I believed that Federation should exercise more control over its agencies.

This book reflects that point of view in many places. Somewhere in Federation's archives my memo lies flat and forgotten.

Ike: Rabbi Isaac N. Trainin

A few years after I arrived at Federation, a new staff member was added to the roster, Rabbi Isaac N. Trainin, known throughout his career at Federation as Ike. A little over medium height, thin (he works at it), beardless, always dressed in high male fashion, smoke issuing from one of his numerous pipes, this traditional Jew with his straw, felt, or woven hat, or indoors wearing a *kippah*, created quite a sensation with his speeches, memos, books, and programs during more than three decades in that singular post. Ike was initially engaged because Federation was in a bitter dispute with the rabbinical and synagogal community over whether a kosher kitchen should or should not be incorporated in the new Long Island Jewish Hospital, and hoped that his presence on the staff might inspire more financial support from the religious community. He fought constantly for the observance of the Sabbath and Jewish holidays in our more than one hundred institutions, the elimination of Christmas trees, and the introduction of kosher food services and kitchens in agencies that had somehow managed to operate without them since the advent of Federation (and even before). On top of this, irrespective of the functions of other staff members, he initiated a series of meetings, seminars, and conferences that had an impact on medical ethics, programs to counter intermarriage, overcome alcoholism and drug abuse, deal more effectively with poverty among Jews, give Jewish neighborhoods more representation through local councils, increase the interest and support for Jewish education, bring to the institution's attention Jewish books and have them establish Jewish libraries, provide awards for those who made contributions to Jewish life as professionals and as laymen, develop better relations between the synagogue and other Federation institutions, and bring more traditional Jews within the leadership orbit of Federation. I am sure the preceding list is not complete, but it will serve in a measure to record Ike's catholic interests and influence.

That he had to counter the leadership everywhere goes without saying. That he often came into direct conflict with his fellow staff members is a gross understatement. In the early years, I found him aggressively approaching the societies within my sphere of responsibility without first consulting or at least informing me. I learned of his incursions when the agencies complained. While I was interested in some of the same ends as he, nevertheless I insisted that he advise me of whatever he was trying to do, and he finally and reluctantly agreed to do so. He found me a sympathetic friend and not a contesting enemy. He is a fiery, independent person, who believes that if you consult, you end up with your hands tied.

Since many of our objectives were similar—we both wanted to make Federation and its constituent societies more Jewish in their philosophy, board, staff, and program—we inevitably ended up working together, but as two freewheeling operators doing it our own ways.

Had it not been for our strenuous efforts in the middle 1960's, Federation and its agencies might well have gone nonsectarian through a revised constitutional charter and outright practice, with substantial government funds. Aided and abetted by the 1967 war in Israel, this unfortunate movement was not only halted but reversed, as we witnessed Federation thereafter taking a Jewish course, which culminated in the merger of the Federation and the United Jewish Appeal.

Ike invited me to speak at a number of his forums. His book committee published my volume *Innovation by Tradition*. He asked me to write a chapter on black Jews for one of his half-dozen historical autobiographical works about himself and his unique department. When my research and writing turned into a small volume, he did not hesitate to have it published by his Commission on Synagogue Relations. He introduced me to Rabbi Charles Weinberg in Jerusalem, which eventually led to my meeting with the Ashkenazi Chief Rabbi, Shlomo Goren, following which Goren joined his Sephardic colleague in the Israeli Chief rabbinate in affirming that the Ethiopian Jews were indeed Jews, an important pronouncement as a forerunner to thousands of them eventually arriving in Israel.

Ike and I have remained friends, see each other socially. I continue to hear him criticize Federation, its institutions, its personnel, for their failure to act immediately on his recommendations. His remarks and writings are as uninhibited and unrestricted as ever. Yet his loyalty and productivity for Federation and its constituent societies have never diminished. Whether one liked what he said, even when it was sometimes in bad taste, he was a fearless champion of Jewish causes. He would go into the ring with the sturdiest personalities—and would usually win. Ike finally retired on June 30, 1986.

* * *

9

Israel: 1955 and 1959

JERUSALEM HAD BEEN in our prayers and Palestine in our family conversations since I was a child. Had my mother not become seriously ill in 1921, I might have gone off with my Hebrew school teacher to Palestine and my entire life would have been different. I belonged to a Zionist organization in my adolescence. I affirmed my interest in Labor Zionism during my last year at the University of Missouri. I suffered vicariously through the 1920s and 1930s as the Zionists, despite pogroms in Palestine, steadily carved out a homeland. The periodic outbursts of Arab violence took their toll of Jewish life. When the vote for participation took place so vividly in the United Nations, I tallied the score as it dramatically came over the radio. I celebrated the creation of the state in a speech that I made as president of the National Association of Jewish Center Workers in 1948 in Atlantic City. Yet when would we go to Israel to see the Promised Land?

The opportunity arose in 1955, when the National Conference of Jewish Communal Service organized the first Jewish social work seminar in Israel. Emma and I immediately signed up, along with twenty-eight others, a miscellany of social workers, Jewish educators, and other workers in Jewish institutions. It was hardly a homogeneous group that was enrolled under the stewardship of Gershon Gelbart, who disappeared in the middle of our six-week journey.

I had arranged a ten-week holiday from Federation, since I had already accumulated a considerable backlog of vacation time. I had never taken my full six weeks vacation each year. We planned a four-week tour of Europe after Israel, our first revisit since 1949. It included Cyprus, Greece, Italy, Belgium, and Holland.

We were still flying in the propeller age. Our Sabena plane lifted off from Idlewild (now Kennedy) Airport, and made stops at Gander, Manchester, Brussels, and Athens before touching down in Lod, arriving at midnight. We sang with joy as we saw the lights of Tel Aviv. Our eagerness to see the land itself would have been more pleasurably fulfilled had we arrived in the daytime. The small airport, the struggle with the porters (Jewish at that) piling our luggage atop a bus, our arrival in Pension Har Aviv in Bet Hakerem, a suburb of Jerusalem, in the early hours of the morning, the disappointment of some of our companions to find they would have to sleep on camp cots covered with army blankets, and with toilets down the hall, temporarily dampened the high spirits of their arrival in Israel. Emma and I were old campers. We understood that this was a Jewish Agency-subsidized trip, so we had not envisioned deluxe accommodations. We accepted this first experience and everything else in the eye-opening six weeks without a word of criticism.

Bet Hakerem, despite the modest amenities, was a delightful setting among the cooling trees. Israelis from hot and humid Tel Aviv came to this pension to spend their summer holiday. This gave us added opportunities to meet Israelis face-to-face for more than a passing *shalom*. We learned how each one had arrived in Israel, how as European refugees with their tattooed numbers and memories of terrible suffering, they had risen in Israeli society, despite all the obstacles confronting a new country that had not attained wealth or self-sufficiency.

Before we could recover from our long flight and get settled, we were briefed on our almost daily excursions, which covered the entire country except Eilat from as far south as Yerucham to Rosh Hanikra and Metulla, from the Dead Sea to the Gaza Strip. Cities, towns, villages, moshavim, and kibbutzim. Every institution that fell into the domain of social welfare, education, religion, and culture. The Hebrew University had only one building on the new campus. The new Hadassah Hospital had not yet been completed. New housing was sporadic. Our visits to *maarbarot*, temporary shelters for newcomers, confronted us with voluble complaints from recent arrivals, who protested the delay in providing them with decent homes and regular employment. While the economic picture was painted everywhere in the darkest hues, we saw evidence of a desire on the part of the government and individuals to make themselves more self-sufficient, trying to lift everyone from permanent dependency on the wealthier Jewish world. On one of our tours, a young sabra guide, who had already fought in the Haganah, led our group up the mountain to Avdot in the Negev. After showing us how the ancient Nabateans had lived in homes carved into the stone escarpment, he pointed to the arid land below, which had once been extensively cultivated, and taunted us with the comment: "We did this long before there was a United Jewish Appeal!"

Prominent Israelis lectured to our group on every aspect of the Israeli commonwealth. By the time we were through, and particularly for those who listened and took notes, it was a four-year college course compressed into forty-two long days. When it was all over, and I sat down with my colleagues to evaluate the experience, we listed twenty-eight suggestions for making the program better in the future. Many were petty, dealing with amenities rather than content.

I know, since I led another group to Israel in 1959, that even with the best will in the world on both sides, these programs cannot meet everyone's expectations. Emma and I came to learn, and we learned. Some came because it was an inexpensive way to see Israel, but they had other agendas. Some wanted deluxe hotels, gourmet food, air-conditioned buses, because they were accustomed to traveling that way on other privately arranged trips. With a "motley" crew, there was no way to satisfy everyone.

I say I led *another* group in 1959, because I literally led this first one for half the excursion, after our leader suddenly left. I was asked to take over, which I did, consulting with a small committee that I appointed.

One of the bright notes on our study tour was having a guide like Zev Vilnay, tall, burly, with a booming voice. This professor of geography communicated his vast and intimate knowledge with force and enthusiasm. His guidebook was the copy of the Bible that he always carried with him. In subsequent years he published his own *Israel Guide,* which I still find the best, because he identifies each site with its historic antecedents. He was always leading us up a steep slope to a new monument, to out-of-the-way places. He described each spot along with Israel's role during the wars before and after the state was established. Vilnay became a good friend; he visited us in the States, and we saw him repeatedly at his home, 15 Radek in Rahavia, usually at his Saturday afternoon open houses, where his charming Egyptian-Jewish wife, who has since passed away, presided over a tasty refreshment table.

Our tour brought us to the excellent Mizrachi school at Kfar Batya. We were so impressed by the school and its director that I offered him a position in the United States as a director of one of our centers.

Although we little realized it at the time, a chance encounter while at Kfar Batya was to change our lives for the next thirty years. At the school we came upon a number of black children, thirteen in all, and upon inquiry we learned that they were Falashas—Ethiopian Jews. They had been brought to the school only a short time before for several years of study in Hebrew, contemporary Judaism, modern farming, and medical care, so that they could return to Ethiopia to improve the lot of their kinsmen suffering from poverty, illiteracy, disease, and discrimination. Emma and I had read about the Ethiopian Jews, but this was our first face-to-face meeting. I took pictures of and with the children. But my only diary notation for the contact was: "Visited Kfar Batya. Saw young Ethiopian Jews. Took pictures."

From then on, we attempted to find out more about the Ethiopian Jews. At the time I did not know about Dr. Jacques Faitlovitch, who for more than a half-century had tried to improve their lot and rescue them from oblivion. Nor did I meet him, although he lived in Tel Aviv, not far from one of the hotels we occupied. He died in 1955, the very year of our visit. When I was told by some Israelis that the Falashas were really *not* Jews, I responded by asking why the government, the Jewish Agency, and Mizrachi had brought them to Israel to educate them. I added, caustically, that I had not known that Israel was interested in teaching and possibly converting native black Africans. At other points in this book, I tell the rest of the grim story of how we became preoccupied with the destiny of the Falashas over three decades.

We had a rewarding visit to the home of the Ashkenazi Chief Rabbi, Isaac Herzog, and his wife one Shabbat after services for *Kiddush*, which they offered to public visitors. We were told to arrive at 11 A.M. Since we are always prompt, we came on the hour. But no other people showed up until a half-hour later. We had a long conversation with the Herzogs. This Irish Jew, who spoke English perfectly, asked me why I did not speak to him in Hebrew. I told him that my Israeli friends thought my Hebrew was atrocious, so I stuck to English. I jokingly added that like Akiba, who did not become a student until he was forty (I was forty-seven at the time), I hoped to improve my Hebrew skills. To which he queried: "But are you another Akiba?" In embarrassment, I had no reply. I mentioned the Ethiopian Jews we had seen at Kfar Batya. He told us that in his view they were authentic Jews. In a letter to the Department of Religious Education and Culture of the Jewish Agency in Jerusalem in March 1954, he told us, he had stated his belief that the Ethiopian Jews were descendants of proselytes, and had written these stirring words:

> Bring them all under the wings of genuine Judaism and in contact with the Chief Rabbinate of Israel and Zion. Have faith in the G-d of Israel. . . . Arm yourself for the difficult struggle against instigators. Let G-d preserve us from them, who like vultures fall upon the remnants of our brethren, the Falashas. May the Lord preserve and keep them alive in Ethiopia. It is a holy duty to help in this pious task. We have only to purify them now, as we accept them and "permit" them to the daughters of Israel without difficulty.

Yet despite the eloquent rhetoric and seeming positiveness about the Falashas as Jews, Chief Rabbi Herzog's letter did not immediately influence the Israeli government to permit them to migrate to Israel, after Israel established formal diplomatic relations with Ethiopia in 1955.

We renewed our relationship with Ralph Goldman, whom I had first met in 1939, when I went to Boston once a month to teach group work. The class consisted of five young men, including Ralph, and one woman. We also reestablished ties with another of the students, Joseph Neipris, who had gone on aliyah to Israel and became the associate dean of the Paul Baerwald School of Social Work at the Hebrew University. Ralph was training for the Jewish center profession. After a stint in center work, he went into the U.S. Army. On discharge, he became involved with the underground movement supporting Israel's independence. When I saw him in Jerusalem, he was representing the United States to the Israeli government in the distribution of grants. Ralph introduced me to Teddy Kollek, who at that time was director-general in the Prime Minister's office. Goldman later returned to the United States to direct the program of the American-Israel Cultural Foundation. He left that position to become the director of the Israeli Education Fund. Then he returned to Israel to become the associate director of JDC-Malben. In 1975, he became the executive vice-president of the overall AJJDC, from which he retired in 1985. When I spoke to Goldman and Kollek in Prime Minister Ben-Gurion's office, it was bare and modest, far from the sumptuous quarters later built for the leader who ran the country. My relations with Goldman continued over the years, our only serious differences being opposite positions on what I believed was Israel's indifference to rescuing Ethiopian Jews and the role that the JDC should play in Ethiopia in bringing relief services to them.

We met Manny Kraicer, head of the HIAS program in Israel, on numerous occasions before his untimely death.

On our tour was a Korean, Dr. Hong Chun Kim, who had been studying Hebrew and the Bible at Dropsie College in Philadelphia. He knew Hebrew well and the Bible by heart, identifying every guidebook reference as we toured the country. A Presbyterian by religion, he planned to return to Korea and publish a newspaper. Our relationship deepened over the summer through many conversations. He invited us to Korea should we ever visit the Orient. When my brother Sam became the U.S. ambassador to Korea, we went there in 1962 for an eighteen-day visit, during which we had a reunion with Kim and met his family, including his well-to-do brother, who was a successful businessman and outstanding collector of Korean art objects.

Several years later, when Kim's brother visited us in the States, he brought as a gift an ancient large jar, unearthed from an old funeral mound. It was from the Koryo dynasty in the tenth century. It turned out to be a valuable addition to our sizable Korean pottery collection.

Speaking of art leads me to recall our visit to the studio of Jakob Steinhardt, whose wood-block prints, some illustrating books on Jewish subjects, had given him an international reputation. His charming, businesslike wife served tea. We bought one of his books. But before we left he printed two of his newest works for the forthcoming "Book of Ruth" and gave them to us as a present.

One evening we spent at the home of the Mohilevers, whose walls were covered from ceiling to floor like an atelier with paintings given to or purchased by them, all from artists they knew. Amongst them was a Polish (non-Jewish) artist by the name of Matoushek, whose colorful and delightful paintings of Jerusalem prominently featured Hassidim. We began to hunt around Israel for one of his works and finally bought one from a shop in Jerusalem. It portrayed several small Hassidim in a stylized version of Mea Shearim, where they live. After some bargaining we bought it for a price we could afford. We wouldn't part with it, as it was the only one we could find; even though it was not one of the artist's greatest paintings, it was typical of his genre.

On an alley off Ben-Yehudah Street in Tel Aviv, we discovered the tiny art shop of Imre Szabo, where we purchased a score of paintings. They included several watercolors by Shmueli Katz, a prominent cartoonist and delightful painter; works of Edward Phillips, who became famous and popular under his new name, Ben Avram; superb paintings by Alex Levy, whose premature death deprived Israel of a fine artist; and the works of young Shlomo Schwartz, who had recently won the first prize in an Israel art exhibit. These became the nucleus of an art collection for ourselves and our children (we usually brought at least three, one for each family), added to periodically by purchases in Israel and around the world in the course of later travels. We could not afford expensive paintings. We never paid more than $100 for any painting on our walls, which are now covered with some ninety works. (Many more repose in the attic.) When we framed and hung our pictures, many of our friends wanted similar art works. Szabo was happy to send some by the same artists, which we gladly disposed of at cost. His shop was visited by friends in later years.

Despite our euphoria about Israel, we sometimes saw the seamier side too. One night with Dr. Leon Feldman, who knew Judge Steinhardt of Tel Aviv, we went on a tour of Jaffa. The jail was crowded with Arabs arrested for a number of crimes. We were unhappy to find amongst them some Jewish inmates incarcerated for misdemeanors and felonies. On the streets, the judge stopped to talk with a young prostitute, a Jew, daughter of a recent immigrant, whose family life and morals had already suffered from the shock of too rapid dislocation from a former closed culture. The Israelis had not yet learned to appreciate the need to maintain something of their previous life and its values which was worth preserving, if for no other reason then to avoid personal tragedies. The Israelis were too frequently heard to say: "We are a pressure cooker, we must make our immigrants Israelis overnight." This lack of initial interest in the cultures and family life of the Jews still streaming into Israel from Arab and other lands was to become a major concern in subsequent years in education, work attitudes, political factionalism, family morals, crime, and emotional breakdowns.

I end this section on a humorous note surrounding my first experience in eating the ovaries and testicles of sheep. Discovering their unique flavor one day in a small Oriental restaurant in Ben-Yehudah Street in Jerusalem, I sought them in various other restaurants, usually without success.

When we returned in 1959 for another six-week visit, we were asked one night by our host in Haifa what kind of food we would like. I suggested some restaurant where they served these delicacies, preferably an Arab-operated dinery, for I had heard that they prepared them best. It was a colorless, whitewashed place, except that while we were having a drink, the owner brought us nargilah pipes to smoke. I had not smoked since 1940, but once assured that the mouthpiece was sanitary, I drew in a few drafts of smoke, held it for a bit, and then puffed it out. I assumed that it would have some narcotic effect, but it didn't. I abandoned this potentially stimulating device, notwithstanding the attractiveness of the bowl and the stem.

The waiter approached us for our orders. He spoke English quite well. Emma and the others, who were less adventurous, ordered the conventional shashlik and shish kebab. I had been told to ask for "sheep's eggs." He assured me by citing his credentials—he had worked in Greek, Turkish, and Arab restaurants—that he understood what I wanted. The other three got what they ordered, but he brought me a large plate of fried eggs sunny side up and potato chips. I stood up in dismay, holding the plate in my hand and almost shouting at him, "What the hell is this?" He took the plate and answered forcefully, like most waiters who will not take an affront, showing me his note pad with the other hand so that I could see that he had indeed written down exactly what I had told him. And there on the slip were my very words, "chips and eggs." It was such a hilarious reply that I laughed, forgave him, and ate what he served. But my appetite for this dish pursued and consumed me.

In a Tel Aviv Oriental restaurant one day, I invited some friends to partake of this *mychel* ("tasty dish"). The male waiter did not understand a word of English, so "sheep's eggs," "Rocky Mountain oysters," and "lamb fry" brought no response. Neither did the Hebrew word *baitzim* ("testicles"), although my Hebrew might have been faulty. So I resigned myself disappointedly to doing without this exotic food. He ushered a young female waitress to our table. I repeated all the English and Hebrew terms, but had no better success. Finally, in desperation, I blurted out, "Sex. You know, sex," gesturing between her body and mine. Whereupon she took me by the hand, led me to the kitchen, and there, reposing coldly and silently in the glass refrigerator, was a whole dish of ovaries and testicles. I left Israel with a feeling that all would be well in a country that could produce and properly prepare such dietary delicacies.

The Jerusalem YM-YWHA

On our first visit to Israel in 1955, Emma and I got ourselves involved with the Jerusalem YM-YWHA. Louis Kraft, after leaving the Jewish Welfare Board in 1947, undertook a mission to Israel in 1948, while death-dealing shells were flying all over Jerusalem, to establish a YM-YWHA. A magnificent YMCA, with its tower making it the highest building in Jerusalem, stood there as a monument of what U.S. Christians had done for the country, sharply revealing that the Jews in the American YM-YWHA movement had never done anything comparable. Kraft managed to find an old Arab building on Rehov Hillel and set up a modest program, but something went amiss with its financing. Israel in its early years as a state, was in no position to support, let alone build, an adequate structure.

We went to see the Y but found that it was closed. Someone directed us to Samuel Behar, manager of the Barclay's Bank branch on Jaffa Street, who was the president of the Y. We walked into the bank, asked for Behar, and after a wait, this swarthy, attractive man of Turkish-Jewish origin, who spoke English impeccably, greeted us with no enthusiasm. "Oh, are you another American Jewish couple interested in visiting the Y, promising to help, and then forgetting about us after you leave?" We protested that we were not like other American Jews, that the Y was my calling, and we'd like to talk with him and determine how we could assist. He then graciously invited us into his office for some Oriental coffee. We talked for a while, then made a date with him for dinner that evening at the President's Hotel, where we spoke further about the Y, danced, and ate. (Ralph Goldman later related to me that when Behar had been in despair about keeping the Y open for lack of money, he had told him that Graenum Berger was coming and would solve the Y's problems. Behar made no reference to this conversation with Goldman.)

We spent the following weekend with Behar and his late wife, Chayuta, at his farmhouse on the road to Tel Aviv, a house built into a hillside looking across an already cultivated valley to the new Hadassah Hospital. They also had an apartment in Jerusalem. We went on a tour of neighboring kibbutzim, where they had friends. We had lunch and afternoon tea and cake, a standard diet in all of Israel whenever you visit someone.

The Y building was almost devoid of furniture and equipment. It was in need of a painting and decorations. It was a temporary, makeshift structure, and with a spare program, not likely to attract young people, nor provide the ambience so essential to influence their lives.

Behar needed $10,000 a year to run the Y. We promised to raise it, although we did not know where or how at the time. We left him with the assurance that he should engage staff and money would be forthcoming within a few months, for we would not be returning to the United States for another six weeks. Emma and I vowed that we would not only find money to maintain the current program, but would start a campaign for a new building.

Among the people that we met in connection with the Y in 1955 was Moshe Levin, the director, and his wife, Miriam. Ever since they are dear friends; we see them on our frequent visits to Jerusalem, and when they occasionally come to Pelham. On that trip we also met Florence Mittwoch, the first director of the Y, and we have also kept close ties with her and her husband, Yaakov.

On our way back to the States we met Ben and Bertha Touster in front of the Excelsior Hotel in Rome. Ben was president of the Boro Park Y, chairman of my center committee at Federation, and also president of HIAS. We told them about the Jerusalem Y and its dire needs. We collectively agreed over lunch to raise money for the Y.

Our first activity on our return was to sponsor a concert. We coaxed all of our friends to buy tickets, and the first thousands of dollars were dispatched to Behar. It was obvious, however, that we could not do the whole job alone and that we needed the support of the Jewish Welfare Board. There is where we ran into heavy weather. Even a small annual maintenance program was not high on its agenda, let alone a new building. The JWB was unhappy—ashamed would be a better word—of the decrepit Jerusalem Y building, its program, and its leadership.

After our pleas, the JWB finally decided to send someone over to study the problem, and this led to further delays. Meanwhile, each year, our small committee raised a few thousand dollars, appealing to family, friends, and center executives over the United States through concerts and raffles. It was not enough. We added appeals at the annual national conferences of Jewish Communal Workers, where we charged admission to the well-attended Gridiron sessions. Rabbi Philip Goodman, a staff member of the NJWB, who as part of his responsibility was charged with maintaining relations to Ys overseas, was helpful with the raising of funds.

In 1957, Mrs. Hugo Dalsheimer, an important, wealthy, and generous

Jewish leader from Baltimore, active in the Y movement, returned from Israel and apparently raised hell at the JWB office about the shabbiness of the Jerusalem Y. I was summoned to meet her at the JWB to discuss the possibility of a new building. When an impecunious professional like me had repeatedly suggested such a development, it was ignored. Now that an outstanding volunteer leader was interested, everyone at the JWB stood smartly at attention.

A meeting was arranged at her sumptuous, suburban Baltimore home that summer to which were invited a large group of people who should have been concerned with the problem. Few appeared. There was too little time for preparation and promotion. The summer season was on, when most people normally abandon all communal interests. Getting to her home was expensive and time-consuming. We raised some money, set up a committee, and decided to press the Jerusalem leaders to find a piece of property.

In 1959, on a second trip to Israel, I spent time with Behar and others, as well as with Mayor Gershon Agron (he died shortly thereafter) and his planning commissioner, to explore sites that might be available free or at little cost. The only parcel I thought large enough was the one that was ultimately selected in Katamon. In 1959, there were no buildings and no decent access roads. I thought it was acceptable nonetheless, because the planners predicted and assured me that this would be the first area of major growth in the city's expansion. They proved right. I came back and recommended the property. Other Jewish Welfare Board committees and architects were dispatched to look it over. My original suggestion was finally confirmed.

We needed $600,000 to build. Sol Litt, president of the JWB, undertook to raise it. Money came in slowly. I agreed to be the guest of honor at a cocktail party sponsored by James Felt and Joseph Willen. We raised $25,000. A year later, I was also the guest of honor at another cocktail party sponsored by Clarence Unterberg and Joseph Willen, and we obtained $70,000 more, $2,500 being Emma's and my contribution. The appeal at the second party was that the money was to be used to build a swimming pool in our names. Construction started in 1963 without all the funds available, although we had reached the $500,000 mark. Philip Goodman was the coordinator and was always pressing leaders to raise more. Individuals in Canada as well as the United States were approached. I finally obtained a gift of $150,000 from Horace Goldsmith, and we named the building for him. All the money needed seemed to be in hand.

I learned that there was a "plot" to give the swimming pool designation to someone else. I took this unkindly and raised a fuss about it, threatening to make the issue public. Whoever made the final decision I do not know, but when the building was dedicated a small plaque in the large pool, high above eye level, bore our names.

When the pool was being constructed, we wanted to put up and pay for tiles in Hebrew, English, and Arabic citing the talmudic statement that amongst other things, a father has the obligation to teach his son how to swim. I encountered resistance all the way from the Jewish Welfare Board to the Jerusalem Y leadership. They preferred apparently to have it bare—and it still is—rather than display this marvelous piece of ancient wisdom and instruction.

Emma and I attended the dedication in 1968, postponed for a year because of the 1967 war, when the building was used for a time as a bomb shelter. It was quite a ceremony in the large gym, with Teddy Kolleck and other government officials present. By the time the building was completed, the entire area was surrounded with apartments, so there was no problem in recruiting membership.

The Jerusalem Y was the first of over one hundred Ys which were established years later under quasi-government boards. I say government, even though the capital funds for the building usually came from private donors, mostly Americans. Except for such income as was generated by dues and fees, the bulk of the budget came from various departments in the government. The Ys, except in their clientele, never became quite the same democratic, middle-class institutions one found in America, but they did serve an important function for the integration of the heterogeneous populations that characterized most Israeli communities.

Some of the Israeli Ys were more akin to the settlement houses in the immigrant neighborhoods of large American cities at the end of the nineteenth and the beginning of the twentieth century. They served the lowest-income groups and dealt with a multitude of social problems, trying to raise the cultural level of their clients and help make them "natives" in the quickest possible fashion. Under the leadership of Chaim Zipori, a strong, untrained professional, with some financial help and the guidance of Ralph Goodman, who was then the number-two man in the American Jewish Joint Distribution Committee's office in Israel, the buildings multiplied and the programs became a major social force. Zipori, whom I met on numerous occasions, died prematurely in 1984.

In 1975, the JDC and the Israeli centers asked me to conduct a six-month training program for directors of centers, teaching them how to recruit and train volunteer board members. The boards were usually chosen from a small group of local politicians appointed by the mayor or representatives of several central government departments—welfare, education, labor, etc.—and they collectively appointed a few friends. It was a self-selected, closed group. Obviously there was resistance from the board and even from some executives, who either liked the system or didn't want to take on extra duties. Nonetheless I introduced the program in Dimona, Ashdod, Jerusalem, Afula, Safed, and Kiryat Yam, traveling to each community twice a month. In a few instances I broke through the obstacles and obtained cooperation. While I do not speak Hebrew, I was able to communicate with the individuals involved. All the directors spoke English. The board system that I tried to introduce was so contrary to Israeli institutional practice that after I left, it was never extended properly to the new centers arising each year. On occasion American-trained directors of these centers recruited interested laymen for their local boards, but it never became a universal policy.

My trips—mostly alone, although at times Emma accompanied me—up the West Bank from Jerusalem, to Jericho, to Beit Shean, were often brutal in the summer heat, driving a non-air-conditioned car. Yet I enjoyed the drive through the barren desert, mostly arid wasteland. Occasionally I passed farms that were being redeemed from the long-neglected soil. I never encountered a single problem with Arabs. On a few trips, I drove down the center of the West Bank through Tulkarm, Nablus, and Ramallah, and stopped for lunch or coffee at an Arab restaurant. While there were no smiles of welcome, neither my person nor my car was ever touched. Several times, when I went into a store to make a purchase and engaged in conversation with the owner, I was even treated to a cup of coffee, Arabic, served in the too tiny cups. When Emma traveled with me, she was in dread of my daring, always fearing that the worst would happen. She, along with Israeli friends, thought I was foolhardy. I never gave a thought to the possible danger, concentrating more on getting back and forth over the shortest and quickest route. Sometimes I had the good luck to pick up a young Israeli soldier, so I was guaranteed further security. The Italian Fiat stood up admirably under the superheated winds, the overly hot roads, and my fast pace.

I made some efforts to get the directors and the board members of the Jerusalem Y, in which I had a special interest, to communicate with its original donors as well as the stream of American visitors, so as to sustain their interest and use the contacts as an instrument for fund-raising. My many attempts failed. The constant change of directors and the board itself militated against the development of such a fundamental medium. I was always told, whenever I made a suggestion, "Why don't you come and live in Israel, and then you can carry out your interesting ideas?" I am not sure that I could have achieved these objectives even if I had lived there.

Cyprus Adventure: 1955

We had finished our first trip to Israel and were about to leave for Europe. On the way back to the States, I wanted to stop for a few days in Cyprus, rich in history and conflict between the Turks and the Greeks. At the moment it was engaged in a struggle to expel the English. Emma was afraid to go to a country in such turmoil. However, I managed to book us on a plane that would make a brief stopover in Nicosia en route to Greece.

As our plane landed in Nicosia, we saw below not only the interesting and varied topography from desert to lush farms to mountains, but also what appeared to be a huge military camp. To my disappointment, we were told that no one was allowed into town during the layover, as there was trouble in the city. We resigned ourselves to a drink at the airport bar, where I bemoaned my fate to the English-speaking barkeep. "If you are not afraid, I can arrange to get you to Nicosia." I looked at Emma and she showed no sign of fear, so we took our hand luggage, walked through the back door into a waiting taxi. The driver spoke creditable English. He turned out to be a first-class guide. As we drove to the city, he showed us the British camp, claiming there were seven hundred thousand British soldiers to keep the half-million Cypriotes under control. We drove into a beautiful, well-kept city with multicolored attractive buildings. We passed the U.S. Embassy, the Israeli Embassy (we had told him that we had just come from Israel), the library, civic buildings, residential sections, when suddenly we came to the start of a large demonstration with marchers carrying signs attacking the British. Stopping the car in front of the demonstrators, he told them I was an American newspaper man and photographer, and it would be good propaganda to allow me to take pictures. I stepped out of the cab, exhilarated, and snapped one photo after another. I bowed and thanked them profusely and we drove on. He stopped at another spot where words had been whitewashed on the pavement: "Eden [Anthony] equals Hitler. British Get Out."

As time was running out, we started to return to the airport, but on the way I shot pictures of the statue commemorating a priest who was martyred in 1821, during an old battle for freedom, of a farmer wearing the unique shirt-pants, and of an English garrison. The driver thought I should not leave Cyprus without a bottle of the best brandy, which he bought for 85 cents. He claimed it was better than the best Scotch. I tipped him handsomely.

At the airport, we were accosted by officials, who, speaking in indignant Greek, demanded to know how we had the audacity to go into the city without a permit. Our airline officials, who already had boarded all the passengers and were in a hurry to get off the ground, for there was a rumor that the demonstrators were heading for the airport, interceded on our behalf. They took us by the hand and rushed into the plane; the door slammed behind us and we sped off. The next day we learned that a number of people had been killed during the demonstration.

When I related this adventurous incident to my brother Sam, who was then in Washington with the U.S. Foreign Service, he replied indignantly: "This is what makes U.S. consular officials get gray hair and have heart attacks before their time, because of stupid Americans, who do not respect the laws of the land and other regulations." I told him, and all others who would listen to this story, that even if we would have landed in jail, it was an unforgettable hour and a half in Cyprus.

Greece, Italy, Belgium, and Holland: 1955

As our plane circled Athens before landing at the end of July 1955, the sight of the Parthenon evoked memories of my year of study of Greek civilization (history, philosophy, literature, and art) in 1928–29 at the University of Missouri.

Our non-air-conditioned room at the Grand Bretagne cost only $6.40 a night, but we overlooked the discomfort of almost unbearable heat and humidity as we later drove around this beautiful city, viewing its historical monuments and eating in savory restaurants.

Louis Shapiro, an American working for the United Nations in Greece as a banking specialist, had arranged to give us a tour up to Delphi. He invited Mario Modiano, a Greek Jew who was the correspondent for the *London Times*. We also invited Dr. Leon Feldman, who had been with our group in Israel, to join us.

Several days before, an El Al passenger plane with fifty-eight aboard was shot down at the Bulgarian-Greek border. In every town, Modiano stopped to check with his office for more details on this tragic incident. We paused in Daphne to see the eleventh-century Byzantine church and its graphic mosaics. At Eleusis, we saw the excavated ruins and sculptures. This was the ancient sanctuary dedicated to Demeter, scene of the Eleusinian mysteries. Through Thebes, which recalled Greek plays that I had read. Up the mountain, higher and higher to Arachova, then to Delphi, where the Greeks traveled 125 miles from Athens to consult with the oracle before they went off to war or embarked on any adventure. Nestled on a cliff under the stark gray-black Mount Parnassus, looking off to the Gulf of Corinth, it is a site to inspire even modern poets. We arrived just in time to see Sophocles' *Ajax* performed in an open theater with the mountains serving as a backdrop. In a modern stylized version, we saw and heard the dramatization of the tragic tale of Ajax, who had been promised the mantle of Achilles, but instead discovered that Ulysses had decided to run a popularity contest for this honorable trophy. Ajax committed suicide. We walked over the restorations and saw the excavated sculptures, before then known to me only in plaster casts or from photographs. We left the inspiring site with photos and memories. We ate a local feta cheese, whose taste and quality I have found in no other place.

On our return to Athens, we dined at an unforgettable seaside restaurant. One fisherman brought us fresh clams that Modiano selected for our first course. Then another fisherman produced some red mullet. A third came with squid. After each purchase, we turned them over to the chef to prepare and serve. All three courses were washed down with Greek white wine, everything consumed slowly at sunset on the shores of the sea. It was another of those romantic events that enticed us back to Greece on many occasions. That night we went to an Athens park to see an extraordinary outdoor vaudeville show with Greek costumes and music. This was a spot where the lower-class Greeks went in droves. They knew where to find a good show. We walked up the rock-strewn Acropolis, visited all the museums, the Olympic stadium, the Temple of Zeus, the Theater of Dionysus.

Our son Michael, who collected old guns, had asked us to bring him firearms from every country we visited. We could not find even one Arab gun in Israel, for the Arabs claimed the Israelis had confiscated their weapons. After a long walk through the streets of Athens, where we could not even read the street signs, and where few spoke English, we finally came upon a shop and bought an old Greek pistol. We bargained with our fingers, writing down the number of drachmas we were willing to pay. Our figures on a piece of paper were scratched out over and over again until we arrived at a mutually agreeable price.

* * *

Then we were off to Rome. The Hotel Massimo D'Azeglio was in the center of the city, from which we could walk everywhere. I had taken courses in Roman history, not as intensive as my studies of Greece, but with Hachette's excellent guidebook (we also used its guidebook for Greece) and reading up beforehand on the areas and buildings we wanted to visit, our stay proved to be another refresher course that made Rome, and for that matter all of Italy, so delectable that we returned many times. It is still our number-one country for travel. It would take a volume to write about all that we have seen. Bernini's sculptures jumped right out of many corners of Rome. As good tourists we saw everything that tourists were told to visit. We had dinner near the Jewish quarter one night, indulging in superb cannelloni. We took in the opera *Lorelei*, extravagantly presented at the Baths of Caracalla. We sauntered through the Roman Forum, went under the Arch of Titus, where the Jews were ignominiously marched in chains after the destruction of Jerusalem in 70 C.E. and to which we were now triumphantly returning after the reestablishment of the State of Israel in 1948. We learned from native Jews how the Jewish community rebuilt itself after their cruel treatment by the Germans during World War II.

We drove out to Castel Gandolfo with thousands of Christian pilgrims to see and hear the Pope address us from his balcony. The ecstasy with which he was greeted in that tiny square, where four thousand, mostly of the faithful, literally pressed upon each other without an inch to spare, was an extraordinary tribute. They prayed, genuflected, and shouted, "Viva la Papa." We met Rabbi Mordecai Waxman of Great Neck in the crowd.

We dined that evening at Alfredo's, where the proprietor mixed our fettuccine with the gold fork and spoon that Douglas Fairbanks and Mary Pickford had given him as a gift decades before. We have never eaten the equal of that dish. The veal and mushrooms that followed, along with saltimbocca, salad, strawberries, and wine was memorable.

The Vatican, the other great churches, including St. Peter in Chains, to see Michelangelo's *Moses,* were our next visits. Since the light was poor in the afternoon, we came back the next morning to witness the formidable figure of Moses with sun shafts striking the massive form.

We went to another dramatic opera at the Baths of Caracalla, *Mefistofele,* the Sistine Chapel, and attended a Friday night service at the ornate synagogue. The poorly dressed worshippers, mostly Italians, contrasted sharply with the pomp and ceremony and the unique attire of the religious functionaries. The chazzan, to the accompaniment of the organ, reminded us of the chanting in a Catholic cathedral we had attended the day before. It was nonetheless a moving Jewish experience as his voice made the interior resound.

That night we dined at La Cisterna on the Trastevere. Located in a narrow court between two tenements, with the neighbors looking out of their open windows, with waiters in white socks, blue and red pants, varicolo ed blouses, and bandannas around their necks, we ate our dinner to the music of a fine orchestra. Some opera stars who had come in after their performance, at the prompting of a diner, arose and sang, to our delight. We ate an excellent steak dinner, other goodies, and wine.

I cannot overlook the fabulous dinner at the Tre Scalini on the Piazza Navona, which included cannelloni, bauletto, broiled shrimps, wine, gelato tartuffe, and demitasse, all for $3.00 each. We came back to this restaurant some years later, ordered a gelato/tartuffe, and paid $2.75.

We talked with many Italians about their economy, their jobs, their religion, their culture, and found them warm and responsive. Their greatest concern was holding on to a job and having enough money to pay their bills.

We dropped coins in the Trevi Fountain and made a vow to return. We drove to the Villa d'Este, built imaginatively and extravagantly by one of the Borgias, scenes made memorable in an American movie titled *Three Coins in the Fountain,* traveled on trolleys and motor-bus trolleys, talked to fellow passengers. During our week in Rome, we walked our feet off; we did not see most of it, but enough to whet our appetite for future visits. Despite its size, we felt that we had grasped something of the city's character.

Packing our bags once again, we took the bus to Firenze, driving through the pines along the hill country, incredibly beautiful in August.

Every inch of the hillsides was cultivated with farms, fruit trees, and grape vines. Spoleto, Trevi, and Assisi with its basilica, the city that St. Francis created following his influential ministry. Through Perugia (to which we would return in 1965 and again during the summer of 1985 to study its art and architecture for a fortnight). On reaching Arezzo, the birthplace of Maecenas and Petrarch, we were taken with this still unspoiled city (a decade later it was smoke-ridden and industrialized), particularly the square with its bougainvilleas, its little restaurants, where nuns in their white hats and gray growns sat and drank coffee in the quiet afternoon. This was the square in front of the church with the extraordinary frescoes that Piero della Francesca painted. I thought then that it was a city that I would like to retire and live in. When we drove through ten years later the square had become an unattractive parking lot. Gone were the colorful bushes and trees, and the nuns. So another Shangri-la was written off our list.

Firenze on the Arno. A veritable outdoor and indoor museum. Smaller than Rome, yet it was more difficult to get to know the Florentines, who seemed to be too busy serving tourists to converse. We ran into Wilfred and Majorie Wyler twice, close associates at Federation, rode around the city in a horse-drawn wagon. Together we ate at an outstanding restaurant, Sabatini, where we topped off an excellent dinner with a cream cake, of which I made a drawing in my travel diary. I never found its equal.

While there were too many pictures on the walls of the dimly lit Uffizi and Pitti Palazzo museums, the works that we could see up close excited us, both the paintings that we had seen in art books and those that we had heard about.

One of our exquisite experiences was to see the works of Fra Angelico in the San Marco Church, in which he lived as a friar, while in his spare time decorating the shrine. His luminous paintings seemed as fresh as when he painted them centuries ago.

We took pictures of the baptistry and the zebra-striped cathedral and entered the mysterious, ornate Medici Chapel, the Tomb of Michelangelo, with the four marble statues representing Dawn, Day, Twilight, and Night. We rushed around from early morning to late at night peering into the shops on the Ponte Vecchio, and tramping through the Piazza of the Signora with slim David always in view, so that not a moment would be wasted viewing the huge collection of art.

Four days were all that we had and then we were off for Venice. Wherever we dined, we always ordered the wine of the region. We nervously sat in a bus making constant hair-pin turns. As we rode through Forli, our guide told us that it was Mussolini's birthplace. At Ravenna we walked to Dante's tomb. As we approached Padua, a city developed by the Romans two thousand years ago, we looked up at the picturesque hilltop castle built by Frederick Barbarossa in the twelfth century, a monument to a memorable figure in medieval Italian history.

Padua was a surprise. Five hundred years older than Rome, with the second oldest university, this was where Dante and Galileo studied. The impressive Basilica of St. Anthony, the marvelous arcades, and the public gardens with over a hundred statues were a tribute to those great architects and artists, and to the leaders, who had the imagination, the wealth, and the sheer power to accomplish these majestic works.

In Venice, we boarded our first decorated gondola. The gondolier, with his red and blue ribboned straw hat, poled us without song at twilight through the murky waters of the Grand Canal, passing one building more handsome than the next, under bridges, darting busy traffic to the landing of the Danieli Royal Excelsior Hotel. Seven white-suited bellhops, each carrying one of our seven bags, traipsed up one flight of stairs and then another with Emma and me trailing at the rear into our large, luxurious mahogany-furnished room.

The Tauber sisters, who had been on our tour in Israel, had left for us a welcome pack of cheese, rolls, and peaches that served as our indoor supper, for we were too tired to seek a restaurant.

Our arrival was marred by news of a tragedy. Old friends and colleagues, Louis and Mina Sobel, had been drowned when their holiday cruise ship sank in the Chesapeake Bay. Louis had once approached me about taking on an assignment with the Joint Distribution Committee to work with Jewish refugees as the war was drawing to a close in Europe. My life might have been vastly different had I bowed to his offer.

St. Mark's Square with its decorated basilica, the Clock Tower, the imposing Campanile, the arcades, cafes, orchestras, the pigeons, and the great cathedral.

Venice on a Sunday was crowded with Italians as well as foreigners. We took the steamer to the Nuovo and Vecchio ghettoes and saw where the Jews at one time had enjoyed wealth and power. We entered the synagogue in a rather shabby building. By contrast, inside, the items were neatly displayed. The custodian was Catholic. Down another alley we went into a rather elegant Sephardic synagogue, then into a typical Ashkenazi *shtiebel*. There we met some Italian Jews, who greeted us with their "Shaloms." The prayerbooks we examined were in Hebrew and Italian.

It was our habit, wherever we traveled, to buy our lunches of rolls, cheese or meat, and fruit in a shop and then eat in a cafe where we could order coffee. Venice had many ideal luncheon spots, either in one of the many squares or sitting on the edge of a canal.

We strolled through the narrow streets and found our way back to San Marco Square in time for the bell-ringing on the top of the palazzo and watched as the pigeons descended by the thousands in a fluttering roar for their feeding by the crowds of pedestrians. We walked through the cathedral, guarded by men in Napoleonic-era costumes, and marveled at the frescoes, mosaics, and paintings which bedecked the interior.

We dined in a small fish restaurant, where the natives went. The menu was in Italian. Finding it difficult to decipher, we gestured to the waiter to serve us what a young man at the next table was eating. Excellent squid was followed by scampi, followed by lobster. When the meal was over the handsome youngish man, in pure English, albeit an Italian, introduced himself, commending us on our selection with a broad smile. He was an artist, took us on a strolling tour into art galleries that we would have missed without him. It was one of the delightful, unexpected events that frequently marked our visits.

Venice cannot be seen in three days. But we had to leave, boarded a gondola to the bus station, and were off on the final leg of our Italian journey. The bus paused at the Villa Pisano, where Hitler and Mussolini had hatched their tragic Axis pact, another stop in Padua to see the mosaics and frescoes at the Cappella Scrovegni, then to Vicenza to enter the first indoor theater (1580) with its fantastic columns and statuary.

Before stopping in Verona, we left the road to the hills, where the Capulets and the Montagues had once carried on their bitter feud. From Romeo's castle, one overlooked a lovely village and *campagna*, and there, in a restored building in a splendid restaurant, we ate one of our best Italian meals. Lasagna, cooked in a massive pan in a huge oven, was followed by cotellete milanese, salad, fruit, rum-maraschino cake, and Italian coffee. No one worried about diet.

Verona, which had taken a beating during the war, rewarded us with a visit to the chapel. According to Shakespeare, this was where Romeo and Juliet were married. Then to the Roman Colosseum, restored to its original first-century character, for outdoor opera where *Aida* was being rehearsed.

As we drove north, we heard more German spoken, and restaurant menus were frequently in both Italian and German. We drove past Lake Garda, the largest lake in Italy, and through Sialo, which Mussolini had used as his capital in 1944. We stopped at Gardone, where D'Annunzio lived and died, finally reaching Milan, a large modern city including a few skyscrapers. Regrettably we arrived there on a long holiday weekend, so most institutions were closed. The La Scala had no performances. Museums were shut. We scaled the immense cathedral, second only to St. Peter's in Rome, with its elaborate flying buttresses and statuary and huge stained-glass windows. We lunched at Biffi's with its celebrated ravioli, the most expensive restaurant we found in Italy. It was worth it.

Holland

We were off on the KLM to Amsterdam, landed at nightfall, the lights shimmering in the canals. We tried to drink Bols gin straight like the natives, but found it hard to down this national liquid. After wading through the overly generous Hollander's breakfast the next morning, we went out to see the city of 900,000 people, 450,000 bicycles, 70 canals, 400 bridges—the entire city built on wooden piles. If you turned it upside down, it would become a veritable forest. We spent the better part of the morning at the Rijksmuseum, with its superior collection of great masters, many paintings with Jewish subjects. The seventeenth century was an extraordinary era for local artists.

After a pause for lunch, we passed the whole afternoon at the Stedelijk Museum to see hundreds of paintings by Van Gogh. I actually cried at the beauty and skill of his works, none of which he ever sold. He died of frustration, driven to the verge of insanity, unheralded. (One could not buy tickets easily for the early-sold-out exhibition of his works at the Metropolitan Museum in New York in 1984–85.) The museum hung other competent artists of the last century, but none could compare with Van Gogh.

We found antiques cheaper in Amsterdam and bought a variety of brass and sterling silver items. But all the Jewish works were far beyond our modest resources. Dealers told us that there was a good market for such pieces. We went to the old Ashkenazi shul, now turned into a museum. We photographed the statue in the park that Christian workers had erected to memorialize the German destruction of a large part of the Jewish community in September 1941.

We toured the famous Sephardic-Portuguese synagogue, guided by the wife of the *shammes*. It was undergoing extensive repairs. It must be a sanctuary of grandeur when the candles light up its interior for worship.

We toured through the countryside with its well-cultivated and tended farms, sleek cows, artistically assembled haystacks, windmills, dikes, and ditches, witnessing the prodigious reclamation of land by filling in and desalinizing the artificial lakes. We bought and ate cheese at the open-air market in Alkmaar, watched the men with their varicolored straw hats carrying hundreds of loaves at a time. We ate marvelous herring, purchased from a street vendor who reminded us of the frankfurter stands on the streets of New York. We watched the metal bugler blow the time at each stroke of the hour promptly at 11 A.M. We rode through Edam, another famous cheese village, with an architectural style that reminded me of Luneburg, Germany. Then to the picturesque fishing village of Volendam, where everyone walked around in old-fashioned costumes clacking away in their wooden shoes. The motor launch took us to Marken, where I bought a pair of wooden shoes for $1.10, and found them reasonably comfortable, parking them at the threshold wherever we entered a building. We went through a cheese factory, where we saw this food processed from beginning to the end product. We strolled into antique shops and picked up interesting items.

One day we took the fast-propelled train to the Hague, the seat of the World Court. We passed through attractive cities like Haarlem and

Leiden, and dikes, farms, and houses with thatched roofs, which had a durability of eighteen years. The Hague was where Spinoza lived in the seventeenth century. His house still stood, as well as a statue of the modest, influential philosopher. We viewed an unusual exhibition of Etruscan art and learned the history of the picture of the frescoed blue flute player that we had purchased in Italy a week before. We saw Andrew Carnegie's Peace Palace, where periodic efforts are made to keep the world from destroying itself. We walked through part of the attractive Parliament, then through the Mauritshuis Museum, where we saw more Rembrandts, several with Jewish themes, along with the art of Fabritius, Stefn, Hals, Vermeer, Rubens, and Holbein the Younger, all treasures. We managed to get along in Holland by speaking our Yiddishized German.

Belgium

We plane-hopped to Belgium, which to us appeared more French than distinguished by a national style of its own. Despite its half-Flemish character, our version of the German language was often not sufficient for adequate communication, but our smattering of French helped in several instances. The Hotel Astoria in Brussels still retained much of its original elegance. As it was situated amidst the great institutions and monuments, it was convenient for walking to many places. Our dinner at the Rotisserie Ardennes was memorable for the quality of food served at the unbelievable cost of $3.50 per person, for which we had a delicious cold soup, eels, steaks, cheeses. Only the apples were not up to the American varieties. There had been surprisingly little destruction during the war, because Brussels had been immediately declared an "open city" and was spared by the Germans. The stone figure of Edith Cavell recalled the brutal shooting of this celebrated nurse during the First World War. We went to Waterloo, where Napoleon's ambitions came to an inglorious end. It seemed that on every block of the city and its suburbs, we were walking on historical ground with an interesting story. The statue of Manneken-Pis, the small boy urinating into the fountain, was superb. A distinguished citizen, his figure is adorned with varied raiment on special occasions. We found a small brass piece in an antique shop.

We took the train to Ghent and Bruges. Until the river silted, these cities were preeminent in the Middle Ages, then Antwerp became the major seaport. Bruges struck our fancy. A beautiful city still preserved as it was of old. Its canals made it not quite the Venice of the north, but with an altogether different charm. The swans swimming in the park-lake gave it a peaceful, pastoral, photogenic appearance. Every building awaits a photographer.

We met Max Gottschalk, a friend of Louis Kraft and Dr. Maurice Hexter. An expert on postwar problems, teaching law at the university, he was the acknowledged leader of the Jewish community, a remnant trying to rebuild itself after the ravages of the war. A train ride brought us to Antwerp, the city of Rubens, where his work was abundantly available, along with that of Rembrandt, Hals, Breughel, Cranach, and Memling. In the cathedral, Rubens's three great paintings enriched the shrine.

Our second European tour was over, leaving us with an unquenchable thirst to come back and see more.

Israel: 1959

In the fall of 1958, I was approached by representatives of the World Zionist Organization to lead a second tour of Jewish communal workers to Israel in the summer of 1959. Since Emma and I were eager to return to Israel, I accepted. I decided to recruit and interview prospective participants well in advance of the six-week study program, and to plan with Israeli officials six months before our arrival on the scene, so as to avoid some of the bugs that had occasionally plagued our 1955 experience. I made candidates fill out detailed forms. I interviewed all those who lived in and around New York. I conducted several orientation sessions. I corresponded with the Israeli director of the institute, indicating what places and institutions we should be visiting, the kind of people to address us, the topics for such presentations. Thirty of us launched our trip with the highest expectations.

I wish I could report that all went well, but that would be untrue. The first two weeks were a nightmare, and I vowed that I would never lead another tour. All that I actually received for my arduous labors was free air transportation, board, room, and travel in Israel for Emma and myself, roughly valued at $1,300.

First, our four-motor El Al plane flew over half the Atlantic Ocean with one motor out of commission. I quieted our group by telling them that planes could fly with only one motor. I proved a good prophet, since the plane landed safely in Orly, Paris. The motor had to be replaced, so we were guests of the airline, fed sumptuously, put up at a good hotel, bused around Paris, taken to the Moulin Rouge for the usual stage-dancing potpourri, all free. So the accident provided a delightful interlude. The plane then took off with a stop at Athens, where during our layover we were surprised to find my brother Sam and his wife Margaret at the airport to greet us. Sam was the acting ambassador at the U.S. Embassy. They looked great, and we arranged to see them at the end of our Israeli tour.

At the Israeli airport, our group was met by Louis Horwitz of Malben-

JDC and Mannie Kraicer of HIAS, official greeters, but also personal friends, and Samuel Behar, president of the Jerusalem YM-YWHA. Rahel Breslau, who would be our Israeli secretary-coordinator, was also there. It was evident from the beginning that Israel was different than four years before, except for the heat and humidity. The airport had been enlarged. Buildings were going up everywhere as we drove through Lod and Ramle. The excitement in the group kept mounting as we began the climb to Jerusalem. For most, this was their first visit to Israel. The magic of the ancient city was evident in their questions and facial eagerness.

We were again staying at Pension Har Aviv in Beth Hakerem. There I had my first arguments with some of the group, who were not content with their assigned rooms. We gave up our room with an independent shower. Usually the tour leader was given one of the better rooms. We turned it over to still the outcries of two obnoxious women. One actually became hysterical, lying on the floor, screaming and kicking her heels like a lunatic. Was it a case of fatigue, separation from home, or a return to infancy? I summoned the group after supper for an orientation session and told them at the outset that I was not providing psychiatric care during the summer. I expected adults to behave like adults. There was no response from anyone. My own spirits were not of the highest. I was not meant to be a tour leader or hotel keeper, despite my long experience in operating a camp for more than 350 persons. I was conflicted between giving people the comforts they expected and their infantile responses to what was being offered. Apparently my picture of the realities of the pension as I had presented it to them in New York had not penetrated. What brought them to silence was my final question: "What did you expect for $860 and six weeks in Israel? The King David Hotel? You'll find some of the accommodations in other cities will be even more modest than this one." This was not the last scene.

We toured Jerusalem the first day. We still could not get into the Old City and had to peer into Jordan from some high buildings on the artificial border. Our guide this time was not Vilnay, but a young sabra, Meron Benvenisti, of mixed Sephardic and Ashkenazi parentage. Tall, handsome, a bit dark-skinned, he was articulate, vigorous, with a touch of arrogance, exuding strength and confidence as he explained and defended Israel.

We now could walk up to Har Zion over a new macadam road, instead of grasping on bushes as we had four years before to reach the citadel. We chanced on the ceremony of Ogden Reid, the new U.S. ambassador, presenting his credentials to the President of Israel, Ben-Zvi. This young, attractive, Foreign Service officer attempted to address the crowd in Hebrew, repeating what he had to say three times, and then gave up. We had coffee at the King David Hotel with David Rose, an old friend and a major supporter of Technion, who was studying sites in

Israel for building apartment houses, a subject which he knew expertly. With Samuel Behar, president of the Jerusalem Y, we toured Jerusalem for potential sites for a new building. Joseph Neipris told us about the new Paul Baerwald School of Social Work at Hebrew University, of which he was a member of the faculty. I recalled our meetings in Baerwald's home in Manhattan in 1948, when I was conducting a study group on Jewish history, with his son and daughter as members.

Whenever we had a speaker, I acted as chairman and coordinated the question period, usually ending with my own summary in an effort to give cohesiveness, continuity, and direction to the lectures.

During the course of the institute, I tried to relate it to our American experience and even to similar activities in other foreign countries where we had traveled. I sought out books for reading and purchased some for the group. Our lecturers covered every aspect of Israeli institutional life—hospitals, aged, child care, family welfare, education, aliyah, housing, army, religion, personnel training, use of volunteers.

One of the new things I brought to the seminars was the cultural life of the Israelis—writers, poets, dramatists, journalism, artists, the dance—so that our group could have some appreciation of what was happening in the creative aspects of Israel. When we were in Haifa, I introduced Yaakov Malkin, the brilliant director of the Haifa-Rothschild Community Center, and his artist wife, Felice, who added another dimension to our knowledge. Their reputations have increased over the years, he as a teacher and writer, and she as an artist and illustrator. Our families have continued an intimate friendship for a quarter of a century. My own background in the humanities would naturally lead me to introduce this element.

I had lunch with Mayor Gershon Agron and Samuel Behar, which led to the selection of a site for the YM-YWHA. Regrettably Agron died in 1959, so that he never saw the new building. When I brought the group to the decrepit Y building, they spontaneously made donations for the operation of the program.

We revisited Kiryat Gat and observed the strides made since our first trip to this burgeoning city, which had sprung out of the desert in 1955. We listened to the problems of creating an industrial-agricultural complex, attempting to integrate Jews coming from many parts of the world, each with distinctions in their history, culture, language, food habits, and outlook.

On our arrival in Ashkelon, despite my advance planning and phoning the day before, the pension was short of space for all of us. Some of us would have to be scattered in private homes, for which no arrangements had been made. At first some of the group refused to go to private homes. I blew my top at their intransigence. Emma and I gave up our room at the pension and said we would accept such emergency accommodations. Four other husbands and wives volunteered to follow us, so another crisis was averted. Private homes gave us a better insight into how the Israelis lived. I was in a bitter mood toward some of our group and with our Israeli coordinator for failing to anticipate this housing problem. But since my temper is usually ephemeral, I became more temperate as the day wore on.

In Beersheba, we spent a pleasant evening with the colorful Mayor David Tuvyahu, who looked like one of our American western pioneers. In four years, this city had spread itself over the neighboring desert. It was no longer a Bedouin town. I ordered brandy for everyone, and we topped off the evening in song and high spirits.

The next day we took in S'Dom, Yerucham, and Sede Boker, Ben-Gurion's favorite kibbutz; in the mid-afternoon of a hot day, we climbed Avdat to see the Nabatean excavations and the remains of a medieval Christian church.

Several members of the group asked me whether we could go farther south to Eilat, a city two and one-half hours away, and not on our summer's itinerary. I asked the driver and guide if it was possible and they assented. I would have to call Eilat to make hotel arrangements and then notify Jerusalem that we would not be returning that evening and to cancel all programs for the following day.

As an efficient but somewhat naive group worker, I did not tell the group this was what we would be doing, but instead presented them with the idea, expecting that the group would receive the suggestion with hurrahs for adding this interesting spot to our route. Three people objected with a storm. One, a young divorcee, had a date that night in Jerusalem. Another couple were expecting a letter from their children and therefore wanted to be back in Jerusalem to read it, providing it came. Twenty-nine people were for the trip. Three against. So I said we would go to Eilat. Whereupon the wife of the couple lay down in front of the bus and dared us to move toward Eilat. It was another disagreeable experience, in which I made an arbitrary decision to return to Jerusalem. The twenty-nine did not speak to me for disappointing them. The three were angry, because I had dared to interfere with their plans. Total alienation.

When we returned to Jerusalem, I called the group together and read them the riot act, indicating that if there were any further exhibitions of such negative, unjustified behavior as I had encountered at Avdat, those people would be immediately severed from the group. I told them that I did not have to undergo this repeated childlike behavior on the part of those who could not accept the wishes of the overwhelming majority, or who would compel the group to be subjected to their whims, their relatively unimportant social engagements, or their expectations of mail, or who were not prepared to share in whatever discomforts might occasionally arise in hotels, at mealtime, etc. I reminded them that several times people had unbelievably complained that food served did not come to them first. I had to point out a simple fact of life: the waiters had to start somewhere, and if they happened to choose an end table, our group might be served a few minutes later. I would not even listen to such stupid comments in the future. My anger and final warning had a decided effect, and except for one other incident, the rest of the trip ran smoothly.

In Tiberias, another blowup was in the offing, and I almost sent two people home. One couple found that their room was very narrow and only had one window. They confronted me with this injustice. We had not yet seen our room, which was slightly larger but had two windows, so we made the exchange. Neither the beneficiaries nor the rest of the group seemed concerned that we would be less comfortable. It was such pettiness that almost drove me to distraction.

On our flight to Israel, we had sat next to Dr. Nelson Glueck, president of Hebrew Union College and a distinguished archaeologist. He invited us to visit one of his digs in the Negev, but we couldn't fit it into our schedule. One Saturday afternoon, as we were approaching the entrance to the King David Hotel, Dr. Glueck emerged with a group of Reform rabbis to whom he had given a luncheon-lecture on his excavations. He was dressed in blue jeans and open shirt, and carrying a shovel. Grasping my hand he said, in everyone's hearing: "Berger, come along with me to the Negev. I'm ready to leave." He pointed to his jeep. Nothing would have given us greater joy, but we couldn't go. The rabbis did not see anything incongruous or irreligious in the head of their religious seminary leaving on a Shabbat afternoon in his working clothes for such a journey, but we did.

That same afternoon we visited our former guide Zev Vilnay, who loudly asserted (he always spoke in a booming voice) that "all Israelis are either archaeologists or snobs." When I told him of our meeting with Glueck, Vilnay, who has decided opinions about everyone and everything, stated for all to hear: "Nelson Glueck is a good archaeologist, but he is given to extravagant, even exaggerated judgments about ancient life in the Negev. Glueck sits for eleven months in Cincinnati dreaming about getting back and digging for one month in the desert." As for Moshe Dayan, Vilnay gave this appraisal: "An excellent soldier. An amateur archaeologist." Vilnay had written an excellent guidebook on Israel, and has also authored a number of other works on Jerusalem and Israeli legends. We have all of his books in our library. When Dayan's collection was exhibited at the Israel Museum in 1986, it proved to be more than the assembly of an "amateur."

One day, Moshe Yakir, head of the aliyah department of the Jewish Agency, was lecturing to our group, and he stressed the need for more immigrants from the Western, sophisticated societies, otherwise Israel might become another Middle Eastern, Levantine country rather than a modern one. He idealized Israel and all that it was doing for immigrants wherever they came from. When I asked whether any Israelis were leaving, he reluctantly admitted that about ten thousand left annually. The emigrants were usually better off economically and educationally, and were seeking more secure residence in the United States, Canada, Australia, or Brazil. This was already an early indication that Israelis were not all necessarily enamored with the future prospects of the country.

An archaeologist taking us through Mount Zion in Jerusalem gave us the disillusioning information that "David was not buried on Har Zion, but probably half a mile away."

We met with Karl Katz, the youthful curator of the Bezalel Museum, and for a few of us he took the museum's treasures out of the safe: the Rothschild illuminated manuscript of Rashi's Commentary, a work estimated to be worth $800,000, and other items from the thirteenth century. In the courtyard, there were sculptured works by Chaim Gross and Jacob Epstein, and the Yugoslavian Ivan Mestrovic's *Moses*. Some years later we visited his home, which became a museum after his death, in Split, Yugoslavia.

During the summer of 1959, the Satmar Rebbe, Joel Teitelbaum, was making his first historic trip to Israel. He arrived in Haifa by ship and was traveling by train to Jerusalem, where he would reside in Mea Shearim with fellow Hassidim. There was tension in the air in anticipation of his coming. The police were alerted in large numbers along the line of march to protect him and preserve order. The streets through which his vehicle would pass were fenced off in the middle.

We decided that the best place to see him was near his synagogue. We repaired to that spot early and waited with thousands of others. The Hassidim, young and old, were running back and forth, gesticulating wildly as the moment of his arrival neared. The scene was charged with an excitement that we could only compare to the devotional ecstasy we had witnessed at Castel Gandolfo when we went to see the Pope in 1955, accompanied by thousands of pilgrims and tourists.

Finally the car appeared at the foot of the narrow street. Devotees with signs and green branches surrounded all sides of the Rebbe's car. His bodyguard was running, pushing, sweating. Suddenly all were brought to an eerie silence in the late afternoon under an orangey sun in anticipation of his presence. The small rabbi was quickly ushered into the synagogue through two lines of Hassidim, their arms linked together in an unbreakable cordon. He appeared briefly on the third-floor tiny balcony, waved his arms, but made no speech to the jam-packed, venerating audience. There were no shouts or hurrahs. Children waved banners quietly. There were no Zionist or Israeli flags. The Rebbe had arrived. The Rebbe and his followers do not recognize Israel as a Jewish state, often publicize vicious and vitriolic and anti-Israel views, give comfort to the enemy, particularly the Arabs, Moslems, and Palestinians.

Yet he was protected by the state's police to assure his safety while in Israel.

We heard nothing but praise for the Yemenite Jews who had come to Israel on "the wings of eagles" under Operation Magic Carpet between 1949 and 1951. Vocationally competent, with traditional backgrounds, some were goldsmiths and skillful in jewelry making; they were quickly taught how to change from handicrafts to a machine-production culture. But there were radical changes in their aboriginal national cultural patterns. Women began to work. Fathers were no longer supreme. All had to learn a new language. Children adapted more quickly than the parents, hence family conflicts. But overall, they made a good adjustment. What helped the Yemenites was the presence of thirty-five thousand of their kinsmen in the country when the state was declared. The political presence of this group in Israel brought about their immediate rescue when they began to suffer from Moslem persecution in Yemen. The old settlers helped in their early adaptation. Despite their darker hue, the Yemenites were brought en masse to Israel without disturbing the national coloration. I cite this because of the different attitude that Israel had toward rescuing the Ethiopian Jews, who lived across the Red Sea from the Yemenites, and who, centuries ago, had intimate contacts with dark-skinned Jews living in southern Arabia.

We learned on our tour that there was a growing problem of juvenile delinquency and serious crime, quite a shock to some of us who had come to believe that the state only produced law-abiding citizens.

We arrived at Kibbutz Urim, where I knew Americans, and to our surprise and pleasure we renewed relations with Dr. Isidore Keyfitz, my mentor and close friend at the University of Missouri. His daughter, son-in-law, and grandchild were living at Urim, at night guarding the southern flank against marauders from nearby Gaza.

A group of us flew to Eilat, this time without incident. It looked like a town trying to find itself. At that time there were relatively few hotels and fewer public buildings, a sharp contrast with what one finds in the 1980s. We drove to Solomon's Mines, picked up pieces of rough copper, and for a moment transported ourselves back to the year 1000 BCE, when these mines and smelters produced a metal at times worth as much as gold. It was shipped by sea as far east as India. (In 1971, when we were in Cochin, India, we read documents that purported that an ancient trade existed with Palestine, although no Jewish community was founded there until 300 C.E.)

In Israel, we renewed our relations with Larry and Marilyn Frisch, formerly of Pelham. He was now producing radio, TV, and movie scripts. Some years later he was a nightly visitor on our U.S. TV set, as he broadcasted Israel's news over Channel 5.

Our visits to Arab villages revealed that they were not as backward as they were painted by chauvinistic Israelis. Many built attractive houses.

They cultivated well-tended farms, utilizing every bit of available land in a rock-strewn country, which produced good and varied foods and fruits. Their small farms sharply contrasted with the large machine-operated, well-watered kibbutz tracts.

While our biblical and archaeological knowledge had been enriched during our first tour in 1955, we drove through new terrain in 1959, and this made both the Bible and Vilnay's guidebook indispensable. Whether one was religious or not, one was always conscious of treading on sacred soil. Yet the reality of modern Jews in Israel was brought back to us one night at a *simcha* in Tiberias. Walking along Lake Kinneret, we heard music. We strolled over to a restaurant, where four hundred Sephardic Moroccan Jews were celebrating a wedding. We were invited to the festivities by the father of the bride. We danced, ate, and kissed the bride, and were quickly made part of the "extended" family. For that brief interlude, we seemed to be part of an old Jewish culture, which offered its hospitality to whoever appeared on its doorstep. It was an experience that was repeated on our trips to Jewish communities all over the world.

At 5 A.M. one morning in Tiberias, I joined a minyan of traditional Jews, mostly Sephardic, at synagogue prayers just as the cocks were crowing. I suspected that some might have been descendants of those who fled from Jerusalem in 70 C.E. or who were driven out of Spain and Portugal by the Inquisition in the fifteenth century, and ultimately settled in Tiberias, made forever a shrine by the presence of Maimonides' tomb. Their flowing dress was distinctly native. Worship was quickly completed. As soon as prayers were finished, everyone disappeared. There were no greetings, no good-byes, no invitations. Here I was accepted as a random Jew who had wandered in to daven.

We walked through Kfar Nahum, dear to the Christians, because Jesus was associated with many religious ventures in the vicinity of Lake Kinneret. The ruins of an old synagogue still gave it a Jewish ambience.

Our visit to Kfar Blum brought another reunion with Saadia Gelb, an American social worker, and with his family. He had pioneered in the development of this kibbutz. I got a different view of kibbutzim when interpreted through the words of an American rather than a European Jew. Europeans seem to emphasize the hardships, while Americans pointed out the achievements. Nestling as this kibbutz does on the narrow Jordan River and looking up at towering Mount Hermon bordering nearby Lebanon and Syria, it was a magnificent site. One could appreciate how a kibbutznik felt as he surveyed what he owned, cultivated, and defended from invasion.

At Metulla we touched the unfriendly border of Lebanon. As we drank tea in the daylight and slept there overnight, we felt that we might be attacked at any moment. We felt the same way as we drove west along Lebanon and observed the kibbutzim and villages being hewed out of the omnipresent rocks to make a home for newcomers and to protect the interior of the country. In Lebanon all appeared peaceful, but we knew this was where rockets were readied to destroy and kill Jews who had dared to move to this marginal area. We passed through territory that reminded us of Leon Uris's *Exodus,* many of whose dramatic scenes were laid in this northern part of Israel. Although a fictional account, I did not hesitate to recommend it to anyone going to Israel in those days.

Safed (Tzefat) took us back to the synagogues made memorable by the medieval cabbalistic rabbis who so deeply influenced our ideology and our liturgy. One cannot recite *Lecho Dodi* on Friday night without thinking of its original chanting in this beautiful hill city. One could almost see Rabbi Solomon Alkabetz (1505–1584) going into the open fields outside of Safed to welcome the Sabbath with psalms and hymns.

We observed the sharp contrast between the religious sector and the host of modern artists who have built studios on both sides of the Safed hillsides, exhibiting their religious and secular works in paint and sculpture for the tourists who daily flocked to this city, a city captured from the Arabs in the first war with the miraculous "Davidka," a phony cannon. One member of our group from the United States had been born in Safed, and it was a glorious homecoming for him.

The Druze intrigued us, because of their intimate cooperation with the Israelis, serving in the army and entertaining our group in their homes. We saw the sharp distinction between them and the hostile Arabs.

The changes in Haifa in the four-year span were phenomenal. An unhappy note was the death of Ashkenazi Chief Rabbi Isaac Herzog, whom we remembered so vividly from our long visit to his home in 1955 and for his favorable memorandum about the Ethiopian Jews. A high point of our visit to Haifa was our meeting with Yaakov Malkin, who introduced our group to the intellectual, literary, and artistic side of Israel. This revealed how little we knew about the country from these aspects, which never received enough publicity in the press. While many of our group were informed about Israel generally before they came, even their knowledge was more political and "romantic" than about the arts. A few resisted to the very end what they termed "Zionist propaganda"; most ended up better instructed and strengthened in their resolve to do more for Israel. I encouraged them, with some success, to buy books, art, and other religious objects made in the country.

Yet I was disappointed in the art work at both Safed and Ein Hod, in contrast to some of the excellent work that I had seen exhibited in fine art galleries in Jerusalem and Tel Aviv.

I was somewhat repelled by the conspicuous opulence of the Rothschild tomb at Ramat Hanadiv, and that included the toilet facilities, which didn't fit the mundane human functions performed in the building.

We met Ludwig Wolpert, the distinguished silversmith, in his studio in Jerusalem. We couldn't afford the price of his beautiful work. When we later acquired some of these objects, a modern Kiddush cup and etrog container as gifts from our friends, I first realized that I had turned down a bargain in that basement in Jerusalem.

In the final evaluation, the group was more positive than I would have expected, in view of the incidents referred to previously. The major recommendation was that they would prefer a five-day instead of a six-day intensive schedule, so as to have more free time to explore things on their own, see their relatives, and shop. They felt that they had not seen enough of kibbutz life. There was little or no interest in studying the economy, industry, farming, or housing. All were willing to pay more for a similar tour in the future. I was convinced that everyone could afford to do so. At our final dinner, while I did not win the love of all of them, I know I achieved their respect, they referred to my compulsive pecadillos, my demands for punctuality, universal participation, to read, to buy good Israeli products—all with good humor. They presented me with a book, *The Saga of Jerusalem: The Holy City* with a simple inscription: "A reminder of the exciting days exploring Jerusalem."

I could not help but recall in reverie the "sacrifices" Emma and I had repeatedly made so that the comfort of the group would be assured. Twice we gave up our hard-to-get tickets to a concert and to meet Ben-Gurion, to noisy protestors who had failed to make the initial requests for attendance and at the last minute literally demanded that I find some way to meet their change of plans. Was this a sign of weakness or of strength in a leader, to satisfy belated and unjustified requests? Perhaps neither the concert nor meeting Ben-Gurion was important enough for us.

Shortly after our return to Pelham we invited most of the group living in the New York environs to have dinner at our house. There they evidenced appreciation of what they had learned on the trip and earnestly thanked both of us for our leadership on the trip and the hospitality that evening. It gave us a feeling again that we had done something substantial for them. We always seemed on the giving end. Over the years, there was occasional correspondence, occasional meetings at conferences and even on the street. Death has taken a number of the group. In retrospect, it was both a pleasant and an unpleasant experience. I have never lead another group again. I have had many requests to do so, to Israel and other parts of the world. I have adhered to that decision. In the long run, we have found that most people want to get whatever they can and really do not want to share. Relatively few appreciate what a leader is investing in such an extended and complicated enterprise. While I knew that I had much to give and gave it, I decided to use my energies in different ways than leading a motley group into a foreign land.

We left Jerusalem by train for the first time en route to Tel Aviv. We rode through Arab country, thrilled by the landscape, enjoying conversations with our fellow riders. We were loaded down with Israeli art, which now adorns our walls in Pelham for daily viewing. It is the land, the people, and their artifacts that we always remember, rather than our transient leadership of a group that may or may not have responded pleasantly to our vigorous and thoughtful efforts.

Emma's Auto License

One night in 1959, when I returned home from work, Emma greeted me with her automobile driver's license. I was amazed. I am not always the most patient instructor, and my attempts to teach her to drive had been unsuccessful. I thought she was much too tense to master the wheel. When Emma made up her mind to achieve something, she never failed. She started taking private lessons with one of the auto schools, and on completing the course, she passed the state test on her first try. Needless to say, she could now drive wherever she wanted without having to wait for me. On occasion, she even relieved me at the wheel when we were driving long distances. She is a careful driver. My only complaint is that she uses the brake too much. Yet what is a brake for, except to be pressed to the floor to avoid an accident? She has had only one mishap in twenty-seven years, when she struck a car: damage to the other car, $46; damage to ours, $900. That is what insurance is for.

Greece, Spain, and Portugal: 1959

After we left Israel in 1959, we flew to Greece, where my brother Sam was ensconsed as the deputy chief of mission at the U.S. Embassy. During his three-year tenure, he was actually the acting ambassador, for the incumbent left shortly after Sam's arrival and his replacement did not come on the scene until just before Sam left Greece. Sam and his wife, Margaret, lived in a magnificent, large white stucco house on a one and one-half acre tract with an immense flower garden which both of them helped tend, since they were interested in floriculture. They had five helpers to run the establishment.

They had planned a three-day trip together with us to Hydra, a tiny island over three hours by boat from Piraeus, so we barely had time to repack. One must read Henry Miller's *The Colossus of Maroussi* to appreciate the boat trip, which passed the islands of Athena and Poros, where you can almost shake the hands of women hanging out the windows on shore. We were awestruck as we approached Hydra, with its natural amphitheaterlike harbor, its stone houses and churches perched perilously on the hillside one above the other. We were met by Ione Georgescu, professor of law and former governor-general of Rhodes, an outgoing, talkative, argumentative Greek, who with his wife and daughter, weekended on the island. It was a delightful few days. The scene was used for a pictorially beautiful movie, *The Boy on a Dolphin*, which we had seen. We swam, boated against strong currents, ate, drank, and talked incessantly. We stayed in a small hotel, built of large gray stones, which high-ceilinged rooms, a huge comfortable bed, a breakfast which would satisfy a major league football player; and when I paid the bill it was $3.50 for both of us. A bargain.

Sam and Margaret had also arranged for us to see parts of Greece that we had not visited in 1955. Sam loaned us his personal car, and with his chauffeur we were off. I have already written about my studying of Greek civilization at the University of Missouri, so I was prepared for the sites we covered. First Corinth, one of the oldest of the Greek cities, where archaeologists were still excavating. Shards were piled everywhere, but one was not allowed to keep them. Then south to Mycenae, where Agememnon and Clytemnestra once reigned, the subject of the fascinating trilogy by Aeschylus, *The House of Atreus*. It was a terrain that looked very much like Israel, as we drove through the rolling hills and valleys. We watched as some archaeologists, digging in an area with third-century B.C.E. remains, suddenly penetrated through a shaft into the thirteenth century B.C.E., the period of the Mycenaean culture. They uncovered a perfect, but still uncleaned, perfume jar. This event made that period come alive. We walked up to the royal palace, the collapsed tomb of Aegisthus, and the still intact tomb of Clytemnestra. The story, as related in the three plays: *Agamemnon, The Eumenides,* and *The Libation Bearers,* was that Agememnon had returned from the Trojan War. His wife and her lover, Aegisthus, killed him while he was bathing. His children, Electra and Orestes, avenged his death by murdering their mother and her lover. Orestes fled, pursued by the spirits, who demanded a life for a life. The play is an appeal by Aeschylus that anyone accused of a crime—and he himself had been so charged, despite the laurels that he received as a foremost poet and playwright—should be tried by his peers and not by an anachronistic tradition. To jump ahead a bit, when we returned to Athens after our tour to the Peloponnesus, we went to see the last two of these plays at the dramatically restored Herodes Atticus amphitheater, following the actors' lines with a little flashlight playing on the English text which we had bought.

From Mycenae, we drove to Naplion, mingled with the natives at the hotel, restaurants, and bars. We ascended the castle citadel built by the Venetians on a rocky bluff, which controlled not only the harbor, but also the roadways leading into this strategic port.

Our next stop was Epidaurus, the site of ancient and even later Greek thermal baths, where the rich came to recover their health and enjoy life. The amphitheater, in the process of restoration, was acoustically perfect. One could speak in a moderate voice on the stage and be heard at the top row of seats, about an eighth of a mile away. This tribute to the god of health, Aesculapius, was in a religious-health resort for Greeks, then Romans, and now tourists.

We stayed overnight and then drove back to a restaurant on an empty beach that stretched for miles, where we had a rendezvous with Henry Brandon, the well-known British journalist and author. The bartender did not know how to make a martini, so I was given the run of the bar. Finding no vermouth, I substituted twelve-year-old Scotch whisky mixed with gin. Brandon and a tall Texan named Monte Rickey, who had driven in for a drink, agreed that it was an unusual concoction, but drinkable, refilled twice. There was much talk, as we ate and drank, about Khrushchev, whom Brandon had recently interviewed. He was on his way to Geneva to talk with Eisenhower. He gave us a sophisticated appraisal of the two world leaders, who dominated the media.

Our chauffeur then drove us through the unrelieved barren mountains running across southern Greece with hairpin turns and roads without side barriers. We stopped in the picturesque city of Tripolis, where one could see Greek life as only the *National Geographic* portrayed these outposts. What impressed us was how hard Greek women had to work to eke out a living from the soil. Our goal that night was Olympia, the seat of the original Olympic games. It was now a huge ruin. Few tourists went there. It was both out of the way and had only a small hotel for overnight visitors. To see with our own eyes the famous pediment, the huge ruined Temple of Zeus, and the statue of Hermes was worth the arduous journey.

Then we turned back to Patros along the Gulf of Corinth. In the market, I bought some fruit and took out some paper drachmas to pay for the modest purchase. A crowd gathered around the vendor and watched as he made change with seeming reluctance, piece by piece, in metal coins. When the onlookers were satisfied that he had given me the proper amount, their faces smiled. They were content with the ultimate honesty of the transaction. I thanked them all in Greek, one of the few words I had learned. Some of them came up to shake my hand. For me, it was a reflection of the integrity of the run-of-the-mill natives.

The scenes throughout Greek were picturesque. The women in funereal black dress, with shawls wound around their heads and necks, always working or knitting, seldom talking. The old men with their skirt-trousers tied in the front and wide-brimmed straw hats riding on overloaded donkeys. The general impression was of an absence of wealth. Churches abounded, with small shrines along the road to remind the indigenous of the need to be devotional. The houses and even the trees alongside were whitewashed almost daily. Food seemed plentiful. We crossed the gulf by ferry and arrived exhausted and exhilarated in

Athens, catching another glimpse of the Parthenon in the late afternoon.

There was no rest for the weary. That evening Sam and Margaret invited Charles Collingwood, the well-known international reporter for CBS-TV, and his attractive actress-wife, Louise, for cocktails and dinner. We then went to the amphitheater to see *The Libation Bearers* and *The Eumenides*. All of us had read Robert Graves's, *The Greek Myths,* so we were reasonably well prepared for what we were to witness in Greek. The plays read better than the performance, although the setting, the lighting, and the recitative singing, dancing, and bodily movements of the chorus, and especially the music accompanying the Furies, kept the play from being stiff and boring.

We walked in the moonlight to the nearby Acropolis and the Agora, as electric lights played dramatically on these ancient structures. It stirred up memories of our readings of what had happened in the days when these monuments were fashioned.

At a coffee shop at 11 P.M., we met Ione Georgescu, and this led to a night of revelry. It began with a visit to Pindos, a bouzouki-music restaurant, where rich men, politicians, and night-lifers escorted their girl friends, not their wives, to drink, eat, listen to the stringed music, and watch the men—and only men—dance. Bouzouki music was not very old. Started in the 1930s at the wharves and revived after the war, it had become part of the Greek national culture, like jazz in America. The varied mandolins and guitars with their high-pitched sounds and rhythms inspired the singers to recite melancholy tales of love. The sadness of the lyrics contrasted with the spirited responses of the participants. Ione translated one song: "Man is made for love. Women are only the recipients of man's love. Woman's role in life is to work and bear children."

We witnessed a scene like the one we saw some years later in the film *Never on Sunday*. Men who became enamored of the music and dancing to the point of ecstasy broke glasses on the floor, the price of which was included on the bill. Ione, in fact, was so overstimulated that he suddenly turned over the table, breaking dishes and liquor bottles, as we scurried out of the way in surprise and laughter. The management took it in good stride, sent over waiters to clean the mess and reset the table. At 3 A.M. Ione ordered spaghetti with a flavorful sauce. Then we left, found a cafe that served tiny cups of good Greek coffee. At 4:30 A.M. we turned in. We had been up for nearly twenty-four hours. (Collingwood died in 1985 with the *New York Times* reporting a fine tribute in a long story on his life.)

We paid a visit to Piraeus and its museum, which was exhibiting five large Greek bronzes and stone statuary, found only a few days before as men were digging to lay sewer lines. We drove over to the street corner, which had been boarded up to keep out potential looters seeking other ancient finds. It was almost like the scene at Mycenae when the archaeologists had unearthed some pottery as we watched them dig. We easily visualized a scene over two thousand years ago, when perhaps Romans or other marauders, surprised by the Greeks, had to drop their booty, instead of transporting these large pieces to their waiting ships. Hurriedly covered over in the event they should be able to return, these statues had lain for several millennia undisturbed, unspoiled, until the mundane accident of improving a sewer brought them in view.

In Greece one could buy all kinds of drugs without a prescription, but to purchase saccharin, one had to have an official slip.

We lunched with Jonathan Prato, the head of Israel's diplomatic mission in Greece, and his wife. Prato, an Italian Jew and son of the Chief Rabbi, was an educated urbane gentleman. We talked about Israel's position in the part of the Mediterranean world that was outside the Arab-Moslem orbit, how Italian Jews fared during and after the war, and he gave us of his considerable knowledge of both ancient and modern Italian and Greek art and architecture. He had a collection of Judaic art. He frowned on the inchoate form of Judaism practiced in Greece. His wife was a German Jew.

An outstanding event was our five-day tour of the islands on the S.S. *Semiramis*. When we docked at Heraklion, we missed the ancient monument, one of the wonders of the ancient world, which once straddled the harbor. We eagerly visited Knossos, the seat of the Minoan civilization, which the archaeologist Sir Arthur John Evans unearthed and restored to its present imaginative beauty. Some years later Sylvia L. Horwitz, a good friend, who had already written and published biographies of Toulouse-Lautrec and Goya, wrote a biography of Evans. As we read it, we relived that day at Knossos.

Rhodes, our next stop, was eyecatching from the boatside and on land. Its fortresses, walled towers, windmills, the mosques with their tall, thin minarets, were imposing. This was where the Knights of St. John had reigned in the Middle Ages. Some of their original structures were now fully restored. The cobblestoned streets had stood the test of time. Mussolini's Fascist architects had rebuilt the island, hoping that it would forever remain in Italy's possession.

Rhodes once had a thriving Jewish population, which established itself in the sixteenth century. All had been destroyed after the Nazi-Fascist invasion during World War II. In reading *The Jews of Rhodes* (1980), written by a friend, Rabbi Marc D. Angel of Shearith Israel—the Spanish-Portuguese Synagogue, the oldest Jewish congregation in the United States—whose parents came from the island to America, I was reminded of our visit to the "Island of Roses." I also learned that an Ethiopian Jew had been educated at its Jewish seminary before the war.

I subsequently received a detailed account of what happened to that student in a letter from Yona Bogale, perhaps the most outstanding Ethiopian Jew now residing in Israel.

We rode through a good part of the island to the Valley of Butterflies and then to Lindos to see the restoration of the ancient temple with its formidable columns. Then to the peak, which looked down to the cove where, legend has it, St. Paul once sailed to preach to the natives. A tiny church marked the spot.

Another day found the boat anchored off Kos, a smaller version of Rhodes, less sophisticated. The island, associated with the god of health, Aesculapius, is where Hippocrates practiced medicine, dispensing his prescriptions under a huge plane tree and composing the oath that physicians still take before entering the healing profession. While he was born in the island, the city which claimed his monument was not actually established until after his death.

During our voyage we read Henry Miller, all the plays of Sophocles, and a good part of the Hachette guidebook with its mine of information.

Patmos was another gem from the bay to the whitewashed monastery of St. John on the promontory, which we finally reached on the backs of donkeys. While waiting for the animals, we wandered into a Greek cottage. The residents had lived in the United States, spoke English, and had returned four years earlier after the male head of the household had retired and now enjoyed a pension and Social Security checks. He was trying to persuade me to live there. One could own a home for a pittance and needed only only about $150 per month for maintenance. As he looked me over, he added: "And we would elect you our mayor." He took me to the seashore where he caught his daily supply of fish and swam for his bathing and health. Then to his backyard with olive and fruit trees and grape vines to provide oil and wine.

Every house was whitewashed, as were the stone streets, giving an immaculate appearance. The donkey droppings were immediately scooped up by boys, not so much to assure sanitation and the removal of the swarms of flies, but because they could sell their spoil as natural fertilizer.

Delos, the island where Apollo was reputed to have been born, was forlorn, devastated long ago by earthquakes and never repopulated. It had once been a major free port and trading center, where the rich and the noble, including Cleopatra, had built fabulous homes with artistic mosaic floors, temples and statuary, and amused themselves in the amphitheater. The ill-kept museum gave evidence that a vigorous and promiscuous sex life was once indulged, for Delos was a sea town given over to the fullest exercise of every voluptuous pleasure. The contemporary barrenness only emphasized the joys once experienced in this tiny island.

Mykonos was not an island, but a movie set, with scores of whitewashed churches and windmills. Because it had become popular for tourists, its streets were lined with stores and cafes. Every household seemed to be a factory making goods sold in the shops. When we had time to catch our breath, we sat down at a tavern and had our usual daily drink of ouzo, the cloudy "pernod" with its sweetish, odd, licorice flavor.

Too soon it was all over. We were back in Piraeus with Sam and Margaret. We walked through the Agora again, almost restored to its original size and beauty, again walked up to the Acropolis, for we never tired of this ancient ruin. We dropped into Pratos' home in Kifissia, a suburb of Athens, filled with Jewish ceremonial objects and wall decorations, many of Italian origin. We ended the day at a Greek dance and song festival, where we were treated to the folk forms of Thessaly, the Dodecanese, Macedonia, Thrace, and Crete.

Another day, we pushed our way through the Plaka, that crowded flea market. We were easy victims for purchasing antiques. Our search for old Jewish objects was fruitless. We drove to Sounion, picking up old shards along the way, wherever we saw a two-thousand-year-old dig abandoned by archaeologists. Some stone statuary protruded from the soil. We ate at a taverna, downing a fabulous lunch, which included native coarse bread, lamb, eggplant. We could not drink the red retsina wine, homemade from the owner's own vineyards, for no matter what the connoisseurs say, to me it tastes like turpentine. The owners ate with us. The Temple of Poseidon at Sounion, eroded by the winds and rains over the millennia, was one of the most beautiful ruins, outlined distinctly as the sun was setting.

Greece was not all ancient ruins. Wherever we drove we saw evidence of new attractive construction in sharp contrast with the absence of such developments only four years before.

That night, we went to see and hear Sophocles' *Antigone,* handsomely costumed, and performed by vigorous actors, although it was dulled intermittently by long declamations. More singing would have improved the production, at least for our eyes and ears. The orchestra, playing modern compositions to support the text, was superb. The audience, mostly Greek, applauded thunderously.

Our second trip to Greece was over.

Spain

Our plane via Rome landed us eventually in Barcelona, Spain, where we stayed at the Arycasa, a pleasant and old-fashioned hostelry. We walked the streets. The markets were piled high with melons in season. The exterior of the huge cathedral never seemed to have been cleaned. The major museum was drab, relieved only by some Picassos that dominated the walls. We had come to Barcelona principally to see the work of Gaudí and his magnificent sculptured conception of the still unfinished Cathedral of the Holy Family (the Sagrada Familia). We went to the Park Quel, another colorful ceramic of Gaudí's creation. The concrete with glazed decorations resembled palm tree bark. Our visit to the National Museum treated us to a prodigious display of religious art, and as always we were moved by the numerous El Grecos.

A seaside restaurant introduced us to zarzuela, the Spanish version of bouillabaisse, and at its best, it does not take a back seat when compared with the French dish. Talked with many Spanish natives in restaurants and on streets and found them amongst the warmest people to strangers.

We flew to Madrid, were gypped by the taxi driver. This had happened to us only twice in our extensive travels. The other time was in Messina, Sicily. We bedded ourselves down in the deluxe Fénix Hotel. Madrid was extraordinary in its architecture, boulevards, and public buildings. Our first day at the Prado Museum was overwhelming, and we decided it couldn't be seen even on an all-day visit, so we came back each day for several hours. We toured the city, mostly on foot, in and out of museums and other buildings.

At the suggestion of Dr. Harry Friedman, a member of the Jewish Federation board in New York and a major collector of Judaica (the Jewish Museum in New York is filled with his benefactions), we went to the Linares Galleries, where they had unusual Jewish pieces, but too rich for our pocketbook. There was a fifteenth-century Spanish hanging brass oil lamp and an early-eighteenth-century Belgian Kiddush cup in the form of a mug matched with a spice box, apparently the work of the same silversmith. There are many fake antiques, and since I could not determine whether these were genuine, I made detailed descriptions and drawings and sent them to Dr. Friedman.

The Museo de Arte Moderne had fine paintings, including some by Dali and Picasso. Modern abstracts were also visible, the kind of art form that usually makes me indignant at the curators who buy such outlandish works.

On Friday evening, we sought the synagogue, which with great difficulty we finally found on an obscure side street. Walking through a court, we ended up in the basement of a building, poorly furnished, but clean. The slim congregation used an American Orthodox prayerbook edited by Rabbi Dr. David de Sola Pool of the Spanish-Portuguese Congregation in New York, whom I had met many times. The Jewish population of Madrid numbers five hundred. About thirty people were in the sanctuary, mostly visitors. The reader chanted in an East European dialect. I detected a dozen different accents in the room as I turned my ear toward the various individuals. The worshippers came from Texas, San Francisco, Detroit, Tel Aviv, Istanbul, Casablanca, and Cairo. I was told that there were only eight children in the Hebrew school, taught by an East European who had come from Warsaw in 1935 and remained. We learned further that the government was not yet willing to give the Jewish community permission to build an attractive and visible building. That was to come within a few years.

After the service we met three young people, two of them Israelis and one from Istanbul, all exchange students studying in Madrid. They lived modestly. They took us to a cafe in Porte du Sol, where we drank manzanilla, ate olives and chips. Then to a cellar, Luis Candelas, off the Plaza Mayor, noisy and crowded with young people, where we listened to singers and guitarists playing native tunes. We drank large pitchers of sangria. The students were our guests and seemingly enjoyed being with somewhat older people.

We went to Spain despite our distaste for Franco's dictatorship, after a struggle with a weak conscience. We found it a pleasant country with everything that a tourist craves. There were some rich and many poor. Prices were cheap. While there were many police on the streets, we never felt that we were in a police state. No one offered to talk politics, and we didn't want to endanger ourselves or them by introducing this perilous theme. We came away with a feeling of having been in a culturally varied and interesting country, with warm people, extraordinary food, wines and sherries. Only one drawback: vile coffee was served everywhere.

10

The Early 1960s

SHORTLY AFTER RAMON was graduated from New York University in 1951, he married Anita Fink, who was finishing her own courses at Brooklyn College. It was a brilliant wedding at the Tremont Temple in the Bronx, with a dinner afterward at the Concourse Plaza.

Ramon was drafted into the Marine Corps. He was one of the first of the young men to be inducted during the Korean War. During his two-year service, he went through the agonies of boot camp at Parris Island, South Carolina, a camp that was then under investigation for the brutality of its training methods and leadership, which had resulted in the death of a recruit. Due to his educational background and typing skills, Ramon was assigned duties as a lecturer and office worker. Marine officers were urging him to remain in the corps and become an officer in the intelligence section. He left the Marines as a staff sergeant, having received quick promotions. While exposure to the military was an invasion of his normal life, it broadened his "experience with people," and it was a "toughening process."

Anita lived with us for a time in our new home in Pelham, while she attended the University of Pennsylvania Graduate School of Social Work in Philadelphia, also a "tough" school, doing her field work in New York. They often talked about which was tougher, the Marine camp or the Pennsylvania school. During the summers of 1952 and 1953, she moved to Morehead City, North Carolina, and lived with Ramon off the base. Some weekends they spent with Sam and Margaret in Washington.

On Ramon's discharge from the Marines, they set up an apartment in Parkchester, the Bronx. Anita went to work as a family caseworker in the

Jewish Community Services of Long Island and later with the Jewish Family Service in New York. Ramon completed a master's degree in camping administration and took some technical-drawing courses at Pratt Institute. He became a temporary journeyman jeweler, making objects in silver and gold, in a shop in Greenwich Village. His talent was professional, and we still have items that he fashioned, but he preferred to work directly with people. For the next two years he taught industrial arts in the Bronx public school system, employing all the skills that he had acquired since childhood.

Eventually Ramon found the school system too circumscribed and stifling. Searching for a freer milieu and wishing to pursue a career in a voluntary Jewish setting, he became assistant executive director of Surprise Lake Camp, the oldest Jewish agency camp in the country. It was located at Cold Springs, near the Hudson River, seventy miles from New York. It was in a hospital in Cold Springs that Elisabeth Harrie, their first child, was born.

After eight years, during which his program and management proficiency were sharpened, Ramon was offered the assistant directorship of the Usdan Center for the Performing Arts, devoted to the dance, music, and arts, one of the most unique institutions in this country. An opening developed in the newly created Association for Jewish Sponsored Camps, a coordinating body for thirty Jewish nonprofit camps, where Ramon provided consultation services. During this period, Ramon and Anita and Elisabeth rented an apartment on East 20th Street in Manhattan, where Elisabeth at first went to a public school and then to the United Nations International School, where she prospered in her contacts with an unusual group of teachers and children from countries around the world. In 1965, Ramon and Anita added another precious child to their family, Gideon Samuel. While working in New York, Ramon received the Cummings Award (money and a citation) from the Commission on Synagogue Relations of the Federation of Jewish Philanthropies for his services to the Jewish community.

The Jewish Center of Greater Buffalo was looking for a camp director for Camp Lakeland (founded in 1910), which had just merged with the center. Ramon accepted the position with the understanding that it would lead to an executive post. He remained there for three years, after which he was ready to become director of his own center.

He was appointed to such a position in the Jewish Community Center of Providence, Rhode Island. The family moved to that quaint old American city. He built up the formerly declining membership, introduced more Jewish programming, was able to obtain personally a large municipal grant to improve the facilities for the aged and the handicapped, developed a relationship with the Orthodox Jewish denominations, so that they built a mikvah on the center's property. Ramon and Anita purchased an imposing home in an excellent residential section.

Ramon's name was included in *Who's Who in the East* (1971) and *Who's Who in World Jewry* (1972).

Upon leaving the center in 1981, Ramon became a community fundraiser and eventually a business broker. He is a volunteer member of the board of a hundred-year-old community center.

Anita, who received a master's degree in social work, and had worked in voluntary agencies in New York and Buffalo, including an assistant professorship at the State University in Buffalo in the Graduate School of Social Work, opened a private practice as a psychotherapist and adult educator in Providence, where she attracted a large clientele and developed an excellent reputation as a therapist, in addition to lecturing in agencies and industrial corporations. She has been the recipient of several awards, including local "Woman of the Year."

Elisabeth completed her high school studies in Providence, where in only one year, she had an extraordinary record: Cum Laude Society, National Honor Society, National Merit finalist, prize for poetry, Shell Oil Leadership Seminar in Virginia, All-State and All–New England actress award.

Then she received a Lyndon B. Johnson Congressional Scholarship and worked for Democratic Congressman Fernand J. St. Germain and Republican Congresswoman Claudine Schneider in their respective Washington offices. Schneider asked Lizzie to work with her permanently, but while Lizzie helped out with her re-election campaign, she preferred New York to Washington. After spending a year in New York City on a Municipal Urban Fellowship, she is now a legislative aide under Mayor Edward I. Koch. She is tall, attractive, bright, articulate, and outgoing—and above all hard-working, so that she has accredited herself well in the public domain.

When Elisabeth was a tiny child and before she went to school, Emma would go to the apartment on East 20th Street in Manhattan and babysit while Anita was at work. A bond grew up between grandmother and granddaughter that has been enriched throughout the years. They share intimacies. Emma has had some influence on her life. When Lizzie was still a tot, she distributed handbills for Ed Koch, who was running for Congress from that district. She assisted Ramon and Anita, who were supporting his campaign. Twenty years later, she would become his legislative aide. The long hand of the past has a way of indenting the future.

Gideon, after finishing his high school studies in Providence, has completed his third year at Skidmore College in Saratoga Springs, New York, where he is showing promise in his study of art and photography. He is usually on the dean's list. During the summers, he was an accomplished waiter at a fashionable restaurant in Providence and earned enough money to buy a car, live in an apartment off campus, and take winter vacations in Florida, the Caribbean, and California.

The Bergers have a handsome house in Providence, decorated with a large collection of furniture and art, a place where Emma and I always enjoy our altogether too infrequent and too brief visits.

Our relationship with all of them has deepened over the years. On several occasions we have gone on holidays together or spent time as a family at our cottage at Sacandaga in the Adirondacks. We spent a week with Elisabeth and Gideon in the Dominican Republic one winter. We have many of the same tastes and interests.

Baruch Michael and Sandra

Baruch Michael Berger usually signed letters as B. Michael Berger or Michael Berger or Mike Berger. He was always called Michael or Mike and never Baruch. Emma and I followed suit, and thus he remains Michael at the age of forty-eight as I write these memoirs.

His high school years were a burden for him. For several years he wore a brace from ankle to hip to correct a knee injury. This kept him out of athletics and limited his social life. The high school, however, provided opportunities for him to be active. He was the manager of the varsity football, track, and basketball teams. This kept him in touch with the machos. He traveled with the players and took care of their gear at home games and meets. He was a member of the Sock & Buskin drama society. As an actor he played a major role as the murderer in *Hangman's Noose*; and he was Mayor Lacade in *The Song of Bernadette*. Critics noticed his histrionic talents. Always a quick study, he learned his lines quickly, and with his good, clear baritone voice, he could be heard anywhere in the auditorium. In his last year, after he had recovered from an operation on his knee and regained full use of this important appendage (Emma always thought his knee injury would keep him out of the army, but it didn't), he was more active socially, dated girls, drove the car. He expected us to give him a car as a graduation present. Many of his classmates received cars, but he was given a watch and money and was told that the first car he would own was the one that he would purchase with his earnings. We were not only frugal, but wise.

Deciding on a university and a field of study was fraught with controversy. We toured a number of colleges, which were ready to enroll him on the spot. Because of his seeming interest in the out-of-doors and camping, following in the footsteps of his father and older brother, and the possibility of getting a sizable scholarship, we suggested and he finally consented to study forestry, and he had no difficulty in matriculating at Syracuse University on a tuition scholarship. Although we provided him with an allowance beyond room and board, his needs were a bit greater, since he joined the Phi Sigma Delta fraternity (which eventually, through a series of mergers, ended up in Zeta Beta Tau, the same fraternity of which I was a member at the University of Missouri). He found jobs, usually in eating joints, which supplemented his income and his weight. He was an average student, despite a very high I.Q. I went up for a weekend to meet his instructors, and while all thought well of him, some observed that he did not apply himself, and others that he was not interested in forestry. At the end of the first year, he changed his major to the social sciences and majored in psychology, English and American literature, thus pursuing an academic career closer to that of his father. This position was never articulated by him and possibly was merely coincidental, or the courses were easier and pleasurable. He was a writer for the *Syracusan,* the campus humor magazine, and participated in intramural athletics.

Michael immediately joined the ROTC, following a bent which had started years before when he became interested in buying, repairing, and collecting firearms, old and new. In high school he had become a leader of the student civil defense rescue squad, maintaining the equipment in good order and accepting his patrol assignments without reservation. In some respects the ROTC provided him with a number of things he liked to live through in fantasy and realistically: physical exercise, the uniform and other military costumes, the drill, the orderliness, the regimentation, the sense of power—all fitted him to a tee. He was elected to the Pershing Rifles, an elite, drill team and honor society, and delighted in executing the intricate movements. On his graduation from Syracuse, he was commissioned a second lieutenant in the U.S. Army Reserve and flirted with making the army his career.

During his college life, he met Sandra Miller, a young Syracuse girl, who had left Penn State to become secretary to the dean of Syracuse University Medical School. When he wrote and told us that they wanted to get married, Emma and I had reservations about such an involved attachment when he was twenty years of age, and she only eighteen. I can still hear him tell Emma in precise language: "Mother, I never expected to hear such an objection from you. How old were you and dad when you were married?" We were exactly the same ages and about as ready perhaps as Michael was. I hurried up to Syracuse to meet Sandra and her mother. Her mother had been divorced for some years. She was an attorney, the first woman to graduate from Syracuse University Law School. In addition, she operated a nursery school and summer day camp. We collectively discussed the pros and cons of such a union. Both sets of parents were of the view that marriage should be postponed until Michael graduated. But there was no stopping their resolve to wed at the end of his junior year. Michael and Sandy used their summers as counselors in camps. In the summer of 1958, Michael was already a camp supervisor and traveled to his post on Lake George on a Vespa motor scooter. He later described it as "fun, but stupid. No one should make such a long trip, over two hundred miles, on an underpowered vehicle." I had bought him one with the proposal that he select one or two friends and I would take them all on a tour of Europe by scooter. Michael obviously did not want to be under his father's close domination for that length of time, so he went to camp instead. Today, he regrets missing that travel experience.

Emma and I toured Israel, Greece, and Spain in 1959 and returned to the States a few weeks before their elaborate wedding in Syracuse. Emma couldn't find a wedding dress in Spain, so there was a frantic, last-minute search for a gown on her return. The wedding took place in the Reform synagogue, symbolically named Temple Society of Concord, where her mother Bertha Miller, some years older than Emma and me, was a member and a teacher. Sandra, in those days a quiet, demure, intelligent young woman, made an attractive bride, and Michael, as always in "uniform," wore a tuxedo. The dinner at a Syracuse hotel was attended by many of our friends, who came from long distances.

They found an apartment in Syracuse. Michael finished his senior year. What to do next was a tough question. He finally decided to study social work, his father's career, and one in which his older brother Ramon and Ramon's wife, Anita, were also engaged. He obtained a handsome fellowship from the Jewish Welfare Board, entered into his graduate studies, and was assigned to do his fieldwork in a public welfare agency. His studies were easy, but he questioned the whole welfare system. Not that he necessarily always sided with the clientele, but he saw it as little more than a palliative and unable realistically to improve the lives of many of the people and make them eventually independent and possibly more satisfied with their lot. He decided at the end of the year that social work was not for him, paid back the scholarship grant, which had been conditioned upon him completing his studies and working two years in a Jewish agency after graduation. Returning to the armed forces, he was stationed in Albany as a personnel psychologist. However, this was not his milieu, because his craving for action and more responsibility could not be satisfied by the job of selecting recruits from an unlikely group of candidates to fill posts in the sophisticated U.S. Army.

Bonnie Lynne, the first of their three girls, was born in Albany, a pretty, outgoing little thing who always sought affection. When an opportunity for further study for intelligence work in the army arose, they moved to the outskirts of Baltimore, where Michael went to a military school. There a second daughter, Judith, was born, pretty, more demure, less outgoing.

Michael wanted real action and finally was assigned for thirteen months to Korea. Separation was something that the family did not take easily. The girls missed their father. Sandra, with her organizing talents, formed the Overseas Wives Club and was its first president. Michael, as he wrote and later related, had a ball in Korea. We had friends in that country, who graciously received him. We had purchased art from a

Korean on our visit in 1962, and Michael decided to promote his pictures by arranging art exhibits at army posts. He got older, more confident, more experienced in the mysterious ways of the army, and returned a captain, still not certain about his future.

The Vietnam War was in progress, and he was eager to serve on that front, in part because of the danger, which he was not afraid to face, and in part as a means of rising in the army hierarchy. When he first joined the army, he was asked what his goals were, and he replied, "To be a general." Vietnam inspired a family conflict. because Sandra did not want him to go, for many reasons, including the high risk. The dispute was finally resolved on a long weekend in Pelham, where he decided to remain in the States.

Michael left the active army as a captain, enrolled in the reserves, and found a position in the Department of the Army as a civilian, where he became a personnel-management specialist in selection, classification, and testing.

A third daughter, Deborah, appeared on the scene, small, feisty, and reserved, completing the family. Each girl was different and bright. This propelled Sandra, apart from her interest in sewing, canning, and tie-making, to get involved with how schools should deal with gifted children. By 1980, she was a leader in her county in moving public schools to make better provision for such students. Eventually Sandy, as we call her, returned to school and earned her bachelor's and master's degrees, so that she would have the academic base for advocating her views. She was no longer the back-seat, quiet wife, but a self-assertive woman on many fronts.

Michael's career with the army gave him an opportunity to study, and he obtained two master's degrees—in personnel and in management. He wrote important papers for his department, was sent off on speaking tours; one included a two-week training program for Egyptian army personnel in that country. With another colleague, he wrote a chapter titled "Occupational Analysis: An Automated Approach," which was published in a handsome volume, *Handbook of Vocational Education Evaluation*. Before accepting the contract for a $500 fee, he called to ask whether it was enough. I told him that I had never received more than $200 for an article, and that while I had written hundreds of articles, my collective earnings from them totaled little more than the sum he was to receive for one.

But the job and the reserve were not enough to utilize his energies. With several friends he set up a business called "System Analysis," which undertook studies in computer analysis for educational and other non-profit organizations. This provided a little more income for the family.

They had bought a small house in Arlington, Virginia, when he found his first job with the army in Washington. This was turned into a larger house, which they built in Vienna, Virginia. In 1984, they built an even larger home in Vienna, where they felt they could live more comfortably. Sandy's mother, in her late eighties, had come to live with them.

Bonnie, who dropped out of college after two years, was working in a synagogue in Virginia. She was married in October 1984 to a young man who went through a full conversion in order to become a Jew. Bonnie is now working for the *Washington Jewish Week* as an editorial assistant.

Judith went off to the University of Virginia, following an unusual high school career as a student, champion swimmer, soccer player, and clarinetist in the high school symphonic band. She now teaches top-level swimmers. I once asked her, when she was eleven years old, what she had been thinking about as she won a swimming race, and her instant reply was, "Winning." She might have gone on to Olympic trials, for she practiced each day at 6 A.M. before going to school, but other interests, as she got a bit older, superseded. In 1985 she transferred to Penn State College, changing her courses from the humanities to the business world, and immediately made the dean's list.

Deborah, who is now in high school, is also a soccer player, also a clarinetist in the symphonic band, and a good student.

Michael felt that his military career would not go ever upward, because apart from Korea, he did not have a war record that would help him to achieve higher rank. He flirted with private industry, but opted for the revitalized Selective Service System, where he obtained a top-level civil service position. He prepared major papers, was sent about the country to give talks, and in 1984 he went to Munich, Germany, to read a paper on the U.S. Army's historical failure to use individuals with handicaps in the service, an interesting document. 1986, he transferred to the Veteran's Administration, where he saw greater opportunities. Sandy became a paid consultant to several organizations.

He had moved up to major, then lieutenant colonel, but despaired of rising higher in the army reserve. Suddenly in December 1984, shortly after his forty-sixth birthday, he was notified that he had been recommended for promotion to full colonel. He finally pinned on his eagles in October 1985.

He is protective of his parents, calls them several times a week, never wants us to go to places which are dangerous—war, revolution, disease. As always we disregard his benevolent counsel, because we have the same streak for adventure that somehow has been imbedded in his own character. He sacrificed such acts for himself in order to provide stability in his own life and household.

A Man Is Killed

It was 6 P.M., dark and midwinter, 1966. The streets were slushy, so I was driving carefully. I had just left one of Federation's agencies on the

Lower East Side of Manhattan. At 11th Street and First Avenue, I stopped for a red light. When it turned green, I resumed driving at low speed to avoid skidding. My windshield wiper was swishing back and forth at full speed. As I reached the other side of the street, I suddenly saw a man start walking across the avenue against the light, and in a second he was lying over the hood of my car. In another twinkle, he was on the ground, the bag of groceries he was carrying scattered over the street in the rain-soaked snow. I was going so slow as to stop immediately. I had not skidded. The man—an old man, I realized, as I bent over him—was obviously hurt and groaning almost inaudibly. Witnesses gathered around to assure me it had not been my fault, that he had run into the side of my auto and was walking against the light, obviously confused, or perhaps he was also a bit blind. I asked bystanders to call an ambulance—Bellevue Hospital was up the street—and to summon a police car. The police arrived first. I was told not to move him. I could not bear his lying in the cold and wet slush. I took a blanket out of my car and covered him. The police took all the information, interrogated some witnesses, took notice that I had not skidded and therefore the car was indeed moving slowly, examined where he had fallen on the hood and noted where the dirt had been rubbed off. The ambulance arrived and took him to the hospital. I followed, going into the emergency room. The doctors saw that he was seriously hurt and didn't bother to undress him; they simply cut off his clothes. There were no identity papers on him, so I could not learn his name. To me he looked like a gentle old Jewish man, perhaps in his early seventies. The doctors told me not to wait around and gave me a number to call for further information. Shaken up by the accident, I drove home. I called the hospital and was told that the patient was on the critical list.

The next day I reached the hospital director, told him who I was and of my interest in this patient, and asked him to give the injured man the best possible care.

He died on the second day. His name was Jewish. He lived alone. He had no family or relatives, according to the caretaker of the apartment house where he lived.

I knew there would be a police investigation, so I called my attorney and personal friend, Joseph Mandell, and asked what I should do. I had already prepared a minute-by-minute memorandum. Joe told me that a police investigator would come to see me. I might also have to appear in court. If called, he would attend with me. The police officer came to my Federation office and asked me many questions, jotting down my answers. He gave no indication as to what would follow. No charges were filed against me. A week later, I received a note to appear before a judge in his courthouse office. He also asked me a lot of questions, which I answered in a low, subdued voice. After fifteen minutes, he told me that the case was dismissed and I could leave. My attorney had not been called upon to say anything.

It was a great relief to learn that I bore no responsibility for the man's death. The memory of his body on the hood of the car, his lying in the slush on the street, my covering him with a blanket, watching the doctors cut off his clothing, has never left me. Everytime I pass East 11th Street and First Avenue in Manhattan, the scene of the accident looms up before me afresh. I will always live with that awful recollection.

Dogs and a Trip to Canada

Emma and I had decided to make an extended trip by car through eastern Canada during the summer of 1961. We had been to Canada for a day or two on several occasions, but confined ourselves to Montreal and the flatlands leading to and from the Adirondacks. The problem was: what were we to do with our two dogs for a month? While I do not dislike dogs, I am not rhapsodic about them either. Dogs have been a part of my life off and on for many years. I have a photo taken in 1912 of my father sitting dignifiedly, as he always did when photographed, on a rocking chair on the porch of our home on Washburn Street, and I, who was then four years old, holding a small white dog with black spots, who was appropriately named Spotty. But I have no recollection of taking care of him as a child. I suspect that he was not my dog.

When Ramon was a child on Staten Island, we bought a big beautiful white Eskimo Spitz, who never should have been permitted by law to live in an apartment. He needed space to just run around. Every night, he insisted on sharing our bed rather than Ramon's, although he was ostensibly Ramon's dog. He barked incessantly, annoying the neighbors and us. One day, when we took him for an airing, he disappeared. I heaved a sigh of relief. Ramon still liked dogs, and whenever one proved friendly, he would pet and play. One day, while he was about to touch a medium-sized dog, the hound leaped up and bit him on the lip. There was panic in our house. He was rushed to the hospital for tetanus shots, stitches on his lip, and we awaited with dread the report as to whether the dog had rabies. Fortunately, he didn't. Ramon made a quick recovery.

No dogs entered our lives again until we moved to Pelham in 1953. We had pledged our younger son, Michael, that if we ever bought a house, he could have a dog. We would not have one in an apartment again. No sooner had we moved into Pelham, and to fulfill our promise, I took Michael to a pet shop. He selected a cuddly, little brown puppy, who the vendor assured me would not grow large and would not shed hairs, neither of which proved to be true. Toughy, as Michael named him, after another Toughy had been part of my sister Rachel's household for many years, and with whom Michael had played on our visits to her home. Toughy, of mixed breed, mostly golden retriever, was handsome, good natured, and barked apologetically whenever someone came to the house, that is, except for the two times when we were burglarized while we were home—once with a house full of company. Whenever we went on trips, we placed him in a kennel. On picking him up, he greeted us in a rapturously pawing way that clearly showed that he really missed us.

The question of what to do with Toughy when we left this summer was solved by placing him in a resident camp with friends. But we had acquired another dog, a well-bred, registered, miniature black poodle, whom we had given the Hebrew name Kton-ton ("The little one"), despite his long pedigree with distinguished names of Scotch ancestry. We called him Tonnie. We had previously been given a poodle by Michael's mother-in-law. We had grown to love the puppy. He had been killed by an automobile in front of our country cottage in Sacandaga, as he suddenly darted from us and dashed onto the road. We cried as we buried him under a large pine tree. Michael and Sandy, who were visiting us from Syracuse that day, felt that our grief had to be assuaged, and drove to Syracuse, 145 miles each way, and brought back another poodle at 1:30 A.M., within less than nine hours of the death of Kton-ton. We were again pleasurably burdened with Tonnie #2. Like all dogs, there were daily problems of feeding and toileting, but what concerned us most was what to do when we had to go away. Kton-ton II had been brought back to life after becoming seriously ill from eating the fiberglass insulation on our washing machine while left in the cellar on one of our all-day excursions. Emma loved the dogs and felt they were both companions to her when I was away all day and a protection on nights when I didn't get back until midnight. They seemed to gravitate toward me whenever I came home from my office, sat at my feet while I was eating, reading, or watching TV. However, I never became dependent on them.

When we were about to go off on an extended holiday to Canada, our problem was what to do with Tonnie, a high-strung poodle. Our friends and family shied away from taking him in even as a temporary boarder. The Isaac Seligsons of Boston dropped in on us one Sunday afternoon with their daughter. I asked her whether she'd like to take care of Tonnie for a month. We'd pick him up in Boston on our way back from Canada. She was playing with Tonnie and obviously cared for her. There had never before been a dog in her life. She said she'd love to, but she didn't think that she could take separation from the poodle after living so intimately with her. Without a moment's hesitation, and without consulting Emma, who never forgave me, I told the child she could have the dog, for I saw not only a good home for her, but I would be relieved of a burden. A dog could be expensive, when you took into account medical care, as well as placement with a veterinarian whenever we left town. I did not realize that in my impulsive, reckless generosity, I had not only made a child happy, but had made it possible for the whole life of the household to take an upward turn. The Seligsons pampered the pedigreed dog and took her to dog shows, where she won prizes. So in God's inscrutable way, I had performed a mitzvah, both for the family and the dog.

Sad to say, Toughy had an unhappy end. Several years later, we gave him to the caretaker of one of Federation's camping properties. He ran off and was killed by a railroad train. Dogs have not entered into our lives since.

* * *

Our journey to Canada started with lunch at Surprise Lake Camp, where Ramon and Anita were working, and where we dropped off Toughy. Overnight we were in Albany with Karl and Evelyn Liss, Emma's sister. Then to Johnstown, where we lunched with my sister Rachel. On to Syracuse to see Michael, Sandy, and our new granddaughter, Bonnie. Drove back to Saratoga Springs for a day at the races, where, after an intensive afternoon of picking horses, we ended up losing only $10. Then back to Gloversville to dine with Milton's family. We left a few things at our cottage in Sacandaga, to which we would return after our Canadian journey. The next day we had lunch with Anita's mother, Saide Fink, who was summering at Lake Luzerne, a beautiful spot in the Adirondacks, then drove on to Norwich, Vermont, and stayed overnight in a hotel built in 1797, in a lovely old New England town with other vintage houses.

The next day we stopped at Dartmouth College in Hanover, New Hampshire, with its attractive campus. We saw the Orozco murals plaster-painted on the basement walls of the Baker Library in 1934. We drove on back roads across mountainous New Hampshire to Lovell, Maine, to lunch with Barney and Evelyn Lambert, who, after many consultations with me, had bought and were running a camp named Kezar Lake. Barney had done his fieldwork for the New York School of Social Work at Camp Bronx House under my supervision during the summer of 1947. The camp nestled on a picturesque lake, surrounded by pine trees, and looked off toward Mount Washington some miles to the west. We continued our camping explorations by staying overnight with Matthew and Mary Penn, who owned and operated a superb girls' camp named after the star Vega at Readfield, Maine. Lizzie, our grandchild, spent part of a summer at this camp.

Then we drove to Bar Harbor, up Cadillac Mountain, took a boat ride to see the view and the homes of the rich and distinguished that decorated the shoreline. It recalled to me conversations with Ambassador Henry Morgenthau, Sr., who summered in that city. The library from his summer home was bequeathed to Bronx House.

We rode along the Maine coast, fell in love with Sullivan, Maine, and vowed to return there for a longer holiday. We never did. Passed by Passamaquoddy Bay, where during Franklin D. Roosevelt's early years in the White House, our government planned to harness the tremendous tides for electrical power. We passed Indian reservations, ate prodigious quantities of small blueberries, which were in season, crossed into New Brunswick, Canada, at St. Stephen, visited St. Andrews, and briefly stopped at photogenic Chance Bay and Dipper Harbour, with their stark churches and spare but colorful painted houses. At St. John, we spent hours watching the falls reverse their flow with the surge of high tide. A day and night were passed at Fundy National Park, where I studied the arts and crafts program, an idea that was later partially incorporated in the Henry Kaufmann Campground program.

As we toured Nova Scotia, we ate blueberries in every conceivable form—fresh, cooked, preserved, in custard, in pies. We ended up in Truro, ate superb broiled halibut and more blueberries. Through a northern highway we arrived at Pictou, a charming fishing village. Here they were harvesting and barreling herring. Played golf on a tiny course atop a hill overlooking the ocean. At Caribou, we took the ferry to flat Prince Edward Island with its many fishing villages, none of which seemed to be prospering. The wide beaches on the north shore stretched for miles, totally unpopulated, the beige sand untouched except for the debris spewed up from the sea, mostly broken lobster boxes. We bathed in the nude indifferent to anyone who might appear. No one did.

We stayed overnight in the dreary city of Charlottetown, whiled an evening betting on the trotters, the only activity patronized by natives or stray visitors at night. While novices at this type of horserace betting, we won some money, proving that there is no skill to either winning or losing. We drove over the island to get a good view of its stark barrenness.

We took a ferry to the mainland, back into the French-speaking country, for the island was conspicuously English. We drove through Rexton and noted that Bonar Law, a former Prime Minister of Great Britain (1922–23), was born there. At Newcastle, we saw a plaque that marked the birthplace of Lord Beaverbrook, the English journalist tycoon, and of Samuel Cunard, the shipping lord. Everywhere along the route, we stopped to eat pan-fried salmon, for lunch, for dinner, and once for breakfast. Despite the prominence of these famous personalities, we got the impression that except for the larger cities, the land was desolate, with poor woodland, houses needing repairs. We boarded a ferry named *Romeo and Annette* at Dalhousie, a thriving lumber and fishing town. The boat pulled into the dock at Miguasha, Quebec, where the land and hills were thickly wooded and came down within a block or two of the shoreline. The villages alternated between English- and French-speaking communities, the French towns distinguished by a large Roman Catholic church with well-decorated interior and stained-glass windows. Thus began the Gaspe Peninsula, a territory described as filled with "mystery and romance." Occasionally one passed an Indian village like Marie, where the Micmacs lived in wooden houses that simulated tepees. We learned that the city of Caplan was not named after a Jew, but after an Indian tribe, or perhaps was a corruption of Capeland, since at this point the land jutted out into the sea. Since we always talked with natives and storekeepers, who gave generously of their time, we picked up many miscellaneous facts about the economy and the culture (or lack of it). As we drove through village after village on a Saturday, weddings were always being celebrated at the churches.

We arrived at picturesque Percé in a drenching rain, with fog shrouding the huge rock in the sea, to which sightseers sailed out in clement weather. For dinner, we climbed up the mountain by auto along a road with a forty-five-degree grade, and arrived at the Gargantua, where we ate an incredible meal. It included tiny snails that had to be extracted with a long hat pin, potato-carrot soup, followed by bouillabaisse with the greatest variety of shell and other fish that we had ever previously consumed. Percé was worth the stop even in the rain.

We rounded the village of Gaspé for the return trip along the north coast, following the St. Lawrence River at its widest. We passed through lovely French-speaking villages at every turn of the road, nestling in coves at the foot of wooded mountains. Stopped for some time at St. Jean-Port-Joli to see an old church (1779) with its pulpit carved with biblical figures, including Moses and Ezekiel. This village was an art center for painters and carvers.

Quebec City, our first visit, was the one genuinely European-like city on the American continent. As in some of the other larger Canadian cities on our trip, we met Jews, who ran stores, belonged to a synagogue, worked for Hadassah, sent their children to Montreal for a day school education. Jews always seemed to be well off. We visited the Citadel, where Churchill and Roosevelt met in 1943 to plot the course of World War II. We learned a great deal of French en route.

From Quebec, we headed south through Vermont, bought good Cheddar cheese and maple syrup, and ended our three-week tour at Sacandaga. A week of partial rest with swimming, golf, and reading helped us recuperate from the 3,500 miles we had driven. While we learned a great deal of local history and geography and saw a part of the world that we had never visited before, we also discovered that such journeys were terribly wearing, when compressed into a limited time schedule. We never took another similar trip in the United States, thus depriving ourselves of seeing at close range a good part of this country. It cannot be viewed satisfactorily out of the window of a train or airplane. Only in Europe have we driven long distances by auto, and it has made a difference.

The Orient: 1962

We frequently discussed flying to the Pacific and the Orient. Emma had fantasized about Japan from her earliest childhood, as a country of beautiful dolls, dressed in ample kimonos, hair artificially coiffured, based on books she had borrowed from the Albany public library. My own view of the Japanese and other Orientals was more prosaic. When my brother Sam was on the U.S. Embassy staff in Japan in the 1950s, his service there was too brief for us to make the long journey. When Sam was appointed ambassador to Korea by President Jack Kennedy, an invitation was extended. The summer of 1962 was set aside for a ten-week holiday to that vast region. I had put in a strenuous year at Federation. I was in need of a long break. Before flying, I spent actually only an hour at Pan-Am working out our schedule. I selected hotels under $10 a double and wrote airmail letters for reservations. We obtained the necessary visas, accumulated a host of names of people to see in Hawaii, the Philippines, Hong Kong, Taiwan, and Japan, read everything we could from Michener's *Hawaii,* Ruth Benedict's *The Chrysanthemum and the Sword,* the unforgettable Oliver Statler's *Japanese Inn,* and above all the formidable and indispensable *Japan Tour Guide.* We consulted *National Geographic* for other countries. Then we took all the injections—smallpox, typhoid, paratyphoid, cholera, polio, diphtheria, and tetanus.

At the airport, as always, we bought maximum flight insurance for each of our sons and their families. Emma always said: "If we leave them bereft of parents, at least let's leave them a small fortune."

We left in mid-August. We spoke at length to a journalist en route about the government's horrible treatment of the Japanese-American citizens on the west coast, who were humiliatingly interned in 1941 for the duration of the war. I had read a book on the subject and wondered how I would explain this to Japanese we might meet, along with the destruction wrought by the atomic bomb on Hiroshima and Nagasaki in 1945. We were hoping to visit at least one of these sites. I was fully aware that the conflict had been initiated by the Japanese, so our retaliation was partly understandable.

We stayed some nights with Dr. Charles and Maryann Ansell, friends and colleagues from the east, who lived in Sherman Oaks, California, an attractive suburb of Los Angeles. Charlie (Bezalel), an Iowan by birth and a lawyer by education, had settled in Chicago, where he married Maryann and became a Jewish center worker. They moved to Yonkers, where he became the executive of the center, and where we first met. Later he directed the Educational Alliance, superintended Camp Bronx House–Emanuel, flirted with the idea of becoming a writer, then seriously studied psychology, received his doctorate, moved to California, and set up a practice as an analyst. He was immediately and immensely successful, taught at several universities and wrote professional and popular articles. The Ansells lived in a charming modern house with an outdoor swimming pool in the side of a hill—with two huge dogs and a talking bird.

As usual I was exploited. I gave a lecture on my Jewish point of view at the Valley Jewish Center. There was a favorable reaction to my position, but it was a self-selected audience, unlike those I encountered elsewhere. The Ansells arranged for us to see a great deal of the region, including the Huntington and other museums. We met with old friends and colleagues, ate in gourmet restaurants. The rush of events up to the last moment got us to the airport a bare ten minutes before take-off.

Hawaii

Our plane to Hawaii was practically empty. There was a threat of a strike. When we stepped down from the plane at midnight in Honolulu, to our surprise and delight we were met by Rabbi Howard Kummer, the Jewish chaplain, resplendent in his immaculate, white navy uniform. He circled our necks with aromatic pink and yellow flowered leis. He then drove us to our cottage-hotel just off the beach, where we exhaustedly fell asleep. Our stay in Honolulu was not to be the rest before the strenuous journey to the west.

Honolulu was not crowded. We found everything lush and attractive. The light, misty rain, often with the sun shining, kept the atmosphere clean and cool. We rented a car and each day toured another section of Oahu, and were able to see a lot more than the touristy part of the island. Talking with representatives of the polyglot Oriental population, we were urged to buy one of the beautiful houses, first being constructed since the war. They appreciated in value forty times within a few years. As a conscientious social worker, I could not resist visiting an old age home, a prison, schools, some of whose directors had been educated on the mainland and knew mutual friends. We watched surfboard riders and the catamarans taking the surging waves. We attended a performance of Polynesian dancers, the hula, and the Samoan fire-and-sword dancers, which as the evening wore on became monotonous, because of the repetitiveness of the routines.

We ate pineapple from the farm, so completely different from the unripened variety that appeared in mainland markets. We satiated ourselves on this delicious fruit every day, along with other fruits like guava, passion, coconuts, papaya, and mangoes. We went to a poi factory, where they made this taro food nostrum, said to be a cure for every ailment. This was one item we rejected at the first taste, but we loved macadamia nuts at the first crackle. We toured the sugar plantations, the museum, the university, the Mormon church, the army, navy and air bases, and the grim Pearl Harbor with memories of the 1941 disaster. We ate every type of local fish—dolphin, striped jack, tuna, and bonita. We dined with Robert and Shirley Kamin, he a brother of Maryann Ansell, and a professor of economics at the local university as well as an adviser to the governor.

I was asked by Rabbi Kummer to speak to the Jewish military personnel and their families on Shabbat eve. My sermon dealt with the *sedra* of the week (Deuteronomy), my work in philanthropy, and how Jewish identity could be furthered even in remote outposts in the Pacific. From the questions following the service, it seemed to have been well received.

When we returned to the hotel, we found a message from my brother Sam, who was in Honolulu, en route to Washington. He was meeting with Admiral Felt, commander of the American fleet in Australian waters. When the admiral left, Sam, who looked tired, unburdened himself of the serious problems he faced, as the new dictator, Park Chung Hee, had not yet been able to reconcile the conflicting parties in South Korea. However, he reported some economic improvement in the country, and if this continued, he thought Park would be able to retain his powerful position resulting from a coup.

On our last night, after another excellent dinner (no dinner cost over $3), we walked to the concert shell to hear Andre Kostelanetz conduct the Honolulu Symphony Orchestra in an all-Tchaikovsky program. It was a romantic ending to our six-day holiday. We heard ukeleles playing on the beach in front of our cottage as we fell asleep.

Philippines

The plane to the Philippines was crowded on the seven-hour hop, with a stopover in Guam, where we talked to natives about the humid climate and their struggling economy.

From the airport to our hotel, the Bayview in Manila, we had the immediate impression of a bustling city, a great deal of construction, beautiful homes and public buildings, wide boulevards and tropical plantings, but squeezed in between these signs of prosperity were makeshift shacks, groups of people sitting around with apparently nothing to do, looking languid and poor, so that the poverty of the country, which I had read about before we arrived, stared at us starkly. Most Filipinos were small, tan, and otherwise vigorous.

Our first walk was an adventure. We met Leopold Hidalgo, twenty-seven, a lawyer, whose father was a doctor. We had stopped and asked him where we could eat good native food. He directed us, joined us, wanted to take us home to meet his family, until he discovered we were Jews and then ran from our presence. We had meanwhile learned about a middle-class Filipino family, his views of the country, its cultural life, and his bigoted religious attitudes. We rode on the colorful, crowded, ubiquitous, inexpensive jeep-taxis, a hangover from the war. We learned that the Filipinos hated the Japanese and the Chinese in that order, and, I suspect, everyone else, including unscrupulous Americans. The day we arrived, the papers headlined the involvement of an American Jew in a widespread bribery scandal. Along with the squatters, there were churches, schools, colleges, and clinics in abundance.

We bought gifts for everyone back home. The prices were cheap. We saw paintings in a window by Serna, liked them, went in to talk with him, purchased three, which hang prominently in our dining room. Serna had visited a small island off the mainland and painted the Igarots, originally black slaves from Africa, who lived in virtual isolation, resorting to cannibalism when crops failed. Serna's work had been praised by critics, we learned later. We had dinner with him and learned more about art and the cultural life in that country.

But what kept oppressing us was the squatters, hungry, lean, and in a state of lassitude. (The same conditions prevailed in 1986 and led to a peaceful revolution in the overthrow of the Marcos regime.)

On one street we noted the Philippine School of Social Work, where we met Dean Dr. Angelina Almanzor and several of her faculty, including Howard Amsterdam, an American, a Western Reserve graduate. He knew our nephew Howard Berger, who worked for the Cleveland Jewish Federation. He also knew all about me. This led to a visit at the Girl Scout headquarters, where we met the beautiful director, Mariquita S. Castelo. The five of us had dinner that evening. The next day Dr. Almanzor took us on a tour of Quezon City and insisted that we visit the Rizal Revolutionary House, which gave us a further clue as to her political views.

While there were few Jews in the Philippines, she gave us the impression that all the Jews she had met were rich and were considered "usurers," irrespective of their profession. Nonetheless she was trying to ingratiate herself with us, because Amsterdam had told her that I was an "outstanding" American social worker. Dr. Almanzor later became an important international social worker, presenting papers and providing leadership at worldwide conferences.

We entered the quite imposing synagogue (it was replaced with an even finer one in 1984), met Rabbi Ephraim D. Shapiro, an American without rabbinical ordination, who had found an Iranian-Jewish wife in Israel. He was the leader and teacher of the congregation. He immediately called Jack Harberer, the president, who rushed to pick us up for lunch, first stopping at the U.S. Army and Navy Club, where he had "privileges," for a drink. Then, joined by the rabbi and his wife, we went to the impressive Polo Club for excellent abalone. Jack related that there were only one hundred Jewish families in the Philippines.

On a tour of the better sections of Manila, he pointed out where both the rich natives and rich Jews lived, revealed that Jews were reasonably well integrated and accepted, that Jews eagerly supported anything that was Jewish and Israeli. They had the best of both worlds. Many were refugees from Germany. He felt that the scandal about Stonehill, so glaringly reported in the press, would not reflect on other Jews. He thought Stonehill would survive the scandal and was not likely to be deported. Stonehill, an American Jew, had served in the Philippines during World War II, then returned to the States, where he divorced his Jewish wife. He came back to the Islands, and married a native woman, who converted to Judaism. She and her three children attended the Hebrew school and the weekly service in the synagogue.

Before leaving Manila, I went to the barber shop in our hotel for a haircut, shave, and manicure, and the three attendants threw in a body massage while I was sitting in the chair. The charge was 27 cents (U.S.). My tip was four times larger than the bill.

Since it was Ramon's birthday, (August 23) we ordered champagne on our flight to Hong Kong. He was thirty-three years old.

Hong Kong

We had not expected anyone to meet us at the Hong Kong airport but there were three different people to greet us: Father Howard D. Trube of the Bishop Ford Refugee Center, who had been alerted to our arrival by Monsignor Philip Murphy, a social work colleague in New York (Murphy is now serving as a parish priest in Pelham); Sheng Hwa Hong a member of the U.S. Embassy staff, who had been informed of our coming by Andrew McKinley of the Bronx House Music School; and J. S. Loh, a Chinese businessman, who had been cabled about our arrival by Abraham Abramson, a New York businessman whom I knew as a member of the Surprise Lake Camp board. All wanted to help, but the task went to the most aggressive Mr. Loh, who drove us to the Imperial Hotel, checked out our room and approved, and then told the manager that we were to be properly taken care of during our stay. Our hotel room viewed the Hong Kong side from Kowloon, and it was breathtaking.

The next day, Loh sent over one of his key employees to take us sightseeing and shopping. Loh checked on us several times each day. We bought hand-tailored clothing, pearls, *chachkes* (trinkets), so as to leave us free for the rest of the week. We dined that night with Loh's assistant, enjoyed genuine Peking duck, and learned about this bustling economy.

The streets of Kowloon were a sight to behold with the varieties of costumes, the ornately decorated building fronts, the myriads of foodstuffs open to the dust of the streets, the humid climate, unprotected. There was the pungent odor of food and people, yet not objectionable.

Most of the people were refugees from China. Every alley had its merchants and small manufacturers of everything from clothing to dolls and musical instruments. Everyone was in a hurry, using the unique gait of the Chinese. Some slept on empty corners, others were cooking, playing cards and mah-jongg.

An hour's boat ride around the harbor gave us a close-up view of the equally busy life on the water. Ships of all nations were berthed, including warships, freighters, junks, and sampans. People were born, married, and died on the boats. There were floating stores, churches, schools, and recreational craft. The beauty of the harbor and the hills rising up from the shore was captivating.

It was Friday evening, and we took the ferry and taxi to the synagogue at 70 Robinson Road. The building was a mixture of Moorish and Oriental architecture. We had persuaded another Jewish couple from the United States, whom we met on the ferry, to join us. Yet with our four, there was a bare minyan. The seventy Hong Kong Jewish families only turn out on the High Holy Days or when celebrities like Golda Meir arrived. None of the Kadoorie family, who run many things in Hong Kong, was present. Rabbi Ralph Adler was leaving Hong Kong. Some weeks later we davened with him as he presided over High Holy Day services in Tokyo.

We went to the Skyroof restaurant for a tea luncheon with the Hongs, a meal worth traveling to Hong Kong for. Dim sin in infinite varieties were served in steaming woven baskets, and the bill was computed by adding up the baskets at the tableside. We visited their home and caught a glimpse of how the upper class lived, in magnificent, protected homes sprawled on the mountainside. They were educated refugees from mainland China who had gone to the United States. He had been assigned to work largely with Chinese who were seeking asylum or permanent residence in the United States. A tour around the inside of the mountainous islands, valleys, and sea revealed a mystic beauty, the kind often captured by Chinese artists.

We dined one night on one of the Aberdeen fishing boats, riding out to the eatery in what we thought was a tippy sampan. From a large wooden tub filled with sea water at the side of the boat, the Hongs selected large shrimps, a tremendous lobster, and garoupa fish, which were converted into ten different dishes.

Loh and his family drove us through the New Territories, so we could see what the farming area was like, the day ended with another superb Chinese dinner at the Metropolitan, an extravagant restaurant.

Father Trube, who called daily, picked us up the following morning for an inside view of Hong Kong, with its poor, its sick, and its serious problems. Originally from New York, he had spent most of his life in China as a Maryknoll priest, but after he was arrested and expelled by the Communists, he settled in Kowloon in 1952 to serve the poor in the "walled city," where few whites ever went. We saw new apartment houses built for the refugees, models of absolute simplicity in facilities and furnishings. We entered a recreation center and a nursery school, both staffed by refugees whom he had recruited and trained. Trube said he did not preach. He "just practiced charity." We toured the walled city with its dingy, dark alleys, unventilated stores, and tiny factories, where they made everything for the international market and were paid a pittance. We observed a dentist repairing someone's teeth in something less than an ideal hygienic setting. It was a world apart from the openness of the rest of Hong Kong. He took us to his rehabilitation center for victims of leprosy, a study in the courage of people who had lost parts of their limbs. Then to his main center with its apartments, school, recreation rooms, workshops. Here, with American-provided eggs, milk, flour, they turned out tons of noodles for free distribution. Trube was thus known as the "noodle priest." Whether in the streets or his workshops, or even as we lunched at the Carlton Hotel with its panoramic view of the city, everyone knew and greeted Father Trube. He drove us to the border of the Chinese mainland, where we peeked at what appeared to be well-ordered and large rice paddies. Trube claimed this was a showpiece for tourists. Naturally, he opposed the developments in China. He pointed out the high price paid in human lives for the collectivization of its citizenry. That is why millions had fled to Hong Kong and elsewhere. Father Trube was a well-read man. We conversed about Catholicism and particularly the famous Catholic author Teilhard de Chardin, who after publishing his *The Phenomenon of Man,* had become much in vogue in the United States and the world during that period. Teilhard had lived in China, and Trube knew him. I had read several of his works.

On another day, we went to an exhibit by David Kwo, an American artist of Chinese ancestry, who was in the gallery with his wife. We rambled with them about art in the United States and in Hong Kong. We went to see *The Dream of the Red Chamber,* a classical Chinese movie done in beautiful sets and color, well acted and sung, even if a bit slow in overall treatment. We took all of our hosts of the week out for dinner at Maxim's, danced to a good Filipino orchestra, met the owner of the club, a Chinese from New York. We said our tearful good-byes as we left after a hectic holiday for Taiwan.

Taiwan

With no room in the economy cabin, they sat us in first-class, and we were treated to a wonderful dinner and service as we flew to and were dropped in very green Taiwan. The ride from the airport through the city gave evidence of its fertility. Taipei was in the process of being built up as a result of the huge influx of mainland Chinese and the presence of ten thousand U.S. soldiers, sailors, and airmen to protect it. Part of the Golden Dragon Hotel had originally been a shrine, hence the brilliantly colored facade with typical Chinese designs. It was owned by Madame Chiang Kai-shek.

A cable from my brother Sam told us to delay our trip to Korea for a week, as he had been summoned again to Washington. We visited Dr. Pardee, a friend of the Hongs of Hong Kong, who was working in the cultural affairs office of the U.S. Information Service. We told him we were social workers and educators and wanted to see Taiwan from that point of view. He contacted Dwight D. Rugh of the YMCA and Mrs. Cho Ying Yang, director of social services at the National Taiwan University hospital.

Pardee's secretary drove us to the YMCA. Rugh, at first, seemed in a hurry to get the visit over with. However, once we learned that he had been in Israel for four years, and that we both knew Ralph Goldman, a former student and colleague of mine, who was then the director of the U.S. Point Four program in Israel, we had all we could do to break away. He defended Chiang Kai-shek, despite his dictatorial practices, and saw no end to the conflict with Communist China.

We ate another extraordinary Chinese dinner at the hotel consisting of shrimp, duck, and pigeons. There were no barefooted human beings pulling rickshaws here. Instead there were bicycle pedicabs. I'm not sure which exploited the human being more.

Mrs. Yang called for us in her car early the next day, and that was the beginning of a beautiful friendship, which continues to this day. She was educated in the United States and had introduced mental health approaches in hospital care, home visits, and rehabilitation programs borrowed from America. She took us all over the hospital, then to a community center, and to the family-planning offices, where we met the articulate and aggressive Mrs. Tze-Kwan. Mrs. Tze-Kwan later came to the United States, stayed with us, and thus we reciprocated her extravagant hospitality in Taipei.

Needless to say, with all these contacts, we were busy seeing museums, crafts displays, institutions. Emily Cho, a friend of our White Plains cousins, Ed and Joy Borgos, came to see us. She was a most attractive and intelligent young woman. On our return to Pelham, we invited Emily and her parents for dinner, along with an interesting group of people, including Bill and Ann Peters (he was a CBS TV producer and a friend of the Pelham Jewish Center), to learn more about the two Chinas. They all preferred to talk about Jews, and thus over a Chinese dinner, the entire conversation was devoted to that subject. Emily later became a well-known designer and writer about American fashions.

Wanting to meet the Jewish community, which consisted of military personnel, we reached Commander William Jasper and his wife Retha, who, with their two small children, lived on Grassy Mountain, an attractive suburb overlooking Taipei. Bill had been in the navy since the age of seventeen, became a dentist, was always active in the Jewish community, and took charge of conducting services for some fifty Jews. He needed a Torah for the forthcoming holidays, and I told him whom to call in the States, and it was immediately airmailed. He hadn't previously received such cooperation.

Since the Jewish constituency was not large, no rabbinic chaplain was permanently stationed at this post. A few years later, we met again in Israel, where the family and Retha's mother had gone on aliyah. However, Bill was not well received professionally.

They returned to the States. Bill taught dentistry for several years, and they now live in retirement in North Carolina. We exchange letters once a year.

We left their home that night by cab for the hotel in advance of a typhoon, which caused considerable damage and pushed our cab from side to side down the mountain roads, driven at a pace that was faster than I travel, and I am not a lagging driver.

We went to lunch with Mrs. Kwan and her guest, Mrs. Pei Yu Feng, wife of a rear admiral in the Free China Navy. The term "Free China" was preferred by the Chinese mainlanders rather than "Taiwan," which gave too much status to the natives. When the admiral joined us for lunch, we learned that he knew Sam from Greece. He asked what he could do for us. I told him that we wanted to visit the island of Quemoy, very much in the news those days, along with the island of Matsu. These islands were the subject of the bitter debate between presidential candidates John F. Kennedy and Richard M. Nixon in 1960. A battle for their control threatened to draw the United States into China's civil war between Mao Zedong and Chiang Kai-shek, for Mao asserted they were part of the Chinese mainland. The United States stated that it would defend those Taiwanese outposts at any cost. The admiral glanced at his watch and said: "We just missed the last plane today for Quemoy." "What about tomorrow?" I asked. "We can't do it tomorrow. We shall then be shelling them and they shell us. It wouldn't be safe. Are you free on Friday?" Regrettably, we were leaving, so that another interesting experience was denied us. We also learned that this was the way some wars were fought.

We met many Chinese. All originally came from the mainland. They occupied important positions in the country. When the mainlanders arrived in 1947–48, they liquidated the native opposition and established their own military and political supremacy and hierarchy. In fact, the political leaders represented provinces on the mainland and reelected themselves to office by proxy. We were approached by a young Taiwanese to help their cause, and he pressed an underground paper into our hands. It was impossible to discuss the problems of the Taiwanese with the mainlanders.

One day, when we left Mrs. Yang and took a taxi to our hotel, she wrote down the number of the cab, and told the driver in Chinese that if anything happened to us, she would prosecute him. We arrived safely.

In Taiwan, they were pirating English-written best sellers and encyclopedias and selling them for very little. We bought a bag full for Sam and Margaret and gave others to Mrs. Yang and Mrs. Kan.

While in Taipei, we printed New Years cards (Rosh Hashanah), which we have done on a few occasions while abroad. The printing used some Chinese characters. We had marvelous reactions from the relatives and friends who received them.

One afternoon, we went on a tour-picnic with the Jaspers and the Millsteins. The latter was a career army man, married to a Chinese woman who had converted to Judaism. Their three children were being raised as Jews. We met other mixed couples in Taiwan and Japan, and in all instances the marriages between American Jewish army personnel and natives were working out quite well. Mrs. Millstein was a professional musician.

We were disappointed not to see the great and old Chinese art. It was hidden in Taiwan, awaiting display when a new museum would be erected.

Our last dinner in Taiwan was at the home of Mrs. Yang, presided over by her husband, who was formerly a teacher and now was employed by the National Bank. We met all five children and two guests. One of the guests was a sociologist at the university. He asked me for material on juvenile delinquency, a growing problem in the country, as the old Chinese family's controls were weakening. He also asked for books on Jewish contributions to civilization, since he taught courses on the history of world thought. I sent them to him. The other guest was a woman cardiologist, who had just returned from the United States. It was clear from the evening's conversation that they really knew little about the United States and absolutely nothing about Jews and Judaism. The children spoke English, behaved beautifully, and were not afraid to ask questions. Two were about to complete their undergraduate college courses. Eleven of us sat around a large table, where we were served fifteen courses of the best Chinese food. The menu included roasted nuts, Peking duck with small pancakes, chicken, shrimp, fish of several varieties, pork, bamboo shoots, soybean shoots, noodles, cucumbers, mushrooms, and several soups, including one made of shark fins. Each item was served separately. We ate each course from a large central dish, picking up large and small pieces with chopsticks. Before each course, we toasted each other drinking a Chinese wine. It was a long, talkative evening, ending with tearful goodbyes and promises to write and perhaps see one another somewhere in the future.

At our final breakfast we were visited by a young Chinese girl who wanted help in coming to the States. She came to us because she had been told that we had influence. We gave her some suggestions.

At the airport, we found the entire Yang family, who gave each of us synthetic leis as a farewell present. In a drenching rain we boarded the plane for Japan.

On our return to the States, we received letters from the Yangs asking us to sponsor their son at the Univerity of Colorado and their daughter at Boston University. I wrote glowing recommendations. Both were matriculated and graduated with master's degrees. We saw the daughter several times on visits to New York. Both now live in Denver and are doing well.

Several years later, Amy Yang came to the United States to study, and we took her out to a fine restaurant, Manny Wolf's, but even at its best, American cuisine does not compare with the feast we enjoyed at her home in Taipei. She said: "You don't think we eat like that every day or even once a year? We hired the chef of the Bank of Taiwan to prepare that special dinner for you."

Japan

We arrived in Tokyo in a downpour. Bedded ourselves at the huge Dai Ichi Hotel. Found a cable from Phil Baskir, a fund-raising colleague at Federation, to contact Dr. Edward Aberlin, an old friend from Staten Island, who was staying at the Hotel Napoleon in Paris, to get his consent to be the honored guest, along with his brother Isidore, at a dinner to be sponsored by Federation. It took me a day and a half, tied to the hotel, before we reached him and received his consent. I should have added this time to my vacation.

On our first night, when we sauntered to the nearby Ginza, what we saw was not Emma's vision of Japan based on her childhood reading. Some men and women still wore kimonos, the women with their more elaborate obis, but in the Ginza, the women were mostly in Western dress, serving as bar girls and prostitutes. We had wandered into the red-light district. Our faith was restored when we learned that they did not represent more than a thin slice of the Japanese population.

Tokyo was then teeming with its ten million people, one million autos, buses, trolleys, subway, overhead rapid transit trains, a bustling city still on the upward move. At the Matuya and Takishimaya department stores we had a taste of what these modern commercial ventures were like, with playgrounds, live pet shops, art, antiques, and whole floors devoted to the sale of kimonos, still fashionable, although being steadily replaced by Western clothes, conspicuous on the street and worn mostly by younger people.

It was dark when we left the stores, and it was time to go to the Kokosai musical-dance theater. We approached a man at the curb, well dressed, carrying a brief case, and asked him how we could get to the theater—taxi, subway, overhead railway? He apparently did not understand me. In a few seconds a car drove up, he opened the back door and ushered us in. He sat in front. Without further ado, the car drove off. I was sure from previous instructions that we were going in the wrong direction. Whenever I said "Kokosai," he would only reply, "Neva mine." After fifteen minutes in busy traffic at the height of the rush hour, I showed him our tickets, which I should have done in the first place. He had the driver turn the car about and drove in the opposite direction for another twenty minutes to the theater. When we got out I tried to put a lot of yen in his hand. He refused to take it, got into the back seat, and drove off. It then dawned upon us that it was his car and chauffeur, not a taxi. What hospitality!

Ruth Benedict, in *The Chrysanthemum and the Sword*, related that you should never do a Japanese a favor, because he will be forever obligated to you to a point of becoming a nuisance. Here was evidence of a courtesy that probably could never be duplicated. Yet the same thing happened to us in Kyoto and Nikko, so it was not a singular experience.

At the theater's box office, we asked the girl, who spoke English, how we could get back to the hotel after the performance. She said that she would escort us. As we had some time before the curtain went up, we walked through the mixed neighborhood from a red-light area to the Asakusa Sensusi Temple. The original, dating to the sixth century, had been destroyed in World War II, and a new one had been built in mammoth Japanese style, ornate, gilded, colorful. People scurried in and out, deposited a coin, prayed briefly and left. There were no visible priests.

The Kokosai reminded us of Radio City Music Hall with its great, precision-line dancers, attractive acts, spectacular stage settings. The cast was all female, including actors who played male roles in masculine dress. The dancers were good, but the routines were repetitive, even if they changed their costumes. The voices were superb. The music was much more melodious than the Chinese musical theater. There was strangely no applause, yet we felt that it was an appreciative audience. The seats were filled to capacity.

We decided not to bother the young lady in the ticket booth and started walking to the subway. We heard someone clacking in high heels pursuing us, calling out: "My American friends, my American friends." Sachiko Miyao, a cute little thing, accompanied us to the subway. She was attending her last year at the university. Her father, although a laborer, was sending two children to college. She gave us an insider's view of what life was like in Japan on a very modest income.

Sachiko took us to the Kabuki theater. She was our interpreter. After the performance, we met the actors backstage, all male this time, most of whom she knew. She came to see us several times and even left a fine gift before we departed.

She later wrote to us in Pelham that she wanted to be a Pan-Am airline hostess and needed a recommendation. I wrote an excellent one. She got the job. Whenever she came to New York she visited us.

In 1971, when we went to Hawaii again, Sachiko was living there. We renewed our relationship. Subsequently she married an American and went into business in Honolulu. From time to time we hear from her.

Rabbi (Chaplain) Herman Dicker, stationed in Tokyo, called and asked us to have breakfast with him at the Sanno Hotel, where military personnel were billeted. German-born, a graduate of the Jewish Theological Seminary, he had been in the army since 1941 and was about to be transferred to Governor's Island in New York harbor. He had spent eight months in Korea. He told us that my brother Sam was doing a superb job as ambassador, that he gave the chaplaincy excellent cooperation, and that he appeared at special Jewish holiday events for the military. Dicker had just published a book, *Wanderers and Settlers in the Far East*, describing a century of Jewish life in China and Japan. He gave us a copy when we invited him to dinner in Pelham. Occasionally, we have spoken over the phone, and he was helpful to me as the librarian at the seminary some years later, when I was collecting material on Ethiopian Jewry.

We toured Tokyo, saw the Imperial Palace, watched the readying of the stadium for the forthcoming Olympic Games in 1964, went through the Happoen Gardens with its attractive and typical Japanese architecture, sculpture, and landscaping.

We participated in a chado (a tea ceremony) with Mrs. Tamaki, the oldest tea mistress in Japan. She sat in her kimono on a low bench, folded her napkin in a carefully arranged pattern before scalding and cleaning the various utensils, including the cups in which the brew would eventually be poured. Mrs. Tamaki meticulously measured out the powdered green tea, added a few drops of water with a spoon, which looked like a bamboo smoking pipe. She held it in the prescribed manner. She stirred the potion, then stopped to turn the bowl halfway around, sipped the tea, made another quarter-turn of the bowl, and finished drinking, making noises of satisfaction. She cleaned all the utensils, restored them to their proper place. Rose, bowed, completing the ritual.

Mrs. Tamaki served us sweet candy, followed by rice tidbits and cups of the green tea, which tasted like the Chinese variety. Then we were served some smoky cold orange tea. Neither tea was to our taste. She runs a school teaching the ceremony she had performed. In the seventeenth century, tea was a religious beverage. It was introduced, I read somewhere, to keep monks from falling asleep.

We met Rabbi Ralph Adler from Hong Kong on the street. He had just moved to Tokyo to take over the rabbinical duties at the Jewish Community Center, a synagogue-center. He said that he had a year's vacation in Hong Kong. The Kadoories, who he claimed were not really interested in Jewish life, nevertheless controlled the small Jewish community, and when they presided at meetings, they discouraged participation.

We went to the USO headquarters and spent two hours with Eugene Schramm, head of the unit. His aide, Mr. Nagai, offered to arrange our trips out of Tokyo. This saved us a great deal of time and money.

That night we had dinner with Alice Boney, a friend of Earl and Irene Morse of New York. The Morses bought Oriental antiques from her studio. At the new Hotel Okura, where she thought we ought to stay, she was giving a party. (The 1986 seven-nation Economic Conference was held at this hotel.) Alice was then sixty-one, tall, with an expressive face, gay and talkative. While married, she lived alone in Japan and ran, as she frankly stated, an "expensive antique shop." The dinner turned out to be a birthday party for Sidney Cardozo, a cousin of the late Supreme Court Justice Benjamin Cardozo. Sidney was a bachelor, ascetic, aesthetic, who remained in Tokyo after the war. A translator, he also listed himself as a professional in Japanese fine and decorative arts. Another guest was a young Japanese tourist specialist who personally supervised guided tours for well-to-do visitors. In the group was Mrs. J. E. Sussman, an American sculptor about to open a show in Tokyo. As we gaily cocktailed, everyone who passed stopped to greet at least one person in this party. The food served was mostly Western style. Champagne flowed like water. The dinner was finally touched off with a birthday cake for Cardozo. There was lots of talk about Japan, art, antiques, and sex, including Japanese geishas. None of the others had ever heard or read of James Michener's reference in *Hawaii* to the use of masks by male Japanese when sleeping with a girl, so that ritualistically she remained a virgin, because she had not been violated by a real person.

Close to midnight, when we were all high, Mrs. Sussman insisted on seeing Boney's house. We piled into two taxis and wended our merry way through the suburbs, through narrow alleys and ended up in a commodious Japanese house with sliding doors, filled with antiques of India, China, and Japan, gotten out in ways that Alice would not reveal, all to satisfy the voracious American market. It was almost dawn when we took a train back to Tokyo proper, exhausted from a long, exhilarating night.

Korea

We left for Korea the next day still half-asleep. On the plane was tall, freckled, vivacious Shirley MacLaine, the well-known American actress, accompanied by her husband, Steve Parker, and their young daughter. We landed in a downpour in Seoul. Sam and Margaret were at the airport to greet us. When an embassy official introduced them to Shirley, she assumed that he, along with a host of reporters and photographers, had come to greet her. She thanked him profusely. Sam's presence in meeting her was accidental.

The embassy house was within a compound. An old-style Korean building, made of wood, cement blocks, adobe, and topped with a thatched roof. A sizable staff was required to maintain it. The grounds included gardens and a tennis court. Sam and Margaret helped tend the gardens and played tennis. The interior was decorated with drawings, paintings, and pottery, the latter from the early Silla dynasty, which ruled the country from the year 300 to 918 C.E.

Sam was entertaining General Maxwell Taylor, chief of staff, General G. J. Meloy, head of the United Nations command in Korea, and Lieutenant General Hugh P. Harris, head of the front line in Korea. All were over six feet tall, in contrast to Sam's five feet five inches. All were in well-starched white uniforms. They were on their way to dinner with the Prime Minister. I was invited by the generals to sit in on the conversation as they drank cocktails. Taylor kept stressing the need to take more imaginative initiatives in solving the highly strained relations with the North Koreans. He stated that during the Berlin Wall crisis with the Russians and East Germans, he had discovered that serving American ice cream to the Eastern soldiers guarding the frontier had eased tensions. Everyone laughed heartily. My inner reaction was that even soldiers at the highest levels still resorted to pleasantries in serious conversation. They were all concerned that Park, the head of the Korean government, who had come to power through a coup, might not be able to control the country. All, except Sam, had underestimated the new, young, powerful leader, who would remain at the helm until 1979, when he was assassinated.

General Harris invited us to visit Panmunjon, where North and South Korea met under the aegis of the United Nations, and we set a date for such a trip to the restless enemy border.

When Sam returned from the embassy, and on other occasions, particularly at night, we had long talks. He unburdened himself of the problems of running an embassy in a country where war and political instability were the order of the day; and where he had to be firm in the execution of U.S. policies. He was trying to prevent the continued Korean postponement of reintroducing civil liberties as well as the restriction of religious freedom to the Protestant missionaries.

Seoul, since Park's takeover, had once again become a thriving city, clean, good traffic control, stores filled with native merchandise. As an ambassador's guest and brother, we were royally received everywhere. Dr. Kim, curator of the National Museum, personally escorted us through its considerable collection, giving us scholarly and historical details about each item. Visiting shrines and palaces, we were surprised to find that they were usually wooden buildings, brightly decorated, but not with the high colors witnessed in Japan. We wondered how they had survived fires and wars, and learned that many of them hadn't.

During the Japanese occupation from 1911 to 1945, Koreans were not permitted to develop their potential industry; thus there was a shortage of technicians and skilled workers. But native intelligence soon made up for this gap, and a decade later, South Korea was a major industrial force.

Sam and Margaret were always having dinner parties for us. One night I sat between the wives of the ambassadors from Vietnam and Greece, both well educated, well traveled, and exceedingly attractive. Shirley MacLaine had a stomach upset and couldn't come at the last minute. The talk was civilized, about art, literature, travel, and of course politics and the future of Korea.

Chaplain (Rabbi) Kleinberg invited us to a service, and before fifty American Jewish servicemen, I was called upon to speak about our visits to other Jewish communities and military establishments around the world. I stressed the need for their retention of their Jewish identity. I referred to the *sedra* (portion) of the week, emphasizing one's Jewish obligations to humanity. It included the biblical reference to the ancient one-year deferment from military service of a newly married man, so that he could properly take care of the initial adjustment to his wife, before he served his country. The rabbi related Sam's recent participation in the dedication of a new Torah. Several soldiers, including dentists and doctors, told me that they had found Judaism a more positive influence in their lives while serving in the army.

We toured markets, streets, and alleys filled with colorful natives, especially the elderly men with their wispy beards and woven, black, small top hats. We bought all kinds of art work and silver objects, including silver chopsticks. Some of the oldest pottery of the Silla dynasty reminded us of basalt bowls of the Chalcolithic period unearthed near Beersheba in Israel.

On one tour, when we asked to see where the native royal art treasures were kept, a curator immediately drove us to the secret palace and gardens, where we ran into Shirley MacLaine, who had made the same request, and where the accompanying photographers took pictures of all of us. The national treasures, made of gold and exquisite jewels, were housed in a wooden building that could easily be destroyed by fire.

One evening we had dinner with the Hendersons, Sam's cultural attaché, who had a fabulous collection of old and new Korean art. His beautiful wife, a German sculptress, had decorated the home as though it were a museum. We took off our shoes on entrance. The guests included the wealthiest Korean industrialist, recently released from jail after paying a $7 million fine, and now back in business. There was a leading Korean journalist, who gave us a set of the photos he had taken while covering stories in Paris. The other guests were the curator of the

National Museum, whom we had met before, and the dynamic president of Ehwa Women's University, Dr. Helen Kim.

When I wrote earlier about our trip to Israel in 1955, I mentioned the presence of Dr. Hong-Chun Kim, a member of our group. He had returned to Korea and became an editor of a newspaper, which went into bankruptcy. He had a Ph.D. in Hebrew studies and was now working on a book about the Dead Sea Scrolls. Kim took us through Seoul University, from which he had graduated. Parents sometimes sold some of their younger children, in order to give their older and gifted offspring a college education, which might ensure them a life devoid of farm drudgery and economic uncertainty. The professors at the university knew a great deal about the United States, but were reluctant to discuss contemporary Korean politics. One could be jailed if he was reported as stating anything that might be construed as disloyal to the Park regime.

We had lunch with Kim's young brother, Won Chin Kim, president of a major paper company, rich, and a premier collector of old Korean art. All the children in Kim's family had been college educated. He was also supporting Hong-Chun. When the paper was still operating, Hong-Chun had interviewed Sam on several occasions, and Sam had told him of our relationship. We ate in a Korean restaurant, indulging in ten different dishes, totally at variance with Chinese food. Spiced, especially kimchi, a pungent, garlic vegetable resembling sauerkraut.

We were taken by the army to a model village, where soldiers who finished their military service spent some weeks before returning to their farms, learning how to diversify their crops by raising chickens and rabbits, how to sanitize night soil (human excrement) for fertilizing their crops.

I was invited to Ehwa University to speak to its faculty on American social work theory and practice. As I concluded my remarks, in came Dr. Kim, whom we had met at a party, and who personally escorted Margaret and me around the campus, so we could see the buildings and the museum. (Later she gave me several pieces of pottery as a present.) She stopped the car in the rear of the large auditorium and asked me to accompany her through the rear door, and before I knew it, she and I were on the stage and I was introduced as Sam's brother, a prominent American social worker, to speak to two thousand girl students in assembly. I spoke briefly about my delight in being in Korea, a remarkable country slowly recovering from enslavement by the Japanese and a disastrous war. I remarked that Korea seemed to be vitally interested in educating its youth. Finally, I hoped that relations would be most cordial between the United States and Korea in the future. While I was speaking, you could have heard a pin drop. Whether they understood what I stated or not, although I spoke slowly and clearly, they all arose when I finished and gave me a long, standing, clapping ovation.

We lunched at Dr. Kim's house with a number of her faculty present. I answered questions about similarities and differences between American and Korean educational polices and curriculum, the kinds of books students read, extracurricular activities, sociology, theology, art. It was quite a workout. After lunch, Margaret took me on a tour of social work agencies—a rehabilitation center, health clinic, and a boys' vocational trade school, where a sign was posted: "Greetings to Mr. Berger's family."

As though the day wasn't complete, all four of us spent an evening hopping from theater to theater escorted by a leading Korean theatrical producer. First we saw a Korean version of Gershwin's *Porgy and Bess*. While we could not follow the words, we knew the music and the story, so that it came off quite well. Then to the opening of a new play, *The Zoo Family*, dealing with the integration of a Korean and Western white, the first time that this theme had been presented dramatically in this country. The voices were good. Acting was superb. The stage sets imaginative. We could follow the theme without knowing a word of Korean.

Sam and Margaret arranged a tour to the south, via Taegu, where we first dined at the USIS with Leaford Williams, head of the unit, saw an exhibit of native Korean artists, and were attracted to the work of Jeomsik Chung and asked Williams if the artist would sell any of his work.

We then drove south through endless rice fields to Kyonju, the seat of the original Silla Dynasty in the third century C.E. There we saw many royal tombs, actually huge mounds of earth, under which the Korean ancients were buried with all their possessions, which when not looted, produced the handsome gray ceramics of that period. We climbed a steep mountain to enter a Buddhist temple, recently unearthed, with a huge statue of the founder of the faith and the entire interior lined with bas-reliefs illustrating Buddha's various roles. The temple, a thousand years old, was in perfect condition. We bought a number of Silla Dynasty clay objects.

When we reached the Taegu airport, we discovered that Leaford Williams had arranged an exhibit of Chung's paintings. We picked out two large ones, which Sam had crated and shipped. We later learned that Chung was essentially a religious painter, and that one of the Piccaso-like works was *Mary and Jesus as a Child* and the other, a magnificent gray painting, was *Flight into Egypt*. The latter is hung at Ramon and Anita's home in Providence. The artist used a bird for his hallmark on both paintings.

On our return to Seoul, we arranged a picnic trip to Panmunjon, where Sam could not go for security reasons. General Harris escorted us to the meeting hall, where representatives of the UN, the United States, North Korea, and South Korea regularly met to discuss issues which never got resolved. We walked to the actual border of North Korea and could see the North Korean soldiers with guns patrolling the area only a few feet away. They eyed us suspiciously and held their guns alertly. We were told not to take notice of their presence, or we might just be unlucky enough to draw fire. We left unmolested. We drove through pleasant hilly country, stopped in a few villages, and ate our lunch in front of a small, decorated Buddhist shrine.

On a Saturday night, I was introduced to a kaising house, the Korean equivalent of a Japanese geisha house. I was taken there by Philip Habib, then Sam's political counselor, who later became ambassador to Korea, held notable high posts in the State Department, helped negotiate the Vietnamese peace treaty with Henry Kissinger, and then attempted to resolve the Israeli-Lebanese War in 1983–84. Phil was the son of a Lebanese shoemaker who later became a shopkeeper. He was born in Brooklyn, college educated, decided to enter the diplomatic service. Gregarious, articulate, good sense of humor. As we sat in the embassy compound before going to the kaising house, he said that he "wished his father could see him now. A diplomat hobnobbing with ambassadors in the far reaches of the world." He sounded like a Jewish boy, proud of his achievements. Born of immigrant parents. Phil always had a sympathetic attitude toward Jews, coming from a Christian rather than an Islamic background.

We drove to the kaising house in the ambassador's car with the U.S. flags flying on the fenders. Sam was not "permitted" to go with us for reasons that I never fully understood. There we met three other men—one, another member of the U.S. embassy staff, and the others journalists, one named Cho, whose byline occasionally appeared on his dispatches to the *New York Times*. We sat on the floor for an hour, drinking and having a most frank discussion on everything pertaining to Korea, the United States, and the world. I wish I could have tape-recorded it, particularly the cynicism of the journalists. But enlightening as all this was, I also knew there was an 11 P.M. curfew and wondered where the kaising girls were, since none had appeared. The men chided me for wanting to interrupt such a verbal free-for-all cum drinking bout, but they gave in to my request for this new experience, although obviously old hat for them. Five charming women entered, sat down next to each of us, forming a circle on the floor. Food and more drinks were served. My kaising was an attractive, small young woman, dressed in something less than the flamboyant artificiality in dress, facial makeup, hairdo, and mannerisms of the Japanese geisha. We graciously toasted each other repeatedly, fed ourselves. None of the girls spoke English; some relied on sign language. They did not object to a hug or kiss on the cheek. They rose to entertain—sang, played instruments, and danced, in a charming, unsophisticated fashion. Their voices were superb. We danced with them to the thumping of a drum played by one of the girls. Before I knew it, it was curfew time. The four pushed me into the ambassador's car, since they had promised Sam that I would not get involved with anything embarrassing. I don't know what they did, but I went back to the ambassador's house to tell Emma, Sam, and Margaret about the night's happenings.

Several nights before we left, we had dinner at the home of Wun Chin Kim, the owner of a paper factory and art collector and brother of the Ph.D. journalist and writer whom we originally met in Israel. While Wun-Chin, Hong Chin, a Korean professor of sociology, Emma, and I sat cross-legged on the floor for the feast and conversation that lasted for more than three hours, the wives, who were college graduates remained in the kitchen throughout the meal, apparently preparing the food, while the numerous dishes were served by their lovely children. We greeted the wives on our arrival, when we presented both families with gifts and bade them farewell when it was all over. We ate an extraordinary meal of many different dishes, all selected from a central bowl, delicately picked up with thin, short Korean chopsticks. The conversation was far-ranging, as we discussed the United States, Israel, Korean education, politics, and art. It was evident that they had some doubts about the stability of the Park regime, but Wun-Chin saw the prospect of making lots of money, despite the austerity decrees which marked the beginning of the reign.

When we arose from the long and rambling discussion, our host took out of many drawers and closets a tiny part of his ancient Korean art collection. He did not reveal how he had obtained them. We were awed with the taste and quality of each item.

Several years later, when he visited us in Pelham, he brought a large piece of pottery from the late Silla dynasty, about one thousand years old, which we now estimate, on the basis of what we have been told by dealers, is worth a small fortune. He also brought a box of ginseng, guaranteed to assure our sexual life forever, which we traded for a pound of good black Chinese tea from our Chinese laundry man.

When Michael, our youngest son, went to Korea in 1965 for a year, as part of his U.S. Army assignment, he was entertained by our Korean friend in his newly built home, where much of his art collection was on permanent display.

We had lunch one day with the Prime Minister, the number-two man in the government, accompanied by his wife. There was a pleasant exchange, but he avoided all questions which called for frank answers. It was a cordial interlude and not much else, although the engraved invitation which came to us before the luncheon seemed to augur something more auspicious than a generalized conversation with our gracious hosts. Sam seemed to be a bit concerned, when I started asking probing questions, but my manner was neither provocative nor indiscreet. He seemed to give off a sigh of relief when our hosts responded with some polite platitudes.

It was a holiday which we thought could never be bettered. (That is, until we met again in Vietnam in 1971.)

Japan: II

On our return to Japan, we were met by Nagai, who had arranged our tour through other parts of the country. First we boarded a train in Tokyo for Odawara, then up the mountain to the Miyanishita-Fugiya Hotel in Hakone, where on a clear day we were told that Mount Fuji could be seen. It continued cloudy, so we didn't get that majestic view. The hot water came from natural hot springs, the steam of which misted from the ground in many places. Emma decided not to take the trip with me to Lake Hakone, because it included a long trip on a cable car. I took the bus to Fora, then a funicular up the mountain to Sountan. I entered a red cable car seating eight passengers, which pulled us across the vast cut with smoking sulphur mines a thousand feet below, that the natives call "The Big Hell." The cable car traversed several miles, swaying gently, but since none of the other passengers seemed fearful, I traveled with equanimity, enjoying the sights below. It finally stopped at Kujiri on Lake Hakone. It had started to pour, so I gave up the boat ride and took a bus back to the hotel via Sengoku-Haro, passing through green tree-covered mountains without a bare spot, farms and attractive villages.

We took a train from Odawara for the five-hour run to Kyoto, spoke to a group of German industrialists, who were impressed with the new Japanese industrial methods and thought they were bright competitors. We stayed at the Hotel Kyoto, toured the historic shrines. We noted again, as elsewhere in the world, that all shrines were approached through endless commercial vendors selling religious objects and food. We saw several museums. We ate dinner in a restaurant which featured shab-shab, wherein you cooked our own meat in a steaming pot, adding all kinds of vegetables. It was then served by waitresses in kimonos, who opened the sliding paper door, fell to their knees, filled our dishes, as we ate sitting on the floor, while listening to a thirteen-string Japanese harpist. It was an event.

Then we joined an all-day tour to Nara, led by an inexhaustibly informed guide, who since no one seemed to ask him questions, spent the better part of the day responding to all the queries I propounded. His name, when translated, meant "Rice." In Nara we walked through unique shrines, some thirteen hundred years old. I noted writings on each of the *torii* ("gates") and learned that they were the names of donors. I laughingly commented to someone that the Jews in the United

States were obviously not the originators of memorializations. I also recalled that at Epidaurus, Greece, rich visitors who recovered from illnesses, put their names on sculptured monuments, commissioned from famous Greek artists. In Greece, I was told that this was an additional form of therapy for the donors. We watched the deer graze in the parks in Nara, a symbol for the city. The deer in the Kasruga shrine were considered sacred messengers of the gods. One would be severely prosecuted for killing them. One shrine had thousands of hanging bronze and concrete lanterns, again with the names of the donors. This proved an ingenious way of decorating and lighting the park with its huge cedar trees, and paying for the illumination. We visited a half-dozen shrines, each different architecturally and having its own singular history.

Back in Kyoto that night, we had a steak dinner at Suehiro, eating matsuzaka beef (Kobe), the cattle were fattened on rice and rubbed down with sake and beer to distribute the fat. The steak was then marinated in onions, carrots, celery, and salad oil for 24 hours. Despite all the preparation in raising the cattle and preparing the meat after slaughtering, it was not up to our best American beef.

After spending another day visiting more shrines and the Imperial Palace, we dined at our hotel with Shichiro Matsu, a professor of economics at Soshisha University in Kyoto, who was accompanied by his wife, a writer of a Japanese column on advice to the lovelorn, like Beatrice Fairfax in the United States. Matsu had studied at Wisconsin. Sam had met him when he was deputy chief of mission at the U.S. Embassy in Tokyo in 1953. He wore Western dress, she a kimono. We thought they might like Western food for a change, but instead we sat on the floor for an evening of talk and Japanese food. He was liberal in his social viewpoint. She resented the fact that her son had chosen a wife without first consulting her.

We told the professor that we were interested in old Japanese prints portraying the excessively overweight Japanese Sumo wrestlers. Though it was 10 P.M., he took us in his car to meet Kondo, who owned the famous Red Lantern Japanese Print Studio. Diminuitive Kondo, in his early seventies, sat in his kimono on a stepped-up pedestal in the middle of the room, while we sat on small, well-worn benches in a semicircle around him. For a half-hour he established his credentials—who he was, how he had become the foremost authority on prints, and why he was sought out by serious collectors. For another half-hour, he showed us a book detailing, who his customers were. They included the Metropolitan Museum of Art, Lawrence Rockefeller, Mrs. Walter Heller, Frank Lloyd Wright, James Michener, and Oliver Statler, the author of the best-selling *Japanese Inn*. We wondered whether we had any right to be in this shop, and whether we could afford what he would show. He tried to put us off with a variety of other works, but finally at 11:30 P.M., he placed before us two woodblock prints, magnificent, dated 1792 and 1841, and we bought them at the unbelievable price of $25 each. We might have gotten them for less by bargaining, but we were satisfied after the long lecture and display of other prints, and the hour. (In 1985, each print was reputed by dealers to be worth in excess of $1,000.)

The evening was not over. The professor and his wife, who were now enamored of us, invited us to their modern, not Japanese, house for tea and cakes. We were served while sitting on chairs at a regular table. They even invited us to stay with them in their guestroom on our next visit to Kyoto.

As in our conversation with the German industrialists on the train to Kyoto, Professor Matsui indicated that the U.S.-Allied destruction of Japan's entire industrial, commercial, transportation, and waterfront infrastructure had given Japan a head start in reordering its total economy with a new plant and a different approach to labor relations, supplanting the traditional obligation of an employer to his workers irrespective of their productivity. Thus Japan was able to compete with any country in the world, including the United States. I recalled this conversation in the days when I was writing this volume, because these developments were a major cause for America's loss of many industries and the overwhelming foreign trade imbalance.

We had been urged to stay in a Japanese inn in the city of Takamatsu on the island of Shikoku, off the mainland from Kobe. We took a train, second-class, from Kyoto to Kobe, and found it comfortable at one-third the cost. We arrived an hour before our boat sailed, but on reaching the landing, to our chagrin, we learned that our tickets were for the following day. The huge ferry staring us in the face was sold out, and there was no way we could get on board. We called several hotels, but they were filled, because three tourist ships had docked in the harbor. Luckily, I had two addresses in Kobe. One should always be prepared for an emergency. I first called J. Gotlieb, a businessman, whose name had been given to me by Rabbi Philip Goodman of the National Jewish Welfare Board, as the leader of the local Jewish community. There was no answer. I called the other person, Hans Selig, a friend of Abraham Abramson, and learned that he was in Gemany, but had received a letter from Abramson indicating that we might visit Kobe. Selig's associate told me that I should not worry, that he would find a hotel for us. He came in a cab, booked us at the Oriental Hotel, the second-best, which we thought was pretty awful, although we learned later that Vice-President Richard Nixon had stayed there a few years before. We wandered through this interesting industrial seaport, ate Japanese food, played pachinko, a "cursed" game introduced by the Chinese and Koreans, which had completely seduced the Japanese. We called Gotlieb, whom we found at home this time; he told us he was busy that night, but would pick us up early the following morning and spend every minute with us until our boat left. We spent the evening at a night club, the Kantino, with a scenic view of the city and inland sea and were entertained with singers, dancers, magicians, good music, and so-so Japanese food.

J. Gotlieb, a youngish-looking man in the forties, appeared at 9:30 A.M. Originally from Pinsk, he had arrived in China in 1937, then moved to Japan, was incarcerated during the war, left for Israel when the war ended, but returned to Kobe in 1950 to enter the pearl business. He was married, had two children, a daughter studying in Switzerland, and a bright boy of thirteen about to become Bar Mitzvah. He liked the Chinese but was suspicious of the Japanese. He was deeply interested in Jewish life. We first went to the Kobe Club for drinks, then a tour of the city, then to the Jewish center, where two Israeli teachers taught fifteen students. Kobe had thirty Jewish families with a count of seventy individuals. Gotlieb drove us to his home, where we drank wine, ate kichel and honey cake. He showed us his extensive collection of *netskes*, miniature ivory pieces, gave us a number of his excellent Japanese prints, and wanted me to market a pearl polish which he claimed to have perfected. He just couldn't do enough for us, even as we said our goodbyes at the boat landing and boarded the *Karenai Maru*. We had a superb lunch aboard with clam soup, raw fish, smoked fish, tempura, vegetables, bean curd, rice, tea, and a pear. The four-hour voyage to the island allowed us to mingle with the Japanese. We were the only non-Japanese passengers. They were most attentive to us, but communication was difficult.

Our hotel, the Tokiwa Honkan, was a phenomenon. We were first met at the pier by a hotel representative, drove though a busy city with its 250,000 people. We approached an unprepossessing building in a cul-de-sac. At the tiny office entrance, we deposited our shoes, and entered a veritable Japanese fairyland. Little bridges over waterways filled with gold and red carp. The walls decorated with excellent, traditional Japanese screens, samurai and geisha clothing, the carpeted walkways separated from the walls with gravel and greenery. We entered our room with its sliding paper doors, with tatamis on the floor, a large low table with pillow backs and arm rests. Several rolled wall paintings decorated the small sitting room, separated from the larger area by a bamboo screen. The only incongruity was a TV set. The waitress in her kimono, always falling to her knees, served us tea. The hostess, who spoke some English, asked us if we wanted to bathe. Emma was concerned, since this was a Japanese inn, that we'd have to get into the larger tubs with other guests. (There was only one other guest, a foreigner, but not American.) "Oh, no. We no do that," replied our hostess. We went into an unusual large bathing room. One wall was an aquarium filled with a variety of fish. Another was a rock wall with hot water tumbling into the oversize tub. We first soaped ourselves, then rinsed off the soap with a showerlike hose, and then soaked luxuriously in the miniature swimming pool. When dried, we donned kimonos and slippers.

When asked what we would like for dinner, we could not read the Japanese menu. Half-facetiously, I turned to Statler's *Japanese Inn*, which listed the menu for each day that the Emperor stayed in that old Kyoto Inn, which he attended during its three hundredth anniversary. We were served in our room, sitting on the floor, small portions (the Emperor apparently was not a big eater) of tempura, baked fish with a delicious sauce, barbecued chicken, tiny vegetables, rice, fruit, ice cream (in combination, enough for a king). Everything was superb except the rice tea.

We put on our Western clothes that evening and went to a movie, the only entertainment in the city. One short piece was *Peg's Show*, an old-fashioned, lascivious burlesque with bumps and bare tits. It was followed by *Red River* with John Wayne, which we had seen in the States in 1947, in Paris in French in 1949, and now in Japanese in 1962. That night we slept on the floor with a head rest. It was quite comfortable.

Our hostess took us to a famous Bunshindo lacquer factory, where we observed men and women applying twenty-four coats of lacquer, brushed down after each application, ending with a covering shiny and hard. They earned $3 per day. We bought two sets of three-tiered, flower-decorated lacquered food bowls including a spoon, which we cherish among our displayed treasures. We also purchased a variety of other large, flower-decorated plates. All are museum pieces.

We awaited our next Emperor's dinner with great expectancy. Sake, clear soup with oysters, prawns with green peppers tempura-style, seaweed, tuna and sea bream shashimi with a tiny radish and baby cucumber covered with green sauce, charcoal-baked baby eggplant with sesame and soy sauce, tiny pickles and cucumbers, rice, fresh soy beans, melon and green tea. Who could ask for anything more? So we got a taste of a Japan off the beaten track, with its crowded alleys and quick-walking people, its lovely parks. Surprisingly, most people wore Western dress.

Hiroshima

We left the island on a ferry crossing the Inland Sea to Uno on the mainland. On a train to Okayama, we ate the best grapes we had ever tasted, akin to the Belgian variety. Boarded another train to Hiroshima, one of the main objects of our going to Japan. Our modern hotel was only a few hundred yards from the epicenter, where the atom bomb fell on August 15, 1945, at 8:15 A.M. The entire area has been rebuilt, largely in the form of a park with various monuments, but the ribs of one building still stood as evidence of the cataclysm. One can visualize the devastation that was wrought in large photographs in a museum. The Children's Peace Memorial was covered with paper doves. It was a site of frequent demonstrations by pacifistic students. As we walked the streets, a few people told us in English to "go home."

We took a tour of the surrounding countryside, visiting shrines. We met many foreigners, including Americans, all of whom had, as we did, a sense of guilt about this horrible event.

Hiroshima was chosen as the first target for the bomb because no one in the United States had any sentimental attachment to this southern city. Henry Stimson, our Secretary of War, was first advised to use Kyoto.

According to Lewis L. Strauss in *Men and Decisions* (1962), pp. 190–191, "Secretary Stimson, when he learned of it, interposed his personal veto.... Kyoto was the cultural and religious center of old Japan. There were located the delicately beautiful palaces of the former emperors... Hundreds of ancient temples and their shrines." The suggestion that the bomb be exploded over an uninhabited area was rejected by the laboratory group, as they "did not think exploding one of these things as a fire cracker over a desert was likely to be very impressive." Hiroshima and then Nagasaki became the targets, with horrendous loss of lives.

We visited a hospital where I had an introduction from the director of Mount Sinai Hospital in New York, a Federation agency, which had taken a group of Japanese victims of the bomb for treatment. The director of the Hiroshima hospital did not show us any patients, but we received a graphic picture of the serious medical problems that had already arisen, and the many more that would occur in future years, perhaps for generations.

As we were walking near our hotel, a Japanese man approached and asked whether he could walk with us, as he wanted to practice his English, which he taught in a local school. We asked him to dine with us. He said he was occupied, but would visit with us after dinner. We found the Amagi restaurant, where we ate twenty varieties of tempura, the best in our experience, a very light batter and deep-fried quickly in sunflower seed oil. It was topped off with the inevitable sashimi and tea.

Yasuhiro Fujikawa came back that evening. He had been a child when the bomb exploded. Luckily his family lived in the mountains several miles away, but overlooking the city, so they witnessed the awesome scene. The waves of radiation did not reach them. As their lives were spared, they became intensely religious. They converted to the Tenrikyo sect, a movement founded by a woman in the nineteenth century. It did not have the medical reservations nor the austerity of Mrs. Mary Baker Eddy's Christian Science movement. Its ceremonial use of song and dance was reminiscent of Hassidism. The church demanded large tithes. Each day an adherent volunteered his services to a good cause. Yasuhiro massaged patients in a hospital. That is why he could not have dinner with us. We roamed over many subjects, including American and English authors. To repay us for giving our time by speaking English with him, he offered us his gift of a massage for both of us. We courteously declined. He promised to send me literature of the movement, and for years I received books and letters from him. I, in turn, kept sending him material on Judaism and Israel.

Tokyo

The eleven-hour train ride back to Tokyo was a scenic event, but much too long and tiring. In Tokyo, we met Dorothy Brickman, a dynamic woman from the United States, who was the assistant director of the USO. She had a backbreaking program lined up for the balance of our stay in Japan.

I had lunch with the president of the Jewish Community Center and arranged to have two seats reserved for Erev Rosh Hashanah. He said we would be billed. We sat down to prayer that evening at a typical traditional service, with men and women separated. The *shammes* called me out and asked me to pay him 3,000 yen, the price of both tickets, before I returned to my pew. He would not allow me to wait until the service was over. So I paid him in shul. After services, we ate a typical Ashkenazi holiday dinner in the center and talked with a number of people, mostly Americans, who were working in Japan. The rest of the worshippers were of European descent, mostly refugees from Germany, with several Japanese women present, wives of American soldiers.

I had promised both Rabbi Philip Goodman of the JWB and Dorothy Brickman that I would accept any assignment over the holidays. I gave a sermon on the first day of Rosh Hashanah at the Yokota air base. Rabbi Charles Zimmelman was the chaplain. On the second day, I made a similar presentation at the Yokohama naval base, where Rabbi Leonard Cahan was the chaplain. In both sermons, I wove in the biblical sections which were part of the prayer service. I referred to our moving, emotional experience at Hiroshima, ending with the benedictory words that we must find ways and means of avoiding armed conflicts, otherwise the use of this volatile weapon would destroy mankind. No militarists arose in either sanctuary to challenge this position. In both congregations, there were Jewish soldiers and sailors with Japanese wives and children, the Japanese having converted to Judaism.

We sandwiched in a visit to the shrine in Kamakura, a one-day trip to Nikko, an evening at a geisha house with two Japanese businessmen, friends of Abraham Abramson. These men did not tell us much about Japan, but questioned me about the Korean economy, because they hoped to establish a branch of their electrical plants in that country. The geishas were picturesque women to be with, but the scene was artificial, including silly games. Were it not for the excellent food and good conversation with the Japanese men, it might have been a boring evening.

Dorothy Brickman arranged two meetings for me with different groups of Japanese social workers, who wanted my opinion on what they should do about the break-up of the traditional Japanese family, due to changes induced by U.S. officials in altering the laws of primogeniture, whereby the older son now inherited only his portion of the father's legacy, and thus no longer had complete responsibility for his mother and siblings. They wanted me to tell them how to deal with the growing problem of alcoholism, with the increase in prostitution, and the pitiable problems of the aged. The latter had been laid off from jobs which before U.S. intervention would have been theirs until they died, or if unable to work the factory owners had to provide for them for life. Now they were a huge number, and the country was trying to fill in their time more constructively by busing them all over the country to visit shrines, palaces, and parks to occupy their empty hours. I unhesitatingly gave them my or the American point of view on everything, later sent them books, pamphlets, and outlines on these and other subjects.

We barely had time to buy beautiful kimonos for each of us, second-hand but in perfect condition, cleaned and sold at a tiny cost. We flew back via Alaska, disembarked at Fairbanks in bitter cold and high snow, covering ourselves with numerous blankets, finally arrived in New York in the morning exhausted, slept all day, then that night went to a party in New Jersey, planned for in advance of our leaving the United States. We arrived a little late, dressed in our Japanese costumes to the delight of many friends, eating our dinner with chopsticks and regaling everyone with our adventure in the Far East.

11

Ethiopia: 1965

IN THE TEN years since we met our first Falashas in Israel, I had been trying to learn more about Ethiopian Jewry. I read everything that was available and attempted to elicit information from Jewish organizations that I thought ought to be concerned with their welfare. People were beginning to turn to me for information, which I did not possess. Emma and I decided to go to Ethiopia to see for ourselves under what conditions they were living. While I offered to pay my own way, I couldn't get any Jewish organization, including the Joint Distribution Committee, to give me credentials stating that I was representing them on an exploratory mission. I made some contacts in Ethiopia, so that I would have assistance on arrival in the villages.

Less than a week before leaving, while putting a box in my car during a few days of visiting with our son Michael and his family in Baltimore, I pulled something in my lower back. I had a painful ride back to Pelham. The next day, Monday, I went to see Dr. Joseph Milgram at the Hospital for Joint Diseases. He told me I would just have to postpone the trip, that I needed a couple of weeks of bed rest. "Doctor, make believe that I am the leading dancer in the Rockettes and that I must perform Friday night." Telling me I was "crazy," he suggested that I buy a Swedish salt pack and put hot compresses on the aching portion of my body. A day and a half passed as I suffered the agony and messiness of this scalding-hot treatment, but the back was no better. Wednesday I went to see Dr. Joe again. He measured me for a corset, which was sewn and ready on Thursday noon. That night we attended a party celebrating Sadie Fink's seventieth birthday, Sadie being Anita's mother, Anita being Ramon's wife. The pain had eased with the corset in place. On Friday at 7:30 P.M., with the corset tight and feeling no pain, we flew off to Athens, our first stop on the way to Ethiopia.

Our neighbors in Pelham, the Berkowitz family, with three children, had been vacationing in Greece. They picked us up at the airport early in the morning. We slept in their room for a few hours. Then arose, the corset still intact, for a tour of Athens, a city which we had grown to love. We stopped in a tavern and Dr. Carl Berkowitz, who enjoys brandy, on learning that the best cost only 7 cents a drink, invited all the bystanders to drink at his expense. Then to a fabulous restaurant on the sea, dining on shrimp, squid, red mullet, and lobsters. After the sumptuous dinner, they put us on the midnight plane for Addis Ababa. During the brief stopover at the Cairo airport, the cheapest duty-free port in the world, we loaded ourselves with Scotch whisky and perfume to be used as gifts in Ethiopia and Israel.

We flew over most of Ethiopia above the clouds, but a half-hour from Addis Ababa, the plane was in sunshine and then in rain. We could see a green countryside. Addis was a busy city. Men and women in their shamas, a white gauzelike material, walked the streets, despite the rain, their heads wrapped in the same cloth. We became used to these sudden showers, for August was still the rainy season. We later learned that not enough rain was falling, which meant that food would be less plentiful. At the hotel I took off the corset after having worn it for four days. There was no longer any pain. The therapy had worked. Since then the corset has reposed in a trunk in our attic.

The Ethiopia Hotel was only second-class, but quite good. Not having slept for nearly two days, we went to bed and were sleeping at 4 P.M. when we were awakened by a ringing phone. It was Shalom Shelemay, originally from Aden, a British citizen and the leading Jew in the small Addis Jewish community, if you exclude the sizable Israeli presence. Shelemay was an importer-exporter of different goods, including leather and auto products. Rabbi Harold Gordon, the executive director of the New York Board of Rabbis, a good friend, who had visited Ethiopia the year before, had written and cabled Shelemay to do everything possible for us, as we were important American Jews. Shelemay and his youngest son, Jack, were waiting for us in the lobby. We dressed hurriedly. Over our first cup of Ethiopian coffee with its interesting flavor, we told them about ourselves.

Coffee originally was grown in the province of Kaffa in Ethiopia, found its way to Saudi Arabia, and the Portuguese brought it to Europe, Central and South America, to make it one of the favorite beverages around the world.

Since it was Rosh Hodesh, the Shelemays invited us to the synagogue, a compound near their apartment house, which looked as if it might have been an abandoned mosque. We climbed to the second floor. It was poorly furnished. The prayerbooks were tattered. Women sat in a back room. About twenty people were present for *Mincha* and *Maariv*. All looked like they might have come from somewhere in the Middle East. There were no Ethiopian Jews nor any Israelis at the service. We went outside to pray directly to the New Moon, an eerie, romantic, ancient form of Jewish worship.

There were twenty Jewish families in Addis, mostly from Aden, a few Europeans. There were also one hundred Israelis, part of the embassy complement, for Israel had many interests in Ethiopia. The Israelis did not always intermingle with the Addis Jewish community. The Shelemays had ten children, all grown up, evenly divided between male and female. Some had married Israelis. Their families lived in Israel and in England. Initially, they had fled from Aden when the Moslems started persecuting Jews after the creation of the State of Israel. A non-Jewish guide told us that the Shelemays were well regarded, as they employed many natives and treated them well.

We ate a good meal at the hotel, which was only spoiled when a passing waiter dropped a bottle of red wine at our feet and discolored my tan suit and Emma's dress. When it came time to pay our bill, we found a cleaning charge on our account, and I had to argue with the top management before this item was removed.

We shopped with Jack Shelemay in the huge market and purchased a number of naive paintings. With his haggling, they cost us practically nothing. A guide took us around the city to see the museum, where pictures of Solomon and Sheba dominated everything on the walls, as these royal figures still do with contemporary artists. The public buildings, old and new (the oldest ones were less than a century in age), were attractive architecturally. Yet two blocks away from the wide, tree-lined boulevard and the imposing structures, one was amongst slums, mud streets, homes without floors, lights, or toilets. We drove to the attractive U.S. Embassy and they graciously mailed all of our purchases to Pelham. Africa Hall with murals by Tekle was an outstanding building. It had not yet become the scene for attacks on Israel by African nations. The thin air due to the elevation of Addis—at its highest point, 8,500 feet above sea level—made it difficult for me to climb the steps of some buildings.

We dined with nine Shelemays at their eldest son's home, a well-furnished apartment with French and Chinese designs. There were no Ethiopian art objects. The meal was Italian cuisine. A number of their Jewish friends were invited after dinner. There was talk of building a new $80,000 synagogue. It was never constructed, because the elder Shelemay died a few years after our visit and there was no one else who could have given and raised the funds. The group read books, were interested in music, were well traveled. They were eager to know about American Jews, for none of them had been to the United States.

When we told them that our only purpose in coming to Ethiopia was to see the Beta Israel, they sought to avoid the subject. Not only were none of the Ethiopian Jews permitted to worship in their synagogue, but no one had ever bothered to visit their villages in the north. None appeared to be concerned with their welfare. They somehow managed to avoid answering any of our questions. Shelemay wanted to know whether we would be interested in meeting the Emperor Haile Selassie, whom he considered a personal friend, and they were surprised when we said we had no such intention. Apparently other Jewish visitors grabbed at such opportunities. All we knew about the Emperor was that he claimed lineage from Solomon and Sheba, that he had the title "The Lion of Judah," that he showed little interest in the condition of the more than 30 million inhabitants, distributing his favors to the court, the military, and the church. He had little interest in the fate of Ethiopian Jewry, although he appeased Jewish visitors by pretending to be concerned.

As we left the Shelemays' house, one of the men, who had said little, told me that he was the treasurer of a fund provided by Israel to help support Ethiopian Jewish schools. Several years later I learned that the money actually came from the Torah Department (traditional) of the Jewish Agency, which had kept this a well-guarded secret since 1951. They must have considered the Beta Israel Jews long before the rabbinical statements of 1973 and 1975. It also proved that the Jews in Addis knew about the Falashas, the pejorative term used by their non-Jewish neighbors since the seventeenth century, a term meaning "landless," i.e., strangers in their own country. They were either ashamed or reluctant to acknowledge any relationship.

We left for the north on a well-used and deeply dented twin-propellor DC-3 (Dakota) airplane, that had no toilets, except a one hole opening in a small room, through which one could see the ground. We were served a sandwich lunch out of a brown paper bag and coffee was poured from a cracked enamel pot. Not elegant or hygienic. We ate and drank and survived. The passengers—thirty of us—included a few tourists, some government and church officials, and a couple of natives in nondescript costumes. The plane stopped en route to Gondar some three hundred miles away on grass airfields at Debra Markos, Bahar Dar (Lake Tana), and Debra Tabar. As we debarked everytime in the treeless countryside, bare-footed natives in ragged dress rushed up to the plane to gaze at the passengers, but not to beg. Cows, sheep, goats could be seen roving the never-ending plateau with sown fields, tukkels (mud huts) with thatched roofs. A few men, tall, lean, carried guns or spears, but we could not determine whether they were there to protect us or themselves. We saw our first Ethiopian Moslems. We noted the elaborate handshakes and kissing that marked their greetings.

We landed on another grass field in Gondar, the capital of the province, and the capital of the country before Addis Ababa. We were met by Dr. Mario Felzer, with whom I had corresponded, his wife and tiny child. Mario in his early forties, born in Poland, educated in Argentina, and a citizen of Israel, was working for the World Health Organization in Gondar and supervising three Ethiopian Jewish clinics. He was jovial, articulate, and attractive. He drove us through villages, past military barracks, into the city of Gondar, which the Italians had rebuilt during their occupation from 1936 to 1941, past a crowded open market, the street of prostitutes, to our hotel, the Integie Menen, perched on a hill overlooking the city and valleys below. It was built and operated by an Italian, and had a garden which provided vegetables and flowers. There was a pool without water. Toilets were in the hall. Showers were out of doors. This was the best hostelry in town.

We toured Fasilie Castle, built by the Emperor in the seventeenth century, employing Ethiopian Jewish laborers. For centuries the Jews had been builders of major monuments, currently important tourist attractions. We visited churches, one with paintings on the doors and walls, on which all the saints had white faces.

We stopped at Walleka, a small Jewish village a few kilometers outside of Gondar, where Yona Bogale was born. It was an unsanitary site. Clothing was far from clean and mostly ragged. There was a *kohen*, poorly garbed. He too had to make a living by working in the fields. Their faces were animated, often beautiful, with those singular Ethiopian eyes that made it easy to identify an Ethiopian, and lighted up as the doctor and we approached. He reminded them to brush their beautiful white teeth, which seemed not to have suffered despite the absence of brushes and paste. They cleaned their teeth, as we have seen natives around the world do, with sharp sticks.

Ethiopian Jews lived on land rented from absentee landowners or the church, the largest landowner. They paid taxes to the province, so only about one-third was left of all they produced from the land or the few cattle they possessed. In Walleka, some had been taught to make primitive sculptured objects, which they sold to the few tourists who occasionally came that way. We bought a lot of these poorly fired pieces, most of which were broken before they reached Pelham. Besides farming, they wove cloth, baskets, made utilitarian pottery objects to carry water and store grain. Some were iron workers, making knives, spears, and plowshares. Others fashioned items out of hides. Despite these diversified activities, they lived on the verge of starvation. The price of their goods was usually set by the purchaser in the markets, because they were Jews, at the mercy of the buyer without recourse to anyone. In 1965, the per capita income for all Ethiopians was $65 (U.S.) per year and probably lower for the Jews.

We had prepared ourselves thoroughly by reading books and articles and obtaining first-hand reports from a few eyewitnesses, but no matter how we tried we could not see the romantic and exotic aspects described by many writers and visitors. Evaluating the scene at first hand, we saw only misery. We came back to Israel and the United States with a different version of the condition of the Ethiopian Jews and a vow to help them in Ethiopia, but we were already of a mind that the only salvation for them was in aliyah to Israel.

Most visitors, we learned, came for a few hours, saw one village, and left some money or some objects, occasionally a toy Torah like those carried by children in the United States on Simchat Torah. Most visitors were overwhelmed with the enormity of the problem, and after discussing it with officials in the Jewish world, were discouraged and abandoned any thought of providing continuing aid as individuals or through their local organizations. A few sent money in small amounts from time to time, but this was never for long. Hence the Jews of Ethiopia realized that any promises made by visitors were ephemeral. We were reminded of such short-lived offers by Dr. Felzer and Yona Bogale.

With Dr. Felzer, I visited the village and clinic at Gedebeque, some seventy-five kilometers north of Gondar, at an elevation of ten thousand feet. The gravel road built by the Italians traversed a constantly rising plateau, with mountains in the distance, comparable to the approach to Denver, Colorado, from the east. We saw occasional villages, cattle, goats, and sheep, ragged children, some naked, adults with spears and guns. With rare exceptions, most were not Jews. Gedebeque was a mixed village. Since it was on the road, there were some rudimentary shops. Some of the huts had tin roofs, always a sign of somewhat better economic conditions. The farmers sowed their fields by hand. Few had oxen. None had fertilizer except human night soil. They complained that the insufficient rain would mean poorer and fewer crops. Cattle, when ready for market, were driven hundreds of miles north to the abattoirs located in Asmara. When we were in that city later, we saw a kosher one. In the villages, when starved, a non-Jew will even cut a piece out of a live animal and eat it raw to satisfy his hunger. Jews were forbidden by the Torah to follow this practice. Natives were severely punished, even put to death, for committing such a crime. The same extreme penalty went for rustling animals, and recently even the killing of wild animals belatedly came under the government's protection.

When we arrived at the clinic at 7 A.M., there were already 150 patients waiting for us on a cold, damp morning. Some had walked 50 kilometers. Some brought sick people on improvised stretchers. Several fathers carried their children around their necks, protecting them from the drizzle with an umbrella.

A smallpox epidemic had broken out in the vicinity. The medical staff was administering vaccinations. I was taught the technique and helped out until we ran out of vaccine. The clinic was run by Getahun Telahun, a twenty-four-year-old Ethiopian Jew, married, with a child, who had as much training for his title of "dresser" as a beginning practical nurse, yet he delivered babies when the midwives were not around, performed surgery, and administered sophisticated drugs by reading the instructions on the bottle label. It was hoped he could be sent to Israel for a year and a half training program, after which he would return to Ethiopia to direct the clinics more professionally, in the event that no doctor was available. Emma and I agreed to fund him if he was sent to Israel. (He finally was brought to Israel by the American Association for Ethiopian Jews, along with his family in 1986.) Other diseases that we witnessed were scabies, eye ailments which often ended with blindness, parasites, and gonorrhea, although this was a rare disease amongst Jews because of strict sexual prohibitions and the rejection of the widespread prostitution found elsewhere in Ethiopia.

For lunch I was served engera, which looked, tasted, and felt like a sour buckwheat pancake. I broke off spongy pieces and dipped them into a pot of wat, composed of onions, hard-boiled eggs, chunks of chicken, and peanut oil spiced with red-hot pepper. I couldn't eat even the first bite. It literally burned my mouth. Messengers apparently were dispatched to other villages I visited later, where they prepared the wat without the red pepper. A *kohen* offered me a bottle of Arak. I could see dead flies at the bottom of the bottle. Out of courtesy, knowing it was alcoholic, and with the doctor's approval, I took a tiny sip. Nothing happened.

We stopped for a second time at Walleka, where we found the Drs. Mollinoff and Rauscher, our flight companions, and I enlisted their aid immediately in raising $1,000 for Telahun's education.

Fleas were everywhere, infesting my clothes and skin. Each day, as I returned from a trip, I would take all my clothes off before entering our bedroom, took an outdoor shower, and had the maid wash and iron all my clothing before wearing them again. It took many days before I was rid of the fleas.

Another shaking trip by Land Rover was made to Ambober, the largest of the Jewish villages. This time there was no smooth, gravel road for most of the forty kilometers. During the last half, I wondered whether we would make it at all. Rains had made deep mud ruts of the path the vehicle tried to traverse. Only the expert navigation of Felzer made it possible to move forward and upward. We came to a waddi, which had been flooded. Not daunted and with the help of a group of *kohanim* on their way to Ambober, we filled the ditch with large rocks and finally crossed the shallow stream.

Ambober was distinguished by a three-room, primitively furnished medical clinic, which boasted a stone floor. Two school buildings, of one and two rooms respectively, with some rickety wooden benches, a few tables, not too many books nor other materials, provided the most advanced school program up to the sixth grade. One other village school went to the fourth grade. An assortment of twenty other schools, some

Graenum's father, H. I. Berger (1906)

Graenum's parents—Bessie and Harry Isaac Berger (1918)

Maternal grandfather—Isaac Cohen (1890)

Paternal grandmother—Nachama Yochevet Berger (1907)

House where Graenum was born, John St. (1908)

Father, Graenum and Spotty, Washburn St. (1912)

Sam and Graenum, Washburn St. (1915)

Rachel, Father, Sam and Graenum, Washburn St. (1912)

Rachel and Graenum, Washburn St. (1914)

Graenum and nephew, Robert Finn (1918)

Graenum (front, second from left) Captain, Gloversville YMHA Basketball Team (1923–24)

Graenum, University of Missouri (1928)

Mr. and Mrs. Graenum Berger

announce their marriage

on

October Sixth, Nineteen hundred twenty-eight

at

Kansas City, Missouri

Rabbi Samuel S. Mayerberg

Miss Emma Finestein   Mr. Graenum Berger

At Home
June First
Albany, New York

Wedding announcement (1928)

After their marriage, Gloversville. (1929)

Milton, Mother, Graenum and Sam, Bleeker St. (1930)

Graenum, President, Jewish Student Organization, University of Missouri. (1930)

JEWISH STUDENT ORGANIZATION

GRAENUM BERGER, President

DR. I. KEYFITZ, Faculty Advisor

The Jewish Student Organization was established on the University of Missouri campus fifteen years ago, when a group of earnest college men and women felt the need of perpetuating the wealth of Judaic culture, which had made up their culture for almost six thousand years.

Through the co-operation of the Hebrew Union College of Cincinnati, Ohio, and the active participation of its faculty leader, Dr. I. Keyfitz, the organization has been able to maintain its high purpose, and join in with the general spirit and work of the Students' Religious Council.

The organization holds weekly meetings on Sunday night at the Bible College of the University. No business is transacted at the meetings; they are solely for the purpose of presenting interesting programs in the form of lectures and other material of interest which has a bearing on the faith. Rabbis from nearby towns, members of the faculty of the Bible college, and others are secured for the lectures.

The entire relationship in the club concerns the practice, rejuvenation, and interest of all the members for which the organization exists.

Brochure—Student Religious Council, University of Missouri. (1930)

Jewish Community Center of Staten Island, N. Y. Graenum was the Executive Director. (1932–38) (Courtesy JCC of SI)

Graenum with Day Campers on Staten Island. Ramon is the youngster with Hazel (Cohen) Fleischman. (1933)

Graenum was leader of the Cardinal Club at Bronx House (1940)

Ambassador Henry Morgenthau, Sr., and Mrs. Josephine Morgenthau, co-founders of Bronx House. Standing: Mrs. Lillian Riegelman, President (1942–45), Graenum, Headworker (1938–49) (photo in 1942)

Graenum playing baseball at Camp Bronx House (1940)

Camp Bronx House, Copake, N. Y. Graenum was Director (1940–48) and Emma was the Administrative Assistant.

Graenum teaching at Education-Social Work Seminar in Germany (1949)

New York Federation of Jewish Philanthropies—Usdan Center of the Performing Arts, a major creation of Graenum, when he was the Consultant on Jewish Community Centers, Camps, Day Camp and Jewish Education (1949–73). Performance by the orchestra, chorus and ballet. (Photo courtesy Usdan Center)

Usdan Center—Art Complex (Courtesy Usdan Center)

A Ballet Studio at Usdan Center, which bears placque honoring Graenum. (Courtesy Usdan Center)

Graenum with Wiener Center students (1973) (photo by Herbert Halweil)

Graenum presenting check to Milton Weill, President of Federation, for Center bearing his name. (1963) (photo by Alexander Archer)

Leonard Block awarding Lehman Medal and $1000 to Graenum at Federation (1968)

Graenum was the Founding First President of the Pelham Jewish Center in 1953

Graenum conducting dedication service at the Pelham Jewish Center (1954)

Graenum and Emma at Pelham Jewish Center annual banquet in 1955. Others left to right: Ethel and Nat Lax, Ruth and Joseph Mandell, Sonia and Tim Gidal.

Graenum (fifth from left) leader of Israel summer seminar (1959)

In front of the new Jerusalem YM-YWHA (1968) (Photo by R. M. Kneller)

Miriam Ephraim presenting Emma and Graenum to the Israeli President, Zalman Shazar (1968) (Photo by R. M. Kneller)

Graenum and Emma in the swimming pool dedicated to them at the Jerusalem YM-YWHA (1968) (Photo by R. M. Kneller)

Graenum visiting Korean Military Educational Center (1962) His brother Sam was then the Ambassador to Korea.

Graenum, as always, writing notes wherever he is traveling.

Village on border of North Korea (1962) (Photo by Graenum Berger)

Ambassador Samuel D. Berger, Graenum, Emma, Henry Kissinger and Ambassador Ellsworth Bunker's grand daughter, Patsy Gentil. Saigon, South Vietnam. (1971)

The day Graenum first met Ethiopian Jews, Kfar Batya, Israel (1955)

Graenum with Ethiopian Kohanim. Ambober, Ethiopia. (1965)

Graenum founded American Association for Ethiopian Jews in 1974 to provide relief, rescue and resettlement. Listening to A. N. Pritzker at AAEJ fund-raising dinner in Chicago, where both were speakers. (1984)

Emma and Graenum with the Wube-Hollander family in Herzylia, Israel. (1979)

Graenum greeting Eddie Cantor at dedication of Cantor Outdoor Playhouse, Surprise Lake Camp, Cold Springs, NY (1955)

Graenum and Emma with Frances and Rabbi Isaac N. Trainin at Khan Israeli Night Club and Theatre. Jerusalem (1975)

Graenum presenting Yona Bogale, venerable leader of Ethiopian Jews with Kiddush cup on behalf of the AAEJ in Petah Tikvah, Israel. (1982)

Graenum with Baruch Tegegne, rescuer of Ethiopian Jews, at AAEJ Conference, Washington, DC. (1984)

Reuben M. Greenberg, Chief of Police, Charleston, S.C. A Black American Jew, who Graenum met and wrote about. (Photo by William Murton)

Graenum inscribing his book "Black Jews in America" (1978) (Photo by Herbert Halweil)

Graenum receiving an Honorary Doctoral Degree from Yeshiva University. (1973) Other recipients included: Elie Wiesel, Senator Henry M. Jackson and Dr. Jean Piaget.

Graenum responding at his New York Federation retirement dinner, holding Sterling Silver Etrog Container designed by Ludwig Wolpert. (1973) (Photo by Herbert Halweil)

Graenum with family and friends at New York Federation Retirement dinner. (1973)

(Photo by Herbert Halweil)

Milton, Graenum, Sam, Harriette, Emma and Margaret. Three brothers and their wives. Pelham (1966)

Graenum, Rachel, Milton and Sam (1955)

Graenum and Emma "remarried" on their 50th wedding anniversary at the home of Carl and Genia Urbont, Larchmont, N.Y. (1978)

Milton, Harriette, Graenum, Emma, Betty Lee and Sam—Washington, DC. (1969)

Graenum chanting prayer for bread at a Berger family Simcha. (1976)

Ceremonial objects given as gifts to Graenum

Playground established in Jerusalem in memory of Graenum's brother, Samuel D. Berger (1983) (Photo by Brian P. Hendler)

(caption) Books Graenum has written

ADVENTURES
IN GROUP WORK

SELECTED WRITINGS

by

Graenum Berger

November, 1948

Graenum Berger

speaks on the

JEWISH COMMUNITY
CENTER

*A Fourth Force in
American Jewish Life*

JEWISH EDUCATION COMMITTEE PRESS

*INNOVATION
BY TRADITION*

Articles on Jewish Communal Life

by

GRAENUM BERGER

NORMAN LINZER, Ph.D.
EDITOR

COMMISSION ON SYNAGOGUE RELATIONS
FEDERATION OF JEWISH PHILANTHROPIES OF NEW YORK, INC.

(Adventures in Group Work (1948)

(Jewish Community Center—A Fourth Force in American Jewish Life—1966)

(Innovation by Tradition—1976)

Black Jews in America
— a documentary with commentary —

by

GRAENUM BERGER

COMMISSION ON SYNAGOGUE RELATIONS
FEDERATION OF JEWISH PHILANTHROPIES OF NEW YORK
130 East 59 Street, New York, N.Y. 10022

1978

(Black Jews in America—1978)

THE TURBULENT DECADES

Jewish Communal Services in America 1958-78

Including selected papers published in the
"Journal of Jewish Communal Services"
with a historical overview

by

GRAENUM BERGER
Editor

Volume I

☆

Published by
CONFERENCE OF JEWISH COMMUNAL SERVICE
5741-1981 — New York

(The Turbulent Decades—1980)

Congress of the United States
House of Representatives
Washington, D.C. 20515

October 31, 1985

Dear Graenum and Emma:

As members of Congress with an abiding concern for the Ethiopian Jewish community, we wish to extend our greetings and good wishes to you on this significant occasion. The long and difficult history of the Ethiopian Jewish people would not have been brought into the consciousness of world Jewry so vividly had it not been for your commitment and determination. For over three decades you have contributed substantially to the dramatic growth in understanding and support for this threatened Jewish community. But, most importantly, the dramatic rescue of thousands of Ethiopian Jews has been accomplished in the last two years.

The success of "Operation Moses" has brought great joy and pride to Jews the world over. That joy, however, must not lead us to forget the years of struggle when few people realized the plight of this very special and unique Jewish community and what needed to be done to ensure their very survival and keep alive their hope of reaching Israel. During those long lean years, you two worked away, writing, speaking, and encouraging others to get involved in this important issue. Those years of steadfastness have paid tremendous dividends to the entire community. We are happy to have this opportunity to publicly acknowledge the important role that you have played in the effort to save the Jews of Ethiopia. At the same time we are mindful that this struggle is not yet over. There are still thousands of Jews who languish today in Ethiopia, not knowing if they will ever again see their loved ones who have already reached Israel.

Citation by U.S. Senators and Congressmen to Graenum and Emma for their labours on behalf of Ethiopian Jews. (1985)

(top) Congressmen Stephen Solarsz presenting citation to Graenum and Emma. (1985)

The most significant honor that we can pay today to you both is to pledge that we, too, will not cease our efforts until every man, woman and child left behind in Ethiopia has been reunited with their family in the freedom of Israel.

There can be no greater reward for the two of you than to know that your commitment to saving lives has produced such marvelous results. We join your many friends and associates in honoring you for this mitzvah.

Sincerely,

RUDY BOSCHWITZ

STEPHEN J. SOLARZ

ALAN CRANSTON

GARY ACKERMAN

CARL LEVIN

BARNEY FRANK

HOWARD M. METZENBAUM

TED WEISS

ARLEN SPECTER

BENJAMIN GILMAN

TOM LANTOS

(bottom—remainder of second page of citation)

Graenum dancing with his youngest granddaughter, Deborah, at her Bat Mitzvah party. (1982) The other grand children:

Elizabeth **Bonnie** **Judith** **Gideon**

without a thatched roof, offering instruction for the equivalent of the first two grades, were scattered in other villages. Ethiopia was a country where 92 percent of the people were illiterate, could not read and write their variegated dialects. This percentage was also true of the Jews. At Ambober, children walked back and forth every day from their villages, some as far as 10 kilometers away. They brought their own lunch, usually a piece of engera. There was no hostel to house them overnight, nor was a hot meal ever provided. This was true even when ORT managed the schools from 1976 to 1981. Some of the Jewish teachers had been trained in Israel during the period 1955–60. Two young men in Western dress were arguing with Yona Bogale about work in the school. They had also been trained in Israel. Yona claimed he had no money to pay them. When we learned that their salaries were $250 per year, Emma and I agreed to support them in the first year and added them to our list of items that we would raise money for when we returned to the States.

Yona Bogale was a man of my age, fifty-seven in 1965, although he looked much older than I did. He had been selected by Dr. Jacques Faitlovitch as one of the twenty-seven young people brought to Europe over the years to be educated as future teachers. He spent ten years in Europe, Egypt, and Palestine, and returned to Ethiopia in 1932 to help open a school in Addis, which would be directed by Emanuel Taamrat, an older and earlier recruit of Faitlovitch. The Italian invasion in 1936 destroyed most of the schools. Yona was a teacher during the Fascist occupation. He knew eleven languages. When World War II was over, he worked for a time with the restored Emperor. In the 1950s, he assumed the responsibility of recruiting and training Jewish teachers and opened over twenty schools for the Beta Israel.

On April 3, 1985 I received a letter from Yona, wherein he recalled our first meeting:

A few months ago, when my son Ephraim went to Addis, I asked him to look for some of my note-books or even calendars that we printed for our people. I used to write some notes on these calendars. A few weeks ago, I received five such calendars. On one of 1964–65, Thursday, the 12th of August 1965, I wrote that I met you in Ambober and the next day, Friday the 13th of August, you came to Tedda with Mrs. Berger. Is it possible? I think it was the first time that we met each other. On the calendar, I wrote in a few words that I detailed to you the problem of Jews in that area.

Yona believed that if the Emperor would give the Jews a large block of land, the Jews could improve their economic lot and sustain their ancient culture. Several years later, such an opportunity arose. Land was provided on the Sudanese border, in part to use as a military bastion. About one hundred young men were recruited to cultivate the crops of cotton, sesame, and sorghum. Shortly after they arrived, they were driven off by Sudanese soldiers, who claimed the land as their own. Once again they cleared and planted land somewhat farther east. No amenities of any kind—housing, clinics, schools, roads, sanitation—were provided. Half of the men were always ill with malaria, for while the land was fertile, it was swampy and mosquito-infested. Some Americans like Lilia Kavey, Jack Fishbein of the *Jewish Sentinel* of Chicago, and Gabriel Cohen of the *Jewish Post and Opinion* of Indianapolis raised money for tractors. After four years, and even after making a small surplus in the last year, the project was abandoned. Unless the Jewish world was prepared to put up several million dollars, and a study was undertaken for such a venture, it could not succeed. The study was rejected by the Jewish Agency and other Jewish organizations. I never had any faith in this program. My solution for the problems confronting the Jews of Ethiopia was aliyah to Israel.

The synagogue at Ambober was made of stone and wattle. It collapsed in the early 1970s and a new one was erected in 1978. It had a corrugated roof made of tin, topped by a crooked Mogen David (Star of David). The interior was an earthen floor. There was no ark for the Torah, nor even a table to read from. Their Bible, leather bound, was handwritten by a scribe on parchment from left to right, in Ge'ez, an ancient Ethiopian tongue. It was wrapped in a *shmotte* ("ragged cloth") and lying on a leather hide on the ground. During services, the women remained on the outside of the sanctuary.

When the new synagogue was dedicated, I obtained a magnificent full-sized Torah and mantle donated by Rabbi Irving J. Block of the Brotherhood Synagogue in Manhattan, and after appropriate ceremonies at his sanctuary, the Torah was airmailed to Ethiopia in time for the new synagogue's festivities.

Eighteen *kohanim* greeted us at Ambober. Some had walked 50 kilometers. Their heads were wrapped in turbans, their bodies covered with clean, white shamas. They stood barefoot. Around their necks they wore amulets. All carried staves. In their presence Yona read a letter of personal greetings and then a letter addressed to the President of Israel, this one in Hebrew, begging to be lifted on the "Wings of Eagles," like their brethren from Yemen, to Jerusalem, the land of their daily and perennial prayers. It was signed "The Remnant of Israel." I knew the contents of the letter to the President, but since it was personal, I never made a copy. It was given to him and, I assume, reposes in his archives.

Several months later, I received a letter similar in content to the one addressed to the President. I assume it was sent me because the one I delivered to President Shneur Zalman Shazar had never been answered. Yona and the *kohanim* wanted me to follow this up.

The letter addressed to me read as follows:

Gondar, Ethiopia
October 24, 1965

Dear Mr. Berger:

First of all we ask about your health and the health of your family. We prayerfully remember your visit with us, despite all the obstacles in making your journey. We were joyous in our innermost being, not only that you came to see us, but that you also gave us some hope about our future.

Despite the good counsel of the late Dr. Faitlovitch and the rebirth of the State of Israel, our worries have not ceased. Again, we repeat to you, as the elders of the community, whose forefathers came to Ethiopia, that to this day we have not forsaken the religion of our fathers, no matter what difficulties we had encountered. Slowly these unhappy conditions are influencing our children, and in the course of time, they are likely to become goyim. We are distressed and shed bitter tears that after this generation has passed there will be no new Jewish generation to follow. As it is said, "If you do not sow seeds, you will reap no crops."

We are therefore requesting you, our honored friend, to extend your help to show us the way to return to Eretz Yisrael. We long for Her day and night and trust that in our names you will request World Jewry to take all of us. If that is not immediately feasible, save at least a small number of our people as a remnant. Don't ever forget what we spoke to you about in the synagogue, when you were with us. We hope you will fulfill our plea with a full heart. God willing, it will be our good fortune to meet together in Israel. Amen, Amen, Selah.

We will be waiting with great longing for your quick response. With our fervent prayers.

(Signed) The Outcasts of Israel
(Three Kohanim)

The letter was written in Hebrew and was translated for me by Jed Abraham, who had spent several years in Ethiopia, and who took up their cause on his return to the United States in 1968.

This letter was displayed in the exhibition on "The Jews of Ethiopia" at the Jewish Museum in New York December 15, 1986-April 30, 1987.

I took many photos of the *kohanim* and particularly of Uri Ben Baruch, the leading *kohen,* with their Sacred Book, and another of him with a *shochet* knife. He asked me what I would like as a gift. I told him that I would like *schochet* and *brith milah* knives. The one-eyed iron worker in a military uniform, gun in hand and barefooted, who made them, presented them to me at the airport before we left Gondar. I wanted to purchase both a *siddur* (prayerbook) and a Bible, but I was told that they were rare and seldom available. It was not until 1985 that I received a magnificent hand-lettered, illustrated *siddur* and Psalms, leather-covered volume as a gift from Rachamim Elezar and Rachamim Yitzhak, both Ethiopian Jews now living in Israel, whom we had seen on our visits to that country, and whom we had entertained in our home on their trips to the United States. Their gift was inscribed with this note:

Dear Graenum,
   The good that a man does should never be forgotten. In your lifetime you have worked without rest on behalf of the Jews of Ethiopia. And we have not forgotten this. And so, it is on behalf of the Jews of Ethiopia that we are pleased to present to you this Siddur, written in Ge'ez. It is a token of appreciation.

I also took photos of the *niddah* hut, where women in menstruation isolated themselves during their "uncleanness." (There was also a child-bearing shelter, where women spent the biblically required forty to eighty days after giving birth.) Other photos showed the preparation of baking of injera, of women making pottery objects and firing them in a charcoal pit, of weaving, of men working in iron, leather materials, and herding cattle, including a cowboy, the construction of huts, medical clinics, schools—all so as to record their life and economy.

Those pictures were later used for lectures. Without demanding fee or royalty, I gave a set with commentary to the Jewish Media Department of the National Jewish Welfare Board, and for twenty years, they have been rented and sold to institutions and speakers. My photos have been reproduced in numerous newspapers and journals. I have since 1965 delivered over seven hundred talks, usually accompanying the slides. In 1984, I made a tape to run with the slides. The new set included photos that I had taken of Ethiopian Jews in Israel to indicate how quickly and successfully they had adapted in the Promised Land. Their accommodation was all the more significant, since most had come to Israel illiterate, impoverished, and lacking in skills considered essential for work in a twentieth-century sophisticated industrial society.

The medical clinic at Ambober was little better than the one at Gedebeque. When the dresser, the person in charge of the clinic, gave some powdered milk to a mother whose child was undernourished, and told her to cook and feed it to the child, I saw her go out of doors and dip a pan in the dirty rain water, in which other children had just urinated. That is how this portion of milk was ultimately served. There was no hygiene. The outdoors was a toilet, breeding insects and disease. While Ethiopian Jews washed before meals and went through total ablution before the Sabbath, cleanliness was not easily achieved in such an environment. Despite these serious lacks, the Amhari term often used with respect to the Ethiopian Jews by their uncharitable neighbors was "The people who smell of water," an indirect tribute to their somewhat higher standards of sanitation.

The life span was then less than forty years. Twenty years after I first visited the country, there were only twenty-nine doctors per 100,000 population, one of the lowest doctor-patient ratios in the world.

A visit to the village of Tedda revealed many of the same features we had seen elsewhere. I noted a woman wearing a cross and was told that she had converted to Christianity. While this was still occurring, it was not as prevalent as in the nineteenth century, when active missionaries literally preyed on the Jews. The Jewish world had offered them too little, so that with or without active groups of missionaries, some took this step in order to achieve a somewhat better life and status. It was for most the only way to get a secondary or university education, to obtain a job in the civil service, to become a soldier in the army, or to avoid the constant discrimination practiced against them every day in the villages and in the marketplaces.

We shipped many items home, but it cost us nearly a full day in the post office, where we were sent from one department to another, unwrapping and rewrapping the same packages. If we had only given a small bribe to the first clerk, we would have been spared the nuisance. No one told this to us until after we related our frustrating experience.

We gave a royal banquet for the Felzers at our hotel on our last night in Gondar. We included a few other Jewish and Israeli tourists. In the following year the Felzers came to the United States, stayed at our house. He was studying in the United States, returned to Ethiopia for another year, and then left for Jamaica, after which we lost contact. But Felzer, like the Israeli doctors who preceded and succeeded him, Dan Harel and Daniel Pridan, for a time tried to introduce higher levels of medical care. Without sufficient funds or the opportunity to train personnel in an adequate way, the clinics provided minimal service for one of the poorest countries in the world economically and medically.

It was clear that visiting more villages would only reinforce our already committed view. It was obvious that the Jewish world had no right to allow Jews to live in such horrible political, social, economic, medical, and even Jewishly religious and educational squalor. Conditions were even worse, if that is imaginable, in the four hundred other remote locales where they also lived and suffered. All the years that Faitlovitch tried to improve their lot were for nought, because world Jewry had not responded, was not interested in investing any substantial sums in the welfare of a black Jewish tribe that was remote from their daily presence.

Bringing them to Israel might present difficulties of which I was not yet aware, but it would mean a vast improvement in the lives and chances for survival of a small ancient Jewish group, which numbered twenty-five thousand to thirty thousand persons. They were physically attractive, apparently intelligent, and if they could be transported en masse would make a contribution to the new and growing state, in need of loyal immigrants. We left Gondar with the resolve to foster their migration to Israel.

On the way to Israel, we decided to spend a few days in Asmara, Eritrea, where the Italian influence was still dominant. A handsome city with many fine buildings, including a large mosque, for many of the inhabitants were Moslem, a large Catholic church, another legacy of the Italians, and an even larger Coptic church. We stayed at an Italian-run hotel, ate Italian food, purchased many Ethiopian artifacts—paintings on wood and leather, scrolls, one an old piece that turned out to be quite valuable. We visited a huge Israeli-operated abattoir, where Israeli *shochetim* arrived periodically to slaughter herds of cattle. The meat was either shipped to Israel frozen or canned for sale in Europe. We visited the local synagogue, which served fifty Jewish families formerly resident in Aden, met some of their leaders in places of business—jewelry, hides, export and import. Although cordial, no one invited us to their homes.

Except for the Sabbath, when they counted forty in the synagogue, it was difficult to get a daily minyan. Few Jewish tourists visited Asmara. They questioned whether the Ethiopian Jews were Jews and doubted that their historical origins really went back to Solomon and Sheba. They had no interest in them, in any event. Few lived in that city. This Adenite Jewish community had its origins in Ethiopia in 1920. They prospered under Haile Selassie. They suffered when the Italians were in power. They had contacts with Israel via business and the nearby port of Massawa. Their fate was later sealed when, after the revolution of 1974, a recurring civil war raged in Eritrea between the secessionists and the new revolutionary government's forces.

In 1976 I was called to a meeting at the New York American Jewish Committee regarding the persecution of Jews in Ethiopia. Thinking that this might be the beginning of a genuine interest in Ethiopian Jews by that prominent organization, I broke another date to attend. To my amazement, the session was concerned with reports that the Jews of Asmara, the former Adenites, were threatened with confiscation of their property and businesses. I pointed out that they could still get out of the country alive, if they wished to, and could go either to Israel or, since they had retained their British citizenship, to some country within the British Commonwealth. It was my judgment that little help could be extended, except to ease travel elsewhere. When I raised the issue of what must be done to rescue the black Ethiopian Jews, who had no money to leave, no friends abroad, no country that was ready to welcome them as citizens, I was told that it was not on the agenda. The committee never undertook a campaign to provide significant help for Ethiopian Jews and maintained at best a distant, intellectual interest.

One member of the committee, who met with an accident on his way to the meeting and could not attend, was so outraged by the committee's failure to act on the real native Jews and their problems that he became a large contributor to the American Association for Ethiopian Jews.

Sitting at the bar in our hotel with several well-traveled Englishmen working in Ethiopia, our discussion led to where we had eaten the best fish soup (bouillabaisse). They contended that it could be found in Massawa, a four-hour train ride down to the Red Sea. We had an off-day with no fixed plans. Always ready for any adventure, including eating, we arose the next day at 5 A.M. It was cold. I wore an undershirt, a shirt, a sweater, jacket and raincoat. Emma was similarly garbed. We caught a 7 A.M. one-car, gasoline-driven train filled with thirty-two colorful passengers. We descended from a 7,500-foot elevation, through picturesque country with terraced farms, drove around hairpin turns through numerous tunnels. At close range, we noted the strange white-marked eyes on most Ethiopians. They nursed their babies. They carried live chickens. They dropped off at various waystations, their seats immediately taken by other natives. Many looked more like the brown-skinned Arabs than the blacker residents. As we rode down the barren, rugged, brownish hills with touches of brush, few trees, the weather became hotter. We began to shed clothing. As we approached Massawa and the sea, it was unbearably humid—105 degrees in the shade. We were carrying most of our clothes.

To our disappointment, the proprietor of the Hotel Savoir restaurant told us that soupa de pesce was not on the menu that day, but if we would come back in an hour (it was now 11 A.M. and our only return train left at 1 P.M.) he would prepare it special.

We walked about this interesting seaport, where the Emperor enjoyed a winter palace. The architecture was distinctly Arabic. For a superb picture of Massawa, see the Israeli Hebrew edition of Shmuel Katz's drawings in *Maseh Laeretz Kush ("Travels Through Ethiopia")*. Emma's beautiful new blue-print dress, which she bought at Lord and Taylor just before we left, guaranteed color-fast, faded to a pure white, so intense was the viscidity. We returned to the hotel before noon for a superb fish soup, among the best we had eaten before and after (the Englishmen were right), topped off with hot rolls and Stracchino, a good goat cheese.

The scenic trip back to Asmara was longer, because the train had to pull itself up the mountains. It had been a long, hot, and tiring ride for an excellent bowl of fish soup. It is a story we've told endless times.

We were warned not to check our bags through to Israel, as airport workers in Cairo were reported to have confiscated such marked luggage when the plane stopped in that city for servicing, so they were labeled only for Athens, where we would change for El Al.

12

Israel: 1965

IN ISRAEL, WE noted that the airport had been enlarged. An enthusiastic cab driver told us that the country was in a building boom, getting richer. In 1955 cars were used mostly for business, so there were few. Now they were being bought and used for pleasure. Boys and girls in sports cars could be seen necking. We noted dogs for the first time, another sign of better times. That night in Tel Aviv, we took in a concert by Isaac Stern, the superb violinist, and the Gadna Orchestra. We went to see *Fiddler on the Roof* in Hebrew, a more sober interpretation than the U.S. version with its ebullient comedian Zero Mostel. We saw some good and mediocre Israeli art at the museum, took in the glass museum, walked through the beginnings of the reconstruction of old Jaffa, bought some paintings from Imre Szabo, the art dealer, which included works by Shmuel Katz, Alex Levy, and Edward Phillips (now known as Ben Avram). We found an old Persian Torah pointer with a spice box at the top, which when cleaned turned out to be not only sterling silver, but an antique.

We went to the opening of the Maccabiad in Ramat Gan, a thrilling event as fifty thousand spectators stood and loudly applauded Jewish athletes from around the world.

Abraham and Anne Covell, from Mount Vernon, members of the Pelham Jewish Center, arrived from Russia. We had agreed to take them on a tour of parts of Israel they had not previously seen. We rented a car and driver-guide, who had a light touch and believed that his job was primarily to amuse American tourists and not to educate and indoctrinate them. He couldn't find a Karaite village near Tel Aviv that I wanted to see. His response was: "No one else has ever asked me to go to such a place." From then on I became more guide than tourist and determined precisely what our route would be. He had to be prepared for anything.

We rode through Ashdod, the land of the ancient Philistines, which was rising from the sands to become a major harbor and industrial town. We ate excellent watermelon at a stop in Ashkelon. We followed the borders of Gaza, trying to get a peak at the Arabs living in that hostile area. We learned from our driver the difference between Ben-Gurion and the Messiah. "Ben-Gurion doesn't want to go, and the Messiah doesn't want to come." We noted the extensive cultivation already taking place on the formerly almost lifeless desert. We stopped at Kissufim, a border kibbutz, where the inhabitants seemed weary from toiling all day and guarding the settlement all night against potential Arab incursions. Then to Urim, where I knew some American kibbutzniks, and admired the progress they had made in farming and industry in such a short time.

The long, hot drive ended at the Beersheba Inn, where we stayed overnight. We decided to have a cocktail with the vodka and caviar the Covells had brought from Russia. We never realized the potency of this liquor, and as a result, when we went to our rooms to rest for an hour before we joined them at dinner, we instead, and so did they, slept through the night.

Since our last visit ten years before, Beersheba had become a growing, lively city with sixty thousand inhabitants. It was no longer a low-key Arab town. On the outskirts, many of the Bedouins were now living in shacks rather than the black goat-hair tents. Dimona, which had not yet been started in 1955, was now a thriving city. A huge fenced-in area elicited no response from our guide when I asked him, "What is that?" I therefore assumed that this was where the Israelis were developing their nuclear reactor—a top secret. The road to Sodom had been widened, and was no longer a hazardous descent. Sodom was brisk with new industrial buildings, an interesting contrast to the fantastic forms that nature had shaped out of the salt hills silently guarding the shores of the Dead Sea.

Massada was formidable as we encircled this ancient citadel. Due to construction, we were not allowed to climb the steep hill. The oasis kibbutz Ein Gedi was a stopover, reminding us that David had fled to this spot to avoid the murderous assault of Saul, who in his madness wanted to do away with the lyrical poet, the slayer of Goliath and next king of Israel. We edged our way along narrow ledges to reach the cool, fresh waterfall. As we peeked into each cave, we felt like we were about to discover another Dead Sea Scroll. To our disappointment, they were all empty. We drove up the barren highway with only a suggestion of vegetation clinging to an inhospitable soil. Windswept Arad had arisen once again from the earth, fighting off the sand, which blew constantly on this rise over the Dead Sea. It covered an ancient village, which archaeologists were unearthing. At night we finished the rest of the vodka in moderation, had a good supper, and an undrunken sleep.

On the road back to Jerusalem, we stopped at an Arab village and studied its buildings and farms, in such sharp contrast to the kibbutzim and moshavim under development in the same areas.

Kiryat Gat, which was only a plan in 1955, was now bustling with many buildings and thirty thousand people, housing twelve ethnic groups. While our guide was not allowed to take us to the excavations of the old Philistine city of Gath, we asked him to stop and Emma picked up a few shards. At the dig at Manesha, we were also prohibited from entering. I remembered reading in II Chronicles 14:9–12 that this was where Asa defeated Zerah the Ethiopian, offering further proof that Jewry had direct contact with Ethiopians in commerce and in battle almost three thousand years ago. Then on to the Valley of Elah, where David challenged and slew Goliath. Before entering Jerusalem, we stopped to see the recently installed Chagall stained-glass windows in the Hadassah Hospital synagogue, windows which we had previously seen on exhibition in New York at the Museum of Modern Art. Although too small to house the windows, it was an impressive building.

* * *

On our arrival in Jerusalem, I found myself immediately immersed with two committees, one to plan the first revived international conference of Jewish Communal Service in Israel for 1967, and the other a committee to start construction and raise the balance of funds needed for the Jerusalem YM-YWHA, a project which we helped initiate in 1955.

In planning the international conference, I gave a preliminary paper stressing the need for more accurate research data on the Jews around the world; how we might keep the menacing personal and social pathologies from destroying the historic Jewish family; and the need for Jewish-oriented education of professionals to assure leadership for Jewish continuity. I was told the paper was more a "sermon" than a social work document. Another said I sounded like an "evangelist." In any event, like most conferences, this one would follow the conventional format: a few prominent names were invited for speaking assignments; an enormous number of committees were set up to prepare special sessions that would entice individuals from around the world to attend; a few top Israeli officials were thrown in and that was it! I was always seeking a more intensive educational experience that would influence the attendees to go home and put what they had learned into action. I was asked to prepare a definitive paper for an interim conference to be held in Washington in 1966 that might be used as a theme and guide for the final program in 1967.

* * *

As to the Jerusalem Y, the committee decided to accept the site that I had recommended in 1959. The cost of the building would undoubtedly be greater, about $800,000 instead of $600,000. Except for the land site, utilities, and roads leading to the structure, there was little money to be obtained in Israel. American Jews had to find the additional funds. The building was obviously not going to match the impressive Jerusalem YMCA, a landmark structure. Yet it was to be an attractive, modern, utilitarian facility, which would be readied in time to serve a neighborhood in the Katamons that had sprung up overnight and within a few years would be a densely populated area. We had not been wrong in selecting this location. There was nothing like a new structure to stir up excitement for a program in which Israelis had previously displayed little interest.

Gettye Benjamin

I buttonholed everyone I could reach about the plight of the Ethiopian Jews. There was considerable initial questioning, but few were interested in doing anything more than listen. I couldn't get the subject mentioned on the agenda for the forthcoming international conference two years hence.

In returning one night to our hotel, we found Gettye Benjamin, an Ethiopian Jew, in the lobby. He had written to Professor Martin Warmbrand in the United States, of the American Pro-Falasha Committee, for help, and had been told we would be in Jerusalem. A short, thin, good-looking, golden-dark-brown-faced young man of twenty five, with a trim moustache and curly hair, he told us he was from Gondar. He was a cousin of Yona Bogale, a relative of Emmanuel Taamrat, the distinguished educator, and was related to Tadessa Yaacov's family, the latter a counselor to Haile Selassie. So he had the best family connections. He had been selected in 1956 to study at Kfar Batya with twenty-six other Ethiopian Jewish young people. He refused to return to Ethiopia on the completion of his studies. He had served in the army, where, he told us, he was intensely happy and where, he said, he should have remained. He had tried to enter Israeli society without success. He had developed a few friends over the years. He was always being released from a job, just before the employer had to assure him tenure. He thought this was prejudicial. His sister, one of the original Kfar Batya contingent, also remained in Ethiopia, where she became a nurse. Meanwhile their parents had died in Ethiopia.

We invited Gettye to dine with us. He ordered in Hebrew and the Moroccan Jewish waiter was surprised to hear him speak Ivrit. The waiter was further overwhelmed when I told him that Gettye was a Jew. At that time, there were no more than thirty Ethiopian Jews in Israel. Except for a few Kfar Batyah students who had refused to return to Ethiopia, the other Ethiopian Jews were families where the mothers, Ethiopian Jews, had married Yemenites who were living in Ethiopia. They came to Israel with the inflow of Yemenites fifteen years earlier.

Gettye ordered the same food that we had asked for, but after tasting it, he put his knife and fork down. I asked the waiter to bring him the spiciest peppers that the hotel had in its kitchen, and then with relish Gettye consumed the rest of the meal. All food served in Ethiopia was garnished with red-hot pepper.

Everyone coming into the dining room approached us as we sat around the table, curious as to our guest. Dr. Aryeh Tartakower, head of the small, active, but ineffectual Israeli committee on behalf of the Ethiopian Jews, joined us, so that I could give him a report on our Ethiopian venture. He told me about the monies being spent in Ethiopia, most of it coming from England and Israel, but the total sum was less than $30,000 per year, I told him that it was insufficient. He had many ideas about how we could raise a lot of money in the United States for educational and medical programs, imploring us to undertake this mission. We promised to raise money.

The next day I called Teddy Kollek and told him about Gettye's need for a job and that Histadrut had not been helpful. Teddy agreed to see him and Gettye was employed at the new Israel Museum, which was arising to the west on high ground of Greater Jerusalem.

Within a year Gettye found an Egyptian girl, Rachel Aboud, who was prepared to marry him. The religious authorities would not give him the necessary license, because he could not show proof that his mother was a Jew. Despite his superb family connections, and the fact that his deceased father had been a kohen, and thus certainly would never have married a woman who was not authentically Jewish, his request was denied.

Gettye took the case to the highest court and lost. He married Rachel in any event, but the whole prolonged battle to prove his Jewishness had a traumatic effect on his life. They had two children, but the marriage did not last. They were divorced. He lives a lonely life in Eilat, having cut himself off from contact with his kinsmen and others.

Turkey

We flew to Turkey in 1965 on a Turkish propeller plane over the sea, avoiding both Lebanon and Syria, which would have been a shorter route. We reached Istanbul with its prominent mosques and minarets, visible as we descended over the Black Sea. We checked into the Park Hotel, where our balcony glimpsed the Bosporus. The huge, heavy Turkish bathrobes with a cowl instead of a towel were a delightful variation, as we sat around in our room or the balcony after a bath. We spent the first evening at an authentic Turkish nightclub, because I did not recognize a tourist in the large audience. The singers, the pantomimic comedians, the orchestra composed of violins, banjos, piccolos and drums were excellent. The ballads were sad, like those we heard in Greece and Portugal. The visiting dancers from Trinidad were poor, but it did not detract from the Turkish performers.

We toured Istanbul, visiting the Mosque of St. Sophia and the Blue Mosque, among the five hundred in the city. All lived up to their advance billing as described in travel magazines and Hachette's guidebook. Our tour included a few churches, like the Byzantine St. Saviour in Chora, now a museum. How any buildings survive in Turkey, where earthquakes occur with frequency, was evidence of the tenacity of the people and the government to rebuild after disaster.

Topkapi Palace, a sprawling museum, had an immense collection of Byzantine and Ottoman treasures. We did not overlook the Chinese pottery or the famous jewel collection. Saladin, Sultan of Egypt and Syria in the twelfth century, was largely responsible for this astounding assembly. We viewed the hall where the thrilling robbery was supposed to have been executed as seen in the well-known movie *Topkapi*. On a visit to the Grand Bazaar with its six thousand shops under one huge arcade, we resisted every solicitor and didn't buy a thing.

We went to Galata, the old Jewish quarter, to see the synagogue, following Bernard Postal's and Samuel H. Abramson's guidebook, *The Landmarks of a People* (1962). The taxi driver couldn't find it, or as we learned later, probably did not want to take even paying tourists to Jewish sites. After walking through many slum streets, full of poor people and poor shops, we found the Jewish Communal Center, but it was not open. We walked on and reached the Neve Sholom Synagogue. The shammes, who spoke English, showed us the sanctuary. What impressed us was the array of collection boxes for the school, the synagogue, for charity, for strangers who came to Istanbul, for poor girls in need of a dowry. We dropped coins in all of them. This was the synagogue where 21 helpless Jews were gunned down by Arab terrorists in 1986.

The street with the synagogue had many Jewish merchants, although few lived there. The languages spoken were Turkish, Spanish, French, and Ladino. In a hardware store, we found a young man who could speak English quite fluently. He spoke openly of the anti-Semitism faced by Jews in Turkey. His brother was one of the few Jews admitted to the navy, yet it was impossible to visit him—and only because his family was

Jewish. It was a daily occurrence for Jewish youths to be beaten on the way to school. Jacob took us to the Beth Israel Synagogue, also recently built, where Jews, on entering and leaving, were often maligned with obscene epithets.

Since it was Erev Shabbat, we returned to the synagogue for services before dinner. No one greeted us. The *shammoshim* wore uniforms with gilded buttons and peaked hats with gilded braid. The congregation of seventy-five men and women sat separated by a *mechitzah*. The young, short, thin, bearded rabbi chanted the service at high speed without a pause. The chazzan, in good voice, tried to slow the pace, but that only seemed to goad the rapid-fire rabbi to read the text even faster in his distinctive Sephardic mode. Many rose after the service, went up to the ark to touch it, to peer into it through the cracks, and to kiss it.

As we were leaving, a young man was loudly admonishing several people for not greeting us, pointing toward us conspicuously. But they rushed out. Moshe Dyl, thirty-two, a tall Afghanistani Jew, who spoke Hebrew and French, a citizen of Israel, in the diamond and rug business, approached us. Between Emma's limited Hebrew and my even more limited French, we carried on a conversation. As we walked out of the synagogue, a Jew took my *kippah* off my head and handed it to me, gesturing that Jews did not wear this gear on the outside.

We asked Moshe to dine with us, but he was kosher and instead invited us to his pension, where we assumed we would pay for our dinner. We found that he was the only resident, and that we were probably eating the meals that he had prepared for the entire Sabbath. He apologized for not having either candles or challah. His landlady was not an observant Jew. He told us that Jews lived in a kind of limbo, playing no part in the general community. When we asked why the Jews had rushed out of the synagogue, he replied, so that they could eat a quick dinner and then play cards, a Friday night pastime. We were leaving for a tour of the country, so we promised to contact Moshe on our return. He was eager to maintain a relationship.

* * *

Our trip was to Troy, Pergamum, Izmir, and Ephesus, starting by boat down the Bosporus, through the Sea of Marmora to the Dardanelles, well known to us through the study of history. Our guide, a man in his sixties, was surprised by my "knowledge" of Turkey (all obtained from previous readings), and he referred to me as "savant" and "professor." He was a liberal Moslem, who prayed only on Fridays. The other tourists in our party of four were Renee Odou and her mother, both from Belgium. Renee was a hostess on Sabena Airlines. Both were well traveled and well informed. Renee became our close friend, visiting with us in Pelham frequently.

The S.S. *Gemlik* was filled to its capacity of five hundred passengers. The sunny day kept us outdoors on deck viewing the flat countryside.

Whenever the boat docked at a village, it seemed that all the inhabitants came down to greet the vessel and those disembarking.

A Gypsy family with six children boarded the ship with apparently all of their belongings. The children danced and sang with good rhythm and voice, and passengers tossed coins at their feet. Gypsies claim a Balkan origin, live a wandering, makeshift life. This family made its livelihood by weaving baskets and their children entertaining.

It was easy to make conversation with the passengers: Turks, Greeks, football players, young couples—although there was more gesture than articulation. I took their addresses and sent them photos I had taken.

At nightfall, we arrived in Canakkale, the busy port near Troy, stayed overnight in a hotel, where the flies and mosquitoes were devastating both in the dining room and our bedroom.

A beautiful morning allowed us to look across the Dardanelles at Gallipoli, where Leander swam the Hellespont. We now understood why this piece of terrain was so important throughout history. Whoever controlled this point was in a position to govern the traffic of the land mass to the east. Troy itself was a *tell*, a high mound, overlooking the straits. We walked over the eight levels of excavation, where Heinrich Schliemann, the nineteenth-century German "amateur" archaeologist, unearthed rich finds in gold and pottery. We also recalled that in ancient Greek lore, this was where Odysseus, Agamemnon, Hector, Ajax, Helen, and Paris trudged, loved, and fought. Despite the extensive and continuous diggings, there were few shards of any significance lying around. We had to exercise our imagination to visualize how Troy really appeared in olden times.

Our next stop was Pergamum, which we reached by riding along the coast of the Aegean Sea. We saw farmers in their odd native dress, eking out a living from the rich soil in plots carved out of twisting mountains with good tree cover. Living in rather primitive huts, they cultivated grain, corn, cotton, tobacco, figs, olives, and the colorful sunflowers, then in full bloom. Camel caravans still plodded along the roadside. There was little traffic. We viewed the island of Lesbos, made famous by Sappho, the sixth-century B.C.E. poetess, whose strophic poems I read at Missouri University. We passed a long line of carriages bearing young males six to eight years of age, who had just been circumcised. The boys wore white suits, small white pillbox hats, and a red sash. It was quite a ceremonial contrast with the Jewish *b'rith milah* taking place on the eighth day of a new Jewish male baby's life.

Pergamum, with its phenomenal stadium ruin situated on a steep incline overlooking the town and sea, was an awesome site. Riding up to the Acropolis was like approaching the palace at Mycenae. The eye-catching view from the top gave one a picture of the many civilizations that had put their stamp on this spot: early Greek, Hellenistic, Roman, Byzantine, and now Turkey. The ancient stone buildings were in surprisingly good condition. We entered the museum and noted the treasures that had been excavated from the surrounding countryside. We peeked into the site of an ancient temple dedicated to Aesculapius, the god of medicine, recently unearthed. Turkey, like much of the Middle East and the Mediterranean, was one vast archaeological dig.

We stayed overnight in Izmir at the beautiful Kismet Hotel. Izmir, much of it rebuilt after a destructive earthquake, still gave evidence of its historical glory. One could see walls built during the reign of Alexander. From the Acropolis, one had a spectacular panoramic view of a fine harbor and a teeming city.

Our goal was Ephesus, where we walked over the restored ruins of this ancient Greek, and later Byzantine, city. It once housed great sculptural works and one of the finest libraries in the world. Parchment (named for Pergamum) had replaced papyrus as one of the new writing materials, and as a result Ephesus became a major cultural center. Lest anyone get the impression that this was only a city of intellectuals, the archaeological evidence graphically revealed that it was also a city of pleasure, devoted to the sex goddess Artemis. We entered buildings which once were houses of prostitution. The museum revealed the work of once well supported artists.

Wanting to spend more time in Istanbul, we skipped Bursa. In our room at the Park Hotel back in Istanbul, we could overhear the conversation of the American black author James Baldwin with his friend sitting on a balcony across the court. We continued with our synagogue explorations and finally found the Orchrida, where Sabbatei Zevi worshipped four hundred years ago, before he traitorously converted to Islam, leaving hundreds of thousands of Jews in despair. The synagogue, recently restored, was built in Sephardic style. It was painted bizzarely. We took pictures of the *shammes* with his Turkish peaked hat.

We stopped at a Greek coffee stand and had a long talk with several individuals who spoke English, learning how deeply hated the Greek population was by the Turks. They compared it to the discrimination and persecution experienced by the Jews in history and in many contemporary lands.

Whenever we talked to a Moslem, we obtained a negative picture of the Greeks. They would also comment on the Jews: "Very rich," "Own much property." There were only thirty-five thousand Jews in all of Turkey, where the population was approaching 50 million.

Moshe Dyl dined with us at the hotel and gave a dim picture of Jewish life in Turkey. Jews were rich, but not generous. They feared, like many Jews in South America, to expose their wealth, so they lived below their proper financial status.

We bought brassware, shipped it home, and were off to Geneva. One gastronomic memory was the excellent, unmatched baklava.

Switzerland

I had been invited to give a speech that night in Geneva at a conference of the Jewish Community Centers of Europe. When we reached the airport in Istanbul, we found that the plane could not leave, because of a missing part. I wired Geneva that I would unfortunately be unable to reach the meeting on time. After some hours at the airport, I finally found a way of getting to Geneva via Vienna, but there would only be a fifteen-minute interval between arrival and departure. When we reached Vienna, we quickly retrieved our heavy baggage and ran like mad. We tried to push ahead of the long line at the customs counter, but were forcefully shoved back by the officers controlling the queue. Happily, the people understood our plight and allowed us to get to the head of those waiting, although we had to face the ugly glances of the officials. Our passports were quickly stamped and then, breathless, we ran another quarter of a mile, each of us weighed down with two heavy bags that were dragging on the ground. We crawled up the steps to the plane just before the doors were closed. It took us a while to recover from the excitement and the exertion, relieved by a good Swiss dinner and the beauty of flying over the Alps and Lake Geneva.

Our taxi dumped us at a quaint hotel, Le Chandelier, recommended by Deborah Miller, the center and camp specialist for the JDC in Geneva, located on a street of antique shops, reminiscent of old Beacon Hill in Boston. Our attic room overlooked the red-tiled roofs of Geneva and then out to the grand lake. We dressed quickly and taxied to the Jewish Youth and Communal Center for a meeting of the American Jewish Joint Distribution Committee's Standing Committee on Community Centers and Camps. In view of my telegram, they were surprised to see me. There was a small European audience, with fifteen Americans swelling the attendance.

I gave a well-formulated five-page speech, some of which was written on the planes from Istanbul to Geneva. I referred to our recent visit to Ethiopia, Israel, and Turkey and the interrelationships of the varied Jewish worlds. I paid tribute to the debt that American Jews owed to European Jews for migrating to the United States during the last hundred years, bringing their rich Jewish culture with them. I reviewed the demographic data on American Jewry—that we were now mostly American born, rich, well educated, but assimilating too rapidly. I pointed out that centers and camps had to concern themselves with the entire Jewish family, our aged as well as our youth; that we needed not only decent buildings, but well-trained professionals, who would be as interested in Jewish culture and continuity as with the long list of items that made up the conventional agenda.

I ended with a plea for more communication and more frequent contacts, now that it had become so easy, what with Telstar providing us with news and pictures in a few seconds, and planes reaching different parts of the world in a few hours. Sol Litt, the chairman, stated that it was a good, succinct speech, as did some of the others. My reaction was that there were too few Europeans. Americans already knew my position.

* * *

I attended meetings the next day about the need for wider participation of European Jewish communities in such conferences. Charles Jordan, head of the JDC in Geneva, gave a lavish cocktail party at his home, filled with remarkable paintings, including some by Chagall and Mané-Katz. Jordan met a tragic death two years later, just before he was to come to the international conference in Jerusalem. I bought Emma a lovely gold Swiss watch with a gold bracelet for her forthcoming birthday. We dined with Melvin and Lana Faigen, friends of my brother Sam and his wife Margaret. He worked for the European Trade center of the United Nations.

Rose Stockhamer, on the staff of Bronx House and a long-time friend, arrived from the States and joined us for the rest of our trip through Europe. We dined with Deborah Miller and lost at roulette at the Rothschild gambling casino over the border in France, where we completed an eventful evening.

Raphael and Esther Spanien, brother and sister, who worked for HIAS in Geneva, a fabulous couple, learned, well read, well traveled, competitive garrulous conversationalists, bubbled over with comments about the Jews, Jewish organizations, the world, literature, and art. They took us under their wing for a few days, including a day trip through parts of Switzerland and France we had not seen. We stopped for lunch at the Café des Gorges in Le Sotty, France, a meal of superb fresh trout caught in the brook that flowed by the restaurant. The luncheon, as was the ride in their Citroen, was punctuated with talk and humor. We drove through Passy opposite snow-covered Mount Blanc, up the steeper, winding road to Assy, to see the famous church built by Ferdinand Leger and filled with religious art created by Chagall, Matisse, and Lifschitz, among others. Thus ended five well-filled days in Geneva.

We rented an Opel Rekord and started our trip through Switzerland, eventually driving all the way to Rome, beautiful Lausanne, lunched at the Garden with a Green Arch in Nyon, saw the old Roman theater in Averches. When we noted a *schloss* (castle) in the distance, we turned off the road into Mertens (Morat), a fairy-tale village with a huge clock over the arched tower, surrounded by Swiss chalets, and with flower boxes everywhere. We decided to spend the night in this attractive spot, sleeping under thick *perenes* (down comforters). We drove to flag-decorated Bern, bought books, and saw the bear pits, as we lingered for a few hours in this attractive community.

As we approached Thun with its haunting, romantic lake, we saw another *schloss*, and having a sentimental fascination for old castles, we turned into a narrow street with curious arcades, and ended up in a picturesque square. We decided to stay overnight at the Hotel Zu Mezgern at the foot of the castle. A fourteenth-century hostelry, rebuilt in 1866, it was once frequented by the barons and their entourages, who occupied the *schloss*.

Our next short stopover was at the overcrowded resort of Interlaken. Then on to Stechelberg, took the cable lifts to the top of the mountain overlooking the snow-capped Jungfrau. Quite a vista. Traveling without reservations was at times frustrating. The hotels were bursting. We finally found a quaint Swiss chalet guest house at Innerkirchen, where we stayed overnight for 50 cents a person, and for another 25 cents, we had a hot bath, making our own wood fire in the copper heater. The beds were covered with huge pillows and comforters.

We drove through the winding, tunneled Sustenpass with unexcelled views of the lofty mountains and stopped to throw snowballs at each other in mid-September. As we began to wind down the St. Gotthard Pass, the country and its people became more distinctly Italian. I had been warned about the difficulties and dangers of driving through the passes, but found them as easy as any other highway with twists and turns.

Italy

At Lugano, I changed to a Fiat 1500 to avoid an auto-return fee. We visited the Thyssen Villa Favorita, a magnificent art museum on the lake, surrounded by well-groomed flower gardens and trees. The paintings were amongst the best we had seen, hung in a large house instead of a huge, walled institutional museum. Our car took us through Como, where we walked in the church in the square and bought books in the stalls.

On these tours, we usually bought our lunch—cheese or salami, fruit, tomatoes, rolls—and ate in a square nearby or in a coffee shop. Occasionally we picnicked on the highway and had coffee later. In this way we tasted a variety of foods, native to each region. We always found a pleasant spot in an inner city park or overlooking the countryside.

Genoa was a large, ill-kept seaport. Even the palazzos, once built and occupied by the rich shipowners, were seedy, except for the Palazzo Bianchi, which had been maintained in good repair and housed a fine collection of paintings and sculptures. We paused at the statue of

Christopher Columbus and wondered, as a result of our extensive reading on this explorer-seaman, whether he really had lived in Genoa. Many cities claimed his birth, his residence, his burial site.

We wound down the Italian Riviera through Comogli and Santa Margherita, stopping overnight at the charming cove of Portofino, where we roomed in a delightfull small hotel, Albergho Piccolo, whose owner, Carlo Tibaldi, not only helped serve, but after dinner regaled all willing listeners with stories of the area, including the history of wine making. This sea village was favored by the jet set and royalty. The Princess of Monaco's boat was anchored in the tiny harbor.

Pisa, and how many photos have we seen of the Leaning Tower (Campanile), with the Duomo, the Baptistry, and Campo Santo, was one of the most aesthetic piazzas we have seen. We just could not tear ourselves away from its pink-white marble, architectural beauty.

In Firenze, we billeted near the Piazza del Signora, and thus had another opportunity to enjoy this notable city. Apart from seeing the museums and churches again, we drank our coffee in the Piazza Republica, listened to the musicians, who rendered in good voice and instruments, popular and operatic selections at our request. We entered the Moorish-styled synagogue, talked with its secretary, who related that the fifteen hundred Jews saw no future in remaining in Italy. There was barely a daily minyan, only forty appeared for worship on the Sabbath, and the large attractive sanctuary could not be filled on the High Holy Days.

When we met Italians on the street or in a restaurant, they questioned us at length about famous Italo-Americans like Perry Como and Frank Sinatra and had no awareness about the significant contributions that other Italians, perhaps more worthy, had made to the development of the United States from its very inception.

Once again we drove through Sienna, stopped to see its black-and-white striped cathedral, and descended the numerous steps to the Campo, always regretting that we were not there when the horses raced through the piazza. We had an unusual lunch of tiny broiled pigeons and baked chicken livers.

We drove up and around the winding road leading to attractive Perugia, which gave such a stirring view of the valley below. We bought some Perugina chocolates and ate them along with lamb sandwiches purchased from a vendor in the street, who cut the meat to order. We vowed someday to return to this exciting city. We did in 1985.

In Assisi, as always, we were intrigued by thoughts of the influential mission wrought on this hillside in the thirteenth century by Saint Francis, who began as a carefree playboy and then became a major religious figure.

Rome, like Firenze, was a street museum. In the few days we were there, we quickly saw once again all that had delighted us a decade before. We purchased seats in the ornate Assyrian-Babylonian Synagogue for Rosh Hashanah, lunched in the nearby ghetto, attended a good performance of Puccini's *La Bohème* at the Eliseo Opera House.

The next day we worshipped with what looked to us like two thousand Italians—all Jews of course. There were few tourists in the congregation. The native Jews, even in their dress, did not give the appearance of wealth. During the service, everyone talked. There was little decorum. It reminded us of the old-fashioned American Orthodox shuls. The children were walking to and fro, greeting their fathers and grandfathers, then to the balcony, where their mothers, grandmothers, and sisters were seated behind a screened *mechitzah* (barrier). A large part of the service was chanted by a chazzan in good voice supported by a fine choir. It sounded more like a Catholic musical service than the typical Ashkenazi ritual. As the Torah was removed from the majestic ark, two children carrying silver Torah pointers led the procession around the synagogue. The religious functionaries and some of the *balebatim* were dressed in a kind of formal uniform with a long silver chain adorning their neck and chest and their heads topped with high hats. It gave the ceremonial walk a festive air. When the coverlets were removed, two of the attendees unrolled the Torah across the length of the *bimah*, then slowly rerolled it and carried it to the slanted rostrum for reading. Many individuals were called up for an aliyah, reciting prayers before reading sections of the Bible.

When the large shofar was blown in short, staccato bursts and long, eerie summoning wails, it seemed that the very walls of the sanctuary shook. It had a reverential impact on me, one that I have never forgotten.

Even another visit to the vast Vatican and the Sistine Chapel, with its many treasures, could not duplicate the awesome synagogue experience.

Portugal

We flew to Lisbon and stayed at the excellent, new, but small Mundial Hotel in the old section of the city. we ate in superb restaurants, usually calderada, a fish soup. Madeira wine was always part of the menu. We purchased gold jewelry, which was available at a low price. We visited all the museums and were delighted with the Calouste Gulbenkian collection of art and furniture, then housed in a pink, stuccoed palace on the road to Estoril.

One evening we took in a program of Fado performed by singers and dancers in a small table-pressed-against-table restaurant, where the food was good and the entertainment superb. Most of the guests were Portuguese and knew the songs being sung and often joined in the renditions. The ballads, when translated to us, were reminiscent of similar songs in other countries—sad, lovers leaving and not returning, death. The dancers were garbed in native costumes. The music was performed by guitarists.

We sat next to a man, a woman, an older woman, and a child. He looked German, but they seemed to be Latins. We carried on incidental conversations during the dinner during which we revealed that we had been to Ethiopia, Israel, Turkey, Switzerland, and Italy. After they all left the table, the man returned alone to shake our hands and say "Shalom." We conjured that he was a Jew married to a Portuguese woman who did not know of his background. Such may be the contemporary "Secret Jews" now living in Portugal, just as they had to survive during the Inquisition.

Lisbon was made for walking. The old Alfama section with its "Thieves' Market." Men were playing dice on the streets. The native markets were filled with a variety of foods.

On our last day, we taxied to the Sefardic synagogue, a fine building in a prosperous neighborhood, protected by a high iron fence, but there was no visible evidence by name or symbol that it was a Jewish house of worship. As we approached, Isaac Toledano, wearing *tallit* and *tefillin*, was standing just inside the gate and apparently was looking for a tenth Jew to provide a minyan for prayer. He rushed us in without introductions. The service began immediately and was chanted at breakneck speed. The reader wore a high hat. During services a collection box was passed around. I put in a number of coins. Later I spoke with Toledano, Moroccan born, educated in England, the leader of the congregation, but not an ordained rabbi. He saw little hope for the five hundred Jews in Portugal. Intermarriage was increasing, and he feared that his thirteen-year-old daughter would become a victim if they remained in the country. Before we left, Toledano asked me to leave some money under the tablecloth in the room where we had been talking. Apart from what I had already put in the collection box, I left several bills. For whom and for what purpose the money was to be used, I did not inquire.

13

South America—Central America—Mexico: 1966

THE INTERNATIONAL CONFERENCE of Jewish Communal Service asked me to prepare a paper for a meeting in Washington in 1966, which might be used as a working document for the convocation in Jerusalem in 1967. After considerable jockeying back and forth, we decided on a formidable title: "Critical Factors in a Consideration of the Role of Jewish Communal Services in Strengthening Jewish Identification." I would have preferred a simpler heading, but the one chosen left me with plenty of leeway to get in what I wanted to write about, namely, a world review of the status of Jewish life, how it compared to the people and nations among whom they lived, and what had to be done to shore up developing weaknesses, so that the strengths of the Jewish experience would not be eroded by inexorable assimilation.

I had collected a great deal of material about Jews all over the world. From one large section of the Jewish landscape, stretching from Mexico to the tip of Chile-Argentina, there was little data, particularly in English. I do not read Spanish. Not having been south of the U.S. border, I decided to make such a trip, covering the major countries, where more than three quarters of a million Jews lived. I had written most of the paper before the trip, but I planned to take the entire script along to fill in any new information that would turn up as a result of my interviews and observations. Since the conference in Washington would take place only a few days after our planned return, I promised to send out the final draft from some spot in the lower Americas, which would then be mimeographed and circulated in advance of the meeting. I had undertaken an assignment that would eventually fill seventy pages in a printed book. Joe Lowenstein, a CPA partner in Loeb and Troper, and a frequent visitor to South America, arranged for a number of Jewish leaders to spend time with me.

Venezuela

What with researching and writing this paper, working at top pitch all year and during the early part of the summer, and in addition writing to a long list of people I wanted to see on our journey, I was depleted by the time the day arrived for our leaving for Caracas, our first stop. I was nauseous and not feeling right when I boarded the plane. I couldn't eat and slept fitfully on the long Pan American flight. The stewardess gave me some aspirin. I knew that I had a fever. The long ride at midnight from the airport to the hotel did not help. It was cold and raining. I fell into bed, taking a terramycin pill, and woke with a raging fever. Emma called the U.S. Embassy at daybreak, and the desk officer sent a native doctor, trained in the United States, who prescribed medicine and told me to stay in bed. I read *Malcolm X* and worked on my paper. I had a terrible second night, until the fever broke. The doctor on his second visit told me I would be O.K., that I didn't have to return to the States, but not to go out until at least that evening. I made a rapid and remarkable recovery. The next day I interviewed Jacobo Schneider, an informed leader of the Jewish community, who filled me in on many things about Venezuelan Jewry. A clue as to the status of Venezuela's Jews was that their Jewish day school was so good that the non-Jewish minister of education sent his children to that institution. The Jewish community was about to build a million-dollar secondary school. Hebrew was compulsory. Nearly all graduates went to colleges and studied for the professions. There was no poverty. Little intermarriage as yet, but increasing. There was almost zero criminality or personal and social pathology. Jews were nationalistically pro-Israel, rather than religious.

While sitting in the lobby, I was paged by a man who was looking for a sick Jew from America. It was Mr. B. Selinowski, secretary of public relations for the Jewish community. Jacobo had told him about us, and he filled me in on a few points that Jacobo had overlooked. Later Jacobo took us on a tour of the city, both the Jewish and the public sites. Our impression was favorable. But I had lost two days, and we had to move on without seeing any part of the country outside of Caracas.

Brazil

Five hours later we were in Rio, having left Caracas at midnight. At the Hotel Gloria, we had a beautiful room overlooking the harbor, the park, museum, and Sugar Loaf, a prominent peak. Josef Steinberg, young, a poet and editor, head of the local American Jewish Committee, joined us for lunch, where we ate excellent barbecued filet of beef. He talked for hours about Brazilian Jewry. Parents and their children preferred the public to the Jewish day schools. Social clubs were organized to keep Jews close to other Jews. There was little Jewish content in their programs. If one wanted to remain Jewish he had to be part of the day schools or synagogues. There was a great deal of intermarriage and divorce. Yet there was little conversion to other faiths. Most Jewish youth went to college. Most Jews were in business or the professions. No one wanted to study to become a Jewish communal worker. Jewish youth were largely politically left-wing. There was little personal and social pathology. Jews followed the life-style of upper-class Brazilians, yet they feared total assimilation, even as they drifted toward secularization. Most spoke Portuguese. Pictures of Zalman Shazar, the Israeli President, were displayed in windows of homes as well as Jewish institutions. While they supported Israel, few went on aliyah. Large assemblies could be marshaled when a Jewish celebrity appeared.

We talked about American Jewish novelists, many of whom he had read. We ranged over poetry, the ballet, concerts, and the arts.

On our own, we toured Rio with its scenic views and monuments. We noted the shanty towns on the hillside overlooking the splendid hotels and beaches. We stopped at synagogues, where all reported the assembly of a minyan each day and good attendance on the Sabbath.

We ate feijoado, the celebrated Brazilian dish of a variety of organ meats and black beans, which Emma claimed poisoned her for six months. I found it quite tasty and suffered no after-effects. We went to a few museums and art galleries, none of which were distinguished.

By contrast, when we reached São Paulo, we found it to be an amazing metropolis. The Jewish community was thriving in its synagogues, schools, social clubs, and charitable endeavors, including a new hospital. This was a city with a superb art museum, galleries, an opera house. We lunched with Rose Neumann, a former staff member of the New York Jewish Federation, who had married and settled in São Paulo. She clued us in on the economic problems of this overly fast growing city, where we saw three score skyscrapers going up at one time for commerce and residences.

I learned about the sociology of the Jewish community in a long talk with Rabbi Pinkuss, Alfredo Hirschberg, and Suzanne Frank. Pinkuss the senior rabbi in the city, headed a Reform synagogue, the largest in the community. Hirschberg was a professor and sociologist, who wrote for the *American Jewish Year Book*. Frank was one of the best-known social workers in the country. They told me that most children went to the public schools. Intermarriage was not yet a serious problem. There was little divorce, in part because it was difficult to get one in a Catholic country. The only adult Jewish crimes they could think of was smuggling, false bankruptcy, and forgery. I asked: "What about bribery?" The answer was: "Since when is that a crime?" When I inquired about prostitution, which had been a serious problem decades earlier in Brazil, when Jewish white slavery flourished, they did not want to discuss it. I subsequently learned that some of the former Jewish prostitutes had obtained respectability later in life and were now listed amongst the "better" families. Few Jewish youth were in radical movements. The majority went to college. Most Jews had a nationalistic rather than a religious identity.

Pinkuss was optimistic about the future of Jewish life in Brazil, but Hirschberg gave me a more negative view of the years ahead as we walked out of the meeting. Mrs. Frank was concerned with the lack of trained Jewish social workers.

When I spoke to Itzhak Levy, who wrote for *Haaretz* (an Israeli newspaper), he told me that while there were few social problems, except in the major cities, there was little hope for survival for the Jews located in small towns. Not enough Jewish youth were affiliated with Jewish organizations. "Cards and sports" dominated the lives of most Jews.

With regard to social and personal pathologies, I had drawn up a list of questions as to how Jews rated in adult crime, juvenile delinquency, poverty, intermarriage, divorce, conversion to other faiths, alcoholism, drug addiction, prostitution, homosexuality, out-of-wedlock births, serious mental breakdowns, affiliations with radical movements. Whenever possible, I attempted to find out what they thought was the relative difference between the behavior of Jews and non-Jews in these various categories.

Since my visits to the three cities had already given me clues as to what I would find elsewhere (and it was subsequently confirmed), I completed my paper for the international conference, had it Xeroxed, and sent it off by air to Miriam Ephraim, the executive secretary of the conference, to have it reproduced for the meetings on August 29–31 in Washingotn, less than three weeks hence.

São Paulo, like many large South American cities, was a community of ethnic diversity. Indians and Spaniards of course, but there was also an assemblage of 650,000 Italians. We saw the new university, the world-famous Butantan Snake Institute, the Albert Einstein Hospital. A journalist we met en route invited us to see his unique collection of hummingbirds. Everywhere there was evidence of the work of the distinguished architect Niemeyer. We enjoyed the celebrated churascaro restaurants which served mouth-watering barbecued steaks.

On Friday night, we went to Rabbi Pinkuss's congregation, which was nearly full. The cantor and choir were excellent. The sermon, in Portuguese, we were later told, stressed, not unexpectedly, spiritual vs. material values. References were made to the writings of Martin Buber, Leo Baeck, and Louis Finkelstein, with whose works we were familiar.

As we were leaving our pews, we were greeted heartily with a "Shabbat Shalom" by a male congregant. As soon as we identified ourselves as tourists from New York, he immediately invited us to dinner. That was how we met Max and Alice Eberhardt at 7:45 P.M. and didn't leave them until nearly 2:30 A.M. Actually Max took us to his widowed sister Lilli's home for dinner. She apparently went through this exercise weekly, because when we reached her house, there were assorted other guests. Twelve of us sat down to a full and typical Friday night feast, except for apple pie rather than apple strudel for dessert.

I was asked to make *Kiddush*. Max's son chanted a long *Birkat* after dinner. Max, a hustler, a textile manufacturer, an officer in seemingly every Jewish organization in São Paulo, kept the evening bubbling with conversation. After dinner he drove us like mad in a Volkswagen to his expensive, well-decorated condominium apartment. In passing, he told us that he and Alice were the only Jewish residents in this deluxe new building, and that he also had a large car and chauffeur. Alice related that she had two maids and how much they were paid per month—as much as Emma paid for one maid for six hours back home. He sought my counsel on how to find funds and support for a hospital, which was more than the Jewish community could afford and I suspect even needed. They hoped it might help solidify their relationship to the non-Jewish community and local government officials. He frankly admitted that many Jews had benefitted from the Material Claims fund established by the German government for German-Jewish refugees. He was unhappy with the local Russian and Polish Jews, who did not seem to be as deeply interested in philanthropy or in keeping the memory of the Holocaust alive. In the early hours of the morning, when his hustling enthusiasm began to wane, he confessed his concern about the future of the Jewish people both in Brazil and elsewhere in South America.

Uruguay

We lost a whole day flying to Montevideo, Uruguay, with the plane late to start off, then a long layover in Porto Alegre. We arrived towards the end of a cold afternoon, and for the first time realized that we hadn't brought the right things to wear, to ward off the colder weather in southern South America, just the reverse of the climate in Pelham. The city was most attractive with its wide, tree-lined boulevards and well-fashioned houses. We stayed at the excellent Columbia Hotel, where there were few guests.

Eryk Kohn told us about the forty thousand Jews, who lived in the country. Seven day schools served only 20 percent of the Jewish children. The cost of living was much cheaper than in Peru, so that his Peruvian brother-in-law had arragned the Bar Mitzvah for his son in Montevideo at a fraction of the price. The Jews had built a large country club and had recently opened a community center, renting quarters in a commercial building. Many Jews had come to Uruguay in the 1890s as farmers, with the help of the Baron de Hirsch Fund. Russian and Turkish Jews settled after World War I. German Jews arrived in the 1930s. After World War II, East Europeans—Hungarian Hassidim and others—appeared.

They were an athletic-minded community and were sending one hundred Jewish athletes to the Pan American Maccabiad in São Paulo. Athletics were a means of preparing themselves for any eventuality.

Kohn's report on the Jewish pathologies was similar to that which I had heard in other South American countries. The recent visit of Israel's President, Shazar, had "raised the status of the Jews." Synagogues have a problem attracting enough worshippers. Eryk was English, a businessman, seemed to be involved with a great many commercial enterprises as well as Jewish organizations. He lived in a beautiful mansion with good art on the walls. Yechiel Reichman, president of the Asociación Hebraica, reinforced most of what Kuhn had told us, but stressed that the Jewish community was still divided amongst its ethnic units and there was an effort to try and coordinate them.

José Sasson, president of the Comité Central Israelita del Uruguay, had been told of our presence. We lunched with this handsome Sephardic Jew and his equally attractive wife. Werner Wolf, an accountant, joined us. We were filled in with more details about the older Sephardic Jewish census and the German-Jewish refugee population. There was a definite allegiance to Israel amongst the diverse constituencies. Their contacts with the United States were minimal. We learned from José that a contingent of Sephardic Jews had arrived in the 1890s. They worshipped in an imposing synagogue. Were it not for the current seemingly uncontrollable inflation, there would be few poor Jews. While Uruguay was a meat-producing nation, meat was rationed in stores and hotels two days a week, so that most of this commodity could be exported for hard currency.

At a cafe we met three young Jewish Peace Corps workers, who had finished their assignment in Venezuela and were touring South America before returning to the United States to study social work. They gave us a tragic view of life in the underclass in Venezuela, which was totally different than the picture we drew from the Jews who enjoyed the benefits of the upper class. Poverty in Venezuela was widespread and creating political instability, since the poor were easily exploited by the revolutionists. This better explained the presence of armed soldiers in front of banks, business buildings, as well as public institutions. The soldiers were there to prevent the frequent holdups that helped finance the undergrounnd. The rich Jews we met never mentioned these conditions and problems.

We bought some unusual silver objects. We left with a favorable impression of the small and attractive country.

Argentina

Buenos Aires was only a half-hour flight away. We were surprised to find a considerable shantytown area for the poor as we approached one of the most beautiful cities in the world. A walk around our hotel revealed a cosmopolitan city with dense traffic and shops filled with good merchandise and art galleries displaying fine art.

Rosita Resnick Helfgot, an American-educated social worker, who was directing a volunteer recruiting program at the Hebraica Community Center, lunched with us the first day. Slight, dark-eyed, vivacious, articulate, acquainted with everyone in social work in the United States, she briefed us on the Jews of Argentina. This country had the largest Jewish community south of the United States. There were 296,600 Jews. She estimated, and this was confirmed by others, that between 20 and 30 percent of the Jews were "Communists." The Jews in colleges were often the leaders of the radical left. As I went over the pathology list with her, the record of the Jews, in contrast to the natives, was exemplary. She revealed that there was a cemetery for Jewish prostitutes outside of Buenos Aires. We attended the Bialik School, where her children were enrolled, along with one thousand other students. Mr. Carp, the principal, looked like the late American Rabbi Joseph Lookstein and acted like the late American Rabbi Alter Landesman, who used to go into the classrooms of the Hebrew Educational Society in Brooklyn and temporarily take over the class. Hebrew was emphasized in this school.

Rosita led us to the impressive fourteen-story Hebraica, one of the largest centers in the world, serving youth from six to twenty-five years of age. Every institution we visited requested materials for programs and administrative operations.

Izaak Kleinbaum, formerly with the JDC and now with Israel Bonds, and his wife talked as we ate in a superb Italian restaurant in the Italian section of the city. He reconfirmed what Rosita had told us, but put the Jewish "Communist" affiliation higher, at one-third of the Jewish population. He was concerned with the sharp divisions in the community and with the future identification of Jewish youth. He was disturbed by the dictatorial trend of the government. We talked with a number of other social workers and rabbis. We had several conversations with Dr. Abraham Monk, who was a professor of social psychology and worked for the American Jewish Committee. He gave us a detailed political, economic, and sociological analysis of Argentina and its impact on the Jews. The recent closing of the Jewish credit banks, from which Jews made most of their loans, was leading to a serious financial crisis. He numbered the radical Jewish element more conservatively at only 15 percent, but whether higher or lower, it constituted a formidable public relations problem for the Jewish community. He believed that the schools, synagogues, and Hebraica had a beneficial influence on Jewish youth, but admitted that most Jews were untouched by such positive Jewish forces.

The Jews were "jittery, but not panicky" was the way he put it. He reiterated the lack of sufficient professionally trained Jewish personnel.

Some years later Monk came to the United States for an advanced degree and is now considered one of the major specialists on services for senior citizens.

Boris Farberman of the World Jewish Congress felt that Jewish organizations, especially from the United States, should not interfere in the policies and programs of native Argentinian Jewish associations. He escorted us to the Escuela Scholem Aleijem, the largest secular Jewish school, with two thousand students, which was managed by the sparkling Jaimé Finkelsztein. It had a Zionist, Hebraic orientation. Jaimé was well known worldwide as an inventive Jewish educator, although he had come to Argentina as an immigrant plasterer and was self-taught.

We visited the impressive Yiddish Folk Theater, which was operated by Jewish "Communists." It produced Yiddish plays and conducted classes in every aspect of the theater. On occasions it produced plays from a political point of view not favorable to the rest of the Jewish community. Other Jewish groups did not patronize this theater, which embarrassingly distributed Communist literature.

An evening was spent at the Odeon Theater, where we witnessed a first-class native folklore program of music and drama.

It was so cold that we bought winter underwear at Harrod's, which I still wear during equally cold Pelham winters.

Another meeting was held with Mr. Triwax, a volunteer leader of the local Kehillah, which attempted to influence the government about policies affecting Jews. The Kehillah had forty-five thousand members, offered insurance policies, pensions, and controlled all cemetery privileges. Less than 7 percent of the Jewish population was poor and in need of financial and other assistance. He was uncertain how the current government would treat the Jews, but as a businessman and communal leader, he thought the most serious problem was not the government per se, but inflation, which could have a ruinous affect on the economy of the Jews. Monk said that the dictatorship and inflation would force many Jews to leave Argentina. We left the country with a feeling that despite the obstacles, even Jews who "had their bags packed" would not leave in large numbers unless the dictatorship became cruel and economically repressive. A number of the people we met asked us in which stocks they should invest their money. I gave them the names of several Jewish brokers.

Chile

Santiago, Chile, was less than two hours away from Buenos Aires over the Andes Mountains. We were met in a downpour at the airport by Rolf

Nathan, a former German refugee, now a successful auto parts dealer, who drove an old car and lived in a modest rented house, not wishing to disclose the state of his real fortune. Since there were relatively few eligible Jewish young men, their daughter was literally compelled to enjoy non-Jewish male company. An older sister had already intermarried.

Our hotel in the center of town overlooked an old church and the snow-covered mountains in the distance. This was the skiing season and North Americans flew down for this sport. We were introduced to a good native drink, pisco. We toured the schools, built by Jews, now integrated, yet they were Hebrew and Zionist oriented with many Israeli teachers. One-third of the students spent at least one year in Israel. There was an inclination toward radicalism among Jewish college youth, but not as marked as in Buenos Aires.

Rolf drove us to the Estadio Israelita, a substantial Jewish sports club, where most of the Jewish community spent its weekends. They were also constructing the "finest" eighteen-hole golf course in the country. Jews were not admitted as members in the other good clubs. Religion was not a major interest of the Jews. Most Jews were well off. There was relatively little pathology.

To keep warmer, for Chile was cold, we bought some wool ponchos. We dined at Rolf's home on Friday night. There was no challah, no candles, no *Kiddush*, although wine was served. There was little talk about Jewish affairs, but we did range over art, travel, which they did a lot, and about investments of money abroad. While he worked in many organizations to keep Jews together, he hadn't the foggiest notion whether Jews would survive in Chile.

My long phone conversation with Rabbi Gunther Friedlander did not alter the picture of Jewry given to me by Rolf.

There was a popular, widespread anti-American campaign in Santiago with graffiti everywhere attacking the United States and its ambassador. The Jews did not share this adverse political attitude.

Peru

The three-hour flight over and along the spectacular Andes Mountains to Lima, Peru, brought us to the Hotel Alcazar, which, like most South American hotels we had been in, were always short of heat. At the hotel restaurant we met an American Catholic social worker, who considered Peru a progressive country. The Catholics in Peru believed that the Jews kept too much apart from the life of the state. This isolation was later confirmed by Gerard G. Astruck, with whom we made arrangements to fly to Cuzco and see Macchu Pichu. A German Jew, he still lived in the shadow of the Holocaust. He did not know where Jews would flee if political problems arose to disturb the Peruvian government. Yet he indicated that Jews presently lived in Peru free of concern and well off financially.

Lima was an attractive city. The square around the Cathedral, Palace, private homes and public buildings was a beautiful site. One noticed prominently the presence of Indian faces, squat, dark complexioned, with large bony features.

Joseph Lemor, a travel agent and leader of the local World Jewish Congress, was a Sephardic Jew, originally from Turkey, but had resided in Peru for forty years. Most of the sixty-five hundred Jews lived in Lima. There were 150 Sephardic families. Seven synagogues, but only one of consequence. The Germans, Ashkenazi, and Sephardi Jews maintained separate organizational lives. Eighty-five percent of the children attended one major day school. High school graduates, if male, entered the universities in the United States, and after graduation returned to Lima. Jews did not fear the Catholic hierarchy, but were concerned about the recurrent political upheavals that usually accompanied a change of leadership in the periodic six-year elections. Jews maintained favorable relations with political leaders.

Israel was well regarded in Peru by Jews and non-Jews. Israelis were solicited for desert research and water exploration.

We had a good lunch with Michel Radzinsky, leader of the Ashkenazi Orthodox group, a wealthy and generous Jew. He was joined by Herman Zvilich, a correspondent for the Yiddish *Morning Journal*. Michel said that only thirty families observed Kashrut, fifteen were *shomer shabbat,* and five closed their stores on the sabbath.

There were few pathologies. Some intermarriage. Missionaries were active in the Jewish community. Jews married off their children quite young to assure Jewish marriages. The day school was partially integrated and directed by a non-Jewish principal, a legal requirement. While the teachers came mainly from Israel, the school was not as strongly Zionist as those in other South American countries. Everyone was concerned about the growing intermarriage and assimilation.

We met Zvilich and Radzinsky again for coffee at a shop where other Jews dropped in. Zvilich told us that twenty years ago, presumably in 1946, two hundred Jewish prostitutes had been driven out of Argentina (hence the reluctance to speak about this issue when I raised it in Brazil and Argentina) and settled in Lima. They filled a need for single men without wives. Some married. There were some offspring of "illegitimate" (his word) liaisons. Some became respectable. A few died and were buried in a separate part of the Jewish cemetery reserved specifically for them.

When Jews were expelled from Brazil in 1654, some settled in Peru, where they were persecuted by the Inquisition. A few were burned at the stake. Some names of places and people in Lima were remembrances of this early presence.

Jacobo Gomberoff, secretary-general of the Union Israelita del Peru, joined us for coffee and took us on a tour of the city. We visited the new Ashkenazi synagogue, where it was still difficult to attract a daily minyan, although it was well attended on Shabbat and High Holy Days. The day school was a superb institution with its up-to-date facilities and equipment. We noted pictures of Eshkol and Shazar, Israeli officials, on the walls. The Jews raised funds for local Jewish charities and institutions and for Israel. He said: "We are not middle class, but rich."

We spoke to an Austrian Jew who was married to a Peruvian non-Jewish woman. While he was "reasonably contented," he would "not do it again," as non-Jews have "different attitudes toward life and justice and suffering."

We arranged our trip to Cuzco, were medically checked by Dr. Holzer. Found we were in good health for this elevation to 12,000 feet. Nonetheless he gave us coramina glucosa pills for relief if we experienced high-altitude sickness. We also bought a can of "Kik," at his advice, to discourage mosquitoes.

This was what it took to make this fascinating side trip: First to a travel agent and sat around for an hour, while he told us of the virtues and caveats of going to Cuzco. It was cold up there. You could get a heart attack. The mosquitoes ate you alive. The rooms in the hotel might have little or no heat. You would need to rest for two hours in bed to be able to move around the city. Don't walk too fast. You must not eat too much. You must get a medical checkup. If you were lucky you would fly in a pressurized cabin. Otherwise you would have to suck oxygen during the two-hour flight. He then told us that it would take two days to confirm whether we could go there at all. Flights and hotels were limited. We wondered whether we should go at all. He called to report that reservations had been made. We flew.

We left Lima, a city where the sun does not penetrate a thick cloud cover for four months. On the way to the airport, we could see the poverty that faced the natives daily in contrast to the glitter of Lima. The four-motor Fawcett plane took off. We sucked oxygen. The other two planes, both pressurized, had been wrecked on flights to Cuzco in recent months. When we pierced the clouds, we flew in dazzling sunshine over a terrain that was rugged, devoid of tree cover, rising ever higher. We looked down on tiny villages, specks in the Andes. We finally appeared over Cuzco, a city of 100,000 people with its many visible brown churches and squares. At 11,500 feet, I could hardly walk, but Emma made it easily. The Indians at the airport, with their round, high felt and straw hats, greeted us with offers of ponchos, rugs, hats, scarves, and knickknacks. One could barely escape their embraces.

Our hotel was built in Moorish design. Room 145 overlooked the Church La Merced, built on the ruins of an Inca temple. Its carillon rang during the day. I took another pill, went to bed for an hour, and was still woozy when I arose. We went on a bus tour of Cuzco, riding higher into the mountains. Saw Incas on their llamas. Others were weaving and spinning. A man was plowing by foot with an instrument we had seen in Van Hagen's book. We stopped at a temple where Incas once performed animal sacrifices. (This was unlike Guatemala and Mexico, where the Mayans and the Aztecs in the same period performed these rites with human beings.) The Indians were poor. Their former culture had been depreciated. The cathedral displayed European, Moorish, Spanish, Byzantine, and baroque influences, but not a touch of the Inca was in evidence. The markets were colorful, dirty, and stank of feces.

Emma discovered paintings by an artist who signed his name Salomon. I was sure that he was a transplanted Jewish artist from Brooklyn. A taxi driver helped us locate his studio. Hamilcar Salomon was slight, dark-hued, and spoke English. On his mother's side, he was one-quarter Indian and one-quarter Spanish. His father made him one-quarter Chinese, and the other quarter was Jewish, hence his last name. We were taken with him and his pictures and bought two large ones with distinctly Inca subject matter—an Indian in traditional headdress and the other of a group of Indians in a market-place. The latter has hung over our fireplace for years.

In this out-of-the-way hotel, where relatively few tourists come, we met Merwin Rosenman, whom I had recruited for the board of Bronx House, and who later became its president. Merv worked out the legal details for Bronx House to handle the funds for the publication of this book and suggested that I set up a private publishing company. We also met Abe Sudran, the executive director of the Essex County, New Jersey, Jewish Federation. Sudran was never interested in my strong recommendations for Jewish content in all Jewish communal services and showed even less interest in my comments on Ethiopian Jews.

Despite the elevation, Cuzco was actually hot and not cold, and we needed neither the long underwear nor the ponchos that we had purchased in Argentina and Chile. We were awakened early on a Thursday morning, with church bells tolling at 4 A.M., when the church across the street opened for any passing worshipper. Few went in. Most just paused and crossed themselves. This was the day for our trip to Macchu Pichu. We descended on a narrow-gauge single-track train from a height of 12,500 feet, with snow-covered mountains in the distance, through narrow gorges sixty-three miles away to a height of only 6,693 feet above sea level, passing through Indian villages, poor and ill kept. A bus took us up a winding mountain road on a perilous ride some 2,182 feet higher. We found ourselves at Macchu Pichu, at a height of 8,875 feet.

As we walked over the inspiring old Inca area, where on a mountain peak, they had carved out of granite rock, terraces for farms, houses, temples, an industrial location, cemetery, we marveled at their engineering and construction ingenuity. The setting looked out on majestic higher peaks, some under cloud cover, completely surrounding this awesome location. Here was where the Incas withdrew to make their last stand, believing they could defend themselves on the inaccessible, isolated mountain.

They perished when the conquering, greedy Spaniards reached and destroyed them. Their unique gold objects were confiscated. Centuries later many were unearthed by Hiram Bingham, an archaeologist, and now repose in a museum in New Haven, Connecticut. It was all overwhelming.

We rode back upwards and talked with our guide, a young Peruvian anthropologist, Julio Sotomayer, who related that the Indians in these regions still worshipped the sun, mountains, and nature along with their Christian Jesus. He did not know if any Marranos (Secret Jews) had accompanied Pizarro on his rapacious conquest of Peru. In fact, he had never heard of Marranos, nor that some of them had been burned at the stake during the Inquisition. He did not know the origin of his last name, which I had noted was one occasionally found amongst Jews. I presume that such information was kept out of native textbooks. Were it not for Jewish historians, who look for every Jewish component in history, I would never have asked the question.

Mountain sickness dogged me during the brief stay. Dizziness, a bit of nausea. I didn't let it interfere with this extraordinary adventure. We sucked oxygen on the flight down to Lima. Our plane was delayed for hours, as we witnessed the ceremonies at the Peruvian airport on the arrival of the President of Chile.

Colombia

We reached Bogota at night, ending up in the splendid Continental Hotel. When we awoke in the morning, it showed us perched at the foot of two mountains with a statue of Jesus at the top of one and a church at the peak of another. The city rested at an elevation of 8,500 feet. It did not have the charm of Lima. It reminded us more of urban Caracas. The mountain background made it different from either. This was the city of emeralds. On the streets we were constantly approached to buy these jewels. Emma bought some from a recommended dealer. The museum had a fine collection of pre-Colombian Indian pottery, many with grotesque human images.

We lunched with José Honlein, a German Jew who had settled in Bogota in 1935. The Jewish community was divided between the Sephardim, who had their own synagogue, and a German-Jewish group, which also had a synagogue and a good school. The Ashkenazim were the largest contingent and had just built another fine synagogue and a social center. There was an old age home, small, well maintained. We were told by everyone that the Jews were "rich." Honlein took us on a tour of all the Jewish institutions and to the new "club," an extraordinary, modern-designed country club for all ages, with special facilities for youth, a soda fountain which duplicated a liquor bar, an indoor pool, and a nine-hole golf course. Completed at a cost of $1 million, the "club" gave visible evidence of Jewish wealth. Adults occupied many of the rooms and did not leave their card tables to eat, since a waiter stood by ready to serve them. Cards and sports dominated their lives.

There were few problems amongst the Jews. Not many children attended the Jewish schools. There was no overwhelming interest in Israel. Few went on aliyah. To the question of intermarriage, Honlein replied: "Yes, there is some intermarriage. The Ashenazim are marrying German and Sephardic Jews." We left with a feeling that they were content, as they were living in what they believed, as one described it, "paradise." We sent a great many Jewish books that Honlein had requested for his synagogue's library.

Panama

A few hours flight brought us to hot, unbearably humid, lush Panama. Nathan Witkin, chaplain and USO director for the Jewish soldiers, took us in tow. Most Jewish servicemen were identified as Jews, in large part due to his influential leadership. The Canal Zone was a U.S. enclave. Jewish soldiers were exemplary in behavior; only one had been incarcerated in the past five years.

The Jewish community was located at the opposite ends of the canal in Colón and in Panama City. Colón was distinguished for still having a small colony of twenty families descended from the Spanish-Portuguese Jews who had arrived in the seventeenth century, coming from Dutch Guiana and Curacao. Both cities were sharply divided between newer Levantine Sephardim and Ashkenazi groups. The Albert Einstein Institute was an exceptional day school. We had lunch and talked at length with its esteemed director Heszel Klepfisz, who filled us in on the demography of the local Jewish community. I read his book *Culture of Compassion,* (1983), in which he described the spirit of Polish Jewry from Hasidism to the Holocaust. Personal and social problems were minimal. Their economic status was high. Amongst the Sephardim, 80 percent kept kosher.

We were taken to a fantastic Sephardic wedding one night and treated as though we were members of the families. These Middle Eastern Jews were the largest and dominant group in Panama. While the ceremony was traditional, it differed from East European practice only in that a veil was draped over the couple just before the ceremony was concluded. There was little drinking, but lots of eating and dancing. The women were dressed in gorgeous gowns. We sat at a table with three young couples in their thirties, who had three, four, and five children respectively. When I asked them why so many, they did not reply that they wanted them, or that they could afford them, or that Sephardic Jews had large families. Almost in one voice, as though it was rehearsed, they replied: "We must make up for those we lost in the Holocaust," adding that they were not done with bearing more children. It was a remarkable statement about a Jew's responsibility to his people.

We bought molas, colorful needlework vestments made and worn by Kuna–San Blas Indian women living on an island off the coast of Panama. One was framed and is part of our art collection.

At a B'nai B'rith meeting we met many of the leaders of both communities, including a member of the old Spanish-Portuguese Fidanque family. The discussion that evening dealt with how to prevent intermarriage with non-Jews.

Mexico

Flight hopping through Costa Rica, San Salvador, and Honduras, we arrived in Mexico City. The 7,500-foot elevation bothered me, but did not interfere with my interviewing Mexican-Jewish leaders. We had a long conference with Dr. B. Ghulgasser, head of the Colegio Israelita de Mexico, which reached fifteen hundred Jewish children, a quarter of the youth census.

The school was forty-two years old, stressed Yiddish during the first three years. In the younger grades, they spoke and sang in Yiddish. Then the school switched to Hebrew. It was not a religious school, for it had a secular-Zionist orientation. Ghulgasser was pessimistic about the future, as only the mothers, not the fathers, were interested in their children's Jewish education. We went to a concert that evening, where Jewish children were performing Yiddish and Hebrew songs and sketches. Sitting in a row behind a number of Jewish parents (all women), we noted that when the children returned to their parents, they spoke only in Spanish. That told us a great deal about the "lasting" Yiddish, linguistic education of the children. It was a good concert.

An interesting afternoon was spent with Tevia Maizel, in the new, handsome, and active Kehilah Ashkenazi de Mexico. Originally a teacher, he later became a rich industrialist and a philanthropist. At the age of seventy, he still taught a course at the seminary. We spoke Yiddish, although he understood English. He was a mine of sociological data about the entire Jewish community. He pointed out that those with a Jewish education had only a 3 percent intermarriage rate. For others, it was already 17 percent. The only hope for Jewish survival was Jewish education and Israel. He would be content with a smaller, better-informed, devoted Jewish census than with mere numbers who were indifferent to their fate.

We spent some time at the largest Jewish social-athletic club in the world. It was evident from our conversation with the young director and a review of the posters on the bulletin board that it was just what it was billed—a social and athletic center with little or no Jewish programming, a well-equipped complex with indoor and outdoor facilities.

I was invited to dine with several other Jewish groups. They wanted me to return and make more definitive studies of the entire Jewish community, to plan for the future. I referred them to other resources. Everyone was ordering books from me, which I subsequently sent. Our last night was spent in a restaurant operated by a former Jewish poet, where we conversed with a number of intellectuals about the cultural life of the Mexican Jew. They reported a limited interest and market for their creative writings and art.

We ended our tour with this evaluation: while there was little personal and social pathology amidst the Jewish population, there was a steady thinning of interest in religious and cultural Jewish matters, an erosion that might accelerate as the current generation received its education outside of the scope of Jewish institutions. How to keep Jews Jewishly identified was their constant question. It was also the subject of my paper in Washington a few days after our return to the United States.

The Washington Conference: 1966

My paper, bearing the formidable title "The Role of Jewish Communal Services in Strengthening Jewish Identification," had been prepared at the request of the International Conference of Jewish Communal Service. The meeting in Washington was organized by a working party in Jerusalem on August 29–31, 1965. My address was to be a trial run for the enclave to take place in Jerusalem in 1967. It was presented before worldwide representatives at the ICJCS in Washington on September 7, 1966, in conjunction with the non-Jewish International Conference of Social Work. The mimeographed version had been sent to the delegates, so that it was not necessary for me to read the 70-page document. I took the liberty of summarizing its contents.

The paper was not discussed. It was bitterly assailed by some of the major professionals in the field, including Sanford Solender, executive vice-president of the National Jewish Welfare Board. This was not the first time that he had taken it upon himself to attack my positions. He did so in 1954, when I presented a paper in New York on "The Jewish Center as a Fourth Force." What bothered my assailants was not the mass of facts that I had assembled about Jews around the world, which had a bearing on our daily practices and the problems that we had to cope with as professionals in Jewish agencies. These data were ignored. The paper indicated that while the Jewish situation was still quite favorable when compared to our non-Jewish neighbors, there were straws in the wind warning that if we did not shore up our constituents, members, clients, and patients with a bastion of intensive Jewish education, we might not be able to hold the line in the foreseeable future. In 1966, we were still living on the euphoria that Jews were well off financially, were better educated, were accepted in the non-Jewish world. We were free to practice variegated forms of Jewish life that each preferred. It was my opponents' view that we did not yet need to be zealously concerned with building ramparts to protect ourselves or to withdraw within ourselves in order to strengthen our identification, our morale, our inner Jewish life. Less than a year later, when we were frightened to death by the possibility of the destruction of Israel and then dramatically found ourselves overindulging in the quick six-day triumph by the Israeli army, the Jewish landscape changed. My paper, if given a year later, might have had a different impact.

That day, few wanted to listen to my recipes for Jewish identity and continuity. The angry attacks resulted in my equally vigorous defense of my position. A few weakly attempted to defend me. Overall, the outcome was inconclusive. The paper, due to the intervention of professional adversaries, was never published. However, when news trickled out about its provocative content, I mimeographed sufficient copies to meet more than one thousand requests.

In 1966 Jews still felt secure in America, in Israel, and in the world. The 1967 war changed Israel radically, a trauma from which it has not yet recovered. As I write this book, the problems that victory engendered have not yet been resolved. It was before the redemption of several hundred thousand Soviet Russian Jews. It was before the unfortunate involvement of Jews with drugs, alcohol, abortion, divorce, and intermarriage, which undermined the character of the Jewish family and Jewish life on the American scene. These unfortunate developments forced our Jewish agencies to develop programs for which they were not prepared, compelling some to employ Jewishly oriented and understanding personnel. Eventually many of the agencies were forced to change their programs, and finally, Federations were influenced to alter their Jewish priorities.

My paper was a portent of what was to come. It was at first ignored, but within a decade was adopted by the very people who had initially and openly opposed it.

Bill Kahn

William (Bill) Kahn, the New York Federation's executive vice-president (1981–1986), with whom I have a warm relationship, reminded me one day at lunch (April 11, 1986) that we had our ideological contretemps in the past.

Back in 1964, Bill had met Martin Luther King in St. Louis. Bill was the executive director of the Jewish Community Centers Association of St. Louis. Amongst other things, Bill was supportive of improved relations between blacks and Jews. King's office, the Southern Christian Leadership Conference, requested Bill to organize a group of social workers, go to Tuscaloosa, Alabama, and develop a student council for black teenagers in a college-readiness program. The social workers would also assist in developing support services for the teachers in this special school. Bill recruited eight colleagues from Jewish community centers. He asked the National Association of Jewish Center Workers to place this item on the 1964 annual convention agenda in Philadelphia. At the Philadelphia meeting, Bill asked the NAJCW to sponsor his participation as well as that of his colleagues.

Caught up in the civil rights elation, few challenged the proposal. I averred that I was for the civil rights program in all of its aspects, but if anyone was to take part in such helpful enterprises, it should not be as a Jew or through a Jewish organization, but rather as a citizen of this country; and that sponsorship should be absolutely nonsectarian. Even if Jews were motivated by the Jewish ethic in their desire to assist this discriminated section of our vast population, it was not a "Jewish" issue, but a national political obligation.

The resolution passed. Again I lost. I wonder whether this same resolution would even be brought up on the floor of a similar Jewish conference today and approved by the delegate body.

I think that Bill now feels the same way as I do.

Papers Written in 1965–66

I cannot explain, even in retrospect, why 1965–66 turned out to be such a very productive year, with many requests to me to read papers at meetings.

I had written a piece on intermarriage in 1964, indicating that if the trends continued, it would be an unhappy omen for the future of the American Jew. In 1965, I participated in another symposium on intermarriage in which I wrote an "Agenda for Tomorrow," which stated that Jewish agencies would have to abandon their free-wheeling, open-ended policies, and undertake drastic changes in order to halt and reverse these unfortunate, inexorable trends. No one was willing to undertake the radical measures I suggested. I ended my paper with the charge that if the Jewish school, the synagogue, the parents, the Jewish centers, the Jewish case work agencies, and Jewish communal relations organizations did not follow my prescription, "Our discussions are another academic exercise at best, or at worst, our indecisiveness or indifference can only result in a further exacerbation of the menacing problem."

As I finished this book in 1986, the problem was out of hand. There were such a huge number of intermarriages that the emphasis shifted to find some way of enticing the intermarried back into the fold, converting the non-Jewish spouse, declaring that the children of mixed couples were Jewish by virtue of having a Jewish father, as against the historical halachic position that the Jewishness of the mother determined the heritage of the children. Efforts were being made to proselytize among the non-Jews to refill our depleting Jewish ranks. Everyone was trying to grapple with an elusive fact of life, after the ailment had spread to epidemic proportions, because none had undertaken the preventive steps I had outlined earlier.

In the Winter 1966 issue of *Tradition*, I published a rejoinder to Charles S. Liebman's "Orthodoxy and the Jewish Community Center." Admitting that I too could offer some criticisms of the Jewish centers in the United States, I nonetheless insisted that the centers were here to stay. Responding directly to the issue Liebman had raised, I said:

> I doubt if orthodoxy and the Centers through dialogue will ever agree on a common philosophy and program. However, there is room for the Orthodox in the Center, if they can tolerate association with other Jews. But if they proscribe the Center's creation of full-scale Jewish programs, it will not contribute to more knowing Jews, nor the professional leadership that makes such knowledge possible. It will not add to the enrollment of existing synagogues, but diminish the numbers of Jews who will survive in the future. (p. 146)

Asked to comment on a paper delivered by C. Bezalel Sherman, "The Last Twenty-Five Years in Jewish Education" (Feb. 7, 1965), I replied with "Who Will Lead the Drive in the U.S. towards a Greater Concern with Jewish Education?" While everyone was seeking another Moses, I stated, I would settle for his father-in-law Jethro's sage counsel: "Seek out from among all the people capable men [and women, I would add], who fear God, trustworthy men who spurn ill-gotten gain; and set over them, to be rulers of thousands, rulers of hundreds, rulers of fifties, rulers of tens. And let them judge the people at all seasons; and it shall be, that every great matter they shall bring unto thee, but every small matter they shall judge themselves; so shall they make it easier for thee and bear the burden with thee" (Exodus 18: 21–22). I indicated that we must carefully recruit, train, and subsidize a large cadre of the ablest of our young Jewish people to become the teachers and leaders of Jewish education tomorrow instead of relying on their chance involvement or a miracle-worker.

On February 19, 1966, I presented a paper entitled "Welfarism" at a conference sponsored by the American Histadrut Cultural Exchange devoted to "Welfare State and Welfare Society." In it I observed that the current American antipoverty program could not succeed unless it was predicated on four cardinal Jewish principles: (1) The attack had to be universal and not local, with the removal of all resident laws. "There shall be one law for the stranger as well as for the Hebrew." (2) Support must be "adequate, not minimal, not marginal, not temporary, but sufficient to maintain the person on a level of dignity." (3) Financial support must be a continuous obligation of the government and society, as poverty could not be eliminated in a year or two. (4) Finally, the object of all welfare should be to make the person economically self-sufficient, so that he no longer had to rely on any outsider or on government. Lyndon Johnson's antipoverty program failed, I said, precisely because it did not fully take into account these basic principles.

Another paper that I was asked to give "The Cultural Life of the Aged Jews," presented in May 1966 at the National Conference of Jewish Communal Service, was not only well received and published, but had some modest impact on providing enriched Jewish cultural programs for the Jewish aged in institutions of all descriptions.

Occasionally my papers were well regarded, when I did not dig too deeply into the errors committed by professionals or challenge their philosophy and practice. However, I could never write a paper unless it had a "message," and that message was meant to correct mistakes or to chart new courses. Doing either was a hazard.

The Brandeis Institute

Dr. Shlomo Bardin, founder and director of the extraordinary Brandeis Camp Institute, came to see me in 1965 to talk about his camp and to tell me that he was seeking an assistant, who would succeed him in the not-too-distant future. He was already past seventy years. A tall, powerfully built, and articulate man, he had established a camp, originally for college youth, then for children, then for their parents and other adults, where they were exposed to a closed and total Jewish environment, which had a decisive effect on their lives as Jews.

Accompanied by the new executive vice-president of the New York Federation, David Salten, I flew out for a long weekend in California at this camp. Like most of the other invited visitors, I was impressed with the setting, the leadership assembled by Bardin, and the program. The camp seemed to be sealed off from the rest of the world. For example, campers had no access to radios or television or movies and even most newspapers for the duration of their four-week stay. The camp was marked with Jewish symbols and Jewish practices. While there was a choice of programs in drama, music, and dance to select from, all were in the Jewish orbit. The campers performed most of the chores, such as cleanup and the preparation and service of food. There was only a small, select staff for the college youth, experts in their own specialties, and they supported the administration's policies without equivocation. The camp brought outstanding, seminal, and inspiring Jewish thinkers and speakers who had a message for young people; and such visitors remained long enough to permit a vigorous exchange of views. The young people, although carefully selected, all had minds of their own. Bardin held the operation together with firmness and his presence almost guaranteed universal success.

I participated in one such weekend, where I gave the young people a description of what youth and especially Jewish youth were in danger of becoming in that turbulent period, ending the 1960s (revolts on the campus, antiwar rebellion, beginning of the drug culture and addiction, challenges to family life through cultistic life-styles). The campers resisted my negative description, in some degree because they were Jews to begin with, and in part because they did not believe that they were susceptible to the pathological forces which were already plaguing American society. Regrettably for them, my predictions proved to be accurate. In the next few years, many Jewish youth succumbed to this epidemic development. Yet I somehow felt that many of those who had come under Bardin's benign influence were able to survive this unfortunate period.

Eli Wiesel also participated on that week-end and as usual mesmerized the young campers with his voice and his stirring message.

In 1968, I brought a group of New York Federation camp directors to Brandeis to observe how a comprehensive Jewish program could be successfully conducted, if they were prepared to operate their own camp services along the controlled lines of a Bardin. They were all immensely impressed, but only one or two had a Jewish and educational background to match Bardin's. None of them had his massive strength, imagination, or influence. All tried to introduce some Jewish elements. Yet none of them were in a position to transform their camps into anything resembling the California Institute. A few other Jewish institutions have since tried to emulate Brandeis, but the leaders did not have the initial ability or never stayed with the enterprise long enough to achieve his results. I wrote a paper on this camp, which was widely circulated.

14

The Latter 1960s.

THE SPRING OF 1967 was a parlous season. Israel and Egypt had reached an impasse. War seemed imminent. The United Nations had withdrawn its protective forces in the Middle East. Egypt, now free to move militarily, closed the waterways which provided economic life-lines for Israel. The mood in the United States among Jews could only be described as despair. Despite Israel's vaunted military prowess, no one believed that it could withstand once again the same consortium of Arab Nations—Egypt, Jordan, Syria, perhaps others, who presumably had taken military lessons since 1948 and 1956. Some were so pessimistic about the outcome that they saw the Jews of Israel veritably facing another Holocaust, the second tragedy in our living memory. Demonstrations were organized in Washington, and over 100,000 of us went to the Capital to urge our President and the government to do everything possible to prevent war, or if war was inevitable, to assist Israel with all means. What was more, it looked as if the International Conference of Jewish Communal Service, scheduled for Jerusalem during the summer, which Emma and I had planned to attend, would have to be canceled.

The miracle of the pinpoint effectiveness of the Israeli air force, followed by its seeming invincible mechanized infantry and artillery, overran the Egyptian forces in a few days, conquering Sinai, Gaza, the West Bank of Jordan, and the Golan Heights, handing the Arab nations a crushing defeat. Israel now controlled a land mass far larger than its own previous limited borders. It had captured a huge population that it would have to police, inheriting a hornet's nest of problems which twenty years later have not been resolved. That world Jewry was not only emotionally relieved, but actually euphoric, would be an understatement. Not only was the conference to be held, but it was to take place in an Israel that would permit visitors to see areas they had never dreamed of seeing before, particularly the Western Wall and the Jewish sector of Old Jerusalem.

Margaret's Death

Before leaving we went to Washington to see Margaret, Sam's wife, who was suffering from terminal cancer. We were not sure that we would see her again. She died shortly after our return, on October 14, 1967. We were at her bedside when she finally passed away. A wonderful woman, who was intimately associated with Sam's rising career in the Foreign Service, her death brought to an end a genuine love affair of thirty years. She never converted to Judaism and wanted her funeral rites conducted at the Washington Cathedral. I wrote a beautiful eulogy for her, which I gave to the priest, who read it at the funeral service. Her body was cremated and the ashes were scattered over a part of New York State which she had grown to love. It was the home of Thomas and Virginia Knowlton in Mill Brook. Thus ended a relationship which was almost as much of a loss for Emma and for me as for Sam, so closely were the lives of the four of us bound together.

* * *

I had another busy year, so that before we left for Israel, I was again in a state of exhaustion. On our return from Washington by train, I had been working up to the last minute on two papers that I was to present in Jerusalem. Thoughtlessly, I left them in my portfolio on the train. When I rushed back only ten minutes later, it was gone. I had to reconstruct these writings from scratch without even the benefit of my notes, which I had also left in the bag.

On the *sherut* from Lydda to Jerusalem, I sat next to an Australian Christian layman, who said out loud, "Now that the Israelis have won the war, recaptured old Jerusalem, it is time for all Jews to accept Jesus Christ." As we taxied through the new and shorter route to Jerusalem via Latrun, I patiently explained to him that most Jews would never accept Christianity, because most of us thought that Judaism was still a superior religion, and had better answers as to man's relationship to God and to our fellow men. His loquaciousness ceased and he did not even bother to say good-bye to any of us when he left the car.

Before reaching our destination, the driver took us through parts of the Arab quarter, where Hassidim in their distinctive garb overflowed the streets. We stayed at the King David Hotel in Room 231, overlooking the old city walls. It was Tisha B'av. Jews did not know whether to weep or laugh over the dramatic turn of events. That night, with the customary solemnity, they recited the Lamentations of Jeremiah. Early next morning we literally rushed to the Western Wall. Decrepit buildings were being demolished. The court before the Wall was being cleared for the crowds that would daily assemble in this historic religious sanctuary.

The Dung Gate looked like its name. The Arabs that we passed were glum. They wore kaffias almost in defiance. They could hardly be enthusiastic about the reversal of their political and geographic fortunes. Israeli soldiers were everywhere on foot, on jeeps, on trucks, in jets overhead. We walked into the Moslem Dome of the Rock and the Mosque El Aksa. We walked through the desecrated cemetery on the Mount of Olives. The Mandelbaum Gate had been removed.

In walking through the Arab quarter, we opened a door and found ourselves in an Arab courtyard. Instead of being driven out, we were invited into a home, where the mother quickly prepared coffee and cakes. A daughter spoke some English. We had no problem in communication. She told us that she now hoped to go to the university. I doubt if their hospitality was out of fear. They may have been one of the families that recognized the reality of Israel's victory and were preparing to make the best of their lot.

We saw many of the former Arab territories overrun by the Israeli army, including the Golan Heights, which once dominated the Israeli settlements. Driving down the back road through Taiyiba, the highway that Jesus trod to the Mount of Temptation near Jericho, we stopped in this Christian village to observe the distribution of food by United Nations trucks. I looked at an interesting Arab house, where the exterior was faced with green tiles. A young man came out to greet us in English. He invited us into the house, where his mother quickly made fresh, hot pitta bread, cakes, and coffee. They were interested in learning about the United States. Not a word was exchanged on the Israeli control over that sector.

After examining the archaeological sites in Jericho, we drove to En Gedi. The road along the Dead Sea was now open. In some places we still saw white flags of surrender protruding from upper-story windows of Arab houses. We meandered around Qumran, desolate, barren, brown-hilled, where the Dead Sea Scrolls had been discovered.

We drove up to Nablus, went to the Samaritan synagogue on Har Eval, held the scrolls, said to be over one thousand years old, went to the house of their *kohen*, browsed through his collection of books, and were served coffee and cakes. The Arabs in Nablus looked upon us with eyes of hatred.

We went to the excavation and museum at Hazor. We visited Kfar Blum, home of old friends. For the first time in the history of that kibbutz, they felt free and secure against the ever-menacing attacks from the nearby elevated Syrian border.

Another day we drove through Gaza as far as El Arish in the northern

Sinai desert, saw the huge collection of captured military hardware that the Israelis were mounting on railroad cars to be removed to Israel proper. The Arabs showed no signs of hospitality, walking away when approached, and one closed his little shop when we wanted to purchase a cold drink. Cultivating relations with Egyptian Moslems after Israel's military conquest seemed to me to be an impossible task.

On another day, we made a trip to Masada, which had just been reopened. We had to approach it via Arad over a stone-strewn road that literally shook us to pieces. We walked up the western path and steps (there was no cable car then) and in exhaustion reached the top on a vary hot morning. We were deeply moved with what the citadel meant as both a castle for the king and a hideaway for refugee warriors. The sweeping view of the Dead Sea and the haze-covered, purple mountains in Jordan, the sheer exhaustion of the soil and the sandy, brown-covered barren hills was a site to remember. Undaunted by our arduous crawl to the top, we ventured down the north face to see the frescoes that had once decorated the palace. Luckily, the sun was not spraying its heat in that area, so the walk up, while strenuous, was bearable.

The sightseeing over, we addressed ourselves to the International Conference, which had attracted a large registration due to the Israeli victory. As usual, there were too many speeches, too many sessions, not enough opportunities for the delegates to talk to one another, not enough time to visit the social welfare agencies in Israel. Yet the universal reaction was one of enthusiasm. I edited and prepared the Conference *Proceedings,* in which I wrote:

> Planned in the days of uncertain calm, it took place in a magnificent setting of recent triumph. Conceived as a modest exchange of professional views on the intriguing subject of "Jewish Identity," it turned into an inner exposure of both the contemporary and historical roots of our people. . . . It demonstrated that despite erosion by acculturation, there was still a strong, unbreakable bond that united, perhaps even could cement, our dispersed, but not so insignificant remnants.

The two sessions in which I participated were on Jewish community centers and Jewish community organization and planning. With too many panelists, there was no time to read the papers that each of us had prepared. I had lost my original papers on the train from Washington to New York and had rewritten them hurriedly before the conference. I summarized in a few minutes what I had laboriously written twice. My emphasis was on the need to study thoroughly our Jewish problems by diligent and reliable research. To stregngthen Jewish identification, we had to abandon our nonsectarian philosophy and practice and devote ourselves to furthering Jewish knowledge and reintegrating ourselves back into the bosom of the Jewish community. Somewhere I said:

I get no comfort in a Jewish case worker making his Jewish client comfortable in his indulgence in adultery, which was destroying his family and denying them the resources needed for their own development. What must be done is to see that he abandons such negative practices, which are contrary to Jewish ethics, rebuilds a Jewish family and participates in the active and vital Jewish community with its variety of institutions and services.

So-called liberal Jewish social workers found it difficult, if not impossible, to buy this concept.

I devoted some time to meeting with a few Ethiopian Jews, who were unhappy with the fact that no encouragement was being given to their kinsmen in Ethiopia to migrate to Israel. In 1967, the Ethiopians in Israel numbered a bare thirty. They visited each other in order to derive whatever comfort they could from intimate association. My suggestion that recognition be given to their plight by the conference was rejected with silence. No one argued for or against the suggestion. They simply and collectively, perhaps conspiratorially, ignored it, as they continued to do for the next two decades.

I met with Dr. Dan Harel and Dr. Daniel Pridan, both of whom had assisted the tiny medical clinics in Ethiopian Jewish villages. They told me of the tremendous unmet needs for medical services in a land where the government spent little, where all kinds of diseases were still unconquered, where the life span was amongst the lowest in the world. Pridan spurred me to try to do more for them when I returned to the States, but I saw little help forthcoming from the organized Jewish world.

The Rones

Before embarking by boat for Sicily, we spent a few days with Rabbi and Mrs. James Ronberg (later he changed his name to Yaakov Rone), our former Pelham rabbi, who was now performing a two-year service mission in a home for children with problems in Kiryat Bialik, just north of Haifa.

We rode out to Megiddo to once again see the always interesting excavations undertaken by James Henry Breasted of the University of Chicago. We spent the rest of the afternoon and evening in Nazareth. After touring the churches, we stopped at an Arab antique shop, which had an unusual brass Syrian brazier on display. I asked the young, attractive Arab dealer for the price and he answered in perfect English "$125." I shook my head, "No." He asked what I wanted to pay. I replied, "$25." We browsed around the shop, talked to him about the United States, about popular music, Israel, art, with all of which he was familiar. When he suddenly said, "$100," I shook my head again and repeated,

"$25." I usually do not bargain. I decide whether I like an object, know how much I will offer, and if the offer is turned down, I walk away. We talked about Arabi-Israel relations. We were getting to know each other's views on many subjects. "$75," he said in a decisive voice. I repeated "$25." It was now 4:30 P.M. "$50." I still held to my offer of $25. Suddenly he picked up the several parts of the brazier and put it in my hands. "I give this to you as a gift. You are my friend." I was momentarily taken aback, but only for a moment. In the palm of my hand I had been holding a U.S. $20 bill and a $5 bill, and I handed them to him. "I give you a present, because we have become friends." He took them. Thus he never sold it to me. Apparently something happened to him over the two-hour period that made him give it to me in this fashion. Maybe he enjoyed our roving conversation in a good, earnest, informed, honest tone. Perhaps he wanted to show that an Arab could be generous and not a bargaining, mercenary vendor.

Now that we had exchanged gifts, I offered to take him to a nearby cafe for coffee. "Oh, no. You are my friend, in my country. I shall take all of you to dinner." We drove out to a restaurant on one of the hills overlooking Nazareth, where we did not leave him until 9 P.M. As a lavish host, he spent far more than the $25 he had received for the antique. We talked again on many subjects, but particularly politics. He thought that Jews and Arabs might work out a more positive relationship. I told him frankly that this would only be possible if Arab leaders abandoned the uncompromising position they had taken since 1948. We left with hearty handshakes. This ended a long and profitable transaction. The brazier reposes in our living room, always an object of inquiry by guests, who have to listen to this story of a most unusual bargaining.

Sicily

We were on our way for a fortnight in Sicily via boat from Haifa. There were a number of Israelis on board, sailing to Canada. Before we disembarked in Messina, we were told that they were migrating, going to a new world for a better and safer life. They never expressed the exaltation of most Israelis and Jews around the world as a consequence of the recent miraculous victory over the Arab nations.

The boat stopped long enough in Piraeus for us to taxi into Athens and take another quick look at the Parthenon with its notable ancient ruins, now regretably suffering from the inroads of pollution. A guide told us there was talk about removing the original Caryatids from the Erectheum and preserving them in a museum. Subsequently, this was done.

On the ship I drank too much wine, as we danced and cavorted with many of the merry voyagers. We disembarked at Messina across the narrow straits from the mainland of Italy, and could easily see Calabria from the boat and the shore. We walked through the city that had been rebuilt after the devastating earthquake in 1908, when eighty-three thousand people perished and medieval churches were destroyed. In a museum, we found a fountain dated 1450 with an inscription in Hebrew letters. As in many other parts of Sicily, we learned that there was a Jewish presence in the country, going back to the ancient days when Greece controlled this substantial island.

Renting a car, we explored the heights around Messina, then drove off to Taormina, a gem perched on top of a mountain overlooking the sea. I woke up the next morning with a painful attack of gout in the big toe of my left foot. I asked the concierge for a doctor and he said that the only one was out of town. He was also the mayor, so he had other pressing duties. I had not taken any colchicine with me, since I had not had a bout with this illustrious ailment in several years. I hobbled over to a shop with only one shoe and bought a pair of oversized sneakers, one of which I wore untied on my ailing foot. I then trudged with difficulty to a pharmacy a block away, but I could not explain to the Italian-speaking pharmacist either what my problem was or the medication needed. I recalled reading about gout in English on a bottle of mineral water the night before in a restaurant across the way. But the shop didn't open for an hour. I waited impatiently in exquisite pain only relieved by a beautiful sunny day. I bought the bottle of mineral water and took it to the drug store and showed the pharmacist what was printed in Italian, but he still shrugged his shoulders and did not give me a bottle of pills. I looked through his volume of pharmacopia in Italian and finally found colchipina, and I could make out that it was for gout. I finally bought a bottle of those curing pills. In the United States, it works within twenty-four to thirty-six hours, and it did the same in Sicily.

One could not get around easily in Taormina by foot. We used the car to see the heights and particularly the ancient Greek theater, where plays were now being performed. I was in a state of sheer torture, for I insisted on climbing up the steep stone steps to the top so as to visualize what it must have been like over two thousand years before, and at the same time to gaze at smoking Mount Etna some distance away.

We drove up the highway to Mount Etna, observed where the lava had hardened from previous heated outpourings over the years. People were still building houses on the sides of the roadway, some of considerable size and style, as though to defy the next eruption. We reached a point beyond which no visitors could go by car. We sat and overlooked the picturesque countryside thousands of feet below.

In Syracuse, we saw the ancient Roman theater. I was still wearing the sneakers, but enduring less pain. We examined the site, where archaeologists were still uncovering ancient artifacts.

We turned, after Catania, from the coast to the interior, drove through beige-gray villages. Neither the people nor their homes looked as though there was wealth. Sicily was grimly suffering from continued economic difficulties. Everything we purchased was incredibly inexpensive. People were most hospitable toward us as strangers. It was the grape season, and we saw carts everywhere piled high with fresh-picked grapes. The wine presses, some manned by donkeys going round and round endlessly, extracted the precious juices. The pears, also in season, were amongst the best we had eaten.

Our destination was Piazza Armerina, brought to the world's attention in 1950. There, at the foot of Mount Mangone, on a large clearing, was revealed the ruins of a majestic country villa, the luxurious hunting lodge of the imperial Roman family of Maximanius Herculius, with the numerous brilliantly colored, African-influenced floor mosaics. The sculptured pieces and the marble columns had been almost totally destroyed. These mosaics alone made our trip to Sicily worthwhile. Each room had a different theme. There were scenes of hunting, of fishermen, and appropriate artistic decorations for the bathroom, bedrooms, children's rooms. The tiles in the swimming pool showed young women wearing bikinis. All of this was made in the third century for the indulgence of an emperor and his entourage for use between August and October.

Moving on to Agrigento on the sea, we quickly learned that there were probably more Greek temples in fair condition in Sicily than we were likely to find in Greece. Resting before a large intact temple of Hercules, we struck up a "conversation" with an Italian family. We showed them Italian words in our Italian-English dictionary. We talked and laughed trying to make ourselves better understood. Before we knew it, we were invited to have dinner with them. We followed in our car, assuming we would end up in a restaurant. Instead, they took us to their luxurious penthouse apartment, located in an unpretentious neighborhood. He was a prominent doctor. The meal was typically Italian with soup, pasta, meat, and dessert. Our dinner conversation was punctuated by frequent passing back and forth of the dictionary. Yet we learned a great deal about the family, the doctor's practice, and the general state of Sicily. For several years we corresponded with them, we writing in broken Italian, they replying in broken English. They promised to come to the United States but never did. Letters ceased.

At another site in Agrigento, we were sitting on the huge, fallen caryatids from the Temple of Zeus when we started a conversation with a young couple, he a lawyer and she a teacher, from Riverside, California. He had brought his wife, who was not of Italian origin, to Italy to see his ancestral village. He had taken her to the church at Palma di Montechiaro, which we had also stopped to visit, because this was the village that Giuseppe Tomasi di Lampidusa, the author of *The Leopard*, a popular historical Sicilian novel published in the 1960s, had so well described. He told us that when the priest showed him the records of the family going back to the sixteenth century, he had discovered that his ancestors were originally Jews, who converted to Christianity during the Inquisition. His name was Mela, the same name as a Jewish family in Pelham, who had an English and also a Sephardic, possibly Italian, origin. Mela. Does it mean salt? Were his ancestors in the salt business, a trade monopolized by the court and at times handed out for lucrative returns to trusted Jews?

We ran into our first Norman church, indicating that these prodigious military and political adventurers had, beginning with the tenth century, conquered everything from England to Sicily and influenced the cultures of these varied countries. Some days later we saw the magnificent church they erected in Monreale on the outskirts of Palermo with its phenomenal mosaics on every wall portraying both the Old and the New Testaments. Another superb creation was the Palazzo dei Normanni in Palermo itself. We were deeply impressed with the artistic abilities of this medieval power.

We could not resist going to Marsala on the west coast, famous not only for its wine, but as the place where Garibaldi landed in 1860 to begin his triumphant march on Rome, which changed the character of Italy for more than a century. In Trapani, as we walked down the via Giudecca (Jews' street), we could see the symbols of a former synagogue now converted into a church. We bought Fragola wine, and finally learned that the name of our next-door neighbor in Pelham, former Sicilians, whose name was Fragola, meant "strawberry."

We stopped at a beautiful Greek temple with its intact unfluted, graceful columns, in Segesta. Nearby were the fairly good remains of a large Greek theater facing the sea. This must have been a substantial ancient Greek settlement.

Along our route we met natives. When we jokingly asked them where all the mafia were, since we had never been molested, they slyly replied: "They are all in America." We were often treated to wine, to coffee, and occasionally to lunch. They always waved us away from the bill when we wanted to pay the addition. We exchanged addresses and on a few occasions we heard from them, including several families that wanted to migrate to the United States and wanted us to be their sponsors. We found a polite way of writing them that we were in no position to undertake and underwrite such a responsibility.

We have inspired many people, who never thought of going to Sicily, to undertake this venture in their European itinerary. We wanted them to see a country that had successively been invaded by the Siculi, Greeks, Carthaginians, Romans, Arabs, Normans, French, and Spaniards, each leaving their own distinctive impress on this attractive island. All of the people we influenced to take this trip came back in raptures.

Students, Teaching

From the instant that I became an executive director on Staten Island in 1932, I conceived that my role was more than administrative, but that I was essentially a teacher. I applied these skills by direct leadership of groups of teenagers, young adults, and adults. I led informal groups and formal courses of study. Within a year after my arrival on Staten Island, and because I was one of the relatively few graduate social workers, and as I was also becoming known in professional circles, I was assigned students from schools of social work. I continued these functions when I was the executive of Bronx House and its camp, and expanded my responsibilities to the supervision of students from a variety of graduate schools. Many of the young people from the groups that I led and many of the students under my tutelage have grown to successful adulthood and have assumed leadership roles in both Jewish and in non-Jewish organizations. I have witnessed former students become executives of institutions and professors and deans in schools of social work. Some became authors of important professional works and experts in their special disciplines.

From 1938 to 1949, I taught group work at the New York School of Social Work (later Columbia), Yeshiva University, and City College of New York. I usually offered instruction in only one course a week in any institution. Occasionally, I participated in seminars in universities in Cleveland, Buffalo, and New York.

At Federation, it was not possible to undertake direct leadership of groups, nor could I teach regularly, or take on the supervision of students, since I was burdened with a tremendous schedule. Instead I maintained a "teaching" role in my relationship with scores of leaders within Federation and its constituent agencies. Some of them have asserted publicly the influence that I exerted on their views and their functional roles. From time to time, I was invited to give a single lecture to fund-raising professionals or to the new leadership (young adults) that Federation was developing for assignment to agency boards of directors and in the fund-raising apparatus. Occasionally I was asked to address adult leadership groups in Federation, and even out of the city, about special developments in the fields of my specialties. In later years, at my own instigation, I gave a series of lectures on the Jewish community, both historically and contemporaneously, so as better to prepare fund-raisers for their role in educating the committees and the communities with which they worked.

I had always been a firm advocate of better and more demanding professional education, along with the Jewish educational development of professionals in the schools of social work and related instruments for study, which eventually led to positions in Jewish communal service.

Thus early in 1967, when Samuel Silberman, known to his friends as Buddy, was the president of Federation, a successful businessman, who was also interested in bettering professional education for both the general and the Jewish communal field, it seemed only natural for him to turn to me to exploit an imaginative idea that had gripped him. He felt that the Jewish agencies had done such a superior job in administration, fund-raising, and public relations that they should use their talents to provide a similar educational exposure for the minority groups (blacks and Hispanics) in greater New York, to enable them to perform much better on the job. The antipoverty program had given a tremendous boost to new organizations in the minority communities. It had become painfully obvious that there was a massive shortage of trained personnel able to manage such new and swelling enterprises. What better service could the Jewish community perform than undertake this mission, was Silberman's thought.

When Silberman broached this subject to me, and indicated that he had access to money for such an undertaking, I told him that it would be a useful program, but that such a service was not the obligation of Federation as a Jewish agency. I was personally not interested in directing such a program for non-Jews. I informed him that there was a chronic shortage of qualified middle-management personnel within the Jewish organizational establishment, that the nonsectarian schools of social work were not preparing Jewish or other students for administration, fund-raising, and public relations, and certainly not preparing them for the Jewish type of community organization. If he was willing to revise his concept of who should be served, I would be interested. We discussed his plan casually on one or two other occasions, but there was no change in his original thinking.

In the summer of 1968, Emma and I decided to go to Helsinki, Finland, for the International Conference of Social Work, in part because we had never been to the Scandinavian countries. We saw this as the beginning of a summer tour that would take us to Sweden, Denmark, Israel, Yugoslavia, and Austria, on a fast-paced six-week vacation. Silberman told me that he would be in Helsinki and perhaps we could discuss the executive-training project again. We met for lunch on August 21, talking about other matters he had gleaned at the conference, such as the wide use of volunteers in countries out of the United States and the differences in funding voluntary institutions. Then, in his usual offhand, smiling manner, he told me that he had given a lot of thought to the training program. He had also learned that there were serious staff shortages in Jewish communal agencies. Now he was willing to go along with my proposal that the educational center be concerned only with preparing Jewish students for the Jewish field. He suggested that we talk about this further when I returned to New York. That is how the Wiener Educational Center was born.

The William E. Wiener Educational Center

By the time I met with Silberman again, I had drawn up a program of the size of the class, what kind of students ought to be recruited, where I should seek them, how the students would spend their two years in training, what kind of subsidies would be needed to attract high-level personnel. I wanted young men and women twenty-five to thirty years of age, preferably who had already completed a master's degree or its equivalent. They could come from the business world, the rabbinate, other professions, and even social work. I hoped to attract the same kind of bright young people that were making their mark in the business and public relations fields. They had to have two specific requirements, apart from being personally attractive: first, to be healthy, for one of the hallmarks of a successful executive is the ability to carry a massive physical load; and second, to be affirmatively Jewish and possess a respectable Jewish background.

Silberman, as president of Federation, found $1 million in three funds, which were to be reserved for this program, but only the income could be indented. This would provide $70,000 to $80,000 a year. Part of my salary would be charged to this budget. All facilities and materials would be provided by Federation. Fellowships up to a maximum of $10,000 per year for not more than two years would be offered.

I was to give up my consultantships of camping and Jewish education, retain my relationship with the community centers and day camping, have the use of the same single secretary, and expand the extensive library, which I had accumulated over the years. I was assigned a somewhat larger office, so that each of the students could have a desk. I was to be given an increase in salary, a matter which had been delayed for several years.

The name William E. Wiener Educational Center was attached to the enterprise, as his estate was the largest benefactor.

It took another year, until 1969, before the first class was matriculated, a task which turned out to be more formidable than I had anticipated. I had written to all the Hillel Foundations. I approached the schools of business administration at Harvard, Columbia, and Pennsylvania. I wrote to graduate schools of social work with large Jewish enrollments, I notified all of the major national and international Jewish organizations and some of the larger Federations. All were contacted in the hope that they would make many and superior referrals.

Believing, as I always did, in volunteer participation in the operation of any program, with suggestions from Federation's leadership and my own contacts, I assembled a sizable board composed of heads of large corporations, foundations, and welfare agencies, representing such diverse fields as Wall Street, real estate, publishing, and insurance, so as to get a mix of people who would do the final selection from the applicants

I had interviewed. Over 150 applications were received. Thirty were chosen to be interviewed. With great difficulty we selected four people, all men. In my estimation they did not meet the high standards we originally affirmed, but I was under pressure to get the school started. One was an ordained rabbi, another a graduate social worker, another a lawyer who was directing a camp, another had a master's degree in sociology.

They were first exposed to the Federation apparatus, meeting with a number of executive and department heads. They attended major staff and board meetings. They were given two five-month assignments, first in fund-raising; and the second in community organization, the latter working in the field rather than in Federation. I met with the entire group each week, and in addition each student had an hour's conference with me each week. I took them with me to important meetings in and out of the building. I gave them books to read. I asked them to submit detailed reports on their total experience for each five-month semester. I invited them to my home twice a year. I sent them to a variety of conferences, local and national. We gave them stipends of $6,000 per year in the first year. This was tax free. We paid for all expenses they incurred as part of their student assignment. If they worked under the supervision of a fund-raiser or a community organizer, I met those individuals from time to time and expected those supervisors to provide a final written report.

It was a demanding schedule. The students literally sweated out the first year, resisting and learning. But I did not recommend that any of them return for a second term. Two obtained positions in Federations after the first year. One returned to law, but several years later became the head of a Federation. The other found a position in social research.

The question they always raised with me was their fear of asking for money. I had urged each of them, apart from their formal assignments, to undertake an independent fund-raising project for Federation. One did so with residents in his apartment house; another with students in the graduate school of social work where he was taking courses and a third amongst his relatives and friends. One, however, procrastinated so long in deciding what group to solicit that nothing materialized. The financial responses in all cases was meager, but what I wanted from them was a planned approach and an evaluation of why their efforts succeeded or failed.

For the second year, the number of applicants was even thinner. We decided to see whether the graduate schools of social work had qualified second-year students who could meet our requirements. Of some seventy applicants, we interviewed fifteen and chose only four students. One was a mature man of thirty, who had not completed his bachelor's degree. At the same time that he was under my tutelage, he received his bachelor's degree and completed his graduate studies. As he was married and had a child, he was the one and only $10,000 per year fellowship awardee. This class included one woman.

The second class went through the same routines, except that some, being younger and less experienced, not yet holding graduate degrees, required a great deal more personal supervision and motivation. Finding desirable placements for them in fund-raising and in community organization continued to be a problem. There were not enough fund-raising personnel capable of helping to "educate" a student. Most were deficient in academic experience and could not conceptualize what they were doing. Most operated within very restricted practices and schedules, where the use of the imagination was held in check. We had to turn to community centers for community organization placements, even though few executives in centers had this technical skill. I had to give a great deal more attention to these field supervisors than I had foreseen, in order to see that my training objectives would be reasonably satisfied. Student fears of the complexities and even of failure in both exposures were another stumbling block with which I had to cope. Only one student, Haim Morag, Morocco-born, Israel-nourished, and now living with his wife and son in the Uniited States, had the natural abilities in both fields. He was aggressive, creative, a bit abrasive and authoritarian. He has proven to be a successful Federation executive for many years and a close friend.

In my third and last year, we enrolled a class of six. They were all students in schools of social work. My experiences were similar to those in previous years. They all came through quite successfully and obtained positions in the field.

In retrospect, the program, as I evaluated it, was moderately fruitful. While I never obtained the kinds of students that I was seeking, a number of them became executives of small federations, a few in other types of Jewish institutions, and one even became a consultant in a national agency.

It was obvious, throughout the three years of working on the Wiener program, that it was difficult to get the high-level students that I had sought, for such individuals did not see Jewish communal work as their professional cup of tea. The cost of training each student, because of the small class size, was inordinately high. I never spent all of the income from the several funds supporting this program. Actually I added to the corpus. I had questions about its continuance, despite the fact that graduates had little difficulty finding good jobs in a field short of executive personnel.

The committee was in agreement with this evaluation. After I retired in 1973, the center engaged another person, who changed it from a full-time student-training program to one that conducted short-term, inservice training programs dealing with management functions that the field required. I lectured before one such group on the Jewish elements in administration, a program that was sponsored jointly by the Wiener project and the New School for Social Research.

I keep in contact with several of the students. From time to time I run into others. Whether one can take what they say at face value, all claim to have received an intensive and varied experience at the Wiener Center, unlike that of most of their colleagues, who entered the Jewish communal field via different routes.

I cannot resist including in this book a memorandum sent to me by Haim Morag, one of my students in the Wiener program, which gives a clue as how I recruited students, my educational methods, my identification with their unique needs and abilities, and how they became in some respects "disciples," but more than that personal friends and cooperating colleagues.

In June 1970, I was working at the JCC in Bridgeport, Connecticut, and was seeking ways to get a higher education and advance in the field. Bessie Pine of the JWB suggested that I call Graenum Berger, who was directing the Wiener program at Federation.

I called Graenum. Despite the fact that he was recovering from an operation, he invited me to his house in Pelham. We spent five hours talking about the program, the requirements and my background. Graenum indicated that he had never accepted anybody without a master's degree, which I did not have. Nevertheless, he agreed to bring me before the selection committee.

The program offered a generous fellowship, that was more than my full-time salary, in addition to tuition for graduate courses. In spite of the investment involved, Federation did not ask for a commitment to work for it upon graduation. Nor did it guarantee a position.

When I met with the selection committee, everything seemed to be working out, until I volunteered that there was a possibility that I could end up going back to Israel after the training was completed. I felt that it would be wrong not to inform them of that possibility, because their intention was to train candidates for positions in the U.S. I was later told by Graenum that my "honesty" split the committee. Half decided to accept me and the other half were opposed. The committee, in view of the tie vote, decided to have Sanford Solender, Executive Vice President of Federation, interview me and make the final decision.

I felt that the interview with Sandy Solender was my last chance, and decided not to "spoil it" this time. Consequently, I volunteered nothing and simply answered his questions. Mr. Solender must have been impressed, because he recommended that I be accepted.

Graenum designed individual assignments and decided on the

graduate courses based on each student's area of strength and weakness. The program was tailored for the individual needs of each student. Standards were very high and Graenum expected a lot of reading and writing about all aspects of Federation and the Jewish communal field. I was weak in writing. My reading was slow, English not being my first language. (It was my fourth.) I worried about my ability to keep pace with the assignments and withstand his pressure. At no time did I feel threatened. I felt many times that I was unable to meet his expectations.

Graenum's interest in me went beyond what was expected of him as a teacher-supervisor, perhaps because of my inadequacies in the fields of administration, fund-raising, community organization and community relations, or perhaps because I showed more of an eagerness to meet the challenge and survive the full two years of the program.

With Graenum's constant encouragement and support, I attended every conceivable meeting that took place in and outside of Federation. I also joined special functional committees in their field trips to agencies of Federation. Knowing that previous students did not make the transition to the second year, I concentrated my efforts during the first year's assignment on succeeding well enough, so that I could be accepted for the second year. I made myself available to participate in meetings, programs and conferences of the Federation, the Council of Jewish Federations and other outside organizations.

Graenum invited me to join him on trips to schools of social work and national conferences, often staying at his house or sharing a hotel room. It was then that I started to feel that he was acting more like a "mentor," looking for "disciples," than a conventional supervisor or teacher. That feeling only added "pressure" and concern as to whether I could meet his standards.

Sometimes I felt that he was a bit "old fashioned." I didn't think that people dwelled so much on theoretical concepts in their daily work. I thought that I would stick to what I knew, I did best, and that was action, not theory. Graenum was resolved to develop my skills, embellish my style and smooth out some of my rough edges.

I don't know if I ever met his expectations, but my success on the first year's assignment was beyond my own projections. The evaluation of my various supervisors as well as that of the teachers in school was positive, so that Graenum and the Wiener committee must have thought that I was worth the investment and accepted me for a second year.

I did not have to work very hard to convince Graenum that eventually I would need a formal master's degree in social work, if I was to expect a respectable position after graduation.

The Wiener program was not designed to give a degree or even allow full time for added study. Graenum was sympathetic to my personal and professional needs and he helped me find a suitable program. I started that second year at the Hunter School of Social Work, which recognized past and current experience in social agencies and enabled the candidate to complete the master's degree in less than the usual required two years of full time studies. With his recommendations, I was accepted as one of four students. I was determined to get my master's degree by the end of the year. I took 23 credits per semester, until I was "caught" by my counselor, who was enraged by my chuztpa of taking so many courses without her prior approval. I managed to convince her that since I was not failing in my work, she should close her eyes until I finished.

With a lot of nerve, a little manipulation and Graenum's moral and the school's financial support, I was able to complete the requirements for a degree by the end of the Wiener program.

By the end of the second year, I felt that Graenum had full confidence in me and my abilities. He took particular "nachas" that when I went for my first job interview, I was offered the position on the spot.

By the end of the program, the relationship had changed from student/supervisor to friend/professional colleague. I was often invited by Graenum and Emma and felt welcome in their home. Throughout the years, I kept in touch with them and was invited to family events. They both had an interest, not only in me, but in my wife and son.

A few years after the program, I became interested in the cause that Graenum had spent years on—solving the plight of the Falasha—or Ethiopian Jews. I knew nothing about Ethiopian Jews, but listening to his lectures and genuine concern for them, I felt that I owed it to him to do what I could. Subsequently, when I moved to the Albany area, he was invited to speak. He asked me to fill in for him sometimes. As usual, he provdided tons of material, which made it easy to prepare a lecture, which I repeated before different audiences. Later on, I was able to interest my Federation's Community Relations Committee to form a sub-committee and study the issues out of genuine concern about their condition. They also wrote letters to the national UJA as well as Prime Minister Menachem Begin in Israel. Later on, I convinced Federation's Allocations Committee to grant a substantial sum to the American Association for Ethiopian Jews.

Because of Graenum's frustration with the lack of progress by Israel and the American Jewish community in rescuing Ethiopian Jews, he became more and more vocal and was labeled a "militant" and probably lost quite a few friends.

There were moments when I felt that my "association" with Graenum might not be "good for my career." Actually I was not concerned at all. As a matter of fact, I felt quite comfortable also being defiant, especially for such a just cause. I felt that he and the AAEJ played a tremendous role in publicizing the plight of Ethiopian Jews and sensitizing the Jewish community. I have watched support for Ethiopian Jews grow to the point that it was taken up by the established Jewish commuity. UJA "packaged" it for fund-raising purposes during "Operation Moses."

Graenum's background, work and interests make him an unusual man. I feel most fortunate with my associaton with him and his friendship throughout these years. I am certain that had he not "discovered" me and taken a personal interest, I would not be where I am today as the head of a Jewish Federation. At the beginning I did not know why he took such a chance on me, till I learned about his compassion for the underdog, the Blacks, the Falasha, the Sephardim and the like. I felt that his work and interest, and yes his fights, were all manifestations of his love for the entire Jewish people.

* * *

During David Salten's brief regime, he somehow never was able to take hold of the organization, neither making an impression on the volunteers nor the professionals. While I tried to be helpful in many ways, it was my early view that he wouldn't last. First of all, he was the successor to Hexter and Willen, both of whom had enjoyed the highest status conceivable on their retirement. They were a tough act to follow. Some volunteers felt that with the strongmen out, this was the time for them to "run the show." Furthermore, both of the erstwhile executives remained on the scene as consultants, and this meant that their shadows would always darken any independent efforts that Salten might have advanced. However, in the last analysis, private social welfare was not his milieu. He came from the school system, where as a superintendent, he was the boss. While he might have been beholden to a board of education, running schools was deemed a professional job, and by and large, it was left to educators. One had to be a pretty poor performer to be dismissed.

The voluntary scene in welfare was different, and more so in the Jewish community. It was dependent on lay leadership and generous donations from private citizens. While contacts with government officials could be an important source of funds, this was not decisive in determining one's value as the chief Jewish communal official. Regrettably, Salten did not establish those necessary, often close, personal relationships with Jewish volunteers, for he did not speak their language and did not understand the philanthropic business. Nor did he develop ties with the rabbis and synagogues.

Moreover, Salten procrastinated in choosing an assistant, essential to strengthening the professional staff. Pressure was exerted on him to appoint a key member of the staff he had inherited, whom he did not want. It was evident that he would be forced to make a decision. The day before he was to make the final determination, he asked me to fill the post. He told me that he had a good relationship with me, thought I would get along better with other staff executives and the rank-and-file staff, and with executives of member agencies. I was qualified for the position. Under other circumstances I might readily have accepted, but I turned it down. Since the rejected colleague would have reacted with bitterness, an internecine battle would have ensued. At the time this was the right decision, but in the light of the events that followed, I realize that I made an error. The job would have given me more instant influence and a substantial increase in salary. With Salten's leaving shortly thereafter, I would have been in a position to put in my bid for the top rank.

Prior to the appointment of Salten, when a committee was choosing a successor to Hexter-Willen, my name was advanced by some volunteers and a few professionals. I knew that I had little chance of being appointed, and never promoted my candidacy either by requesting an interview or by approaching influential laymen. I was never interviewed.

* * *

After Salten vacated the executive position, there was an interregnum as the board began to seek a successor. Candidates had to be interviewed, evaluated, and if chosen, allowed time to leave their incumbent positions. Thus an instant replacement could not be made. Federation's president was George Heyman, Jr., an able volunteer, who had risen phenomenally in Wall Street and always made precise speeches spiced with appropriate quotations from literary sources. He decided that he would take a turn running the complex operation until a professional was engaged. It wasn't working. Many of the pros needed someone to consult with at length, often required quick answers to knotty problems; and as a busy person in his own business, Heyman just didn't fill the bill, even though he was giving up a great deal of his time in both capacities. He was also not a person with whom most professionals could develop intimate relations.

The professionals at the top level of Federation met on several singular occasions to discuss this lacuna. Some were for writing Heyman a detailed memorandum of their concerns. Others didn't want to put anything on paper with their names attached, because it might be used against their personal ambitions. There was no unanimity. The stubborn problem persisted. Finally Robert (Bob) Smith and I decided to approach the lion. Bob had been the director of the public relations department for many years, in fact had seniority amongst the upper-echelon staff.

We met with Heyman in his apartment early one morning. We told him we were not spokesmen for the other executives, but represented only ourselves. We pointed out the inadequacies of the existing situation. He told us that an executive would soon be engaged, although we were given no names or dates for such an appointment. There was no predisposition on Heyman's part to ask either one of us or any of the other executives to assume even temporarily some of the duties of the top executive. We were left no better off than when we came. I inferred that we were advised to mind our own affairs.

Some of the staff resented our daring overture to the president, interpreting it as a sneaky effort to insinuate ourselves into his good graces, and even promote ourselves as candidates for the vacant post. I doubt that Bob had such pretensions. I know that I didn't. Yet if designated, I would have been ready to serve in an interim capacity. I knew from the grapevine that I had been ruled out. My unequivocal personal views on Jewish life, on Jewish education, on aiding Soviet Jewry, on developing Jewish neighborhood communal groups, on Israel, on merger with the United Jewish Appeal, on opposing government aid to voluntary agencies, had not sat well with members of the search committee in its earlier selection of Salten, and in this subsequent scurry for his replacement. I wasn't interviewed for this opening either.

Why I Never Wanted an Assistant at Federation

Over the course of my work history since 1932, during all of which I was always an executive, and from 1932 to 1949, the top executive, I had known lean budgets and insufficient staffs. On Staten Island, it was five years before I could persuade the board of directors that we had enough money, actually $1,800 per year more, to engage another full-time program worker. So for the six years that I spent in my executive apprenticeship, I learned how to get along with less and less, and assumed all the burdens of an executive, including administration, fundraising, plant management, public relations, community organization, program creation, supervision of paid and volunteer personnel, and providing direct leadership for a variety of groups.

At Bronx House, during the next eleven years, I came into a reasonably well staffed agency with a full-time assistant director, who obviously relieved me of many administrative and program responsibilities. Yet my belief that the executive must also be an educator, so that he could have more direct contact on a program level with the membehrsip, compelled me to keep my hands in every aspect of the institution. While I had a number of superb assistants, several of whom went on to become national and international leaders of reknown, they had minds of their own and frankly wanted to impose their own philosophies of purpose and practice on the agency. Had I been a weaker person, they might have bent the agency, the board, the staff, the program, even the community in a different direction than what I envisioned. That my views prevailed, and the agency began to enjoy a widespread reputation, was in great part because my assistants left for greener pastures, and because the institution chose to follow a course that I had outlined and found the resources and staff to execute those goals.

At Federation, my final post for twenty-four years, I was not the top executive. My responsibilities increased enormously in dimension and diversity over that period. As I added function upon function, I seemed to be able to encompass these multiple duties by dint of my own well-organized mind and my capacity for high productivity. While the volume of work grew, I only enjoyed a second secretary for a brief period, and got rid of her when I found the first one was spending too much time supervising the work of the other. Together they did not produce more than what one had before.

I have always been an early riser. I usually took work home with me. I read and wrote on the railroad, thus isolating myself, so as not to waste time talking to a neighbor or acquaintance who might be riding in the same car. People I knew began to respect this practice, and often remarked on my diligence and concentration when they saw me at some social event in Pelham or elsewhere. Literally every minute was precious. Thus when I reached my office, I usually had already written enough material to keep an ordinary secretary fully occupied for the better part of the working day. I disliked dictating to a secretary, except for the briefest of last-minute letters or memos, because it took her away from the machine and tied me up when I could be meeting with people, teaching students, or getting out into the field. I disliked talking into dictaphones and even later into tape recorders, because I found that my spoken words often had to be retyped, which I considered an expensive waste of two people's time. My written script—and I always had to find secretaries who could read my rapid, often illegible writings—was usually final copy.

As my work load increased at Federation, and as a few other departments underwent similar expansion and added assistants, some of whom would have preferred to work under me, professionals and volunteers often asked me why I didn't request additional aid. At moments, when the pile of work was overwhelming, I had such fleeting thoughts, but they were quickly dispelled. I just didn't want an assistant, who would take too much of my valuable and accountable time in teaching him what to do and then making sure that he performed as he was instructed and up to my professional and productive standards. I also assumed that as soon as he learned the business, he would be gone, and I would have to start all over again. I didn't mind supervising students and being tolerant of their inexperience, their mistakes, their lack of high productivity, even their failure to be punctual (in my schedule this was more than a misdemeanor, bordering on high crime), because I looked upon the students as just that—students, who would be under my sway for a short period and then leave to test themselves in the workaday world. Although the standards that I wished them to attain were high—approximately mine—I could accept their invasion of my time as a task that I voluntarily assumed. I was educating executives for the future and elsewhere. I could not have tolerated such behavior in a paid professional whom I had engaged to perform specific jobs day in and day out, not only to relieve me, but to add to the volume of work performed through my office.

The life of an executive can be a good one in terms of financial rewards, perquisites, and status. I must, however, confess that over a lifetime, most of the work was perforce routine. What made it enjoyable was the 10 to 15 percent that was creative, where I was innovative and introduced new and exciting ventures. I often told this to my students and others, who only saw the glamour of the office and not the repetitive, tedious aspects that consume most of the working day. Assigning these mundane duties to another person might have given me more time for creativity, but I preferred to see the position as a whole, rather than made up of discrete elements that could be parceled off to others.

Thus I was willing to take on the additional burdens, usually volunteering, or better yet creating and assuming them and somehow incorporating them in my always overloaded schedule. Being in reasonably good health most of my life helped. One of the marks of a successful executive is physical, having the stamina to take on ever-enlarging loads. Selecting out what was most important was another necessary trait. I set a time goal toward the completion of any program that I undertook, even if it was a matter of several years. I persisted in anything that I undertook, precisely because I thought it was essential. This valuable characteristic made me press for its resolution and fulfillment, for I did not like to suffer any defeat.

These things I was always able to do better alone. I believe that it was my largely one-person approach that enabled me to achieve so much. While I used other individuals, if needed, to complete my programs, and was fairly good at finding and exploiting such individuals, I preferred to do things my own way, unencumbered. This usually proved, by time-test and result, to be successful, despite frustrations and occasional delays.

I have often wondered why it was always difficult for me to get a salary commensurate with my skills, my overlong hours of work, my single-minded devotion, my achievements, and my reputation. I was admired by the boards of directors and the constituents I served. Was I afraid to demand an increase, perhaps for fear that I would lose my job? Was I more concerned about the overall needs of the organization and the inadequate salaries of lower-level workers, for whom on many occasions I made personal sacrifices? Did I secretly think my work was already sufficiently rewarded? All I recall is that in order to get results, I either had to tell my board or the upper-echelon professional chief that I had been offered a higher salary elsewhere, or I had to press my case through long self-evaluations and other subtle forms of coercion. In any event, the increase was never up to what I wanted, nor commensurate with the contributions I was making.

Conference in Helsinki: 1968

Helsinki, despite the rain and the grayness of the skies—the sun came out only grudgingly for part of each day—was a city of gray-stoned old buildings and modern architecture. It was experimenting with new types of housing and developing suburban communities like the attractive Tapiola. It was stamped as the city made famous by Sibelius, the great composer.

Our hotel reservations had been fouled up, and since rooms were not available, we had to be billeted in a university dormitory, simple and clean, with a sauna (a luxury each day), very good, and fair food, all at unbelievably low prices. We rode a bus to the university where the conference sessions were held. Regrettably, this convocation was no different than others I had attended over the years. Rather dreary papers, few original or challenging.

What outraged some of us in Helsinki was the Russian takeover of Czechoslovakia. The diehard pro-Soviet attendees, however, were not disturbed by this perfidious event, and did not cancel the side trip that had been planned to Russia, the huge bear bordering on tiny Finland. Some of them also took a side trip to Czechoslovakia after the conference. Finland was visibly affected, because it never knew what it might do unwittingly to give Russia an excuse for overrunning its territory.

In Helsinki, we went to see *Fiddler on the Roof* in Finnish at the new, lavish Kaupungin Teateri. The Yiddish musical version on tape was playing in the lobby. Since we knew the script by heart, we could follow the native text without difficulty. The dancing was poor. The singing was fair. The humorous parts evoked instant laughter and applause. The middle-class audience knew the actors, particularly the one who played Tevye, who seemed to be addressing them directly by word and song. When the Russian hooligans upset the tavern and the wedding, there was a tense, eerie silence in the audience. I watched their faces and the handkerchiefs wiping away their tears. The Czechoslovakian rape had touched them deeply, and they easily identified with the Jewish characters and the story. We had now seen three versions of this musical play in the United States, Israel, and Finland.

The Russian circus was in town and the performers had been put up in our college quarters. On our return from the theater, a group of young adult Finns were standing in front of a building next door. As we passed, they shouted "Russians go home" in good English. They obviously thought we were Russians, as the Russians and the Bergers were the only adults occupying the dormitory. The others were only young students. This incident further emphasized the often unexpressed attitude of the Finnish population toward the Russians, which otherwise was publicly repressed.

We visited the Jewish community complex consisting of a synagogue, school, center, and old age home. There were one thousand Jews in Helsinki and three hundred in the rest of the country. All were descendants of Jews who originally migrated from Russia. A musical reception was tendered the Jewish delegates to the conference. We once again met Max Jakobson, Finland's Jewish representative to the United Nations in New York, and a resident of Pelham. (He was a member of our Pelham Jewish Center. When his son was Bar Mitzvah at our center, we were invited to his home for the reception that followed.) We met his mother and father, who a year later came to their grandson's rite in Pelham. It was obvious from the remarks and the songs, all in Hebrew, that the orientation of the Jewish educational program for children was definitely Israeli. The Jewish delegates listened to a paper on "The Status of Jews the World Over." In light of Russia's infamous invasion of Czechoslovakia, the delegates were concerned with what would happen to the Jews still left in that country. (Some weeks later, when we were in Yugoslavia, we met a number of Czechoslovakian Jewish refugees, who had fled for their lives and were being supported by the small Jewish community in Dubrovnik.)

We toured and shopped in Helsinki and its environs. What bothered us most was the large number of drunks, including youth, that we saw in restaurants and on the streets, confirming the published reports about the excessive use of alcohol in these bleak Scandinavian countries.

Stockholm

We were so busy talking in the small, crowded, and noisy airport lounge in Helsinki that we missed the announcement of our flight to Stockholm. Luckily, we managed to get on a plane many hours later. The short flight gave us an opportunity to board a boat and see the handsome city from the waterfront just before nightfall. We ate at Riche's restaurant that evening, one of the best. We were served a tiny piece of hazel hen, of the game variety, in a huge silver-covered platter. The food, wine, and service were superior.

The next day we saw the city, with its fourteenth- and nineteenth-century buildings, and visited the Royal Palace where the assassination of Gustavus III took place in the eighteenth century, an event that later inspired Giuseppe Verdi (after David Auber) to compose the lyrical drama, *The Masked Ball*. Gustavus had founded the Academy of Letters and wrote and acted in dramas.

We were intrigued with an apartment house built for the aged with the proceeds from a *blumen* ("flower") fund. People were urged to send money instead of flowers for deceased friends and relatives, so that this necessary facility could eventually be constructed.

Stockholm was rather free with its sexual literature and, we were also told, equally free with its sexual practices. Adults with whom we talked were outraged, but there seemed to be no movement to counteract these liberties.

We were impressed on our visit to the Jewish center and the synagogue at Wahrendorffgatan, no. 3. Here was a modest-sized Jewish community, struggling against intermarriage and assimilation, maintaining an institution in the finest manner.

The Carl Milles sculptured garden displayed many works of a native artist, who had to live abroad in the United States and France before his creative works were recognized. It was an outdoor museum worth a visit.

One night we heard *Tosca* at the ornate Opera House, where the voices, particularly those who sang Tosca and Scarpia, were excellent, but the acting was laughingly marred by a too-short tenor, who kept stumbling over Tosca's long, trailing red velvet gown.

In the States we had befriended a Swedish representative to the United Nations, married to an American woman, a schoolmate of our sister-in-law Margaret. We were invited to their home in Stockholm for dinner. The taxi driver lost his way. We were late. When we knocked on the door, Lars greeted us with a cocktail shaker. Before we had taken off our raincoats, he hurriedly introduced us to the others in the room and martinis were forced into our hands. From the hilarity, we could see that the party was well underway and everyone already had downed several drinks. Lars offered a simple toast to his American friends: "Skoal." I paused before drinking, still wearing my coat, to ask him what *skoal* meant. "Graenum, when my Viking forebears licked another group in war, they cut off the head of the defeated chieftain, scooped out the skull, filled it with aquavit, and drank a victory salute until they were drunk. *Skull* was translated into *skoal*. By the way, what do you Hebrews say?" I told him: "L'chaim—to Life." "I like that better," commented Lars. Throughout the evening, whenever he had a fresh drink, it was "L'chaim." I mused that maybe that was the reason Jews were generally more abstemious, while Scandinavians were known to consume inordinate quantities of hard liquor and become at times unbearably intoxicated. "Life versus Death" were thus appropriate symbols.

Whenever I told this story later on, everyone thought that what I had said was apocryphal, that I had made it up, even though my readings of

Scandinaivan literature reinforced this tale. The *National Geographic* (March 1985, p. 282) related a story of the Vikings who fought marauding tribes along the Dnieper between Kiev and the Black Sea. "Most fearsome of all were the Turkic Petchenegs, who in 972 slew Prince Svyatoslav of the Rus and made a drinking cup of his skull." Now the legend was reconfirmed.

Denmark

In Copenhagen, we stayed at the Palace Hotel with easy access to every part of the city and country. We visited the synagogue, where we were told once again of the vicissitudes of the Jewish community during the Hitler epoch, and how the Danes had saved them. There was a torchlight demonstration in front of the City Hall for Freedom and Democracy. Speakers harangued a large crowd. We went to the Freedom Museum, where it clearly exhibited how the Danes stood up to the Nazis. We saw the actual spot from which the boats departed with the fleeing Jews to Sweden. The lesson of the Nazis and the Jews became firmly stamped on our consciousness.

Touring Denmark was fun. As we approached the Palace in Frederiksberg, we saw the King and Queen each driving separately in their own small cars. At Elsinor we saw the drab castle which inspired Shakespeare's *Hamlet*. We paused before the statue of Hans Christian Andersen, whose fairy tales we had read as children. It was an attractive country of legend and lore.

Israel

We had come to Israel in 1968 specifically to attend the dedication of the Jerusalem YM-YWHA, for we had played a conspicuous part in bringing it into realization. The festivities included a cocktail party and dinner at the King David Hotel. We were photographed with the President of Israel, Zalman Shazar. The dedication ceremonies were stirring, starting with three anthems—Israel, the United States, and Canada. Tribute was paid to Horace Goldsmith, for whom the building was named, but no mention was made of my obtaining the sizable gift from him that made it possible. Our names were displayed in the lobby among other donors. On a tiny plaque, our names were also evidenced on the wall of the magnificent swimming pool. Altogether it was a large and attractive building. But it had no sooner opened, than the U.S. committee was faced with requests to double its size by adding an auditorium and more classrooms. We had raised $240,000. Emma and I contributed $500 more at a fund-raising luncheon, so that our personal gifts to this building fund totaled $2,500, a large sum for a social worker of modest earnings.

Our role in the resurrection and the creation of the Jerusalem YM-YWHA has been all but forgotten except in our own immediate family. One good friend who knows the story intimately is Ralph Goldman; on a number of occasions, both in writing and verbally, he has made reference to the role that Emma and I played in reviving and sustaining this institution and initiating the action that brought about the construction of the building.

A Menorah and a Psalm

Walking down Sholom Zion Road in Jerusalem, we always stopped to rummage through the antique shop of Abraham Peretz. It invariably looked as though he was going out of business. The shop had not been painted or dusted in years. If you couldn't find what you wanted in the way of precious and semiprecious items or jewelry in the one small glass case, Peretz would disappear in the recesses of the back room and emerge with gold and silver and stones, "objets d'art," as he termed them. If you were interested, the items were weighed on a tiny scale and you paid for their value at the going price for the metal or stones. During a purchase, the shop would be visited by Arabs in their traditional garb topped by a *kaffiyeh*, bringing him items that they had inherited, dug up, pilfered, or bought for resale. He shifted from Arabic to Hebrew, to French, to Yiddish, or to English, depending on the customer. Thin, frail, gaunt, aging, his face marked by a thin moustache, he radiated a feeling of patient kindness, as he discussed the object for trade or sale. His prices were always bargains. He never pressed you to make a quick purchase. A native of the city, he had seen it go through many changes in his more than seventy years. Full of stories, if once prompted about a date, an incident, a person, he talked interestingly and endlessly. He was in no hurry. It was apparent that he might have prospered enough to maintain himself in his declining years, although there was no visible evidence in exhibited wares to demonstrate the size of his fortune.

On this day, I was poking around in a cabinet, when I saw an envelope, and upon opening it, found a small parchment, 4 inches by 7½ inches with Hebrew inscriptions illuminated in several colors—gold, purple, red, green, and black. What struck me was the Hebrew lettering in the form of a menorah, written vertically. Peretz explained that he had obtained it from an Austrian Jew who had settled in Israel. He did not think it was very old—perhaps one hundred years or less. As I started to read the words, he interrupted by stating that it was David's sixty-seventh Psalm. We bought it, took it home, put it over green velvet in a gold and black frame. It is in our library den. Peretz, a scholar of sorts, believed that my name, Graenum, was derived from Gamaliel, but he had no specific source to prove it.

In art galleries, we learned that Edward Phillips, whose art adorns our walls, had become successful and had Hebraized his name to Ben-Avram. We attended a cocktail party at the Inter-Continental Hotel overlooking the Mount of Olives. In the late afternoon, before sundown, we were inspired by the orange-toned views of the Old City of Jerusalem. It was a rushing seven days in which we saw a score of our Israeli friends at breakfast, lunch, over coffee, for cocktails, and at dinner.

We met our longtime Staten Island friend, Dr. Edward Aberlin, in Jeruselem. He had been in Prague the day the Russians took it over. He asserted that the Czechs welcomed the invaders warmly. There was no opposition. The Russians had simply prevented, in his view, a takeover of the country by the American CIA and the Green Berets. Ed was an ardent pro-Soviet supporter, who made frequent visits to the Soviet Union, returning full of praise for their regime and style of life.

Yugoslavia

On our way to Yugoslavia, we had a day's wait in Athens. We rented a car, drove down the coast toward Sounion, then returned to the Parthenon, had another view of it from the Hill of Phillipia, then up the mountain to Lycabettus, and finally rushed off to the airport with pleasant memories of our renewed quick review of Athens.

Arriving in Dubrovnik at 11 P.M., we took a bus into the city, where we changed to a taxi to reach the pension where we had made reservations. The house was dark. Left with our bags on the street, I finally found a bell, rang it, and after a wait, Rahela Radojevic, the proprietress greeted us in her nightgown. She had been awakened from her sleep. It was 1 A.M.

We awoke in a large, high-ceilinged bedroom, having slept in a king-sized bed. It was furnished with antique native furniture; and elaborately framed tapestries, which our hostess had made, to embellish the room and every other room in the pension. There were four guest bedrooms. Everyone had to share a single bathroom. We bathed at 5 A.M. to be sure we had hot water. We breakfasted on an awning-covered porch overlooking the sea. The house was situated on a high bluff. The water below, even from a height of several hundred feet, was a clear light green and we could see the bottom near the tiny sand beach. The pension, very inexpensive, had been recommended to us by Deborah Miller, on the staff of the European Joint Distribution Committee, who had stayed there on one of her trips. Ralph and Luba Baum of Mount Vernon joined us and together we later traveled to Austria.

Rahela had prepared a breakfast of fresh-squeezed tomato juice, grapes, prunes, marmalade, all grown in her garden and orchard, plus meat, eggs, toast, and coffee. Rahela's mother was a Jew. Rahela had married a Serbian engineer. Being a non-Communist, he was unemployed and had constant problems with the regime. Rahela considered herself a Jew, and as she put it: "I only eat fish with scales." I was fighting off a head cold. She gave me a stiff drink of native brandy, which cured it within a day. We learned that Rahela was considerd one of the great cooks of the country and that photos of her in native dress were featured in a cookbook about the country published by *Time* (1968).

Despite its being a country in the Communist orbit, Yugoslavia did not have quite so rigid a dictatorship as we had been informed was associated with all such states. Nuns, many of them, were seen walking to church. Church bells were ringing everywhere. It was Sunday. We watched processions of worshippers from our high perch overlooking the roadways below and around our pension.

After such a heavy and what we were told was a healthy breakfast, we had our first lunch, consisting of stuffed egg plant, salami and green peppers, capon with spiced rice, pastries stuffed with a light cream sauce, and a good white, native wine. Other meals were comparable, unusual, of gourmet quality. Rahela went out of her way to please us. Elaborate dinners and luncheons cost only $2 each.

While we were living with Rahela, she introduced us to some natives, young and old, some of whom were anti-Communist. Some were knowledgeable about the United States and its literature. Some resented the unrelieved party line of six newspapers and one TV channel.

Old Dubrovnik was magnificent. Originally built by the Venetians, when they dominated the coastland, it had been restored as a major tourist paradise. Rahela insisted on being our guide. She knew every place and everyone.

One day she steered us to narrow Jew Street, and at 3 Zulica Zudioska, we walked up the steep stairs to the narrow synagogue, flush against the residence of the Tolentino family. Originally from Spain, they had lived in that house since the fourteenth century, leaving Spain before the expulsion of the Jews. In the current generation, there had been fourteen children, most of whom died in concentration camps during the war. We first met two brothers, the remaining sister a few days later. Another sibling lived in Israel. All were over sixty-five. None were married. This was the end of an ancient family line. There were only seventeen Jews in the city. The synagogue was furnished in an Italian Sephardic style with ritual objects, including a Torah scroll, dating back to the thirteenth century. Tolentino wrote a book about the tragic disappearance of most of the Jews during the Nazi occupation, which I purchased. We attended a Friday night service with a few natives and tourists, barely a minyan. The service was Sephardic. A speech-sermon was read by a tourist. The melodies had more of an Arabic than a Mediterranean tone.

Rahela invited three Tolentinos for dinner along with a Communist woman judge, who was a strict party-liner. Everyone tried to keep me from asking sharp questions, which happily provoked one of the most interesting discussions they had in years. This was told to me after the judge left. They lived in fear of discussing anything that might impugn Tito's regime and indict them.

We toured the southern Dalmatian coast, stopping at Igalo to see the radioactive mud, taken from the beach and used for treatment of children with orthopedic ailments. We went through the ruined city of Perast, which was not being rebuilt by the residents because of an excessive tax on construction. Then through Kotor with its medieval walls rising to the peak of the mountain, once used to ward off incursions by the Montenegrins. Through Budva, a beautiful but smaller version of Dubrovnik. Then to the Royal Palace near St. Stephen, where we saw how a decrepit island taken from poor, resident fishermen had been converted into a splendid resort. We bought a small painting on wood, which looked like an icon, from Father Daniel, a priest-painter, who was exhibiting his work in a seventeenth-century church.

When we asked where we could buy art, Rahela took us to see the paintings of her nephew, Jovan Obican. His father and his son were also artists. Before we left, we purchased more than a dozen paintings, large and small. They painted native subjects—folk art, dancers, musicians, singers, chicken thieves, magic carpets, all very colorful with a touch of humor. Emma commissioned a painting, which the Obicans brought to Pelham one night and dined with us. It flamboyantly adorns our dining room. We have met them in New York at annual exhibitions of their work. The father's and the son's paintings are in the private collections of many individuals and in museums. The paintings have materially appreciated in value over the years. I suggested that he paint Jewish and Israeli subjects, which he did with great success.

One night Obican took us to a folklore concert and dance festival. The performers were the best folk dancers that we had ever seen in our travels. Unhappily, Jovan died in 1986.

Another excursion was taken to Trebinye, overlooking Dubrovnik, where one could see the influence of the Moslem religion and culture on a great part of Yugoslavia, where the dominant religion was still Eastern Orthodox Christian. The women, in their baggy bloomers down to the ankles, were a curious sight.

We stopped at Caftat to see the unique mausoleum built by a wealthy shipowner for his family, all of whom died suddenly and mysteriously, and were buried at the same time.

We left Dubrovnik and Rahel with tearful thanks, for it was such a pleasant experience. We drove north through the Moslem city of Mostar, up the steep mountain east to Sarajevo, where the Archduke Ferdinand was assassinated in 1914, the spark that ignited World War I. We had been told by Irwin and Doris Rosenberg, good friends and Federation volunteers, to look for an elderly guide named Dusan Brkic. To our amazement, at our hotel, he came up to me and asked if I was Graenum Berger, stating that he was expecting us. Tall, thin, white-haired Brkic took us on a tour of the Jewish museum, formerly the synagogue, where there were mementos of the Jewish past. Then to the Jewish cemetery, where gravestones were so old and eroded that the names were unreadable. There was a huge memorial for the forty thousand Jews, who were killed during the Nazi occupation.

The highlight of our visit to Sarajevo was the National Museum, where Brkic persuaded the curator to take out of the vault the famous Sarajevo Haggadah. This superb medieval codex was written and illustrated on parchment in northern Spain about 1350. It went through a remarkable journey. It was deemed so valuable that when the Germans invaded Sarajevo, they searched high and low for this text. It was well hidden. The curator permitted us to hold it in our hands and to turn each precious page, some with the doodles made by readers, perhaps children, over the years. Shortly afterwards, the Haggadah would no longer be available to visitors. It is now displayed under glass in a cabinet maintained by temperature control. I have a copy amongst the Haggadahs in my collection.

Our drive took us north to Split. We visited the home-museum of Yugoslavia's greatest sculptor, Mestrovich, where many or his monumental works can be found. One imposing piece was in the outdoor Billy Rose Garden of the Israeli museum in Jerusalem. Mestrovich, who could design the most tender works, was largely an artist dealing with powerful, massive subjects. In his garden were works with a sensuous beauty unlike his more prominent heroic pieces. He lived a lusty life. Since his wife produced no children, he brought in a mistress as part of his household to bear him a family. He introduced them jointly to all and sundry with the words: "This is my wife, and this is the mother of my children."

Along the coast, we ran into old churches, some dating back to the ninth century. We drank slivovitz, the national beverage, at every opportunity. It was tasty, hearty, and inexpensive. Part of the highway was along a barren, gray stone, uninhabited coastal road, hugging the sea, but with too many sharp curves to allow one to see anything. We had to keep mind and eye on the wheel and road.

After Ljubljana, we drove up into the mountains, crossed the border into Austria, where the towns, the buildings and churches, the forests and farms took on a richer and more formal character. Klagenfurt was a superb example with its onion-domed churches.

Austria

In Graz, we visited a new synagogue, not yet dedicated, located on the second floor of a nondescript building, an inadequate replacement for the handsome edifice destroyed by the Nazis. It housed a small collection of Jewish ritual objects. The small Jewish community was composed entirely of pensioners.

At Mariazell, a famous Christian shrine, we found every hotel occupied by a farmers' convention. We had to rest overnight in a little *gasthaus* overlooking a lake and mountains, a picture-book scene. In the city we heard good guitarists, watched the natives dance their polkas in the street, and heard a typical Austrian band, dressed in lederhausen and hat with a feather, play in the square before the architecturally garish church.

For our first visit to Vienna, we selected a small hotel, the Kaiserin Elisabeth, in order to be situated in a place from which we could see this beautiful city as much as possible on foot. We were entertained by natives in superior restaurants, one where the violinists played Zigeuner music, another on the lofty moving tower Donauturm, which overlooked the city and the Danube, and where we ate the best venison in our memory, from deer raised for the table and not shot wild. At the Grinzing, we joined scores of merry, young people who were welcoming and imbibing the new white wine. We heard and saw a dramatic production of Mozart's *The Magic Flute* at the famous opera house. We hard Kahlman's *Countess Maritza* at the Volksoper and joined with the audience in demanding an encore for "O Gypsy, O Gypsy." We also heard and saw Johann Strauss's *A Night in Venice*. We had Sachertorte at the Sacher Hotel. We lunched at Demel's with its fabulous pastries. We saw every palace, museum, park, statue, as well as the famous Lippizaner horses.

Two days were spent in the synagogue. It was Rosh Hashanah. We bought our seats in advance, worshipped in the beautiful, restored Stadttempel's sanctuary with its three-story circular balconies. The chazzan was a man of excellent voice as he petitioned God. The shofar-blowing was impressive. We read the service from a Hebrew-German Mahzor printed in 1862. No one said hello or *gut yom tov* to us before or after the service. We dropped into a Hassidic synagogue, where they were observing the holiday in a demonstrative fashion. We ate in a kosher restaurant, which also provided food to Czechoslovakian Jewish refugees for a small fee.

While we did not personally experience any anti-Semitic remarks, we were told by Jews and some non-Jews that anti-Semitism was a fact of life in Austria, and that little had been done to eradicate this unfortunate attitude.

After 11 P.M., prostitutes freely plied their trade on the streets of Vienna. It was interesting to see them competing for customers and bargaining about their fees in vestibules of the most expensive shops closed at that late hour.

We left Vienna full of its rich food, full of its serious and joyous music, marveling at its sumptuous art, parks, buildings, but with the memory that Jews were living under sufferance and there was little that this socialist-run country was doing to eliminate this hostile spirit. It was manifest during Kurt Waldheim's run for the Presidency of Austria in 1986.

Developments on Long Island

I was one of the very few at Federation, who saw the growth of the Jewish community in Nassau and Suffolk as a reality that we would have to plan for in the way of services and facilities and not simply use as another resource for fund-raising.

I had a difficult time persuading the building and the communal planning committees to include center services for both burgeoning counties. We finally included three areas, although there was little disposition to provide any capital funds for this section of Greater New York. I finally found a well-endowed and capable chairman to head a committee that developed YM-YWHAs for greater Long Island, and managed to keep this organization out of the grasp of the Associated YM-YWHAs, which still believed, before and after I left Federation in 1973, that all new Ys should properly fall under its jurisdiction. As a result of the independence of this eastern Long Island unit, by 1985 there were several major buildings in Nassau-Suffolk conducting large and important programs.

After Federation established its day camp facilities in western Suffolk County, my frequent visits to that area, my readings of the local press and meetings with some local Jewish leaders, convinced me that Suffolk would increasingly house an ever-larger Jewish population. I pressed this idea before the distribution and communal planning committees in the hope that Federation would reach out with services and support. Every effort was made, as always, to delimit Federation's expanding farther and farther from Manhattan. When I left Federation, the so-called Manhattan complex still dictated how far Federation extended its arms. I pursued the matter persistently, and we finally drew a line at Smithtown (Suffolk County), but I was warned, "No further."

Peggy Tishman, who became president of Federation in 1986, was a valuable aid in getting recognition for Nassau and Suffolk Counties as legitimate locations for Federation activities. We traveled out to that part of the island on numerous occasions and prepared reports which influenced Federation to move in that geographic direction.

There were no regrets on the part of Federation leaders about earlier delays. Only a few knew how hard a couple of us had to labor to make sure that Federation adopted the correct, forward-looking course.

I only wished that Federation had listened to me about moving into northern Westchester sooner, going into Rockland County, and entering northern New Jersey and making it part of Greater New York. Into all three areas, former New Yorkers were constantly moving. This was where new services and facilities were needed, and there was where a great deal of the wealth of former New Yorkers was being created and could have been tapped for the support of such programs.

Labor Zionism

In the early years of my life, I became a Zionist due to the influence of my father. He was not simply interested in Palestine as a fulfillment of our religious prayers, but sought to help this far-off land by modest contributions and investments in its budding industries. How he would have loved to see Israel. Regrettably, he died just before the state was established.

One of my Hebrew school teachers was a convinced Zionist, and if things had gone differently in my family in 1921, I might have ended up on aliyah with him. My family was sympathetic, but my mother's illness changed many of our family plans. I was a member of Young Judea, and when the field worker from the national office would appear at least once a year, we were subjected to jingoistic speeches not only to support Palestine, but also go there to live.

I formally joined the Labor Zionist movement in my final year at the University of Missouri under the influence of Dr. Isidore Keyfitz, whom I had been instrumental in bringing to the campus in 1929. I continued my affiliation, read literature, occasionally went to meetings, listened to speakers. Yet I did not become too active. After I became an executive of Jewish community centers in Staten Island and the Bronx, my sympathies with Labor Zionism grew, along with my interest in labor and the unionization of workers, my preference for socialism as a political philosophy until 1936, and my interest in cooperatives, which I helped to establish at Bronx House. Since I was concerned with creating a homeland for Jews in Palestine, the program of the Labor Zionists was more appealing in what they were doing to develop the country, particularly through kibbutzim, the Histadrut, and the creation of a defense force that could withstand the continued hostility and assaults of the Arab population and neighboring Arab countries. While I gave little thought to going on aliyah for myself and my family, I was supportive of those who made this decision.

When I was approached in the early 1950s to organize Jewish communal workers to work on behalf of Israel, now a full-fledged state, with the stimulation of the persistent C. Bezalel Sherman, a talented Jewish sociologist, writer, and devoted supporter of Israel, we managed to create an organization that met periodically during the years to listen to important Israelis. Moshe Sharret, Abba Eban, Yaakov Morris, Saadia Gelb were some who appeared at our meetings. We established a resident fellowship fund that enabled us to send two American Jewish social workers to Israel for a period of six months each, to contribute their skills in our American professional specialties. We held a luncheon session at the annual Conference of Jewish Communal Service to spread our message to a somewhat wider audience. I regret to say that with all of our vaunted efforts and those of my successors to the chairmanship, we were never able to recruit more than fifty members. Despite the political liberalism of Jewish communal personnel, neither Israel nor Labor Zionism obtained their support. Most of them were more interested in the problems of the larger society, native and foreign, and did not want to associate themselves with what they deemed a parochial cause. Some of them changed their minds during the 1967 Arab-Israeli war, but most did not move in that direction until 1973, when it looked as if Israel was facing disaster. Only those who had a longtime ideological commitment to Labor Zionism or Zionism, some who had been to Palestine-Israel, some who were involved in Jewish education, some of whom had a good Jewish background, became members. Otherwise there was almost nothing that we could do or say that would entice them either to join our group or to make a contribution toward the projects we initiated.

I was elected to the central committee of the organization, but I had precious little time to get deeply involved in the too frequent meetings that were called or the duties they wanted me to assume. The central committee included people who devoted practically all their spare time and energies to the movement.

I was honored by the organization, if that is the proper term, when it conducted its annual dinner for the Israel Bond drive. Individuals in the Jewish organizational spectrum were often asked to be honored guests at fund-raising events, in order to attract their friends and relatives to attend, and, perforce, contribute—a device that has proven rewarding. I learned that my "affair" attracted the largest attendance up to that time, June 14, 1962, selling several hundred thousand dollars' worth of bonds to a great many new purchasers, who had come to this event only because of me. Ironically, the main speaker was no less than Member of the Knesseth Dr. Joseph Burg, who has been a member of every cabinet since the state was established, and with whom those of us concerned with the rescue of Ethiopian Jews were to have many quarrels in later years, because of his apparent indifference and foot-dragging on this issue. I received a handsome, modern sterling silver *bezumin* (spice box) as a gift that evening, which I treasure amongst our modest collection of Israeli and other Jewish ritual objects.

Returning to Burg, I remember that when I went to see him in 1975 on the subject of the Ethiopian Jews, he asked me who I was. I recalled his having sat next to me and spoken on my behalf at the Israel Bond dinner. "Oh, yes. I remember you well. You have that interesting name, Graenum." But it had little effect on his attitude and efforts on behalf of the Jews suffering in Ethiopia.

Except for an article that was published in the *Jewish Frontier,* a Labor Zionist periodical, I could not get the support of this American organization to use its influence on the Israeli Labor Zionist parties, which dominated the government, to do anything on behalf of Ethiopian Jewry.

When the American committee asked me to be one of its delegates to the World Zionist Conference in Jerusalem in 1974, I was prepared to accept the assignment, but on one condition—that the American delegation would present a strong resolution demanding that the government of Israel undertake an immediate and massive rescue program designed to bring the Ethiopian Jews to Israel. Apparently the American committee was informed that such a resolution would not be welcome, so I took this occasion to resign from the Labor Zionist organization. My statement was subsequently printed in an issue of the *Jewish Frontier* (September 1974). The article, "Falasha—An Open Letter to Labor Zionists," is worth reading today, because it not only indicted the Labor Zionist movement for failure to act on its published principles, but also gave a historical account of the Ethiopian Jews and the need for their expeditious rescue.

I can state categorically that the Labor Zionist movement and party in Israel, in control of the government from 1948 to 1977, never had the slightest interest in the plight of the Ethiopian Jews at a time when it could have saved all of them.

So I terminated my formal relationship of fifty years. I knew of no better way to show my disapproval of what I considered an immoral position than by severing ties with an organization that had the power and should have been in the forefront—on its own initiative, not needing any promptings from me, to save a beleaguered remnant of an ancient Jewish tribe.

Camping

I had been formally out of the camping field for a year when my good friend Matthew Penn called me one day to tell me that the New York section of the American Camping Association was honoring me at a luncheon. Matt was always seeking to have the world give recognition to my contributions, knowing that I had been deeply involved in this specialty for more than thirty years, a unique educational and social welfare service in which I had made a number of significant innovations. I had also written extensively and given a number of major addresses, which at one time I thought I would compile and publish as a book. I never got around to putting the material together.

On January 30, 1970, I addressed the ACA and at the same time was presented with a handsome plaque by Henry Wellman, the president, whom I had known from his early days as a professional in YM-YWHAs and camping. Henry read the citation aloud; amongst other things it stated:

> *Graenum Berger*
> Articulate spokesman and writer,
> Inspiring leader, teacher, and innovator,
> Searcher for excellence,
> Challenger and critic.

15

Around the World—1971

ROMANTICALLY, EMMA AND I had envisaged a trip around the world. Unlike the rich and the more adventurous, we never could sit down seriously to plan and finance such a venture. But life has a way of offering unforeseen opportunities, and when it arose we seized it. My brother Sam had been appointed deputy chief of mission in Vietnam during the height of the war, working with the able Foreign Service officer, Ambassador Ellsworth Bunker. Sam invited us to come to Vietnam, and without a moment's hesitation we accepted. Our son Michael, who was in the military and who had wanted to serve in Vietnam, was the only one in the family who objected. He feared it might be dangerous.

* * *

I had another busy year at Federation covering my multitudinous duties. As usual, I also accepted a number of invitations to speak, which required considerable time for preparation. One asked me to address myself to a subject with a long, questioning title: "Will YM-YWHAs and Synagogues Work Closer Together in the 1980s Than Today?" It also had a subtitle: "A Strategy for Joint Ventures in the Next Decade." In my speech I observed that while diversity may be a fact of Jewish life, it was not necessarily a divine virtue that guaranteed our existence in the future. It was my contention that Jews must reverse the trend toward more diversity, which seemed to threaten integration. I quoted from the Apocrypha: "Observe the waters. When they flow together, they sweep along stones, trees, earth and other things; but if they are divided into many streams, the earth swallows them up, and they vanish. So shall ye also be, if ye be divided."

For several years, I had been providing direct supervision to the nursery school directors operating in community centers associated with Federation. My emphasis had been on making them more consciously Jewish on a personal level and making the ambience and the programs under their direction more Jewish for both the children and parents. In 1970–71, I was endeavoring not only to emphasize Jewish themes, but to bring the directors more closely to an Israeli experience. Instead of approaching them politically or ideologically, I decided to reach them through music and dance, two art forms with which they were sympathetic. In an interesting paper, which began with King David, the psalmist and sweet singer, who brought the ark to Jerusalem three thousand years ago with song and dance, I ended with the following:

> Israel should not be taught apart from the Jewish educational experience we give all of our children. It must be woven in, made integral, be normal. Otherwise, it will become at best no more than another interesting country. It must be part of the Jewish person, as though he himself actually went on aliyah. It is not mere subject matter, it must be a "soul" experience.

That workshop had a decided impact on future programs in the nursery schools.

The Ansells

Planning a trip around the world was a vast project, particularly if you wanted to cover it in only ten weeks. Which countries do you include, and which do you leave out? How long do you stay in each one? We realized that we might never go over this route again. While we made some minor changes en route, we conformed to the original schedule. After planning at home, I worked it out in an hour and a half sitting on a stool at a Pan Am counter in Manhattan. We tried to pick up as many addresses as possible from friends, and they stood us in good stead in India, Nepal, Iran.

Our first stop, to break up the long flight, was with Charles and Maryann Ansell in Sherman Oaks, California, where after a day of activity, we talked each night until the weary hours of the morning about the past, our mutual friends, and about developments in contemporary social work and psychology. The first night we met with a group of well-to-do American Jews, who had given up on the drug and hippie culture, alcoholism, the decline in values in American society, and were flying to Israel to give their children an opportunity to develop in a "normal"

Jewish environment. They objected vehemently to the American youth movements, which had become obsessed with a culture that affected their children's speech, dress, sex, dance, music, art, drama, literature—best symbolized, as one put it, in the "invention of the water bed." They argued that America had been unable to resolve the serious problems of poverty, race, housing, education, pollution, drugs, transportation, and could no longer inspire loyalty in its citizens. They saw all of these negative trends as having a pathological influence on the behavior of their children in their choice of educational goals and professions, premarital sex, deferred marriages, intermarriage, divorce, abortion, pornography—all inimical to the Jewish family and the future of Jewish life. The group included a research scientist, doctors, psychiatrists, businessmen, teachers, and social workers. Even the Ansells were flirting with aliyah, although they had no children of their own. Eventually, some made it to Israel. A few returned in a few years, but were not totally disillusioned with Israel, for they continued their intimate association with and support of that country.

The Ansells assembled an interesting luncheon party for us, where we met a major-general in the Israeli army, Mattityahu Peled, who was completing his Ph.D. studies in California. Sitting around and in the swimming pool on a sunny day, we got a full presentation of his "radical" views. He maintained that Israel should make immediate peace with the Arab countries, starting with Egypt, and then Egypt would get rid of Russia. He had a poor estimate of most Israeli leaders, except Pinchas Sapir. We met Peled later in Israel, where his views were being adopted by a small group of followers. In 1984 he was elected to the Knesset and could vote officially on how Israel should act. He boldly met with Arabs and even with Arafat.

I expressed my own views that afternoon. It was time for American Jews to fight for their continuity, and this could only be done by "withdrawing" from concerns of the larger world and devoting themselves principally to perfecting their institutions, emphasizing Jewish education, and developing a more disciplined, singular point of view. Everyone present took exception to such a reactionary solution to the Jewish problem.

* * *

My brother Sam had married Elizabeth Lee Pressey, the widow of an admiral in the U.S. Navy, who had three grown daughters. Sam had known Admiral Pressey and Betty Lee when he had served as ambassador to Korea from 1961 to 1964. On our arrival in Hawaii, after flying there on our first 747, we found a pleasant hotel near the golf course. Unlike 1962, no one greeted us at the airport, for no one had been apprised of our coming.

In Honolulu we renewed our relationship with Sachiko Miyao, our friend from the 1962 trip through Japan. We ate at several superb Japanese restaurants that she recommended. Honolulu had gone through a building boom since our visit nine years before. There was a new superhighway. We were again impressed with its cleanliness and courtesy to pedestrians crossing the streets. It was, however, overrun with ill-clad hippies, who had finally found this warm paradise as a place to loaf. We ate pineapple and mangoes and enjoyed the fragrance of the plumeria flowers.

* * *

Our 747, the first 747 flight to Vietnam, was late. This was a bad omen. It was filled with Japanese and Philippine civilians and many soldiers returning to Vietnam for either a second or third tour of duty. They had not found Vietnam the evil war portrayed in the U.S. press and on TV. Some miles out of Hawaii, something went wrong with the plane. It dumped its gasoline, and returned to Honolulu for repairs. After several hours' delay, we were off again. No one openly displayed any fear during this episode.

Our next stop was Guam, a flat island which, we were told, grew nothing but coconuts. Large numbers of natives and officials noted the arrival of the first 747. En route to Manila, we spoke to many soldiers and some officers at length. They expressed it this way: "This is not a war. Just guerillas and skirmishes." One claimed that the soldiers were instructed never to shoot first. "You could never tell a friend from the enemy when you entered a village. If Calley [who had been indicted for killing Vietnamese wantonly] did it deliberately, he should be punished." Sam told us in Vietnam that scores of U.S. soldiers had been court-martialed for violations of "strict army regulations." As to the use of drugs, it was the result of "sheer boredom." We were also told that most of the soldiers who used drugs had been exposed to them in the States and had not become novitiates in Vietnam. Yet drugs were said to be easily available and cheap in Vietnam. They sniffed, drank and main-lined heroin. They got hooked. Those who wanted to go home clean, laid off the drugs several months before their tour of duty expired. At Manila, where three-quarters of the passengers disembarked, there was a colorful reception for the first 747.

Saigon, Vietnam

In Saigon, we landed at the huge airport, which seemed to be overrun with G.I.s and Vietnamese officials to celebrate the arrival of the first 747. Sam and Betty Lee led us through immigration quickly without inspection, although the functionaries at the terminal were doing a thorough job of examining everyone's luggage to prevent the smuggling of drugs and other articles.

A police car escorted Sam's chauffeur-driven vehicle through a city crowded with people, bicycles, motorcycles, and cars. Women were dressed in slacks with a long slit on the side almost to their hips, worn with an over blouse. Men wore Western clothes. The city appeared prepossessing in its temples and public buildings, but the stores were mean. The exposed overhead electric and telephone lines were ugly intrusions on the palm-tree-lined boulevards.

Sam's house was surrounded by a high cement-block wall with an iron gate guarded by marines. In the attractive building, originally erected by a rich French banker, and formerly the residence of the U.S. ambassador, some marines slept indoors, protecting it around the clock. Ellsworth Bunker, the current ambassador, occupied a dwelling that was rented, closer to the U.S. Embassy offices. Sam had restored the outside gardens with grass, shrubbery, and with his current plant hobby of growing scores of varieties of orchids, some hanging from the trees, or else shooting out of nests in the trees. He played tennis on his own court, but had to use a neighbor's pool for swimming. The interior was filled with mementos—paintings, sculpture, ceramics, rugs collected on previous assignments abroad, as well as his and Betty Lee's combined assembly of native antiques, particularly Annamese (old Vietnam) china. Visitors came and went continually, each one telling us a bit about their various roles in Vietnam—military, political, cultural. Our store of information accumulated daily. We were introduced to new fruits like marguettes, which had sections like an orange, but tasted more like a banana. Fresh litchies were served at every dinner.

Sam told us a story of a "stupid" U.S. congressman who talked and never listened. In an interview with the press he had said that Bunker should be dismissed and Sam put in charge of the embassy. It was embarrassing for Sam.

I asked Sam about an article I had recently read in the *New York Times* by Ivor Peterson, who claimed that Sam had driven his own car out to a reception for the Prime Minister and had gotten out of his small vehicle to take pictures of the scene. Sam said he never drove himself in Vietnam. The bulletproof vehicle was always chauffeured by a well-armed Vietnamese. Furthermore, he always had an official photographer who took pictures. He wondered whether Peterson had even attended the ceremony. He felt the U.S. press always sought out the worst events in the Vietnam war rather than presenting the story in an objective manner. For example, while he did not approve of the prison cages in which prisoners were housed, he told me that they were not in dungeons, but open. Yet when photographers took pictures only from the top, they appeared to be encased in buried cells.

One night Sam had at dinner another well-known American reporter, who had written about the easy availability of drugs in Saigon and that anyone could buy them openly in certain alleyways. I told the reporter that on that very afternoon, I had walked through these alleys with a young marine in civilian dress, who was escorting Bunker's granddaughter, a tall beautiful girl, wearing the briefest of miniskirts. Nobody had approached any of us. Maybe we didn't look like drug buyers. But I saw no evidence of any street salesmen with their wares in the area he had described. I admitted that the military police might have cleaned up those streets, but I wondered what value the story had apart from sensationalism. I indicated that the soldiers on the plane had told me that many of the men were already drug users in the States before coming to the Orient. While military life, whether boredom or to forget the gruesomeness of the combat experience, led soldiers to a first or expanded use of drugs, the situation ought to be portrayed more accurately rather than as a consequence only of the U.S. venture. He listened patiently. His only reply was that he reported what he had seen. No further discussion.

While we expected to be filled in with a good deal of on-the-spot information about how the war (still undeclared) was proceeding, we had not expected to be taken by plane, helicopter, and P.T. boats into the interior, which at the moment of our visit was still largely under the control of government forces. Sam had a typed itinerary of six pages, which we studied in amazement, but accepted without question and without fear.

One morning we drove to the Free World Forces Helipad (named for other nations supporting the war) and took off in a helicopter. They kept the doors open, so we could get a better view of the terrain and take clearer pictures. Emma confessed later that she was scared stiff, but like a good trooper said nothing. Soldiers with heavy-caliber rifles sat on each side of the plane with guns pointed downwards, ostensibly to protect us. We flew at an elevation of 1,500 feet, said to be out of the range of most arms borne by the enemy. We could easily see the rice paddies, the meandering streams, the lush tropical fields and forests. We could also observe the numerous pockmarked bomb craters.

At Bing Duong, we stopped for a briefing on who controlled what parts of that province. We saw a museum of captured guns. Many U.S. government officials had been visiting the country. The briefing area was covered with maps and full of movable pins. A nearby village was functioning normally. Emma and Betty Lee visited a lacquer factory and made some purchases. Once a locale for large rubber plantations, the area was now being protected as the main entry point to Cambodia. Other crops had been substituted. It was clear that only Vietnamese forces controlled this sector. We did not have to worry about sudden guerilla attacks. The province was populated by a quarter of a million people.

We flew to the Tay Ninh province, but flying at a higher elevation, because here there were Viet Cong infiltrations. We were again briefed on landing about the 735,000 people who dwelt in this region. The inhabitants belonged in the main to the Cao Dai sect. They worshipped Laotze, Buddha, Confucius, Jesus, Sun Yat Sen, and Victor Hugo, a potpourri of Eastern mysticism, Christianity, and modern progressive universalism. They were vegetarians and cultivated their own communal gardens. The religious ceremonies in their garishly designed and oddly decorated temple included rows of barefoot dancers, a children's chorus, and an array of musicians. When I walked up close to one of them to take his picture, a priest literally grabbed me and took me to the side, where he forced me down on my knees to pray. I satisfied his request without resistance, reciting some Hebrew prayers which no one understood. We later ate an excellent vegetarian lunch. The nearby village was alive with a lumber yard, a flour mill, and a brass factory, where they were manufacturing vases made out of heavy, expensive, spent American brass shells.

At Long Hai, we saw the effects of the war, with a refugee settlement providing facilities for part of the 250,000 currently displaced persons.

We flew to an area on the numerous canals and waterways, which frequently changed hands as one or the other army took over. Now it was well protected by both Vietnamese and American soldiers. We rode on boats, so that we could see where the enemy frequently invaded that territory from streams flowing in from northern parts of the country. We were always well guarded by armed personnel scouring nearby areas.

Whenever we ate in Saigon's better and excellent restaurants, it was always a feast. One night was memorable for the seafood soup, skewered broiled, marinated steaks, fried crab in sugar cane, braised pigeons, and unusual fruits.

We spent an interesting morning talking with Richard Hughes, an American actor who had organized a local "Boys' Town" for abandoned street urchins. He was then getting a good press around the world. We visited his facility, where Gene Aynsworth, an ex-G.I., was in charge. We were impressed with what he had already done to rehabilitate a large number of tough kids.

With friends of Sam's we took a boat trip up the Saigon River, where the wharves were lined for miles with U.S. Army equipment of every conceivable type. Docked along this river were boats, small and large, discharging equipment for the war arsenal.

While Vietnam was quite a "modern" country and one could see evidences everywhere of the French influence, in Saigon, you could not escape a host of fortune tellers, who quickly foretold what would happen to you, using all kinds of devices, including chicken feet, to bolster their prophecies. You were importuned to light candles and light up incense pots to save and cleanse your soul, so as to obtain long life and prosperity. Despite the decisive religious and political influence of Catholicism, it was abundantly clear that the country was still largely Buddhist and superstitious.

Henry Kissinger

Henry Kissinger arrived in Saigon. He was meeting with all the Untied States ambassadors accredited to neighboring countries in a room directly across from our bedroom in Sam's house. Not only was that room guarded, but Sam's entire grounds were surrounded with scores of additional soldiers carrying heavy arms.

Sam had arranged for us to meet Kissinger at lunch. Apart from Betty Lee, the only others present were Ambassador Bunker and his granddaughter. Cocktails were served. The irrepressible, garrulous Kissinger did all the talking, regaling us with stories about Nelson Rockefeller, Richard Nixon, Jack Kennedy, and Lyndon Johnson. Johnson was "arrogant," and "his administrative style was to use his key people as adversaries." Nixon only asked for options and made his own decisions. All Presidents had to combat the tyrannies of the bureaucrats, who not only dominated their own departments but also tried to influence policies for the country over which they had no jurisdiction. Emma thought that some of the personal stories Kissinger related about the Presidents were in bad taste. None of us made any comments during this monologue.

When he finally deserted these personalities, Kissinger went into a tirade against the *New York Times* for having printed the Pentagon Papers. Neither Bunker nor Sam disagreed with him. I finally broke the soliloquy by stating that in preparation for my visit to Vietnam, I had read all of the *Times* copy, and although I admittedly lacked expertise in reading between the lines, there didn't seem to me to be anything in the report which gave away state secrets. Bunker, who was lean and over six feet tall; Sam, who was five foot five and in good physical shape; Kissinger, who was my height of five foot eight and inclined to a bit of portliness, descended on me like an avalanche. "No foreign country will have confidence in our government. No one in government circles will any longer write what he truly knows and believes." They gave me no chance to reply, as though the final word had been uttered and I should accept their positions. (In 1984, when a reporter asked Kissinger whether he would have the same reaction today to his rage against the printing of the papers back in 1971, he replied that the papers were really unimportant.)

When we sat down to lunch, Sam and Bunker remained laconic. To avoid what might have been a silent and uninteresting meal, I asked Kissinger a question: "Tell me, Dr. Kissinger, why does the President need the National Security Council, which you are now heading, when he has the Department of State, the Department of Defense, the CIA, and the Secret Service? I understand that you have a staff of over one hundred people and a budget that runs in the tens of millions."

Kissinger answered me in a professorial voice with a trace of German accent. He admitted everything that I said, but added that each of these departments competed with one another. One could not always trust the dispatches that were cabled or arrived by diplomatic pouch from generals and Foreign Service officers. It was necessary for an objective outside body to assemble these miscellaneous reports, evaluate them, then draw up brief summary statements with options and the consequences of taking one position as against another, from which the President could bring his recommendations to the cabinet or make his own final decision. We listened to a rather lengthy explanation without interruption or comment. Kissinger was indicting two of the most prestigious ambassadors in the State Department.

Contrary to Kissinger's opinion, Bunker has been referred to as a man of "integrity," who might have "lacked flair," but nonetheless was one of the greatest statesmen of our times and perhaps any other time. He was "possessed of two qualities, deliberateness and inner security. He was able to do what few ambassadors can afford to do, he could tell the President of the United States to get off his back" (Martin F. Herz, *Resolution of the Dominican Crisis*, Georgetown University, 1980). A successful businessman turned mediator on the international scene, Bunker was without peer.

As to Sam's status, on May 23, 1986, in an article entitled "Journey Among Tyrants," A. M. Rosenthal, executive editor of the *New York Times*, referred to Sam and Bunker.

> I was always struck by the fact that so many American diplomats seemed to get along easily with the generals and civilian dictators. I suppose it was because they could go right in and get a yes or no instead of going through all that bother of dealing with political leaders, who had to explain to their own people what they were doing. There were exceptions of course—Ellsworth Bunker, the elegant Ambassador to India in our time, who seemed to get along with the troublesome Indians quite well; Samuel D. Berger, the quick-minded former labor attache who became the United States Ambassador in Seoul and soon convinced the local generals not even to think of

pushing him around. (Philip C. Habib, who went on to become a Presidential trouble-shooter in the Middle East, the Philippines and Central America, was Sam Berger's deputy in those days. One day, when the generals were attempting one pressure tactic or another against the embassy, Mr. Habib shook his head in mock sorrow and said they didn't have a chance, not in an embassy "where the ambassador is a Jew, his deputy is a Lebanese and the C.I.A. station chief is a Greek.")

As Kissinger was talking I could not bring myself to watch either Sam's or Bunker's face. They must have felt uncomfortable. Neither commented about his remarks after the luncheon.

Then, out of the blue, Kissinger literally fired a direct question at me: "Since you seem to be so knowledgeable about the operations of our government and its foreign affairs, what would you do to stop the war in Vietnam?"

Without a moment's hesitation, I replied: "If I was the President of the United States, I would go to China, because I think that is the key to the solution of this problem."

There was silence around the table. I thought that I had made such a stupidly fantastic comment that they all thought it was not worthy of reply.

The rest of the lunch was spent in chitchat.

I did not realize that I had touched on the very reason for Kissinger's being in Vietnam. *He was on his way to China for the very purpose I had propounded.* Subsequently we read in the press that Kissinger had gone to Pakistan. There was a blackout on news about him, except that he was not well and had to be hospitalized. A few days later, the media startled the world. Kissinger was in China on behalf of the President.

Some weeks later, we were in Nepal having lunch with Carol Laise, Bunker's wife, who was ambassador in her own right to that mysterious land. When I walked in, Bunker took me aside and asked what had prompted me to make that reply to Kissinger's question. Kissinger and he thought that someone might have overheard the secret plan. I answered that what I had said was my independent view. He was happy that there were no consequences of my remarks. We left it at that. I was then concerned about how it might affect Sam, because the suspicion might be that he had given me some inkling of the discussions going on in his residence. It was just not so. Sam never told me anything before, after, or since that luncheon. I am not even sure that Sam even knew about Kissingers's projected visit to China. That secret might have been limited only to the ambassador. While I had mentioned to Sam off and on, even before we went to Vietnam, that the Chinese would be an important element in deciding the fate of the unfortunate conflict, Sam had not agreed with me, or if he really held the identical view, he never revealed what his personal outlook was on this issue.

I always had my own perspective about the need for the United States to control, if necessary, and not merely assist, Vietnam in its ordeal. As far back as 1941, we learned that our Western border was vulnerable. As a consequence it was necessary to have a connecting military line from Alaska, through Korea, Japan, Taiwan, the Philippines, Vietnam, and Indonesia, to Australia at the other side of the Pacific. Vietnam was a key, because it offered control over the entrance to the Indian Ocean, where we had vital interests. The question was: Were we doing enough and the right things to keep Vietnam in our orbit? To fortify our presence in Vietnam, it was necessary to improve our relations with China, so that it would not consider our presence there a threat.

I recall being in Sam's house in Washington in 1967, when he was deputy assistant secretary for the Far East. We had come to Washington for a long weekend, the day American citizens "assaulted" the Pentagon (October 21–22, 1967). That night Sam gave a dinner party at which were present a former ambassador, who was now writing foreign policy speeches for President Johnson, Sam's boss in the Far East Department, an admiral in the navy, and a prominent federal judge. There was a spirited debate as to why the U.S. government was not getting its message across to the American people. They were upset that tens of thousands of Americans would even assemble to picket the Pentagon in order to get the United States out of Vietnam. Finally the speech writer turned to me and asked: "Graenum, you are not part of the establishment. What do you think went wrong?" I told him that I had asked that same question of the cab driver who drove us from the station to Sam's home, and that he had replied, without hesitation, that what we needed was a line of defense on the other side of the Pacific, a point of view similar to the one I held. So I replied to the query adding: "That is a position that Americans can understand. Bringing democracy to a land and a section of the world that never practiced such a civic philosophy was a slogan, not a program. Plain, simple defense should be our position, or some day, perhaps in the not too distant future, we would have to fight another costly war in the Pacific for which we were again, like in 1941, unprepared." They turned to each other and one said: "We thought of that approach, but we didn't use it. Why?"

We went to a July Fourth celebration at the U.S. Embassy, where I met ambassadors, generals, and personalities from dozens of countries. The only strange aspect was that everyone there wore a dark suit and I had come dressed in a light, blue-striped cord. Oh, yes, we ate an ice cream cake decorated with the red-and-white stripes and white stars on a blue field—the American flag.

At a briefing one day by the U.S. civilian adviser to the city of Saigon, which has become one of the most densely populated cities in the world, I was told that Saigon would be defensible against any enemy. He proved to be wrong. During our visit to Vietnam, I was advised that the Vietnamization program for the native army was working well, that the government would be able to protect itself against the Viet Cong and the North Vietnamese forces. Somehow I carried away an impression that while mechanically things were going satisfactorily, thanks to the massive American presence, there was serious question about the native leadership of the country and whether the army and the people would support the administration if things really got tough. My own pessimistic assessment was that they would not. No one could assure me that popular morale was high enough to justify such a permanent claim on their loyalties.

In replies to some of my questions, I gathered that the G.I.s liked the Vietnamese girls, who were strong, devoted, and traditional. There were thirteen hundred marriages in 1970. However, there were also thousands of out-of-wedlock children, who had to be absorbed in the already overcrowded extended families. Black soldiers were not socially acceptable to Vietnamese parents. Racial prejudice existed even amongst those who were themselves victims of bias.

We took another trip in a single-motor plane and by helicopter to the Mekong Delta, where six mllion people lived, and where the turning fortunes of war gave the enemy control over many parts of this vast waterway. We were always well protected by numerous security forces, who spread out to perimeters far beyond that which we were traversing. As we flew over some areas, our guide pointed out villages under V.C. control. This time we went to Kien Hua province, which had a history of pirate lawlessness, rich in fisheries and farming. While we floated on P.T. boats in marshy areas, from which any guerilla could have sunk the vessel or killed the passengers with relative ease, we went through unscathed, as though we were on a holiday, without any thought of the possible tragic consequences. Being so well guarded, the V.C. probably decided not to molest us that day.

Sam was eager for us to see some of the social welfare facilities and for me to meet the officials in charge. We visited child care centers, where tiny tots were well taken care of by Catholic nuns assisted by the wives of foreign embassy personnel. We entered a home care center, where women from the farm areas were being vocationally retrained for other types of work in the city. These institutions were products of the continuing war, dislocation, and the presence of foreign soldiers.

We sat down to a lavish lunch with the five top Vietnamese welfare officials around a large table. In between snatches of conversation about their welfare problems—and they were numerous—we consumed over a dozen dishes, which included bird's nest soup (men risk their lives to obtain this gelatinous delicacy from the little caves where the birds nest in the high sea cliffs), quail eggs, duck legs, roasted pigeons, monkey cervelle, fish in ginger and black beans, plankton soup, seaweed and mushrooms with livers, and so much more.

I was asked to breakfast with several Americans, including Wells Klein, son of Dr. Philip Klein, a professor at the Columbia University School of Social Work and a former board member of Bronx House, about the resettlement both of refugees and of soldiers during and hopefully after the conflict ended. They wanted to know what Israel was doing. I indicated how some soldiers who completed their service helped to establish kibbutzim around the undeveloped borders of Israel, so as to provide security for the country and a livelihood for themselves.

I also referred them to what the Koreans had done a decade ago, after their war, in retraining soldiers for a different kind of self-sufficient farm program, which assured better health measures in the use of night soil along with a more diversified type of farming to improve their diet and their fortunes.

It was unbelievable how much we had packed into a short visit to Vietnam.

Cambodia

While events were getting rougher in Cambodia, and the Red Army's shelling could be heard in Phnom Penh, the capital, Sam thought we ought to go there for a glimpse of the country. He made arrangements for us to stay overnight at the U.S. ambassador's residence with Ambassador Emory C. Swank. It was only a half-hour flight on Air Vietnam. We were greeted at the airport by some of the ambassador's aides, who first drove us to an excellent French restaurant for lunch, then took us on a shopping tour. The beautiful city was deserted. The stores were empty of customers, but still well stocked. We bought some silver objects. Our only regret was that we could not carry more. Storekeepers wanted to get rid of everything. We were given a quick look at the major Buddhist temple, the Palace with its famous dancing hall (we had seen Cambodian dancers in New York), and the museum.

The ambassador joined us at dinner, relating the trip he had made during the day to the outskirts. He was pessimistic about the future, although the Cambodian regulars were still putting up a stiff defense of the city. At night we heard the shelling not too many kilometers away. We left his beautiful residence the next day wondering how long it would last.

A few days later, we heard that an attempt had been made on Swank's life, as his car, in which he was riding, left his driveway. He escaped unscathed only by seconds. It was a dangerous place in which to dwell.

We couldn't visit Angor Wat and its historic ruins, temples and palaces. A sign at the airport read: "Angor Wat is not safe."

Thailand

We flew out of Phnom Penh on Air Cambode and landed in Bangkok, 335 miles west. Sam picked us up and drove us to the U.S. ambassador's residence, where we would stay for several days, while Ambassador Leonard Unger was away. We had use of his house with its art collection and large garden, where friendly monkeys abounded. We were professionally and warmly served by his white-coated housemen.

We toured the crowded city, had a Thai dinner at a hotel, watched the delicate Thai dancers in their colorful costumes and exquisite movements. The half-naked male dancers performed the violent sword dance. We visited all the well-advertised Buddhist temples and the Royal Court. We went on a motorboat ride on the *klongs* (canals), bought and ate the best bananas we had ever eaten. We noted the active life on and along the shores of the canal beautified by thousands of variegated orchids.

Edward Rosenthal, my sister Rachel's oldest son, had just arrived in Bangkok the day before, with his wife, Amy, to assume his duties as a U.S. Foreign Service officer. He was assigned to see what could be done to control the endless flow of opium from the Triangle of Cambodia, Laos and Thailand that was flooding the American market, after having been converted to heroin. A year later, while on a helicopter mission, Edward's plane was shot down; his companions and he were arrested and held in prison for weeks until the U.S. government obtained their release. A harrowing experience.

There were many soldiers in U.S. uniforms in Thailand shoring up the shaky regime and protecting it against potential invasion from Cambodia. One day as we were walking through the flower market, we ran into General Creighton Abrams, supreme commander in South Vietnam, in mufti, visiting with his family, who were billeted in Bangkok. Abrams was in charge of the American forces in Vietnam. I knew that Bunker was in Nepal. Sam was with us on a trip through Thailand and then into Burma. So when I greeted the general, I asked him: "Who is minding the store in Vietnam?" He smiled most genially and replied: "Nothing catastrophic will happen while we are away." We had met him on several occasions in Thailand, and he always seemed more like a gentle father than a tough soldier.

Abrams died before Sam. In 1980 Betty Lee, Sam's wife, and I selected a site for Sam's grave in Arlington Cemetery in Virginia, where he now lies next to his Vietnam colleague, General Abrams.

Burma

Sam and Betty Lee continued their journey with us into Burma. From the air, it looked like one huge rice bowl. Burma had undergone a socialist revolution in 1962. Only in recent months had foreigners finally been permitted to remain in this mysterious country of Chinese and Buddhist origins for more than twenty-four hours. With nationalist fervor, the Burmese had thrown out the Chinese and Indians. Even the Russians did not believe that socialism could be foisted on this quaint country. Socialist measures were introduced at the same time that an open, official black market and a great deal of small private enterprises continued.

The Burmese were short in stature, with shorter names, quiet, swarthy, and pleasant. The men wore longhis, a long skirt. I bought the cloth and had one sewn for me by a street tailor. It prevented the mosquitoes from eating me alive one night.

Ambassador Arthur Hummel was packing to leave for another assignment, so we did not spend too much time with him. Hummel was born in China, the son of missionaries, and was a prisoner-of-war during the Japanese occupation. He knew the people of the Orient intimately. (In 1975 I visited with him in Addis Ababa, Ethiopia, where he had been assigned as ambassador, and we talked about the Ethiopian Jews.) Hummel's staff in Burma outdid itself in hospitality, dinners, and providing opportunities to meet native Burmese and make purchases.

If a visitor did nothing more in Rangoon than climb to the Shwe Dagon Shrine with its scores of Buddhist temples and thousands of varicolored Buddhas, the trip would be well rewarded. We walked up the interminable staircase. Then onto the holy area in bare feet, according to the religious custom. It was a rainy day.

At the suggestion of U.S. officials, Emma and I met with the Israeli Ambassador Arieh Elan. He greeted us warmly, took us on a tour of the city, and spoke of the aid Israel was providing by way of economic assistance, construction of roads, and training of the military. Yet at that moment, relations between the two countries were strained. The Jewish community was tiny, less than two score Jews, mostly elderly.

We flew to Pagan to see the remains of the four thousand Buddhist temples that had been built on a vast flat plain from the tenth to the twelfth century. Some were still standing almost intact, each different, with their interior frescoes, even though a bit faded, providing a picture of the religious and secular life of that day. They gave graphic evidence of earlier creative artists. We also dropped in to watch native makers of lacquer ware using the distinctive decorative colors that marked their products.

Then we flew north to Mandalay, where we found Kipling's poem wrong in its geography, for the city is well situated on the muddy Irrawaddy River. From the air it seemed to be a city composed largely of Buddhist temples. There was one shrine with a hundred spires. We found a well-known artist, Paw Oo Thet, who painted this scene and his work is hanging in our hallway.

We stayed with the young consul-general, Carl Taylor, an informed and generous host. He had written books for children on Indonesia and Burma. He escorted us to the Maha Muni Pagoda, reminiscent of Rangoon's Shwe Dagon, but smaller, austere, and without the flamboyance. We saw palaces and other pagodas. We bought antiques and original paintings from young artists. We visited a home factory, where a whole family had been working for months on an order for a large, uniquely designed fabric, which used gold and silk threads to give it richness and a sheen.

One night we went out to what was reputed to be the "best" and most typical native restaurant in Mandalay. It had an earthen floor, one unshaded bulb for light, uncovered wooden tables, no screening to keep out ravaging mosquitoes, where we ate the worst meal in our memory. The duck, the chicken, the prawns were all undercooked, cold, and undistinguished.

Another night we met a few formerly well-to-do Burmese intellectuals, now sadly reduced economically because of the socialist revolution. The educated class had been replaced by the self-appointed dictatorship. Economic conditions were sluggish. Yet it was a pleasant country with a quiet, gentle people, all busy in city and countryside trying to make a living and the best of their unhappy situation.

Calcutta

Leaving Sam and Betty Lee in Burma, we continued our journey westward and reached Calcutta at 3:30 A.M. At the airport we learned about Kissinger having gone to China to arrange for a visit by President Richard Nixon. So my suggestion to Kissinger in Saigon had been coincidentally fulfilled.

Riding in a bus to our hotel, we noted that people were sleeping on doorsteps and window sills. At the Oberei Grand, where we were stopping, hundreds were huddled together under the porticos. They were allowed to sleep there between midnight and 6 A.M. Calcutta, unable to provide housing for one quarter of its ever-growing population, was besieged with one million refugees as a consequence of the India-Bangladesh crisis. Skin-and-bone refugees could be seen everywhere, sitting on the street curbs, cleaning their teeth with little sticks dipped in dirty water, and searching for accumulations of water puddles, where they could wash themselves and their clothes. Some had died of hunger and disease on the streets, and their bodies were carted away daily for burning.

The streets were filled with people buying from the numerous shops, all of which seemed to be thriving. Sacred cows wandered aimlessly through the busy thoroughfares leaving their soil for someone to pick up and either sell or use for garden fertilizer. Emma bought saris for herself, Anita and Sandy, our daughters-in-law, and Doris Rosenberg, a good friend. While beautiful fabrics, did they ever wear them?

Before we left the United States, I had become friendly with Monica Ghosh, an Indian woman from Delhi, who was working at the Jewish Federation as a secretary while chaperoning her daughter studying at a New York college. This beautiful woman, whose husband, a prosperous businessman, lived in Delhi, had written to friends and family in Calcutta, Bombay, and Delhi to take care of us on our arrival. On our first night in Calcutta, we were taken out by a young couple, Mr. and Mrs. Surrenda Rampira. She was a beauty, dressed in an imported French embroidered sari, with jewelry in her ears, nose, around her neck, both arms at the wrists, all fingers and both ankles, which extravagantly added to her native charm. Emma had purposefully dressed simply without jewelry, because she could not see herself displaying a well-to-do appearance in a city where abject poverty stared her in the face at every turn. While in the car, we passed huge mounds of garbage piled on the sides of the street, where ragged people were searching for morsels of food.

Despite this widespread poverty, Calcutta was the city of culture in India. It was the city of Tagore, the famous poet. Our hosts offered us the choice of many dramas and dance recitals. We chose a drama by Shankar, about whom we had read, and we were well rewarded. It was a combination of the traditional and the modern innovative theater, in which drama and dance were woven together. Suddenly the actors were curtained off-stage and a movie showed them in a black-and-white film environment, appearing on more panoramic landscapes. We were intrigued with the technique. The audience, which we were told only showed approval when something they witnessed was very good, only applauded twice.

After the theater, we drove through crowded streets, at some points blocked by political demonstrations of the "Communists," so that the car's driver had to detour. Refugees, beggars, and cripples abounded everywhere. Our young hosts were both accustomed to and annoyed by these scenes, spoke of moving their business and residence elsewhere, because Calcutta was becoming an impossible city in which the educated and rich found it difficult to live.

They took us to their swanky country club for a sumptuous vegetarian dinner. They ate no meat, no fowl, no fish, no eggs. Yet the meal, consisting of pancakes, a variety of thin, crusty breads, fresh vegetables, lentils, beans, custard, and tea, was different, tasty, and filling. Sitting in the midst of these luxurious surroundings of beautiful flowers and abundant trees, with music being wafted through the air, and served by white-turbaned waiters wearing white gloves, it seemed impossible to believe that we had just seen people dying in the streets, eating out of piles of garbage and sleeping in the rain. Despite the hygienic food and the service, Mrs. Rampira did not hesitate to stop the car and buy from an old woman, not particularly clean, some betel nuts and lime leaf to chew on to cleanse her mouth and teeth, and, as she said, aid her digestion. She forced some of it on me, so that I could not refuse. It was something that I could do without and quickly disposed of same through the car windows, praying that I had not contracted some untreatable disease.

We had already seen the sharp contrasts in India in a single day. With plenty of money, our new friends could enjoy the best of the city's resources, homes, restaurants, country clubs, entertainment. The unique orchestras, singers, and dancers were superb.

On another day, we visited the Queen Victoria Memorial, the museum with good collections of native art, and began to feel India's varied, mysterious culture. We began to understand the antagonistic differences between the Hindus, the Moslems, and the Sikhs. While on the street, I had my shirt pocket picked. Thereafter we took pains to conceal our valuables and did not permit strangers to jostle us, usually two people, who walked on both sides of you and engaged you in conversation, asking you for the time, and then wanting to know if you wished to exchange dollars.

We did not have time to see our friends again, nor did we have time to seek out the tiny Jewish community, but within a few days, what with the reading we had done about India beforehand, we had a glimpse of a city unable to cope with its massive problems, yet carrying on like any huge metropolis. We did not find it unduly depressing, but rather a vital city with its contrasts and ferment.

What can you do about a city which displayed a large advertisement with several women and men sitting on a large mattress under which was written: "Save, Rave, Misbehave"—an appeal no prospective buyer could resist. Or another sign with the hammer and sickle in each corner: "Two or three more Vietnams—That is our purpose." It gave you an indication of the Communist desire to strike at American capitalism from an Oriental position without fear of reprisal.

Nepal

We flew on a new, clean, crowded Thai airplane to Kathmandu, the capital and major city of Nepal. French caterers had prepared a meal worthy of only the first class, though we were traveling, as always, in the economy section. Nepal was a country living in the shadows of the lofty Himalayas, but except for a few quick seconds at sunrise, we could not see these massive peaks, for they were hidden under a gray-white cloud bank.

Kathmandu was a kind of bazaar sandwiched in between the streets and the temples *(stupas)*, where some still worshipped the monkey and the phallus. It was an ancient country with ancient symbols and practices that had shown no sign of disappearing, even with the new hotels, buildings, and hordes of foreign tourists. It was best understood when you visited the Temple of the Living Goddess, where a five-year-old girl had been rigidly selected and scrupulously trained to carry out a three hundred-year-old myth of religious adoration.

On the plane, we met Ralph Lippman, a New York photographer, who had been assigned by United Press International to do a photographic story on the hundreds of American hippies who had found their way to Nepal, where hashish was "good, cheap, and legal." He had not yet met any of these vagrants. The three of us were walking one evening when we spotted a group, all with their long hair tied in the back with a ribbon, wearing odd outergear, including typical Indian dress. When I began to quiz one of them, he turned out to be Allan Horowitz of Staten Island, whose father and mother we had known when I directed the Jewish Community Center in that city in 1932–38. He knew all about me. "You are a household name in our home." They had reached Nepal by the most economical and bizarre routes—ship, plane, railroad, bus, oxcarts. Hostels had been set up by Western "missionaries," who wanted to bed, feed, and get them off drugs. They existed quite inexpensively, spending as little money on food as possible. The next night we invited four of them to have dinner with us at the hotel. When the food appeared, they asked whether they could look at it for awhile, because they had not feasted on such victuals since they left the United States. One was a girl from Panama. Allan had $1,000 in American Express checks in his pocket, but he did not want to use them, because he was trying to prove to his parents that he could support himself.

Several weeks later, Allan met us in Bombay, when he wished to make a phone call to his mother on her birthday. He just assumed that we would be staying at a fine hotel—the Taj Mahal. The hotel would not let him in at first, because of his peculiar long hair and dress, but when we approved of his visit, he was allowed to come to our room. We offered to pay for the phone call, knowing how little money he was living on, or at least urged him to reverse the charges, as his parents were well-to-do and would have spent any amount just to hear from him. He refused, telling us that it was his mother's birthday and he wished to pay for it himself. He called his mother. We also spoke to her. It was only our word that he looked well that made her stop crying.

Emma had a habit of temporarily adopting many of the sick, hungry, or lonely young people whom we sometimes met in off-beat parts of the world. She would feed and talk with them, take their parents' phone numbers, and called them when we got back to the States to say that we had seen their wandering or wayward children alive and reasonably well.

Ambassador Carol C. Laise, the wife of Ellsworth Bunker, invited us to lunch, which included an interesting group of people—an anthropologist, a Catholic priest who ran a school for boys, and a native artist. I have already written that Bunker, on my arrival, took me aside and asked what had made me blurt out, at the luncheon in Sam's house for Henry Kissinger, about sending the President of the United States to China to stop the war. I told him that I hadn't had the foggiest idea why Kissinger was in Saigon, but had expressed my views spontaneously. I told him that now I understood the ominous silence which greeted my remarks. I hadn't known I was so prescient.

When Emma asked Carol to recommend a hairdresser, Carol told us a funny story about Mrs. C., one of the best-groomed women in America, whose husband was also a prominent ambassador. While Mrs. C. was visiting in Nepal, Carol had referred her to the same, very modest place which she used, and where Emma went later that day. Mrs. C. had been featured in the *New York Times Magazine* as one of the best-dressed women in the world and a great hostess in Washington. She asked for an egg shampoo with fresh eggs. Her hair was washed in scalding water on which the eggs were broken. As Mrs. C. described it later to Carol, she was shampooed with scrambled eggs running down her face.

* * *

I arose one morning before 5 A.M. and went to the roof of our hotel to catch a glimpse of the Himalayas just as the sun rose on the far distant peaks. It was only a glimpse, but a magnificent one, for the clouds immediately enveloped and obscured the snow-covered majestic mountains.

We took a tour into the interior, where we saw how the natives lived in small villages on the sides of mountains, their strange temples with the peaked roofs and the huge eyes built into the steeples surveying and perhaps protecting the landscape and anyone who looked upward at them. One of the temples was devoted to phallic worship. Several had curious erotic sculptures. All had their bizarre designs. The monkey and the elephant were prominent figures of worship. We purchased a few paintings and other curios. In visiting a well-known native artist, we found his style universal, showing nothing of what we would call a Nepalese character.

We had enjoyed Lionel Davison's novel *Rose of Tibet,* an absorbing adventure story of that region. We found a copy in Kathmandu and sent it to Ellsworth Bunker, who had not read it, although his wife Carol had and strongly recommended it.

We left Nepal with a feeling of awe for the industrious people on farm and workshop, still living with religious concepts that seemed unmodified by Western influences. Buddha was born in Nepal. India seemed to have had the major impact on Nepal's culture. Despite the intensity of the religious activity, the temples were poorly maintained. There was a lack of hygiene all over the country. Streets were untidy. People lined up to buy the uncovered foods first tasted by hordes of flies and sometimes coated with dust of the streets. A curious country. It was necessary to have a doctor's prescription to purchase an aspirin, but hashish was available over the counter.

Benares

Benares, India, on the Ganges River, was a famous holy city. Here was where Guatama Buddha lived and preached, establishing it as the religious center of a vast country. We saw the *stupa* built to commemorate his history-making philosophical address, to five friends, uttered in the sixth century B.C.E., a little later than the historic outpourings of the Hebrew prophets. Buddha did not become embodied as an object of worship until the first century C.E. Temples and images of Buddha were in abundance. It was impossible to escape his influence.

I took a photograph of a handsome monk named Yuda Tulka in his saffron robes. I later sent it to him, and we developed a correspondence. He wrote that I was the first foreigner to send him a copy of his image after photographing him. One of his relatives, who knew how to write English, sent me the letters. Yuda also mailed me several original and beautiful small paintings that he had created.

* * *

We undertook a "pilgrimage" to the Ganges, passing hundreds of beggars, the deformed, and lepers, who patiently sat on the ground in the rain, in long lines, into whose outstretched cups Indians put money and food. On the walk to the river with our guide, we had to step very carefully to avoid the feces that covered the ground. The sitting priests, wearing only a loin cloth, with stripes of mud on face and arms, were photogenic. They harangued anyone who would listen. We saw people who were bathing in the Ganges to purify themselves. When we took a large rowboat out on the river, we saw bloated dead bodies floating in this holy stream. We observed the crematorium, where the dead were ceremoniously burned, to the wails and moans of the surviving women relatives. Later the ashes were strewn on the river of life and death.

We went to the old city of Varanasi with its bustling alleys, filled with merchants, buyers, beggars, cripples, priests with painted faces, flower salesmen, with its penetrating smell of incense and the fumes from fried foods. The streets were filled with debris, often excrement, cleaned only by the daily rainfall at this season. At the same time we passed schoolchildren well dressed and singing lustily. There seemed to be no cultural-artistic life apart from the religious establishment. We were pulled everywhere by men with their bicycle rickshaws. There was no other way to get around the overcrowded city streets.

Our British hotel, Clark's, was on the edge of town, where the setting was tropical and verdant. The furnishings in our room would give delight to any collector of nineteenth-century antiques. The electrical wiring was so primitive that it gave us an uneasy feeling that any minute something might catch on fire. The food was good, and the mangoes, which I ate at every meal, were the best I had ever consumed.

We visited the few and limited museums and scarce art dealers. One came to our hotel room and we purchased a nineteenth-century Indian painting, which adorns our dining room.

Khajraho

At the suggestion of Ambassador Carol Laise, we altered our flight route in order to visit Khajraho. A major religious center from the ninth to the eleventh century, it was built by the Chandella kings, whose thousands of workmen carried huge stones twenty miles to erect an array of temples. They were decorated with sculptures on the exterior and interior with amazing erotic figures displaying every form of sexual activity. Abandoned and overgrown by forests it was uncovered in 1884 by a British archaeologist. These Hindu temples were dedicated to Brahma (the creator), Shiva (the transformer, the reincarnator), and Vishnu (the preserver) in innumerable forms. Here was where the Sain religious ascetics revolted against the excessive ritualism of Hinduism. A short, but visually important visit, to learn about a distinctive period in India's history.

Agra

We obviously came to Agra to see the Taj Mahal. Even though we had only a few days, we saw it three separate times. It was as beautiful as it has been endlessly described and portrayed. No one should ever miss this memorial of a Rajah for his wife. We learned that Agra had other aspects. It was an important shoemaking and marble-manufacturing city. We took a bicycle rickshaw over the bridge to the Tomb of Itmad Ud Davla on the left bank of the Jumna River, which some call the little "Taj." There was hardly any comparison. We saw the industrial and commercial parts of the extended city where tourists seldom travel.

* * *

Whenever we traveled on plane, bus, rickshaw, or were in a hotel, temple, museum, we met scores of people, with whom we talked, made tours, and ate in restaurants. Some were natives, often business people or tourists.

We exchanged experiences of our travels in other faraway places.

Occasionally we exchanged addresses. In the main these were pleasant, transient relationships. Several times some of our acquaintances asked us to send them information about my profession of social welfare, books we had read, about Ethiopian Jews, or a special recipe. All of these contacts were noted in our travel diaries. Usually Emma made the initial contacts. I was always a bit more reticent.

* * *

One side trip by car was taken to see the palace at Fatehpor Shikri, built in 1575. Twelve years in construction on the backs of thirty thousand workers, it constituted a remarkable series of buildings with unusual art decorations curiously many in violation of Moslem law. Alcabar, a liberal-minded ruler, issued his own legislation. He had separate apartments for Hindu, Moslem, and Christian queens along with rooms for his five hundred concubines. He erected a special hospital, where numerous babies were born. The five-pointed star noted on one building was the sign of Vishnu and not of Solomon.

One night we stayed in the Rambagh Palace, so we could get a taste of how a Maharajah once lived. For a higher fee, we could have slept in one of his ornate rooms, but we chose more modest accommodations. The palace was in need of considerable refurbishment, having obviously seen much better days. The grounds were still populated with peacocks and other unusual birds, which gave one a temporary feeling of princely grandeur. The Maharajah had obviously lived very well.

Jaipur

Jaipur, the Pink City, with its terra-cotta facades, was a thriving town. The observatory gave evidence of an early scientific interest on the part of its rulers. Museums were well stocked with artifacts and art. It was a photographer's paradise. Wherever you turned there was an interesting shot: elephants, camels, horses, donkeys, ox carts, bicycles, and autos. Peasants came to town with their garments of many hues, begging to be photographed.

Bombay

At the airport in Bombay we were met by Feroze Netervala, a twenty-year-old student, studying in Scotland, who had been notified of our coming by our friends the Ghoshes. He was a Parsee, sometimes called the "Jews of India," because they resemble Jews in their business precocity, wealth, separateness, and family integrity. This did not include their mysterious religious rites. We were stopping at the Taj Mahal, a superb hotel where we ate an Indian buffet lunch, the equal of any food served elsewhere in the world. With Feroze and his mother, we went on a "commercial" tour and took in an Indian fashion show modeled after Western styles. In the evening we dined and were entertained by India's music and dancing, which after a while had, like music and dancing almost everywhere, a note of repetition and monotony.

Our tour the next day noted a well-kept city, which apparently forced its very poor, except for itinerant beggars, to live outside of its inner-city borders. We had seen them on our way from the airport living in swamps and in large pipes that had been placed along the roadside in preparation for laying water mains. We saw the Jain temple, where Gandhi and Nehru had worshipped. Both were of that faith. The monkey and the elephant were prominent idolic symbols. A visit to Gandhi's home in Bombay was imperative, for it was a model of the simplicity with which he chose to identify his life.

Every man on the street wanted to change rupees for dollars at very favorable rates. Fakirs sat on the roads enticing small crowds with their pipes and stand-up cobras.

We saw the Tower of Silence, which the Parsees used for their death rites. Placed in the tower, the bodies were picked of their flesh by ever-present vultures. The Parsees neither intermarry nor permit conversion to their faith. It was indeed a closed religious society that faced the possibility of extinction.

While in Bombay, I received a letter from Dr. Nahum Tim Gidal of Jerusalem, a good friend, who wanted me to buy a statue he had seen on his visit to the country a few years before, when he was gathering material for one of his many books. He enclosed a picture and authorized me to pay up to $1,200. He was not sure of the location of the shop. Since there were scores in the area he mentioned, it was no easy task to find the owner of the piece. Regrettably for Gidal, it had been sold for $1,800 six months before. The lesson that one learned from this experience was that if you see something you can't live without, buy it impulsively on the spot, even if you cannot afford it, or it will forever haunt you. We had such regrets many times.

In making arrangements for our flight to Aurangabad, in order to visit the famous caves at Ellora and Ajanta, I dealt with a young woman in a sari with a black dot on her forehead, who I thought was a native. The next day, when I returned for my tickets, she asked me a personal question: "Are you Jewish?" "Yes. Why do you ask?" "I am a Jew. I told my parents about you and they want to invite your wife and you for dinner." I readily accepted. Their names were Gubbay. A long time ago, their forebears from Baghdad had gone to Rangoon, Burma. They fled to India in 1943, when Burma was overrun by the Japanese during World War II.

In going to their home, we were picked up by an American girl from Washington Heights, who was wearing a sari. She had met and married an Indian non-Jew at the University of Wisconsin. She was having a difficult time remaining a Jew and bringing up her children Jewishly while living in an Indian household that held strong, contrary views. She described herself as a "Yankee with a Sari." The Gubbays were a most genial family. He was the public relations director of the hotel where we were staying, the president of the B'nai B'rith, and his wife had a similar role with B'nai B'rith Women. He described the Indian Jews in villages as mostly poor, often uneducated, but they have a *mezzuzah* on their doorposts. No one saw a future for the Jews in India. The youth were leaving for Israel, England, and Australia. Often, if they remained, they had no alternative but to marry non-Jews. Several young people at the party confirmed these views. One was a daughter of Professor Walter Fischel, who was in India researching its Jewish history for a book, which he later published.

We drank Scotch and soda, and ate a partly vegetarian dinner, except for kosher chicken, which had been flown in from Hong Kong.

* * *

Aurangabad was a large city in the interior. It was not distinguished for anything except as a marketplace for the surrounding villages. The non-air-conditioned room left much to be desired. We were off early in the morning on a government tourist bus, which cost only 55 cents to Ellora some fifteen kilometers away. Getting on the bus was a battle, and holding on to your seat, if you just arose for anything, was a comedy act. To say the least, it was overcrowded.

The Ellora caves, carved out of the volcanic basalt rock between 500 and 1300 C.E. by the Jain priests, were a remarkable array of sculptured pieces, friezes, columns, testimony to the Indians' devotion to the idols of the past and their skill as artists. We entered many caves. At one time, these figures were painted, which would have made them more luminous and lifelike, as well as eerie, as the only light available was from the outside. Thus the workmen who created these treasures had literally worked in semidarkness. Some of the sculptures were erotic, and in one cave there was evidence of worship of the phallus.

The guide asked us whether we would want to see a temple devoted to phallic worship. A few of us joined him to see the small temple with a long Indian name built in the eighteenth century. We followed a number of men wearing only loin cloths and bearing flowers, who entered a small, open door, then went into an interior chamber, lit only by candles shining on a phallic stone. At each of the four corners, squatted women chanted, presumably prayers, as the men bowed on their knees, their heads touching the floor, after which they deposited the flowers around the phallus, rose, and left. When they came out, they broke open a coconut and drank the milky fluid. No one could explain the meaning of this ritual, except that it was a custom. Why worship the phallic symbol? To restore fertility to the soil, which had gone without rain for more than a year. Apparently with the incredibly high national birthrate, there was no need to stimulate the human being through any additional fertility rites. We saw it in all of its stark primitiveness.

Some of the caves at Ellora were also used as tombs. Those took on a more elaborate character, since they commemorated deceased leaders. Overall, one could only be awed by their immensity and creativity.

We were too exhausted the next day to make another trip in the overcrowded public bus, so we slept another hour and hired a taxi to take us to the caves at Ajanta. En route we watched the women working on the maintenance of the highways for 25 cents per day. The parched soil gave wider evidence of the ravages of the drought. The monsoon did not come this year.

Unlike Ellora, which was built by the Jain sect, Ajanta was constructed and decorated with brilliant frescoes by the Buddhists between the second century B.C.E. and the seventh century C.E. It was lost to history from the eighth century until 1819, when it was accidentally rediscovered by British soldiers. While sculptures guarded the outside entrances, the interior wall paintings related stories of this ancient religion, and its gods and its secular personalities. The painting of these walls in the limited light issuing through the entrance was evidence of artistic imagination and skills. Our guide chanted Buddhist prayers to give poignancy to this part of our tour. We bought an artist's oil rendering of a section of one of the frescoes. We have a volume on Ajanta to which we periodically refer, recalling each time that stimulating day in this out-of-the-way religious museum.

* * *

On our return to Bombay, we visited the Jewish club, where a dozen men and women, all past middle age, were playing cards. The club served kosher food. The secretary told us there were 350 members. There were no small children or youth. Only seven thousand Jews were left in Bombay out of an original thirty thousand, mostly elderly and poor. Nearly all were workers. Few were in business or the professions. Two schools served fifty children. The Joint Distribution Committee and ORT supported educational and vocational programs in Bombay. The six remaining synagogues had difficulty in attracting a minyan even on Saturdays. We entered several synagogues in between drenching rains. They were located in crowded ghettos, where we saw only Moslems and Hindus. From the number of plaques, scrolls, and other symbols on the synagogue walls, it appeared that these sanctuaries had seen better days. The Gates of Mercy Synagogue was 250 years old.

Cochin

We decided to fly to Cochin to see the region where, it was said, Jews had lived for at least two thousand years. Some claimed that King Solomon's ships landed their goods in the ports of the Malibar Coast three thousand years ago. We changed planes in Goa, going through a most thorough security check, because the Indian airline had just lost a plane to a Pakistani hijacker.

Cochin was green, tropical, and humid. Our Hotel Malibar on the bay gave us a picturesque view of the busy seaport. We rushed off to see the world-famous Kathakali dancers in nearby Ernakulam. When asked at the box office which class of tickets we wanted, we chose the second of the three types offered. We found later that only six seats had been sold for the evening performance. Before the show, we were taken into the dressing room to observe how the dancer-actors made up their fantastic masklike faces and put on their elaborate costumes. They do not wear masks. All were males; the skills of dancing, acting, makeup were passed from father to son. In many respects they reminded us of a similar experience with the Kabuki actors in Japan in 1962.

The three characters—a man, a woman, and a demon—chanted their story like a small Greek chorus, accompanied by three musicians—a finger drummer, a stick drummer, and a cymbalist. They used rolling eyes, facial grimaces, graceful movements of the fingers and hands to spell out through physical actions, different meanings and moods. A prince was seeking love. A demon fell in love with him by changing into a woman. At the last minute the demon changed his mind and reverted to his original character. It was dramatic and novel as a dance form. Like so much other folk dance and music, it was repetitive. The drum thumped throughout the performance. The drummer's fingers on the right hand were taped with cloth made rock-hard by a plaster of rice paste and lime. The one-hour performance was just enough.

I cannot resist including in this brief account of the dancers a perceptive comment by Carl G. Jung, in his *Psychology and Religion: West and East* (p. 559), on his reactions to these performances:

> If one carefully observes the tremendously impressive impersonations of the gods performed by the Kathakali dancers of southern India, there is not a single natural gesture. Everything is bizarre, subhuman and superhuman at once. The dancers do not walk like human beings—they glide; they do not think with their heads but with their hands. Even their human faces vanish behind blue-enamelled masks. The world we know offers nothing even remotely comparable to this grotesque splendour. Watching these spectacles one is transported to a world of dreams, for that is the only place where we might conceivably meet with anything similar. But the Kathakali dancers in the flesh or

in the temple sculptures, are not nocturnal phantoms; they are intensely dynamic figures, consistent in every detail, as if they had grown organically. These are no shadows or ghosts of a bygone reality, they are more like realities which have not yet been, potential realities which might at any moment step over the threshold.

Apart from this artistic event, which we had planned for in advance, our major purpose was to visit the shrinking Jewish community. I had made arrangements beforehand by writing to Shabbatai S. Koder. To reach Cochin, where he lived, we had to take a crowded ferry and then waved off a host of rickshaw drivers after we stepped off the boat. We walked down Jews Street into Jew Town, the places well defined by large signs, passed a row of houses all with Magen David labels on the windows and a *mezzuzah* on each door. Mrs. Joseph Cohen, looking out of the window as we were passing, engaged us in conversation and directed us to the synagogue. The modest synagogue was built four hundred years ago, when the Dutch briefly controlled the province. Indira Gandhi visited it when the anniversary took place in 1968. A commemorative stamp had also been issued by the government, testimony to the curious influence the remaining Jews had on the leaders of this country. The courtyard was filled with old plaques, the remains of earlier structures. The interior was shown to us by a *shammes* named Cohen, who had been alerted to our coming. Not too many visitors reach this isolated portion of India, far off the main tourist arteries. He showed us through the garish interior. Women prayed from a balcony behind a screen. We bought copies of the original copper charter given to the Jews in 379 C.E., when Jews had already been living in Cochin for three hundred years. The clock tower with Hebrew letter-numbers was another sign of the Jewish presence.

Mr. Koder's chauffeur brought us to the Koder store, which sold a miscellany of items. To our surprise we found the Koders living over the shop in a large rambling apartment overlooking the Arabian Sea. Koder was a tall, stout man, with an albino white skin, about sixty, who was not only a businessman but a scholar, an author, a book collector, and a diplomat, representing the Israeli government. The family originated in Baghdad two centuries ago. His wife was a buxom Jewish housewife, who also minded the store. Both were totally Westernized in their views. The Jewish community of Cochin was now reduced to ninety-five souls and declining. (It numbered twenty in 1986.) We saw no very young people. There was no intermarriage between the Cochin white Jews and the other brown or black Jews of India. There appeared to be no Jews with those darker hues left in Cochin. There were no old or new Jewish ritualistic objects for sale. One came away with the distinct feeling that this once large and prosperous community was conducting a death watch.

While Koder claimed that the small community had excellent relations with the Indian natives, contributing generously to all local ventures, we had an experience that evening, while walking along the waterfront near our hotel, which belied this contention. We were approached by two Moslem men, who wanted to row us across the river at any price "you choose." We had no interest in such a boat ride, but engaged them in conversation at some length, as they spoke English and seemed knowledgeable about the economy and politics. While they belonged to Mrs. Gandhi's political party, they thought a man could do a better job as head of the government. With encouragement, they began to speak about the Jews. Koder was a "millionaire." The ninety-five Jews "own everything." They reluctantly admitted that there were rich Moslems and rich Indians. They told us all young Jews were leaving for Israel, a country of which they disapproved. I am not sure how much Koder really knows or wishes to publicly admit about the true attitude of the average Indian toward the Jewish people. Mrs. Koder rode to the airport with us, and it was a pleasant goodbye.

We changed from a small to a larger plane at Goa. On the plane we were given such an abundant lunch that we saved the extra sandwiches, fruit, and candy to give to a woman begging at New Delhi. This was a common sight. We watched as she immediately sat down with her two children to share this gift. Whenever we traveled by plane in India, we were always besieged at the airports by begging—women carrying babies with small children trailing behind. They never asked for money. They just pointed to their mouths and stomachs to give evidence of their hunger. Emma always carried food off the plane and gave it away.

New Delhi

The day after we arrived in New Delhi, we lunched with Wolf Isaac Ladejinsky, who was working for the Ford Foundation, and another night we dined together. He was a close friend of my brother Sam. We had met him in Washington, after Margaret, Sam's first wife, had died in 1967. Already in his seventies, European-born, a bachelor, he had become a world-famous expert on agricultural economics. He was the principal architect of land reform in Japan after World War II. He had spent the greater part of his latter life serving in Indonesia, Korea, Nepal, Malaysia, Taiwan, and now in India. With a strong identification to the State of Israel, after his death in 1975, he left his vast collection of Asian art to the Israel Museum in Jerusalem. No one ever learned where and how he obtained his unique collection. When asked, he said: "I bought it all in marketplaces." Wolf had a pessimistic attitude about the United States as a country steadily losing its historical value system. He predicted that North Vietnam would conquer the South when the

American forces left. Whenever you asked him questions about art, politics, India, he would give detailed, carefully measured replies in a soft, low voice. He was a pleasant man.

Ghosh picked us up after lunch and took us on a tour of what he called the "real" India. He introduced us to S. M. Ghose, Mohandas Gandhi's closest confidant. Garbed in traditional Indian dress, he discussed Indian philosophy for more than half an hour in response to my question whether India had actually improved after Gandhi's death. At eighty-four, he was chairman of the cottage industries department in a large store, where our meeting took place. I was assured that this was no sinecure.

We then saw the elaborate Parliament, the President's house, other government buildings, and the Birla Lakshur Temple. In the temple, where we had to walk in our stocking feet, I noted a quotation on the wall written in Sanskrit, Hindi, and English: "Though men call it by many names, it is really one." It was a quotation from the *Upanishads*, originally written by the Vedic priests. I remarked to Ghosh that it paralleled in some respects the *Shma* in the Hebrew Bible: "Hear, O Israel, the Lord our God, the Lord is one." A man standing behind us overheard my remark and volunteered: "But who said it first?" I indicated that the statement had been written about the same time in both countries, somewhere between the thirteenth and eighth centuries B.C.E., when the Hebrew Bible began to attain its close to final formulation and the Vedic writers were establishing the principles of monotheism in their land. This was before Buddha came on the scene. Then, in an off-hand commment, I said: "If Abraham had gone east instead of south, India would now be Israel."

When I returned to Pelham and browsed through my library on India, I found a curious reference in A. L. Basham's *The Wonder That Was India* (1954) indicating that my chance remark might have some substance. The Panis, wealthy Semitic traders from the same region as Abraham, went east to trade and not south to help form a new nation, in about the same time frame as Abraham. They had difficulties with the Vedic priests and disappeared from the scene about the thirteenth century B.C.E. Had they brought monotheism to India?

* * *

When Mrs. Hema Gupte, a friend of Ghosh, asked us whether we would like to meet her swami, we immediately accepted. Hema was married at eighteen. Her husband was a well-to-do industrialist and government official. She was a follower of the Jain sect, rising at 6 A.M., meditating until 7 A.M., then going to the temple for one hour of prayer. She spent much of each day working as a volunteer in a child care center and managed her household with the aid of a number of servants. She went to bed at 11:30 P.M. and was a strict vegetarian, the only one in her household.

Swami Vivikananda lived in the Sri Rama Krishna mission. Tall, shaven bald, in saffron robes and sandals, he sat in a modern office, an elegant figure, dispensing wisdom. I observed as a petitioner came in to consult him, bowed to the floor, and kissed his toe. He had spent fifteen years in the United States, where he was sought out mostly by Protestants who were searching for meaning for their lives and were looking into the mysteries of this Eastern religion. They often affiliated, as did some Catholics. "Jews invite me to speak, but do not join." Hippies were not serious in their "search," because they were unwilling to accept the disciplines and particularly patient meditation. They wanted a "quick fix," a few rituals like flowers, dress, incense, and to learn a few quotations from the *Gita, Upanishads, Veda,* and *Kuma Satra.* Like any competent, contemporary psychologist, he did not believe there was any possibility of instantly transforming someone who did not fundamentally want to alter his life's content and style of living.

In this connection it is worth noting Carl G. Jung's comment in *Psychology and Religion: West and East* (p. 568) on the difficulties of a Western mind trying to become an Eastern religionist:

> I particularly warn against the oft-attempted imitation of Indian practices and sentiments. As a rule nothing comes of it except an artificial stultification of our Western intelligence. Of course, if anyone should succeed in giving up Europe from every point of view, and could actually *BE* nothing but a yogi and sit in the lotus position with all the practical and ethical consequences that this entails, evaporating on a gazelle-skin under a dusty banyan tree and ending his days in nameless non-being, then I should have to admit that such a person understood yoga in the Indian manner, but anyone who cannot do this should not behave as if he did. He cannot and should not give up his Western understanding; on the contrary, he should apply it honestly, without imitation or sentimentality, to understand as much of yoga as is possible for the Western mind.

What surprised me was that as we entered the temple, Hema bowed and prayed before the statue of the founder of the movement—Bhagavan Sri Ramakrishna (1836–86). A flower petal was offered for each verse chanted. Incense was pervasive. I left loaded with literature, but not one whit persuaded that I could ever consider this esoteric religion.

Some weeks later, when I was in Israel, I met a man who told me that his son was an addict of one of the Indian sects, and he was deeply concerned about losing him as a son and as a Jew. I gave him the pamphlets I had received in Delhi to read, so that he would better understand how difficult it was for a Western mind and a Jew to be overwhelmed by an occult Eastern religion. My observation to the father was that the son, who had been raised in a secular Jewish home, was seeking a deeper and more disciplined faith and that he might find it in one of the ultra-Orthodox Jewish sects abounding in Israel. I learned subsequently that the son made such an affiliation and became a devoutly religious Jew. He lived in Israel with a wife and children.

Another incident occurred when Emma and I were invited to a party on Long Island at an Indian home, but where the guests were apparently mixed. When we arrived, I noted a young woman sitting in the lotus position in a corner praying before a photograph of a man, the picture decorated with candles and flowers with incense burning at the base. I quietly sat down on the floor next to her and waited for her to complete her devotions. When she finally looked up, I could readily see that she was a Jewish girl. How had she come to this pass? "My home was not Jewish. There were no beautiful rituals. I needed a religion that would give me those things. India offered it."

Sitting one day at a dinner party in Herzlia, my partner was a young woman in her early twenties. When I asked about her life, she excitedly told me that she had joined a Hindu sect and finally found some meaning and purpose in her life. When asked why she hadn't found such satisfactions in Judaism, since her father was a prominent Jewish social worker, her answer was that her parents were not affiliated with a synagogue and never believed in or practiced any form of Judaism. She had been driven by the need to find a religion of beauty and rituals that would "nourish and discipline her soul."

A well-to-do supporter of the Jewish Federation in New York called me one day and asked me to speak to his son, a young man in his late twenties, who had gone through the hippie episode, was in and out of various cults, went on drugs, and now was slowly finding his way back to a normal life through Judaism. I saw this man. He seemed distraught. He still dressed lilke a hippie with a band around his forehead. After telling me the story of his disorganized life, he now wanted to set up a temple, where he could recruit young Jews like himself, straighten out their lives, and make them Jews again. He was learning more about Judaism by dipping into a variety of texts, none of which he studied thoroughly. Although he was no academic, he wanted to be the leader, or "rabbi," of such a temple. One of his innovations would be to have incense burning during the religious service.

I took a book off my shelf, which revealed that Jews had used incense in ancient days. Many pages were devoted to the techniques of preparing various kinds of incense, but that we had given it up millennia ago, because it was a practice adopted by other religions, and was no longer necesary to impelement Jewish rituals. It had become taboo. He was amazed and irate at what I read and asked why his Hebrew teachers hadn't ever told him this, when he was going to synagogue schools. Growing impatient with his nonsense, I saw that he was really unstable, and advised him not to establish his own congregation, but to affiliate with one of several traditional synagogues that catered to young Jews seeking to be "born-again Jews." I learned afterwards that his parents, while nominally affiliated with a Jewish congregation and active in Jewish affairs, had little learning and did not practice Judaism in their home.

* * *

The day we left New Delhi was a public holiday in India. Gromyko, the Russian foreign minister, had been in India for several days, and this was the day on which Mrs. Gandhi and he signed a friendship pact between India and the Soviet Union. Workers were given a day off and villagers were bused into town for a free lunch and for an informal parade and massive rally estimated to number more than a million people. Our friends warned us to stay off the streets and not go shopping (in fact many stores in the area of the rally were closed). Yet we ventured out. We found most of the huge crowds composed only of men. They were orderly. Despite the violence attributed to the Indian masses, there were no incidents. We spent part of the day visiting the Red Fort and Jama Masgid, which some consider not only the biggest but the most beautiful mosque in India. We enjoyed a gourmet vegetarian dinner with the Guptas and Ghosh, topped off with lotus blossom pudding and coffee. Then we flew off.

Iran

On our arrival in Teheran, Iran, we first roomed at the Hilton, which was located on a beautiful site overlooking the city. It was so far out of the center of Teheran that we changed hotels in a few days, moving into the Oriental. We had a drink with Daniel Chester Cochran, third secretary of the U.S. Embassy, and he agreed to send home some of the things we had lugged from India. He was being reassigned to Vietnam to work with Sam. He gave us an excellent book, *Iran: The Land of the Great Sophy* (1962), which we read with interest.

Dr. Ben Mussaf of the Joint Distribution Committee office arranged for our visits to installations it was supporting in Teheran and Isfahan. We went to the Family and Youth Educational Center, sat in on a teenage and college youth group planning a benefit musical show, spoke to several social workers, learned about the lives of their clients. While we saw services, we did not see any poor Jews.

We toured the nineteenth-century Golestan Palace with its ornate museum objects, such as the Peacock Throne. Then to the Bazaar with its hundreds of shops seen through a maze of alleys.

We were impressed with the beauty of the city, the wide bouelvards, tree-lined and decorated with flowers, excellent buildings, and its absolute cleanliness. The country was getting ready to celebrate its 2500th anniversary, commemorating the founding of Persia by Cyrus. Jews were part of the scene in that ancient period, for after the destruction of the First Temple, they were enslaved and brought to that country. We visited a few rug shops owned by Jews, but after extensive bargaining and getting nowhere on a fair price, we decided that it was better to buy them in the United States, for there was no way of evaluating the quality of the rugs we wanted to purchase. We visited the Iraqi synagogue and found no visible indications of its existence either architecturally or by any sign on the outside. Jews had low visibility.

We flew to Shiraz, the City of Roses, lying, like most of the larger cities, in a huge oasis surrounded by a treeless desert. It was one of the hottest days we had ever experienced. We drove to Persepolis, some fifty-five kilometers away through a countryside with little rain and where crops had to be artificially watered. We reached the ancient site, once a palace in the spring and fall, being readied for the anniversary. Officials had set up a huge, gaily colored tent with red-and-white stripes. On the old site, the remnants of sculptured friezes and other stone objects had a magnificence in size, quality, and story that must have been overwhelming millennia ago. They still retained that aura.

We also took in the Nagh-E-Rustantomas of Darius with its impressive friezes and sculptures. There was talent, creativity, mystery, and wealth in abundance in the olden days.

There was no time to visit the facilities that served the six thousand Jews living in Shiraz, as we had to take off by plane to Isfahan to conform to our tight schedule. In Isfahan, Yitzhak Golan of the Joint Distribution Committee staff arranged our visits to Jewish installations, and we were taken at our request to see where and how the Jewish poor lived. In slums, in poverty, with a well in a courtyard only a few feet away from the latrine. It was not a pretty sight. A thread maker with eleven children, who worked from 6 A.M. to 7 P.M., with wife and children helping out, earned $1.00 (U.S.) and was a ward of the JDC. There were many Jews living in that condition.

We stayed at the Shah Abas Hotel, more like a museum with its distinctive decorations, where the food matched the beauty of the place—both interior and exterior—in quality and taste, particularly the caviar and the wild duck. It had been built in the seventeenth century as a caravanserai by the king's mother. It was recently refurbished into a modern hostelry. Isfahan was filled with mosques. We visited all the distinguished ones.

At the market, we bought many brass trays decorated with biblical and other themes. We purchased a painting on ivory from the artist and learned that only an expert could tell the difference between work on expensive ivory or cheap bone once the base had been covered. We found other Jewish objects and amulets in antique shops by diligently searching the dust-covered wares.

At the airport, officials took my knife away and made me shoot all the film in my camera to prove that it was not a bomb. I must have looked like a very suspicious character. It took an hour to get my knife back after we reached Teheran.

On our return to the capital, we had an opportunity to attend a Jewish wedding in the hotel, to visit a Hebrew school with fifteen hundred students, a Jewish hospital, and an ORT school.

Emma had her hair done in a shop and the color was all wrong. She was irate all day and for some weeks thereafter until the color finally washed out. The problem was that they did not speak English and misjudged the instructions she tried to impart.

We went to a synagogue on Friday night. Again there were no signs of its existence. Our guide was Ezra Kushki, the young man at the desk of our hotel. About two hundred Jews were present at a long service, where the Haham Shofet, head of all Iranian synagogues, was present. Children participated. Ezra himself recited a long prayer in Hebrew. At the end, women went about the room sprinkling rose water from bottles on the worshippers' hands. One had a "white silver" bottle; another, a beautiful one of sterling silver. Those who recited *Kaddish* performed this interesting rite. We acquired an attractive white silver bottle.

As we walked out, another synagogue across the street was also discharging its worshippers. All were well dressed. Apart from Ezra, no one greeted us. The more I talked with Jews I met in a variety of other settings, the more I was convinced that of the eighty thousand Jews, most were well off, that the poor did not constitute as much as 10 percent of the community, and that the Jewish population was providing little for its own poor, since the JDC and ORT were assuming this major responsibility. On my return to New York, I spoke about this to JDC officials, who promised to look into it. Subsequently the grant to Iran was substantially reduced. Prior to our return to New York, and while we were in Jerusalem, a prominent Jewish leader from France, told me that "we don't mind giving them $2 million a year, for it gives us an opportunity to visit that part of the world from time to time." No professionals had ever been sent to Iran with firm instructions to encourage the local Jews to develop a sense of financial responsibility for the needs of their own kinsmen.

Ezra Kushki, our guide in the synagogue, wrote to us for several years, asked us to send him typical American jeans and jackets, which we did. He wrote and asked whether we could find a kosher, observant family, where he could live, if he chose to come to New York to study. I made inquiries and sent him the information, but he decided to attend a university in Iran. We lost touch with each other. I have often wondered what happened to him after the Khomeini regime assumed reactionary and ruthless power.

At the airport, we had an interesting experience. Across the room, I saw a man who looked like Milton Olshon, who ran the mail room at the Federation in New York. I could not bring myself to believe that Milton could actually be in Iran. The longer I sat and observed him, the surer I became that it was indeed Milton by his gestures as well as his face. Finally, I got up to check, and it was Milton. He had married a girl from Iran, and they had returned to the country for a holiday and to be with her family.

Israel

On our many trips to Israel, Ralph and Helen Goldman, old frineds from the States, would frequently see us off at the airport, and what is even more pleasurable, greet us on our arrival in Lod. So it was when we came from Iran. We stayed overnight, and the next day they invited a number of people we knew from the United States, with whom we exchanged travel experiences. Then we moved on to Jerusalem, where we would be stopping with Dr. Nahum Tim Gidal.

As always when visiting Israel, there were new things to see. From Mount Scopus, as the sun was setting, Jerusalem became a study of haunting landscapes.

We were in Israel primarily for the International Conference of Jewish Communal Service. This time I had relatively little to do, unlike four years earlier, when I had occupied a prominent role in the program and edited the *Proceedings*. A note of pessimism about Jewish life was sounded at meetings, because Jewish youth and Jewish families had begun to be immersed in the pathological trends that were intruding on our societies—drugs, cults, intermarriage and divorce disrupting Jewish family life. Regretably the agencies had been ill prepared to counter these sickly forces, or worse, were ambivalent about what to do. It was obvious that the use of Jewish values to combat these invidious developments was still not a major interest or medium for most Jewish communal workers. They were not intimately informed or involved in that aspect of Jewish organizational life. It was observed that some did not even know how to discuss our Jewish problems, because we were so assimilated to the life-styles of the Western world that we could not distinguish one ethnic group from the other. Jewish youth were speaking up and demanding more support for their Jewish interests, particularly on the campuses, which would give them an opportunity to learn about their people, to be active, and to assume roles that might ultimately provide a more affirmative Jewish leadership. Perhaps many more of the ablest would study and practice within the Jewish community as professionals—rabbis, educators, communal workers.

There was general criticism that the conference was not profound enough, that the major papers were neither new nor stimulating, that there was an absence of sufficient Jewish substance. Furthermore, that the smaller sessions did not achieve the objectives of getting the limited themes analyzed adequately and prevented the international colleagues to get to know each other better.

This time we went to see Masada again, reaching the top by the convenience of the new cable car. This was Emma's first visit. She did not have to undergo the exhausting climb that I did in 1967. We also visited the caves at Qumran, where the Dead Sea Scrolls were found. While at one time there was life in these hills, now it was a treeless, brown sand, lifeless desert. We made our first visit to the Rockefeller Museum in East Jerusalem, the part of the city formerly controlled by Jordan. A treasure trove of ancient excavations, it had not been open on our last visit in 1968. We went to see the Arab mosques again and the Western Wall, the latter now facing a broad plaza. Underground it was undergoing extensive excavations.

We met a few Ethiopian Jews, who wanted to know what could be done to bring in their families. We promised to pursue this further, although those Israelis interested in their plight were more concerned with offering some modest help for them in their native country.

In walking down the streets, black market operators were everywhere offering us better shekel rates for American dollars. This was getting to be a practice that almost had official sanction. Black market rates were published in the press. There was already talk about growing inflation and the devaluation of the Israeli pound. The cost of housing was rising. We left Israel again with many concerns on our mind. Was it losing its pioneer, idealistic spirit?

Rumania

We arrived in Bucharest at 1:30 A.M. We had to go through a cholera check by white-coated medical personnel. They gave us tetracyclin to take for three days to prevent the disease from taking hold and made us down the first pill on the spot.

Arnold and Sofia Arnovici were waiting for us, although our plane was over four hours late. Arnold was the uncle of one of my former students, Mircea Samoil. When we couldn't obtain hotel reservations in Bucharest on our own, Samoil wrote to his uncle, who invited us to stay with them in their "new and large" apartment. Since it was only for a night or two, we accepted the invitation. We also asked Arnold to arrange to rent a car and chauffeur, as we wanted to tour the country. The Arnovicis spoke Yiddish (no English). We got along famously, although we had to dredge up Yiddish words from our memories that we had not used for over forty years, actually since my parents passed away. Arnold was a tall, heavy-set man, who had retired after serving as an accountant for the state-supported Yiddish theater. They had no children.

As we drove through the city, even in the dark, there was evidence that the municipality was preparing for the twenty-seventh anniversary of the Republic (August 23, 1944). Apart from stands and bunting, huge signs with pictures of Marx, Engels, and Lenin were displayed in the main square.

The apartment turned out to be new, but not large or grand. Built for lower-income workers, it actually had only one bedroom, and we slept on a converted couch in the living room. The Arnovicis placed before us huge quantities of food at every meal. They had bought so much that they did not even permit us to take them out for lunch or dinner. We rode through the city, which was attractive. Whenever I wanted to take a photo, they dropped me off and drove away some distance, because if the police should interrogate me or even arrest me, they did not want to be implicated. Thus we got an immediate feeling of the semi-terror of citizens in a dictatorship. This was somewhat like Yugoslavia, in that the country had an independence from the overall tyranny exercised by the Soviet Union. The government implanted fear in the citizenry, and this made them behave in conformity with the regulations, so that threats of force were not always needed. I took fewer pictures as a consquence.

The Arnovicis also warned us not to buy too many items in any one place. Otherwise, we might be reported as having an excess of lei, the native currency.

The city was pleasant in buildings, squares, and parks. There were relatively few automobiles. People appeared to be well dressed, perhaps because this day was a holiday. We visited the 116-year-old, handsome synagogue and the Yiddish theater. Jews were steadily leaving Rumania, whenever they could get permission. Most went to Israel, with which Rumania had satisfactory relations. There were only thirty-five thousand Jews left in the country, in contrast with the hundreds of thousands before World War II.

At the synagogue we met Rabbi David Moses Rosen. Our conversation was brief, as he had to rush off to perform a wedding. He was not only the Chief Rabbi but a representative of the Jewish community in the government's parliament. He was both respected and feared by the Jews. We walked into the synagogue to observe the preparations for the wedding. The bride proudly told everyone that her wedding dress had been made in the United States.

Several years later I had lunch with Rabbi Rosen in New York to see if he could be helpful thru the Rumanian government in arranging for the exodus of Ethiopian Jews. Rumania had good contacts with Ethiopia. Although this squat, bearded, impressive man promised to look into it, nothing came of our conversation. I presume Rumania didn't want to get involved.

In the evening we attended a performance of three Yiddish plays ostensibly written by Sholem Aleichem: *People, Doctor,* and *Divorce.* They were presented before stylized, modernistic backdrops, and the actors also wore similar patched costumes and grotesque makeup. All the plays had political implications, with the villains invariably bosses or rich men. The actors used exaggerated gestures. There was enough humor expressed to tickle the adult audience, which only partly filled the small theater. An orchestra added to the performance, for there was occasional singing in the script. Although many Yiddish words were unfamiliar to us, we could follow the action. The Yiddish theater was experiencing a slow death. The children, when there were any, were no longer learning this tongue. After the performance, Arnold introduced us to the director and the leading actors.

We learned on the day of our departure that the Arnovicis were joining us on the trip around Rumania. While it was pleasant having their company, for they could be our guides and interpreters, the car was a tiny one, a Czechoslovakian Skoda. Arnold, because of his size, sat in front with the driver, while Emma, Sofia, and I squeezed into the back seat with our knees actually pulled in and almost touching our chins. What could we do? We stopped frequently to stretch our limbs.

Our long ride through the countryside revealed how individual farms had been turned into huge industrialized agricultural establishments. They grew grain and raised cattle, used the latest types of farm equipment. Large dormitories housed the workers. By contrast we also passed villages that continued to exist in their original quaintness. Elderly women were selling vegetables and fruits from makeshift stands at the roadside. We noticed women drawing water by hand from centrally located wells. I could not make up my mind whether the government was punishing them for not joining the huge farm cooperatives, or whether the natives preferred to continue older technical devices which were cheaper and for whose modernization they would have to pay excessive taxes. The well, we noted, served as a social gathering place. Wherever we drove we found houses and shops well kept, with an abundance of flowers to brighten the otherwise staid buildings. The ride was long, hot, and for the most part unrelievedly dull. This could not be the romantic Rumania we had read about in books and manuals.

We stopped at the Hotel International in Mamaia on the fabulous Black Sea, where the sandy beaches have a spread of hundreds of feet from the water's edge and stretched for miles in either direction. Hotels were as dense as those along the eastern Florida coastline. The tourists flocked not only from Rumania, but from Germany and Bulgaria. Menus were usually printed in both Rumanian and German.

The waiters in the larger hotels were really something. They were totally indifferent to the customers. You had to wait for your menu. You waited even longer for each course of your meal to be served. If you asked for anything not on the bill of fare, you could wait interminably, it seemed, for an answer, and it was usually "no." Finally, you had to wait impatiently for your bill. We found that eating in larger restaurants could cover quite a span of time. There was obviously no tipping, so why give the customer more than dilatory service? This was not true in smaller, owner-operated eating places, where the service was often too quick, as though they wanted to get you out and make room for another group of diners. There were often lines in such places.

The same attitude was present in shops, small or large. All goods were standardized, marked with a government label listing the price. None of the sales persons urged us to buy. They were completely indifferent. You could, however, find the same goods in most stores around the country, so if you couldn't locate all of what you wanted in one place, you could pick it up elsewhere.

When we left Rumania on its own airline, we received the same treatment. There was no cheery greeting when we came on or smiling goodbye when we got off. Food, quite good, as it was all over the country, was served without a gracious word. During the entire flight, except when performing their duties, the hosts (male and female) sat in their seats almost unaware of our existence. They had not bothered to check whether we were properly strapped. Signs indicated where the oxygen masks were located and when to stop smoking. There was otherwise no warning of our landing. Fortunately it was smooth.

At Mamaia, we went to other hotels to listen to music, watched young people dancing to rock and roll.

Leaving the sea resort, we drove to Histria to see the ruins of ancient Greek and Roman structures. It was once a busy seaport that declined when silt clogged the harbor. The ruins reminded us of Delos, the island off the Greek coast. We then rode to Constanta, the largest port city, with a history that boasted a Greek origin twenty-seven hundred years old. Some of the archaeological sites were covered to preserve them from erosion. The excellent museum gave us a good picture of the type of life and art of those ancient days. Whenever we talked to people—native or tourists—they were eager to meet us again, pressed on us addresses in Prague and Sofia, should we ever travel to their cities.

We drove another long distance northwest into the interior, through the oil town of Ploesti; then, twisting and turning into the mountains, we finally arrived at the beautiful city of Brasov with its medieval buildings.

We bedded ourselves in the superb Hotel Carpati, where the service, the food, the setting, and the music were top-flight.

We visited the fine synagogue. Kosher meat was being cut up and sold that day to the twelve hundred Jewish survivors of a community that once numbered fifteen thousand. Most were pensioners. Some asked whether we were Israelis and were surprised to learn that we were American. Few foreigners came to this out-of-the-way city. On the streets, we watched long lineups for the purchase of vegetables and fruits. Then the queues suddenly disappeared, as all the items had been quickly sold. Women seemed to perform all of the duties of keeping the streets tidy.

On our way to Bucharest, I noted some Gypsies off the road cooking a meal, their wagons and unhitched horses nearby. As I went up to photograph them, a swarthy man with a large black moustache and a slouchy black hat tilted on his head, came up to me menacingly with a knife. He was the typical Hollywood version of the Romany. Instead of coming to my aid, our chauffeur drove off a bit and left me alone. When I handed him some money, he turned quite courteous, allowed me to take pictures, and even offered me some maliga, which I never liked and politely refused. The Arnovicis were concerned by my reckless behavior and indicated that I was taking unnecessary risks. I told them that the knife was being used by the Gypsies in preparing their food and not as a weapon to threaten me.

We saw Arnold in the States, after his first wife died. Regretably he too has passed away, leaving behind memories of an interesting excursion in Rumania. Emma did not like the country in any respect and kept repeating that this was the one country she would not care to revisit.

Rome

We had a day's layover in Rome on our final leg to Portugal. We rented a small Fiat, drove into the city, parked our car near the Colosseum, walked under the Arch of Titus, which was built in part to commemorate the destruction of Jerusalem in 70 C.E., and spoke to a Jewish peddler, who asserted that Italian Jews would slowly and surely go to Israel. We saw other familiar sights which we had grown to love on previous trips: the Forum, Bernini's statues, the Trevi Fountain, the Baths of Caracalla, Borghese Park, the Ghetto. The Piazza Navona was full of hippies—American and European. We ordered gelatis and cappuchino, both very good, at the Tre Scalini, a favorite dining place, and the price was equal to a dinner for four in Rumania the night before, and was equivalent to a full dinner for two in the same eating place when we were first there in 1955. Rome exuded a charm even on the run.

Portugal

The superior South African plane with its perfumed toilets and first-class dinner arrived in Lisbon after midnight. We taxied to the fine Tivoli Hotel, our room overlooking the scenic Avenida da Liberdade. We visited the Thieves Market the next day, where Emma haggled, but did not buy a sterling silver lorgnette for which the woman wanted $30. Emma's best offer was $15, claiming she was about to leave Portugal and had no more money with her. The woman dismissed her with "boa viagem" (bon voyage). Several days later, we were in Sintra. There was another flea market and Emma saw the same lorgnette, which she had regretted not having bought in Lisbon. This time a man was in charge, and she finally bargained the glasses down to her original tender. Emma always wondered what the woman, perhaps his wife, had said, when she learned that the ultimate purchaser was a blond-haired American woman.

Sintra was a hill town with an old palace, castles, and museum, all worth visiting. Then we drove to Cascais, where we took in a horse show and our first bull fight. Despite all the noise and cheering from the stadium, the actors in the ring went through a farcical charade of first taunting the seemingly reluctant bull, then sticking darts into his hide, which tortured and slowed rather than maddened him into action. Finally with dramatic bravado the ornately dressed *cavaliero* stabbed the still uninfuriated and defeated beast to death. An empty gesture. Then the *forcados* dragged the animal off the field. The only excitement occurred when a bull broke out of his hold and nearly trampled an unsuspecting *cavaliero,* who was looking up at admiring ladies rather than protecting his rear.

We drove to Sesimbra, an entrancing fishing village south of Lisbon, where the fishermen repaired their nets on the streets, where women seemed to wear nothing but black gowns (they can't all be widows?), and where there was an auction on the beach before sundown, after the fishing boats brought in their daily catch. When you turned your back on the sea, you saw the semi-barren hills that enveloped the village, one with an old Arab fort at the very top. We usually ate with the natives in their familiar restaurants, filling ourselves on the warm bread and the heaping plates of caldeirada, a fish stew, and Portuguese wine. Sometimes we would have a few broiled sardines before the main course. On later trips to Europe, we stayed in Sesimbra to rest for a few days before returning to Pelham.

Each day we toured a different part of this region. Whether in a village at the sea or in the interior, we always found the local people easy to meet. When they could speak a little English, we learned a great deal about their life, the economy, and the general culture. This was before the revolution. Despite the dictatorship, people talked freely. Wages were low. Prices for foreigners were even lower. Emma bought some beautiful clothes, table cloths, and other woven items. Since the manufacturers were sewing the same clothes for Bergdoff-Goodman in New York, Emma was dressed in high style.

Ramon waited for us for four hours at the airport—our plane was late.

* * *

It was a trip around the world. We saw so much that was new, exciting, and rewarding, filling in ten weeks of our life with memories only partly related in this book.

16

Readings and Travels—1972

As a pre-teen child, I remember going to the handsome Carnegie Library in Gloversville and borrowing books to read at home, although I cannot recall any of their titles. When I earned a few pennies, I bought books written by Horatio Alger, or about Tom Swift and Frank Merriwell—adventurous, inspirational, yet I do not recall ever rereading them. There were not many books in our home. A bookcase housed prayer books in Hebrew and Yiddish works. While my father and mother occasionally read a Hebrew or Yiddish volume, they were much too busy or wished to spare their dimming eyesight. They both wore glasses bought in Woolworth's only for reading. Both perused the Yiddish paper daily and often read portions of it to us. My sister Rachel was the bookworm in the family and went to the library regularly. She always tried to improve herself by reading in her own limited leisure time, and encouraged me to do the same.

During my four years in high school, I did not read or borrow a single book, except those that were assigned by teachers. While some Shakespeare plays linger in my memory, even those works or the novels prescribed in English classes did not stir me intellectually.

At New York University, I lived with a few men, several of whom were readers, but they were given more to poetry, particularly of an erotic nature, which they occasionally recited out loud, when we did not have a host of visitors. I was so busy studying, working, going to the theater, socializing, that general reading suffered.

When I worked on the *Morning-Herald* in Gloversville in 1926–27, I had plenty of time to read. There was little to do between midnight and 3 a.m., when the presses started to run. I covered a number of Jewish and general volumes, including novels and nonfiction. I even found time to review several books for the local paper. I realized that no matter how much experience and even formal schooling I might have in the future, books were perhaps the major way to fill in the vast lacunae in my self-recognized limited background.

From the day that I entered the University of Missouri in 1927, books became almost a mania. I read and collected them with such fervor that I would often spend my last few cents on a book and then have to wait in virtual poverty until my next check, days later. I tried to conceal this indulgence from Emma, after we were married, when we could ill afford to buy books. Emma was always a constant reader, her selections based on my suggestions or picked up out of curiosity or from reading book reviews. As a child she was also a steady user of the library in Albany, enjoying romantic volumes about far-off places, which she ultimately visited. Emma's neighborhood library, realizing that children of poor families owned no English books, awarded prizes to the child who read and could review the books for the librarian after a vacation period. Emma proudly won many times.

Over the course of years, we gathered thousands of volumes. Many were bought, some were given, some earned as a reviewer for a periodical or for reviewing the volume before specific audiences. Books were the most frequent gift I received on birthdays, when someone came to the house for dinner, or when I was honored at some event. I always kept lists of my readings, and still do. Apart from the fugitive perusal of the press and periodicals, some years I read one hundred volumes, although the average was closer to fifty.

I read histories, biographies, other nonfiction, novels, short stories, poetry, drama. When Emma and I went on a holiday, we would take an armful of books, sometimes by a single writer, so that we might know his writings better. Upton Sinclair, Thomas Wolfe, Herman Wouk, Eugene O'Neill, Lawrence Durrell, James Michener, to mention but a few.

On short vacations, it was more likely to be a miscellany. While I always read Jewish books, I concentrated more on such writings after 1945. Frequently my reading was determined by an interesting review or by the suggestion of friends, who wanted to know what I thought of a book they had just read. A friend who worked for a publisher sent me a dozen volumes on religious subjects—Christian, Moslem, and Jewish—which I read over a period of one year. Before we went to an art exhibit, we would usually read about the artist, so that we might better understand his works. We would do the same about a play that we were about to see in the theater. I have reviewed a hundred books during the years for magazines, the bulk of them on Jewish themes or social work.

If one examined the papers that I have written for more than fifty years, one will find them heavily documented with footnotes of my extensive reading. My writing has forced me to peruse and research books, articles, magazines, and tapes, and to reread books and other items I have collected. Frequently their presence on my shelves and in my files saved me valuable time, for I did not have to turn to other resources. My files are cluttered with clippings and correspondence on many subjects.

While I made notes on some of my readings, more often I lined or underlined the books I was examining. By and large I remembered somewhat more of what I had read by talking about the subject to family, friends, colleagues, and whoever I could buttonhole. Many of my letters reflect my reading. Some thought that I was showing off. Perhaps this was in some ways true. I often introduced the book I had just read at a group sitting around a dinner table. I brought it to the fore when I was teaching or lecturing. I believe that this was an effort to reinforce the content of the book in my memory bank.

In later years, when my memory sometimes failed me, and I had to force the memory "tape" to give forth with its hidden treasures, the effort was usually rewarded. I could recall names of books, titles, and authors, as well as much of the content that I had once discussed or written about.

Reading led to collecting, although I do not consider myself a serious assembler. Our shelves in many rooms are lined with Judaica—old and new, Haggadahs, histories, biographies, classics, poetry, drama, English literature, American novels, social work, travel books, art. There are twenty cartons of books in the attic, which I shall someday have to give away, but I cling to them, because they are part of my early purchases or other acquisitions.

For the last ten years, I have been giving away books to universities, institutions, libraries, and frequently to individuals who have an interest in a special subject. Hundreds of our books are on the shelves of our children and grandchildren. Except for our granddaughter Elisabeth, an omnivorous reader, who outdoes her grandfather, few in our family seemed to have the same passion. Yet the libraries in their own homes are large. When the children and grandchildren were young, we gave them books along with money on their birthdays and Hanukkah (Jewish books, of course). We always told them not to buy a book for school until they had checked to see whether we had it on our shelves. I wish they had taken many more.

I am often asked whether I have a favorite author. I must confess no. I read with a purpose to find out more about something. I am not inclined to reread whole books. I have only done so on rare occasions, when I had to review a book that I had previously finished. When I had to refer to it, I could usually find the passage I wanted without too much difficulty. I often found an author so stimulating that I recommended the book to everyone who came in my presence. I liked certain books written by an author better than others, but I haven't embraced anyone completely, particularly after I have found that the quality does not stand up when one examined most of their writings. It is similar to my feelings about a retrospective art exhibit of an artist's total work. There was variation in quality and too much repetitiveness.

Yet books have been a good part of my life. I can read a book a day on a ship or on a holiday, or when I have to do so rapidly while doing research, or for an oral or written review. I usually read three or four books at a time, in part depending where I find them—in the den, the kitchen, the living room, bedroom, and of course the bathrooms. As a companion, a book is unbeatable. It demands only one's individual attention.

In renting a furnished apartment on our travels, we always looked to see what kind of works were on the shelves. We have often stayed in the apartments of distinguished scholars, where we found an intellectual mine. In hotels, I have always read the Bible, usually Gideon and Christian, when there was nothing else. On sea voyages I have spent much time reading books from the ship's library to while away the boredom. Whenever I visit someone's home, I inspect the library, which gives me a good idea of their intellectual interests, and if I stayed over, I could always find enough to keep my eyes and my time occupied. Since I usually rose between 5:30 and 6 A.M., while the family was asleep, this filled in an hour or two. Sometimes such a visit was an intellectual holiday. I recall one, where Emma and I read all the plays of Oscar Wilde and George Bernard Shaw, along with their biographies, because the apartment had a collection of their respective works.

Ten years ago I initiated a book readers group at the Pelham Jewish Center. We read only books on Jewish subjects. The four to six sessions per year are considered one of the major activities of the synagogue. I convinced two of our members, the late Charles Bernstein and Celia Greenfield to create a fine Judaica Library.

When I worked on a book like *Black Jews in America*, I read hundreds of volumes of history, biography and novels to seek material. I did the same extensive research, when I was compiling material for a pictorial history of American Jews between 1776 and 1976, a book, which I finished was paid for, but was never published.

The book which I reread annually was the Pentateuch and Haftorahs, along with different translations of the Bible, both from Jewish and Christian sources. Usually I will reread a play of Shakespeare before attending a performance in the theatre or watching it on TV. The Humash and Shakespeare are amongst the greatest writings.

Am I wedded to my books? No. I am eager to loan them or even give them away. In fact I often say that if a book was stolen or borrowed and not returned, the thief or the borrower might have actually read it and learned something. That was the only reward I would want for finding it missing.

Who will want them when we are gone? Perhaps our granddaughter Lizzie, who has already started to take them by the bagful. Many are valuable, like my collection on the Ethiopian Jews and Black Jews in America. They will be willed to the American Jewish Historical Society, which will receive them along with the 18 file drawers of papers, to be used by scholars, who may wish to research these subjects in the future.

* * *

I had finished another hectic year at Federation and was in need of another long vacation. I had also decided that I would retire on June 30, 1973, after I became 65 years of age. I had enough, wanted a change of life style in my remaining years. Before I left on a holiday, I wrote to the Executive Vice President, Sanford Solender, to that effect, that on my return I would want to discuss with him about recruiting a replacement or replacements, since I did not believe that one person could assume these responsibilities, I also wanted to talk with him about my pension. Having made the decision, I knew I would not be burdened with indecision on my holiday and when I returned for my final year.

England

We had worked out a trip to England, Israel, Capri, Sardinia, Corsica, Southern France, Spain, and Portugal. It would be a full and busy schedule from June 26 to September 1.

When we reached the BOAC counter at Kennedy Airport to check our tickets and baggage, we learned to our chagrin that Emma's passport had expired, and they wouldn't let us board. We returned to our son Ramon's apartment, to his and his wife's surprise, for an overnight stay. The next morning we spent many harassing hours overcoming long lines at the New York passport office, finally getting a new one in the midafternoon, changing our tickets for that evening's flight; and luckily there was space, even though this was the busy tourist season. In between waiting for our passports to be processed, we took in an exhibit at the Museum of Modern Art, where I once again decided that Matisse was not the great artist that others, including Emma, who has taken many courses in art appreciation, so vehemently affirmed.

We arrived in London a day late. Unfortunately our baggage was not on our plane. We sat at the airport waiting several hours, praying that the bags would be on the next one, and to our relief they were.

While waiting, I met Rabbi Haskel Lookstein, who had come to Europe for a meeting on Soviet Jewry. I tried to enlist him in the problems of Ethiopian Jews, but he smiled kindly and said it would have to wait, as there were other items higher on his agenda. As usual, he, like so many other Jewish leaders, commended me for my zeal, but he was expressing the typical attitude of most American rabbis and Jewish establishment leaders in the United States and abroad, including Israel—indifference.

David Kessler

This was my first opportunity to meet David Kessler, the publisher of the oldest and one of the best Jewish newspapers in the world, the *Jewish Chronicle*. Kessler, of medium height and slender, reminded me of Leslie Howard, the late British actor, by his looks, speech, and manner. He had assumed the chairmanship of the Falasha Welfare Association, following the death of Norman Bentwich.* The association was a consortium of several British organizations, which collectively gave or raised a modest sum of money for work with the Jews in Ethiopia. He had written several sympathetic articles. He had visited the Humera-Abderafi area on the border of Sudan, where the emperor had provided a 5,500-acre tract, where the potentate hoped Ethiopian Jews would settle and cultivate the land—and, not so incidentally, act as a buffer against the Sudanese. Although the Jews were driven back many kilometers by Sudanese soldiers in 1968, when they first moved to this outpost, Kessler did not believe that this would happen again. He hoped that a development committee could be created by world Jewry to provide funds for the farms. I told him that a study had already been made by ORT, but it had been rejected by the Jewish agency, in part because of the high cost, approximately $2 million. Yet he believed Israel might become involved. He thought that the World Bank and the United Nations might also be approached as a way of dealing with the whole area for the benefit of all Ethiopians. These hopes were never realized. The land was 150 miles from Gondar, where most Jews lived, not easily accessible, but Kessler still felt that sooner or later a road would be built from Asmara, farther north in Eritrea. Kessler admitted that the climate was hot and humid, the area malaria infested, and reliable water a chronic problem, but he pointed out that two tractors had been provided by American Jews, that the farmers were already growing cotton, sesame, sorghum, and durra, and that a small flour mill had been constructed. I told him that of the one hundred young men recruited each year, half of them were usually laid up with malaria and could not work. There was still no clinic or adequate medication, or for that matter any other amenities—decent housing, cultural programs, synagogue. I noted further that not more than 50 percent of the young men volunteered to return for a second year. Yet despite my pessimism, Kessler believed that this locale offered a future for some, perhaps even a great number of Ethiopian Jews, once facilities were provided. He did not want to consider aliyah to Israel as the only alternative. He wanted me to help him raise at least $100,000 a

*Shortly before he died, I met Norman Bentwich in New York. We agreed that the only solution for the Ethiopian Jewish problem was immediate aliyah to Israel.

year to aid the existing and other projects in Ethiopia. He thought we must try and find someone who could be an overall supervisor for an expanded educational and agricultural program in Ethiopia. I promised to see what I could do, since the Ethiopian Jews were likely to remain in Ethiopia for the foreseeable future, as no Jewish world leadership wanted to contemplate their settlement in Israel.

Several days later, Emma and I had lunch with Kessler and Joseph Linton, a member of his board and former Israeli ambassador to England. They shared similar views about the agricultural development. Despite Linton's statement that Eliah Elath, the current Israeli ambassador to England, was opposed to the project on the Sudanese border, they both felt that U.S. Jews and the government of Israel could ultimately be persuaded to find funds for its development.

The land project in Ethiopia terminated in 1973, due to lack of funds and no amenities, even though in the fourth year the operation produced a small surplus. Its termination was about to take place even as we were talking.

I left Kessler on the best of terms. Despite the substantial differences in our views we maintained a letter correspondence for several years.

One dividend was that I was able at long last, to obtain a much-sought-after copy of Henry A. Stern's *Wanderings Among the Falashas in Abyssinia*, which had been reissued by a British publisher in 1968. The original edition, printed in 1862, related how this *meshumad*, a Jewish convert to Christianity, had undertaken a mission to Ethiopia to proselytize amongst the Ethiopian Jews on behalf of the Christian faith. In 1983, I purchased the original from a rare-book dealer in Iowa.

* * *

Apart from museums, like the Tate and National, and other sights, like the Tower of London, we saw *The Canterbury Tales*, a play which had been running for its fifth year, a delightful bawdy musical with good acting, voices, dancing, and staging, as pieces of the Miller's, Priest's, Steward's, Merchant's, and Wife of Bath's tales were unfolded. These rollicking stories were a reminder of the course in Chaucer I had taken at the University of Missouri in 1928. *London Assurance,* an early-nineteenth-century imitation of the comedies of manners that had reached a high point in drama during the eighteenth century, did not prove diverting and actually seemed kind of silly. Reading Leon Edel's *Henry James,* I noted that James had seen the play in New York one hundred years earlier with no comment.

We attended a long Sabbath service at the handsome traditional Marble Arch Synagogue with its many columns on the exterior. An excellent hazzan was accompanied by a choir with fair voices. There was no sermon, so we had no basis for evaluating the young Rabbi Unterman, a son of the Ashkenazi Chief Rabbi in Israel, who was a stumbling block in permitting Ethiopian Jews to come to Israel. I worshipped with Maurice Bernstein, an old friend and colleague going back to my days at the Graduate School of Jewish Social work. He was spending a year in London trying to fashion an American-type federation for a foot-dragging Jewish leadership.

* * *

At the modest hotel where we slept, there were also a large number of Moslem families from Kuwait, including its minister of defense and the director of the free cinemas in that oil-rich land. We became friendly, had a few drinks together, received a favorable picture of their country. Emma and I were enthusiastically invited to come to the country and be entertained by them. The next day, when we met them again in the lounge, they asked us where we were going after London. When we frankly said we were on our way to Israel and that we were Jews, their mien changed suddenly. The Jews had "robbed" the Arabs of their land; the only solution was for the Israelis to capitulate or better yet leave the country. When we invited them to come with us to Israel, be *our* guests, and see for themselves what kind of country it was and how they treated the Arabs within the original partition zone, the minister of defense, a young man, indicated that if he did, they would, as he gestured, cut his throat. I'm afraid that we made no converts in this two-time exchange.

* * *

I had read in a catalogue published by the Hirschler Book Shop that it had books on Ethiopian Jews, so on a cold, rainy day we took two long Underground trains and a bus trip to reach the shop. He had advertised a book by Flad, another Christian missionary to the Jews of Ethiopia, for 5 pounds. He now wanted 15 pounds, I presume because he had us as a live customer, who would buy it at any price. While I wanted this book, published in 1869, I was outraged by the change in price, from which he would not deviate. I walked out disgusted with his nonethical deportment, a man dressed in typical Jewish traditional style with hat on head. Afterwards, I regretted not having made the purchase. I only have a Xeroxed version of this interesting volume.

Israel—1972

In Israel we attended a week-long conference on the "Communication of Values," sponsored by the New York Board of Rabbis. By and large the content was more ethereal than practical, although there was general agreement that unless Jewish institutions communicated basic Jewish values for the daily living of Jews in more effectual ways, they would fail in their mission. Thus one could question their validity as instruments for Jewish survival. A number of tours were organized by the conference. We found the Jerusalem YM-YWHA a crowded institution. We went to the newly built Metseveret Zion Absorption Center outside of Jerusalem, which was occupied principally by Russian Jews. We were bused to the excavations at Beit Shean to see the Roman theater and the mosaic floor at Bet Aleph, an extraordinary archaeological discovery.

On the Sabbath, we walked to the Old City of Jerusalem. On another day in the Arab *shuk*, we found a folding table for the large brass plate we had bought the year before in Iran. At Tim Gidal's apartment, we had dinner with Geoffrey and Devorah Wigoder, he the scholarly editor and writer, and she a Catholic convert to Judaism, and the author of *Hope Is My House*. A friend saw her having lunch with a nun in Jerusalem, and when told that the nun was her sister, her friend, assuming that Devorah was born a Jew, replied: "My, my, your mother must have been devastated." Devorah frequently lectured on why she became a Jew and why Israel had become her permanent home. We once met her brother, a Catholic priest at a dinner party in Pelham, at the home of a Jewish family related to Wigoder. Incidentally Wigoder, like our hosts that night, had originally come from Ireland. I spent a good part of the evening talking with an urbane, educated, liberal Catholic, the sort of person one now occasionally finds in that formerly hidebound church.

I conversed with Wigoder about the Ethiopian Jews, and he told me there would be a long section on this subject in the forthcoming edition of the *Encyclopaedia Judaica,* published later in 1972. He was the co-editor with Cecil Roth of this tremendous undertaking. I have all the volumes and supplements, and not a week goes by, but I find recourse to its contents. I have many books written by Roth, to whose volumes I frequently return. On occasion Wigoder wrote pieces about Ethiopian Jews, toward whom he expressed a great deal of sympathy, yet he was inclined to follow the Jewish establishment on this issue and never became an activist on their behalf.

* * *

The rest of the conference was devoted to visits to social welfare institutions, finally ending up with a session on how we could better use the press, radio, and television as instruments to promote the Jewish value system—not only to reach Jews, but for the edification of the general public. Prominent broadcasters who were present indicated that it was difficult to determine in advance what position and what content would or would not "sell" over the air or image on the screen. They pointed out that many "good" programs fold up shortly after being aired. By contrast, so many lowbrow productions succeed. The public evaluated every program with a turn of the knob (or today with the remote control button). The question that plagued everyone was how to reach the people who "needed" such value-laden programs, rather than continue "talking" to those already converted.

I privately evaluated the conference with Rabbi Fred I. Hollander, a promoter of this event. I felt that it was disjointed, as many speakers did not pinpoint their remarks to the theme. There was too much diffusion of definition on values, which were more relativistic than singularly Jewish. There was no consistency of attendance by the Israelis, with only the Americans turning up for all sessions. Yet Hollander hoped to follow it up from the States with greater use of the media, since he directed the media program for the New York Board of Rabbis. Hollander was giving some thought to having his family go on aliyah. In the following year he made that decision, and they settled in Jerusalem. In 1974, he invited me to evaluate the Keren Yaldenu program, of which he had become the director.

We also toured the Keren Yaldenu centers being erected around the country to better educate and absorb children who had come from Mediterranean and Near Eastern lands. I thus had an introduction to the institutions that I would later study.

* * *

I met with Aryeh Tartakower and his committee, which was interested in assisting the Jews in Ethiopia. The committee felt that greater support should be given to the land project in western Ethiopia, following the lead of David Kessler. The local committee looked to the United States, England, and me, to supply the $100,000 for this venture. All agreed that a good full-time person was needed to supervise the several programs in Ethiopia. The committee felt that most obstacles could be overcome with good supervision, money, and time. When I raised the issue of a large-scale aliyah to Israel, there was only support for a "select" group of young people being brought into the land.

I met privately with Lieutenant Colonel Yitzhak Paz, who had served in Ethiopia with the Israelis, and with Dr. Daniel Pridan, who had spent nearly a year in Ethiopia supervising the clinics in three Ethiopian villages. Both had been to the Humera settlement. They asserted that unless sufficient money was poured into that venture, directed by an organization and a professional with authority, all the money invested would be wasted. They reported that the area was malaria-infested and required many amenities to attract people to work there and to keep them well. I agreed.

Eventually the Falasha Welfare Association found a well-meaning, underpaid young man, lacking in most of the skills that were needed, who was ready to go to Ethiopia to undertake this difficult mission.

Capri

We embarked at Haifa on the S.S. *Dan,* an Israeli ship. As usual we talked to many of the passengers and found out who they were and where they were going. For some strange reason, people rarely asked us about our history, our views, or our interests. I decided to do without Dramamine and was seasick. By avoiding most liquids, at the suggestion of the purser, I reduced the severity of the malaise of the last part of the voyage. Captain Albert Wetzler, master of the ship, invited us to sit at his table the last night, and it was a merry evening of drink, food, and dancing, starting with a cocktail party in his cabin-office.

The ship docked at Naples, where we took the hydrofoil to Capri. When the funicular brought us up the mountain and deposited us on the square at sundown with the lights just beginning to shine, it looked like an Italian opera set with the orchestras, restaurants, adults walking about, and the children everywhere running, playing, and dancing.

We traversed every part of the small island with its many levels, mostly on foot, partly by bus and taxi. Goods in the shops were cheap. I had a pair of leather sandals made at a cost of only $3.50. (Over the years, I had them duplicated in the Christian Arab section of Jerusalem by a native shoemaker, whose prices escalated from $7.50 for the first pair, to $12.50 for the second, and then to $25.) We visited Anacapri and Axel Munthe's house, about which we were then reading in his excellent book, *San Michele.* It was perched on a rock overlooking Capri and the sea. We climbed up to see the ruins of the Villa Jovis, the palace Tiberias built almost two thousand years ago.

One day we made a side trip to Pompeii and Vesuvius on the mainland, entered the top of the crater, still smoking in various places, descended to the excavated ruins of Pompeii destroyed by the flow of superheated lava millennia ago. The bus drove us to Sorrento on the twisting Amalfi drive along the scenic coastline, that has made the peninsula a popular tourist resort.

Capri should be on every tourist's agenda. A romantic spot, celebrated in song as the "Isle of Capri" and in photos for its sheer loveliness and isolation, yet not too far from the coast.

Sardinia

To reach Sardinia, we sailed on a boat from Naples. We met people from around the world, but most were Italians going to or from the great island. At Caligari, we stayed at the attractive Hotel Jolly, rented a car, and spent the first day visiting villages outside the city. We could not find an English guidebook of the island. Luckily we carried our own *Hachette,* and that served. After a day-long tour of the city to its ancient and contemporary monuments, we were off to the north. We learned about and saw for the first time remnants of the pre-Christian Nuraghi, pagans who controlled the island and left examples of their primitive but well-built stone houses, their curious idols, and other artifacts. We stopped overnight in Nouro, a city without distinction. We were beginning to feel that Sardinia was not a place for serious travelers, but only for those who wanted to swim at the growing number of new seaside hotels and resorts being built in the northeast.

When we reached Olbia, as we were drinking coffee in a square, we struck up a conversation with a handsome Englishman named Tancred, who not only persuaded us not to go to Corsica—"Worse than Sardinia" was the way he put it—but to leave Sardinia the very next day. Our only adventure was to be stopped by the police, who were looking for a kidnapper of a wealthy Sardinian, but we did not fit the description. Although all flights out of Sardinia were booked for several days, Tancred managed to talk the airline into flying us first to Milan and then to Nice, our destination after Corsica. While this roundabout route was less convenient and more expensive, we took it.

France

We left Sardinia, saw Corsica only from the air, changed planes in Milan, and by noon we were in Nice. We rented a Renault, learned of a room available at the Hotel Regina in Vence, which turned out to be a charming chamber overlooking a flower garden and offering a superb cuisine.

Vence was a hillside Provençal resort in the Maritime Alps with a population of ten thousand, overrun by visitors during the summer because of a cultural festival, its fine wines, and its accessibility to other interesting points on the French Riviera. From Vence we drove to the picturebook walled village of St. Paul de Vence, with its striking architecture and art. We easily drove in a slightly different direction to the modern Maeght Museum with its marvelous, diversified collection. In the mood for a bit of gambling, we drove to Monaco a short ride away along the coastline, stopping for some superior bouillabaisse at a restaurant facing luxurious ships of the rich and famous, docked at the pier. We had our coffee at Oscar's in Monaco. We lost some money at the Casino, but it was worth just seeing the much-gossiped-about place.

Another day, when we wanted to see the collection of Léger's diverse works, we drove to Biot. Nice itself had a few museums, including one dedicated to Matisse along with many antique shops, where Emma made a few purchases. In Cagnes-sur-Mer we visited the house where Renoir lived, now a museum. At Antibes, after a look at Picasso's works, many of which had been painted on brown paper bags, we sat on the sea wall overlooking the Mediterranean musing about our art exposures in this small area around Vence.

To see the Matisse decorated Chapelle Du Rosaire in Vence, we sat through an hour-long Catholic service one Sunday morning. If we closed our eyes, to blot out the sanctuary with its Christian symbols, we might have been in a synagogue with the singing of the choir, the responsive readings, getting up and sitting down, the priest's sermon. It was all in French, of course, easy to follow in the prayer book. The church walls were painted in a severe white, with Matisse's paintings in stark black, the large figures drawn quite crudely, but it had an imaginative charm. The only color was in the stained-glass windows and ceramics, the latter on the exterior. It relieved the starkness of the black and white.

As we went west, we did not hesitate to pick up hitchhikers, most of whom spoke English, and they filled us in on their experiences touring France on less than $5 per day. At every restaurant, coffee shop, or gasoline station where we stopped, it was easy to engage in conversation with people, who gave us leads as to places to see, inexpensive hotels, and excellent eating places. We found the French more open and warmer than in the north and in Paris.

In Aix-en-Provence, when we went to the home where Cezanne once lived, it was closed. So was the synagogue. But we did find excellent pâté and pears for a lunch in partial compensation. Our objective the next day was Arles, to see the city which Julius Caesar founded in 46 B.C.E. and to live for a few days where Van Gogh had exhausted himself in a burst of some of his greatest paintings. While we saw the drawbridge which he painted in 1888 on some of his celebrated canvases, in daylight, it was dull and gray contrasted with his brilliant paintings. Although we knew that Arles was an ancient Roman town, we were not quite prepared for the extraordinary amphitheater, the baths, the theater, and other equally well-preserved remains.

An hour away was Avignon, a completely different city from quiet Arles. Many outdoor shops were clustered around the Papal Palace, which had been set up in 1309 to compete with the Papacy in Rome. The palace was formidable in size and austerity. An over-enthusiastic guide told us more minute details than we wanted to know or had time to digest. We stayed in a medieval Crusader-built hotel, modernized to suit the most fastidious contemporary tourist.

Our road took us through Pont-du-Gard, where we saw the three-tiered Roman aqueduct going back to 19 B.C.E. In Nîmes, founded by the Roman emperor Augustus, we ate our lunch sitting on the steps of the Maison Carrée, a Roman temple built by Agrippa in the second century. We walked through the pleasing gardens of La Fontaine. We passed through elegant Montpellier. We drove along the sea with its beaches running for miles, crowded with campers and bathers. We finally stopped overnight in Beziers, which was preparing for its annual wine festival and bullfights. Our car took us through scores of miles of grape-growing country. The villages from higher levels looked like freshly painted Cezanne landscapes.

Carcassonne, an old city going back to the second century, which Charlemagne failed to conquer, had restored its fortresses, walls, and towers, a commanding sight. We bought a stained-glass piece, "The Troubador and His Girl," crafted by Elizabeth Brenas. It hangs in Ramon and Anita's home in Providence.

Descending from Carcassonne, perched in the Pyrenees, we made hairpin, twisting turns through a rock defile until we eventually reached Perpignan. We found lodgings in the Hotel du France in the center of town, astride a canal that ran through the city. In the evening we went to a square amidst striking buildings from the fourteenth through the eighteenth century. A band of musicians played with old Catalan instruments. We joined the natives in dances reflecting that distinctive district. This city had an old fortress, a cathedral, a palace, a citadel. Yet for us, it was the city of Malliol, one of the greatest of modern French sculptors. It was a pleasure to touch his statues in public places.

Driving without advance reservations sometimes paid dividends with the surprisingly good hotels and restaurants we chanced on throughout this trip. One of the superb hotels and eating places we encountered was at Foix, where we stayed overnight at the Hôtellerie de la Barbakane de Chateau. After a fine meal and a good night's sleep, we visited the castle-fortress built over Roman ruins in the twelfth and thirteenth centuries, which controlled traffic between France and Spain in medieval times.

Lourdes was more than we had expected with its huge crowds, a parade of the severely handicapped, with a large choir singing and marching around the shrine dedicated to Bernadette. While it smacked of commercialism, like all shrines we have seen around the world, with their shops and street salesmen, there was a note of solemnity that was different, since the purpose of the shrine was healing, with an expectation that miraculous cures would be found for the incurably ill.

At Pau, we found another fine hotel. In the morning, we visited the elaborate chateau built by Henry IV, brought up to date by Louis-Phillipe in the nineteenth century with its famous Flemish and Gobelin tapestries and at its peak a spectacular mountain panorama.

We changed autos in Biarritz, a crowded resort town on the Atlantic Ocean, and immediately departed for Spain. We ran into heavy, slow-moving traffic, not having realized that this was the height of the holiday season.

Spain

By the time we reached San Sebastian, we couldn't find a room at any hotel and ended up with a chamber in a private apartment. We could not sleep; the room was on the street side, and every truck seemed to pause in front of our window to shift gears as it moved uphill. Next day we toured the old churches and a museum, the latter displaying a few El Grecos. We made arrangements with a hotel in Bilbao. We did not want another sleepless night.

The road west was along the coast, up and down hills, with twisting, treacherous curves. The beauty of the sea and the attractiveness of the villages made the journey, though difficult, worthwhile. We purposely drove through Guernica, but could find no tribute to Pablo Picasso, who made the city famous with his extraordinary painting of the Spanish Civil War. It is now in Barcelona in the Museo Picasso, after hanging provocatively in the Museum of Modern Art in New York, where we saw it on every visit over recent decades.

While Spain continued under the dictatorship of Franco, we could find little visible evidence of his strangling rule. With new construction everywhere, stores filled with goods, well-kept farms, and unusually well maintained highways, the inhabitants had come to accept their lot no matter what we foreigners thought of the regime. There was surprisingly little criticism of the government or of Franco by the natives we met; and when there was criticism, it was not a complaint about lack of freedom, but only lack of work or not having sufficient money.

Bilbao was a seaport and industrial town. Facing another rainy day, we decided to move on to see the famous prehistoric cave paintings at Altamira west of the city. On our arrival we discovered tickets had been sold out for the next two days. The nearest hotel with accommodations was far away. Because of the waiting crowds. Some tourists slept in their cars. That was not for us. It was still pouring. We pushed south. In Madrid we saw a facsimile of the caves in an underground museum, dimly lit to portray more of the reality of the real cave with its prehistoric frescoes.

We picked up two young French women teachers, who were hitching south. We began to climb a mountain on a narrow road, when in the middle of the day a dense fog turned day into the blackest of nights. I followed the tiny tail light of a truck in front of me for miles, for I feared to turn off the road, since I could not see a thing. There were no siderails. A wrong turn would hurl us down the mountainside. On top of the foggy darkness, a tremendous hail storm began to strike the car. We thought that the thunderous pounding of large balls of ice would be the end of the vehicle and the four of us. I was concentrating too much on the road to have more than rudimentary fears, but Emma and the two women were reciting prayers, awaiting the end. Emma vowed never to travel that road again and has warned everyone we know to avoid it. Suddenly the fog lifted and sunlight appeared with a beautiful double rainbow, revealing that we were traveling through a magnificent gorge with its unique rock formation. My passengers were restored to life.

We drove into Burgos, which was dominated by its famous thirteenth-century Gothic cathedral. We were overwhelmed by its architecture and art. We visited a museum and the Monasterie de las Huelgas, a Cistercian convent founded in 1180, where we sat through a religious service attended and conducted only by nuns. Two sudden hail storms interrupted all traffic for the rest of the day.

Our route took us through Palencia, the residence of Castilian kings in the thirteenth and fourteenth centuries and where the first Spanish university was established. Then through Valladolid, the former capital of Spain, where Cervantes lived, Ferdinand and Isabella were married, and Columbus died.

When we approached Segovia, around twists and turns, we suddenly came on the spectacular presence of this beautiful city founded by the Romans. We entered the walled town with its narrow, ever-turning streets, its enchanting plazas, its buildings of Moorish design, with its startling high aqueduct. We went to the Alcazar, a fortress palace built in the eleventh century. After knocking on the door for some time, we were allowed to enter the Corpus Christi Church, formerly a synagogue serving a once-important Jewish community before the Inquisition brought it down. It was located on Vielle Juderia calle (Jews' Street). There was little change in its interior, except for the placement of Christian symbols on the *bimah,* where once reposed the ark. To a stranger, the city looked as though it had undergone little change over the centuries.

Not too far away was the Santa il Defonso, a town built around a palace and its gardens, which Phililp V hoped would upstage Louis XIV's Versailles. We continued on the road to El Escorial, a monumental sixteenth-century domed monastery, now a museum, decorated in part by Cellini, housing some of the greatest European artists—El Greco, Bosch, Titian, and Tintoretto, to name but a few. We also took a peek at its collection of rare books and manuscripts.

After this long ride, we finally arrived in Madrid for a few days of rest and some local sightseeing. On our very first evening, just outside of our hotel, we were swept by crowds into a fiesta, were invited by some of the merrymakers into a large house, and urged to drink wine out of a uniquely shaped bottle with a long spout, hygiene totally ignored. After the adoration of the Virgin of Paloma, the natives were enjoying an evening of abandonment.

Each day we set aside two hours to visit the Prado Museum, so that we could enjoy its immense treasures without exhaustion. This was our second visit to Madrid, and we had seen the museum before, so we could now choose what we would want to view more closely. Madrid was a city full of museums. We took in a few others that we had previously missed, such as the Monasterio de las Descalzas Reales, which suffered, if I may use that word, from having too much of everything. We visited, the

Museum Lazaro Galdiano, where both the building and its contents were art gems.

We walked to the new synagogue, where the *shamas* gave us a V.I.P. tour of the interior. What a contrast between its open presence on a busy street and the previous one hidden in a building, and which one approached only after walking through a maze. The new synagogue was guarded by a soldier.

The Palais Royal was another extravagant museum relieved only by King Alfonso XIII's sparsely furnished room, with the unadorned bed in which he once slept. The simple washstand was memorable. He did not live like a king.

Passing Racomer, a Jewish-owned gift shop, we noted a silver object in the window. We bought a replica in sterling silver of an old Hanukah menorah of unusual design, as though it had been used by secret Jews, who wanted to conceal its religious purpose from the eyes of inquisitors. We dealt with the owner's son, Braulio Samuel Leon Pil (of mixed Italian-Jewish and Spanish-Jewish parentage) and made such a good impression on him that he invited us to join him along with two Jewish girls from Australia, who had wandered into the store, on a visit to a nightclub called the Meson del Segoviho, where there were only young people. Dirty, smoky, noisy, crowded, we were entertained by friends of Braulio, who played their guitars and sang, with everyone in the restaurant, with its broken furniture and indented wooden tables, joining in the chorus. We treated the group composed of nine people to cheese, bologna, chicken, and sangria until we were all sated, weary, and finally retired to our respective beds well after midnight.

We took the flat, treeless, uninteresting road to Toledo. Like Segovia, it was a city to behold first from a distance or from the overlooking heights. Unable to find a room at the Parador, we were recommended to a very, very modest hostel, Los Cigarrale (The Cricket), where for $2.50 for two per night, we had a room, breakfast, and an unparalleled view of Toledo, which at night blinked like a jewel. By day, Toledo lacks color; it is drenched in too much sunlight.

We visited the synagogue (El Transito) built by Samuel Levi about 1350, adjacent to El Greco's home. It has a lofty interior hall with handsome carvings. Then to the synagogue of Santa Maria la Blanca (1405), which the anti-Semite Ferrer, accompanied by a mob, attacked one night, when the synagogue was filled with worshippers, tossing all the unprotected Jews over the city walls to their death.

At the Museo de Santa Cruz we saw more El Grecos in one place than ever before. While we marveled at his ability to paint figures suffering, in agony, in his sombre gray-colored tones, after a while they seemed to be more alike than creatively different.

At the Zocodover Square we were reminded that this was where the autos-da-fé took place during the Inquisition. Reminders of that tragic historical past were everywhere in a city that now radiates so much beauty.

* * *

We drove through Spain's agricultural bread basket and olive groves to Granada, visited the cathedral with its art and curios, the museum at the monastery, walked through the Gypsy quarter to observe their way of life and watch them entertain. The better part of the day was spent at the formidable Alhambra, after reading Washington Irving's *Alhambra,* a good part of the previous night. Our enthusiastic guide, Aragon, imparted a lot of information to our group of ten, most of whom wanted to move on rather than listen. When he reached the Salon where Queen Isabella gave Christopher Columbus the "charter" and "money"—that was the way he put it—to seek a western route to India, I asked Aragon how could she have given him money, when the court was bankrupt following its extended wars with the Spanish Moslems. "Do you want to hear the true story of Columbus?" Everyone suddenly became alive and shouted as if in one voice, "Yes!" He took us to a corner and told this curious story, which Emma and I had known from our previous extensive readings about Columbus. "Columbus was a Spanish Jew, not an Italian. He obtained his maps from Jews. All the money was given to him by Jews. Many of his crew were Jews. He gave his first reports on his return to his Jewish backers. They were "Secret" Jews, Marranos. You can see that the true story is different from what you read in history books." How much of this was retained by the listeners, I do not know, for there was no discussion. Everyone else, we presumed, were non-Jews. Aragon's thesis was held by Spanish historians as far back as 1892 in an attempt to prove that Columbus was a Spaniard, perhaps a Converso, rather than from another country. These assertions were made on the occasion of the four hundredth anniversary of the discovery of America. From my extensive readings, from books that are on our shelves, I am persuaded that he might have been part Spaniard, but I question any Jewish origin, although several Jewish writers have written to that effect. The guide showed us Queen Isabella's jewel box. Perhaps she wasn't totally impoverished. Somewhere I have read that "not Spanish jewels, but Jews" financed Columbus's voyages. A fanciful story, even if not quite true. The Alhambra (Palace of the Red) should be a must for any visitor.

When we went to the site of an old synagogue in Granada, we saw that it was now the Church of St. Cecilia, another sad end for an old Jewry.

* * *

Cordoba was different. They were trying not to forget the Jewish past, but rather reviving it. The statue of Maimonides sat somberly in an attractive plaza. They were restoring former Jewish houses with garden courts, as well as a synagogue, in which Jews once prayed. The old Moorish mosque with its incongruous add-ons as a Christian cathedral was worth a glance for the curious mixture of architectures that don't blend.

* * *

Seville seemed deliberately determined to block out its Jewish past with its infamous treatment of the Jews. The huge and formidable cathedral, which displayed two keys given to Ferdinand III in the thirteenth century by the Jewish citizens after the capture of Seville, cannot erase this historical obliquity. While the city is Christian it could not altogether eliminate its rich Moorish heritage. The city itself was another handsome museum.

Portugal

Our travels took us into Portugal. We passed Roman ruins; and olive orchards in neatly planted rows extended for miles. Small villages were harvesting melons for the market. Sesimbra was our destination. Every hotel was filled. We spent the first night in a pleasant Portuguese house. The next day we obtained a room at the Hotel Espadarte ("Shark"), our room overlooking the ocean. Fishermen still took over the streets and alleys by day with their enormous nets, making repairs, unraveling lines, baiting hooks, getting ready for the next morning's catch. We had lunch and dinner at the Virgilianda, filled with noisy natives, and indulged ourselves with heaping portions of coldeiradas, fish and potatoes, always accompanied by excellent white port wine.

At the hotel we met Jack and Rita Swinburne. (He claimed to be a descendant of Algernon, the English poet.) Their home was in Auckland, New Zealand. She was Jewish on her father's side. Jack, in his sixties, could drink a bottle of wine at a meal, and even stronger stuff if it was served, but retained his sobriety. He boasted of his large sheep hold, fine home, many cars, membership in the best clubs. We got chummy for several days, and they invited us to come and stay with them in that faroff country. One night at dinner, Jack asked me what I did for a living, and I replied that I raised money for philanthropies, I explained about our card-calling techniques, which literally compelled a donor to get up and announce his gift publicly. His curiosity aroused, he asked me how much he would be expected to contribute at such an event. I commented on his flocks, his private dwelling, his many vehicles, his clubs, and his travels, and said, "Jack, as an initial gift, I'd expect you to give $10,000." He leaped from his chair. "You can't come to New

Zealand. Our invitation is cancelled." He meant it. We never got to New Zealand. However, we almost made it when my brother Sam was the deputy chief of mission in that country from 1956 to 1959.

We suspect that Sesimbra will never be the same isolated fishermen's village in the future. They were building a modern road that could handle large buses. That meant crowds of people during the day, unlike the serene atmosphere that prevailed on our visits. No longer would we be able to walk the mile-long beach in bare feet without stepping on innumerable bathers, unleashed dogs, and scattered garbage.

On our return to Lisbon, we visited the new Gulbenkian Museum, a tribute to modern architecture. It was not as interesting as the pink palace in which these art treasures were formerly housed.

17

The Dyarchy

My autobiography would not be complete without some comments on my bosses at Federation—Dr. Maurice B. Hexter and Joseph Willen. There is not sufficient space or time to relate their life histories. As I write this, Hexter at ninety-five is as vigorous as ever in mind, in the articulation of his views, and with his chisel in stone. Willen recently died at the age of eighty-eight, incapacitated and silent for the last decade of his life.

When I became an executive at Bronx House in 1938, they were both assistant executives in Federation. In 1942 they simultaneously became co-executive vice-presidents. Hexter directed the institutional side, with Willen finding the funds to support this largest of all Jewish philanthropies in the world. Men of completely different backgrounds, training, and experience, they became dyarchs, and for the next thirty years, until they jointly retired, they witnessed Federation and its constituent societies rise in numbers, in wealth, and in influence in the lives of millions of Jews and others in the New York area.

I was directly responsible to Hexter, who as I have written before told me at the outset that Federation had only "one boss." He was. He always called me "Mr. Berger" until he retired, after which both of us ascended to the more intimate first-name relationship, although this actually never brought us any closer together. Imperious as a person, he nonetheless allowed me and my immediate colleagues all the latitude we wanted or needed, provided that we made no mistakes. Since I made few if any blunders, and my tenure was accompanied by substantial successes, I had little need for his protection. In the few instances where I was under attack, he stoutly defended what I had done, and in all instances I was vindicated. He did not always go along with my views on the institutions, the Jewish community centers, Jewish education, nor the way the Jewish community was to be organized, nor Israel, or not accepting public funds, and certainly not on a merger of Federation with the United Jewish Appeal, which was finally accomplished in 1986. He never differed with me publicly when I asserted these views, whether orally or in writing. What he might have said beyond my hearing I do not know, nor did I ever make inquiry. I never showed him anything that I was writing in advance; and he never asked to look over anything.

I might say. I suspect that his views were somewhat closer to mine on the "Jewish character" of Jewish institutions, for on more than one occasion he said or wrote that "only Jewish eyes could treat another Jew." That was enough for me.

Hexter never gave me any advice on how to enrich myself financially, although I know that he had done so for at least one other colleague. He once told me that I was a "poor businessman." I probably was for myself, for I never could devote any of my waking hours to plotting how to get wealthier. His charge had no merit with respect to my enrichment of the Federation treasury by many tens of millions, through my astute purchases of properties for camps and day camps, and through obtaining foundation grants, legacies, and other properties of people with whom I had developed personal contacts. At times I had to overcome the resistance of Hexter himself in the acquisition of some of these land sites.

He sought my counsel whenever requests came into the Henry Kaufmann Foundation, on which he was a most influential board member, and my recommendations were usually honored with the Foundation's allocation of its substantial resources. I never received a penny for these extensive professional services. I once found in my mail a letter of appreciation.

Several times, when I was offered positions outside of Federation, he fumed bitterly, not at me, but at the people who had made me generous offers, which I had already turned down on my own decision. I preferred to complete the agenda which I had written for myself while on Federation's payroll, much of which I accomplished by the time I retired. When he was about to leave Federation, he suggested that I make inquiries about another position, one of which I followed up, but decided not to pursue. I assumed then that he was not recommending me as a possible successor to his post.

While my salary steadily grew over the twenty-three years, I had to fight for raises, when the periodic increases were not forthcoming nor sufficient. I never felt that either Hexter or Willen had done enough to assure an adequate pension for the key staff, who merited it. Thus there was insufficient reward, at least in my instance, at the end of my working trail. Both could have improved our lot, but for obscure reasons, they never chose to confront the lay leadership with the need to provide for this due bill.

On occasions I run into Hexter since my retirement. He is always pleasant. He disagrees with many of the ways that Federation has been going since he lost control of the scene. I differ with him on the direction Federation has taken, for much of it is in fulfillment of my own agenda, even for directions in Federation over which I never had any jurisdiction. Federation has become more of what I wanted it to be—Jewish, worldwide—something that might not have happened at all. Larger events over which we had no dominion determined the character of Federation. If Hexter and Willen had continued at the helm, they would have resisted the inevitable until the end.

Willen from the outset was different. He was a talkative man and liked an appreciative and argumentative audience. He asked questions about one's family and personal life. While he had diametrically opposite views on the direction I wanted Federation to take, he delighted in debating these issues with me. When I needed money to buy a home in 1953, it was Willen who told me of a Federation fund that would loan me part of the money, so that I could make a more satisfactory deal on the purchase price and interest rate. Yet, he was never concerned with my financial status otherwise, for technically that was not in his domain. He admired my liberalism rather than my brand of Judaism. Occasionally, when I showed him that both were intertwined and compatible, as in the need to support Jewish college youth, he went out of his way to persuade the Council of Jewish Federations to reverse its rejection of these young people protesting against the leadership of the national Jewish community for neglecting their need for greater Jewish knowledge, which would assure their identity and support for Jewish causes. Willen saw me as a kind of fellow intellectual, for I had read and in some cases had met the heroes of his early life in the Jewish, general, and socialist spheres. He always boasted of his intimacy with important ideologues. While I did not go along with a great deal of his casuistry, he was always an interesting person to listen to and for the imaginative plans that he wanted to execute. He liked to get things over with and go on to the next challenge.

Regrettably, he had a stroke in his latter years, which left him without speech, a terrible fate for a man who liked to engage everyone in conversation.

Hexter and Willen worked together with a harmony that was extraordinary for two such different personalities. Yet perhaps they were not so different. They were twinly devoted to Federation in the realization of the objectives that they both had envisioned. The organization prospered during their leadership years. They were also men interested in their own welfare, and both retired from Federation well endowed from their own earnings, their private investments, but with the added assurance that Federation would support them handsomely for the rest of their lives. They made an impression during their generations of service. The legacy will endure for a long time.

* * *

Charles S. Liebman in an evaluatory article "Leadership and Decision-Making in a Jewish Federation" *(American Jewish Year Book—1979)* had this to say about the Hexter-Willen epoc.

"At the helm of Federation during this period stood two great leaders, each with the title Executive Vice-President. Joseph Willen was responsible for fund-raising, and Maurice Hexter for administration. Serving under Hexter were three professional consultants: Maurice Hinnenberg in the health and aging field; Graenum Berger in the community centers and camp field; and Martha Selig in the family, social-service, and child-care field. Hexter and his three lieutenants have been described by a number of respondents as 'giants.' They combined intelligence, detailed knowledge of their fields of service, dedication to Federation, and political savvy. Agency executives gave them genuine professional deference, had difficulty resisting Federation staff recommendations, which were practicable and well-informed.

"All of this stimulated an élan among Federation's lay leaders, especially among those on the Distribution Committee. They felt that they were participating in an exciting, challenging, and supremely important enterprise. . . . There was a sense that Federation's professionals, agencies and lay leadership were the very best."

"There were some lay leaders, most likely of East European origin, who had deeper Jewish concerns, specifically that of Jewish survival. One of the professional consultants, Graenum Berger, had become, within a Federation context, radically Judaized, and he influenced others. Federation files from the late 1960's include many memoranda from Berger sharply objecting to the direction in which Federation was moving. On the other hand, the Jewish universalist outlook of the majority of Federation leaders was shared by most agency executives."

Federation Leave–Taking

I had made a decision long in advance of my reaching sixty-five years that I would retire in 1973. While I derived satisfaction from my work, had accomplished a great deal, and had received considerable recognition for my services from both volunteers and professionals, I'd had enough. Although I had a relatively free hand in 95 percent of what I was engaged in and was even able to challenge the administration when I disagreed with its policies or plans for altering certain basic principles, I yearned for a change of scene and of pace. I wanted to travel more. I wanted to write. I wanted to see what could be done to bring the Ethiopian Jews to Israel. There was enough to keep any normal person busy twenty-four hours a day for the rest of one's life.

A year before my sixty-fifth birthday, I notified the executive vice-president that I would leave on or about June 30, 1973. I also wrote that I would expect certain benefits as a consequence of my long and productive services to Federation and to the two agencies affiliated with Federation, the Jewish Community Center of Staten Island and Bronx House, in each of which I had been the executive director.

There were efforts during the last six months to make me change my mind, to stay on for another year or at least the summer. I was not dissuaded.

As is my wont, I set about writing detailed memos on the centers and day camps for whoever would be my successor. I wrote short histories of each agency, indicating the major issues it faced, the problems in the areas in which the services were located, brief biographies of the leadership of each agency with whom the new incumbent would have to work, an evaluation of each executive director. I wrote a less-detailed report about the New York Board of Rabbis. I prepared an elaborate document about the future of the Wiener Educational Center, which I had directed for four years. Sundry other statements were written about Federation itself and the directions in which I thought it ought to move in the coming decades, suggesting greater emphasis on the Jewish component, the elimination of agencies not devoted to Jewish purposes, greater concern with Jewish college youth, assuming greater responsibilities for Suffolk and Westchester Counties and even reaching out and incorporating Rockland County and northern New Jersey in the Federation orbit, because these sectors of Greater New York were still growing and taking many of our existing Jewish residents away from where we had been operating since the advent of this philanthropy. I once again emphasized the need to merge with the United Jewish Appeal. Furthermore, I advocated that Federation take in a number of nonaffiliated Jewish organizations—camps, centers, homes for the aged, child care—that would strengthen both Federation and these independent agencies, often struggling to survive.

While I looked forward to finishing up the year in good spirits, I found that my negotiations about my final pension—and not so incidentally, rewards which I recommended for all retiring employees—were not meeting with favor by the administration. Federation had taken into account the services rendered by a few retiring employes in organizations that subsequently were admitted into the Federation family, thus increasing their pensions. This was so, not by rumor, but because I had fought for these benefits on behalf of some of my colleagues, who would otherwise have retired with but a pittance.

I have no hesitancy in recalling my labors on behalf of a number of my colleagues in the Federation family, who would not have been able to live on the pensions they received, had it not been for my one-man intervention. I insisted that they receive at least 50 percent of their final salaries, and between Federation and the agencies which they directed, this sum was attained. Those executives included Samuel Solender, head of the Washington Heights YM-YWHA; Rabbi Alter Landesman of the Hebrew Educational Society; Ben Fox and Harold Morris of the Jewish Community House of Bensonhurst. I was not able to receive anywhere near 50 percent of my final salary, when I retired.

I had worked six years in Staten Island when it was not a part of Federation, and I wanted that counted in my final portion. The same courtesy was not extended to me. It would have meant several thousand dollars additionally each year, not an inconsiderable sum.

After several appeals, I was permitted to appear before three members of the pension committee, all of whom I knew intimately, to present my case, but I soon found that agreement had already been reached that I should not receive a penny more than was already calculated. One said: "We cannot do any more for you, Graenum, than for anyone else on the staff." I was outraged, but controlled myself. I was not an ordinary employee. I had entered a job with literally nothing to do and had made it into a force for Federation. Each year new duties were added, and I had absorbed them. I never complained about assuming additional responsibilities; in fact, I welcomed them. I never made a request for an assistant or even for a second secretary, although I could easily have used both. Through my land acquisitions for day camps, for which I conducted a one-man campaign, I had added tens of millions of dollars to Federation's assets. I had personally inspired the writing of wills by a number of people that ultimately brought millions of dollars in legacies. So from the financial side alone, I had added substantially to the Federation treasury. But the few thousands of dollars annually that I thought I should receive as just compensation, irrespective of these extraordinary services, was turned down.

I was so angry after leaving the meeting that I sent a letter to the executive director, stating that I was retiring earlier, on April 21, 1973, my sixty-fifth birthday, ten weeks before the June 30 date which I had previously used as a final day of work. Suddenly a way was found to add some additional retirement compensation, but not the full amount due me. I agreed to stay on to June 30, but no longer.

I thoroughly enjoyed working at Federation. Above that I only wanted to work in greater New York, which I still consider the most interesting locale for an imaginative executive, who not only could conjure innovative projects, but could find the manpower and funds with which to translate them into reality. Yet, if I had left New York, I am sure that my personal fortunes would have grown considerably.

There were a number of retirement parties by my colleagues in the larger field, by lower-echelon Federation staff, by the distribution committee, and by Federation itself, the latter a well-attended gala with poems, humor, singing, and chiding. Gifts included a 19-inch Sony TV with remote control, a valuable sterling silver citron holder for Sukkot, a magnificent copy of the Darmstadt Haggadah (since I was a modest collector of Haggadahs), and the full set of the new *Encyclopaedia Judaica*, volumes which I have used constantly. A copy of the speech that I gave on the occasion of my colleagues' party, which also celebrated my sixty-fifth birthday, was subsequently printed in my book *Innovation By Tradition* (1976).

My last day was spent taking down the eighteen paintings that had decorated the walls of my office. Regrettably I took only a few personal files. There were no tears. Lots of hugs and kisses. As I walked out, I felt that I had sloughed off an enormous burden.

I left behind scores of files, mostly bound in hard folders, which were a gold mine of information on all that had happened at Federation since the day that I arrived on September 15, 1949. I don't know what happened to this valuable material. For years afterwards, whenever I was called for information about a certain past happening, I was told that none of my professional remains could be found in the so-called "morgue," which I had always presumed had been set up to retain archives. What a waste of time on my part to have written and husbanded such materials.

Did Federation find one person to take my place? No! That would have been impossible under any circumstances. While one person, starting from zero could somehow, if he was productive, inventive, and ambitious, absorb what I had accumulated over twenty-three years, no new person could possibly assimilate so much coming to the post for the first time. I have heard that four people were ultimately engaged to take over my duties. Several of them even had assistants. All had their own secretaries.

As I left Federation, I was informed that a retiree was cut off from major medical services, a costly item if one cared to take out such insurance on his own. After being deprived of this financial aid for twelve years, I am happy to say that William Kahn, the incumbent executive vice-president of Federation, restored me to this service, when I brought the injustice of this earlier decision to his attention. It only included me as a recipient for whom Federation assumed financial responsibility. I am paying for Emma's coverage separately.

When I was leaving, I was asked whether I would take on any assignments as a part-time consultant. I said I might, but that my fee would be $500 per day. I received a letter asking whether I would reduce it to $250. I wrote back, "No." I was engaged for three and a half days, received a check for $1,750, and that was the end of that relationship. I wanted out, and a high fee assured the cut-off. I was also asked whether I would continue my volunteer services to the Henry Kaufmann Foundation, to which I had given considerable time for twenty years without compensation. I wrote that my fee would also be $500 per day. I received a note to the effect that the Foundation would find other means of evaluating organizations that sought funds.

* * *

On the eve of my retirement from Federation, I was asked to prepare a paper on the occasion of the fiftieth anniversary of the Metropolitan Association of Jewish Center Workers, a professional body with which I had been affiliated since 1932 and had served as its president. It was titled "A Personal Perspective—Past and Future." When printed in a small booklet, it had a wide circulation.

I ended that paper by noting the changes that had taken place over the half-century from 1923 to 1973, where from being immigrants we had become predominantly a native-born population, and had developed a native American Jewish culture.

From an institution for Americanization, into one that must concern itself primarily with Judaization; from one where Jewish families were intact, to a period when families are in crisis; from a world where the Balfour Declaration was a paper of hope, to the reality of Israel; from a period when the centers were institutions seeking a more permanent foothood in the American scene, to one where they constituted a major force in Jewish life.

The New York Board of Rabbis

The New York Board of Rabbis became a member of Federation for reasons which were still unclear to members of the distribution committee when I arrived at Federation in 1949. Its attitude, when not outrightly hostile, at best remained lukewarm throughout the years of my incumbency. Federation did not provide any support for the general services of a professional rabbinical body. It only aided those items which could be encompased in some way under the rubric of "welfare." This covered chaplaincy services in hospitals, homes for the aged, child care institutions, and prisons.

The portfolio was handed to me, since now that Federation had a second-tier professional staff, such a responsibility had to be allocated to someone, and I seemed the appropriate person. I immediately wanted to find out what the board was doing in the areas we funded. How many rabbis were involved in the chaplaincy program? Which ones were paid a salary? How many were volunteers? How many clients were served? What were the accomplishments? Were there any unmet needs? As a consequence, for the first time, the board itself began to maintain better records, so as to provide evidence of its achievements. Annually, I took the chairman of the appropriate sub-committee of the distribution committee, perhaps the most powerful arm of Federation, since it was the allocator of funds, to visit the board's offices, so that he or she could see how and where the board functioned. At the distribution committee hearing each spring, the board representatives were given a sharp going-over by the sub-committee. I always had the feeling, as I sat in on these sessions, that there was little empathy for the rabbis and their work.

One year the board came in with a proposal that it would like to introduce a training program for *mohelim* (circumcisers), because they were in short supply. The board wanted to upgrade the training of *mohelim* by having them obtain first-class medical exposure and supervision. Otherwise *mohelim* would still only be able to acquire their skill from observing others in this profession. An arrangement had been worked out with Mount Sinai Hospital, a respected Federation Agency, as the host for this innovative venture. At first there was outright opposition on the part of the distribution committee, although the auspices were of the best and the sum involved was modest, $25,000 per year. A grant was finally made after Rabbi Isaac N. Trainin and I made repeated appeals to the committee to support this scientific approach for the realization of an ancient Jewish rite.

Needless to say, the program, while supported by most rabbis, was opposed by private *mohelim,* who felt that Federation was encroaching on their domain and bringing unnecessary competition into this field. They claimed that circumcision was already in decline, because of the lower birthrate amongst Jews, the wider use of physicians to perform the surgery involved, usually in the hospital where the child was born, and the abandonment of the rite by some Jews, who did not believe in this ancient covenantal practice, or where intermarried couples did not want it at all.

While all of these observations were true, nonetheless, the fact remained that there were also fewer *mohelim.* The use of a fine hospital and modern scientific medicine to train new people would force all existing *mohelim* to reexamine their own methods. If nothing else, it would promote higher standards of hygiene. Even at best the program could only enroll a few candidates. So it was initiated.

The board was still receiving support from Federation when I left. Changes in the composition of the distribution committee made that body more sympathetic to the program. The board found in me, one who understood how essential the rabbinate was in assuring a future for Jewish life in Greater New York. I understand that its membership in Federation is no longer questioned.

A War Disrupts Our Travel Plans - 1973

Six months prior to my retirement on June 30, 1973, Emma and I started to plan our first extended travel holiday, which was to have begun on Yom Kippur night, October 6, 1973. The trip was to extend over six months, beginning with our journey to Israel, where we would spend nearly three months, working primarily on the business of getting Israel to start admitting larger numbers of Ethiopian Jews. I suspected that this would not be an easy task, having already found Israeli officials and the leaders of other Jewish organizations in Israel and the United States indifferent or resistant on this issue. Now we would have time to pursue the matter with diligence.

As a follow-up to such a restful sojourn in the Promised Land, where we also hoped that we would really learn to speak conversational Hebrew, we would tour Africa, starting with another visit to Ethiopia. The rest of our trip, worked out in detail with a local travel agent, included Kenya, Tanzania, Uganda (the latter three on a safari to see the wild life in their natural habitat), Mozambique, Rhodesia (now Zimbabwe), and a great deal of South Africa. Then we would turn north to what is now Namibia, having been invited there by a Jewish mining developer who happened to have lived in Mount Vernon, a city contiguous to Pelham. The other countries in West Africa that we would cover were the Cameroons, Nigeria, Ghana, Ivory Coast, Sierra Leone, and Senegal, ending in Morocco, where we planned to catch our breath before returning to the States. As we planned our tour, we became overwhelmed with the size of the continent, the long distances we would have to traverse, the many different countries with their distinctive cultures. But none of this, as we studied books and maps, daunted us.

Over the summer of 1973, as we began to read more materials about each of the countries, we also began to gather addresses from friends, mostly Jews and Jewish institutions, although here and there names of natives, mostly officials or professionals, some in government and social welfare, were added to our address book. We submitted to all the shots necessary for Africa, smallpox, yellow fever, cholera, bubonic plague, typhoid, paratyphoid, and tetanus, and bought a supply of pills to prevent malaria. This alone took weeks during which we used our own doctors and United States public medics.

All the farewell parties had been attended. We said goodbye to our children. The day before our departure, we were mentally, emotionally, and physically prepared for a journey of half a year that would cover nearly 25,000 miles.

Yom Kippur day arrived. Our bags were packed, for we were leaving that night. I was up early and off to the Pelham Jewish Center for services. Emma would come a bit later for this all-day ritual observance. I had not turned on the radio that morning. When I entered the synagogue, I was greeted by several members, who told me the unhappy news that the Arab nations had attacked Israel on this holiest day of the year. For me, the implications were obvious. Would El Al take us on that evening's flight in view of the ominous developments? I ran home, tried in vain to reach the El Al office. It was hours before I finally got through. No. Our seats had been preempted for returning Israeli soldiers. I offered to go as a volunteer. They still had no room. They didn't know when they could accommodate us on any future flight. They could not get us a seat on any other airline, as those companies were either cancelling their flights because of the war, or if flying would take only those passengers who had a valid reason for going to Israel. The U.S. government was advising U.S. citizens not to go.

So there we were bemoaning our disappointment. But that was only momentary, for it soon gave way to concern about what was happening to Israel. The news was dire: an Egyptian breakthrough on the Suez Canal, attacks by the Syrians in Golan. In the first days, Israel suffered heavy casualties, largely because it had refused to undertake a preemptive strike, even though it had been made aware that the Arab-Moslem countries might engage in a surprise attack. This time, unlike 1967, it preferred to wait, so as not to alienate anyone, particularly the United States. Although it eventually triumphed, it paid a heavy price in death, injuries, wealth, and the loss of the belief in its military invincibility engendered six years earlier by its 1967 victory.

After several hours, I returned to the synagogue, but it was difficult to keep one's mind on the Yom Kippur prayers. When I read Maftir Yonah, as I had been doing every year since the synagogue was founded, I felt the call to do something for Israel. If we couldn't fly to Israel, we would instead spend our energies for the coming months raising funds. We rejected any thought of going to Africa. We were angry at the African nations for severing relations with Israel because of Arab pressures. Instead we began to make plans to go to Israel in 1974 for an extended period of six months.

Despite the need to raise funds for Israel, we found, to our dismay, that many people refused to give money. They had serious reservations about Israel's future. They thought Israel would lose the war, so why send money at all! We have many odd Jews in our midst, but those I encountered then were the strangest of all.

Honorary Degree

At the graduation exercises of Yeshiva University in New York, in 1973, Dr. Samuel Belkin, the President, awarded me an Honorary Degree, Doctor of Humane Letters, for my services to the Jewish community at home and abroad. Other awardees were Senator Henry Jackson and Elie Wiesel.

18

The Formation Of The American Association For Ethiopian Jews

BETWEEN 1955 AND 1965, we were never approached to give money to an Ethiopian Jewish organization. The American Pro-Falasha Committee, founded in 1922 by Dr. Jacques Faitlovitch, had ceased to exist in the 1950s, and no other group took its place.

After we returned from Ethiopia in 1965, we started to raise money for educational and medical programs there, as we had promised. All checks were made out to the World Jewish Congress for tax-exemption purposes, and the proceeds were mailed to Dr. Aryeh Tartakower in Jerusalem, who assumed responsibility for transmitting these funds to appropriate Ethiopian Jewish sources. We assumed that the money was sent to Yona Bogale, who supervised the schools. Tartakower subsequently formed the Relief Committee for the Falasha Population in Ethiopia, which became the formal instrument for the receipt and transmission of such monies as were sent from the United States through our efforts.

In 1969, Jed Abraham, who had recently returned from Ethiopia, where he had worked as a lawyer in the U.S. Peace Corps, and who had become concerned about the fate of Ethiopian Jews, organized The Friends of the Beta Israel (Falasha) Community in Ethiopia, to solicit funds and aid Ethiopian Jews. After meeting with him, I began to use his organization as the instrument of dispensing such monies as I raised for Ethiopian Jewry. Abraham and I appeared at a number of meetings pursuing the Ethiopian Jewish cause.

Meanwhile the old American Pro-Falasha Committee had been reactivated by Mrs. A. H. Kavey, who had been an ardent member of the original committee in the 1920s, and Martin J. Warmbrand, along with a small group of interested people, to obtain money for the Humera-Abderafi Jewish settlement in Ethiopia. Mrs. Kavey had visited Ethiopia and was concerned with their welfare. She campaigned for money for a tractor. At the same time Gabriel Cohen of the *Jewish Post and Opinion* of Indianapolis solicited money for a tractor through the pages of his national newspaper, as did Jack Fishbein editor of the *Chicago Jewish Sentinel,* who had visited Ethiopia.

As more people went to Ethiopia, like Lester and Sylvia Gerson of New Orleans and Bernard and Frances Alpert of Highland Park, Illinois, they immediately contacted me on their return. I saw the need to consolidate whatever had to be done on behalf of Ethiopian Jewry, and initiated discussions with the American Pro-Falasha Committee and Abraham's organization, out of which emerged a new body in 1974, the American Association for Ethiopian Jews. I stressed the need to use the words *Ethiopian Jews* rather than *Falashas,* because *Falasha* was a pejorative term. It was equally important and essential to emphasize the Ethiopians historic connection with world Jewry.

While some preliminary meetings took place at Federation before I retired in June 1973, the first formal meeting occurred in Chicago in November 1974, where a board of directors was elected, based on invitations which I had extended to supporters of previous solicitations, the entire board of the American Pro-Falasha Committee, and members of Abraham's small group who chose to identify with the new association. Apart from Abraham, Jeffrey B. Stone, a young attorney, became secretary of the new organization, and helped to arrange the merger of the several societies and to obtain IRS tax exemption. I was elected president. Dr. Theodore Norman, head of the Baron de Hirsch Fund, was chosen treasurer.

For several years, the annual meetings were held in our home in Pelham, until the change in the presidency and the enlargement of the board membership necessitated finding larger quarters. We then met at the Brotherhood Synagogue, where Rabbi Irving J. Block, a member of the board, officiated. As of the last election, in November 1985, fifteen of the thirty original board members continued to serve on the board, which has been increased to fifty individuals. The board now meets in hotels in New York, Chicago, and Washington, as its constituency has become national.

Lebanon?

At a party given by Sam and Betty Lee in Washington in early 1973, we met G. McMurtrie Godley again. He was a great bear of a man with a good sense of humor. Mac, as we called him, had been ambassador to Laos when Sam was serving in Vietnam, and they had become good friends. He had just been appointed ambassador to Lebanon. When he learned that we were going to Israel, he extended a hearty invitation to visit him in that land. Before we had a chance to take him up, the war of 1973 broke out, and we didn't go. We always regretted having missed this opportunity to see that country, before the process of destruction and disintegration set in. Under his auspices we would have been permitted to see that unfortunate state from the inside. Mac now lives in a small town in the middle of New York State.

Do I Want to Be a Banker?

Early in 1974, I was approached by three men, all Orthodox Jews, who were establishing a new bank in one of the suburbs of Greater New York. The bank would be closed on the Sabbath and Jewish holidays in conformity with Jewish tradition. It would cater to that sector of the religious Jewish population that was growing rapidly in that county. They invited me to be one of the organizing board of directors. My name had been given to them by the bank's attorney, a former student at the Wiener Educational Center. They felt my name would be an "asset," in view of my many connections with prominent Jewish individuals and Jewish institutions. I would have to invest only a small sum of money. If the bank thrived, and as I purchased additional stock, it would be a way of ensuring added resources during my retirement.

After I read the voluminous material they left with me and learned of the obligations I would have to assume as a board member, should the bank lose money or become insolvent, I decided that banking was not for me. Furthermore, I would have to attend too many meetings and undertake other responsibilities, such as soliciting depositors and even prospective borrowers. After all it was a bank. They tried to talk me out of the decision, but I stood firm.

In 1985, I read in the newspapers that this bank was ordered closed by state investigators, because it was insolvent. Luckily, the bank closed its doors just before the Sabbath and Rosh Hashanah, so that there was no run on its holdings. A purchaser was found overnight, hence the bank did not actually "fail." The only losers were depositors who had over $100,000 in their accounts. The government insured all the rest up to that amount.

As I read the newspaper account, I was happy with the decision I had made eleven years before, even though many of my friends then thought I had made an egregious mistake. I really was never cut out to be a banker.

Spring of 1974: England and Israel

While our first traveling abroad since the cancellation of our six-month trip to Israel and Africa was only to Israel, with a brief stopover in England, it was to be an eventful month. I had been invited by Rabbi Fred I. Hollander, who left the New York Board of Rabbis to become the head of Keren Yaldenu in Israel, a substantial youth-serving educational and recreational organization. He wanted me to make a quick survey of his agency. Our expenses were paid. There was no other stipend.

We stopped in London to break up the long flight. We took along for reading, Meyer Levin's *Obsession* and David Halberstam's *The Best and the Brightest*. We were met by Dr. Leon Feldman, who was on leave from Rutgers University, and teaching at Jews College in London and at Oxford. Britain was in the midst of another election, and it looked as though the Labour Party would suffer a defeat, for the workers were dissatisfied and divided with their party leaders. We went to the theater to see Ingrid Bergman in *The Constant Wife*, an excellent comedy directed by John Gielgud, that played to a full, enthusiastic house.

We met with David Kessler, president of the Falasha Welfare Association, and several members of his committee, to discuss Ethiopian Jewish matters. He appeared content with the modest program undertaken in Ethiopia, which I saw as inadequate and not even a stopgap for meeting the suffering and abject needs. I stressed aliyah. The revolution had not yet taken place in Ethiopia. If we were to provide aid in Ethiopia, the sums required would have to be substantially greater. I raised the need to get the Joint Distribution Committee and the Jewish Colonization Association (ICA) more deeply involved in the Ethiopian undertaking, for they had both the resources and the professional knowhow. He listened, but had his own ideas about what should be done.

* * *

After our arrival in Israel, I met with Mordecai Paran, head of the Jewish Colonization Association, and reviewed my meeting with Kessler. He felt that Kessler was a "dilettante amateur" and not a professional on this issue. He told me that Sir Henry Avigdor Goldsmid, president of ICA, was going to the United States this very month, and suggested that on my return to meet with him and possibly with Samuel Haber, executive head of the JDC, to see whether they would support a more generous program in Ethiopia.

Such a meeting was arranged in New York, six hours after we returned from Israel on April 2. Goldsmid could have been type-cast as an English lord. After my presentation and plea, he agreed to contribute $25,000, and Haber of the JDC reluctantly consented to follow suit with a similar sum. While the total of both donations was still insufficient, it more than doubled the annual amount of money that had previously been spent for the twenty-eight thousand Jews in Ethiopia.

I had bought a stereo-radio for Tim Gidal, in whose apartment on 16 Nili Street in Jerusalem we would be staying. The cost was $85.56. The customs officials were stubborn about allowing me to bring it in as a gift, and after several hours of at times violent argument, I had to pay $147.90 duty. The bargain instrument eventually turned out to cost $233.46. It was still cheaper than one purchased in Israel.

For a few days we took in the sights, visited "our" swimming pool at the Jerusalem YM-YWHA, drove up to Herodium to see the excavations of this ancient palace, fortress, and tomb situated amidst the bleak hills just east of Bethlehem. That evening, at Gidal's apartment, we had a long talk with Boris Levin, the son of Shmaryahu Levin. He told us about his father and the early days of the Zionist movement. We discussed the future of Israel, along with his own field, pharmacology, where we learned a lot about pills. Gidal was bound to have us meet everyone he knew in Israel. Since he was a social animal, our stay was dotted with enjoyable parties where we met many Israeli celebrities.

Israel—Keren Yaldenu: 1974

In 1974, after Rabbi Fred Hollander, formerly with the Board of Rabbis of New York, became the director of Keren Yaldenu, a youth service organization in Israel with numerous buildings, he invited me to study his organization. I had worked closely with him when he was in New York. He knew that I had considerable experience in the administration of centers, which were akin in purpose and program to his collective. He felt the need for a review of its structure, which had grown like Topsy and was presenting him with difficulties as the new executive.

Keren Yaldenu had been created by a small group of traditional Jews, originally immigrants from Germany, in the period before World War II. They wanted to serve the poor, the needy and neglected, usually Jews who came from non-European countries. They wanted to help them in an atmosphere that would maintain and keep them within the traditional religious fold. The founders had obtained considerable sums from generous philanthropic donors in both Europe and the United States. This was supplemented by grants from the religion and education ministries of the Israeli government, as was characteristic of most associations in Israel.

My examination over a period of six months revealed that the board itself was too small and inbred and needed an infusion of new blood. I prepared a long list of potential board members.

In the main, most of the paid directors of the score of centers were neither well trained nor, in most instances, qualified for the work they were doing. They needed either intensive retraining or equally intensive supervision, and in some cases should have been replaced.

The buildings were actually being used only for afterschool programs and occasionally for some special event, usually around the holidays, to which parents were invited.

Despite these deficiencies and limitations, some parts of the program were of good quality. There was an emphasis on prevocational education, hoping that this would inspire the youngsters, most of whom would probably never have entertained the idea of higher education, to go on and obtain the kind of training that would enable them to make a better living. The courses offered were in electronics, ceramics, and the use of simple computers. The instructors in some instances were young men who had been recruited from the streets only a few years before. The Hebrew and Jewish studies were all in the traditional vein and usually led by competent, traditional young women. Here was a case where the program was better than the management and the supervision, largely by dint of the luck of obtaining good teachers, who were dedicated to their work, albeit these were second jobs and not their primary source of work and income.

I felt that the facilities would easily lend themselves to use as preschool programs, for which there was an unsatisfied demand. I made overtures to Jerusalem public officials, through contacts that I had made on previous visits, and obtained a grant for initiating an early childhood educational enterprise. I contacted architects to redesign the buildings at little cost and approached an organization where all the furnishings could be acquired at low prices, some of it as a donation. I arranged a meeting with parents of potential preschool enrollees to obtain their reactions to the development of such a service. The response was affirmative, even though the parents were suspicious, since no one from the agency had ever consulted them on what they wanted or needed.

I also saw the use of these underutilized facilities for older adults, for they too were in need of more activities than the country was then providing.

In addition, I prepared a detailed manual on the total operation, the overall program, which included sound administrative practices and stronger financing.

Since Keren Yaldenu was involved in rapidly opening one building after another, I wrote a manual on what should go into the initiation of new buildings. I was invited to the inaugural of the building in Kiryat Shemona. I flew up to that unhappy northern city beset with constant bombing raids by Arabs from either Lebanon or Syria, both not distant, to see the mayor. There I ran into the usual waiting and interruptions that characterized any conference with Israeli officials. Finally I had to tell the mayor that my time was as important as his. He smiled, told his secretary not to interrupt him, as she had already done on five occasions during our presence, closed the door, and we finished our business with dispatch.

At the opening ceremony, a young Moroccan Jew, the deputy mayor, made the welcoming speech. His mother, who worked in the kitchen, *kvelt* at her son's status, telling everyone who would listen—in Hebrew: "My son, my *shelli*," a tribute to the rapid assimilation and improvement in status of her kinsmen.

Despite all my writings and reports, several of which were presented before a small group of the board, there was no disposition to alter the way in which the organization functioned. It never attained the status it should have enjoyed, through the excellent work that it could have done had the board not been so limited and arbitrary. For my services, I received only transportation and a small stipend for expenses.

The Tel Aviv University Institute

The year 1974 provided me with another experience in Israel. Apart from my work with Keren Yaldenu, I had been invited by Dr. Emanuel Rackman to attend a meeting at the home of George S. Wise, one of the top lay leaders and supporters of Tel Aviv University, where I found on my arrival my former mentor, Dr. Salo W. Baron, the world's outstanding Jewish historian, and Dr. Harry M. Orlinsky, a biblical scholar and professor at Hebrew Union College, to see whether I could help them recruit graduate students for a three-week seminar they were planning for Tel Aviv University at its Ramat Aviv campus.

It was not clear what the subject of the seminar was to be, but I do recall throwing into the hopper a suggestion that it might focus on how Jews had coped with violence against them over the millennia. The 1973 war was still fresh in my mind. While the Israelis finally won, it was a bloody victory. Questions had already arisen as to how they could assure more permanent fruits for this latest triumph, since they seemed no closer to assuring their own security than before the conflict. Some felt that the conditions of Jewish life, not only in Israel but elsewhere, had been painfully compromised. Jews found that they had no allies this time, except for the major assistance of the U.S. government. Israel and Jews had been deserted by American blacks, by the white churches, and by most countries, because the Arabs had used their most potent weapon, withholding oil, raising the price outrageously for this essential commodity. Our small group talked about how the Jews could and did defend themselves. A title emerged: "Violence and Defense in the Jewish Experience."

The participants were to be limited to post–master's degree holders, young Jewish professors, social workers, and educators. The actual enrollees included some with Ph.Ds. Thirty students were accepted from all over the United States. Their expenses were paid. When they arrived in August 1974, they were housed at the Ramat Aviv Hotel, a long walk or short bus ride from the university, where all sessions were held.

A distinguished faculty of fifteen people was recruited, and I was delighted to be one of them. The others were Yohanan Aharoni, Salo W. Baron, Haim Cohn, Michael Confino, Ben Halpern, Joel L. Kraemer, Yuval Ne'eman, Harry M. Orlinsky, Emanuel Rackman, David Schers, Shimon Shamir, Shlomo Simonsohn, Uriel Tal, and Ephraim Urbach. Some of the lecturers dwelt on the ancient and medieval periods, and others covered the modern and contemporary years. The presentations were scholarly, followed by long discussions, usually ending with a summary by Professor Baron. I sat in on all the sessions.

My paper, "The Role of Communal Workers in Jewish Self-Defense," was unique in that the subject had never been assembled and presented in that form before. It was well received. The discussion was spirited.

I was dealing with a time and situation that all the participants were familiar with, as against historical material and events with which none of them had any personal contact.

In addition, I was asked to conduct a special session, quite apart from the seminar, on Ethiopian Jewry, and introduced the seminarians to their first exposure to this subject. Only 175 Ethiopian Jews lived in Israel at this time. None of the students had ever met one before. None of them had visited Ethiopia.

The seminar culminated in a volume under the aforementioned title, published by the Jewish Publication Society in 1977. Reviewers remarked that while various scholars had pointed out that counterviolence was at times essential to defend Jews under assault, usually Jews were defenseless, and as one reviewer put it: "The voice of judicious, socially responsible Halacha emerges clearly from the pages."

Most American Jews, influenced largely by the major Jewish communal relations organizations, put their faith in the support of democracy, advocacy of civil liberties and individual freedom, combating prejudice and discrimination, and coalitions with other American minorities, particularly blacks, who constituted the largest bloc in the American polity. Other Jews have taken a more conservative stance, stressing self-interest, which at times means identifying with the conservative Republican Party, as against the conventional Democratic Party with which they have been for decades aligned, on the theory that this is a better social, economic, and political association for Jews. There are strange bedfellows in this loose amalgam of high-level intellectuals, well-to-do-business and professional men, the right wing of Orthodox Jewry, including Hassidim, all lumped together under the banner of Neo-Conservatism.

As I stated at the seminar in 1974, and still believe: . . . there are others, still a minority amongst American Jews . . . who are demanding a halt to indiscriminate total involvement in all sorts of issues. They want

... more selectivity of interests ... greater consolidation of the efforts of various agencies often doing much the same thing; they want a turning inward, perhaps even withdrawal in some areas. ... the Jews, numerically fewer and quite assimilated to the Western mentality, are losing their specifically Jewish intellectual, moral and emotional strengths, their financial base, and their always uncertain political influence. If so, as in the past, when the world has grown either indifferent or hostile, it may be necessary for Jews to build new walls around themselves to defend against the threat of violence to their lives and their civilization.

Ethiopian Jews

I became much more involved with Ethiopian Jewish affairs than I had intended on this short visit to Israel. The 165 Ethiopian Jews in the country, nearly all of whom had come to the land illegally, since Israel, despite having an embassy in Ethiopia, would not grant any visas for migration, had organized themselves under the influence of Hezi Ovadia. After his recent retirement as the top sergeant in the Israeli army, Ovadia, a Yemenite Jew born in Ethiopia, had decided to devote his energies to improving the lot of the Ethiopian Jews in Israel and in promoting aliyah for those left behind. He had already achieved a major objective in asserting their authenticity as Jews when he elicited a formal statement to that effect from the Sephardic Chief Rabbi, Ovadia Yosef, in 1973. The actual document was incorporated in a letter to Bernard and Frances Alpert, founding members of the American Association for Ethiopian Jews, who were in Israel on business and had met Hezi Ovadia.

Emma and I contacted the organization and its young and vital leadership. We visited some of them in their homes, which gave evidence of their having already made reasonably good economic adjustments in the country. We urged the local volunteer committee, headed by Dr. Aryeh Tartakower, a Polish-born sociologist, who now in his older years was director of cultural affairs for the World Jewish Congress in Israel and writing a history of that organization, to press the government and the Jewish Agency to undertake an immediate aliyah or rescue program, if the latter was indicated, of those in Ethiopia. I spoke to everyone who would listen in the upper levels of Israeli society and politics. While my views received a polite reception, many were skeptical, despite the Chief Rabbi's decree that they were indeed Jews. I had no offers of assistance to aid in alleviating their plight in Ethiopia or to bring them to Israel.

The rabbinate insisted that the Ethiopian Jews on arriving in Israel would have to undergo a quasi-conversion rite. If they refused, they would be granted status as permanent residents, but not as bona fide Jews. Rabbi Yosef's decree, instead of clearing the air, in some respects complicated the situation, since the government itself had not yet decided that the Ethiopians were Jews, and thus they were not eligible to enter under the Law of Return.

The Chief Ashkenazi Rabbi, Shlomo Goren, had refused to associate himself with his colleague's manifesto. This was also used as an excuse for not acting on anything connected with the rescue or status of Ethiopian Jews. I was instrumental in overcoming that obstacle a year later (1975), when I personally persuaded the good rabbi to co-affirm their Jewishness and welcome their immigration and absorption.

I met Rabbi Yosef and was interviewed on Israeli radio with him, each of us speaking in our own language. Both of us urged the government to help more Ethiopian Jews reach Israel.

I met several young Ethiopian Jews who had just arrived and were being cared for on an Orthodox Jewish kibbutz, where they were well received.

A few days before we left, we attended a meeting of the Ethiopian Jewish organization in Tel Aviv at the handsome Beit Faitlovitch in Tel Aviv, where in the presence of sixty Ethiopian Jews and other Israelis I was surprised to find myself the honored guest and was presented with an attractive parchment statement lauding my work on their behalf.

It was brought to my attention that evening that Faitlovitch House might be sold by the city of Tel Aviv. We considered ways to preserve it for use by the Ethiopian Jews in Israel and to keep intact his extensive library. Unfortunately, the library was soon scattered to several Israeli universities. The house, while used for several years by the Ethiopian Jews, was suddenly taken from them following an altercation between the Gondar and Tigrenean Jews at a meeting in 1978. Efforts were still being made in 1986 to keep it as a memorial to Faitlovitch and as a central meeting place for the sixteen thousand Ethiopian Jews now in Israel. I had told the group then, and on several occasions since, that if the house could be turned over to the Ethiopian Jews for permanent use, the American Association would find money to maintain it from year to year.

At the meeting in Tel Aviv, it was reiterated by several speakers that help for those in Ethiopa was only a band-aid. What was needed was wholesale aliyah, since all Ethiopian Jews wanted to settle in Israel permanently.

I was the *sandek* at the *brit milah* of the first son of Michael Tesfaye and Rahel Wube. It was a beautiful ceremony attended by as many non-Falashas as Ethiopian Jews, testimony to the successful social integration that the few who had managed to reach Israel had already achieved.

* * *

On several occasions I met with Haim Zipori (he died in 1984 after a short and illustrious career), who had just been selected to develop what eventually turned out to be over one hundred community centers in Israel. A young, healthy-looking, dynamic, goal-oriented individual, he was a happy choice to realize this ambitious program. It necessitated large-scale capital funds, which were solicited primarily in the United States. Substantial annual support from the government was obtained in Israel. Zipori was opposed to Keren Yaldenu, because it was religious, separatistic, and competitive with his burgeoning enterprise.

* * *

We spent a day at Kibbutz Givat Haim-Ihud, as a favor to Dr. Tim Gidal, to help them think through the intended expansion of a special school they had established for brain-damaged and other exceptional children. While I helped them prepare a letter of appeal to some foundations that might be interested in supporting this specialized program, I begged off becoming as intimately involved as the leadership had hoped. The school was performing an unusually good job.

When I chose to drive back to Jerusalem via Tulkarm, Nablus, and Ramallah, a beautiful part of the West Bank Arab world, Atte Meron, head of the school, who had asked me to give his daughter a lift to Jerusalem, strenuously opposed my taking this route. When I stubbornly persisted, he permitted his daughter to go along. We had no untoward experience. When we reached home, the telephone was ringing. He wanted to make sure that she had arrived safely. The next day, we read in the *Jerusalem Post* that a bomb had been thrown at an Israeli vehicle passing along this highway.

* * *

I gave a lengthy interview to Louis Rapaport, who was writing his first article on Ethiopian Jews for the *Jerusalem Post*.

* * *

As we were leaving Israel for the States, Ralph Goldman approached me about coming to Israel in 1975 to do an extended workshop for the executive directors of the twenty-nine centers already established in the country. I told him I would think about it and send him some suggestions.

Funerals

I saw Samuel Taylor's play *Sabrina Fair* in 1953. I have laughingly recalled the opening scene, after the father's return from a funeral, when his daughter asks him why he is so preoccupied with attending these deathly rites. He answers that when one reaches his elderly years, dying becomes a part of one's daily life. He likes to attend funerals early, so as to get a "good seat." When he has only two funerals over several days, "It's been a damned slow week." These references were from a comedy that was described as the "best in a decade." It is not the humorous aspect about which I write.

Until my mother died in 1938, I had given little attention to death, funerals, cemeteries. Over the course of years few of my family, friends, or other people I knew had died, so that I do not have any intimate recollections of attending funeral rites. As a *kohen*, a descendant of the first high priest, I had learned all the taboos surrounding death. I should not touch the dead. I should not go on a cemetery. No one of our family had died up until my mother passed away. Thus I had no need to visit a cemetery, to recite *kaddish*, observe *Yahrzeit*. At my mother's funeral, my father and I stood outside the iron gate surrounding the Knesseth Israel cemetery in Gloversville, while the final prayers were chanted and her casket was lowered into the ground. My brothers and sisters, who apparently were not bound by the same taboos that I had accepted, were at the graveside. Perhaps I chose these ancient biblical practices, reinforced by later rabbinical laws and customs as a way to avoid death and all of its implications. I gave little thought to immortality of the body and/or the soul. We never discussed this at home, nor was this a topic of conversation amongst my contemporaries.

After I completed my studies in geology in 1925–26, I had a view of the creation of the world that didn't quite square with the Jewish interpretation, but I reconciled the two positions by putting them in two different intellectual spheres. At that time, I also came to the conclusion that when one died and the body was interred, that was the end. It literally turned to dust, unless the body was miraculously preserved by embalming. Memories of the deceased lived on in other ways: things one had done, letters one had written; gifts one had given. These were tangible evidences of one's once earthly presence. Memories could be strong or weak depending on former relationships. I can still "see" my parents, my brothers and sisters, relatives, friends, almost pictorially in my mind, in some once fixed stance. These images were "resurrected," when I observed their *yahrzeits*. For some of the death rites, I followed my father's practices, although he never commanded me to do so.

The first time I actually went on the cemetery was when my father died. Perhaps his kohanic influence disappeared with his passing. Now I could do what I pleased. It was the first time that I saw a body lowered into the grave. It was the first time that I cast a shovel of earth on the coffin as a mark of assisting in the burial. It was the first time I saw my mother's grave, the large, unevenly cut granite stone with the name Berger incised in the rock, which my father had commissioned to mark the family plot. It was the first time that I saw Sam Finn's headstone. He was the late husband of my sister Sadie.

Since then I have attended scores of funerals in homes, in funeral parlors, in synagogues. I have been a witness in rain, snow, and sunshine, when the chest was lowered into the grave.

What has often disturbed me are funeral services conducted by a rabbi who was brought in at the last moment by the family, never knew the deceased, and was paid to deliver an eulogy that always lacked any sense of how the individual had lived as a person. The rhetoric extolled virtues which the deceased may or may not have possessed. Such services were often short, not always well attended, and seldom served more than a perfunctory exercise. They did little to comfort the bereaved if they needed such comfort. Often such funerals were of individuals, who were not members of a synagogue, who may not even have owned a cemetery plot, so that the last rites were hurriedly arranged without pre-planning.

On occasions, when listening to such an exposition about a person I knew quite well, I was almost impelled to get up and say, "Let me give the eulogy." Sometimes he or she were both virtuous and iniquitous. They were once real and alive with all of their foibles. That was the image that should be conveyed in the last moments, so that the family and friends will not have a stereotyped portrait that fitted any passing character.

On a number of occasions, I have been asked to give the eulogy at a funeral, both for members of my family and for friends. In some instances, I was called by the family to make such a final presentation because the deceased had requested it before his death. Some living individuals, having heard me deliver such an historic evaluation, have approached me with the request that if I am around when they pass away, they hope that I would undertake this solemn task.

In such instances, I have taken into account special things which illuminated their lives—their family ties, their work, their philanthropic acts, their creativity—and have always embellished these aspects with mundane recollections of ways in which my life and theirs had crossed. It was these concrete albeit transitory illustrations that gave poignancy to the eulogy and made a person memorable for the survivors.

I still prefer to have members of the family of the deceased give a eulogy. When there was forthrightness in their presentation, all received a sharper view of what a father, mother, brother, or sister was like. Once, when I was called by a son to deliver a eulogy of a man I knew intimately, I convinced him, a distinguished educator and competent poet, to undertake the act. It was one of the most ardent and emotional eulogies I had ever heard. While I would have liked the *kovod* of speaking on such an occasion, I knew that I had again made the right decision and suggestion.

The saddest act I ever performed was to accompany the body of an infant named Jennifer, the less-than-a-week-old baby of my son Ramon and his wife Anita, who had died too soon. I went with the undertaker in a private car, which carried the tiny basket for 200 miles, and saw the beautiful child properly buried with the attendant rites in the cemetery in Gloversville near our family plot.

I don't know what will be said about me when I am gone. I hope my survivors will speak well of me but tell the story of a complex life. I want to be buried in a simple pine box in the Berger plot in Gloversville next to my parents. Hopefully my sons will recite *Kaddish* on the anniversary of my passing, thus carrying on both an old and a family tradition.

The Cemetery

Whenever I was in Gloversville over the past twenty years, my late brother Milton would always raise the question about having enough cemetery plots for members of the family who wanted to be buried there. This subject always annoyed both Harriette, Milton's wife, and Emma, who never wanted to face the inevitability of death. Milton always raised the subject in the most matter-of-fact way.

In the course of years, apart from the original plots that I thought had been purchased by my father, a section was acquired by my brother Morris, and still another four units by Milton and me, rounding out what I thought were twenty-two graves. I had also assumed that the lots were contiguous and that we owned all of them. After Milton's burial, the synagogue advised us that we did not hold title to four plots in the middle of the family complex, including the one that my brother Morris occupied. Since Morris was one of the most careful purchasers that I ever heard of, it was inconceivable that he could have made such a mistake when he acquired his parcels. What is more, I wondered why the synagogue had approached us only after Milton's death.

Milton had been a president of the synagogue and knew all the details of the cemetery, which was part of the synagogue's holdings. He would have had the answers. So we were in dispute as to who owned the four plots. There were no deeds, except for the four lots that Milton and I had acquired. We finally purchased them, for what I believe was a second time, in order to bury other members of our family in the future. The acquisitions were made by contributions from my parents' grandchildren, all arranged through my nephew Howard Berger and Ramon, who in the distant future will also be interred with their successors and family. This would make an excellent piece for the *New Yorker*.

In any event, the lots have been allocated. Only Ramon and Anita eventually want to be buried in Gloversville. Michael and Sandy believe they have time to make a decision. Michael, as a high officer and veteran soldier, could be buried at Arlington, as was my brother Sam.

What of the succeeding generations of Bergers? They will be scattered all over the map. The family unity, so carefully nurtured in the past, will come to a generational end—at least as far as burial in one cemetery is concerned.

Burglaries—Security

When I was a child, I do not recall ever carrying a key to open or close our house in Gloversville. I assume that we locked the doors when we left, but the matter of security never arose. When we left for trips, I don't recall any fuss being made as to whether all the doors and windows were shut tight and fastened. In recent years, in contrast, I have driven back fifty miles to check doors and make sure the gas was tightly turned off. While burglaries were occasionally reported in the press, and I wrote such stories as a reporter for the local newspaper, no one seemed to be unduly security minded, an obsession which has possessed us since the 1960s. While we locked our doors when we lived in apartments in Columbia, Missouri, in New York, on Staten Island, and in the Bronx, it was a matter of course, rather than an elaborate ritual. In all those years, our houses and apartments had never been burglarized. So our minds were relatively at ease as we left the homestead—even for extended periods.

The same was the case, when we first moved into our two-story house with cellar and attic in Pelham in 1953. While we normally turned the single key in our one-lock (not even a dead-bolt lock) doors, front and back, whenever we went away, we also left a window or two partly open on the second floor to keep the house airy. It would have been a simple matter for any thief to climb up to the second story and enter our household.

About a year after we moved into the house, we had a large dinner party. All the women had conveniently put their bags on the radiator cover in the hallway. When it came time to leave, the bags were missing. Some laughingly said the Bergers were playing a practical joke on their guests. The truth was that the bags were gone. I quickly discovered that the back door had been open. What was more, the back hall carpeting had been muddied by someone's shoes, for it had rained that evening. I called the police. They found a small stepladder next to the kitchen window, which the burglars had climbed to watch our movements, before boldly entering and stealing the bags. Furthermore, the bags were visible from the front door, which had also been left ajar to ventilate the house. Sad to say, the bags were never recovered. Every one was inconvenienced replacing keys, driver's licenses, charge cards, eyeglasses, and other personal items that women endlessly carry in their oversize bags. Some had sums of money too. What of our dog, Toughy? He had been put in the basement, because two women were scared to death of dogs. He had barked, but we paid no attention, as we thought he was annoyed at being locked up.

We should have learned a lesson, but we didn't. There was no need to change locks, since entry had not been made that way. There was no necessity to alter our habits. One night when Emma and I were watching *Hamlet* on TV, then in the den on the first floor, with our dog Toughy at our side, we thought we heard the door open. It might be Ramon, who often came to visit us unannounced, as he lived not too far away in Parkchester in the Bronx and had a key. When he did not respond to our call, I reluctantly left the tube and turned on the wall lights in the foyer, only to find the door wide open. Emma's bag, also left on the same radiator cover, was missing. We suspect the thief had been frightened off by Emma's call. He must have entered by picking the simple lock, for it had been closed. After calling the police and giving them a report, we resigned ourselves to the usual troubles after a theft, replacing many objects, and feeling personally guilty for not having been more careful. Again Toughy, our faithful hound, never uttered more than a low-decibel growl, which we had ignored.

The only changes we made then was to add a second dead-bolt lock on the front door and insert screw bolts for all the downstair windows. We continued to naively believe that we would statistically not be hit again. However, we were now more concerned about security, because burglaries were more frequently reported in the local press, and a couple of muggings had taken place in the village. While I frequently came home by train late at night and walked the half-mile to our house down Corlies Avenue, not a well-lighted street, I radically changed my habits in the late 60s, either taking the car to work, when I was going to return home late, or else extravagantly jumping into a taxi for the short ride.

We returned from a trip out of town in the year 1980. As we drove the car into our driveway about 11 A.M., Emma noticed that one of the rear windows of the dining room was open, the curtain flapping in the breeze. I rushed into the house, found the upper bathroom window had been broken, glass all over the bathtub, and the house burglarized. A quick inspection revealed that the thieves had taken our expensive Pioneer stereo radio, phonograph, stolen a new Minolta camera which I had decided not to take at the last moment and left on the bed, and an antique Korean jewelry chest with some of Emma's less valuable jewelry. These items had been removed through a rear window. The thieves had left it partly open, because they obviously planned to return and take the silver, which was visible all over the place, and perhaps even remove some of our good paintings. Some months later the police caught up with two burglars who confessed to this entry, but we never retrieved the stolen goods. The insurance company paid for the stereo and camera, but we received only a fraction of the value of the jewelry and the antique chest.

Then we decided it was time to enter the modern age of security and install an electronic system. Thieves had been around since the advent of man, and there was no sign that this ancient blight was likely to disappear in our lifetime. Besides, we were frightened that more than thievery wa involved, as the papers constantly reported such entries were often accompanied by physical attacks and murders. We called friends, inspected their systems. Everyone swore theirs was the best. Most had key systems that worked from the outside. We asked what happened when one dropped a key in the dark and couldn't easily retrieve it. No one had an answer for that except "Don't drop your key." Some did not have protective controls on all their windows and doors. Some preferred beam systems or under-the-carpet devices. We were interested in security and an alarm to go off before the burglars entered the house. We found that in the main, price often determined what our friends installed. Often the equipment was installed by someone they knew, who would come in and repair whatever went amiss. We wanted security and not personal relations.

We finally bought the most expensive system, wiring throughout the house from cellar to attic, covering all the entry points—doors and windows. We preferred to hook into a central station rather than the local police. It cost us much more, including a monthly charge, but all service charges and repair costs were met by the installer and not the buyer. The touch buttons were on the interior; you had 30 seconds to turn on the system and get out, and the same limited time span to get into the house and turn it off. If the alarm went off, within a minute the telephone rang from the central station asking for the code word to establish our identity. We selected an unbelievable one so as to ensure that no one else could possibly guess it. If the central station was satisfied that there was no illegal entry, the bells would stop ringing and the system restored to normalcy. If there was no answer, or an unsatisfactory answer, one of our neighbors would be called, after which the police were notified, and officials would be there in minutes with their flashing lights and guns drawn, searching the house.

During the first two years, the alarm went off too frequently; the police arrived faithfully, but there was no sign of burglars. Nearly every week, sometimes twice, the installers sent a man around to check. While they found no fault in the wiring, they always tightened and replaced a wire or two. Frequently the alarm rang when we were away. It was becoming a nuisance for our most friendly neighbors. The police began to complain. We thought we had purchased, albeit the best, a lemon. One day, when a new man was checking the wires, I suggested that he look at the outside bell, high up on the outside of the house, and which no repair man had bothered to recheck. Believe it or not, that was the culprit, and since then we have had little difficulty. The few times that it went off, I had failed to turn off the system when I arose in the morning and blithely opened the rear door to take out the garbage, as the inside and outside bells clanged away.

Can't a thief cut the outside electric wires and enter by once again breaking a window with no alarm going off? No he can't. There is a stand-by battery to replace the electrical inlets. It is supposed to provide absolute security.

However, to make doubly sure we are safe, we make the nightly or departure rounds by seeing that all doors and windows are shut, locks are keyed. We inspect the controls to see that all is in order, then finally push the button to turn on the fixed red light; then we are hopefully safe when we leave or fall asleep. It is quite a routine.

That is, unless the alarm should suddenly go off when we are home and asleep. We rouse ourselves and wonder, sometimes in fear, whether there is any absolutely dependable device to make sure that security is perfect. Did you ever come down the stairs in your pajamas with a flashlight in your hand, wondering whether a thief is lurking just around the corner ready to pounce on or kill you? It is frightening! When you have made the rounds from cellar to attic, found nothing, finally went back to bed, sleep was usually over for that night, for you lay there wondering whether the bell would ring again.

Israel: Summer and Fall 1974

We returned to Israel in the summer of 1974, so that I could participate in a seminar at Tel Aviv University and resume my consultation services for Keren Yaldenu.

When we arrived at Kennedy Airport for the 11:45 P.M. flight on El Al, we found that the plane would not leave until the next morning. We checked into an airport hotel to await the departure, annoyed and impatient. At 3 A.M. we were awakened and informed that the plane would leave at 6 A.M. We didn't get a good night's sleep.

On arrival in Israel, our calendar was immediately filled from early morning until late at night with considerable Ethiopian Jewish business impinging on my official reasons for coming to Israel. Meetings were held with the Ethiopian Jewish committee and its individual members, with Israeli and Jewish Agency officials, and with a number of Ethiopian Jews. There seemed to be some prospect of aliyah, but in the end it once again proved to be illusory. One of the happy by-products was to meet Meyer and Tereska Levin for the first time, after which we developed a close friendship, seeing each other in Israel and the United States, and frequently writing letters, until Meyer suddenly died in 1982 while in Israel covering the Lebanese War. We still continue our contacts with Tereska, who has devoted herself to the cause of Ethiopian Jewry. Meyer frequently sent me sizable checks he received for his lectures, so that we could rescue individual Ethiopian Jews and bring them to Israel. On several occasions, we both addressed audiences interested in this problem. The Levins usually showed the film they had taken in Ethiopia in 1969. I followed, answering questions from the audience.

I gave interviews on the Ethiopian Jews to several journalists and free-lance writers, most of whom never could get the articles published either in Israel or the United States. On a number of occasions, I showed my excellent slides of Ethiopian Jews, taken in Ethiopia in 1965, before interested audiences of professionals in the Jewish world, but nothing came of that either. I spent time with Arnold Sherman, a writer and executive at El Al, who had demonstrated a direct interest in Ethiopian Jews and had been to Ethiopia several times. While his interest was genuine, there was little that he could do, except at the risk of his livelihood.

We attended an exhibition of Ethiopian (not Jewish) art at the Ten Fingers Gallery in Tel Aviv, run by Ruth Hefer, which attracted attention, but did not advance the Ethiopian Jewish cause. After the showing, we asked nine Ethiopian Jews, two families, to have dinner with us in a Tel Aviv restaurant. We walked our feet off until we found one they approved as kosher. Even then, they were selective about what they ordered, avoiding anything with meat, because they were not absolutely sure of its religious acceptability.

Emma attended a daily ulpan and her conversational Hebrew was prospering. Every Sabbath we attended services in the Conservative synagogue, where we developed relationships with a number of the congregants. We were invited to their apartments, where inevitably the conversation turned to our interest in Ethiopian Jews. They listened, but did nothing to advance this mission. We visited the excavations taking place under the Western Wall, a locale still not open to the public. It was stirring, reaching back two thousands years.

On Rosh Hashanah and Yom Kippur we attended services at the Jewish Theological Seminary in Jerusalem. Although conservative, there was still a separation of men and women, the service was entirely in Hebrew and completely traditional. Only the sermon was in English. The *kohanim* in the congregation arose and walked up to the *bimah* at the appropriate moment and collectively performed the priestly rites of duchening, praying to God for the benefit of the worshippers. It was a moving moment. As a result of the Yom Kippur War the year before, armed soldiers and reservists were present in and outside the synagogue to prevent a surprise Arab terrorist episode.

From time to time I was asked to meet with Israelis to talk about the aged, child care, community centers, building construction and management, since services in these areas of communal work were burgeoning over Israel.

We were invited to the wedding of Hezi Ovadia's daughter. She, half-Yemenite, was marrying an Ethiopian Jew, also half-Yemenite. The ceremony was performed by Sephardic Chief Rabbi Ovadia Yosef in the presence of five hundred guests, before a representation of Israeli society.

I heard a story while visiting Givat Brenner which I must record. It has the ring of genuineness. The year was 1956. Ben-Gurion was visiting this kibbutz, with which he had historical ties. Several Ethiopian Jewish teenagers studying at Kfar Batya had been invited to spend the Shabbat at Givat Brenner. As they were passing by, Ben-Gurion overheard several white Israeli children refer to them disparagingly as *kushi* ("black ones"). He was reputed to have remarked to those gathered around him: "Israel is not ready for the Falashas." If the story was true, it may be one of the reasons that he never did anything to bring Ethiopian Jews to Israel, during the years when he was the most powerful leader Israel ever had.

Yitzhak Navon

I had told Haim Zipori, head of the community centers in Israel, about my interest in Ethiopian Jews. He thought he might help by arranging for me to meet Yitzhak Navon, a member of Parliament and chairman of committees that had a bearing on migration and absorption. Haim was a close friend of Navon. On a pleasant Shabbat, Navon and his beautiful wife, Ofira, Haim and his wife, Rifka, Emma and I had lunch at Zipori's house. I gave a lengthy account of Ethiopian Jewry. Navon, short, articulate, with a good sense of humor, was patient during my tale. He gave visible evidence of excited interest. He told me that he would immediately look into the matter and see what could be done about expediting their admission to the country. He promised to be in touch with me the next night (Sunday), following a meeting of the Knesset. I left this friendly Sabbath luncheon conversation with a feeling, also shared by Zipori, that Navon would act affirmatively.

When I did not hear from him Sunday night, I called his office on Monday. His secretary told me he was not in. I called on Tuesday, Wednesday, and Thursday, and was given the same answer. Each time I left my name and phone number, but received no response. On Friday, I decided to call his home. He lived just around the corner from where we were staying. His wife answered. We had a pleasant conversation. She also told me he was not in. She was surprised that he had not returned my calls. She would give him a reminder.

I never heard from Navon in 1974 or thereafter. I concluded that like most, if not all, Israeli leaders, he took the official position of not doing anything for the Ethiopian Jews and ignoring Berger.

In 1982, when Navon was president of Israel and visiting the United States, it was suggested that I approach him at a private reception being held at the Spanish-Portuguese Synagogue in Manhattan. I put pride in my pocket and decided to go. Since I doubted that I would be able to talk with him alone, I wrote a long letter bringing him up to date on the issue. It urged him once again to use his influence for a massive and expeditious rescue. I squeezed up to him on the reception line, introduced myself. Whether he remembered me or not was immaterial. It was just not the place for an embarrassing confrontation. I handed him the letter. He put it in an inside pocket and thanked me. I never heard from him.

As the President, he did attend a Seged of Ethiopian Jews, his first and, as far as I know, his only public affirmation of their presence in Israel.

This was the summer when we met Esther Wube, an Ethiopian Jewish young woman. She had come into the country illegally and gradually rose from a lowly job to a better post in the Daniel Towers Hotel in Herzlia Pituach. She was being courted by Aaron Hollander, the sabra son of a Polish-Jewish family that had come to Israel after World War II. Aaron was a fine young man, a tinsmith by trade. He spoke Yiddish, while Esther conversed in English. In 1976, they were married. She bore him two children. They had to live in Arad, as the government could find no place for them that was closer to where their respective families resided—Herzlia. The AAEJ was instrumental in helping other members of her family finally reach Israel, where all the living members now reside.

Since I have already mentioned one President of Israel, I recall an incident with Haim Herzog, before he attained that rank, which involved the Wubes. The father had left behind in Ethiopia two young boys and a girl, just before he flew to Israel for medical care.

Ethiopian officials would not allow them on the plane even with all papers in order. Every pressure was being put on World Ort, which at that time was operating a program in Ethiopia, to find some way of getting them to Israel, since they were virtual hostages. Mr. Wube had worked for ORT as a schoolteacher. Muherta, one of the young Wubes left in Ethiopia, had been detained by the police for no crime, except talking to other youths on the street in Addis Ababa. Their rescue was now more urgent. They had no funds. Muherta was in jail. When ORT's office in Addis Ababa wrote that it could do nothing about getting them out, I suggested to the Wubes, who had all approached me in tears, that they see Herzog, who by coincidence happened to be president of World ORT. I also suggested that they all wear their Israeli military uniforms and go to his house in nearby Herzlia Pituach. On a Shabbat afternoon, they went to his home. Mrs. Herzog opened the door and told them that her husband was not home, although they had seen him sitting in the garden as they neared the house. She said that her husband could do nothing. It was not in his province. "He had no influence." She referred them to other governmental departments, where they had already paid frustrating visits. She finally closed the door. After he became President, Herzog made a number of favorable statements on Ethiopian Jews for the first time.

After this heartless tale, Emma decided that it would be her mission to see that the three children were saved. Henry and Edith Everett, two generous supporters and leaders of the AAEJ, who were active in ORT, were importuned by Emma to pursue this issue. When results were not forthcoming immediately, Emma began to pressure them incessantly, until they were able to persuade the executive director of World ORT, their personal friend, to rescue these helpless children. After months of delay, a way was finally found to bring them, via a roundabout route, to Israel, where the family was reunited.

Uzi Narkis

Before coming to Israel, I had heard that Uzi Narkis, head of the immigration and absorption department of the Jewish Agency, was in New York. With some difficulty I arranged to meet him. Narkis had been a general in the Israeli army and enjoyed some fame as one of the conquerors of the Old City in the 1967 war with Jordan. Short, slender, curt in manner, he listened to my plea for a larger-scale Ethiopian Jewish migration to Israel. There was some discussion as to whether they were really Jews. As we came to the end of our tense conversation, where I had consciously spoken in a restrained, nonbelligerent tone, he finally blurted that "the Falasha would only come to Israel over his dead body." I rose and gave him the conventional answer: "Maybe we'll have to see how this could be arranged." I left in an angry mood.

An Ethiopian Jew was in my home in Pelham in 1985. He had studied at Kfar Batya in the 1950s, but was forced to return to Ethiopia. He came back to Israel illegally in 1965. I met him in 1974 and tapped him as one of the future leaders of the Ethiopian Jews. Since 1977, he had been deeply involved in the Jewish Agency absorption program for arrivals from Ethiopia and some of the subsequent rescue missions. On May 13, 1985, he told me that in 1971–72, several young Ethiopian Jews approached Uzi Narkis at his Jewish Agency office in Israel appealing for help in getting their kinsmen into Israel. Narkis gave them the same reply: "Over my dead body." His morbid, prejudiced imagery had not changed over the years.

Pinchas Sapir

After many conversations with various Israelis, I came to the conclusion that Pinchas Sapir, the newly designated head of the Jewish Agency, might be sympathetic to the migration of Ethiopian Jews, but I could find no way of meeting him. When I returned to the States I addressed a letter to him early in 1974. He replied that he was attempting to make arrangements for the migration of four hundred Ethiopian Jews. I learned that he was coming to the United States and that a reception would be given for him at the Jewish Agency office in Manhattan. I wangled an invitation. As he entered the room, a tall, rather heavyset man with a Junker-like body, neck, and head, he was escorted by Uzi Narkis and Charlotte Jacobson, two individuals who had never lifted a finger to help the migration. Both were dwarfed by Sapir's height and size. After I introduced myself, we had a brief talk, during which I thanked him for his promise. I did not acknowledge the presence of the two standing at his sides, but Narkis extended his hand, asking me to come and see him on my next trip to Israel. Jacobson nodded.

When I reached Israel later in the spring, Pinchas was not available. He died suddenly on August 12, 1975. I attended his funeral. Although no Ethiopian Jews had arrived in Israel at the time of his death, I always felt that the Ethiopian Jews had lost a potential rescuer.

* * *

To be in Israel during Sukkot was a memorable experience. Sukkahs abounded everywhere in front lawns, back yards, gardens, on porches and on rooftops. They were most picturesque in the crowded sections of Mea Sheraim, the most traditional section of Jerusalem. The holiday ended with joyous dancing with Torahs in synagogue and on the street during Simchat Torah. There was a parade at midnight to the Western Wall, followed during the day by separate dancing marches by different ethnic groups to the same sacred site, each carrying their unique Torahs and celebrating this festival in their specialized styles.

* * *

We attended the opening of the new Islamic Museum with all the distinguished Israeli and English Jewish families who had made possible this singular collection of art and the building to house it. It was an added attraction for all who came in increasing numbers to this beautiful city. It was located near the President's Mansion and the new Jerusalem Theater, an area marked with attractive public institutions.

* * *

Henry and Edith Everett of Brooklyn, long-time friends, invited us to the dedication of the handsome school they had donated to the village of Hazor in the northeastern sector of Israel. It gave us an opportunity to see the archaeological excavations nearby. Hazor had a history going back to the nineteenth century B.C.E. and was among the important cities conquered by Joshua in the fourteenth century. Some of the finds were in the museum on the grounds of Kibbutz Ayelet Hashahar ("Morning Star"), where we stayed overnight. It was on the shore of Lake Kinneret. I was one of the speakers at a meeting following the dedication ceremonies and spoke on education in development towns. I touched on the need to train teachers to work with parents and whole families, an oversight in Israel's educational practices, and stressed the necessity to coordinate the work of teachers with social workers, so as to anticipate and minimize problems before they became serious and often could not be dealt with at all. Finally, I urged the use of the school from early morning to late at night, year round, in order to get maximum benefits from an expensive facility.

* * *

Before we returned to Pelham on November 20, 1974, we packed in a busy concluding month. First, I finished up my work with Keren Yaldenu, preparing reports on administrative practices, personnel, opening of new buildings, and detailed programs for preschool children, family education, and the aged. I found the board resistant to changing anything, even when I obtained the money to initiate activities like preschool care and funds for furnishing such a facility.

There were a dozen emergency meetings on Ethiopian Jewry, as plans seemingly were being jelled to bring in groups of young Ethiopian Jews, who, it was intimated, might be let out of Ethiopia, if they were to be trained in industry and nursing skills, which that country needed. We had no intention of letting these young people return to Ethiopia. Only one of these projects for seven young men materialized. Plans were formulated for setting up an office for Ethiopian Jews at ICA in Tel Aviv to house a tiny staff of Ethiopian Jews to coordinate all programs to be conducted on behalf of the 165 who lived in Israel. I promised to support such a venture through the AAEJ.

To top off our long stay with a bit of a holiday, we flew to Eilat to enjoy the warmer climate, where we rested and read. While there, we discovered the presence of three Ethiopian Jews, who later became active in the Ethiopian Jewish organization. One, who worked on ships, would call us every time his vessel berthed in the States. We received and welcomed collect calls from New Orleans, Mobile, Boston, and Montreal.

I wrote over a hundred letters during this long stop as well as scores of memoranda, mostly on the Ethiopian Jews, apart from a diary that daily recorded an exhausting schedule seven days a week from early morning to late at night. This material was important, for it demonstrated the constant struggle to create an organization of Ethiopian Jews and the diligent efforts of a few of us to bring about the migration and/or rescue, with all the frustrations we encountered from officials in Israel.

American Jewish Pictorial History: 1776–1976

During most of our six months stay in Israel in 1974, we lived in the luxurious apartment of Dr. Professor Nahum Tim Gidal. Tim had purchased a penthouse apartment in a new building at 16 Nili Street, overlooking a good part of the western section of Jerusalem. We looked out from his roof on the Knesset, the Israel Museum, the Church of the Holy Cross, and the green belt, which would soon disappear. He had recently been divorced and was reestablishing his life anew as a writer and a lecturer on photo-journalism, a field in which he had been a pioneer. He had not yet obtained the honors and recognition that would be heaped upon him within the next decade. His apartment was furnished with a collection of art works gathered around the world, along with an excellent library.

Tim approached Dr. Raphael Posner, an important editor at Keter, which had just published the *Encyclopaedia Judaica*. He proposed that Berger and he write an illustrated volume on Ethiopian Jewry. Posner, who lived a few houses away, dropped in for a drink. He told us that there was no market for a book on that theme, but that he was looking for someone to write a one-hundred-page photo-history of the Jews in the United States for the period 1776–1976, which the company would print in time for the bicentennial celebration of the United States two years hence. Tim looked at me. "Graenum can do it!" I agreed. Posner, a bit taken aback, queried how long before he could have an outline. Without a moment's hesitation, I answered: "Tomorrow!" Posner was incredulous. "You can take a few days longer." Again I replied: "No, you shall have it tomorrow."

Over the years, I had read extensively in the field and had lectured on American Jewish history on numerous occasions, so that the outline was already being formulated in my mind as we were talking. I was concerned about gathering the pictures to illustrate the volume, but decided to worry about that after I had a contract. Posner told me he had to have the manuscript by September 1, 1975, in order to have it ready before the spring of 1976. I assured him he would have it.

After Posner left, I immediately sat down and wrote a five-page outline for the book, chapter by chapter, and suggested pictures to illustrate the text. The next day, I retyped it, and called Posner to tell him it was ready. When he came by for another drink at 4 P.M., I gave him the outline. He looked it over carefully for about ten minutes, while Tim, Emma, and I waited in anxious silence. When he finished, he asked how much I wanted for writing the book. Tim had advised me to ask for a low fee, as it was more important that I establish myself as a writer than get full value for my services. Besides, he said, Keter paid poorly. He had received small sums for his work from that company. I decided to ask for $2500, hardly enough for a work that would take nine months to prepare. Posner answered: "Fine. I'll send you a contract tomorrow." He took the outline and left. After his departure, we all had a drink to celebrate. Tim thought I had achieved a great deal and gotten a good price for my eventual product.

When I returned to the States, I immediately set to work collecting pictures appropriate for the text that I would later write. Apart from looking through my own collection of American Judaica, I wrote to relatives and friends, seeking old pictures of their Jewish ancestors in the nineteenth century. I uncovered a number of excellent photos and manuscripts. I spent days at the New York Public Library, the Museum of the City of New York, and the B'nai B'rith library in Washington; three days poring through the files of the American Jewish Historical Society in Waltham, Massachusetts; then to the Leo Baeck Institute, the Library of Congress, and the AFL-CIO library, the latter two in Washington. I checked the Jewish War Veterans library in that city. I wrote to most of the smaller Jewish historical societies around the country and to a number of Jewish newspapers for old pictures. I followed up references that I came across in reading scores of histories of local American Jewish communities, and contacted Jewish institutions that had photo collections, like the YIVO Institute for Jewish Research, where I nearly froze to death going through their files in the basement of their building on Fifth Avenue in New York. Synagogues and temples were also helpful, for a few had histories going back to the American Revolution and the early nineteenth century, and I also found useful items in books and magazines. My book would have had a full page in the tiniest print listing credits for picture sources.

Finally, I selected three hundred potential pictures, filling two large boxes with negatives and two prints made from each negative. The work was done at Ralph Baum's famous photographic studio, Modernage. The bill for this alone was $1,000. I spent at least another $1,500 in travel, purchase of pictures and books, interviewing people, letter writing. There wasn't going to be much profit.

I began to write the chapters in the United States and did the final editing in Israel, selecting about one hundred pictures to accompany each of the twenty-four chapters. At the time we were living in an apartment rented from the late Professor Jacob Talmon, the eminent Jewish historian, on Ben-Maimon Street in Jerusalem, directly across from the residence occupied by Golda Meir when she was Prime Minister. Living in an apartment contiguous to ours in the same building was Sylvia Horwitz, a writer. She painstakingly looked over my text and helped me tighten up the writing, since it had to be as compact as possible to fit into the projected format. I also began to work with the graphics editor of Keter, and a number of layout pages were prepared to show prospective purchasers.

I had quite a time getting paid, Keter was in financial trouble. They finally paid me in shekels rather than dollars. I had some difficulty getting rid of them before we left Israel.

Promises that had been made by American co-publishers fell through even before they saw my book. The presidents of two American publishing companies that were at first interested in the book told me they could not get guarantees that the book would be ready before the bicentennial celebration in 1976. There was talk of a thirty thousand first-edition run. I also had some problems with Keter getting the money to pay for the pictures I had assembled. After a few threatening letters, I received a check.

To my everlasting regret, the book was never published. I could not get a release from Keter for several years, and then it was too late for the anniversary event. It would have taken a complete rewriting before submitting it to other publishers, who were interested only in a larger book. The book in manuscript reposes on my shelf. Occasionally I turn to it, if only to recall the amount of time that I spent in what ended up as a fruitless enterprise.

* * *

It had been another busy year with many lectures on behalf of Ethiopian Jewry, trips out of town to be interviewed for local radio and TV programs. I was always trying to persuade prominent American Jews to become interested in saving Ethiopian Jews or at least helping to support them while they were still in Ethiopia.

* * *

On March 7 the Meyer Levins and I recruited Henry and Mildred Rosenberg of Manhattan for the Ethiopian Jewish cause. The Rosenbergs saved hundreds of Ethiopian Jews over the years, and are still doing so even as I write this. Their selfless, courageous, and heroic labors are worthy of a book, and perhaps I shall write it one day.

* * *

I selected and assembled papers I had presented or published in recent years and turned them over to Rabbi Isaac N. Trainin and Dr. Norman Linzer, the latter on the faculty of the Wurzweiler School of Social Work of Yeshiva University, for publication in early 1976 under the title *Innovation By Tradition*. My essential thesis was that creativity would stem largely from our involvement with the past.

Guatemala, Mexico, Yucatán: 1975

Despite being so busy in 1975, and our plans to get off to work in Israel in the latter half of the year, Emma and I found time to join my brother Sam and his wife, Betty Lee, on a three-week adventurous trip to Guatemala and Mexico, including the Yucatán. Our primary emphasis was to study the Mayan culture and see the extensive archaeological restorations in those countries. We read a number of texts on the

Mayans written by Von Hagen and Popenoe as well as on the countries to be visited, which incidentally added to our knowledge about the Aztecs and Incas, part of whose ruins we had seen before on trips to Mexico and Peru.

Our plane took off from Kennedy Airport in New York and stopped in Washington, where Sam and Betty Lee joined us. After an unusually good meal on board, initiated with several martinis, we leaned back, read, and dozed until we landed in Guatemala City. This was a tropical country with six million people, mostly poor Indians, living under a "liberal" dictatorship. A chauffeur-guide by the name of Reuben Hernandez picked us up, and for the next ten days we were entirely in his hands as our driver and interpreter. The short, squat, stoic Indians, whose faces had not changed from those portrayed in the friezes carved by their ancestors, chiseled out hundreds of years before, impressed us.

We immediately left for Antigua up a winding mountain road, rising thousands of feet, and arrived at this town of twenty thousand Indians. At the market, on the streets, going in and out of the large churches, we saw Indians living at the foot of an active volcano, Fuego, which in 1541 had devastated what was once one of the most magnificent cities in the Western world, with huge, handsome churches and homes. It was never rebuilt in the same fashion.

The church of San Francisco, which had survived the volcano's destructive fury, had some interesting sculptured decorations in the entrance hallway. They included the Star of David, a menorah, the Ten Commandments, and depictions of the twelve tribes. I conjured that perhaps a Marrano might have carved these Hebraic symbols and somehow gotten away with it, for there had been no effort to destroy them over the years.

Our guide told us that the Indians were reputed to be descendants of the Lost Tribes. Such imaginative inventions were part of the literature in the American colonies, England, and Holland during the seventeenth and eighteenth centuries. References to the Indians as Jews can also be found in the writings and speeches of Mordecai Manuel Noah in the early nineteenth century.

I liked sun-beaten Antigua. When I learned that one could buy a fine hacienda with a walled-in garden covering a quarter of an acre of land for $6,000, and that maintenance, taxes, insurance, and a caretaker would cost only $600 per year, I mentally flirted with the idea of purchasing a piece of this isolated paradise. Emma's usual good sense wouldn't hear of such a preposterous proposal, particularly since the house was situated at the foot of smoking Fuego. I reluctantly abandoned another romantic real estate venture in a far-off land. Shortly after, a volcanic eruption destroyed part of the town.

Colorful handicrafts abounded, including clothing and straw hats, so all of us had a field day buying things, which we never thereafter wore, not would our children and grandchildren, except for Lizzie, who was always excited by something different. The paintings and sculptured pieces we acquired are displayed by our children as mementos of this trip.

We flew into the interior to Tikal, a major old Mayan site, on an old DC-3, like those that had moved us about in Ethiopia in 1965. There were no instructions to passengers. No air compression. No food and no heat. We landed on a tiny dirt runway cut out of the rain forest. Our accommodations were in thatched huts. No hot water. Electricity was shut off at 10 P.M. We were told to light our way by candles. Regretfully the dampness made it impossible to strike a match. We lived out the night in darkness. No one had told us to bring a battery flashlight. We had been warned against the mosquitoes. We brought a spray can and had relief from the bites of thirsty insects, who penetrated parts of our skin not covered by the spray.

The food served at dinner and the next day's breakfast and lunch was Spam, rice and carrots, an orange, bread, and coffee. Having never tasted Spam, after a test, we left it uneaten. Meals were nothing to look forward to. We met a bird-watcher couple, who had returned to Tikal for several seasons to see the unusual, colorful varieties, who told us that they would have stayed longer, but they too couldn't eat Spam for more than a week.

Tikal was a must. A vast forest, dampened by rain, included an excavated temple area, now a necropolis, with scores of handsomely designed buildings. It had been suddenly abandoned about a thousand years ago, overgrown with dense vegetation and earth, only to be uncovered in recent years to reveal the splendor of this fabulous people. Why they settled there, nobody knows. Why they disappeared was also a mystery. Perhaps they ran out of water. Perhaps the people rebelled about the extravagant extent of human sacrifices to propitiate their gods. They built temples and playing fields, and cultivated farms to provide an adequate food supply. Despite all of the discomforts, it was an unforgettable experience of a people with astronomers, architects, and artists, equal to many cultures.

The rain and fog prevented our leaving the following morning, as no plane could venture into this blind airfield. We finally took a bus and rode for 34 miles to Flores over a road that would make a washboard seem flat. We saw ususual birds, ate fresh chicle, and saw close up how the natives, mostly non-Indians, lived and worked. A plane finally arrived through the clouds and flew us to Guatemala City.

Our driver picked us up and drove for two and one-half hours up to heights of 9,200 feet until we reached Chichicastenango, another half-Indian, half-mestizo town, virtually given over to a huge marketplace. The quaint Mayan Inn was another delight in accommodations, food, costumed waiters, and native music.

We observed both Indian and mestizo religious services in the church in the market square, an effort by the Catholic church fathers to meet the spiritual needs of the aboriginal natives. The Indian service was more colorful, with candles and flower petals. There were no Indian priests.

What struck us about the huge market was that it was set up largely for the 250 tourists who arrived daily from Guatemala City. Otherwise they sold goods to each other or the peasants who came in from the hills. We drove deeper into the interior and saw farms and villages and peasants in costumes that varied from village to village, a kind of competitive fashion show.

We then drove down the mountains around hairpin turns to Lake Atitlán, formed from an extinct volcanic crater, until we reached Guatemala City for a night's rest. The next day we traveled 140 miles on the Atlantic highway through scenic mountains, turned off onto a good dirt road, which deteriorated into a dust bowl until we reached Honduras, where the farmers seemed even poorer than in Guatemala, less colorful, had faces that resembled the Mexicans.

Honduras was half mestizo, part Caribbean blacks, who were also part Indian, but from India, not America. For four and one-half hours we drove through more dust-covered roads until we arrived in Copan, a lovely town in the midst of nowhere, where a local guide, a young man who smelled of liquor on his clothes and breath, took us to the Mayan ruins. There we found well-preserved figures, in highly decorated stelae, some of which had a distinctly Oriental cast. There was speculation that some or all of the sculptors might have navigated the Pacific Ocean to reach this land and influenced the design of the pillars. Each Mayan site had its own characteristics. Each exhibited a history of wealth and talent in the creation of their religious communities. Our guide pointed out a wall with a frieze that included the six-pointed Star of David. This symbol we have seen in many countries around the world. I suspected that he thought we were Jews. A Catholic bishop and an Irish lord wrote books to prove that the Mayans were aboriginally Jews.

On our way to Quiriqua, Emma fell on a muddy road, breaking her left arm at the wrist, so we could not see the ruins, nor stay at the Hotel Catamaran on romantic Rio Dulce Lake. We drove with speed to Puerto Barrios, hoping to find a doctor to set her arm, but the best he could do was to put her arm in a splint. She was given pills to endure the excruciating pain. We stayed overnight in a hotel and undertook the 200-mile ride to Guatemala City in the morning. Luckily we found an able surgeon and orthopedist at the Privado Hospital—Bella Aurora, where her arm was set. He had been educated in the States and spoke English fluently. (On our return to the States, Dr. Joseph Milgram reset it permanently at the Hospital for Joint Diseases.) This delayed our trip to Mexico City by a day. Sam and Betty Lee went on ahead. Clark Tours paid all the hospital bills. We had been invited to have cocktails with the U.S. ambassador, Frances E. Meloy, Jr., in Guatemala City, but couldn't make it. Tragically, Meloy was killed in Lebanon by Arabs in June 16, 1976.

With Emma in the hospital, I took a look around the city. I passed the locked Ashkenazi Reform temple built by Mayer, the celebrated architect who created Brasília, the new capital of Brazil. The six-pointed star dominated the pagoda. The Sephardic Orthodox synagogue was a conventionally designed building. Both were closed.

We decided to continue the trip despite the accident. I helped Emma get washed and dressed. She had her hair done in a beauty shop. We were off to Mexico City. In order to reduce pain, she continued to take pills. Coming a day late, we found that our hotel room had been booked, so late at night we had to find a new place to sleep, which turned out to be even better than the original. We had difficulty getting our deposit back, but we persisted and it was returned.

The next day, with Sam and Betty Lee, we went to the San Juan market, where we bought dresses and paintings. We had dinner at the extraordinary Hacienda Restaurant, ate new and strange foods, such as fish baked in banana leaves and chicken in chocolate sauce. We topped off the evening with four thousand Mexicans at the spectacular Mexican folklore dance festival, which we had seen before in New York.

We viewed the outdoor works of the great Mexican muralists and then more art works in the Museum of Modern Art. We never could get our fill of the paintings of Tamayo, Rivera, Orozco, Sequeiros and Martinez.

We watched with wonder the natives approach the Church of Guadalupe Hidalgo on their knees, cutting their skin and tearing their clothing. We went to the Aztec pyramids and stayed to see the light and sound show, which ended suddenly in a lightning-thunder downpour, which made the ancient story realistically alive with nature doing the acting.

We drove to Cuernavaca along a scenic highway to see the historical location of Cortés and Maximilian and Carlotta, with its fine churches, hotels, houses and shops. Then proceeded up the mountains to the silver city of Taxco with its busy, multicolor-dressed natives. The churches were historically and architecturally different, particularly the one dedicated to the Miners' Saint. A huge, imaginative O'Gorman mural made our hotel an outdoor museum. Sterling silver proved to be as costly as in the States, and our purchases were minimal.

The last leg of our trip was to the Yucatán to explore more Mayan sites. We stayed over night in Mérida, a sprawling city on the never-ending flat landscape. We visited a sixteenth-century church, observing the large congregation at mass on a Sunday afternoon. Here, too, many of the buildings were decorated with excellent murals. We ate a superb dinner at the hotel and watched folklore dancers and musicians perform across the pool from our tables.

Our new guide took us to Uxmal through numerous villages, where native women wore elaborately embroidered dresses, while performing their daily chores. The Hacienda Uxmal was one of the finest hotels we had ever occupied. From there we walked to the nearby Mayan temples, pyramids, palaces with their corbel arches. Friezes covered large parts of the structures with curious abstract designs. Kabah, another Mayan site, was composed of mounds, palaces, mostly dedicated to the rain god, often with grotesque friezes emphasizing the fertility character of their dieties.

Taking our daily malarial pills, we made a second tour of Uxmal, seeing another array of buildings with their phallic symbols, the House of Pigeons, the House of Turtles. It reminded us how birds and even small animals played a role in their religious life. The structure with the Jaguar, the Governor's Palace, the Pyramid of the Nunnery gave us a view of the Mayan site as a religious sanctuary as well as a necropolis.

Our final visit was to Chichén Itzá. We saw the Temple of the Jaguar, a thousand years old, and what remained of the once elaborate friezes. We walked along the ball courts, where they played for their lives; the altars, where human beings were sacrificed; the thousand-column Temple of the Warriors decorated with endless frescoes; the Caryatids supporting the altar; the Observatory.

Our education in Mayan life had just begun. We acquired books en route and made a list of those to be read on our return. In New York we attended lectures to deepen our knowledge of these native American Indians, who had such great creative talent and then suddenly disappeared.

It was a tough trip for healthy people. Sam somehow survived. Emma made it despite her arm in a sling.

New Orleans

On the way home, we stopped for several days with our friends Lester and Sylvia Gerson in New Orleans. They were amongst the most active helpers in the Ethiopian Jewish cause, having made several trips to that country. We went through the city, ate in its famous restaurants, bought paintings by Allan Gerson, the Gersons' youngest son, who gave up a career as a philosopher to be an artist. We met him painting and displaying his work in Jackson Square Park.

* * *

We stayed in Washington with our son Michael and his family. We met with Gilbert Kulick of the State Department. He had served in Ethiopia and was involved in the AAEJ. We agreed that the lot of the Ethiopian Jews had not improved, but had actually worsened since the revolution the year before. Kulick informed me that Ambassador Arthur Hummel, whom we had met in Burma and in Washington, had been assigned to Addis Ababa, where I hoped to meet him in the fall, following our visit to Israel and the safari in other parts of Africa.

Chapter 19

Israel: 1975 and a Safari

OUR REASON FOR going to Israel for a long period in 1975 was due largely to Ralph Goldman, the assistant executive director of Malben-JDC in Israel. I had first met Ralph when I traveled to Boston in 1939–40 to give instruction to a small group of bright students in social group work. Our paths did not cross until we met again in Jerusalem in 1955. Since then our lives were intertwined. He usually consulted with me whenever he was thinking of taking on a new position. We helped him find a house in the neighboring city of Mount Vernon. During his residence our families saw each other frequently. Ralph moved from one important position to another, finally returning to Israel to work at Malben. Whenever we went to Israel, we saw a great deal of his family and their three children. It was most convenient being picked up by the Goldmans or the Malben driver on our arrival and our leaving the country. Through the Goldmans we met many prominent Israelis, David Ben-Gurion and Teddy Kollek to mention but two, as well as many American Jews visiting or living in Israel. Their homes in Kfar Shmaryahu and Herzlia Petuach were meeting places for scores of visitors and residents.

For several years, Ralph had indicated that he would like to get me involved in the Malben apparatus as a consultant and teacher. An invitation was finally extended to me in 1974 to serve them for six months during the following year. I suggested a training program for executives in community centers, which were rapidly expanding, wherein I would help them recruit, train, and use high-level volunteers, who might eventually serve on the boards of these institutions.

The centers, an American import, had been established to assist in the absorption and integration of the millions of newcomers in Israel.

Whereas most educational instruments were designed to make them instant Israelis, what they needed was an agency to respect their individual and familial requirements, give recognition to the cultures from which they came, and opportunities to express themselves in many ways ranging from socialization, athletics, and artistic creations to leadership development. In this respect the centers resembled the settlement houses originating in England and emulated in the United States, which made a decided contribution to the development of immigrant Jews as individuals and in communities in the latter part of the nineteenth and the first quarter of the twentieth century.

The boards were essentially political. The mayor and his cohorts controlled about half the board, and the rest constituted individuals representing the government departments—labor, welfare, education, etc.—which provided funds for the program. They did not parallel the boards of similar institutions in the United States, where nonpolitical lay people legally controlled these enterprises. For new, usually untrained Israeli executives, the current arrangement was convenient, since they had to deal only with a small group of people, all of whom were in a position to do something, usually financial, for the agency. That the board members knew little of the indigenous community's real needs, less about programming, and nothing about administering such institutions was of no consequence. The executives learned about these essential matters through periodic meetings with other administrators or from the knowledgeable overall executive, Haim Zipori, who made frequent visits to the centers and for whose development he was responsible.

I believed that educated laymen, young and old, male and female, a cross-section of the diverse ethnic groups populating the cities and development towns where the centers were located, could offer original notions of what the community's varied ethnic groups, the family and individuals, really wanted and needed. Such a board could eventually pressure the governmental bodies to provide additional support, where indicated. They could recruit more members for the institution, could better interpret the role of the center to the population which had not yet learned how to use these excellent facilities.

We arrived in Israel in early May, rented the late Professor Jacob Talmon's top-floor flat at 25 Ben-Maimon Boulevard in Jerusalem. Our next-door neighbors were Louis and Sylvia Horwitz. Louis was the former director of Malben, and Sylvia was already a published writer (biographies of Toulouse-Lautrec and Goya) and was working on a book about the archaeologist of Crete and the Minoan civilization, Sir Arthur John Evans. Ben-Maimon Boulevard was populated with members of the government, professors, and upper-class Israelis. From our porch we looked down on the Tomb of Jason, a second-century burial cave of the Hasmonean period on nearby Alfasi Street. It had been dug up in

1956. It was a fine neighborhood in Rahavia within walking distance of the center and the Old City.

Malben provided me with a car, paid our expenses traveling to and from the States, and gave me a modest stipend, far from a salary, to cover some out-of-pocket expenses.

London

On our way to Israel in 1975, we stopped in London for a few days. As company, we had Maryann Ansell, our good friend from Sherman Oaks, California. In London, we saw Arthur Shaffer's play *Murderers,* which, while literate, would do much better as a movie than a stage drama. Through a newspaper advertisement, we went to a pub that presented noonday plays. It turned out to be a meeting place for homosexuals. This did not deter us. In order to see the play, we had to become members. So we joined, giving our true names. We walked up a steep flight of stairs to a tiny theater, where we sat on benches, close enough to touch the actors. The play, *Thinking Straight,* was about a writer who couldn't make up his mind whether he was heterosexual, homosexual, or bisexual. He moved from his typewriter desk to a bed with a woman, enjoyed sex, then to a bed with a male. The male stripped all of his clothes off within inches of Emma, who didn't know whether to stay, stunned, or to flee. The play was brief, poignant, and if you like that sort of drama, well done. There were eight other people in the audience.

I had breakfast with Jeremiah Kaplan, head of the London office of Macmillan Publishers, whom I knew from New York. He was a member of my former Wiener Educational Center board. I left his office with a gift of a good Chaim Bermant book on English Jewry.

I spoke to David Kessler over the phone about the Ethiopian Jews. He was still hyped up on trying to aid the Jews in Ethiopia by improving their facilities rather than promoting their aliyah to Israel. He felt the revolution would give the Jews land, and this would ease their economic insecurity. I indicated that revolutions were never good for Jews, that there would be pressure on them to adandon their religion and culture, to assimilate, so that the future for Ethiopian Jews would be catastrophic. Unhappily, my evaluation proved correct.

Israel

For the community center project in Israel, I had suggested in a prospectus that I use a half-dozen centers to demonstrate by my direct presence how each executive and his board could recruit and obtain future board leadership. The selection of centers had not been made in advance and was determined only after I outlined the program to all the executives, who were called to a meeting in Givat Olga, a soldiers' resort on the beach near Hadera. My criteria for selection of centers were an English-speaking executive with whom I could communicate, a local board that approved and would participate in the four-month demonstration, and a center which had not involved the community in board selection.

The final selection included the Jerusalem YM-YWHA and the centers in Afula, Kiryat Yam near Haifa, Safed, Dimona, and Ashdod.

I first made a preliminary visit to each community, met the executive, examined the latter's facility, program, and staff, and studied the community. With two exceptions, I met no volunteer board members at the initial session. I outlined what I wanted from the executive. He was to recruit up to twenty-five volunteers who met the criteria. Such individuals should be interested in the center, reflect the community's composition of age, sex, and ethnic background. Each should be prepared to attend meetings that would be held every two to four weeks, would undertake assignments such as attempting to recruit members, and report their successes and failures. Each participant was given a notebook to keep a running account of his experiences, along with a number of papers that I had prepared in advance on such subjects as: the meaning of leadership; what is a center?; the functions of a board member; how to recruit members; and sundry other matters that a board member should know about himself as an individual and his role as a potential leader in a community enterprise.

I set up a schedule of visits. Except for Jerusalem and Dimona, all travel involved staying overnight. I usually arrived hours before the meeting to brief and dine with the executives. I always brought additional articles and books. Occasionally on my way up or from these pinpointed centers, I would visit other similar institutions. During the summer, I looked in on a dozen, thus broadening my own knowledge of what each one was doing or had to contend with.

I wish I could report that the program was a howling success. It was not. In the middle, one executive was dismissed, after a quarrel with his board on other matters. Another, as the program developed, was seen as indifferent to this project by his own active board, and when the program terminated, his services were ended, because they learned that he was not executive caliber. A third, who was doing quite a competent job, decided to go abroad in the winter and thus could not carry out what he had learned. Several were resistant to involving more volunteers, either out of fear of their interfering with their current unrestricted freedom or because they saw that this program would make demands on their time that they preferred not to assume. In only one instance did the program meet with an excellent response from the outset. There was general recalcitrance on the part of the existing board leadership to widening their ranks with more community participation.

If I had to evaluate the program on the basis of what I achieved, I would not give myself high marks. Perhaps none of them were ready for this type of experience. Perhaps I had selected the wrong centers, or the wrong boards, or the wrong executives. Yet for all that, from comments made to me in subsequent years, after my original plan and the final detailed written report to Zipori had been circulated to the entire executive staff, I learned that some of my efforts began to take effect. In some instances, particularly when better trained executives were engaged, some were able to translate the plan that I had initially envisioned. On a longer-term basis more was achieved than what I saw during the strenuous summer months. Zipori and Goldman were reasonably satisfied.

Driving from Jerusalem to Jericho to Beit Shean along the windswept sand over the tar roadway of the West Bank in a non-air-conditioned car with temperatures soaring more than 100 degrees was sweaty and arduous. Yet it gave me a chance to see a portion of the country that was slowly being brought back to agricultural life as Israelis and Arabs worked diligently on this stubborn soil, which needed above everything else lots of water. The military kept a constant guard against terrorists, who might try to enter from Jordan, whose purplish hills I could see along the entire route. I often picked up soldiers as companions to ride on these lonely treks, particularly when I drove at night. On some occasions, Emma did not accompany me.

These lonely rides jogged my memory about a quotation from Laurence Sterne's *A Sentimental Journey,* written in the eighteenth century: "I pity the man who can travel from Dan to Beersheba and cry 'tis all barren'; and so it is: and so is all the world to him who will not cultivate the fruits it offers."

After the unhappy Yom Kippur War, Israelis and world Jewry no longer expressed the same euphoria that we had found following the unprecedented victory in the Six-Day War in 1967. Too many soldiers had died or were permanently disabled. The economy was sluggish. The war brought no resolution of the political problems with neighboring Arab states. People wanted to take their minds off these dismal memories. They wanted to concentrate on improving their fortunes—buying cars, buying larger and better apartments and homes, furnishing them with costly modern equipment and attractive art. The day of poverty, sarcrificing, and doing without are a thing of the past for hundreds of thousands, who had the ability to make it. Yet whenever I traveled about the country, I could still see large pockets of poorer Jews, who did not have the wherewithal to add to their meager possessions, let alone luxuries. The contrast was widening. Hopefully community centers could prevent and overcome the breach.

Chicago Black Israelites

While in Dimona, I met Ben Ami Carter, the imperious leader of the Black Israelites, dressed in his white robe, turban, girdle, jewelry around his neck, carrying a staff, in the lobby of the center. From the original small group of twenty that had arrived in Israel in 1968, they numbered six hundred in 1975, including an influx of more illegals. Being fruitful, they increased with a large number of children born in Israel. Carter claimed they were discriminated against. True, these blacks were unwanted by the Israelis and presented serious social problems, but Israel had yet found no way of ousting them, due in large part to the intervention of American Jewish communal relations organizations that felt such a move would exacerbate fragile relations between Jews and blacks in the United States and give Israel another black eye amongst many of the world's nations. The Black Israelites did not claim to be Jews, but asserted they were the predecessors of the original Jews who inhabited ancient Israel. They professed no loyalty to the state, yet they wanted to live there and enjoy all the benefits of residence.

Carter was reluctant to be interviewed. I confined my conversation to listening to what the Chicago Israelites were doing within their own segregated community in Dimona. I could see that some were in the center that morning to do their wash in the automatic machines the center had installed for the benefit of its members. The women, despite the workaday tasks, were dressed in colorful costumes and turbans. According to the center's director, none of them ever presented behavior problems when they used the center's facilities. They did not join any other activities, under orders from Carter. Carter told me that he did not know any Ethiopian Jews in Israel and had no contacts with them.

I have written about the Chicago Israelites in my book *Black Jews in America* (1978).

* * *

We went to the Har-El Reform synagogue in Jerusalem on a Friday night for services. On a previous visit, several years before, the service, attracting mostly Americans, was largely in English. There was mixed seating. No *kippahs* were worn. A few donned *tallesim*. In other words, it resembled a classic Reform congregation in the States.

This evening, all had changed. The entire service was in Hebrew, including the Dvar Torah. The rabbi wore a *kippah* and *tallit*. Most of the men in the congregation wore a *kippah*. There was still mixed seating. More Hebrew was chanted than in many of the Conservative congregations we attended in the States. Reform Judaism in Israel, despite its inability to obtain formal recognition by the traditional rabbinate, was obviously moving, in speech and costume, to the religious right.

As we left the synagogue, we asked a young couple in Hebrew how to find a certain street. He gave us instructions in excellent English. Emma asked him where he had learned to speak it so well. "In America, where I was a shaliach for several years." "Where in America?" asked Emma. "It is a place you never heard of," he replied. "Try me," she responded persistently. "Gloversville, New York" he replied. We then greeted each other with enthusiasm, for they had lived in my hometown. They knew my family intimately; in fact, he considered my brother Milton, who was the president of the synagogue, his best friend. It is a little Jewish world after all.

* * *

The Jewish Agency had a conference in Israel during June 1975. No mention was made of Ethiopian Jews at the meetings, although I raised the subject with a number of delegates.

* * *

I attended a meeting at the Journalists House in Jerusalem on June 22, where the topic was "Are Samaritans, Karaites, and Falashas Jews?" The chairman was a white-bearded rabbi from Natanya. In his opening comments, he stated the following: "The Samaritans are not Jews. The Falashas are Jews. The only question to consider this evening is whether the Karaites are Jews." No Ethiopian Jews were invited to the meeting. None were in the audience. Karaites attended in large numbers, and carried on a vigorous debate with the chairman and hecklers during the entire evening.

* * *

Herman (Hy) and Janet Sainer were in Israel. They are old friends and professional colleagues going back to the 1930s. We drove together to Kfar Blum and stayed overnight. Saadia Gelb, an old friend and member of the kibbutz, in surveying the land and the scenery, while standing on the walk of the handsome swimming pool, told me: "I am a wealthy man. My chaverim and I own all this." He swept his arms in a complete circle. "What more could a man want in this world?" Before 1967, the kibbutz members had to defend themselves day and night from the Syrian soldiers and terrorists shooting down from the heights that bordered their well-cultivated land and fine buildings on the edge of the Jordan River.

While in the area, we drove up to the top of Mount Hermon for the first time. As we rode up the mountain roads to the ski lift, we passed Israeli military outposts. Not too far away, we could see where the Syrians had dug in with their own observation posts. Not a shot was fired that day on the beautiful and quiet mountain.

In the Druze villages we drove through, the people were occupied with their own affairs and no one paid any attention to our passing vehicle. We did not see another civilian automobile going up or coming down Mount Hermon.

Dr. Salo Wittmayer Baron

On July 1, 1975, there was a party at Hebrew University honoring Dr. Salo Wittmayer Baron, the distinguished Jewish historian, on his eightieth birthday. Having studied under Baron at the Graduate School of Jewish Social Work in 1930–32, I was asked to represent his former students and speak on this occasion. I recalled Baron as a sterling lecturer, who never came to class with notes but spoke without interruption for an hour and a half, then answered our questions during the last thirty minutes. I have previously mentioned that he had given me an assignment to read all of Graetz and Dubnov, eight volumes by two eminent Jewish historians, which I did during the summer of 1931, so that I could fill the vast lacunae in my limited knowledge of Jewish historical events. Thereafter whenever we met from time to time over the years, he always greeted me with cordiality.

Baron had invited me to be a participant in the 1974 Tel Aviv University seminar on the subject *Violence and Defense in the Jewish Experience* (a volume printed in 1976). I confessed to owning all the books he had written, as well as those about him, and to having read great portions of all of them. As I write this, he has passed his ninetieth birthday, universally receiving all the well-deserved honors. Unhappily, his wonderful wife, Jeanette, whom I also knew quite well, passed away in 1985, depriving him of a loving companion and literary collaborator.

On Friday, July 4, I might have been killed, had it not been for a fortunate meeting with Jeanette Baron. She stopped me on upper Ben-Yehudah Street in Jerusalem and asked me to write a paper on Jewish social work in the United States for *Jewish Social Studies*, which she edited. She was also its president. Standing together, we spent some time talking about the paper, which was eventually presented and published under the title "American Jewish Communal Services: 1776–1976" in vol. XXXVIII, nos. 3 and 4 (Summer–Fall 1976). While engaged in conversation, we heard a blast, and ambulances with sirens shrieking at the other end of the street—Zion Square—a quarter of a mile away. If she had not detained me, I would have been in a shop in the square picking up a travel bag which I had left for repairs, a shop whose windows and facade were shattered. Thirteen people were killed and seventy-five wounded.

* * *

On July 11, while in Jerusalem, I received a cable that Louis Kraft, a former Pelham resident, a long-time colleague, and in later years an intimate friend, had died. The cable asked whether I could return to the U.S. and deliver the eulogy. It was impossible. Yet I wish I had told the story of his life and where our fortunes intersected. While I knew Louis since 1930, he had in the early years unstated reservations toward me, when he headed the National Jewish Welfare Board. His attitude changed radically once he left that post. He told me that he should have hired me for the staff in a top position. It might have made vast differences in my career as well as the character of the organization. As a resident of Pelham, we saw each other frequently. We conducted programs together at our synagogue.

Louis was a warm, informed, hard-working expert, who was largely responsible for the shape and growth of the Jewish Community Center movement. He sent me lengthy letters from Geneva, when he worked there for the Americn Jewish Joint Distribution Committee, reestablishing Jewish communities and building Jewish communal centers in Europe after the war. He wanted me to succeed him in that post, but I could not leave my work with Federation, which was just beginning to bloom. He gave me some books that I treasured. His letters to me are important, and someday they should be published, perhaps after the people he referred to have passed away.

Ashkenazi Chief Rabbi Shlomo Goren

I had been trying for several years to get prominent American traditional rabbis to approach Ashkenazi Chief Rabbi Shlomo Goren to associate himself with the statement issued by his colleague, Sephardic Chief Rabbi Ovadia Joseph, that the Falashas were Jews. I hoped that if they were to make this a joint decree, the government of Israel would be forced to declare the Ethiopians Jews and thus eligible to come to Israel under the Law of Return. This would then hopefully initiate the long-neglected and delayed aliyah for Ethiopian Jews. All of these "emissaries" returned from Israel indicating that Goren would not issue such a ukase. Since his appointment to the highest rabbinical post, he had been feuding with Joscph, so he had no disposition to join his rival even on this stubborn human issue.

Rabbi Isaac N. Trainin, my former colleague at Federation, was in Israel and told me that he and others had also tried to influence Goren, but without success. Trainin, however, gave me a lead that ultimately changed the situation completely. He told me to contact Rabbi Charles Weinberg, an American, who had become an important aide of Goren. I sent Weinberg a letter and received a call inviting me to meet him in Goren's office at the Hechel Shlomo, the seat of the Chief Rabbinate in Jerusalem. I assumed that I would be meeting Goren personally, but instead found Weinberg alone. He asked whether I would like to sit in

Goren's chair. I declined with the comment: "I'm not seeking the Chief Rabbinate post, but only a meeting with His Eminence". Apparently other visitors like the distinction of briefly occupying that seat.

Weinberg, an articulate, gracious, insinuatingly persuasive, man—and, I understand, wealthy besides—told me how sympathetic he was to my concern for the Ethiopian Jews, Nonetheless he made an outrageous proposal: that Goren would probably find it easier to join the crusade if all doubts as to their Judaic authenticity could be dispelled. He said that if I issued a statement that the Falashas were *not* Jews but wanted to become Jews, thereafter they would simply go through a formal conversion, and there would then be no further question as to their status. They would come to Israel without fetters.

The enormity of this outrageous proposal must have shot my blood pressure up to threatening heights. I rose from my seat, livid with rage. "You tell the rabbi that if he dares to set foot in the United States, I will see to it that every meeting at which he appears is picketed with signs testifying to his prejudical views that the black Beta Israel of Ethiopia are not Jews. Furthermore, I am sending a letter to the Internal Revenue Service of the United States, informing them that all religious institutions under the domain of Goren are unworthy of receiving tax-exempt funds, because they are glaringly prejudiced against accepting black Ethiopian Jews in Israel on racial grounds."

Weinberg thought I would have a heart attack. He quieted me down and tried to appease me by saying that he would arrange a meeting with Goren as soon as possible. My anger was not abated. I was not sure whether Weinberg would or could carry out his promise. I misjudged him. Several days later, he called to tell me that he had set up a meeting with Rabbi Goren for August 10.

Emma was afraid that I would so antagonize the rabbi that he might excommunicate me from the Jewish fold. Several days before, another rabbi had placed a Jew in *cherem* (excommunication) for daring to challenge a statement that the rabbi had issued.

In any event, when I told Dr. Aryeh Tartakower what I had accomplished, he was amazed and told me that since I had achieved the impossible, he would like to be present. I took him along, hoping he would say nothing. He was silent throughout the session.

Goren was a short but imposing man, with a photogenic black-and-white beard. He greeted me effusively. What language should we speak—Hebrew, Yiddish, English? I told him I preferred English. What would I like to drink—coffee, tea, soda? I answered coffee. Weinberg, Tartakower, and I were seated in a semicircle around his desk, but he remained standing. Suddenly, he raised both hands and face heavenward and almost shouted: "All my life I have had a vision of the return of the Falasha to Israel"; then turning toward me, he said in a lower voice: "Do you know that three years ago, I wrote a memorandum to the government urging them to bring the Falashas to this country?" This was to inform me indirectly that he had been a friend of a Falasha aliyah before Rabbi Joseph. I did not ask for a copy of the memo.

While I had not expected either of these statements, I was still not taken aback. I replied in a clear and calm voice: "I had come to quarrel with you, but now I find that you are on my side." He quickly responded: "It was always so. What can I do to help?"

I told him that we had seven Ethiopian Jews in Beersheba. They had been in the country for more than six months, learning skills in a chemical plant, and that the local rabbi was holding up granting them official residence cards. They had also completed their Jewish studies, including Hebrew-language instruction. He reached for the phone, spoke to the rabbi in Hebrew. The next day, the young men became bona fide residents of Israel.

He said that the Falashas—that was the term he used throughout—would need my help in recruiting Israelis and American Jews to make sure that the newcomers—I presumed that he meant those who would be coming in the future—would not only receive instruction in Hebrew and preparation for a vocation, but would be taught what was necessary to keep them in the traditional Jewish fold. I offered to assist in that effort.

When I asked him for a formal statement reiterating what I had just heard from his mouth, he took my arm and replied that it was not necessary. What he had said in the privacy of that room was now public, having been made in the presence of three witnesses—Berger, Tartakower, and Weinberg. I reluctantly accepted this as final and didn't pressure him. We left with great cordiality. I have never seen Goren since.

Yet, I don't trust officials. As it says in the psalms, "Put not thy faith in princes." I hurriedly returned to our apartment, gave Emma the good news, and typed up a letter of thanks, which incorporated what he had said. Tartakower was impressed with what I wrote, did not suggest any changes, and asked whether he could sign it with me. I agreed.

This was the letter:

August 15, 1975

His Eminence Rabbi Shlomo Goren
Chief Rabbi of Israel
Jerusalem.

Dear Rabbi Goren:
On behalf of the Israeli and American committees for the Ethiopian Jews, we wish to thank you for your gracious reception on our visit to your personal headquarters last Sunday, August 10.

We were uplifted by your eloquent remarks that you have long had a messianic vision of the return of the Falashas to Israel and that three years ago, before your elevation to the Chief Rabbinate, you had written a memorandum proposing that steps be taken to achieve this laudable objective.

Your plan for bringing them to Israel and providing them with instruction in Hebrew and Judaism following which they would automatically receive the certificate of conversion, is one to which we subscribe.

Your suggestion that there be recruited a group of inspiring teachers from amongst the Ethiopian Jews, Israelis and Jews from other foreign lands, to assist in their educational development is also a plan which we heartily endorse.

As we pointed out, the Ethiopian Jews have already made an excellent aliyah. They have a capacity for the most rapid acquisition of the Hebrew language. They are now prospering in schools and universities, on jobs and in the assimilation of Israeli customs and religious practices.

The government ministries have affirmed their right to immigrate to Israel and will assist them in their absorption. The Jewish Agency has agreed to fund the costs of their immigration. Industrial, commerical and communal institutions have offered to provide them with specialized training and employment.

So with your valuable collaborative efforts, there should not be a single voice of dissent with respect to bringing this too long isolated section of the Jewish world to Israel. They have suffered every disability—political, economic, educational, medical—for their strict adherence to our ancient faith. The utmost speed is essential before revolution, civil war, Arab-Moslem persecution and Christian Missionaries liquidate their existence in Ethiopia.

Your humane leadership in this noble venture is reverently appreciated.

Shalom:

Graenum Berger, Chairman
American Association for Ethiopian Jews

Dr. Arieh Tartakower, Chairman
Israel Association for Ethiopian Jews

Thereafter, whenever Goren was asked what his policy was on Ethiopian Jews, he showed them the above letter. Later he issued a number of affirmative statements to the press. He could no longer contain it as a private matter. Even the mighty can eventually be conquered.

My only regret was that I assented to the concept of "conversion." When I met with Goren, he implied that all he meant was their obtaining a knowledge of Hebrew and of contemporary Judaism, but it turned out to be something more—taking a drop of blood from the males and immersion, *mikvah,* for both men and women. It became a sticky issue in later years.

Rabbi Mordecai Menahem Kaplan

In July 1975, I was walking in Rahavia, when I saw shuffling up the street the familiar figure of Rabbi Dr. Mordecai Menahem Kaplan, my teacher at the Graduate School of Social Work in 1930–32. Rabbi Kaplan introduced the revolutionary ideology of Reconstructionism into Jewish life and for more than half a century had shaken up the religious Jewish world by emphatically preaching that a new approach would have to be made to the Jewish people, if they were to continue as a life force into the future. Kaplan was ninty-four years old when I blocked his path. He stopped, lowered his glasses, and peered at me for a second. "Berger," he alertly said, as if he met me every day, "Are you writing?" "Yes, Rabbi Kaplan." "Then you will be remembered." There had been no "hello" or "shalom." As always he got right to the point. I told him what I had been writing and what was now on my agenda—chiefly the Ethopian Jews. He told me that had it not been for his writings, his views would not have been so universally noted and accepted. Then he moved on to the post office.

I recalled his having told his students in 1930–32 that unless they wrote what they had to say and had it published, they would have little influence on the course of events.

While Kaplan was always in the public eye, my impression of him was that he was a private man, with a tendency to withdrawal. I met him many times over the course of forty-five years, but I never really knew him intimately. Even when we spoke on a common platform, our conversation was "shop" and not about our personal lives. I always regarded him as one of the few influential Jewish leaders and intellectuals of the twentieth century, particularly for his evaluation of the condition of the Jewish people and offering a prescription for the resolution of their inner problems. He saw Jewish life as an ever evolving religious civilization. He died at the age of 103 in 1984.

Henry and Mildred Rosenberg

Henry and Mildred Rosenberg, of Manhattan, whom we had inspired with the Ethiopian Jewish cause, and who together went to Ethiopia to see if they could rescue some of them, after which they flew to Jerusalem, rented the apartment next to ours. We saw this energetic couple daily. More and more they grew in heroic proportions as they rescued hundreds of Ethiopian Jews during the next ten years. They had a host of friends in Israel. Mildred, as a nurse, had served in the Haganah before and as the state was being established in 1948. Her first husband was an Israeli physician. Henry, an attorney in Manhattan, had also been divorced. They married, sharing many similar interests and adventures.

They had arranged for two young Ethiopian Jews to come to Israel. Working with Israel and the Jewish Agency was at best an uncertainty when dealing with Ethiopian Jews. When the two young men arrived in Athens, while a promise had been made, no one was there to meet them. Greek officials forced them to return to Addis Ababa.

One of them had the courage to try again. This time, with a new ticket, provided once more by the AAEJ, he was met in Athens. If not, we would have made it a public issue. He changed planes to Israel. He was given a rough time at Lod, was interrogated at length. Finally, near midnight, after we had been waiting for more than four hours, he emerged. Hezi Ovadia, Henry, Mildred, Emma, and I greeted him. We were told to take him to a hotel in Jaffa, where the Jewish Agency housed new immigrants. It was not a prepossessing hostelry. Emma, over the manager's objections, inspected his room and found clean sheets on the bed in an unattractive chamber. The proprietor was not amused by her investigation and asked her: "What were you expecting, the Hilton?"

Most restaurants were closed. We took him to the only one that was open, a crummy place next to the hotel, which had not been swept all day, and was populated at this hour of the morning by whores and pimps. Our new friend was so delighted to be in Israel, the land of his prayers, that everything astonished and pleased him. He kept asking: "Are all these people really Jews?" We shamefacedly acknowledged that they were. We did not reveal the nature of their questionable professions. The next day Hezi saw to it that he was billeted with an Ethiopian Jewish family.

The JDC Breakthrough

While my diary and files indicate that I had scores of meetings in Israel with the local committee, with officials, with prominent American Jewish leaders, and that all kinds of promises were being made to bring about an Ethiopian Jewish migration, nothing came of all these sessions. Increased activity was taking place in Ethiopia, as a result of the additional funds the AAEJ, the JDC, and the Falasha Welfare Federation of London was providing, yet even this was hardly enough, about $2 per capita. To perform the tasks properly would require the presence of an international organization like the JDC. It could attract funds, had contacts and knowhow. My efforts to get such involvement had so far failed, although in 1974 the JDC had upped its stipend to $25,000 per year.

On October 9, I was at the King David Hotel on other business, when I was tipped off that the top leadership of the JDC was holding a meeting at the hotel. I learned the room number, took the elevator to the third floor, rapped on the door, and opened it to find Jack D. Weiler, the president, before a mound of papers. Donald M. Robinson, the treasurer and president-elect, was there along with Samuel Haber, the executive vice-president, Harold Trobe, Ralph Goldman, and Arnulf L. Pins, the professionals in charge of the Israel-JDC-Malben offices.

Weiler, whom I knew quite well, looked up: "Graenum, what do you want?" I replied: "Thirty minutes of your time to tell the Ethiopian Jewish terrible story." "I'll give you fifteen minutes. Talk fast. We are busy." I was there for forty-five minutes. Robinson, who had never heard about the Falashas, was responsible for prolonging my stay, as he wanted to know more details. Weiler finally asked: "How much will it cost the JDC?" I answered: "$250,000 in the first year." Weiler laughingly replied: "You'll take less." I left feeling I might have broken through. At the annual meeting in December 1975 in New York, the JDC appropriated $100,000 and agreed to set up an office in Ethiopia.

* * *

It was a busy six months in Israel. We met old and made new friends every day. We ate prodigious quantities of food as hosts and as guests. We bought scores of paintings, artifacts, and religious objects for ourselves, our family, and friends. We went to the theatre, concerts, ballet. We took a few days off for a holiday in Sharm Es Sheikh—Ophira, a paradise Israel had conquered in 1973, built up, then abandoned with the Camp David peace agreement. We celebrated Rosh Hashanah, Yom Kippur, and Sukkot in several synagogues, getting the flavor of the different ethnic groups and how they each uniquely approached these holy days. We found time to read books, which we took off the shelves of the several apartments we occupied.

I wrote letters by the score, kept detailed typed records on all meetings, so that the Ethiopian Jewish story would be as accurate as the human pen and mind would permit. We entertained Esther Wube, an Ethiopian Jew, and Aaron Hollander, a sabra of Polish-Jewish parentage, on many Saturdays for lunch on their days off, as they struggled to find a way of getting married in a country that still frowned on such an interracial Jewish union. They were married the following year.

While I tried shuttle diplomacy to settle the contentions between three conflicting Ethiopian Jewish factions, I was unsuccessful. While different, the problem had not been resolved in 1986, when they numbered 16,000 and not 165 as in 1975.

Despite bouts with a variety of not-too-serious illnesses, we ended a glorious half a year with some important tasks completed. However, the aliyah of Ethiopian Jews was immobile.

A Safari, an Accident, Ethiopia

Emma and I had decided months before to complete our six-month working holiday in Israel with a safari to Kenya and Tanzania (one could not get into Uganda), then fly to Ethiopia for a week, followed by a meeting in Paris with the Jewish Colonization Association (ICA), which wanted my report on Ethiopia. The association, at the stimulation of Mordecai Paran, its director for Israel, was considering the possibility of setting up a moshav for Ethiopian Jews once they arrived in Israel. We had taken our medical shots, which included vaccination for smallpox, bubonic plague, cholera, tetanus, and typhoid, and had bought malaria pills. To obtain visas to Kenya and Tanzania, we had to go to the British consulate in East Jerusalem, for Israel had no formal diplomatic relations with these countries. I did not ask for a visa to Ethiopia, because I had been informed that one could have his passport stamped at the airport on arrival in Addis Ababba. I dealt mostly with Arabs rather than Britons in the consular office. A strange experience as they questioned me as to my mission. "Purely as a tourist," I emphasized. Israel's El Al, despite the break in relations, was still flying to Nairobi en route to its final destination in Johannesburg, South Africa.

We flew directly from Lod to Nairobi. From the airport the terrain appeared to be a vast plain with little tree cover. A few animals—giraffes, antelopes—appeared out of our taxi window as we sped to the Norfolk Hotel, a famous older hostelry. Kenya, as we were to observe later, was one huge unfenced zoo. The center of the city itself was modern, displaying the pronounced influence of the English. Hundreds of the smaller shops were owned and operated by Indians. In the epicenter, there were a few skyscrapers and a new hotel-convention complex. Across from our hotel was the university. A new synagogue nestled nearby.

Our hotel room was located in a court and most pleasant. The food, and especially the coffee, was superior. As we drank our first cup of Kenyan coffee—and I drank six cups a day—the flavor was of a character that we had never tasted. Emma and I agreed that this was the best coffee in the world. Subsequent meals in Kenya and Tanzania provided further confirmation. As we had only a week, we made immediate arrangements to go on a six-day safari with a small group.

The next day we left for the south. The Land Rover had a top that slid open, so that when we reached the wild-animal terrain, we could stand up to take closeups of every animal that ventured close enough. Some, like the lions, did. We were not wearing the conventional khaki clothing that marked the sophisticated safariite, but relied on our lightweight, miscellaneous wardrobe, easily washable. We soon learned why khaki was preferable gear. The vehicles were not tight enough to keep out the seeping dust. Each night when we reached our destination, we had to bathe and wash our clothes, since we could not shake the khaki-colored sand off or out. With khaki we could have worn the same garments for several days.

Our driver, a Kenyan named Thomas, drove us through Masai country, where we saw the almost naked natives, in colorful dress, necklaces, spears, and earrings, hung through their carefully nurtured, elongated ears. They drove their cattle, a mark of their wealth, over a countryside that looked overgrazed, a veritable dust bowl. Thornwood and acacia trees were the only flora. Impala gazelles were everywhere. The giraffes kept their distance, but they could not hide their long necks in the bush. We stopped at a Masai village at the border of Tanzania, bought some crude jewelry, and took some pictures. All had to be paid before their images were snapped.

Tanzania was another adventure. It was a primitive state going through a socialist revolution. Villages and farms were being collectivized under the supervision of Chinese advisers. It was difficult to determine whether the natives appreciated the change, because they did not respond to our questions. We bought two pieces of Makonde carvings from ebony wood. He wanted to sell me another in exchange for an Arab-made belt for which I had paid $3 in a shuk in East Jerusalem. The belt, not money, enticed the carver. Since I couldn't find a belt to hold up my pants, the deal had to be called off. Animals and birds, which we had never seen before, included ostriches, red-eyed deer, and yellow-necked fowl. We ended our day's trip at the Ngorongoro Crater Lodge, at the peak of the Ngorongoro crater, not far from the Uganda border. As we drove up the twisting, ever-turning spectacular mountain road to an elevation of 9,000 feet, water bucks and water buffaloes greeted us at the roadside.

The hotel bedded down 120 guests drawn from over the world, mostly from Europe. We drank a native vodka before dinner and then ordered the local special, zebra steaks, which proved to be tougher than the deer and horse meat that I had eaten elsewhere. Guards were posted around the well-lighted outdoor area surrounding the hotel, and guests were warned not to go out at night as dangerous animals prowled about the building.

A local driver steered us down a treacherous path of the crater, which stretched east, north, and south beyond our ability to see its perimeter, bringing us to its 102-square-mile bottom, 2,000 feet below the rim, to the greatest outdoor zoo on this globe. Wildebeests, zebras, Thompson gazelles by the thousands, jackals, hippopotammuses, hyenas, lions, water buffalo, guinea fowls, ostriches, cheetahs, and many others were seen and photographed. We envied the families in other vehicles, who had brought their children. While wonder was discernible in the faces of the adults, it turned into ecstasy as the children stared at the animals. We watched a cheetah stalk a gazelle, catch and rip the body to pieces. We saw lions finishing the remains of a meal, a large wildebeest, who could with patience be run down. We listened to tales of former hunters, who had come years before, when shooting animals was permitted. It was now strictly forbidded by law. Poachers, when caught, were severely punished.

We left the crater too soon. It would have been worth another day or even two, even though we would see the same scenes. It was an unforgettable sight. We drove through the mountainous, dusty roads to the Ngorongoro Safari Lodge near Karafu Gibai, run by a Scotsman. He had served in the Royal Air Force, came to Tanzania, bought a 250-acre estate, raised coffee beans. The coffee that evening was of the same delicious quality and taste that we had enjoyed in Nairobi. They had built cottages to accommodate ten guests. Isolated, we felt that it was as much to have someone to talk to as to derive additional income. The meal, served in family style with them at the table, was deluxe. The hosts didn't mind talking about their life. The collectivization of the estates was going apace and would envelop them. They were planning to leave and go off to Australia to start life anew with another farm.

The next morning our Land Rover took us through the dense rain forest, grasslands, and marshes, where we saw baboons, lions, velvet monkeys, maribou storks, pelicans, herons, bushrocks, huge lizards, more impalas, and our first elephants. The elephant herd was startling. The huge masses of gray-tan-covered hard flesh moved ponderously with great noise, overturning small trees in their path. Yet as the young ones rubbed close to their parents, they hardly seemed like live monsters.

Over the stretches, we saw relatively few people. Occasionally, despite the dustbowl, with the whirling spirals that blotted out the land in every direction, one did see what appeared to be cultivated farms and coffee plantations. We stopped at one collective village, where some central facilities had been provided for marketing. Other amenities seemed to be lacking.

After lunch at the Lake Manyara Lodge in the midst of a well-wooded area, we rode through Arusha, a modern city, exactly halfway between Cairo and Capetown, and then eastward toward Mount Kilimanjaro, passing red bucks, giraffes, and warthogs. We ended our trip in the middle of a flat prairie facing the peak from the picturesque Momella cottages with thatched roofs, built by a studio to house the staff and actors for a movie titled *Hatari*. A talkative French hunter kept us up for hours relating tales of the region.

The next morning we visited a fenced-in animal farm, where we saw animals that were not visible to us in the wilds, but gave us an added dimension of wildlife still roaming in this region. We then twisted and turned on dusty roads, where the land was abundant with wild animals like the gorex, zebras, gazelles, cheetahs, until we reached the famous animal reservation (without fences) across the border in Kenya at Amboselli, spread over 1,000 square miles. A herd of elephants greeted us, while drinking at the waterhole near the hotel, with a dramatic view of Kilimanjaro in the background. After changing from our quarter-inch dust covered clothes into fresh gear, we had a sumptuous dinner, listened to a lecture by Professor S. Altman of the University of Chicago on "The Social System of Baboons," a perfect intellectual way to end a strenuous day.

When we toured this region we added to our list of animals and birds the rhinoceroses, crested cranes, foxes, cobras, black-breasted bustas, egrets, and ugly scavenging vultures swooping down to feast on carrion.

The people on our tight little bus were pleasant. We drank to each other before meals, ate at the same table, related personal histories. While we exchanged addresses and wrote a card or two after we returned home, we never developed any long-term relationships.

An Almost Tragic Accident

We returned to Nairobi to learn that the next day, a Monday, was a holiday. It was the anniversary of Kenyatta's assumption of power. Everything would be closed. The only event was a big parade, and we were advised to get to Kenyatta Park early if we wanted to find a place to sit on the hillside. The following morning we were scheduled to leave for Ethiopia.

Emma and I walked leisurely to the viewing grounds, where VIPs with tickets had reserved seats on a large reviewing stand. There were few people on our arrival. We met four young Ethiopians, whom I easily recognized, having been in that country in 1965. They had escaped from Ethiopia, because young people were not safe if they assembled on the streets. During the first year of the revolution (1974), the military dictatorship was fearful of demonstrations by the young. If they came from families which had connections with the former Emperor Haille Selassie, or had a college education, they were suspect. The universities had been closed to control student activists. If they did not immediately join the revolutionary movement, they were in trouble. The young men fit these categories. They described their escape route of some two thousand miles. I took detailed notes and immediately sent this information to Dr. Aryeh Tartakower and Hezi Ovadia in Israel with the recommendation that this route be used by Ethiopian Jews who were prepared to leave that country for Israel. I mingled with the assembling crowd. Except for one other white family, the throng was entirely black. I took photos. Later I read that several hundred thousand people were gathered to greet the presidential parade. By the time his car passed us, the hillside was filled. We sat at the bottom with good visibility.

As Kenyatta's car passed us in a colorful parade, everyone on the hill stood up. A swarm of bees appeared. Someone lost his footing at the top of the hill above us. Suddenly there was a snowballing avalanche with hundreds of people rolling down. This took only seconds. Before we could even turn around, we were hit. I was thrown forward and free, but Emma was buried in the bottom of a heap. I knew where she was because she was wearing a red jacket. There must have been twenty people on top of her. The Ethiopian young men, also thrown forward, but free, began to pull people off the pile, and we finally reached her. Her face was in the earth, dirty and bloody. Her glasses were broken. She was obviously hurt and in pain, suffering from shock. We carried her to a first aid tent a hundred feet away, where I washed her face. An ambulance arrived within a few minutes.

I rode with Emma to the Kenyetta public hospital, where hundreds of people were already lying on the floor as a result of the tragic slide. Emma was placed on a rolling cot. I could see at a glance that this was no place for her and asked where she could get good and immediate treatment. A doctor suggested the English Nairobi hospital. Luckily a cab was there, and the Ethiopians and I carried her to the taxi and rushed to the hospital, thankfully a short distance away.

Emma was remarkably controlled despite the excruciating suffering. As we came into the hospial, a Sikh ophthamologist was at the desk. He took one quick look, and before she was even registered, he rushed her up to the operating room to treat her eye, which had been damaged by the broken glasses frame. Luckily for her he was there and competent, so that her eye recovered and he could remove the bandage in a few days. It was splendid and successful, albeit delicate surgery. X-rays revealed two broken ribs and a slight fracture of the skull. The orthopedist, an Englishman, was also excellent, as was the internist, another Indian. Four people were killed and over one hundred injured in that accident.

To make sure that I had the best physicians, I called the U.S. Embassy, informed them I was both an American citizen and a brother of Ambassador Samuel D. Berger, whom the American ambassador knew. It never hurts to call this office. His wife came to see Emma and sent flowers. Lisa Rozsa, a Jewish woman who was a volunteer visitor to the sick, on learning that Emma was Jewish informed the town and a stream of visitors arrived. Rachela Szlapak, the owner of the Fairview Hotel, a motherly type, took over completely. She brought Emma chicken soup and challah on Friday night.

Ethiopia

We were due in Ethiopia. I wired that we were delayed. When I learned from the doctors that Emma was going to make a good and rapid recovery, I decided to fly to Ethiopia for a couple of days and learn more about the condition of the Ethiopian Jews under the revolution.

Gershon Levy, director of the Falasha Welfare Association's operation in Ethiopia, whom I had met in Israel and recommended for this position, a program which the American Association for Ethiopian Jews was also supporting, met me at the airport. I checked in at the Hotel Ghion, where except for one other guest, I was the only tenant. Yona Bogale, the distinguished supervisor of education for the Ethiopian Jewish schools, whom I had met in Ethiopia in 1965, and with whom I corresponded, joined us, and for the next few hours they briefed me on what the revolution had wrought. The Jews were not better off, as some had thought or predicted. They told me that I could not get permission to fly into the interior, where the Jews were living in fear and harassment. Their hope of obtaining the individual tracts of land promised by the revolutionary regime would be unfulfilled in most cases, because the landlords had organized a counterrevolution. Other landless Ethiopians asserted that since their ancestors had once owned the land on which the Jews were now tenant farmers, they enjoyed historic prior rights as first claimants on the property. The areas in which the Jews lived were in political disarray, due to the counterrevolutionary and antigovernment groups seeking independence for Eritrea and Tigre. Guerillas were operating everywhere, intimidating peasants who did not immediately side with their efforts to control these regions. In this chaos, Shiftas, roving bandits, also preyed on whoever was helpless. They grabbed anything, everything, and ran.

Levy hoped to continue operating the Jewish schools and clinics in the villages, but everything was uncertain. He told me that he needed a lot more money than his current budget provided.

We had to talk in my hotel room, because Levy and Bogale were in fear that our conversation might be overheard. We searched my room for bugging equipment and found none. Nonetheless we talked in low voices. I was told not to use the phone, as every call was recorded.

I phoned the U.S. Embassy and spoke to the new ambassador, recently arrived, Arthur W. Hummel, Jr., whom I had met in Burma in 1971, where he occupied the same position. He was a friend of my brother Sam. We met at his office in Addis Ababba and conversed for several hours. I had learned more about the area from Levy and Bogale than he and his staff knew, because the embassy was fearful of sending anyone into the interior, as some foreigners had been taken hostage in recent weeks. He called a secretary to take down my comments. I gave him the names and addresses of Levy and Bogale, who somehow managed to go back and forth into the northern regions. It was clear that the United States did not look with favor on the revolution, hoped it would be short-lived. This error in judgment about the future ultimately led to the Ethiopian take-over of the major electronic surveillance bases that the United States had built, to the refusal to pay debts due the United States, and the cooling off of diplomatic relations as each country pulled out its respective ambassadors. The relationship had not improved in 1986.

I dined that evening with Jack and Kay Shelemay in another hotel, where we also had to speak in low voices, as they feared we might be overheard. Kay had come to Ethiopia some years before to study Ethiopian Jewish music and received a Ph.D. for her study and publication of that work. She received a grant from the National Foundation for Jewish Culture. I am a member of its board. She married Jack, who originally came from Aden along with his parents and siblings, after the Aden-Yemenites made it impossible for Jews to live at the tip of the South Arabian land mass following the creation of the State of Israel in 1948. A British citizen, well educated, he had been in a thriving family business in Addis Ababa, which along with considerable property was being gradually confiscated by the government. Emma and I had met the Shelemays on our previous trip to Ethiopia in 1965, so my visit was a reunion. Kay was leaving soon for the United States to take up a teaching career and hoped Jack would follow thereafter. The Shelemay brothers were literally held as hostages until they trained Ethiopians to take over their business—chiefly in leather. It would be several years before Jack and Kay were reunited in New York. Their contacts with the bulk of Ethiopian Jews were minimal. They did not know whether the Ethiopian Jews would be worse or better off as a result of the revolution. It was too dangerous for them to help the Ethiopian Jews leave the country.

I told Levy and Bogale that only a wholesale aliyah to Israel would save the Ethiopian Jews, that during the current political turbulence, it might be possible to get many of them out, and that they should work on that goal. Such a proposal fell on deaf ears, as far as Levy was concerned, but I suspected that Bogale probably agreed with me, although he did not know how to go about it. He had finally come to the unhappy conclusion that there was little possibility of developing an Ethiopian Jewish community of consequence in Ethiopia under a Marxist regime. My predictions proved true.

Kay Shelemay took me shopping, and I bought a number of excellent Ethiopian paintings and a beautiful native silver necklace for Emma, from which, with other African beads, Anita,, our daughter-in-law, eventually strung three exquisite necklaces for Emma, Sandra, our other daughter-in-law, and herself. Yona gave me a native basket made by his daughter.

I had no trouble flying in and out of Ethiopia, and felt that if I had more time, I would have found a way of getting into the interior around Gondar. While I called Emma each day at her hospital bed and learned that she was recovering quickly, I was eager to get back to be with her.

* * *

On my return, I learned that many of the two hundred Jews in Nairobi knew about Emma's accident, my presence, as well as my trip to Ethiopia. Emma would have to spend at least another week at the hospital, after which she would have to recover at a hotel for another ten days. On the very night of my return from Ethiopia, I had been invited to dinner at the Roszas. He was an architect and president of the synagogue, and she was in the business field. Seventeen people came after dinner to listen to my report on Ethiopia, among them Michael R. Kaufman, the East African correspondent for the *New York Times*, who had arrived in Nairobi a few days before. He was intrigued more by me than about the Ethiopian Jews and asked whether he could interview me the next day. When we met he told me that he had never thought that the first article he would dispatch to the *Times* would be about an American Jew and black Ethiopian Jews. His long, one-column story appeared in the *Times* on November 2, 1975. I received numerous inquiries following its publication.

To be closer to the hospital, Mrs. Szlapak recommended that we move into the Fairview Hotel, where she gave us a beautiful apartment at a cost far below the Norfolk. That is where Emma and I remained until we left Nairobi. When Emma could move around, we dined at several homes, including the Dovers, Israeli's unofficial "ambassador" to Kenya, where I pressed for the rescue of Ethiopian Jews. We attended the synagogue on Friday nights.

Andrew Torchia, the East African representative for the Associated Press, invited us for lunch, so he could interview me for a story on Ethiopian Jews.

Meanwhile I sat down with Professor Irving Gershenberg, an American teaching at the university, Mrs. Szlapak, and the Rosazas, and persuaded them to take care of any Ethiopian Jews who might escape via Nairobi. They were to provide housing, money for food and clothing and other incidentals, and airfare to Israel. I met with the Director of El Al in Nairobi to be sure he would issue tickets for travel to Israel and waive all formalities. I assured everyone that they would be reimbursed. Regrettably, they were not called upon to render any actual help. It was not until 1982 that Henry and Mildred Rosenberg, members of the AAEJ Board, who rescued hundreds of Ethiopian Jews from both Sudan and Ethiopia, used such facilities.

I bought a magnificent brass Ashanti group of figures of the king and his native servants, actually pieces used as "gold weights," for Emma, who collected such items. I tried to purchase old Ethiopian Bibles, but I could not get any confirmation of their Ethiopian Jewish authenticity. They looked too good and too new to be genuine antiques. I also suspected from a few signs that they were Christian Coptic. Obviously I could not read the Ge'ez script.

In Nairobi I developed vertigo. The doctors thought it might be a prelude to malaria. I was given medication for both ailments, which I consumed for some weeks after I returned to the States, when the vertigo disappeared and malaria never materialized.

Kenyan Jews, like all people with money, had difficulty in getting their money out of the country. I arranged to have all of my bills—and they were considerable—paid with money offered to me by Jewish friends in local currency and sent the dollars to various addresses in England and Israel.

I phoned Paris that I would not be able to meet with the board of ICA, and as a consequence nothing was done to provide a fund for the creation of a moshav for Ethiopian Jews in Israel.

We left behind friends with whom we have been corresponding for years. We flew first to London to break up the flight and to give Emma more rest. We then took a plane, or rather planes, which eventually came down in Buffalo, where Ramon lived. He had borrowed our car, after his own was demolished in an accident. We decided to give him our car, and after a few days of rest, bought a new Plymouth and drove back to New York.

While in Buffalo, I gave an impromptu lecture at the Jewish Community Center of Buffalo, where Ramon was the assistant executive director. This lecture, along with another at Ramon's home before a group of his friends, was on Ethiopian Jews. I had a number of acquaintances in Buffalo as a result of three previous visits, when I spoke to their boards on camps, centers, and social work.

By the time we reached Pelham, after an absence of seven months, Emma had completely recovered from an experience that she and I recall with horror, but which miraculously turned out well.

1976: The Bicentennial Year

After the years 1974 and 1975, with extended responsibilities abroad, travel over long distances, and Emma's injuries, the Bergers needed a rest. The Bicentennial year kept us in the States, except for a short visit to Canada on Ethiopian Jewish business. This didn't mean that it was without a great deal of activity, much of it centering around Ethiopian Jewry. I was frequently on the radio, on TV, writing articles, lecturing over many parts of the eastern seaboard, appearing at synagogues, universities, and private groups. Journalists, writers, photographers, students doing research visited our home.

That was how I first met William Patrick Halpern, a Jewish young man working on his Ph.D. at Berkeley, who researched a great deal of material from my copious files. He convinced me that Ethiopian Jews might be rescued via Sudan, suggesting that if they became refugees, they might eventually reach Israel. As one of a tiny team of two that we sent into Sudan in 1979, he initiated the rescue of thirty-two Ethiopian Jews, proving first of all that they were there, and demonstrating that they could be taken out and eventually land in Israel. Both views and facts were categorically opposed by Israeli and American Jewish leadership. Bill was tragically killed in Kenya in a motor accident. His last act there was to arrange for an Ethiopian Jewish young woman to leave the country.

* * *

It was the year that John A. Williams, the distinguished black writer and professor, came to my home to be briefed in detail about Ethiopian Jews, because he had been commissioned to write an article on the subject. In 1981, he wrote a play, *Last Flight from Ambober,* about Ethiopian Jews, in which I am one of the characters, named Gerber from Gloversville, New York.

* * *

Yehudah Avner, then in the Israeli Prime Minister's office (in 1984, he became the Israeli ambassador to Great Britain), called, and we met on several occasions while he was in New York. He assured me that the Israeli government was exploring all possible avenues for taking the Ethiopian Jews out of Ethiopia, but to no avail. Later I put him on my blacklist as an apologist for the do-nothing policy of the Israeli regime.

I attended major Jewish conferences, where it was still impossible to get the Ethiopian Jewish subject on the agendas. Emma and I, along with a few die-hards in the AAEJ, like the Gersons of New Orleans, would arrange a rump session and attract a small group to listen to our report on the plight of Ethiopian Jews. The General Assembly of the Council of Jewish Federations and Welfare Funds, meeting in Philadelphia, ironically on the anniversary of the American Revolution, was a prime example of the indifference of the Jewish leadership to this ever-serious problem.

* * *

True, the JDC had agreed to go into Ethiopia to expand services in 1975, but World ORT persuaded the JDC to relinquish this role and turn the burden over to them. ORT had projects in other African countries, so that it claimed it knew the terrain. What is more, it would be able to attract large-scale funds from a variety of governments, including that of the United States, which would preclude soliciting and using Jewish money. Both ideas were enticing. A year later, we began to regret supporting this change, because ORT had made the project nonsectarian and not in the exclusive interest of Ethiopian Jewry.

I was invited to Montreal to speak to Canadian ORT leaders, who had previously raised funds for the AAEJ. ORT had brought two Ethiopian Jews to Canada, employees of ORT in Ethiopia, to tell the story nationwide and thus help Canadian ORT raise funds both from Jews and from the Canadian government. On meeting the two Ethiopians, I quickly learned that one was not a Jew. A few days later he defected. He is still in Canada. I had all I could do to restrain the Jewish member of the team from doing likewise. He wanted to go to Israel. I argued at the time that if he did so, along with the defection of his companion, it would injure the ORT program in Ethiopia. Had I anticipated what would befall Ethiopian Jews under ORT's Ethiopian dominion, I would have counseled a different course. Since I believed in aliyah as the only way to save them, I should not have let another unworthy "loyalty" swerve me from that path. He eventually returned to Ethiopia.

Philip Habib

I met socially with Philip Habib at my brother Sam's home in Washington. Phil had risen to the third highest post in the State Department. I wanted to enlist his aid in getting Jews out of Ethiopia. We talked at some length. He gave me excellent counsel, but it involved having either Israel and/or several prominent American Jews, who were highly regarded by the Republican Administration, request the United States to undertake this task. Obviously, neither the AAEJ nor I stood high enough in Jewish communal circles to influence this course of action. I communicated this information to Yehudah Avner. Nothing was done about it. It would have to await my contact with the newly elected senator from Minnesota, Rudolph Boschwitz, in January 1979, through Bill Halpern, who was a personal friend of the senator, before any concrete rescue operations were undertaken, at first by the AAEJ and a few years later with the assistance of the U.S. government.

On April 30, 1985, I was to have attended the annual lecture at Georgetown University's Institute for Diplomacy in memory of my brother Sam. The speaker was Philip Habib, who had been Sam's political counselor in Korea in 1962, where I first met him, and a close friend of Sam's ever since. I could not attend, because of a sudden medical problem, which turned out to be a superficial phlebitis. Ramon represented me at the lecture and the dinner that followed. Habib met Ramon and said: "Tell your father that I spoke to Menachem Begin about the Falashas, as he had requested. I guess it helped save Ethiopian Jews." I had made this request to him in 1980 at the funeral of Sam in

Washington. Habib followed this up when he was shuttling between the various Middle Eastern countries in 1982, after the Israeli incursion into Lebanon. I always considered Habib a person who would carry out a serious request from me if he had the opportunity.

* * *

I presented a paper at the Conference on Jewish Social Studies on April 26, 1976, also as a kind of Bicentennial piece, entitled "American Jewish Communal Services 1776–1976: From Traditional Self-Help to Increasing Dependence on Government Support." It was widely distributed in a special printing. It was translated into Hebrew and circulated in Israel. It has been used by instructors in various graduate schools educating Jewish communal workers. The article was condensed and printed in the *Jewish Digest* (February 1978).

* * *

Jacob Behrman of the Behrman Publishing Company approached me to write a history of the Jews in America. He had read some of my writings and felt that I could assemble a work that could be used in Hebrew high schools as well as for the adult market. While I believe myself knowledgeable about the Jewish experience in America, this would have been a formidable task, requiring a great deal of additional research and writing, which would have taken several years out of my life. I turned down the offer to the regret of the publisher, who had more faith in me than I had in myself for creating such a volume.

* * *

While we were in Israel in 1975, we met an interestingly costumed character, an American black who had converted to Judaism. He had come to Israel, married a white woman, who prior to the marriage, had also been converted. He was preparing himself to be the "savior" of Ethiopian Jewry. He knew little Hebrew as yet and was equally deficient in knowledge of Jewish history, customs, and practices. He hoped to learn within a matter of months how to become a *mohel* (ritual circumciser) and a *shochet* (ritual slaughterer of animals and poultry), so he could perform these rites in Ethiopia. He knew nothing of Ethiopian Jews. He kept coming to our apartment each Saturday afternoon, although not invited, stayed, ate, drank too much, and entertained, in his amusing style and speech, whoever happened to be our guests. I finally ended these intrusive visits by telling him that I would not recommend him for any position in Ethiopia.

He subsequently left his wife, went to Ethiopia, and managed to enchant and persuade some Ethiopian Jews that he was genuine and influential and they should accredit him as a rabbi (they do not have rabbis in Ethiopia) and delegate him as their official and only fund-raiser in America.

When he showed up in the States, he called to tell me about his new credentials. I decided to meet him in Manhattan, where he showed me his papers, officially stamped by an Ethiopian Jewish priest. He was lavishly dressed in a blue-and-white robe with a massive turban topping his head. After reading his material, I told him that the documents were fraudulent, and if he attempted to raise any money on behalf of Ethiopian Jewry, I would expose him. He took my threats without a battle. On the way to the subway, where everyone on the streets looked at him with his outlandish garb, he told me he was penniless. I gave him $10, telling him that this was the last sum I would ever give him and the final contact we would ever have.

He tried to make some speeches on the west coast. I sent out a notice to likely prospects not to engage him. He had a gift for ingratiating himself easily with people. If left unchecked, he could do great harm to the Ethiopian Jews. I have not heard anything about him for many years.

* * *

After wearing the golf shoes I had bought in 1946 until they were worn out, I purchased a new pair. It did not improve my game, although they bore the name of Arnold Palmer. They did keep my feet dry. I liked golf, but with or without a cart, it required at least six hours of traveling and playing, much too much time to devote to a recreational pursuit. I dragged my clubs around each year in the car, but rarely swung more than a round or two each season. I have found it better to watch the experts play on TV than to get out on the course myself and struggle with a small ball and a heavy bag full of clubs.

20

Israel: 1977

WE WERE EAGER to return to Israel in 1977. Despite promises and promises, no Ethiopian Jews had arrived in Israel. My voluminous correspondence with Dr. Aryeh Tartakower constituted a mass of words, plans, meetings, but no aliyah. How much more I could do if I was on the scene in Israel, I did not know, for frustration had marked my previous labors. With the generous benefactions of several friends, we found a way to go to Israel within our modest resources. Louis and Sylvia Horwitz offered us their beautiful apartment on Ein Rogel Street, which gave us an unparalleled panoramic view of the Old City from the southern side. They also gave us the use of their car. They would be away for a month in Crete, where Sylvia was researching her forthcoming book on Evans, the archaeologist who rediscovered the Minoans. Then Tim Gidal tendered us his equally beautiful penthouse apartment on Nili Street, while he would be away in Europe for a month. For the third month, we rented an apartment on Alkalai Street in Rehavia, spacious, on the first floor with a nice garden. All three had extensive libraries.

Soon after we arrived on June 8, we plunged into a number of meetings with local committees, government officials, Jewish Agency bureaucrats, the American Jewish Committee, Ethiopian Jews, and representatives of the Falasha Welfare Association in England. Dr. Theodore (Ted) Norman, treasurer of the AAEJ, was in Jerusalem, so he joined me at many of these sessions. There was talk about absorption, perhaps establishing a kibbutz or a moshav, of making the Faitlovitch residence in Tel Aviv a permanent national Ethiopian Jewish headquarters, creating a scholarship fund for Ethiopian Jewish students entering higher education, of obtaining a Jewish Agency grant for the support of the local Ethiopian Jewish organization, such as it had done for other ethnic groups, and of arranging a mission to Ethiopia. At every meeting, secrecy and quiet diplomacy were stressed. No publicity was advocated. That is, by everyone except me. I thought the subject should no longer be under censorship, for keeping it secret had saved no lives, and if we were to obtain widespread support for rescuing Ethiopian Jews, the whole story must be widely ventilated in the press and other media, not only in Israel but abroad. I influenced no one.

At several private parties, where I broached the subject to high officials in the Israeli government, I found no enthusiasm, not even a lukewarm response, for aliyah. Worse still, there had been no improvement in the lot of the Ethiopian Jews in the three years since the revolution, even with ORT's presence in the country.

ORT

We were already getting disquieting news from Gershon Levi, who was directing the ORT program in Ethiopia. Gershon, a German Jew who settled in Israel, became an expert on agricultural programs in Ethiopia, where he had previously been assigned by the Israeli government. After meeting him in Israel, I strongly recommended to the Falasha Welfare Association that he head its program in Ethiopia. From Ethiopia Gershon warned us that ORT had adopted a nonsectarian path, was opening up all Jewish schools to the general population, and was employing more non-Jewish teachers; moreover, a non-Jew whom it had appointed to the top level of its administration was not favorably disposed to the Jews. Even the itinerant executive that ORT sent from Geneva to establish and supervise the project, while efficient, was not looking with favor on the extraordinary needs of Ethiopian Jews. ORT had already been assured of substantial support from non-Jewish sources, on conditions that contractually called for a nonsectarian approach. Because of the source of financial support, Gershon and I felt, that ORT would then not have to be accountable to the Jewish world.

Tartakower and I immediately brought these matters to the attention of the Jewish Agency and the Israeli government officials, who listened to us in silence and did nothing about our complaint. It is a fact of Jewish organizational life that one agency does not like to criticize another except privately and off the record. The leaders, both volunteer and professional, meet together regularly to decide the fate of Jewish affairs, divide the turf, and develop a clublike relationship. They know each other by their first names; their families socialize. I suspect that even if they feel a colleague might be doing something not necessarily in the Jewish client's interests—notwithstanding that this is or should be their major, perhaps only, reason for being—they also know that if they ever get into a jam, they may need the unswerving aid of that colleague. Thus they not only avoid being critical of one another, but they end ganging up against any outside critic, particularly if he or his organization was not part of their circumscribed establishment, seemed to be encroaching on their terrain, and not responding to the disciplines that they have set up to patrol one another.

Gershon ultimately was forced to resign, because he would not repudiate his criticisms. Vicious but untrue canards were circulated about his character, his integrity and honesty—and his insubordination. The AAEJ and I did not become more deeply involved in this crucial issue until the following year.

* * *

I had already raised the possibility of bringing one or more Ethiopian Jews to the United States to tell the inside story of the grave plight they were facing in Ethiopia and why aliyah, more than aid in Ethiopia, was essential. I urged a few of the local Ethiopian Jewish leaders in Israel to improve their English, so that when they came, they might be more effective in communication. The first one arrived in the United States in 1978.

* * *

Yoseph Adane, the first Ethiopian Jew to become an ordained rabbi in Israel, was attempting to advance their cause, but tried to do it circumspectly. Being a member of the rabbinate imposed constraints on what he might say and do. We had tried to bring him to Canada for a conference, but he could not obtain an exit release from Israel.

During the demonstrations in Jerusalem on the High Holy Days of 1985, when thousands of Ethiopian Jews and others protested the decision of the Chief Rabbis and other governmental religious officials to impose *mikvah* as a condition for accepting them as Jews, Adane was quoted as supporting the rabbis rather than the Ethiopian Jews. For a time, he was persona non grata amongst the activists of his own people.

Adane visited our home in Pelham in April 1986. He was endeavoring to raise money for a new seminary in Israel, which would educate Ethiopian Jews for the rabbinate. He told me that his position the previous year had been misinterpreted by the demonstrators. While I could not get him to say so explicitly, I inferred from other remarks that he was not happy with the rabbinate's treatment of the status of his kinsmen.

When I asked him whether he could give me the name of a single member of the Knesset or Cabinet who unequivocally favored aliyah for those Ethiopian Jews still suffering in Ethiopia, he paused. I thought at first he did not want to answer my query. Then he said that he couldn't name one.

Several Israeli teachers, who had been to Ethiopia in 1976 to train teachers in contemporary Judaism, did not see a role for Adane in Israel, but told me in 1977 that I should urge him to go back to Ethiopia and spread modern traditional Judaism amongst the Jewish villagers. The 165 Ethiopian Jews then in Israel were fearful, did not know whose advice to follow. Few, if any, were prepared to demonstrate publicly, although they did not hesitate to state their views vigorously before their own membership or in the presence of a few trusted friends like myself. They lived in a fantasy hope that what they were being told by Israeli officials would be realized, although with one delay after another, they slowly began to doubt the unfilled promises.

* * *

I met with the four teachers who had gone to Ethiopia in 1976 to educate the sixty-two teachers conducting classes in twenty schools. They had found the native teachers, albeit not scholars, quite satisfactory, and potential leaders, even Zionist leaders. They encountered some opposition from the native *kohanim*, whose role and knowledge the teachers questioned, not directly, but simply by introducing Hebrew instead of Ge'ez, and initiating modern religious customs, which obviously challenged older Ethiopian Jewish practices. It was clear that the young Ethiopian Jews were being directed toward modern Judaism and Israel, which gave them a broader Jewish identity, different from the past. This trend had been initiated a hundred years before, when sporadic contacts were made by Western Jews traveling into Ethiopia, the most important of which was the visit of Joseph Halevy and the direct influence of Faitlovich. It was now coming to a head with the failure of the revolution to improve their lot. The native Jewish teachers began to advocate aliyah, even though they took little initiative in pressing this policy with ORT officials, who would have punished them for "disloyalty" to the state's policies and ORT's own contractual obligations to the government.

* * *

When Begin issued a statement for the press of the government's aliyah policy on June 21, 1977, and made no reference to the Ethiopian Jews, I sent him a special-delivery letter noting the oversight and the need to include them specifically in an immediate aliyah program. Begin had only been Prime Minister for a few months. It was my hope that since he was an ardent Zionist and believed Israel should be a haven for all Jews, especially those in jeopardy, he might alter the do-nothing program of the Labor Party, which had been in power since 1948, until his succeeding incumbency.

All news about Ethiopia and Ethiopian Jews was under strict military censorship. I had become convinced that censorship was not for the benefit of the Ethiopian Jews, nor with the purpose of keeping Ethiopia, the Arabs, and Soviet Russia in the dark, but rather, to keep the Israeli public from knowing more about them or that the government was even thinking of promoting their migration. I was beginning to think of ways by which I might break through this blockage.

The Ethiopian Jews were quarreling amongst themselves for leadership of the organization. The struggle was between those who came from Tigre as against the majority, who had come from the Gondar region. The Tigreneans charged that all Jewish organizations and the Israeli government were partial to helping and saving those from Gondar. When a list of sixty names was drawn for the first prospective migration, they were all from Gondar, who were more accessible for travel to Addis Ababa and were better prepared for life in Israel; all of them had relatives who had established themselves in Israel and could be more helpful in their integration.

The Jewish Agency sent Haim Halachmy, head of HIAS in Israel, to Ethiopia ostensibly to see what could be done about arranging the movement of the three score to Israel. This was happening at the same time that independent individuals, who sought information about Ethiopian Jews from government sources, were being told, nothing, because the subject was most "sensitive." I received the distinct impression that officials did not want any more Ethiopian Jews. Some would even have liked to send those in Israel back to Ethiopia, giving as an excuse the need to use them to improve the lot of their undereducated, unskilled kinsmen. It was certainly not to prepare them for migration. They had this attitude, actually a position, despite the fact that every Ethiopian Jew in Israel had made a satisfactory accommodation with little or no help from either the government or the Jewish Agency.

* * *

Aharon Cohen, principal of an important traditional school in Jerusalem, a brother of Geula Cohen, the fiery Herut member of the Knesset, and one of the Israelis who went to Ethiopia as a teacher in 1976, introduced himself to me with a bang. Articulate, equipped with batches of Xeroxed documents proving that the Ethiopian Jews were indeed Jews, he wanted to be part of the small inner group promoting aliyah to Israel. He had been a student at Kfar Batya when the first Ethiopian Jewish students arrived in 1955. He had scores of ideas, which he shot out in rapid fire, most of them impractical. He introduced me to Geula, his sister, who was chairman of the aliyah committee in the Knesset. He thought judicious pressure should be exercised on the government, but not by those in Israel. It had to come from the Jews in the United States. He really knew nothing about American Jewish leaders and their views on this subject. His plans were of no account. His influence proved to be zero. When confronted with a crisis, he supported the Israeli establishment rather than the Ethiopian Jews.

I told him, at a meeting on July 5, that I had lost all patience, and that unless there was action very soon, I was prepared to blow up the issue in the Israeli media, if I could only find a way of overcoming its rigorous censorship. I told him American Jewish leadership was completely subservient to the Israeli policy on Ethiopian Jewry and that no help would be forthcoming from such a source.

* * *

Some months before, a good angel had turned up in George Levinrew, a social work colleague whom I knew from the early 1930s, who had settled in Israel and was conducting a weekly forum for Hebrew University on topics of the day. George also wrote a bridge column for the *Jerusalem Post*. He invited me, in fact pressed me, to give an academic lecture on Ethiopian Jewry on August 15. I proposed that I speak together with persons like Aharon Cohen, who had recently been to Ethiopia and seemed to have connections, and an Ethiopian Jew such as Zimna Berhane, who had been in Israel off and on since 1955, and who was the elected leader amongst the Ethiopian Jews, and perhaps the closest to being an activist. I suggested that we invite another long-time friend of mine from the States, Dr. Bernard Reznikoff, head of the American Jewish Committee in Israel, to be the chairman. All accepted the invitation.

In back of my mind was to see what would happen by August 15. If no Ethiopian Jew had arrived from Ethiopia by that date, I would change my "academic, historical" account to an outright accusatory one. I knew that the forum usually attracted forty-five to fifty older people, mostly English-speaking Americans. I wanted to change the audience. I told George I would pay for several advertisements beyond the single one that his budget provided.

I composed an advertisement to read as follows: "Will the 28,000 Ethiopian Jews experience a Second Holocaust?" The word *Holocaust* was immediately deleted, as that was a sacrosanct term reserved only for the white European Jews who were murdered during the Hitler-Nazi mania. A more innocuous sentence was substituted. "Will Ethiopian Jews Face Extinction?"

* * *

During the summer of 1977 an Israeli ship, the *Yuvall*, picked up sixty-six Vietnamese refugees, whose desperate situation had been deliberately ignored by ships of other nations. These unfortunates were given asylum in Israel, and they are still there. I wondered then why the same helping hand was not being extended to the Ethiopian Jews. So did others, as reflected in letters to the editor of the *Jersualem Post* and cartoons in the same newspaper.

* * *

In the intervening weeks, my diary indicated a schedule from morning until night, always pressing the government and the Jewish Agency on the aliyah issue, harassing the Jewish Agency, the JDC, and ORT not to change the program for Jews in Ethiopia. I tried to compose the differences between the several Ethiopian Jewish factions in Israel. I met with William Halpern, who introduced me to Baruch Tegegne, one of the Kfar Batya students of 1956, who had been forced to return to Ethiopia after he completed his studies. Baruch escaped from Ethiopia in 1975. He saw no future for his people in that unfortunate country. He could not obtain a visa to reach Israel directly. After traveling halfway around the world, he finally landed in Israel. His story has been reported many times in the American press. I have the whole story on tape, taken in Jerusalem in 1977. Halpern and Tegegne both advocated a rescue program over the route Baruch had taken from Ethiopia via Sudan. There were numerous meetings with professors, rabbis, government officials, journalists, writers, who expressed a reserved interest in Ethiopian Jewry. Any lead was followed up. I obtained a copy of a 1975 government-authorized survey as to whether Israel should encourage the migration of Ethiopian Jews. The reactions were overwhelmingly favorable. The contents never saw the light of day in the public media.

* * *

I had been insisting for months that an appointment be arranged between the Israeli committee and Prime Minister Begin to discuss the Ethiopian Jewish crisis. After many delays, such a meeting was scheduled with the Prime Minister for September 1. I was to be included in the small group.

* * *

I advised Dr. Tartakower that if no one arrived from Ethiopia by August 15, my speech at the forum would be revised to an accusatory statement on the indifference and prejudice toward them on the part of Israeli officialdom. Other members of the Israeli committee and he vehemently opposed such a speech. I indicated that it was a personal statement and that I was not asking for the committee's sanction. It was at this point that my relations with Dr. Tartakower began to deteriorate and shortly thereafter were permanently broken.

August 15, 1977

As August 15 drew near, no one had arrived from Ethiopia. There were official off-the-record statements that there were political difficulties at the Ethiopian end, and that Israeli representatives were having problems implementing a rescue program. I did not believe this was true. I decided to rewrite the original speech. Efforts were made by Israeli officials to sabotage the meeting by discouraging Ethiopian Jews from attending and pressuring the other participant speakers to withdraw. The night finally arrived. About 250 were in the audience, including government officials, the press, Ethiopian Jews, personal friends, mostly people who had never attended these forums before.

The chairman, Dr. Bernard Reznikoff opened the meeting and introduced Zimne Berhane, an Ethiopian Jew, and Aharon Cohen, an Israeli, as the first speakers. Both urged caution. No one should criticize Israel. No one should protest against Ethiopia. In fact to say anything openly might jeopardize whatever was being done to save Ethiopian Jews. It was a sorry spectacle. It was an attempt, under duress from the outside, to keep this subject under wraps.

My speech was a long one—about forty-five minutes. I reviewed the history of the Ethiopian Jews, but placed emphasis on the current problems—poverty, disease, illiteracy, persecution. I noted that Ethiopia was suffering another of its periodic droughts and famines during which hundreds of thousands of people had already died. I revealed that no serious efforts had ever been made to bring them to Israel; that up to this very moment—I looked at my wristwatch for dramatic impact—no Ethiopian Jew had ever come to Israel legally. I ended with a ringing statement:

> "Even if rescue should eventually—even tomorrow—produce a few score—what of the rest of the 28,000? Must they be left behind, sacrificed and disappear from the face of the earth after 3000 years of courageously clinging to the Jewish faith? Is this their final reward?
> The restoration of diplomatic relations with Ethiopia is a most desireable policy for Israel.
> The furtherance of trade relations are most desireable economically for Israel.
> Permitting Israel to fly over their territory is of immense value to Israel.
> Continuing to have a toehold on the Red Sea is essential for the security of Israel.
> But are all of these valid governmental policies inconsistent with or even more important than saving 28,000 Jewish lives?
> Or are there other unspoken reasons why no official bodies in Israel or the rest of the Jewish world are not lifting more than a little finger to bring them to Israel?
> I leave the answer to that searching question up to you!

Despite the severance of diplomatic relations, Israel had daily contact with Ethiopia. It was supplying, amongst other items, military parts for the Ethiopian war machine and keeping Ethiopian equipment in good repair. Israel had not used its presence and its influence to rescue any Ethiopian Jews, when it could have taken a full load back with every empty plane that returned from that country.

There was a lot of applause. Many commended me on the speech. Yet not a single member of the Israeli committee was present. The next day I heard that I had been put in Coventry, excommunicated by those who were allegedly doing something for this critical cause. Not a word appeared in the paper. When I called Louis Rapoport of the *Jerusalem Post*, who had sat through the meeting taking copious notes on my speech, and asked why he had not filed a story, he replied defensively: "Everything about Ethiopia was under censorship. Furthermore, if I told your story, there would be a pogrom in Ethiopia. I don't want that on my conscience." I told him it was "sheer nonsense" and "outright cowardice" on his part, and hung up.

Ethiopian Jews Arrive

Ten days later, on August 25, in the early hours of the morning, a lone Israeli military airplane landed in the far corner of the Lod airport, carrying fifty-nine Ethiopian Jews from Addis Ababa. A historic moment. No top officials, no reporters greeted them. No red carpets were rolled out. In their native garb, some barefoot, without baggage, they descended. A bus drove up to the plane and the Ethiopian Jews were loaded on the vehicle and driven to Tiberias Illit, several hours away, to an absorption center that had been hastily reopened to house them.

Dr. Tartakower did not apprise me of their arrival, nor did he send me a copy of his confidential memorandum, which indicated that they had come and that additional Ethiopian Jews would be rescued in "due course."

However, I did receive a call from Zimna Berhane to come to Tiberias immediately to see the Ethiopian Jews, because several had asked for me. He had been hastily recruited along with other Ethiopian Jewish volunteers to help, since the Israeli staff was totally ignorant of the newcomers' history, customs, dress, food habits, and life-style. The volunteers were relatives of the newcomers. Emma and I immediately hopped into a taxi and took the long ride from Jerusalem to Tiberias to see with our own eyes the fifty-nine, for whose welfare we had been working and struggling since 1965, following our first visit to Ethiopia. Yehudah Dominitz of the Jewish Agency and Haim Halachmy of HIAS were there. Neither had informed me of their arrival, although I had been meeting with them for months on this matter. Dominitz said: "Aren't you happy about the arrival of your friends." Note the emphasis on *your* friends. I simply replied: "Yes" and walked on. I never had any use for either of them thereafter.

Did it really require months of political maneuvering and processing to get them out of Ethiopia, as the bureaucrats claimed? I learned that the new arrivals had been apprised of their selection only several days before. They were quickly packed into buses and taken on the two-day ride to Addis Ababa airport. They were secretly loaded aboard the planes. Paperwork had actually been done on the plane.

Who gave the order to bring them at this moment? I believe that the constant pressure on the Prime Minister, my letters, including the speech that I made ten days before, forced the government's hand. There was fear that the real reason for the long delays might be made public.

Could they have been rescued before? Of course. Even in 1948, when the state was born. But there was no predisposition to perform this mitzvah, despite rabbinical and governmental decrees. I still felt that the test of the government's sincerity woule be a continued flow of Ethiopian Jews. It didn't happen. In December, I addressed another letter to the Prime Minister that a token rescue was not enough. A week later, another sixty-two arrived in the cold of winter. There was insufficient warm clothing for them. They were hastily billeted at Afula, a distance from where their kinsmen in Israel resided. Was this also a coincidence? No preparation. Keep them isolated. No one was rescued in all of 1978.

* * *

Dr. Tartakower's committee was to meet several days before our meeting with Prime Minister Begin to go over the agenda. When I walked into his office, he looked up at me with hostility in his face and voice. "What are you doing here? You are not welcome! I called the Prime Minister's secretary and told her to scratch your name from the conference list on September 1st. You had no right to make any speeches in Israel about the Ethiopian Jews without my consent." I listened until he was finished. I thought he was mad. I left his office.

Before we left Israel, a week later, he attempted to make amends, stating that he was sorry for what he had said and done against me. He wanted to have coffee with us. I refused to meet with him.

Dr. Tartakower wrote me a letter wanting to meet with me again, but I never answered. He asked mutual friends to see what they could do to reestablish our relationship. I refused to have any further contact with him. I considered his offense forever irreparable. He died in 1982. It was my conviction about him and other members of his committee that they did not mind bringing the Ethiopian Jewish problem to the attention of the government, but they were unwilling to press it to a point where it might injure them. Every Israeli was somehow dependent on the government officials for favors for themselves and/or their organizations. They were afraid that such connections might be severed. I had learned long ago that unremitting pressure finally paid off. One had to be prepared to jeopardize his position and status, even alienate long-time friends, if a life-saving issue was involved. That, none of them were prepared to do.

"May Have to Kill You"

One other side note: On August 3, twelve days before I made the speech, we had several friends over for dinner, one of whom was connected with the Jewish Agency. He could not believe the stories we piled up one on another of the perfidy of the government and his own organization on the Ethiopian Jewish issue. He knew me well enough, so that he knew that I would not give up on this cause until it was finally settled. He told me: "Graenum, if you continue to attack Israel about the Falashas, they may have to kill you." I laughed. I later briefly noted his remark in my diary. Then I forgot about it, for I could not believe that anyone, let alone a bureaucrat or a government, would go to such lengths to silence a critic.

On March 24, 1985, in London, Emma and I met Professor Tudor Parfitt of London University, who was writing a book on Operation Moses, the airlift of thousands of Ethiopian Jews from Sudan to Israel. He asked: "Have you ever been threatened by anyone because of what you were trying to do to rescue Ethiopian Jews?" I looked at him increduously. "No! Why do you ask?" He repeated the question. Again I answered in the negative.

I came across the August 3, 1977, memo, as I was preparing this book. I then wondered where and how Dr. Parfitt had obtained the information that prompted his query. Was he told this by someone? Did he read it on file in someone's archives? He would not tell me the reason or the source for his question. At the outset of our conversation, he told me that he had access to all Israeli files.

* * *

In 1977, I presented a paper at the twenty-fifth annual meeting of the Henry Kaufmann Campgrounds board and told them what I knew as to the true origins and development of this phenomenal institution in the New York Jewish community. From time to time I heard others claim credit not only for its creative initiation, but even for its step-by-step development. People, even of high degree, like to attach their names to programs and institutions which proved successful, although their role in its growth was secondary. Thus they try to rewrite history. I prefer to portray events as they occurred, often with the blemishes, so that some researcher in the future would have the facts. I was its creator. I assembled the tracts. I found a great deal of the money to purchase the land and build its incumbrances. I got the properties off the tax roles.

These efforts were not spasmodic, but continual from year to year for two decades. The results were testimony to this prodigious outpouring of energy.

* * *

Somehow, I permitted myself to get involved with trying to resolve the institutional problems of the Gloversville Jewish Community Center and the Knesseth Israel Synagogue. Both were faced with an unrelieved, declining population and ever-rising costs. I devised a plan for a joint venture, which would have led to the consolidation of these two shrinking institutions. While it was never fully implemented, some recommendations I made managed to produce additional funds: thus both could continue to function with somewhat greater security. The center has actually outlived its usefulness to Jews, except for preserving, through its fine building, a positive Jewish image in a Christian city.

Emma and I traveled to Los Angeles and San Francisco on Ethiopian Jewish business, hoping to help both Jewish communities determine a correct course of action on an issue that was beginning to disturb Jewish leaders. Regretfully, both cities ultimately preferred to follow the well-formed and protected line of the Israeli-U.S. establishment. The vaunted "independence" of the west coast was suppressed. It adopted the conventional, supine position that did nothing to advance the rescue of Ethiopian Jews.

One executive of a small branch of a national agency was threatened with the loss of his job if he dared once again to advocate the rescue of Ethiopian Jews. Thereafter, he too was silenced.

* * *

While on the west coast, we flew up to Portland to see my aging sister Sadie and her children and grandchildren. This was the last time we would see her alive. It was, as always, a beautiful reunion. We had loved each other deeply. She also loved Emma from the start. Once again we ate her specially baked lemon meringue pie, crusty, thick, sweet, and lemony. I still have graphic memories of our contacts as a small child and as grown-ups. I can smell the savory foods that she competently prepared in her kitchens in various places and on numerous occasions, wherever we visited her. She died in 1980 at the age of eighty-seven, and was buried in Gloversville, where I gave a eulogy on her long and active life.

* * *

It was a great year for Bonnie, our grandchild. She had been confirmed in the synagogue in McLean, Virginia. Emma and I were present. I gave a brief talk. Then she went on a two-week trip to Israel with a youth group from the Reform Jewish movement. She earned most of the money for this journey. It reinforced her identity with the Jewish people.

* * *

Lest we forget. Emma bought her second fur coat with her own money. This time it was a good one. She bought it from an independent furrier and not from a close furrier friend, who told her he was doing her a favor.

21

The Year 1978

ETHIOPIAN JEWRY HAD begun to take more of my time. We had prayed for a greater movement of Jews out of Ethiopia, but it did not materialize. In February, Moshe Dayan revealed publicly that Israel was supplying arms to Ethiopia. This was now cited as an additional excuse why Ethiopia refused to allow any more Ethiopian Jews to leave the country. I never put much credence in this lame myth. From all other indications, there was no new evidence that Israel was seriously concerned with rescuing them in small or large numbers. In Israel, there was no hint of planning to receive them. The 121 that had arrived in 1977 were being absorbed with the help of the government and the Jewish Agency, but primarily through the wholesome aid of their families, who played an active assisting role. This latter factor would be absent when Ethiopian Jews arrived in larger numbers via Sudan beginning with 1980.

I lectured over the U.S., appeared on radio and TV, telling the story of their horrendous condition and to raise more money for the expanding AAEJ.

Changing of the Guards

I had served as president of the AAEJ for four years. As one who believed in rotation of leadership, I was happy to turn over the reins of office to Dr. Howard M. Lenhoff of Costa Mesa, California. Howard, a professor of biology and related sciences at the University of California at Irvine, had become interested in the Ethiopian Jews several years before and was already giving evidence of the special kind of leadership

ראש הממשלה
THE PRIME MINISTER

Jerusalem, March 9, 1978

Dr. Graenum Berger
American Association for Ethiopian Jews
340 Corlies Avenue
Pelham
New York, 10803

Dear Dr. Berger,

As you are well aware, the Government of Israel is committed to the rescue of the Falashas of Ethiopia. However difficult the obstacles in carrying out this sacred task, we shall persist in exploring every avenue to bring our fellow Falasha Jews home.

I have been told of your years of dedicated service to help the Falashas. Israel is grateful to you and to the American Association for Ethiopian Jews for your help. We look forward to your continued cooperation with the Government of Israel and with the Israel Committee for Ethiopian Jews until all the Falashas return to their homeland.

May the forthcoming years bring peace to the Falashas and to all Israel.

Sincerely yours,

Menachem Begin

that he could provide. He wrote well, had a superb public relations sense, saw the need for broadening the base of support and making it a real national organization. He knew many of the Ethiopian Jews intimately in Israel and had spent time with the group that arrived in Afula in December 1977. In the four years that he occupied the post, the organization advanced tremendously in the number of donors and in its budget. Chapters sprang up, and knowledge of both the Ethiopian Jews and the organization spread.

Howard supplied something which I either lacked or did not comprehend. I thought of the Ethiopian Jewish problem as one that could easily be resolved by Israel and the existing world Jewish communities. All it required, as I saw it, was getting the subject on the agendas of those bodies, particularly in the minds of the top leadership. That is where I concentrated my energies. Howard saw the need for having this kind of pressure exerted not by a few upon a few, but as a massive assault from the grass roots on the indifferent and resistant leaders and their organizations. He had learned something of what large groups could do through his association with the Soviet Jewry movement. He thought it could be applied to the Ethiopian Jewish issue as well. He was correct.

In 1978, we also won the support of a young businessman from Highland Park, Illinois, Nathan Shapiro. He had concluded his presidency of a Reform synagogue and was undoubtedly marked for larger Jewish communal posts in the Chicago region. He suddenly found an absorbing interest in Ethiopian Jews, after reading one of my articles that the Alperts, his neighbors, had given to him. Since then, as a vice-president and from 1982 as the president, he has moved the AAEJ into even higher spheres of operation. As his influence grew from year to year, the results were phenomenal in pressure, fund-raising, and rescue.

Howard and Nate, although at times working with the Jewish establishment, did not avoid their wrath. This was true of other individuals in our organization. They discovered, like myself, that world and American Jewish leaders were in a conspiracy to do as little as they could get away with respecting Ethiopian Jews. They too learned that we had both to attack the opposition and go around it, if salvation was to come to the African Jews. The three of us earned the enmity of both Israeli and Jewish establishment leaders. They couldn't influence us. They couldn't buy us. They finally capitulated and did what they should have done at the outset. That would come later. They demeaned us publicly. They never gave us credit for anything.

* * *

While I already disliked some of the unhealthy practices World ORT had introduced in Ethiopia, it had not reached the point of making me openly critical. I first tried to get the leadership to change its ways. I attended the annual meeting of ORT in New York and was called on to speak from the floor. I found Simon Guedj, the director of the Ethiopian project, an "engaging" person, smooth as silk, who painted a prettier picture than the true conditions warranted. Women's ORT invited me to speak at its annual meeting. My slide lecture ended with the advocacy of wholesale aliyah rather than raising money to provide additional services in Ethiopia. Later I was interviewed at some length for a major article in the Women's ORT magazine. The editor failed to include a single critical comment I had made about ORT's program. She was selling only ORT's positive involvement only for fund-raising.

* * *

Leonard Fein, editor of *Moment,* finally printed an excellent major article on Ethiopian Jews, which I had submitted. He did this only after he was importuned by a member of his board, a close friend of both of us. At first he did not want to print it at all. As the issue began to heat up, Fein approached me at a breakfast at the annual meeting of the Council of Jewish Federations and asked me to prepare for immediate publication a second "hard-hitting" statement on the same subject. He needed it within a few days. He received my copy in that time frame. When weeks passed and I did not hear from him, I wrote to find out what was holding up its publication. I have his long reply. He said that while what I had written was probably true, it was too critical of Israel, and he would not publish it. I wrote him a stinging note that I had considered him an editor of creativity and courage, now I found him only a mere man, who easily knuckled under to the Jewish organizational position. The cause that I espoused was saving Jewish lives and not trying to correct relatively minor administrative policies which preoccupied the Jewish world.

* * *

For years, I had been urging Jewish organizations to set up a committee to save Ethiopian Jewish lives, but had not succeeded.

The Council of Jewish Federations and Welfare Funds had appointed a phony committee, largely to placate me, to explore the issues superficially, but to do nothing to resolve the serious problems confronting the Ethiopian Jews. Philip Bernstein, the retired executive vice-president, gave an exaggerated account of the role of his organization in his volume *To Dwell in Unity* (1983).

* * *

In the fall of 1978, the National Jewish Community Relations Advisory Council, which had only added the word *Jewish* to its title a few years before, assembled representatives of various Jewish organizations, which eventually led to the formation of a committee to deal with matters concerning Ethiopian Jewry. It was composed, on the basis of attendance, mostly of professionals from the major Jewish organizations. It did not become formal until the spring of 1979. During its initial stages, I was never invited, but when meetings were held, I appeared, welcome or not. When the committee was formally established, the AAEJ was asked to be a member. We preferred, at my instigation, to attend only as observers, as we did not want to be bound by its decisions. It was evident that the committee had been set up to contain the AAEJ and not to advance the rescue of Ethiopian Jews. A member of the Israeli consulate in New York attended all meetings and sat at the head table. Every other member of the committee, with the exception of the AAEJ observers, deferred to him. Instead of dealing with the crucial issue of how to save Ethiopian Jews massively and expeditiously, the representatives usually attacked the AAEJ for being too activistic and public about its positions, and for raising money that properly belonged to the United Jewish Appeal (although the UJA had no program to raise funds for the relief, rescue, or resettlement of Ethiopian Jews). It was also charged at one meeting that we had contributed to the death of several Israelis trying to rescue Ethiopian Jews. At this meeting, I rose in a rage, accusing the committee of being accessories to the demise of thousands of helpless Jews. I walked out. The AAEJ did not attend meetings thereafter. The two organizations became not merely adversaries, but sworn enemies.

* * *

Over the years I approached the American Jewish Committee leadership to do something about this cause. I was called to one meeting where the committee was concerned about the status and property of the few score of non-Falasha Jews in Addis Ababa and Asmara, whose possessions were being confiscated by the Revolutionary Socialist Dergue. The fate of the Ethiopian Jews was not on its agenda. Marc Tanenbaum periodically showed some ephemeral interest. He invited me to a meeting of a subcommittee and interviewed me for a TV and a radio program. That was all. I was also interviewed for a tape to be sent by the committee to its affiliates around the country, but it was never issued.

* * *

Requests were coming in for more visual material about Ethiopian Jews, and at the request of the Jewish media department of the Jewish Welfare Board, I prepared a set of slides of photos I had taken in Ethiopia and in Israel along with a script. I did not ask for or receive any royalties. Hundreds of these sets were sold and/or rented for presentation around the country. In 1984, I revised the set of slides and taped my own interpretation, making it easier for viewers to learn the story. This was also turned over to the JWB. I received no compensation or royalties for this generous gift of my slides, voice, and time.

My slides and photos have been used extensively in newspapers, magazines, books, and TV throughout America, but only rarely was there any attribution of the photographer. When I wrote letters to the responsible parties, I received no replies.

Ethiopian Jews in Sudan

The most important development regarding the Ethiopian Jews occurred on September 8, 1978, when I was badgered to come to the Israeli consulate in New York, where some of its top officials tried to persuade me not to print an advertisement that I had prepared for the major American newspapers. They begged me to be less strident in my blame of Israel for any failure to rescue Ethiopian Jews. The headlines of the advertisement, which alone covered half a page, read:

> WHY DOESN'T ISRAEL,
> THE JEWISH AGENCY AND
> AMERICAN JEWISH LEADERSHIP
> RESCUE LEGITIMATE BLACK JEWS
> FROM EXTERMINATION?

I informed them in polite but no uncertain terms that neither the AAEJ nor I could stand by and allow Jews to be arrested, tortured, raped, sold into slavery, and killed without registering our most vigorous protest against the indifference, even prejudice, of the names mentioned in the advertisement.

When they did not succeed in shaking me from my position, they all walked out, leaving me alone with a junior member of the consulate's staff. After they left, he told me that he was sympathetic to my position. I thought this was a scheme to soften me up through another tactic. Suddenly he picked up a paper and started to read it, revealing that there were eighteen Ethiopian Jews in Sudan. This was the first official information that I had of this salient fact. Then he stopped: "Oh, I made a mistake. I had no right to read that to you." I said nothing, for I knew he had purposely leaked this vital data. Why? He would not give me a copy of what he had read. Did he want me to do something about helping them get out of Sudan? Guilt?

Without revealing my source, I immediately dispatched a letter to the Jewish Agency and the Israeli government officials, indicating that my informtion was impeccable, and that I expected them to rescue these Jews, who were now refugees and had a radically different status from those in Ethiopia.

I heard nothing further for several months. Then I received a letter from an Ethiopian Jew in Sudan. My name and address had been given to him by some tourist visiting Ethiopia. He had kept the information, wrote, and asked for help in getting to Israel. He noted that his letter to

Israel making the same request had gone unanswered. Now I had the Smoking Gun, confirming what the consulate member had merely read to me about the presence of Ethiopian Jews in that country. I sent a copy of this letter to Israel. No answer. When I received a second letter from Sudan indicating that he was still waiting for action, I contacted Israel by phone. They claimed they had lost his original letter. No answer was given as to why they had not followed up my inquiry. I gave them all the information again. Nothing eventuated.

Several years later, just before the annual meeting of the Council of Jewish Federations and Welfare Funds, we attempted to place advertisements in the American Jewish press about the serious plight of the Ethiopian Jews. While they were accepted as paid advertisements, not as news stories, some prominent newspapers associated with local federations did not print the advertisements. When called, we were told the copy had been "lost." Strange how items which affect the lives of Ethiopian Jews could be either ignored or disappear. Careless or deliberate?

* * *

My book *Black Jews in America* was published in 1978. It was properly dedicated at a cocktail party, received several reviews in the Jewish press, and precipitated a number of invitations to lecture about it live, or on TV and the radio. I was subjected to a grueling interview by three sharp black editors on the Black Radio Network. They were more concerned with Ethiopian Jews than with black Jews in America, and asked one hard question after another: If the Ethiopian Jews were Jews, why didn't the Jewish world take care of them properly? Why were only a few hundred permitted into Israel? Were Jews and Israelis racists? They then switched course and wanted to know why Jews should leave Ethiopia altogether. Wasn't Ethiopia their native land? Shouldn't they stay and fight for black freedom side by side with their black brothers? Apparently I handled myself commendably, for I got praiseworthy comments from the three black editors after the interview was completed, as well as favorable reactions from a few Jews, who heard the program and called in or wrote to me. They commented that I had stood up for Israel, for the Jews, against what they deemed "savage" questioning. The book gradually sold out its first printing, but I doubt if it will go into another. Actually, I sold half of the printing. Wherever I gave a lecture on black Jews in America or on Ethiopian Jews, Emma and I disposed of books. There was no other promotion of this documentary volume. The only revision I would make, if there was to be a further edition, would be to indicate that some of the black people mentioned, whom I then did not believe were authentic Jews, had since converted to Judaism. My prediction that there would be no substantial influx of blacks into the Jewish fold has so far stood up. Becoming a Jew was still an individual matter, sometimes occurring around marriage to a white Jew, sometimes to escape their own unhappy relationship with the black community, sometimes to take advantage, often for their children, of the better opportunities that the Jewish institutions offered.

The book was published by the Commission on Synagogue Relations of the Federation of Jewish Philanthropies of New York, with the blessing of Rabbi Isaac N. Trainin, who was also concerned with the destiny of black Jews in Greater New York. I received no compensation for writing the book, and all profits were turned over to Federation.

The black Jewish subject also put me in contact with Jan Frederick Heijbroeck from the Netherlands, who decided to write his Ph.D. dissertation on the same subject. He has toured the United States on several different visits to gather material for his volume, spending many days at our home in Pelham, reading my files and books. His views were at complete variance with mine, for he believed that there are many times more black Jews in the United States than my estimate of only five thousand. He gave credence to sects and cults that claimed they were Jews. Their say-so was sufficient for him. Yet these individuals and groups had never converted nor met the prime test of having a Jewish mother, black or white. Their leaders, despite their rabbinic titles, were not trained or ordained rabbis. I await the publication of his volume with interest. Meanwhile, he is a respected curator at the Rijksmuseum in Amsterdam, Holland.

Dr. James E. Landing of the University of Illinois is working on a book that will be titled *Black Judaism: The Story of a Movement*. We have been in frequent consultation, and I await the fruits of his research.

* * *

Ralph Goldman, who now headed the American Jewish Joint Distribution Committee, tried to entice me into a study of aged Jews around the world, a program that his organization thought it might want to pursue on a global scale. I drew up a prospectus for such a study, but withdrew further consideration of my involvement when I learned I might have to work with one of the professionals in that organization, a burden that I did not care to bear or share.

* * *

The Commission on Synagogue Relations of the Federation in New York presented me with the Hurowitz Tzedakah Award for my publication of books on Jewish life and my overall contributions to the Jewish communal welfare scene.

* * *

Dr. Azriel Eisenberg, formerly head of the New York Bureau of Jewish Education, approached me one day with a mass of material that he had accumulated on the Jewish aged. He felt he needed a co-editor, who had some expertise with that age group, to assemble his material for publication. He had published many volumes, often working with collaborators. I was fond of Azriel. I had read, admired, and owned many of his books. I did not want to get involved in any partnership arrangements. I settled the matter by saying "no" and suggested a number of other people who might work with him. The work was never completed. Azriel died in 1985 at the age of eighty-one. The Jewish world lost an important author and a champion of Jewish education.

The Turbulent Decades

The National Conference of Jewish Communal Service was about to celebrate its eightieth anniversary. Its leaders wanted some fitting memento to commemorate four score years of contributions to the American Jewish community. A volume had been published in 1958 titled *Trends and Issues in Jewish Social Welfare in the United States: 1899–1958.* Some of the NCJCS's officers thought that a follow-up edition was needed to bring the story up to date. I was approached by its executive director, Matthew Penn, a close personal and professional friend for forty years, to undertake this formidable task. I turned down his ambitious tender. If I wouldn't write it, what did I think should go into such a volume? I am a sucker whenever I am asked for counsel. It did not take me long to dash off an outline. The next thing I knew William Kahn, president of the NCJCS, and Penn asked me to lunch, where they put the screws on me from both sides, flatteringly insisting that I was the only one who could produce the book that I had outlined. I had also included a budget, which provided for a $10,000 stipend for an editor. Before I knew it I had agreed to prepare the work.

For two years, I was burdened with the tremendous task of assembling major papers written during that twenty-year span. I wrote a 78-page overview of the Jewish communal historical scene from 1654 to 1978. I edited more than one hundred papers, prepared the index, found a printer, read proof. Finally a work of two volumes, 1,557 pages, was finished. It had doubled from my original prospectus of one volume with only 750 pages. I happily turned it over to the conference in June 1980 under the catchy title *The Turbulent Years,* one that I fought for against dozens of pedestrian titles suggested by the publication management committee. As the volume grew, more money was needed. I had no difficulty in getting the committee's support, largely the work of Matthew Penn, Sanford Solender, and Sanford N. Sherman. In addition I had twenty-two aides, who helped select the papers included in this work. The three thousand copies were readily disposed of in advance purchases by members of the association and to various individual and organizational contributors. It was a heavy work to carry around. It has already demonstrated its value for universities in educating workers for the Jewish communal field. Parts of it, including my "Overview," have been translated into Hebrew for use in Israel.

I was asked, when I presented the volume to the conference, what had I learned from my twenty-four months of labor in editing twenty years of written material. My instant reply was that the Jewish communal workers have "few creative people and writers" and that the overwhelming numbers were "followers" of a few original minds.

Would I undertake such a tremendous task again? I would say no. Not at my age. Except that in writing my own autobiography, the task was in some respects as sizable and equally formidable.

* * *

I was invited to participate in an arbitration involving a worker who felt she had been dealt with unjustly by her Jewish communal employer. The other arbitrator, Dr. Harold Kase, a friend, colleague, and neighbor, and I listened to the several parties. We agreed that the employee, while not particularly competent in all respects, had been treated unfairly. We adjudicated the issue to the satisfaction of both parties in the dispute. It was relatively easy to slide back into former professional practices after being away from the field for five years.

* * *

The year brought joy to Emma and me as we attended Gideon's Bar Mitzvah in Providence and Judith's Bat Mitzvah in McLean, Virginia. Elizabeth graduated from Providence High School with several awards. We were delighted to visit her at Yale, where she would spend four years. When she was graduated, she claimed they were the most rewarding years of her life.

* * *

I thought I was getting a bit deaf. An expert decided that it was not yet time for me to get a hearing aid. As the years rolled on, the condition worsened. I had difficulty hearing in the theater, in the cinema, even over TV, unless it was turned up high. Worst of all I couldn't easily hear questions addressed to me from the floor after I had given a lecture. I was presenting more than fifty lectures a year. Finally, in 1984, I went to another audiologist, who agreed with my perception of the problem, and I now wear a tiny piece in my right ear. It has vastly improved my hearing. Yet, when I want to hear, I reserve front-row seats in the theater or seek theaters where they offer an auxiliary hearing instrument. It is fun being a bit deaf. Everyone defers to you. You can turn the aid off and avoid listening to so much nonsense. Sometimes deaf people do have advantages.

Morocco

This was the year we decided to spend five weeks in Morocco. Everyone wanted to know why would anyone want to devote that much time to any country and particularly Morocco. Five weeks turned out to be not quite long enough.

Our decision about Morocco was prompted not only by our reading about the country, a land which we were to have seen at the end of our postponed six-month journey in 1973–74 to Israel and Africa, but by the presence of Mircea Mark Samoil, an excellent student of mine in the Wiener Educational Center, who was then directing the AAJDC operation in that northwestern African state. That settled it. We were in correspondence, asked him to make the necessary hotel and travel arrangements. We knew his wife, Rosalie, and their two children, Grace and Donny. We were sure our visit would be pleasant and instructive. All of them spoke French, and they would be helpful interpreters.

My own readings on Morocco had disclosed that Jews had been there at least since the Roman period. Thus we would be looking at sites where Jews have lived for more than two thousand years. At times they prospered; at many other periods, they suffered dearly for their faith, particularly after the Moslem invasion and under barbaric rulers bearing the Islamic banner. In recent years, since the creation of Israel, their lot has been precarious. We would be in Morocco during Pesach (Passover), and we were eager to learn how the Sephardic Jews celebrated this ancient Jewish festival. We left the States on March 30 and returned May 2.

Our plane was filled with elderly passengers going to Tunis and Morocco on a three-week tour. Mircea and his driver, Moshe, a Moroccan Jew with a cap, turned out to be a mine of information about the Jews of that country. Moshe had been a chauffeur for the JDC for many decades. We discovered that instead of making arrangements for us at a hotel, Mircea expected us to stay in his handsome residence. We protested, but we were helpless, and they were hurt even at our questioning their plans. Rosalie was a great cook and baker. Needless to say, the table was overly abundant.

Moroccan Jews, since the major exodus to Israel and France in the early 1950s, had been on a continuous population decline. About twenty thousand were left, mostly in Casablanca, a handsome French-designed city. The young Jews were leaving for France, Canada, the United States, and Israel. While anti-Semitism was almost official and was experienced by many Jews every day, and the movies had a 4 percent tax to support the PLO, Jews were nonetheless tolerated. Some were in business with the King or his family or his cronies. Visiting a number of Jewish homes, we had the vivid immediate impression that Jews were prospering.

On our first Saturday in a Moroccan synagogue, filled to the rafters with worshippers, I was kissed by the Bar Mitzvah, invited to his parents' home for Kiddush, where a group of twenty men were served a meal as sumptuous as a wedding feast, while the women, including the wife, sat in the kitchen. The color of their faces was light, like the French and Spanish, contrary to the description of Moroccan Jews as dark. The host was darker, and he was kiddingly called *negre* ("Negro"). His origin was in the southern part of the country.

Morocco, despite its surprisingly modern facade, was trying to retain its traditional image. Women's faces were usually covered. They wore the long, ill fitting djallabahs with full sleeves and hood in somber colors. Yet we saw one woman trying to hitch-hike on the highway. All Jews except a few of the aged opted for Western dress. There was a clear separation of men and women in public places. Polygamy was permitted. It was whispered that a few Jews had more than one wife.

I was told about, but did not witness, the Hillulah, a candle-lighting ceremony, often a major fund-raising event for Jewish causes, performed in memory of Jewish "saints," or better yet, "sanctified Jews," usually rabbis of great merit, who were reputed to possess miracle-working powers. Tall candles, works of color and of art, were lighted at these events.

Mircea told me he had introduced American methods in fund-raising for Jewish welfare needs and had succeeded in obtaining larger sums each year. He had learned these methods when he was studying with me. Despite the wealth of many Jews, they were content to put the burden for supporting their own poor, including education, on the treasuries of the JDC, ORT, British OSE, and the Lubavitch rabbis.

We were driven to Marrakesh, the beginning of the south, on well-constructed highways. Since this was early April, the snow-covered mountains could be seen in the distance. Marrakesh was a charmer, quite different from other major cities. The Jemac el Fna, a huge square, which served as an entrance to the thousands of small vendors in the souk, was a carnival with entertainers and their solicitors holding their hands out for a donation. We saw every type of market, the manufacturing of all kinds of items in metal and weaving. Prices asked were initially high. One had to bargain long and hard, and could usually purchase the object for half the asking price. We purchased rugs and metal teapots. Even though we thought we watched our rugs being wrapped, we found when we unwrapped them at home that a switch had been made to an inferior fabric. We had been warned that this sleight might happen.

Being in Marrakesh with representatives of the JDC, we were invited to the typically ornate house of the president of the Jewish community in the heart of the Mellah. We were also guests at a henna party for a bride-to-be, shortly before her wedding. It appeared as though only rich and prominent Jews were present, along with important government officials, non-Jews. Native musicians played their unique melodies. Dancing was performed in regular Western style, until the music for belly dancing poured forth. Then the women, most of them dressed in elaborate Moroccan and French gowns, took over. The bride-to-be, in her richly designed dress (she wore two different ones during the long evening), was adorned from head to toe with gold, including a wide belt of the precious metal. She was finally given a dish of henna, which was rubbed into the palm of her hand to ensure her wifely virtues and fertility after marriage. The mother of the bride equaled her daughter in the quality of her robes. Not a single woman, except Emma, had gray hair, although many were much older. It was the custom to dye one's hair until the end.

The food was memorable in this two-tiered Moroccan hall with its multicolored, painted walls. Scotch was drunk like water. The costumed waiters brought in huge platters of b'stila, a crisp, philo-dough pie crust in which had been baked bone-free pigeons with the taste and aroma of many spices and sugar. With our hands we dug huge pieces out of the tremendous pie and ate this choice morsel. No dishes. No utensils. Huge cloth napkins were served to wipe our fingers and lips. Another course appeared on immense platters consisting of mishoui, a quarter of a lamb. It was not cut up. There were no plates or knives. We pulled off a piece at a time and ate this tender meat in Moroccan style. It was a party the likes of which we had never observed or attended, where Jews in their finery were simulating customs that went back to a tent culture centuries old. An appeal was made for charity, and many responded. I don't know how much was pledged, since the gifts and the final sum were announced in rapid French. I was simply told that it was considerable.

As we toured from city to city, it was clear that my friend Mircea wanted us to see not only the historical Moroccan sites, but also the Jewish ones. Synagogues, cemeteries, schools, homes for the aged, medical clinics, playgrounds, eventually even a campsite, so that in some instances I could give him my objective professional appraisal of what I saw and how the facility and the services might be bettered. I was introduced as an expert. So I gave advice whenever it was requested.

In some communities we were given valuable Jewish religious artifacts, items I had planned to purchase if they were available. In Meknes, I received a two-hundred-year-old Megillot Esther with the Hebrew lettering handprinted on cowhide. In Tetuán, I was presented with two mid-nineteenth-century sterling silver finials, a unique Northwest African creation. In Fez, I was given a turn-of-the-century glass memorial lamp covered with gold leaf, hung on a beautifully formed brass chain. In Rabat, a grateful Jewish leader gave me a number of textiles. We gave the finials and memorial lamp to the Knesseth Israel synagogue in Gloversville, which was assembling a collection of Jewish religious art objects.

The departure of hundreds of thousands of Jews had forced the closing of numerous synagogues and the closeting of a rich array of ritual objects that should already have been distributed to museums or to new congregations arising around the world. This would keep them fresh and clean and utilized for the furtherance of Jewish worship.

My observations were used by Mircea to effect certain improvements. Some were done within a day or two after my comments. I was not happy with some of the facilities for the aged, which required instant remedy. Improvements were made somewhat later. After returning to the States, I gave a verbal evaluation to Ralph Goldman, head of the AAJDC, at no variance with what I had related to Mircea. I praised his Moroccan director for his administration and influence in such a short time, which improved both facilities and services; and for getting the native Jews to donate a larger part of the bill. I witnessed Mircea actually soliciting their support, but along with the money, like a good communal worker, getting individuals more deeply involved in the program. It was a mistake for the JDC to let him leave that organization, for he could have continued to make a contribution whereever he was posted.

In every school that I entered, in every community I visited, the principal and teachers were eager to show off the knowledge of their pupils. The children rose and stood during my presence in the classroom. The schools were well organized, and the teachers appeared to be interested. Often students were called on to recite something or go to the blackboard and comment on what was written. This was usually done in either French or Hebrew. In one school, a tiny tot, who could not have been more than five years old, began to recite the Haggadah from memory. I am sure she would have finished the lengthy text had I not said it was enough and patted the child on her head. All classes were preparing for Pesach. Nothing about Israel could be openly taught in the schools. I saw no pictures or other symbols of Israel.

When I went to the synagogues on several Shabbatim, I also marveled that most of the worshippers, old and young, were praying without a *Siddur*, a prayerbook, or even looking at it when they held one in their hands. They had memorized the book. I presumed that this was partly due to the absence of sufficient books to begin with.

There was little personal or social pathology in the various communities, unlike the growing problems amongst individuals and families that had emerged in American Jewish communities in the middle sixties and seventies. This was partly due to the absence of large numbers of children, and partly to the tight control that was exercised in some mysterious way on all the Jewish residents. It took place despite the absence of any significant social work program and personnel.

The word *mellah,* designating the ghettolike neighborhoods in which Jews had lived, meant "salt." Jews often enjoyed almost a monopoly on the sale of salt, the taxes on which were used to enrich the royal treasuries. I read that the Jews of Morocco once had the contract to salt the heads of victims killed in battle by Sultans and brigands, who hung these gruesome pieces in public view as a sign of victory and as a lesson to all challengers of their military and political control.

We rode deep into the Atlas Mountains, climbing to elevations of 8,000 feet until we reached Telouet, where we saw the partial ruins of the once-fabulous Glaoui Castle, a monument to the bandit chieftain who had saved the King's life. Jews had lived in this area for centuries, making their living as craftsmen, but all left on the exodus to Israel twenty-five years before. We purchased many sculptured figures made out of soapstone and semiprecious stones at some of the roadside markets. There was little traffic.

We went to a lavishly decorated Moroccan restaurant to eat typical native foods such as b'stila, couscous, lamb, and were entertained by musicians and shapely belly dancers, whose bodies shook and tremored at your side, so as to make the tables piled with food rattle. Food, whether Moroccan or French, was universally good.

I added to my Haggadah collection by purchasing an old Moroccan work, a Tunisian-Arab-Hebrew print, a French-Hebrew work, and a new Casablanca publication. Emma bought Moroccan embroideried gowns, after watching the girls in basement and back-alley shops sewing these fancy dresses with skill and speed.

Despite a decline in the number of Jewish students and with no prospect of their increase in the future, despite posters which I saw everywhere soliciting Jewish students in every Jewish community we visited, ORT had just built a handsome new brick school to replace (or add to) the older stucco one across the street. It was furnished with the finest modern mechancial equipment. When I asked why it was needed, the reply was that this was a gift of the West German government and ORT never turned down any donations.

Our trip to Fez was through the attractive Moroccan countryside with its rolling hills, cork forests, flower cover, and well-groomed farms and villages. We usually ate many meals with native Jews, discussed their youth needs, and what they might do for the poor Jews, usually older people. Fez was once a great Jewish city. Now it was in decline. The remaining Jews were planning to leave.

I attended the synagogue in Fez on the Sabbath. It was inconspicuous from the outside, modest and well-designed on the second-floor interior. There were only twenty people present. No women. I was given an aliyah, called to the Torah, but unlike the Moroccans, who when completing this ritual would each go up and kiss the Rabban Yedida Monsanego, a venerable elderly man in fine robes, I simply shook his hand. He would soon assume a new post as the Chief Rabbi of Casablanca.

In Meknes, we dined at the home of a wealthy Jewish family, which owned a number of farm-produce canning factories. The house was a walled-in estate. In a typical Moroccan home, we sat on wide, pillowed benches that were built around an entire room. Kiddush was made in elaborate fashion over one long and one round challah. Their grown children were being educated for professions in France and Italy.

The following morning, as we were leaving the luxurious Palais Jamais Hotel in Fez, one of the grandest we have stayed in, Moshe, our driver, nudged me, so that I could see the clerk behind the desk in the midst of reading Hitler's *Mein Kampf*. He told me that he had overheard the clerk say to a guest: "This is what Morocco ought to do to the Jews." Even the twenty thousand Jews were, for some Moroccans, an intrusion in a country of 22 million Sunni Moslems.

The young men who ran a shop at the hotel asked us where we came from in the United States. We decided to answer Texas rather than New York to draw them out, because we suspected, and we were right, that they identified New York with everyone being Jewish. "Have you ever been to Israel?" We lied: "No." Then one of them uttered a bitter attack against Israel, Jews, and above all, Moshe Dayan. We did not defend the duo, not because we were afraid, but because we knew it would immediately clam their vicious language. This further confirmed our view that the general populace was more anti-Semitic than the top layers of government.

One Friday night in Casablanca we attended services, where the rabbi told the congregants not to leave in large groups, so as not to be too conspicuous on the street. He told the men to take off their yarmulkes. Hopefully these two gestures would protect them from assaults by Moroccan hoodlums, who frequently preyed on the Jews.

In the following weeks, we found all Jews in the midst of preparing for Pesach. They literally turned their houses upside down almost a month before the holiday, even doing extensive interior redecoration. They cleaned all their clothes. Entertainment during this period was minimal. Except when we were alone or with the Samoils, we usually ate in kosher restaurants. As Pesach approached, we were told that Moroccan Jews would be inviting us to their homes, since all kosher eateries would be closed. They just assumed we would be observant of Pesach dietary regulations.

The morning before the Seder was also my seventieth birthday. The Samoils wanted to celebrate with a luncheon in a restaurant. In walked Moshe, the driver, with a whole dressed lamb, a gift for the holiday. No one knew what to do with it. Frankly, neither did I, but I am never daunted in an emergency. With a sharpened knife, I carved it into two legs, chops, kidneys, testicles, and a variety of other cuts, most of which could be stored for future use. I suggested that instead of going out for lunch, we have a party in the backyard of barbecued lamb chops along with the kidneys and testicles, a delicacy which I had learned to eat in Israel. So we ate this delicious meal on the patio with a birthday cake that Rosalie had prepared in advance. Champagne was provided by Maurice, an employee at the JDC, whom we had befriended.

In the evening we went to the Jewish old age home for services and watched as the elderly walked into the dining room for their own Seder. Then we went over to the home of Elie Benaouish, a well-to-do businessman, who had invited the Samoils and the Bergers to the first Seder. Twenty of us sat around a huge table. Elie, with a shawl-covered plate of matzohs, at the beginning of the service, went around the room, briefly holding the plate over each person's head, as he recited the *Holachmah* from the Haggadah. The rest of the ritual was in most respects similar to that of the Ashkenazim. The Haggadah was entirely in Hebrew. However, the food was radically different. The wine was dry and not sweet. Incidentally, Morocco produced its own Pesach kosher wine. We also drank mahia, a sweetish Arab drink akin to ouzo, as well as a green liqueur similar to slivovitz and equally powerful. The *haroshes* used dates instead of apples. A huge hors d'oeuvre plate included radishes, peppers, tomatoes, cooked celery and onions, eggplant, and beets. The baked fish oriental was unique, in contrast with gefilte fish. This was also true of the traditional fava bean soup, different from our chicken soup and matzo balls. It was made and served only on Pesach. Other dishes included tripe, meatballs with celery, and assorted other loaf meats, French and Dutch matzoh, ending with fruit, which completed the dinner menu. They asked us what we ate in America and we told them that our Seders consisted of sweet wine, chicken soup and matzo balls, hard-boiled eggs in salt water, a Hillel sandwich of *haroshes* and horseradish, gefilte fish, chicken or turkey or crown of lamb, tzimes, topped off with fruit, sponge cake, compote, and tea.

* * *

With the Samoils, we took the long auto ride north to Tangier in "Spanish" Morocco. The Jews of Tangier made sure we observed the Pesach diet by inviting us to lunch and dinner. We had taken along boxes of matzos for any meals we might eat elsewhere. At lunch we ate at the home of Yamin Soudry, a businessman. There were twenty-four people present, mostly their own family and relatives. I listed thirty-nine items on the varied and elaborate menu. After lunch we listened to the finals of the International Music Festival, where the Israelis won the first prize. The Moroccan TV omitted any reference to the triumphant Israelis.

At dinner with the Samuel Kelassy family, who were in the gold and jewelry business, the food was similar to what we consumed at lunch, except for a few extra items like lamb and other meats. We were again surprised by the amount and variety of liquor consumed. This time we ate sparingly, since we were not accustomed to the heaviness of their generous servings. The next day it was the same for lunch and dinner, but we picked and chose instead of permitting our plates to be piled high with everything.

We were warned not to buy Jewish ritual objects from any Moslem, no matter how cheap, since these items were invariably stolen from empty synagogues and private homes.

While these Jews did not consider themselves wealthy by American standards, we would have had to classify them among the upper middle class.

The Jews of Tangier, like those in Casablanca, maintained homes for the aged and several schools, all in good condition, reflecting a little more care and generosity. The large Jewish communtiy of the past was gone. In one alley we visited four synagogues still being used, but five others were padlocked. While there was joy in the household, when the family assembled from near and far, yet there was a pall, as the older children were about to return to other countries for study. "We will stay in Morocco as long as King Hassan treats us well." We heard this over and over again. A fragile source of comfort.

The four of us took a hydrofoil boat, skipped over the rough Mediterranean Sea to Gibraltar to see the Rock sticking out from the coast of Spain. Gibraltar is British, and physical barriers existed. They were finally removed in 1984. The Rock was a shopping paradise along with its picturesque natural landscape, preserved by the long presence of the English army and navy. We met a number of Jews, who spoke glowingly of life on this tiny point.

The next day we drove to Tetuán, an old Jewish settlement, where I helped the leaders plan for better youth facilities and services. The first Alliance Israélite Universelle French schools were established there in 1862. The city did not have the same air of prosperity as Tangier. This was the community where I was given two handsome *rimmonim* in "payment" for the services I rendered.

On our return to Casablanca, we drove through Larache, once a prosperous Jewish community of seven thousand, now reduced to eighty-two persons, and the birthplace of our driver, Moshe. Mircea took us to see a family of two sisters and a brother, all over seventy, who lived in a cluttered, filthy cellar apartment in the former Jewish Mellah. One sister was sick and in bed. All refused to move to an old age home, because they wanted to live and die where they and their ancestors were born. My own inclination was to move them out by force, if necessary, because the conditions under which they were existing was the worst I had ever seen. I have seen how poor Jews lived in other countries, but there was no comparison. No Jewish organization wanted to take the responsibility for uprooting them.

Back in Casablanca, we were invited to lunch with Rabbi Aaron

Monsanego. It was in his father's synagogue in Fez that I had prayed and was given an aliyah some weeks before. While he had been to Israel many times, we saw no symbols of Israel in his home. A picture of the King adorned the wall. There were Jewish books and other Jewish objects made in Morocco. He gave me the most authoritative account of the present condition of the Jews in Morocco, from which I could only draw one conclusion: that the future could never be bright, even for this more privileged family with its eleven children.

The U.S. government enjoyed a good relationship with Morocco. I suspect that it might use its influence with the King if any demonstrations were undertaken against the Jews. At the U.S. Embassy, I was told that the Jews were well regarded and were well treated, and, the official added without questioning, that they were "prosperous."

On the last night of Pesach, we went to a home where the family ushered out the festival with aplomb. Each Jewish house was supposed to be open to any Jew who wanted to enter, but the practice in recent years was to invite only friends. In this well-furnished home of a successful businessman, the table was laden with assorted and unusual foods. The featured attraction was a deep dish with dough and eggs waiting for the baking of bread on the next day. The bowl rested on a shining silver platter, decorated with flower petals and a gold coin.

I was informed that the parents were not generous to Jewish community appeals. The father told me, in the presence of his son, that the poor were receiving enough and should never be indulged. When the father left my side, the son told me he disagreed with everything his father said about the poor. There was therefore hope in the next generation.

We drove up to Rabat, the capital, to have lunch with Fortune Moreno, by contrast a genial, generous Jew, who lived in a splendid house, whose walls were lined with pictures. He set a grand table. Fortune was a friend of the King. When not occupied in his huge store, where he sold textiles, he was busy visiting the local Jewish charitable institutions. He kissed all the old ladies in the home for the elderly. He bemoaned the fact that they had so few Jewish young people. Rabbi David Sabbah, head of the school system, was moving his family to Montreal, Canada, to become the Chief Sephardic Rabbi for the large Moroccan immigrant population. The Jewish leadership in Rabat, mostly businessmen, all seemed to be cut from the same cloth. Smart, well-groomed, articulate, outgoing, and well-to-do. But they had no heirs for their business properties. All the children were leaving.

In Casablanca we purchased many brass objects, which now adorn our home and those of our children. We took account of the enormous quantities and varieties of food we consumed in five weeks. I started to make detailed notes for an article which I might write for the travel section of the *New York Times* with the gustatory title: "Eating Our Way Through Morocco," Like many other writing plans, the article was never written, but some of the notes found their way into this volume.

22

1979—A Breakthrough

As I reviewed each calendar year, it was difficult to visualize how the next one could be packed with more activity and even higher drama. The year 1979 more than fulfilled any expectation I had that my life was slowing down at the age of seventy-one. Most of the year pertained to Ethiopian Jewry. Events would not permit any lessening of concern, even if I wanted to do so, which I didn't, because the task I had set for myself—and everything included Emma—had not been realized.

The AAEJ had made a decision to do something about getting those Ethiopian Jews who were now refugees in Sudan out of that miserable country. While there were still relatively few refugees from Jewish Ethiopia, and since no one could be stirred to rescue them from Ethiopia directly, other options had to be explored.

Young and eager William Halpern, whom I had met with periodically over the last four years, was certain that he could round up Jewish refugees, if he had the help of Baruch Tegegne. Obstacles were immediately put in Tegegne's way in Israel, when he revealed his intention to go to Sudan. The Israelis invited him to work for them and asked him to obtain a visa to Sudan. He went to Athens, made an application, and in a few days had the stamp on his passport. The Israelis then tried to divert him from the Sudanese mission and offered an assignment in Europe. Baruch was not interested. He wanted to rescue his own people. Finally he left Israel. His Israeli passport was confiscated at Lod, so he had to travel on his original Ethiopian passport, joining up with Halpern in Germany, where officials of Jewish international agencies attempted to dissuade them from going to Sudan. They threatened them. The AAEJ, fearful that something might happen to both young men, took out huge insurance policies for their benefit. Halpern and Tegegne told me that they slept with pistols under their pillows.

In order to get into Sudan, they needed a "cover," and found two; one was a sympathetic businessman who had interests in Africa, and I was responsible for the other, a global rescue organization that wanted to establish a clinic in Sudan for the growing refugee population. The organization used telex facilities in Khartoum to facilitate communication with its office in America and with me.

Halpern and Tegegne encountered unforeseen difficulties in Sudan after their arrival. We and they were not prepared to find an Israeli presence there. The Ethiopian Jew who had written to ask my help in getting from Sudan to Israel had been hired away by Israeli agents in Sudan and told to counter anything that we would be doing. Halpern and Tegegne rounded up a few Ethiopian Jews at a time from eastern Sudan and placed and fed them in a safe house in Khartoum. I was given their names and other information via telex. Occasionally I received a call directly from Halpern. The data were immediately communicated to the Jewish Agency via HIAS in New York, which volunteered to serve as an intermediary, although it would take no direct responsibility for their rescue. There should have been no delay in getting them out even singly or in pairs on commerical airlines flying to Europe, where they could transfer to planes an route to Israel. There was no possibility of direct flights to Israel, because Sudan had no diplomatic relations with Israel, nor did any of the many airlines leaving Sudan have any direct connections with Israel. Weeks passed and there was no pick up and delivery. We kept pressing without success.

On May 15, 1979, Aryeh Dulzin, head of the World Zionist Organization and Jewish Agency, came to New York and wanted to meet me. I agreed to see him, providing I could be accompanied by other members of the AAEJ board, and took along Henry Everett, Dr. Theodore Norman, and Henry Rosenberg, all personal and generous supporters of Israel. Dulzin, with his customary arrogance, asked us why we were so concerned about eight (later he changed it to eleven, indicating that he was not properly briefed) Ethiopian Jews in Sudan, when there were many more important problems in Jewish life. I sternly reminded him that I would be concerned if there was only one Jew involved, but there were not the numbers he cited, but thirty-two, and they had been waiting for months under our care to be taken to Israel. The exchanges became somewhat heated. To placate us, he even offered to reimburse the AAEJ for our expenses if there were more than the eleven. I finally had to threaten him: "If you don't take them out within thirty days, we will tell the story of your inhuman indifference to these black Ethiopian Jews to the *New York Times*." We left not sure what he would do. I was prepared, despite calming counsel from my colleagues, to act on my threat, if necessary.

A few days later, there was a meeting on Ethiopian Jews at the NJCRAC office. I had not been invited, but nevertheless went and sat at the end of a large horseshoe table. Most of the forty people present were representatives of major Jewish organizations, but not always their top leadership. The only key leader present was Charlotte Jacobson, a powerful political force in American and Israeli affairs, who was head of the World Zionist Organization's American Section. Sitting next to her was Benjamin Abileah, of the New York Israeli Consulate. I always thought that he was a secret Mossad representative on that body. At the meeting, both declared that there were only eleven Ethiopian Jews in Sudan, supporting Dulzin's erroneous count. I jumped up to state categorically that there were thirty-two, and if they were not rescued in the next few weeks, the dirty story would be told to the *New York Times* in an article and an advertisement.

In June, within the thirty-day limit, sixteen were taken out of Sudan by Israel, but the price the AAEJ had to pay was to abandon our operation in that country. If I had been in Israel when AAEJ representatives agreed to that condition, I would have strenuously objected. Israel flew out the other sixteen in July. It then claimed that there were no other Ethiopian Jews in Sudan.

As to repayment by the Jewish Agency on our bill of $85,000 for the Sudanese operation, it took a lot of pressure by some of our board members, and even then we received a check for only $9,000. I didn't want to accept it, but other members on our board decided to take it. I knew then that the word of Dulzin was not exactly a bond.

To Israel

Emma and I went to Israel on July 18 for a two-month stay, during which I engaged one of the new *olim* from Sudan whom we had helped to rescue, who spoke English, to submit a questionnaire I had prepared to the thirty-two new arrivals. The last question, and for me the most important, was: "Do you know any other Ethiopian Jews left in Sudan? Give their names and location." From this I discovered that there were at least forty-two others. The list was later expanded to ninety names. Some of them had been in Sudan for two and three years, arriving shortly after the revolution of 1974. The names were turned over to Israeli and Jewish Agency officials. Nothing was done to move them out immediately.

Montreal

The AAEJ began to step up its propaganda in the United States. We forced the laggard CJFWF to include a program on Ethiopian Jewry for the first time at its general assembly in Montreal. The AAEJ brought four Ethiopian Jews to the conference: Yona Bogale, the most distinguished of the Ethiopian Jews, who together with his wife and two children we had managed to bring from Ethiopia to Israel only a few weeks before; his son, Zechariah Yona, Rachamim Elezar, and Baruch Tegegne. The meeting was scheduled for a medium-sized room, but a growing interest among the three thousand delegates at the Assembly crowded 350 into the space, most standing, with hundreds waiting in the hallway to get a peek at the proceedings. The meeting quickly got out of hand when some activists, including myself, demanded that wholesale rescue be undertaken of the twenty-eight thousand Ethiopian Jews in Africa, that $20 million be raised in the 1979–80 campaign by the UJA to rescue and absorb them; that Yona Bogale be allowed to sit on the dais along with Menachem Begin, the guest of honor for that evening's plenary session, and that he should be invited to speak. There was widespread approval of these demands from a surprisingly sympathetic audience.

The conference officials at first refused to allow Bogale either on the podium or to speak. Unremitting pressure all afternoon brought about a change. Bogale sat with the dignitaries and did speak, although every word of his speech was rigorously edited. A handsome, dignified figure, he managed to depart from his text and made a dramatic appeal to the hushed listeners for his kinsmen. He was enthusiastically applauded.

Even this prodigious maneuver did not bring about the rescue of more Jews. A month later we had to inspire demonstrations in Israel. The three hundred Ethiopian Jews in Israel were now prepared to become much bolder in asserting their cause.

While we had agreed not to operate in Sudan directly, we had not promised to cease all activities that would save them. When no more were taken out, early in 1980, Nathan Shapiro, the AAEJ president, initiated another rescue operation, working out a deal with an Ethiopian performing such clandestine services in Sudan, and we agreed to pay him $2,000 a person for every Jew he delivered to us in Frankfurt, Germany. I handled the details in Pelham, buying the round-trip tickets from Sudan to Germany. They were ostensibly going to Germany to work, like many other Ethiopians who were brought to that country. Tegegne and Zechariah Yona were recruited to handle the refugees arriving in Germany. On arrival, they would inform the Israeli consulate and the Jewish Agency, so that arrangements could be made to put them on a plane to Israel.

The first six arrived, consisting of two families, husband, wife, and child in each. Israeli officials apparently wanted or were instructed to keep them from going to Israel. They charged that none of the six were Jews, that they were not married, that the women were prostitutes, the children bastards, and refused to send them on. When impatient German officials finally gave the six a choice of remaining in Germany or returning to Sudan, they opted to stay in Germany. At this point, seeing that their plan to keep them out of Israel had been frustrated, the Jewish officials offered to send them to Israel. The Ethiopian Jews asserted that their names had been besmirched; therefore they didn't want anything further to do with either Israel or Jews. They have remained in Germany ever since. This is a tragic commentary on the perfidious behavior of officials of a Jewish state.

Not deterred, we asked our agent to send more. Two young men arrived in Frankfurt. The Israelis interrogated them. One was found acceptable, but a seventeen-year-old was rejected when he refused to divulge anything about his mother. Out of shame, he apparently did not want to acknowledge that she had been forced to turn to prostitution to support her starving family in Sudan. In tears, he cried that nobody wanted him in Ethiopia, in Sudan, and in Israel. Our representatives in Germany had not yet had time, because all of these events took place in a matter of hours at the airport, to pick up his return ticket to Khartoum. He slipped away, managed to get on a flight back to Khartoum, and committed suicide on arrival in that city's airport. The other young man flew to Israel.

Undaunted by these recreant mishaps, I arranged tickets for fourteen more to leave Sudan for Germany. Believing that efforts might be made to prevent their departure and arrival on any direct flight from Khartoum to Frankfurt, I arranged transport via Zurich. There the refugees changed planes for Frankfurt. This time our agents were told to advise the Israelis that if the refugees were not put on the next plane to Israel, we would tell the unsavory story from the very beginning to the *International Herald-Tribune*, so that the entire world would know how Jews treated fellow Jews in jeopardy. The Israelis sped them off to Israel.

We were then persuaded for a second time to agree that we would cease our operation in Europe. We assented on the condition that Israel would start a major and continuous rescue operation out of Sudan, where we believed there were ever-growing numbers of Ethiopian Jewish refugees. I questioned our withdrawal until refugees actually began to arrive in Israel. Our rescue demonstrations and our threats of exposure had their effect, and 679 were taken out of Sudan in 1980. It was still a foot-dragging exodus. We never were able to relax our pressing tactics. Yet we were heartened that the Ethiopian Jews, at great peril, had at last found a way of eventually reaching Israel.

U.S. Senators and Congressmen

The year 1979 marked beginning of our AAEJ campaign to enlist the aid of U.S. senators and congressmen in the cause of Ethiopian Jewry.

My own view was that we should start working only with the Jewish representatives in both Houses, and induce them to pressure Israel to undertake a large-scale rescue program. Time was running out on the fortunes and future of the Ethiopian Jews. While the U.S. government did not have a great deal of influence on Ethiopian officials, since it had completely misjudged the continuity of the revolutionary regime and was viewed with suspicion by the leadership of the Dergue, the United States did carry a lot more weight in Sudan, where it had for years literally underpinned the always shaky Numeiri regime.

Before Halpern went to Sudan, I went to Washington with him and met Rudolph (Rudy) Boschwitz, the new Republican senator from Minnesota. He was a friend of Halpern. A genial, outgoing individual, who proudly asserted on every occasion that he was a "refugee" from World War II's Europe, a successful businessman who used billboard advertising to promote himself into the Senate, Boschwitz and I hit it off right away. We liked each other's candor on all kinds of issues. At lunch in the Senate dining room, he asked me over a bowl of its famous bean soup what he could do. I suggested a meeting with the new Israeli ambassador, Ephraim Evron. He asked me to ride and walk back to his office, called the ambassador, and arranged a date in the senator's office at 8:30 the next morning. He did not tell the ambassador what it was all about. Boschwitz wanted me to be present.

I arrived, as is my wont, at 8:20 A.M. The senator was not yet in. His secretary told me that the Israeli ambassador had called and canceled the date. When I told this to Boschwitz on his arrival, he went into a rage, literally pulled me into his inner office, phoned the ambassador, and shouted: "No one cancels a date with me ten minutes before the meeting is to take place. I want you to know that you need me more than I need you, and we had better get our relationships straight at the outset. I want to talk with you about Ethiopian Jews." A meeting was set for 4 P.M. that afternoon.

Evron, a short, pleasant, but not particularly prepossessing man, but one with enough talent, perseverance, and connections to rise in the hierarchy of Israeli politics, arrived with two aides: Hanon Dar-on and Zvi Rafiah. Boschwitz opened the discussion by referring to the serious condition of Ethiopian Jews in Ethiopia and wanted to know why Israel had done so little, and why the two modest rescues in 1977 had not been continued. Evron admitted to being no expert on the subject and called on Dar-on, who had served in the Israeli Embassy in Addis Ababa, to give a historical review. Dar-on lapsed into a detailed geopolitical analysis of the Horn of Africa. He stated that it had been almost impossible to take any Ethiopian Jews out of the country since 1973, even though there had been a breakthrough in 1977. He omitted any reference to Israel's restrictive policy when it had formal diplomatic relations, or why the 1977 lift out was not continued. It was "complex," it was "difficult."

Everything must be "shrouded in secrecy." Boschwitz turned to me for comment. I disputed Dar-on's statements, indicating that in the political and military chaos which persisted in Ethiopia, it was possible to bring out thousands, providing there was a policy and a will to do so. I stated that I knew there was still an unofficial Israeli presence in Ethiopia. I referred to the possibility of rescue through Sudan and that Israelis were known to be in that country this very moment on other business.

The discussion that followed appeared to be getting nowhere. I decided to leave Boschwitz with the Israelis, to see what he could work out on his own.

As I rose to leave, standing behind Evron, Boschwitz scribbled his private home telephone number on a piece of paper, and over Evron's head, handed it to me and told me to be sure and call him the following morning. I surmised this was a calculated piece of drama to emphasize to the Israelis that I wasn't to be ignored. I did not shake hands with the Israelis as I left, although we had done so when introduced, and simply uttered "Shabbat Shalom," because it was almost Sabbath eve.

A year before I had attended a cocktail party in Washington with my brother Sam, at which I met Dar-on and his wife. A charming woman, she asked me whether I had ever been to Israel. I replied: "About a dozen times." "What brought you to Israel so frequently?" While I could have replied in many ways, I chose to say that I went there with the hope of bringing Ethiopian Jews to Israel. She turned away from me and then turned back: "Do you know anything about Ethiopian Jews? My husband and I lived in Ethiopia, and we question whether they are Jews and whether any effort should be made to bring them to Israel." He said nothing. I told them that I had been to Ethiopia twice, that I knew they were Jews, that I had seen the terrible conditions under which they lived, that they wanted to go to Israel and that I was giving a great deal of my time to seeing that they were brought to Israel. I then turned away to talk to others at the party. So I knew Dar-on's views in advance of our meeting in the senator's office.

I maintained a relationship with Boschwitz, sent him detailed memos on the subject, urged him to call a meeting of Jewish senators and congressmen at the earliest moment. Such a meeting finally took place on June 7. The NJCRAC and the Israeli Embassy learned about the session and asked to be present. They were invited. The meeting was attended by Senators Boschwitz, Stone, Metzenbaum, Ribicoff, Wolpe. Several other senators sent their aides. Also present was Congressman Stephen Solarz.

The meeting turned out to be disastrous for the NJCRAC and Israeli point of view. There was sharp criticism of the Israelis lack of helpfulness over the years. I had informed the legislators about the thirty-two Ethiopian Jews we had assembled in Sudan, who had not yet been flown to Israel. The Israeli representative replied that his government never did anything illegally. Metzenbaum reproached him: "Then how did you and so many Jewish refugees ever get to Israel? Was it always so legal?" Each of the officials in his own way addressed the Israelis, insisting that something had to be done.

I maintained my contact with Boschwitz for a time. Later, others, including non-Jewish congressional officials, began to play even more important roles in forcing the rescue of Ethiopian Jews. They eventually caused the dramatic rescues of 1984 and 1985.

World ORT In Ethiopia

Reports began to circulate about World ORT's program in Ethiopia and the negative reactions of the Ethiopian Jews to their presence. When I raised these issues with Paul Bernick, head of American ORT, at private luncheons, he tried to put a better face on my information, indicating that it was difficult to deal with some Ethiopian Jews. He asserted defensively that his organization had a competent team in Ethiopia, including non-Jews, who were carrying out the agreement with the Ethiopian government to develop a sound, nonsectarian program. He told me that if he had known that I was going to monitor everything that ORT was doing in Ethiopia, he would never have recommended that ORT get involved. I told him that the AAEJ and I would continue to play that role of "monitor."

When I raised some of the shortcomings of ORT at a meeting at the JDC with a number of individuals representing Jewish organizations seemingly interested in the welfare of Ethiopian Jews, I was given, actually thrown, a pile of charts, indicating how well things were developing. Building plans. Statistics. Expenditures. Was I aware that ORT was building synagogues, schools, clinics, making loans to farmers and students. When I pointed out how pitiably few Ethiopian Jews were receiving these services, less than 10 percent, while a great deal of money was being expended for buildings and vehicles and offices, I was told—for I was the lone critic—that they would look into my comments and see what they could do to enlarge the program. Some changes were made as a consequence of my criticisms.

Bernard and Frances Alpert of Highland Park, Illinois, who had been to Ethiopia and were members of our board, returned from Israel with detailed written charges against ORT's program in Ethiopia, reports which had been prepared by Eli Turgeman, an Israeli who had been engaged by ORT as an expert in rural development. It was not clear whether Turgeman resigned or was fired, but in any event he decided to reveal the unhappy story of how little was being done, how officials, and particularly a non-Jewish official of ORT, were notably prejudiced against the Ethiopian Jews. He claimed that the non-Jewish official had been responsible for informing on some Jews, who were subsequently arrested and tortured. Two of them had been killed in prison.

The AAEJ invited Turgeman to New York where he stayed at our house. We asked for a meeting with ORT to present Turgeman's and our observations on the Ethiopian program. We decided to do everything verbally, presenting no written statements, taking no minutes, because our clear purpose was to have ORT internally correct the situation. We had no intention initially of making this a public affair. I was so irritated by the snide remarks of the American ORT chairman of this session that at one point I could have choked him. He kept on questioning the motives of the accusers rather than dealing with the unpleasant issues we presented.

With the encouragement of several members of the AAEJ who were present, I was inveigled into preparing a written statement to American ORT, so that it could examine the charges and determine how these assertions could be remedied. The president of ORT spoke of the possibility of going to Ethiopia himself to determine whether Turgeman's and our statements had any basis in fact.

I worked night and day, prepared a carefully phrased 11-page memorandum, assembling a pile of documentary evidence, which was read and approved by nine members of the AAEJ board, most of them on the executive committee. It listed twenty-two indictments of the ORT program in Ethiopia, with footnotes supporting every allegation.

I said inveigled, because despite the names of other members of the AAEJ on the document, I was singled out for attack by ORT, the Jewish Agency, the Israeli government, and others, with the distinct hope on their part to wean other members of the board away from associating themselves with the report and with me.

The document was presented to Sidney E. Leiwant at a meeting on April 3, which he chose to attend alone. This was calculated. He read it through as we watched. He was obviously stunned. He told us that he would initiate an immediate investigation and go to Ethiopia personally. Members of the AAEJ were content with his serious mien and decision. We had no intention of circulating the memorandum. We would await ORT's reply, especially how it would remedy our charges.

We did not suspect that ORT had no intention of investigating the indictments. Instead it turned the document over to Simon Guedj, the ORT director of the program and himself named in several of the allegations, to answer. On May 14, 1975, in a memorandum of 17 pages, ORT denied every charge, stating that it had no need to make any changes and would not withdraw from the Ethiopian project.

ORT in addition sought the help of the Falasha Welfare Association, the Jewish Agency, the Israeli government, and others in countering these charges and did a perfect job of maligning the critics rather than dealing with the issue. As a consequence, the controversy via ORT was brought to the attention of a larger Jewish public, and we belatedly had to send out our memorandum to inquiring organizations and individuals, who wanted to know what it was all about.

There were consequences. Guedj was removed from his post. A more hospitable attitude was exhibited toward the Ethiopian Jews. Some additional programs were introduced. However, the nonsectarian program was continued and even expanded. Kebede, the Ethiopian non-Falasha administrator, still occupied a powerful job in the organization and grew rich as a consequence of his strategic position. ORT still refused to provide outright relief to the growing number of needy Jews, sticking to loans, clinics, and education for a small sector of the total Jewish population. It refused to intervene when Jews, even its own employees, were arrested and imprisoned and tortured. Until we pressured, it refused to provide funds to families of employees who were jailed and could not support themselves. It refused to assist in any way, directly or indirectly, any program of aliyah to Israel. It claimed this was not its mandate.

Our position indicting ORT was supported only by Tartakower's Israeli committee and by the Israeli Association of Ethiopian Jews. Otherwise we were left to fight the battle on our own. The usual "clubby" negative attitude taken by Jewish organizations toward the AAEJ and me made them either defend ORT or do or say nothing else.

During the fall of 1979 a report was issued by a special investigating committee appointed by no less than the Israeli Prime Minister's office to inquire into the AAEJ's complaints about ORT's handling of Ethiopian Jewry. It concluded: "There is no basis for the charges levelled against ORT and they derive from the impure motives of the accusers." The statement referred to the "irresponsible and counter productive activities of Mr. G. Berger (USA) and Mr. E. Turgeman (Israel)," stating that "their activities have resulted in the withdrawal of aid. . . . and their public statements are also liable to bring about a change for the worse in the attitudes of the local authorities towards the Falashas." Neither of these dire predictions about the results of our memorandum came to pass. If anything, the lot of the Ethiopian Jews became for a short time somewhat better.

As for the Israeli committee, it never called me as a witness, although I was in Israel at the time it was meeting. I would have been instantly available.

With regard to my so-called prejudiced attitude toward ORT, the facts were otherwise. I had always had a positive respect for the work of this hundred-year-old organization. I had visited its installations in many countries and was favorably impressed by its personnel, facilities, and programs. I was one who approved of ORT's assuming responsibility for the enlarged services that would be provided for the Jews in Ethiopia after 1976, even though I would have preferred the JDC as the managing agent. My disillusionment with this single program in Ethiopia appeared as a result of the unhappy reports that I and others were receiving from a variety of sources. I wasn't gunning for any individual or the organization out of spite, but out of the gruesome facts.

I wanted to sue the Israeli committee, ORT, and the *Jewish Chronicle* of London, which had printed a story defending ORT and attacking me, for libel. Sober legal heads talked me out of such an audacious venture. They told me that even if I won the case, it was of no consequence. I think the advice was *not* sound.

The events clearly revealed the perfidious, conspiratorial practices of Jewish organizations, when accused of deleterious acts, which were supposed to be in the interest of the clientele served rather than the agency's image in the public mind. I've never had anything to do with any of the organizations involved since that unhappy experience.

* * *

To step up immigration from Ethiopia to Israel, the AAEJ organized a demonstration before the Israeli consulate in New York. Rabbi Avi Weiss and others spoke fervently at the United Nations Isaiah Plaza.

At Nathan Shapiro's invitation, I flew to Chicago for a four-day speaking tour in synagogues, awakening interest and raising some money. Meetings with Philip Klutznick and Chuck Hoffberger, with Nathan Shaprio present, could not elicit the support of these top Jewish leaders. I made another three-day speaking tour to Minneapolis and St. Paul for the same cause. I returned with a few more friends, but the key people could not be enticed into supporting this cause.

Two Lubavitcher representatives invited themselves to our home to be educated about the Ethiopian Jews. After several hours, they asked me for money to go to Ethiopia, so that they could make their own determination as to whether they were indeed Jews and thus objects of interest for their movement. Regrettably, the Lubavitcher Rebbe has never spoken out on their behalf, and as a consequence no help has been forthcoming from this influential worldwide Jewish sect. In 1985, the Lubavitch schools in Israel refused to accept Ethiopian Jewish children, because they still questioned their Jewish authenticity.

This was the year when for the first time the AAEJ brought an Ethiopian Jew to the United States for a speaking tour. While Zechariah Yona met with favor in some communities and youth groups, he was shunned by the establishment, an indication that at this time there was no genuine interest in helping Ethiopian Jews in any manner.

Dan Ross, a writer, spent some time at our home obtaining background material on Ethiopian Jewry, for an excellent book, *Acts of Faith* (1982), in which he devoted a chapter titled: "Falashas—Is Zionism Only for White Jews?"

Baruch Tegegne

When Baruch Tegegne went to Canada with me for the General Assembly of the CJFWF in November 1979, I asked him whether he planned to call his future in-laws, who lived in Montreal. Susan Migicovsky, the daughter of a middle-class Jewish family, had gone to Israel after finishing college, and there she and Baruch had fallen in love. Their efforts to get married in Israel did not materialize. Furthermore Susan was not happy with the attitude of Israelis, particularly young men, because of her relationship to Baruch, a black Ethiopian Jew. When Baruch left Israel to work for the AAEJ in Sudan, Susan awaited his return in Italy, where he joined her in the summer after completing his duties in Africa. She remained in Italy when he went to the United States and then to Montreal. Baruch was uncomfortable about calling Susan's parents, because they were opposed to the union of their daughter with a black Ethiopian, even if he was a Jew and an Israeli. So I undertook, with his consent, the delicate job. We arranged to meet at our hotel for lunch the next day. The Migicovskys were an attractive middle-aged couple and greeted both of us quite formally.

I wish I had recorded the conversation, most of which was addressed in my direction: Could a black and white marriage work out? There were no such marriages in the Canadian Jewish community. How would they be able to develop friends amongst Jews, who would see any fraternization as an encouragement for their own children to do the same? Would I want such a marriage for my own daughters or granddaughters?

While not advocating the marriage, or any kind of marriage, including an interracial one, I tried to deal with the subject with some degree of objectivity. I told the Migicovskys that on principle I was opposed to any form of racial discrimination, particularly by Jews toward other Jews. I said that I would have no objection to my granddaughters—and I have four of them—marrying a black Jew, but I hoped that there would be a great deal of common interests between the two parties, before blessing such a union. The questions I put were: was Baruch a good man? Would he be a good husband and father? Could he support a wife and family? Could they both be helped by her parents to make an accommodation in the Montreal Jewish community? When we said goodbye, Mr. and Mrs. Migicovsky kissed both Baruch and me.

Baruch and Susan were married in a private ceremony and a year later had a beautiful child. The Migicovskys set them up in a small business, which despite their heroic efforts did not thrive, because the neighborhood changed as a result of the shutdown of a number of industries. Baruch actually wanted to serve and work for his people. He accepted invitations to speak on their behalf, often only for his expenses.

He was brief in speech and effective emotionally. He changed from job to job. He did not improve himself by any university or technical training. While there was love, the marriage did not work out. In 1984, when Baruch indicated that he wanted to go to Israel to work for his kinsmen, Susan sued for divorce. They maintained communications, but their life-styles and abiding interests were not compatible. He could not make an adequate living for all of them. She became a schoolteacher. It was an unhappy ending to a dramatic romance. In Israel, Baruch was still footloose. He accepted an assignment in Africa, but that did not work out. What he will do with his life in the future is still an uncertainty.

* * *

When Baruch Tegegne and Rachamim Elezar were in New York in November 1979, they were invited to the wedding of the daughter of Henry and Edith Everett. It was a beautiful affair in a prominent Brooklyn synagogue with several hundred guests. Both sat at our table and engaged in conversation with the others. Out of courtesy to me—and they always treat Emma and me as though we were their parents—they left the table to smoke in another room. They were immediately besieged by a large number of young people, who wanted to know from whence they came, and when had they become Jews. Baruch, who has an excellent sense of humor, quipped: "Thirty-three hundred years ago, when Moses *verblunzhet* ("wandered off the beaten path" or "got lost") in Ethiopia." He was asked if Tegene was a Jewish name. He replied, "Yes, the same as Migicovsky," his future Jewish wife's name. When he returned to our table, he told us of this exchange and then added: "Why do they ask me such a question, when did I become a Jew? It would never occur to me or any other Ethiopian Jew to ask a white person when he became a Jew."

* * *

The United Jewish Appeal was planning a large public meeting to be held in Lincoln Center on December 7, 1979, in honor of Jacobo Timmerman, who had recently been released from prison in Argentina and was now living in Israel, where he was writing books and lecturing worldwide as a celebrity. A Russian Jew, living in Israel, was also to be feted. Eli Rockowitz, a young activist on the AAEJ board, undertook a one-man campaign to see that Baruch Tegegne was also honored at the same convocation. At first this suggestion was rejected. Eli persisted, emphasizing that Baruch and his family had personally been in jeopardy because of their Jewishness and finally he prevailed. At the last moment, it was agreed that Baruch would be part of the ceremony, but he would be permitted to give only a two-minute speech and it was not to be provocative. While there was time to print his name on the elaborate program, there was no time to have his photograph included along with the others.

Both Timmerman and the Russian spoke at length, but Tegegne was a hit with his brief speech, presented with deep emotion, pleading for the rescue of his unfortunate brethren.

I don't know what happened to the Russian. Timmerman ended up in disgrace in the world Jewish community for his inhosptable, graceless, and vicious attacks on Israel. Baruch barely survived, devoting his time and energy to saving his people and trying to bring them to Israel.

I often wonder whether, in light of the mass rescue and absorption program of 1984–85, the top leaders of American Jewry, who planned and presided over this event, recall their initial rejection of this lone Ethiopian Jew, at a time when the cause of Ethiopian Jewry was not even on the agenda of either Israel or the world and American Jewish community.

* * *

In 1979 Louis Rapoport started working on his book *The Lost Jews*. I was not satisfied with the draft he sent me and wrote detailed comments about the content and the style. He heeded some of my observations about content but persisted with his own style, which made the book less effective than it might have been. It went into a second edition and was also published in a French version, *Les Falashas D'Ethiopie*. I personally sold more than fifteen hundred copies during my lectures on Ethiopian Jewry.

Caribbean Research

At several of my lectures on *Black Jews in America,* blacks (Jews and non-Jews) in the audience were critical of my historical treatment of how American blacks had become Jews. In my view, some had become Jews by conversion, but most asserted that they were Jews simply by self-declaration. They had come chiefly from the Caribbean region, did not want to identify with a black slave ancestry, and claimed that they were aboriginally Jewish. My critics insisted from the floor that I had not done enough homework, and if I gave the matter further study, I would find colonies of black Jews in that section of the world to disprove my thesis. I had read a number of books about each Jewish settlement in the islands. While Jews settled there in the sixteenth century and were slave owners, there is no record of their converting their chattel to Judaism. It was not in their economic interest to do so, since being Orthodox Jews, they would have had to free them after six years of servitude. Furthermore, the Jews did not enjoy full political and civil rights in most of these countries until the end of the eighteenth and the early part of the nineteenth century, so there would be no civil benefit to a black who became a Jew. Jewish congregations in those countries and in the southern part of the United States, where slavery was the practice until the Civil War, did nothing to encourage blacks to become Jews.

Yet, when challenged, Emma and I decided to take an extended holiday in the Caribbean, visiting those islands that still had or once had a Jewish settlement of consequence. On January 18, forsaking the cold spell in our area, we flew off to Curaçao. We had prepared ourselves by reading about each island and collecting names of Jews, Jewish organizations, and others who might be helpful in our search for black Jews. I had decided to pose as a writer who was collecting material on exotic religious sects, particularly the Rastafarians. This black religious sect, founded in the 1930s in Jamaica, held the strange belief that Haile Selassie, who became Emperor of Ethiopia in 1930, and thus the only contemporary black ruler of an African nation, was the living Christ. The movement was described even more interestingly as "Black Zionism." Selassie, who traced his ancestry back to the biblical account of the union of King Solomon and the Queen of Sheba, disliked being considered a black or Negro, but this had no bearing on the group's views, which had their roots in the teachings of Marcus Garvey, who urged his followers to look to Africa for the coming of a black king who would be their redeemer. The cult had other odd practices, like using marijuana as part of its service as well as its economy. They combed their hair in a curious style—dreadlocks. I thought it would be easier to get information if I started with the Rastafarians (Selassie's original name was Ras Tafari) and then slid into a discussion of black Jews.

Walking into the courtyard of Mikve Israel–Emanuel, one of the oldest synagogues in the Western world, which still covered its floors with sand, I saw a black, who I presumed was a goy-shamas, sitting on a bench. He was a Jew. I immediately learned his history. While he claimed to have been a Jew all his life, and he was a man in his late sixties, he actually did not convert to Judaism until 1964. His parents were not Jewish. His mother had been a cook in a Jewish household, and these were the closest ties that any of them ever had with Jews. The rest of his family, wife and children, remained Roman Catholics, had never been interested in becoming Jews. So he was a lone black Jew, who found fulfillment in this ancient faith and its rituals.

He told me about two black Jewish women. I subsequently interviewed them. One had been converted in 1975, the only one in her family. She was seeking a Jewish husband, so far without success. She found her Jewish life only in the synagogue.

The other woman related a strange tale. She formerly lived in Surinam, which had an interesting Jewish history. She claimed an Indian (Oriental not American) Jew as a grandfather, and a grandmother who was Palestinian-Israeli and white. She had a deep-brown-black tincture. Her father and she were the only black Jews in Surinam. She had no need to convert, for she was already a Jew. She made a trip to Israel, but could not find any trace of her grandmother's family. I found it hard to believe this fantastic tale.

Curaçao proved my thesis. None of the black Jews were descendants of black slaves owned by Jews. Two were recent converts.

I met all the leaders, some descendants of original Jewish settlers, and the rabbi of the synagogue. None of them could provide me with more information than I had already assembled. They told me that few whites in Curaçao, let alone blacks, had ever been converted to Judaism.

* * *

My diary recorded that I had dreams two nights in a row about Golda Meir and Yitzhak Navon in which they had worked out a deal with Ethiopia to rescue twenty-eight thousand Ethiopian Jews and bring them to Israel. During my dream I tried everywhere to get confirmation of their actions, but awoke each night having found no answer, I still do not know why this dream occurred, and of all places, in Curaçao.

* * *

Several people in Curaçao and from Surinam told me that they had met blacks in both countries who greeted them with "Shalom." Some wore a Star of David on a chain. It has been my experience that when such persons politely were questioned as to both practices, it invariably turned out that they were not Jews. The Mogen David was an ornament, often given to them by a Jewish friend or employer. For them it was a talisman to bring good luck and good fortune.

* * *

We reached Port of Spain in Trinidad via Caracas, after a day's delay, when the airline blithely cancelled a scheduled flight. Trinidad was a country living off and dependent upon its underground oil. Just above the equator, it was both tropically green and hot. Sugar plantations and water buffaloes gave it a quaint character. English memories were still present, as traffic followed the left-side driving pattern.

I had been given the name of Mr. Stecher, a Jew, who ran a large, expensive jewelry and imported china store. He only knew of one black Jew, who was a recent convert. The white Jews could barely corral a minyan for prayers.

Four young Americans took me to a calypso theater, where singers offered endless verses, accompanied by a brassy orchestra (all the good steel drum bands were on tours out of the country), to an appreciative, nonstop applauding audience. The songs, dealing with politics, love, and sex, were familiar to the listeners. During a few numbers, the seatholders actually went into ecstasy or laughed uproariously. I was told these were extra-sexy tunes.

Further research revealed that there were no black Jewish groups on the island.

* * *

Grenada, the nutmeg island, was lush in vegetation and proved to be the most beautiful of all the islands we visited. The tiny country was in the throes of conflict. A bomb had been thrown against the wall of the Barclay Bank the night we arrived. A few years earlier Grenada had become independent. The moderate government was overthrown by a socialist dicatorship with an actual Cuban presence. In 1983, the United States invaded the island and restored democracy to that problem-ridden country. Walking and riding through the mountainous country and St. George, the capital, gave one no outward impression of unrest. Talking to natives revealed an undercurrent of discontent. They couldn't make a living.

We contacted Dr. Morris Alpert, dean of the local medical school, and a former classmate of mine at Gloversville High School, who knew nothing of black Jews. He had to spend the next few days at a hospital on the nearby island of St. Vincent, so we could not meet. The presence of numerous American students attending this medical school, and their need for protection, offered U.S. soldiery a pretext for invading this handsome spot.

This was the kind of romantic island we loved. The beaches, extending for miles, permitted us to walk barefoot for exercise and the sheer almost silent pleasure of the sea.

We spent some time with the editor of the major newspaper and his assistant, trying to find out about various cults. It was clear that intellectuals were not identified either with formal church organizations or with the sects. He dismissed the cults as "fads," coming and going without permanence. They had never heard of a black Jew.

The music in Grenada was marengue. Orchestras played these tunes for dancing in the evening during and after dinner. The music was different from what we had heard in Trinidad in content, melody, and rhythms.

* * *

An hour away was Barbados in the Atlantic, the farthest east of the West Indies. It was by contrast a busy island, with shops that made it a tourist paradise. I had been informed that there was a black Jewish congregation headed by "Rabbi" Philip Evelyn, whom I invited to lunch. Evelyn, seventy-nine, medium-brown complexion, spoke vaguely of his father and mother, who had told him of their Judaic ancestors in Africa. Originally from Barbados, he had gone to the United States to work.

There he joined the Ethiopian Hebrew Congregation in Harlem, learned Hebrew and Jewish rituals. He never became a Bar Mitzvah. The Harlem congregation was never recognized as Jewish by the New York Board of Rabbis. (Read my book *Black Jews in America* for a more detailed history of this congregation.) Evelyn's first wife was not a black Jew, but his second wife was. None of his siblings pursued a Jewish life. Evelyn returned to Barbados, along with a few other American blacks who had similar Judaic interests, and they had formed a separate black Jewish congregation, worshipping in a building provided by one of the richer members. The synagogue was established in 1960 and called itself the Zion House of Israel. It had ten members, but could rarely muster enough for a minyan. Since it was difficult to get kosher meat in Barbados, they ate fish. During the year they did not maintain two sets of dishes, but on Passover, they used separate dishes and ate distinctive holiday foods.

We called Stanley and Joan Kaufman. He was a young, successful American businessman, manufacturing children's clothing. He conducted services at the "white" synagogue with its membership of twenty families, and was known, as he laughingly told us, as its "rabbi." The original Jewish community of Sephardic Jews had expired in 1832, the Kaufmans told us, but they knew of a black man named Pinheiro, a practicing Christian, who was supposed to be a descendant of the original Jewish residents. We visited an older synagogue, that had been sold, because there were not enough Jews to support it. The cemetery at its side was still used for burial purposes. The synagogue has become a landmark, restored for its original purpose as well as an attraction for tourists.

The white Jewish community had no contact with the black Jewish congregation, for they did not believe that they were authentic Jews. I would agree with this evaluation. A young Jewish woman in the United States Peace Corps had spent time with the black group and wrote an account for the *Cleveland Jewish News*. The Kaufmans described her report as "replete with errors." There were no references to the black congregation in any Jewish guidebooks.

I visited the local newspaper office. No information. I spent a number of hours in the library, where I read a number of books dealing with the Jews of Barbados. It was evident that the Jews never proselytized among the whites nor the blacks. In the eighteenth century, Jews on the island were severely limited as to the number of slaves they could own, often limited to only one. As one writer put it: "The Jews were allowed one slave, and as they could not employ Christian servants, they had to make use of their poor fellow religionists" (Rev. Canon P. A. Farrar, *The Jews in Barbados*, 1941).

* * *

After hopping on a small plane from island to island, we reached Antigua, where we rested for a few days in a handsome hotel on a quiet beach, on which ripe coconuts dropped into your lap. My search for black Jews proved fruitless. There were no Jews of any kind, according to the natives.

* * *

Nevis was our next stop. Here Columbus landed in 1493. Alexander Hamilton was born on that cloud-capped volcanic island. We stayed in a former sugar plantation, Golden Rock, converted into a hotel through the addition of sufficient lodges for twenty-eight guests. It was run by a young woman and her husband, whose ancestor owned the property in 1815.

I spent some time in the newspaper office and the local library in Charlestown looking up references about the Jewish community that once dwelt on this island. They had built a synagogue. One could still see the ruins of the building and the contiguous cemetery. We visited the home of Robert Abrahams, a Jewish lawyer from Philadelphia, who had built a museum, also his home, to house his collectables dealing with the English admiral Horatio Nelson, who was married to Fanny Nesbit in a local church in 1787. Abrahams's research disclosed no black Jewish converts or heirs of early Jewish settlers, although he found that in their wills—and this was true in other places as well—some black slaves were manumitted and inherited some money from their former owners. He assured me that there were no black Jews on the island currently.

* * *

Before reaching the Virgin Islands, we had to change planes in St. Kitts. With several free hours, we walked the streets and stopped in an antique shop. The woman owner told us she had married a Jew, but that she and her husband were now both Roman Catholics. When asked about the presence of black Jews, she referred us to Ian Peter Mallialseu, who ran the Town House bakery. He left his oven and related this tale. About 150 years ago, a Miss Scofield, a young Jewish woman from England, came to the island and married into his family, a mixture of Negro, French Huguenot, and English. Miss Scofield was of Sephardic origin. She became a Christian and was buried in the Moravian cemetery.

Apart from this slight Jewish intrusion on the family escutcheon, he and his father, who joined our conversation, told us that they had never heard of any blacks or colored Jews on St. Kitts. He thought that the blacks who went to New York in recent decades and became Jews must have been converted, for they had no Jewish ancestry.

* * *

St. Thomas in the Virgin Islands, proved a bit more fruitful in our pursuit of black Jews. First we saw the sights of this bustling city. Then we visited the synagogue and talked with Rabbi Stanley Relkin. He told us there were three blacks in his congregation. He had never questioned them about their Jewish origin. Why the lack of curiosity? One was a teacher in his religious school. The Rabbi told us that he had refused to marry a black couple in his synagogue, because he was unsure of their Jewish status. I was told that there might be several other black Jews on the island, former members of a black "Jewish" congregation in Harlem, New York City.

I spent several hours in the library, where the librarian brought me everything listed under "Jews." It was evident from the texts and the clippings that the colonial Jews had not married blacks or converted them to Judaism. The laws of the synagogue dating from 1848, did not permit the rabbi to perform any marriage which "may contravene the laws of our religion or the state." It was not clear what Judaism had to say about this type of marriage, but the state abjured such unions.

I spoke with Isidor Paiewonsky, the most prominent Jew on the island and its historian, who told me that as far as his records revealed: "No blacks converted to Judaism in the history of the islands." While Jews may have had children by black women, they were never considered or raised as Jews. Some blacks claimed a Jewish ancestry, but were not identified as Jews. There was no record of any black Jewish congregration. He doubted the Jewish authenticity of any blacks on the island.

Dominican Republic

Santo Domingo impressed us so much that we returned on two later occasions, once with two of our grandchildren, Elisabeth and Gideon, for a seven-day holiday. It was an interesting city with old monuments, a good museum, fine restaurants, shops full of amber and native art. Predominantly white and Spanish, the Dominican Republic put up barriers against any influx of French-speaking blacks from Haiti, with which it shared the large land mass of Hispaniola.

A Friday night in the synagogue counted more tourists than natives, who together provided a bare minyan. As far as we could learn from the Santo Domingo Jews in the synagogue that night, there were no black Jews in the country. They had heard that a few Jews had married natives, but the families no longer considered themselves Jews.

We had a pleasant meeting with Bruno Phillip, eighty-nine years of age (he died in 1982). He was amongst the German Jews who were provided a haven in the Domincan Republic in 1938 during the Trujillo regime. They set up a colony of Jewish refugees from Europe in Sosua on the northern shore. Dr. Maurice Hexter, my former chief at Federation, and James Rosenberg, a New York attorney, had told me a great deal about the colony, which they helped establish. Phillip subsequently prospered, moved to Santo Domingo, and lived in a luxurious villa. Two of his children lived abroad, but an unmarried son, Thomas, resided with him and ran the businesses in which they were involved. On our subsequent trips to Santo Domingo, we met with his son. Both the father and later the son served as vice-consuls at the Israeli Embassy and enjoyed a special diplomatic status. Both knew nothing of any black Jews in the republic.

My historical readings about this land revealed that the Inquisition was introduced there in 1517. There was no evidence of a Jewish presence until recent decades.

Jamaica

To reach the island of Jamaica, we had to fly via Haiti and spent several hours in the airport to be sure we had a seat on the first plane out. We had seen the colorful, imaginative works of Haitian native painters in the Dominican Republic's fine art shops. The airport was filled with these paintings. We made up our minds to go to Haiti and see the country and its artists at first hand. We did in 1983.

Unlike most tourists, who go to the beaches on the north shore, we stayed in Kingston, the capital, in a hotel that was flooded with Cubans, living in the United States, who had finally obtained visas to visit relatives in their native land, from which they had fled after the Castro revolution. They were loaded with radios, electrical appliances, and toys.

After making many calls on the phone, we traced down Ernest H. De Souza, a photographer by profession (he fixed my nonworking camera), the acting rabbi of the Shaare Shalom synagogue, as well as its instructor in Hebrew. He was a delightful, middle-aged, youngish-looking man, who traced his ancestry to the early Sephardic settlers hundreds of years ago. There were 350 Jews in Jamaica. They could barely attract a minyan for services, except on the High Holy Days. Most of the old Jewish families over the years either moved elsewhere or intermarried with the colored. Several years ago, a census revealed that there were six hundred Jews, but it included several hundred Rastafarians, who had classified themselves on the demographic register as "Israelites." He told us that the Rastis were generally pro-Israel.

Souza's extreme religious liberalism was reflected in his willingness to be a party to an intermarriage even in a church. He admitted that no active rabbi in this congregation would do so. As a justice of the peace, Souza performed every variety of marriage. He asserted that an intermarriage could be performed in the synagogue if the non-Jewish partner, whether white, colored, or black, vowed to live as a Jew and raise the children as Jews. His experience was that they did, although he admitted that the quality of Jewish life was not very deep either in support of the synagogue or for other Jewish causes abroad. The synagogue was fortunately well endowed.

Jews participated in Jamaican life and had held important posts as governor, mayor, and ambassador.

Several black Jewish families were members of the synagogue. Not all had converted. They attended religious services. One claimed by his name, Mudahy, that he was a descendant of an original Sephardic family, but apart from the name, the succeeding generations had never had any connection with Judaism. A Bar Mitzvah of a black youth had recently taken place. Apart from these instances, Souza had never heard of any other black Jewish individuals or a black Jewish synagogue, nor was anything of the sort related in any book on the Jewish community of Jamaica. While he was sure that there had been many sexual unions between Jews and blacks over the centuries, there was no reference to any of their offspring following the Jewish religion.

We took advantage of our stay in Kingston to buy books about the Rastafarians, met a number of them personally, went to an interesting exhibit of their art work, which had a resemblance to the bold strokes of a Rouault. A number of pictures had Christian-like themes of blacks being nailed to crosses in imitation of the crucifixion of Jesus Christ. We listened to and purchased reggae records in their shops and heard this melodic beat, which is different from calypso and merengue.

* * *

Our island-hopping three-week journey, which introduced us to the warmth and variety of natives in their distinctive settings, left us with a resolution to return to the Caribbean during our cold northern winters. But by count, we could only find seventeen black Jews; some were converts of recent vintage, some were of questionable Jewish status, although I have included them in the count because they were members of synagogues. Thus my book was accurate. Jewish slaveowners did not convert their chattel to Judaism. When they intermarried with blacks, they did not remain in the Jewish fold. Most of the seventeen, nearly all of whom had doubtful Jewish credentials, were actually transplanted from the United States.

1980

My involvement with AAEJ affairs took the better part of the year, starting with our second mission out of Sudan. I spoke in such diverse places as Wilmington, Delaware, and its environs, seeing for the first time some towns and cities that had been among the earliest English settlements in the New World: Teaneck, Livingston, Montreal, New Haven (twice), Providence, Albany, Schenectady, Buffalo, New Rochelle, Philadelphia. I made a number of trips to Washington, meeting with senators and congressmen. When Rachamim Elezar came from Israel for a lecture tour, I accompanied him to several synagogues in the New York area, where for the first time white Jews saw and prayed with a black Ethiopian Jew, who spoke Hebrew fluently, and knew the prayerbook by heart. I flew to Williamsburg, Virginia, with Baruch Tegegne to educate a group of seasoned, eastern seaboard Hadassah women, who were enthralled with our presentations, but regretfully, for reasons not made known to us, did not follow up on those inspiring two days of face-to-face discussions of the plight of Ethiopian Jewry. I suspect that their national office dampened their enthusiasm.

I met with researchers, journalists, photographers, including Yoav Levy, who brought back an excellent collection of photos from the Ethiopian villages, photos which gave a truer picture of their lives than those of most photographers, who went there with some other public relations purpose in mind.

The Synagogue Council of America had a brief flurry of interest in Ethiopian Jewry, but it rapidly died down to nothing but the issuance of an innocuous memorandum

The NCJCRAC continued to meet. Nothing materialized, since the committee had no intention of pressing Israel to rescue larger numbers out of Sudan or to initiate a life-saving program out of Ethiopia.

At the annual meeting of the CJFWF in Detroit, a reference to Ethiopian Jews was thinly sandwiched in between programs referring to other Jewish groups, who were hardly experiencing the same frightful conditions as those in Ethiopia. An effort had been made by our organization to bring Rabbi Yosef Adane, the only Ethiopian Jewish rabbi in the world, and now an Israeli, to the conference, but even this mild mannered, nonactivist young man was refused an exit visa at the last moment, because the Israelis feared that he might say something inimical to their political image. Rabbi Charles Weinberg, who arranged the meeting for me with Chief Rabbi Shlomo Goren in 1975, made an attempt to get the Israelis to let Adane go to the United States., but sad-facedly told me that he had failed to move the officials.

Ethiopian Embassy

Brant Coopersmith, a former Washington Jewish communal worker, arranged for Emma and me to meet with Demeke Tesfaye, the Ethiopian chargé d'affaires in Washington. Together with Brant, we were entertained at his home, where we drank his Scotch and met his beautiful wife, who Tesfaye told us originally came from an Ethiopian

Jewish family. When I asked whether I would have any difficulty getting into Ethiopia and visiting the Ethiopian Jewish villages, Tesfaye replied that he would arrange it. Might it be possible, I asked, to permit the reunion of seventy-five Ethiopian Jews with their families in Israel? He paused and said that if I gave him such a list in advance, he was confident that that too could be managed, providing it was done without publicity. While nothing came of this meeting, since the AAEJ decided not to follow up on his affirmative replies at this time, it was evident that arrangements could be worked out with the Ethiopian government, if overtures were undertaken by responsible parties. Neither Israel nor the leadership of the American Jewish community appeared to have any intention of taking such initiatives with Ethiopia. In 1985, Tesfaye defected to the United States.

* * *

The Jewish Museum in New York showed some casual interest in mounting an exhibit of Ethiopian Jewish artifacts, providing that the AAEJ found substantial funds to underwrite the venture. Since this was not a high priority with us, nothing happened. In December 1986, such an exhibit was launched by the Jewish Museum in New York.

A similar exhibition will open in the museum of the Diaspora in Israel in the fall of 1987.

I spoke at the opening of an Exhibit of the Art works of Ethiopian Jewish children in Israel at the Board of Jewish Education in New York in January 1987.

Sam's Death

Tragically, my brother Sam died of cancer on February 12, 1980. A serious illness had been stalking him for more than a decade. I went back and forth to Washington in the last months of his life to be with him in his final days, during which he spent much of the time in a hospital or lying on his sofa. Sam welcomed old friends. I listened in on reminiscences of the good and former days, as well as the vital international current events that always concerned everyone connected with the Foreign Service.

Sam told me that he had willed most of his estate to me. I was surprised at his testamentary decision, but was also pleased. Having many of his prized possessions in our home, items that he had collected or had been given while serving abroad, gave Emma and me daily reminders of how much he meant to us.

Shortly before Sam died of incurable cancer, he wanted to make sure that all his funeral arrangements were in order. Though on the verge of death, he was still vital and in charge. So at his request, I made preparations with a Washington undertaker to have his body eventually transferred in a simple pine box with the Star of David to Gloversville for burial in the family plot. On a second visit to Sam's house, while I was present, the undertaker advised Sam, since he had obtained a great deal of information about him on his initial interview, that he was eligible for burial in the National Cemetery in Arlington, Virginia. Sam looked at me and said: "That might be nice for the family, wouldn't it?" While I would have preferred Gloversville, I did not say so, knowing that Sam had already changed his mind. I accepted his decision. Together with Betty Lee, his wife, whose first husband, an admiral in the U.S. Navy, had already been laid to rest in that cemetery, I went to Arlington and selected the grave site.

Thus Sam was buried in Arlington with full military honors. He had been a captain in the army as well as an ambassador. Dr. Daniel Polish, who met Sam before he passed away, and whom I selected to preside and perform the sacral functions, chanted the Jewish ritual in the chapel. Tributes honoring Sam for his distinguished diplomatic career and the valued services he had rendered his country on many difficult assignments were given by Averell Harriman, Ellsworth Bunker, Philip Habib, and me. Hundreds came to bid him farewell and walk behind the caisson, drawn by eight well-groomed horses, which bore his casket, as mourners and friends walked behind from the chapel to the grave. I felt that Sam would have smiled in satisfaction as he contemplated all of us being so ceremoniously involved in his last rites.

A modest gravestone marks the site. Incised is a Mogen David.

On Sam's passing, friends and the Berger family established a memorial lecture series at Georgetown University, devoted to labor and foreign affairs.

The six lectures were given by prominent personalities: Roy H. Jenkins, president of the Commission of European Communities; Leonard Woodcock, former U.S. ambassador to China; Dr. John T. Dunlop, professor of economics at Harvard University and former U.S. secretary of labor; Irving Brown, AFL-CIO director of International Affairs; Ambassador Philip C. Habib, former undersecretary of state for political affairs; and Lane Kirkland, president of the AFL-CIO.

Emma and I have met all of them, along with scores of other officials in government and labor circles. Ellsworth Bunker, president of the Institute for the Study of Diplomacy, recently passed away. His post has been filled by Senator Edmund S. Muskie, former secretary of state.

Sam's Letters and Mine

My sister Rachel, who loved all of her younger brothers, Graenum, Sam, and Milton, probably in that order, and who never felt that any of them could do anything wrong, wrote me many decades ago—I think when I first became an executive—that I should keep all of the letters I wrote to my brother Sam, and of course keep copies of his to me, because someday both of us would be famous and our correspondence would be worth publishing and reading.

It was natural for me to file all letters I received and wrote. Mail from Sam was obviously treated in the same organized fashion, although in searching my files I find gaps, which means that I may have filed them somewhere else, and thus they got lost. I never asked Sam what he did with my missives. The question of whether we would be famous or not really never occurred to me. Our mail was normally related to the routine pursuits of day-to-day living, including travel, people we met, books we read, family matters. Occasionally they referred to the theatre, movies that grabbed me. Sometimes there were comments on the larger events—political, economic, cultural—that impinged on our lives at home or abroad. I was not above making suggestions to him about the course of action the U.S. government should take on foreign policy. This occurred only after Sam became part of the diplomatic corps in the early 1940s. My file during the years got thicker, as I never got around to sorting or thinning out was what or was not worthwhile keeping.

In the last months of Sam's life, I would visit him frequently in Washington. One day, he said he wanted me to go through his papers. As I took folder after folder out of his cabinets, he told me that some items were confidential, but he wanted me to keep them and read them, and perhaps at some future time determine whether they should be preserved and placed in the public domain through a university or a research department in some other institution that collected specialized data. These papers reveal much of the agony Sam had to undergo to prove he was not a Communist or associated with known Communists. The FBI and the Foreign Service investigators seemed to be constantly probing into his past to determine whether he was a security risk and not worthy of higher office. He was eventually cleared of every suspicion and evaluated as a reliable American citizen and deserving of trust and responsibility in the higher echelons of the Foreign Service. Yet there was a period when he questioned whether he wanted to remain in a system that put a person under constant and unnecessary scrutiny. He was persuaded to stay, and it was lucky for him that he did, for he would have borne those scars throughout his life. He was vindicated. I have those papers in my possession.

As I sat next to his couch, we decided to just throw away some of the material he had assembled. Other important papers, speeches, and articles, including some photographs, were bundled off either to the Institute for the Study of Diplomacy at Georgetown University or, when they dealt more with labor and economics than with foreign affairs, to the George Meany Institute for Labor Studies in Silver Springs, Maryland, along with his considerable collection of relevant books. Sam knew the key people in both institutions, including the late George Meany.

What I also found in Sam's accumulations, was that he had kept my letters as I had kept his, some going back for decades. I read through a few of them with a smile, for they revealed how prescient I had been with respect to some global events and how hopelessly wrong I was on others. On balance I seemed to have been more often correct than in error. Sam told me to keep them. I took them home and put them in a cabinet, with the thought that someday I might go through all of them and see whether they were worthy of a book, which might include what we had both written to each other. I had written an article about Sam, "The Quiet Envoy," for the *Jewish Digest* (July 1968), and that along with my eulogy and our letters would make interesting reading in a slender volume.

Books of letters by famous people are frequently of great interest, because when the letters are honest and detailed, they reveal a great deal about these distinguished personalities. Yet in reading such books I have sometimes felt that they were written by their respective authors, not as private communications, but with a view to having them appear in print sometime during or after their lifetime.

Sam and I had no such motives. He was too modest, to privatistic, to think of such an eventual exploitation of his random thoughts and writings. As for myself, I must confess that it never occurred to me that my personal letters might find their way into a book. I certainly never composed them with that conscious thought, even though my sister Rachel had urged me to write and keep every missive for posterity. I have written my views and expressed them publicly in the open forum. I assumed that these formal statements, often provocative, were all that would remain of my efforts to say something to the world.

After I complete this autobiography, I will find some time to sort out our respective correspondence and see whether any of it is worth an article, let alone a book. If I keep our letters unpublished, will my children or grandchildren ever read them? Will one amongst them, perhaps as a writer or researcher, think they merit a memoir—"Letters of My Grandfather and His Brother, Our Granduncle"? I presume that if I write a short tract, some of them will eventually read it. Or perhaps, after reading the letters, they will put them in a clean folder and send them on to the American Jewish Historical Society—and let some latter-day author discover them, evaluate them for whatever worth they might have in recording the correspondence of two Jewish brothers, who achieved some eminence in the twentieth century.

* * *

A friend offered us his handsome apartment in Fort Lauderdale, Florida, which Emma and I occupied for three weeks. Florida has not been a favorite vacation resort for us. On previous visits, it always seemed to rain or was too humid. Once Florida experienced one of its periodic freezes while we were there. This time it rained, was hot and humid. When it stopped raining, we took long walks along the sea, the canals, and the streets lined with magnificent homes and palm trees. We saw a few friends and relatives, but in the main read one book after another on the balcony of the apartment, which overlooked the ocean and the winding canals with their heavy traffic.

* * *

We spent a long weekend with Robert and Peggy Wolf at their summer home in Marlborough, Vermont, walking through the country roads, listening to a concert at the nearby music festival, playing bridge, and reading books. We found time to drop in and visit Ellsworth Bunker and his wife, Carol Laise, who lived nearby on a large and old attractive farm-estate.

* * *

While at Sacandaga, where we spent six weeks during the summer, we drove up to Montreal to see friends and visit its interesting antique shops. In one shop, Emma discovered a Wavecrest biscuit jar similar to one that Irving and Faye Epstein had given us as a gift when we moved into our new home in Pelham in 1953. Emma had given it to Anita, our daughter-in-law, who filled it with ordinary cookies, and it stood on her kitchen counter amongst assorted other containers. When Emma was told that the jar could be purchased for $475 Canadian (about $425 U.S.), she immediately called Anita in Providence, to take it off the kitchen counter and put it amongst her expensive trinkets in the china cupboard in the dining room. Emma kept reminding me, whenever she chanced upon some bargain, that you could never know how valuable an odd item in your home was until you saw the prices quoted in an antique shop.

23

In Search Of The Origins Of Graenum

"GERANIUM!" "GRAHAM CRACKERS!" How would you like to have been taunted by your preteen peers in the streets of Gloversville, New York, a small town in the Adirondack Mountains, because your parents had chosen to name you Graenum in memory of your grandfather, *olav hashalom* ("May he rest in peace"), seventy years ago?

The name is not only different, one in 45 million (counting my four cousins with the same cognomen), but strange. A moment after being introduced—at a conference, across a desk, holding a cocktail in my hand, or just as I am about to place the napkin on my lap at a dinner table, whenever I find myself between or among new people, there is a surefire ice-breaker, "Where did you ever get that unusual (uncommon, rare, quaint, unique, odd, interesting—even beautiful) name? How do you spell it? Is it Latin?" The *ae* conjures up memories of a high school course in that ancient tongue.

And so, I hold everyone in earshot in rapt attention as I rapidly unravel the mystery of how Graenum came to be my name.

Sired by immigrant parents, who had migrated from Russia at the turn of the twentieth century, I was actually called Abram for the first eight years of my life. How that patriarchal name came into being has ever remained an enigma to me and even to my parents, and I have never been able to establish its accidental origin. But that was it "officially," shortened to Abe (not Abie) in the confines of our home, amongst relatives, friends, and villagers.

In the third grade, I was summoned one day to the teacher's desk and without ceremony was asked to write my name on a piece of paper. Not knowing what it was all about, but nonetheless having been brought up in a Jewish home to be responsive and respectful to a teacher, who might only have been testing my writing ability, in elegant, disciplined penmanship (a far cry from my present undecipherable script) I cursived Abram Berger. As I stood stiffly, actually terrified, awaiting her verdict, she reached for a letter lying on her desk, that had been written by my older sister Rachel, of blessed memory, who had revealed, after a typical sibling quarrel, that my real name was Graenum, and that I was to be so dubbed on all future official documents and intimate associations. To say that I was at first traumatically distraught and then uncontrollably angry would hardly define my emotional reactions. While confusion as to my name reigned at home, at school, and amongst my companions—and the jeering appellations referred to in the opening text constantly mocked me—I finally settled for Graenum A. or Grae, and somehow learned to survive with the new title. An older cousin, an esteemed college student preparing for a professional career, already bore this name, and my fondness for him assisted in my acceptance of the inevitable. Three younger cousins had also been named Graenum at birth, so that I had comfort in knowing that I was not alone and that it was not really such an oddity. I must add that two of them later changed their names to the nondescript George, albeit one later restored Graenum as the distinctiveness of the name began to spread.

Subsequently, *A* for Abram was dropped on my first employment certificate (1922) and on my high school diploma (1925), and only the pristine Graenum remained. Inquiries as to its origin had to be constantly satisfied. I told them it was a family name. I was named after my sainted grandfather. Curiosity had not yet driven me to a fuller investigation of its etiology.

In my final year (1929–30) at the University of Missouri, a distinguished professor, the late Dr. Isidor Keyfitz, a scholar in Hebrew and antique languages of the Middle East, conjectured that I probably bore an ancient name—Aramaic, possibly Phoenician, possibly Latin—the meaning of which might be translated as "fertile," "seed," perhaps even "grain"; and for many years thereafter I enthusiastically added these academic facts to the grandfather legend. I never bothered to check the sources.

In 1949, when I applied for my first passport and had to establish proof of my American birth, the Bureau of Vital Statistics, to my consternation, reported that the name recorded at my blessed beginning was neither Abram nor Graenum, but Geneshon. (Having read into Hindu mythology, my fancy unveiled a connection with the legendary god of wisdom, Ganesha, even if he was portrayed as short, fat, with a large belly, yellow and an elephant's head.)

My parents had already passed away; my older sisters and brother could not recall such a designation, so we wrote it off as one of those aberrations that occur when an immigrant family tried in fractured

English to make a foreign-sounding name intelligible to a native American bureaucrat. The State Department accepted Graenum as my bona fide first name—and that ended that.

May 3, 1956 was a red-letter day that began the earnest search for the origins of my name. I was sitting next to the late Dr. Joshua B. Block, chief librarian of the Judaic section of the New York Public Library, when my other luncheon partner asked the inevitable question. Dr. Block's ears perked up. This is what he wrote to me by hand that very day:

> It was a wonderful, indeed a memorable function, which we were privileged to attend today. I have just arrived home and before I turn to the dinner table, I hasten to pen these few lines to explain, to the best of my ability, the derivation of the name GRAENUM (in Hebrew the letters are: Gimmel, Raish, Vov, Nun, Mem). It is ultimately traceable to a distinguished name in church history, the church father called in English, St. Jerome, who lived from 337 to 420 A.C.E. The translator into Latin of the Bible officially used in the Roman Catholic churches bore the Latin name—Hieronymus, which subsequently was frequently spelled GERONYMUS and as such found its way in Jewish usage in various phonetic variations including the one which you bear. I take it that you must be of Austrian origin, since your name was rather "standard" among Jews in the seventeenth and eighteenth centuries, perhaps even earlier in Austrian Jewries.

Somewhat nonplussed that my name might have been quite common two hundred years ago, and stunned by the christological aspect, my curiosity was not dimmed, so I replied to Dr. Block on May 8, 1956 as follows:

> I am grateful to you for the explanation that you gave of the origin of my name, because someone at our table had been skeptical as to where a Jew could have acquired such an odd one.
>
> My family came from Vilna, where they had lived for a great many years. The name belongs to my grandfather. The legend on my late father's tombstone is inscribed in Hebrew letters: YITZHAK BEN GRAENUM FALK BERGER. I do not recollect anyone in our family referring to some earlier sojourn in Austria, although it is plausible that my forebears might have come from there.
>
> Many years ago, when I met Dr. Isidor Keyfitz of the University of Missouri, he told me that the name could be traced to Phoenician and Aramaic sources. Some derivates are Gershon, Gershuna and even Geronim. The latter is, of course, somewhat akin to Geronymus, to which you refer in your letter.
>
> Having an obscure Hebraic origin may not seem as exciting as being

named after the distinguished Christian St. Geronymus, which I understand means "Holy Name," but my ancestral nostalgia begs for an earlier and Jewish identification. Can you help?

In my imagination, I transported myself back to Austria in the eighteenth century, where Joseph II, in the spirit of the rising local nationalism, was carrying on a program of Austrification, which mandated that all Jews assume names other than the traditional "Yitzhak ben Yaacov," and my progenitors, acting in accordance with the Emperor's decree and wishing to be up-to-date at the same time, yet mindful of the fact that they were also descendants of *kohanim* (high priests), took on for, at least one male heir, the popular name of Graenum, a variant of Hieronymus, a high priest in his own right, albeit of the Christian faith.

If one had to adopt a Christian name, he could take some satisfaction in accepting that of Eusebius Sophronius Hieronymus, who had visited the Holy Land, and had mastered Hebrew from friendly and scholarly Jewish teachers, so that when he translated the Greek text of the Bible into the official Latin Vulgate, his faithfulness to the lost and original version earned him the respect of later exegetes.

Since Jews also had to take on last names, my ancestors assumed the designation Berger. It could have meant "shepherd on the hill" or "resident of a city"; or according to Dr. Norbert Pearlroth, it was "a Galician Jewish surname, merely an elaboration of the Hebrew name Baruch (Blessed). The name Baruch was usually changed to Benedict or Behrend. Some families when commemorating an ancestor named Baruch, assumed the name Berger."

But Dr. Block liked to tangle with scholars, particularly where the past is both esoteric and exotic, and so he expanded on his initial response with a second letter a fortnight later dated May 20, 1956:

I am reasonably certain that Phoenician does not even enter the situation. I know of no Aramaic source that is older than any of the extant sources in Hebrew. Moreover, Aramaic is so close to Hebrew as to present no variation other than phonetic in the spelling and pronunciation of your name. If the name was actually used that early, it would have survived in one form or another in early Jewish and Christian Aramaic writings. Neither the Targum nor the Talmud and Midrash offer it. I am sure it does not exist in Christian Aramaic (often called Syriac).

The more I think of the explanation I furnished you, the more convinced I am of its accuracy. The fact that you came from Vilna only confirms my claim that it was widespread in Austria. Many Jews from Austria and Germany found their way to Lithuania and Poland at an early date. It is this fact which explains the vast number of Germanic names and family names they bear.

The famous Harkavy of Petersburg once wrote a book showing beyond any doubt that the rapid growth of the Jewish population in Czarist Russia was largely due to the gradual but persistent migration of German and Austrian Jews into the territories (beginning with the 13th century) which then comprised Russia. They retained not only their Germanic names, but also their Germanic rites in worship and religious practice. How else would you explain the prevalence of Minhag Ashkenaz in Russia, Poland, Lithuania and their neighboring areas?

Let Gershon and Gershuni alone, they have no connection with your grandfather's name. I am sure that when he was called up to the Torah in Vilna, he heard his name pronounced "GRONAM." That's what it is. The word sounds Hebrew, it is derived from (Gimmel, Raish, Vov, Nun) "throat," the plural form of which sounds like your name. But all this is coincidental with its use as a proper name among Jews. They borrowed names from their non-Jewish neighbors. In good English your name should be Jerome.

I was disappointed that his second thoughts had not confirmed that my name was derived from Gershom, for then I would have been able to associate it genealogically with an ancient personality in Jewish history. Gershom was the son of the greatest Jewish prophet, Moses, and his Midianite wife, Zipporah. True, the name means "Stranger in a foreign land" (Exodus 2:21–22), a not uncommon designation for "The Wandering Jew" since the dispersion; but we all, so to speak, live in "Exile." In earlier interpretations, I had been deprived of an alliance with Abram (or Abraham), the "exalted father" and founder of the Jewish nation with its "multitudes."

Nataniel Cohen, a prominent Jewish educator, refuted Block in a letter (December 24, 1978) and supported Keyfitz, thus restoring my name to venerable biblical sources. He believes the name is derived from the Hebrew word (Gimmel, Raish, Nun), found in Genesis 50:11, Numbers 15:20, Ruth 3:2 and Jeremiah 51:33, the translation of which could be either "threshing floor" or "heap of corn," both allied with grain, seed, fertility. Some of the larger dictionaries include Grannum and define it as the Latin word for "grain." So the name has a leguminous ancestry.

Though rare, the name was not totally unknown. Further written testimony was forthcoming which confirmed variants of Graenum. Groinem (Reb Groinem in fact) was a teller of jesting *mysehlach*, tall tales, according to Nathan Ausubel (*A Treasury of Jewish Humor:* Doubleday, p. 594), and he turns up as the Beadle Grunam in Isaac Bashevis Singer's *Satan in Goray* (p. 29).

In 1949, Saul Bellow wrote *The Adventures of Augie March*. Granum, without the *e*, was a character in the book. For a while I enjoyed private, literary fame, even though the figure in the novel—like most of Bellow's imagined personalities—never attained heroic proportions. Strangely not a single soul ever brought this reference to my attention, which leads me to conclude that no one I knew ever really read the book.

As a modest collector of Haggadahs, the ritual story read on Passover, I was gratified to find an article by the late Cecil Roth on *The Illustrated Haggadah* in *Studies in Bibliography and Booklore* (Library of Hebrew Union College–Jewish Institute of Religion, Cincinnati, volume VII, 1965). Referring to a text produced in Prague in the year 1526, Roth wrote:

> The magnificent work, with its superb borders, its poised lettering, its stately initials, its marginal cuts and decorations, and its assured balance, is among the most distinguished productions of the sixteenth century press. The printers and publishers were Gershom ben Solomon Katz (= Cohen) and his brother GRONEM (Geronim?), who had already shown their taste in other productions.

While flattered in this association with an artistic namesake and the confirmation of another variant spelling or pronunciation, it also established that Gronem or even Geronim was not the same as Gershom or Gershon, which other learned Jews have from time to time asserted was probably my true name. It was unlikely that two brothers could bear the same designated name. It also disposed once and for all any Mosaic ancestry.

A most curious aspect of the origins of my name took an international twist. While opening an account for me in the Bank Leumi in Jerusalem in 1975, the teller, a young, blond, bearded traditional Jew with a marked English accent showed no surprise when I said that my name was Graenum. He asked whether my family or I came from Wales. He told me that he had met Welsh people with the same name.

Returning to the United States shortly thereafter, I was in a funeral cortege motoring down Eastern Parkway in Brooklyn, when we paused briefly at the intersection with Utica Avenue. Looking out of the window, I noticed a shop near the corner with the legend "Grannum's Jewelry." When I returned home, curiosity led me to phone the store, where a distinctive West Indian Negro accent greeted my hello. I told him briefly that I was trying to check on the origins of his and my name. He told me that it was his last and not his given name. To the best of his knowledge it had not only been his father's family name, but also that of his paternal grandfather, who had migrated to the islands from Wales. He suggested that I write to his brother, who was a judge of the Supreme Court in Kingston, Jamaica, where other relatives also lived. My letter to his brother was returned—address unknown.

When friends went to Jamaica for a holiday, I asked them to look him up, but they too had no success in locating him. In the telephone book, they discovered a number of Grannum(s). They brought me the ripped-out page.

This lead prompted me to examine the New York area phone books, and to my amazement I found scores of Grannum(s) living all over the area, and curiously enough living in what I suspect, even in this day of integrated neighborhoods, were sectors more densely populated by blacks. Did they come from the West Indies? Were they all descendants of this fertile Welsh grandfather? Was Rex Granum (one *n*), President Jimmy Carter's press secretary, also part of the same *mishpachah* (Hebrew for "extended family")? Was the original Grannum a white man? Was he Jewish?

That the name Graenum is still odd is attested to by this reference in a professional journal. A social worker by the name of Morley L. Torgov wrote an article in the spring 1975 issue of the *Journal of Jewish Communal Service* (vol. 51, no. 3), which invited a response from the editor, who thought that the name was a nom de plume. Whereupon the editor received this reply: "I am puzzled by your comment repeated several times, about the unlikelihood of Morley Torgov as a name. . . . Why, I ask, is it any less likely a name than others I've seen in the *Journal*, *lemoshl* (for example): . . . Graenum Berger?" to which the editor noted: "Well, they're not so likely either." (*Journal of Jewish Communal Service*, Fall 1975, vol. 52, no. 1, p. 101).

Benzion C. Kaganoff, in his *A Dictionary of Jewish Names and Their History* (Schocken, 1977), wrote that "Gronim is an abbreviated form of Geronymos," which literally means "the old man." Thus it would *not* be derived from Hieronymus after all. Gronim falls "in the category of religious names. . . . not only old and new Hebrew names, but also all the Aramaic and Greek names that had been sanctified by constant usage." Kaganoff went on to say that Gronim and its variant Gronimann, derived from the Greek Geron ("old man"); "Another name used in the apotropaic ritual of changing names to ward off the evil spirit." The name was "given to a child because of its dual therapeutic qualities. First of all, it expressed the hope that this child would live to attain the age of an old man. Secondly, it could be used in a ruse. If the Angel of Death came to claim the child, he could declare. 'You have the wrong person. There is no child here, only an old man.' "

It was consoling to know that I had been protected against the Angel of Death in my childhood. How do you fend him off when you have become a septuagenarian?

Lest I get carried away only with the praiseworthy, exotic, literary, sociological, and historical, I must relate that when I read Isaac Bashevis Singer's *When Shlemiel Went to Warsaw and Other Stories* (1968), he deflated my ego. Singer wrote: "It was known that the village of Chelm ruled by the head of the community council and six elders were all FOOLS. The name of the head was GRONAM the Ox."

If you rummage around old barns in the Adirondacks or read the *New York Times* faithfully each day, you will come across other items bearing on my name.

The *Ladies Home Journal* (January 1896) carried the following advertisement:

> World's Fair! Highest Award
>
> IMPERIAL GRANUM
>
> Mothers know its value preceding child-birth and while nourishing their offspring. INFANTS from birth thrive on it!
>
> IMPERIAL GRANUM
>
> Is pure and unsweetened and can be retained by the weakest stomach. A safe, easily digested FOOD for DYSPEPTICS!
>
> Sold by Druggists Everywhere!
> John Carle & Sons, New York

William Safire, in the *New York Times* (October 27, 1983, p. A31), wrote in his essay column about the invasion of Grenada:

The resistance put up by hundreds of Cuban soldiers shows that Grenada was already under the military domination of another country, with more troops probably on the way. That island (its name from the Latin *Granum,* meaning grain, which led to "pomegranate" and then to the similarly shaped "hand grenade") had already been invaded.; our objective, as in Lebanon, is to get foreign forces out and leave.

Over the years I have heard that other people bear the same given name, even with the same spelling, but I have never met them.

Do you know a Graenum or one of its variants?

My Brother Milton's Death

One of the unhappiest events in my life was the passing of my brother, Milton on September 12, 1981. It had become obvious that the medication which had worked so well for him at the outset of cancer in 1980, was losing its effectiveness. He came to New York for a week of injections each month. I picked him up at the train either at Grand Central or Croton-on-the-Hudson. I would visit him daily at Mount Sinai Hospital, and then put Harriet and him on the train back to Schenectady or Amsterdam, from where they were driven to Gloversville. Harriet always accompanied him, gave him support, and kept him alive. His once constant cheerfulness was deserting him. A talker, he spoke less. Although he tried to maintain a firm front when friends came to visit—and there were so many—he was no longer in command. We conversed, as we always did when together, about everything except his impending death.

In April, the Gloversville Jewish community honored him at its annual Jewish National Fund dinner. Thin and pale, he gave a stirring speech. I also spoke at this function and paid tribute to the contribution he had made to the community—Jewish and general—over his lifetime.

In August, he began to fade. He had to be hospitalized. He ate little and his body shrank. He had little energy to talk. In September, I had to return to New York to take care of some personal business. We were delayed by a day. We drove up to the Nathan Littauer Hospital in Gloversville at 7:30 P.M. and went to his room. It was dark and empty. We learned that he had passed away silently at 6:15 P.M.

I delivered a eulogy for Milton at the Knesseth Israel Synagogue, an encomium to him as a person, a family man, a community leader, and a Jew. I recalled that a similar service had been held for my father in the old synagogue in 1947, an honor conferred only on the Jewish community's most distinguished citizens. I had delivered eulogies for Sam and for Sadie, all within a year and a half. As I spoke about each of them, it was like reviewing my own life as well as theirs, lives which were intimately interwoven. Now I wondered, for the first time, how many years I had left. I was seventy-three. Close friends of mine were steadily dying. I attended their funerals. I spoke on several occasions. Was this what was left in the twilight years of one's life?

When the funeral was over, we mourned for seven days. One cannot grieve too long. We are commanded to resume our life's work. There was still so much that I had to do. But I could not forget him, and his image appears before me daily.

Orphaned: As the Family Dies One by One

Death, the final of all events, came early in my life. While my mother recovered from her first bout with cancer when I was a teenager, she had a foreboding that she did not have long to live, and that pall hung over her and all of us for seventeen years. Only in the last two years did she openly suffer as she underwent a variety of radical treatments in different medical settings in an attempt to forestall the spread of the malignant disease.

I was always close to my mother, even though I never made her the confidant of my innermost thoughts, feelings, and acts, and she knew nothing of my vagrant activities. I did not share my intellectual interests with her as much as I did with my father: nonetheless I felt an intimacy, being deeply concerned with her welfare, trying to be helpful in every large and small way, even though the assistance I provided could not prolong her life for a single day. Her death was not a shock, but a profound loss, as part of my life was being severed. I have tearfully mourned her many times since her burial. The image of my mother appears before me not in ghostly form, but as a living person, even today and most poignantly whenever I recite *Kaddish* on the anniversary of her death or during the several holidays when the *Yizkor* rite is chanted during the Jewish year. Strangely, I never recall her as wan and sickly, bundled up and sitting in a wheelchair on the porch, when the days in Gloversville grew a bit warmer in the late spring, or lying in bed as she shrunk in her illness. I remember her always as dressed, her hair set, her face pink, radiant, and vivid, talking. She was a good conversationalist, charitable to some and cutting to those she did not like. There was a reinforcement of her once precious presence rather than a dimming of her being as I grew older.

Yet I took my father's death somewhat harder. After my mother died, I had made every effort to see a great deal of him either in Gloversville or in the Bronx, or at Camp Bronx House, where he visited with us for several weeks each summer. He had never been ill, except for the flu during World War I, until the last year of his life. I almost had a sense that he would live forever. He seemed invulnerable, all of his faculties intact, except for one vagary—that the cleaning woman was stealing things from his household. Some things disappeared. I did not try to read more into these occasional expressions than a little loss of memory—forgetfulness about where he had put things away. He had grown mellower with the years, seldom critical of anything or anyone. He did not live in the past or try to recall his early years—many of them; for he was approaching eighty-one years. Whether he blocked out the early years for any convenient reason, I never learned. I left the subject with the unasked question, which in turn was unanswered. He always preferred to deal with the present—the future. He derived great joy from his family. He had done whatever he could for them. All of us had done quite well, and he was proud of our accomplishments. He related our successes to his friends in the neighborhood, in business, and in the synagogue. When I met them they always seemed to know about my work and my achievements. Freed from any economic worry, in good health, reasonably active in the out-of-doors as part-time farmer and part-time fisherman, he had reached a stage of tranquillity which I have not yet found, as I approximate his years, but am still seeking in my own life.

When he was felled with a stroke, I was shocked. I came to see him at the hospital, where I would sit at his bedside for the better part of the day holding his warm hand as he from time to time squeezed mine. But he could not talk, although I felt somehow that he was able to hear what I was telling him. The weeks brought no relief. He died. I think about him as I do of my mother—alive, vigorous, always well groomed even if his hat was often askew, his ruddy color, his warm smile and animated conversation. Yet I remember him most often in my childhood years, his taking me by the hand and walking by my side to the synagogue a mile and a half away on Sabbaths and holidays. Or I think of him during his horse-and-wagon days coming back to the house on Washburn and Lincoln Streets and allowing me to mount the animal and steer her into the barn. I recall his quarrels with his contemporaries in the synagogue and his ferreting out any unethical conduct among the officers. I wonder whether he had bequeathed to me that sense of justice and righteous indignation which has marked much of my life. It may have been more profound than I ever realized. Just as my mother unconsciously taught me to reach out to people, to be philanthropic, my father more didactically gave me lessons in ethical conduct and an example I inherited by ingrained habit of being morally piqued at any wrong.

When my brother-in-law Sam Finn, Sadie's husband, died at an early age from a sudden heart attack, I took it sadly. Sam and I had done many things together. Despite being the entrepreneur of a capitalist ice cream parlor, he was still the embattled socialist and pro-labor advocate of his younger days. I suspect that some of my sympathies for both labor and this brand of politics came from fervent discussions with Sam. I missed him, but not in the same ways as my parents, although he died in between their demises. My sympathies were with my sister Sadie, who deeply loved Sam and chose to remain a widow, because no man could ever replace him. She lived to be the oldest of us, eighty-seven. Over the years we saw each other frequently until she moved to Portland, Oregon to be close to two of her three children. We still talk of Sadie as though she were in the next room. Emma uses her recipes for pot roast, lemon meringue pie, and kichel. Sadie, like my sister Rachel, were profoundly devoted to Emma, for which I have always been grateful. Sadie had a sharp tongue, as she evaluated people and events. She had a beautiful physical presence. Her face lighted up when she appeared anywhere and when she spoke.

When my brother Morris passed away, it was a solemn event, but I did not grieve. Our relationship had grown a bit warmer in the last two decades of his life, but we were never close, even when I was a child. I always felt that he had not given me the support that I desperately needed, and which he could easily have afforded. He disapproved of my marriage and our having a child so soon after our marriage. He thought I was not ready for either. Thus I did not seek to maintain closer contact with him. As our marriage proved to be durable, as my career and my reputation kept rising, he began to take some pride in the achievements of his younger brother. Yet I was never held by him in as high esteem as my younger brother, Sam. Later, it was not unusual for the four brothers to play golf together. During the course of our walk around the course, there was much serious conversation and some idle banter. Morris's son, Howard, who always looked up to me and aspired to become a Jewish communal worker, contrary to the wishes of his parents, came to see me the afternoon following the funeral to tell me that he had decided to become a social work professional and abandon the business world. I helped him achieve that goal. Howard is currently a top Jewish communal executive in Cleveland and has never regretted following in my, rather than his father's, footsteps.

When my sister Rachel died—and we knew it was coming, as she suffered from the same cancerous ailment that took away my mother—I wept. Rachel and I were united in many ways all of our lives. If we were not six years apart, we might have been twins. Since childhood we had played together, danced together, talked books together. She came to see me at college in New York and was always amazed, yet pleased, by my adventurous nature, something she herself exhibited before her marriage, and carefully sublimated thereafter. I followed her as a reporter on the *Morning-Herald*. She did not disapprove of my marriage or our having a child. She gave great comfort and assistance to Emma. Their mutual affection deepened over the years.

Rachel had great wit, at times biting, held herself with great dignity, but put on no airs. She could have achieved any place she wanted as a volunteer or professional, but believed that her first responsibility was to her husband and their three children. Her correspondence was crisp, usually confined to a postcard, in which she wrote all that had to be said. A beautiful, sprightly person. When she left, it created a vacuum, never filled.

When Sam died, it was not a shock, for I was well prepared, since for more than a year we had known that his days were numbered. I grieved. It sundered a very important, long, intimate, intellectual association. Our letters, our visits with him in Washington, London, Athens, Korea, and Vietnam, were major experiences in my life and helped me see the world in a more comprehensive light. Both of his wives were close to me. We have kept his memory alive with an annual memorial lecture at Georgetown University in Washington, and by creating a children's playground in Jerusalem. I miss the lengthy, brotherly conversations over the phone, and the letters we wrote to each other. Sam, despite his high station in the Foreign Service, had an unusually lofty regard for me, for my thoughts and my insights, and for what I had achieved, like him, on my own. Whenever he introduced me to "the best and the brightest," he always did it with extended, dignified remarks, with a sense of pride. Usually they greeted me with some foreknowledge, for he had already spoken to them about me and my life beforehand.

Sadie's death saddened us. Yet she had lived to a ripe old age, had fulfilled her life through her children, grandchildren, and great-grandchildren. Her own progeny had grown up and prospered. She lived close enough to two of her children in her later years, so that we never felt she had been abandoned.

Milton's passing, so close to that of Sam and Sadie, left me an "orphan." Milton and I had seen a great deal of each other over the years, because we were frequent visitors to Gloversville and Sacandaga. He was not a letter writer, although he could write well, but he was an excellent communicator in other ways. I always said that he was the best of the Bergers. We had deprived him of a college education, since, being the last, he was literally forced to stay home, enter my father's business, and take care of our parents. Beyond high school, he was self-taught, knew everything and knew everybody. While he reveled in the success of his two older brothers, Sam and me, and I presume envied us, he became a successful businessman, raised a family, became president of the synagogue (twice), and helped build the beautiful new one during his incumbency. He was president of the Jewish Community Center of Gloversville. He was a superb elected councilman, acknowledged as the leader of that body. While he ran unsuccessfully for mayor (Emma and I spent that day in Gloversville trying to get him elected), he never compromised his integrity and refused to make preelection deals that might have elevated him to that office. He learned belatedly and painfully that excellent and honest public service and political probity did not necessarily endear one to the voters, who apparently preferred to have a person in office that they could personally corrupt, if the need should arise.

I was with him during the year and a half of his bout with cancer. The doctors I found for him seemed for a time to give some promise of good health, but the rampant, malignant disease would not permit any remission from its devastating course. I watched daily as this vital and outgoing man wasted away without the strength to even speak to hosts of visiting friends. Emotionally I was more attached to Milton than to the others, because he was the youngest, and he took over burdens that I should have shared more extensively with our parents. I lovingly watched him grow up from an infant, whose very birth I witnessed, who struggled back to life through the dreaded diptheria as a child. He always anticipated what I might need. I was never out of any kind of leather goods. He was my partner in the ownership of our cabin at Sacandaga, and there, too, he took care of it. We were in the same field of Jewish communal service, he as a volunteer, so we had plenty to talk about. When he left, I was bereft.

Other uncles and aunts and cousins have passed away, some of whom I knew intimately. They too left voids. Viewing the picture of the first cousins' club meeting in 1937 revealed that few were alive in 1986, some fifty years later. I have pleasant memories of most of them. I cannot recall ever quarreling with any of them, testimony to our respective tolerance. With their deaths, the family unity, once so strong, has been weakened. With the passing of the first and now most of the second generation, we do not see much of each other, except at funerals, and occasional *simchas,* providing, of course, we are well enough to attend these ceremonial events.

As other friends and colleagues pass away, it was often with sorrow, because in so many ways our lives had been interwoven. I have delivered eulogies at some of these final rites for family and friends. I reviewed their lives, how we interacted, and expressed my solemn views on what they meant to me. I read the obituary column of the *New York Times* each day and sigh with relief when the names are unknown to me. I find myself writing letters to the survivors, indicating how the life of the deceased had intersected with mine. Regretfully, I erase their names from our address book.

That was why the subject of death was often on my mind. How many more years do I have to go—at seventy-eight? The cold actuarial tables give me another decade or so, but who knows? That is the mystery that one never quite resolves. Our only hope is that when the end comes it should be, as everyone prays, painless and quick. What will they say about me after I am gone? I am writing no advance eulogies. I rest my case on my life and my works. Even if they said nothing, I would have no regrets. I wouldn't have wanted to live it differently, except for eliminating any pain that I might have inadvertently caused my beloved Emma and my sons. I hope I made up for it in my later days.

24

Ethiopian Jewry

ETHIOPIAN JEWS WERE still my major concern. Israel had rescued 679 Jews via Sudan in 1980. The AAEJ and I were now shouting, "This is not enough." We claimed that thousands had been left behind. We learned from those who arrived in Israel that they were suffering terribly and many had died. Yet we were told by the Israelis, and by their supine following in the American Jewish establishment, to be quiet, that only secret diplomacy would save the Ethiopian Jews, and our raucous voices were interfering with such efforts. We knew this was untrue. We could find few officials who believed what we were relating. Only thousands of independent-minded Jews supported the AAEJ financially. They placed the saving of Jewish lives at the top of their agenda. They remembered the Holocaust. We turned elsewhere and arranged meetings in Washington with senators and congressmen. Henry Rosenberg and Nathan Shapiro recruited the highly influential Alan Cranston, Democratic senator from California, to our ranks. I was one of those who went to Washington to brief him. He proved to be a major factor in the rescue of Jews from Sudan in 1984–85.

Once again, I flew and drove everywhere. I spent several days in Baltimore with the Board of Jewish Education, which had prepared a manual for teachers and students on Ethiopian Jews. I was introduced in the New York Reform Temple Emanu-el by Rabbi Ronald B. Sobol to address a large turnout of his membership on a Sunday morning. I spoke before groups in Washington, Hartford, Metuchen, Mount Kisco, New Haven, Providence, Montreal (twice), Omaha, St. Louis, and numerous other locations around New York. Usually, I dined with the rabbi or the chairman of the lecture committee. Often I stayed in their homes rather than a hotel. I helped train young speakers to talk to audiences of young people, particularly in the universities.

I met with all kinds of officials, alone or with others, in an attempt to persuade them that it was imperative to step up the rescue operations in Sudan, and to initiate a similar clandestine program in Ethiopia. New initiatives to influence the leadership in the Orthodox Jewish movements once again failed. Their excuse was that there was still a question as to whether the Ethiopians were really Jews. All the responsa and decrees over the years, the statements of the two current Israeli Chief Rabbis, the formal declaration by the State of Israel that they could now migrate under the Law of Return, were rewarded with deaf ears and little action.

In the summer there was a flurry of excitement by the Union of American Hebrew Congregations about doing something to rescue the Jews out of Ethiopia. That too soon passed without result.

Rachamim Yitzhak, under the pseudonym Nahum Ben Yosef, came to the United States from Israel to lecture for the AAEJ. He was a prime example of one who had escaped from Ethiopia via Sudan and finally reached Israel. A college graduate, teacher, engineer, personable, who spoke English with eloquence, he made an impression on all his audiences. Yet he was shunned by the Jewish establishment, which did not want the gruesome story of the misery of Ethiopian Jewry to be revealed to the Jewish public. They wanted only their own distorted point of view known to the bulk of the Jewish community.

A prominent Israeli journalist was persuaded to interview me. While he took copious notes, I could detect no real interest on his part from the weak questioning, as though he wanted to avoid hearing and having to write about the truth of the Ethiopian Jewish condition. His story did not appear for nearly a year. After the situation grew more acute in Africa, he wrote a sympathetic account, actually reflecting my point of view and quoting me, albeit anonymously.

Even Abie Nathan got into the act for a few days. He looked more like a businessman than the flamboyant ship "captain" and radio operator, who used his sailing vessel to try and bring peace between the Arab-Moslems and the Jews. He told me with assurance that he could rescue Ethiopian Jews, but it would take money. "How much?" I asked. He quickly answered: "Two million dollars." "You've got it." I instantly replied that if he could save large numbers of Jews, the AAEJ would find the money. He wanted to know how he could reach the Ethiopian ambassador in Washington. I gave him the name of the chargé d'affaires, since there was no ambassador, and his phone number. He called him in my presence and arranged a date the following day. But Abie bungled the meeting and nothing happened. His name was given to me many times subsequently, but I never followed up, because I lacked faith in him and his methods on this issue.

* * *

Efforts were made by Israelis to divert me from the Ethiopian Jewish cause. A prominent Israeli rabbi visiting the United States, called on the phone to say that he must see me at once, as he felt I could be helpful to him. He was vague, but left the impression that he wanted to discuss Ethiopian Jews. It was inconvenient for me, but I went to Manhattan to meet him in his splendid suite at the Waldorf-Astoria Hotel. He was on the phone for half an hour and kept me waiting. Annoyed, I brusquely asked him how long his conversation would go on. From what I overheard, it was not business, but personal chitchat.

When he finally gave me his attention, he made it clear that he had no interest in Ethiopian Jewry, and in his opinion a talented and concerned man like me was wasteing his time on this "trivial" issue. He had a cause that was more worthy of my attention. The Israelis had recently learned that there were hundreds of thousands of "alleged" Jews in Afghanistan. We must rescue them and bring them to Israel. I got up from my chair, indignantly told him I wasn't interested, and left the suite. He didn't know what hit him.

The frustrations of dealing with the official leaders of traditional religious organizations were exemplified on May 19, 1981. Rabbi Yaakov Pollack, a leader of the Young Israel movement, who had become interested in the Ethiopian Jewish problem, arranged for a few of us to meet with Rabbi Moshe Sherer, chairman of the Agudath Israel World Organization, perhaps the largest and most powerful of the Orthodox associations. We wanted his support in fostering the immigration of Ethiopian Jews to Israel. Sherer questioned the authors of recent statements with respect to their Jewish authenticity. He urged us to obtain a more profound and scholarly statement from rabbinical scholars like Rabbi Joseph Soloveitchik. He passed over statements issued by rabbis like Rabbi Moshe Feinstein, who was considered, even in his venerable old age (he died at the age of ninety-one in 1986), as one of the greatest of halachic sages. While he admitted that Rabbi Ovadia Yosef, the Sephardic Chief Rabbi of Israel, was a *hacham* ("scholar"), he felt that the responsum he had issued in 1973 was not scholarly enough. After a long harangue, because it was not a graceful discussion, it was agreed that if Ovadia Yosef would prepare such a definitive statement, Sherer would take it up with his organization's leadership and seek support for our cause. After listening and closely observing Sherer for well over an hour, I came to the conclusion that we could never satisfy him with any document from any source.

Nonetheless, no stone could be left unturned, if we were to save Jewish lives. The AAEJ sent Rabbi Pollack to Israel at its expense to meet with Rabbi Ovadia Yosef and obtain a revised and fuller document. Rabbi Pollack returned with the identical decree that Joseph had issued in 1973. Joseph had told him that nothing further was needed. We turned it over to Sherer. He used this as an excuse for doing nothing then and since on this vital subject.

Meyer and Tereska Levin

Emma and I saw a great deal of Meyer and Tereska Levin in 1981. We not only met socially, if you can call an evening with the Levins merely social. We roamed over the world and protested its ills. We relived his obsessive battle to present his own version of the original play, *The Diary of Anne Frank*. We talked about Ethiopian Jews, our mutual concern. On several occasions, we made joint presentations on the subject before audiences which had initially invited him to show only his film.

Emma and I listened to his powerful, emotional speech, again reviewing his struggle anent *The Diary,* as he was inducted as a fellow into the Jewish Academy of Arts and Sciences.

I have read most of Meyer's books, including the autobiographical *In Search* and *Obsession*. I have also read a great deal about his efforts to obtain justice after writing the original play dealing with Anne Frank. I am persuaded by the facts, not by friendship, that he was done in by left-wing Jewish intellectual elements in the theatrical world, because his play was "too Jewish" and "Zionist." He could not obtain the support of conservative Jewish leaders when he sued in the courts. While he won the case, he was persuaded by Jews of some eminence not to pursue the matter of presenting his play. Only in the last few years have a few groups in Israel and elsewhere dared to produce his version without fear of court injunctions. I have distributed scores of copies of his drama to Jewish-sponsored amateur theater groups. With a few exceptions, most were too timid, or were intimidated, so his writing has not been seen too frequently on the stage.

A year later, in his late seventies, Meyer was stricken with a heart attack and died, as he began to cover the war in Lebanon. We lost a valued friend. For years he had supported the Ethiopian Jewish cause, often sending me checks he received from lecture fees, so that we might save more Ethiopian Jews. His will left the AAEJ the royalties from the sale and rental of his Ethiopian Jewish film. Tereska has undertaken missions to Africa to help them. The Jewish world lost an important defender of the Jewish way of life, of Israel, and of Ethiopian Jewry.

How U.S. Jewish Organizations Treated Ethiopian Jews

The initially callous attitude of a U.S. Jewish organization is reflected in this tale. A young Ethiopian Jewish woman and her eight-month-old child were brought to the United States by a well-meaning person. After several weeks, he did not know what to do with them. He called a national Jewish organization that had as its prime function the settlement of Jewish refugees who came to these shores. He was told that it could not assist Ethiopian Jews. He had heard about the AAEJ and phoned me. I immediately called the organization's executive director, whom I had known for nearly fifty years, and asked for her help. I was given the same incredible story—it had "no policy" on assisting Ethiopian Jews. I warned her that if the woman and child were not aided within three days, I would tell the press the whole story of how a Jewish organization that assisted all other Jews, and even non-Jews, would not help the first Ethiopian Jewish refugees in the United States. It had been and still was AAEJ policy not to bring Ethiopian Jews to this country as immigrants, because they all wanted to go only to Israel, where they would find kinsmen and be able to establish their own ethnic community. Since we had not brought the woman and child, and coming here had been her choice, I wanted to be helpful. Within twenty-four hours I received a call from the agency: They would make an exception in this case on "humanitarian" grounds. The board of directors had not yet developed a policy for aiding Ethiopian Jews as Jews. I was outraged by this rationalization. Yet I decided temporarily to accept the procedure. I was told that the agency would only take them if I brought them personally and not with that "other terrible man," who had apparently spoken to the workers in not very flattering language.

I met this timid, tiny Ethiopian Jewish woman of twenty-eight, who was a trained surgical nurse, and her beautiful child, took them to the agency. It was arranged that they would be given a room in a hotel and money for food for a limited time. The hotel room, on the West Side of Manhattan, was as bare as could be. No provision was made for the child, for cooking, for eating utensils. Emma and I shopped with her for food and equipment. As I held the child in my arms, while the women were in the store, strangers came up to me and asked who the beautiful child belonged to. I answered: "He is my grandson." Most were taken aback. While they admired his beauty, they visibly disapproved of black-white unions. I assumed they knew I was a Jew.

When I asked the young woman why she hadn't gone to Israel, she replied that she was awaiting the arrival of her husband and four-year-old son before making that decision. As we were leaving the city for an extended period, we notified another member of the AAEJ to look after her. During our absence, she was moved to an apartment in Far Rockaway, which was cheaper than a hotel. She was placed there without a shred of furniture. Luckily, the late Mrs. Rosalind Roy, an octogenarian, and her daughter, could not tolerate such treatment and partially filled the four rooms with a bed, crib, table, some chairs, a used TV set. When we visited them on our return to the city, we noted that she had no chest. We bought a large one, so that she did not have to keep her clothes in boxes. We noted that the apartment house was occupied entirely by blacks. I visited the local Jewish Community Council and told them to arrange to have her involved in a YM-YWHA a couple of blocks away and in a local synagogue, which was nearby. Such contacts were made, but neither institution followed up the initial interviews. A black Jewish family that lived in Laurelton, a few miles away, took an interest in them, and each Sabbath brought them to a mixed black and white Jewish congregation.

Meanwhile I designed a plan to get her husband to the United States by inviting him to attend a conference on public relations, a field with which he was familiar and employed in Ethiopia. All of his expenses for travel and living would be paid by the "university" which sponsored him. Actually, the AAEJ assumed all of these obligations. He was able to get permission to leave, but was informed that he had to leave his four-year-old son behind, presumably as a hostage to guarantee his return. This he could not live with. He found a way for this child to leave the country for Europe. The child had to be "drugged," so that he would not cry out while going on a voyage without his father. Four months after his wife arrived in the United States, the father got off the plane in New York, a handsome, English-speaking young man about thirty. I picked him up at the airport and witnessed the happy reunion with his wife and child.

The family immediately approached an international Jewish agency to help them bring their child from Europe. The "case," for that is what it was, dragged on for months until I called and indicated that this was unconscionable and I wanted action. Shortly thereafter the child arrived. He traveled a good part of the world unescorted. Airline hostesses took care of him.

Living in Far Rockaway did not make it possible to find work. I obtained the help of the Jewish Community Council of Parkchester in the Bronx, which located a fine apartment in that huge private housing complex, where we had lived from 1940 to 1953. The children were enrolled in a local day school. I escorted the mother to a major city hospital not far from their residence, where she was hired on the spot. The father found temporary work with a local Jewish doctor, but when the doctor moved, he was engaged by a New York State agency, which had been set up to assist the thousands of Ethiopian refugees (none Jewish) who had settled in New York. The family became self-sufficient and required no further Jewish organizational support.

While a few of us, mostly members of the AAEJ, welcomed them, the rest of the Jewish community has not been hospitable, so that most of their friends are not Jews. They now want to move to a better section, more heavily populated with Jews, and thus transfer their children to better Jewish day schools. Their children are bright.

In Ethiopia, both were descendents of Jewish families that had lived in

Addis Ababa for a hundred years, families which had never converted to Christianity, but like so many other Jews around the world, became fully assimilated. With few Jews in the capital, their Jewish knowledge and Jewish practices were marginal. When they arrived in the United States, they had to learn Judaism from scratch, now following the Western Jewish pattern. They know the history of their Jewish forebears in Ethiopia in full detail.

They have kept a low profile in the United States. They rarely make appearances to speak on behalf of Ethiopian Jews, although when he does, for he is a good speaker, he has received a good response from the audience, all Jewish listeners. The reason for this reluctance to appear in public is that after nearly four years, they had not yet obtained the "green card" that would assure them of permanent residence status in this country. The delay, I regret to say, was due to the negligence of a Jewish agency that had undertaken the responsibility for such processing, but had not pursued it with diligence. The official form was finally obtained in the spring of 1986, due to the intervention of a person in Washington close to the AAEJ. Although they have relatives in Israel, they do not want to settle in that country. They hope to bring other members of both families to the United States.

The only Ethiopian Jewish family in New York City has been beset with difficulties by Jewish organizations from the beginning. The agencies only moved to help them when threatened with exposure of their policy-practice prejudice.

A year later, the same reception agency for Jewish refugees, called me to report that another Ethiopian Jew was arriving via a nonsectarian international rescue organization. Unlike the first family, this man was coming from Sudan. I told the worker to first establish the fact that he was a Jew and gave her some suggestions on how to do this. If he was, I proposed a plan for his absorption, providing that he did not want to go to Israel.

He was not Jewish, so the agency had no further responsibility for him as a Jew. However, it is curious that the agency, based on the first experience, not only had done nothing to rescue Ethiopian Jews, but did not even know what to do with them should one have arrived.

Matti Elias and the Mizrachi

Matti Elias, an Ethiopian Jew who lived with his family at Kibbutz Nezer Sereni in Israel, was brought by the AAEJ to the United States and Canada to tell the story of the plight of his kinsmen in Ethiopia. He had been one of the original students enrolled at Kfar Batya in 1956, a school supported by American Mizrachi Women. That organization graciously accepted our invitation to co-sponsor his tour. Matti was one of the courageous students who had refused to return to Ethiopia after completing his studies. He served in the army, married an Ashkenazi young woman, daughter of a Holocaust survivor from Germany, and was raising three girls, or as he described them, *madelech*. They were fully integrated into the kibbutz and Israeli society.

The Mizrachi Women went all out to promote his appearances in cities where they had chapters. A farewell party was given by the officers and board members to which I was invited. Since the Israeli rescue operation from Sudan was going weakly in 1981, over the entire year only 598 were saved, less than the year before. And since the Israelis were taking none out of Ethiopia, I pleaded that Mizrachi, which had some influence in Israel, particularly with Dr. Yosef Burg, a member of the Cabinet, to appeal to the government of Israel to undertake such a rescue effort. More than that, I suggested that the Mizrachi Women, on their own, undertake a special mission to bring out the remaining Ethiopian Jewish young men and women and their families, Jews whom they had helped educate at Kfar Batyah, but who had been forced to return to Ethiopia on the completion of their studies. Of those who returned to Ethiopia, a few had become Christians. They could find no work as Jews. We had reason to believe that twelve of these former students and their families would be overjoyed if they could reach Israel.

At first, the women raised questions as to who would finance such a venture, because their funds were solicited for other purposes. I would have thought that saving lives was far more important than conducting educational, recreational, and even religious programs in Israel. To make it easier, because I was more interested in their influence than their money, I said that the AAEJ would provide the funds.

Then one important officer arose to jettison the undertaking before it began. She indicated that there must be some good reason why Israel could not take them out of Ethiopia, and for Mizrachi to try to pressure such a course of action might jeopardize all the good work that it was supporting in Israel. She revealed that Israel provided far more money for Mizrachi's various undertakings than they were able to raise in the United States. Therefore it would be in the organization's best interests not to do anything that might disturb the flow of Israeli support. The Mizrachi Women never undertook a program to save their former students. The AAEJ brought out some of them during the succeeding years.

I had always known about the stranglehold that Israeli ministries had over American Jewish institutions, so that their leadership never did more then perform minimal, often only verbal, acts on behalf of Ethiopian Jews. This was the first instance where the nefarious connection was revealed in all its pristine, self-interested immorality.

The St. Louis General Assembly

As the year was winding to a close and the record of rescue was even lower than a year before, despite information that the AAEJ had received that there were now thousands of refugee Jews in Sudan, I prepared another advertisement, with the aid of several friendly experts in the advertising field. The AAEJ threatened once again to place and run full-page ads in the major newspapers across the land—the *New York Times*, the *Washington Post*, the *Los Angeles Times*, and *Chicago Tribune*—with specific dates for publication listed on the ad itself. The shrieking bold headlines, surrounding a photo of a child with flies all over his face, accused the leaders of Israel, American Jewry, and world Jewry of failing to rescue Ethiopian Jews in large numbers and thus being accessories to their suffering and death.

Several copies were given to members of our board, who would show, but not give, these copies to selected American Israeli officials. The result, as once before, was devastating, with frantic appeals to us, and particularly to me, to refrain from such publications: It was costly; it was a waste of money; it would not achieve the desired effect; it would only blaspheme Israel and respected Jewish organizations. *Don't do it*!

The annual CJFWF general assembly was to be held in St. Louis. No significant program regarding Ethiopian Jewry had been planned by the assembly. At the last minute one was improvised, but we were not invited to participate. Something more drastic and dramatic was needed. The Candian AEJ asked us to help pay for a hotel room for a special meeting it wanted to arrange. We paid. Less than twenty-five people showed up at the meeting hall, which unfortunately was at some distance from the conference headquarters.

An Israeli official sought me out and pleaded with me not to publish this "scandalous" advertisement. I told him that Israel could rescue three hundred per month out of Sudan; and if it did, that we would withhold printing the provocative advertisment. He never said that Israel couldn't do it, but repeated the same refrain that I had heard from others: that printing the copy would be a disaster for the Jewish people.

I met with Irwin Cotler, head of the Canadian Jewish Congress, who tried to impress me with his concern for Ethiopian Jews, while at the same time he attempted to persuade me not to go public with such an inflammatory advertisement, or for that matter any kind of a statement. He unmasked his own position on the issue of rescue when he staunchly defended everything that Israel was or was not doing. In the last analysis, this all demonstrated that Israel dictated the size and time of the rescue program and how Western Jews should think and act.

That evening, Emma and I were invited to the apartment of the president of the NJCRAC, whose organization claimed that Israel and American Jews were doing all that was possible to save Ethiopian Jews.

The discussion, which began in gentlemanly fashion, soon shifted to bitterness. In the face of such apologetics and indifference, I accused American Jewish leadership of failing to go to Ethiopia or Sudan to observe at first-hand the parlous lot in which they lived. When I asserted that Israel and American-Jewish leaders including our host, were guilty of moral bankruptcy and being accessories to Jews suffering and dying, he told me in no uncertain terms to leave his room—which Emma and I did.

"Last Flight From Ambober"

One night in early November, I received a phone call from Brett Goldberg (since going to Israel on aliyah he calls himself Haim Brett Goldberg), a young Yale graduate, who knew Amharic and had become deeply interested in the problems facing Ethiopian Jewry. "Graenum, do you come from Gloversville?" I replied affirmatively. "I just saw a play in rehearsal in Cambridge, Massachusetts, in which you are a character under the name of 'Gerber.' " He told me the play had been written by John A. Williams. Williams had visited our house to obtain background on Ethiopian Jews in advance of a trip he was making to Israel and possibly Ethiopia. Williams was a distinguished black writer and a professor at Rutgers University.

I called John. He admitted to having me on his mind for a long time. He told me that his play *Last Flight from Ambober* covered the story of the Ethiopian Jews in historical-dramatic terms up to 1977, when the first group was actually flown out of Ethiopia to Israel.

On November 30, Emma, Ramon (we were staying with my son in Providence overnight), and I drove up to Cambridge, had dinner with Williams, and witnessed the opening formal reading of the play. Knowing the story, we found it a stirring drama. It portrayed the conflicts that had surrounded the Ethiopian Jews since Jacques Faitlovitch came on the scene in 1903. "Gerber" was an American Jew who constantly irritated the Israelis by pleading and demanding that Ethiopian Jews be rescued and brought to Israel.

> *Man # Two:* Ha. Ha. But this old man, Faitlovitch, and the American, Gerber, and the Falasha, Rahamim—they're persistent.
> *Man # Four:* You've come about the Falasha and the Law of Return. When are we going to bring them home?
> *Gerber:* Yes, of course, once more.
> *Man # Two:* What a curious crew! A broken-down Frenchman and an African who thinks he's a Jew and you! Don't you have a family, Gerber? A business? Things to *do* in America?
> *Gerber:* Yes, I do.

Man # One: Then why aren't you doing them? Why are you *here* getting in the way?

Gerber: Because this is important. Because too few people got in the way in Germany. Because I am a Jew. [A silence follows.]

Man # Four: [Wearily.] Do American Jews even know about the Falashas?

Gerber: Like Jews anywhere, some do, some don't, but those who know seem to care.

Man # One: About the schvarzes? You're joking! You want us to have the same problems here you have in America with the black people?

Gerber: I'm going to visit them in a couple of days. I'll take pictures, assess their current needs—if one teacher needs $200 a year, why shouldn't we fill all the villages with teachers? Do they need farming equipment? What kind? How much? Grain? Medicine? Books? Canned and dried food? Wells dug? Building materials—*but only until they're brought home to Israel!*

While the writing was dramatic-fiction, it was accurate.

After the performance, the actors and especially the man who played "Gerber" were astounded to learn that some of the people involved in the drama were alive. The play went through several rewritings, was almost produced in California. The AAEJ was prepared to underwrite part of the costs. At the last moment, it was withdrawn from presentation. I suspect this was due to pressures from Jewish leadership.

I saw to it that the play was published. Many copies have been sold as the Ethiopian Jewish issue became public. Perhaps one of these days it will be produced on college campuses or in some Jewish community center's playhouse.

* * *

At the annual meeting of the Conference of Jewish Communal Services, I formally presented my two-volume work, *The Turbulent Decades*, to the officials of that body, which had sponsored its publication.

At this same session, several prominent Jewish professionals strongly advocated the need for Jewish participation once again in the remedying of problems confronting minority groups in the United States, particularly blacks. Not a word was said about aiding Ethiopian Jews suffering and dying in Africa. Afterwards I admonished one of the speakers (the other had disappeared) for his omission of any reference to the black Ethiopian Jews. He stumblingly tried to apologize. I had approached him shortly before about marshaling his large organization for this cause. He did nothing. Apparently non-Jewish American blacks still had a high priority of concern amongst most Jewish professionals, for the applause which followed the presentations had turned into a standing ovation.

* * *

The Jewish Community Center of Staten Island's board of directors was honoring Lillian Schwartz for fifty years of service. Emma and I drove out to tell a dinner party of several hundred people how I had recruited her as a young college graduate to work at the summer day camp, how she became a member of the Friday-night study group that met in our apartment, a group that eventually produced a number of leaders for the Jewish and general community. Lillian and her husband, Arnold, an attorney, had played a major role in the Jewish organizational life on the island. Lillian, a retired executive for Macy's department store was an able, articulate, and influential woman, who always made her views and her presence felt.

* * *

Sol Rafel, whom I recruited to work at Bronx House in 1940, and who succeeded me as its executive in 1949, intimate friend and colleague, suddenly passed away, almost on the eve of his own retirement. I delivered a eulogy at his funeral. His wife, Ruth, continues to be one of our close friends.

* * *

Emma and I went to see the play *Amadeus*, written, acted, staged, and produced most brilliantly. It was the best play we had seen since the Pulitzer Prize–winning drama *Death of a Salesman* (1949), and that was quite a span of time. That was our enthusiastic judgment and we defend it against all opposition of our evaluation. The movie which followed the play in 1984–85 was easily one of the best movies of all time and merited all the honors awarded.

* * *

At the end of the year, we flew off to the Dominican Republic with our grandchildren, Elisabeth and Gideon, to enjoy the sun, shop, visit historical sights, and browse in the art studios. We ate graciously. I tried to read books while sitting at the pool, when not interrupted by other tourists, who preferred to talk.

* * *

We spent most of the summer at our cottage at Sacandaga, where we could visit my brother Milton during the terminal days of his life. It was not a happy summer. My sister-in-law Florence, the widow of my late brother Morris, died. She was in her late eighties. I read. I walked. I wrote many letters. We took occasional side trips to the beautiful mountain and lake region to the north. We ate the wonderful corn, picked daily, that grows only in the area, and topped off our daily salads with fresh-picked dill. It turned out to be a healthy summer, despite the pall of death that hung over part of our daily lives.

25

1982

FOR THE AAEJ and for us, there was no diminution of activity on behalf of Ethiopian Jewry in 1982. In fact there was only heightened concern as we put increased pressure on Israel. We were disappointed—yes, angry—about the lessened rescue operations from Sudan in 1981. Our threatening advertisement in the major U.S. newspapers disturbed the Israelis, and a few of us were called to the Israeli consulate in New York on January 27, where we heard the officials rationalize why the lifesaving program had not expanded but decreased. It was another charade from beginning to end, for more than an hour of aimless conversation. Finally, fed up, I said that in order to keep us from printing more advertisements, Israel would have to rescue at least three hundred per month. I felt that they could rescue more, but if they would take out that number, we would be partly satisfied. I gave them one month to start the operation. The Israelis, when threatened, always came through. A ship arrived in Israel at the end of February with 375 Ethiopian Jews. This was another indication that whenever it was forced, Israel performed magnificently. We did not become euphoric, for we had a premonition of what to expect. For the entire year of 1982, Israel saved 742 Ethiopian Jews. As soon as their officials saw that we did not print the advertisements, they lapsed back to their previous foot-dragging tactics.

I stepped up my own speaking campaign to propagandize and raise money. Before the year was out, I had spoken in Englewood (four times), Croton, Riverdale (twice), Brookline, New Haven (twice), Summit, New Jersey, Washington, Gloversville, Bronx, Norwalk, Connecticut, Charleston, South Carolina, Providence, Denver, Chicago, Harrison, Plainview, San Diego, Los Angeles, San Francisco, Oakland,

Harrison, New York, Montreal, Pittsburgh, Mobile, New Orleans, Malboro, New Jersey, Monsey, as well as many other locations in New York proper. I was seventy-four years old. This was a heavy schedule. These lectures were in addition to radio and TV appearances and numerous interviews at our home in Pelham by journalists and researchers.

Mayor Koch

Mayor Edward Koch's aide phoned. The mayor wanted to issue a proclamation on rescuing Ethiopian Jews. I helped prepare the document. When I arrived at the mayor's office the morning it was to be proclaimed, I was told the mayor was not present and had decided to postpone making the statement. Tremendous pressure had apparently been put on him to withdraw it altogether. A year later he finally issued the proclamation. It was appalling to me that Israel and American Jewish leaders would go to almost any length to keep any story or action about Ethiopian Jewry out of the media. We issued our own release. It was printed in a few papers, but it could never be as effective as the coverage that might have been obtained if the mayor's statement had been printed in all the newspapers and transmitted over the wire services.

We did get resolutions passed and published from the New York State Legislature and the Board of Aldermen of Chicago.

Simon Wiesenthal

Simon Wiesenthal, the Nazi hunter, was in town. A friend arranged a fancy luncheon, so that I might try to get his assistance on behalf of Ethiopian Jewry. While he was a world-famous name for his unrelenting pursuit of living Nazis, I had no illusions about what he might do. He had his own specialty, and that consumed his attention.

Several years before I had delivered to him a pack of material on Ethiopian Jews. It was done at his request. I never heard a word from him after that meeting.

At the luncheon I reviewed the situation, indicating that the entire redemption program was in the hands of the Israelis, who wanted to rescue them at their own pace, and didn't want anyone else to go into either Sudan or Ethiopia. They insisted on no publicity, either on how Jews were suffering in Africa or how many had arrived in Israel. I told Wiesenthal that since 1977, only sixteen hundred had reached Israel, while twenty-four thousand more were living in jeopardy. He listened to me, asked a few questions, wanted suggestions as to what he might do.

My only thought was that he meet with Menachem Begin and persuade him to expedite the take-out operations. I insisted that Begin could do much more than he had, but needed "pressure" from important people.

Wiesenthal was a tall, heavy-set man, his face dominated by a prominent moustache. He never smiled throughout the excellent meal, which he ate with relish. I told the person who had arranged the meeting that I had not moved Wiesenthal. He thought differently. Neither he nor I heard anything further from Wiesenthal. For him hunting Nazis was still more important than saving Ethiopian Jewish lives.

Moshe Gilboa

Moshe Gilboa, minister of Diaspora affairs for the Israeli government, blew into town and called. He wanted to meet with me at once. Talkative, boastful, unctuous, he first tried to cajole me into believing that Israel was doing everything possible. I insisted that this was not true. He blurted: "Israelis are endangering their lives to save *your* Falashas." I told him that this was another lie. I twinged every time an Israeli or an American Jewish leader referred to them as "your" Falashas. I had no hesitation in acknowledging the kinship, but it further indicated that Jewish leaders had not yet identified themselves with their black fellow Jews in Ethiopia. Gilboa, aware of my forthcoming trip to Israel, invited me to his office in Jerusalem, promising that I would have access to information on all the wonderful things that Israel was doing for the Ethiopian Jews after they arrived in Israel.

A month later, I received the red carpet treatment from the Israeli government for the first time. I first had to listen to a long harangue from Gilboa, as he moved from chair to chair, he answering the phone, briefly interviewing intruders, and never looking at me directly, although I stared directly at his face all the time I was in his office.

He started off by telling me that his superiors, whom he did not mention by name, but implied that they were at the highest levels, thought I was an "evil man," a "hater of Israel." He really didn't know why he was "bothering" with me. In jumbled remarks, he said that he had read my books on "The Fourth Force" and "Black Jews," and had discovered that I was a "good Jew" and wrote "favorably" about Israel. "Ralph Goldman (JDC) and Manny Wiener (Montreal Jewish Federation) spoke well of you." Then he jumped to an article by Hadar, an Israeli journalist, where I was quoted as having made remarks about Israeli "racism" and "using Moroccans as cannon fodder." I denied having said anything about Moroccans, since the subject had never come up in our interview. As to "racism," I thought it was one of the factors in not aiding or rescuing Ethiopian Jews earlier and in significant numbers at the present time. Poverty, illiteracy, and lack of good working skills were other elements in their rejection.

He gave me a thick folio of material on Ethiopian Jews. Whether he had read all the material or not, I do not know.

When I asked him to arrange a meeting for me with the Prime Minister, he said he couldn't do that, but suggested my meeting with lower-echelon officials. I told him I wasn't interested. I brought up three Ethiopian Jews who were in jail in Ethiopia, whose only crimes were being Jews and Zionists, and insisted that they must be released. He said he'd look into it. (Nothing happened. The AAEJ was later instrumental in getting them out of prison and eventually to Israel.)

He wanted to know why I didn't work with Bennet Janowitz and his NJCRAC. I told him that the committee was worthless, because it was not interested in helping Ethiopian Jews in Ethiopia and definitely not interested in rescuing them. The organization followed the Israeli line one hundred per cent.

He referred to the enemies of Israel in the United States, who were using the Falashas as a way of attacking Israel. He referred to critical statements made by Edgar Bronfman, Philip Klutznick, and Rabbi Arthur Hertzberg. I told him that his statement about their use of the Falashas was nonsense. None of the articulate trio had ever helped the Ethiopian Jewish cause by speeches, with money, or by contacting Israelis, other Jewish leaders, or foreign governments.

Then he praised the excellent work being done by the American Jewish Committee, the American Jewish Congress, and the Anti-Defamation League on their behalf, to which I replied in indignation that they paid some periodic lip service, but had spent most of their time as apologists or trying to discredit the activistic role of the AAEJ.

Once again he rose to defend Israel's rescue efforts, citing all the difficulties claiming that Israelis were risking their lives in trying to save Ethiopian Jews. I again questioned his remarks, but thanked him for not repeating that Israelis had died on these missions, as some of the American Jewish leaders, Israel's best friends, had stated at open meetings in the United States.

Gilboa thought I ought to spread my interests to other causes. "I want you to meet Mrs. Shcharansky and help her get her husband out of a Soviet Russian prison." I told him I had formerly assisted Soviet Jewish programs in the United States, but I wasn't interested in meeting her. "Everyone is thrilled to meet her." I told him that I would not get involved in any other issue until the last Ethiopian Jew was out of Africa and settled in Israel. It was a trying meeting.

Three hundred thousand persons, mostly Jews, greeted Anatoly Shcharansky, at the annual Solidarity Sunday for Soviet Jewry in New York on May 11, 1986. It was a merited response. But no large delegation ever greeted any of the Ethiopian Jews on their arrival in Israel.

While I would have had no difficulty in visiting the absorption centers on my own, I decided to accept the VIP treatment generously offered by Gilboa, the first time we have ever been so favored by a government department. Emma and I visited a number of these locations and schools accompanied by and driven in the car of Ambassador Aharon Lopez, Gilboa's assistant, altogether covering four centers. Later we went to other centers with Zimna Berhane, an Ethiopian Jew who worked for the Jewish Agency as its specialist on Ethiopian Jewish problems. We were impressed with what we saw. While there were gaps in the services, not enough to do after Ulpan classes, lack of books and play equipment, not enough help for individuals with special needs, not enough Ethiopian Jewish employee translators, I could not bring myself to be critical, for the larger needs of the Ethiopian Jews were being met with reasonable effectiveness.

At the end of our last visit, Gilboa wanted me to issue a public statement that Israel was doing everything to rescue and absorb the Ethiopian Jews. While I would have happily provided an affirmative statement about its absorption efforts, I was unwilling to state that Israel was doing enough to liberate them. This was my last contact with Gilboa. I was told that he was not happy with me, having failed in his peculiar way, which I found distasteful, to make me succumb to his blandishments.

With Zimna, I learned more about the unmet problems of absorption, and this confirmed my own earlier impressions. The Israelis were still unprepared for the coming of so many Ethiopian Jews by the end of 1982. That year 742 arrived. Israel had not yet recruited and trained a sufficient number of Ethiopian or non-Ethiopian Jewish personnel. They were still using methods employed previously for Jewish immigrants with better educational backgrounds and skills. They were not co-opting enough resident Ethiopian Jews to help, although they would have provided a closer link between the native condition and what newcomers must absorb in Israel to make the best accommodation.

My judgments were confirmed in an issue of *Israel Social Science Research* (Ben-Gurion University, 1985) devoted to "Ethiopian Jews and Israel." The article by Jeff Halper, an anthropologist, "The Absorption of Ethiopian Immigrants: A Return to the Fifties," is the most graphic description of what was *not* done to assist Ethiopian Jews in the most constructive fashion. The gaps in essential services were also indicated in Shmuel Avraham's *Treacherous Journey: My Escape from Ethiopia* (1986), written in collaboration with Arlene Kushner, and in Louis Rapoport's *Redemption Song* (1986).

While Zimna believed that some of the needs could be resolved by money and services provided by such an organization as the AAEJ, I insisted that this must be the responsibility of the government, the Jewish Agency, and other institutions set up to help all Israeli citizens, including new immigrant Ethiopian Jews. While the AAEJ might provide some supplementary assistance, such as scholarships, books, dictionaries, etc., at best these would be only modest enrichment programs. In time, even such assistance should become the total obligation of the trio of existing Israeli operations mentioned above. That was still my point of view in 1986.

If the AAEJ was to have any continuing role, at best it should be to provide Ethiopian Jews with an ombudsman, who would report to the AAEJ what gaps in service must be filled, and then we would exercise pressure on the appropriate Israeli instruments to see that these deficiencies were corrected.

It has been my contention that when the last Ethiopian Jew has been settled in Israel, the board of the AAEJ ought to convene and determine whether it has any further function. Too many agencies don't like to go out of business, even when they have completed their task. I believe we should terminate. As individuals we might then assist other organizations operating in Israel that are aiding the integration of Ethiopian Jews. Our task will have been accomplished.

* * *

We secretly brought an Ethiopian Jew to the United States to plan an independent rescue program out of Ethiopia and Sudan. He had such experience before, knew every bit of the terrain, and had the courage and savvy to carry out a clandestine operation. Israeli officials in the United States phoned Henry Rosenberg and me daily, demanding that we turn him over to them, so that he could be warned not to work for us and learn the personal consequences of his going into African countries without their permission. The Israelis believed we might use him for a venture in Sudan, which was not our intention. Somehow we managed to keep him "concealed," although we were guided entirely by his wishes. He didn't want to meet with any Israeli officials, even if he was now an Israeli citizen.

This Ethiopian Jew tried to persuade me to allow him to remain in the United States, which he was visiting for the first time. He wanted to complete a four-year college education. I bluntly told him that this was not our policy, and he could obtain a comparable education in Israel at a fraction of the cost. What is more, in the United States he would be considered a black, even if a Jew, and that was not an additional burden we wanted Ethiopian Jews to assume. Let me illustrate.

Our Ethiopian Jewish friend was staying with us in Pelham. After breakfast he wanted to smoke. Emma and I discourage—at times forbid—smoking in our house for health reasons. So he walked out on the street just as our black mailman (a non-Jew) delivered our daily mail. Since it was a cold day, I invited the mailman in to have a cup of hot coffee. Shortly thereafter our Ethiopian Jewish guest returned and joined us. A moment later the doorbell rang. I went to the door and found several policemen with drawn guns standing at the threshold. Several police cars were at the curb. "We just had a call that a black man went into your home. He has been walking up and down the street in front of your house." I laughed and invited the officer in. "I have two black guests. They are friends of mine." "That won't be necessary, if you say so." I thanked him for being so vigilant. As I walked out with him, I found the house surrounded by three other policemen, who also had guns in their hands.

I told my Ethiopian Jewish friend that this would probably never have happened if he had been white. He shook his head in resignation. The incident most poignantly underscored my previous point about his not coming to the United States to study.

The NJCRAC Mission to Ethiopia

A mission sponsored by the NJCRAC finally went to Ethiopia. It included representatives of a number of Jewish organizations. Henry Rosenberg of the AAEJ was amongst them. The report issued by the mission indicated that while conditions in Ethiopia were poor politically and economically, the Ethiopian Jews were not suffering as much as they had in the past, and seemed to be no worse off than their neighbors. The mission never fully or sympathetically explained why if things were so good, hundreds of thousands of Ethiopians were leaving Ethiopia and becoming refugees in Sudan and elsewhere, amongst them thousands of Ethiopian Jews. Not far away from Gondar, the very time the mission was there, several Jews had been killed for no other reason than that they were Jews, but the mission had not even heard about this tragic incident. In interrogating several Jews who had been arrested and tortured in Ethiopia, some members of the mission questioned them as sharply as if they were culprits and not victims, as is revealed by the following extract from a secret tape that was provided to me:

Q: How long were you hanging upside down?
A: I don't know. I didn't have a watch.
A: Weren't non-Falashas in jail?
A: Yes, but they were not accused of being Zionists and Jews.
Q: Weren't they tortured, too?
A: Yes, but not as severely as the Beta Israel.

The members of the mission had agreed not to record the proceedings, but *one* of them could not resist, in light of what he observed to be the prejudicial attitude of some of his fellow members. Not surprisingly, the mission's report did not clamor for a larger-scale and immediate effort to rescue Ethiopian Jews from either Ethiopia or Sudan.

Israel: 1982

We stayed at the new Windmill Hotel in Israel and enjoyed its favorable location, facilities, and food, the latter not as elaborate or as expensive as the King David and other five-star hotels.

We visited the playground that Emma, Betty Lee Berger, her daughter Sheriden Collins, and I had provided for Jerusalem in the Liberty Bell Park, near our hotel, in memory of my brother Sam, and enjoyed watching the children use it. Emma and I subsequently provided additional funds for equipment, benches, and tree shelters, so that even better use could be made of these excellent play facilities. Richard Collins, Sheriden's husband, who worked for the U.S. Senate Committee on Foreign Aid, was in Israel with his senatorial committee. We visited the site together. He told me on several occasions then and later that the Senate was most sympathetic toward Israel. Later, Senate support was extended specifically for the rescue and absorption of Ethiopian Jews.

* * *

On behalf of the AAEJ, we purchased five Yemenite sterling silver *Kiddush* cups, had them suitably engraved, and presented them to Yona Bogale and four other Ethiopian Jewish *kohanim* in Israel, for the extraordinary leadership they had provided for the Ethiopian Jewish community in Ethiopia. The *kohanim* had been practically ignored since arriving in Israel; thus their previous status was being questioned by the Ethiopian Jews. We wanted to tell them in some concrete form that at least we were aware that their inspiring role had sustained Jewish life in their native land.

* * *

We had our first Passover Seder in Israel at the home of Bernard and Frances Alpert, charter members of the AAEJ board, who had made aliyah. Twenty of us crowded around the table in their quaint, reconstructed home in the old Jewish Quarter of Jerusalem to read the Haggadah and supplementary materials, eating and singing and talking until midnight. I read an Ethiopian Jewish prayer, in which the theme pleaded that the Ethiopian Jews should not be abandoned by God and the rest of the Jewish world. The points of view that evening on Israel's policy toward the Arabs varied from extreme hard-liners to avowed peaceniks.

* * *

Wherever we went during our three-week holiday, we were engaged in discussions on politics, economics, military affairs, cultural activities, so that each meeting was a thorough and often trying experience.

Everyone expected us to bring them up to date about Ethiopian Jewry, since the media censorship provided little information. Except for those already involved, we were not able to recruit any new supporters for a larger rescue program. Israelis didn't like to demand anything extraneous of the government, except benefits for themselves. They made their private views known when they cast their vote at election time or by writing letters to the newspapers. Occasionally an Ethiopian Jew was invited to speak before some Israeli group, but nothing further came of these initial contacts. A few tiny groups were interested in their welfare, but seemed to compete with one another rather than work collectively. Israelis naively asked me again and again what was the real reason that more of them were not brought to the country. Was it racism? I gave them my standard reply: "They are poor, illiterate, unskilled, and black," enough excuses why Israeli officialdom never expressed an interest in rescuing them massively. Most Israelis and American Jews winced at the mention of "racism," because they were not willing to believe that either Israel or Jewish leaders would be negatively influenced by the Ethiopian color. All urged me to be less critical and more statesmanlike in my approach. They felt I would be more successful as a patient quiet negotiator rather than as a rabid activist. I disagreed. I had tried that tactic for years, and it hadn't worked.

* * *

We went to a friend's home for a Shabbat luncheon, where besides their children, one married to an officer in the Israeli army, there were a number of guests, young and middle aged. A discussion arose as to the "cruelty" of the Israeli soldiers to the Arabs in the occupied territories. What struck us was that most asserted that the soldiers' conduct was standard practice, and not exceptional; and that it violated the spirit of the Judaic, Zionist, and Israeli moral codes. The officer, with some help from me, defended the Israeli soldiers, who, he claimed, were provoked at every turn by the inhabitants of the conquered areas, and therefore had to resort to force to protect themselves. This was the first time I had ever heard the Israeli army attacked by Israelis. It came as a surprise. The conversation was a portent of the explosion of inflamed passions that occurred after the incursion into Lebanon.

* * *

We had friends who were ardent supporters of the settlers who refused to evacuate Yamit in the Sinai Desert as a consequence of the Israeli-Egyptian peace treaty. Other friends would have permitted the Israeli soldiers to shoot these fanatics. We defended those who did not want to leave Yamit, first as being the victims of an equivocal Israeli government, which at first urged them to settle and develop the site, then reversed itself and forced them to leave. After some demonstrations, the settlers finally left, and were adequately compensated. We continued to distrust the Egyptians, just as we distrust the whole Arab-Moslem complex.

We were in Israel on April 25, 1982, the day when the Israeli evacuation of the Sinai began. Many Americans in Israel were opposed to the evacuation. Most Israelis accepted it philosophically, as the only road to peace.

* * *

One problem about rescuing larger numbers from Sudan was the unwillingness of the Israelis to involve more than a few Israeli Ethiopian Jews in the undertaking. A white Israeli, or even a darker-skinned non-Ethiopian Jew, could never determine who was and who was not a Jew. Only Ethiopian Jews could reliably carry out the detection and the selection. Keeping the operation secret meant using as few Ethiopian Jews as possible. As a result, vast numbers remained in Sudan and suffered.

* * *

There was some criticism by Israelis and a few always fearful Ethiopian Jews regarding the advertisement AAEJ had placed in American Jewish newspapers about the several hundred Jews who had died in Sudan. They all felt that we had revealed a well-kept secret—the presence of Ethiopian Jews in Sudan—and this would interfere with rescue procedures. I replied, as usual, that this was sheer nonsense. It was only another excuse for not doing more. The death of any more of these helpless Jews was a tragedy that should not be permitted to continue. Besides, the Sudanese not only knew that there were Ethiopian Jews in the country, but they also were fully aware of the presence of Israelis. What concered Jews and Israelis was that we were trying to stimulate them by guilt, for they didn't want to admit to any negligence on their part.

Sometime later, we printed a second list with even more names of those who died. Efforts were made by Israelis, including a few Ethiopian Jews working for the government and the Jewish Agency, as well as Jewish leaders in the United States, to discredit the list of 214 names by pointing out that six of the names were alive and in Israel. The list was compiled by Ethiopian Jewish refugees who had just arrived in Israel from Sudan. While an error might have crept into their memories, it was also possible that more than one person bore the same name. This nasty effort to dispute the death list, while expressing no concern for the 208 others who had died, was an obscenity.

* * *

We went to Lod to attend the Bar Mitzvah of Daniel David, whose father we had first met in Ethiopia in 1965. The entire nuclear family was now in Israel, eight children, all very bright.

The AAEJ, through private donors in the United States, was helping the two oldest, Zvi and Ruth, with educational scholarships, while they attended high school. Daniel conducted the Minha-Maariv service in beautiful Hebraic diction, after which some forty-five people, all Ethiopian Jews except for Emma and me, joined in the collation. They had prepared some dishes without the inevitable red pepper spices for us. It was a memorable affair.

* * *

We visited two absorption centers in Beersheba and Ofakim, where we learned at first hand, from recent arrivals from Sudan, about their suffering in Africa and the difficult trek from Ethiopia to Sudan. We took a sherut back to Jerusalem over the Hebron-Bethlehem road. At several places we noted piles of stones on the roadside. It meant nothing to us. One of the passengers wrote down the location of these piles. When we left the sherut, he told us that these were often used to attack Israeli buses, sheruts, and private vehicles. Emma had held my hand in fear during the entire trip. I had not previously informed her that we were passing through territory that from time to time proved dangerous. Otherwise, it was uneventful.

* * *

Some sharp divisions had arisen among the newly arrived refugees. These conflicts were exploited by a few Ethiopian Jewish malcontents, who were out of favor with the government and the majority of Ethiopian Jews. Several new, small non-Ethiopian groups had sprung up, concerned with their personal welfare. All the groups, at one time or another, appealed to the AAEJ for financial help. We turned them all down on the ground that we wanted to deal with one united organization. This had still not come into being as of 1986.

After the airlift of November 1984, new units sprang into being among the Ethiopian Jews to protect their status as Jews, to lash out at prejudicial rabbinical decisions, and to advocate rescue for those kinsmen left in Africa. There was an outburst of interest by officials and voluntary organizations, whom the government involved in various absorption functions, and by volunteers who arose in one community after another to help the newcomers. All this was a few years off. The point I wish to make is that there was really little effort by the government to bring about an orderly development of both leaders and organizations. Such steps would have warded off future demonstrations.

I asked Teddy whether he would accept an invitation to give a memorial lecture at Georgetown University in Washington, D.C., in memory of my brother Sam, whom Teddy had met in London in the early 1940s, when both were stationed in England. Their friendship continued throughout Sam's life. I suggested that he speak on "Can Jews, Christians, and Moslems Live Together in Peace? The Jerusalem Experience: Implications for American-Israel Foreign Policy." He agreed to accept such an invitation. Regrettably, the university and Teddy could never work out a mutually convenient date, so we never had the pleasure of listening to his always cogent observations.

* * *

One day we had lunch with Rabbi Philip and Hannah Goodman, whom Emma and I had known and worked with since the early 1930s. Phil, whose wife was an Israeli, had retired and settled in Israel, where their two children and their grandchildren lived. Phil was one of the few courageous Jews who, over fifty years ago, was not afraid to accept converted black Jews into his white congregation in Harlem. We had worked together on the creation of the Jerusalem YM-YWHA. I had kept him informed on the Ethiopian Jewish issue, but he never became involved until he went to Israel. He had become the consultant for the Israel Philanthropic Fund, an American Jewish organization which had received, through legacies and gifts, large sums to aid individuals and groups in Israel. I asked him to see what he could do to help the Ethiopian Jews. In 1985, after the large influx of Ethiopian Jews, he wrote me that his fund had allocated nearly $100,000 for a variety of programs directly benefiting them.

* * *

While I was in Israel, I celebrated my seventy-fourth birthday. Dr. Bernard Reznikoff, a former student and professional colleague for over thirty years, and then the director of the American Jewish Committee in Jerusalem, invited a few friends for a cocktail party at the Jerusalem Plaza Hotel. Bernie was trying to tell some Israelis, who had doubts about me only because of my deep concern for Ethiopian Jews, that I was a "good guy," a "good Jew, who "loved Israel" and had a "lot of fine Israeli friends."

* * *

At the Israel Museum, we finally found a newly made silver-on-copper container for the Moroccan Megillot Esther that Haim Morag, Moroccan-Israeli-American, had given me a decade ago for being his mentor and good friend. Another Megillot Esther, also Moroccan, was already housed in our home in an olive wood box made in Israel.

Rabbinical Assembly

The day after our return from Israel, I was scheduled to address the Rabbinical Assembly at the Concord Hotel in the Catskills. On my arrival, I was told that attempts had been made to cancel my lecture on Ethiopian Jews. The chairman, Rabbi William Frankel of Illinois, who was most sympathetic to the AAEJ program, had rearranged my presentation for an hour alone instead of my being part of a panel. He had been unable to get anyone to debate my position. Several hundred rabbis heard me cite the problems of getting Israel to rescue Ethiopian Jews in significant numbers, of their sufferings and death in Ethiopia and Sudan, and the need to provide more services for them in Israel after their delayed arrival. There was some response from individual rabbis, a few invitations to speak before their congregations, but there was no gung-ho feeling on the part of the assembly that this was an issue that must become number one on their agendas.

* * *

As a consequence of my speaking at the Rabbinical Assembly, Rabbi Bernard Eisenman, who was the rabbi of the Pelham Jewish Center when he was starting out in the rabbinate, and who became a good friend, invited me to speak before his congregation in Denver. Efforts were made by prominent Jewish leaders in Denver to have him cancel the invitation, but he refused. One of the Denver leaders was chairman of the national United Jewish Appeal. They finally persuaded him to broaden the base of the meeting by having a chairman from another Jewish organization and by inviting two other panelists. Eisenman insisted on his right to have a small separate meeting for his own congregation, and several score of people appeared at a luncheon meeting, where I spoke and raised some money for the AAEJ.

At the evening meeting, there were fewer than one hundred people in the audience. I was told that Federation leadership had urged everyone to boycott the meeting. There were no prominent local leaders in attendance.

The evening program turned into a charade. The American Jewish Committee representative briefly related his recent trip to Ethiopia, reporting that life was poor and turbulent all over the country, and Jews were suffering like the rest of the population. He made no plea for either greater relief for them in Ethiopia or for their rescue. As to Sudan, where thousands of Jewish refugees existed on the brink of death, he briefly commented that Israel was doing everything that could be done for them. He stressed that there should be no publicity about their condition in either country, or about their arrival and the numbers living in Israel, as this would interfere with the rescue process.

The other speaker, who spoke anonymously, giving neither his name nor the organization that he worked for, was a young man whom I had helped get a position with ORT in Ethiopia in 1976, a man whom I had sheltered and fed in our home in Pelham and in our apartment in Jerusalem on several of our visits, whom I had allowed to read my extensive files and correspondence without reservation. He arose and told the audience that the AAEJ had never rescued anyone from either Ethiopia or Sudan. He impugned the honesty and integrity of our organization as one not worthy of receiving any aid from the Jewish community. Having been on the Ethiopian trip, he reaffirmed what the previous speaker had said.

When I arose to reply to both of them, I spared neither the young man, his older colleague, nor the rest of the American Jewish organizations, nor Israel for failing to aid the Jews in Ethiopia and to rescue them in larger numbers. I accused them of covering up the tragic situation, of censoring information about the true condition of Ethiopian Jewry, of issuing inaccurate reports. I indicated that Israel must undertake an all-out rescue effort. I opposed quiet diplomacy, which only delayed saving them, and reminded the audience of the European Holocaust and the death of six million Jews at the hands of the Nazis, in part by the neglect of World Jewry. I am happy to relate that in this limited audience my words rather than theirs were believed. The AAEJ received substantial support from a few people in Denver, but the key Jewish leadership prevented every effort to develop a large local group by refusing to give this issue their blessing. The same could be said of many other communities around the country.

The Congressional Hearing

On August 4, the House Committee on Human Rights held a hearing in Washington regarding the violation of Ethiopian Jewish rights. The hearing had been inspired only by the AAEJ through its sustained contacts with congressmen like Barney Frank, Stephen Solarz, Tom Lantos, all Jews, and a non-Jewish representative, Don Bonker, who headed the committee. Invitations had been sent out to the major Jewish organizations to attend and make presentations. Not a single Jewish organization, except the AAEJ, put in an appearance. Strenuous efforts were exerted by various Jewish groups to cancel the meeting. What could have been their motives? Had the issue been concerned with any other country where Jews were also in jeopardy, whether Russia, Argentina, Iran, or Syria, the Jewish organizations would have flocked to attend, to be first in line, and their statements would have flooded the Jewish and the general press. With respect to Ethiopian Jewry, there was no interest. This was another piece of evidence of what I term the negative, conspiratorial aspect of everything associated with Ethiopian Jewry.

The AAEJ brought an Ethiopian Jew, Rachamim Yitzhak, who was now living in Israel, to testify. Statements were made by Henry Rosenberg of the AAEJ board and chairman of its rescue committee, and by the above-named congressmen. I was not scheduled to speak, but when certain questions arose, everyone turned to me to answer. The printed text of the hearing, which occupied forty pages, made good reading. The meeting should have been carried in the Jewish press with front-page headlines. The meeting and the subsequent printing were never publicized in the Jewish media.

* * *

Dr. Simon D. Messing, a professor at Connecticut University, who had served in Ethiopia in the 1950s, where he worked closely with the Ethiopian Jews as a medical anthropologist, had written a book on the Ethiopian Jews. He had not succeeded in getting a publisher. I urged him to complete the slender volume and publish it himself, since most of his costs would be covered by the large number of books that the AAEJ would purchase for resale. I found a printer for him and the paper-backed, illustrated volume of 134 pages was published in 1982 under the title *The Story of the Falashas*. It included important details not found in other volumes. It has enjoyed a good sale due largely to my promotional efforts.

Los Angeles

The annual General Assembly of the CJFWF in Los Angeles in November again demonstrated that American Jewish organizations and their leaders were showing only feigned interest in Ethiopian Jewry, but were still doing nothing to mitigate their problems in Ethiopia and Sudan by not advocating more aid for them in Ethiopia or greater rescue operations out of Sudan. Jewish leaders, after their visit to Ethiopia, had become apologists for the footdragging tactics of the Israeli government and were now widely urging silence rather than raucous protests.

While a program was planned at the assembly, the AAEJ was neither involved nor invited to participate. Since it was to be an unusually large gathering, and Los Angeles Jewish leaders were both defending Israeli policies and attacking the AAEJ, the AAEJ decided to depart from its previous restrained practices and become demonstrative. We urged our board members to go to Los Angeles. We printed large placards, which graphically revealed the serious plight of the Ethiopian Jews and demanded immediate rescue. We printed thousands of leaflets, which amplified the tragic story.

On the opening day of the assembly, we gathered in the lobby, held up our placards, and handed out leaflets. We were told to cease. We held fast, pointing out that other groups were doing the same thing; but the causes they advocated—anti–nuclear energy, environmental protection, the rescue of Soviet Jews—were appealing to the council's leadership, and thus they were unmolested. The Ethiopian Jewish cause, on the other hand, stirred their fury, but not in a positive direction.

Suddenly Nate Shapiro, the AAEJ president, was ushered out of the hotel by the hotel security guards, when he refused to remove his placard. Then, out of the blue, one of the council professionals rushed over to Emma and tried to take her poster away. Emma, a "gray-haired activist," as she was later described in the press, resisted, and as the pulling match continued, she was thrown back, barely caught from falling to the floor by friends who had come to her rescue. Emma had been greeting and kissing scores of people, whom she knew from our years of association with Jewish communal work. We had to abandon our inside publicity campaign or face exclusion from the hotel and the conference, for which we were all properly registered, having paid our $100 per person fee. We even faced the possibility of arrest.

I was in a rage when I heard what had happened to Emma and immediately wrote a letter to the executive vice-president of the CJFWF, a man I had known for decades and a man who usually referred to me as his "mentor," demanding an apology for the brutal, goonlike actions of his staff. We never got the courtesy of a reply, nor did we get even a word of regret from other top-level staff members of the council, some of whom had been good friends and guests in our home. Since then, they have all been on our black list. I ran into the man who attacked Emma and was about to strike him with my fists, when I found my arms pinned from behind by friends, who strongly felt I should not get involved in such an unseemly altercation. The man disappeared. My anger has never been assuaged.

At a meeting on the subject of the Ethiopian Jews at the same conference, the speakers' table included representatives of the Israeli government and the Jewish Agency, leaders of several Jewish organizations, and a young Ethiopian Jew, who had been brought to the assembly and given a written speech to read to an audience of over 350 people, dotted with top leaders of American Jewish organizations. He read several pages haltingly and was heard with difficulty. When he had finished, he took a folded sheet out of the inside pocket of his jacket and to the embarrassment of the entire dais presented "Twelve Demands" of the Ethiopian Jews in Israel, among them the immediate rescue of his kinsmen, the need for better absorption programs, and a plea for the involvement of world Jewry in saving them from extinction. His voice and English were now loud and clear. The Jewish leadership had planned a tour of the United States for him, but in light of his eccentric behavior, he was quickly dispatched to Israel.

During the meeting, a young Ethiopian Jew arrived directly from Ethiopia. He came through the combined efforts of the Los Angeles Federation and the AAEJ, one of the few occasions when we worked together for the benefit of Ethiopian Jews. He walked across the crowded hall to greet some of us sitting on the other side of the room, temporarily interrupting the proceedings. As I put my arms around him in greeting, I heard a well-dressed, portly Jewish woman say out loud: "Another one who just came out of the trees." Prejudice was sometimes unrestrainedly vocal. I wondered how many others felt as she did, but did not openly express their views.

Not allowed to speak from the podium, several of us asked for the microphone from the floor during the question period. We were admonished to be brief. I approached the instrument with a six-inch sheaf of documents in my hands, in case anyone challenged whatever I would say. Brief I was, but I was accusatory toward Israel, the Jewish Agency and American Jewish leaders. The Israeli and Jewish Agency spokesmen interrupted me to challenge what I had to say, but I put them in their place by a succinct recitation of the facts, pointing to the documentation. No one asked to see the papers.

These exchanges were no-win for the AAEJ. We were not allowed to occupy or even share in the driver's seat. We found, as always, almost a phalanx of solid opposition. There were a few courageous delegates who later invited us to speak in their communities, but they wouldn't get up and speak at the convention. We alienated others, who literally hated us for both creating a disturbing atmosphere and for daring to question the elite leadership of the American Jewish and Israeli organizations.

We left Los Angeles with a resolve that our work to save Ethiopian Jewry had just begun.

* * *

After the General Assembly in Los Angeles, Emma and I took a combined holiday and trip on behalf of Ethiopian Jews through the coastal parts of California, some of which we had never traveled. Renting a car, we drove south to Costa Mesa to spend a night with the Lenhoffs, then to San Diego, where I have several talks before Ruth Benett's active committee. As in many places throughout the country and the world, people who had known me on Staten Island, at Bronx House, in Pelham, and/or at Federation came up to greet me. I brought them up to date on friends they asked about. They had come to the meeting because they had seen my odd name in the local Jewish press.

On a nasty rainy day, we visited the fantastic San Simeon Castle and

Estate which William Randolph Hearst had created to partially satisfy his extravagant interests. Having recently read W. A. Swanberg's *Citizen Hearst*, the place reflected an obsessed collector and a man with a need to be surrounded with scores of people constantly at his beck and call. I liked the story that while entertaining in the vast dining room with its extraordinary long table and furniture, reflecting an English baronial mansion with a vintage several hundred years old, he always insisted upon having an ordinary bottle of ketchup on the table, a condiment to garnish his prodigious appetite.

We continued up the highway, which became more picturesque as we approached Carmel. We spent several days in this attractive but reserved holiday resort. We had a reunion with a creative and successful cousin of mine, Harry Hamburg, who had started out as a photographer, then turned to making TV ads with prominent people, which under his hand had become not only an art form but a lucrative profession. It was his idea to use the sonorous voice and portly presence of Orson Welles, who had portrayed Hearst in the movie *Citizen Kane*, in that highly successful and often-repeated ad that went: "We will sell no wine before it's time."

In San Francisco and Oakland, I gave several talks about the Ethiopian Jews. The response and attendance was poor, there was no cooperation from the leadership of the organized communities. While the AAEJ had committees in both cities, they had never been able to achieve effective results. I met several Ethiopian Jews who had lived anonymously in these cities for a number of years.

Once again we had a pleasant reunion with Dr. Harry Specht, dean of the School of Social Work at the University of California in Berkeley. He was one of the prize alumni of Bronx House, demonstrating that an agency and its staff could make a major impact on a human being's life. Despite his straitened origins, he was now a distinguished teacher and author. We cherish his friendship.

* * *

Nicki Tanner, a volunteer at the Federation of Jewish Philanthropies of New York, spent many hours at our home interviewing me for a long oral history about my twenty-four years at Federation as well as my earlier experiences as an agency executive. It was a candid interview in which I did not hesitate to evaluate a number of issues as well as lay and professionals leaders at Federation. I understand that one has to obtain permission to read my historical account. I had put no such restrictions on its availability to any reader.

* * *

A study was being made of the Jewish community in the Bronx House area of the Bronx. Interviewers from Federation spent several hours in Pelham asking me for my recollections of the community and my recommendations for its future. Many of my views were incorporated in the printed document. I had given a training program for Bronx House community leaders several years before, in which I had already projected my position on the future of that Jewish neighborhood and how to keep it both from declining and within the Jewish fold.

* * *

This was a year for recollections. A young man from Staten Island came to our home in Pelham and quizzed me about the six years that I spent there from 1932 to 1938 and my views on what had happened since then. He was part of a group that had organized a Staten Island Jewish Historical Society. The study of local history was becoming a phenomenon around the country as natives assembled material on the roots of the original Jewish community and its development over the last century.

* * *

I was inducted as a fellow into the Jewish Academy of Arts and Sciences, presumably for my contribution to the field of Jewish communal service and for the several books and many articles I had written on this subject and other themes. The certificate read: "In recognition of his literary attainments and important contributions in the special field of endeavor with which his name is associated, thereby adding to the sum total of human knowledge."

* * *

We had the enormous pleasure of attending the graduation of our granddaughter Elizabeth from Yale University, not deterred by the pouring rain that doused us to the skin. We also attended with great pleasure the Bat Mitzvah of another granddaughter, Deborah, who like her two older sisters, Bonnie and Judith, before her, conducted a beautiful service at the synagogue Temple Rodef Shalom in Falls Church, Virginia. We danced to exhaustion at the party that followed these impressive ceremonies.

* * *

I traveled to Charleston, South Carolina, where I spoke before a Jewish Federation committee for the American Association for Ethiopian Jews and raised a great deal of money.

There I met Reuben Greenberg, the black Jewish commissioner of police, about whom I had written a section in my book *Black Jews In America*. He was an interesting personality, who had attracted many articles in magazines and the press. He was both Jewish and a most competent police official. (In 1986, he was interviewed on the *60 Minutes* CBS TV program as a cop and a Jew.) At that meeting in this charming southern city, he told me that he had recently undergone formal conversion, so that there was no longer any question about his being a Jew. I will have to make a correction in any subsequent edition of my book.

Ireland, Scotland, and England

Emma and I invited Michael, Sandy, and Deborah to join us on a two-week holiday that would include Ireland, a bit of Wales, Scotland, and England. It was a delightful journey that took us to places we had never visited. We ate native foods and drank liquors, especially different varieties of beer. In Dublin we went to the synagogue on Friday evening, where we learned about the problems of living as a Jew in the Irish Republic. While friendly to Jews, the country has never been kind to Israel. We visited the National Gallery of Art with its superb collection of classical paintings. At the Abbey Theatre we attended a presentation of the Irish Ballet. They were terrible in the ballet's traditional form, but eloquent in modern dances based on the poems of James Joyce.

Our visits to Scottish castles and the home of Robert Burns, the poet, revived memories of my college days, when I had to learn a number of his poems for an examination in English poetry. At one castle, we met four young women school-teachers all from Gloversville, on the same search for knowledge that had attracted us to this spot. Glasgow and Edinburgh were cities worth visiting for much longer periods than our brief stay. London was, as always, a stupendous city. We've been there six times, yet even cumulatively, we have not seen all of its vastness. We went to see the play *Another Country,* which won the top prize in the theater season. It dealt with England's exclusive all-male public schools, whose graduates invariably seemed either to become violently radical, usually Communists (and generally homosexuals as well), or staid and ardent supporters of the Conservative Party. We finally saw *Evita,* the story of the infamous wife of the Argentinian dictator, Peron. It had the musical quality of a tragic opera.

While in London, I met with a man who formerly worked with the Ethiopian Jews in Ethiopia. He told me there was little interest in Ethiopian Jewry in England, despite the presence of the Falasha Welfare Association. I acquired David Kessler's new book *The Falashas.* Kessler, the president of the FWA in Great Britain and publisher of the *Jewish Chronicle,* had written a worthy book, except for the last chapter, where he gave a distorted vision of what actually took place during the period in which he was involved, condemning the AAEJ and me for "sensational and ill informed articles" and "vicious attacks . . . on ORT personnel." Contrary to Kessler's claim, all of our public statements had been designed to reveal the truth about what was *not* being done for the

Jews in Ethiopia and the failure of Israel to bring about a wholesale rescue operation. On the other hand, he attributed to me correctly the belief "that the only positive way to help the Falashas was by aliyah. All else, in his [Graenum's] view, simply led to assimilation and, therefore, hastened the extinction of the community." These were views that Kessler did not share at that time. In recent years, he changed his mind.

* * *

During the greater part of the summer, we again went to Sacandaga for meetings with our family and friends. I took long walks each day. There was a rash of reading and catching up with months of accumulated corresonndence. Being out of Pelham, away from the telephone, improved both my mind as well as my body.

There was one unprecedented event. On August 31, at 7 A.M., I heard what I thought was an accident, like a heavy vehicle hitting a tree or pole. The dishes rattled in the closet. I rushed out to see what had happened, but there was no evidence of any accident, major or minor. I turned on the radio and learned that an earthquake had occurred, and I was standing almost at its epicenter, feeling the low-rated Richter scale shock about as much as anyone. This was my first experience with such tremors.

At the request of the public authorities, I sent in a detailed account. What surprised me was an earthquake in the Adirondacks, which I always believed was the safest part of the United States. This was the place we always planned to flee to, if there was any possibility of nuclear war. It now seemed that every part of this country was subject to natural as well as manmade hazards.

* * *

I completed the year with a flight to Canada to talk before various groups, Hillel, synagogues, even though the Canadian leadership would not share a program with me. I attended a meeting, where after listening to a report from the head of the Canadian Jewish Congress on Ethiopian Jewry, I was asked to comment from the floor. I gave such a straightforward, objective statement, without rancor or emotion, that the executive apologized publicly for not having wanted me on his program. I was then invited to meet with a CJC committee the following day. While there was much conversation, note-taking, and promises to become more active on behalf of the Ethiopian Jews, nothing came of it. The key leadership, lay and professional, vetoed any action recommended by lower-level people. That is why I have contended that sweetness on my part attracts no favors. Only castigation works. It was left to student groups and the CAEJ to carry on a vigorous public campaign, which actually rescued a number of Ethiopian Jews and brought them to Canada. (There were fifty Ethiopian Jews in Canada in 1986.)

26

1983

As we entered the year 1983, I, as well as the leadership of the AAEJ, were still tormented with how little had been accomplished in rescuing Ethiopian Jews. About twenty-three hundred were now in Israel. Most news about their ordeal in Africa, or even about their happier existence in Israel, was censored or not deemed worthy of major coverage. We knew from interviews with recent arrivals that there were thousands suffering in Sudan. We published the names of hundreds who had died from hunger and disease, but it seemed to have little impact on the leaders of Israel and American Jewish organizations. On three different occasions, we brought Ethiopian Jews to the United States to tell the frightful tale to receptive Jewish organizations, occasional receptive conferences, to the press, radio, and TV, but little of consequence resulted from our noble and expensive efforts. The AAEJ finally engaged a public relations firm. We issued news releases on a national basis. I stated that we had little consequence, except for the growing following and numerous financial supporters that we were slowly continuing to attract, to fund the major projects we would undertake that year. Support came almost entirely from the grass roots.

A controversial report had been issued on how American Jews had not done enough to help the Jews of Europe during the days of the Nazi Holocaust. I arranged lunch with the professor who had directed that research undertaking and asked him to do a study of how little the Jewish world was doing to save the lives of Ethiopian Jews, showing how we had learned nothing from our horrible World War II experience. He begged off on the ground that he had no time to undertake such a study. He suggested that this would be a good project for a master's student.

Apparently he thought it was not worthy of a Ph.D. candidate. This response was as good as any evidence I could present that the lives of black Ethiopian Jews meant little even to a sophisticated scholar, who had invested several years of his life and time in a study of the historical consequences of our neglect of Jews who died only forty years ago.

I accepted invitations to speak in Albany, Stamford, Madison, Connecticut, South Brunswick and Tenafly, New Jersey, Providence, Staten Island, Highland Park and West Orange, New Jersey, New Haven, River Edge, New Jersey and Montreal, appearing on TV and radio on several occasions. I also referred many requests for speakers to other members of our association. Nothing seemed to step up the tempo of rescue.

I received a call from NBC-TV. They had seen some clips of a film being prepared by Simcha Jacobovici of Toronto, in which I was shown in four different segments, and they wanted to talk with me about a national TV presentation in the United States. Tom Tomizawa, the producer, came to Pelham and interviewed me over lunch for three hours. Next I was invited to his office to meet with Stephen Delaney, the field reporter–interviewer. Over a couple of drinks and a luncheon in an expensive restaurant, I satisfactorily answered all their searching questions. I gave them names of people to be interviewed abroad, if Delaney went to Ethiopia and Israel. A few days later a crew of five showed up in Pelham at 10 A.M., turned our living room upside down, and after interviewing me for hours with the TV camera rolling, they finally packed up at 3:30 P.M. Now I know why it costs so much to produce a TV film. Emma served a delightful lunch. I believe in meeting people for lunch either in our home or elsewhere. I find that business gets transacted in a more intimate and candid fashion through this medium.

A twenty-minute film was shown on NBC-TV on June 4, when Emma and I were in Israel. Was it seen? While walking in Liberty Bell Park in Jerusalem with Lester and Sylvia Gerson of New Orleans on June 6, they encountered a neighbor from that city, who after saying "hello," started telling the Gersons about the NBC production, for they knew the Gersons were deeply interested in Ethiopian Jewry. Lester turned to the man and asked whether he had seen me on the TV broadcast. "Of course." He then turned to his wife: "Here is Dr. Berger, who was in the TV film we saw two nights ago in New Orleans." The TV film had an impact on what Israel and American Jews were forced to do later in the year.

In April, shortly before we left for Israel, we had two visitors. One was an Ethiopian Jew, a friend since 1974, who now worked with the Jewish Agency. The other was his white American Jewish wife, who also worked for the Sochnut. They tried to persuade me that Israel was doing everything possible to rescue the Ethiopian Jews, and that Israel was meeting with difficulties that they couldn't share with me. The Ethiopian Jew had been used by Israel to identify and bring out some of the Jews in

Sudan. I argued that I did not believe what they told me. I knew there were thousands in Sudan, that they were coming over the border from Ethiopia every day, yet in the first four months of 1983, a bare four hundred had been flown out. Meanwhile Israel, through its tight censorship and its own propaganda agents had convinced the universe that this was all they could do.

The AAEJ had begun to plan for an independent rescue operation in Sudan itself, headed by Henry and Mildred Rosenberg, vice-presidents of the AAEJ, two people whom I had recruited for the movement in 1975. The AAEJ wanted to demonstrate that amateurs were prepared to undertake rescue efforts, even though it might be a dangerous and difficult enterprise, since our volunteers would not be representatives of a government or an acknowledged international rescue organization. They used only one vehicle, had to traverse thousands of miles over difficult terrain with few gas stations, operate clandestinely, drive mostly at night to avoid running into military patrols. It was a saga worthy of a book. They rescued 135 persons, who reached Israel. But I am getting ahead of my story.

Were There Any Ethiopian Jews in European Concentration Camps?

In March, Michael Allegro, a Dutch Jew who migrated to the United States after World War II, came to see me about an important incident in his life. His wife and he had been arrested in Holland by the Nazis and taken to the Bergen-Belsen concentration camp, where he recalled the presence of Ethiopian Jews. He brought me two signed affidavits testifying to their presence. I had never heard of any Ethiopian Jews having been in such custody, but it was a possibility. Perhaps they were soldiers in the British army in North Africa captured by the German or Italian forces, brought to Italy for imprisonment, and because they were black and because someone learned they were Jews, they were inevitably transported along with other Jews to Bergen-Belsen. The affidavit stated that they lived apart, eating a special kind of bread. This could be injera, the staple carbohydrate consumed in Ethiopia, but where would they have obtained the flour and other ingredients?

Allegro told me that he could not elicit any interest or information from Jewish Holocaust survivor organizations, including the one made up of those who luckily survived Bergen-Belsen. I tried to find out more about this intriguing matter by writing to the military archivists in Washington, Great Britain, and Germany. No one could confirm or deny the substance of my inquiry, nor could they give me further leads, except to make use of their extensive libraries and files in a personal investigation. I tried to learn whether any of the generals or other officers who had entered Bergen-Belsen had mentioned them in published biographies or histories. I came up with another zero. Could the Allegros have imagined all this? What would have been their motives? No one, except the AAEJ or me, had any interest in this odd story. The Holocaust had been portrayed only as a deathly attack on white Jews. No one wanted to be associated with a sudden revelation of a black Jewish presence in this historic event.

When we went to Israel, we decided to visit Yad Vashem and speak to their archivists. We had a pleasant hour with a woman, herself a refugee, who told us she had never heard of black Ethiopian Jews being in any of the concentration camps. She told me that if anyone was prepared to do the research, it would be necessary to go through millions of names and thousands of other items. Although I later discussed this with an Ethiopian Jewish student at Tel Aviv University, I questioned whether anyone would profit from this probing into the past.

I would not have written about this incident in such detail had it not been for one remark made by this archival director. She doubted that the records would reveal anything. "The Ethiopians were not Jews until 1975, when the State of Israel made a declaration that they could come to the country under the Law of Return. They couldn't have been registered as Jews during the Holocaust." This would have been an unbelievable comment even for an uninformed person. From a respected researcher, it was incredible. Nothing further has been done on this curious matter to date.

The Jacobovici Film

One other event also forced the Israelis to act. In September, the first showing in a commercial theater of Simcha Jacobovici's film, *Falasha: Exile of the Black Jews* took place in Toronto, Canada. Simcha, born in Rumania, was educated in Israel and later migrated to Canada. A leader in the North American Jewish student movement, deeply touched by the plight of Ethiopian Jews, he undertook on his own to film their shabby lives in Sudan, Ethiopia, and then more happily in Israel. He interviewed prominent individuals in the respective countries, including several in the United States and Canada, and produced a prize-winning documentary. Officials in Jewish organizations and Israel considered it anathema, tried to keep it from being shown anywhere, and boycotted it before audiences over which they had control. I was interviewed and was included in four segments.

Originally I recommended that the AAEJ help finance the film. Before it was finished, it cost us a considerable sum of money. Despite my plea for aiding Simcha, I had serious doubts at the outset whether he would be able to penetrate the interiors of Sudan and Ethiopia, and whether he could get prominent Jewish, American, Israeli, Ethiopian, and Sudanese personalities to sit for interviews. The film was a blockbuster. Despite efforts to prevent its showing, it received considerable and favorable coverage in the press over the world. Critics described it in such vivid terms as "passionate," "heart rending," "remarkable," "moving," "searing," and "incisive." It proved once again what a single person's efforts could do toward saving the lives of a remnant of Israel.

Newspaper Advertisements

We were to have combined a holiday in Egypt and Israel, but our doctors persuaded us to forgo Egypt (heat, food, potential illnesses), so we spent the entire month in Israel, our seventeenth visit to that country. We stopped overnight in London just to break up the long flight, because that was what Emma preferred.

Tim and Pia Gidal picked us up at the Lod Airport in Israel and drove us to Pia's extra Jerusalem apartment in Rehavia at 18 Metudela. As it was Shavuot, we took them out for dinner at the Moriah and ate walnut blintzes. We talked about possibly meeting them in Bad Gastein, where Tim goes for his annual therapeutic baths and massages. Once again we could not make it in the fall; a disappointment, as we too were looking for the elixir that might assure us of a better and longer life.

The first thing I did was to arrange with Murray Greenfield, our AAEJ representative in Israel, to have advertisements placed in the major Israeli newspapers each Sunday morning for one month on the front page, to read:

> WHEN WILL ISRAEL RESCUE THE REMAINING 20,000 Ethiopian Jews suffering and dying in the Horn of Africa?
>
> AMERICAN ASSOCIATION FOR ETHIOPIAN JEWS

Regretably, Murray got hung up arguing price with the newspapers, so we lost a week. I insisted that he go ahead at the newspapers' standard fees. The ad appeared in a few, but not all the papers. The advertisement had some impact. A number of people called me after having read the brief text. It would have accomplished even more if I had arranged to place the ads myself.

Israel officials were concerned about our rescue operation, which began at the end of May with an AAEJ volunteer, the daughter of Henry and Mildred Rosenberg, taking a group to Khartoum, then Paris, and finally to Israel. A letter was sent by an Israeli official to Nathan Shapiro, demanding that we cease our operation. To avoid any further excuses by the Israelis for doing so little, we changed our routes out of Sudan.

Strangely the same cease-and-desist letter asked us for information about the effect of the drought on Ethiopian Jews, an odd request, as the Israelis had a continued presence in Ethiopia, which could easily provide them with this data. They could also have spoken to the refugees, who knew the situation intimately. The Israelis always maintained the fiction of not being in Sudan and Ethiopia, and not quizzing the refugees for information.

* * *

We were impressed with the recent excavations and restorations in the old Jewish sector of Jerusalem: the walls of Hezekiah, the rebuilt synagogue, the old Roman road from gate to gate.

* * *

We spent a great deal of time with ten Ethiopian Jewish students at the Etzion Ulpan. Before reaching Israel via Sudan, all had completed a high school or higher education in Ethiopia. Most spoke English. All wanted to go to college and be either engineers or accountants. I told them politely but firmly that making it in Israel was uncertain and difficult. They should think about scaling down or deferring their ambitious goals and seek vocational training as carpenters, electricians, plumbers, and bookkeepers, then plan to study at night. The economic rewards would be greater and quicker. Yet the status of a college student was what all of them aspired to, and some put in a great deal of extra study effort to make it to the university.

We entertained them at our apartment as a group. Some came to see us after that singly or in pairs, asking special help in rescuing their families still in Ethiopia or in Sudan.

One was a particularly attractive and well-dressed young man, who not only spoke English with fluency, but had learned to speak Hebrew equally well. Emma, he, and I had been invited to a Bar Mitzvah of an American boy, whose grandfather and grandmother had recently returned from a trip to Ethiopia. The young Ethiopian Jew, without prior notice, was suddenly called on to speak. With extraordinary savoir-faire, he strode to the microphone and, speaking in Hebrew, told the gathering of several hundred that he prayed that the grandson would be like his grandfather—adventurous, traditionally Jewish, and interested in all Jews whether white or black. He was given a stand-up, handclapping ovation.

* * *

Some Ethiopian Jews were recruited to work in the expanding number of absorption centers. After many years of indifference, the government and the Jewish Agency finally admitted that they could work more effectively with the new immigrants from Ethiopia if they employed interpreters who knew how to converse with them in their native tongue.

The Gersons had returned from their trip to Egypt. Led by Zimna Berhane, we were driven to the absorption centers in Afula and Pardess Hana, where we met recently arrived Ethiopian Jews. I knew and had previous correspondence with several of them. The first thing they asked, after embracing me, was our help in getting their families out of Ethiopia or Sudan. That was a recurring appeal wherever we went. We were impressed with the rapid progress made by these individuals.

At Pardess Hana I photographed a grandmother of ninety-one, her daughter, the daughter's husband, and a small child born shortly after their arrival from Sudan. The grandmother had made the perilous journey from the Semien Mountains, across the rugged terrain of northwestern Ethiopia, to parched Sudan over a period of two weeks, mostly walking, but occasionally riding on a donkey. All managed to survive and finally reached Israel. They seemed to be thriving. Every family we talked with had a similar heroic tale to relate.

* * *

Louis Rapoport, journalist for the *Jerusalem Post,* called and came for lunch one day with a gift, an inscribed copy of his book on Ethiopian Jews, *The Lost Jews,* now in its second edition. At this point I was still suspicious about his interest in Ethiopian Jews, as he had not filed copy of the speech I gave on August 15, 1977. To me, he was ambivalent. I felt pity for his lack of journalistic integrity and personal courage. He agreed with my assessment that the Israelis really did not want to save the Ethiopian Jews in great numbers. He even admitted that Israel brought in as many as it did only as a result of pressure from the AAEJ. He thought I ought to write a book about the Ethiopian Jews, since I was so knowledgeable on the subject. He said that he would speak to the editor of the *Jerusalem Post* about his writing a story on the Ethiopian Jews and me. Nothing came of it. When I pressed him as to whether he knew of any member of the Knesset who was genuinely interested in the Ethiopian Jews, he paused thoughtfully, but could not give me a single name.

* * *

While walking in Jerusalem, we dropped into the Safrai Gallery, from which we had occasionally purchased paintings. I fell in love with a Castel, in brilliant red and black, painted on sand ground down from basalt rock. In bold, quaint, almost undecipherable Hebrew script, it was overwhelming. Safrai wanted $9,000. It could have been bargained down, but Emma would not hear of our spending such a huge sum for a painting. Besides, we would have to buy two, which would ultimately be inherited by each of our sons. I argued that it would not only be an investment for our children, but something we could enjoy in our own lifetime. There was another, smaller painting in blue-black, for which the dealer wanted $6,000. Now we were getting far beyond our financial means. We didn't buy either. I have regretted it. I would have liked a Castel and would have looked at it daily as it hung on our already crowded walls.

* * *

We attended services at the new Hechel Shlomo Synagogue. An impressive entrance. An extravagant, garish interior. One forgot about the questionable architecture as one worshipped in the huge, populated sanctuary with a superb chazzan and choir; the ritual procession in taking out and returning the Torah was spiritually moving. While there was no sense of intimacy in its vastness, it was quite a stirring dramatic Sabbath service.

* * *

We had a wonderful evening at the Jerusalem Theater watching the Pilobulus dancers. Coming early for a bite of supper, we sat at a table with some of the dancers. They related the company's history, how they were recruited, and what a joy they derived from their imaginative sensitive, graceful, athletic dancing. The accompanying music was electric. The final number, "God Makes the Seas," was one of the most theatrical dance performances we have ever witnessed. The audience clapped until everyone's hands were sore. A great show.

* * *

We were invited to a rabbi's home, a rabbi whom we had known for many years. It was Shabbat afternoon. He wanted us to meet an Israeli rabbi who had just returned from Ethiopia. After a handshake introduction, he blurted out: "What makes you think the Falashas are Jews?" I was taken aback for a second. I facetiously replied: "Do you want me to start with ancient history or go backwards from today?" Belligerently, he replied: "There is nothing you can tell me that will convince me that they are Jews." We had not yet sat down. His wife, seeing that he was in a combative state, took him by the arm, said they had to leave, and they departed. It was a brief but stirring scene. The attitude expressed by this young, American-born traditional rabbi was one that I suspect was shared by many other prejudiced religious Jews.

* * *

We were visited one day by a higher-level representative of the Jewish Agency. He first called on the phone: "Graenum, I heard you wanted to see me." Since I had never met him and didn't even know who he was, I replied: "You are mistaken. If you want to talk to me, I shall be available tomorrow at 4:30 P.M. I have another date at 5:30." He greeted me by my first name, extolling me to the skies as a person whose name would go down in history as the savior of the Ethiopian Jews. I interrupted his effulgent remarks by telling him that flattery was no way to soften my critical attitude or dull my activities on behalf of Ethiopian Jews. "What do you want?" He then tried to persuade me that I was wrong in my criticism of Israel, that Israel was doing all that it could, that the AAEJ was endangering Ethiopian Jewish and Israeli lives by its current mission in Sudan, and that it was about time that the AAEJ and I desist from our destructive remarks and activities. I listened to the same litany of complaints that I had heard from other officials before. Then I gave him a succinct, sharp, historical review of what Israel had *not* done, how it had permitted Jews to suffer and die, and that Israel was guilty of influencing world Jewry not to do anything either. I told him categorically that Israel could have and even now still could save thousands from Sudan, if it only wanted to. Israel had a presence in Sudan, which it had exploited spasmodically, when the AAEJ put pressure on the regime. He blustered a weak and repetitive defense. I finally warned him that if Israel didn't save all of them in Sudan this year—we estimated that there were three thousand—we would be forced to do two things: continue our independent rescue operation and go to the press with the unhappy story.

When he left, he was no longer praising me. I could see from his face and his voice, that he was disappointed at having failed with his mission. I might have told him that his betters had tried and flunked. I felt so sorry for him that I refrained from such a parting shot.

* * *

While in Israel, I visited the Ethiopian Jewish section of the Tel Aviv University library and selected some material for reproduction. The books were part of the Faitlovitch collection, which had been scattered amongst several Israel universities. Thus I added to my ever-growing personal library, which will someday be given to the American Jewish Historical Society.

* * *

Our next-to-the-last meal in Israel was a full Ethiopian luncheon including ingera and all the other spiced dishes at the home of Yona Bogale. Once again I urged him to dictate his memoirs. Several researchers were recording aspects of Ethiopian Jewish life through taped interviews with Yona and others, mostly *kohanim*, who had recently arrived in Israel and had prodigious memories about the past. Once they are gone, treasuries of material will be forever lost. Yona had a great story to tell, and at seventy-five years of age, he had to tell it soon or it might be too late.

Finally, we had a sumptuous dinner with Aaron and Esther (Wube) Hollander, where as always we brought and in turn received many gifts.

Someday a writer will tell the story of the Bogale and Wube families, who in their separate histories reveal a great deal of what Ethiopian Jews, coming from one of the most underdeveloped countries, were able to achieve in their lifetimes.

* * *

In between scores of breakfasts, luncheons, afternoon teas, dinners, and afterdinner meetings, where we met friends, new people, and many Ethiopian Jews, Emma and I managed to read a lot of books in one short month. Somerset Maugham's *Summing Up* (his autobiography); Vincent Brome's *Frank Harris;* Frank Harris's *Oscar Wilde:* four of George Bernard Shaw's plays; Ruth Bondy's *Emissary,* the life of Enzo Sereni. In addition Emma read Nancy Mitford's *Zelda,* and Gilot and Laka's *Life of Picasso.* We didn't waste one moment of our brief journey.

* * *

The AAEJ brought another young Ethiopian Jew, who had escaped with his family from Ethiopia, Sudan, and finally reached Israel, to the Council of Jewish Federations General Assembly in Atlanta. No place could be found for him on the program devoted to the subject. He had to speak briefly from the floor. A showing of Jacobovici's film attracted fewer than fifty people. Every effort was made to disparage it. This was November 1983. I decided this would be the last general assembly I would ever attend. The apathy of Jewish leadership, its indifference and prejudice, had hardly been dented after a decade of relentless pressing. I'd had enough. I was embittered with respect to both Israel and the organized Jewish community. It was at this very moment, after the AAEJ had agreed to withdraw from Sudan, that the Israelis began the rescue of three thousand Ethiopian Jews.

* * *

In November 1983, as part of its annual meeting, the AAEJ mounted its first open conference in Washington, attracting several hundred people. The conference was addressed by a number of congressmen, but did not entice a single national American Jewish leader, even out of curiosity. Several Ethiopian Jews spoke. Jacobovici's film was screened. I presented a handsome sterling silver plate to Henry and Mildred Rosenberg for their heroic rescue of hundreds of Ethiopian Jews out of Sudan and Ethiopia. We received only fair coverage in the non-Jewish press, and hardly a mention in the Jewish weeklies.

* * *

Despite the adverse attitude of official Jewry, the demand for materials on Ethiopian Jews was mounting. Our campaigns were paying off.

The JWB's Jewish media department was receiving numerous requests for my slides and Meyer Levin's film. The director, Eric Goldman, thought the slides required a soundtrack commentary. I trekked down to a studio for several days and voice-recorded the slides as they flashed on the screen. This was a volunteer service for which I never asked nor received compensation. Requests began to flood our office for the new Jacobovici film. The public was being educated despite the boycott of major Jewish organizations.

* * *

Emma and I got a scare in August, when after a routine breast examination, she went to a specialist, who ordered all kinds of X-rays, and unhappily diagnosed her as having cancer. She entered Memorial Hospital in New York to be operated on by a famous breast cancer surgeon, with anxiety and fear, which affected all of us, but distressingly more so for Emma. She was always apprehensive before an operation. She had gone through a number of them successfully. The surgeon came down to the lobby after the operation looking for me. He put his arms around me. He had tears in his eyes as he whispered that it was *not* malignant. He regretted the inaccurate diagnosis. I thanked him in a husky voice, because I had been expecting the worst. I could not upbraid him for the error. Even with the use of every modern technological device and the employment of different medical experts, mistakes were still being made. It took Emma awhile to get over the shock.

* * *

One morning I awoke with pains in my chest and my left arm, notable symptoms of a potential heart attack. I said it would pass. Emma was concerned. Our doctors were on holiday. She called a cardiologist and insisted, over the objections of his nurse, on an immediate examination. He found nothing wrong with me after a thorough physical checkup and a cardiogram. He gave me pills in the event that symptoms recurred. They didn't. I never took a single tablet. What brought it about? I do not know. What I do know is that if you think you are ill, consult a good physician. Don't wait. I'm told over and over again that I am not a candidate for a cardiac disease. Who knows? I am overweight, always a hazard. I do get overly concerned about the Ethiopian Jews to the point of open rage against those I deem their enemies. I no longer exercise sufficiently. I stopped shoveling snow from our walks and driveways. But who knows when and where?

27

1984—Haiti

TRAVEL WAS ALWAYS on our mind. We decided to go to Haiti for two weeks during February. Everyone warned us against going to this Caribbean country. It was under a dictatorship. The poverty was visible and painful. Strange diseases emanated from the tortured Haitian half of Hispaniola, the island it shared with its inhospitable neighbor, the Dominican Republic.

We were persuaded to go there by a few people who loved the country and returned regularly. We were attracted by the naive paintings which we had seen in the Dominican Republic and at the airport in Port-au-Prince while changing planes several years ago. We had heard and read about voodoo from Lizzie, our granddaughter, who curiously studied this phenomenon at Yale, and we wanted to observe at first hand how this occult movement, a combination of religion, medicine, and entertainment, had captured the minds and bodies of the Haitians as well as people in other countries like Brazil. Poverty was evident along the road from the airport to our hotel in the center of town. We have seen poverty everywhere from the United States to India to Ethiopia, so that was no novelty. The streets were jammed with people, for Haiti is one of the most densely populated countries in the world. Many made a living street-selling their wares, from food to clothing to toys. Odors emanated from the wayside cookeries, pungent but pleasant. In between we saw evidence of greater wealth in public buildings, parks, and fine homes. This contrast would be repeated on later trips to other parts of the land.

Our travel agent had neglected to tell us that we would be there during the Mardi Gras carnival, nor that the balcony of our hotel overlooked the street where hundreds of thousands assembled, danced, and paraded. But there it was before us. Band music played with an extraordinary beat. Voices in song filled the air from the slow-moving throngs. We watched the building of the decorated stands where people would gather in their finery, drink, and enjoy the never-ending parade, which stretched out over a four-hour period late in the afternoon and early evening for three successive days. Many were in costume, some quite original. Groups of paraders representing workers' organizations, lodges, and religious associations wore uniforms. A vast amount of food was sold to seemingly ever hungry and thirsty participants, who watched from the streets and balconies. While the police were everywhere with their ready truncheons, we saw little evidence of disorderliness. It was quite a remarkable event, part religious, part social, part fun, and part madness.

Despite prior warnings not to walk in the streets at night and even in the daytime in certain areas, we were not molested; no one tried to rob us. During the daytime, young men attached themselves to us, and when we couldn't shake them off, we took them along. They proved to be helpful in finding out-of-the-way places for shopping. They carried our bulky purchases, found a cab to take us back to the hotel, and even wrapped our packages for shipment. We paid them a few dollars for their services.

While generally at night, unless the restaurant was nearby, we traveled by cab, we were never accosted even as we sauntered through well-peopled but ill-lighted back alleys. The natives, both white and black, told us that Port-au-Prince was safer than any city in the United States, because criminals who steal or mug were dealt with harshly. The one danger in Port-au-Prince was to fall into a hole in the sidewalks, which they never repaired.

Shopping was a bargaining enterprise, unless you shopped in a one-price store. What you eventually paid was at least half the asking price. After bargaining, you had not alienated the merchant, even the young ones, when you walked off with your purchase. They liked the game and would then try to sell you something else, once again starting at a price that would ultimately be shaved to its proper proportions.

We toured the country, entering some of the gingerbread, wooden houses of the nineteenth and twentieth century, now landmarks, sometimes even meeting the current owners, who delighted in relating the building's history—who built it, who lived within it, gossip and mysteries associated with it. When we drove into the mountains, we saw villages and the sharp contrast in the homes of the rich as against the poor. We traveled on new, superior, hairpin, twisting roads to the southern side. We inhaled the aroma of coffee beans drying everywhere on the streets. The museums were filled with striking art, painted by some of the country's best. The graphic arts were comparatively new in Haiti, having been initiated only in the last five decades. There was little talk of politics, a subject which could easily get a resident into difficulties with the authorities. Most young people talked about their schooling—and wanted to know about schools abroad, which they would like to attend, if they could earn and save enough money to get to the United States. They spoke of the lack of jobs and earnings which were a pittance.

We went to a voodoo performance one night with a dozen other American tourists. They rushed to sit on the front benches, close to the performers. We preferred to be seated a few rows back. It took place in a large shed with a concrete floor, the roof supported by a single center pole painted in bright red. Various ritualistic symbols were chalked on the floor and pole. Five drummers performed during the forty-five-minute presentation, as a dozen actor-dancers, male and female, went through a routine build-up climaxing in a frenzy. Candles were lit and placed on the floor in a ceremonial act. The leading male drank from a bottle throughout, and to reveal that he was not drinking water or tea or soda, he spilled some of the liquid on the candle, which flared into a large flame as the alcohol touched the lighted portions.

The dancers were in constant motion, varying their steps, back and forth, in circles, often with sexually suggestive movements, while they sang various verses. The highlights occurred, when one of the female dancers feigned, but realistically executed, a fitful delirium, rolling on the ground in seeming madness, putting a whole egg into her mouth, eating the shell and yolk. Then she walked on burning sticks. The act culminated when the leading actress took a live chicken, executed a number of incomprehensible ceremonies, then twirled it around and around until the chicken was apparently dead, finally biting into the feathered neck and sucking out its blood. Gruesome. A goat was brought into the arena. The dancers threatened to kill it with their machetes. The goat was spared. In a sexually exultant and exhausting dance, the program was brought to an ecstatic finale.

The whole performance was primitive, pagan. It could be revolting, if seen only as a show. Voodoo was said to be the religion of the poor, who looked forward to these sessions to forget their poverty, overcome their illnesses, and as a form of entertainment. For people who had little joy in their lives, the music, the dance, the rituals were meaningful. The role of the priest was crucial, as he represented the ancient African spirits. In a sense it was also a protest against the formal rites and control of the official Catholic church, which constantly warned the natives against this insidious rival.

As I sat there watching the ceremonies with the chicken and the goat, I could not help but recall the Judaic primitiveness of *Shluggen Kaporoth* and the scapegoat, which traditional Jews practice in connection with our holiest of days—Yom Kippur, the Day of Atonement.

When we rode back to the hotel in the bus, one of the tourists called out: "Who is having chicken for dinner?" There was hysterical laughter. In a chorus, they shouted: "No."

At one of the old houses, now converted into a museum, the woman who supervised the building showed me a picture of her great-grandmother, who she claimed was born in Ethiopia. She herself was almost white, in sharp contrast with her ancestor, who was jet black and looked nothing like the distinctive natives of Ethiopia. She also said her husband believed that the family—generations before—had a Sephardic Jewish origin. I thought both stories fanciful but interesting, and wanted to interview her for an article I might write. She had to leave the country within an hour and would not return until after we were gone. I left my name and address and told her to write me the details of both the Ethiopian and Sephardic origins. I never heard from her.

We met a young Jewish woman married to a native doctor. She hungered for Jewish contacts and associations. There was no evidence of any organized Jewish life in the country.

It was a restful, albeit active, holiday in the sun. Everywhere we went we were told of American and English actors, writers, TV and stage producers and directors, and politicians who went to Haiti for their holidays. What better credentials than going to a place with the jet set? We were entertained at hotels by native dancers and singers in their colorful costumes, accompanied by vigorous bands, which repeated the same rhythms until the dancers and the audience, who responded to the rhythms, were exhausted.

Emma and I read amongst other things during this trip, Gabriel Garcia Marquez's great novel, *One Hundred Years of Solitude,* which fitted into our vacation perfectly.

We brought back a lot of paintings, a hand-carved trunk, some good Haitian rum, and excellent guava preserves.

As I finished typing this section on Haiti, the radio announced that President Jean-Claude Duvalier, "Baby Doc," as he was called by his unhappy citizens, had fled the country after a series of revolts. He thus brought to an end thirty-five years of tyranny, first introduced by his late father-dictator. They had mulcted the country for their own benefit, reducing it to one of the poorest nations in the world and governing with a ruthless hand.

Back to School?

As late as 1932, when anyone asked my mother what I was doing, she would invariably reply: "First, he didn't want to go to school at all, but when he started, he wouldn't stop, even though he is now married and father of a child." I might add, that when I stopped my formal studies I never returned to anything resembling a formal classroom, except as a teacher. While I taught for many years and theoretically had no objection to college offerings, yet I had mastered, or so I believed, the trick of learning by myself, and therefore I did not have to sit in a didactic setting any longer. I was a wide reader, knew where and how to find material in which I was interested, and that filled any lacunae in my background. I didn't want to go through some of the tediousness associated with the classroom. I had found relatively few instructors inspiring over this long educational trek. I felt no impulsion toward obtaining a higher degree. I thought I knew as much as the prospective teachers, and in many instances more, so there was no incentive to be subjected to those who could not guide me to knowledge that I couldn't find at my own pace and leisure. Thus I abjured the formal structure.

Occasionally I would sit in on a single lecture of an eminent scholar, writer, poet. Sometimes it was a delight, as when I heard Dylan Thomas literally sing his own poetry. More often it was a disappointment. Some read their own works badly. Others gave such a superficial lecture that I was tempted to walk out. Sometimes I did. It became a point of my pragmatic philosophy as an administrator to avoid sponsoring single lectures on anything by anybody. Instead I preferred to sponsor a series of lectures; and similarly I always insisted on doing a series whenever I was asked to give a talk. Only through a series could the speaker get to know the participants and at the same time be able to give them a better and more thorough grounding in the subject.

Emma was always enrolling in courses of study—French, art, music, current events, foreign affairs, Jewish studies; so whatever I missed she related to me from her retentive memory.

After I had been retired for a few years, the thought occasionally occurred to me that maybe we ought to go back to "school," particularly when we were traveling, for this might give us a great deal more information than we might otherwise accumulate, even if we were traveling on our own and did some reading in advance. We always bought the best guidebooks. Sometimes we seemed to know as much as the guides, who often would rather entertain than educate their charges. In very few instances have we found guides who were deeply informed and could satisfy our questions.

Elderhostel

In 1983, we decided to enroll in a three-week Elderhostel program. These courses in universities in the United States and other countries in the world were designed primarily for the elderly, the retired. We selected England and attended universities in Cambridge, Birmingham, and Brighton. Our subjects were the development of these cities, with additional trips to the surrounding countryside, where we could learn more about the origin of villages, types of architecture and art. The students were all in their sixties and seventies, mostly women, a few married couples, coming from all over the United States. They were urbane, upper-middle-class, college-educated, well-traveled, so we had much in common.

The universities provided us with individual rooms. Washing and toileting were down the hallways, not an inconvenience for former campers like us. Three meals a day were served—of average quality, but sufficient and nourishing. Wine was available for luncheons and dinners, and a bar was open for those with hardier drinking tastes.

The courses were another thing. At Cambridge, that magnificent city and university, we had a different instructor each day, who usually delivered a slide lecture and fled. We never really knew them, even when they were interesting. The trip leaders were equally superficial. Cambridge was disappointing academically. However, just to roam around the city, listening to the youth choir at King's College Chapel and sitting in the chapel itself, rummaging in old book shops, seeing a fine collection of Korean pottery in the Fitzwilliam Museum, taking side trips to Bury St. Edmunds and Lavenham, gave us a good exposure to old English monuments and the earliest developing villages. The King's College student chorus provided us with a marvelous performance of classical tunes and then switched to modern popular music with original jazzed-up antics. Their solemn rendition of Lamentations coincided with the forthcoming Tisha B'Av memorial Jewish holiday commemorating the destruction of the ancient Temples in Jerusalem. While radically different, it reminded us of sitting on Har Zion in Jerusalem with Yemenites in 1955 where we chanted the Lamentations attributed to Jeremiah, although modern scholars question his authorship. We walked down William Wordsworth's Lane, where I could not help but recall his definition of poetry as "powerful emotion recollected in tranquillity." We were on our way to see an outdoor version of an Elizabethan play, *The Mock Astrologer*. I found old books on Ethiopia. We read E. M. Forster's novel *The Longest Journey* about his early life at Cambridge as a student.

I wrote a long critique of our week's program, suggesting that there should be only one lecturer throughout the session and hopefully one who could accompany us on our trips. I suggested a program of major works written by famous graduates of Cambridge, which would also give us a review of Cambridge's influence on the intellectual political, economic, and religious development of England. Elderhostelers should be encouraged to read such selected works in advance, so that the lecturer could concentrate his energies on a stimulating discussion.

When my grand-nephew, Mark Miller of Scardsdale, after graduation from Haverford, was awarded a three-year all-expense graduate fellowship to study architecture at Cambridge University in England, his parents asked him why he had selected King's College as his residence and study hall. Mark replied: "What would Uncle Graenum have thought of me if I had chosen one of the other colleges: Christ's, Corpus Christi, Jesus, Magdalene, Peterhouse, St. Catharine's, St. John's, or Trinity. It had to be King's!" Who would have thought that a granduncle's views would have an effect on a contemporary college student's decision?

Birmingham, an industrial city, gave us another view of England. We were housed in new college buildings, unlike Cambridge, where our entire program was centered in Victorian structures. Our rooms had low ceilings and individual washbasins, an additional amenity. Here we had an ideal learning situation with an enthusiastic thirty-five-year-old instructor, who not only lectured, but took us on the tours, just as I had recommended in my critique on Cambridge. He was a battler for maintaining landmark buildings, and injected emotion as well as information in his talks. We purchased his books, so that we could learn more about old towns and the canal system of earlier England. We had never realized that one could navigate a good part of the country through its elaborate canal system, developed before the days of the railroad and the modern highways. Birmingham was largely a product of the nineteenth century with its unique dark-red-brick Victorian architecture, due in great part to the residence of eminent architects in that industrial town.

Lewis C. Braithwaite, our sterling teacher, gave us a lecture on timber-framed Stratford, which would still be a remarkable town even if a Shakespeare had never lived there or had never written and produced a single play. We visited the Wedgewood pottery factory and saw how they designed and fashioned this unique ceramic ware. We went to Litchfield, a city with a fabulous cathedral, and the birthplace and residence of Samuel Johnson. I had taken a course in The Age of Johnson at the University of Missouri, and some of his writings and those of his biographer, Boswell, were recalled as we strode through his home and the town. We went to Warwick with its excellent castle and Leamington with its Regency architecture. The usual view held that Birmingham was a city not worth more than a pass-through, but with Braithwaite as teacher and guide it took on another dimension. While there, Emma went off with some of her fellow students, who also came from Pelham, to see an English version of *Amadeus*, which she found as thrilling as the one we saw together on Broadway.

Our third week was spent in the seacoast town of Brighton, which the Prince Regent George IV, in the early part of the nineteenth century, had transformed into a magnificent city, rivaling London for a while as the "second capital." There we had several teachers, one of whom both lectured and took us on tours, and proved to be the more influential.

The new university buildings provided us with the comforts experienced in Birmingham. We saw Brighton inside and out, and the more we saw, the more we were taken with this municipality. It combined a certain elegance with shades of Coney Island and Atlantic City, both of which were partially patterned after Brighton. Even the monstrous overly ornate Pavilion could not remove the spell of its original grandeur.

Side trips were made to Battle, where we were reminded of the invasion of England by William the Conqueror, Lewes, then Rye, where we passed the residence of Henry James, Hastings, the chalk cliffs at Burling Gap, and Arundel Castle, where the Norfolk family had lived continuously for seven hundred years.

We learned a great deal about three sections of England, not only from the lectures, but from seeing them closely and intensely, and from our supplementary readings. We have recommended the Elderhostel program to others, who are more serious in their travels seeking knowledge as well as entertainment.

This was our sixth trip to England. We became more impressed with the country on each visit. The countryside was varied, beautiful, and magnificently maintained. The villages and towns were a delight with their historic origins, their unique architectural development, their fine shops and interesting places to eat—from the old-fashioned pub with its odd foods to restaurants of glamor and special-quality foods like the memorable luncheon we had at Litchfield. Sitting under the portrait of King Charles—"Poor Charles," as the waitress put it—in almost silence, for the other guests and we spoke in whispers. We were served an unusual luncheon topped off with fresh raspberries and a superb apple pie, which we always thought was an American monopoly. While there was a bit of rain—not unusual for England—it was the hottest summer on record, for once we had an abundance of sunshine. The people everywhere were friendly, but it still took a bit of motivating to turn their friendliness into an interesting conversation.

* * *

28

Operation Lion's Cub

Operation Lion's Cub

THE EMPTYING OF the refugee camps and villages in eastern Sudan of Ethiopian Jewish refugees in the last months of 1983 was a substantial achievement for which we were grateful to the Israelis. I had always believed that Israel could perform this life-saving task, and under constant pressure from the AAEJ it moved in to solve the problem. Now there were seven thousand Ethiopian Jews in Israel. Unhappily, the Israelis wiped their hands as though they had finished the task. There were still upwards of eighteen thousand Jews in Ethiopia, but except for the AAEJ, they seemed to have been forgotten.

The Jews in Ethiopia had learned something from this large exodus at the end of 1983: that there was little hope of ever reaching Israel if they chose to remain in their native land, now suffering from one of the worst droughts and famines in its calamitous history. In 1984, spontaneously, twelve thousand Ethiopian Jews left their villages, abandoning places where they and their ancestors had lived for centuries, and moved stealthily at night over the border to Sudan, the next stopping place on their road to freedom and Israel. They left behind their meager possessions. They carried children and the elderly on their backs. They walked for days, stretching into two weeks. Some became ill and died. They buried their dead in no-man's land in unmarked graves. Many were robbed by the Shiftas (bandits). Young women were raped. They straggled into Sudan starved and sick, expecting an immediate rescue. They left behind in Ethiopia pregnant mothers, small children, and older people, who could not make this strenuous journey to eventual liberation.

Rescue did not come easily or quickly until the unprecedented airlift on November 21, toward the end of the year. Although the airlift has been termed Operation Moses, the Israeli name for it was Gur Aryeh (Lion's Cub). Up to that date only seven hundred had been taken out for nearly eleven months. Food and water were scarce and often contaminated. They died of hunger and disease at the rate of fifteen to twenty a day. There was a lack of doctors, nurses, and medicine. They buried their dead at night in hastily dug graves, so that no one would know that they had been interred with Ethiopian Judaic rites.

When reports of their agony reached the United States from tales related by the few hundred who managed to reach Israel, and from statements of field workers in international rescue organizations, who could no longer contain the gruesome facts, they were not, for some incomprehensible reason, printed in the press. When I called the Jewish media to print these terrible facts that two hundred, then four hundred, then eight hundred, then twelve hundred, and finally two thousand Ethiopian Jews had died, as one prominent Jewish editor put it to me over the phone: "Your information is fictitious. I have more reliable sources which refute these figures." I hung up on him in anger. That two thousand died was not published in the Jewish press until Judith Miller wrote the story for the *New York Times* (January 20, 1985).

How to get the world, at least the Jewish world, to respond to this tragedy in early 1984 was a problem? The Canadian B'nai B'rith delegation to Ethiopia concluded that the Jews in Ethiopia "do not live worse" than other sectors of the population and attacked the AAEJ and the CAEJ for "biased and tainted" reporting. "The delegation encountered Israeli businessmen in Ethiopia's capital, Addis Ababa" (*Jewish Floridian,* April 6, 1984). I assume that this was to counteract the stirring editorial in the *New York Times* (March 2, 1984) under the heading "Exodus for a Twice-Lost Tribe," which stated in part: "Only a pathetic trickle of Falashas managed to reach Israel by 1982. Only when their plight came to the public's attention was the number of refugees allowed to grow, to about five thousand." The AAEJ was responsible for that editorial, as it was for the *Wall Street Journal's* long article "The Endangered Falashas" (March 13, 1984). I was interviewed for the latter article. We pushed the showing of Jacobovici's film *The Falashas.* We brought several Israel Ethiopian Jews to the United States for press conferences and lectures. We met with Israeli officials, who shrugged their shoulders and stated over and over again that they were doing all that was possible. We stepped up our campaign to obtain the help of the United States State Department, senators, and congressmen, all because we knew that more were dying than were being lifted out of Sudan.

I undertook a strenuous campaign of speaking and raising money, which took me to Milburn, New Jersey, Boston, Trenton, Washington, Great Neck, Upper Nyack–New City, New York, Binghampton, Staten Island, New Haven, Bel Aire and Encino, California, Scranton, and

Wantagh, New York, apart from many communities in New York City proper.

Before the magnificent airlift, such articles as appeared in the Jewish press about Ethiopian Jews did not mention their suffering and death. They usually reported the relatively successful absorption of those who had managed to arrive in Israel. They now numbered seven thousand and were no longer inconspicuous dots on the landscape. Yet all articles were not favorable. Some insinuated that the Ethiopians were bringing in strange diseases, that they would require a long and expensive absorption at a time when the Israeli economy was in dire straits, thus further emphasizing the negative aspects of this immigration. No national campaign was suggested to raise the additional money necessary for this absorption program. No Jewish newspaper proposed that large-scale funds should be raised. The United Jewish Appeal, which always benefits from any kind of Israeli crisis, still kept mum about the need for more and special contributions.

My own rage was rising daily as the months progressed. Meanwhile the leadership of the AAEJ was working quietly and intensively with U.S. officials to break the impasse. I felt that we should take out advertisements in the American Jewish, Israeli, and even the general press to reveal the death of two thousand Jews and that ten thousand others were waiting in Sudan in hunger and sickness for a massive exodus. It was not easy, even for our own board leadership, to go public, because they too felt it might interfere with behind-the-scenes plotting. I managed to win a close vote at a meeting of the board of directors in October 1984, and an advertisement was inserted in over thirty American Jewish newspapers. The papers would print a paid advertisement, but would not publish the grimly newsworthy story for nothing. The ad read:

> 2000 ETHIOPIAN JEWS DIED OF STARVATION AND DISEASE IN AFRICA AWAITING RESCUE BY WORLD JEWRY.
>
> ARE WE GOING TO PERMIT THE SAME GRUESOME FATE FOR THE REMAINING 10,000?
>
> CABLE OR WRITE PRIME MINISTER SHIMON PERES.
>
> CONTACT YOUR SENATORS AND CONGRESSMEN TO PRESS FOR MASSIVE RESCUE WITHOUT DELAY.

In addition, the AAEJ mailed out tens of thousands of letters urging our supporters to write to the State Department and to their senators and congressmen to save Ethiopian Jews. All this, *before November 1984*, began to have a cumulative impact. When these officials received sizable batches of mail, they raised the issue with appropriate representatives of Israel, in the State Department, in the highest offices of the land, the

President and the Vice President, to undertake a bold and large-scale operation. I presume they also advised Sudan not to interfere with such an exodus.

Yet I suspect that all this in itself might not have been enough. A third, a natural element arose that no one had planned for—the creeping drought and famine, which now embraced seven million Ethiopians. This became first-page news in late October 1984, and the world was daily exposed to graphic presentations of misery on the nightly TV stations. Even Israeli citizens became aware of the major calamity taking place in Ethiopia. Despite the economic pinch, Israelis began to raise money for humanitarian relief. I believe that many were motivated by the belief that fellow Jews were also affected by the consequences of lack of food, water, and medical aid.

Collectively our educational advertisements, the Jacobovici documentary film, the pressure of the U.S. government, the granting of millions of dollars for rescue and absorption, grimly highlighted by the gruesome photos of famine-ravaged Ethiopia, finally forced Israeli officialdom to open their minds and their doors for a massive, albeit secret, airlift beginning on November 21, and when it ceased on January 4, 1985, seven thousand Ethiopian Jews had been brought to Israel, in rags, sick, impoverished, but doubling their population in less than seven weeks.

Why it stopped before all the Ethiopian Jews vacated Sudan has been explored in the world and Jewish press. All the blame fell on the Israelis, the Jewish Agency, and on American Jewish leaders who could not wait until all were airlifted out of Sudan. They saw a "crisis" opportunity to raise millions through the UJA campaign, so Operation Moses was hastily conceived. While tens of thousands involved in this nationwide fund-raising effort, which speedily raised $60,000,000, were sworn to secrecy, the news could not help leaking. The Belgian airline, which had the contract for the airlift, refused to continue, due to Arab-Moslem pressures, for the airline also flew Moslem pilgrims to Mecca, and that was a larger and more permanent source of income. No other airlines were approached to finish the job. The Israeli Prime Minister stopped the mission.

Between January 4, when the operation ceased and March 21, another fifteen hundred Ethiopian Jews died of hunger and disease in Sudan. Then a singular, one-day, U.S. government airlift was carried out on March 21, which saved 920 more Ethiopian Jews from Sudan. Thus of the twelve thousand Ethiopian Jews who had left Ethiopia in 1984, thirty-five hundred died. Eighty-five hundred miraculously reached Israel. Sudan was now said to be clean of any more Jews. Actually about several hundred were still there.

Now our concern was how to save the remaining six thousand to ten thousand still in Ethiopia.

* * *

In March 1984, I received a call from Puerto Rico to come down for a weekend of lectures and fund-raising for Ethiopian Jews. I asked for a formal letter of invitation. When I received no confirmation, I phoned the organization and learned from its executive director (an Israeli shaliach) that it had been persuaded by world Jewish leaders who had been consulted in Israel and the United States, not to invite me, nor to raise any money for the AAEJ. The conspiracy that I always felt behind the world Jewish policy of doing as little as possible for Ethiopian Jews, was once again demonstrated even on this island in the Caribbean.

* * *

At the suggestion of one of the board members of the Baron de Hirsch Fund, I met with its representatives, submitting a request for a scholarship program for Ethiopian Jews in Israel, and in due course, the AAEJ received a substantial grant. This was renewed in 1985.

A notable event occurred, which as far as I have been able to determine, has not been commented on by anyone in the general and Jewish world. Salo W. Baron, the most distinguished of living Jewish historians, published the eighteenth volume of his *A Social and Religious History of the Jews*. He devoted 43 pages in text and notes to Ethiopian Jewry, the first contemporary, serious treatment of the subject by an outstanding historian, apart from the *Encycleopedia Judaica* (1973). Baron was more hospitable to many of the oral traditions of Ethiopian Jewish origins and development, even though they had not yet been verified by archaeological artifacts, such as those which have periodically turned up to confirm many aspects of other ancient civilizations, including the Judaic.

While he encouraged more scholarly research, Baron noted that "to shun the required strenuous effort and to hide behind a wall of allegedly impenetrable darkness can turn into sheer escapism" (p. 588). Had it not been for the same encouragement for the intensive study of early Jewish history, Jews elsewhere would not have had anything but myths to explain their origins—not unlike the Ethiopians Jews.

* * *

The Young Israel of Staten Island invited me to give several lectures on the Ethiopian Jews over a weekend. Dr. Robert Dublin, his wife Cathy, and their four sons, who had inspired the invitation, asked us to stay at their home over Shabbat. Dr. Dublin, disturbed by the neglect of Ethiopian Jewry, had been the spearhead for substantial fund-raising for the AAEJ. We arrived before sundown in this recently developed community of traditional Jews, who observed the Sabbath with all the restraints and religious obligations along with its joys. No one used a car on the weekend. There was no turning on of lights after sundown. Lights, once illuminated, burned throughout the Sabbath. There was no fresh cooking. Once cooked, hot foods were maintained on low burners in the oven until consumed. Nose tissues substituted for rolls of toilet paper.

We went to the synagogue before the Sabbath meal, davened, and returned for a festive dinner with prayers and chants. I returned to the synagogue about 9:30 P.M. for a lecture and discussion before an assembly of several hundred people.

On the Sabbath itself, apart from cogent remarks made by the rabbi in his introduction, I delivered a sermon before four hundred worshippers, relating the plight of the Ethiopian Jews to the portion of the Torah that had been chanted earlier.

At a luncheon in the Dublin home to which sixty people were invited, I spoke informally to many of the guests, answering their queries about Ethiopian Jews.

In the mid-afternoon, Emma and I visited some friends, where we talked about personal matters and Ethiopian Jews.

In the late afternoon between the Mincha and Havdalah services, I answered questions raised by those who wanted to know more about Ethiopian Jews. Some fifty people participated in this session.

On the whole, I found a most sympathetic response, unlike the indifference exhibited by most traditional congregations. It was further reflected by the considerable sums that were subsequently donated to the AAEJ.

It was a rewarding Shabbat. Even though we are not observant, we appreciated the sacrifice and devotion and the self-imposed restrictions on their lives, that each made in order to fulfill the commandments in the contemporary world. Yet, they all lived well and probably denied themselves little.

The Dublins represent a family that made the decision to live as traditional Jews, for they were not born that way. Dr. Dublin came from a conventional Jewish home that did not follow all of the traditional practices. Mrs. Dublin was of Filipino Catholic origin but converted to Judaism, and for twenty years had been a faithful, practicing Jew. She told Emma that her four sons would never marry out of the faith of Judaism, because they have "no opportunity to meet anyone but Jews." The family chose to live in a total Jewish neighborhood. Their children studied only in day schools on all levels of education. They spent part of each year in Jerusalem, where the Dublins owned an apartment. When they went to the Philippines to visit Chaty's family, they lived as Jews, attending the synagogue and bringing sufficient kosher food with them to fulfill their special diet. In 1985, their youngest son had one of several Bar Mitzvahs in the Philippines.

* * *

We stole away for a week in the Dominican Republic, once again to enjoy the warmth and the quietness of a holiday. This time my nephew Edward Finn and his wife Harriette were living in the country, where, as a volunteer, he was assisting a local business to introduce modern American business practices. Edward had retired from the presidency of one of the largest department stores in Portland, Oregon, and each year undertook such assignments in different parts of the world. It was a pleasant holiday. We visited museums and art galleries. We brought back some excellent native guava preserves and coffee.

Illnesses

Until my prostate operation and treatment in 1984, I had never been seriously ill in the seventy-six years of my life. As a child I suffered from some periodic stomach ailments, nausea, vomiting. I was finally taken to a specialist in New York. He told my sister Sadie, who accompanied me, that it had something to do with my liver. He prescribed a horrible-tasting mineral oil, which I took for a while. The illness did not recur. I don't know whether it was the oil, or my distaste for the medicinal lubricant, or that I just grew out of it.

When a baseball batter in the school gym swung so wide of the plate that he found the bridge of my nose as a target, I was only temporarily "knocked out," quickly recovered, and was sent home for a day. No one bothered to X-ray me or ask whether everything was O.K. Today, a clever negligence lawyer would have suggested that I sue the school system for at least half a million dollars.

My tonsils and adenoids were removed in a doctor's office, and after a half-hour wait, he sent me home alone, with the tempting suggestion that I eat lots of ice cream. This would never be done today. At least a ride home, if not in an ambulance, then by one's parents. Medicine, even this type of surgery in those days—1918—was more casual.

My eyes went bad when I was ten. I could not even read the blackboard in the classroom. When I was sent to an optician, he prescribed glasses. "Four-eyes" had to live with that mockery for a while. It didn't interfere with some of my athletic activities, as I wore a leather-and-metal eyeglass guard while playing basketball. Now I could see and read. It never bothered me in future years. I went from simple frames to rimless, then reverted to the brown plastic type. Despite changes in frames, I have always sought only conservative patterns. Then I added bifocals, both for daily use and for walking in the sun. As an avid reader, they were essential to my life, my comfort, and my knowledge. I was never tempted by contact lenses. I didn't want to be bothered, and besides, I thought I looked as well as I ever would with frames wrapped around my eyes and behind my ears.

I broke my leg on several occasions, a green stick fracture while playing baseball in camp with the children; and another time, while making an extra skip as I stepped over a high curbstone. I used crutches, went to work every day, used a cane for a time, but in a matter of a few months the bones healed and I was back to normal.

In 1965, just before a ten-week trip to Ethiopia, Israel and Europe, I ripped something in my back.

For a number of years, I suffered from periodic blackouts. The doctors on examination could find nothing wrong, but told me that I probably had Mëniêre's disease, otitis media, an illness associated with the middle ear. I had endured seasickness on several occasions, and this confirmed their imaginative diagnosis. I took Dramamine when I sailed on the sea, which partially reduced the dizziness, but abstaining from too much liquids, and particularly liquor, eliminated the vertiginous episodes almost entirely. After another attack, a thorough examination in a hospital over six days revealed that I had problems with an artery serving my brain. Salt was the nemesis. I had to eliminate it from my diet. It had nothing to do with my middle ear. I banished salt and have never had another serious attack. However, I travel with capsules. Gout struck me a number of times. It was an initial relief to learn that it was a disease associated with high intelligence. History records all the famous names that endured this ailment. Colbenimid was prescribed, based on colchicine, an ancient Egyptian remedy. It is a poisonous alkaloid extracted from the corms of the meadow saffron and used on mitotic cells to induce polyploidy in the treatment of gout. I carried the pills with me to relieve the exquisite pain that usually lodged in my left big toe, where the uric acid crystals rubbed against the interior flesh.

Once I came back from Europe with trouble in my interior tract. After many examinations, it was diagnosed at first that I had diverticulosis, which I considered nothing serious, but the discomfort did not disappear. Finally, after a few more doctors, it was pinpointed as "parasites," and once this was determined, it was easily cured. I was warned not to eat any kind of raw seafood, ham, or pork. The physician was a Christian. Now I could be an observant Jew by medical injunction.

I went through an emergency prostate reaming in 1970, after first trying to solve the problem with hot baths and electrode therapy.

The problem did not disappear. I became another of the confirming statistics that all or most males have to endure. I watched the operation performed by two doctors, for they only gave me a lower, partial anesthetic. I took three months off from the office, but did as much, if not more, work both in the hospital and at home as I would have accomplished during those summer months on 59th Street. People came to see me, and it was a delight talking with them at a leisurely pace, uninterrupted by the telephone, usually sitting under a crab apple tree that shaded my backyard's green lawn. I incidentally raised a lot of money for Federation projects.

My doctor discovered a hernia in 1975, and so I was hospitalized for the new Schuldice treatment of lapping over the flesh and covering the wound with a large band aid, instead of sewing it together. In a few weeks I was as good as new, but I cut down on the size and amount of luggage we used in travel, a caution given to me by my surgeon. We found—something that we knew before but never pursued—that we just didn't have to take so much clothing with us, no matter how long we were away. Wash-and-wear clothing that had come into fashion also helped reduce the volume and the burden.

My teeth have held up pretty well. A broken tooth, when I was in my middle twenties, had to be replaced. Some root canal work in my forties. The removal of three back teeth in my middle seventies was the only sizable repair that was ever done, apart from the usual fillings. Had we put fluoride in the water earlier as well as in our current toothpastes, even these cavities might never had developed. I have done without dentures and the other difficulties that face many human beings in a dental lifetime. I understand from my dentist that I brush the wrong way, that I should undertake a daily practice of using dental floss and toothpicks, but I perform these cautionary elements rarely. I used a special toothpaste to reduce the occasional sensitivity I felt in one of my teeth. When that tooth was removed, the sensitivity disappeared. I am back to the ordinary and less expensive varieties. Who knows, I may still make it with the mouthful of remaining second teeth which came forth in my early youth. Altogether, not yet a bad record.

Cancer!

The year 1984 did not prove to be all work or fun. In April I had a routine annual medical examination. My doctor since 1953, when we moved into Pelham, Morris A. Goldberg, whom we affectionately call Murray, thought my prostate was enlarged again and referred me to a urologist. I had a prostate operation in 1970 by the eurethyma method and had no trouble since with an ailment that plagues most men as they grow older. I made an appointment with Dr. John Coleman, an eminent urologist, who discovered a growth near the prostate. He sent me for X-rays, after which I went into the hospital for an exploratory biopsy, which required anesthesia. I learned that the tumor was malignant. I was not happy with the result, knowing that so many members of my family had died of cancer. Yet I was not devastated.

I subsequently returned to the hospital for another drilling of the prostate, but nothing was done about the tumor. A bone scan revealed that the disease had not spread into any other organs or my bones.

Dr. Coleman, after a postoperation examination, went over all the modalities for treating the malignant tumor. He strongly advised surgery and the insertion of radioactive seeds in the tumor, which would hopefully, but not absolutely, destroy the treacherous cells or at least keep them from spreading. It involved hospitalization for fifteen days, a long stretch in the operating room, and a recovery period that might take a month or longer.

Since my mother and siblings had all died of cancer, I had to do something. I was advised to make up my mind quickly. I spoke to Dr. Coleman about other options. He told me you can do nothing and take your chances statistically. I reminded him that I had read that twenty-five thousand males died of cancer of the prostate each year. He told me that I could also subject myself to weeks of radiation treatment or undergo some form of chemotherapy by pills or injection. Or, and he put this last, you could have your testicles removed to inhibit the growth of cancer cells. The prospects were not pleasant.

Dr. Goldberg and I went into a huddle. He and I began to make inquiries wherever advanced research was being done on this ailment. Contacts were made in Israel, Canada, Houston, New Orleans, Baltimore, Buffalo, and Boston, with varying recommendations.

In reading an article on the subject in the *New York Sunday News*, which our neighbors bring in on Tuesday after they have finished reading this newspaper (Emma likes the crossword puzzles and the bridge hands in its weekend edition,) I came across a reference to research being done by Dr. Jack Geller at the Mercy Hospital Center in San Diego, California, where by a combination of radiation, estrogen hormones, and a pill, Megace, they had extraordinary success in treating cancerous tumors of the prostate. I called Dr. Geller on the phone and talked to this friendly physician and endocrinologist, who described his treatment plan. We spoke at some length. Dr. Goldberg called him and was given the same counsel.

I returned to Dr. Coleman with this information. He still preferred surgery and seeding. I then asked Dr. Coleman who was the outstanding authority in the field, and told him I would fly to Australia if necessary. He said it wasn't necessary, because the best man was in New York, across the street at the Memorial Hospital, Dr. Willet F. Whitmore, one of the original advocates of seeding-surgery for this type of cancer. With some influence, I arranged an early meeting with the busy Dr. Whitmore. He confirmed the existence of the tumor, but absolutely forbade surgery. He thought Dr. Geller's plan would probably work. I reported this to Dr. Coleman, who was not exactly pleased, and told me that there might be some side effects—phlebitis, heart attacks, to mention the most serious—but the chances of success were something like 80 percent.

After a search for the ablest radiologist, I finally put myself under the care of Dr. N. A. Ghossein, an Egyptian-born radiologist, who was the clinical professor of radiotherapy at nearby Albert Einstein College of

Medicine in the Bronx. I preferred this treatment only fifteen minutes away rather than going downtown, which would take the better part of a day. I underwent 35 two-minute treatments five days a week. At 8:30 A.M. each morning I watched the cobalt machine cast its healing rays on four corners of the region of the tumor. Blood tests were taken each week to check any possible side effects. Except for a day or two of diarrhea, I weathered the treatments without any other discomforts. Along with the radiation exposure, I was taking three Megace and one estrogen (disethylstilbestrol 0.5 mg) daily. The latter pill would gradually destroy the emissions from my testicles, the evil source of the malignancy, and lead to medical castration. While the prospect was unpleasant from a masculine point of view, at my age of seventy-six, I took it in stride, even as it slightly enlarged my breasts and reduced the quantity of hair under my arms and chest.

The treatments, always complemented by my battery of physicians, after examinations by my internist, my urologist, and my radiologist, proved successful. The tumor disappeared. Subsequent tests, such as testosterone and acid phosphatases, confirmed the negative findings. So everything was working. I would have to take those pills the rest of my life. I would have to undergo the above tests regularly, have a bone scan every year or two, as well as submit to other blood tests with some regularity. I would also have to return to my three major (or at least two) physicians for physical checks at least twice a year. All were minor inconveniences on my calendar. All assured me that when I died, it would not be of cancer of the prostate. So here in detail I have written about the anatomy of my own illness and how with some extensive research and the daily help of my personal physician, Murray Goldberg, I found an easier and what might prove to be a better way than dramatic surgery, to solve my first serious medical problem.

In April 1985, I decided that I ought to see Dr. Geller, on whose prescribed pills, I was continuing my campaign to see that any cancer cells were either destroyed or else kept dormant. I flew out to San Diego and spent an hour and a half with him. Geller was an easterner, tall and white-haired. He looked completely different from my picture of him through phone conversations. He thought I had made extraordinary progress, advised me to take certain tests twice a year, and predicted that I was likely to go on forever. I had now touched base physically with all my medics, and felt greater confidence that I had looked into every nook and cranny to ensure reasonably good health in the future.

My treatment with diethylstilbestrol, a female estrogen hormone, for the containment of any cancer cells that might grow in the region of my former malignant tumor on the prostate, was changing me into a eunuch, a castrated male. The medication destroyed the function of the testicles, the evil source of trouble. While I was curious as to what effect it would have on me physically as well as on my psyche, I was prepared to do anything that would prevent the spread of carcinoma. I watched as it slowly increased the size of my breasts. Hairs were fewer and lighter under my armpits and on my chest. I appeared to be a bit rounder about my stomach and hips. Apart from these observable physical changes, there appeared to have been a total cessation of sexual arousal. Although this was a radical alteration of my vigorous life pattern, I accepted it with philosophical equanimity.

I had been active sexually since my adolescence and enjoyed the excitement and fulfillment of the sexual act. A decline in frequency began to occur in my early seventies, and I accepted this as another fact of life, and did not read or seek out those clinics, usually in Europe at some famous spa, or native elixirs, those advertised panaceas, that would assure an endless sexual life.

During my lifetime, I never resorted to or purchased sexual devices to stimulate myself or my loving partner in the sexual act. I never bought or even read a book that purported to tell me how to get some additional or new pleasure out of sexual contact, for my satisfactions were realized without external professional or pseudo-professional counsel. While I did acquire a few art books—Indian and Persian—as gifts, with their graphic, but artistic, not pornographic, exotic sexual practices, my viewing of these extraordinary paintings was more as a transient delight than to seek other sources for sexual stimulation. It was like the naughty viewing of the sexual motifs of the exquisite sculptured works that we found in the temples of Khujaraho or in the Indian religious-sexual portrayals on frescoes in the Ajanta caves.

I enjoy a sexual joke and do not mind telling them, when they are good, even before a mixed audience. But I never tell them to my children or grandchildren, who observe the same self-imposed decencies to me. While I have no hesitation in appreciating feminine beauty, I have never viewed women primarily from a sexual perspective.

I have enjoyed a long and reasonably fruitful sexual life. Now that was coming to an end. There were no regrets or disappointments. Advertisements and books may be written to prove that elderly people can enjoy an active sexual life to the end of their days, and certainly in their eighties and nineties; mine was over. I can say that I have only the most pleasurable memories. I may have been done in by a prostate. Maybe it was time. I have other things to do in my waking and bedtime hours. Long ago, I discovered that there was more to love than physical sex. Living with a loving, devoted, caring partner was now enough.

* * *

Our intimate friends, Dr. Charles (Bezalel) and Maryann (Miriamne) Ansell, were celebrating their fiftieth wedding anniversary and Charlie's seventy-fifth birthday. We had promised to attend the "bash" which they planned for the weekend of September 28–30. It looked as though we would not be able to make it because of my radiation treatments. But as luck would have it, the cobalt machine broke down and it would take a week to repair. The week coincided with the California party, and we were off, a bit weakened, but still bold. The dinner–wedding party that the Ansells tendered for 125 relatives and long-time friends was memorable. A marriage ceremony was reenacted under a chuppah. They both spoke words of love to eternity. After all, fifty years had already proven that married folks can live together in peace and comfort, despite families disintegrating all around them. I learned on my arrival at the dinner that I was to be the master of ceremonies and introduced twenty-five individuals with a few words of fact and wit, who in emotional warmth spoke of their long and rewarding relationship with the Ansells. I have never before experienced such a response at what we sometimes call testimonial events. That is the impact that the Ansells have had with their generous hospitality, their keen intellectuality, their entertaining humor, and their capacity for sustained relationships with all kinds of people of high and low degree.

While in California, I gave a fund-raising talk on behalf of the Ethiopian Jews. On Yom Kippur, we attended a synagogue service. The rabbi became indisposed, and while he could sit on the pulpit and perform certain rites, he did not feel up to delivering the morning sermon. He called me to the podium and asked me to perform this mitzvah. "Say something about the Falashas." It was no great feat for me to improvise even at the last moment. I spoke for twenty minutes, interweaving the seriousness of the holy day with the plight of the neglected Ethiopian Jews.

Friends in Palm Springs, Harold and Yvette Arian, invited us to visit with them for several days. Accompanied by Ruth Rafel, we took the bus to that famous resort in the desert and drenched ourselves in the unrelieved sunshine. Their magnificently located and decorated apartment overlooked the swimming pool and was shaded in the late afternoon by the mountains a short distance to the west.

So a fortuitous breakdown in a cobalt machine made it possible to cross the country, be with intimate friends, and observe our holiday rites, and at the same time serve the Ethiopian Jewish cause.

* * *

On November 28, in Chicago, I was one of the featured speakers at the first major fund-raising dinner ever tendered by the American Association for Ethiopian Jews. Despite efforts by Jewish organizations to boycott the event, eleven hundred people appeared, and we raised $450,000, a significant sum. The master of ceremonies was Philip L. Klutznick, a distinguished American and Jewish leader of national and international renown, and a public servant as ambassador to the United Nations and secretary of commerce. I had known Klutznick for forty years, but I could never get him closely identified with the Ethiopian Jewish issue. J. N. Pritzker, lawyer, real estate and corporate developer, billionaire, philanthropist, cigar-smoking octogenarian (he was eighty-nine), sat at my left, and we talked about the Hyatt Hotels and Braniff Airlines, some of the ventures in which his family both prospered and lost money. I had met him several years before, after which he became a major supporter of the AAEJ. Unhappily, he died in February 1986 in his ninetieth year. Senator Alan Cranston, one of our staunchest friends in Washington, pledged his devotion to our mission, a pledge that was fulfilled shortly afterwards, when the U.S. government, assisting in two rescue operations, flew eight thousand Ethiopian Jews to Israel. I paid tribute to our young and inspiring president, Nathan Shapiro, of Highland Park and Chicago, without whose influence and relentless pressure such a dinner outpouring could never have taken place in Chicago or elsewhere. I introduced two Ethiopian Jews, who spoke briefly. The AAEJ had recently brought them and their families out of Ethiopia to Israel. Both had been arrested in Ethiopia and jailed. One had been severely tortured in prison. They had suffered because they were Zionists and advocated aliyah to Israel. In my estimation they were heroes ignored by the rest of the Jewish world. Their sad fate in Ethiopia was equivalent to that suffered by Jews in Soviet Russian prisons. People resented it, when I compared them to Anatoly Shcharansky, who was finally released in February 1986 and given a tumultuous welcome when he arrived in Israel. No red-carpet treatment was accorded Uri Ben Gad and Rachamim Ben Yosef (both pseudonyms) when they reached the Promised Land.

* * *

In October, our granddaughter Bonnie, twenty-three, daughter of our youngest son, Michael, was married to George Ruby. What was memorable about this marriage, the first of our grandchildren, was that George had become a convert to Judaism before the union. The marriage was formalized in a synagogue, under a chupah, with Bonnie's rabbi performing the marriage rites.

* * *

One night we went to see and listen to Stephen Sondheim's *Sunday in the Park with George,* which won the coveted Pulitzer Prize in drama. An inventive work, based on a painting by Seurat, the music aptly fitted the pointillistic technique that the artist employed, yet only the first act deserved consideration for an award. Emma and I thought the second act was a boring disaster. Award committees have their own unique standards, that often make them arrive at peculiar decisions.

* * *

On a plane coming back from Washington, my neighbor across the aisle was Mike Wallace, the celebrated TV commentator of *60 Minutes*. He was then immersed in a major court trial for libel versus General William C. Westmoreland as to who had told the truth about the Vietnamese War. We had read Wallace's life's story in a book titled *Close Encounters*.

I had been planning to contact Wallace about televising the Ethiopian Jewish case on *60 Minutes*. When I first broached the subject across the aisle, he threw up his hands: "You want to get me in more trouble with Jewish organizations?" He had weathered a wordy storm after he had done a story of Syrian Jews. Undaunted, I continued to talk. He showed interest and gave me a handwritten address, where I should send him material, as he excitedly said, "Immediately!" I sought the opinion of the AAEJ leadership, some of whom were at that moment working on the airlift programs. The board was not eager for the kind of melodramatic coverage that Wallace was wont to present. I did not follow up on his invitation. The major airlift took place within a month after our chance meeting, and I dropped the matter. During this period, Wallace devoted one of his Sunday night programs to the famine in Ethiopia. No mention was made of the Ethiopian Jews.

We may still have to seek Wallace's help to get the remaining thousands of Jews out of Ethiopia. It may have to take the shock of a Mike Wallace TV program to finish this overly long delayed life-saving task.

In passing, I might add that the public relations organization we had hired would have paid an arm and a leg to achieve such a dramatic publicity coup.

* * *

After driving a car since the age of eleven, that is, since 1919, I was motivated to take a senior citizens driver's reeducation course, prompted by the promise that our ever-rising insurance costs would be lowered by 10 percent. Emma, who had only been driving since 1965, also attended. We learned nothing that we did not know before. We listened to a teacher who tried to be more amusing than informing. The course was completed after eight tedious hours of sitting impatiently, half listening, and filling in numerous forms. Our insurance was reduced.

On the Writing of More Books

While I had assembled files of material on the Ethiopian Jews, about my work, my writings, diaries of my year-round activities, and detailed notes on all of our travels, I had never thought seriously about writing an autobiography. The mere thought of the arduous work involved turned me off. I had thought of writing brief memoirs on various topics, even a modest book on the Ethiopian Jews.

In February 1979, I received a letter from Dr. Jane S. Gerber, a professor at the Cuny Graduate Center in New York City, specializing in Jewish studies. She asked me to contribute a chapter on the "Falashas" for a volume she was editing, *The Jewish Peoples: An Ethnographic History.* I had met Jane in 1974, when she was one of the students attending the Tel Aviv University seminar, where I was one of the lecturers.

I agreed to do it, although when the contract came, the only compensation was *one* copy of the book. When I protested, the contract was changed to four books. I began to write the manuscript immediately. It grew far beyond the forty pages originally requested. The years went by, and when finally pressed for it, I turned it over to her in September 1984. It was seventy-two pages. Jane thought it was too long, too strident. She said she would try her hand at editing it down and making it more diplomatic. I haven't heard from her.

As a result of the major rescues in 1984–85, the sizable population of Ethiopian Jews now in Israel, the issues that arose during their absorption, and the failure of Israel and world Jewry to save those thousands still in Ethiopia, my work is incomplete. I have no idea, when and if the book will be published. The content of what I wrote is different from what I have included in the autobiography. If not otherwise published, I may revise and expand it one of these days, and print it as a separate volume.

An Autobiography

But an autobiography, that was just too much.

Matthew Penn, of Chevy Chase, Maryland, a colleague and friend of some forty-five years, would not have it that way. He had previously talked me into editing and writing a long foreword to the two-volume *The Turbulent Years*, a review of Jewish communal services from 1959 to 1979, which took two years of my life. During an overnight visit with us, he again tried to convince me to write an autobiography. He wanted the emphasis put on my contributions to Jewish communal service rather than an overall review of my history and my interests in a multitude of other events. He thought I should tape-interview a number of people who were associated with me over the course of many decades, so that it might reveal a spirited two-way discourse on whatever role I might have played. I gave the matter some thought and hastily abandoned that approach, because it might be too talky and would not elicit the material I sought. I have found few people willing to talk frankly, hopefully honestly, of events and individuals. In testing this out, I found several horrified at the thought of relating what they really thought and believed when their voice was committed to a permanent tape. I have read enough oral histories to know that the authors rarely told the whole story, almost never related the behind/scenes role which they played or were a party to. Most were pathologically fearful of being critical of anything or anyone, and preferred to present a prettier, positive picture of what they did. If I had followed that procedure, it would have provided an autobiography without a blemish.

I came to the conclusion that this book, if I did it at all, would have to be a straight history, recording the struggles, if any, in my own life and work. While I would not necessarily emphasize only the pleasant features, I would only leave out those embarrassing, personal events, dramatic as they might be, and show more of my total life, hoping that it would not give offense to my family, especially my wife and children. I still was reluctant to undertake it, because there was little likelihood of getting such a work published. I didn't have enough relatives and friends that would purchase the book. Most would expect me to give them a free autographed copy. It would not be commercially worthwhile for any printing company.

Matt, always ingenious in overcoming my resistance, offered to raise the money, which I estimated at $15,000, since there would be no fees or royalties for the author, and I planned to do the typing, proofreading, and indexing. I was weakening. He quickly wrote to about thirty individuals, mostly volunteers with whom I had worked over the years, and raised the money in a matter of weeks. A few other people heard about the book and also became patrons; thus some additional sums were added to the treasury. Since contributors usually preferred to make their donations to bonafide tax-exempt philanthropic organizations, Matt and I approached Bronx House, where I had spent eleven years of my professional labors. Some of the board and staff still remembered me. The agency agreed to assume the modest burden of taking care of receipts and expenditures.

Mervin Rosenman, an attorney, whom I had recruited for the Bronx House board in the mid-1940s and later its president, suggested that I form my own publishing company. I filed papers at the county clerk's office in White Plains, New York. I invented the company name of the John, Washburn, Bleeker, Hampton Publishing Company, Pelham, New York, which intrigued the clerk. When she took my filing papers and check, she asked: "Are you English?" I replied: "No. These are just the names of the streets where I was born and lived during my early days in Gloversville and Sacandaga, New York."

With money in the bank and a legal publishing company, I was in business. What should be the title of the book? Several friends suggested pedestrian titles like "The Autobiography of a Jewish Communal Worker," which I dismissed out of hand. While still not sure what prompted most people to buy or read books, I am often attracted to a book by a provocative title. I flirted with the idea of using words like "Maverick" or "Curmudgeon," even in their Hebrew version. While some view my life and work in those terms, occasionally using the term *provocateur*, it would not be quite true to give such a jolting emblem to my definitive work.

In discussing Mayor Koch's recent work *Mayor* with Herman (Hy) and Janet Sainer (Janet is the commissioner for the aging in Koch's cabinet), Hy blurted out his suggestion, also a kind of critical comment on my egoism, "Why not *Graenum?* The idea grabbed me and that is what the book will be labeled. The name Graenum is unusual. It was rare for me to meet anyone who was not curious about its origin and how I acquired that name.

I gave some thought about how to collect material, examined old pictures in the attic, sought photos from relatives as well as other relevant information, scribbled notes, made outlines, began to put together some of my files. There were some interruptions, travel and a major illness that made me temporarily postpone any painstaking efforts to assemble material. I decided to write it, as I have written most everything else, chronologically, hoping that this method would stimulate further memories of past events and lead me to papers in my filing cabinets.

I started typing on September 1984, and unless I was sidetracked with other matters, I usually wrote from 6:30 A.M. to 10:30 A.M., covering ten pages of copy. It was a wonderful, quiet part of the day. The sun streamed in through the windows. The phone rang occasionally, and I was tempted not to answer. Everyone who called knew that I arose between 5:30 and 6 A.M. and was always home in the morning. While I typed, I found that the clicking interfered with my mental and memory processes, that I was inclined to overwrite with too much detail. After a few weeks, I decided to use the pen, which wrote slower and produced matter, which I hoped would be closer to the finished product. I confined my writing to the chronology of events, and did not roam too far from year to year, nor resort to flashbacks. My mind had always been retentive, yet I was surprised how much I remembered as the mental tape began to unspin. Events that I had not thought about for decades—and I started writing this book at the age of seventy-six—were as vivid as though I had experienced them a moment before. Things I did, ate, or clothes I wore were recollected and described with reasonable accuracy, some later confirmed by pictures which I assembled. Wherever I went, I took a pad and wrote sections for the book, so the pages began to fill, and at much greater length than I had anticipated. When I finished the initial writing in June 1985, it covered a thousand pages of hand-written material. Since my letters were small, it would be the equivalent of that many pages in a book. Obviously no one, except a handful of faithful family and friends, would read a book of that length about me, and the costs would be beyond the funds I had in hand. What to do? When I began typing the manuscript in August 1985, I decided to prepare a complete copy (with some discreet omissions) which I would Xerox and make available in about thirty copies to those with an appetite for detail, an editor, the Library of Congress, and members of my family, the latter to go over it for their own emendations.

If I elected to print one volume, the task of editing it down to a publishable size—not more than 350–400 pages, I would first try the cuts myself. I was sure, and others counseled me as well, that I should engage a competent, objective editor to make that drastic reduction and effect other improvements in spelling, language, style, and organization.

In any event, I wanted the book finished and printed by the end of 1986, when I would hopefully, with God's influence, good medicine, and self-discipline, have passed my seventy-eighth birthday.

* * *

Meanwhile Emma and I became involved in the presidential campaign of 1984. We did not like Reagan, nor the Republican Party, nor its platform. We bent our energies and donated a bit of our fortune to elect congressmen, senators, and, somewhat reluctantly, the Democratic nominees for the highest offices. Frankly, we were not enamored by the Democratic candidates. We preferred Lee Iacocca, head of Chrysler autos, who we felt would make the best candidate and suitable occupier of the White House. We had been impressed with how he turned Chrysler around from a bankrupt to a profit-making company within a short time. He knew how to deal with government, with labor, with finance, with public relations, and with the technical aspects of production and distribution. We thought the country needed more of a humanistic technician than a manipulating politician, one not too intimately associated with cronies and the hyped communication media. Iacocca was of Italian origin. We liked his humbler and foreign past. While he was no "expert" on foreign affairs and relations, neither were most incumbents of the presidential chair when they first came to office. I put forward his name on numerous occasions to our Democratic Party leadership, which was constantly soliciting funds for the campaign and at the same time asked our opinions about the candidates who had already elected to run for the presidency. While others also raised his name as a potential leader, he was never seriously considered, either because of his own personal affairs or because of the inability of the Democratic Party hacks to accept an outsider and an independent.

Consequently the Democratic candidate suffered an ignominious defeat. The victors, despite their overwhelming scores in the vote, have not yet led us down the parlous path, partly because a resistant Democratic Congress and a divided Republican Senate have forced the second-term Republican President to compromise or defer some of his wildest plans for both a super military build-up and a sharp reduction in services in education, welfare, and medicine for the lower-income sections of our population. Doubts were arising about the President's strategies even on international issues. We felt that we had been right in our analysis before the election.

29

1985

THE YEAR 1985 opened with so much promise.

During the first four days of January the airlift for Ethiopian Jews continued. The number of Ethiopian Jews in Israel had doubled to fourteen thousand within six weeks. Over half of the total Ethiopian Jewish population now lived in Israel. Then it stopped suddenly. Some blamed the Jewish Agency's leaders for talking too much, and the United Jewish Appeal for permitting a public campaign for funds for the absorption of the newcomers in Israel, which additionally revealed the existence of the rescue operation. Others blamed the Sudanese government, the Arab world, and Ethiopia. The fault lay entirely with the Israeli government. Prime Minister Peres made the decision. If Israel really wanted them, it could have made standby provisions with other airlines, when the Belgian-Jewish owner of the airline bowed out of the contract. It was whispered out loud that Israel had enough Ethiopian Jews. It had been totally unprepared to receive them on their arrival in November. Why, if the plans had been in the offing for months, was there so much initial negligence? How could it stop, when there were still upwards of thirty-five hundred more in Sudan? When there were some six thousand to ten thousand suffering in Ethiopia?

Of the twelve thousand who trekked to Sudan in 1984, two thousand had already died. Seven thousand had been saved. By the time the U.S. government stepped in again and airlifted nearly a thousand on March 21, another fifteen hundred died of disease and starvation in the intervening two and a half months. The task was over—a miraculous salvation for those who made it. The rest suffered a terrible end.

The AAEJ played an influential role in getting the United States to act—a story which has not yet been acknowledged. The only reference was in the *Jewish Week* (New York) of March 29, 1985, when it reported the role played by Senator Alan Cranston of California, whose "view of the plight of the Black Jews was sharpened by conversations with Nathan Shapiro and other officials of the American Association for Ethiopian Jews that began at a luncheon in Chicago last November (1984)," before the first airlift took place.

Tudor Parfitt

Emma and I learned about the U.S. airlift on March 22, the day we arrived in London, when we spoke to Professor Tudor Parfitt of the University of London. He told me on the phone of the arrival in Israel of eight hundred Ethiopian Jews from Sudan that very morning. When I asked him about the remaining fifteen hundred, he replied: "That was all there were left." I claimed that there were many more. I told him that they must have died of hunger and disease. Later that week, in another phone call, he said that my view was "probably correct."

Parfitt, a Welsh non-Jew, pro-Zionist and pro-Jewish, had been commissioned to write a book on Operation Moses. He had been to Sudan, to Israel, spoken to many of the important Israelis and others involved in the airlift. He had read a great deal of historical material—apparently almost entirely from Israeli sources. He now wanted to know more about the AAEJ's views on this sparkling enterprise. We spoke for four hours fact-to-face and about three hours in three separate calls over the phone.

When we first met, he looked me up and down physically, as though he could not believe that he was gazing on a mild-mannered, elderly man. I had been portrayed to him as a "monster," one who "hated Israel," one who had "interfered with the Israelis in their efforts to save Ethiopian Jews." The two portraits didn't match. He warmed up to me as we continued our long exchange, during which Emma and I gave him in most instances a totally different version of events dealing with Ethiopian Jews since the birth of the state. He wrote it all down, eventually filling some fifty pages, often shaking his handsome face, topping a man over six feet tall, in disbelief. When Emma asked him toward the end how much of what I had told him he would use, he replied, almost in a voice of despair, "If I have to choose between your version and that of the Israelis, at this moment, I would favor the Israelis." When she persisted: "Why not?" He said: "I'd be crucified." He used a gesture of a finger cutting across his throat. Emma then sadly commented: "That means history will be rewritten." He simply said: "Yes."

I received a letter from Parfitt dated June 18, 1985 in which he wrote: "I changed my text somewhat after meeting you here, but I felt forced to stick with my original thesis for the reasons that I mentioned to you while you were here. You do not come out of it badly, I think, although you may well not agree with that assessment." He promised to send me a copy of the book and a report for the Minority Rights Group, which he had written in cooperation with David Kessler, publisher of the *Jewish Chronicle*. I never received either. He had added in a postscript: "I am trying to set up a lecture tour in the states. Given my criticism of the AAEJ, you probably would not feel inclined to help with that. If you do, please let me know."

I wrote that neither the AAEJ nor I would sponsor him. After I read his book, with its omissions, errors, distortions, and outright misstatements about the AAEJ, I would use all my energies to condemn the book or his appearance in the United States.

He mentioned me a number of times in the text, including one complimentary remark. He referred to the Ethiopian Jews still left in Ethiopia: "Their situation . . . is critical and those whose responsibility it is to rescue them and get them to Israel should not tarry. Graenum Berger, now in retirement, will no doubt ensure that they do not."

Moment magazine printed a damning chapter from Parfitt's book, to which Nathan Shapiro replied. Several reviews of the book written by Jesse Zev Lurie, former editor of *Hadassah* magazine, and no friend of the Ethiopian Jews or the AAEJ, have appeared. I have sent their editors a reply condemning not only the book but Lurie's perfidious comments. "Why has Lurie chosen to continue his vindictive campaign against the AAEJ? Perhaps it is because he cannot bring himself to reveal his own failure as a journalist, who chose in the past to ignore or conceal the horrible facts behind the Ethiopian Jewish issue." The AAEJ prepared a detailed refutation to Parfitt's work, but no Jewish newspapers have published it.

* * *

Louis Rapoport, an editor for the *Jerusalem Post*, has referred to my role with the Ethiopian Jews in two books. In *The Lost Jews* (1980), he acknowledges me as a source of information and also says:

> The American Association for Ethiopian Jews—headed by Graenum Berger, a long-time activist for the Falashas, and Professor Howard Lenhoff—has been the most militant of the groups in campaigning for aid to the Falashas. It has also been a bone in the throat of ORT and the other large Jewish organizations that became involved in aid to the Falashas after 1976. The American Falasha Committee urged the Israeli Falashas to make their struggle public and to demonstrate in front of the prime minister's office and the Knesset, or parliament; so after years of being told that quiet diplomacy would solve their problems, the Falashas decided to follow a more activist line, and they made their protest public.

Louis and I have had our differences over the years, because he thought I was too critical of Israel. In his second book, *Redemption Song: The Story of Operation Moses* (1986), he made a number of references to me.

> Aid would also come from an American support committee that Faitlovitch had started in the 1920s to "rehabilitate our co-religionists" and that was rejuvenated in April 1974 by an elderly Zionist fund-raiser and firebrand, Graenum Berger, who called his group the American Association for Ethiopian Jews.

Later he wrote:

> The small, activist AAEJ was a mixed bag. . . . The establishment had to be goaded constantly; and for years, the AAEJ was all alone in its concern for the Beta Israel. AAEJ founder Graenum Berger and the group's successive leaders, Professor Howard Lenhoff of California and Nate Shapiro of Illinois, devoted their personal fortunes and years of their lives to rallying support for the Falashas.
>
> Only the AAEJ was warning in 1983 that thousands of Jews were facing death by disease and starvation in the refugee camps of Sudan. In early September 1984 Berger said, "We know hundreds are dying now. Israel could get them out." Even in their negative activities, the AAEJ seemed to serve as a catalyst, causing Israel to accelerate its efforts to save the Ethiopian Jews.

Critical or not, perhaps even grudgingly, Rapoport included in his book a State Department official's assertion that while "the AAEJ people suffered from overzealousness, the airlift would not have happened without them." Our zeal paid off.

The need for a definitive and accurate history of the Ethiopian Jew is evident. That story still has to be printed. A number of writers are preparing books, including one being written by Professor Howard M. Lenhoff, a former president of the AAEJ. Lenhoff, having access to all the material, will hopefully produce a book comparable to David Wyman's *The Abandonment of the Jews,* an account of what was *not* done by the United States, Britain, and the rest of the world, including the disunity amongst the Jews themselves, which impeded the rescue of European Jews during the Hitler-Nazi regime, resulting in the death of six million Jews. The Ethiopian Jews, if the remaining eight thousand can be taken out of Ethiopia, would have suffered the death of six thousand, nearly 21.4 percent of their census in 1976. Simcha Jacobovici is also writing a book to supplement his superb film *Falashas.*

* * *

I undertook a number of trips to talk about the Ethiopian Jews in 1985. Now it had become a number one topic on the Jewish agenda. My visits included Schenectady, Scarsdale, Pelham, Riverdale, Staten Island, Lakewood, and San Diego. Other demands were made for speaking on the radio and over TV. ABC-TV interviewed me for fifty minutes over the phone. USA-WEEK was another long phone interview. CBS-TV followed. BBC called from London, as did the French TV from Paris. WNEW-TV taped me for a half-hour, parts of which were presented for several nights over its tube. Everyone wanted stories. A half-dozen writers appeared at my home to ask me scores of questions. A long interview when I was in San Diego subsequently appeared in several editions of *Israel Today*. I was invited to speak before the Jewish Public Relations Professionals organization. Less than a dozen appeared at the luncheon. I have not been popular with the Jewish establishment representatives on this issue for many years. Most of them would rather distort or even omit what I said rather than present my remarks faithfully.

* * *

Ruth Gruber, an important American Jewish writer, a friend of nearly forty years, spent an afternoon (May 3, 1985) at our home in Pelham getting background for a book she has contracted to write about Ethiopian Jews. For years I have been trying to get her to visit Ethiopia, so that she might expose the tragic conditions under which they were forced to live. Ruth plans to tell their story now, through the lives of several families who came from Ethiopia to Israel. I suggested names of families that she might interview as well as material that she might read to gather background on the subject. She will not be critical of any of the Israeli officials and Jewish organizations with whom she had a close relationship. She told me that she had heard the best and the worst about me from many sources. Yet even those who disliked me still had a great deal of respect for my long interest in bringing the Ethiopian Jewish issue to the attention of world Jewry. She would not reveal the source of these hostile or favorable reactions.

I have known Ruth since the early 1950s, when she was first married to Philip Michael, a socially minded merchant who had become a member of the Bronx House board of directors.

An irony worth relating: A handful of people, who knew how long and hard I had labored on behalf of this frustrating cause, took the trouble to send me notes of congratulations now that my thirty years of advocacy was finally bearing fruit.

I was always amused, when I read in these notes or in the press, that the Zionist program of rescuing Jews in jeopardy was now being fulfilled again. If rescuing all Jews everywhere was really the Zionist program, I asked, why was the rescue of Ethiopian Jewry not undertaken decades ago, when the state was first established? Or why had not the Zionist organizations assisted in saving them in the hundred years since their presence was first widely publicized through the writings and speeches of Joseph Halevy and Jacques Faitlovitch? The truth is that the Israelis and the Zionists were literally forced to save them by pressure of the AAEJ and contemporary events, which had nothing to do with any humanitarian, Zionist, millennarian philosophy of the redemption of the Jewish people.

* * *

A prominent organizational executive invited me to lunch. He had always been sympathetic to the Ethiopian Jewish cause, but had never used his influence to pressure either the Israelis or the American Jewish establishment to expedite the movement of Ethiopian Jews to Israel. Now he felt that his Jewish colleagues should honor me and proposed a luncheon at which such tributes would be expressed. He mentioned a few names. I told him that I did not want to listen to their belated hypocritical remarks. I sent him a letter as follows:

> I appreciate your wish to give me some kind of recognition for the role that I played in the long history of trying to get the Ethiopian Jews to Israel. I am not seeking anything of the kind. I would not want to be honored by colleagues, and particularly some of the names that you mentioned yesterday, because they have not only been indifferent to this cause, but have actually placed every obstacle at their leadership disposal to see that as little as possible should be done for them. Over the course of years, I have been invited to speak in few Jewish Community Centers on this subject. . . . About ten Federations have asked me to speak on this issue, but all of them were in small communities. I knew efforts were made by the Council of Jewish Federation and the NJCRAC to discourage and cancel some of these invitations. Not even ten professionals have ever made contributions to the AAEJ, and they were all either personal friends of mine, who knew of my intimate involvement, or a few were moved by some story about them and wanted to help. I had to recruit totally new people, mostly laymen, only occasionally identified with the major Jewish organizations, and a small group of Rabbis, who to this day do not understand why the Jewish world and its leadership never took up such an imperative life-saving mission. So I could hardly sit in an audience that for the most part would be hypocritical and I would have to review their late conversion with unrelieved irony. So it is best that I receive informally the warm comments of friends like you, rather than any public tributes which would not sit well with my views of this historical record.

I will have to live with my own recollections of these heartrending events, the abuse that I had to take, and the unsparing retorts that I handed out in return on the pulpit and in the press.

What I resented more than anything was the unwarranted credit every organization was taking, heaping fulsome praise on themselves because of what they claimed to have done for the Ethiopian Jews, when the objective evidence in my files was to the contrary. Regretfully history will be rewritten, as it usually has been, to justify virtuous conduct that was never exhibited. I doubt whether the AAEJ and some of us personally will get the proper recognition for our sustained efforts. As I write this, over six thousand Jews in Ethiopia are still suffering inordinately, and no one, except the AAEJ, seems to be concerned with their rescue.*

Recently some Israeli visitors in Pelham, who have been deeply involved with the rescue and absorption of Ethiopian Jews in Israel, confessed to some disillusionment that Israel was never properly prepared for serious large-scale rescue operations, that it had responded only to pressures, and that it was never prepared to receive the Ethiopians in Israel, having to improvise at the last moment, when they appeared on the doorstep. I wish that I had their permission to reveal their names, for it would establish the complete credibility of everything that I have been saying and writing over the years.

The Testimonial Dinner

Edith Everett called me one night to say that the AAEJ wanted to honor Emma and me for our long and sustained efforts on behalf of Ethiopian Jewry. She suggested a dinner on November 2, 1985, the evening before the annual meeting of the AAEJ. Although I had run many dinners of this character over the years, and knew how pleasant it could be to hear one's own acts and virtues extolled, I at first said no, but later recanted, if the event could be used as a means of raising money for Ethiopian Jews. It was agreed that a fund would be set up, and at Emma's suggestion, it would be devoted to providing scholarships for some of the fifteen hundred Ethiopian Jewish children now in Israel, who had been orphaned as a result of the death of their parents en route to Israel via Sudan.

It was not a high-pressure dinner. Vast numbers of invitations were not sent out, and unlike most such affairs, the guest list did not include the usual cadre of prominent American Jewish leaders. Their presence

*On January 2, 1987, *The Jewish Week* of New York had a long account about me as one of the "unsung heroes of 1986." I was a driving force in a group battling on behalf of Ethiopian Jewry, therefore singled out by the newspaper for its "annual homage to people whose good works are done without thought of honor and glory."

would have been inappropriate, since most of them had never done anything to help Ethiopian Jewry and indeed had actually obstructed the rescue operations.

One hundred and sixty people attended the banquet. The food and decorations were deluxe; and with Edith as chairman, the proceedings were conducted with warmth, dignity, and dispatch. When our son Ramon spoke, he looked around the room and stated: "I'm surprised that my parents still have so many friends, after all they have gone through trying to save Ethiopian Jews."

Ramon, with the support of Anita, has been an interested and a generous supporter of the Ethiopian Jewish issue for many years. He has promoted this cause through speakers and fund-raising activities in Buffalo and in Providence. At the dinner both made a major contribution to the Scholarship Fund.

Apart from Edith and Ramon, other speakers included Congressman Stephen Solarz, who gave a moving tribute, and presented us with a long letter signed by a number of senators and congressmen involved in this important cause. They included Senators Rudy Boschwitz, Alan Cranston, Carl Levin, Howard M. Metzenbaum, and Arlen Specter, and Congressmen Solarz, Gary Ackerman, Barney Frank, Ted Weiss, Benjamin Gilman, Tom Lantos, Sam Gedjeson, and Mel Levine. Amongst the things they wrote were:

> The long and difficult history of the Ethiopian Jewish people would not have been brought into the consciousness of world Jewry so vividly had it not been for your commitment and determination . . . for over three decades. . . . The most significant honor that we can pay today to you both is to pledge that we, too, will not cease our efforts until every man, woman and child left behind in Ethiopia has been reunited with their family in the freedom of Israel. . . . There can be no greater reward for the two of you than to know that your commitment to saving lives has produced such marvelous results.

Other speakers were: Nathan Shapiro, Daniel Rose, Jane Norman, Dr. Charles Ansell, Mildred Rosenberg, Rabbi Isaac N. Trainin, Rabbi Irving J. Block, our other son, Michael, who presented his mother with his gold colonel's eagles, having recently been promoted to that high rank in the National Guard, and our granddaughter Elizabeth. Esther Wube Hollander, a young Ethiopian woman whom we first met in Israel in 1974, and who had since become a close friend, not only spoke but presented us with a candelabra made by Ethiopian Jews in Israel. Eli Rockwitz topped off the evening with an original song that he had written with his wife, Fern, accompanied on his guitar. Following all the speeches, I replied on behalf of Emma and myself.

In a long report on the dinner in the *Jewish Post and Opinion* (Dec. 18, 1985,) Jean Herschaft wrote:

> Graenum, for his part, termed the affair in honor of the organization AAEJ. But, unlike other acceptance speeches, Graenum told the whole aching story, brushing aside polite distruth in favor of a searing truth, which the Jewish establishment has found difficult to give an honest ear to. And, perhaps it accounts for their almost united effort in ignoring the herculean efforts of Graenum and his AAEJ crew that led to success in spite of their indifference to the cause, early in the game and later.

She quoted me:

> World Jewish leaders would like to have us believe today, that the fault in not saving them lay only on Ethiopia and later Sudan. That portrayal is based on an invented, fanciful myth. Israel and world Jewry could have gotten them out of the Horn of Africa long ago. They didn't, by their own deliberate decisions. So thousands of Jews had to die of discrimination, persecution, hunger and disease. For the 16,000 that finally reached Israel, the AAEJ, made the difference, and no books or phony scholars can prove differently, no matter how they try to rewrite and falsify history.

Herschaft went on:

> Graenum wove in a parallel to the recent revelations that Jews did not do enough to save the Jews that were threatened and killed during the Holocaust, noting that it has taken four decades to unmask, with many Jews still trying, but in vain, to hide these facts. He concluded: "We pray that someone will have the courage to write an accurate, honest account of what Jews did not do until forced, to rescue Ethiopian Jewry. . . . Being maligned is not so bad, if you can take it. Emma and I have not only been calumniated, but libeled, threatened, and she [Emma] was even assaulted. As soon as we became critical of Israel, we were labeled anti-Israel, that we 'wanted to destroy Israel,' as important Israelis put it nastily."

The writer ended with the validictory: "*Graenum Berger* is our choice for Man of the Year, indeed Man of the Decade."

The entire program was taped for video, and we received as a gift a VHS video cassette recorder to play back and recall this memorable evening.

The Racism Issue

In 1975, the United Nations General Assembly, with its substantial majority of Arab-Moslem and pro-Arab countries, passed a resolution condemning Israel and labeling it as a state which was "racist." Since then it has repeatedly suffered from this charge. I tried to point out in many ways to both Israeli and American Jewish leaders that Israel could counteract this accusation with one stroke, by admitting black Ethiopian Jews in large numbers, even if it was not then prepared to rescue the entire community of less than thirty thousand Jews. This appeal went unheeded. Israel and its supporters in the Jewish world denied the racism charge. They argued that Black Jews had been admitted from countries like Yemen and India. My suggestion might have influenced the Begin administration in 1977, when for the first time, Israel rescued 121 Ethiopian Jews directly from that country. There appeared to be no exploitation of the presence of some black Ethiopian Jews in Israel nor any public declaration for their rescue in substantial numbers.

In 1985, approaching the tenth anniversary of this blot on its escutcheon, Israel and its Jewish supporters in this country made another effort to get the United Nations to abrogate the resolution which remained on its books and was regularly reiterated by Israel's enemies in the vitriolic debates that took place on the floor of the General Assembly. One day in November 1985, I received a call from one of the Israeli representatives at the United Nations, a man whom I had met in 1975–77 in Israel, when I was promoting Ethiopian Jewish immigration, but getting nowhere. He asked me whether I could contact Rachamim Elezar, an Ethiopian Jewish young man who had attained some status in Israel, a college graduate, a frequent speaker abroad (at the moment he was in Brazil), a leader amongst his own people, explaining that he wanted Elezar to attend a meeting planned by Israel at the United Nations, in an effort to quash the unhappy resolution. I told him that Elezar might come to the United States, but even if he did not come, I had in my home Esther Wube Hollander, an Ethiopian Jewish woman who had established herself as a worthy representative of Israel at the recent International Women's conference in Nairobi, Kenya. The AAEJ had brought her to the United States for a lecture tour. Elezar arrived in New York a week later. Esther and he were both invited to attend the meeting held by the Israeli delegation, where they were shown off as "black" Jews, citizens of Israel. I was not invited to the meeting. I was told there was no room.

Martinique

In February 1985 we stole away for a week to the French Caribbean island of Martinique to catch a bit of sun in the midst of a cold winter.

Martinique, a volcanic island, where a devastating eruption some years ago had burned and killed tens of thousands of natives, was a green-covered tropical rainforest that nourished every kind of flower and tree. We made a tour of its interior. Most of the time we sat on our balcony, overlooking the park below, the bay, and the mountains in the distance, with the sun pouring down on us from sunrise to sunset. We read books. We used our minimal French to make purchases in the shops and order our meals. We listened to the mixture of native music and old-fashioned American tunes from the 1920s and 1930s played by steel-drum bands each evening during and after dinner.

Emma, who had been trying for years to get me to dance, whenever music was played in a restaurant with a dance floor, remarked about an elderly, white-haired Frenchman, eighty-two years of age, who was dancing every night with young women, every dance, whether the music was an old-fashioned waltz or fox trot, jazz, or with a Caribbean beat. The man told Emma, in broken English, that dancing was healthy and kept him young. I promised her that once we were home again, we would begin a daily routine of turning on the radio in the kitchen after dinner and dancing for an hour. She laughed. We never adopted this regimen.

* * *

Just before the High Holidays in the fall of 1985, the Ethiopian Jews, under the leadership of some activists, both old and new residents of Israel, undertook sit-in demonstrations across the street from the seat of the Chief Rabbis in Jerusalem to protest the insistence by the religious hierarchy that the Ethiopian Jews undergo *mikvah* before becoming full-fledged citizens and before marriage. The protest went on for weeks, receiving international news coverage on all media, but the picketers, even with the intervention of the Prime Minister, received little reward for their efforts, although some concessions were made, since the rabbinate had complete control over who was a Jew and who could get married officially.

Again there were writers, Israelis and others, who charged the strikers with ingratitude, with being Marxists who were trying to transplant the Ethiopian socialist revolution in Israel, of having ignored the leadership of their own *kessim* (priests) and of other Ethiopian Jews who fearfully followed the establishment line. They were also accused of being dupes of groups that were "anti-Israel," of Reform Jews, of extreme left-wing Israeli organizations. There was a view that they had alienated all the goodwill that had been offered to them since their massive arrival in Israel only a year before.

Their battle for equal Jewish status must go on, and it will not be resolved until the Israeli religious leadership does what it is morally obligated to do—affirming that this ancient Jewish group, which suffered for millennia to remain Jewish, must be accepted as it is and not by questionable interpretations of the Halakhah. I side with the pickets.

* * *

One day we took in the latest Kandinsky exhibit at the Guggenheim Museum. While we could not help admiring the creativity of this artist of the first half of the twentieth century, we became aware, perhaps for the first time, since we had never seen so many Kandinskys together, that he repeated himself over and over again, even as he partially changed his colors and the size of his canvasses in later years. It is best, I believe, to see a few of the great paintings of an artist, rather than to be overwhelmed with the completeness of his works, poor, good, and great.

A Brand-New House

Michael, our youngest son, and his wife Sandy, decided to build a larger house, three hundred yards from their former home on the outskirts of Vienna, Virginia. When it was finished, we drove down to attend the housewarming on March 2, 1985. It is a grand and beautiful home, a third larger than the old one. It is better able to accommodate their collection of art, a great deal of which we had given to them, as well as scores of pieces of antique cut-glass and other bric-a-brac, which Sandy's mother, Bertha Miller, eighty-five years of age and an ardent collector for decades, had given to them. Bertha was living with them, having recently given up her home in Syracuse. It was a great house party; the liquor flowed, and the varied foods prepared by Sandy were eaten in abandon. They had a large number of friends from Michael's office and from Sandy's volunteer corps, as well as neighbors.

Unhappily, Bertha suddenly become seriously ill. After a long hospitalization, she died on January 31, 1986. Her long life had been marked by a career as a lawyer, as an owner of a nursery school and children's day camp, and as a collector of American antiques. She was one of the first women to graduate from the Syracuse Law School and was honored as a Woman of Achievement in 1975 by the *Syracuse Post-Standard*. She did not live to see Halley's comet again, which she had first observed in 1910, when she was ten years old.

* * *

Our joy after the housewarming was short-lived. On our way home, a car skidded into the right side of our Toyota Cressida, hitting us twice and shoving us off the road. I managed to keep the car under control and brought it to a halt. Eleven cars behind us were involved in a pile-up. Yet, the greatest damage to any car was ours. Luckily we were both strapped in. Emma, who was sitting on the right, felt the impact most, was terribly shaken up: "Like my insides were falling apart." A hospital visit in an ambulance and subsequent medical check-ups revealed no external or internal injuries. It took her several weeks to get back to normalcy after suffering pains in her head, back, and sides. The car had $3,500 in damages, most covered by insurance. Thanks to a talented auto body mechanic, it looked after repairs as though it had never been touched.

When we purchased our Cressida in 1981, I was intrigued by the name given to this top-of-the-line Toyota. It had an ancient and royal history. Cressida was a Trojan woman, according to ancient legend, who pledged herself to Troilus, a son of Priam. While a captive of the Greeks, she gave herself to Diomedes, a Greek hero of the Trojan War. Priam, King of Troy, was also the father of Hector and Paris. This ancient story was the background for one of the most modern vehicles.

London Interlude

An inexpensive trip to London was available through Emma's membership in the Stamford theater group. It included three theatrical performances and three side trips, all in eight days. We decided to take it, even though we knew that the weather in England in late March would be wet and cold. Despite the severity of the climate, it turned out to be a delightful week.

We went to four plays: Shakespeare's *A Comedy of Errors*, brilliantly staged, accompanied by a heavily weighted brass orchestra, that made you jump. It was costumed in colorful garb and humorously acted. The story of the two sets of twins who constantly get mixed up delighted a full house. Shakespeare himself would have laughed uproariously at the antics he had invented.

The prize-winning *Benefactors* was a bit wearing on the audience, waiting for the few laughs that emerged from the endlessly talky script. The two families, strangely dependent on each other, suffered through an evening that somehow worked out better than it deserved. We have been in England three times during the past four years, and attended prize-winning plays on each trip. The others were *The Real Thing* and *Another Country*, all well acted, but hardly deserving of the coveted awards they received. Who is to judge the judges?

A spectacular presentation was *Starlight Express* in a theater that had given up a thousand seats, so that a good part of its three levels could be converted into a roller-skating track. This musical, with tones drawn from rock, ballads, and Negro spirituals, introduced a large group of actors and singers, who performed throughout on roller skates. When the black skaters triumphed over their white rivals in the final act, the play ended on a note of spiritual triumph. An interesting venture, a sellout, but we still hesitate to recommend it except for young people or those who like to see something different. It is a novelty with elaborate costumed actors riding on tiny wheels.

We also saw one of the earliest Neil Simon musicals, *Little Me*, which turned out to be a surprisingly well done farce that had most of the audience in stitches. We witnessed the story of the two main characters unfolding from rags to riches, and vice versa, in every type of setting, costume, and skit. A pleasant evening in the theater, that one could comfortably forget about the moment one left and still not feel cheated.

Chagall

We managed to get into the jammed Chagall exhibit during a driving rainstorm that had not deterred the hundreds who joined us. A day later Chagall died, so that in retrospect our tour became a sentimental journey. We had never seen most of the works well displayed in the Royal Academy of Art. That he was a great colorist no one could ever deny. That he captured the inner spirit of the Jews of Vitebsk, his art still affirmed. Yet like any major retrospective, we saw the repetitiveness of theme in this great collection, by a master, now past ninety years. He had moved from the fixed smaller canvas to the large paintings needed in the ballet, the opera, and for the spacious walls of major institutions, then onto the majestic stained-glass windows in religious and quasi-religious institutions. As usual I came away with a feeling that he had come upon a successful subject and type of art form, and had not hesitated to repeat it over and over again with modifications. Audiences and buyers apparently liked them. We have seen much of his work in singular settings, as in the Ferdinand Leger Church on top of the mountain in Passy, France, and his stained-glass windows in Metz, France, where in both settings the work fits.

I recall seeing one of his shows at the Museum of Modern Art in 1946. When I arrived in the middle morning, Chagall was alone. We spoke in my limited Yiddish, he responding in soft but expressive tones. At that time, he was living in the United States. Our conversation was interrupted when Ilya G. Ehrenburg, the well-known Russian journalist appeared. They greeted each other with enthusiasm and immediately lapsed into Russian, of which I understand nary a word. Ehrenburg was interviewing him for an article in the Soviet Russian press.

When I was a very young child, my father often drew pencil pictures for me as we sat around the kitchen table after supper. I vividly remember the Roosters with their beaks, combs and feathers, and the sleek cows, large and fat, with their udders almost touching the ground. They had a naive quality, akin to subjects painted by Chagall, which I saw and admired in later years. Ramon and Michael told me that my father rendered the same drawings for them in the early years of their lives, 1930–31 and 1939–41, respectively, as he had entertained me in 1909–1912 and for my younger brothers thereafter.

* * *

One of our tours took us to Stonehenge and to Bath. Stonehenge, that stark outline of massive stones assembled thousands of years ago eerily guarded an almost barren landscape. No one knows what it was built for—perhaps as a religious shrine, or for political assemblies, or as a sacrificial altar. These stones sat lonely and majestically on a treeless English countryside.

Bath, that old Roman city, resurrected and transformed into a spectacular residential city by an eighteenth-century British architect, intrigued us. We vowed to return there to study sometime in the future.

Another tour took us through gray, staid Gothic Oxford and then to Stratford with its Elizabethan wood-frame, stucco houses. I had seen both cities on previous trips, although Emma had missed the Oxford visit back in 1949. We ate in English pubs, tasted the varied dishes that the pubs in different regions cooked up. While in some instances the food was unusual, flavorful, nourishing, and inexpensive, I would not give any Michelin ratings to any of them except the superior pub in Brighton, where we lunched several years ago. Visiting England in the cold and rain and biting wind only whets your appetite for a return when the weather is salubrious.

No matter how many times we have been to England, we always found new neighborhoods to explore which evoked our admiration for the planning, the taste, the architectural decorations, and the solidity of their structures. London is a vast city. Yet apart from the postwar repairs to the extensive damage caused by German bombing raids, and the visible evidence of many new buildings, most of the scaffolding we witnessed was for the repair of older structures, all worth preserving. What a place to shop in! What a magnificent city!

Thyroid

A holiday is not always a lasting pleasure. Several days after our return, Emma developed a fever, cough, and overall malaise. The ordinary aspirins, Tylenols, and antibiotics prescribed did not mitigate the illness nor the fever, albeit low grade, which persisted for weeks with its debilitating effects. Her attitude grew more pessimistic. She resigned herself to the belief that no remedy would be found to restore her to good health. Her physician, a personal friend, then took her to a throat specialist, who could not find anything to treat. He suggested blood tests and a chest X-ray. The blood tests revealed a possible sedrate problem, a revelation appearing for the first time and contrary to all tests taken previously. The reading of the X-rays disclosed a few spots on the lungs. Both reports disturbed Emma and worsened her growing fatalistic attitude that this was a portent of the end. We immediately arranged for her examination by a chest specialist, who carefully examined not only these new X-rays, but others that had been assembled in 1983, plates made at Memorial Hospital before she underwent some breast biopsies. While the doctor could see nothing ominous, for Emma this was further confirmation that something was seriously wrong. He had felt something in the thyroid region. The doctor ordered both a CAT scan and a thyroid scan, which Emma underwent a few days later at the New Rochelle Hospital. The chest specialist's readings of these scans ruled out any problem in the chest and lungs, but aroused his suspicions that something might be wrong with the thyroid.

Our next step was to have an intensive examination by an endocrinologist, who took a biopsy and diagnosed it as a Hurtle Cell, probably malignant, tumor, as large as a golf ball, which had to be surgically removed at the earliest moment. While the thyroid was one of the locations with which medicine has had overwhelming success in removing cancerous elements, with few if any fatalities, this gave Emma further cause for gloom, since she saw no end to the maladies which had now consumed her energies for over a month. While low fevers had intermittently reappeared on the thermometer, the cough persisted. She had never felt the presence of the tumor, despite its size, and the prospect of anything going wrong while the Hurtle Cell tumor was being removed during surgery, further deepened her despair.

The operation was successful. The whole cell was removed encapsulated. The surgeon was confident that everything would be all right in the future. There was a delay of several days in getting the final laboratory report. The report proved negative. He told Emma she could leave the comfort of the hospital, and she decided, on the instant, to return home. There were no more fevers. The cough disappeared. There was some residual headaches and sleeplessness, which had been part of her life for decades, easily treated with medication. The scar around her neck was healing perfectly, the surgeon having chosen creased areas around the front of her neck to make the cuttings. It was concealed by a necklace and scarf. In time it completely disappeared, testimony to the skill of the surgeon. One thing he assured her, was that she would never die of this ailment in that location. Her only reminder of its presence now is that she must take thyroid pills every day for the rest of her life. Our thanks to the chemists who invented Levothyroid.

Bonnie Widowed

Good fortune doesn't always last too long. The year 1985 proved to be inauspicious. On May 27, we received a frightening call from our son Michael, that his twenty-four-year-old son-in-law, George Ruby, had accidentally died of asphyxiation. He had been alone at home over the Decoration Day weekend, as he didn't want to go to the beach with his wife Bonnie, our granddaughter, who went instead with a girl friend. He was fooling around with nitrous oxide, the inahling of which led to his death. Alerted by the sound of the TV, which had been playing uninterruptedly for twenty-four hours, his landlord kicked in the door to discover his body, after phone calls and knocking brought no response.

Bonnie and George had been married seven months. They had known each other since high school days. While he had not yet found the kind of employment that might bring some measure of prosperity, between the two of them, they eked out a living. George had been in the Navy. He had gone through conversion to Judaism before Bonnie would marry him. He was buried as a Jew and a military man, with their rabbi performing the funeral ceremony, at the Quantico National Cemetery in Virginia. The American flag was draped over his simple pine coffin decorated with a Star of David. A rifle salute was fired. The bugle sounded taps for a life that had never really begun.

Bonnie is a Berger and a survivor. Although grief-stricken as a young and loving bride, after Shiva, she once again became involved in her work on the *Jewish Week* in Washington and is managing well.

Phlebitis

But one never knows when something will appear in the body, particularly when one is seventy-seven years old. I had been feeling well since my last ailment, taking care of Emma during her persistent illness, which we finally conquered. Our Drs. Goldberg came over to visit with Emma. I was about to leave for a dinner meeting in New York. Emma asked them to look at my left calf, which had given me a little discomfort but not enough for me to call a physician. They immediately diagnosed phlebitis, inflammation of the veins, and told me to get off my feet, bathe my leg with wet packs, and see a specialist at once. I not only abandoned my trip to the city, but cancelled my trip to Washington the next day to attend the annual lecture at Georgetown University in memory of my brother Sam.

I saw a specialist the next day. He described the condition as a superficial Thrombophlebitis and said I should go about my business as usual. However, just to make sure that his diagnosis was correct, after strapping me up lightly with an Ace bandage, he told me to get a venogram and made an appointment for me with a doctor in New York the following day.

At the office in New York, the nurse buckled heavy equipment around both of my legs from the ankles to my crotch, a larger version of what one undergoes when a check is made of one's blood pressure. They blew air into these weighty straps and something registered on an electrical chart too far away for me to read, even if I could translate the up-and-down lines similar to a cardiogram. The doctor later told me I was O.K. It was superficial. What was I to do about it? He said: Listen to both of your doctors. Put wet packs on your leg when at home. Otherwise go about your work as though nothing was wrong. My personal doctor, Murray, didn't agree. "Graenum, you are not forty-seven, but seventy-seven. Follow my advice." I did. I even drove down to the store, half a mile away, to get my daily *New York Times*, a distance I had always walked for air and exercise. The question arose: How would I get myself ready for Perugia in June if I practically immobilized my legs? On June 1, I started to walk again. I was a bit tired, but I knew that in the intervening three weeks, I would somehow make it.

Perugia

In the fall of 1983, shortly after we received the catalogue from the Elderhostel, we registered for a two-week course of study at Perugia, Italy. Our study trip to England the past summer had whetted our appetite to study in Italy, a plan that we had made as far back as 1965, when we briefly passed through the city on our way to Rome. This study tour was very popular, so we never got beyond the waiting list at numbers 3 and 4, so near and yet so far. In the fall of 1984, we again signed for Perugia, and luckily, along with Charles and Maryann Ansell, we were accepted. We planned what we would do together, once we reached Perugia and after it was over. We agreed that following the study sessions, we would rent a car and travel to Belgium, after which they would embark on a ferry for a stay in London, while we would remain in Belgium for another week, spending the time with Renee Odou Smith, an old friend, who was living in her native city of Brussels.

With Emma just getting over an operation, and with my quirky phlebitis, we were never sure until the last moment that our doctors would permit us to make this journey. When they did, although Emma had many reservations, we flew off on June 21 for Rome. There we were joined by others, spent some hours in Rome visiting the Vatican, had lunch, and then were off to Perugia, nestling in the hills about halfway between Rome and Florence.

The program was directed by Paul Leopold, a remarkable younger man who also taught one course. A caring director, he overlooked no detail, all of which added to our pleasure and comfort, and he was also a superb teacher. He taught a course "Vernacular (Folk) Architecture," and led us on all the tours. Thus he did what I had missed in England at Cambridge, a person who tied the whole experience together.

We were housed at the Hotel Della Posta, located on the Corso Vannucci, the main Esplanade in the old city, resting on top of the mountain, at whose end were located medieval and Renaissance buildings with their historical and artistic lore. In between were shops and restaurants, where we enjoyed many a gelati and good patisserie. We had a nice apartment with all facilities, enjoyed an abundant continental breakfast each morning in the small dining room, taking our midday and evening meals at the Ristorante Priori, off the Esplanade on one of the downhill side streets, about a quarter of a mile away.

The other courses were given by Charles Cooper on Italian history from Garibaldi through the years of Mussolini's Fascistic dictatorship. Cooper had served in the U.S. Embassy in England during the war and had worked under my brother Sam. The other instructor was a native Italian, Bruno Dozzini, who with a delightful accent taught "Art in Umbria," illustrated by walking tours in Perugia and other cities: Spoleto, Sienna, Gubbio, and Assisi.

Leopold asked us to prepare a brief report on some piece of architecture in Perugia. Emma and I selected a small building which required some research. It was originally constructed by Pope Paul III in 1549 as a porch to overlook the deep valley and the Apennine Mountains in the distance "for the benefit of the people." A portico extended down into the square, connecting the old buildings. Subsequently a fire destroyed most of the long portico. The porch was enclosed and turned into a small church by Cardinal Tiberius Crispus. In recent years it had become an annex of the Biblioteca, across the street. Some of this information we gleaned by translating the Roman lettering on the front and the side of the building. The rest we obtained by going to the Biblioteca and conferring with Dozzini. Before we assembled all this data, Emma and I romantically contemplated purchasing and remodeling this delightful structure and living in it in the future. Italy has a way of romanticizing every experience. I made drawings of the building and gave a good, brief lecture at one of the sessions.

We learned a great deal of Italian history from these classes. The town had its origins during the days of the Etruscans, a fabulous civilization that had a striking culture before the Romans overran the interior.

Although we knew that Perugia was hilly, it actually proved too steep for the many excursions that were planned, so that we did not always participate. It was wearing. Not so for the rest of the thirty people in the tour, most of whom were about our age, some a little younger, a few even older. They were a pleasant group, including a number of Italians, often intermarried with non-Italians in the States, who came back to their "roots" in Italy, where their parents had been born and raised.

The side trips to the other cities, which were also hill towns, were too much for our weary bodies and feet. We sat out Assisi altogether, since we had seen it in 1955 and 1965. The experience of studying Perugia will be an enduring one. We purchased lots of books, so that we were able to enjoy everything over again in later readings.

The restaurant was an enjoyable experience, as we ate veal prepared in infinite varieties, pastas that never had the same shape and taste twice a day, usually downed with some light Italian wines, although we did little more than taste the wines, since alcohol was proscribed in our diets. Shopping was fun in the shops, including Gucci, which had an extraordinary display of its wares in our hotel.

We recommend Perugia as a site for historical study and to witness how the middle class of Italy lives. Each night on the Esplanade thousands of young and older Italians gathered for the nightly promenade, to talk, to sit at the many cafes to enjoy a drink, a piece of pastry, a gelati. Well behaved, well dressed, in informal wear, few in the extreme, it was enjoyable to be there in good weather, only one day clouded by rain.

Some nights we went to a concert, and once we attended a movie, *Assisi Underground,* a film about how a cardinal, one of his priests, and some nuns, aided by a German general, protected a number of Jews during the Nazi occupation. It was a stirring movie, there were familiar shots of Assisi and Perugia. Every free night we played bridge with the Ansells, after teaching Charles this intricate game soon after our arrival in Perugia. We talked with Ethel Abrams, another student on the tour, who had worked for me at Camp Bronx House and Bronx House in the 1940s. She later became a well-known camp director. Since her retirement, she had taken to travel and study, collecting art and jewelry, items that she once made, for she was also a talented art and crafts person.

From Italy to Belgium

We hired a car and started our journey northward, driving both on the express highways and off the beaten paths until we reached Pacienta and stopped overnight at the Hotel Milan. We walked into town, listened to a concert by a youth band, gazed at some of the old buildings. The next morning we were off early. After replacing a dead battery in a small town that fortunately had a garage, we drove through the Piedmontese Alps, where the industrial towns, attractive villages, and well-groomed farming country turned into beautiful mountains. Grenoble was out of the question for an overnight stay, so we headed for Oulx, ski country, where, after making some hairpin turns up the mountainside, we reached the Hermitage Hotel at Sauze d'Oulx, which served skiers in the wintertime. At five thousand feet, it overlooked the snow-covered mountains (in July!) surrounding our lodgings. As Maryann put it: "God directed us here. Maybe we ought to stay longer." That night, since it was Shabbat, we made Kiddush in the goyishe dining room over sips of good Italian wine.

The next morning with Charlie and me alternating at the wheel, we crossed the French border into Besançon, changed our lira to French francs, and walked through this old town, once a fort, with its narrow streets, where the savory smells of cooking made us stop to buy a wonderful roast chicken, with rolls, tomatoes, and peaches. Washed down with orange juice it made a nourishing lunch in the out-of-doors. As we approached Le Grave, we stopped for coffee and watched hundreds of bicyclists pass us on an annual race that ended near Grenoble. Since it was still daylight, we continued on the road until we found a motel in Bourgin l'Isle d'Abeau that had excellent rooms, good food, offered a tremendous breakfast, all very reasonable.

The next day we continued on the Peage express highway, driving through good towns, passing well-cultivated farms, lots of new buildings, many painted in pastel shades, finally reaching Dijon, which we associated with a famous mustard. It was a handsome city. In the Center its public buildings were structures of beauty. We had an excellent lunch at the Café Théâtre, met and talked with tourists and natives, and decided to head for Neuchâtel. On the way we stopped in small villages to see if there was a suitable hotel, but found none inviting. We drove to Campanile, just before Nancy, and found the mate to the hotel we had stayed in the night before. Each day the weather remained beautiful.

After fixing a flat tire, we decided to drive on to Luxembourg via Metz. We visited the Cathedral Etienne, a massive Gothic church, built over a period extending from the thirteenth to the sixteenth century, with tremendous stained-glass windows, including a number by Chagall. We bought lunch and ate it in the big park alongside Prince Henry Boulevard in Luxembourg. The city was overrun with wall-to-wall tourists. No rooms were available, except a few luxuries, where the prices were prohibitive. We finally left town, found a room for $100 per night in the beautiful new Hotel Inter-Continental on a rise in the outskirts. In this lush hotel with its elegant dining service and gourmet food, including an unusual raspberry pie, we lived it up for a night. But we didn't see Luxembourg.

The next morning we found a little bakery shop, where we had a breakfast of fresh croissants and rolls, juice, good coffee, butter and jam for 65 cents (U.S.), so we learned that the poor can live as well as the rich. Since Metz, we had been in German-speaking regions, more pronounced in Luxembourg, and more so as we went over the border into eastern Belgium, where Flemish was more dominant than French. We stopped in Bastogne. Here the American soldiers fought a fierce battle in 1944, where MaAuliffe, the general who refused to surrender to the overwhelming German counterattack, replied "Nuts!" to the Nazis. We bought our lunch and headed for the farm country of Belgium and ate in the village square of Ceney. Since the Ansells wanted to be in Ghent, which they had never seen, and I recalled it as a city of charm with a cathedral that had art of Rubens, we drove into town, but found the cathedral and other important buildings closed for repairs, Hotels were impossible to find as the tourists were there en masse, so we bedded down in the Holiday Inn, dining on unusual foods like wild boar pâté on crackers, bisque of snails, raspberry duck, and the famous Belgian dish, chicken waterzooi.

We drove speedily to Bruges, that beautiful city, which in medieval times was more important than Paris. The silting of the river had interrupted its growth and importance. It has remained as it was hundreds of years ago, a relatively small city of charm. Yet it had changed so much since our visit in 1955, with dense traffic and hordes of tourists. We stopped overnight in a Holiday Inn, formerly a monastery. We walked about the town, visited the two cathedrals, found the Memling Museum unfortunately closed, for we had looked forward to seeing its handsome paintings once again. It was the first time during our trip that I began to feel tired, as though a cold was coming on. I tried to anticipate its development by taking Vitamin C and Ascriptin. We had dinner in the fabulous market in the Cuiviere d'Orn, an elegant old place, where the watercress soup, the fish, and the chicken waterzooi, each topped with a creamed soup concoction, finished off by raspberries covered with schlag made a delectable meal.

The next day we left this quaint city with its narrow, ever-curving cobblestoned streets, its many canals, and drove the Ansells to the ferry in Ostend, that sailed to England. It was a tearful goodbye, after a wonderful three weeks.

Brussels

We returned to Brussels, 110 kilometers away, in one hour, where Renee Odou Smith took us on an immediate tour of the city, somewhat changed in the thirty years since our last visit. Her lovely home was filled with antiques that she had acquired over the years, twelve of which had been spent as a constantly traveling hostess on the Sabena Airlines. A woman of many talents, in the arts and fine crafts, a writer and illustrator, skilled with the needle, she was finding it difficult to make a career. She had inherited some money from her American husband of only two years, who died of cancer. She lived and traveled simply. She had worked out a detailed schedule for our week's stay. In my fatigue, we told her that we would take it easy. We ate spicy Thai food the first night in an interesting, Oriental-decorated, busy restaurant, then had a tour at night around the city.

The following day we visited some museums. Reading the Paris edition of the *International Herald-Tribune,* we found that our Merchants Bank of New York stock had risen phenomenally from \$63 to \$102½, so we celebrated our paper "richness." We had lunch in a *bierstube* overlooking the elegant market square, and ate a delicious raspberry tart for dessert in a grand *patisserie* in the original galleria. For dinner we went back to town in one of those alleys off the square, for a superb bouillabaisse, stopped to listen to groups of musicians, and in exhaustion went to bed.

The next day, when we were walking through a flea market, I felt a tightening in my left leg, and wondered whether the phlebitis had returned. We ate in that evening. I went to bed early.

The next day the pain in my leg continued. When I went for a little walk, on my return, I could hardly climb the stairs. For the first time, I felt a distinct shortness of breath. Emma decided we must go home the next day. Renee, who knew the ways of Sabena, took her to the airport, where we secured tickets. I rested most of the afternoon, but we went out for dinner to a unique restaurant, where the customers could eat and drink all the food and liquor they could consume for \$12 per person. The catch was that you had to make your own food over the charcoal fire. There were at least twenty kinds of meats, an equal number of vegetables in every possible form, after which you had a choice of twenty kinds of desserts. It was all good. Renee, who drank at least five large glasses of wine (we had none), showed no signs of even the beginnings of inebriation. As it was still light, she took us on another tour of the finer sections of the city. There was confirming evidence that Brussels was a town of considerable wealth. I bought a copy of Uris's book *Haj* in French for Renee. When we picked up the *Herald-Tribune* at the airport, we found that it carried an article by Charlie Ansell about crime in high places. The Met baseball team was two and one-half games out of first place in the eastern division of the National League. We bought Scotch, Chanel no. 5, a fine scarf, and a cap at the airport. The pain in my leg continued. For once Emma had a better flight than I did. We decided that such strenuous vacations were getting to be too much at our age, and that we would plan differently in future years. Despite it all, it had been a good three and a half weeks.

Pulmonary Embolisms

The day after we returned from Europe, I saw Dr. Murray Goldberg. He examined and told me that the phlebitis had returned and that I should see a cardiologist immediately. He was concerned about my shortness of breath and the pain in my leg. The following day I was scrutinized by Dr. Julien Frieden, a cardiologist whom I had seen a couple of years before, when I thought that I had a heart attack. It wasn't. He went over me thoroughly. Said nothing, because he is a man of few words. He sent me down to the nuclear unit for a lung scan. Then he gave me the bad news. I had developed pulmonary embolisms, induced perhaps by the phlebitis, which had thrown off clots that filled my lungs. Having expected a benign report, I was unprepared for his decision that I must enter the New Rochelle Hospital immediately for at least ten days. I was to lie on my back, not cross my legs, not leave the bed except for the inside bathroom, and not leave the room. He informed me in solemn tones that this ailment had been caught in the nick of time. Otherwise, if neglected, it might have led to serious complications, even sudden death. That sobered me. Yet I must confess that I did not feel sick in the common sense of that word.

I was put to bed. The doctor took me off the estrogen pills, which I had been taking daily for almost a year, as he believed, and later confirmed, that they might have been a contributing factor to the clots in my lungs. I had originally been told that there was a 20 percent chance of this side effect. I was unlucky enough to be in that statistical range. I laughingly told Dr. Frieden that I now had a choice between dying of cancer and dying of heart disease. A laconic man, he did not reply.

However, I was informed that without the estrogen capsules, I would have to undergo the surgical removal of my testicles, those appendages being a potential contributor to cancer in that region. Not looking forward to that prospect, I decided to pursue the question further with all my physicians—endocrinologist, radiologist, urologist, internist, cardiologist. Happily, by a majority of four to one, the decision was that there would be no further surgical alteration of my body. During my stay in the hospital, subsequent lung and other tests on the most modern equipment revealed that the clots in my lungs had disappeared.

I'm an excellent patient. I took my medicine, ate the proper foods, rested in bed. After ten days, I was discharged and was restricted in exertion and travel, could only climb the stairs once a day, could take no long walks, could not drive a car. My medication was Coumadin, a blood thinner, in 5 mg capsules which I will probably have to take all my life to keep the blood thin enough to prevent or at least inhibit blood clots.

Curious about this life-saving Coumadin, I mentioned it by chance to my friend Bert Jahr, who had worked with me at Bronx House in the 1940s. He told me this interesting tale. When he was director of the Jewish Community Center in Madison, Wisconsin, in 1945–50, an unknown plague began to destroy herds of cattle, a serious blow to commerce in this dairy state. A research team determined quickly that it was due to internal bleeding; but it took three years of study to isolate the fact that it was due to the fodder the cattle ate. Each item of food was analyzed for clues, their essences extracted and chemically probed. The extracts were tested on rats, and they too died of internal bleeding. The flower that contained the chemical that caused the deaths of the cows was an innocent and useful plant, clover. This leguminous herb, valuable for forage and attractive to bees, the four-leaf variety a symbol of good liuck and a charm for the Irish, turned out to be the culprit. The scientists, one a friend of Jahr, thus indirectly discovered an anticoagulant that proved to be a boon to mankind. The resulting medication was first called Warfin, for the Wisconsin Alumni Research Foundation.

Except for this brief episode in Brussels, I never felt ill. The same was true during my stay in the hospital. Some suspected me of malingering. I have reasonable faith in modern, technological instruments. They may be costly. They usually don't lie. I began to walk up and down the stairs, take longer strolls, drove the car—all as though nothing had happened. I knew that I must slow down appreciably, watch my food intake rigorously, travel only for leisure and not for exertion, that is, if I want to live something like the approximate 120 years of our ancient sage—Moses.

30

Cancun, Mexico

IN 1986, OUR latest journey, to Cancun, Mexico, started off marvelously. Emma had brought every conceivable type of medicine to ward off those ailments that were associated with Mexico—diarrhea, or "Montezuma's revenge," as the travelers put it. There was no discomfort during the first four days. In our euphoria, we even decided to buy a time-sharing condominium, so that our children and grandchildren might visit this stretch of sand and nine-mile beach overlooking the Caribbean and enjoy the sun and warmth in the middle of February. Then Emma became ill. We will not return to Mexico.

Forced to reconsider our more extravagant travel itineraries, and realizing that maybe we would have to cut down for both our physical and mental tranquility, we began to take counsel from Miguel Cervantes (1547–1616), the author of *Don Quixote*, namely, to "journey over all the universe on a map, without the expense and fatigue of travelling, without suffering the inconveniences of heat, cold, hunger and thirst." If we had followed his advice in our earlier years, we would never have reached Spain nor walked through fabulous Granada, where Cervantes was once a tax collector (Pt. II, bk. II, chap. 6). His thought brought me back to my elementary school days, when I was permitted to sit at the table in front of the class in the Estee Junior High School in Gloversville, turning the large globe, locating far-off countries, cities, rivers, and mountains, dreaming of the journeys that I might take to these far-flung places when I grew to manhood.

JDC and Ethiopia

The JDC has had an off-and-on affair with Ethiopia and its Jews since 1919, when it sent a medical mission to examine their condition. From

1922 to 1932, it allocated funds, at first quite substantial for those days, and then diminishing to nothing, to aid the educational programs that Dr. Faitlovitch developed. Until I importuned the organization to resume its concern with the Ethiopian Jews, it did naught. The year was 1975. However, despite making large appropriations each year in sums of $100,000, it actually spent little until the year 1981, because it had turned over its franchise, so to speak, to World ORT, which obtained funds for its programs from non-Jewish sources, namely several governments, including the United States. In the year ORT was forced to end its program, JDC claimed that it picked up the tab.

For reasons that I have never been able to determine, the JDC made application on its own to the Ethiopian government about 1983, and subsequently established a program of building a medical clinic located in Gondar Province, where the remaining six to eight thousand Jews still reside. The programs are nonsectarian. Despite the fact that JDC raised over $1 million in 1984–85 for the relief of Ethiopians suffering from the famine and drought, it has not provided any direct relief to Ethiopian Jews per se, nor has it undertaken an obligation to support any Jewish educational or synagogal activities, nor has it involved itself in assisting their exodus from the country.

At its annual meeting in December 1985, the JDC presented the head of the Ethiopian mission to the United Nations with a plaque extolling the assistance that the Ethiopian government had given to the JDC operation. In the spring of 1986, a high-level mission of JDC officers went to Ethiopia. They were welcomed by government officials, and in turn, Elaine Winik, leader of the mission, praised the officials highly at the quarterly meeting of the JDC in New York on May 21. When Ethiopian Jews asked Mrs. Winik and her entourage when the JDC was going to help them get out of Ethiopia and be reunited with their families in Israel, she told them that that was not within the province of the JDC. When a similar question was addressed to her group by the United States chargé d'affaires in Addis Ababa, he received the same answer—that was not JDC's function.

While it is probably true that JDC would also be expelled from Ethiopia if it engaged in any activities exclusively for Jews, including Jewish education and religion, and if it tried to help them leave the country, one wonders what they, as an international Jewish organization, were doing there. That is, unless they have some secret mission, which has nothing to do with Ethiopian Jews.

How We Financed Our Way Through Life and in Retirement

Money had not been a concern of mine in my early days. The table in my childhood home was always laden with ample and varied foods. I always had enough and the right clothing for the varying seasons in a climate that included both cold winters and warm summers. The homes in which we lived gave more than adequate shelter and in later years were substantial. Entertainment out of the home was limited and inexpensive. If I needed money for candy, an ice cream cone, or the movies, it was provided. A baseball and a mitt could be obtained, if I saved my money. I never thought of buying athletic uniforms except to play basketball. When I started to earn some money after the age of eight, I didn't have to ask my parents for extras. As a teenager, I bought some of the necessities—clothing, shoes, haircuts, toothbrushes, cologne, talcum powder, a bicycle. When I wanted to buy an old Ford car for $35, I saved up the money, spent it, and my treasury was temporarily empty.

While going to college, my parents paid for my tuition and a good deal of the room and board. I earned money in one way or another to supplement these monthly grants. After my marriage to Emma, money was always tight. Somehow we managed each month, occasionally by small borrowings from friends, which we instantly repaid when money came in. I did not like to be in debt. Buying clothing during our early marriage years, and when Ramon came onto the scene, often was postponed. Eating out, going on holidays was rare. Such excursions not even planned. We welcomed invitations to dinners, and when I became an executive of the Jewish Community Center of Staten Island, they happily came frequently. We welcomed these parties, where we ate a sumptuous meal and saved some money at the same time.

Marriage made money become exceedingly important. Unhappily my earnings were small, and in Staten Island, during my six years, I was unable to obtain my modest salary on time and had to resort to regular short-term borrowings from a few friends and/or the bank to tide us over. Emma and I often said that if we had five dollars more per week, we could live like millionaires. We just did without necessities in furniture, clothes, entertainment, and holidays, except when my parents made such holidays possible, usually at their home in Gloversville or in Sacandaga.

When I started working at Bronx House in 1938, I was in debt, which I managed to pay off in three years out of a salary of $4,000. We finally began to accumulate our first savings in 1945, when my wages were raised to $6,000 per year. We kept some liquid money in the bank, but saved through the purchase of government bonds. We bought our first new car in 1948 with $2,000 willed to me by my father and a $600 gift given by the board of Bronx House on the occasion of my tenth anniversary as its executive. When we decided to buy a home in 1953, I had only managed to accumulate $6,000. This plus a noninterest loan from Federation in an equal amount enabled us to purchase the property for $24,000, assuming a mortgage of $12,000, payable over seventeen years. Interest rates then started at 4.5 percent and for the last ten years were only 3.5 percent. My salary in 1953 was $13,000.

My wages increased steadily over the course of years at Federation. However, after my salary reached $25,000, I put all of the excess into tax-deferred annuities, so that we had the prospect of living almost as well after retirement as during my better-paid working days. Emma constantly complained that the monthly allowance was insufficient. I put her off by promises of Nirvana. It was not that we did without, for we lived quite well, traveled, vacationed, added to our furniture, bought new cars every six years, saw our children through college and marriage, but we did not live extravagantly. I did not want to go into debt. I mowed our lawn. Did a good deal of the repairs around the house. We had a girl come in once every two weeks to do the heavy cleaning. All within our means. Emma never had her own savings or checking account until after I retired and she began to receive her Social Security stipends in 1973.

While I was at Federation, we had invested a modest sum in a joint stock account held by the top executives of Federation. This was added to each month. While the fund had its ups and downs, when I left Federation, it provided us with a substantial sum, supplementing our overall resources.

Another sum had been invested in stocks, under the generous supervision of a friend, who managed my account. On retirement, this became significant.

The lack of boldness in money making, or perhaps lack of a genuine interest in getting rich quickly, may have contributed to my timidity. Perhaps if I had been envious of my associates, friends, and colleagues, for I was surrounded by great wealth during my long working years, I might have become more of a plunger.

Yet, as I look back, we denied ourselves comparatively little. Our two sons went through college with help from us, but both, being industrious, prudent, and thrifty, worked during their college years to help support themselves. Michael was married in his junior year, so that he had to assume some additional burdens over and above our stipends and gifts.

We began traveling in 1949, and if there was one luxury we indulged ourselves, it was to continue this exploration of the world. While in some instances, I was able to obtain assistance for travel, as the leader of a group, as a benefit of working at Federation while attending a conference abroad, this covered only a small portion of the costs. I could deduct part of the outlay as a legitimate expense in filing our annual income tax statement.

Gradually our home was completely and tastefully furnished with new and antique furniture. The art and artifacts were assembled mostly by Emma from our travels abroad and by occasional purchases at auctions and shops. Apart from many books purchased, a sizable part of our vast library consisted of books I reviewed for periodicals and gifts from family and friends, who knew we were a bookish family. When a car wore out after six years, it was replaced and always paid for in cash.

We were able to help our two sons, their families and grandchildren, but until I retired, our gifts were modest. These have been increased substantially over the years.

How did we manage after retirement, when my salary dropped to a pension one third of my salary? The annuities, Social Security payments, income from other savings in banks, bonds, and stocks brought our disposable income up to a level where it was almost what we were indenting before I gave up working. Some prudent investments and rising interests rates eventually made my retirement income even larger than my final salary, although part of its value was eroded by inflation.

When my brother Sam passed away in 1980, he willed me some magnificent art (Japanese, Korean, Vietnamese), silver, and his Washington home, which we sold.

We began to give a portion of our capital accumulation each year to our two sons and their families. We substantially increased the gifts we gave to each of them at birthdays, wedding anniversaries, Bar and Bat Mitzvahs, confirmations, graduations from high school and college, and even the marriage of one of our grandchildren. We gave generous gifts to our grandchildren whenever they went on educational tours to Europe and to Israel. On a few occasions we took our children and grandchildren with us when we went on extended holidays abroad.

During our entire lives, and certainly after 1945, when we had paid our debts and began to add to our fortune, we contributed handsomely, for people in our income bracket, to philanthropy, admittedly mostly to Jewish associations, some to the general community, and to our synagogues in Pelham, Gloversville, and Jerusalem. It represented at least 10 percent of our gross income, and some years even more, as we began to add to our philanthropic list, the AAEJ and the Jerusalem Fund. Our friends thus believed that we were wealthier than we really were. This sense of communal responsibility we have successfully taught to our children, and they have followed our example of generous tzedakah.

Somehow, by dint of hard work, careful husbanding of our resources, conservative investment, the benefits of a legacy, high interest rates, at my age of seventy-eight, we are able to live well, with memories of our difficult earlier days, but with the knowledge that we have enough to live out our alloted time on this earth without the need of having to call on our children for anything but their time, devotion, and love. We never give a thought to having to resort to public welfare. Needless to add, Medicare and two major medical plans also ward off the full cost of expensive medicine and hospital care. It is a very comforting feeling.

When we are through with this world, although this had never been our original plan or intention, we will probably leave behind a handsome legacy, which we hope that they will all use prudently for themselves and for the benefit of the Jewish and general community.

Helpful Friends

From the outset of my professional career, I was always surrounded by people of wealth. Yet while I always aspired to higher salaries, I never envied by volunteer associates for the homes they lived in nor their style of life. I will confess that I liked to hold meetings in some of these homes, where I could glance up at a Van Gogh self-portrait. I never coveted such art and believed that such works should be in museums rather than private homes. Most of the great works, including that Van Gogh, ended up in one. Even a few major art works in our own home, I believe, should really be in a public art gallery, and I know museums that would be delighted to have them. Emma felt the contrary, and our children feel as she does, so they will eventually move from one house to another. Mere possession of objects, except for temporary use and pleasure, was never part of my psyche.

What surprised me over the years was that despite my intimacy with men and women of wealth—realtors, stock brokers, accountants, lawyers, jewelers—none of them with three exceptions, ever suggested that they would like to help me obtain some additional wealth. All others, when I hinted, but never directly asked, about ways and means of improving my assets through businesses in which they were involved, discouraged me from making such investments.

One of my Federation associates, an outstanding, generous, and educated Jewish leader, and one of my firmest supporters for the development of Jewish education and the Judaization of our institutions, was a leading partner in a stock brokerage firm. One day, he asked me to send him several thousands of dollars for investment, but on condition that he manage the purchase and sale of all stocks, and I forget about the reinvestment of any assets that might accrue. Some fifteen years later, when I left Federation, the fund was worth many times what I had originally sent to him. It added immeasurably to our retirement years.

In recent years, another friend, who amongst other things is an astute stock investor, asked me to send him some money for investment in stocks. He also exercised sole control over the way the portfolio was managed. Some years later, when I needed the money, he sold my holdings for many times the original outlay.

One other friend's advice was worthy of note. Twenty years ago, while we were bicycle riding together, he urged me to buy the stock of a bank on which he had recently become a director. Over the course of two decades, while the market has risen and fallen and risen, it has appreciated many fold, perhaps more so than any bank in the country. Emma keeps throwing it up to me that we should have purchased a lot more of the stock when it was offered to us years ago, but that my conservatism prevented us from actually becoming wealthy in our own time and in our own right. She was correct.

These are the only direct benefits I received from my associations with some of the rich. The magic touch was due to others, not to any wise investments of my own. While I read the financial pages of the *New York Times* and the *Wall Street Journal* and occasionally magazines like the *Economist*, *Forbes*, and *Fortune*, I have never bothered to master the intricacies of the marketplace. My own initiatives were and are conservative. I want respectable returns from moneys put into various avenues with little possibility of risk. I prefer government guarantees in case anything goes wrong. Under such circumstances, I slept well each night of my later life and had no dreams of either sudden riches or economic disaster.

Birthdays—Simchas—Gifts

When I was a child, even an adolescent, I do not recall any special ceremonies or gifts on my birthday, nor any comparable celebration for any other member of my family. Annual events or other personal anniversaries seemed to be ignored. Before Rosh Hashanah in the fall of the year, we were outfitted with clothes. There might have been a modest gift on Hanukkah and on Purim, when Jewish custom called for the exchange of benevolences, but I have no such recollections. A bicycle, a sled, a watch, a baseball glove, a musical instrument, even special articles of clothing were given, if given, as needed, and not on any unique, life-cycle occasion. I didn't get anything on graduation from elementary school, junior high, high school, college, or graduate school. So I have nothing associated with these academic completions.

Recognition of annual recurrences of a date-marking event began to take place after Emma and I were married. While our resources were meager, somehow we tried to chronicle these dates with a bit of festive giving—clothing, a book, jewelry, or dining out in a restaurant. The favorite gift for me, if anything was given at all, was a book, usually a precious, sometimes an expensive book, and I still have a number of them in our collection. Emma once gave me for a birthday a magnificent edition of Honoré Daumier's caricatures, because I had become rhapsodic about his works that I had seen in an exhibition. As I got older the family seemed to think that I had enough books—although one can never really buy, receive, and read too many books—so they began to give me clothing, such as cashmere sweaters, fine shirts, innumerable ties, and finally cosmetics and perfumed soaps. When I take one of these items out from a drawer or closet, it immediately brings back memories of the distinctive occasion when it was given.

Collectives of friends also took note of my birthdays, especially milestones—fifty, sixty, sixty-five, seventy, seventy-five—so I have two magnificent sterling silver *Kiddush* cups, the latest *Encyclopaedia Judaica,* the expensive Darmstadt Haggadah, a handsome collection of Bialik's poetry, a number of works of art. As with the clothing gifts, whenever I look on our walls, bookshelves and cabinets, there is an immediate flashback to the generous donors and the memorable occasion.

Frequently, on returning from abroad, we brought gifts to a few personal friends, usually a work of art or a Jewish ceremonial object. We note with pleasure, on our visits to their homes, that they are exhibiting these wares in perpetuity.

Emma and I, however, always found it difficult to determine the right gift for someone else, especially our own children and grandchildren. At times we discovered that the articles of clothing we gave them were not worn. Not everyone liked exotic items purchased in some out-of-the-way place in India, Guatemala, Mexico, Chile, or Peru. Art works they can hang or put in a cupboard, and it becomes a family rather than a personal present.

Hence we began substituting money for tangible objects. As Emma frequently repeats: "It is always the right size and the right color." Such monetary gifts have increased in magnitude, depending on the event.

Thus from no recognition of annual or special events in our early days, now, in the advancing years of life, we have accepted the more traditional view that gifts do remind us of hallmarks in one's life and deepen our memory.

Art

In my parental home, I was not surrounded by art. Two large pictures in handsome gilt-and-black frames adorned our living and dining room. European scenes, one of the daily life in a village, and the other a romantic night view with the moon reflectings its silvery light over a lake as people were launching a boat at a primitive dock. My parents purchased them on time payments, but I have no recollection of what they might have cost. They are still hanging on the walls of our cottage at Sacandaga. Visitors are more attracted to these two large objects than to the score of other pictures—many very good—that decorate the other rooms.

I do not remember art, as such, being taught in the schools. Yes, we had drawing lessons, but somehow it was never connected with classical art or even the artists of the day. I never went to an art exhibit until I attended college in New York in 1925. In fact I don't recall any such exhibitions having taken place in Gloversville. I was never inclined to study art in any form, nor do I recall reading a book on art in my adolescence. I would have flunked any test where I had to name five well-known artists in history or the contemporary world.

My interest in art was aroused suddenly as a student at the University of Missouri. In order to use the spacious museum for quiet study, one had to register for a course. Furthermore, to get out of doing household chores at the ZBT fraternity house, I enrolled in a class on art on Saturday mornings, the very time that these cleaning activities took place. So a place to study and to avoid an unwelcome task thrust upon me, an interest in art developed, and it has never ceased. In my second year at Missouri, I decided to study Greek civilization, and one of the courses was in Greek art. I was exposed to the creative productions of that period in history, plaster copies of the most popular sculpture being available in the college museum. The table where I placed my books and pen were under the testicles of the huge figure of the Discobolus, the athlete who threw the discus. Each semester I pursued another era, thus covering the entire spectrum up to modern times.

A single stimulating professor, Dr. Pickard, made the subject live. His mane of white hair and long white mustache, and a booming voice spoken with intensity, demanded the fullest attention. His field trips, one in particular to the State Capitol in Jefferson City, to witness the frescoes that Thomas Hart Benton, a native of the state, had painted, deepened my curiosity. The knowledge of those courses never left. Becoming a collector would still not occur for some time. We had no extra money to indulge in such luxuries.

Some years later, I went to an exhibit of Benton's paintings in New York, where I found Benton himself present. I told him of my courses with Pickard and having seen his work in the Missouri State Capitol. He was most pleased, treated me as a serious student of the subject. We have books about Benton in our library.

On Staten Island, to cover the bare walls in our apartment, Emma and I cut out a dozen modern French impressionist painters from *Vanity Fair*, shellacked them, framed them with Woolworth's Best for 10 cents apiece, and hung them conspicuously. In that obtrusive way, we introduced art to the many young people we constantly entertained.

At the center I arranged periodic art exhibits. I also introduced art classes, about which I have written earlier, telling how I became a student sculptor and painter in those classes in order to stimulate registration. I sculpted and cast three pieces and painted two oils. Located in the New York area with its vast museums, I occasionally took groups to these extraordinary places. I began to read books on art in my leisure and even reviewed several for the Staten Island Library book-study group. I was a founder and first vice-president of the Council of the Arts on Staten Island, an effort to inspire an interest in this field in the 1930s. I learned a great deal more about art and was invited to homes where interesting art works were displayed. At the Marchais-Glauber home I was introduced to Far Eastern art, developing an interest that was further deepened when we made trips to those regions in 1962 and 1971.

Except for my own works which adorned our house, and a few we had obtained from WPA artists who worked for me at the Staten Island center and Bronx House in the 1930s, we had bought little else.

Our first serious purchases started in Israel in 1955. Apart from gifts from artist-friends, and my own painting of "Emma," in our travels we have acquired paintings, sculpture, wood carvings, silver objects, because we liked them and because they would become mementos of our trips.

While a few were purchased from dealers, we have bought many works directly from the artists in Israel, Korea, Burma, India, Mexico, Guatemala, Haiti, Philippines, Yugoslavia, Tanzania, Ethiopia, Nepal, and Thailand.

My brother Sam added to our collection before and after he died, so that we have a fine display of Korean pottery, screens, and other art forms, along with a magnificent screen from Japan, which covers an entire wall.

Our house is a veritable museum, and whenever we held meetings, we took the newcomers on a tour of the several floors. There are more than a score of paintings in the attic, because the atelier has no place to hang them.

While adding to our own collection, we would also purchase paintings and pottery and other objects for our two sons and their families. As a consequence, their homes are equally decorated with interesting pieces of art, along with items that they acquired themselves, which further enrich the displays. They too have little museums. Sandy, Michael's wife, has also acquired her mother's extensive collection of antiques, and they are distributed about the household.

Several of our grandchildren have developed an interest in art. One is a college student studying art as a major. Some of his paintings are already in Pelham.

We know that our children are interested in eventually obtaining most of the items in our home, on walls, shelves, and in cabinets.

We were never in a position to pay a great deal of money for any of the items we acquired. We were not interested in prominent names, for by the time these artists became famous, the prices were far beyond our reach. Our emphasis was also on folk art, usually subjects with people rather than with scenery, giving one a more intimate picture of what the people looked like or were concerned with in the countries we visited. Most are colorful, although color in itself was not our criterion for selecting them.

In recent years, I have been tempted to purchase expensive pieces from established artists. Walking along Madison Avenue in New York, I have seen attractive paintings in the window, and after a moment's hesitation decided to enter and make an inquiry about its value. They have ranged from $8,000 to $180,000, the latter for a small painting by Modigliani. We have never paid more than a few hundred dollars for any item in our collection, including antique furniture. Some of our art is worth a great deal more than we paid, although we never bought them as an investment. In one instance, an artist from whom we once purchased a picture at a cost of $75 has since offered to buy it back for $1,500. We kept it.

We have great joy in looking at them daily, recollecting the interesting places and the events that accompanied their acquisition. Hence we constantly relive and reinforce our memory of earlier experiences.

Art is decoration. Art is stimulation. Art is education.

* * *

Emma always contended that had I been more temperate in my presentations and less accusative, angry, and bitter in the way that I wrote or orally expressed my ideas, I might not have alienated so many of my listeners, colleagues, and even lay people, although she admitted that in the course of time my ideas were finally accepted. She believed that the interval before acceptance would have been shortened had my approach been more diplomatic. Thus instead of immediately winning friends and allies for causes, my strong positions literally pushed them away from an open-minded reception of my notions. She told me that if I had done as she indicated, I might have become a greater leader. Thus I got only their grudging respect and not their willingness to translate good proposals into immediate action.

My differences with Emma's position were that both the field and my profession were locked into ways of doing things that were historically restricted and conventional. I always believed that to move people quickly, you had to shock them into the realities of the current situation and the limitations of their fixed points of view. They had to be shown that they were wrong on their facts, that they had not sufficiently analyzed the positions under which they were operating; they had to be told that they did not have foresight, or a sufficiently prophetic strain, nor even what I call the simple imaginative boldness to venture into programs that were better for their clientele and better for their communities. One's temperament always intruded on both the content and manner of presentation. My temperament, whether inborn or developed, controlled my life, and not always in my own short-term best interests.

I wanted the power of my ideas to prevail, even though I did not trust people who had too much power, even if such power was in my own hands.

* * *

The summer of 1986 was spent largely at Sacandaga, where I finished the book, before shipping it off to my editor. It was also an occasion for meeting once again with some old friends from Gloversville: Jack and Lillian Muskin Shwartz, Essie Nissenbaum Lazarus, David Frisch and Dr. Morris Alpert. While we talked about the "good old days," I could not get a single critical comment about my early life from any of them.

* * *

Then we were off for our first trip to Cape Cod, where we spent a pleasant four days at Wellfleet, attending an exhibit of the paintings of Seymour Kameny, who is married to Emma's niece, Frances. Then we renewed friendships with a number of people, one of whom we had not seen in nearly 50 years. The sand dune Cape is crowded, except for some isolated parts, which, those who can afford it, have found ways and means of separating themselves from the traffic and hordes of visitors. While we do not have any prejudices against the seashore, we are mountain people, where the elevation is higher, the air seemingly purer and less humid and the population less dense.

A Medal

In the spring of 1986, I received copies of several letters that had been sent to congressmen and senators recommending me for the Medal of Freedom, which the President of the United States periodically bestows on citizens who have made meritorious contributions to the national security, the national interest, world peace, culture, or other significant public or private endeavors. The several people who sent me copies of their letters did not tell me how this movement started.

One day I received a visit from Larry Rothbaum, a youngish man with family living in Riverdale, who had been interested in the Ethiopian Jewish issue, had promoted a number of meetings in his neighborhood, distributed literature, raised and gave money. As a result of his self-initiated efforts I had proposed his name and he was elected to the board of the AAEJ.

Larry turned in a folder of letters that had been sent to prominent elected officials in Washington, Jewish and non-Jewish, recommending me for the award based on what I had done for the Ethiopian Jews for the past thirty years. In addition he gave me a Resolution passed by the Assembly of the State of New York making a similar plea to the President of the United States. Larry had inaugurated the entire program.

Naturally I was both surprised and delighted, even though I had no illusion that such a distinguished honor would ever be given to me, since hundreds, perhaps thousands of names are submitted each year, and from what I have read about past recipients, they all had outstanding reputations and were widely known. While their honors had been for labors like mine, what they did had been heralded repeatedly in the public media. Yet it is good to know that there are people who respect the work that I and others have done to save the Ethiopian Jews from extinction.

* * *

Older professionals tell me that they are too quickly forgotten after they retire, unless they find some way of continuing to work in some consultant relationship. That has not been the case in my life. While I chose to pursue other avenues of activity, I have written extensively, have laboured domestically and abroad, have been called for counsel. At the age of 78, the bell has not stopped ringing.

Apart from the requests for speaking and conferring on the problems confronting Ethiopian Jews, and the stream of visitors who come to our home for material on this subject, I have within recent months been asked to write a section for a forthcoming volume for the Encyclopedia of Jewish American History and Culture, the topics covering: Jewish Communal Organizations in America, the Ethiopian Jews and Black Jews in America. I'm compiling notes for two more books.

I assume that when one has been active in a variety of fields throughout a lifetime, which included readings, studying, writing and speaking, that these skills do not become readily moribund, but can easily be reactivated as long as there is a will to respond to invitations as well as self-motivation. Even if one's body and spirit flag for a bit, there is always "one's second wind," as William James wrote in *The Energies of Men* (1913), "That 'second wind' is a reality in the mental as in the physical realm and can be found and used when needed." I have needed it and have found it.

31

Summing Up

How does one label his life, when it comes time to sum up? Have I always been the same since my earliest days, developing patterns of thought, feelings, and behavior that were relatively undeviating during a comparatively long life? Have I shown evidence of growth, with corresponding accommodations, so that I could live out my days normatively, as psychological theorists expect from most human beings? Have I periodically undergone radical changes in my views about the nature of man and society, so that my attitudes took decidedly different forms in the early, middle, and later sections of my many days?

While I could have written an autobiography from any one of these perspectives and perhaps stoutly defended each one by selective evidence, I am inclined, on later and longer reflection, and with the use of hindsight, to conclude that the third position has marked my three score and eighteen years.

While I may have been a bit challenging and provocative in my earlier years, I would contend, by and large, that I was basically idealistic. I saw my family, my friends, the tiny society in which I hospitably operated as essentially good. While I heard of evils—murder, war, treachery, infidelity, deceit—very little of this tinctured me. What I saw, by contrast, was that if your own needs and desires were modest, and not too demanding, nor envious, they could be realized with the assistance and advice provided within one's own family or by dint of one's own productive labor, seizing opportunities afforded from the outside world. Despite the vagaries of the larger universe, there were periods of optimism in my youth. Labor was beginning to be recognized, even if it had to fight for every right and privilege. Rapacious trusts were being contained by federal legislation. The government had courageously decided to step in and pass a somewhat more equalizing income tax. Women were about to obtain the suffrage. Even war, when it affected the United States in 1917–18, a short span, was seemingly fought more for human values—democracy, freedom of the seas, self-determination for minorities, suppression of a growing tyranny—than for sheer bloodletting to ensure a victory over a temporary enemy. Wilson had a vision. Even the Russian Revolution appeared on the surface as a crowning victory for the common peasant and soldier, long-suffering and persecuted during the entire history and over vast stretches of that nation. My family probably played a major role in shaping these early, cheering attitudes.

The middle years of my life brought home realities with which I had to cope; I had to recognize and find realistic ways of combating them or else make the necessary accommodations. My mother's illness, the temporary decline in our family fortunes after the war, the reactionaries that sprang up in America, the recrudescence of anti-Semitism, the quotas for Jewish student selection in Ivy League universities, the unbridled gambling in the marketplace, the impotence of a wealthy nation to deal with the tragic human problems of poverty and unemployment during the depression, the unwillingness of the Great Powers to prevent or contain the dangers inherent in German Nazism, Japanese expansion in the Far East, Italy's insidious conquest of weak, underdeveloped Ethiopia, and the cruel dictatorial takeover of a nascent democratic Spain—all culminated in the need once again to resort to a destructive global war in order to destroy temporarily these menacing developments. I watched these calamitous unfoldings with horror, with sporadic and weak efforts to find some way of stopping them, but like most everyone else, I too was overwhelmed by the flood-tide of seemingly inexorable events. All led to a conscious review of many of my first-stage values. Although I still had the notion that with intelligence man could master most of these invasions of a decent and peaceful life, I began to realize, perhaps for the first time, that political leaders were not fundamentally interested in improving the lot of the citizens they represented, let alone of mankind. Greed, self-interest, and cruelty were omnipresent, more than generosity, goodwill, and self-sacrifice. I witnessed our teachers, our professionals, our scientists, our intellectuals, at times even our artists, becoming more interested in their own careers than in remedying society's ills. Money and power were their goals rather than the creation of a more ethical earthly kingdom. I found it harder to be aligned with any political party, although by and large, I eventually, after flirting with socialism, found the expressed goals of the Democratic Party more acceptable among invidious choices. I ignored party lines and pulled down the lever for the man, or sometimes the woman, who I felt had a greater sense of righteousness—a vote which I often found later was unrewarding, for all too often elected representatives in high places discovered that their own powers were transient, or were forced into compromises. They quickly learned how to make deals, if they were to continue in office. I shifted uncertainly with the political and economic winds in a world suffering from ever greater disequilibrium. Yet I formed opinions after considerable contemplation, rather than impulsively, although my initial view was the one that I finally adopted and advocated.

In this latter, middle period, I began to find more satisfaction in returning to the teachings of my Judaic ancestors, because I became more convinced that history repeats itself. While it was clear even from the biblical text that our forefathers were not always exemplary men, I was impressed with the destinations they had sought as far back as thirty-three hundred years ago, ends that eventually were written down, and which succeeding generations tried repeatedly to put into practice; ends that began to influence the ethical outlook, if not always the conduct, of Jews and other people for millennia. I was impressed that these lofty principles also kept alive a people without a land and without military power for two thousand years, while they endured suffering and death rather than succumb to missionary appeals by other faiths. The Jews did not disappear unlike other, larger, and more powerful civilizations, which are only known today as a consequence of archaeological artifacts and pieces of salvaged writings on stone, clay, papyrus, and parchment. I saw in the Jewish people and their historical struggle some evidence of the idealism that I had gradually foresaken since the days of my youth.

Recent decades have been disillusioning. They have given me no comfort that man was embarking on an ever-improving road for all the peoples around the globe. Nor has Judaism either, through its diasporic leadership and in Israel, given me a strengthened inner feeling that we as a people are doing everything that we can to add to man's betterment and, for that matter, even to the welfare of Jews. As I write, Jews are experiencing menacing disunion in Israel and in America.

As to the larger society, it has produced the unbelievable possibilities of nuclear energy alongside the ever-present danger of atomic conflict that for the first time could actually destroy the entire world. Even the benefits of domestic, nuclear energy are now suspect, because of careless construction and management, so that few communities want such advanced instruments built in their localities. Our vaunted scientists have not yet provided all of the protective safeguards against the accidental release of death-dealing radiation in the atmosphere. We are despoiling, if we have not already done so beyond remedy, our environment—animals, fish, air, lakes, forest, farmlands, drinking water, even the once pure and expansive oceans. A government allegedly created to protect the hapless citizens, instead of providing the measures to prevent such hazards, seems to legislate and supervise the creation of more pollution, and drags its feet when it comes to investigating and prosecuting malefactors. Hunger has not been appeased or resolved. The world, and particularly wealthy nations like the United States, has the capacity—fertile land, scientific and technological knowledge, safe fertilizers and pesticides—to feed everyone with nourishing foods and prevent starvation. Yet hundreds of thousands of people die annually from lack of sufficient nourishment. Lands in underdeveloped nations are permitted to erode. Rich and productive agricultural properties are turning into arid deserts. We have not fully shared our reserves, our funds and knowhow, with the many poor nations that have not yet learned how to husband their own vast lands.

Easy divorce, for there is no longer sanctity or a sense of support for permanence in marriage, is undermining family life, and we accept currently permissive familial trends as inevitable, not reversible, all in the shrill cry of freedom, apparently for women as well as men. We treat inebriated drivers, who kill, as though they were mere everday drunks—"Don't we all drink?"—more to be laughed at and pitied than jailed for long terms. We still permit the tobacco and liquor industries to write their own ticket, futilely trying to "control" their lethal ravages on our lives by high taxes on the consumers, who continue to indulge, get ill, kill, and die, despite the plundering of their pocketbooks. The public is waking up to the menace of inhaling smoke, alcoholing their innards, abusing drugs, but the epidemic is still out of control, and no one prophesies when it will be managed and outlawed. Crime is rampant. One is afraid to use unpatrolled parks for leisurely walks and picnicking, or to traverse our streets. It follows us into transportation arteries, into the guarded city apartments of millionaires and the luxurious homes in suburbia, to which we initially fled for more decent living, and where we still remain, although safety there now is more questionable. Our schools struggle to produce literate college and postcollege graduates, but the young people they turn out do not seem to be able to cope with these serious problems, nor have our schools, public and Jewish, reared a higher ethically practicing person, who is prepared to give more than the minimum to our society, rather than seek profit for himself. Individualism was never more rampant.

What is there to be happy about as we look forward at least to the end of the century, which may accompany my latter days?

In our Jewish communities, all these evils are duplicated, as we follow trends rather than exert ourselves as an ancient, ethical community to steer a different course for ourselves and perhaps for the world to emulate. Rabbis preach academic irrelevances or what their congregants want to hear, for the limited number who attend. Other communal workers do not take leadership roles, because they might lose their prestigious, well-paid positions. Different ideological groups are more concerned with elevating and preserving their images and staking out large claims for Jewish communal support, than with trying to use the essence of our historic teachings to bind us together and make us more perfect citizens. We suffered the Holocaust. We were then mightily inspired to keep ourselves alive by restoring Israel. We write and publish books, hold mass meetings, build monuments, all to burn into our consciousness the memory of the six million Jews who died. Yet none of this had carry-over value in the early saving of the lives of twenty-eight thousand Ethiopian Jews. If it had not been for the role played by a handful of Jews, who had to confront the leadership of Israel, Western and American Jewish organizational leadership, all would now be dead. Only unremitting pressure by a few Jews on most Jews forced the issue, so the sixteen thousand, in extremis, eventually found a safer haven in Israel. This was one of the happier occasions in a lifetime always devoted to serving what I believed were the best interests of the Jewish community, rather than my personal benefit. I witnessed one of the sorriest exhibitions in my life. I have since seriously questioned the role of Jewish leadership worldwide in being able to preserve the Jewish people from extinction.

I have come to a time of life when disillusionment rather than hope, cynicism rather than idealism, begins to occupy my daily ruminations. This mood is reinforced by the press, the TV and radio, and books I read. It is not because life has not been kind to me personally, for it has. There is a rot in our civilization which no society, no religion seems to be able to stem. Educate yourself, be more active politically, become a participant in a cause, were slogans that I once used with promise that something good would eventuate. When I see education failing, when I see political parties and officials only interested in getting elected and reelected, repudiating the campaign promises that ensured their getting into high office, then turning their jobs into extravagant profiteering, and when caught, indicted for fraud, bribery and perjury, I wonder about the abiding values of our free, but extravagant, electoral processes. I see causes, good and bad, being exploited equally with all the talent that modern public relations can muster. Few care about the consequences of their donations. Many of the voluntary agencies are no longer designed to help the poor, the needy, the helpless. That has become the burden of the government alone, where bureaucrats ape the voluntary sector. I question with failing energies how future generations will fare.

Yet I await the coming years, hoping that I will be around to usher in the twenty-first century and have the mentality and agility at that time to evaluate whether life is better than it was once (for one's past is always more nostalgic), the same, or steadily worsening.

As I review the above, I am forcibly reminded that our sages admonished us not to finish reading any portion of the Torah on a downbeat note.

Our shakily romantic marriage fifty-eight years ago has been durable, mutually sitmulating. Since my retirement thirteen years ago, it has become ever more interdependent, as we live out our twenty-four hours a day at home or abroad with love. Our relationship to our children and grandchildren has grown freer and closer. Our original and subsequently augmented educational underpinning has been a continued stimulant to our readings, our cultural and art interests, and our widespread traveling. Our circle of real friends keeps increasing and, if anything, has become more intimate. Our battles, for I can find no other words to describe them, for decent causes show no signs of weakening. These are all to the good.

I pray that somewhere amongst our unknown Lamed Vovniks, the thirty-six super-virtuous men and women for whom God was always prepared to sustain the world, a seer will arise to bend the present, unhappy, headlong course of life, as a few Jews have done in the past, and etch a design that will resolve some, if not most, of the grave problems confronting mankind; and bring, if not for eternity, at least an epoch of tranquility and more equitable, dispersed prosperity to an ever larger body of people in this untidy globe. Then my coming into this world wet and bloody in 1908 might have had some purpose.

Index

Aberlin, Edward, 473
Abileah, Benjamin, 652
Abraham, Jed, 405, 557
Abrahams, Robert, 668
Abrams, General Creighton W., 496
Abramson, Abraham, 390
Abramson, Samuel, 415
Acne, 33
Adane, Rabbi Joseph, 620, 672
Adler, Rabbi Ralph, 373, 380
Advertisements, 729
Aged, 170
Agra, 504
Agron, Mayor Gershon, 323, 337
Albany, N. Y., 179
Allegro, Michael, 727
Almandor, Dr. Angelica, 371
Alpert, Bernard-Frances, 558, 565, 657, 711
Alpert, Dr. Morris, 666
Ambober, 402
American Association for Ethiopian Jews (AAEJ), 557, 657, 756, 763
American Camping Association, 232, 480
American Jewish Committee, 223, 265, 273, 408, 635
American Jewish Congress, 265, 273
American Jewish Joint Distribution Committee (JOINT, JDC), 153, 324, 419, 515, 590, 603, 657, 788
"American Jewish Pictorial History," 580
American Pro-Falasha Committee, 557
Angel, Rabbi Marc D., 349
Ansell, Charles-Maryann, vi, 176, 368, 484, 592, 755, 770, 780
Amsterdam, Howard, 371
Antevils, 60
Antigua (Caribbean), 668
Antigua (Guatemala), 584
Anti-Defamation League (ADL), 265
Anti-Semitism, 52, 116, 258, 646
Arnovici, Arnold, 520
Argentina, 431
Arlington Cemetery, 674
Art, 103, 731, 795
Arian, Harold-Yvette, 756

Asmara, 408
Assistants, 156, 465
Associated Ys, 218
Association of Jewish Camps, 232
Atlantic City, 186
August 15, 1977, 624
Austria, 477
Autobiography, 759
Ausubel, Nathan, 682
Autonomy or Centralism?, 310
Avner, Yehuda, 614

Bain, Gene, 70
Banker, 559
Barbados, 666
Bardin, Shlomo, 444
Barkin, Mike, 104
Barnes, Edward Larrabee, 242
Barnesboro, Pa., 1, 6
Baron, Salo W., 89, 563, 597
Baron de Hirsch Fund, 748
Barron, Harry, 94
Baruch, Uri Ben,
Basketball, 41
Baum, Ralph-Luba, 473
Bavli, Hillel, 250
Beckelman, Moses, 151, 207
Beckerman, Stanley-Ruth, vi, 250
Begin, Menahem, 621, 624, 627, 632, 653
Behar, Samuel, 321, 337
Behrman, Jacob, 616
Beierfeld, Isidor, 95
Belgium, 334, 784
Bellow, Saul, 682
Benares (Varanasi), 503
Benda, Dr. Clemens E., 195
Ben Gurion, David, 590
Benjamin, Gettye, 413
Bennet, Ruth, 720
Benton, Thomas Hart, 86, 796
Bentwich, Norman, 531
Bergen-Belsen, 727
Berger
   Baruch Michael-Sandra, v, 129, 161, 201, 357, 365, 387, 723, 770, 774
   Bessie, 32, 120

Bonnie, v, 359, 629, 757, 779
David, v
Deborah, v, 360, 722, 723
Edwin, vi
Elisabeth, v, 355, 640, 669, 722, 770
Emma, v, 68, 75, 76, 120, 201, 345, 608, 719
Fanny, 2
Gideon, v, 355, 640, 669
Harry Isaac, 2
Howard, 371
Hyman, 2
Judith, v, 359
Max, 2, 121
Milton-Harriet, 7, 31, 127, 365, 674, 685
Moe, 2
Morris-Florence, 2, 28, 703
Pauline, 2
Rachel-Sidney (Rosenthal), 31, 82, 129, 674
Ramon-Anita, v, 82, 146, 199, 354, 613, 770
Sadie-Sam (Finn), 2, 14, 44, 629
Samuel-Betty Lee, 485, 558, 583, 656, 673, 674
Samuel-Margaret, 16, 67, 75, 128, 130, 202, 345, 370, 381, 447
Stanley-Sally, vi
Cousins, 5, 121
Berhane, Zimna, 623, 626, 708, 731
Berkowitz, Carl-Miriam, 397
Bernheim, Elinor, 176
Bernheimer, Charles, 179
Bernstein, Blanche, 222
Bernstein, Charles-Celia (Greenfield), 263, 266, 529
Bernstein, Ludwig, 91
Bernstein, Philip, 634
Black Israelites (Hebrews), 296, 301, 595
Black Jews, 296
"Black Jews in America," 296, 637, 663
Black Radio Network, 637
Blacks (Negroes), 42, 73, 108
Block, Rabbi Irving J., 297, 404, 558, 770
Block, Joshua B., 680
Block, Leonard-Adele, vi, 230
Bluestein, Milton, vi
Bluhm, Walter, 250
B'nai Torah (Highland Park, Ill.), vi
Bogale, Yona, 400, 403, 610, 653, 733
Bombay, India, 505
Boney, Alice, 381
Bonker, Congressman Don, 717
Book Readers (PJC), 529
Books, 526, 533, 734
Borgos, Edward-Joy, 375
Boschwitz, Senator Rudolph, 655
Bragdon, Claude, 102
Boy Scouts, 42

Brandeis Institute Camp, 444
Brandon, Henry, 347
Brazil, 426
Breslau, Rahel, 336
Brickman, Dorothy, 394
Brodsky, Irving, 220
Bronx House, 133, 216, 722
Bronx House Camp, 159
Bronx House Music School, 148
Bronx YM-YWHA, 212
Brown, Beatrice (Chapman), 171
Brown, Irving, 203, 674
Bunker, Ellsworth, 487, 502, 674, 677
Burg, Joseph, 699
Burglaries, 571
Burlesque, 270
Burma, 496
Buttenwieser, Lawrence, 286

Cahan, Rabbi Leonard, 394
Calcutta, 498
Cambodia, 495
Cambridge (England), 740
Camping, 69, 225
Canada, 363, 724
Cancer, 120, 752
Cantor, Dr. Ben, 100
Capri, 536
Card Playing, 55
Carnovsky, Gertrude, 95
Caroga Lake, 44
Cars, 47
Case Work, 92
Case Work—Group Work, 139
Casseres, Benjamin de, 102
Catholics, 111
Cemetery, 570
Central Jewish Institute, 95
Chagall, 776
Charak, Jean, 71
Charleston, S. C., 722
Chaucer, 87, 532
Chile, 432
Cho, Emily, 375
City College of New York, 175
Civilian Defense Volunteer Organization, 153
Claremont House, 141
Closing Centers, 272
Coffee (Kaffa), 397
Cochin, India, 509
Cochran, Daniel C., 515
Cochran, Prof., 83
Cohen
  Aharon, 622
  Elliott, 257
  Gabriel, 404, 558
  Geula, 622
  Isaac (Grandfather), 2

Ike, 6, 26
Jacob, 175
Nataniel, 682
Dr. Nathan, 172, 176
Philip, v, 28
Wolf-Batya, 2
Cohn, Peter A., 174
Coleman, Avraham R., 298
Coleman, Dr. John, 752
Collingwood, Charles, 348
Colombia, S. A., 437
Columbia University, 52
Communism, 114, 257
Community Chest, 118
Conference Jewish Social Studies, 616
Congressional Hearing, 717
Coopersmith, Brant, 672
Cotler, Irving, 700
Council House, 97
Council of Jewish Federations, 634, 652, 672, 700, 718, 734
Council of Jewish Women, 97
Covel, Abe-Anne, 411
Cranston, Senator Alan, 692, 757, 764
Cullman, Joseph III, 174
Curacao, 664
Cyprus, 325

Dalsheimer, Mrs. Hugo, 323
Dammann, Richard, vi, 151, 188
Dar-On, Hanon, 655
Darrow, Clarence, 54, 63
Deafness, 640
Delaney, Stephen, 726
Delhi, India
Demographic studies, 222
Denmark, 471
Denver, Col., 717
Dicker, Rabbi Herman, 380
Dogs, 363
Dominican Republic, 669, 703, 750
Dominitz, Yehudah, 626
Dublin, Dr. Robert, 748
Dulchin, Arye, 651
Dumpson, James, 294
Dunlop, Dr. John T., 674
Dyl, Moshe, 416

Earthquake, 724
Edwards, Dean G. D., 80
Ehwa University, Korea, 384
Eisenberg, Dr. Azriel, 307, 638
Eisenman, Rabbi Bernard, 266, 716
Eilat, 580
Einstein, Albert, 102
Elderhostel, 740, 780
Elezar, Rahamim, 406, 653, 662, 672, 722
Elfers, Jack, 163
Elias, Matti, 698

Elson, Matthew, 176
England, 203, 530, 560, 592, 723, 740, 775
Ephraim, Miriam, 95
Epstein, Irving-Faye, 677
Erdman, Edna, 230, 250
Erlin, Al, 89
Ethiopia, 396, 610
Ethiopian Embassy, 672
Ethiopian Hebrew Congregation, 243
Ethiopian Jews, 11, 304, 316, 349, 519, 565, 629, 713, 773
Ethiopian Jews—U. S. organizations, 695
Evelyn, Philip, 666
Everett, Henry-Edith, vi, 297, 579, 651, 662, 769
Evron, Ephraim, 655

Faitlovitch, Dr. Jacques, 403
Falasha (see Ethiopian Jews)
Falasha Welfare Association, 531, 658
False Arrest, 124
Family Membership, 109
Fane, Irwin, 76
Father Divine, 144
F. B. I., 113
Federation Jewish Philanthropies of N. Y., 209, 282, 549
Federation Settlement House, 213
Fein, Leonard, 634
Feinstein, Charles-Pearl, vi, 263
Feldman, Dr. Leon, 253, 319, 327, 560
Feldman, Yonata, 141
Felt, James, 237, 323
Felzer, Dr. Mario, 399
Finances, 789
Finestein, Emma (See Berger, Emma)
Fink, Dr. Julius, 263
Finkelstein, Dr. Louis, 182
Finkle, Charles, 42
Finland, 468
Finn, Edward-Harriette, 750
Finn, Natalie (Oppenheimer), 147
Finn, Sam (see Berger, Sadie)
Fishbein, Jack, 404, 558
Florida, 676
Fleischman, Abraham-Hazel, 101
Fogel, Jules, 77
Fogg, Helen, 191
Fonda, Johnstown and Gloversville Railroad, 23
Food, 12, 42, 320, 402, 409
"Fourth Force," 252
Fox, Ben, 551
Frank, Congressman Barney, 717
Frank, Suzanne, 427
Frankel, Rabbi William, 716
France, 198, 205, 537, 770
Free Funds, 212
Frenkel, Leo E., 211

Frieden, Dr. Julien, 786
Friedman, Rabbi Hillel, 266
Frisch, David, 49
Frisch, Larry-Marilyn, 341
Friedman, Dr. Harry, 352
Fuld, James, vi
Fund-Raising, 274
Funerals, 567
Furman, Roger, 142

Gaitskill, Hugh, 204
Gambling, 106, 289
Gelb, Saadja, 342
Geller, Dr. Jack, 753
Georgescu, Ione, 346, 348
Georgetown University, 674
Gerber, Dr. Jane, 758
Germany, 191, 653
Gershenberg, Irving, 612
Gershowitz, Samuel, 179
Gerson, Lester-Sylvia, vi, 558, 588, 726
Ghosh, Satya-Monica, 512
Ghossein, Dr. N. A., 753
Gibney, Carroll, 114
Gibraltar, 648
Gidal, Dr. Nahum Tim-Pia, v, 262, 506, 518, 561, 580, 618, 729
Gifts, 794
Gilboa, Moshe, 706
Ginzberg, Dr. Eli, 154
Glazer, Nathan, 257, 283
Gloversville, N. Y., 1, 34, 119, 629
Gluckman, Ernest, 104
Glucksman, Harry, 114
Glueck, Dr. Nelson, 339
Goetz, Norman-Mildred, 236, 250
Goldberg, Brett Haim, 701
Goldberg, Drs. Morris and Rose, vi, 260, 264, 752
Goldman, Eric, 735
Goldman, Ralph-Helen, 318, 375, 518, 567, 590, 604, 638
Goldsmid, Sir Henry Avigdor, 560
Goldsmith, Horace, 248
Goldsmith, Jerome, 152
Golf, 24, 617
Goodman, Rabbi Philip-Hannah, 108, 322, 390, 715
Gordon, Rabbi Harold, 357
Goren, Chief Rabbi Shlomo, 566, 598
Gotlieb, J., 390
Gottlieb, Samuel, 265
Gould, Samuel, 162
Government Funding, 277
Graduate School Jewish Social Work, 85, 89
Grainger, Lester, 143
Granada, 543
Grant, Hyman, 32, 95
Greece, 327, 345, 397, 473

Greenberg, Reuben, 722
Greenberg, Rabbi Yitzhak, 287
Greenfield, Murray, 729
Greenwich Village, 56
Greifer, Julian L., 186
Grenada, 666
Grossberg, Louis C.-Celia, vi, 2
Gruber, Ruth, 766
Gruen, Dr. George E., 303
Guatemala, 583
Guedj, Simon 658
Guggenheimer, Elly, 176
Guggenheimer, Randolph III-Elizabeth Miller, 176
Gupta, Hema, 512

Haber, Samuel, 560
Habib, Philip C., 386, 492, 615, 674
Haggadahs, 645
Hadassah, 672
Haham, Abraham, 175
Hall, Helen, 188
Hall, Noel, 204
Hallowitz, David, 152
Hallowitz, Emanuel, 152
Haiti, 736
Halachmy, Haim, 622
Halpern, William P., 614, 624, 650, 655
Hamburg, Harry, 721
Handlin, Oscar, 178
Handwerker, Murray, 219
Harberer, Jack, 371
Harel, Dr. Dan, 450
Harris, General Hugh P., 382
Harrison, Frances, 86
Hatzaad Harishon, 297
Hawaii, 368, 485
Hebrew School, 8
Hechel Shlomo, 732
Heijbroeck, Jan Frederick, 638
Helfgot, Regina Resnick, 431
Herschaft, Jean, 771
Herzog, Chaim, 577
Herzog, Chief Rabbi Isaac, 317
Hess, Marian, 230
Hexter, Dr. Maurice B., 189, 210, 246, 546, 669
Heyman, George, Jr., 464
H.I.A.S., 223
Higgins, William, 237
High School, 40
Hinenberg, Dr. Morris, 549
Hiroshima, 165, 392
Hirschberg, Alfredo, 427
Hirsdansky, Simon, 146
Hodson Center, 172
Holland, 332
Hollander, Aharon-Esther (Wube), 577, 734, 770, 772

Hollander, Rabbi Benjamin, 266
Hollander, Rabbi Fred I., 535, 561
Holman, Nat, 42
Holocaust, 168, 725
Hong Kong, 372
Hong, Sheng Hwa, 372
Horowitz, Allan, 501
Horowitz, C. Morris, 222
Horwitz, Louis-Sylvia, 335, 349, 591, 618
Housing, 155
Hughes, Richard, 489
Hummel, Ambassador Arthur, 497, 589, 610
Hurowitz Award, 638

Illnesses, 17, 452, 735, 750, 777, 779, 785
India, 498
"In Search of Origins of Graenum," 678
"Innovation by Tradition," 583
International Conference Jewish Communal Service, 412, 425, 440, 449, 518
Iran, 515
Ireland, 723
Isaacs, Edward, 309
Israel, 314, 335, 410, 447, 471, 518, 533, 574, 590, 592, 618, 653, 711, 726
Israel government, 658
Italians, 149
Italy, 328, 421, 523, 780

Jacobovici, Simcha, 726, 728, 734
Jacobs, Dr. Morris, 239
Jacobson, Charlotte, 579, 652
Jae, David, 262
Jahr, Bert, 786
Jakobson, Max, 469
Jamaica, 670, 683
Jameson, Samilla Love, 105
Janowsky, Dr. Oscar I., 177
Janowsky Survey, 177
Japan, 378
Japanese Inn, 391
Japanese Prints, 389
Jasper, Dr. William-Retha, 375
Jenkins, Roy H., 674
Jerusalem playground, 711
Jerusalem YM-YWHA, 248, 321, 413, 471, 561
Jewish Agency, 596, 652, 658, 732
Jewish Association Neighborhood Centers, 216
Jewish Academy of Arts and Sciences, 722
Jewish College Youth, 286
Jewish Community Centers—YM-YWHAs, 64, 84, 94
Jewish Community Center of Staten Island, 99
Jewish Community Council of Parkchester, 697

"Jewish Digest," 676
Jewish Education, 306
Jewish Flag, 165
Jewish Museum, NY, 405, 673
Jewish Student Organization—Missouri, 79
Jewish poor, 291
"Jewish Week," 769
Jewish Vacation Association, 231
Jewish Welfare Board, 635
Jordan, Charles, 420
JOTS, 253

Kaganoff, Benzion C., 684
Kameny Seymour, v
Kansas City, Missouri, 168
Kaplan, Irving, 152
Kaplan, Jeremiah, 592
Kaplan, Lawrence J., 222
Kaplan, Rabbi Mordecai M., 90, 602
Kahn, William, 442
Karpeles, John, 219
Karpf, Maurice, 85
Kase, Dr. Harold, 640
Kathakali Dancers, 509
Katz, Arthur, 152
Katz, Karl, 340
Katz, Shmuel, 409
Kaufman, Michael R. (N.Y. TIMES), 612
Kaufman, Stanley-Joan, 667
Kaufmann Campgrounds, Henry, 235, 628
Kaufmann, Edgar, 238
Kavey, Lilia, 404, 558
Kenworthy, Dr. Marian, 91
Kenya, 605, 612
Keren Yaldenu, 535, 561
Kessler, David, 531, 560, 723
Keyfitz, Dr. Isidore-Sarah Feder, 83, 88, 341, 479, 679
Kfar Batya, 316, 413
Khjraho, 504
Kheel, Theodore, 175
Kibbutz Givat Haim, 567
"They'll Kill you," 628
Kim, Dr. Hong Chun, 318, 384
Kim, Won Chin, 384
Kim, Dr. (Ehwa University), 384
Kindergarten trauma, 15
King's College, Cambridge, 741
Kirkland, Lane, 674
Kissinger, Henry 489, 502
Klein, Philip, 172
Klein, Wells, 495
Kleinberg, Rabbi, 383
Klutznick, Philip, 756
Kolleck, Teddy, 318, 414, 715
Koch, Mayor Edward, 705
Koder, Shabbatai S., 510
Kohs, Samuel, 94
Kolodney, Nathan, v

811

Korea, 381
Kraft, Louis, 263, 597
Kraicer, Mannie, 336
Kramer, Rabbi Simon, 250
Kulick, Gilbert, 588
Kummer, Rabbi Howard, 368
Kushki, Ezra, 517
Kushner, Arlene, 708
Kuwaiti, 533

Labor Zionism, 479
Ladd, Edward, 194
Ladejinsky, Wolf I., 511
La Guardia, Mayor Fiorello, 155
Laise, Ambassador Carol C., 501
Lambert, Barney, 220, 365
Landau, Gertrude, 173
Landesman, Rabbi Alter F., 188, 551
Landing, James E., 638
Landman, Beatrice, 176
Langman, Anne W., 173, 181, 210
Lantos, Congressman Tom, 717
Lawes, Warden, 77
Lazrus, Julian, 174
Leather business, 10
Lebanon, 558
Lee, Porter, 91
Lemberg, Samuel, 244, 309
Lewis, Dale, v
Lenhoff, Dr. Howard M., 631, 720
Lerner, Joseph, 168
Lese, Bill, 241
Levin, Harold, 211, 242
Levin, Meyer-Tereska, 574, 583, 695
Levin, Moshe-Miriam, 322
Levine, Harry, 171
Levine, Hillel, 288
Levine, Samuel, 151
Levinrew, George, 623
Levy, Bernard, vi
Levy, Gershon, 610, 619
Levy, Yoav, 672
Lewis, Salem L., 220
Lichtenstein, Howard, 175
Liewant, Sidney E., 658
Liebman, Charles S., 443, 549
Linton, Joseph, 532
Linzer, Norman, 254
Lippman, Leon-Hortense, vi
Lippman, Ralph, 501
Liquor, 36, 76, 411
Liss, Karl-Evelyn, 365
Litt, Solomon, 323
Littauer, Lucius, N., 65
Loh, J. S., 372
Londow, Ezekiel J., 94
Long Island, 478
Lookstein, Rabbi Haskel, 530
Lopez, Ambassador Aharon, 708

Lourie, Norman, 157
Lurie, Harry L., 255
Lurie, Jesse Zev, 25, 765
Luxembourg, 783

Macbeth, Wallace, 104
MacLaine, Shirley, 381, 383
Malkin, Yaakov, 343
Man is Killed, 361
Mamlok, Dr. Hans, 103
Mandell, Joseph, 262
Marchais, Mrs. Jacques-Harry I. Klauber, 102
Marcuse, Corinne (Dolly), 151
Marlborough, Gibson, 163
Martinique, 772
Massada, 449, 519
Matsu, Shichiro, 389
Matthew, Wentworth Arthur, 243
Mayer, Myron, 229
Mayerberg, Rabbi Samuel A., 77
Mayor Wagner's Committee on Poverty, 293
McCloskey, Mark, 113
McKinley, Andrew, 243
McNeil, Hector-Sheila, 203
Meir, Goldie, 665
Melamed, Monte, 238
Meloy, General G. J., 382
Menorah-Psalm, 472
Messing, Dr. Simon D., 718
Metropolitan Association Jewish Center Workers, 115, 553
Mexico, 439, 587, 788
Milgram, Dr. Joseph, 396
Miller, Deborah, 419
Miller, Dr. Jacob, 174
Miller, Mark, 741
Missouri University, 68, 70
Mitchel, Viola M., 147
Mittwoch, Florence-Yaakov, 322
Mizrahi, American Women, 698
Miyao, Sachiko, 379, 485
Modiano, Mario, 327
Monk, Abraham, 431
Morag, Haim-Judith, vi, 459
Morein, Teddy, 44
Morgenthau, Henry Sr.-Josephine, 133
"Morning-Herald" Reporter, 61
Morocco, 641
Morris, Harold, 551
Morse, Earl, 253
Moss, Ira, 262
Murphy, Monsignor Philip, 372
Muskie, Edmond S., 674

Nadel, Jack, 176, 188
Narkis, Uzi, 578, 579
Nathan, Abie, 693

National Assn. Jewish Center Workers, 185
National Conference Christians and Jews, 265
National Conference Jewish Communal Service, 256
National Foundation Jewish Culture, 310
National Jewish Community Relations Advisory Committee, 634, 652, 656, 672, 700, 710
National Jewish Welfare Board, 109, 406
National Youth Administration, 112
Naumburg, Frederick, 246
Navon, Yitzhak, 576, 665
NBC-TV, 726
Neipres, Joseph, 318
Nemser, Charles, 95
Nepal, 500
Nevis, 668
Newark YM-YWHA, 114
Newhouse, S. I., 112
New Delhi, 511
Newspaper Reporter, 61
New York Board of Rabbis, 533, 553
New York Philharmonic Society Orchestra, 249
New York School of Social Work, 53
New York University, 52
Nineteen Hundred and Eight (1908), xiii
Norman, Theodore-Jane, vi, 558, 618, 651, 770
Nissenbaum family, 60

Obermeier, Minnie, 146
Obican, Jovan, 475
Odou, Renee (Smith), 784
Olshon, Milton, 518
O'Neill, Eugene, 57
Operation Lion's Cub (See Operation Moses)
Operation Moses, 744
Oral History, 721
Orchestra, 42
Orenstein, Max, vi
Orlinsky, Harry M., 563
Orphaned, 686
ORT (World ORT), 614, 619, 633, 645, 657
Ovadia, Hezi, 565, 575

Pacifism, 131
Paiewonsky, Isidor, 669
Panama, 438
Panmunjon, 382, 385
Papers written, 442, 483
Paran, Mordecai, 560
Parfitt, Tudor, 628, 764
Parsee, 505
Patri, Angelo, 146
Paz, Col. Yitzhak, 535
Pearlroth, Norbert, 681

Peled, General Mattiyahu, 485
Pelham, Jewish Center, 258
Penn, Matthew-Aviva, v, vi, 365, 759
Peretz, Abraham, 472
Peru, 433
Perugia, 780
Peterson, Ivor, 487
Philip, Bruno, 669
Philip, Thomas, 670
Phillipines, 370
Phillips, Edward (Ben Avram), 410, 473
Pilobulus Dancers, 732
Pinkuss, Rabbi, 427
Poison Ivy, 239
Politics, 19, 78, 98, 279, 762
Polish, Rabbi Daniel, 674
Pollack, Rabbi Yaakov, 694
Pope (Castel Gandolfo), 328
Portugal, 423, 524, 544
Posner, Dr. Raphael, 581
Postal, Bernard, 415
Pozefsky, Mary, 6
Prato, Jonathon, 349
Pridan, Dr. Daniel, 450
Pritzker, J. N., 757
Proskauer, Joseph, 242
"Professional Training for Jewish Communal Service," 254
Public Schools, 146
Puerto Rico, 748

"Rabbi Berger," 181
Rabbinical Assembly, 716
Rabinowitz, Samuel, 89
Racism, 772
Rackman, Rabbi Emanuel, 254, 563
Radojevic, Rahela, 473
Rafel, Sol-Ruth, v, vi, 158, 216, 703, 756
Rafiah, Zvi, 655
Ramsay, Prof., 86
Rand, Michael, 152
Rappaport, Israel, 182
Rapoport, Louis, 567, 626, 663, 708, 731, 765
Rastafarians, 671
Raucher, Dr. Fred-Lois, 402
Relkin, Rabbi Stanley, 669
Resnick, Hyman M., 174
Reznikoff, Dr. Bernard, 623, 715
Riegelman, Lillian, 151, 172
Riesenfeld, Victor, 311
Roberts, Beatrice, 172
Robinson, Donald M., 604
Rockowitz, Eli-Fern, 662, 770
Rone, Rabbi Yaakov, 266, 450
Roosevelt, Franklin D., 146, 154, 162
Rose, David, 247
  Daniel, vi, 211, 247, 770

Elihu, 247
Frederick P., vi, 241, 247, 250
Rosen, Ellie, 295
Rosen, Leah, 185
Rosen, Rabbi David Moses, 520
Rosenberg, Henry-Mildred, 583, 602, 612, 651, 692, 709, 729, 734, 770
Rosenberg, Irwin-Doris, 230
Rosenberg, James, 670
Rosenman, Merwin, v, 174, 436, 760
Rosenson, Lillian, 147
Rosenthal, A. M., 491
Rosenthal, Abraham W., 189
Rosenthal, Edward-Amy, 496
Rosenthal, Sydney, 125
R.O.T.C., 73
Rothbaum, Larry, 799
Rothman, Harry, 219
Roshgolin, Rabbi, 250
Roth, Cecil, 683
Roy, Rosalind, 696
Rudavsky, David, 105
Rumania, 519

Sabbah, Rabbi David, 649
Sabbath, 250
Sacandaga, 22
Sachar, Abram L., 81
Safire, William, 685
Sainer, Herman-Janet, 254, 596, 761
Saint Kitts, 668
Saint Thomas, 669
Salomon, Hamilcar, 436
Salomon, Julian, 238
Samoil, Mircea-Rosalie, 641
Samuels, Ralph, 210
Samuelson, Aaron, 174
Sandmel, Rabbi Samuel, 87, 146
Sanchez, Amelio, 142
Sanger, Margaret, 111
Sapir, Pinchas, 578
Sardinia, 536
Schachter, Rabbi Herschel, 251
Scheuer, Simon, 217
Schools, 38
Schrag, Louis, 262
Schwartz, Lillian, 703
Scotland, 192, 723
Seasonwein, Roger, vi
Selig, Martha K., 549
Seligson, Isaac, 364
Sesimbra, 524
Sex, 46
Shapiro, Judah-Ida, 205, 256
Shapiro, Louis, 327
Shapiro, Nathan, 633, 653, 692, 719, 757, 764, 770
Sharpe, Dr. William, 226
Shazar, Zalman, 471

Sheep's Eggs, 320
Shelemay, Jack, 398, 611
  Kay Kaufman, 611
  Shalom, 397
Sherer, Rabbi Moshe, 694
Sherman, C. Bezalel, 443, 480
Simkovitch, Mary, 188
Shore, Dr. Maurice, 157
Shufro, Jacob, 146
Shwartz, Louise, 229
Sicily, 451
Siegel, Rabbi Seymour, 291
Silberman, Samuel J., vi, 456, 457
Singer, Isaac Bashevis, 682, 684
Sklare, Marshall, 175
Slave Market, 145
Slavin, Simon, 101
Slawson, John, 223, 287
Slutzker, Ruth, 141
Smith, Robert, 464
Sobel, Louis-Mina, 331
Sobol, Rabbi Ronald R., 692
Solarz, Congressman Stephen, 717, 770
Solender, Samuel, 551
  Sanford, 156, 440, 539
Soleveitchik, Rabbi Joseph, 254
Soltes, Mordecai, 91
Souza, Ernest H. De, 670
Soviet Russia (ICOR), 110
Spain, 351, 539
Spanien, Raphael-Esther, 420
Spanish Civil War, 111
Specht, Dr. Harry, 175, 721
Spelling Bee, 50
Spellman, Frances Cardinal, 219
Spinacks, 9
Springfield, Mass., 115
Starr, Harry, 69
Staten Island, 99
"Staten Island Advance," 112, 115
Stein, Dr. William-Phoebe, 174, 181
Steiner, David, 152
Stettenheim, Frederic R., 122, 163, 175
Stockhamer, Rose, vi, 420
Stolzenberg, Lewis, v
Stone, Jeffrey, 558
Strook, Alan M., 288
Strook, May, 220
Stoughton, Clarence C., 117
Student training, 305, 455
Staff training, 304
Sudan, 636, 650, 652
Summing Up, 801
Swank, Ambassador Emory C., 495
Sweden, 469
Switzerland, 419
Synagogue Council of America, 672
Szabo, Imre, 319
Szlapak, Rachel, 609, 612

Taiwan, 374
Talmon, Prof. Jacob, 582
Tamis, Dr. Abraham B., 174
Tannenbaum, Rabbi Marc, 635
Tanner, Nikki, 721
Tanzania, 605
Tartakower, Dr. Aryeh, 535, 565, 599, 624, 659
Tauber sisters, 331
Taussig, Frances, 140
Taylor, Carl, 497
Taylor, Katherine, 191
Taylor, General Maxwell, 382
Tegegne, Baruch, 624, 650, 653, 661, 662, 672
Teitelbaum, Satmar Rebbe Joel, 340
Tel Aviv University Institute, 563
Tenth Anniversary—Bronx House, 176
Tesfaye, Demeke, 672
Testimonial Dinner—1985, 769
Thailand, 496
Theatre, 56
"The Quiet Envoy," 676
"The Turbulent Decades," 639, 702
Timmerman, Jacobo, 662
Tisch, Mrs. Lawrence, 230
Tishman, Peggy, 478
Tokyo, 394
Tolentino Family, 474
Tomizawa, Tom, 726
Torchia, Andrew, 612
Torgov, Morley, 684
Touster, Ben-Bertha, 211, 212, 322
Toyota Cressida, 774
Trainin, Rabbi Isaac, N., 231, 288, 296, 312, 638, 770
Trinidad, 665
Trube, Father Howard D., 372
Trubin, John, vi
Tulka, Yuda, 503
Turgeman, Eli, 657, 659
Turkey, 414
Tze-Kwan, Mrs., 375

Union American Hebrew Congregation, 693
Unions, 134
Unitarian Service Committee, 191
United Jewish Appeal, 662
United Nations, 772
United States Senators and Congressmen, 654
Unterberg, Clarence, 309, 323
Urbont, Carl-Genia, 175, 207
Uruguay, 429
Usdan Center Performing Arts, 243

Vence (France), 537
Venezuela, 426

Vietnam, 486
Vilnai, Zev, 316, 339
Vivikananda, Swami, 513
Voodoo, 736

Wales, 683
Wallace, Mike, 758
Warmbrand, Martin J., 413, 558
Warburg, Felix M., 92
Watson, Sam, 203
Weil, Frank A., 224
Weil, Frank L., 169
Weil, Morris A., vi
Weiler, Jack, 276, 604
Weinberg, Rabbi Charles, 598, 672
Weintraub, Anne, 175
Weisberger, L. Arnold, 122
Weiss, Rabbi Avi, 660
Wien, Lawrence A., 233
Wiener, William E., Educational Center, 246, 457, 641
Wiesel, Elie, 287, 445, 556
Wiesenthal, Simon, 705
Wigoder, Geoffrey-Deborah, 534
Willen, Joseph, 176, 211, 287, 310, 323, 546
Williams, John A., 614, 701
Willner, Isadore, 74
Wilson, Harold, 204
Winik, Elaine, 789
Wirth, Prof. Louis, 178
Wise, George S., 563
Wise, Rabbi Stephen S., 117
Witkin, Nathan, 438
Witty, Helen, 230
Wolf, Robert-Peggy, vi, 211, 677
Wolpert, Ludwig, 344
Woodcock, Leonard, 674
World War I, 18, 22
World War II, 150
Wube, Esther (See Aaron-Esther Hollander)
Wyler, Marjorie, vi, 230

Yad Vashem, 728
Yale University, 722
Yang, Amy, 375
Yeshiva University Honorary Degree, 556
Yitzhak, Rahamim, 406, 693, 718
Yom Kippur War, 555
Yona, Zachariah, 653, 660
Young Israel—Staten Island, 748
YWHA of New York, 216
Yoseph, Chief Rabbi Ovadia, 565, 694
Yugoslavia, 473

Zeta Beta Tau, 70
Zimmelman, Rabbi Charles, 394
Zionism, 167
Zipori, Haim, 566, 576

Books by Graenum Berger

Adventures in Group Work (1948)
The Jewish Community Center: A Fourth Force in American Jewish Life (1966)
Innovation by Tradition (1976)
Black Jews in America (1978)
The Turbulent Decades—Editor of two volumes (1980)